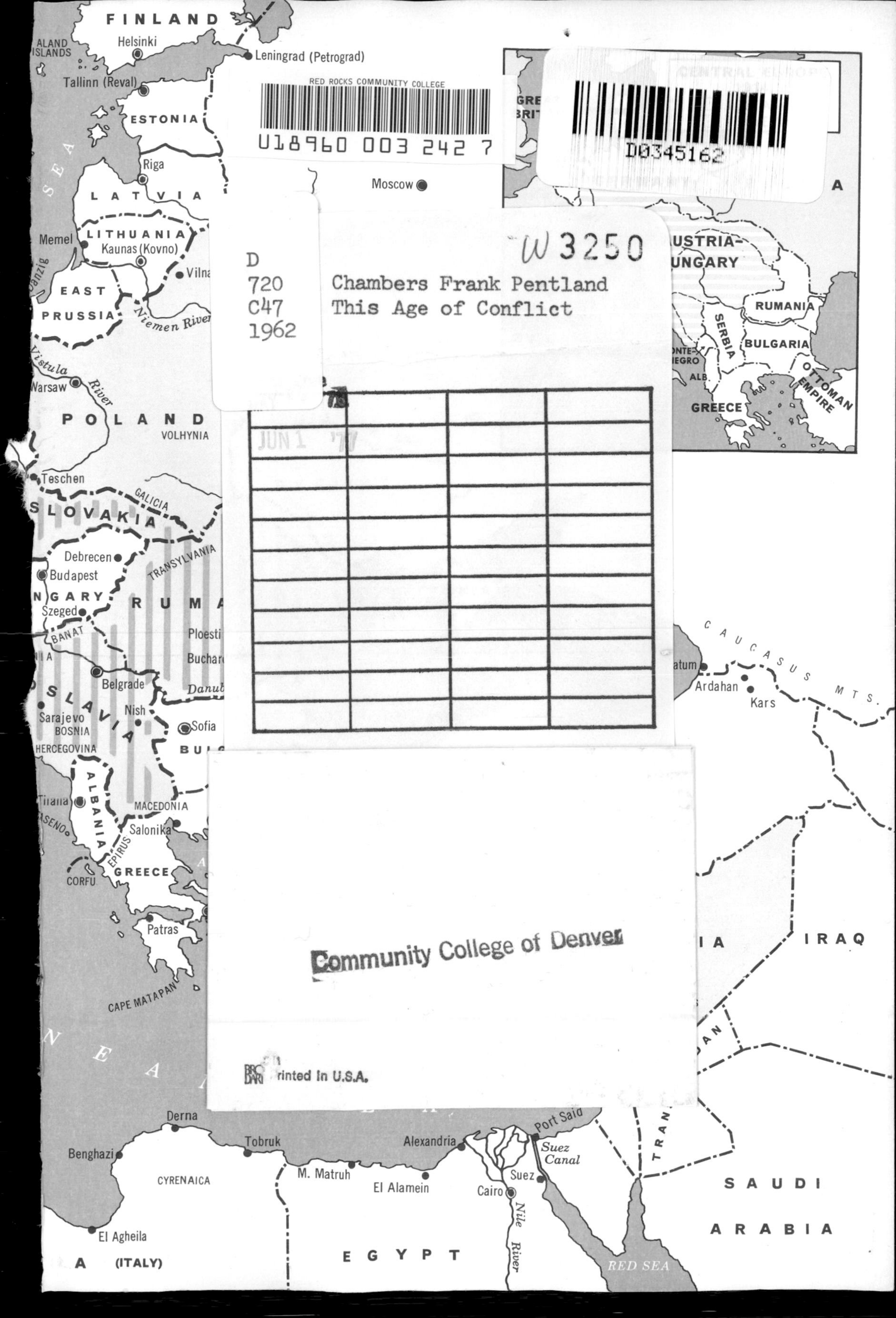
FINLAND
ALAND ISLANDS
Helsinki
Leningrad (Petrograd)
Tallinn (Reval)
ESTONIA
Riga
LATVIA
Moscow
Memel
LITHUANIA
Kaunas (Kovno)
Vilna
EAST PRUSSIA
Niemen River
Vistula River
Warsaw
POLAND
VOLHYNIA
Teschen
GALICIA
SLOVAKIA
Debrecen
Budapest
TRANSYLVANIA
Szeged
BANAT
Ploesti
Belgrade
Danube
Sarajevo
BOSNIA
HERCEGOVINA
Nish
Sofia
ALBANIA
Tirana
MACEDONIA
Salonika
EPIRUS
CORFU
GREECE
Patras
CAPE MATAPAN
AUSTRIA-
HUNGARY
RUMANIA
SERBIA
BULGARIA
GREECE
OTTOMAN EMPIRE
CAUCASUS MTS.
Ardahan
Kars
IRAQ
Derna
Tobruk
Alexandria
Port Said
Suez Canal
Benghazi
CYRENAICA
M. Matruh
El Alamein
Suez
Cairo
Nile River
SAUDI ARABIA
El Agheila
(ITALY)
EGYPT
RED SEA

This Age of Conflict

Third Edition **THIS AGE OF**

FRANK P. CHAMBERS

LONDON SCHOOL OF ECONOMICS AND POLITICAL SCIENCE

CONFLICT

The Western World—1914 to the Present

Maps by Lilli Mautner

Harcourt, Brace & World, Inc. New York Chicago San Francisco Atlanta

BY THE SAME AUTHOR

The War Behind the War: The Political and Civilian Fronts, 1914-1918

Perception, Understanding and Society: A Philosophical Essay on the Arts and Sciences—and on the Humane Studies

Printed in the United States of America

Library of Congress Catalog Card Number: 62-12186

FOR FRANCES

Ogni vera storia è storia contemporanea.
(Every true history is contemporary history.)

—BENEDETTO CROCE

PREFACE

The present edition is a complete revision of the earlier editions of the same title and brings the narrative down to 1961. The emphasis this time has been somewhat shifted. Whereas the earlier editions attempted an overall history of the international world, the present edition has concentrated on Europe, the United States, and the British Dominions. In other words, it has attempted the history of the "West" in this twentieth century Time of Troubles. The other parts of the world have been included insofar as they seem to have contributed to the main theme.

Very regrettably, two of the former team of authors, Professor Christina Phelps Harris and Professor Charles C. Bayley, have withdrawn. But Professor Harris has continued in an advisory capacity, especially in those chapters touching her special fields, and several portions have been rewritten by her.

The manuscript was circulated among several specialists before going to press, and parts of it have been read and checked in detail. The author, of course, remains responsible for his book, but he is very well aware of the help he has had, and he makes grateful acknowledgments to the following: Mr. Hedley Bull, Mr. James Cameron, Mrs. F. P. Chambers, Mr. R. P. Dore, Mr. Geoffrey L. Goodwin, Miss Muriel Grindrod, Mr. R. M. P. Hawkin, Professor Robin A. Humphreys, Mrs. M. MacGibbon, Mr. D. T. Muggeridge, Mr. William Pickles, Dr. Richard Pipes, Professor Theodore Ropp, Dr. Ernst W. Sander, Mr. Leonard B. Schapiro, Mr. J. E. Spence, Mr. Brian Tunstall, Dr. S. V. Utechin, and Professor Henry R. Winkler. Also to be mentioned are Mr. A. W. Butler, Professor Michael Florinsky, Professor David Harris, Dr. Veit Valentin, Mr. Sydney Walton, Professor George A. Washburne, and Miss Elizabeth Wiskemann, who read the earlier edition and whose contributions of that time have been carried over into the present edition.

Note on Arrangement

The division of the book into five Parts explains itself, and to some extent the former nation-by-nation treatment has been retained:

Part One	The First World War
Part Two	The Period of Settlement
Part Three	The Period of Crisis
Part Four	The Second World War
Part Five	The Cold War

But the old problem of closing dates has become even more difficult. Parts One and Four on the two World Wars can be ended with some precision, but not so the other Parts. The chapters on Part Two have been rounded off as far as possible with the economic breakdown of 1929 and the Depression which followed, Part Three with the outbreak of the Second World War, and Part Five in 1961. But chronological neatness has not been attempted, and generally each separate episode in the narrative has been allowed to work itself out to its own appropriate conclusion. Often in Part Five even this could not be done; the European integration, the "retreat from colonialism," rearmament, the Cold War itself, are all unfinished business and must so be written.

Note on Spelling

The spelling of persons' names and place names is one of the minor difficulties in a project of this sort. *Webster's New International Dictionary*, the National Geographic Board, and the Index of the *Encyclopaedia Britannica* have been the main guides. But familiarity has been the overriding rule. Beneš appears with his *š*; Pashich without his *š*. Most first names, other than French and German ones, have been anglicized. Stepan becomes Stephen, Grigorii becomes Gregory, and so forth. But now and then Andrei or Georgi or Josef have been used for no better reason than that they "looked right."

For place names familiarity has again been the rule. Thus Teschen is used, for example, not Těšin or Cieszyn. Many place names have changed during the years covered by this book. Lwów, Istanbul, Cóbh, Oslo, Peiping, and many others were unknown a generation ago. Generally, where it seemed important, the names used are those of their respective times. Thus St. Petersburg, Petrograd, Leningrad change with their chronological context. In the same way, ranks and titles of persons, where mentioned, are also those of their respective times.

CONTENTS

Part One

THE FIRST WORLD WAR

Part Two

THE PERIOD OF SETTLEMENT

Part Three

THE PERIOD OF CRISIS

MAP LIST

This Age of Conflict

Part One

THE FIRST WORLD WAR

1. The Outbreak of the War
2. The Opening Phases — 1914-15
3. "The War Behind the War"
4. The Middle Phases — 1916-17
5. The Closing Phases — 1918

The lamps are going out all over Europe.
We shall not see them lit again in our life-time.
— EDWARD GREY

IMPERIAL WAR MUSEUM

1. THE OUTBREAK OF THE WAR

The World of 1914

From time to time in the course of history human affairs reach an equilibrium, an equilibrium so stable as almost to give the illusion of permanence. The ages come to their sum and apex. Institutions, manners, conventions, the entire sociocultural complex, seem fixed and final. Yet, in fact, behind the façade the structure may be already creaking to its collapse, and whatever survives or is rebuilt from the ruin is very different from what has gone before.

Such was the Western world of 1914. Here too was an unquestioned, an almost unconsciously accepted stability; here was confidence and boundless optimism; here did man think of change only in terms of perpetual progress. Yet here too the structure crashed, and the design of what is to come, different though we know it will be, is not yet clear to us.

By any standard the European century that stretched from 1815 to 1914 was among the most expansive, teeming, and varied of any equal period of time. Man, it seemed – at any rate Western man – was coming to control his own fate. Science promised new material conquests and the answers to nature's riddles. Mechanized industry poured out its products in rising volume and at falling cost. New modes of transport and communication made all men neighbors. Exploration opened up the last unknown tracts and corners of the globe. Medicine and public health increased the length and enjoyment of life. Education brought literacy and widened interests to multitudes. Women were emancipated from age-old disabilities. Missions, social services, insurance, and laws for the protection of children and animals signified a new humanitarianism. Slavery and the slave trade were generally abolished. Penal codes were constantly revised in the direction of leniency and reclamation. The world's rulers were learning at last that politics is the science of welfare. Recreational facilities for people of all classes were available as never before. Culturally, the century was extraordinarily rich. There were brilliant minds at work in every art and discipline – in poetry, fiction, drama, music, history, philosophy – and, outstandingly, science. Printing was cheap, and books had never been so plentiful. Historians have hardly yet appreciated the sheer efflorescence of creative genius in these years.

But there was another side to the picture. Even in the eyes of its most conservative contemporaries, the Western world of 1914 was still far from the earthly paradise. With all its technological advances, poverty and social injustice were still the lot of many. The century's triumphs had been won partly as the result of, and partly in spite of, an economic system that often made the individual little better than a commodity. Only perpetual expansion had disguised the defects and deficiencies of the system — but expansion had its physical limits, and the limits might soon be reached. Science had brought new things into the world, new powers and new luxuries; but old habits sometimes failed to respond to the many changes. Large-scale industry had upset the balance of town and country, and the land was losing its cultivators to sprawling, urban growths which demanded novel social and hygienic readjustments. The phenomenon of mass politics was appearing. Meanwhile, for those who held the purse strings, the struggle for markets and for overseas possessions continued — was indeed intensified. Territories and populations outside Europe were being drawn into Europe's economic and political rivalries. Especially since 1900 several of the more "advanced" nations, having industrialized themselves, were competing to their mutual exasperation in fields which till then had been the preserve and monopoly of England. Many political leaders and economists in Europe had lost faith in the classic virtues of free competition and had turned to the cartel and the combine as the proper policy for their respective countries.

Yet there were very few who conceived of a state of affairs radically different from that existing. Marx, Nietzsche, and their prophetic brethren may have a little pricked the conscience of the world but hardly moved its deep complacency. Genuine reform, so most men believed, was still achievable by peaceful means within the established order; revolution could still take place without subversion.

Europe was then the political and military center of world power, and she was aggressively expanding. In the course of the century, from 1815 to 1914, her population had increased from 200,000,000 to 450,000,000, and Europeans outside Europe had increased from 20,000,000 to 200,000,000. Europe was the fertile motherland of an irrepressible migration. Every one of the four other continents was brought under the influence or actual control of Europeans or of men of recent European origin. The plains of America and Siberia, the larger islands of Australasia, and the southern tip of Africa were colonized; tropical Africa was partitioned; India lay under British rule. Even lands nominally independent, like Turkey or Persia, China or Japan, felt the impact of Western ways and Western acquisitiveness. War and peace for millions were decided in the six great chancelleries of Vienna, Berlin, Rome, St. Petersburg, Paris, and London. "When Europe sneezed the whole world had a cold."

Nationalism was the characteristic ideology of the day. Since the French Revolution it had come to absorb all Europe and was now beginning to spread through the rest of the world. Nationalism was a passion that ruled men's lives, gave them a new egotism, glorified their histories, and rationalized their conflicts. Even trade followed its respective flag. "Submerged" nationalities demanded independence as a right. In the course of the century nationalist revolts had occurred and recurred from Poland to Ireland, Finland to Greece. In 1914 it was estimated that, of Europe's population, one man in four lived under a hated and alien rule. Countries outside Europe – in the Near and Far East, in Latin America, as far afield as the Pacific Philippines – had their versions of nationalism, ironically often enough as the result of European tutelage and in protest against European domination.

The contemporary attitude toward the problem of war was curiously contradictory. On the one hand, war was accepted as a legitimate instrument of national policy, and, popularly, was still hung about with glamour and romance. Diplomats and general staffs made their alliances and their "Plans" with the ultimate eventuality constantly before them; for the wider public world, which only recently had rung with the names of Napoleon, Nelson, Wellington, and Blücher, the soldier and sailor were still the national heroes. The century, in fact, had been far from peaceful; wars had been frequent enough. Somebody was always fighting somewhere. The new Germany and Italy, the United States and Japan had all been born or matured in war. In Germany, particularly after 1871, war was almost a philosophy of life. War was the test of national virtue, ardently wished for; it was history's forge and workshop – as witness Germany's own history. The current economic doctrine of competition and the current biological doctrine of the survival of the fittest seemed to support the view that war was a necessary, natural, and beneficial form of human behavior. In the fifteen years prior to 1914 there had occurred the South African War, the Spanish-American War, the Russo-Japanese War, the Tripolitan War, and the two Balkan Wars – altogether no mean catalogue of conflict.

On the other hand, though the century's wars were frequent, they happened to be localized and of short duration. None of them could be said to have greatly disturbed the overriding stability and permanence of the time. They might bring about a change of dynasty or government, a cession of territory, a limited impoverishment or gain – results which were often admitted to be desirable. Certainly no one in those days spoke darkly of a crisis of civilization or the annihilation of man. Despite its wars, it has been called the century of the Great Peace, the *Pax Europeana*. By 1914 masses of mankind no longer remembered what war was, and in the great European armies even senior officers were living out their professional lives without sight of violent death on the battlefield.

There was indeed some hope – almost a silent assumption – that a new enlightened internationalism might gain on nationalism, that nationalist passions, like religious sectarianism formerly, might learn to coexist without intolerance, and that the romanticism of war, wherever that romanticism was still cultivated, might not spill over into action. It was possible to cite several minor triumphs of international cooperation – notably the postal service and the Red Cross. Latterly a number of international disputes had been successfully arbitrated. The powers had partitioned Africa without recourse to war. Science and scientific research had developed a great international freemasonry. Music and the arts were cosmopolitan and belonged to all peoples. Interesting peace movements and institutions, such as the Carnegie Endowment and the Nobel Prize, had been founded. Socialism in all countries was internationalist and pacifist. High finance was a mysterious, invisible, but generally pacifist force; for high finance, though it had been known to support a small war and certainly supported armaments, was averse to risking damage to the system of which it was so integral a part. Diplomacy, that delicate art practiced by a small aristocracy of careerists, could be relied on to adjust a difference or redress an incident. For a humane and progressive civilization, general war indeed had become "unthinkable."

More sinister than the possible "causes" of war were the increasing elaboration and enlargement of modern life. The Western world of 1914 was like a cosmic system, able to maintain itself only in perpetual and accelerating motion. If it slowed, or if its finely balanced interplay of forces was tampered with, it might break down. Cities were bigger; governments were assuming greater responsibilities; industries were more monopolistic; national budgets were higher; armaments were increasing fantastically; for everyone the business of living was becoming more complicated and expensive. Peoples could no longer live to themselves. Distances were shrinking. "One World" was almost a practical conception. A famine in India, a flood in China, a financial panic in the United States, an assassination in the Balkans, started a circle of widening repercussions.

Here indeed was an additional argument for peace. But if war on an extended scale should ever come, then, quite apart from its technological frightfulness, it would involve human life and wealth in ways unimagined hitherto. Not only would it mean unprecedented financial loss – financial collapse was the favorite "expert" prophecy before 1914 – but it would be a peoples' war, fought with an almost religious fanaticism, absorbing every man and woman and all the resources of the nations in it. German military theorists had coined the term "total war"; but the coming war was to have a "totality" which even they, these professional philosophers of war, had not conceived.

Such was the Western world of 1914. It is an academic question to ask whether, by any chance, it could have continued to exist, whether the particular turn of events that brought it down could have been prevented. The real inwardness of the predicament is largely hidden from us, and we still ask, in all humility, by what reason or unreason does a great civilization at the height of its maturity seem suddenly to go berserk and destroy itself? Yet this world of 1914, to all appearances, so progressive and secure, so rich in accomplishment, so full of hope and promise, was now to enter upon one of those intervals of general war which have sometimes marked the close of an old historical phase and the beginning of a new. Mankind was in the presence of events which for significance and magnitude can only be compared with such transitional epochs as the Fall of Rome or the Reformation. The Great Peace dissolved in an Age of Conflict, the course of which, it seems likely, is not yet fully run.

The Last Years of Peace

In the century from 1815 to 1914 four new states had arrived at the front rank of importance – two in Europe, one in the Far East, and one in the Western Hemisphere. At the beginning of the century Germany and Italy were geographical expressions; Japan was an unknown fastness; and the United States, not long since emerged from colonial status, still lay within 500 miles of the Atlantic seaboard. At the end of the century these four states were Great Powers. At the same time four other states were gradually falling into decay and anachronism – Imperial Austria, Tsarist Russia, Ottoman Turkey, and Manchu China. Mercifully history's troubles usually come singly. But it was now one of her major misfortunes that these eight states should all represent "problems" simultaneously crying out for a "solution."

The interests of Imperial Austria, Tsarist Russia, and Ottoman Turkey crossed and clashed at one particular point – the Balkans. Here lived a cluster of peoples who had felt all the storms and stresses of contemporary nationalism. Since the seventeenth century, Ottoman Turkey had been receding from her former conquests in the Middle Danube; and Austria, once Europe's defender against the Turk, had fallen heir to the evacuated territories. In theory, Turkish recession and Austrian advance might have continued indefinitely. But south of the Danube, in the Balkans, in the line of Austria's advance, lay an area of some wealth and strategic importance. Some of the Balkan peoples, notably the Serbs and Bulgars, were Slavs, and looked to Russia for support. Constantinople, the Turkish capital, was both the Rome of Russian Orthodoxy and Russia's hoped-for outlet to the Mediterranean Sea. Russia therefore was also a claimant to the residual Ottoman estate. Furthermore, two other Powers, Britain and France, themselves strongly entrenched in the Near East, were striving to keep the Ottoman Empire alive, not out of love for the Turk as such, but to contain the Russian encroachment. The Crimean War of 1854-56 was evidence of the lengths to which Britain and France were prepared to go to keep Russia at a safe distance from their preserves.

In 1878 Bismarck, the German Chancellor, had sponsored the Congress of Berlin in an attempt to stabilize this complex of contending forces, the "Eastern Question" as it was called. But Balkan pacification, for Bismarck, was only incidental to a larger policy, designed in the main to weaken France and to protect his own great political creation, the German Empire. In 1879, he brought Germany and Austria-Hungary into a Dual Alliance, and in 1881 he concluded the League of the Three Emperors – the German Kaiser, Austrian Emperor, and Russian Tsar. In 1882, he further fortified his system by bringing Germany, Austria-Hungary, and Italy into a Triple Alliance. In 1887, when the line between Berlin and St. Petersburg seemed to be breaking down, he entered into a "reinsurance treaty" with Russia. By 1890, thanks to Bismarck, Germany was hedged about with friends and allies, and France was Europe's diplomatic outcast. With herself the strongest Power in the continent, her one most likely enemy weak and isolated, and the Balkans quiescent, Germany's barometer of state should have set fair for many years to come.

But, in 1888, William II became German Kaiser. Under the German imperial constitution of the day he enjoyed all but absolute power, and every major act of German policy was executed in his name. Yet, with all his faults, William II was never the ogre of iniquity he was once made out to be. No one man could have loosed on the world all the ills of 1914. He is more to be condemned for what he represented than for what he was himself; for there is a curious way in which a monarch's character often reflects his people's. He was born and bred to military heroics. He adored the pomp and plumage of the parade ground. Photographs of himself with bristling mustaches, belligerently postured, in full military regalia, were to be seen in every shop and home of his Reich. Brilliant he was, gifted and versatile, but boisterous, touchy, and irresponsible. Impulsive arrogance was followed by timid withdrawals and indignant denials. His public speeches – and he spoke on every possible occasion – were awaited with anxiety throughout Europe. In 1890, this man, chafing under Bismarck's domination, dismissed him from the chancellorship.

Almost at once the Bismarckian alliance system went to pieces. France came out of her isolation to enter into an alliance with Russia, to be followed in 1892 by a precise military convention. Slowly but surely, Britain began to fall into line with France and Russia – Britain, who till then had been well disposed to Germany, whose blood and language were partly German, whose royal family was of German origin, who admired German culture and science, and who had even made offers of a German alliance. And, by a further strange and evil fate, as if to complete the European transformation, the affairs of the Three Emperors passed into the hands of advisers – Bülow in Germany, Aehrenthal in Austria, and Izvolsky in Russia – who were dilettantes in brinkmanship and who played politics as if it were a colossal game of chance.

Germany, Bismarck had once said, was a "saturated" power, averse to foreign adventures. Yet German colonial expansion had been proceeding during his later years in office, and, in 1890, when he was dismissed, the bulk of the German empire overseas had already been acquired. Various patriotic associations, such as the Colonial League, the Pan-German League, and the Navy League, came into existence in Germany to provide the necessary imperialistic ideology; and their efforts were often financially supported by German industrial magnates and armament manufacturers. The old Hanseatic cities, Lübeck, Hamburg, and Bremen, were reviving their traditions of maritime enterprise. But Bismarck, much as he may have encouraged Germany's "forward" *Weltpolitik,* had never permitted it to jeopardize his main European settlement, and Germany's colonialism was confined to areas in Africa and the Pacific relatively free from possible diplomatic complications. Under Bismarck it had been Germany's remarkable achievement to have seized a million square miles of territory overseas without exciting British suspicion – and to have done so sometimes even with British encouragement and good will.

By the international standards of the day Germany's imperialism was perfectly correct and meritorious. But, even if it had continued to be conducted with Bismarckian caution, it would probably have reached a stage at which, sooner or later, it must have encountered the opposition of Britain and, to a lesser extent, of France and Russia. It was now conducted, however, with the gratuitous tactlessness and intimidation which was coming to be associated with German foreign politics, and the Kaiser and his post-Bismarckian ministers reveled in a colonial diplomacy that succeeded in alarming and antagonizing all their European neighbors. Thus, in 1896, over the Kaiser's signature, a telegram was sent to Kruger, the Boer President, congratulating him on the repulse of the Jameson Raid. In 1897 Germany made use of the murder of two German missionaries in China to seize Tsingtao, to the extreme annoyance of Russia, who had promised that outpost to herself. Meanwhile German agents were busy in Turkey, building stretches of the Berlin-to-Baghdad railroad, acquiring an influence in the country which was virtually converting it into a German economic dependency, and realizing in a new direction the *Drang nach Osten* (drive toward the East) which was always supposed to have inspired the Teutonic conqueror. In 1898 the Kaiser, on a visit to Palestine, only a couple of years after the Armenian massacres, offered his protection to the Ottoman Sultan, "Abdul the Damned," and to the thirty million Moslems of the Near East. In the same year came the first of Germany's dreadnought navy bills, inspired by the Kaiser's redoubtable State-Secretary of the Navy, Admiral von Tirpitz – again perfectly correct, if it had not been simultaneously made plain that Germany was challenging the supremacy at sea which Britain had enjoyed since the Battle of Trafalgar and creating a High Seas Fleet to be the special toy of the Kaiser himself. During the South African War the German Government's attitude was officially circumspect, but no attempt was made to soften German public opinion in its most vehement pro-Boer moods or to hide the inference that, but for British sea power, German aid would have been sent to the Boer republics.

By the turn of the century the great Anglo-German naval race was on. Britain, perceiving that her former "splendid isolation" was no longer serving her so well, began to cast about for allies by revising her traditional foreign policy and by patching up her differences with her former rivals, France and Russia. Eventually France, Russia, and Britain entered into a Triple Entente. The newspapers of the day used to talk of an "Entente Cordiale," a looser association than the Triple Alliance, but the foundation of a progressively closer diplomatic and military collaboration. Germany, of course, complained of "encirclement"; Britain, she declared, "was pursuing her ancient policy of opposing whatever Continental Power happened momentarily to be the strongest." By 1907 the powers of Europe were marshaled into two potentially hostile camps – the Triple Alliance of Germany, Austria-Hungary, and Italy and the Triple Entente of France, Russia, and Britain.

Yet even then, to the average European citizen, general war seemed entirely remote and unreal. His mind was not conditioned to its possibility; responsible civilian leadership scarcely gave it a thought. The much-advertised armaments race – though the military expenditures of the Powers doubled between 1900 and 1914 – was little more than a budgetary annoyance. The Briton, for instance, might well wail at the recent increases in his income tax; but, in 1914, with the biggest navy in the world to support, he was still paying only 9 pence on the pound.[1] The illusion of perpetual peace was now confirmed by the successful circumvention of three penultimate minor crises and three penultimate minor wars which preceded the final catastrophe — the Morocco crisis of 1905, the Bosnian crisis of 1908, the Agadir crisis of 1911, the Tripolitan War of 1911, the First Balkan War of 1912, and the Second Balkan War of 1913.

In 1905 came the Morocco crisis. France regarded herself as having prior claims in Morocco. The territory adjoined her Algerian colony, and she contemplated its eventual annexation. But German commercial interests had also gained a foothold there. At the height of the crisis the Kaiser, with his unfailing instinct for provocative situations, paid a visit to Tangier and offered the Sultan of Morocco his championship. Britain took the part of her new ally, France, and would certainly have gone to her aid in the event of war. A conference of the powers was called together at Algeciras, with President Theodore Roosevelt interceding from a distance; Morocco was confirmed in nominal independence; the scare of war passed.

In 1908 came the Bosnian crisis. In that summer a revolution occurred in Turkey, the government of "Abdul the Damned" was overthrown, and a new political party, the "Young Turks," with a zealous program of reforms, seized control. Bulgaria made use of the occasion to revolt from Turkish rule and proclaim her independence. Austria, fearing changes in the Balkans that might aggrandize Serbia and thereby encourage unrest among her own Slavic subjects at home, proceeded formally to annex the Turkish provinces of Bosnia and Herzegovina, of which, since 1878, she had been in military occupation. The provinces were largely inhabited by Serbs, and Russia, protectively inclined toward them, looked as if she might intervene in force. As it was afterward revealed, Aehrenthal, the Austro-Hungarian Foreign Minister, had secured from Izvolsky, the Russian Foreign Minister, his secret connivance in the annexation — though, in public, Izvolsky roundly accused Aehrenthal of trickery. In any event, Russia, just recovering from the recent Russo-Japanese War, was in no fit state for new military adventures. Germany gave notice that she would support Austria; Bülow, the German Chancellor, induced Izvolsky to recognize the annexation. Once more the scare of war passed; Austria kept her provinces; Russia swallowed a diplomatic defeat; Germany had the satisfaction of standing "in shining armor" beside her Austrian ally; Serbs in Bosnia and Herzegovina stored up their hatred and frustration for another day.

In 1911 came the Agadir crisis. France and Germany again clashed over their interests in Morocco. The French marched into the Sultan's capital at Fez. Germany protested that the recent Algeciras agreement had been broken. A German gunboat, the *Panther,* appeared off Agadir, ostensibly to protect German nationals in Morocco. Britain again took the part of France. In a famous speech at the Mansion House in London, a speech that was all the more significant because of his pacifist reputation at that time, Lloyd George, the British Chancellor of the Exchequer, warned Germany that Britain would not buy peace at the price of humiliation. Once more the scare of war passed; Germany recognized France's right to a protectorate over Morocco and received in compensation a strip of the French Congo.

In 1911 also came the Tripolitan War. Italy, jealously eying the recent British and French colonial successes in North Africa and considering that she too deserved a share of the receding Ottoman Empire, declared war on Turkey and seized the Turkish dependency of Tripoli in North Africa and the Dodecanese Islands in the Mediterranean. She had previously secured British and French consent to the acquisition, and her own allies, Germany and Austria, could hardly say her nay. Tripoli was surrendered to her after an unexpected and embarrassing resistance. Italy undertook to withdraw from the Dodecanese Islands, but in 1915, when she entered the First World War, she was still in occupation.

In 1912 came the First Balkan War. The Young Turk revolution, the Bulgar revolt, and Italy's Tripolitan War were a tempting revelation of the weakness of the Ottoman Empire. Serbia, Montenegro, Greece, and Bulgaria banded together as the "Balkan League of Christian States" and resolved to complete the expulsion of the Turk from Europe and to free the remainder of their respective countrymen from the Turkish despotism. They declared war on Turkey, and in a short triumphant campaign drove the Turks back into their capital, Constantinople. The European Powers, profoundly concerned over the deterioration in the Balkans after years of quiescence, called a conference in London – a poor imitation of Bismarck's Congress of Berlin. Austria, seeking as always to curb the vaulting ambition of the Serbs, recognized the insurgent Albanians and sponsored an entirely new state of Albania under a German prince, thereby blocking the Serbs from access to the Adriatic Sea. Otherwise Serbia, Montenegro, Greece, and Bulgaria benefited by various extensions of their territories. Turkey lost her remaining Balkan possessions except the small strip of Thrace which covered Constantinople and the Dardanelles.

In 1913 came the Second Balkan War. The four victors of the Balkan League fell to quarreling over the division of the spoils. The London agreement was ignored. War broke out between Serbia, Montenegro, Greece, and Rumania on the one side, and Bulgaria on the other. Turkey returned to the charge, herself declared war on Bulgaria, and recaptured Adrianople. Bulgaria, overwhelmed by so strong a coalition, made peace at the cost of heavy concessions.

The War Begins

The several incidents of the "international anarchy" up to 1914 may have been of relatively small importance. They were like the sharp, painful twinges, ignored as soon as gone, which a man who has enjoyed a normal and scarcely conscious habit of good health feels, but which are in fact the warnings of a mortal sickness. There was no theoretical reason why the crisis of 1914 should have led to general war any more than the crisis of 1905 or 1908 or of any other intervening year. But each successive incident wore away a little more of the patient's margin of resistance, and the time would come when the hidden consumption suddenly took full possession of his members.

The Bosnian crisis of 1908 had left the Serbs in a state of extreme unrest. Serbian irredentism had suffered a blow to which the Serbian patriot could only give one answer. Serbs in Serbia and their brothers under Austrian rule were soon in full conspiracy for their national unification and independence. Their spearhead was the secret terrorist society, the Black Hand, recruited from Serbian army officers, civil servants, and students. Among its members were Colonel Dimitrievich, chief of the Serbian Military Intelligence, and probably Alexander, the Serbian Prince Regent. Covert Russian support, threats of Austrian countermeasures, and political intrigue in Serbia kept the temperature at fever pitch. Then, on June 28, 1914, the Archduke Francis Ferdinand, nephew and heir of the Austrian Emperor Francis Joseph, paid a ceremonial visit to the Bosnian capital of Sarajevo, and, on that fatal day, he and his wife, the Countess Chotek, were shot by a nineteen-year-old Bosnian student.

By a tragic irony the Archduke Francis Ferdinand had been a liberal-minded man who, had he come to the throne, would have made a genuine trial of racial conciliation in Austria-Hungary. His assassin was a certain Gavrilo Princip, armed and trained by the Black Hand. The complicity of the Serbian Government has never been satisfactorily confirmed. The Serbian Premier, Pashich, through the Serbian minister in Vienna, tried to inform the Austrian authorities that a plot was afoot in Sarajevo, but the minister, himself a frenzied Serbian nationalist, failed to deliver the warning. At the time, however, no one on either side was in any mood to consider too judicially where the real guilt lay. The crime was barbarous enough, and even in Sarajevo crowds were soon parading the streets, singing Austrian patriotic songs, shouting "Down with Serbia!" and raiding Serbian shops and hotels. Anti-Serbian demonstrations occurred over the length and breadth of Austria-Hungary. Obviously the Austrian Government would have to take some sort of "punitive action" against the "focus of criminal agitation in Belgrade" and against Serbia herself "as a political power factor in the Balkans."

Meanwhile in Belgrade there had been unconcealed rejoicing. The crime had been committed, it so happened, on St. Vitus' Day, a Serbian national holiday, and the coincidence was too much for a people of primitive tempers, not given to hiding their feelings. The Serbian Prince Regent addressed his formal condolences to the Austrian Emperor, and the holiday celebrations were officially called off. But no one was deceived. In the Serbian press the assassin of Sarajevo was already a martyr and hero. Irritation fed on irritation, and the peoples of the two countries were almost surprised when war did not immediately break out between them.

However, the Austro-Hungarian Government seemed in no hurry to move, and the rest of Europe was reassured by the evident relaxing of a crisis which at first had looked hardly more serious than other international crises of the past decade. The European press was content to condemn this new Balkan atrocity and to trust that, as seemed already likely, time would heal the injury. The Balkans would always be the "turbulent" Balkans, liable to recurrent "imbroglios." For the average citizen of 1914 peace was a habit, and summer was the holiday season. Surely the most lurid prophets of doom in their wildest fantasies could not have foretold that a sordid political killing in a remote Balkan town was to let loose upon the world such wars and revolutions as it had never known before, or could have conceived a fraction of all the woes and agonies that were now to be crowded into the experience of a single generation.

On July 5, 1914, the situation took a more serious turn. On that day, at Potsdam, the Kaiser received at lunch the Austro-Hungarian ambassador in Germany, Count Szögyény-Marich, bearing a personal letter from the Austrian Emperor together with a strong memorandum setting out the Austrian view. The Kaiser, at first correct and cautious, but then warming to the excitement of the occasion, impulsively assured his guest that Austria-Hungary could reckon on Germany's "full support . . . even if matters went to the length of a war between Austria-Hungary and Russia." The Kaiser had little trouble in bringing round to his point of view Bethmann-Hollweg, the German Chancellor, who was also at Potsdam later the same day. The Kaiser then consulted his military chiefs and, on the morrow, to allay disquiet, went off on his holiday cruise in the North Sea.

Such is the usual story of the Kaiser's famous "blank check" to his Austrian ally. The impression prevailed in Vienna that Germany would endorse strong action, even war, on the part of Austria-Hungary against Serbia — and the sooner the better. Count Berchtold, the Austro-Hungarian Foreign Minister, considered that "the moment had arrived to render Serbia innocuous once and for all by a display of force," and he resolved to present her with an ultimatum that would give her the alternatives of vassalage or extinction. Count Tisza, the Hungarian Premier, alone offered Berchtold any determined opposition, but even Tisza withdrew his objections when convinced of Germany's attitude. Berchtold's ultimatum, after calculated delays, was delivered to the Serbian Government in Belgrade on July 23. It demanded the suppression of all subversive nationalist propaganda and of conspirative societies in Serbia, the dismissal of officials in the Serbian Government who were suspected of connivance in the assassination at Sarajevo and whom the Austro-Hungarian Government would afterwards name, and the collaboration of Austrian representatives in investigations to be conducted by the Serbian police. A time limit of forty-eight hours was given for the unconditional acceptance of the terms.

The tenor of the ultimatum had been known in Berlin, and its actual text was seen by the German Foreign Minister, von Jagow, twenty-four hours before it was delivered. The German Government at once addressed notes to Russia, France, and Britain asserting that the Austro-Hungarian demands were no more than "fair and moderate" and urging a "localization" of the crisis. Sazonov, the Russian Foreign Minister, when he first heard of the ultimatum, exclaimed, *"C'est la guerre européenne!"* and at once demanded partial Russian mobilization against Austria. Sir Edward Grey, the British Foreign Secretary, avowed that the ultimatum was "the most formidable document" he had ever seen addressed to an independent state and proposed a conference of mediation between the Powers not directly involved, namely Germany, France, Italy, and Britain. The proposal was accepted by France and Italy, but rejected by Germany on the plea that "she could not drag Austria in her conflict with Serbia before a European tribunal." Sazonov would have preferred a "private exchange of ideas"

William II, German Kaiser, in the uniform of Chef (Colonel in Chief) of the Garde-Kürassier Regiment

RADIO TIMES HULTON

with Austria through the Austrian ambassador in St. Petersburg. But, in any event, it was clear that Russia would not now stand by while Austria-Hungary subjugated Serbia, a kindred Slavic state, and played havoc with Russian interests in the Balkans. If Russia fought, Austria's ally Germany would fight; if Germany fought, Russia's ally France would fight. Berchtold, it seemed, had unstopped the European dike. Austria's "punitive action" against Serbia bade fair to become a European war.

The Serbian Government's reply to the ultimatum was delivered in person by Pashich, the Serbian Premier, to the Austro-Hungarian minister at Belgrade on July 25, within five minutes of the time limit. It was a capitulation on all but one or two points of detail. But the Austro-Hungarian minister, instructed to receive unconditional acceptance or nothing, broke off relations there and then, and hurried home to report to Berchtold and to the Austrian Emperor. Certainly the Serbian order for mobilization on July 25, before the reply was delivered, had not seemed like the act of a penitent asking for clemency. Berchtold himself may still have hoped for peace, but he was not now to be balked of his "display of force." On July 26 the Austrian Emperor consented to order partial mobilization. On

July 28 Austria-Hungary declared war on Serbia. On July 29 Austrian artillery bombarded Belgrade.

There were two unforeseen factors in the situation as it had now developed. One was the detachment of civilians and soldiers from each other's business; the other was the extreme rigidity of the war plans of the various general staffs. The mobilization in whole or even in part of a great European army was a stupendous administrative undertaking; yet a Berchtold or a Sazonov labored under the delusion that this or that military threat, commensurate with this or that political situation, could be ordered at will. Berchtold, clinging fondly to the doctrine of "the localization of the conflict," wanted a "display of force" against Serbia without in the least understanding what it really meant. Sazonov wanted partial Russian mobilization against Austria and was amazed to be told, too late, that the Russian General Staff had no plan for partial mobilization. For Russia it had to be general mobilization, or none. The Tsar, fighting weakly for peace, bewildered by events, and perhaps deliberately misled by his advisers, signed two orders, one for partial and one for general mobilization. On July 30 it was his order for general mobilization which was issued. The Kaiser replied by proclaiming a "state of danger of war." At midnight on July 31, Germany dispatched an ultimatum to Russia demanding the suspension of "all war measures." On August 1 the Kaiser ordered general mobilization, and Germany declared war on Russia.

Meanwhile France, Belgium, Luxembourg, and Britain were being inexorably involved. On July 29 the French President and Premier, Poincaré and Viviani, returned to Paris from a state visit to St. Petersburg, whither they had gone for a ceremonial confirmation of the Franco-Russian alliance. The crisis indeed had mounted to its climax while they were still at sea. On July 31 a German note to France demanded to know the French attitude in the event of hostilities between Germany and Russia, but the most the German ambassador in Paris could elicit was the short answer that France "would have regard to her own interest." If France on this occasion had offered to remain neutral, the German ambassador had been instructed to make the impossible demand that she surrender the fortresses of Toul and Verdun as a "pledge." But on August 1 the French Government ordered general mobilization — actually an hour and a half before the German mobilization order on the same day. On August 3 Germany declared war on France.

Belgium and Luxembourg in 1914, wedged between France and Germany, were states whose perpetual neutrality and inviolability the Powers — Germany among them — had solemnly guaranteed.[2] But early on August 2, German troops invaded Luxembourg. Later the same day Germany sent the Belgian Government a twelve-hour ultimatum demanding a free passage for the German Army across Belgium to the French frontier. She offered to reward Belgium's compliance with a pledge of independence and integrity, but would treat her resistance as an act of war. The Belgian Government refused the German demand, and appealed to her guarantors, Britain, France, and Russia.

In Britain, all through these strenuous days, opinion had been vacillating and divided. In that insular and complacent realm there were few indeed who had so much as heard of guarantees to Belgium or of naval commitments to France. The Labor party, in so far as it was interested in international affairs at all, was doctrinally pacifist. There was an important isolationist element in the Cabinet itself. Sir Edward Grey, the Foreign Secretary, ingenuous and high-principled when ingenuousness and high principles were at a discount, at first tried to take the view that the Austro-Serbian quarrel was no concern of Britain. But, even had he desired otherwise, he could do little but wait on developments. The one positive action was that of Winston Churchill, then First Lord of the Admiralty. On July 26, on his advice, the British Navy, already mobilized for the Royal Naval Review at Portland, was ordered not to disperse, and on the 28th the main battle fleet proceeded to its war station at Scapa Flow in the Orkneys. But the German ultimatum to Belgium, no less than the peremptory tone in which it was couched, decided the swing of public opinion, and on the morning of August 4 the British Government, with the full support of Parliament, dispatched an ultimatum to Germany demanding to know whether Germany would respect her treaty guarantees to Belgium. The German Chancellor, on receipt of the ultimatum, asked bitterly if Britain, "just for a word 'neutrality,' . . . just for a scrap of paper, was going to make war on a kindred nation who desired nothing better than to be friends with her," thus uttering what must surely be one of the most famous and revealing lapses of the tongue in history. An hour before midnight on August 4, Britain was at war with Germany.

Of the powers of Europe, Italy alone stood aloof. Deeming that her German and Austrian allies had provoked an aggressive war without consulting her, in violation of the precise terms of the Triple Alliance, Italy declared her neutrality on August 3.[3]

The British Dominions and India responded to the crisis spontaneously and ardently and made ready to give the mother country every support in their power. The little Balkan state of Montenegro made common cause with Serbia. Portugal proclaimed her fidelity to an old alliance with Britain. Finally, on August 23, Britain's ally in the Far East, Japan, declared war on Germany. In Europe, Asia, Australasia, and Africa, populations aggregating nearly 1,000,000,000 were at war.

It is hard to comment on events of which so much is known and so much is still inexplicable. Yet this may still be worth saying: The earlier European crises of 1905-13 had blown over because, every time, someone had given way. The settlements had been marked by what in later years would have been called appeasement. But appeasement generates its own intolerance. By 1914 the parties to the new dispute were too much touched in that imponderable value, their prestige. Austria had to prove to herself — and to her German ally — that she was stronger than her nationalist elements, or else accept disruption at their hands. Germany could not afford another diplomatic setback like those of 1905 and 1911. Russia could not afford a repetition of 1908. France, in exhorting Russia to "firmness," could herself show no less a virtue. Soberly, none may have wanted war; but all wanted the emotional self-reassertion which, ultimately, only war could give. Professional misinformation and administrative rigidity did the rest.

THE NATIONS AT WAR IN AUGUST 1914

The Central Powers	*The Allies*
Austria-Hungary *	Serbia
Germany *	Russia †
	France †
	Luxembourg
	Belgium
(Italy, neutral) *	Britain and the British Empire †
	Montenegro
	Portugal
	Japan

* The Triple Alliance   † The Triple Entente

Yet prestige on this particular occasion perhaps went deeper. It was almost as if the peoples of Europe, with some collective sixth sense, realized that they were at the turning of an epoch. The old order was slipping away, and there were many who would have been false to themselves if they had not tried to seize it and stop its going. There was an overbearing fatality in the air, an Either-Or, between whose horns the existence of a world was in suspension. Statesmanship seemed to be under some kind of compulsion which was beyond its experience to resist or even to understand.

Among the peoples of Europe at large, however, when the sticking point came, the mass response was all but unanimous. The "causes" of the First World War have too often been described in terms of diplomatic notes and conversations, as if a few gold-braided, bemedaled gentlemen, seated at half a dozen tables in half a dozen chancelleries, had had it in their power to order 1,000,000,000 human beings to kill or to be killed. The mass passion in that July and August 1914 was less palpable than the documents which historians have since pored over so diligently, but it was nonetheless a historical fact, a fact deserving of more attention than it has usually been given. Profound as the Great Peace may have been, the First World War, at its outbreak, was undeniably a popular war. In 1914, in no nation affected, was there an important antiwar party. Pacifists and socialists disavowed their faiths, or were driven from the field in confusion. The International Socialist Bureau, meeting at Brussels at the end of July, was entirely ineffective in the face of the crisis. Political parties of every belligerent country, in the midst of domestic strife, declared their *Burgfriede* or their *Union Sacrée*.[4] The British House of Commons, the German *Reichstag*, the French Chamber, the Russian Duma expressed their respective wills with hardly an adverse vote. For the men and the women who lived through that August week, the outstanding impression was of the cheering, singing, marching masses. It was the same before the Winter Palace in St. Petersburg, on the Unter den Linden in Berlin, on the Champs Elysées in Paris, in Trafalgar Square or the Mall in London. Far from being innocents led to the slaughter, the peoples of Europe led their leaders. Ministers of Emperor, Tsar, Kaiser, King, and President watched the press and the streets during these demented days and fell victim to the hysteria as helplessly as any of the nameless multitudes about them.

2. THE OPENING PHASES—1914-15

The Campaigns of 1914 on Land

The war plan had been the professional peacetime preoccupation of every European general staff. It was constantly revised according to circumstances—changes in rates of mobilization or in strengths of reserves, new weapons and tactics, new alliances, and all predictable political complications. It was rehearsed at annual maneuvers. In the first week of August 1914, four great general staffs, by the dispatch of a few sheaves of telegrams, set in motion colossal dispositions long prepared and practised in the minutest detail. The common belief at the time was that the war would be a short, orgiastic episode. At the signal, armies of millions rushed into their schedules in a huge gamble for lightning Napoleonic victories. Europe, which had not seen a major battle since 1877,[1] was led by officers for whom war was largely a matter of staff-college manuals into campaigns comparable with the Mongol ravages of the fourteenth century.

The German plan, inherited in part from Count von Schlieffen, Chief of Staff from 1891 to 1907, was designed to take advantage of the slow Russian mobilization by throwing the main weight of the German Army against France and defeating her in a campaign of six weeks. It counted on Germany's efficient railroads for the rapid concentration of seven out of the eight German armies—not only front-line troops but reservists—in the initial offensives. It would outflank the French fortification system between Verdun and Belfort and invade the open French country by way of the comparatively unfortified northeastern frontier, thus involving Belgium and Luxembourg, of whose neutrality Germany herself was a guarantor.[2] The operation would take the form of a huge encirclement, hinging on Verdun, pushing up the Belgian Meuse and across the Champagne. Once France had been eliminated, the victorious Germans would then turn at leisure against the now gathering Russian hordes on the East Prussian frontier.

The first part of the plan went like clockwork. Five hundred German troop trains a day ran up to the Belgian frontier. The Belgian defense was stubborn, especially round the fortress of Liége, and must have been very disconcerting to the "paper" strategists in the German High Command,[3] but it did not seriously delay the invasion timetable. The French

Army, meanwhile, in accordance with the French "Plan 17," had attempted the invasion and reconquest of the lost provinces of Alsace and Lorraine and had been repulsed in some of the heaviest fighting to occur in the war. The British Expeditionary Force, successfully shipped across the Channel, saw its first action at Mons against divisions of the German right wing.

The German plan failed. To do him justice, Schlieffen himself had predicted that it would fail. It attempted too much, and too quickly. Even in the Second World War, with all the motorized forces, air reconnaissance, and radio that were then available, a division was not expected to advance more than two hundred miles without pausing to re-form. Yet the German High Command now forced its famous right wing to cover four hundred miles. In 1914 a million Germans poured into France, sometimes marching twenty to thirty miles a day on foot, and a campaign which had been perfectly prepared and perfectly begun was soon a swarming, headlong, rather tired mass of men which any setback would throw into complete disorder. In those days communications were kept by cavalry and motor cyclists, many of whom now lost their way in the pace and confusion of the advance. By the last week in August, German corps commanders were often out of touch with their headquarters and with one another. Several divisions had outmarched their artillery, their supplies, even their field kitchens. Unbelievable though it may be, General von Moltke, the German commander, hardly knew for days on end where his armies were.

Yet France came very close to defeat. By the first week of September the Germans had reached the River Marne. Paris was in a panic. The French Government was evacuated to Bordeaux. Then the French and British forces counterattacked on the German flank, and they counterattacked an enemy who had already lost his original cohesion and momentum. General Joffre, the French commander, had waited for the right moment, and, when he struck at last, struck for a decision. The First Battle of the Marne occupied five days, from September 6 to 10. It was one of the great deliverances of history. The bewildered Germans, who had tumbled irresistibly through Belgium and northern France, halted and drew back, hardly understanding what had beaten them or whether indeed they had been beaten. The success of the action persuaded Joffre to repeat it, and the opposing armies entered upon a competition in flanking and counterflanking ever more westward and northward, a competition which developed into what has since been called the "Race to the Sea." Joffre sent General Foch to coordinate the heterogeneous group of French, British, and Belgian divisions which now concentrated in the Nord. By mid-October the combatants stretched from Flanders to the borders of Switzerland, locked in that curious tactical immobility in which for the next four years they were fated to remain.

On September 14, 1914, General von Falkenhayn, former Prussian Minister of War, had superseded the discredited Moltke. During October and November, the new commander, paying a last despairing homage to Schlieffen, delivered against the British forces in Flanders a series of attacks which have become known as the First Battle of Ypres and which were intended to turn the British flank and seize the Channel ports. But the British line

THE GERMAN INVASION OF BELGIUM AND FRANCE, 1914

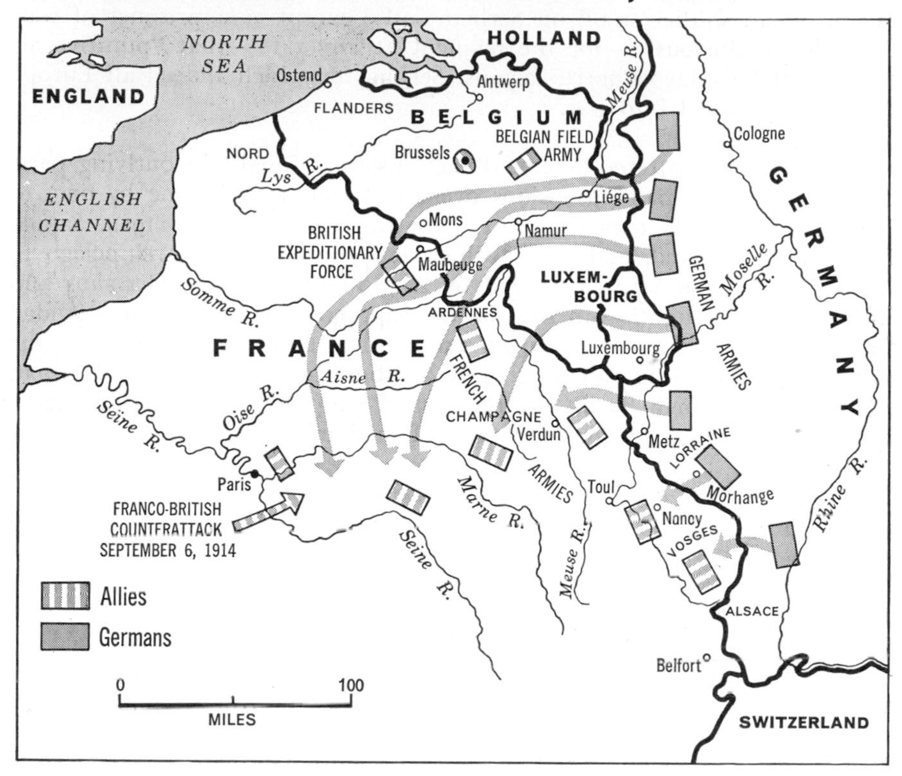

held fast, and the last chances of an early German decision on the Western front irrevocably faded away.

Meanwhile operations had been proceeding along the Eastern front. Here, in accordance with the contradictory fortunes of war, the Germans compensated for their failure in France by a victory for which Schlieffen had not provided. Between August 25 and 30, 1914, Field Marshal von Hindenburg and General Ludendorff, the German commanders in East Prussia, with the eighth of the German armies – the only army on that front – fought the Battle of Tannenberg, one of those perfect, chessboard Hannibalic set pieces which are "the joy of military historians and the grave of nations." The opposing Russian army was annihilated.

Further south, along the Polish-Ukrainian borderlands, the Austro-Hungarian Army under Field Marshal Conrad von Hötzendorf was engaged in a confused series of battles and was steadily borne down by the greater Russian numbers. In two months of this "Unknown War," as Churchill has called it, the Austrians were driven out of their fertile province of Galicia, and, in casualties, the two combatants together lost half a million men.[4] On the Serbian front the Austrian forces, depleted by withdrawals to the Russian front, at last launched an attack across the Danube upon the Serbian capital, Belgrade. But the Serbian defenses held, and, on Christmas Day 1914, the Serbian commander was able to report that not one Austrian soldier stood on Serbian soil — except as a prisoner of war. So ended ingloriously — for the moment at any rate — that "punitive action," that "display of force" against Serbia, for which indeed all Europe had been plunged into war.

A number of scattered "colonial" actions were fought in outlying parts of the globe. German possessions overseas began to fall, one by one, to British and French expeditions. In August and September 1914, Samoa fell to New Zealand, and New Guinea and the Bismarck Archipelago to Australia. Togoland was occupied by Anglo-French forces. Germans and Portuguese were fighting in Angola. On September 2, the Japanese landed in Shantung, and in a hard-fought campaign of two months they took the German port of Tsingtao. During November they occupied the German islands in the North Pacific. By the end of 1914 only the American hemisphere had escaped the omnipresence of military operations.

The Beginning of the Allied Naval Blockade

Naval power rested predominantly with the Allies. From the start Britain was resolved that her traditional strategy of blockade should go into effect. In July 1914, the British Navy had already been mobilized for the Royal Naval Review at Portland, and by the first week of August it was at its war stations — the Grand Fleet, under Admiral Sir John Jellicoe, at Scapa Flow, and the First Battle Cruiser Squadron, under Admiral Sir David Beatty, at Rosyth. By the end of August, German merchant ships were swept from the seas. German warships were sunk or chased to home or neutral ports. The German battle cruiser *Goeben* and the light cruiser *Breslau* made good their escape into the Dardanelles, there to participate in an episode which we shall shortly relate. (See p. 24.) The cruiser *Emden* was run aground in the Indian Ocean. In December Spee's squadron, with the new armored cruisers, *Scharnhorst* and *Gneisenau,* was destroyed off the Falklands. The last German surface ship on the high seas, the light cruiser *Dresden,* was sunk in March 1915 off the coast of Chile. The total siege of the Central Powers, Germany and Austria-Hungary,[5] was gradually established. In the whole course of the war, except for sporadic cruiser sorties in the North Sea and except for the one great Battle of Jutland in 1916, the German Navy made no attempt to break out of the cover of its home bases and mine fields.

The blockade was the supreme economic weapon of the war and soon developed into a ramifying political struggle which involved belligerents and neutrals alike. For as soon as her own seaports were rendered idle, Germany had recourse to those of her neutral neighbors. Norway, Sweden, Denmark, Holland, Switzerland, the Balkans — and Italy till her entry into the war — became backdoor entrances for a suddenly expanded transit trade with the Reich. Christiana, Copenhagen, Rotterdam, and Genoa took the place of Hamburg, Bremen, Antwerp, and Trieste. The Allied blockade, already successful in the stoppage of German commerce, developed perforce into the stoppage of abnormal neutral commerce as well.

The step thence into the erudite complexities of international law was a short one. Today a cynical world can almost marvel at the reams of paper that were once so closely written and closely argued upon the interminable topics of visit and search, continuous voyage, and contraband. Britain and France, supposedly in the interests of safety, adopted the practice of diverting neutral merchant ships to their own ports for purposes of search, and they proceeded to seize any goods whose "destination, ownership, or origin were presumed to be hostile." They continually added to their lists of contraband, till there was hardly an importable commodity which, if found on a neutral ship near German waters, was exempt from seizure. Foodstuffs, as well as the more obvious materials and munitions of war, were made subject to the most rigorous control. By 1916 and 1917, Britain and France were even "rationing" neutrals and seizing any goods which appeared to be entering neutral ports contiguous to Germany in excess of former peacetime quantities.

The blockade tactics of Britain and France were highhanded in the extreme, but it was never easy to establish against either power literal or explicit breaches of international law. In particular the United States – a neutral till 1917 – whose trade with European neutrals was thus arbitrarily intercepted, protested with the greatest vigor; and had it not been for Germany's more criminal and spectacular malpractices at sea, Britain's and France's conduct might not have escaped so lightly. We have only to read the diplomatic correspondence between Britain and the United States in 1915 and 1916 to realize how fine was the edge of friendship and rupture between the two Atlantic nations. But we must defer this part of the narrative to a later page. (See pp. 62ff.)

The Entry of Turkey into the War

A local quarrel between Austria and Serbia had been the immediate occasion of the European conflict, but the sympathies of the other Balkan states were not yet evident. The Balkan Wars of 1912-13 had weakened them, but left them with unsatisfied antagonisms. They all had wrongs to right and scores to settle. Their friendships had been sought after by the European Powers and were already mortgaged under loans and military missions. Their royal families had devious links with those of Central Europe. Their active alliances might now be purchasable with promises of territory. Meanwhile they watched the opening battles of 1914 on the Meuse, the Vistula, and the Danube, and wondered whom among the giants it might soon be most expedient to support.

Yet, of all the states in this area, Turkey was the first to forsake the straight and narrow way of neutrality. For many years past she had been subject to the attentions of Germany. Her loans had been floated in Berlin; her new railroads had been built by German engineers; her army had been remodeled by a German military mission. The Young Turk "Triumvirate," Talaat Pasha, Enver Pasha, and Jemal Pasha, who shared the chief offices in the Turkish Government, were ambitious place seekers and probable Germanophiles if the right kind of persuasion was applied.

Two German warships, the *Goeben* and the *Breslau,* finally tipped the Turkish scales in favor of Germany. The outbreak of war found the ships cruising the Mediterranean, and early in August they appeared at the mouth of the Dardanelles. By the Treaty of London of 1871 that waterway was closed to battleships in time of war. But Enver Pasha, without consulting his cabinet, acceded to the pressure of his German advisers and ordered the forts along the Dardanelles to allow the *Goeben* and the *Breslau* an unchallenged passage.

The *Goeben* and the *Breslau* at once gave Turkey the control of the Black Sea – the Russian fleet had no ships of like armament – and they could even terrorize Constantinople in case of need. The Allied ambassadors protested and threatened. The Turkish Government went through the form of purchasing the ships for its own navy, the German sailors on board were fitted out with fezzes, and the ships remained. Events now moved quickly. On October 29 an engagement between the Russian and Turkish fleets took place in the Black Sea; the *Goeben* and the *Breslau* participated, and the Russian ports of Odessa and Sevastopol were bombarded. During early November, Russia, Britain, and France formally declared war on Turkey. An Allied squadron bombarded the outer forts of the Dardanelles; a British submarine torpedoed a Turkish battleship in the Narrows. A British-Indian force landed in Mesopotamia. Britain declared a protectorate over Egypt. The "Anzacs" – the Australia-New Zealand Army Corps – began to arrive in the Suez area for the defense of the Canal.[6]

The Turkish Sultan proclaimed a Holy War, and some halfhearted demonstrations were staged in Constantinople. But the Arabs and the Moslem world as a whole ignored the call. The Arabs nursed anti-Turkish grievances of their own; the Sherif of Mecca had already made secret contacts with the British High Commissioner in Cairo. Meanwhile the Young Turk leaders, Enver and Jemal, left for their respective fronts. Enver's forces attacked Russian Armenia – the first step, he claimed, in an Alexandrian advance on India. Jemal's forces attacked the Suez Canal. Both attacks, after initial successes, were brought to a halt. In 1915, as we shall see, Turkey was engaged in a much more significant campaign in the Dardanelles. (See pp. 29-31.)

The Entry of Italy into the War

In 1914 Germany, Austria-Hungary, and Italy were members of the Triple Alliance. But the alliance was defensive, one of its provisions was a guarantee of the *status quo* in the Balkans, and it was specifically understood not to be directed against Britain. The Austrian ultimatum to Serbia in 1914, however, presumed an offensive war; it bore all the traces of having been hatched by Germany and Austria-Hungary in secret without consultation with their Italian ally; it patently disturbed the *status quo* in the Balkans; and it led indirectly to the involvement of Britain. Every obligation that had bound Italy to the Triple Alliance had been incontinently broken, and on August 3, 1914, she declared her neutrality.

Thereafter, till her entry into the war, Italy played a tantalizing diplomatic game. "Compensations" from either belligerent group to entice the hesitant nation into the fray became larger and more pressing with repetition. Baron Sonnino, the Italian Foreign Minister, bargained with skill, but it was very clear, as time went on, that Italy had ambitions far beyond what Austria-Hungary would ever be willing, or able, to satisfy. Italy not only wanted the liberation of those of her nationals who were still subject to Austrian rule, but she also wanted a general extension of her interests and influence in the Adriatic, Balkans, and Near East, and only the Allies, Britain and France, if victorious, would be in a position to meet her full demands.

On April 26, 1915, Britain, France, Russia, and Italy signed the secret Treaty of London. Italy engaged herself to enter the war jointly with the Allies "against all their enemies." In return she was to receive the Trentino and the Tirol up to the Brenner Pass, Trieste, Gorizia, Gradisca, the Istrian Peninsula and Dalmatia; the sovereignty of Valona and Saseno, and of the Dodecanese; a share in the eventual partition of Turkey, namely Adalia; and compensation in Africa, if Britain and France should, at Germany's expense, increase their colonial territories there. The Holy See was to be excluded from the peace negotiations at the end of the war. Fiume, it is interesting to note in view of its later importance, and certain other Adriatic ports were to be assigned to "Croatia, Serbia, and Montenegro."

To many an observer, Italian affairs in 1914 and early 1915 were moving not to war but to revolution. The condition in which the country found itself was not unlike the condition in which it was again to find itself after the war, just before the Fascist seizure of control. Yet in the end, in the name of "sacred egoism," Italy achieved the transition to active belligerency with something of the zest of the other nations in the conflict. On May 20, 1915, the Italian Premier, Salandra, asked the Chamber for extraordinary powers. Of a full roster of Deputies present at the session, the only notable absentee was the noninterventionist, Giolitti. Salandra's bill was adopted by an overwhelming vote. The Deputies rose to their feet, cheering and singing wildly. On May 23, 1915, Italy declared war on Austria-Hungary. Two days later the King left for the front. But though Italy had engaged herself to enter the war on the side of the Allies "against *all* their enemies," she showed a remarkable reluctance to break with her former German ally, and she seemed at first to be trying to fight a lesser war of her own within the greater one. She did not declare war on Germany till August 27, 1916.

The Campaigns of 1915 on Land

The First World War was fought in the main by the massed armies of great industrial powers, and its curious tactical novelties were missed at first by all the combatants. A century's growth of population and industrial expansion created its appropriate warfare. The numbers of men in the field were enormously increased. Waterloo was fought by 170,000 men; Sedan by 300,000; the First Battle of the Marne by over a million. Increased numbers required increased armament, and the result was a kind of congested siege. After the Marne in 1914, the battle lines hardened into a "front," which was almost a scandal and offense to the professional military conscience of the time. Moltke and Falkenhayn, no less than Joffre, had been schooled in the war of maneuver. British commanders, like French and Haig, had been cavalry generals in the recent South African War. All thought in terms of deployments, communications, envelopments – not of trenches and week-long artillery bombardments with their vast material expenditure. Even Lord Kitchener in Britain, who had had the exceptional imagination to foresee a four-year conflict and to demand a British Army of the unprecedented size of 70 divisions and 3,000,000 men, could not appreciate the altered tactics which these masses of men were to use. It was left to a few civilians of genius, like Rathenau in Germany and Lloyd George in Britain, to rise to the real needs of the situation.

On the field of battle the rapid-firing rifle and the machine gun were the "dominant" weapons, and their "fire power," when both sides possessed enough of them, all but reduced the combatants to immobility. On the Western front, from the end of 1914, millions of infantrymen crouched in earthen ditches from which they could emerge only at the cost of prohibitive casualties and then after intensive "artillery preparation." Two lines of trenches meandered through Belgium and France, and between them lay the ragged, shell-pocked, wire-entangled isthmus of "No Man's Land," sometimes widening to several hundred yards, sometimes narrowing to as little as fifty feet. Behind the lines, concentrations of artillery sought to redress the excessive fire power of the infantry. Cavalry, the old mobile arm, was completely useless. By 1916 barbed-wire entanglements had become great belts, thirty yards broad, laced to iron stakes and trestles, three to five feet high; front lines had grown from a single trench or breastwork into a system of triple trenches one hundred and fifty to two hundred yards apart; dugouts were tunneled to depths of twenty to thirty feet, each capable of sheltering twenty men or more; concrete machine-gun nests were strewn in the rear; and behind all this again lay second and third lines of support trenches and artillery positions. Developments in 1917, for instance the Hindenburg Line, were even more formidable.

The soldier living under such conditions suffered appalling hardship, especially in low-lying country when his trenches were waterlogged. Only efficient medical services – and his own incredibly stubborn morale – saved him from being swept away by sickness. This was the pattern of warfare on the Western front, and the situation was soon analogous in different geographies and terrains, as in Gallipoli or the Italian Alps. On the Eastern front the same rigid conditions did not obtain. The lines were thinner; the Russian technical resources were less developed. In 1915, as we shall relate, the Russian army went down to virtual defeat in the field. But where arms and manpower on either side bore any equivalence, there the trench deadlock automatically supervened.

An inventive age, which gave so much of its best intelligence to military

THE EASTERN FRONT, 1914-17

science, might have been expected to discover a solution. What technology had made it should have been able to unmake. The Germans, for example, tried the flame thrower, a not very successful device, dangerous to its operator. They tried poison gas, a weapon depending on the surprise of its first employment, after which its effectiveness was largely lost to appropriate protection and to retaliation. The hand grenade, trench mortar, and steel helmet were added to the equipment of the infantryman. In 1917 the British in Flanders dug tunnels under the German positions which they then mined.

But in the main the generals, German, French, and British, came to rely more and more on their artillery. The enemy's barbed wire and trenches, rifles and machine guns were to be battered into total demolition. *"L'artillerie conquiert, l'infanterie occupe,"* as the French put it. Tactical discussions ranged around the weight and duration of the bombardment. The expenditure of shells led to industrial crises on the home front. Even in 1915, 250,000 shells could be fired in a single offensive and, as if to make a virtue of necessity, it was already normal to talk eruditely about "attrition" or *"la bataille d'usure."* But the time was to come when the British, for example at the Somme in 1916, used one gun for every twenty yards on a fourteen-mile front and 1,500,000 shells; and at Vimy in 1917, one gun for every nine yards on an eleven-mile front and 2,600,000 shells. In April 1917, during Nivelle's offensive in the Champagne, on a twenty-five mile front, the French Fifth and Sixth Armies fired 6,000,000 shells. And these figures were surpassed in 1918. Yet, despite all the metal thus squandered and the casualties thus caused, the gains in ground were strategically negligible. The Germans used to refer to the "field of corpses" (*Leichenfeld*) in front of their trenches after an Allied offensive. Pacifists might argue — as many did at the time — that modern warfare was not only inhuman, but had become impossible. The tank — a "self-propelled, bulletproof landship," virtually an armored car borne on caterpillar tractors — the most promising solution of the trench deadlock, though it existed in embryo in 1914, was being built in 1916 and went into action for the first time in a British sector of the Western front in September of that year.

But we anticipate. In the spring of 1915, on the Western front, the combatants delivered their offensives against their opponents' trench systems — the French in the Champagne, the British at Neuve-Chapelle, the Germans in what has since come to be known as the Second Battle of Ypres — the action in which they used poison gas for the first time. But in 1915 the most significant fighting was on the Eastern front. The German High Command turned toward Russia for the decision which it had been denied in France. On May 2, 1915, in northern Galicia, Falkenhayn and Conrad launched a great offensive with one of those concentrations of artillery which, as we have said, were now to be the tactical feature in every theater. Here, on the Eastern front, was no bristling trench system with machine-gun nests at every hundred yards. The Russian line was pierced, and the great Russian retirement began. In July Hindenburg and Ludendorff struck across the river Narew. Fighting became general along the entire eight hundred miles of the Eastern front. Warsaw, Bialystok, Kovno, Grod-

A "self-propelled, bulletproof landship": a British tank of 1917, the beginnings of armored warfare

IMPERIAL WAR MUSEUM

no, and Brest Litovsk fell in August. Vilna fell in September. For a time it seemed that Petrograd was in danger. Winter in its rigors at last descended upon the front, and the exhausted Russian armies came to a rest along that dreary, indefinite morass that lies between Poland and White Russia.

The Russian retirement of 1915 resembled the campaign of 1812 – and the campaign of 1941 of more recent memory. But in 1915 there was no Russian recovery. The retirement cost Russia 15 per cent of her territories, 10 per cent of her railroads, and 30 per cent of her industries. Of her population, 20 per cent were dispersed or passed under Austro-German rule. "Scorched earth," in these days, was not the thorough operation it was to become in the Second World War, but the retirement nevertheless was marked everywhere by extensive and deliberate devastation. The Russian Army's casualties are said to have amounted to 2,500,000 in killed, wounded, and prisoners.

The Dardanelles and the Entry of Bulgaria into the War

There was one attempt in 1915 to circumvent the impasse on the Western front. Thanks to the British Navy, the Allies held the initiative at sea and could make a strategic descent wherever the sea gave access. The Baltic and the Eastern Mediterranean both offered tempting possibilities. The assault on the Dardanelles was first mooted at the end of 1914 by Winston Churchill, First Lord of the Admiralty, and independently by Maurice Hankey, Colonel of Marines, secretary to Asquith's War Council. (See p. 40.) Lord Kitchener and Lloyd George were also canvassing ventures in Syria and Palestine, and the Russian Government was appealing for a diversion in the area. The objectives at the Dardanelles were sufficiently enticing. Such an assault, if successful, would force Turkey to sue for peace, open up a highway to beleaguered Russia, and probably secure the whole Balkans and Near East in the Allied interest. Moreover, such an assault, it seemed at first, could be carried out with auspicious economy. It would be a naval action using ships which for fleet operations were obsolete; and only such land forces would be put ashore as would be subsequently required for occupation and policing.

On February 19, 1915, combined British and French fleets began the bombardment of the outer forts of the Dardanelles. The entire operation was then hopefully expected to take a month. The political effects were immediate and encouraging. The Greek Premier, Venizelos, pro-Ally in his sympathies, urged his country's instant declaration of war on Turkey. But almost at once the difficulties piled up. General Liman von Sanders, head of the German military mission in Turkey, took command of the Turkish defenses. Trenches elaborately crisscrossed every vulnerable point on the Gallipoli Peninsula. On March 18, as the Allied fleets were beginning the second phase of their bombardment in the Narrows, six of their heaviest ships were mined – three sunk and three disabled.

The assault was evidently developing a magnitude and hazard beyond all expectation. It could now have been broken off without reproach. But with perverse, if admirable, magnanimity Kitchener at the War Office in London declared that the fighting must go on. If resolution ever won a battle, this one would not be lost for want of it. General Sir Ian Hamilton was sent out to lead a full-scale military campaign with two British divisions and the Anzacs[7] from Egypt. The French sent a division. At daybreak on April 25, 1915, the first landings were carried out, the British on the Gallipoli Peninsula and the French on the Asiatic mainland. Two hundred ships, men-of-war and transports, participated; and there began a siege of eight and a half months, which ultimately brought together on these rugged tongues of rock and scrub 500,000 fighting men.

The Fall of Serbia

The Dardanelles was Britain's greatest failure of the war. It was a failure of substance – and, even more so, of prestige. Further landings on Gallipoli in August had met with no better success. The earlier political effects in the Balkans had worn off; doubtful governments were leaning toward the more successful side in the conflict. In particular, Bulgaria, lying astride the road between Turkey and the Central Powers, was in a painfully ambiguous position. She was in a dangerous, gamblesome mood. Her Tsar, Ferdinand, was a German prince, and her Premier, Radoslavov, was a prominent Germanophile. Bulgaria's diplomatic history in 1915, not unlike Italy's, consisted of a repetition of offers and inducements, now from the Central Powers and now from the Allies. In the end it was the old hatred of Serbia which was decisive. In September 1915, Bulgaria signed a secret agreement with Germany and Austria-Hungary to make war on Serbia in return for slices of Serbian territory in Macedonia and along the Morava. Venizelos, the pro-Ally Greek Premier, meanwhile continued to try to bring his country into the war, virtually flouting the authority of the more cautious and pacific Greek King Constantine. But, instead of Greek troops being dispatched to help the Allies, Allied troops were now dispatched ostensibly to help the Greeks. On October 2, 1915, a largely French force landed and occupied the Greek port of Salonika. This was more than Venizelos had bargained for. He resigned office, and a new government was formed in Athens which declared itself neutral. Greece remained for the time being an inactive but uncomfortable spectator of the fall of Serbia.

That fall came quickly. On October 7, 1915, a combined German, Austrian, and Bulgarian army began a convergent offensive against the little country. In 1914 the Serbs had beaten off an Austrian invasion, but the odds were now overwhelming. They put up a gallant fight, but they fought alone. The townspeople of Nish, the temporary seat of the Serbian Government, hung out their flags in hourly expectation of Allied relief from Salonika, which never came. By the end of October, the Serbian forces were in full retreat through the defiles of the Albanian mountains. Some 100,000 survivors reached points along the Adriatic coast, whence they were rescued by Allied ships. It has been estimated that Serbia lost one-sixth of her population by enemy action, flight, epidemics, and famine in the course of the campaign. The Bulgarian Government declared that the Kingdom of Serbia had ceased to exist and announced an ambitious program of annexations. Austria toyed with schemes of a new Yugoslav state under Hapsburg rule. But, for Austria at least, her Serbian enemy had been suitably chastised; the original object, for which she had gone to war in 1914, had been achieved.

Meanwhile the Allied force in Salonika, weak and ineffective, was left undisturbed by the triumphant German, Austrian, and Bulgarian armies. Both sides, in fact, were immobilized by the fear of spreading epidemics.

The fall of Serbia ended the isolation of Turkey from her European allies. The four Central Powers — Germany, Austria-Hungary, Bulgaria, and Turkey — now constituted a continuous geographical block, a single Quadruple Alliance.[8] The immediate consequence, as far as Britain and France were concerned, had to be the abandonment of the Dardanelles. If Britain and France could not defeat Turkey when Turkey fought alone, they could hardly expect to defeat her now that German and Austrian units and munitions were available to stiffen the Turkish defenses. German guns, manned by German gunners, were in position by November. General Liman von Sanders was evidently planning a counteroffensive that would end the campaign. Britain and France were consoled perhaps by the skill and cheapness of their eventual withdrawal. There was no dreaded "Coruña."[9] But it was a sad and mortifying conclusion to a great enterprise. In the first week of January 1916, 135,000 men were re-embarked from the Dardanelles with hardly a casualty.

The Beginning of the German Submarine Campaign

By the end of 1915 the war was assuming global proportions. The countries of the Balkans, the Mediterranean, and the Near East were all involved.[10] Only Greece and Rumania maintained a formal, precarious—and temporary—neutrality. But, even more than this, the Allied naval blockade, whose beginning we described earlier in this chapter, had brought home the presence of war to nations far outside the immediate theaters of hostilities. No part of a world that lived by commerce and industry could be indifferent. Early in 1915, Germany had thrown her own maritime weapon, the submarine, into the scales and had thereby challenged the United States.

On February 4, 1915, in a note to the United States, the German Government announced that, in retaliation for the Allied blockade, any Allied merchantmen found in a "war zone" comprising the coasts of Great Britain, Ireland, and northern France would be destroyed without warning and without consideration for the lives of crews and passengers. Neutral ships in the same area would also be exposed to danger so long as the ruse, which allowed a belligerent to fly a neutral flag, made it impossible to identify a ship's nationality. Britain may sometimes have sailed very close to the legal wind at sea, but here in the German note were crimes in contemplation which at that time no law or necessity could admit. President Wilson replied to the note in terms about as severe as the diplomacy of those days allowed one friendly power to address to another and gave clear warning that the United States would hold Germany "to a strict accountability" for the resulting losses of American vessels or American lives on the high seas.

The German Government pleaded with great adroitness that it had to find some defense against the increasing traffic in American munitions to the Allies. But the actual sinkings at sea left President Wilson with no choice but to take further and further refuge in the absolute legalities and to lose sight of those extralegal merits which, on calmer reflection, might have been conceded to the German case. One American life was lost on the British liner *Falaba,* torpedoed on March 28, 1915. Three American lives were lost on the American oil tanker *Gulflight,* torpedoed on May 1. Then on May 7, the British Cunard liner *Lusitania* was torpedoed off the southern coast of Ireland and sank in eighteen minutes. Of her 1,959 passengers and crew, 1,198 were lost; of 159 Americans, 128 were lost; of 129 children, 94 were lost.

Mere description, mere quotation, can give no idea of the reaction in America and in the non-German world to this supreme outrage. For once in contemporary journalism the histrionics of the headline artist were neither exaggerated nor insincere. James W. Gerard, the American ambassador in Berlin, Walter Hines Page, the American ambassador in London, and President Wilson's adviser, Colonel House, then in London, all counseled and expected war. Meanwhile the extreme isolationists, though shocked, struck an attitude of "I told you so!" But President Wilson remained cool and collected. Never did his much-maligned aloofness stand him in such good stead. Congress was not then in session, or its floods of oratory might even then have swept him into war. On May 10, 1915, at Philadelphia, he delivered himself in these words:

> The example of America must be a special example. The example of America must be the example not merely of peace because it will not fight, but of peace because peace is the healing and elevating influence of the world, and strife is not. There is such a thing as a man being too proud to fight. There is such a thing as a nation being so right that it does not need to convince others by force that it is right.

The abuse and ridicule with which this speech was received by large sections of the American press may have persuaded the President to bend a little to the popular storm, and his note to Germany on May 13 barely avoided the finality of an ultimatum. The harassed German ambassador in Washington, Count von Bernstorff, tried to make his superiors in Berlin aware of the intensity of feeling in the United States and sadly likened himself to "another Sisyphus," who had hardly composed one German outrage before another one was committed. At all events he was able to give assurances that attacks on "liners" would cease. In the late summer and autumn of the year there was an over-all decrease in the number of sinkings.

Meanwhile a lesser irritation had started up. German agents were engaged in sabotage in American munition plants. American freighters went to sea carrying infernal machines which exploded mysteriously in mid-ocean. There were reports of bridges and canals being blown up in Canada. The German military and naval attachés, Captain von Papen and Captain Boy-Ed, were sent home for espionage. President Wilson rounded off the events of the year with his "Preparedness" speech to Congress in December. But it was still to be another fifteen months before the United States was to declare war against the disturber of its peace and security.

3. "THE WAR BEHIND THE WAR"

The Home Front

The standard history book of a generation ago, when describing a war, was apt to limit itself somewhat schematically to the "causes," "course," and "consequences" of that war. The causes and consequences would generally be political; and the middle part of the treatment would be "about battles." No such history of the First World War would be remotely adequate. The First World War was fought as much behind the lines as at the front; its history was in its politics and economics and in its revolutionary social changes, no less than in its Marnes and Tannenbergs. And, in this respect, what the First World War began was continued in the Second.

We have already remarked on the mass emotion at the outbreak of the First World War. (See p. 18.) All sections of opinion and all political parties in the belligerent countries in August 1914 supported their respective governments with nearly absolute unanimity. In the new ardors of the war, former social discontents somehow lost their relevance and rationale. Poincaré declared a *"Union Sacrée"*; Bethmann-Hollweg declared a *"Burgfriede."* [1] "I know parties no more," said the Kaiser; "I know only Germans!" "I am in perfect union with my united people!" said the Tsar. Individual opposition to the war — such as that of Ramsay MacDonald in Britain, or Kerensky in Russia — looked like eccentricity, or worse. Only in Turkey, already exhausted by three previous wars, was there no great martial enthusiasm for yet another one; and only in Italy in 1915 did there arise organized anti-war parties, composed of extreme clericals, who were pro-Austrian and anti-French, and of extreme Socialists, who were pacifist.

But once the shouting died down, it behooved governments and peoples to set about the less exciting domestic tasks of the war. By common popular expectation in 1914, the war was going to be a short one — "a brisk and merry war" (*ein frischfröhlicher Krieg*), as the Germans had it. "Home by Christmas!" sang the soldiers on their way to the front in those early days. But four Christmases, nearly five, were to pass before the war ended; and home by then was changed out of all recognition.

The average Western citizen of today almost looks upon total war as a normal national experience. But in 1914 no human mortal could have foreseen its real character. The domestic emergencies, as they crowded upon harassed governments – the allocation of raw materials and food, the efficient employment of man power, the reinforcement of morale, and particularly the expansion of the supporting bureaucratic structure – all these things had to be matters of improvisation, experiment, and often failure. Many of the industrial and administrative innovations of the war were carried over afterward into peacetime ways of life. It is important that we should devote a chapter to "the war behind the war" as it was waged on the home front if indeed we are to form a balanced picture in our minds as to how our fellow men were really occupied from 1914 to 1918.

Even so, our survey will have to be confined to the more obvious aspects of that picture. The First World War – and the Second – were the great agents of revolution. European society, if not the whole world, was transformed by them. The devastation of the battlefield, like a natural wound, might almost be left to heal itself and, in a few years, show no visible scars. Deterioration of the public services, railways, and roads, the disrepair and destruction of buildings could be made good. Despite the unprecedented loss of human life, there were few "centers of habitation" which, within the decade, were not as populous as they had been in 1914, and most were more populous. But the deeper effects of the war in the manners and mores of civilization were permanent. There are books still to be written on the transvaluation of values in these four years. The old social structure of Europe was largely broken up. The war developed into a war for "democracy," and, in such a war, even without military defeat or political subversion, the so-called upper classes of society had to sink and the so-called lower classes to rise. "Edwardian" Europe vanished. Its gilded scions, who contributed the officer corps of the original European armies, were just those who fought most recklessly and sacrificed themselves most prodigally. In the world that emerged in 1919 anything that smacked of royalty or aristocracy was at a discount. It was a world of new parliaments and liberated nationalities, and, at least in Europe, the real political power and privilege had come to rest with a very different breed of men.

In this chapter we shall consider the home front in Germany, Britain, and Russia, partly out of regard for the intrinsic importance of these nations and partly as illustration of the kinds of domestic problems with which, sooner or later, all the belligerents had to deal. We shall also consider certain local incidents, falling properly within this chapter – incidents which were to have far-reaching consequences in the postwar era – in Ireland, Poland and the Baltic, and Turkey. Generally our account will go up to the year 1916. But, as we shall see, it will become more and more difficult from this time onward to separate the twin aspects of the war, the war on the fighting front and the war on the home front, and the next two chapters will further develop many of the themes contained in the present one. Of all wars, the First World War was preeminently the continuation of politics.

Germany

In a military sense Germany entered the war better prepared than any of the belligerents – but prepared for a short war. The blitzkrieg had always been the ideal of the German General Staff. Questions of raw materials, noncombatant man power, and food for a longer war had not been considered. The Allied naval blockade quickly destroyed the greater part of Germany's overseas commerce, and she found herself alone – with the burden of weaker allies – in an encirclement of hostile forces. There were many materials essential to existence, and to war, which could not be won from the soil of the Fatherland. Coal and iron were in good supply; but copper, manganese, gasoline, lubricants, and tropical or subtropical products like rubber and cotton were not obtainable. Agriculture for years had depended on fertilizers and fodders from abroad. Yet the German Army marched off gaily to battle in 1914 oblivious of the certain famine in all those resources without which it could not have held the field beyond the first winter of the war.

On August 9, 1914, Rathenau began discussions with General von Falkenhayn, then Prussian War Minister. Walther Rathenau was one of Germany's leading magnates, a director of the AEG (*Allgemeine Elektrizitäts-Gesellschaft*), the largest industrial combine in Europe, and of some eighty other companies, a man of Jewish stock, loyal to his race and country, philosopher and poet, and now to become the chief organizer of the German war economy. Undeniably he emerges after all these years as one of the great national war leaders. His particular creation in 1914 was the War Raw Materials Department, the KRA (*Kriegsrohstoffabteilung*), administering a chain of "companies," on the lines of the usual German cartel, but working under central government supervision, issuing no shares and making no profits. To each such company was assigned the sequestration and allocation of a group of materials – the War Metals Company, the War Chemicals Company, and so forth – till not a single essential raw material was uncontrolled. Rathenau devoted nine months to the establishment of these organizations. In April 1915, he handed them over to the Prussian Ministry of War. Germany's supplies, he declared, were secure; the blockade had been defeated; a shortage of essential materials no longer threatened the outcome of the war. But, as it turned out, Rathenau judged too optimistically.

Germany meanwhile overhauled such of her trade with her neutral neighbors as still survived. In 1914 purchasing missions, German and Austrian, civil and military, scrambled in the same neutral markets, driving up prices and depressing the rate of exchange. Karl Helfferich at the Imperial Treasury gradually worked out a system of cooperative purchase and formed a Central Purchasing Company, ZEG (*Zentral Einkaufs-Gesellschaft*), somewhat on the lines of one of Rathenau's companies, which thenceforth controlled all German purchases and sales abroad. Similar companies were formed in Austria and Hungary. The ZEG and its ancillaries fought as difficult and complicated a battle as any on the home front. It was the greatest trading organization in the world. For a time it enabled Germany to compete successfully even with Britain in Britain's accustomed markets in Holland and Denmark. Germany's exports to neutrals could not always be maintained, but imports remained tolerably steady throughout the war. It is certain that without the ZEG what was left of Germany's foreign trade would have been swallowed up by the neutral speculator and profiteer.

Food supplies proved to be more difficult than raw materials, if for no other reason than the existence of an absolute shortage which no amount of organizing would resolve. The government in 1914 began by issuing simple decrees – prohibiting the slaughter of calves, prescribing methods for milling flour, and so forth. In the winter of 1914, the German people began to make trial of "K-bread," a name conveniently ambiguous, as it could signify either "war bread" or "potato bread" (*Kriegsbrot* or *Kartoffelbrot*). Then, during 1915, the government began to set up a series of offices, once more after Rathenau's prototype, such as the Imperial Grain Office, and the same system was gradually extended to cover more complex and perishable foods, such as fruit, meat, fish, and dairy produce. Shortages were threatened here and there, or some particular depredation of the profiteer was discovered, and one by one almost every kind of food was brought under the surveillance of an appropriate authority. Sugar was the one foodstuff which, thanks to the intensive cultivation of the sugar beet, was never rationed.

Outside government controls lay the numerous substitutes, or ersatz materials, which now appeared on the market. The days before the war had already known such preparations as margarine, artificial honey, artificial coffee, gravy tablets, and puddings, which were made from substances far different from what they appeared to be. But preparations which had once been made for cheapness were made now because no better could be bought at any price. In course of time, substitutes multiplied and took a recognized place in the nation's diet. The housewife and chef learned a new culinary lore and produced attractive meals out of materials that once would hardly have been given to cattle. There were cakes from chestnut flour, chops from nuts, coffee from barley, rye, chicory, and figs – and even from acorns. There were preparations representing sausages, soups, beer, and lemonade, and various new dehydrated and "stretching" materials. Meanwhile the civil authorities organized patriotic drives against waste. Parties of school children collected potato peel, fruit parings, and paper.

Ersatz processes were soon being extended to industry. German science and invention undertook a colossal program. Human ingenuity was never so taxed nor yet so resourceful, and many a wartime makeshift afterward became a commonplace of peace. Aluminum was extracted from native clays and largely took the place of copper in electrical fittings. Calcium carbide provided illuminants and replaced certain hardening metals in the manufacture of steel. Wood-pulp products saved the textile industry from a complete breakdown and were used for paper, artificial silk, and army sandbags. There were processes for regenerating rubber, and a beginning was made in the production of synthetic rubbers. Perhaps the greatest achievement of German science was the manufacture of nitrates from the air. Huge government factories were built, sufficient to supply the nitrates for explosives and in part also for agricultural fertilizers.

Rathenau's KRA, Helfferich's ZEG, the Imperial Grain Office and their several subsidiaries throughout the Reich made up a vast interrelated system for the prosecution of total war. German officialdom accomplished a heroic undertaking with its customary efficiency and without favors or corruption. But by 1916 the system was beginning to fail. The Allied blockade was causing shortages which even German organization could not make good. Clothing and leather were scarce. Wool was a luxury, and cotton was not to be had. The better stocks of leather went to the army, and the civilian had to be content with what was left. Substitute leathers appeared on the market, and many people were clattering about the streets ingeniously shod with wood. In February 1916 available stocks of clothing were sequestrated, and thenceforth an Imperial Clothing Office rationed all supplies for civilian consumption.

Worst of all was the food shortage. The press agitated for a "Food Dictator," and in May 1916 the government appointed Adolf von Batocki-Friebe director of a new War Food Office (*Kriegsernährungsamt*). Batocki, as president of the local administration of East Prussia, had recently carried out the reconstruction of the areas in East Prussia which had been ravaged during the campaign of 1914, and he now came to Berlin with a record of unusual capacity and the reputation of a strong man. But the situation was stronger than Batocki. He could only see justice done, and, if he could not create plenty from shortage, he could at least bring the cold comfort of an equal misery for everyone.

In the beginning, privations accumulated so slowly that their first ill effects had passed unnoticed. There was then a joy in asceticism and a companionship in the common discomfort. But the very monotony of hunger can wear away a man's resistance. Food becomes an obsession; evading the regulations is the serious business of life; old disciplines lose their force; and any chaos seems sweeter in the prospect than this ordered and unending want. Patience is on edge; some stupid, worried official loses his head, and a dangerous riot breaks out. The whole people seems to suffer from a sort of mass claustrophobia, and the tangents of its moods or of its weariness may take an unforeseen direction. The year 1916 closed with the horrors of the "turnip winter." Premature frosts spoiled the potato harvest, now the basis of so many substitute foods, and the humble turnip became the staple diet of the German people. The soldier home on leave from the front found his wife and children not only undernourished, stretching their rations with substitutes, short of fuel, needing almost all the things that make life tolerable, but looking drab and shoddy, their clothes two, three, and even four times made over.[2] When a state like this is reached, pride of race, self-respect, all human dignity are wearing thin, and a helpless, consuming poverty is laying its hold upon the nation.

By 1916 the most difficult of all shortages, a labor shortage, was appearing in Germany. The outbreak of war had resulted in a sharp unemployment crisis. Hundreds of businesses had closed, thousands of men had been thrown out of work, and neither the mobilization nor the new war industries had immediately rectified the situation. But gradually, in 1915, unemployment was transformed into its reverse. The labor market in the autumn of 1916 was such that two men applied for every three vacancies. Women and children and prisoners of war were put to work. But the shortage gathered momentum, and a labor shortage, as the nation was soon to learn, becomes a vicious circle growing ever wider and more ruinous as it persists. Coal seams, however rich, are of small value when there are not miners enough to mine them. Railroads, however efficient, will wear out if there are not maintenance men enough in the yards and on the road bed. Coal, railroads, and industry are interlocked; the deterioration of any one of them will react upon the other two. Agriculture will suffer not only from a loss of fertilizers, but from the loss of able-bodied hands. A nation engaged in total war virtually blockades itself — unless it has external and sympathetic allies, willing and able to supply it. While its millions are fighting at the front, its economy in the rear breaks down for mere want of workers to keep it going.

The great "battle of material" on the Somme in 1916 first convinced the German High Command of the need for an increase of munitions to offset the unexpected British production. But more munitions meant more munition workers, and more munition workers were not to be had. In August 1916, Hindenburg and Ludendorff replaced Falkenhayn in the High Command. The two soldiers were economists enough to realize that the problem at bottom was a labor shortage, and they were prepared to order a labor levy tantamount to the conscription, on military lines, of the entire population of the Reich. Civilian ministers protested, Social Democrats and trade unions grumbled, but all acquiesced in the end.

The result was the creation, in November 1916, of a *Kriegsamt* (War Office), under General Groener, attached to the Prussian Ministry of War and invested with wide powers, especially in respect to labor. An Auxiliary Service Law provided for the compulsory employment of every male German citizen between the ages of seventeen and sixty who was not already in the combatant forces. At the same time several industries, "not important for war purposes," were "silenced." These measures were collectively called the "Hindenburg Program." At the end of 1916, so serious had the situation become that the *Kriegsamt* was forcibly deporting local labor from Belgium and northern France, whose peoples, under the German occupation, were then suffering from acute unemployment. A "Polish Army" was recruited in Poland for service against Russia.

German munitions production trebled during the ensuing year, but the burden of effort on the nation was more than it could safely bear. The High Command had expected that the Hindenburg Program, under the name of the great national hero, would go into effect with a supreme patriotic outburst, but it had not the psychological skill with which the Nazis afterwards managed these things. As for Belgium and northern France, despite the miseries of the enforced "Deportations," they yielded disappointingly little in the way of the desired labor corps; and Poland yielded little in the way of a "Polish Army." In 1917, for the first time in the war, coal was short in Germany, and the High Command had to choose between cutting munitions or releasing former miners from the army. A special Coal Commissioner was attached to the *Kriegsamt* with absolute powers over the nation's coal supplies. But the problem of coal, like the problem of food, had one cause and one solution. Man power was exhausted. The Hindenburg Program in fact was Germany's point of diminishing returns.

We continue our account of the German home front in the next chapter and discuss there in particular the political repercussions of the situation in the *Reichstag* at the time of the "July Crisis" of 1917. (See p. 70.)

Britain

For Britain, the outbreak of war brought immediate peace at home. In the face of the German invasion of Belgium, Irish Home Rule, women's suffrage, trade-union unrest, all the strikes and factions of the previous months, ceased to be political issues. On August 5, 1914, Asquith, the Prime Minister, appointed Lord Kitchener Secretary of State for War. In October he appointed as First Sea Lord, Lord Fisher, a vehement old sailor and one of the creator's of Britain's dreadnought navy, a fitting colleague for Winston Churchill, then First Lord of the Admiralty.[3] In November, Asquith created a War Council, chiefly of Cabinet ministers, under the secretaryship of Colonel Maurice Hankey, as a sort of political general staff for the conduct of the war.

Leadership and authority were thus secured. But long-term policies were harder to come by. The British people, and all but a few of their leaders, had no comprehension of the real nature of the struggle to which they were now committed. For Britain, hitherto, wars had been the business of the navy and of a small professional army. But, in August 1914, Kitchener issued his "Call to Arms," and Britain, for the first time in her history, began to build up an army of Continental proportions. Enlistment at first was voluntary, and the recruiting offices were soon besieged by the nation's youth. In November 1914, Asquith gave out in the House of Commons that the British regular army then numbered over 1,000,000 men and that 700,000 recruits had joined since the outbreak of war, not including 200,000 Territorials. Finding the men, it seemed, would be easy—at this stage it was too easy. But supplying them with arms and equipment for the kind of war it was going to be turned out to be much more difficult.

Lord Kitchener was one of the few men to have foreseen neither a short war nor a traditionally limited one, but he was slow to appreciate the technical requirements of the fighting which now developed on the Western front. His own professional experience hitherto had been in fields where mobility counted for more than munitions, and many of his subordinate commanders had been cavalry generals on the South African veldt. Yet, from the First Battle of Ypres in November 1914, Field Marshal Sir John French, the British Commander in Chief, was already dunning the War Office with daily telegrams, pleading for shells and yet more shells. Asquith resorted to the usual tactics of government leaders in a quandary and turned over his problem to a committee. Between October 1914 and April 1915 he successively created a Cabinet Committee on Munitions, an Armaments

Output Committee, and a Munitions Committee. Not without reason were these early days of the war called the "golden age of committeedom."

The press became restless, and in May 1915 Lord Northcliffe, through the columns of his *Daily Mail,* began to attack Kitchener in person. Copies of the offending newspaper were ceremoniously burned on the London Stock Exchange. But the great "Shell Crisis" was on. Tongues and pens were loosed; old fears and discretions went by the board. Lurid stories appeared of batteries at the front which had existed for months on two rounds per gun per day. British artillery was outclassed by the German in caliber and range; British machine guns, trench mortars, hand grenades, all the paraphernalia of the new war of position, were disastrously insufficient and inefficient. At Neuve-Chapelle, it was said, British infantry had "gone over the top" behind a scant one-hour or two-hour artillery preparation and had been slaughtered by the thousand. Meanwhile the Dardanelles had become an additional anxiety. Fisher resigned from the Admiralty in May 1915, after a somewhat petulant quarrel with Churchill. Asquith was persuaded at last to reconstruct his government. On May 25 he announced a coalition to include all parties, and appointed his former Chancellor of the Exchequer, Lloyd George, to a newly created department, the Ministry of Munitions.

Coalitions in wartime had historical precedents. At great moments of national emergency it was a natural wish to invite the counsel of acknowledged leaders irrespective of party. Churchill, paying the price for the ill success of the Dardanelles campaign, of which, reputedly, he had been the principal inspirer, was the most notable absentee in the new combination. Grey remained Foreign Secretary, and Kitchener remained Secretary for War. Curzon, Lansdowne, Balfour, Bonar Law, Austen Chamberlain (Conservatives), Simon (Liberal), and Henderson (Labor) received posts. The War Council, Asquith's creation of November 1914, continued to meet under the name of the Dardanelles Committee – a sufficient indication of its main interest at the time – again with Hankey as its secretary.

Britain, in short, was about to institute her version of the wartime administrative reformation already effected by Germany, and her leader in the process was her great war minister, David Lloyd George. He was now a man at the height of his powers. He had followed a varied political career of pronouncedly radical leanings. He had risen from poor beginnings, through an apprenticeship in law, to represent his native Welsh constituency in the House of Commons. For two decades there was not an important political fight in which he did not figure and in which he did not take sides against established wealth and privilege. He was an unconventional but magnificent orator, deadly in repartee, and a born master of mass emotions. In 1908 Asquith had made him Chancellor of the Exchequer, a post which was no more than his evident abilities deserved, but he was a mercurial, troublesome colleague and already too much of a "mirror to public applause." He is said to have at first opposed Britain's entry into the war, but after the German invasion of Belgium he inevitably felt the compulsion of crowd magnetism and threw himself into the crusade against Germany with the same ardor with which he had formerly thrown himself into crusades against the social evils of his day. His irrepressible energies craved to be occupied, and he was soon putting a busy, probing finger into every administrative problem which the Asquith government appeared to be meeting with insufficient determination. In May 1915, he became Minister of Munitions and faced a work as huge and as anxious as his heart could desire.

Lloyd George, against all precedent, appointed several businessmen and professional experts as his ministerial colleagues. He had surveys made of the industrial potentialities of Britain — and of America — and laid his plans to equip a British army of seventy divisions for a prolonged campaign in the trench network of France. He toured the manufacturing centers in England and Wales. He met representatives of owners, trade unions, and workers. He secured the passage of a Ministry of Munitions Act that gave him a virtual dictatorship over British industry.

Statistics sometimes give a good idea of the facts. During the war British factories produced, in round numbers, 4,000,000 rifles, 240,000 machine guns, between 200,000,000 and 250,000,000 shells, and over 40,000 planes, and it fell to Lloyd George to be the director of this huge productivity at that most difficult stage when it was being organized and developed. In June 1916, he left the Ministry of Munitions to succeed Kitchener at the War Office. The great "Shell Crisis" was a thing of the past. In July 1916, the British Army fought the battle of the Somme, that first of the great "battles of material," as the Germans called them, and inflicted the first lasting wounds on the body and soul of military Germany.

In 1915 and 1916 there began to appear in Britain that concomitant of total war, a labor shortage. The pace of recruiting and the production of materials and munitions approached the point beyond which further augmentation seemed to be physically impossible. Enlistment in 1915 had been particularly heavy in the big industrial districts, and the more intelligent and skilled workers had always been the first to answer the "Call to Arms." Kitchener objected to restrictions upon recruiting and objected even more to returning a man to civil life once he had joined the colors. Attempts to transfer workers from one occupation to another, or from one locality to another, were regarded by the workers with suspicion, and generally failed. The "dilution" of skilled workers with unskilled or semiskilled workers seemed to offer one solution of the labor shortage, but a special agreement had to be made with the trade unions to lay their traditional fears of scab labor. The workers found themselves, for the first time in their history, in a strong bargaining position, and both government and employers were afraid of incurring disputes with them in the midst of a national emergency. In July 1915, 200,000 coal miners in South Wales went on strike and incidentally demonstrated how thin was the happy truce under which all the pre-1914 discontents were supposed to have been so safely buried.

In July 1915, Parliament passed a National Registration Act, providing for a thoroughgoing census of the population for military and industrial purposes, and it is again a reflection on the novelty of the situation that the bill was stubbornly contested in all its stages. In August 1915, Asquith appointed a Cabinet committee to investigate the nation's resources of man power. At that time 3,000,000 men had offered themselves for military service, and casualties in killed and wounded had already exceeded a tenth of the number. At the end of the year, Lord Derby was directing an intensified recruiting campaign, the "Derby Scheme," as it was popularly called, which was in effect a last despairing effort on behalf of voluntary service.

In January 1916, Asquith introduced conscription for single men and childless widowers. In May 1916, under the Universal Military Service Act, he introduced conscription for all men, married and unmarried, between the ages of eighteen and forty-one. Ireland was excluded from the act, and special tribunals were set up to grant or withhold the exemption of "conscientious objectors." Labor and the trade-unions made some show of resistance, but Asquith succeeded in obtaining that "progressive general consent" he had hoped for, and the British people, in a spirit of grim acquiescence, bowed to the new discipline and to the absolute reversal of every tradition and principle for which they had stood in the past.

From 1915 onward, women were increasingly employed, not only in munition factories, but in all branches of the war effort — as agricultural workers in the Land Army and Timber Corps, as drivers and conductors in the transport services, and in the police — to say nothing of the nursing and ambulance services. By mid-1916 nearly 350,000 women and girls were thus employed, and by the end of the war their number was well over 800,000. Women's auxiliary services were attached to the armed forces. They provided cooks, canteen workers, secretaries, telephonists, interpreters. In 1917 the Women's Army Auxiliary Corps (WAAC) and the Women's Royal Naval Service (WRNS) were formed and, in 1918, the Women's Royal Air Force (WRAF) — with a total enrollment of over 90,000. We have somewhat forgotten today what an extraordinary novelty a woman in overalls or uniform must once have been. Certainly the First World War, on the home fronts of all the belligerents, was the great emancipator of women. The Representation of the People Act, passed by Parliament early in 1918, adopting women's suffrage, was an inevitable recognition of devoted service.

Food shortage in Britain in 1916 was not yet a serious problem. Except for sugar, there was no food rationing in Britain for the first two years of the war. Oddly enough, as we have noted above, sugar was the one food never rationed in Germany. Anxieties over the situation were sometimes voiced in the House of Commons. Churchill, for one, who was out of office after the failure of the Dardanelles, made it his business to take an interest in the nation's food. The dreaded bread line — or "queue" as the British called it — was only a sporadic infection, as yet mainly confined to a few Midland cities. At the end of 1916 the dragon of want was already consuming Germany and Central Europe; but at that date a British government department could still report that there was "less total distress in the country than in an ordinary year of peace." The situation, however, changed suddenly for the worse in 1917, when Germany's unrestricted submarine campaign was launched. But this development will be described in the next chapter. (See pp. 67-69.)

We have briefly considered Germany and Britain. But much the same story could be told of all the major European belligerents. In every case, blockade or no blockade, the same series of crises – a munitions crisis, a food crisis, a man-power crisis – occurred, though not always in the same order or with the same severity. It is no disrespect of the fighting man of 1914-18 to say that his victory or defeat in the end rested as much on the outcome of these crises on the home front as on his conduct on the battlefield. Oddly enough, finance, despite the dire predictions of the experts before 1914, proved a far lesser problem and never an insuperable one. In no case was a belligerent seriously handicapped by want of money, and none suffered panic, bankruptcy, or other decisive financial setback in the course of the war.[4]

Individual home fronts showed obvious national variations. In France, for example, the mobilization of resources was affected from the start by the fact that the German invasion of 1914 cut off the whole of the industrial Northeast departments. For four months in 1914, the French Government moved to Bordeaux; on its return to Paris, it found a munitions crisis already in progress. Typically France had to fight out her problems on the home front amid the usual round of ministerial changes, and she needed six governments in the course of the war, the last being Clemenceau's, which saw out the war to its conclusion. In Russia, with her relatively primitive industrial development, a munitions crisis was perhaps to be expected. But even Russia, by 1916, with all her vast prairie agriculture and her millions of population – and indeed with her ready-made bureaucratic structure – also found herself with shortages of food and man power. We shall describe Russia's wartime domestic affairs in a subsequent section of this chapter. Eventually the regime broke up in the Revolution of 1917. The double war on the fighting front and on the home front was more than the Russian Tsarist state had the power to survive. (See pp. 46ff, 73ff.)

Ireland

In August 1914, the British Dominions and India had all responded loyally to the call of the war and had sent their quotas of men and material without stint or question. And in that spirit, generally, they bore the struggle to the end. But it was hardly to be expected that within these far-flung and varied territories dissident elements should not have occasionally appeared. Indian independence still lay in the future – though there were some rumblings of discontent in 1917. In South Africa, Boer and Britain made common cause in the conquest of the colonies of German Southwest Africa and German East Africa (Tanganyika). The South African leader, General Smuts, visited Britain and became one of Lloyd George's most trusted advisers. But for South Africa, even so, the war was not all amity and comradeship. A short-lived rebellion broke out in the former Boer republics. General Hertzog's Nationalist party was anti-war and anti-imperialist. Nor in Canada – after the first flush of enthusiasm had subsided – could it be said that the French-speaking minority in Quebec Province unreservedly supported the war. In 1917, during the so-called Conscription

Crisis in Canada, serious rioting broke out in the city of Quebec in protest against compulsory military service overseas. And it is perhaps worth noting, in passing, that in the same year, in Australia, a similar Conscription Crisis, touched off by Australian Labor, split the country into two opposing political factions.[5] But the most critical division on the British home front occurred on the very doorstep of the mother country – in Ireland.

In the summer of 1914, Ireland had been in the midst of a more than usually acrimonious crisis in her affairs. Asquith's Home Rule Act had just been passed – the royal assent was given after the actual outbreak of the war – and then another bill was hurriedly pushed through suspending it "for the duration." In northern Ireland, before the outbreak of the war, the Ulster leaders, Sir Edward Carson and F. E. Smith, had been building up bodies of volunteers of a type we have since come to recognize in the Fascist squads; while in southern Ireland similar volunteers were drilling, gun-running, and generally matching the inflammatory tactics of their northern antagonists. It needed the greater war in Europe to distract the Irish people from their lesser war in Ireland and to induce them to make the same kind of truce as had stilled other domestic conflicts in Europe. And, for the first two years of the war, Ireland was unwontedly quiet and markedly prosperous. The war had driven up the prices of agricultural produce, and the Irish counties seemed almost like favored neutrals living off the necessities of a warring neighbor. Meanwhile British Army recruiting in both northern and southern Ireland had been good, and no one could complain of the spirit of the Irish regiments at the front in France.

The Easter Rebellion in Ireland in 1916, therefore, did not arise from those economic aggravations to which so many of the country's ancient troubles have so often been charged. It was essentially a conscription crisis, similar to the conscription crises which were also shortly to divide Canada and Australia. Early in 1916 there were recurring rumors that the British Government meant to extend some sort of compulsory military service to Ireland. Sinn Fein, the Irish Volunteers, and the Citizen Army[6] planned revolt, and they were probably not innocent of German aid. They planned secretly and with great daring. The police warned the British authorities, but the warnings were not taken seriously. The outbreak, when it came, therefore came as a complete surprise. It looked like another of those flank attacks upon the tyrant England for which Irish history has several precedents. England's misfortune, once more, was Ireland's opportunity.

But the plans went wrong. A German freighter was to land munitions near Cork; Sir Roger Casement, late of the British consular service and recently engaged in Germany in trying to subvert the loyalty of Irish prisoners of war, was to be put ashore from a German submarine and was presumably to act as a sort of liaison officer with his German aides. But the freighter was intercepted by British destroyers; Casement was duly put ashore on a lonely stretch of the Kerry coast, but lost his way and was arrested. Nevertheless, on Easter Monday, April 24, 1916, the Sinn Feiners issued a call to the Irish people to support their "Provisional Government" in Dublin. The British Government rushed reinforcements to Ireland and proclaimed martial law. After a week's fighting the Rebellion was suppressed, and its leaders were safely under lock and key.

It is far from easy to estimate the seriousness of the Irish Easter Rebellion in 1916. About a thousand of the "Irish Republican Army" were said to have been engaged, and the loss of life among British troops, mostly half-trained youngsters, amounted to nearly a hundred. The figures were not very formidable. But the British Government took a grave view. Fifteen rebel leaders were executed. Casement was taken to London, tried for treason, and hanged. Eamon de Valera, a young schoolmaster, was among those whose sentences were commuted to penal servitude. Asquith, then Prime Minister, visited Dublin for a series of conferences. A royal commission was appointed and held numerous sittings during the summer. There were debates in the Commons and the Lords, and negotiations with Nationalist and Ulster leaders. But no settlement was reached. On the contrary, the situation, whether or not it had been serious in April 1916, was certainly serious enough later. The execution of the rebel leaders, though perfectly in accordance with the law, revolted many Irishmen otherwise loyal to Britain, and, "by a masterpiece of British callousness and ineptitude," the Ulsterman Sir F. E. Smith was prosecutor at Casement's trial — a "shocking conjunction," as one historian has described it.[7] The more moderate Nationalists as a party, from this time onward, began to lose their hold, and extreme Sinn Fein was well launched upon its career to ultimate power in southern Ireland.

Russia

Politically, Tsarist Russia may be said to have consisted of three powers: the bureaucracy, the Tsar, and the Duma; and it was out of the complex interplay and counterplay of these three powers, under the unprecedented hardships of the war, that there arose in these years the country's domestic conflicts — and eventually, in 1917, the Revolution.

The bureaucracy was the ruling class of old Russia. Peter the Great, at the end of the seventeenth century, bent on centralizing all authority in himself, but mistrusting the existing lordlings of his realm, who were either too independent or too provincial for his purpose, had had no option but to pick his own officials and work out his own official system. The great hierarchy which he then bequeathed to his successors was subjected from time to time to reforms of detail, but never lost its original character. In 1914 it was made up of a vast corps of "professional administrators," a tenth of the urban adult male population — meticulously ranked, titled, and uniformed — and included the Council of the Empire, the Council of Ministers, the ministries, the judges and the courts of justice, the police, the provincial governors and governments — all controlled from a single center and responsible to a single autocrat. Its ranks, to a considerable extent, were recruited from the universities and no doubt contained men of culture and ability. But it suffered from all the vices of long-entrenched privilege; it was rigid and cumbrous, indolent and corrupt. In that fateful year 1914 it was confronted by an emergency which was too big for it.

Tsar Nicholas II was the inadequate figurehead of this massive system. He had been bred in the school of his redoubtable sire, Alexander III. He believed as a matter of course that autocracy and orthodoxy were the twin pillars of the Russian fabric, and that their preservation was his God-appointed task. He was Autocrat of all the Russias, absolute ruler of 175,000,000 human souls and of one-sixth of the earth's surface, "Supreme Defender and Preserver" of the Orthodox Faith, and Commander in Chief of the Russian Army and Navy. But he had not one natural qualification for the office. He was, we suspect, one of those listless, almost vacant characters, which are often the result of generations of inbreeding, obstinate without understanding, charming without sympathy, a slave to privilege and ceremonial, but otherwise happy and unrepressed within the circle of his own family. Such men, in their very blamelessness, invite the tragedies that engulf them.

The Tsaritsa Alexandra, formerly Princess Alix of Hesse-Darmstadt and a granddaughter of Queen Victoria of England, was a woman of great beauty but peculiar mental processes. German by birth and English by upbringing, she never overcame, or even seemed to try to overcome, the strangeness of her surroundings in Russia. Gradually shunned, yet blaming others, impassive, haughty, and cold, she seemed almost to defy the approaches of other human beings, and the imperial family virtually imprisoned itself in the Palace of Tsarskoe Selo, twenty miles from St. Petersburg, away from friends, from advice, and even from current information. There, during her many hours of solitude, she gave herself up to a sort of pietism, not always of the healthiest. She became nervous, hysterical, and sometimes very ill. Her son, the Tsarevich Alexis, her fifth child, was a hemophiliac, and it did not help her psychological condition to have to realize that she herself had been the transmitter of his ailment. She befriended a stupid, characterless woman, Anna Vyrubova, as self-persecuted as herself, who assisted at her religious exercises, and she became the infatuated disciple of the monkish charlatan, Gregory Rasputin, whose hypnotic gifts had sometimes been able to relieve the hemorrhages of the suffering little Tsarevich.

In this crazed household rested the fate of an empire. A popular legislature, which could have acted as a corrective, did not exist. The Duma of 1905 had been a half-hearted concession, extorted by military defeat. The Tsar confessed that he had been forced to create it "in a moment of fever." He feared it, and he was glad enough, whence chance offered, to retract its more radical powers. In the years following, the curtailment of the electoral laws left the Duma a very parody of what a parliamentary assembly should have been. On the outbreak of the war in 1914, the Duma was convened for a short session of one day, August 8, and the Deputies, forgetting their grievances, surrendered to the passion of the moment and pledged themselves body and soul to the support of their Tsar. Thus for a time Russia too achieved her *Union Sacrée*. Only a small, despised group of Deputies on the extreme Left had the temerity to vote in opposition – Kerensky, one of them, on this occasion abstained.

The Duma then obediently adjourned for six months, and the Tsar's ministers, under the emergency of the war, ruled virtually by decree. But the Duma reconvened in February 1915 to pass the budget estimates and at once broke into long-repressed uproar. The war was going very badly. There was no news from the front but news of disaster. The shortage of munitions was almost an accepted condition. A great part of wartime needs, notably of the hospitals — and, in 1915, the care of the refugees of the great military retirement of that year — had been met by popular voluntary organizations, such as the Zemstvos,[8] outside the official departments which should otherwise have been responsible. Liberal Deputies in the Duma formed themselves into a Progressive Bloc frankly demanding "the creation of a government enjoying the confidence of the country." Rodzianko, the President of the Duma, persuaded the Tsar to dismiss some of the more obstructive senior officials and to set up a Special Council, somewhat on the lines of the Ministry of Munitions then being mooted in Britain. Some of these reforms and proposals were indeed put in hand. General Polivanov, an officer popular with the Duma, was appointed Minister of War. Then suddenly, in August 1915, apparently under the influence of that evil genius Rasputin, the Tsar dismissed the Grand Duke Nicholas, who since 1914 had commanded the army in the field, and announced to his astonished ministers that he would assume the supreme post himself. In his curious, half-mystical way he seemed to think that his own self-sacrifice would restore the situation at the front. "A sin offering is needed to save Russia," he said; "I shall be the victim. God's will be done!"

The Tsar could hardly have made a worse decision. At the front the real direction of the war no doubt would fall to the Tsar's Chief of Staff, the very capable General Alexeyev, and the more serious consequences were not to be anticipated there. But, at home, in Petrograd, the Tsaritsa — and, of course, Rasputin — would be left with a virtual regency. While the Tsar ensconced himself uselessly at Headquarters at Mogilev, the Tsaritsa played her own political game with impunity. In September 1915, at her insistence, the Tsar ordered the suspension of the Duma.

Polivanov at the Ministry of War, and the new Special Councils — there were ultimately four of them — exerted themselves against crushing frustration, and did indeed effect some heartening, but transient, improvements. The "Polivanov drafts" at the front were noted for their good morale. Munitions were more plentiful and, in the course of 1916, the Russian Army was even able to take the offensive and to fight that unexpected action under General Brusilov, the last and most spectacular military effort of Tsarist Russia. But there was now a serious shortage of food in the big towns, not only because of the deterioration of the farms and estates, but because of breakdowns of transport and distribution, especially in wintertime. And then it was reported that there was a shortage of men. The army required 300,000 recruits a month to maintain its current strength of 14,500,000, and the Special Councils could no longer find labor for their industrial programs. Unbelievably, the "Russian steamroller," once so belauded in the British and French press, was running down for want of its human fuel.

But the Tsaritsa now held the reins. Daily she plied the Tsar at Headquarters with those strange, passionate letters of hers, in half-literate English, referring constantly to the two main prepossessions of her mind, the sickly little Tsarevich and Gregory, "Our Friend," "Man of God," and recommending this or that ministerial change, which the Tsar, that docile autocrat, invariably ordered to be made forthwith. Thus in February 1916, Goremykin, an ornamental, courtly, entirely ineffective octogenarian, President of the Council of Ministers, resigned and was followed by a succession of the Tsaritsa's nominees, one of whom, Stürmer, was probably pro-German. In March 1916, Polivanov was dismissed and in July Sazonov, the Foreign Minister and one of the original architects of the Allied Entente. In the weeks immediately preceding the Revolution, the Tsaritsa's favorite political mentor seems to have been Protopopov, Minister of the Interior, at one time a safe and well-respected administrator, but later a protégé of Rasputin and probably afflicted with a serious cerebral derangement.

The sequel in the Russian Revolution will be described in the next chapter. (See pp. 73-77.)

Poland and the Baltic

In 1914 Poland was but a memory and a name. The Poles were one of those unhappy peoples whose loyalties the war had torn asunder. Polish conscripts fought in three separate armies, often against one another and on Polish soil. In 1914 Joseph Pilsudski, one Polish patriot, at the head of his "Polish Legion," went off to fight on the Austro-German side, and Roman Dmowski, another Polish patriot, at the head of a similar "Polish Legion," went off to fight on the Russian side. In the course of 1915, as a result of the Russian retirement, the whole of Poland fell under Austro-German occupation, and the "Polish Question" for the future disposal of the territory became one of the recurrent political issues in the chancelleries of the Central Powers. One compromise, much mooted in 1915, would have made Poland a German dependency with an Austrian archduke for its puppet king.

But in 1916 occupied Poland felt all the repercussions of Germany's man-power crisis, which we described above. The German High Command did not demand deportations of Polish labor, as it did in the case of Belgian and French labor; but more subtly, it tried to exploit the traditional anti-Russian sentiment in Poland to recruit a Polish army for service against Russia. In November 1916, the Central Powers solemnly proclaimed the "independence" of Poland and set about organizing a "Polish Government." Pilsudski became the Minister of War in the new regime. But then the trouble began. Pilsudski's Legion, while eager enough to shed its blood for the Polish fatherland, refused to take an oath of "fraternity of arms" with Germany and Austria-Hungary. Pilsudski was arrested by his German sponsors and spent the rest of the war a prisoner in the fortress of Magdeburg. The Polish army in the end proved to be, in Ludendorff's phrase, "a plowing of the sands."

In September 1917, the Central Powers created a Regency Council in Warsaw, composed of Poles, to exercise supreme authority until such time as a Polish king might be installed. A popular legislature, or Council of State, was to follow. But these measures were entirely theatrical. The real power remained with the German High Command. At the end of 1918 Pilsudski emerged from his confinement to lead the Polish national revolution. At least it can be said of Polish affairs in 1914-18 that Germany behaved with tolerable, if self-interested, friendliness. Germany's grim attempt to destroy the Polish nation was to come twenty years later.

In 1915 the Germans also invaded a large part of the Baltic provinces of Russia, and in September 1917 they captured Riga. During their occupation they made every effort to cajole the people of the area into forming some sort of political union with themselves. Conservative opinion in Germany had always regarded the Baltic as a special Teutonic preserve, ripe for annexation. The Baltic ports, Libau, Riga, and Reval were virtually German cities, and throughout the Baltic hinterland were prosperous landed communities of "Baltic Barons" of German extraction. The German Government now planned to create a Duchy of Courland and a Duchy of Estonia-Livonia in personal union with Prussia, and early in 1918 the Kaiser graciously accepted the grand-ducal crowns of both territories. Meanwhile an independent Lithuania was to be formed in alliance with Germany under a princeling of the House of Württemberg, allegedly descended from ancient Lithuanian royalty.

Also early in 1918 Germany signed the treaties of Brest Litovsk and Bucharest and thus completed her chain of annexations in the East. But all these fine plans were abruptly terminated by events elsewhere in November 1918. The whole episode, nevertheless, illustrates the endemic German ambitions in this historically amorphous "Debris Zone" in Intermediate Europe. As we shall see, 1918 was not the end of the story. (See pp. 79-80 and 150ff.)

"The Revolt in the Desert"

Turkey came out of the great trial at the Dardanelles with a well-deserved, if short-lived, enhancement of morale. The Turkish soldier earned himself a pride and prestige he had not known for a century. Unhappily the Turkish Government found it necessary to sully its army's record, even while the campaign at the Dardanelles was in progress, by persecuting its Armenian subjects who lived in and near the Russian frontier in Asia Minor and who were alleged to have shown treacherous, pro-Russian sympathies; and hundreds of thousands of these unfortunates were ordered to be removed en masse to less strategically dangerous districts. "The existence of Turkey," Talaat Pasha is reported to have said, "must outweigh every other consideration." The so-called Armenian Deportations, during the spring and summer months of 1915, were carried out with organized brutality. Armenian labor battalions in the Turkish Army were slaughtered in cold blood. One estimate put the total loss of Armenian lives at 500,000. But this was not the first time in history – or the last – that a war has been used as an opportunity for the "final solution" of a minority problem.

The whole evil episode was a sign, if sign were wanted, of the general deterioration of the Turkish home front at this time; characteristically, despair had turned into fear and cruelty. The Turkish people at large were suffering all the stringencies of the war, and, in a situation in which more efficient governments had failed, it was unlikely that the Turkish Government would signally succeed. The effort at the Dardanelles was not to be repeated. After 1915 the requisite domestic support was no longer forthcoming. In 1916 Russian forces invaded the now derelict districts of Armenia; British forces took the offensive in Mesopotamia and from across the Suez Canal. Meanwhile the Arabs of the Hejaz were in revolt.

Arab nationalism had predated the war and, like the Young Turk movement, was a part of the general political unrest in the Ottoman Empire at that time. Hussein, Sherif of Mecca, was early marked out by his unique position in the Arab world as one of its logical leaders. He was ruler of the Hejaz, protector of the Holy Cities, descendant of the Prophet, and pretender to the Caliphate. He had probably been meditating revolt against the Turks since 1910. In February 1914, his second son, Abdullah, had already had a secret interview with Kitchener, then in Cairo, and had sought his active sympathy. Thence, from the outbreak of the war, had followed lengthy negotiations which concluded in October 1915 in letters from Sir Henry McMahon, the British High Commissioner in Cairo – the "McMahon Pledge" – to the effect that the British Government, with certain "modifications," would "recognize and uphold the independence of the Arabs" in return for an open rupture with the Ottoman Empire. The Arab Revolt, the "Revolt in the Desert," accordingly began in June 1916.

Indirectly linked with the same episode were two other Arab chieftains, Ibn Saud and Ibn Rashid. Ibn Saud, Sultan of the Nejd, leader of the fanatical, revivalist Wahhabis, whose territories were nearer the Persian Gulf, had entered into a treaty with the Government of British India by which his independence was recognized in return for his benevolent neutrality during the war. Ibn Rashid, Emir of Hail, whose territories were nearer Syria, was loyal to the Turks. These two chieftains spent the war years in the prosecution of their mutual rivalry. On the whole, British policy was well served, and the complex of forces in Arabia – for the moment – worked out to the British advantage. Hussein, the greatest of the Arab leaders, whose territories lay alongside the important highway of the Red Sea, was Britain's ally; Ibn Saud and Ibn Rashid were conveniently preoccupied with their own private raids and skirmishes against each other.

Meanwhile the Allies had been considering the future disposal of the Ottoman Empire in the event of its defeat and dissolution in the war. During 1915 Britain, France, and Italy agreed to Russia's possession of Constantinople and the Dardanelles. The Treaty of London in 1915 recognized Italy's interest in the Dodecanese and Anatolia. From time to time attempts were made to bribe Greece into the war with offers of Smyrna. France had traditional claims in Syria and the Levant. In 1916 it fell to Mark Sykes and Georges Picot,[9] representing respectively the British Foreign Office and the French Foreign Ministry, to reduce this many-authored essay in imperialism to some sort of precision, and the Ottoman Empire was parceled out among the prospective victors, leaving a Turkish rump of some 20,000 square miles round Angora (Ankara). The Sykes-Picot Agreement provided for an independent Arab state or confederation of states, for British, French, and Russian acquisitions, and also for the international control of the Palestine area. Finally, in November 1917, Balfour made his famous declaration: "His Majesty's Government view with favour the establishment in Palestine of a national home for the Jewish people." (See Appendix, p. 833.)

Of this since controversial diplomatic interlude it is perhaps only necessary for us to say, at this point, that there was no double-dealing or explicit contradiction in any of its terms. Certainly the Sykes-Picot Agreement was secret, it could be described as cynical, and its conditions were soon outpaced by events; but secrecy, cynicism, and impermanence were not blameworthy qualities in the political usages of the time. Also there was deliberate vagueness and much misunderstanding. Aspirant nationalism is liable to be more interested in the spirit than in the letter of pledges meted out to it, and probably not more than a handful of British and French officials were fully conversant with the precise content and intent of the various documents in question. The consequences were to appear after the war when the settlement of these Near Eastern territories and their many problems had to be made. (See pp. 184ff.)

From the start of the Arab Revolt, the British Government supplied Hussein with what has alliteratively been called a constant stream of corn, cash, and cartridges. T. E. Lawrence, formerly a roving Oxford archaeologist studying Crusaders' castles in the Near East, made his first unobtrusive visit to the Hejaz in October 1916. His mission was military, not political; he had no part, then or since, in "promises" to the Arabs. But he acquitted himself brilliantly as a resistance leader, as he would have been called in a later war. With Feisal, the third of Hussein's sons, he directed the Arabs' campaign, especially their raids on the Turkish railroads in the Hejaz and in Syria. He cooperated throughout with General Allenby, then commander of the British forces in Palestine, up to the final capture of Damascus.

4. THE MIDDLE PHASES—1916-17

The Campaigns of 1916 and 1917 on Land

The years 1916 and 1917, on the Western front, brought their repetition of trench battles, expensive of life and material, strategically sterile, morally wasting – Verdun and the Somme, the Nivelle Offensive, Vimy Ridge, Messines, and Passchendaele. On the Eastern and Italian fronts they brought two sudden and unexpected open battles, the Brusilov Offensive and Caporetto. And we have also to include in the series the one great naval battle of the war, Jutland. We begin this chapter with a brief description of these actions. We then resume the political story with the entry of Rumania and Greece into the war, and move on to Germany's unrestricted submarine campaign and the reactions thereto in the United States, Britain and, eventually, in Germany herself. We continue with the Russian Revolution; and we conclude the chapter with the peace proposals and discussions at the end of 1917, and with the peace treaties of Brest Litovsk and Bucharest early in 1918.

In February 1916, the German High Command, under General von Falkenhayn, ordered the attack on Verdun and initiated round that celebrated hillside fortress the greatest of all trench battles – in point of duration and casualties, it was, and still is, the greatest battle of all time.[1] Far from trying to overcome the trench deadlock, Falkenhayn planned a campaign which accepted it and tried to exploit it. He planned not so much to capture the fortress as to inflict on France, at a vital point, a wound which would not be allowed to heal. Weeks of continuous shelling and short advances by infantry would conform more nearly to the spirit of such an operation than a great Sedanesque victory on the upper reaches of the Meuse. Verdun was easy to attack and hard to defend. It lay less than ten miles distant from the nearest German railhead and, thanks to the salient of St. Mihiel, which had remained in German hands since 1914, it was connected with its own bases in France only by a single road and rail line. The terrain was dry and elevated, and unaffected by vicissitudes of weather. Verdun would make an ideal laboratory for a supreme experiment in the tactics of attrition.

Joffre gave the command of the sector to General Pétain, and under

Pétain's leadership Verdun held firm. But Falkenhayn came within an ace of the objective he had set himself. In France, with the first news of the German attack, all the panic of the early days of the war surged up again. The French people by now had grown so conditioned to the war of position that they magnified the smallest retirements into disasters. In 1914 they had accepted the loss of thirty miles of Picardy with greater calmness than they now accepted the loss of a single strong point. As Falkenhayn had well calculated, the moral effect of a French defeat at Verdun could have been decisive. Yet, as the fighting continued, reports began to come in of the incredible heroism of the defense. "They shall not pass" became all at once a sort of sacred incantation by the mere repetition of which a man could cast out fear and horror. In the end the Battle of Verdun lasted seven months. Falkenhayn had chosen his weapons and his ground and was more deeply and inextricably committed than perhaps he had desired. When it was all over, the total casualties, German and French, amounted to nearly 700,000 men; the territorial change was negligible. The greatest battle of all time was one of the least decisive.

One military historian has described the year 1916 as the "Dog Fall" of the war, the moment of supreme effort in the contest which results in nothing.[2] We still marvel today at the great offensive battles at this time, so confidently launched on so many fronts—at so much cost—against stubborn and immovable defenses. Thus the Austrian commander, Conrad von Hötzendorf, planned an all-out assault on the Alpine front against Italy. Now that Russia and Serbia had both fallen, there seemed no reason why he should not quickly dispose of "this most traitorous of Austria's enemies." Falkenhayn discouraged the project and would have preferred Conrad to maintain the Eastern front against a possible revival of Russia. But Conrad was not to be denied, and his assault duly took place in the Trentino during the late spring.

On June 4, 1916, General Brusilov, commanding the Russian armies facing Galicia, launched the celebrated offensive, which the Allies named after him the Brusilov Offensive, and which the Austrians called the Battle of Luck, the small town round which the offensive began. The whole operation was intended at first to be no more than a feint to divert the Germans and perhaps relieve the pressure on Verdun. The Russian Army after its defeats in 1915 was in no great state to take the initiative in any major campaign. But here, for once, the offensive battle seemed to succeed. The Austro-Hungarian divisions in Galicia, weakened by withdrawals for Conrad's operation against Italy, deceived by the long inactivity of winter and spring, and showing signs of progressive moral decay, "broke like a piecrust" on a 200-mile front. The Russian High Command, after some hesitation, ordered Brusilov to advance to the limit. But there was now no real sustaining power on either side. The offensive petered out in confused fighting over the old Galician battlefields. It was the last great campaign of the war on the Eastern front. Meanwhile Conrad's offensive in the Trentino had made no progress whatever and was called off. But then, in the same June, on the Western front, the British launched their offensive on the Somme.

Canadians on the Somme, October 1916

IMPERIAL WAR MUSEUM

For the Battle of the Somme, General Sir Douglas Haig, the British commander, disposed of twenty-four divisions of Kitchener's "New Army" – "every man a volunteer" – and the products of Lloyd George's munitions campaign. He is said to have entertained the most vivid hopes of the battle and held three cavalry divisions in reserve to exploit his success. The offensive began, at the end of June 1916, with a bombardment of the German lines of eight days' duration, and the fighting lasted thereafter for nearly five months. The British gained a total of 120 square miles for the loss of over 400,000 men. The cavalry divisions were never used. But the Somme was the first of the great "battles of material," and it was also the first battle in the war in which the German Army was forced to stand on the defensive. It broke Falkenhayn's reputation – even more than did Verdun. In August 1916, he was succeeded jointly in the German High Command by Hindenburg and Ludendorff, the victors of Tannenberg in 1914 and of the great Russian campaign of 1915. German military literature in later years constantly referred to the devastating effect of the British bombardments in 1916 and harked back to this supreme trial of the German soldier with the almost nostalgic remark, "He never fought so well again!"

The story continues into 1917. Joffre, discredited like Falkenhayn, had now retired and was replaced in the French High Command by General

Nivelle, recently one of Pétain's most successful subordinates in the Battle of Verdun. But there was little change in military policy. In April 1917, Nivelle's offensive in the Champagne suffered one of the sharpest repulses of the war. The British took Vimy Ridge at a cost – in great part to the Canadian Corps – of 100,000 men. In May the French soldier called a momentary halt to the whole madcap massacre. Mutinies broke out in several French divisions in the offensive sectors. Two regiments at Soissons threatened to evacuate their lines and march on Paris. There was wild defeatist talk even in the Chamber – "Let's have done with it!" *"Il faut en finir!"* – followed by an outcrop of political scandals, some of them treasonable. Pétain succeeded Nivelle as French Commander in Chief, with Foch as his Chief of Staff, and the two leaders addressed themselves to a thorough disciplinary and psychological recuperation of the French Army. But they essayed no major action for the remainder of the year. The France of 1917, in more than one way, presaged the France of 1940.

Haig, however, kept up the offensive on the British sectors and fought the short, seven-day Battle of Messines, followed by the long, three-month Battle of Passchendaele, sometimes called the Third Battle of Ypres, the most melancholy operation in British military history. The British gained fifty square miles at the cost of 240,000 men. Passchendaele, by then an unrecognizable heap of mud and rubble, was announced as captured by the Canadians on November 6.

Then, suddenly, in that autumn of 1917, the Alpine front flared up. Here, since 1915, in the mountainous terrain round about the River Isonzo, dividing Italy from Austria, the Italian Army had fought eleven offensive battles, with great loss of life and little gain of ground. The city of Gorizia had been the single, inadequate prize of more than two years of war. Equally had Conrad's offensive on the same front in 1916 been a miserable failure. Military opinion among the Allies dismissed the Italian front as being as uselessly and irremediably deadlocked as the Western front itself. But, on the morning of October 24, 1917, the Battle of Caporetto, or the Twelfth Battle of the Isonzo, as it was called in Italy, began. The assault by six German and nine Austrian divisions had been planned in complete secrecy. By evening the Italian position on the Isonzo was broken. The Italian Second Army in the sector had become a "fugitive rabble." The entire Italian front gave way. The Italian High Command tried to make a stand on the Tagliamento, and then on the Piave, where at last during mid-November the opposing lines were once more stabilized. Italy lost 6,000 square miles of territory and 600,000 men, and for a few chaotic weeks it seemed as if she had gone down to final defeat.

Certainly in Italy conditions in 1916 and 1917 had not been happy. The country was suffering all the usual domestic difficulties of the war. There was, of course, a shortage of food, and, in Italy's case, there was the much more serious shortage of coal. The harvest of 1917 had been a partial failure. "Unreliable" political elements – notably the pro-Austrian clerical groups – were said to be exploiting the situation to their own ends. Caporetto, like other defeats in other countries, no more than reflected the deterioration of the home front.

But the very completeness of the disaster at Caporetto was in some ways

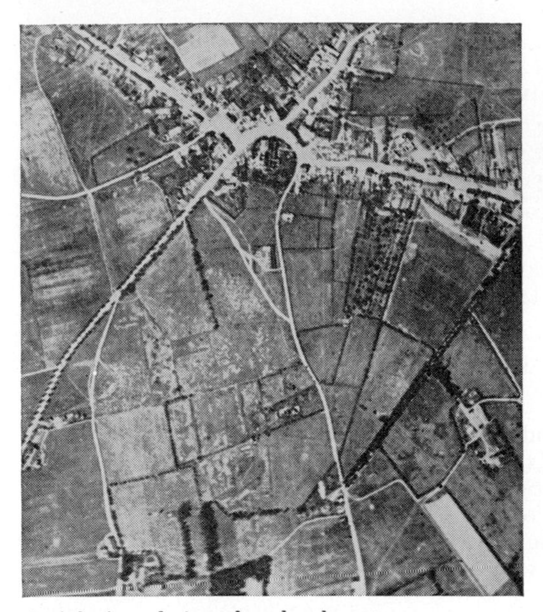

Aerial view, before bombardment

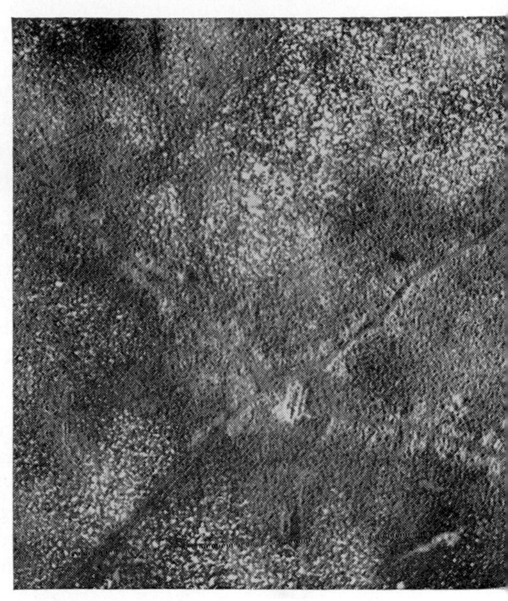

The same, November 1917, after bombardment

Artillery in the First World War: Passchendaele, Flanders

IMPERIAL WAR MUSEUM

its salvation. It was not only that Venezia and Lombardy might once more become Austrian provinces, or that all the labor and sacrifice of Italian unification might be undone. The very nationhood of Italy was under challenge in the eyes of the world. Caporetto stung the pride of a people but recently restored to political self-respect, reminiscent of a former servitude, and fiercely sensitive of their reputed lack of martial qualities. The King invited Orlando to form a new government. The Chamber, normally noisy and obstructive, gave Orlando its united support. Giolitti, the non-interventionist, after months of unsympathetic silence, appeared dramatically in the Chamber and gave one of the bravest speeches of his long political career. The King appointed General Diaz his Chief of Staff, "Italy's Pétain," as he was sometimes called, then a corps commander in the Carso sector.

Meanwhile French and British divisions had been hurried to the Italian front. American and British relief organizations went to work among the refugees who had fled before the Austro-German advance, and did much to counteract the panic of the civil population. On November 5, 1917, Allied premiers and military chiefs met in conference at Rapallo and discussed not only the reorganization of the Italian war effort but the entire question of military cooperation between the Allies. Under the driving initiative of Lloyd George, the conference finally drew up an agreement to establish a Supreme War Council at Versailles. Caporetto was an expensive lesson, but it was the precursor of unified command on the Western front.

The War at Sea

We interrupt our narrative to describe, almost in parentheses, the one great naval battle of the war — the Battle of Jutland.

Naval operations in 1914 and 1915 had been confined to cruisers and submarines, and meanwhile the great British and German battle fleets, which had been built at such cost before 1914 and had caused so much political turmoil, had nowhere been engaged. For their part, Admiral Jellicoe and the British Admiralty had resolved to preserve their existing favorable balance rather than risk a fight for the mere sake of fighting. They maintained the blockade, they renounced the cherished offensive traditions of their service, but they kept the command of the sea. As Churchill once put it:

> The standpoint of the Commander-in-Chief of the British Grand Fleet was unique. His responsibilities were on a different scale from all others. It might fall to him as to no other man — Sovereign, Statesman, Admiral or General — to issue orders which in the space of *two or three hours* might nakedly decide who won the war. The destruction of the British Battle Fleet was final. Jellicoe was the only man on either side who could lose the war in an afternoon.[3]

Early in 1916, Admiral von Tirpitz, architect of the German Navy and the alleged instigator of the German submarine campaign, resigned from the German Marine Office where he had been a baleful influence for so long. His protégé, Admiral Scheer, was now Commander of the German High Seas Fleet, no less aggressively inclined, but his aggressiveness was at last to take the more spectacular and audacious form of surface fighting, and he was anxious to provoke the British Grand Fleet into action, not all at once, but if possible piecemeal. The German High Command in France was appealing for a naval diversion which might embarrass the British Army, then known to be preparing its offensive on the Somme.

Late in the evening of May 30, 1916, Scheer sent out his force of cruisers and battle cruisers under Admiral Hipper toward the Norwegian coast, and himself followed with the High Seas Fleet fifty miles astern. German submarines were already lying in wait in positions off the Scottish coast. Jellicoe, at Scapa Flow with the Grand Fleet, put to sea. Admiral Beatty with the Battle Cruiser Squadron simultaneously sailed from Rosyth with the object of baiting the High Seas Fleet into battle with the Grand Fleet. Beatty sighted Hipper off Jutland in the late afternoon of the 31st, and in the subsequent encounter his flagship was disabled and two of his other ships were sunk. Hipper emerged without a major casualty. The British Grand Fleet and the German High Seas Fleet sighted one another in the evening, and there followed confused partial actions, hampered by mist and defective signaling. By sundown the German High Seas Fleet had escaped. Desultory cruiser and destroyer action continued during the night. But the final tally rested with the Germans. In twenty-four hours the British had lost roughly double the tonnage of their enemy and more than double the lives.

It was a gloomy Britain that read the first reports of the Battle of Jutland. On June 2 the Admiralty bluntly announced the facts, and with sailorly candor mentioned only those German losses which it had definitely ascertained. It did not mention – it could not then have known – the damage, amounting to disablement, which many of the surviving German ships had suffered. On June 5 came the further news that Kitchener had been lost at sea while proceeding on a mission to Russia. The double blow was very hard. In Germany, the *Skagerrak,* as the Germans called it, was celebrated as a victory, the veritable dusk of the Nelsonian legend. But neither side, in fact, had gained its objective. The British had failed to destroy the German High Seas Fleet; the Germans had failed to reduce the overwhelming preponderance of the British Navy and to disconcert the blockade. A month after the battle, Scheer reported to the Kaiser, somewhat platitudinously, that surface action would not compel England to sue for peace, but he added the much more significant rider that Germany's only chance at sea lay in renewed submarine warfare against British commerce. The German High Seas Fleet retired indefinitely to its minefields and harbors. In October 1918, its final "death cruise" was frustrated by mutiny and revolution.

The Entry of Rumania and Greece into the War

At the outbreak of the war Rumania, like her Balkan fellows, had been an uncertain and hesitating neutral. But, as time went on, Rumanian public opinion veered more and more toward the Allied cause. The people prided themselves on their "Roman" ancestry, and they had some rather tenuous claims on Hungarian Transylvania – the ancient Roman province of Dacia, partially inhabited by Rumanians. Rumania had almost followed Italy into the war in 1915. Ion Bratianu, the Rumanian Premier, however, resisted the pressing courtships of the two belligerent groups, and certainly, while the armies of the Central Powers were winning victories in Russia and Serbia, no other policy seemed possible. Rumania possessed immense natural resources, especially grain and oil, and she had none too efficient an army with which to defend them; her position was most delicate. But in June 1916, when the Brusilov Offensive galvanized all southeastern Europe with expectations of a certain Austrian collapse, Bratianu began to think that he might have held off Rumania's suitors too long, and that she had better yield now or lose her chance forever.

On August 17, 1916, Bratianu concluded an alliance with the Allies in return for large accretions of territory in Transylvania and Bukovina. It was a preposterous bargain, for the greater part of which there was no justification, ethnic or strategic. But belligerents in the middle of a war cannot always be too squeamish about the disposal of their enemies' territories. By the end of that August Rumania was in the war. But, as it turned out, Bratianu had sadly miscalculated. The Rumanians had assumed Germany to be fully committed at Verdun and expected to conduct a grand military promenade into the broad Hungarian plains. Nevertheless, the German High Command detached four divisions for service against Rumania; the Brusilov Offensive failed at the critical moment; a joint Franco-British operation against Bulgaria, based on Salonika and reinforced by refugee Serbian units, amounted to little more than heavy raids and counterraids. The Austro-German "punitive expedition" under Falkenhayn descended on Rumania with humiliating speed and power. Bulgarian forces invaded the Dobruja. By the first week of December 1916, Rumanian resistance had miserably collapsed, the Rumanian capital, Bucharest, had surrendered, and the greater part of the country was in occupation.

On December 12, 1916, the Central Powers celebrated their Rumanian victory by issuing a general peace offer to the Allied governments. It was a vague but strident protestation of innocence in the war and a disclaimer of further responsibility for its continuance; but no hint was vouchsafed as to those specific objects — notably Serbia and Belgium — for which the Allies had originally taken up arms. It was the first overt peace offer of the war. It was rejected by the Allied governments out of hand.

Meanwhile the situation in Greece had been steadily deteriorating. There were two main parties contending for power. One was led by Venizelos, Greek Premier at various times — though at this precise juncture, out of office — a tempestuous, headstrong patriot, a passionate supporter of the Allies, a dreamer of a Greater Greece which should include a Hellenized Constantinople and ambitious acquisitions in Asia Minor. The other was led by King Constantine, a much maligned monarch, not pro-German, as he was so often accused of being — though he had married the Kaiser's sister. On the contrary, he was much more inclined toward the Allies; but he was cautious and pacific. Salonika was now occupied by a largely French army, reinforced by British units and by remnants of the defeated Serbs and Rumanians, all under the command of Sarrail, a typical French "political" general. By the end of 1916 the country was virtually divided between Venizelists and Royalists, with Sarrail openly supporting the Venizelists.

We have not the space, nor is it necessary, to describe in detail the intrigues and "incidents" of which Greek affairs at this moment were composed. The eventual outcome, as we should expect, was dictated by the power on the spot — that is to say by Sarrail and his strangely heterogeneous forces in Salonika. Germany, after her successes in Serbia and Rumania, disdained to invade Greece; German writers referred ironically to Salonika as their "biggest internment camp." Consequently Sarrail and the French Government, in the name of the Allies, were left to reshape the Greek world to suit themselves. In June 1917, King Constantine abdicated in favor of his second son, Alexander, and Venizelos was installed in Athens as Premier. Greece's formal entry into the war on the Allied side followed in due course.

The German Unrestricted Submarine Campaign

The year 1917 has been called "The Year of Agony" — *"L'Année d'Angoise."* For Germany it brought increasing austerity; for Austria, racial disintegration; for France, mutiny and defeatism; for Italy, a military disaster. For Britain, as we still have to relate, it brought near-starvation;

for Russia it brought revolution. It was, as might be expected, a year of many peace intrigues and peace rumors. It was a year of the weighing of many imponderables, and its military events, as we read them today, are understandable, not so much as "battles," but as extensions of an ever-widening, all-consuming siege of peoples in which fighting fronts and home fronts were merged in a single, indivisible ordeal. Its only independent event that was, so to speak, still prompted by free will and not by necessity, and ultimately its outstanding and decisive event, was the declaration of war on Germany by the United States.

Germany had entered 1917 under extreme domestic hardship. The battles of 1916, Verdun and the Somme, had added to the existing moral and material strains. The war with Rumania, though a lesser episode, had been even more disturbing to confidence. All Germany's former victories on the Eastern front had not deterred a Balkan state of no military importance from joining the enemy.

Hindenburg and Ludendorff were in supreme command. The partnership which had begun at Tannenberg in 1914 had now assumed the virtual dictatorship of the Reich. The first act of the new leadership had been the reorganization of the home front under the so-called Hindenburg Program, which we have already described. (See p. 39.) On the Western front, meanwhile, the two soldiers elected to stand on the defensive. Early in 1917 an arc of territory facing the British sector was laid waste and evacuated, and the German forces were voluntarily withdrawn to a new fortified position, the Siegfried Line — or, as it was called more familiarly, the Hindenburg Line. Caporetto was the only offensive action in which the German High Command participated during the year.

At the same time Hindenburg and Ludendorff were coming around to the view that submarine warfare would have to be intensified. Theirs was a counsel of despair, but still plausible and persuasive. The Western front, they argued, had degenerated into a dreary stalemate. Military action on land, in the current state of military science, could no longer be expected to bring the war to a conclusion. But the Allied naval blockade remained. All the resources of the outer world — even time itself — were on the Allied side. "Unrestricted" submarine war — that is, total war at sea, the sinking without warning of all merchantmen, belligerent and neutral — only this could provide a way of escape. It would be directed particularly against England, the spine of the Allied coalition and the heart of its economic and moral strength. It would employ that arm of the fighting services, the German Navy, that — with the glorious exception of the Skagerrak — had scarcely had the chance to show its mettle.[4]

Into these considerations international law and humanitarian principles hardly entered. Indeed there was a certain grim justice in hoisting upon England the cruelties of her own hunger blockade. It only remained to make allowances for the reaction of neutrals. The fate of Serbia and Rumania should act as a sufficient deterrent to Holland and Denmark. And as for the Americas, plainly they were averse to war. The United States had tried to avoid a war even with Mexico. But, even if the United States, under President Wilson's prompting, should take the unexpected course and enter the war against Germany, the power of England would certainly be broken before American aid could become effective. And finally, in view of the existing flow of munitions to the Allies, the United States at war could hardly be more dangerous than the United States at peace.

So argued Germany's military leaders, and there was little that the Chancellor and his civilian colleagues, for all their fears and doubts, could offer in reply. Peace overtures in December 1916 by the Central Powers and by President Wilson of the United States had been useless. There was nothing more to wait for. The final decision was taken by the Kaiser on January 9, 1917, and the unrestricted submarine campaign opened on February 1.

We have now to consider three consequences of this new turn of affairs, that is to say, the reactions to it in three different countries: the United States, Britain, and — when its ill success had become evident — in Germany herself. Our next three sections accordingly will describe the entry of the United States into the war and the crises of 1917 in Britain and Germany.

The Entry of the United States into the War

Germany's unrestricted submarine campaign was the occasion of the entry of the United States into the war. Thus far, mention of the United States has only been incidental. But perhaps we should now examine, if briefly, the entire American attitude toward the war and President Wilson's statesmanship during the first three years of it. We return for a moment to 1914.

At the start of the war, President Wilson had at once taken a correct neutral attitude. In his message to the American people in August 1914, he urged them to avoid impulsive prejudices and excitements:

> I venture to speak a solemn word of warning to you against that deepest, most subtle, most essential breach of neutrality which may spring out of partisanship, out of passionately taking sides. The United States must be neutral in fact as well as in name during these days that are to try men's souls.

But the American people did take sides, and they took sides passionately. For nearly three years of technical neutrality, the United States, like a great tree with its roots deeply sunk in tradition, was violently buffeted by the winds of circumstance, and at last wrenched bodily into the universal storm. Strong isolationist sentiment going back to the eighteenth century, a hostility to the old tyrant England, a profound contempt for the European order — as well as the active pressure of organized German-American groups and, to some extent, Irish-American groups — all this seemed to do battle against the shock and horror of Germany's conduct of the war, her invasion of Belgium and reported atrocities during that invasion, her submarine campaign, her use of poison gas, and the crowning folly of her note to Mexico. (See pp. 65-66.) There was also an influential group which feared that Germany's victory in Europe would have to be

German Submarine U-9 going to sea

CULVER

met by the permanent militarization of the Western Hemisphere and that the consequent heavy financial and political burden would have to be borne by a hitherto pacifist American people.

At the same time, however, the British waged a propaganda war of great psychological skill. The British press service in the United States was well organized. The transatlantic cables were under British control, and their use was supervised by British censors. American correspondents were not allowed at the front, and American papers could only reproduce communiqués and the comments of British writers. British diplomacy was in the cautious, competent hands of Sir Edward Grey, the British Foreign Secretary, a great Liberal and a great admirer of American democracy—and, it must be admitted, in the hands also of that complete Anglophile and Grey's personal friend, the American ambassador in London, Walter Hines Page. We need not enter here into all the legal and diplomatic complexities of the war at sea and its effects on American maritime interests and American maritime pride. At least Grey nowhere allowed the British Admiralty to exasperate American patience beyond its limit, and Page manfully came to his aid whenever the extreme of discretion seemed sometimes to have been overpassed. Grey steered his diplomatic ship, in his own words, "through uncharted seas, perilous with shoals and rocks and treacherous currents." But he kept his course, and he brought his ship to port.

Finally, there was the American financial and industrial commitment to the Allied cause. It is a fact that Germany was the first belligerent to borrow money in the United States in 1914. But thereafter all but a very small fraction of American funds went to the Allies. William Jennings Bryan, then Secretary of State and a leading isolationist, tried to have imposed a "moral embargo" on loans to belligerents, but the embargo was quashed by President Wilson in October 1914. By the end of 1914, the House of Morgan was already "coordinating" Allied purchases of war material and munitions in the United States. Natural sympathy, the passionate taking of sides, may have largely determined the direction of "this vile traffic," as Bryan called it, but Allied blockade effectively discouraged the attempt to divert any part of it to Germany. Isolationist sentiment in 1914-17 was a powerful force in American affairs, and the American people were never unanimously pro-Ally at any time during the First World War. Indeed, when they did enter that war, they did so pointedly, not as an "Ally," but as an "Associated Power." Yet it is undeniable that a certain moral predisposition existed in favor of the Western democracies, Britain and France, and it is also undeniable that the increasing and one-sided financial involvement was also a force in the same direction.

Throughout America's neutral period President Wilson was constantly exercised over the problems and prospects of peace. His ambition to be the impartial mediator between the belligerents at some greater Portsmouth Conference of the future amounted to an obsession, in which it is sometimes difficult to say whether humanitarianism or vanity was the real motive. President Wilson offered to mediate in August 1914. In January 1915, he sent his friend and adviser, Colonel House, to Europe to visit the belligerent capitals and sound out the belligerent statesmen as to their views on war and peace. Colonel House's discussions ranged over the blockade and freedom of the sea, international arbitration and collective security. He made valuable contacts and friendships, and he gathered information which was afterward useful to Wilson. But it was a forlorn quest. The sinking of the *Lusitania* in May 1915 brought his efforts to an abrupt end. In January and February 1916, House went on the second of his pacific itineraries, with much the same results. German militarism, at the time, seemed more intractable and oppressive than ever. The Kaiser was in one of his lofty moods and spoke as if the great dynasts of Europe, "I and my cousins, George and Nicholas," would confer the boon of peace as soon as it suited them to do so. In France the situation was as difficult, if for quite other reasons. Nor even in Britain did the Colonel find statesmen or people too eagerly disposed toward his ideas of a "reasonable" peace. At the moment the Battle of Verdun was infinitely more important to the warring world than the peace plans of Colonel House.

President Wilson barely escaped defeat in the presidential election of November 1916, and, though shaken in political prestige and in his own self-esteem, he resolved on one more effort for peace. On December 18, 1916, he sent identical notes to all the belligerent governments inviting them to state their war aims. "An interchange of views would clear the way at least for a conference," ran the note, "and make the permanent concord of the nations a hope for the immediate future, a concert of nations immediately practicable." But President Wilson had been rudely anticipated a few days earlier by the peace offer which the Central Powers had issued just after their triumphal entry into Bucharest. (See p. 60.) In the highly wrought psychology of the time the two peace notes, appearing almost simultaneously, merely nullified each other. Britain, France, and Russia reacted angrily toward what appeared to them to be an untimely attempt of the American President to "inject himself" into the peace intrigue of their enemies. Nevertheless, on January 22, 1917, in a message to the Senate, the sanguine President reviewed the replies of varying degrees of militancy or evasiveness which he had received from the belligerents and appealed with great eloquence for a "peace without victory."

One week later Germany launched her unrestricted submarine campaign, and ten weeks later the United States itself was in the war.

On the afternoon of January 31, 1917, at Washington, Count von Bernstorff, the German ambassador, handed Robert Lansing, the American Secretary of State, the note of the German Government announcing its immediate intention to wage unrestricted submarine war. The note referred to the Allies' "brutal methods of war" and then proceeded:

> Germany will meet the illegal measures of her enemies by forcibly preventing after February 1, 1917, in a zone around Great Britain, France, Italy, and in the eastern Mediterranean, all navigation, that of neutrals included, from and to England, from and to France, etc. All ships met within the zone will be sunk.

Though the general decision of the German Government may not have taken Washington by surprise, the precipitance with which that decision was now to go into effect made the worst possible impression. "To give only eight hours' notice without any previous warning of intention," wrote Lansing, "was in my opinion an unfriendly and indefensible act."

The United States had no alternative but to break off diplomatic relations with Germany. On February 3 Bernstorff was given his passports, and Gerard, the American ambassador, was recalled from Berlin. The same day President Wilson addressed Congress. Deeply moved as he was, he still hoped that the German announcement might prove to be no worse than a diplomatic threat, and he was resolved to postpone a declaration of war until some "actual overt acts" had been committed by German submarines at sea.

But on March 1, 1917, Germany's note to Mexico, the notorious Zimmermann telegram, appeared in the press. It had been picked up by British Naval Intelligence and was handed over to the American government on February 24. Upon the publication of the telegram, Arthur Zimmermann, then German Foreign Secretary, far from seeking to disown it, put the question of its authenticity beyond all doubt by acknowledging his responsibility and by attempting to brazen it out in the *Reichstag*. The telegram, addressed to the German minister in Mexico City on January 19, had been routed in code, through Bernstorff, over the American State Department's cable from Berlin — thereby abusing a courtesy that President Wilson himself had recently extended to the German Government. The text was as follows:

> We intend to begin unrestricted submarine warfare on February 1. Efforts will be made, notwithstanding, to keep the United States neutral. If we are not successful in this, we propose an alliance with Mexico on the following basis: We shall make war together and peace together. We shall give generous financial aid.

Mexico will reconquer her lost territory in Texas, New Mexico, and Arizona. The details are left to you for settlement. As soon as the outbreak of war with the United States becomes certain, you will disclose the foregoing, in strict secrecy, to the President of Mexico; you will add that he should invite Japan to immediate adherence and at the same time use his good offices to mediate between us and Japan. Please call the attention of the President [of Mexico] to the fact that unrestricted submarine warfare promises to compel England to make peace in a few months. Acknowledge. [Signed] Zimmermann.

The people of the eastern United States, who lay in more immediate contact with the submarine war, had clamored with increasing vehemence for a break with Germany. The reference to Mexico and Japan now fired the lagging resentment of the Pacific coast and the Middle West. The whole Zimmermann telegram, in letter and spirit, shocked American susceptibilities where they were most sensitive. All the evils of European statecraft in their most disingenuous form were thrust upon the American system. Monroe had come face to face with Machiavelli. By the same March the submarine sinkings had begun, and the overt acts for which President Wilson had waited were committed beyond question. Then the first news of the Russian Revolution arrived. On March 19 Wilson held one of his semiweekly cabinet meetings, and it was as clear to him as to his colleagues that war could not be avoided. On March 20 the United States recognized the Russian Provisional Government. Even Russia was now a land of free men battling the autocracies of Central Europe.

Congress was convened for an extraordinary session on April 2. President Wilson read his "War Message" to the assembled legislators:

We are glad to fight for the ultimate peace of the world and for the liberation of its peoples, the German peoples included: for the rights of nations great and small and the privilege of men everywhere to choose their way of life and of obedience. The world must be made safe for democracy. Its peace must be planted upon the tested foundations of political liberty. We have no selfish ends to serve. We desire no conquest, no dominion. We seek no indemnities for ourselves, no material compensation for the sacrifices we shall freely make. We are but one of the champions of the rights of mankind. We shall be satisfied when those rights have been made as secure as the faith and the freedom of nations can make them.

On April 4 and 6, 1917, the Senate and the House passed a joint resolution declaring a state of war between the United States and Germany. The presidential proclamation followed.

Crisis in Britain

In December 1916, Asquith and his Coalition had been forced out of office by the growing public criticism of his evident want of initiative and energy. His policy of "wait and see" had been poor comfort to a nation that had just watched its sons fighting the Battle of the Somme and was shortly to face worse terrors. He was succeeded as Prime Minister by Lloyd George at the head of a second Coalition, mainly of Conservatives. The core of the new government was a War Cabinet of five members: Bonar

Law, Lord Curzon, and Lord Milner (Conservatives), Arthur Henderson (Labor), and Lloyd George himself (Liberal), with Hankey as secretary. Britain, in effect, had completed her transition to a war basis. She had built up a great Continental army, and she had solved the problem of munitions. She now had a worthy leadership. But she was feeling the first sharp pinch of privation and the first dull ache of weariness; and losses to her merchant shipping were already very heavy, when, on February 1, 1917, the German unrestricted submarine campaign began.

Losses to British merchant shipping in 1914 "from acts of war" had amounted, on the average, to 51,000 tons a month, in 1915 to 74,000 tons a month, and in 1916 to 103,000 tons a month. The losses for February, March, and April of 1917 are shown in the following table:

SHIPPING LOSSES IN 1917 [5]

	British	*World Total*
January	154,000 tons	369,000 tons
February	313,000	540,000
March	353,000	594,000
April	545,000	881,000
May	352,000	597,000
June	418,000	688,000

In the first week in February 1917, 35 ships, British, Allied, and neutral, were sunk in and near the English Channel alone. In the first three months, 470 British ships were sunk. Neutral ships began to abandon the North Sea, and those in British ports refused to clear. The press raged and railed as if the mere violence of words could conjure away the new affliction. Cabinet ministers hastened to assure the country that its supplies were safe. Shipping returns were deliberately ambiguous and confused. But the losses continued to pile up.

Orthodox methods of defense proved to be nothing better, in the Admiralty's phrase, than "palliation." Merchantmen had already been armed, but the bigger submarines now carried a heavier surface armament or resorted to torpedo attack. Camouflage, "dazzle-painting" as it was then called, was an interesting experiment, more interesting than effective. Mine fields were laid down, for instance in the Heligoland Bight, but they were difficult to maintain. Decoy ships, heavily armed and disguised as tramps, hunted up and down the sea, but, for all their ingenuity, it is doubtful if they accounted for more than a dozen of the enemy's undersea fleet. Sir Joseph Maclay, Lloyd George's Shipping Controller at his new Ministry of Shipping, was squeezing every ton of usefulness out of the country's diminishing resources. The strictest priorities were enforced; all unessential imports were prohibited; heavy purchases of shipping were made abroad; a shipbuilding program of over 1,000,000 tons per year was laid down. Finally, the government approached Japan for a destroyer flotilla for convoy operations in the Mediterranean. Japan complied but exacted a secret treaty, by which Britain and the Allies engaged themselves to support Japan's claims to the former German possessions in the North Pacific—a treaty which, as will be related in another place, was to have some unfortunate consequences. (See pp. 104-05.)

A screen of destroyers as protection to a battle fleet had long been a commonplace of naval warfare. The principle was as old as classical antiquity. But there seemed, at first, good reasons against using the same principle for the protection of merchant convoys. Admiral Jellicoe, for one, lately transferred from the Grand Fleet to become First Sea Lord, was pessimistic in the extreme. The necessary escorting craft — and time for experiment — were both in short supply. The task of forming the convoy at the port of departure would be slow and difficult; the delays involved by ships waiting for the convoy to assemble would entail serious economic loss; the speed of the convoy would be governed by the slowest ship; the convoy would be dispersed by fog or storm; the convoy would offer an enlarged target to the submarine; the convoy, especially in the North Sea, might be raided by units of the German Navy in strength; the final arrival of the convoy at the home port would result in undue congestion; and so on.

But good reasons must give place to better. The opponents of the convoy system had gone astray in their estimate of the number of ships requiring escort. Perhaps 140 merchantmen arrived at British ports per week, and the tactical and administrative task of convoy therefore lay within manageable proportions. The Ministry of Shipping was in possession of daily, almost hourly, information regarding the positions of ships in every part of the world and could quickly organize the assembling of convoys at convenient points. Direct routing compensated for slow speeds; individual ships lost more time warily zigzagging across the sea than did the convoy sailing at the pace of one sluggish tramp. Furthermore, the convoy gave its members a sense of security, and the moral effect on the group was profound. If a ship was hit, rescue was assured. The masters consigned their worries to their escort and devoted themselves, with benefit to all concerned, to their proper task of navigation. Far from being a larger target, the convoy escaped the notice which the old "protected approach areas" invariably attracted. The secrecy of routes and destinations could be far better kept than when individual ships wirelessed for instructions and instantly betrayed their whereabouts. Finally, the convoy constituted a strong combatant force. Surface attack was impossible, and torpedo attack exposed the submarine to the deadly retaliation of the depth charge.

Beatty, who had succeeded Jellicoe in the command of the Grand Fleet, was one of the few ranking admirals who believed that the convoy must be given a trial. Admiral Sims, commanding American naval forces in European waters, who visited England shortly after the American entry into the war, was similarly persuaded and reported favorably to his government. Lloyd George, Maclay, the Shipping Controller, and that unfailing adviser of the British Government in difficult moments, Sir Maurice Hankey, were all supporting the convoy with increasing force and impatience. Early in May 1917, if we are to believe Lloyd George's account of the dispute, the government virtually ordered the Admiralty to initiate convoys, at first from Gibraltar. In mid-May the Admiralty set up a Committee on Convoys, and by June and July the system was in full and regular operation on most routes in the North Atlantic and North Sea.

The final establishment of the convoy system determined Lloyd George to reshuffle the team at the Admiralty which he considered had blocked its adoption. In July he appointed Sir Eric Geddes First Lord, and in December Admiral Wemyss replaced Jellicoe. Under Geddes the convoy system was extended and developed in every direction. It was instituted for outgoing as well as incoming voyages. It insured an ever increasing immunity from submarine attack. Between midsummer 1917 and November 1918, 16,657 ships were convoyed to or from British ports with a loss of less than 0.75 per cent.

Food crisis was the obverse of the submarine war, and its main battles were fought out along with the convoy controversy. The crisis was slow to develop. As we have said, for the first two years of the war, sugar was the only foodstuff that needed to be rationed. (See p. 43.) But, even before 1917, it was becoming all too clear that food control would have to come, and come soon.

But food control was new. It required, like the convoy, considerable experiment — and occasional failure — before it could be perfected, and experiment which concerns the lives of nearly 50,000,000 human beings is a formidable affair. Lloyd George's first appointee as Food Controller was not a success. Lord Devonport was then Chairman of the Port of London Authority, an experienced business executive; but he had no flair for dealing with "the masses," and food control — we understand these things better nowadays — needed efficient propaganda as well as efficient organization. In June 1917, Devonport resigned, and Lord Rhondda took his place. Rhondda may have been a man of far less executive ability, and he was not in the best of health, but he appreciated the value of a "good press," and he was never one to chase away a useful journalist. During his term of office the Food Ministry built up a huge network of food commissioners and Food Committees throughout the country, and ultimately nearly 95 per cent of everything eaten and drunk in Britain was made subject to their controls. By April 1918, a complete rationing system of all foods — except milk, fish, and fresh vegetables — was in force and running smoothly.

The British people little knew and, once their daily portions had been assured, little cared about these huge transactions and the exact manner of their working. They bore their restrictions with their characteristic blend of grumbling and patience; but the margin of their safety in 1917 had been desperately narrow.

Crisis in Germany

In Germany the unanimity of the *Burgfriede* of 1914 had long since gone.[6] Politically, the national deterioration was taking the form of a revival of the old prewar agitation against the semi-autocratic constitution of the Reich. By 1917 the demand for "democratization" was as loud and clamorous as it had ever been.[7] The Social Democrats in the *Reichstag* in increasing numbers were voting against the war budget and against the supplementary credits. They had formally spit into "Majority" and "Minority" factions — the Majority supporting the government's war policy, and the Minority opposing it — and, by 1917, the Minority had grown more numerous than the Majority. Further, party lines were aggravated by the question of war aims. The Right and the Conservatives subscribed to extravagant programs of conquests and annexations; the Left and the Social Democrats, to a peace of reconciliation and of the *status quo*.

The Chancellor, Bethmann-Hollweg, was persuaded that the Kaiser must make a voluntary gesture promising the common soldiers of the army increased rights in the state they had victoriously defended. On March 14, 1917, in a memorable speech in the Prussian *Landtag*, the Chancellor broadly hinted at the "transformation of our political life which must result from the experiences of the war," and he referred in particular to reforms of the Prussian suffrage system. By one of those accidents of history which seem almost preordained, the first news of the Russian Revolution arrived in Berlin an hour or two after the Chancellor's speech. Then, on April 6, the United States declared war. The impact of these events in Germany was tremendous.

On April 8 came the Kaiser's long heralded gesture in the form of an "Easter Message" guardedly promising "the extension of our political, economic, and social life" after the war. Three months later, on July 12, he officially pledged new suffrage laws in Prussia "before the next elections." But these patronizing concessions encouraged rather than quieted the growing unrest. The *Reichstag* appointed a Constitution Committee; but Matthias Erzberger, a member of it, a Deputy of the Center party, not content with discussing the constitution, used the occasion to open up the whole question of the unrestricted submarine campaign, whose ill success was now becoming more than a little evident. Obviously, if the war could not be won on land or at sea, it behooved the representatives of the people to consider other possibilities of making peace. Accordingly, several Deputies of the *Reichstag*, mainly of the Left and Center – with Erzberger among them – resolved themselves into a committee to draft a formal Peace Resolution. (See Appendix, p. 831.)

The Kaiser and the Chancellor, Bethmann-Hollweg, and the Conservatives were now thoroughly alarmed. Peace talk would dangerously intensify the party cleavages. Hindenburg and Ludendorff telegraphed from the front tendering their resignations if the impending Peace Resolution was not stopped. But instead Bethmann-Hollweg resigned, and the Kaiser, on Ludendorff's recommendation, appointed Georg Michaelis, a Prussian food official of no great distinction, to the chancellorship. However, the Peace Resolution was brought before the *Reichstag* and, on July 19, 1917, was passed by that assembly by 212 votes to 126. Michaelis, the new Chancellor, in his maiden speech agreed to support the Peace Resolution, "as I interpret it" – a lame reservation indeed, the evasiveness and prevarication of which the *Reichstag* was not slow to perceive. Michaelis did, however, make a gesture toward "democratization" of the government by appointing one or two *Reichstag* deputies to minor ministerial posts. For the first time in history Germany came before the world with the makings of a cabinet.

So ended the July Crisis in Germany, as it was called. The Kaiser had made his promises, the *Reichstag* had passed a Peace Resolution, the Chancellor had accepted deputies as administrative colleagues. The Peace Resolution, however, was not followed by peace; the German Government made no attempt to translate it into an offer to the enemy. The country's attention was momentarily diverted by a new crisis – this time, insubordinate conduct among the lower naval ratings, who had been too long idle under the blockade, and were allegedly subject to revolutionary propaganda on the part of certain *Reichstag* deputies of the Left. The affair could have ended in an inquiry and, if necessary, in disciplinary action. But Michaelis, in the heat of a debate in the *Reichstag* during October, suddenly blurted out charges against Social Democrat deputies, mentioning several by name, and, without proof, accused them of stirring up mutiny in the navy.

Michaelis confessed afterwards that he had committed a "tactical error." But there was more in the incident than the maladroitness of a harassed chancellor. Germany and her leaders were not a happy company in 1917. Nerves were tense, tempers were short – and stomachs were empty – and it is not difficult to read into the *Reichstag* debates of that summer evidences of a very serious political demoralization. Michaelis was dismissed by the Kaiser on November 1, 1917, and was succeeded by Count von Hertling, the elderly Premier of Bavaria.

Crisis in Austria-Hungary

Austria-Hungary had gone to war in 1914 with a semblance of the patriotic unanimity of the other belligerents. Nationalist unrest throughout the Monarchy was suddenly quieted. The military situation was not too bad, and even a shaky political regime responds to success. The early reverses of 1914 against Serbia had been repaired; the hated Italians had made no appreciable progress on the Alpine front; the subsequent victories of 1915 in Russia had been entirely convincing. Count Stürgkh, the Austrian Premier, had already suspended the Austrian legislature, the *Reichsrat,* before the war broke out, and he now kept it suspended. For two years the peoples of Austria-Hungary passed through a sort of history-less phase, patiently accepting the depletion of their industries and farms, the loss of their overseas commerce, the controls and corruption of their officials, and the growing shortages in all the necessities of civilized life.

Then, in midsummer 1916, occurred the disaster of the Brusilov Offensive in Galicia, the Battle of Luck as it was called in Austria. (See p. 54.) On October 21, 1916, Stürgkh was shot in a Vienna café, not by a nationalist, but by the Austrian Social Democrat Friedrich Adler. It was one of those almost symbolic assassinations which come at critical junctures to release overcharged popular emotions. On November 21 the aged Emperor Francis Joseph died, and the last restraint on the nation's traditional loyalties seemed to be removed. All at once, there arose unmistakable signs that the two components of the monarchy, Austria and Hungary, were turning sour toward each other. Austria, with the main industrial areas, and Hungary, with the main agricultural areas, were waging a minor economic civil war, each trying to blackmail the other with embargoes on their mutual trade. Count Tisza, the Hungarian Premier, established a "customs barrier" along the Austro-Hungarian frontier.

The new Emperor Charles who succeeded to the throne was young, warm-hearted, companionable, and personally well liked. Given reasonable odds he could have brought his peoples a well-deserving, prosperous reign. But he had come into a debtor's inheritance, and his country's predicament would have broken a stronger man. It was relatively easy to reform some of the ornate rigidities of Viennese court life — all this was long overdue anyway. It was relatively easy to dismiss several of the senior officers of the Austrian High Command — even the redoubtable Chief of Staff, Field Marshal Conrad von Hötzendorf, who had led the Austrian armies with such consistent ill success since 1914. But Vienna's food shortage was much more important and much more difficult. Austria and Hungary persisted in their private economic feud, and Tisza persisted in his mood of typically Hungarian egotism and obstinacy. Meanwhile, the subject races of the monarchy — Poles, Czechs, Yugoslavs, Rumanians, and Italians — were clearly becoming restive. Units at the front that contained nationalist elements could no longer be considered reliable. Already, during the Battle of Luck, Poles and Czechs had "deserted" to the Russians by whole battalions.

Count Czernin, the Austro-Hungarian Foreign Minister, seems to have been Charles's principal political mentor at this time. He was profoundly pessimistic, and predicted a nationalist revolution if the war was not stopped. Early in 1917 he and Charles were involved in secret peace talks with the Allies, using as intermediaries the Bourbon Princes Sixte and Xavier, who were brothers of Charles's consort, the Empress Zita, and who were serving at the time in the Belgian Field Artillery. The Princes duly made contact with Poincaré and Briand in France — but nothing resulted. Czernin also advised that the *Reichsrat* should be reconvened. The renewed nationalist agitation, he argued, could no longer be safely repressed, though it is doubtful that he expected the explosion he now invited. The *Reichsrat* eventually met in Vienna in May 1917. Several of the deputies were in jail on charges of sedition or had fled the country. Those who remained immediately used the *Reichsrat* sessions to deliver revolutionary manifestoes. The Czech and Yugoslav deputies demanded the creation of autonomous democratic states. On the Russian front it was currently reported that "desertions" were now taking place by evident prearrangement; Czech troops were marching over to the Russian lines under the white flag, singing patriotic songs.

In Budapest, meanwhile, the Hungarian Diet was in its own toils. Here the agitation was taking the form of demands from the non-Magyar minorities for electoral reforms. Tisza resigned at the end of May 1917 and went off to the front "to seek a hero's death." The Hungarian administration from then onward fell to a succession of Magyar oligarchs of the same breed as Tisza who either would not, or could not, bring themselves to realize the strength of the nationalist revolt.

Abroad, groups of nationalist "emigrants" from Austria-Hungary foregathered in neutral and Allied countries, formed themselves into centers of propaganda, presumed an authority over their brethren at home, recruited contingents to serve in the Allied armies, and demanded the diplomatic recognition of the Allied governments. Czechs and Yugoslavs established in Paris committees that were the nuclei of future national governments. In Russia in 1917, after the Revolution, a Polish Corps and a Czech Legion were formed out of Polish and Czech prisoners of war. At the end of 1917, Polish and Czech forces were being organized in France for service on the Western front. Yugoslav divisions fought with the Allies at Salonika.

Franz Borkenau has written:

> War is the strongest test to which a political system can be subjected. War is the only event which puts before the average citizen the question whether he is ready to die for the sake of his country. If the answer of the great majority, given not in words, but in acts, is in the affirmative, the fate of the country is not yet secure. But if the answer is in the negative, the country is doomed. The majority of Austrians were no longer ready to die for Austria. They were only forced to die for her, against their will, with hatred for the Empire in their hearts. This is what made the war for Austria a horror beyond all horror experienced elsewhere. In Austria, for the majority of her citizens, the war was not invested with the dignity of a grandiose though ghastly sacrifice for a sacred cause. It was a simple butchery in defense of a cause which the majority did not want to defend.[8]

The Russian Revolution

We have elsewhere described conditions in Russia in the first two years of the war. (See pp. 46ff.) By the end of 1916 the regime was clearly at the point of collapse. Corruption and incompetence at home, defeat and demoralization at the front, had done their work. "Revolution was in the air," wrote Buchanan, the British ambassador in Petrograd, "and the only moot point was whether it would come from above or below." Petrograd throbbed with rumors. The Tsar's dethronement by force was the open topic of conversation everywhere. His own royal brother and uncles – and, on one occasion, the British ambassador – appealed to him to save the dynasty by instituting some form of popular government. General Alexeyev and officers of the High Command were said to be planning a military coup. On the night of December 29, Rasputin was assassinated.

The first stages of the Russian Revolution developed, without plan, aim, or leadership, from the food riots and street demonstrations which were taking place in Petrograd in the early days of March 1917. Nobody expected it, least of all the several revolutionary parties which had so long agitated for it. There were some clashes, but the bloodshed was small compared with many another less momentous upheaval in Russian history. The fearsome Cossacks fraternized with the crowd; the police fled; the Petrograd garrison "demobilized itself." The Revolution, as one observer put it, "just walked into empty trenches." In the course of a week, the other cities of Russia revolted with as little effort, and as few excesses, as the capital.

The Tsar was at Headquarters at Mogilev when the news of the outbreaks in Petrograd arrived. A battalion was dispatched to the city to restore order, but the men deserted en route. The Tsar tried to dissolve the Duma, but it disobeyed his decree and continued its sessions. The Tsar then set out for Tsarskoe Selo himself, where the Tsaritsa and the imperial family were in residence, but soldiers and workers along the railroad diverted his train to Pskov, and he was there placed under virtual arrest. The Duma, however, was entirely unprepared for the Revolution. Far from welcoming the turn of affairs, it found itself virtually forced to take power and to set up a Provisional Government. Prince Lvov, the popular director of the Zemstvo relief organizations, was chosen Premier. The first care of the new government was to send a deputation of two of its ministers to the Tsar at Pskov, and at Pskov on March 15, 1917, undramatically and unprotestingly, the Tsar signed his abdication.

Meanwhile the workers, soldiers — and sailors — had been erecting their own impromptu hierarchy of committees, or "soviets," which more than anything else was to give the Russian Revolution its peculiar character. The Petrograd Soviet was soon holding a key position in the country. It accepted the authority of the Provisional Government and to some extent dictated its program. At the end of March 1917, the body politic of Russia presented a curious "dual power." On the one hand was the Provisional Government, a creation of the Duma, and on the other the Petrograd Soviet, a creation of the workers and soldiers. Oddly enough they were meeting in the same building, the Tauride Palace — with Kerensky, a member of both, acting as liaison between them.

Abroad, the democratic world hailed the Russian Revolution fervently. Britain, France, and Italy — and the United States, which was then about to enter the war — at once recognized the Provisional Government, believing that the overthrow of the old autocracy would release the suppressed patriotic passions of the Russian people and inspire them to greater efforts in the war. But, as was too soon to appear, the Provisional Government was woefully weak. It rested on the sufferance of the workers; the bourgeois elements, of which it was composed, were without real leadership and without numerical strength. The police had vanished; the army was still an unknown quantity; the instruments of authority in the state were uncertain or nonexistent. Lvov himself was a kindly Tolstoyan type, who believed in "nonresistance to evil" and "bloodless revolutions." In the circumstances, fundamental reforms were not in prospect. The workers wanted the factories, the peasants wanted the land, the soldiers wanted peace; but the Provisional Government tended to defer decisions to a future Constituent Assembly. Fortunately, winter, both in the trenches and at home, imposed its own armistice. The German and Austrian High Commands preserved a quiet front — we are told they were chiefly interested at this time in preventing fraternization between the opposing troops — and the peasants were hardly able to seize land that was under several feet of snow.

Hence the Provisional Government consented to reforms which were harmless or which it could not prevent. It declared an amnesty for all political and religious offenders; freedom of speech, of the press, and of assembly; removal of racial and religious distinctions, and so forth. But the more explosive questions of the moment, land and peace, it left untouched. It enunciated no agrarian policy and no plan for parceling out the estates. It sought to hold the army together and to prosecute the war in accordance with the commitments made to the Allies by the former Tsarist government. On May 1 Milyukov, Lvov's Foreign Minister, addressed a note to the Allies to the effect that Russia would remain faithful to all her obligations and that indeed the Revolution had only strengthened the determination of her people to achieve a final victory.

May 1, 1917, was revolutionary Russia's first Labor Day, and it was celebrated in every part of the country. But the publication of Milyukov's note to the Allies came as a bitter anticlimax. The Soviets denounced "this imperialistic war." Riots broke out in Petrograd. Lvov was forced to replace his pro-Ally ministers by men who were supposed to be more interested in the cause of peace. Kerensky became Minister of War and the leading power in the new combination. Brusilov, who of all the Russian generals had taken most kindly to the Revolution, was appointed Chief of Staff in the High Command. But Kerensky, for all his former pacifism, was now as bellicose as any Tsarist minister. He toured the front and made a series of flaming speeches intended to restore the morale and discipline of the army. French and British Socialist leaders, then visiting Russia in the interests of Allied solidarity, sent home the most enthusiastic reports about him. An American mission of very mixed political coloring, under the elderly Republican Senator Elihu Root, was also in Russia, partly to get "the facts" and partly to try to put new heart into the Russian war effort. On July 1 the Russian southwestern armies actually launched a minor offensive in Galicia, the theater of Brusilov's triumphs in 1916, but after some initial successes against Austrian troops as demoralized as themselves, they encountered German reserves and retired in disorder. The Czech Legion covered itself with useless glory on the famous field of Zborow. Brusilov, discredited, relinquished his command to General Kornilov. On September 2 the Germans, as if to remind the Russians who the real masters of the situation were, attacked and captured Riga.

Profiting by the Provisional Government's amnesty for political offenders, members of revolutionary parties lost no time in making their way home from their various places of exile. Of the Bolshevik party, Molotov was already in Petrograd when the Revolution broke out, mainly engaged in the editorship of *Pravda.* Stalin and Kamenev joined him in March. Lenin, Zinoviev, and Radek left Zürich, passing through Germany in a sealed railroad car, under permit from the German government, which was anxious to introduce these likely troublemakers into the rear of its enemies, and, traveling by way of Sweden, they arrived in Petrograd on April 16. Trotsky – not yet officially a Bolshevik – arrived in May. At this time the Bolshevik following in the Soviets had been inconsiderable. But Lenin quickly realized – though not without some opposition from his party – that the Soviets were the only organizations with the promise of a future in the new Russia, and, under his famous watchword, "All Power to the Soviets," he began to foment the revolutionary potential in them and convert it to his own purposes. In June the Petrograd Soviet called together the first (All-Russian) Congress of Soviets; but at this Congress the Bolsheviks were still greatly outnumbered by other left-wing parties, notably the Social Revolutionaries and the Mensheviks. (See p. 222.)

Whether or not the Bolsheviks provoked the fresh wave of rioting that broke out in Petrograd during the so-called July Days, just after Kerensky's ill-fated offensive in Galicia, has never been proved. The Bolsheviks did, however, participate in some of the demonstrations – as did other parties also. But obviously no one was yet prepared to take over control from the

Provisional Government. Indeed the Provisional Government for once felt itself strong enough to act, and the rioting was suppressed. The Provisional Government went further; it published evidence that Lenin had been in receipt of German funds and was to all intents and purposes a German agent. But by then Lenin and Zinoviev had escaped into hiding. Kamenev and Trotsky were arrested. The offices of *Pravda* were broken up by the crowd. The Bolsheviks seemed to have sustained a decisive defeat. Greatly encouraged, Kerensky set about to consolidate his position. He assumed the premiership of the Provisional Government and declared Russia a republic. During August, at Moscow, he organized a monster State Conference, representing all classes and communities — with the exception of the Bolsheviks — and tried strenuously to round out his authority with the moral sanction of a spectacular fete in Russia's ancient capital.

The State Conference was Kerensky's apogee. He was already at odds with Kornilov, who was determined to use his own methods for restoring discipline in the army. In September, Kerensky dismissed Kornilov from his command, but not before Kornilov attempted, unsuccessfully, to save himself by setting up a military dictatorship. In an effort to gain wider support, Kerensky made a number of concessions, notably the release of the Bolshevik leaders arrested after the July Days. He called another conference, a "Democratic Conference," a sort of rehearsal for a Constituent Assembly. But the unpleasant feeling had got about that Kerensky was no better than many a lesser place-seeker in the hustings at Petrograd. The Revolution, which till now had been remarkably free from terrorism, took on an uglier aspect. The workers sacked the food shops and bakeries; the peasants plundered the land, burned the manors, and murdered the landlords; there were massacres of officers in the army and navy; the army itself resorted to mass desertion, and the High Command expected it to withdraw from the field of its own volition. The non-Russian nationalities manifested a tendency to secede and form themselves into independent republics — notably Finland and the Ukraine. German agents were already making contact with separatist groups in the Ukraine.

The Bolsheviks took quick advantage of their restored freedom; Bolshevik papers reappeared. On October 23 the inner circle of the Bolsheviks formed a permanent action committee, or Politburo as it was called, "for the purpose of political guidance during the immediate future." It consisted of Lenin, Zinoviev, Kamenev, Trotsky, Stalin, Sokolnikov, and Bubnov. Three days later the Petrograd Soviet set up a Military Revolutionary Committee under Trotsky, ostensibly for the defense of the capital. The Congress of Soviets was planned to reconvene in Petrograd in November, and it was expected that the Bolsheviks this time not only would have a majority at its meetings but would use the occasion to proclaim a new Russian Government.

Kerensky spent the first week of November hunting for a body of troops to defend his regime. On November 7 he left for the front, where prospects of finding reliable men were still said to be good. Almost at that hour, the Military Revolutionary Committee issued a manifesto, "To the Citizens of Russia," written by Lenin, declaring the overthrow of the Provisional Government and its own assumption of power. Late in the evening of the

7th, at the Smolny Institute in Petrograd, the second (All-Russian) Congress of Soviets opened its sessions. During the same night, after a short scuffle, the Bolsheviks occupied the Winter Palace and arrested some of the ministers of the Provisional Government who were sheltering there. The Winter Palace was the "Bastille of the Russian Revolution."

Lenin addressed the Congress of Soviets on the evening of November 8. He read a "Decree of Peace," addressed to "the peoples and governments of the belligerent countries" and proposing "a just, democratic peace without annexations or indemnities." He read a "Decree on Land" abolishing landlord property without compensation and transferring it "to the whole people." The Congress then appointed a Council of People's Commissars (*Sovnarkom*) as the new organ of government in Russia, "pending the convocation of a Constituent Assembly," with Lenin as President, Trotsky as Commissar for Foreign Affairs, Rykov as Commissar for the Interior, and Stalin as Commissar for Nationalities. The Bolshevik triumph was complete. Social Revolutionary and Menshevik opposition at the last moment had been conspicuously disunited and ineffectual. The most serious act of resistance by young army cadets was easily suppressed. But Lenin was now taking no chances; in December he created the Cheka, the "Extraordinary Commission for Combatting Counterrevolution."

Trotsky opened the Russian peace offensive on November 22 with a note to all Allied ambassadors in Petrograd proposing "an immediate armistice on all fronts and the immediate initiation of peace negotiations." A few days later the Bolsheviks began to publish the secret treaties concluded by the Allies between 1915 and 1917, texts of which they had found in the Russian Foreign Ministry.[8] The Allies made a last attempt to enlist the support of the Russian High Command. But the Bolsheviks replied by making one of their party, an ensign named Krylenko, Commander in Chief of the Russian Army, and the High Command was virtually dissolved. On December 5, at Brest Litovsk, Bolshevik envoys signed an armistice with the Central Powers.

Peace Aims and Peace Offers

The general war weariness of the belligerents in 1917 expressed itself in various peace offers and peace intrigues. The Austro-German peace offer of December 1916 was a maneuver dictated more by military than genuine pacific considerations; but the German *Reichstag's* Peace Resolution of July 1917 was of a very different character; it arose from a desperate popular agitation momentarily breaking through the restraints of patriotism and authority.

As mentioned earlier, the Austrian Emperor Charles used intermediaries to make secret contacts with Allied statesmen, notably Poincaré and Briand. We are given to believe that neutral countries, such as Switzerland and Holland, were at that time full of intermediaries, some self-appointed, some with better authenticity, but all carrying messages of peace. International Socialist peace conferences had already taken place in Switzerland — at Zimmerwald in 1915 and Kiental in 1916. In June and July 1917, at Stockholm, Socialist leaders of Holland and Sweden organized a conference that was attended by a smattering of Socialists from various belligerent and neutral countries of Europe. None of these conferences produced the least practical effect.

It was hoped at one time that more substantial success might have resulted from the intercession of the Vatican. Pope Benedict XV's political antecedents well qualified him for the role of mediator, and he had in Pacelli, his nuncio at Munich, a diplomat of infinite tact and experience. But the Vatican's position was never a strong one. The war cut across religious allegiances of every kind. The Vatican's every move, however discreet, was open to misconstruction. Nevertheless, in 1917, with so much peace talk in the air, an effort seemed more timely and worth making. On August 1, 1917, the Pope addressed a peace note to the belligerents:

> In the presence of anguish and peril, we, who have no special political aim, who heed neither the suggestions nor the interests of either belligerent party, but are impelled solely by the consciousness of our supreme duty as the common father of the peoples, by the prayers of our children who implore us to intervene and give peace, by the very voice of humanity and of reason, we raise again a cry for peace and renew a pressing appeal to those in whose hands lie the destinies of nations.

The note then referred to disarmament, to an international court of arbitration, and to the freedom of the seas. The question of reparations for war damage could only be solved "by laying down the general principle of complete restitution of occupied territories," in particular the evacuation of Belgium and northern France by Germany, and of the German colonies by the Allies. The note begged for a spirit of conciliation and equity in the matter of territorial questions between Italy and Austria, between Germany and France, in Armenia, in the Balkans, and in Poland. "As for us, closely united in prayer and penitence with all faithful souls who sigh for peace, we pray that the Divine Spirit grant you light and counsel."

Official replies from the belligerents to the papal note were courteous and evasive. The British Government tried to make use of it to extract from Germany a definite statement of her war aims, especially in regard to Belgium, but no such statement was forthcoming from Berlin, and the German Chancellor, Michaelis, appears to have taken it upon himself to notify Pacelli in a personal letter that "conditions" did not make it possible for him "to issue a decisive declaration of policy." Whether or not the papal note could ever have induced the belligerents to come to terms – or even formally to make known their terms – seems doubtful, but Michaelis' obtuse diplomacy was certainly one reason for its failure to do so.

The winter months of 1917-18 were used by the statesmen of the belligerents for a new kind of diplomacy of "long-distance debate" by speech and press. The feeling that the war was now rushing to a final decision perhaps induced a certain mood for apologetics. At least the great climactic effort on the Western front, which all expected in 1918, could not be made without clarification of objectives. Lord Lansdowne, the British Conservative leader, opened the debate in his letter to the *Daily Telegraph* on November 29, 1917, appealing for a negotiated peace. Lloyd George, Balfour, Hertling, Czernin, and Sonnino made their several statements on their national war aims. Finally, President Wilson, in his address to the joint session of Congress on January 8, 1918, enunciated his Fourteen Points and imparted a definitive literary form to all the searching, groping ideologies of the Allied cause.

The Fourteen Points represented President Wilson's "program of the world's peace." They were "essential rectifications of wrong and assertions of right." They were couched in the form of categorical demands: Point 1, for "open covenants of peace" and for the abolition of "private international understandings" and of secret diplomacy in general; Point 2, for the freedom of the seas; Point 3, for the "removal of all economic barriers and the establishment of an equality of trade conditions"; Point 4, for the reduction of armaments "to the lowest point consistent with domestic safety"; Point 5, for "a free, open-minded, and absolutely impartial adjustment of all colonial claims"; Point 6, for "the evacuation of all Russian territory" and for the settlement of Russian questions in a spirit of "intelligent and unselfish sympathy"; Point 7, for the evacuation and restoration of Belgium; Point 8, for the freeing of invaded French territory and the retrocession to France of Alsace-Lorraine; Point 9, for "a readjustment of the frontiers of Italy . . . along clearly recognizable lines of nationality"; Point 10, for "the freest opportunity of autonomous development" for the peoples of Austria-Hungary; Point 11, for the evacuation and restoration of Rumania, Serbia, and Montenegro; Point 12, for the separation of non-Turkish nationalities from Ottoman rule and for the establishment of the Dardanelles as a free international waterway; Point 13, for the creation of "an independent Polish state . . . which should include the territories inhabited by indisputably Polish populations, which should be assured a free and secure access to the sea"; and Point 14, for "a general association of nations . . . for the purpose of affording mutual guarantees of political independence and territorial integrity." As addenda and amplification of these Fourteen Points, President Wilson, in the course of 1918, further enunciated Four Principles, Four Ends, and Five Particulars. The whole constituted the formal basis for the Peace Conference of 1919. (See Appendix, pp. 831-33.)

The Treaties of Brest Litovsk and Bucharest

This is perhaps an appropriate point for mentioning the two peace conferences and treaties of the war, Brest Litovsk and Bucharest, both of 1918. Obviously it behooved Germany to wind up the war on the Eastern front if possible—and then concentrate her forces for a final decisive campaign in the West. The Bolsheviks were eager for peace, and it was folly to refuse them. On December 5, 1917, the Russians and, on December 9, the Rumanians signed armistices which were tantamount to military surrenders. Negotiations for a peace treaty between the Central Powers and the Soviet Government opened at the old Polish fortress town of Brest Litovsk a few days later.

One writer has called Brest Litovsk "the forgotten peace," and he might have described Bucharest in the same words.[9] Both treaties were renounced by Germany after her defeat, and, except among historians whose business it is to remember these things, they have become truly forgotten peaces. Both treaties were cynical to a degree and were an undisguised fulfillment of Teutonic annexationism in the Baltic, the Ukraine, and the Balkans. They foreshadowed the acquisitions which Germany once more tried to make in 1941-45.

The negotiations at Brest Litovsk brought together an interesting galaxy of conflicting personalities — Kühlmann, the German Foreign Secretary, whose great ambition was to show the world what a model German peace could be; General Hoffmann, the special representative of the German High Command and former staff officer at the Battle of Tannenberg, who steadily refused to renounce one meter of the conquests of the German Army; Czernin, the Austro-Hungarian Foreign Minister, who wanted nothing so much as the wheat of the Ukraine for his starving Vienna; Radoslavov and Talaat Pasha, the Bulgarian and Turkish Premiers, who were after territory — and finally Trotsky, the Soviet Foreign Commissar, who tried to play off one party against the other and to indict the imperialistic, warmongering belligerents. But military power won, and not all Trotsky's sharpened wit and dialectical skill could secure him from the stolid dictation of the German High Command. Probably Trotsky would have preferred a last-ditch resistance with what Russian forces still held the field. But Lenin advised peace, even a model German peace. In the end the Soviet Government agreed to cede Poland and the Baltic states and to evacuate Finland and the Ukraine. An Austrian commission was to be sent to Kiev to requisition wheat. Turkey received Kars, Ardahan, and Batum. The Treaty of Brest Litovsk, on these terms, was signed on March 3, 1918.

The Treaty of Bucharest gave legal form to the Austro-German conquest of Rumania. It granted the victors a monopoly of Rumanian oil and wheat and the lease of Rumanian ports. Hungary secured a frontier which would protect her from future Rumanian aggression. The Dobruja, although claimed by Bulgaria, was allotted to the joint administration of the four "Allied Powers," namely, Germany, Austria-Hungary, Bulgaria, and Turkey. Bessarabia, largely populated by Rumanians, was permitted to join herself to the Rumanian territories. The treaty, on these terms, was signed on May 7, 1918.

World War

Several Latin-American republics followed the lead of the United States into the war, some in a spirit of "continental solidarity" with her, some in protest against specific outrages by German submarines upon their shipping. Between April 1917 and midsummer 1918, Panama, Cuba, Brazil, Nicaragua, Guatemala, Costa Rica, Haiti, and Honduras declared war on Germany. Bolivia, Peru, Uruguay, Ecuador, and the Dominican Republic severed relations. Argentina gave the German envoy his passports, but did not proceed to a complete rupture.

China severed relations with Germany in March 1917, partly as the result of Anglo-Japanese pressure and partly as the result of the German submarine campaign, and in August of the same year the Peking Government, on behalf of all China, declared war on Germany and Austria-Hungary. In July 1917, Siam (Thailand) declared war on Germany and Austria-Hungary, and in August, the African republic of Liberia declared war on Germany.

Twenty-four states — as shown in the accompanying table — thus came to be ranged against four: Austria-Hungary, Germany, Turkey, and Bulgaria — and we may add Albania and Persia, which were variously engaged. Russia and Rumania made peace, as has just been described, early in 1918. In the end, out of a then-estimated world population of 1,600,000,000, it may be said that 1,400,000,000 were involved.

THE NATIONS IN THE FIRST WORLD WAR

WITH DATES OF ENTRY INTO THE WAR

The Central Powers	*The Allied and Associated Powers*
Austria-Hungary (July 28, 1914)	Serbia (July 28, 1914)
Germany (August 1, 1914)	Russia (August 1, 1914)
Turkey (Ottoman Empire) (October 29, 1914)	Luxembourg (August 1, 1914)
Bulgaria (October 7-15, 1915)	France (August 3, 1914)
	Belgium (August 4, 1914)
	Britain and the British Empire (August 4, 1914)
	Japan (August 23, 1914)
	Montenegro (September 9, 1914)
	Portugal (November 23, 1914)
Albania and Persia occupied (November 1915)	Italy (May 23, 1915)
	Rumania (August 27, 1916)
	Greece (June 30, 1917)
	The United States of America (April 6, 1917)
	Panama (April 7, 1917)
	Cuba (April 7, 1917)
	Siam (July 22, 1917)
	Liberia (August 5, 1917)
	China (August 14, 1917)
	Brazil (October 26, 1917)
	Nicaragua (March 18, 1918)
	Guatemala (April 23, 1918)
	Costa Rica (May 23, 1918)
	Haiti (July 13, 1918)
	Honduras (July 19, 1918)

5. THE CLOSING PHASES—1918

The Campaign of 1918 on Land

In 1918 Germany staked everything on a final decision on the Western front. Thanks to the Russian collapse in 1917 and to the treaties of peace at Brest Litovsk and Bucharest, the military situation had turned momentarily to her advantage, and for the first time since 1914 the German High Command could concentrate a superiority, or at least a favorable balance of numbers, in France. The unrestricted submarine campaign still continued, though it had long since fallen short of its first fine prospects, and the transportation of American troops across the Atlantic had proceeded without the loss of a ship.[1] If there was to be an offensive, then, it was imperative to launch it before the Americans arrived in force; if one last effort was to be made to break the deadlock on the Western front, the time was now or never.

The German Army in the main was still sound, and the home front had lately given cause for greater confidence. The economic situation at the end of 1917 was better than it had been at the end of 1916, and the appalling shortages of the "turnip winter" had not returned. (See p. 38.) The Allied blockade, despite its growing thoroughness, had bred its own resistance, and the German people – so the High Command believed – had become so inured to a state of chronic want that they could be relied upon to hold out for another year's campaign. The conquered territories in the Ukraine and Rumania – so it was then hoped – promised a vast storehouse of supplies. Workers' strikes in Germany in January 1918 had been settled – or at least the trouble had blown over.

Germany's allies, however, were fast approaching exhaustion. The Austro-Hungarian Army no longer possessed its old fighting quality, though it would probably suffice for the occupation of the Black Sea provinces and for defensive operations against Italy. The release of prisoners from Russia had added greatly to its numbers, but little to its morale. The Emperor Charles had prayed insistently for an end to the war and had gone so far as to compromise himself in secret peace overtures with the enemy. (See p. 72.) Bulgaria was in a parlous state. The Bulgarian Government and people had always taken a parochial view of the war and could see no reason for prolonging it now that their own objects were attained. For

Bulgaria the war had ended with the Treaty of Bucharest. Turkey was fighting losing campaigns in Palestine and Mesopotamia, and her Arab subjects were in revolt. The very continuance of the weakening alliance depended on its senior member bringing off a spectacular success. As Ludendorff later wrote:

> The state of our allies, of ourselves, and of our army, all called for an attack that would bring about an early decision. This could only be effected on the Western front. Everything that had gone before was a means to the one end of creating a military situation which would make it possible. Until now the situation had not arisen.[2]

In January 1918, preparations in Germany were going forward. The entire Reich was combed for effectives and supplies. Intensive training and even "patriotic education" were carried out in all units. A corps of "storm troops" was created for "shock tactics" and "infiltration." By mid-March 1918, three German armies totaling 70 divisions, 1,700 batteries, and over 1,000 planes were poised on a 45-mile front below Arras. "These were figures no man had credited before," wrote Ludendorff; "still less had any one ever imagined the weight of ammunition to be hurled upon the enemy. Here were massed effects indeed!" Defeat he appears not to have taken into account. Supposedly the German Army could at any time break off the battle, resume the defensive, and hold the enemy as firmly as it had done hitherto. If the new offensive failed, the only deduction would be that, under tactical conditions in the West, the offensive was still not a practicable operation. But Ludendorff had not realized how deeply Germany's morale, as well as that of her allies, was now committed to the decision he promised. In a war of nations there is no middle term between victory and defeat, and the alternative to the offensive this time was not to be a return to position warfare, but utter and irretrievable ruin.

The situation on the Allied side was difficult. The French Army was still shaken from the mutinies of 1917. The British Army was sadly depleted by its losses at Passchendaele, and there was not a division in it but needed rest and training. In January 1918, the British Fifth Army took over twenty-five miles of the French front—the very sector, in fact, which was to bear the brunt of the coming offensive. Administrative friction in Britain, evidenced by sudden and mystifying changes in the higher offices and commands, and even by scandalous "revelations" in the press, was certainly not being helpful. But there was a brighter side to the picture. The political and economic organization of the Allies, since the American entry into the war, had reached a point of high efficiency. Meetings of the Imperial War Cabinet in London in 1917 and the establishment of permanent Inter-Allied Councils for the allocation of raw materials and shipping had integrated the entire Allied war effort. The unification of command on the Western front had been partially achieved by the Supreme War Council at Versailles. (See p. 57.) Propaganda against the enemy, especially against Austria-Hungary, was being coordinated and was known to be effective. All the peoples of Central Europe had heard of President Wilson's Fourteen Points. American divisions were arriving at the front, but to date were being assigned to quiet sectors. Eventually, from May 1918 onward, American divisions were sustaining major actions, and their arrivals in France rose to the rate of 10,000 men a day. But so stupendous an achievement of training and logistics had been beyond all expectation at the time the German offensive began.[3]

"Operation Michael," as the Germans called it, opened at dawn on March 21, 1918, with what Churchill, then visiting the front, has described as "the most tremendous cannonade I shall ever hear." Legends have grown up around the offensive even as they have grown up around the First Battle of the Marne. It was said that the British Fifth Army was badly led and practically annihilated, or that Field Marshal Haig, at the height of the action, gave orders to evacuate Amiens and retire to the Channel, or that the field was only saved in the nick of time by a hastily collected force of 3,000 engineers and railroad men. Official accounts from both sides have given us somewhat less dramatic views, as official accounts invariably do, but they have not detracted from the gravity and anguish of the great battle. In round numbers, between March 21 and April 5 the Germans gained 1,500 square miles between St. Quentin and Amiens on the British front, inflicted 160,000 casualties, and themselves lost as heavily.

These March days now lie before us as a simple story; but for their protagonists they were days of chaos and indecision. The Cabinet and War Office in London appear to have been more sensitive to the seriousness of the early incoming news – or lack of news – than the generals on the spot. An Allied conference was held at the little Picard town of Doullens in an atmosphere of deepening gloom. Both Haig and Pétain were pessimistic. Milner, representing the British Government, could only defer to military opinion. Even Clemenceau was at a loss. But it was the moment Foch had been waiting for. He rose to the occasion like a man called to his destiny. When generals and statesmen, grown old in the hard school of leadership, were all faltering, his was the one driving, chiding voice among them. The conference, at Milner's suggestion, appointed Foch "to coordinate the action of the Allied armies on the Western front." No American was present, but General Pershing, the American commander, afterwards wrote to Foch in cordial terms, accepting the agreement in its entirety. Finally, on April 14, Marshal Foch was invested with the formal title of General in Chief of the Allied Armies in France.

Ludendorff once called the German Army's task in 1918 the "greatest in military history." But the task proved far too great. He had tried to destroy the British Army in France; he drove it back some thirty miles on a sector of its front. His effort in March was his most successful, and in four more offensives in as many months he did not approach even these imperfect results. In April he attacked the British on the Lys in Flanders; in May, the French on the Chemin-des-Dames; in June, the French around Compiègne; in July, the French around Reims. "If my attack at Reims succeeds," he said on the first day of the last offensive, "we have won the war." "If the German attack at Reims succeeds," Foch is reported to have said on the same day, "we have lost the war." The attack did not succeed. At one point the Germans reached and crossed the Marne, but they got

THE WESTERN FRONT, 1914-18

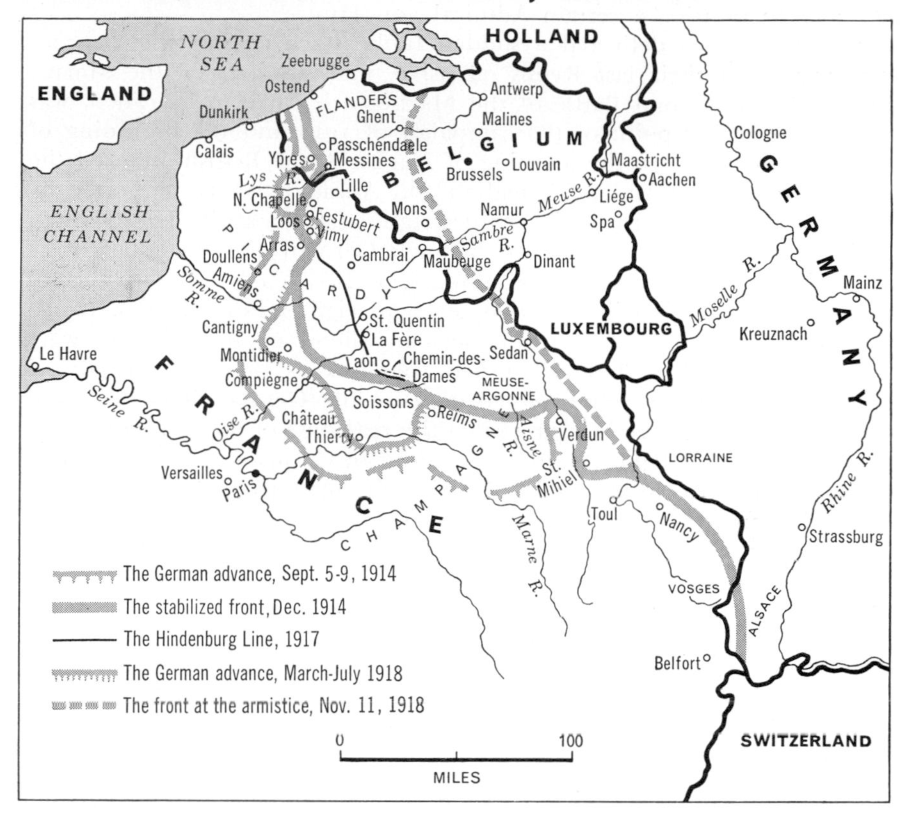

no further. Ludendorff had exhausted his reserves – what was worse, he had exhausted what was left of his army's morale – but at no point had he stretched the Allied line beyond its limit of resistance.

That Ludendorff was not entirely happy with his workmanship was indicated by the diplomatic "feelers" permitted by the German High Command and Government – and indeed by Ludendorff – during the midsummer of 1918. The maneuver was clumsily managed and is mainly interesting today as revealing the German leaders' total incomprehension of the psychology both of the German home front and of the Allies. Kühlmann, the German Foreign Secretary, raised the question in a speech in the *Reichstag* toward the end of June:

> In view of the magnitude of this coalition war, in view of the numbers of Powers engaged, here and overseas, an absolute end to the war, by military decisions alone, without an exchange of ideas and without diplomacy, is not to be expected.

German public opinion in that summer, still being led to expect an ultimate victory, was entirely unprepared for so sobering a shock as this. Kühlmann, even though he had spoken with the approval of his Chancellor and in honest interpretation of the views of the High Command, was dismissed. The Kaiser appointed in his place a somewhat picturesque newcomer to politics, a certain Admiral von Hintze.

On July 18 Foch delivered a sudden tank attack against the German forces which, in their last Reims offensive, had just crossed the Marne. The attack, the Second Battle of the Marne as it came to be called, was in fact the turning point of the campaign of 1918 and the beginning of the end of the war. On the morning of August 8, the British attacked the German lines before Amiens. Canadian and Anzac divisions, supported by a fleet of 450 tanks, formed the main weight of the assault. The German positions on the Somme were overwhelmed; German divisional staffs were surprised at breakfast at their headquarters. In a day's fighting, the attacking forces made a drive of from seven to eight miles and took 16,000 prisoners. Measured by the recent German offensives, these battles were not considerable. But they established the tank as the final weapon of trench warfare – the weapon, moreover, that the Germans had neglected to adopt themselves – and they revealed the real state of the German Army. In the course of the fighting whole battalions of Germans had surrendered, sometimes to single infantrymen. Retiring German troops, meeting fresh units going up into the line, had greeted them with shouts of "Strikebreakers!" and "War-prolongers!" (*Streikbrecher, Kriegsverlängerer*). Well might Ludendorff call August 8, 1918, "the black day of the German Army."

The German High Command was in consternation. Ludendorff demanded an end to the war. For some days he was entirely irresponsible and, we are told, suffered a hysterical breakdown. The Kaiser held a Crown Council on August 14 at Headquarters, then at the Belgian watering place of Spa. The High Command's report spoke of "wearing down the war-will of the enemy by a strategic defense"; the Kaiser remarked that "we must seize the opportune moment for coming to an understanding with the enemy"; Hertling, the Chancellor, added that "such a moment might come after our next successes at the front"; Hintze suggested further diplomatic "feelers"; Hindenburg, like a schoolmaster trying to soften a punishment, hoped that he could still finish the war on French soil. The Austrian Emperor Charles, who had also come to Spa with a new Austro-Hungarian Foreign Minister, Count Burian, pressed – as usual – for an immediate appeal for peace. The Crown Council's deliberations, crassly, criminally, pathetically unreal, reached no conclusion. But in the course of the next few days steps were taken, guardedly and still reassuringly, to make the German people aware of some of the facts. "We have, it is true, suffered some minor checks," read Hintze's report to the Bundesrat, "but not such that we need describe our military situation as bad or desperate." The German press was full of consolatory comment.

But in August 1918, the inwardness of the great conflict in all its gauntness rose to the surface, and the war became nakedly a war of morale. The Allied tank, formidable though it was, would never have so easily overrun the German positions if their living defenders had had any heart left in them. The Allied peoples in their homes were too wrapped up in their own tribulations to give a thought to those of their enemies, and after four years of static warfare they had hardly the mental resilience to comprehend that the German Army was at last in the midst of a general

British fighter of 1916-17 (F.E. 8 single-seater pusher biplane)

IMPERIAL WAR MUSEUM

strategic retirement. Nor, perhaps, did the Allied leaders see more clearly. The rot in the German Army quickened as August passed. Several German divisions "obviously showed a disinclination to attack." The dressing stations were crowded with men who hurried out of the trenches without orders. Offenses were committed "to escape duty by undergoing punishment." There was a good deal of disease, especially influenza and dysentery, both exceptionally weakening to the patient and hard to throw off without those dietary comforts which could no longer be obtained. Numbers of men from the last comb-out in Germany were the dregs of the industrial districts and were dangerously affected by revolutionary socialism. The old officer corps, once the framework of the army's spirit and discipline, had long since been decimated, and the new type of officer had none of the same training or authority.

The Collapse of Bulgaria, Turkey, and Austria-Hungary

The rest of the story can be told quickly. Bulgaria was obviously ready for peace – at any price. In June 1918, Radoslavov, Bulgarian Premier for the past five years and the chief representative of Germanophilism in Sofia, resigned and was replaced by Malinov, a statesman of liberal sympathies, well disposed toward the Allies. The Bulgarian press was openly discussing a separate peace. The American chargé d'affaires traveled freely about the country and, according to the common belief, did not disdain to advance subversive propaganda with American gold.[4] The Bulgarian Tsar Ferdinand, ostensibly in poor health but really in fear of a popular uprising, left for medical treatment in Austria and, while protesting his loyalty to the Central Powers, did not fail to impress upon the Viennese statesmen whom he met in the course of his tour the extreme weakness of his country. Suddenly in mid-September, General Franchet d'Esperey, commanding the Allied forces in Salonika, attacked and broke the Bulgarian lines, and in four days was advancing into Serbia. Bulgaria had no choice but to sue for an armistice. Salonika, that "unwanted" front, had at last been justified. On September 29, 1918, at Franchet d'Esperey's headquarters, the Bulgarian armistice was signed. On October 3 Ferdinand abdicated in favor of his son Boris. Bulgaria was out of the war.

In Turkey, British forces under General Allenby had advanced deep into Palestine and in mid-September 1918, at the Battle of Megiddo, decisively defeated the Turkish Army under the German commander, Liman von Sanders. Simultaneously, British forces in Mesopotamia had reached Mosul. With Bulgaria's capitulation, Turkey was once more isolated; an Allied force from Salonika was marching on Constantinople. The Turkish Government, in an attempt to fend off a revulsion of public opinion, such as had just occurred in Bulgaria, encouraged the formation of a moderate Opposition and allowed political exiles to return home. But the inevitable could not be put off. Early in October, Talaat and his old cabinet resigned. The Young Turks called a congress and voted the dissolution of their party. Talaat and Enver were already in flight to Germany. On October 30, 1918, at Mudros in Lemnos in the Aegean Sea, delegates of a new non-party Turkish Government accepted armistice terms from Admiral Gough-Calthorpe, commander of the British Mediterranean Fleet. Turkey was out of the war.

It was now the turn of Austria-Hungary. On September 14, 1918, Count Burian, the Austro-Hungarian Foreign Minister, issued an invitation to all belligerents to meet in a neutral country "for the purpose of a confidential and noncommittal exchange of views." It was a lame and desperate gesture, and it received a cool reception. President Wilson, according to one story, needed exactly twenty-five minutes to reject it categorically. Austria-Hungary was patently in dissolution. National assemblies were springing up and arrogating political authority to themselves. The Emperor Charles stooped to fervid and futile audiences with nationalist and party leaders; but it was clear that his royal title was no longer recognized. The German-Austrian Social Democrats were talking in terms of a republican German-Austrian state. Early in October representatives of the Serbs, Croats, and Slovenes met in Agram and asserted their right to regulate their own affairs. The Polish Regency Council in Warsaw proclaimed its independence.

On October 4, 1918, Burian appealed direct to President Wilson for an armistice and peace on the basis of the Fourteen Points. In his reply—which arrived in Vienna on the 18th, after considerable delay—the President deemed it his duty to say that the peoples of Austria-Hungary must themselves be "the judges of what action on the part of the Austro-Hungarian Government will satisfy their aspirations and their conception of their rights and destiny as members of the family of nations." But, by this time, even Hungary was cutting loose. In the Hungarian Diet, Count Michael Karolyi, leader of a pacifist and secessionist group, was demanding the recall of "our Hungarian Army" and the abrogation of the alliance with Germany. With amazing naïveté patriot Hungarians believed that they could still get out of the war and preserve their domain intact. At least Tisza, the old autocrat, was more realistic. "I must acknowledge that we have lost the war!" he said. President Wilson's reply made it abundantly plain that Hungary, like Austria, would be shorn of her ethnic appendages.

Allied forces from Salonika under Franchet d'Esperey were now advancing through Serbia; the Rumanians were back on the Danube. On October 24 the Italians launched their offensive on the Piave and in the Battle of Vittorio Veneto broke up the last resistance of the Austro-Hungarian Army. On October 25 Charles appointed a new Foreign Minister, Count Julius Andrassy, whose main function in office was to send one more note to President Wilson, accepting the President's political philosophy in its entirety. On November 3 at the Villa Giusti near Padua, an Austro-Hungarian Armistice Commission signed the terms of the Italian High Command. Franchet d'Esperey reached Belgrade on November 6, and there concluded with Karolyi a separate armistice on behalf of Hungary. On November 11 the Emperor Charles renounced his sovereign rights. Austria-Hungary no longer existed.

The Collapse of Germany

Meanwhile the German position on the Western front had steadily deteriorated. Since August 8 fighting had developed all along the line. Foch had struck where and as he pleased. The British had advanced over the old Somme battlefields and were astride the Hindenburg Line. The French were advancing in the Champagne. The Americans, now established under General Pershing in their own sector of the line on either side of Verdun, won their first action as a united army against the Germans in the old salient at St. Mihiel, and in the last week of September began their offensive in the Meuse-Argonne. Since the opening of the campaign in March the Germans had lost 1,000,000 men, and casualties were now fast gaining on replacements. German divisions were at half strength, and some had been continuously in action for weeks. The depots and railroad stations swarmed with deserters. The Americans were landing at the rate of 250,000 men a month, and to date there were 3,000,000 in France, a number equivalent to the then total strength of the German forces on all fronts. In 1919 an American army of 5,000,000 might be expected, trained, fresh, and equipped with all the wealth of the Western Hemisphere. On September 29 the Kaiser held a second Crown Council at Spa, and this time there was no self-deception. The High Command could only think in terms of an appeal to President Wilson "without delay." Hertling, the Chancellor, an amiable scion of the old school, had no stomach for a development of this sort and resigned.

In view of the controversy that afterward grew up around the precise events of the collapse of Germany in 1918, it is important to note that the decision to appeal to President Wilson was demanded by the High Command irrespective of political developments in Berlin and in the country, concerning which the High Command was profoundly unaware and profoundly uninterested. There is no question but that the soldiers insisted on an armistice and forced the Kaiser to appoint a chancellor who would get it for them. Revolutionary talk was in the air; the Social Democrats in particular were improving the occasion by reviving all the old cries for electoral reform in Prussia and for cabinet responsibility in Germany. Every German knew by now the text and import of the Fourteen Points. The Wilsonian propaganda, with relentless repetition, had made it plain that no peace was to be expected till Germany had transformed herself into a genuine parliamentary state. The Kaiser himself made the first move. On September 30, immediately after the Crown Council, he left for Berlin and issued a proclamation promising the "rights and duties of government" to men "who have the confidence of the people." On October 2 he appointed his cousin, Prince Max of Baden, the new Chancellor, and on the 3rd Prince Max dispatched a note to President Wilson requesting the initiation of peace negotiations on the basis of the "President's message to Congress of January 8, 1918 [the Fourteen Points] and his subsequent pronouncements."

Prince Max, heir to the grand-ducal throne of Baden, had the reputation of a liberal and pacifist, and his war service with the Red Cross had been unexceptionable. To both friends and enemies he seemed an appropriate leader of the new "democratized" Germany and collaborator in a peace of the Fourteen Points. He included a wide selection of *Reichstag* Deputies in his cabinet, and the *Reichstag* at his behest rushed through a series of enactments designed to invest the country with the forms of a responsible, popular constitution. Between October 3 and November 5 the German Government sent four notes to President Wilson and received as many replies. All four notes pressed for an armistice and sought to give to the great transatlantic democrat convincing assurances of the far-reaching changes being carried out in Germany's political life.

But, in the midst of the exchange, the *Leinster,* a steamship plying between England and Ireland, was torpedoed with the loss of hundreds of American and British lives. The sinking, whether accidental or deliberate, instantly hardened President Wilson's attitude. Even in the moment of defeat and retribution, it seemed, Germany had not the wit to forswear her old vileness. On October 14 President Wilson dispatched to Berlin "that terrible document," as Prince Max was to call it:

> The conditions of an armistice are matters which must be left to the judgment and advice of the military advisers [of the American and Allied governments]

. . . and no arrangement can be accepted which does not provide absolutely satisfactory safeguards and guarantees of the maintenance of the present military supremacy of the armies of the United States and of the Allies in the field.

And he added further in his reply of October 23:

The nations of the world do not and cannot trust the word of those who have hitherto been the masters of German policy . . . In concluding peace and attempting to undo the infinite injuries and injustices of this war the Government of the United States cannot deal with any but veritable representatives of the German people . . . If it must deal with the military masters and the monarchical autocrats of Germany now, or later, it must demand not peace negotiations but surrender.

On October 26 Ludendorff, the first of the military masters, resigned. Hindenburg elected to remain and was associated in his command with General Groener, Ludendorff's official successor and formerly director of the *Kriegsamt.* (See p. 39.) But the chief of the monarchical autocrats was harder to get rid of. The Kaiser seemed, of all men, to embody in himself

Some of the 8,500,000: a field cemetery in France, 1918

IMPERIAL WAR MUSEUM

the arrogance of Prussian Germany, but he was now stricken with an obstinacy which neither reason, nor entreaties, nor threats could shake. He returned to Headquarters at Spa, where he basked in the reverence of Hindenburg and dreamed dreams of riding home at the head of loyal troops to suppress the German Revolution.

At this point the German Admiral Staff issued orders for the High Seas Fleet to put to sea. For the crews the operation could only be a "death cruise" by a vanquished navy seeking to evade in suicide the dishonor of surrender, and they mutinied. Dock laborers and garrisons ashore made common cause with them. On November 4 the port of Kiel was in revolt. The government sent Gustav Noske, the Social Democrat, to treat with the mutineers, who at once elected him Governor of the port and, under his authority, restored the port to some semblance of order. But the dam could hold no longer. Noske might patch up one crack; the torrent broke through at another. On November 5 Lübeck was in revolt, on the 6th, Hamburg, Cuxhaven, and Bremen. On the 7th, at Munich, Kurt Eisner proclaimed an independent "Republic of Bavaria." By November 8 the revolution had swept through the entire Rhineland and had reached the very outposts of Spa. The King of Bavaria, the Duke of Brunswick, and other potentates were abdicating or in flight.

On November 9 at Spa, it fell to Groener – significantly not a Prussian – to undertake the unpleasant task of informing His Majesty that his power was at an end, his army no longer able to fight, and even his officer corps suspect in its loyalty. "The soldier's oath is now a fiction," said Groener. (*Der Fahneneid ist jetzt nur eine Idee.*) For a moment the Kaiser, scenting a means of escape, proposed that he could abdicate as "German Kaiser," and retain the title of King of Prussia, and this preposterous compromise was actually telegraphed to Berlin. In the end Prince Max acted on his own responsibility and issued the announcement that "the Kaiser and King has decided to renounce the throne." At daybreak on November 10 the Kaiser crossed the Dutch frontier into exile. Yet years afterward he still protested that his Chancellor, without consulting him, had announced an abdication that had never taken place! [5]

Allied discussions on the German armistice terms began informally at Paris at the end of October and were continued thereafter at the Supreme War Council at Versailles. Colonel House arrived in Paris on October 26 to persuade the somewhat fractious and sceptical Allied premiers to accede to the Fourteen Points, even as the German Government had done. With his last note to Germany on November 5 the President forwarded a "Memorandum of Observations," by which the Allied governments accepted the Fourteen Points – but with a reservation on Point 2 concerning the freedom of the seas and with a demand that Germany make reparation "for all damage done to the civilian population of the Allies and their property."

The German Armistice Commission, headed by Erzberger, was received by Foch on November 8 in a carriage of his special train on a siding near Rethondes in the Forest of Compiègne, and early on the morning of November 11, after two days' negotiations, the terms were signed. Hindenburg and the German High Command approved the signing.

Germany agreed to the evacuation of all territories invaded by her, and of Alsace-Lorraine; the evacuation of the left bank of the Rhine and of three bridgeheads at Mainz, Coblenz, and Cologne; the Allied occupation of this area and the support of the Allied Army of Occupation; the establishment of a neutral, demilitarized zone ten kilometers wide along the right bank of the Rhine; the surrender of military equipment and railroad stock, amounting to virtual disarmament; the surrender also of surviving warships and all submarines; the restitution of gold reserves removed from Belgium, Russia, and Rumania; the repatriation of all prisoners of war without reciprocity; and the annulment of the treaties of Brest Litovsk and Bucharest. At the same time, the existing blockade conditions would remain unchanged, but the Allies would consider such provisioning of Germany during the Armistice as should be found necessary.

Sporadic fighting still continued in Eastern Europe and Russia, and in parts of the Near East. But the First World War may be said to have ended with the German Armistice on November 11, 1918. It had lasted four years and three months, involved thirty sovereign states, overthrown four empires, given birth to seven new nations, taken 8,500,000 lives on the field of battle and perhaps 10,000,000 noncombatant lives by privation, disease, and revolution, and wasted incalculable wealth. The civilized world might well believe that it deserved a new era and a millennial peace.

Part Two

THE PERIOD OF SETTLEMENT

We are glad to fight for the ultimate peace of the world and for the liberation of its peoples, the German peoples included: for the rights of nations great and small and the privilege of men everywhere to choose their way of life and of obedience. The world must be made safe for democracy. Its peace must be planted upon the tested foundations of political liberty.

— WOODROW WILSON

NATIONAL ARCHIVES

6. THE PEACE CONFERENCE AND THE PEACE TREATIES

Preparations and Preliminaries

The First World War had ended in November 1918 with the complete defeat of the Central Powers — Germany, Austria-Hungary, Bulgaria, and Turkey — by the twenty-four Allied and Associated Powers. Armistices had left the vanquished nations disarmed and impotent; revolutions had expelled their former rulers. Austria-Hungary and Turkey (the Ottoman Empire) had dissolved into their elements. Subject nationalities from Finland to Arabia had set up independent governments. A new Poland, Czechoslovakia, and Yugoslavia were in process of formation. Soviet Russia, which had withdrawn from the war early in 1918, was already fighting for survival against counterrevolution.

The peace conference, which was to attempt to inject some stability and legality — and perhaps some justice and hope — into this situation, met with little preparation for its task. In the heat of the war there had been pronouncements on war aims by representative statesmen. But war aims belonged rather to the category of morale and propaganda; they were not the precise agenda for a peace conference. Certain of the Allied governments had bound themselves with secret treaties. The participation of Italy and Rumania in the war had been purchased at a price, and the payment, no one doubted, would be demanded in full. There was an agreement over the partition of the Ottoman Empire, there were pledges to the Arabs, and there was an agreement with Japan over the disposal of the German possessions in the North Pacific. There was the proposal for a Jewish National Home. More recently the League of Nations had been a topic of official consideration, especially in the United States, Britain, and France. But in general, Allied governments in their wartime dealings with one another had fought shy of questions of peace and had avoided risking their hard-won military and economic unity in irrelevant conversations which could so easily have led to disagreements among themselves. Moreover, the collapse of Germany at the end of 1918 had surpassed the most sanguine expectations. Allied commands at the time, far from preparing for a peace conference, were laying plans for the big offensive of 1919.

Among the Allied statements of war aims, however, the addresses of President Wilson had come to occupy an exceptional and predominant place. Germany had originally requested an armistice and peace on the basis of the Fourteen Points and of the President's "subsequent pronouncements." The pre-Armistice exchange of notes had implied that the object of the ensuing peace conference "would be only to agree upon the practical details of their application." The European Allies, in their Memorandum of Observations, had made important reservations in regard to the freedom of the seas and reparations, but they had otherwise accepted the Wilsonian philosophy. Even so, the Fourteen Points and the Memorandum of Observations were a long way from forming the text of a peace treaty, and the practical details of their application could allow of many interpretations. (See pp. 79, 92, and Appendix, pp. 831-33.)

Organization and Procedure

There was never much doubt that Paris would be the place of the Peace Conference, though there were many who would have preferred a neutral city, say Geneva or The Hague, free from the overpowering psychosis of the war. But the choice was a compliment to France, and there were also practical reasons for it. Many of the Allied and American organizations, the subordinate offices of the Supreme War Council, as well as "governments" of the new states, such as Czechoslovakia and Yugoslavia, were already congregated there. Hotel accommodation and transport for the peace delegations were in adequate supply. Yet, if Paris was a mistake, the eventual signing of the German treaty at Versailles was even more a brutal and miserable blunder.

The organization and procedure of the Conference were not expected to be difficult. The Allies had been holding conferences for four years and should by now have become adept in negotiation. In the event, it happened that the first peace meeting in Paris on January 12, 1919, was a continuation of the Supreme War Council, and the so-called Council of Ten, which assumed the initiative and direction of the Conference during its early stages, developed naturally from that body. This arrangement was all to the advantage of the five "Principal Allied and Associated Powers" – Britain, France, Italy, Japan, and the United States. The smaller powers were sometimes to complain that they were excluded from important discussions and that they were then expected to subscribe to decisions affecting their vital interests, decisions to which they had contributed nothing. The war had been a war of liberation, and the Peace Conference, they argued, should have signalized the triumph of the smaller powers. But, as Clemenceau remarked, the five principal Powers at the time of the Armistice had twelve million men under arms – and he added laconically, *"C'est un titre!"* There would be occasions enough for disagreement without throwing open the Conference to the politics and propaganda of every minor pleader that came to it.

But the most important question of procedure to be left unsettled was whether the peace should be preliminary or final. Many of the delegates favored a preliminary peace and indeed had come to the Conference with that end in view. Such a peace would have been a frankly dictated peace, containing military, territorial, and reparations clauses alone; and a second peace, quietly and honorably negotiated between victors and vanquished, would then have worked out the larger problems of economic reconstruction, disarmament, and the League. But public opinion was impatient and imperative and would never have borne so protracted a business as a double peace conference with each of the defeated powers. The principal delegates at the Conference were politicians, for whom a long absence from their homes and constituencies might have been very irksome. Probably it was President Wilson himself as much as anyone – though at first he too had been in favor of a "preliminary military convention" – who was determined that there should be one peace and one peace only with each of the defeated powers, with his own historic creation, the League of Nations, as its cornerstone.

Yet we know that for weeks after the Conference had met several of the delegates had not entirely freed themselves from the idea of a preliminary peace. Clauses in the treaty were sometimes hastily adopted, or sometimes adopted for no better reason than to maintain unity among the Allies, but adopted with the tacit reservation that they could be revised at a future date. And there was always Article 19 of the League Covenant to fall back on, expressly providing for the "reconsideration of treaties which had become inapplicable." The peacemakers of Paris, certainly the Britons among them, in their moments of discouragement – and there must have been many such moments – took refuge in the thought that their labors made no claim to finality, and they were afterward appalled to discover that clauses they had recommended during the negotiations were intended not merely to implement an armistice, but to be written into a permanent and definitive settlement.

Manifestly a conference of such size and importance needed time, time to assemble and time to deliberate. Peace conferences of the past had sometimes lasted years. The mere geographical difficulties of assembling a great number of men, some of them from countries as far away as America and Japan, called for weeks of careful staff work. Some delegates wished to consult public opinion before leaving home. Lloyd George went to the length of a general election. President Wilson felt obliged to give his annual message to Congress. Delegates also had to come from the new nations, nations in many cases hardly yet delivered from the matrix of revolution, and their dates of arrival were not always matters of easy calculation in advance.

The work of the Conference could not but be delayed by the unstable condition of Europe. Although the war was over in the West, other little wars were in progress or impending in eastern Europe and Russia. The new nations were not a happy family. Peoples suddenly liberated from centuries of subjection seemed more anxious to try to recapture the glories of some mythic national existence in the past than to submit gratefully and peacefully to their status in the present. Wherever and whenever they could do so, they tried to anticipate the decisions of the Conference by seizing debatable territories on their own account. Even when it had at last assembled, the Conference found its authority far more often and far more dangerously defied by the new smaller powers than by all the sullen, growling resentment of defeated Germany herself.

So many things conspired to delay and obstruct. Yet never did a conference work under such pressure. Diplomacy in Paris in 1919 was no longer the classic art of the leisurely. A war-torn world was trying to repair its social and economic life; nations were waiting almost hourly for the official proclamation of peace. Demobilization could not safely be completed, nor the naval blockade be raised. Indeed the demobilization of the British and American forces proceeded at such a rate that the French High Command feared the Allied military predominance over Germany was being seriously jeopardized. And every day the unsettlement was allowed to continue, Bolshevism, that creeping paralysis, might spread into Europe. Hungary succumbed to it in March 1919; Austria and Germany were gravely menaced. To the delegates in Paris, as they surveyed their tasks in the early months of 1919, it seemed as if the forces of peace and the forces of anarchy were engaged in a desperate race for the possession of Europe.

Yet, for all the "dawdling" of which it was accused, the Conference's timetable in the end was not discreditable. The first plenary session of all the delegates was held nine to ten weeks after the Armistice of November 1918, and less than four months later the text of the German treaty was ready. When we consider the intricate problems that had to be resolved and the precarious state of Europe, we cannot but regard these dates as representing a prodigious achievement.

States of Mind

Yet, while so much was uncertain, the delegates themselves at least knew their own minds. All came formally committed to the Fourteen Points; all had mental reservations of one kind or another. And wonderful were the rationalizations by which the reservations were defended. The Italians, for example, demanded the cession to them of territory inhabited by several thousand German-speaking Tirolese. Their demand contradicted the principle of nationality in Point 9 of the Fourteen Points. But, in the view of the Italians, a single exception made in their favor – and a minor one at that – could hardly be said to vitiate the general settlement. Should a few thousand Tirolese, who happened to live on the wrong side of the Brenner Pass, balk a "strategic rectification" essential to the security of forty million Italians? Every delegate, it was said, wanted to apply the Fourteen Points to every country but his own. Lloyd George was always accused of being statesmanlike at others' expense. General Smuts planned the most ambitious Utopias, but excluded German Southwest Africa therefrom. Hughes, the Australian Prime Minister, bluntly defied President Wilson to impose a mandate on the Australian-occupied islands in the Pacific.[1] President Wilson himself, however zealous to condemn "special covenants" and "regional agreements," would allow no aspersions to be cast on the Monroe Doctrine.

Then behind each delegate at Paris was a nation. The Peace Conference was a democratic conference, the first of its kind in history, and however well- or ill-intentioned the individual delegates may have been, they were still "delegates." They were answerable to governments and to peoples at home, and they were sensitive – extremely sensitive – to their national presses. And perhaps never before or since have the press and the great press correspondents enjoyed so much sheer political influence. Democracy, in 1919, was in a strange, abnormal mood. Propaganda, which had once done excellent service for wartime morale, could not suddenly be switched back to the service of peace. The Frankenstein monsters of hatred and terror that the war had raised up could not be expected to die just because the angels of love and brotherhood had suddenly been invited to take over the guidance of human affairs. Throughout the Conference the delegates were dunned by their respective national presses at home to show no "weakness" to either defeated enemies or jealous allies.

> It must be admitted that after a war in which seventy million young men had been mobilised, in which ten million had been killed, in which thirty million had been wounded, it would be unreasonable to suppose that any democracy could regard with unclouded nerves the spectacle of four gentlemen sitting in a guarded room together, discussing the result. Nor would it be sensible to expect a population which had been appalled by naval and military defeat, terrified by aerial bombardment, anguished by the dread of starvation, to behave in a moment of unimagined victory with the feudal chivalry of the Black Prince.[2]

The realist and idealist states of mind at the Conference – as they might be called – were embodied in two of its leading personalities, Georges Clemenceau and Woodrow Wilson, the principal delegates of France and the United States. Clemenceau brought to the Conference the disillusioned wisdom of an old man who has seen all the evil of the world. He regarded war as the eternal pattern of human society – certainly of European society. Peace, he said, "is the continuation of war by other means" or at best "an equilibrium of forces." The French and German peoples had always contended for supremacy, and their long histories had swung back and forth between their successes and failures. In 1918 France was the victor – temporarily perhaps – in a war, the greatest war, in a perpetual series. It would be criminal folly for her not to use the opportunity she now enjoyed to extend for as long as possible the period of her advantage. Fourteen Points or no Fourteen Points, the Conference in her eyes would be a miserable betrayal if its eventual terms did not ensure the military disablement of Germany, the imposition of punitive and crippling indemnities, the permanent occupation of the Rhineland, even the dismemberment of the Reich into its components of 1815, and the creation of a ring of strong new border states in vigilant alliance.

President Wilson's character is more difficult to draw. He came to Europe bearing the gravest responsibility, to face the greatest opportunity, that ever befell a man. Here, for the first time in history, was the philosopher-king with a Maxima Carta in his hand and the military power to enforce it. The common people of Europe were ready to worship the very ground he trod. The victors hoped for his justice, the vanquished for his mercy, and all for his peace.

> He was received in Paris on his first appearance with an organized adulation of applause in the streets and in the press which was intoxicating . . . Streets were named after him, Senate and Chamber of Deputies gave him an official welcome, a palace was placed at his disposal, the picked regiments of France provided his escort, and their best bands played him through the most impressive avenues of the city.[3]

And in like manner he was received in Rome and London. There was not an honor, not a mark of trust and devotion, that was not laid at his feet.

But Wilson had his weaknesses and contradictions. Like so many introverts he was complex and elusive, withdrawn and solitary. Great natural endowments, literary power, a burning moral fervor, deep religious convictions, and a touch of the visionary were combined with unreal, academic habits of mind and a sensitive, humorless vanity. He believed in his political philosophy with all the inflexibility of his Presbyterian upbringing; he believed no less in himself as its chosen mouthpiece on earth. But he never seemed to understand that other men could be so ungrateful or obtuse as not to believe in it also. Latterly he had grown difficult to advise, unapproachable, and suspicious in his dealings with his colleagues, and he preferred to overwork himself to the point of collapse rather than delegate his business to aides and subordinates. In the end he became estranged even from his old friend, Colonel House.

For President Wilson the League of Nations, *his* League of Nations, was to be the supreme product of the Peace Conference. The Covenant embodied all his idealism and took precedence over all his other pledges and pronouncements. It was, as Lloyd George put it, "if not a whole Treaty, at least the only part of the Treaty in which he was interested." The Treaty, in short, might have its faults – the Treaty could not be expected to be perfect – but the Covenant would compensate for everything. The Covenant would be the nucleus of a new corpus of legislation, a veritable constitution of mankind. Just as a new age had dated from the Fathers of 1787, Wilson doubtless pictured a new and greater age dating from himself.

To this end was Wilson now in Paris – against the advice of many of his colleagues. In the first place, it was then unprecedented for a President of the United States to travel abroad during his term of office. In the second place, the President's high status at Washington, above the battle, three thousand miles away, would have put him out of the reach of the local antagonisms of Europe. If he spoke for a superhuman cause, he could not help prejudicing his position by consorting with lesser breeds of men at a cosmopolitan convention. The American delegates at Paris could have referred back their difficulties to Washington, as occasion required, and called in the distant oracle to strengthen their hands. But, worst of all, Wilson's entire position in Paris was false. He, the great democrat, did not really represent his people. The Congressional elections of November 1918 had resulted in Republican majorities in the Senate and the House. Yet he took only one Republican representative in the American delegation to Paris. Perhaps he thought that Congress, like Europe, would not dare to oppose his righteousness. But, as time was to show, Congress did dare, and we may hazard the guess that Clemenceau, for instance, would not have treated him so cavalierly, nor would Lloyd George have been so smug, had they felt that he could have claimed undisputed support at home. Americans might sometimes blame Europeans for their cynical diplomacy; Europeans could now blame Americans for turning the grandest occasion in the history of diplomacy into a domestic party issue.

The First Period of the Conference

Twenty-seven powers were represented at Paris, and they took seats at the plenary session of the Conference in rough accordance with their military strength — seventy seats in all.[4] Clemenceau and Pichon were the delegates of France, Lloyd George and Balfour of Britain, Orlando and Sonnino of Italy, Wilson and Lansing of the United States, and Saionji and Makino of Japan. These used to meet as a so-called Council of Ten during the first period of the Conference. Colonel House, in his curiously anomalous, unofficial position, was President Wilson's constant adviser. Maurice Hankey, that obscure, ubiquitous figure, formerly Secretary of Lloyd George's War Cabinet, acted as secretary to the Ten and probably exerted an immense influence in questions of procedure. There were also various experts, permanent officials, interpreters, clerks, and typists attached to each delegation to the number of several hundred. It was remarked that the professional diplomat was conspicuously absent. Some of the most distinguished and picturesque personalities were found among the smaller powers: Dmowski and Paderewski of Poland, Beneš of Czechoslovakia, Pashich of Yugoslavia, Bratianu of Rumania, Venizelos of Greece, and the Emir Feisal of the Hejaz. And to these we may add Borden of Canada, Hughes of Australia, and Botha and Smuts of South Africa.

A host of more or less unofficial and unrecognized delegates came streaming to Paris — Finns, Balts, Ukrainians, Ruthenes, Georgians, Armenians, Kurds, Lebanese, Syrians, Persians, Egyptians, Koreans, Albanians, Sinn Feiners, Zionists, counterrevolutionary and White Russians. All the world brought its troubles to Paris and to President Wilson, the prophet and intercessor of the new order. Many of these delegates did indeed get hearings, some were admitted to the regular meetings or commissions, but most of them went away afterward with heavy hearts and empty hands.

Delegates of enemy powers were not admitted to the Conference. The Allies were resolved that there was going to be no German Talleyrand at Paris to sow dissension among them. Nor were delegates of Soviet Russia invited. Russia was in the throes of civil war. White Russian armies were fighting with the aid of Allied munitions; Allied forces were occupying vantage points on Russian territory. Paris was already the refuge of Russian *émigrés,* all lobbying for their respective doctrines and interests. Opinion in Britain and the United States, and in France and Italy, held Bolshevism in abhorrence. A proposal to hold a sort of annex to the Peace Conference at some safe and isolated spot — the Island of Prinkipo in the Sea of Marmora — where a Bolshevik delegation might be invited without fear of contagion, was soon abandoned.

The Peace Conference formally opened with its first plenary session on January 18, 1919, in the Salon de Paix at the Quai d'Orsay. Its history thereafter falls into two periods. Its first period was mainly taken up with the appointment of various commissions for the study of specific problems — a Commission on the League of Nations, a Commission on Responsibility for War and Guarantees, a Commission on Reparation for Damage, a Commission on International Labor Legislation, a Commission on Minorities, and so forth. The commissions were set up at different dates, as they seemed to be wanted, their terms of reference were not always precise, and their coordination was effected by the Council of Ten. Most of the detailed, technical work of the Conference was done by them. Eventually there were over fifty commissions of various kinds. The Commission on the League of Nations consisted of the delegates of fourteen nations under the chairmanship of President Wilson.[5] The first period of the Conference concluded with a plenary session on February 14, when the draft of the Covenant of the League was discussed. The next day President Wilson left for the United States, where Republican opposition to his policies was already becoming too serious to be ignored.

The Second Period of the Conference

The Council of Ten dominated the first period of the Conference, but the more abbreviated and informal Council of Four dominated the second. The change was not deliberate. At the end of February 1919, Lloyd George and Orlando, like Wilson, had been absent from Paris. The Japanese delegates were following a policy of noninterference in European discussions and, though they remained in Paris, they had been keeping away from meetings. Then, on February 19, Clemenceau was shot at by a half-witted anarchist. He was not seriously wounded, but he was confined to his apartment for some days. House, Balfour, and Sonnino visited him there, and the prototype of the Council of Four thus came about almost by accident.

President Wilson returned to Paris on March 14, and he, Clemenceau, Lloyd George, and Orlando at once constituted themselves the "Big Four." Hankey was their secretary and constant attendant. During the ensuing two months, all the main decisions of the Conference were reached, the commissions submitted their reports, the terms of the five treaties were agreed, and the text of the German treaty was drafted in detail. But it was during these two months that the bigger crises of the Conference occurred, among them three in particular: the crisis over the Rhineland, the crisis over Fiume, and the crisis over Shantung.

The first of these crises arose from France's demand for a frontier on the Rhine. A demilitarized Rhenish buffer state, controlled by French forces, would have solved France's strategic problem vis-à-vis Germany. The project had been canvassed at Allied conferences during the war, Marshal Foch had been its consistent advocate, and Marshal Foch exerted enormous influence. But no logic could have reconciled a French Rhineland with the Wilsonian philosophy. Lloyd George showed every sympathy for France's temporary occupation of the Rhineland, but he stoutly opposed the creation of another Alsace-Lorraine in Europe. Clemenceau fought with every weapon in his armory. An open breach between him and President Wilson and a disruption of the whole Conference seemed unavoidable. The French press attacked Wilson viciously. Wilson threatened to leave Paris. Clemenceau eventually gave way, but he obtained from Wilson and from Lloyd George a pledge of American and British aid against Germany in the event of a future aggression, a pledge which was afterward written into formal treaties of assistance and signed concurrently with the Treaty of Versailles. French opinion bowed to the compromise, but it was a compromise which was fated never to be implemented. (See pp. 259 and 293-95.)

The second crisis, over Fiume, arose out of the secret Treaty of London of 1915, under whose terms Italy had entered the war. (See p. 25.) Orlando put forward the argument that if Dalmatia, which that treaty had assigned to Italy, were now to be incorporated in the new state of Yugoslavia, Italy deserved a "compensation" in the shape of the Adriatic port of Fiume. The British and French had little patience with the Italian claims. They had originally had to "buy" Italy's alliance, and her military performance had hardly seemed to justify the price. The Americans left no doubt of their repugnance for the Treaty of London, as for all the secret treaties. The Yugoslavs, for their part, insisted that Fiume was their only practicable harbor and that the possession of it was vital to the economy of their new state. In an attempt to break the deadlock, President Wilson took the extreme step of appealing to the Italian people in a public statement over the heads of the Italian delegates at Paris. Orlando in high dudgeon left Paris, and the public statement, far from appeasing the Italian people, roused them to a fury which must have given the President a most painful surprise.

In the absence of Orlando, the Four became Three, and the conversations continued. In fact, the Three rather gained than lost by the withdrawal of Italian obstructionism. On April 28 at a plenary session, the Covenant of the League of Nations was adopted, and its text published to the world. Two days later the German delegates arrived at Versailles. The Italians put on the best face they could and hurried back to Paris in time to show a "united Allied front" at the plenary session on May 6, when the German treaty was approved. But the question of Fiume was left in abeyance. (See pp. 235-36.)

The third crisis, over Shantung, was President Wilson's most serious defeat at the Conference, a personal defeat and a defeat of principle. Japan was at Paris to secure three things: first, the cession to her of the former German islands in the North Pacific; second, the cession to her of the rights formerly exercised by Germany in Tsingtao and Shantung; and third, the inclusion of an article or clause in the Covenant of the League of Nations recognizing the "equality of races." Japan had continued to occupy the islands in question, Tsingtao, and a considerable part of Shantung since seizing them in 1914. She now claimed the territories *in perpetuo* under her agreement with Britain in 1917. (See p. 67.) The islands were eventu-

The Big Four at the Peace Conference, 1919:
(left to right) Orlando, Lloyd George, Clemenceau, and Wilson

RADIO TIMES HULTON

ally ceded to her as Class C mandates. But Tsingtao and Shantung were undisputably Chinese and, in the Wilsonian view, should unquestionably revert to China – to China who, moreover, had been an ally in the war. In regard to the article on the equality of races, the Americans and British were sympathetic. But Australia, in the person of her Prime Minister Hughes, vehemently objected, fearing that such recognition might afterwards be used as a lever against her "White Australia" policy. It looked indeed as if Japan would fail in all three of her most cherished objectives at the Conference.

The Japanese delegates threatened to leave the Conference and to decline membership in the League of Nations if their demands were not satisfied. The Chinese delegates were as importunate in the opposite direction. The Rhineland crisis had only just been settled; the Fiume crisis was at its height; and President Wilson, exhausted by two heavy disputes, agreed to compromise. Where indeed would the peace treaty and the League have been if both Italy and Japan had withdrawn from them? Japan was therefore confirmed in "temporary" possession of Tsingtao and Shantung; but she conceded that it was her "policy" to hand back the territory to China at a date not specified, "retaining only the economic privileges [hitherto] granted to Germany." The compromise cost President Wilson the friendship of China, and Chinese delegates did not sign the Treaty of Versailles.

The Treaty of Versailles

On April 30, 1919, Count von Brockdorff-Rantzau, at the head of the German delegation, was received at Versailles with proper, if frigid, courtesy, and on May 7, in the Trianon Palace Hotel at Versailles, in the presence of Allied representatives, he was given the text of the treaty from the hands of Clemenceau. He was notified that he would have fifteen days for written observations, but that no oral discussions would be allowed. The occasion did not pass off without its incident. The Count was quick to react to the prevailing temper around him, and, disdaining to rise from his seat, he delivered a biting, truculent speech on the subject of Germany's war guilt, a speech which at one point at least was a malicious misconstruction of the facts. (See p. 132.)

> We have no illusions as to the extent of our defeat and the measure of our impotence. We know that the power of German arms is broken, and we are aware of the fury of the hatred which greets us. We are asked to assume the sole guilt of the war. Such a confession from my lips would be a lie. We have no intention of absolving Germany from all responsibility for the war. . . . But we expressly contend that Germany, whose people was convinced that she was fighting a defensive war, should not be saddled with the whole responsibility. None of us will argue that the mischief began with the murder of the Archduke. In the last fifty years Imperialism has poisoned the international position of all European states. The policy of revenge, the policy of expansion, and the flouting of the rights of self-determination have contributed to the crisis. The Russian mobilization gave the decision to the military authorities.
>
> Public opinion among our foes dilates on the crimes committed by Germany during the conflict. We are not here to deny the responsibility of the men who directed the war, or the violations of international law. We repeat the declaration that wrong was done to Belgium, and we are ready to make it good. But in the waging of the war Germany was not the only offender. . . . Crimes in times of war may be unpardonable, but they are committed in the heat of the contest. The hundreds and thousands of noncombatants who have died of the blockade since November 11 were killed in cold blood after the victory had been won. Think of that when you speak of crime and punishment.[6]

The German written observations on the treaty were made as directed. The Allies conceded a few minor points. But the text was left substantially intact. It was returned to the Germans with the threat that war would be resumed if it was not accepted within five days. Brockdorff-Rantzau resigned, and a new government was formed in Berlin which sent to Versailles Hermann Müller and Johannes Bell, its Foreign and Colonial Ministers. The significance of one being "Colonial Minister" did not pass unnoticed. On June 21, as a prelude to the ignominy of the peace to be, the German warships, interned at Scapa Flow under the terms of the Armistice, were scuttled by their crews. The signing of the treaty took place on June 28, 1919, the fifth anniversary of Sarajevo, in the Hall of Mirrors of the Palace of Versailles, where forty-eight years before, in its moment of triumph, the German Empire had been proclaimed.

The Treaty of Versailles was a formidable document of 15 parts and 440 clauses. Part I was the Covenant of the League of Nations, which was an essential component of the treaty as drafted. Several clauses named the League as the executant of their provisions. Questions still unsettled were referable to it; certain plebiscites were to be conducted by it; the new administrations of Danzig and the Saar were vested in it; the new mandatories were answerable to it; minorities could plead their grievances before it. The remaining parts of the treaty prescribed Germany's frontiers in Europe, her territories and rights abroad, the disbandment of her armed forces, penalties for her transgressions, reparations for damage, and guarantees for the future.

To read the "retributive" clauses is almost to read the history of imperial Germany. Not a crime of the past was left unmentioned or unredressed. The spoliation of Denmark in 1864, of France in 1871, of Belgium in 1914, of Russia in 1917 – and even of the old Kingdom of Poland of the eighteenth century – were put to rights. Trophies and works of art captured by the Prussian Army in 1870-71 were to be restored to France. Books were to be furnished to the University of Louvain sacked by the German Army in 1914. Allied tribunals would try the Kaiser "for a supreme offence against international morality and the sanctity of treaties" and other German nationals for "acts in violation of the laws and customs of war."

Under the political clauses, Germany ceded to Belgium small areas round Eupen and Malmédy. She returned to France the "lost provinces" of Alsace and Lorraine and agreed to the liquidation of all German property therein. She undertook not to build fortifications or assemble armed forces on the left bank of the Rhine or within fifty kilometers of the right bank. She transferred to France the coal mines of the Saar for a period of fifteen years "in full and absolute possession . . . as compensation for the destruction of the coal mines in the north of France." During the fifteen years the Saar would be administered by the League of Nations "in the capacity of trustee," and at the end of the fifteen years a plebiscite of the inhabitants would decide the future status of the territory. Germany recognized the independence of the Austrian Republic, and agreed that "this independence shall be inalienable, except with the consent of the Council of the League of Nations." She ceded to Czechoslovakia a small frontier district near Troppau. She ceded to Poland the so-called Corridor, comprising the greater part of Posen (Poznań) and West Prussia. Plebiscites were to be held in East Prussia and Upper Silesia. Danzig was created a free city to be administered by the League of Nations and was to serve as Poland's access to the sea. Memel was placed at the disposal of the Allies, eventually to serve as Lithuania's access to the sea. Plebiscites were to be held in Schleswig to determine the new frontier with Denmark. The naval base at Helgoland was to be demolished. Germany recognized the independence of all the former Russian territories and confirmed her annulment of the Treaty of Brest Litovsk. She renounced "all her rights and titles over her overseas possessions."

Under the military clauses Germany was to reduce her army to 100,000 men, recruited by voluntary enlistment and serving for twelve years. After the defeat at Jena in 1806, the Prussians had evaded Napoleon's terms of demobilization and had maintained a large army by putting successive batches of men through short periods of intensive training. The twelve-year stipulation was intended by the Allies to prevent a repetition of any such subterfuge. Officers would serve for twenty-five years. Military equipment and the manufacture of munitions would be proportionate to the size of the new army. The General Staff was to be dissolved. Germany was not to maintain a navy in excess of six battleships of 10,000 tons, six light cruisers, twelve destroyers, and twelve torpedo boats. Germany was neither to manufacture nor to possess submarines, military aircraft, heavy artillery, tanks, and poison gas. The Supreme Council — the name under which the Supreme War Council at Versailles was now known — decided at a later date that, in compensation for the ships scuttled at Scapa Flow in the week before the treaty was signed, Germany was to surrender certain ships, floating docks, tugs, and dredges. The military clauses were to be carried out under the supervision of Allied Commissions of Control.

Under the reparations clauses, "the Allied and Associated Governments affirm and Germany accepts the responsibility of Germany and her allies for causing all the loss and damage to which the Allies and Associated Governments and their nationals have been subjected as a consequence of the war imposed upon them by the aggression of Germany and her allies." The Allies recognized that the resources of Germany were not adequate to make complete reparation. But they required of Germany every reparation within her capacity, in money and in kind, for damage to civilians, and they included in this category "all pensions to naval and military victims of war . . . and allowances to families and dependents of mobilized persons." The Allies also required of Germany the reimbursement of all sums which they had loaned Belgium during the war. A Reparation Commission was to be appointed to determine the amounts of all these sums and to arrange for their transfer, so that Germany's entire obligation might be discharged "within a period of thirty years." "In order to enable the Allied and Associated Powers to proceed at once to the restoration of their industrial and economic life," Germany was to pay the equivalent of 20,000,000,000 gold marks by May 1, 1921. She was to deliver coal and timber to France and livestock to Belgium. She was to deliver ships, principally to Britain, "ton for ton and class for class," to compensate for the havoc of the submarine war.

Under the financial and economic clauses, Germany agreed to make reparations a first charge upon her national revenues, to bear the costs of Allied armies of occupation, to acknowledge her prewar debts, not to increase her tariffs above their prewar levels, and not to discriminate against Allied trade. She undertook to internationalize the four rivers serving states beyond her frontiers and passing through or by her territory — the Elbe, the Oder, the Niemen, and the Danube — and granted Czechoslovakia certain harbor facilities in the port of Hamburg. She undertook to maintain the Kiel Canal "free and open to the vessels of commerce and of war of all nations at peace with Germany on terms of entire equality."

Finally, under "Guarantees," the Allies declared that their occupation of the Rhineland would be continued for fifteen years, but they affirmed their intention to reduce the area of occupation by successive withdrawals of their

GERMANY, 1914-19

SHOWING TERRITORIAL CHANGES UNDER THE TREATY OF VERSAILLES

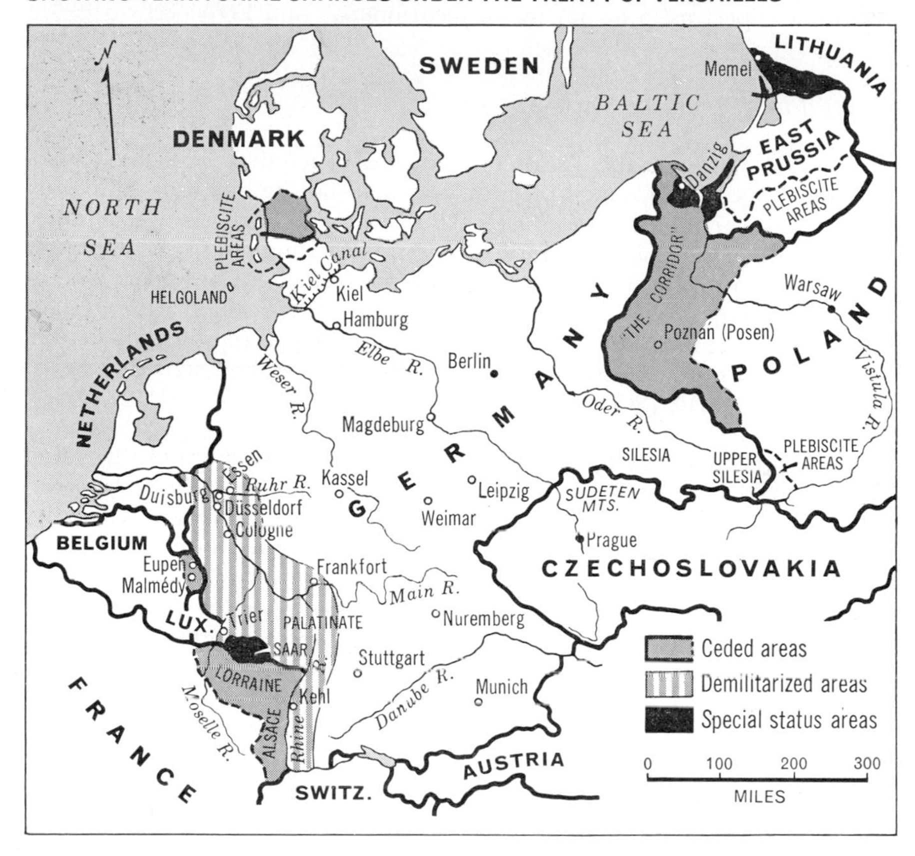

forces every five years, according as Germany fulfilled the conditions of the treaty.

"I should have preferred a different peace," said Colonel House.

"I think it will be found that the compromises, which were accepted as inevitable, nowhere cut at the heart of any principle; the work of the Conference squares, as a whole, with the principles agreed upon as the basis of peace as well as with the practical possibilities," said President Wilson.

"It is a stern but just treaty," said Lloyd George.

"The day has come when might and right—terribly divorced hitherto—have united to give peace to the peoples in travail," said Clemenceau.

"This is not peace; it is an armistice for twenty years," said Marshal Foch.

"The promise of the new life, the victory of the great human ideals are not written in this treaty. . . . The real peace of the peoples ought to follow, complete, and amend the peace of the statesmen," said General Smuts.

"What hand would not wither that signed such a peace?" said Scheidemann.

"Do not expect us to be our own executioners," said Erzberger.

The Treaty of St. Germain

The signing of the Treaty of Versailles concluded the main work of the Conference. The Council of Four ceased to be the organ of Allied discussions, and the treaties with Austria, Bulgaria, and Hungary were framed by the Supreme Council at Versailles. Questions arising out of the execution of the Treaty of Versailles were afterward referred to a Conference of Ambassadors sitting at Paris and consisting of the American, British, Italian, and Japanese ambassadors in France and a French representative. The treaty with Turkey was drawn up in London in 1920 and signed at Sèvres on August 20, 1920. (See pp. 184-86.)

The Austrian delegates, headed by the Austrian Chancellor, Dr. Karl Renner, arrived at St. Germain-en-Laye on May 14, 1919, where they were lodged under the same conditions of restraint as the Germans at Versailles. There was some difficulty over their credentials. The Supreme Council would not admit their claim to represent "German Austria," a state distinct from the old Austria of Austria-Hungary, and made it clear that they dealt with "Austria" and "Austria" only. There was also some delay while the final act at Versailles was being played and the patient delegates at St. Germain were suffered to wait ignominiously for almost three weeks before their own treaty was handed to them. Renner and his aides were indefatigable with "observations" and protests, and important concessions were allowed them. But the Supreme Council admitted no commutation of the bigger issue. Austria was not, as Renner argued, a new nation, as truly new as any "succession state," and therefore deserving of friendly treatment. Austria was still Austria, the old Austria, with whom the Allies had gone to war in 1914, and now come to St. Germain, as Germany to Versailles, to hear sentence. And on this basis, at St. Germain on September 10, 1919, the treaty was signed.

The Treaty of St. Germain was modeled on Versailles. Whole clauses were reincorporated into it without the change of a word. Part I was the Covenant of the League. Under the territorial clauses, Austria ceded to Italy Trieste, Istria, and the Tirol up to the Brenner Pass; to Czechoslovakia she ceded Bohemia, Moravia, Austrian Silesia, and parts of Lower Austria; to Rumania she ceded Bucovina; to Yugoslavia she ceded Bosnia, Herzegovina, and Dalmatia. Only from Hungary did she receive a small strip of territory, which came to be known at this time as the Burgenland. A plebiscite was to decide the future Austrian or Yugoslav allegiance of Klagenfurt. Union (*Anschluss*) with Germany was prohibited in a clause stating that "the independence of Austria is inalienable otherwise than with the consent of the Council of the League of Nations." Austria was to reduce her army to 30,000 long-term volunteers, and to limit her navy to three police boats on the Danube. The penalty, reparations, and financial clauses of the treaty were similar to those of Versailles.

In sum, Austria survived as a relic of her former self, shorn of her empire and shorn of her minorities. Her prewar area (excluding Hungary) was reduced from 115,000 square miles to 32,000, and her prewar population (again excluding Hungary) from 30,000,000 to 6,000,000. The old historic frontiers of Bohemia, including their 3,000,000 Germans, would be the frontiers of the new Czech state.

The Treaty of Neuilly

The Bulgarian delegates arrived in Paris in July 1919, but the presentation of the Allied terms was again delayed, and the delegates waited nearly two months for their treaty. They affected to be surprised that they should be treated as enemies and argued, much as Renner had argued, that the Bulgaria they represented was a new Bulgaria, a regenerated democracy, deserving of a temperate peace. But the Supreme Council gave them small consolation. In October, Stambulisky became Bulgarian Premier and at once gave out that "he had no illusions" and "would sign even a bad peace." The treaty with Bulgaria was duly signed by him at Neuilly-sur-Seine on November 27, 1919.

The Treaty of Neuilly was again modeled on Versailles. Territorially Bulgaria survived with much the same frontiers as she had had in 1914. Her one big cession was that of Western Thrace to Greece. Her forces were reduced to an army of 20,000 and to a *gendarmerie* and frontier corps of 13,000, all long-term volunteers.

The Treaty of Trianon

The Allies had intended to conclude a treaty with Hungary simultaneously with Austria. But Béla Kun's Communist revolution broke out in Budapest in March 1919, and no agreement could be reached with him. The Supreme Council accordingly drew up the frontiers to be assigned to Czechoslovakia, Yugoslavia, and Rumania, and duly notified Béla Kun of its decisions. Hungarian forces were eventually ejected from the territories by force. When Count Apponyi arrived in December 1919, representing a Hungarian government that the Allies felt they could recognize, important and irrevocable commitments regarding the future frontiers of Hungary had already been made. The treaty — also modeled on Versailles — was signed under protest at the Grand Trianon at Versailles on June 4, 1920.

Territorially the Treaty of Trianon was the harshest of the postwar treaties. To Rumania alone Hungary ceded an area larger than the total territory left to her. Her prewar area was reduced from 125,000 square miles to 36,000, and her population from 21,000,000 to 8,000,000. Three million Magyars passed under alien rule. The Hungarian Army was reduced to 35,000 long-term volunteers.

7. THE LEAGUE OF NATIONS AND THE ORGANIZATION OF PEACE

The Origins of the League

The League of Nations was no new idea in the world. Rather it was the synthesis and climax of a long historical development. Perpetual peace was a theme that had long been pondered by churchmen and philosophers. International law in the modern sense, doctrines of mediation and arbitration between states, doctrines of inquiry and delay in international disputes, doctrines of safeguards and sanctions had been familiar since the seventeenth century. The Holy Alliance and the Concert of Powers had been leagues of a kind. The Danube Commission, the Red Cross, the Universal Postal Union, the Pan-American Union, and other bodies were examples and lessons in international cooperation in being. The conferences at The Hague in 1899 and 1907 had set up the Hague Court of Arbitration and had amended the "Laws of War." Peace movements and foundations – such as the Carnegie Endowment and the Nobel Peace Prize – showed the trend of public opinion and philanthropy. International socialism was strongly pacifist. All this was a mass of precedent which gave the framers of the Covenant of 1919 inspiration and authority for their handiwork.

The idea of a league had been canvassed during the war. A "League of Nations Society" had been founded in Britain, and a "League to Enforce Peace" in the United States – both in 1915. President Wilson, in his note of December 1916, had suggested a "concert of nations." Pope Benedict XV, in his peace note of August 1917, had pleaded for "the institution of arbitration." As the war approached its end, several Allied statesmen were giving earnest thought to the future organization of peace. The French Chamber debated a league in 1917, and the British Imperial War Cabinet discussed it at the same time. Lord Robert Cecil, then British Under Secretary for Foreign Affairs, and General Smuts, then South African Minister of Defense, were busy with tentative constitutions and memoranda. On January 8, 1918, as Point 14 of his Fourteen Points, President Wilson declared that "a general association of nations must be formed under specific covenants for the purpose of affording mutual guarantees of political independence with territorial integrity to great and small states alike," and from that moment he became, in the eyes of the world, the great apostle of the League.

When the Commission on the League of Nations at the Peace Conference began its meetings, it was therefore in possession of several proposals. As was so often said, the League was the only problem of the peace on which, before the Armistice, any real forethought had been expended. The draft of the Covenant was adopted at a plenary session of the Peace Conference on April 28, 1919. Its main composers were the American David Hunter Miller and the Englishman Sir Cecil Hurst. In general, the American experts contributed the principles and the British the legal framework.

The Constitution of the League

In the words of the Preamble:

> The High Contracting Parties,
>
> In order to promote international co-operation and to achieve international peace and security—
>
> by the acceptance of obligations not to resort to war,
> by the prescription of open, just and honourable relations between nations,
> by the firm establishment of the understandings of international law as the actual rule of conduct among Governments, and
> by the maintenance of justice and a scrupulous respect for all treaty obligations in the dealings of organised peoples with one another,
>
> Agree to this Covenant of the League of Nations.

In a world made safe for democracy—as was then hoped— it was proper that the League should adopt the standard democratic pattern of parliament, cabinet, and civil service. The Assembly was the League's parliament, and consisted of the representatives of all the members of the League. The Council was the League's cabinet, and consisted of the representatives of the "Principal Allied and Associated Powers"—of which the United States was originally intended to be one—each with a permanent seat, and in addition the representatives of four other powers, "selected by the Assembly from time to time in its discretion." The Council was thus an inner circle of Powers with special executive functions, in many ways reminiscent of the Council of Ten of the Peace Conference. The Secretariat was the League's civil service, and consisted of a Secretary General and staff. The seat of the League was Geneva, where in due course the magnificent Palace of Nations was built to house it. The League also created, or associated with itself, a number of organs such as the Mandates Commission, the International Labor Organization, and the World Court.

The League held its First Assembly in November 1920, after the exchange of ratifications of the Treaty of Versailles. There were forty-two original members, signatories of the Treaty of Versailles and "neutrals, invited to accede." China had refused to sign the Treaty of Versailles, but joined the League in July 1920, upon the ratification of the Treaty of St. Germain, and was counted among the "originals." The United States and the Hejaz, both signatories of Versailles, failed to ratify and never subsequently became members. Germany became a member in 1926, and the Soviet Union in 1934. Up to 1936, nineteen additional states had become members, and six – including Japan, Germany, and Italy – had seceded. The Soviet Union was expelled in 1939, the only member ever to be so treated. The last Assembly of the League was held in April 1946.[1]

The Covenant of the League is printed in part in an Appendix of this volume. Articles 1 to 7 concern the terms of membership, the powers and functions of the Assembly and of the Council, the procedure for convening meetings, and costs of administration. In Article 5 we read:

> Except where otherwise expressly provided in this Covenant [for example, in matters of procedure] . . . decisions at any meeting of the Assembly or of the Council shall require the agreement of all the Members of the League represented at the meeting.

Article 8 enjoined the members of the League to reduce their national armaments "to the lowest point consistent with national safety" and required the Council to formulate plans for such reduction "for the consideration and action of the several Governments." From this auspicious and plausible text was to arise the ill-fated Disarmament Conference. Article 10 was a mutual guarantee of territorial integrity and political independence, and was the cornerstone of the entire security edifice. Articles 11 to 17 concerned the prevention of war. Of these, Article 15, recalling Article 5, prescribed that the dispute could only be settled on the basis of unanimity:

> If the Council fails to reach a report which is unanimously agreed to by the members thereof, other than the representative of one or more parties to the dispute, the Members of the League reserve to themselves the right to take such action as they shall consider necessary for the maintenance of right and justice.

Article 16 specified the sanctions to be applied by members of the League against any one of their number resorting to war "in disregard of its Covenants" and the support which the members would then render one another. These articles may have seemed wanting in forcible phrasing; but it is to be remembered that they were the synthesis of several contributions, and they represented a compromise, the best compromise then possible, between collective action among nations and noninterference in the sovereignty of any one of them. Furthermore, the requisite unanimity was – and, for that matter, still is – a normal diplomatic rule, and in this regard the League was doing no more than conforming to contemporary practice. International conferences of the time always tried to reach agreement, however watered down that agreement might eventually have to be – or else "adjourned."

Article 18 embodied Point 1 of the Fourteen Points, demanding "open Covenants of peace," and provided for the registration and publication of all treaties and international engagements entered into by member states. "No such treaty or international engagement shall be binding until so registered." Article 19 provided for the "reconsideration of treaties which have become inapplicable and the consideration of international conditions whose continuance might endanger the peace of the world." The framers of the Covenant were well aware that their institution might become the refuge of conservatism and that every *status quo,* as soon as it has become a *status quo,* tends also to become a *status sacrosanctus.* The British delegates at the Peace Conference in particular regarded Article 19 as an escape clause under which the defects of the peace treaties might be legally and peaceably redressed. Unhappily the British delegates counted without the unanimity principle, and, as was so often to happen, "the right" lay in the hands of the party most interested in blocking a revision.

It was hoped by many that the League might supersede the old systems of alliances and ententes which they considered had been so fertile of wars. But Article 21, inserted at the behest of the American delegates, made an exception of "regional understandings like the Monroe Doctrine, for securing the maintenance of peace"; and, within a couple of years of the signing of the Treaty of Versailles, the nations of Europe were once more as busy with their regional understandings as ever they had been in the past, all of which they too asserted were for securing the maintenance of peace. Far from being a superalliance, an alliance which obviated the need of all others, the League was soon to be strenuously buttressed about with alliances and ententes, pacts and protocols, such as made the ensuing twenty years the most active and complicated in the history of professional diplomacy.

Perhaps it was in France that criticisms of the "weakness" of the League were most persistent. The French, with their essentially military conception of international relations, had always wanted a military league — a league with "teeth" in it. Léon Bourgeois, the French delegate on the League Commission at the Peace Conference, had pleaded interminably for the inclusion in the Covenant of definite military clauses or at least for the international "surveillance" and "verification" of armaments. But it was hard to see how any sovereign member of the League — least of all France herself — would have been willing to accept in advance the controls that such clauses would have entailed.

Far from accepting the additional severities of a military league, certain member states were soon chafing under even the mild and equivocal obligations of the Covenant as it stood. From the very First Assembly, in 1920, amendments were proposed, notably in regard to Article 16. At the Fourth Assembly, in 1923, the Canadian delegate brought forward an interpretative resolution in respect of Article 10 to the effect that every government should itself be the judge of the extent of its military commitments. The resolution failed of adoption, but it was significant nonetheless. We might remark, incidentally, that the same Article 10 had been most vehemently opposed in the United States.

The inescapable fact remains that no nation entered the League, just as no nation had originally come to the Peace Conference at Paris, without mental reservations of one sort or another. Local needs, local prejudices, local habits of thought contributed variously to the way each of the nations interpreted its rights and duties under the Covenant. When all was said and done, France measured the usefulness of the League in proportion as it could be turned into an instrument for the suppression of Germany. Fascist Italy regarded the League as a standing obstacle to her expansionism. Republican Germany looked to the League as an aid to her liberation from Versailles, but at the same time she could never reconcile herself to the fact that the Covenant had been written into the text of the Treaty of Versailles, and that her great hope and her great humiliation were most diabolically intermixed. British Commonwealth countries generally regarded the League as a European affair which, as far as they were concerned, asked much and gave nothing. America's reservation was her old abhorrence of European entanglements. We shall describe elsewhere the American repudiation of President Wilson and Versailles – and the League. (See p. 294.) But we should observe here that America's reservation was, of all the reservations, the one that mattered most. The absence of the Great Power, which had done so much to create the League, was a fatal limitation of the League's prestige and usefulness.

Yet for all these criticisms and for all the League's failures in the major crises of the Period of Crisis to come, it is unfair and unhistorical to forget the concrete achievements of the League in its best days. Up to the Manchurian crisis in 1931, the League dealt with 28 political disputes between states, and from 1931 to 1939 with 15; and, of this total of 43 disputes, it successfully settled 12, left 12 unsettled, while the remaining 19 were afterward withdrawn, directly negotiated between the disputants, often with the participation or advice of the League Council, or else referred to the World Court. Many of the successful settlements were models of their kind, examples of the function that a world institution like the League was eminently fitted to perform. The total record is no mean one. Moreover, the League administered the Saar and Danzig under the terms of the Treaty of Versailles; it assisted the financial reconstruction of certain states, notably Austria; it supervised several plebiscites; and it engaged in humanitarian, health, and educational work, notably in regard to the drug traffic, slavery, and refugees. Some of these matters will be considered in other contexts elsewhere in this book. The League's activities in regard to mandates and minorities, humanitarian work and intellectual cooperation, the International Labor Organization, the World Court, and finally disarmament will be discussed in the remaining pages of the present chapter.

The Mandates

Article 22 of the League Covenant, the Mandates Article, provided for the disposal and distribution of the foreign and overseas territories of Germany and the Ottoman Empire under a system of mandates. The territories were forfeited by Germany and the Ottoman Empire by reason of their defeat and their deplorable record as rulers of subject races. Open annexation of the territories by the victor Allies would have contravened the high purposes of the Wilsonian philosophy. Yet the territories, inhabited as they were "by peoples not yet able to stand by themselves under the strenuous conditions of the modern world," could not be expected to exist without the tutelage of "advanced nations." Under the mandates system, the territories would be granted to colonial powers – or rather, those Allied Powers which had occupied the territories in the course of the war would now be confirmed in possession – but the territories would be held in trust on behalf of the League, and the worst abuses of the old imperialism, it was hoped, would be avoided. The Mandatory Powers, according to the "character of the mandate" and "the stage of the development of the people," would then be obligated to respect freedom of religion, to prohibit the slave trade, to prevent the building of fortifications and the military training of the natives, and finally to "render to the Council [of the League] an annual report" upon their stewardship. A Mandates Commission was created to sit at Geneva, to receive the annual reports of the Mandatory Powers, to submit its own observations to the League Council, and generally to supervise the mandates system.

There were three classes of mandates, A, B, and C, differing roughly in accordance with the political development of the people in question. To Class A belonged the former possessions of the Ottoman Empire, inhabited by newly liberated peoples who were expected eventually to become independent. Of these possessions, Mesopotamia and Palestine were allotted to Britain as the Mandatory Power, and Syria and Lebanon to France. To Class B belonged the former Central and East African possessions of Germany, inhabited by people who were not expected to become independent. Of these possessions, the greater part of Tanganyika was allotted to Britain, the remainder to Belgium, and Togoland and the Cameroons were divided between Britain and France. Finally, to Class C belonged former German possessions which passed wholly "under the laws of the Mandatory as integral portions of its territory." Thus the former German Southwest Africa was allotted to the Union of South Africa, the former German islands in the Pacific north of the equator were allotted to Japan, and those south of the equator to Australia and New Zealand.

The allotment of these mandates was made at Allied conferences, notably at the Peace Conference in 1919 and at the San Remo Conference in 1920. (See pp. 107 and 184.) In general it may be said that the mandates system worked very well. The mandates in Syria and Palestine proved most troublesome – as we shall relate. (See pp. 194ff.) Japan abused her undertakings in respect of her mandate over the former German islands in the North Pacific, erecting fortifications and refusing to permit League inspection. (See pp. 105 and 297-99.) In 1932 Iraq (Mesopotamia) was the first state to be emancipated from its mandatory status to become an independent kingdom and a member of the League of Nations.

The Minorities

The peace treaties of 1919-20, as one historian has said, represented "the closest approximation to an ethnographic map of Europe that has ever been achieved." [2] The variegated peoples of that restless, fluctuating continent, it seemed, had really found at last an appropriate political geography. Nationality and self-determination, twin ideals, were largely coincident and mutually satisfied. Yet, in places, there were still "minorities" on the wrong side of a frontier. It was estimated that 30,000,000 of Europe's population would still be compelled to live under alien rule. Austria-Hungary and the Ottoman Empire had both been reduced to their national elements, and the new states arising out of them could not always be homogeneous. The new governments were inexperienced; sentiments everywhere were inflamed by war and by long, embittered historical memories; it was impossible to expect that several nationalities, once repressed and now dominant and revengeful, would not wreak their hatred on "islands" of their former overlords which the peace treaties would leave within their borders. Other communities, notably the Jews, created special problems.

There is no mention of minorities in the League Covenant, for the Covenant was drawn up and published before the minority problem had begun seriously to disturb the Peace Conference at Paris. But the five minorities treaties of 1919 and 1920 all subsequently cited the League as the trustee and court of appeal of the populations whose rights they sought to protect. The treaties were largely the work of the Minorities Commission of the Peace Conference. The smaller powers, on whom the necessary legislation was to be imposed, naturally enough were not slow to protest against the implied derogation of their sovereignty, and it needed all the tact and authority of the Great Powers to smooth their ruffled pride.

The Polish Minorities Treaty was the first to be drawn up. For obvious reasons it had to be ready at the same time as the Treaty of Versailles. It took the form of a treaty between the five Principal Allied and Associated Powers and Poland. Poland obligated herself to give her citizens "full and complete protection of life and liberty . . . without distinction of birth, nationality, language, race, or religion," to permit them "the free exercise, whether public or private, of any creed, religion, or belief," and to provide "in the public educational system in towns and districts, in which a considerable proportion of Polish nationals of other than Polish speech are residents, adequate facilities in primary schools . . . for instruction to be given to the children through the medium of their own language." All these clauses constituted "obligations of international concern and shall be placed under the guarantee of the League of Nations." Any member of the League Council might bring to the attention of the Council "any infraction, or any danger of infraction, of any of these obligations." The Polish Minorities Treaty was signed concurrently with the Treaty of Versailles on June 28, 1919.

Similar treaties were signed during 1919 and 1920 with Yugoslavia, Czechoslovakia, Rumania, and Greece. Special minority clauses were inserted in the peace treaties with Austria, Hungary, Bulgaria, and Turkey. Albania and the new Baltic States made declarations recognizing their obligations to their minorities. But it cannot be said that all these treaties and declarations were conspicuously successful. Complicated, ancient hatreds were not to be written off just with the stroke of a pen. Later, as the League system weakened, so also its more precarious injunctions weakened, and in the era of the dictatorships, so soon to arrive, the minorities became convenient pawns in the renewed game of power politics.

The Humanitarian and Intellectual Work of the League

Various ancillary organs and committees of the League were devoted to international health; the traffic in drugs; the traffic in women; slavery; obscene publications; the repatriation of prisoners of war; and the relief of refugees and of communities stricken by epidemics, flood, and earthquakes. In 1921 the Second Assembly created a Committee on Intellectual Cooperation "to secure for intellectual work the place which befits it and to assist in the freer and more rapid circulation of the great intellectual currents of the world." The Committee included such eminent names as Einstein, Millikan, Gilbert Murray, Bergson, and Madame Curie. These many organizations left a record of great accomplishment, and they were precursors of enterprises of the same kind in the United Nations.

The International Labor Organization

The International Labor Organization, the ILO, was brought into existence at the Peace Conference under the benevolent direction of the Commission on International Labor Legislation. Its purpose and constitution were set out in the peace treaties and in Article 23 of the Covenant of the League. It recognized the world-wide interest in social and labor problems which the war and the postwar revolutionary movements had stirred up. It would help, it was sincerely hoped, to remove the "injustice, hardship, and privation" which had involved such large numbers of people and had imperiled "the peace and harmony of the world." It would be "established at the seat of the League of Nations as a part of the organization of the League," and it would endeavor to "secure and maintain fair and humane conditions of labor for men, women and children, both in their own countries and in all countries to which their commercial and industrial relations extend." By its agency, the peace treaties would not only create in the world a better political order, but a better social order as well. It became in addition a valuable central clearinghouse of a vast mass of world-wide economic and social information.

The ILO consisted of a General Conference, a Governing Body, and an Office, departments analogous to the Assembly, Council, and Secretariat of the League itself. All member states of the League were members of the ILO. Brazil and Japan, on withdrawing from the League, remained members of it. The United States became a member in 1934. The first General Conference was held in Washington in 1919. From 1921 to 1939 it met regularly in Geneva. In 1940 the Office was moved to Montreal, where it occupied modest premises in McGill University. A conference was held in New York in 1941, and the regular sessions of the General Conference were resumed in 1944. Up to 1939, the Conference had adopted 73 recommendations and 67 conventions, dealing with working hours, night work, woman and child labor, the weekly day of rest, workmen's compensation, sickness benefit, occupational diseases, minimum wages, unemployment, and so forth. Over 900 ratifications had been received from more than 60 states.

The ILO was the one organization of the League to survive the Second World War under its original name. At the time of writing it is still in existence.

The World Court

The Permanent Court of International Justice, or the World Court as it came to be known, was not an immediate product of the Peace Conference. The framers of the League Covenant at first expected that arbitral tribunals created *ad hoc,* or else the former Hague Court of Arbitration, would deal with future international disputes. Article 14 of the Covenant, which became the basis of the Court's existence, was a highly technical and controversial issue, and in the form in which it was inserted in the Covenant it left room for future discussion and development. A committee of eight eminent jurists, among whom were Elihu Root and Lord Phillimore, was set up at a second meeting of the League Council in February 1920. The committee sat at The Hague for two months and eventually drew up a draft statute which was duly referred back to the League Council. After exhaustive examination, the statute was approved in detail in December 1920 by the First Assembly of the League. The Permanent Court of International Justice, or World Court, was formally opened on February 15, 1922.

The establishment of the World Court at The Hague instead of at Geneva was a tribute partly to the long tradition of international jurisprudence in Holland and partly to the American donors of the Peace Palace. The Court was not intended to supersede the Hague Court of Arbitration, which actually continued in independent existence. It was, as its name implied, a permanent court, holding annual sessions and convenable for extraordinary sessions at short notice. Normally disputes could be referred to it only by states signatory to its Statute, and the disputes had to be specifically "legal or justiciable," for instance, those arising out of an interpretation of international law or an alleged breach of treaty. The Court therefore in no way duplicated or superseded the League or the League's functions in regard to political disputes under Articles 12, 13, 15, and 16 of the Covenant. The Court had no power to require a state to appear before it, nor to enforce its verdict afterward. An "Optional Clause" was inserted in its Statute, to which states were invited to adhere, thereby bringing themselves into a system for the compulsory settlement of legal disputes. The World Court was undeniably one of the greater creations of the peace settlement, but it suffered from the weakness of all "League Institutions." In the last analysis, it relied wholly upon the tenuous constraints of good will and good faith.

The World Court began with thirty-four participating states. It eventually had fifty. By a resolution of the League Council, eleven states, though not members of the League, were entitled to appear before it. In course of time, forty states subscribed to the Optional Clause.[3] More than four hundred international treaties and conventions of various kinds contained clauses providing for the reference of disputes to the Court. The United States, after a long controversy, declined to become a member. (See pp. 295-96.)

The Draft Treaty and the Geneva Protocol

It was in France, we have said, that criticisms of the weakness of the League were most persistent, and it was French diplomacy which, during the interwar years, was most exercised with the task of surmounting that weakness. Clearly the League must be used – for what it was worth; but clearly also the League by itself could never be the only line of defense. We shall describe elsewhere the alliance system which France constructed in Europe against a future German aggression. But we should also note at this point those other more general international agreements by which the League members, largely at the behest of France, tried to inject a little more reality into the organization of peace. We refer to the Draft Treaty of 1923, the Geneva Protocol of 1924, and the Locarno Pact of 1925. And we might include the Pact of Paris of 1928.

During 1922 the British and French Governments each approached the other with proposals for mutual assistance treaties within the framework of the League. In particular the British Government was anxious to find a replacement for the treaty of assistance of 1919, which the United States had failed to ratify and which had consequently lapsed. (See pp. 104, 259, and 293-95.) Eventually a Draft Treaty of Mutual Assistance, was debated at the League's Fourth Assembly in 1923. A Protocol for the Pacific Settlement of International Disputes – the Geneva Protocol, as it came to be called – was drawn up at the League's Fifth Assembly in 1924. Each of these instruments denoted a step forward; but they failed to define the precise nature of the assistance that Britain should be called upon to give. It was easy enough to name the arbitrator in an international dispute; the arbitrator would be the League Council or such other body as the League Council might appoint. It was easy enough to name the aggressor; the aggressor would then be the party which refused arbitration. All this was good diplomatic logic. What was not so easy was to give an unconditional military undertaking in advance. But these three years of patient discussion were not wasted. In 1925 the European Powers concluded the Locarno Pact.

The Locarno Pact

Thrice had Britain declined commitments on behalf of France. The treaty of assistance, the Draft Treaty, and the Geneva Protocol had all failed because of her attitude. Britain by her position and responsibilities in the world was already sufficiently committed to maintaining the *status quo*. There was not a breath of unrest in the five continents or on the seven seas which did not inevitably touch her interests or prestige. There was not a war which might break out, which she could ignore. Moreover she had domestic and imperial troubles of her own, in Ireland, Egypt, and India, in lands outside the ken of Continental Europe, where she needs must struggle alone. Her homeland was sunk in its postwar economic lethargy and wanted not an increase, but a relaxation, of international responsibility. To give a blanket guarantee to the Polish Corridor or Danzig, for example, or to the new frontiers of Bohemia or Rumania or Silesia, or to any of the dozen "danger spots" of Europe – for all that Britain was signatory of the treaties that had created them and must continue indirectly to be concerned in their preservation – was more than the British Parliament and public, with the best will in the world, could afford to do.

Furthermore the British Dominions had their particular interests – or lack of interests – and frankly expressed themselves as averse to involvement in any instrument which in practice could never be much more than a European regional understanding. As the Canadian delegate at Geneva once said, "In this association of mutual assistance against fire, the risks assumed by the different states are not equal. We [in Canada] live in a fireproof house, far from inflammable materials." In 1925 Austen Chamberlain, then British Foreign Secretary, made a statement before the League Council intimating his government's "insuperable objections to signing and ratifying the [Geneva] Protocol in its present shape."

Nevertheless, the British Government felt that a fourth attempt must be made. It wanted a treaty which would satisfy opinion in France, but which would not look, as the French-sponsored schemes always looked, like an alliance of the Versailles Powers for the perpetual subjugation of Germany. In the end, curiously enough, the solution was found in a return to the idea of a treaty of assistance, and the initiative came from Germany herself.

The moment was hardly propitious. As we shall relate elsewhere, the German reparations problem had at last reached what was hoped would be a settlement in the Dawes Plan, and early in 1925 the first stages of the Allied evacuation of the Rhineland should have begun. (See p. 146.) But the Allied Control Commission had reported unfavorably on the progress of German disarmament, and the evacuation was called off. The German press reverted to its old tone of aggrievement and defiance, and the French to its interminable thesis of a Rhine frontier. Nevertheless, in February 1925, with bland indifference to the situation as it appeared to be, Gustav Stresemann, the German Foreign Minister, transmitted to Édouard Herriot, the French Premier, proposals for a regional pact of nonaggression and arbitration to include France, Britain, Italy, and Germany and, if possible, to find a general solution of current international disagreements in Western Europe.

Complicated negotiations followed. Britain relented to the extent of accepting commitments for the Rhineland, but she was still averse to guaranteeing the whole mixed ragbag of Intermediate Europe. In April 1925, the Herriot government fell in France, but Painlevé succeeded, with the moderate Aristide Briand as Foreign Minister, and the continuity of the negotiations was not interrupted. In October the Powers – France, Britain,

The signing of the Locarno Pact, London, December 1, 1925: Luther, the German Chancellor, facing the camera, addressing the conference; Stresemann at his right; Baldwin, the British Prime Minister, and Austen Chamberlain at the head of the table; Briand at the top right-hand corner of the table

RADIO TIMES HULTON

Italy, Germany, Belgium, Poland, and Czechoslovakia – met in the Swiss town of Locarno on Lake Maggiore. Austen Chamberlain, the British Foreign Secretary, represented Britain; Briand represented France; Hans Luther, the German Chancellor, and Stresemann represented Germany; Mussolini, the Italian dictator, was present during the concluding stages of the conference. The pact was initialed at Locarno on October 16 and signed in London on December 1, 1925.

The Locarno Pact comprised a whole series of interlocking treaties. In a "Final Protocol" the Powers declared their intention to "seek by common agreement means for preserving their respective nations from the scourge of war, and for providing for the peaceful settlement of disputes," and pledged themselves to cooperate sincerely in the League's endeavors toward disarmament. The first of the treaties was a Treaty of Mutual Guarantee, the Rhineland Pact, as it was popularly known, under which Britain, France, Belgium, Italy, and Germany, collectively and severally, guaranteed the western frontiers of Germany and the demilitarization of the Rhineland. France, Belgium, and Germany agreed "in no case to attack or to invade each other or to resort to war against each other," except in a flagrant breach of the Protocol, or in fulfillment of League action against an aggressor state. The responsibility for determining the flagrant breach devolved upon the League Council.

There then followed four arbitration treaties between Germany on the one side and France, Belgium, Poland, and Czechoslovakia severally on the other, providing for their disputes to be submitted to a Conciliation Commission and thence, if need be, to the World Court or the League Council; and two treaties of guarantee, virtually defensive alliances, between France and Poland, and France and Czechoslovakia.

Locarno made a tremendous impression at the time. The whole setting of the conference had been skillfully stage-managed to banish the psychology of Versailles. The delegates met informally at country inns and on boating excursions on Lake Maggiore. The very words "ally" and "enemy" were ruled out of their vocabulary. On his return to England, Chamberlain declared the Locarno Pact marked "the real dividing line between the years of war and the years of peace," and a grateful King created him Knight of the Garter. Briand, in the eloquent French of which he was so great a master, apostrophized the new era of "conciliation, arbitration, and peace"! Even Stresemann felt it incumbent on him to say: "We are citizens each of his own country . . . but we are also citizens of Europe and are joined together by a great conception of civilization. We have the right to speak of a European idea."

In 1928 was signed that greater Locarno, the Pact of Paris. This time, the United States was also drawn into the vortex of peace. (See p. 305.)

The Pact of Paris

As far as France was concerned — and, in particular, as far as Aristide Briand, the French Foreign Minister, was concerned — the Pact of Paris was originally intended to be no more than a gesture. The idea was rumored to have been suggested to him by a friendly American professor.[4] On April 6, 1927, in a statement to the press, Briand proposed that France and the United States should celebrate the tenth anniversary of the entry of the United States into the First World War by subscribing to an engagement outlawing war between themselves. Briand doubtless expected that the affair would begin and end with an exchange of courtesies of the type he and his countrymen knew so well how to make. A couple of speeches, a couple of signatures cost nothing, and it would all be very pleasant mummery among friends.

The reaction in the United States was slow in coming, but it gradually gathered force, and before many weeks had passed the "outlawry of war" had become a national movement of extraordinary power. Washington was overwhelmed by petitions and deputations from all over the country. In December 1927, having waited some months while the tide of popular pacifism swirled round his Department, Secretary of State Frank B. Kellogg replied to Briand's proposal by suggesting a world-wide multilateral pact binding all nations "to renounce war as an instrument of national policy."

This was far more than Briand had bargained for. The French Government at once took the line that so universal an engagement might conflict with France's own treaty system in Europe. But in April 1928, Kellogg circulated among the British, German, Italian, and Japanese governments the draft of a pact which, in his view, met the needs of the case. The German Government was the first to accept the draft, and it accepted it with alacrity. The Italian and Japanese governments also accepted. The British Government appeared to hesitate – like France, it also had prior commitments to consider, and perhaps it was a little cynically inclined toward what it felt to be a piece of American naïveté and exuberance – but it was soon forced to fall into line by demonstrations of popular enthusiasm in Britain as impressive as any in the United States. Some time was consumed, nevertheless, while official French and British "reservations" were reconciled with the Kellogg formula, and by the end of June 1928 a more acceptable draft had been sent, for final consideration and comment, to the governments of all the Locarno Powers.

On August 27, 1928, the plenipotentiaries of fifteen powers met in Paris to conclude a General Treaty for the Renunciation of War, the Pact of Paris, or the Kellogg-Briand Pact as it was familiarly called.[5] Among them were Briand, Kellogg, and Stresemann. It was the first time since 1870 that a German Foreign Minister had been officially received on French soil. The ceremony was staged in the Quai d'Orsay. All the little properties of the occasion were chosen with tact and taste. The plenipotentiaries signed with a gold pen presented to Kellogg by the city of Le Havre and bearing the inscription *"Si vis pacem para pacem."* The inkstand was the inkstand used in the signing of the treaty of 1778.[6] Said Briand:

> In the face of the whole world, by means of a solemn covenant, involving the honour of great nations that have behind them a past heavy with political conflicts, war is unreservedly renounced as an instrument of national policy, that is to say, war in its most specific and dreaded form, egotistic and willful war.

In this festival of nations the most important absentee had been the Soviet Union. Chicherin, the Soviet Commissar for Foreign Affairs, naturally regarded as suspect a pact to which all the world was party but his own country, and pronounced it a typical capitalist intrigue. He recalled with some asperity that the Soviet Union had also been absent from Locarno. Nevertheless, with the good offices of the French Government, one of only two signatories of the Pact of Paris then maintaining diplomatic relations with Moscow, the adhesion of the Soviet Union to the pact was secured within a couple of days of the main event in Paris. The Soviet Union, in fact, went further. Having at first condemned the Pact of Paris, the Soviet Union was shortly constructing a pact of its own. Maxim Litvinov, Chicherin's successor, proposed that the Soviet Union, Poland, and Lithuania should recognize the Pact of Paris as binding on themselves. Eventually, on February 9, 1929, the Litvinov Protocol, as it was called, was signed in Moscow and was afterward ratified by the Soviet Union and eight other states around its littoral.[7] The whole world, it seemed, was being bound, pact by pact, to peace.

Disarmament

Disarmament had been a frequent theme in peace proposals during the First World War. It received canonical form in Point 4 of the Fourteen

Points. Article 8 of the Covenant laid it as an obligation on all League members. The Treaty of Versailles imposed unilateral disarmament on Germany "in order to render possible the initiation of a general limitation of the armaments of all nations," and the Allied treaties with Austria, Hungary, and Bulgaria contained similarly worded clauses. In reply to one of the German "observations" at Versailles, the Allies declared further:

> Their requirements were not made solely with the object of rendering it impossible for Germany to resume her policy of military aggression. They are also the first step towards that general reduction and limitation of armaments which they seek to bring about as one of the most fruitful preventives of war, and which it will be one of the first duties of the League of Nations to promote.

Yet, while the arguments might be incontestible, the "practical details of their application" were not so easy. For fifteen years, from 1919 to 1933, some of the best minds in the world were trying to devise the ways and means for preventing another 1914 and the armaments "race" which had led up to it. Never did men seem so much in love with peace; never did they seem so ready to take action against war. None of them believed any more in the vicious old maxim *Si vis pacem para bellum.*[8] Yet the story of disarmament – or, more correctly, the limitation of armaments – was one of failure.

The conspicuous feature of the problem, as it then seemed, was its extraordinary complexity. Louis XIV in his day had stopped dueling by forbidding the carrying of swords. But the nations of this Age of Conflict carried more than swords in their belts. Their armaments varied so greatly in type and function as to defy comparison in any sort of workable legal formula. The real military power and potential of nations depended on their geography and way of life, on their isolation and vulnerability, on their raw materials and industries – on their geopolitics, to use a later term – as well as on even less ponderable factors, the intelligence and literacy of their peoples, their birth rate, their national pride and prestige, their ideology, even their religion. It was difficult to find a common denominator, a "yardstick," by which to assess a nation's effectives. Armies could not be measured by divisions, nor navies by tonnage, nor air forces by the simple computation of the number of planes.

It was difficult to assess the respective requirements of a naval power like Britain, with scattered possessions and widely flung trade routes, and a naval power like the United States, with a concentration of interests in two oceans. It was difficult to assess the requirements of an inland state like Hungary, crowded about with potentially hostile neighbors, and of a state in a strategic lee like Canada, with one neighbor and that a friendly one. It was difficult to assess the real strength of a state like the Soviet Union, supported, as it then was, by an agrarian economy, and a state like Britain, supported by an industrial economy, and states like France or Germany, supported by a combination of both. It was difficult to assess the budgetary expenditures on armaments of a state like Japan, with a low standard of living, and a state like the United States, with a high standard of living. It was difficult to assess the budgetary expenditures on armaments of states having different systems of taxation or accounting. It was difficult to assess the value of secret armaments or of newly invented and untried weapons. It was difficult to assess different methods of training, speed of mobilization, and availability of reserves. It was difficult to assess the value of an industrial plant, say a dye factory, convertible at short notice to the manufacture of poison gas, or of a fleet of commercial aircraft convertible at short notice into a bombing squadron, or of a luxury liner convertible at short notice into an auxiliary cruiser or an aircraft carrier. It was difficult to assess the degree of "offensiveness" or "defensiveness" of particular weapons; one power might regard the submarine as offensive and therefore propose its abolition, whereas another power might regard it as defensive and therefore propose its retention; one power might regard the tank as offensive, whereas another power might regard only heavy tanks above 70 tons as offensive. And so forth. If, in addition to all these difficulties, there was also a lack of good will on the part of certain national governments, a future World Disarmament Conference would hardly meet under the most favorable prospects.

In the actual history of disarmament in the interwar period, naval disarmament did achieve, if only temporarily, a certain measure of success. Naval disarmament was perhaps the simpler problem, as only three principal powers were involved, and the categories of ships were relatively easy to define. The history of naval disarmament begins with the Washington Conference of 1921 and continues through the conferences of Geneva and London in 1927 and 1930. As American initiative and influence were here so strong, we leave the discussion of these conferences to Chapter 16 on the United States. (See pp. 296ff.) The responsibility for disarmament on land fell to the League of Nations, and the League's early discussions in this field we should now relate.

In 1920, in accordance with Article 8 of the Covenant, the League Council appointed a Permanent Advisory Committee on Armaments, to which were successively added the Temporary Mixed Commission and then, in 1926, the Preparatory Commission for the Disarmament Conference. Meanwhile, a further conference had been convened at Geneva to examine that vexatious and delicate problem, the private traffic in arms, and it eventually drew up a convention recommending a system of supervision and publicity in the private traffic in certain types of arms. It also drew up the so-called Gas Protocol condemning the use of chemical and bacteriological warfare. At the end of 1925, twenty nations had adhered to the Gas Protocol, including Italy, who was to repudiate it ten years afterward. (See p. 409.)

The Preparatory Commission began its sessions in Geneva in May 1926 and confined itself at first to questions of procedure, terms of reference, and the collection of evidence. Discussions and hearings continued at a second session in September 1926. The German delegate, who now attended for the first time, recalled to the attention of the Commission the Allied pledge at Versailles to initiate a "general limitation of the armaments of all nations," and asked his fellow delegates to consider, as their "final objective," the removal of "the existing disproportion between the armaments of the League's members," thereby raising an issue which, with increasing emphasis, was to haunt the disarmament conversations at Geneva till their final breakdown seven years later.

Third and fourth sessions of the Preparatory Commission were held in 1927. The Soviet Union sent a delegate for the first time to the fourth session, in the person of Litvinov, who enlivened the proceedings with attacks on the "capitalist powers" and then proposed a sweeping and immediate disbandment of all armies, navies, and air forces, the destruction of all war materials and manufactures, and the abolition of all war ministries, general staffs, and military colleges. The Preparatory Commission, it may be said, did not take Litvinov's thunderings very seriously. It prepared a Draft Convention in the form of the text of a treaty between the powers, but left blank spaces in regard to the actual effectives and matériel. A World Disarmament Conference was then to be called, with the Draft Convention as the basis of its discussions, to fill in the blank spaces with exact figures. The history of that Conference we defer to a later page. (See pp. 376-78.)

8. GERMANY: REVOLUTION AND THE WEIMAR REPUBLIC

The German Revolution

In the pre-1914 German *Reichstag,* there had been three main party groups: the Right, a middle group, and the Left. The Right comprised the Conservatives and the Reich party (*Junkers,* court society, and landowners); the middle group comprised the National Liberals (big business) and the Center party (Roman Catholics); the Left comprised the Progressives (intelligentsia and certain radical banking and commercial circles) and the Social Democrats (labor and trade unions). In general terms, the Right supported the monarchy as it existed, the army, and the policy of imperial expansion; the Center largely represented local and provincial interests; the Left inclined to "democratization," to antimilitarism, and to anti-imperialism. In August 1914 at a meeting of their party caucus, a small dissident faction of Social Democrats had hesitated and havered; but afterward they had fallen into line and joined the other parties of the *Reichstag* in unanimously voting for the government's war policy.

In the course of the war, as we have already described, the party truce, or *Burgfriede,* began to break down, and the old party strifes were gradually resumed.[1] The dissident faction of the Social Democrats withdrew from the party to form the Minority Social Democrats – or, as they were known later, the Independent Social Democrats – in opposition to the government. The loyal remnant under the Majority Social Democrats continued to support the government. In 1916 a small "International" group, popularly called the Spartacists, under the leadership of Rosa Luxemburg and Karl Liebknecht, moved still further leftward and openly agitated for revolution and peace. In 1917 the Center itself split on the war issue and precipitated the July Crisis of that year. Thereafter the retreat from Right to Left, from loyalty to revolution, was a gathering process, which reached its conclusion at last in the Revolution of November 1918. (See pp. 69-70 and 90-92.)

The German Revolution as such was the work of the Left, and the Left was the logical successor to power. On November 9, 1918, Prince Max of

Baden announced the abdication of the Kaiser, himself resigned the chancellorship, and handed over the government to Friedrich Ebert, leader of the Majority Social Democrats. Ebert chose to assume office at the head of a cabinet or council of "Six Commissars" – three of them Majority Social Democrats and three Independent Social Democrats. The further shape that the Revolution would take, however, was still far from predictable. For himself, Ebert would have been content with a limited monarchy. "I hate the social revolution," he once admitted; "I hate it like sin." Meanwhile Workers' and Soldiers' Councils, patterned on the Soviets of the Russian Revolution, were starting up all over the country and even at the front, and it looked for one doubtful moment as if Germany might go Communist. Philipp Scheidemann, a Majority Social Democrat and one of the "Six," alarmed by reports that Liebknecht was trying to bring off a Communist coup, took it upon himself, without consulting his colleagues, to proclaim Germany a republic. Workers' and Soldiers' Councils at a mass meeting in Berlin sealed the issue by voting overwhelmingly in Scheidmann's – and Ebert's – support.

Such were the surface events of the German Revolution. Looking back upon it from this distance, we are struck by its moderation. The crowds that surged through the streets of Berlin on November 9 seemed to be entirely without organization or purpose. It would have been hard to call them a revolutionary "mob." If anything, they resembled the Armistice crowds of the Champs Elysées, or Piccadilly, or Times Square. Some shooting occurred. Army officers who chanced to be in the streets were sometimes assaulted and their decorations and epaulets torn off. There was some looting of government property. The Red flag was hoisted on public buildings, and hawkers appeared miraculously from nowhere selling red rosettes, red ribbons, and red tags of all descriptions. But in general the people had not forgotten their characteristic German orderliness, and after four years of war they were in no condition for new excitements. So far, the transfer of power had been smooth, almost anticlimactic. The first spasms of violence were soon to occur.

Underneath, other forces had been at work. Ebert had found an unexpected ally in the High Command. He had been in direct touch with General Groener by private telephone between the Chancellery in Berlin and Headquarters at Spa and had arranged a secret bargain. (See p. 91.) The government and the High Command mutually pledged themselves to suppress Bolshevism in Germany, to maintain discipline, to secure the provisioning and uphold "officers' superiority of rank" – and incidentally to eliminate the Independent Socialists and the Workers' and Soldiers' Councils. Thus was a pact concluded "between a defeated army and a tottering semirevolutionary regime," an accommodation between two parties that, in principle, were supposed to hold each other in abhorrence, but which, in practice, needed each other for their survival.[2] The first result of the pact was Ebert's formal authorization to Erzberger to sign the Allies' Armistice terms. (See p. 92.) The second was the dispatch of ten divisions under General von Lequis to Berlin and Potsdam for what amounted to the military occupation of the capital. On the morning of December 11, just a month after the Armistice, Ebert went in person to meet a contingent of these troops — which included regiments of the Prussian Guard — making their ceremonial entry into Berlin by the Brandenburger Tor and greeted them with the ringing words: "I salute you, who return unvanquished from the field of battle!"

And then came Spartacus Week.

The Spartacists had not been represented in Ebert's Council of Commissars, and they now staged a series of riots, which for a time looked like a dangerous revolutionary movement. Many of them were in receipt of funds from Joffe, the Soviet "ambassador" in Berlin. On December 31, 1918, at a party convention attended by Radek as Soviet "representative," they had formally assumed the name of the "Communist party of Germany." Their principal armed reinforcement was the so-called People's Naval Division, a pretty draggletailed gang of impromptu mercenaries, mainly made up of naval mutineers from Kiel who claimed to have brought the revolution to Berlin. This force had since occupied the Royal Palace in Berlin and refused to disband till it had received its arrears of pay.

Ebert at last appealed for help to Groener, now installed in the High Command's new Headquarters at Cassel — once more all complete with private telephone. The Independent Socialists denounced him as a lackey of the High Command and resigned from the Council of Commissars. Ebert appointed two Majority Social Democrats in their place, one being Gustav Noske, revolutionary Governor of Kiel and queller of mutinies. (See p. 92.) But Noske turned, not to the divisions under Lequis, which were now alleged to be uncertain in their loyalty, but to those irregular bodies of troops, the so-called Free Corps — the flotsam and jetsam of the demobilizing army, which still retained their weapons and something of their corporate spirit. The Free Corps asked for nothing better. Most of them, in the nature of things, were reactionary and not averse to a bit of bloodshed. From January 6 to 15, 1919 — Spartacus Week, as it came to be called — Noske's irregulars and the Spartacists were fighting it out in the streets of Berlin. Karl Liebknecht and Rosa Luxemburg, the Spartacist leaders, were captured and shot "while trying to escape." Casualties were said to have exceeded a thousand. Spartacus Week was the whiff of grapeshot that destroyed the extreme Left in the German Revolution.

Meanwhile, in Bavaria, a complementary series of events was in train. Bavaria, the second largest of the Federal States that composed the German Reich, had always had strong particularist traditions. On November 7, 1918, in the Bavarian capital Munich, Kurt Eisner, with the support of the local Workers', Soldiers' and Peasants' Councils, had proclaimed an independent "Republic of Bavaria." Eisner was a Socialist and a Jew, perhaps the one man produced by the German Revolution who bears comparison with the great Russian revolutionaries. In the few weeks that he enjoyed power he made his mark as a practical and forceful administrator. But on February 21, 1919, he was shot to death by a counterrevolutionary student.

At this moment the National Assembly, as we shall shortly relate, was meeting in Weimar and debating the new liberal constitution for all Germany. The country as a whole, after its experiment with Workers' Councils and Commissars' Councils, was feeling its way back to normal bourgeois respectability. Bavaria alone grew more and more revolutionary and more and more separatist, and characteristically resented Berlin's centralizing tendencies. Bolshevik rule was set up in Hungary in March, and it looked as if "permanent revolution" might soon sweep through Europe. (See p. 99.) At the end of April, Munich was staging its own version of Spartacus Week; political adventurers and visionaries, many of them pathological types, were thrusting themselves forward, claiming to be People's Commissars; the Munich district was virtually an independent soviet state.

Noske in Berlin was determined that Bavaria should be saved from chaos and secession. Bodies of Free Corps, assisted by Bavarian volunteers, descended upon Munich. Anything that smacked of sovietism in the city was crushed without mercy. There were the usual cases of execution "by mistake." An unexceptionable democratic government was reinstated in Munich when the bloody work was done.

The continuation of the Allied blockade after the Armistice led to a good deal of embittered propaganda in Germany at the time and to mystified comment in Allied countries. The Armistice had stated that blockade conditions would remain in force, but that the Allies would consider the provisioning of Germany during the armistice period "as shall be found necessary." It is said that Churchill, on the morrow of the Armistice, wanted to send food ships to Germany, but was overruled by French objections. The whole question was formally raised in January 1919, at Trier, when Allies and Germans met for the first of their periodic renewals of the Armistice. The Allies made the very reasonable proposal that the German Government should employ its own ships, long lying idle during the war years, to obtain the required foodstuffs, and should pay for the foodstuffs out of the considerable surviving German gold reserves. But this the German Government refused to do. Presumably the German High Command regarded the nation's ships and gold as war potential, or as a bargaining point of possible usefulness at the Peace Conference, not to be released for a mere commercial transaction. Meanwhile, the German people in the winter of 1918-19 suffered worse privations than in any winter of the war. It was not till March 1919 that the German Government at last acceded to the Allied proposals, and foodstuffs, carried in German ships and paid for in German gold, began to arrive at German ports. Count von Brockdorff-Rantzau at Versailles berated the inhumanity of the Allies; but the German people had no one to blame for their sufferings but their own government —and the High Command.[3] (See p. 106.)

Such events only partially describe the condition and mood of Germany at this point of time. The real balance sheet of the war was not written in political, or even military, terms. The defeat of a proud nation is a terrible thing and produces its own peculiar pathology. Combatant casualties had been 1,800,000 dead and 4,300,000 wounded. Shortage of labor and four years of blockade had exhausted the people and their economy. The cash costs of the conflict have been estimated at $30,000,000,000. Wastage and wear and tear of the necessities and amenities of life were beyond calculation. Wartime "silencing" had decimated the consumer industries. Home-grown cereal crops between 1914 and 1918 were nearly halved, and the supply of meat and fats had fallen even more steeply. The population as a whole was 20 per cent underweight. The moral disintegration was complete. All the more unlovely features of the German character seemed to be on exhibition. Visitors to Berlin and other German cities at this time came back with gruesome tales of the license and perversion they saw there, the spate of pornographic literature, the vicious night life, and the gross productions on the stage. The Teutonic fury, balked of its victory, seemed to have sublimated itself into still uglier forms.

The Weimar Constitution

On January 19, 1919, just after Spartacus Week, elections were held throughout the Reich for a National Assembly. With the exception of the Spartacists, all parties put forward candidates. The parties were the old parties of the *Reichstag*, now emerging from the bewilderment of the Revolution and preparing to resume their place in the political life of the nation. But some of them, to avoid the stigma of the prerevolutionary past, took different names. The Conservatives and the Reich party thus appeared as the Nationalists, and the right wing of the National Liberals as the People's party. The Catholic Center appeared as the Christian People's party, but later reverted to its old name. The left-wing National Liberals and Progressives appeared as the Democrats. The Social Democrats dropped the wartime label "Majority." The seats in the National Assembly were distributed by proportional representation, and 85 per cent of the electorate voted, a figure significant of the returning political vigor of the country. The results were overwhelmingly in favor of the moderate Left. Thirty-six of the elected deputies were women.

The National Assembly was summoned to the old Thuringian city of Weimar, partly to escape the disturbances of Berlin and partly to advertise to the world the attachment of the new Republic to the memory of Germany's more peaceful heroes, Goethe and Schiller, and the Grand Duke Charles August, sponsor of one of the first liberal constitutions in Germany. The meetings were held in the Weimar National Theater. Ebert was elected "Provisional" President of the Republic. Scheidemann headed the first government, with Noske as Defense Minister, Gustav Bauer (Social Democrat) as Labor Minister, Matthias Erzberger (Center) as Minister without portfolio, Hugo Preuss (Democrat) as Minister of the Interior, and Brockdorff-Rantzau (no party) as Foreign Minister. The Assembly's first business was to draw up a constitution for the new German Republic. But debates were interrupted by the crisis over the Treaty of Versailles.

Count von Brockdorff-Rantzau led the German delegates to Versailles and received the text of the treaty there on May 7, 1919. (See p. 106.) The terms had been expected to be harsh, and circumstantial rumors regarding detailed decisions of the Peace Conference had begun to circulate in Germany soon after President Wilson's return to Paris in March. But the reality surpassed the gloomiest expectations. The German people were sick and weary, yet they found energy in their tired spirits for something very like defiance. The National Assembly, now back in Berlin, went into continuous session; its debates were long, anxious, and bitter; the struggle for rejection or acceptance cut across all party lines. From Versailles, Brockdorff-Rantzau counseled rejection. Erzberger counseled acceptance and seemed to become spokesman for all those of like mind. Rejection, he contended, would only bring the Allies to Berlin to enforce the terms at the point of the bayonet and result in the complete dissolution of Germany as a nation. Patriotism, like misery, makes strange bedfellows, and Erzberger's arguments found support in an unexpected quarter — again the High Command. Groener, and even Hindenburg, after a dispassionate appraisal of the military situation, could offer no advice but capitulation. But Scheidemann could not stomach the treaty, and he and his government resigned. The Social Democrat Gustav Bauer became Chancellor of a new government pledged to acceptance, with Erzberger as Vice-Chancellor. Hermann Müller and Johannes Bell, the Foreign and Colonial Ministers respectively, were sent to Versailles, where they signed the treaty on June 28, 1919.

In January and February 1919, shortly after the elections for the National Assembly, parallel elections were held in the Federal States, again generally resulting in victories of the Left, and each state duly drew up a democratic constitution of its own. Prussia, that onetime bastille of reaction, from this moment till the final collapse of the Weimar Republic in 1933 was governed by a Social Democrat ministry under the Social Democrat Premier, Otto Braun. (See p. 357.)

The Weimar Constitution was eventually approved by the National Assembly at the end of July 1919. Its main author was Hugo Preuss, Minister of the Interior, a former professor of constitutional law. It was a complex document of many compromises. The difficult problem of state rights in a country of federal structure was adjusted with the greatest delicacy and skill. Whatever the result of the war and revolution might be, Germany could never revert to her pre-Bismarckian particularism. The central government in Berlin was vested with considerable powers: it had the right of veto over state legislation affecting the national interest, it could alter state frontiers and even create a new state, and it could levy direct taxes. But the Federal States, the *Länder,* as they were now called, were left in the enjoyment of autonomous functions not very explicitly defined.

In the words of Article 1 of the Constitution, "The German Reich is a Republic. Constitutional power proceeds from the people." Every German citizen was secured his "fundamental rights" — liberty of person, liberty of speech and of assembly, and inviolability of private property. The *Reichstag* was the lower chamber of the parliament; its deputies were to be elected for a term of four years by the universal, equal, direct, and secret suffrage of all men and women over twenty years of age, on the principle of proportional representation. The *Reichsrat* was a sort of upper chamber and represented the *Länder;* its delegates were members of the *Land* governments, and would vote in the *Reichsrat* in rough proportion to the population of their states. The President of the Reich was to be elected for a term of seven years, again on the basis of universal suffrage. The President appointed and dismissed the Chancellor, and the Chancellor required the confidence of the *Reichstag* for the exercise of his office. In certain circumstances the President could call for a national plebiscite, and in grave emergencies he could suspend the Constitution. In the words of Article 48, later to be so famous:

> Should public order and safety be seriously disturbed or threatened, the President may take the necessary measures to restore public order and safety; in case of need he may use armed force, . . . and he may, for the time being, declare the fundamental rights of the citizen wholly or partly in abeyance.

Weimar changed many things; but, as has so often been argued, it preserved more than it changed. The old symbols had been torn down. The Kaiser and the German princelings had gone into exile. But there had been no dispossession of the former castes and classes. The great landed estates, even the Kaiser's properties, were not parceled out; the industrial cartels and monopolies were not broken up. Little new legislation was introduced except in the field of labor relations and welfare. The bureaucracy, the judiciary, and the police remained intact. German officialdom, the pride of Bismarck's Reich, emerged afresh, rather strengthened by its sense of indispensability to the new order than discredited by its connection with the old. The golden opportunity for effecting long-needed reforms in the universities was lost; the principle of academic freedom required that even the most antidemocratic and anti-Semitic faculties and fraternities should not be touched. Finally, as we shall see, the new *Reichswehr* was the old army in miniature. In her own way, like so many other countries after the First World War, Germany too tried to return to the "normalcy" of 1914.

The Execution of Versailles

For the moment, more urgent than exercises in constitution building were the stark facts of the Treaty of Versailles. "Democratization," genuine or fraudulent, had not exempted the German people from the vengeance of their enemies. For the next few years their lives would be governed by the execution—or evasion—of the treaty's terms. In due course Posen and the Corridor were handed over to their new Polish owners. The League administrators of the Saar and of Danzig entered upon their duties. The plebiscites were held in Schleswig and resulted, as was expected, in the assignment of the northern part of Schleswig to Denmark and the middle and southern parts to Germany. The plebiscites were held in East Prussia, and both parts of the territory in question voted overwhelmingly for adherence to Germany.

The penalty clauses of the treaty were the most passionately resented in Germany, and were, in fact, clauses that remained almost wholly inoperative. The former Kaiser was not brought to trial. The Netherlands Government, which had given him sanctuary, refused to allow him to be extradited, and the Allies were probably much relieved to acquiesce in its decision. In February 1920, the French Premier, Millerand, presented the

German Government with a portentous list of the other "war criminals," a list which included Hindenburg, Ludendorff, Tirpitz, Bethmann-Hollweg, several princes of the blood, and 900 officers and soldiers. The German people to a man rose against this monstrous indictment. A government that attempted to arrest and hand over the nation's heroes to the judgment of its enemies would not have lasted a day, and clearly the Allies were averse to enforcing their claims if it meant a renewal of hostilities. The list was gradually cut and cut, till a mere twelve cases were left, mostly submarine officers and prison commandants. The twelve were eventually tried in May and June 1921 before the Reich Supreme Court at Leipzig and either acquitted or let off with farcically light sentences.

The settlement in Upper Silesia was deferred till 1921. Plebiscites were eventually held there in March of that year and showed German majorities in the north and west, Polish majorities in the south and east, and a center inextricably mixed. Both Germans and Poles, of course, contended that the Silesian coal fields made a single economic unit which would be ruined by division. Both sides carried on a furious propaganda supported, as seemed necessary, by terrorism. The French members of the Allied Boundary Commission sent to Silesia were not the most impartial of judges and tended to give their Polish friends the benefit of the doubt in all the disputed communes. The Boundary Commission, in the end, failed to reach a decision and referred the whole case to the League of Nations. In October 1921, the League Council announced an award apportioning the area between the claimants, an award perhaps as fair and neutral as any that could have been devised in the circumstances. The Germans, who traditionally despised the Poles, were hardly placated. A convention between Germany and Poland, regulating their Silesian affairs, was signed at Geneva in May 1922.

The execution of the military and reparations clauses of the treaty will be discussed in the following sections of this chapter. But we should first consider the incident known as the Kapp Putsch.

The Kapp Putsch

The Free Corps, which have already been mentioned, were irregular military or paramilitary bodies of demobilized soldiers who had found no proper civilian employment. It was perhaps to be expected that they would exist and flourish at a lawless time, especially in a country long accustomed to militarism and now under sentence of disarmament. Some were organized in support of a political clique or faction; some owed the government itself a provisional allegiance, notably the Free Corps used in more than one punitive foray by Noske; but many were no better than gangs of young hotheads denied legitimate military careers. The *Reichswehr,* as the German Army was now to be called, cast a somewhat indulgent eye upon them, and frankly regarded them as recruiting agencies, a convenient circumvention of Versailles. The courts of justice quite shamelessly protected them in whatever incidents came to their notice. The Allied Control Commission in Germany could do nothing with them.

Hitler's National Socialists in Munich were at first just such an organization.

The Kapp Putsch of March 1920 was a fair demonstration of Free Corps tactics. It was the Conservative counterpart of Spartacus Week. The political leader of the putsch was a certain Dr. Wolfgang Kapp, an agricultural finance official from East Prussia, hitherto active in various reactionary patriotic and propagandist associations. The military leader was General von Lüttwitz, commander of the Berlin district. Ludendorff was also more or less directly implicated. The force employed in the main was Ehrhardt's Free Corps, remnants of the German occupation forces in the Baltic, which had refused to disband and had taken up quarters, within striking distance of Berlin, in the military depot of Döberitz.

Kapp and his fellow conspirators evidently hoped to exploit the unpopularity of the Bauer government and of its most influential minister, Erzberger, an unpopularity that had been growing ever since the Treaty of Versailles had been signed and especially since the delivery of the Allied note of February 1920 on war criminals. Their aims included the repudiation of Versailles, the end of demobilization and of disarmament, and the establishment of an authoritarian state. Their choice for the presidency was the former Crown Prince. Far from making their preparations secret, they resorted to so much open bluster that it was some time before the government was roused to take them seriously. But their intentions were clear enough on March 1, when Lüttwitz paid a formal visit to the depot at Döberitz to attend a review staged for his benefit. On March 10, Lüttwitz called on Ebert and Noske with demands for new *Reichstag* elections, new presidential elections, the formation of a cabinet of "experts," and, of course, a halt in demobilization and disarmament. Ebert, an old hand at negotiation, temporized, but he was determined to fight for his government if need be. The next morning Noske, with Ebert's approval, dismissed Lüttwitz from his command.

This precipitated the crisis. On March 13, 1920, Ehrhardt's Free Corps marched into Berlin and seized key positions in the city, everywhere flaunting its badge, the swastika – the first apparition of that strange device. Ebert, Bauer, Noske, and the government fled to Stuttgart. Erzberger resigned. Kapp formed a "government" of his own in Berlin. But within a few days it was clear that he had none of the essentials of power. He might be a competent putschist, but he was no revolutionary. He had little popular support. The ordinary people of Berlin, so far as could be observed, were either frightened or bored; the workers were hostile. The bureaucracy refused to obey Kapp's orders; the Reichsbank would not honor his checks. Far more serious than these entirely unexpected rebuffs, Kapp failed to enlist the support of the *Reichswehr*. Many *Reichswehr* officers were of the same mind as Kapp but considered his action rash and untimely, and could do little but wait and see how the putsch fared before they committed themselves. General von Seeckt, the *Reichswehr* commander, had no wish to get his forces involved in an affair which was almost sure to provoke Allied intervention. However, the *Reichswehr* at least did not oppose the putsch; it was not to be expected that soldiers of the *Reichswehr* would be called on to fight their comrades of the Free Corps.

From Stuttgart the government retaliated by proclaiming a general strike. The workers responded with almost complete unanimity, thus giving the world a classic illustration of "direct action" — that dream of Socialists, perhaps only this once ever carried to complete effect. The British High Commissioner in Berlin curtly denied that the British Government had ever promised Kapp its diplomatic recognition. Berlin was without public services; water, electricity, streetcars, newspapers, even the transport of foodstuffs had stopped. The Free Corps took its revenge in desultory shooting. On March 17 Kapp and Lüttwitz were in flight, and the Free Corps evacuated the city. A detachment of the Free Corps, retiring by way of the Brandenburger Tor, fired point-blank into the jeering bystanders who had collected there to speed its departure. It was significant of the state of Germany that none of the participants in the putsch was ever punished.

The Reichswehr

The conception of an army as a political force in a nation's affairs is foreign to the Anglo-Saxon mind. The Praetorian Guard of the Roman Caesars is the classic example, and once only, in the time of Cromwell, had the phenomenon appeared in an English-speaking country. But the army as such was common enough in modern times in countries having standing conscript armies, even if it was sometimes difficult to identify its effective personalities. Thus the army had won itself an unpleasant notoriety in France during the Dreyfus scandal in the 1890's; it had been all-important in Prussian Germany; it wielded considerable, if obscure, power in interwar Italy, Poland, Spain, Turkey, and Japan. Far from being destroyed by the Armistice and Revolution in 1918, the German Army emerged with fresh power. As we have seen, Ebert had struck a bargain with Groener, a bargain by which the new *Reichswehr* was to become the German Government's spoiled and petted problem child.

In August 1919, Germany's military rehabilitation began with the auspicious episode of the Commission of Inquiry, set up by the Weimar government to investigate the war-guilt question and the responsibility for the Armistice. Ebert, like any good German, had been motivated no doubt by genuine scholarly curiosity, and he had also hoped that the Commission might bring discredit on the old regime. But on both counts his expectations misfired lamentably. The Commission, from its first sessions, turned into a theatrical and triumphant vindication of the most reactionary wartime policies. Bernstorff, Bethmann-Hollweg, Helfferich, and then Hindenburg and Ludendorff, one after the other, made public parade of their past innocence and betrayal. As for Hindenburg, his testimony was historic. He came from his home in Hanover to Berlin by special train; he was met on arrival by a guard of honor; two aides-de-camp were attached to him for the duration of his visit; steel-helmeted sentries were posted outside the villa where he stayed — trains, guard of honor, aides-de-camp, and sentries all being laid on by the *Reichswehr*. His every public appearance was greeted by cheering crowds. Before the Commission he acted as if he were addressing not its president but the German people. The upshot of his speech was that the German Army had not suffered defeat in the field in 1918, but had been basely dealt a "stab in the back" (*Dolchstoss*) — and thereby a new word was added to the Teutonic mythology. Shortly after this scene the government suspended the Commission for some months.

Meanwhile — and afterward — the army preserved itself and even grew. Under the Weimar Constitution a single National Defense Force, or *Reichswehr,* under a single *Reichswehr* Minister, took the place of the Prussian, Bavarian, Saxon, and Württemberger contingents of the old army. Its titular Supreme Commander was the President of the Republic. From July 1919, its professional commander and presiding genius was General Hans von Seeckt. Under the military clauses of the Treaty of Versailles this force was to be made up of not more than 100,000 long-term volunteers, without tanks, planes, or heavy artillery, and an Allied Control Commission was to be responsible for seeing that these restrictions were observed. But in the summer of 1919 the number of men under arms in Germany was believed to be 400,000. The destruction of fortifications and of heavy arms and the inspection of armament works were relatively easy, and the Control Commission soon learned the tactics of surprise visits. But there were hoards, especially of rifles and machine guns, which no skillful probing and no surprise visits could have unearthed, and any systematic checkup on man power was quite impracticable. The Free Corps, which we have mentioned, were beyond supervision even by their own government — even had that government desired to supervise. From 1920 onward, the so-called *Arbeits-Kommandos,* later known as the "Black *Reichswehr,*" were being organized, ostensibly for a civilian labor corps — but a corps whose members wore uniforms, were barracked and rationed by the *Reichswehr* Ministry, were commanded by regular officers, and were given such military training as could be carried out in secret. They were protected against informers by their own private criminal courts.

Seeckt, the "sphinx with the monocle," had been one of the ablest technicians and organizers of the General Staff. Descended from an old military Prussian family, he was a man of wide culture, well read and well traveled beyond what was normal for his caste, with a flair for the kind of politics in which he was now to be engaged. He was assisted by the compliant Otto Gessler, who succeeded Noske as *Reichswehr* Minister in 1920, after the Kapp Putsch, and who held that office till 1928 through six changes of government. With complete coolness and precision, and virtually by converting the restrictions of Versailles into opportunities for innovation, Seeckt set about the prodigious task of building up a modern army. It was a "nonpolitical" army — that is to say, it was untainted by current revolutionary ideas — and its officers, noncommissioned officers, and men were carefully recruited for their professional potentialities as soldiers. It nourished all the old Prussian traditions; each of its companies or batteries preserved the honors, and even the mess-room etiquette, of one of the former regiments. It was moreover an "army of leaders" (*Führerheer*), with an unusually high proportion of noncommissioned officers, virtually a cadre for instant expansion. It was minutely trained in the arts of mobility and mechanization, in which Seeckt already saw the pattern of future warfare. Its supplies and munitions were secured — if not at once, at least prospectively — by the gradual reconstruction of heavy industry at home, such as Krupps, and by the establishment of factories abroad, outside Versailles controls, notably in Russia, Sweden, and Spain. Its General Staff, prohibited by Versailles, was kept in being surreptitiously in the so-called Troops Office (*Truppenamt*) attached to the *Reichswehr* Ministry. It maintained curious, secretive links with the Red Army, and numbers of its senior officers regularly attended Red Army maneuvers in Soviet Russia.[4]

By 1933, when Hitler came to power, the *Reichswehr* was qualitatively the finest army in the world. Perhaps some of its arms were lacking; but they existed in blueprint, and the factories were ready to forge them. In political spirit, however, the *Reichswehr* was reactionary, if not monarchical. As the Free Corps were disbanded, their former "front fighters" found their obvious asylum in its ranks, while many of its officers were still drawn from those *Junker* families that regarded military service as the highest, if not the only, profession for a man. In its midst were the Roehms and the Schleichers, political soldiers of a type unknown to the German Army of an earlier day, men for whom there was no dividing line between military service and underground conspiracy. The Weimar Republic acquiesced in the character of the new army, and its own form and fortune indeed were largely shaped by it. In 1926, it is true, Seeckt went a little too far when he allowed a son of the former Crown Prince to take part in summer maneuvers, and he was dismissed. In 1928 Gessler was replaced as *Reichswehr* Minister by Groener. By then, the *Reichswehr* was beyond change or reform, even if anyone in Germany had been minded to change or reform it. For better or for worse, it had become "a state within the state," a stronghold of all that was least republican in the Republic.

Reparations, Rapallo, and the Ruhr

The Kapp Putsch in 1920 left a wake of disturbances behind it. In Bavaria a group of army officers forced the local government to resign — the government, that is, which had succeeded the Soviet experiment there — and installed a certain Gustav von Kahr, a civil servant and an extreme Conservative. There was a "Red" scare in the Ruhr. Units of the *Reichswehr* marched into the district, in violation of Versailles, ostensibly to restore order. The French replied by occupying Frankfurt. Unsettled by these events, Bauer resigned the chancellorship and was followed by Hermann Müller at the head of an interim government. Müller acknowledged the justice of at least one of the demands that Lüttwitz had made and called for *Reichstag* elections. The National Assembly had completed the Constitution, and the new *Reichstag* was due to be brought into existence. The elections were duly held during June 1920 and were disastrous to the "Weimar parties." Reaction was in full cry. Konstantin Fehrenbach of the Center party became Chancellor; and with Fehrenbach began the series of middle-class governments lasting from 1920 to 1932 that were preoccupied, almost to the exclusion of everything else, with the problem of reparations.

President Wilson's Fourteen Points had called for Belgium, northern France, Rumania, Serbia, and Montenegro to be "restored." The Allied Memorandum of November 5, 1918, had stipulated that "compensation will be made by Germany for all damage done to the civilian population of the Allies and their property by the aggression of Germany by land, by sea, and from the air." Finally inserted in the armistice text was a somewhat obscure clause in regard to "reparation for damage done" and in regard to the restitution of all gold reserves and all documents taken in the invaded countries – "with the reservation that any subsequent concessions and claims by the Allies and the United States remain unaffected." These few utterances made up the total "legal" anticipation of the reparations clauses in the Treaty of Versailles. (See p. 92 and Appendix, p. 833.)

Technically, the problem of reparations was of unexpected novelty. The obvious precedent was the French indemnity of 1871, and it was generally assumed that the imposition and collection of the German indemnity of 1919 would be analogous. Few then foresaw the close relation of reparations with inter-Allied debts and with the wider postwar economic recovery. Nor were Allied policies united in their essential objects. Generally, France regarded the Treaty of Versailles as an instrument for the permanent enfeeblement of her hereditary foe; Britain regarded it as a judgment and a penalty to be alleviated in proportion as the culprit gave evidence of repentance. France would have treated Germany as a bankrupt whose assets must henceforth be administered by and for her creditors; Britain, though glad enough to transfer to Germany as large a portion as possible of her own wartime indebtedness, was far more anxious to restore Germany to her prewar position of a good customer. The United States, meanwhile, more interested in Allied debts, considered reparations as a purely European affair. As for Germany, Versailles was a *"Diktat,"* and, as Erzberger put it, "a treaty signed under compulsion is a treaty which it is our duty to evade."

Except for the deliveries in kind and the initial payment of 20,000,000,000 gold marks to be paid by May 1, 1921, the Treaty of Versailles had given no definite reparation figures. Estimates bandied about in Paris in 1919 started as low as John Maynard Keynes's "safe" $10,000,000,000 and went up to more than ten times that figure.[5] Between Germany's capacity to pay and the astronomic expectations in Allied countries no discoverable mean seemed to exist. Clearly a proper and reliable assessment would have meant sending committees of investigation into the devastated areas and giving hearings to the thousands of claimants for damages, and the Peace Conference did not have the time for so protracted a proceeding. In the end the Peace Conference passed the whole question to a Reparation Commission which was to be composed of Allied delegates, and which, but for the nonratification of the treaty by the United States, would have had an American chairman; this body was to determine the amounts and methods of payment and supervise the discharge of the entire obligation within a period of thirty years. (See p. 108.)

In the early interwar years there was hardly an Allied conference at which reparations were not discussed. In July 1920, Allies and Germans met at Spa, and the figure then mentioned was 269,000,000,000 gold marks ($64,000,000,000) to be spread over thirty-five years. This was the first time that Allies and Germans had sat at the same table, but it could not be described as a happy reunion. Hugo Stinnes, who accompanied the German delegation as the representative of the German coal owners, made a belligerent speech which began with the words, "I rise to look my enemies in the eye. . . ." Fehrenbach, the Chancellor, was afterward at pains to explain that Stinnes did not express the views of his government. In January 1921, the Allies presented Germany with the Paris Resolutions, which fixed the reparations figure at 226,000,000,000 gold marks ($54,000,000,000). The German press raved and railed. Walter Simons, the German Foreign Minister, was so impolitic as to repudiate Germany's war guilt. Lloyd George curtly characterized the German attitude as "an offense and an exasperation." Meanwhile, the Allies at their conference at Spa had reached an agreement among themselves for the division of reparations receipts, France being allotted 52 per cent, the British Empire, 22, Italy, 10, Belgium, 8, and the other Allies lesser shares.

By now the crucial date, May 1, 1921, was approaching — the date when, under the treaty terms, the 20,000,000,000 gold marks were to be paid. But the Reparation Commission, adding up the account, calculated that the receipts from Germany by that date were less than half the stipulated sum. The Commission then assessed the total reparations figure at 132,000,000,000 gold marks ($32,000,000,000), and this assessment was duly forwarded to Berlin. Fehrenbach thereupon resigned, and his successor, Joseph Wirth, formed a government with a declared policy of "fulfillment" for no better reason than to show that fulfillment meant collapse. That Wirth was not wide of the truth seemed evident when the mark dropped to 100 to the American dollar. The first phase of the inflation had begun. Germany at the time was fiercely agitated over the plebiscite in Upper Silesia and the trial of the war criminals at Leipzig. A fresh outbreak of strikes was unpleasantly reminiscent of Spartacus Week. On August 25, 1921, however, came one encouraging item of news — the formal conclusion of peace between Germany and the United States — but the date was marred by the assassination of Erzberger at the hands of two Free Corps troopers.

Lloyd George, the British Prime Minister, was then working out a grandiose scheme, a "European Consortium," a kind of economic League of Nations, which would undertake the reconstruction of Europe with the collaboration of Soviet Russia. It would be the crowning glory of his career. To this end he planned a monster international conference, to be second in impressiveness only to the Peace Conference of Paris, and it eventually assembled at Genoa in April 1922. Poincaré, the archenemy of Germany, had just become Premier of France, and he sent Barthou to represent him; Soviet Russia sent Chicherin, Litvinov, Krasin, and Joffe; Germany sent Wirth and Walther Rathenau, now German Foreign Minister. The touchy subject of reparations for once was debarred from the agenda; but even so Genoa never caught the proper spirit of high purpose Lloyd George had intended for it. The delegates consumed their time and tempers discussing Russian debts and British oil concessions. Chicherin, far from showing gratitude for Soviet Russia's readmission to Europe's common councils, presented the Allies with a bill for 50,000,000,000 francs on account of damage done by the Allied intervention in the Russian Civil War. To cap the tragicomedy, Chicherin and Rathenau drove out to Rapallo on Easter Sunday, April 16, 1922, and there, over a quiet luncheon in that delectable Mediterranean spot, signed a consortium of their own.

On the surface, the Treaty of Rapallo between Germany and Soviet Russia was innocent enough. It provided for the mutual resumption of diplomatic relations, the mutual renunciation of reparations, and the mutual facilitation of trade. But Rapallo was a sinister reminder of Bismarckian *Realpolitik,* and it was undoubtedly a coup, not unlike other coups with which Germany and Russia would again startle the world. The two pariahs of Europe had come together. The treaty also reflected the curious underground liaison which existed between the *Reichswehr* and the Red Army. France's greatest fear, a German-Russian *rapprochement,* this horrid, spectral shape, had been conjured up under the very noses of the Genoa delegates. The Allies addressed some acrimonious notes to Germany, upbraiding her for her underhanded behavior, and the German delegates thereupon withdrew from the conference. Lloyd George's great scheme for the recovery of Europe was finished.

Rathenau himself did not long survive his triumph. On June 24, 1922, he was shot to death as he was being driven in his car in Berlin. He had been a national figure in finance and industry, a man of many gifts and interests, liberal in politics, organizer of Germany's war economy, and lately advocate of a "reasonable" reparations settlement. His murder was in line with other recent political crimes, and it was almost beginning to look as if achievement in public life in republican Germany was tantamount to inviting the murderous attentions of some crazy young Free Corps trooper.

For Poincaré and Barthou the Rapallo incident was proof positive, if proof they wanted, that France would get no satisfaction from Germany on reparations without recourse to force. Barthou was now the French delegate on the Reparation Commission. In July 1922, the German Government requested the Reparation Commission for a moratorium on the next two years' reparation payments. The mark already stood at 500 to the dollar and was declining fast. Poincaré countered with talk of "productive pledges." If Germany could not pay in currency, she could pay in mines, forests, and chemicals; she could buy her moratorium with securities. In November 1922, the Wirth government resigned and was replaced by a "business government" under Wilhelm Cuno, manager of the Hamburg-America Line. In December the Reparation Commission unanimously reported that Germany had defaulted in deliveries of timber. The British delegate on the Commission characterized the default as "almost microscopic," but it was enough for Poincaré and Barthou. Then came further reports of a default in deliveries of coal. On January 10, 1923, the American Army of Occupation began its withdrawal from the Rhine. The next day French and Belgian troops, with a "token" contingent of Italians, marched into the Ruhr. The British took no part in the invasion.

The Ruhr district, which Poincaré had now seized in reprisal for Germany's reparations defaults, contained 10 per cent of Germany's population, 80 per cent of her coal, 80 per cent of her iron and steel industries, and the most intricate railroad system in the world. It was therefore a "productive pledge" of considerable value, and its occupation must soon have disabled the entire economy of the Reich. Poincaré declared that he would create such a state of suffering in Germany "that she will prefer the execution of the treaty to the conditions produced by the occupation." The German Government retaliated with a policy of passive resistance. The German ambassador in Paris and the German minister in Brussels were recalled. All reparations payments and all deliveries in kind to France and Belgium were stopped. Railroad employees in the Ruhr refused to take orders from the French authorities. Postal and telegraph employees refused to transmit French and Belgian letters and telegrams. Local newspapers refused to publish French notices and ordinances. Officials of all ranks "affected to be unaware of the presence of the invaders." The French counterretaliated. They set up their own central administrative agency, the *Mission Interalliée de Contrôle des Usines et des Mines,* familiarly known as MICUM. They seized the local customs. They confiscated anything from foodstuffs to cash deposits. They deported recalcitrant workers. They arrested leading industrialists and tried them before military courts. By the end of February, the directors of Krupps and the mayors of almost every town and city in the district had been imprisoned. Riots were a daily occurrence. French colonial Negro troops were said to have been a constant cause of troublemaking.

The mark collapsed altogether. In January 1923, it had dropped to 20,000 to the dollar, in April to 100,000, in August to 5,000,000. The situation was fantastic. Wages and salaries had to be revised monthly, then weekly, then daily, and still could not keep pace with rising prices. The German worker never knew what his pay was going to be or what he could buy when he got it. His wife went out to make her household purchases with a basketful of notes that might well fall further in value as she stood waiting in the shopping line. A tourist with a few francs or dollars lived like a prince. A postage stamp or glass of beer cost millions. Paper investments, bank balances, savings, mortgages, annuities vanished. Those classes of the German population whose stabilizing influence the country so desperately needed were pauperized. But the big magnates, indeed any possessors of real property, made fortunes. In after years Germans used to speak of the inflation of 1923 as a more terrible experience than the war and the revolution.

The Cuno government resigned in August. Gustav Stresemann, leader of the People's party, succeeded as Chancellor and Foreign Minister and resolved to give up the contest in the Ruhr as lost. On September 27, 1923, Ebert signed a decree rescinding all ordinances passed in support of passive resistance. Poincaré had seemingly won all along the line.

The surrender in the Ruhr, however, was the signal for the outbreak of new disturbances. Separatists in Düsseldorf and Aachen, with French support, tried to set up an independent "Rhineland Republic." The Palatinate was declared "autonomous." Strongly Communist governments, with Moscow support, and designed to be the spearheads of the belated Communist revolution in Germany, enjoyed a short life in Saxony and Thuringia. The most serious of these disturbances occurred in the old storm center of Munich, now the headquarters of several extreme patriotic associations, mostly indefinite as to their ends, but very definitely violent as to their means.

Gustav von Kahr, head of the Bavarian Government, had lately resigned in favor of more moderate successors, but in September 1923, in view of the unrest in Munich, had been recalled as State Commissioner with dictatorial powers. He was already the focus of a ramifying movement whose object was said to be the restoration of the former Bavarian royal family. He had somewhat lukewarm aides in General von Lossow, commander of the *Reichswehr* in Bavaria, and Colonel von Seisser, the Munich Chief of Police. He had gained the support of Ludendorff, then living near Munich, and of a certain Adolf Hitler, a fanatic leader of a new National Socialist Workers party. Kahr built up a formidable organization and showed himself strong enough to go about his business without concealment and in defiance of all the threats that Ebert and Seeckt hurled at him from Berlin. Kahr evidently had some putsch in preparation for early November 1923. But his plans were rudely anticipated by this same Adolf Hitler.

On the evening of November 8, 1923, Kahr, Lossow, and Seisser were holding a mass meeting of their followers at the Bürgerbräukeller, a beer-house in east Munich, when Hitler's troopers surrounded the building. Hitler himself forced his way into the middle of the hall, fired his revolver dramatically at the ceiling, mounted the platform, quelled the meeting with the words, "The National Revolution has begun. . . . The Bavarian Government is deposed. . . . The Reich Government is deposed," and then summoned the astonished Kahr, Lossow, and Seisser to a rear room where, at the point of his revolver, he proceeded to assign them to posts in his "government." Ludendorff, nonplused and irate, joined them.

Seeckt in Berlin was holding detachments of the *Reichswehr* in readiness for emergencies. But the putsch in Munich collapsed without his intervention. As soon as the meeting had dispersed and Hitler had gone, Kahr, Lossow, and Seisser recovered their senses; Kahr announced in a public proclamation that "promises extorted by force were null and void." Hitler and his associates — among them Ludendorff — thus left in the lurch, decided nevertheless on action. The next morning, November 9, they collected their troopers and began their march from the Bürgerbräukeller across the river and into the heart of Munich. They overcame some police cordons without bloodshed, but the inevitable shooting began when they reached the Feldherrnhalle, the Hall of the Generals. In a confused fusillade Ludendorff was captured unhurt; Hitler fled with a wounded arm; sixteen of his troopers and three police were killed. The famous "Beer Hall Putsch" was over. Arrests and trials followed. Ludendorff was acquitted; Hitler served less than nine months of a five-year sentence. For a time, the National Socialist party was proscribed, and its literature suppressed.

By October 1923, the mark stood at 25,000,000,000 to the dollar. All the German Government's efforts to open negotiations with France were unsuccessful. Poincaré rejected its most contrite overtures so long as the stoppage in reparations payments continued. The unhappy German people, it seemed, could look forward only to a future of perpetual and ravaging conflict with their Gallic taskmasters. Yet, when hope was darkest, there came the first glimmerings of a solution. The British Government had constantly exerted itself to bring the estranged parties together and was able at last to persuade the United States to forsake its official aloofness to the extent of participating in a conference of "impartial" experts to investigate Germany's finances. For Poincaré the prospect of joint Anglo-American intervention was decisive. He could not afford diplomatic isolation, especially as returns were beginning to show that the entire Ruhr adventure was far less productive than he had promised. In November 1923, a new government was formed in Germany under Wilhelm Marx of the Center Party, with Stresemann as Foreign Minister. It issued a *Rentenmark* (one *Rentenmark* being equal to a trillion marks) as an emergency currency guaranteed by a general mortgage on the country's real estate; it balanced the Reich budget by the imposition of new taxes and a drastic cutting of expenditures; apparently it succeeded in doing everything that had previously been declared impossible. At least Germany seemed now to want to show that she herself was leaving nothing undone to restore her financial stability.

In December 1923, the Reparation Commission appointed a committee in Paris, which eventually drew up the Dawes Plan, so called after the committee's American chairman, General Charles G. Dawes. Hjalmar Schacht, the new president of the Reichsbank and future "wizard of German finance," made his first international appearance and acted throughout the discussions as the principal German representative. In May 1924, Poincaré and his government in France fell, and a more liberal French premier, Herriot, bent on conciliation, accepted the Dawes Plan in its entirety.

The Dawes Plan still left undetermined Germany's total reparations liability, but it fixed the annual payment at 1,000,000,000 gold marks ($238,000,000) for the first year, rising to a "standard annuity" of 2,500,000,000 gold marks ($595,000,000) in the fifth year. The "standard annuity" could be reduced or increased in accordance with an "index of prosperity." Securities for these sums would be met in part in the first year by an international loan of 800,000,000 gold marks ($190,000,000), and subsequently by taxes and a mortgage on the German railroads. A Transfer Committee would be set up to supervise the conversion of the sums into foreign currencies. Finally, the Reichsbank would be reorganized as a central bank and empowered to issue an entirely new monetary unit, the *Reichsmark,* equivalent to 23.8 United States cents and bearing a stable relation to gold. The Dawes Plan became effective on September 1, 1924.

and the evacuation of the Ruhr began at once. The international loan of 800,000,000 gold marks was successfully subscribed, 55 per cent being raised in the United States. (See p. 304.)

The Stresemann Era

The Dawes settlement in May 1924 coincided with the *Reichstag* elections which then happened to be taking place in Germany. It was hardly a time for cool decisions, and the elections were rowdy enough. The Social Democrats lost heavily; the reactionary parties gained; Hitler's National Socialists scored their first electoral success, with 32 seats. The new *Reichstag* ultimately ratified the Dawes Plan by a margin of three votes. Fresh elections in December 1924 tempered the extremism of the earlier election and succeeded in returning a *Reichstag* of more moderate, but still reactionary, composition.

The general trend of feeling in Germany soon had another opportunity to declare itself. On February 28, 1925, occurred the death of Ebert, President of the Reich. There was at first no obvious successor. Gessler, Wilhelm Marx, the Communist Ernst Thälmann, and even Ludendorff were all prominently mentioned. The first ballot of the presidential elections in March was indecisive, and so also might have been the second, had not a deputation of Nationalists, headed by Admiral von Tirpitz, gone to Hindenburg and persuaded him that it was his duty to step into the breach. Hindenburg was now seventy-seven, living in retirement. He acceded to the new summons with genuine reluctance, and on April 25, 1925, was elected President by a fair majority. There is no reason for believing that he entered upon his office with any other resolve than to serve his country and obey its constitution as best he might. But he was a Prussian born and bred and as good a representative of the old monarchy and the old military spirit as could have been found, and his election was an unmistakable sign of the growing conservative and nationalist humor in the country.

It is not necessary to take the reader through the subsequent German chancellorships of the 1920's. Hans Luther, Wilhelm Marx, and Hermann Müller successively held office till March 1930. The real force in German politics throughout these years was Gustav Stresemann. He had become Chancellor and Foreign Minister in August 1923, and he remained Foreign Minister until his death on October 3, 1929. For six years he was the protagonist of every event and transaction of importance in which his country took part. It was he more than any other man who called off the campaign of passive resistance in the Ruhr, introduced the new currency and obtained the ratification of the Dawes Plan in the *Reichstag*. He then applied himself to the tortuous struggle for the political and economic rehabilitation of Germany.

In October 1925, as related elsewhere, Stresemann attended the Locarno Conference and afterward signed the Locarno Pact. (See pp. 121-24.) He drew from that instrument the conclusions which suited him. If the new peace in Europe was to be a real peace, then the Rhineland must be evacuated and the Allied Control Commission must go home; further, Germany must now become a member of the League of Nations and must be granted a permanent seat on the League Council. Consequently, the evacuation of the Rhineland began in December 1925, after the final signature of the Locarno Pact. Meanwhile Stresemann strengthened his hand by bargaining simultaneously with Chicherin, the Soviet Foreign Commissar, who was on a tour of Warsaw and Berlin in the autumn months of 1925; and, when there was some obstruction at Geneva over Germany's permanent seat on the League Council, Stresemann retorted, in April 1926 in Berlin, by entering into a German-Soviet treaty of friendship and neutrality. (See pp. 156, 218, and 431.) In September 1926, Stresemann went to Geneva to assist at Germany's admission to the League – and to a permanent seat on the League Council. In January 1927, the Allied Control Commission was withdrawn. In August 1928, Stresemann was in Paris to sign the Pact of Paris. All in all, Stresemann's record, whatever methods he chose to achieve it, was no mean one. He found Germany in 1923 an outcast among nations; in five years he had made her a power.

THE GERMAN ELECTIONS — 1919-39 [6]

	NATIONAL ASSEMBLY	REICHSTAG							
	Jan. 1919	*June 1920*	*May 1924*	*Dec. 1924*	*May 1928*	*Sept. 1930*	*July 1932*	*Nov. 1932*	*Mar. 1933*
Nationalists (*Deutsche-Nationale Partei*)	42	66	106	111	78	41	40	54	53
People's Party (*Deutsche Volkspartei*)	22	62	44	51	45	30	7	16	2
Center (*Zentrum*)	90	69	65	69	61	68	75	70	73
Bavarian People's Party (*Bayerische Volkspartei*)		20	16	19	17	19	22	20	19
Democrats (*Deutsche Demokratische Partei*)	75	45	28	32	25	14*	4*	2*	5*
Social Democrats (*Sozial-Demokratische Partei*)	164	113	100	131	152	143	133	121	120
Independent Social Democrats (*Unabhängige Sozial-Demokratische Partei*)	22	81							
Communists (*Kommunistische Partei Deutschlands*)		2	62	45	54	77	89	100	81†
National Socialists (*National-Sozialistische Deutsche Arbeiterpartei*)			32	14	12	107	230	196	288
Minor parties	7	8	19	21	46	78	8	5	6
Total Members	422	466	472	493	490	577	608	584	566

* Renamed *Deutsche Staatspartei*
† Did not sit

Yet Stresemann never won gratitude or popularity at home. The Left considered him reactionary; the Right disliked him for his support of the Weimar Constitution and the League of Nations; patriots of all parties chafed at his policy of seeking the restoration of Germany by truckling to her enemies. To the outside world he posed as a man of peace, and the outside world was perhaps overdesirous of accepting him at his face value — especially when, after Locarno, ordinary diplomatic courtesy required that German good faith must not be impugned. It was conveniently forgotten that in the First World War Stresemann had been one of the extreme annexationists, and that he had supported unrestricted submarine warfare — his nickname in those years had been "Ludendorff's young man." In the National Assembly he had voted for the rejection of the Treaty of Versailles; in the *Reichstag* he was leader of the People's Party, the party of big business and therefore of the armament manufacturers, the inheritor of the old National Liberal economic expansionism. It is also known now that, despite his protestations, he was very well aware of the real strength of the *Reichswehr* and of the various paramilitary organizations, and of the military liaison with the Soviet Union His German-Soviet treaty of 1926 recalled the Treaty of Rapallo of 1922. Among his private papers was afterward found his correspondence with the Crown Prince, Ludendorff, Lüttwitz, Brockdorff-Rantzau, and others of the same persuasion. Oddly enough, he and Seeckt were never on friendly terms; but it is hard to believe that the public attitude of these two men to each other was not also part of the general game of deception which both were playing.

All these things, it could be said, were forced upon a man devoted to the welfare of his country and condemned by circumstances to duplicities which would otherwise have been unnatural to him. Yet, in character, they undeniably foreshadowed the next major political development in Germany. The fact that Hitler afterwards used to refer to Stresemann's memory with the deepest reverence is of some significance.

9. INTERMEDIATE EUROPE: POLAND AND THE BALTIC

Intermediate Europe

We need a name for the belt of territory in Europe extending, north to south, from present-day Finland to Greece. We could call it "Intermediate Europe" and divide it into four parts: The Baltic, the Polish Plain, the Middle Danube, and the Balkans. In ancient times it lay across the track of the barbarian wanderings; and, unlike Western Europe, which in course of time achieved a degree of ethnic and geographic stability, this remained a sort of "debris zone" (*Trümmerzone*), perpetually fragmentary and shifting.[1] It always missed the greater European movements, like the Renaissance or Reformation; even its forms of Christianity were somehow provincial. Its political history was largely the history of external powers — Turkey, Austria, Sweden, France, Germany, Russia — which at one time or another dominated it or tried to dominate it. Only once, during the Polish-Lithuanian episode in the fifteenth century, did a power arise from within it.

At the end of 1918, the territory consisted of thirteen states, newly constituted or reconstituted by the war. Finland and the Baltic states of Estonia, Latvia, and Lithuania, all formerly Russian provinces, achieved their independence; Poland re-emerged united after a century and a half of "partition"; Austria and Hungary were the defeated and separated remnants of the Austro-Hungarian Empire; Czechoslovakia and to a lesser extent Yugoslavia were creations of the Peace Conference of Paris; Rumania was very greatly expanded; Greece rather more moderately expanded; Bulgaria, defeated a second time, was again reduced; and only Albania, established in 1913 at the behest of external powers, remained as before. In effect, Intermediate Europe was broken into its elements, and perhaps for the one and only time in its history revealed its true ethnic composition. In no other area of Europe had nationalism and self-determination, the ideals of the day, found so complete an expression.

The outcome, as we shall see, was not stable. Poland tried momentarily to reassert her fifteenth-century hegemony — and Lithuania likewise. France played the role of the dominating external power. Then, once more, the area became the sport of greater contestants on either side of it – Nazi Germany and the Soviet Union. Today the thirteen states – or what is left of them – measure their political significance in the world by the degree to which they have been forced to accept, or have been able to resist, the despotism of the Soviet Union.

In this and the next chapter we shall review these states during the earlier interwar years – in the Period of Settlement.

Poland

On October 6, 1918, the Regency Council threw off the pretense of submission to Germany and proclaimed a "free and united Poland." (See p. 49.) On November 10, Joseph Pilsudski, the Polish national hero, released from his confinement in Germany, returned to his homeland in triumph and assumed the titles of Chief of State and First Marshal. He entrusted Andrew Moraczewski, a Socialist, with the formation of a provisional government and the holding of elections for a Polish legislature, the Sejm.

Without the simultaneous collapse of her three former overlords, Russia, Austria, and Germany, an independent Poland could never have arisen, but that collapse – miraculous historical coincidence though it was – now left the war-devastated country suspended, so to speak, in an amorphous sea of dissolution. The all-important access to the outer world of the Allies was momentarily blocked by the hostile ports of Danzig and Memel. For over a century Poland had had three administrations and three systems of law, and these had somehow to be taken over by wholly new and hastily constituted authorities for whom political responsibility was an entirely novel experience. The Regency Council had proclaimed a "free and united Poland," but freedom and unity did not result automatically just because foreign oppressions had been removed, and, in the present hard circumstances, freedom and unity were soon proving themselves to be principles not easily reconcilable.

Abroad the Poles were always regarded as men of piquant and exotic culture, often wearing the cosmopolitan charm, and speaking the language, of Paris. Their history was written in terms of their great soldiers, artists, and scientists – Kosciuszko, Sienkiewicz, Chopin, Rubinstein, Paderewski, Korzeniowski, Madame Curie, and many other names as glittering. But the Poles of popular story were not the only Poles of Poland. At home the central, elemental fact of Polish life was the peasantry, the predominant mass of the population, living in small primitive hamlets, cultivating "dwarfish holdings," illiterate and burdened down with debt. Parts of the country, Poznan (the former German Posen), for instance, were tolerably fertile; but the northeastern provinces belonged to the worst of Europe's "poverty corners." Moreover, the Polish birth rate was the highest in Europe, and the pressure on the land increased alarmingly year by year.

Over and above this dead level of destitution and misery existed a "gentry," the descendants of the petty nobility before the Partitions, and the repository still of Polish historic tradition. In this group, perhaps 5 per cent of the entire population and making up the core of the Rightist parties, was concentrated the agrarian wealth of the country and all its most ultraconservative forces. Nowhere, except in Hungary, was the squirearchical system so strongly established as in the new Polish Republic. A long period of alien rule in a country often has a curiously petrifying effect, and in many ways even prerevolutionary Russia had been more "advanced" than its own Polish provinces. It was as if, through the nineteenth century, Poland had stood still while the world with all its material and social changes had passed her prison, and then suddenly in 1918 she re-emerged to live — or to try to live — the same old feudal life she had lived more than a century before.

Among the more articulate elements of the population there appeared three main party divisions. On the Left was the Polish Socialist party, nationalist, anti-Russian, and often terrorist. Pilsudski was a product of it, and he eventually became its leader. On the Right was the National Democratic party, reactionary, Catholic, anti-Semitic, supported by the propertied classes and the universities, with Roman Dmowski as its leader. In the 1930's, its extreme wing could almost have been called Fascist. In the Center was a group of peasant parties — small, as would be expected from the condition of the Polish peasantry — led by men like Vincent Witos. In addition, there were the Christian Democrats, inclining to the Right, resembling the Christian Socials in Austria. There were some "Independents," Communists, Jews, and minorities. The whole formed a variegated and unpromising texture out of which to design a responsible democracy.

Typically Pilsudski and Dmowski had had to be on opposite sides in 1914. (See p. 49.) Pilsudski had led his famous Polish Legion against the Russians; Dmowski had led another Polish Legion against the Austro-Germans. In 1916 Pilsudski had held an important office in the German-sponsored "Polish Government"; Dmowski had continued to collaborate with Russia and the Allies. Dmowski eventually became a principal figure in the Polish Committee in Paris and one of the organizers of a Polish force on the Western front. In 1919, when the Allies assembled for the Peace Conference in Paris, they had long been accustomed to Dmowski's expositions of Polish affairs and regarded him as the official spokesman of resurgent Poland, and they were disinclined to "recognize" Pilsudski, now installed in Warsaw as the Polish Chief of State.

In January 1919, Paderewski, the great pianist, arrived in Warsaw on a mission of reconciliation, bearing the good wishes of the Allies and of Dmowski. He was invited by Pilsudski to become Premier of a new government, and he then returned to Paris, where he and Dmowski represented Poland at the Peace Conference. The general elections, promised by Moraczewski, took place according to plan and passed off without disorder, and Pilsudski opened the first session of the Polish legislature, the Sejm, in February. But Paderewski's truce lasted barely a month. Questions of foreign policy, agrarian reform, labor laws, and in particular, the future constitution, all sundered the young assembly. In December Paderewski was forced to resign. Observers at the time cynically remarked that the Republic in one year of existence was already displaying the qualities that had destroyed the old kingdom a century and a half before.

POLAND AND THE BALTIC, 1920-38

While Dmowski and the Allies at the Peace Conference of Paris were deliberating the future frontiers of Poland, Pilsudski at home was already consulting more direct ways of securing and extending them. As soon as he had arrived in Warsaw he had set about recruiting an army. The remnants of his Polish Legion and Poles demobilized from the former Austrian, German, and Russian armies were drafted into it. In March 1919, the Sejm passed a universal service law. Within a few months the strength of the

Polish forces under arms reached the handsome figure of 600,000, a motley, polyglot host, but full of a militant energy that it was to take three years of fighting to satisfy.

Most of the new nations in 1919 were engaged in frontier warfare of one kind or another. There were old enemies to be expelled; there were the awards of the Peace Conference to be anticipated; there was future security to be considered. All the peoples of Intermediate Europe looked back to a golden age, and the postwar revolutions seemed to offer them a chance to realize visions of half-mythical greatness in their pasts, visions by which, during the darker years, their hope and courage, their entire nationalist ideology had been nourished. They had "historic rights"; they had "cultural missions"; they were the defenders of their particular civilizations against "hereditary enemies." Liberation in Europe in 1919 was a heady wine, made headier by the long starvation of so many of its drinkers.

In December 1918, the new Polish armies were already in Galicia. In January and February 1919, a stubborn battle was fought for the capture of Teschen from the Czechs. In April, Vilna and Grodno were wrested from the Bolsheviks. Pilsudski, it was evident, was forging a long-term policy of expansion and seeking to reconquer the area of the former kingdom of Poland at its greatest extent. Indeed he could lay historic claims of some sort to all the lands from the Oder to the Dniester. He seemed ready to pick a quarrel anywhere with anybody, and in the end there was not one of Poland's six near neighbors, except Rumania, whom he had not attacked or was not attacking. Clemenceau in Paris gave a tacit encouragement to a series of campaigns which were aggrandizing a prospective ally of France and setting up a *"cordon sanitaire"* against Bolshevik Russia. President Wilson and Lloyd George, appalled at these indiscriminate hostilities so soon after the Armistice, were soon threatening Pilsudski with blockades and embargoes.

Early in 1920, in accordance with the Treaty of Versailles, the Free City of Danzig came into being under a High Commissioner appointed by, and responsible to, the League of Nations. The Poles took over their new territories in the so-called Corridor. The question of Upper Silesia was left to a plebiscite, whose eventual results satisfied neither party. (See p. 136.) Eastward the Peace Conference had left the Polish frontiers undefined. Meanwhile the Russian Civil War had broken out, and the government of Lenin and Trotsky was fighting for its life against a ring of counterrevolutionary uprisings. In an attempt at least to clarify the situation as far as Poland was concerned, the Allied Supreme Council, in December 1919, laid down as the eastern frontier of Poland a tentative line, corresponding roughly to the ethnical division, a line that later came to be known as the "Curzon Line" after the British Foreign Secretary at the time. But it was soon evident that neither the Poles nor their French allies had the least intention of recognizing so limited an interpretation of Poland's aspirations. In April 1920, Pilsudski entered into agreements with Petlyura, leader of the Ukrainian Nationalists, and with General Wrangel, leader of the White Russian forces in the Crimea, and, under the patronage of France, plans were made for a concentrated attack on Soviet Russia by Poles, Ukrainians, and White Russians. (See p. 214.)

A major Russo-Polish war broke out, a war of the strangest reversals of fortune. In two weeks the Poles had advanced deep into the Ukraine and taken the Ukrainian capital of Kiev. But, by June and July, they were in headlong rout. Ladislas Grabski, then the Polish Premier, hurried to Spa, where the Allies were holding a conference on reparations, to appeal for help. He was received "very coldly" and was told to accept the Curzon Line. The Poles were then in a mood to accept any line. The Russians were driving the last remnants of Polish resistance before them, and it seemed as if the whole of Intermediate Europe, if not the entire Versailles settlement, would be swallowed up in Bolshevism. The summer of that year, 1920, was as cruel and anxious a time as any that this generation of many crises was to survive. General Weygand, formerly Foch's Chief of Staff on the Western front in 1918, arrived in Poland at the head of a French military mission and organized the defense of Warsaw. The British Government threatened naval action against the Russians in the Baltic. The crisis passed; Warsaw was held. The Polish forces began a triumphant counter-advance, and soon it was the Russians who were suing for peace. The Russo-Polish War was eventually terminated by treaties at Riga in October 1920 and March 1921. Poland acquired a frontier a generous 150 miles east of the Curzon Line, a frontier that she was to hold till 1939. Meanwhile, in October 1920, General Zeligowski, himself a Lithuanian Pole, had marched into the ancient Lithuanian city of Vilna, and against all protests, including protests from the League of Nations, had taken it in the name of Poland.

Poland emerged from the Battle of the Frontiers, as these events have been called, a victorious power, and one to be respected and courted by the nations of Europe. She confirmed her new status in 1921 by alliances with France and Rumania. (See pp. 174, 176, and 259-60.) She had acquired an area of 150,000 square miles, about four-fifths the area of republican Germany, of which only 90,000 square miles could be described as "indisputably Polish," and a population of nearly 30,000,000, of whom only 20,000,000 could be described as indisputably Poles. Of 2,000 miles of frontier, "75 per cent were permanently menaced, 20 per cent were insecure, and only 5 per cent safe."

The military achievements of Pilsudski might have been more impressive had they been built upon a foundation of real strength at home. But beneath them lay the extreme poverty and the cleavages of class and nationality that we have described. They had been won in defiance of neighbors temporarily weak — notably Russia and Germany — and the balance of forces they had created was, in the nature of the case, unstable in the extreme. There was always something fictitious in the restless, quenchless vitality of the new Poland. The minorities problem would have been acute in any event, but it had been greatly aggravated by Pilsudski's sweeping acquisitions. A Polish Minorities Treaty had been signed at Versailles in 1919, and its terms were written into the Polish constitution of 1921, but it can hardly be claimed that the terms were always respected.

The financial instability and the ministerial instability were further indexes of the real situation. The Polish mark and the German mark seemed to operate in unison; in 1923 the Polish mark responded to the inflationary collapse in Germany. Meanwhile Polish cabinets rose and fell in a way reminiscent of France, except that Poland never boasted the bureaucratic substructure that gave the toughness and continuity to French politics. Between the resignation of Paderewski in 1919 and Pilsudski's coup in 1926, thirteen premiers held office, the longest term being that of Ladislas Grabski from December 1923 to November 1925. Grabski was granted special emergency powers and succeeded in putting into effect financial reforms not unlike Stresemann's in Germany and in introducing, with the help of French loans, a new monetary unit, the zloty.

The constitution, delayed by the Russo-Polish war, was adopted by the Sejm in March 1921, almost the same day as the signing of the second Treaty of Riga. Pilsudski's popularity evidently had not survived the Battle of the Frontiers, and he now found a constitution modeled somewhat on that of France, with a deliberate limitation of the presidential prerogatives. Not unnaturally, in December 1921, when the presidential elections were held, Pilsudski refused to stand, though eventually a close friend, the Socialist Stanilas Wojciechowski, was elected. Six years of parliamentary turmoil followed. Pilsudski, out of office, was as much the storm center of Polish politics as Pilsudski in office.

Foreign relations, however, were in good shape. It was the heyday of the Franco-Polish alliance. France had won her Battle of the Ruhr, even as Poland had won her Battle of the Frontiers, and mutual congratulations were in order. French statesmen and soldiers, including Foch, made state visits to Warsaw. In 1925 Poland shared the benefits and felicities of Locarno.

Poland at this time has been compared with pre-Fascist Italy. Both countries had reached a point at which they were wearied beyond endurance with the impotence, futility, and corruption of the democratic system as that system appeared to them. There were many signs that the inevitable explosion would occur in 1926. Early in that year Germany imposed heavy restrictions on the import of Polish goods and touched off a veritable German-Polish tariff war. Then, in April 1926, Germany and the Soviet Union signed a treaty of "friendship and neutrality"; but even friendship and neutrality between Germans and Russians was sinister and suspect in Polish eyes. (See pp. 148 and 218.) At the same time it appeared that Germany was to be admitted to the League of Nations and to a permanent seat on the League Council; but the latter privilege would not be extended to Poland. Early in May, Vincent Witos, the Peasant leader, succeeded in forming a coalition government with the extreme Right, mobilizing in effect all the anti-Pilsudskian parties. Then, as if in deliberate provocation, he appointed an anti-Pilsudskian general as War Minister. Pilsudski raised his standard and, after the style of the Fascist revolt in 1922, marched on Warsaw. He was reinforced by a contingent from Vilna under an old comrade in arms, General Smigly-Rydz. After three days of fighting, Witos and President Wojciechowski resigned. Warsaw surrendered unconditionally.

Pilsudski still declined the presidency, though the Sejm and the Senate went through the form of electing him to that supreme honor. There was some loose talk about a monarchical restoration – which Pilsudski promptly quashed. In June 1926, Ignatius Moscicki, a university professor and a personal friend of Pilsudski, was elected President. Pilsudski himself was less interested in offices than in reforms that would restore the presidential prerogatives and rid the legislature of the "eternal quarrels and eternal discords" of the parties. Appropriate amendments to the constitution accordingly enabled Pilsudski, with good face, to become Premier and War Minister in October 1926.

Pilsudski may have honestly deplored the violent coup for which he had been responsible. Yet, by his action, chaos had given place to order, the old haunting fear of Polish disunity – the disunity which, as he believed, had been the cause of Poland's self-destruction in the eighteenth century – was momentarily overcome, and the country found itself able to participate in the general economic betterment of the later 1920's in Europe. It cannot be said that the fundamental questions of the Polish body politic were any nearer a solution. The peasants remained in their destitution, and the minorities in their oppression. But, for the moment, the budget showed a surplus, trade showed a favorable balance, the zloty was stable, and these were joys and triumphs exhilaratingly new in the experience of the republic. The port of Gdynia, the pride of the nation, recently constructed wholly upon Polish soil and therefore free from the restrictive complications of Danzig, was handling increasing shipments of goods. First-class Atlantic liners were being built for the Polish merchant fleet. Foreign policy was continuing to enjoy its "French period" under the sound and able pro-French Foreign Minister, August Zaleski.

For the next few years Polish politics revolved in the main around a new constitution to legitimatize the Pilsudskian autocracy. The moving spirits in the Polish Government were now the so-called "Colonels" of the old romantic days of the Polish Legion, but it cannot be said that they had much of a program beyond an almost mystical idolatry of the all-puissant Marshal. The required constitution was eventually adopted by the Sejm in January 1934, by which time Poland had passed into the world-wide economic depression of the 1930's and into a new phase of foreign policy. On May 12, 1935, Pilsudski died. Almost his last act had been to appoint Smigly-Rydz Inspector General of the Polish Army and the virtual executor of his political legacy.

Estonia, Latvia, and Lithuania

On the east side of the Baltic Sea is a low-lying, once marshy and forested land, since brought under partial cultivation by a peasant people of primitive and mixed origins. Through the centuries the land was successively ruled by the Teutonic knights, Poland, and Sweden. From the time of Peter the Great, it fell under the sway of Russia, and Russian it remained till the end of the First World War. Its population consisted in the main of an indigenous peasantry, still feudatory to landowners of German extraction — the so-called Baltic Barons, who claimed descent from the Teutonic knights. Its chief ports, Reval (Tallinn), Riga, Libau, and Memel, were largely German populated and German built. Its more recent history had been marked by the rise of a national consciousness and by the consequent revolts and repressions common to the lesser peoples of Europe. From 1915 to 1918, the territory as far as Riga had come under German military occupation. At the end of 1918, the aboriginal races emerged in sharp distinction as the three new republics of Estonia, Latvia, and Lithuania. For a time German Free Corps and Bolsheviks disputed the land anew. Yudenich, the Russian counterrevolutionary commander, used Estonia as his base during the Russian Civil War. Peace and independence were not established till 1920. Estonia and Soviet Russia signed a treaty of peace at Dorpat (Tartu) in February 1920, the first treaty of peace to be signed by Soviet Russia with a border state. Similar treaties with Lithuania and Latvia followed in the same year.

Of the domestic history of Estonia and Latvia it is enough to say that both states had the usual minority problems, and both introduced far-reaching agrarian reforms which, in practice, meant the dispossession of the old landowning classes, notably the Baltic barons, for the benefit of the landless peasantry. Both set up democratic constitutions which, for one reason or another, did not function very smoothly. The all too common faults and failings of young republics in these interwar years, inexperience and egoism, the multiplication of parties and the frequency of cabinet changes, and the inevitable experimentation in government by blocs — all this was sadly manifest in the two countries. When we read that, from 1920 to 1934, Estonia had 18 cabinets and some dozen political parties, and Latvia had 16 cabinets and between 20 and 30 political parties — and this in populations of only 1,100,000 and 1,800,000 respectively — we might well despair of democracy in the Baltic. Eventually both Estonia and Latvia produced their brands of Fascism, and, in 1934, both established dictatorships, or at least governments with strong executive powers.

Yet, in respect to foreign policy, the interwar careers of Estonia and Latvia were relatively quiet and exemplary. They presented no special international problem. They had signed treaties, as we have seen, with the Russians, their only possible hereditary enemies. With Lithuania it was otherwise. Lithuania was the *enfant terrible* of the Baltic. She was one of those liberated states that remembered too well a once great and glorious past. In contemporary Europe her population exceeded only that of Albania and her two neighbors, Estonia and Latvia. Yet she arrogated to herself the ambitions of a power. In the first decade of her existence she antagonized Poland, Russia, and Germany, and, though a Catholic country, broke off relations with the Vatican. Fortunately she lay outside the main international danger zones — for the moment. A state of the same pretensions in the Middle Danube or the Balkans would not have survived the adventure of independent nationhood a single year.

With Poland, Lithuania's relations were obstructed by the stumbling block of Vilna, Lithuania's ancient capital. The seizure of the city by the Polish General Zeligowski has been mentioned. (See p. 155.) A "state of war" between Lithuania and Poland continued thereafter, the frontier remained closed, and all economic intercourse was halted. In 1925 Poland signed a concordat with the Vatican which "recognized" Vilna as a Polish diocese, and Lithuania retorted by breaking off relations with the Vatican. With Soviet Russia, Lithuania's relations would have been delicate in any event. The propertied classes of the country regarded Bolshevism with abhorrence, an abhorrence which was all the fiercer for their actual experience of it in 1919 and 1920 and for their continued proximity to it thereafter. But so long as Poland held Vilna, there would at least be a protective buffer between Lithuanian and Soviet territory. In 1920, as we have said, Lithuania signed a treaty of peace with Russia; in 1926 she responded to the blandishments of that persistent architect of peace pacts, Litvinov, and signed a second treaty with Russia.

With Germany, Lithuania's relations were obstructed by that other stumbling block of Memel. Like other Baltic ports, Memel was an essentially German city on the littoral of a non-German hinterland, and its citizens made no secret of their desire to return to the Reich. Under the Treaty of Versailles, Germany had renounced her rights in the territory, and French troops were sent to garrison it. Though Lithuanian jurisdiction was clearly intended, a settlement was postponed until the general situation in the Baltic had been stabilized. But the Lithuanians were not a people to acquiesce in delays. They had before them the example of Zeligowski in Vilna—and D'Annunzio in Fiume. In January 1923, at the time of the Ruhr crisis, when both France and Germany were otherwise preoccupied, Lithuanian troops took possession of Memel by force. In May 1924 at Paris, a convention regulating the status of Memel was signed by Lithuania and the Allies. For Germany the settlement was a bitter, unforgivable blow. But so long as Versailles was Versailles she had no legal grounds for protest. The day of restitution would come later.

Domestically, Lithuania followed courses similar to those of her northern neighbors. Clerical and Socialist blocs divided the electorate and contended for office. In December 1926, the year of Pilsudski's coup in Warsaw, a group of landowners, industrialists, and army officers under a certain Augustinas Voldemaras, an old fighter for Lithuanian independence, seized control. There were arrests of opposition leaders; a semi-Fascist troop, the Iron Wolf, was organized. Lithuania assumed all the trappings of an authoritarian state. But changes in the respective methods of government did not prevent the two dictators, Pilsudski and Voldemaras, from continuing to glare at each other belligerently over the question of Vilna.

Finland

In December 1917, after the Russian Revolution, the Finns threw off fifty years of subservience to Russia, and the Finnish Diet proclaimed the independence of the country. But the type and style of government were not decided without a struggle. The Russian Soviet recognized the independence of Finland with seeming revolutionary alacrity, but it was soon supporting a Finnish Socialist Workers' Republic which seized power in Helsinki at the end of January 1918. General Mannerheim, a Swedo-Finn, formerly of the Russian Tsarist Army, organized a White Guard and, with the help of a German contingent, drove the Soviet forces out of Finland.

These four months of fighting in the spring of 1918 were afterward called the Finnish War of Independence. They cost the Finns 24,000 lives and left a trail of embitterment and class hostility behind them. A subsequent "White Terror" is said to have cost another 10,000. German intervention was symbolized by the election of Prince Frederick Charles of Hesse as King of Finland and, but for the Armistice of November 1918, the country must soon have been reduced to a military and economic dependency of the Reich.

In December 1918, the German forces were withdrawn, and Mannerheim temporarily assumed the regency. Finland then entered upon a phase of constitution building and of acute party strife, but she eventually appeared in formal democratic guise and, in July 1919, was declared a republic. The Treaty of Dorpat (Tartu) in October 1920 defined her Russian frontier. She renounced her claims to Eastern Karelia; the Soviet renounced its claim to Petsamo, which became Finland's ice-free port on the Arctic Sea. The long quarrel with Sweden over the Aland Islands was referred to the League of Nations, and in June 1921 the League Council awarded the islands to Finland, but later added the important stipulation that they should not be fortified.

For the remainder of the 1920's, the main problems of the young republic were very similar to those of all the other states of Intermediate Europe — and, in this case, they were tackled with fair success. The Swedo-Finns presented the inevitable minorities and language problems. Legislation passed in 1927 marked the beginning of a comprehensive agrarian reform; by the late 1930's it was estimated that one family out of every three owned the land it tilled. On the whole, the interwar years were promising and prosperous, the people were at peace with themselves and with their neighbors, and the world had good reason to expect well of Finland — until, once more, she became a frontier outpost in a new conflict of Intermediate Europe's external powers.

10. INTERMEDIATE EUROPE: THE MIDDLE DANUBE AND THE BALKANS

The Middle Danube and the Balkans

In the previous chapter we described the northern parts of Intermediate Europe: Poland and the Baltic. In this chapter we shall describe the southern parts: the Middle Danube and the Balkans, geographically and ethnically a highly complex area, once united under Ottoman rule, and in recent history the field of Austrian and Russian rivalry. Here in 1914 was played out the prologue to the First World War. Now in 1919, newly made, unmade, or remade by that war, lay eight sovereign states – in the Middle Danube, Austria, Hungary, and Czechoslovakia; in the Balkans, Yugoslavia, Rumania, Bulgaria, Albania, and Greece.

In 1914 the Middle Danube was the domain of the Austro-Hungarian Empire – the Dual Monarchy, jointly ruled by Francis Joseph of Hapsburg-Lorraine, Emperor of Austria and Apostolic King of Hungary. Austria, one autonomous half of that monarchy, was then an aggregation of nationalities – Czechs, Poles, Italians, and Slavs – grouped round a German core. Even at that time it had become customary to speak of the "ramshackle Hapsburg Empire." Emperor, aristocracy, bureaucracy, army, and Catholic Church made a five-pillared structure, once beautifully interbalanced like a system of Gothic arches, but since crumbling with time. The German bureaucracy of Austria, tolerably efficient and incorruptible, had been extended in recent years to meet the innovations of a progressive century, and it was now not only overstaffed but staffed to an increasing degree with non-German personnel. Experiments in parliamentarianism had adulterated the exclusiveness and the authority of the old order. The subject nationalities recked nothing of German organization, Austrian benevolence, or Hapsburg romanticism. They would rather govern themselves than be governed well. Half a dozen Irelands were in revolt against a power that had nursed them for generations. New political parties to meet new political and social conditions, the Christian Socials [1] and the Social Democrats, made fresh fissures in the already complex strata of the state.

In 1914 the other autonomous half of the Monarchy, the proud and ancient kingdom of Hungary, occupied the great plains in the very heart and center of the Middle Danube. Her frontiers had existed, with only minor variations, for nine hundred years. As a self-conscious unitary state she was older even than England or France. But even here the ethnic pattern was not simple, and it is doubtful whether at any time the great plains had been inhabited by a single Magyar race. The Turks had retired, leaving waste spaces that were often replenished by non-Magyar colonies. In 1914 the "ruling" race of Hungary, the stubborn chauvinistic Magyars, amounted to only half the population then included in the Hungarian frontiers, and, not only around the periphery of the Kingdom, but deeply penetrated into the great plains, were numerous outcroppings of Germans, Slovaks, Rumanians, Croats, Serbs, and Ruthenes.

In 1914 this Monarchy entered a war which, won or lost, would have made an end of it. In 1916 the Emperor Francis Joseph died, and his grandnephew Charles succeeded; it was now only a question as to how long the end could be, or would be, delayed. In 1918, as we have related elsewhere, the final revolution was at last enacted. The monarchy's northern areas were assigned to a new republic, Czechoslovakia, and other slices went to Italy, Yugoslavia, and Rumania. Austria and Hungary survived, severed and shrunken, deprived of their monarch, themselves as much "succession states" as the nationalist elements that had broken away from them.

South of these territories, across the rivers Drava, Sava, and Danube, lay the Balkans, so named from the formidable chain of mountains stretching across its eastern part, a rugged, highland country, at once a barrier and a highway at the meeting place of two continents. Anciently it had been Greek, then Roman, and thereafter Byzantine. The South Slavs had filtered into it early in the sixth century, and the Bulgars in the seventh. The Ottoman Turks, a Central Asian horde, converts to Islam, and the last of the historic Oriental empire builders, arrived in the fourteenth century. In 1453 the Turks eventually captured the city of Constantinople and made it their capital; they had thence spread northward into Europe and were repulsed at last before the very walls of Vienna. As they once more receded, Austria and Russia contended for their vacated possessions. By 1914 five independent Balkan states had come into being, originally rebels against the Turks, often threatened in part but protected in part by the two rival powers to their north and west. These states were of as mixed a racial, social, and religious composition as in any equal area on the world's surface – Greek, Roman, Byzantine, and Turk; Slav and Bulgar; Orthodox, Catholic, and Moslem. But they were all alike in one respect – they were all passionately nationalist.

Austria

After the revolution of 1918, there were many in Austria who hoped valiantly that they might be permitted to begin their political life afresh, freed from the burden of the past and freed from all legal connection with the old Hapsburg Empire that had been dissolved. Republicanism was in the air, and, to the Austrian Social Democrats, in particular, union with their neighbors of the new German republic seemed an eminently desirable and practicable course. Accordingly, on November 12, 1918, the Provisional National Assembly in Vienna, consisting largely of Austrian Social Democrats of the former Austrian *Reichsrat,* issued a declaration to the effect that "German Austria is a component part of the German Republic." The Allied Supreme Council categorically quashed these optimistic pretensions and insisted that it was dealing with a defeated belligerent and a relic of the former Austro-Hungarian Empire. Democratic Austria was born into the interwar world with an unwanted birthright and in an environment of guilt and intimidation.

Elections for a Constituent Assembly, however, took place throughout Austria early in 1919 and resulted in the return of a small Social Democratic majority. The Communists, contrary to expectation, made no showing at all. Dr. Karl Renner, a Social Democrat, became Chancellor. He represented his country at St. Germain-en-Laye and put his signature to the treaty of peace. (See p. 109.) A democratic constitution for the new state was completed and promulgated during 1920. Austria took the form of a federal republic of nine provinces, each with its local Diet. The federal legislature at Vienna was a bicameral body, with a president, chancellor, and ministry of the usual democratic pattern. In December 1920, Austria was the first of the nonoriginal states to be admitted to the League of Nations.

Such are the bare facts of the new Austria's political establishment; but they hardly touch the realities of the situation. The German remnant of a once extensive empire was reduced to a demoralized capital city and a truncated, inadequate hinterland. What was left of the old charm and culture, arts and music — the "wistful romance and nostalgic legend" — was a sorry mockery in a life that had become dreary and futureless. The Treaty of St. Germain wrote the inexorable finis, not only to imperial glory but even to an economically wholesome existence, and its ratification crushed the spirits of those Austrians who, in the revolutionary excitement of November 1918, had persuaded themselves that some kind of national reconstruction and recovery was still possible.

Since the Peace Conference of Paris, a great deal has been written on the "viability" of states. Many factors can bring a state into being and make it viable — a dynasty, a military campaign, an economic need, a popular revolution, even an idea. But Austria's entire rationale seemed to have disappeared with the fall of the Hapsburg Monarchy. Political union (*Anschluss*) with Germany was forbidden. A Middle Danubian customs union was often discussed but never realized. For the new Austria there was nothing left but an all-pervading negation of purpose. If she was now to continue to exist at all, she was to do so at the behest of a group of powers that found it politically convenient to keep her alive.

The usual economic hardships of the war were now aggravated by the peculiar political situation. The return of the armies from the front took place in the midst of the political reorganization. For weeks, in 1919, the country swarmed with soldiers of many nationalities demobilizing themselves, and with prisoners of war releasing themselves, all ransacking the shops and farms, trying to find their way back to their homes on congested roads or on broken-down railroads. Private levies of troops, especially in the rural areas, claiming authority to maintain law and order, often enough were fighting among themselves. While the city of Vienna tried to feed and house its thousands of refugees, its own citizens were scouring the countryside hawking any portable article they could lay their hands on for a loaf of bread or a pint of milk. Outside Austria lay the ring of the new succession states, already reinforcing their frontiers with prohibitive tariffs, and beyond them again lay the ring of the victorious Allies maintaining, with occasional charities, the rigors of the wartime blockade.

The government in Vienna continually exerted itself to relieve the public distress by spending money it did not possess. During the first three years of the Austrian Republic, the state revenues were less than half its expenditure, and the expenditure could not have been described as lavish. A few people with the right kind of property or the right kind of wits speculated feverishly, especially in foreign exchange. The total result was inflation, and then more inflation. The huge middle class of Vienna – the official, the *rentier,* the professor, the artist, the writer – was pauperized. What cultured life survived – and it is surprising how much survived – did so by the sheer force of tradition.

In 1914 the Middle Danube had had a single currency and a single customs union. Industrial Austria in many ways had complemented agricultural Hungary. The Dual Monarchy, with all its faults, at least constituted a logical economic unit. Now the Middle Danube was divided into a number of national states, each one of which seemed to be motivated by a long-repressed hatred of "Austrianism." In their determination to be independent of the city that had once held them in thrall, these states even withdrew their banks and places of business – Czechoslovakia, for example, made it illegal for a Czech firm to maintain a head office in Vienna. All of them resorted to policies of self-sufficiency, or autarky, as it was called. States that were predominantly agricultural built up industries at uneconomic cost; states that had been developing industries were forced to revert in part to agriculture; and in either case they set up mutually ruinous tariffs. New fears and hatreds distorted even those problems to which an elementary common interest should have pointed obvious solutions. Many restrictions on foreign trade, and also on foreign travel, could not even be justified as protective and looked more like reprisals, reciprocally increasing. Meanwhile Vienna was left with services, industries, and a huge bureaucratic apparatus, once designed for an empire and now a useless liability – like a staff without an army, a board of directors without a company, a head without a body.

One feature of postwar Austria was the division that arose between the city and the country, between "Reds" and "Blacks," as the parlance of the time had it. For not only did the succession states put themselves in irreconcilable antagonism toward Vienna, but so also did the very provinces of Austria. At the end of 1918 many of the provinces had set up their own administrations, each enjoying a distinct local autonomy. The federal constitution of 1920 indeed recognized the situation and in some ways legalized it. And the party system in Austria reflected it. There were two main parties, the Social Democratic party, which was the Left-wing party, the party of the urban workers, and the Christian Social party, which despite its misleading name was the Right-wing party, the party of the peasants – and of the Catholic Church.[2] As a further complication, the Social Democratic party was the political home of the Viennese Jews, who amounted to a fifth of the city's population and who had always made a large contribution to its intellectual and artistic life; while the Christian Social party was inclined to anti-Semitism, and afterwards to Fascism.

The two parties inevitably were divided over the question of the *Anschluss,* or union with Germany. The Social Democrats wanted it – at least as long as Germany remained a like-minded democratic republic – and they believed that the new principle of self-determination in Europe should assure it to them. Members of the Christian Social party, who had inherited all the old Austrian distaste for Prussian Germany, were indifferent or adverse. How strong the *Anschluss* movement was at any time is difficult to say. It was never tested by a free vote. Such as it was, the movement was always frowned upon by the Allies, especially by France, ever watchful of any accession of strength to her defeated enemies. By a clause in the Treaty of Versailles, Germany acknowledged the independence of Austria as "inalienable, except with the consent of the Council of the League of Nations," and she was afterward compelled to expunge a clause from the Weimar Constitution anticipating the eventual incorporation of Austria into the Reich. The Treaty of St. Germain prescribed similar conditions. The succession states, Czechoslovakia, Yugoslavia, and Rumania, which were afterward allied in the Little Entente, would have regarded the *Anschluss* as a justification of war. (See p. 110.) Italy was always fearful of it. A certain amount of popular agitation in Austria in favor of the *Anschluss* continued in spite of these summary prohibitions, though the agitation usually took innocent "cultural" forms. Successive governments in Vienna did what they could to suppress any too inconvenient outbursts of self-determination. Later Allied loans to Austria were always coupled with some sort of anti-*Anschluss* proviso that threatened the direst consequences if the movement were not kept under control.

Government after government in Austria struggled with the financial situation. Successive chancellors seemed to be always begging from one European capital to the next for loans and commercial treaties. In 1921 Britain, France, and Italy agreed to suspend their claims to Austrian reparations. Then in May 1922, Ignaz Seipel, one of the most remarkable figures of the interwar era, became Austrian Chancellor. As a Catholic priest and a man of unworldly learning and ascetic life, he cut a strange, detached figure in the seething world of politicians, diplomats, and bankers. Yet he was just as shrewd in temporal affairs as they. He entered public life through the Christian Social party, and gradually became its recognized leader. His appointment as Chancellor signified the eclipse of Social Democracy and the beginning of the conversion of the Austrian Republic to a clericalized authoritarianism.

For the next seven years the history of Austria, in great part, is the history of Seipel's financial program. In August 1922, he appealed to the Allies, then holding a reparations conference in London, and the Allies finally referred the whole case of Austria's finances to the League of Nations. Between the London meeting and the League's meeting, Seipel visited Prague, Berlin, and Verona. At Verona he went so far as to propose a currency and customs union with Italy and to accept the "protection" of Italy in return. Eduard Beneš, Foreign Minister of Czechoslovakia, unwilling to tolerate any such newfangled Italian *Anschluss* or the further penetration of Italy into the Middle Danube – of an Italy, moreover, just then going over to Fascism – at once came out strongly for a League loan to Austria. Seipel's maneuvering had not been without astuteness.

At a later date the League organized financial help to other states, but in 1922 the appeal to the League on Austria's behalf was an original, unexpected move. No one till then had ever considered the League's possible usefulness in the field of international finance. The League Council set up an Austrian Committee at Geneva, and in October 1922 the Geneva Protocols were signed, under which Austria was granted a loan of 650,000,000 gold crowns (nearly $130,000,000), guaranteed in the main by Britain, France, Italy, and Czechoslovakia. Austria undertook drastic retrenchments, established a virtual financial dictatorship, and of course once more pledged herself "not to alienate her independence . . . and to abstain from any negotiation or from any economic or financial engagement calculated directly or indirectly to compromise this independence."

The stipulated retrenchments were harsh enough. A legion of supernumerary state employees, to the number of 80,000, many still uselessly surviving from the old imperial bureaucracy, were pensioned off or dismissed. A new bank of issue, the Austrian National Bank, was set up. Exchange was stabilized, and foreign capital began to be attracted to Vienna. The Social Democrats abused Seipel for selling his country to the Allies. They pointed to the facts that unemployment showed little diminution and that strikes were as frequent as before. But elections in October 1923 resulted in no big changes in party strengths and were considered to have confirmed Seipel's policies. In 1924 the budget was balanced for the first time, the feeling of stability returned, and in 1926 the recovery of Austria seemed to be so far advanced that the League control was withdrawn.

Seipel, in or out of office, continued to be the moving spirit in all these events. His career corresponds in some ways with that of Stresemann in Germany. At the end of 1924, an attempted assassination left him with a serious injury that forced him for a time to retire from active politics, but his work was carried on by a faithful disciple, Rudolf Ramek. Seipel was reappointed Chancellor in November 1926 and held office till April 1929. He died in August 1932.

Yet Austria's recovery was perhaps more apparent than real. The exchange and the budget may have looked good on paper, but they did not mend the fundamental weaknesses of the new state. Vienna was still the overgrown city, parasitic on a reduced and hostile countryside. The conflict of worker and peasant still kept breaking out. The practice of raising private levies of troops, a practice that we noticed in the rural areas just after the Armistice, became a matter of very serious concern during the later Seipel administration, especially as it was evident that urban and rural forces were tending to coalesce into two main opposing camps. In the later twenties, an urban Social Democratic *Schutzbund* and a rural Christian Social *Heimwehr,* both well armed, well officered, and well trained, were engaging in open forays against each other. As we shall see in another chapter, the government, far from suppressing them, seemed to provoke the one and encourage the other, and by 1933 the then Chancellor Dollfuss was governing dictatorially with the exclusive support of the *Heimwehr.*

Hungary

On November 16, 1918, Count Michael Karolyi had proclaimed a Hungarian Republic. He was himself an aristocrat of socialist and pacifist leanings, and in the last weeks of the war he had founded a party advocating severance from Austria, collaboration with the Allies, and a Wilsonian peace. Traditionally in Hungary, none but a titled member of the Magyar squirearchy could aspire to political eminence, and the new party was doubtless well pleased to have a ready-made count as its leader. But Karolyi was soon to find that his good will was lost on the subject nationalities of Hungary. Czechs, Yugoslavs, and Rumanians wanted their freedom and were resolved to take it, and, without their territories, Karolyi's Hungary would be a poor rump of its former extent. His good will was also lost on the Allies. Karolyi had rejected the Austro-Hungarian armistice of Padua because of the severity of its terms, believing he could negotiate better with General Franchet d'Esperey, commander of Allied forces from Salonika, who had now established himself in Belgrade. But the General imposed terms worse than those of Padua. The new armistice had not even delimited the areas of occupation by foreign troops, and Czechs, Yugoslavs, and Rumanians were soon taking advantage of the elasticity thus afforded them to push their own prospective frontiers ever more deeply into the rich lands of Hungary. (See p. 176.)

In the circumstances it was impossible for Karolyi to keep up the fiction of government. The real power of the moment was passing into the hands of Workers' and Soldiers' Councils in Budapest. In March 1919 Karolyi threw in his hand and left the country, and Béla Kun, with the support of the Workers' and Soldiers' Councils, set up a Soviet Republic. Béla Kun was a middle-class Jew, successively a reporter, secretary of a workers' benefit society, soldier, prisoner of war in Russia, and friend of Kerensky and of Lenin. He had returned from Russia at the end of November 1918, a trained professional revolutionary, deputized to foment Bolshevism in Hungary. Normally he should have found the stoniest soil for his seed, and it is doubtful if even in the Hungary of 1919 his influence spread much beyond the streets of Budapest. The peasants, for all their grievances, were never very deeply touched by "these scoundrels from the city."

Béla Kun followed the usual Communist program – expropriation of banks, industries, and land. But, even with his "Red Terror" and his genuine revolutionary zeal, he could not conjure away the dread economic and military realities. Budapest was starving, and the armed forces of the Allies and of the succession states still laid siege to the country's frontiers. In April 1919, the Allied Supreme Council sent General Smuts to treat with Béla Kun – a strange conjunction of personalities – and, not surprisingly, Smuts returned to Paris to advise the Supreme Council to wash its hands of Hungary for the time being. In the end Béla Kun owed his removal to a Rumanian invasion. During the summer months a full-scale Hungarian-Rumanian war broke out. King Ferdinand of Rumania advanced in triumph and occupied Budapest. Rumanian troops "confiscated" Hungarian property wholesale, grain, railroad cars, machinery, and household booty, protesting that they were recouping themselves for the similar spoliation of their country by the Austro-Hungarian invaders of 1916.

But a counterrevolutionary movement was already organizing. The old Magyar lords of Hungary, bewildered and scattered by the collapse of 1918, were slowly recovering their self-possession. In May 1919, Count Julius Karolyi (a distant cousin of the luckless Count Michael), Count Bethlen, and Admiral Horthy, raised their standard at Szeged in the French-occupied zone, formed a national government, and began to muster loyal forces. In November the Allied Supreme Council at last induced the Rumanians to retire from their conquests, and Horthy, at the head of his new army, returned to Budapest. He was received with hysterical rejoicings, and, of more immediate importance, he was received with something like "recognition" by the Allies. Even so, peace was not restored at once. A disorderly "White Terror" beset the country in retaliation for the Red Terror of Béla Kun. Patriotic gangs, such as the "Awakening Magyars," "executed" some 300 to 400 adherents of the former regime, mostly Jews.

Yet, after all the blood and tears of the past months, at least a stable government had been installed in Hungary, albeit it was the rule of the old Magyar magnates in its most conservative form. The Allied Supreme Council intimated that it would accept the credentials of the new government, and early in 1920 a Hungarian delegation was sent to receive the peace terms. Elections were held in Hungary for a National Assembly, and large reactionary majorities were returned. The government proclaimed that Hungary would remain a kingdom, though without a king, and on March 1, 1920, the new Assembly elected Admiral Horthy "Regent."

The signing of the Treaty of Trianon has been described elsewhere. (See p. 111.) It was ratified in Budapest in December 1920, in an atmosphere of protest and crisis. In respect to its territorial terms, it was the severest of the European peace treaties, and the Hungarian people were never reconciled to it. Hungarian "revisionism" became a popular cause more insistently pleaded and more empoisoning to international relations in Europe than even the revisionism of Germany. "No, no, never!" (*Nem, nem, soha!*) was a rallying cry overriding all the lesser causes of party, class, and creed.

A curious episode occurred in 1921. In March of that year Charles, former Emperor of Austria and King of Hungary, left his exile in Switzerland, crossed the Hungarian border, and, accompanied by a few supporters, reached Budapest by automobile. His arrival was entirely unplanned and unannounced. He had evidently counted on the support of monarchist elements in the Horthy regime. Horthy, good monarchist though he was himself, was placed in a most painful dilemma. He could only refuse to hand over the government to its new claimant without the consent of the National Assembly. Fortunately there was no popular outburst to complicate the situation. France, Italy, and Britain, in a joint note, protested that a Hapsburg restoration contravened the solemn assurances of the Hungarian Government and must jeopardize the very basis of peace. Hungary's neighbors, Czechoslovakia, Yugoslavia, and Rumania, threatened military action. Charles returned once more to Switzerland.

It is characteristic of dispossessed royalty to cling to lost causes. Far from taking his rebuff to heart, Charles made a second attempt in October 1921, this time with better preparation and in the company of his consort Zita, who was probably the real inspirer of the adventure. He reached Budaors, a few miles from Budapest, where he encountered some government troops under a Major Julius Gömbös, sent to oppose his progress. Czechoslovakia, Yugoslavia, and Rumania again threatened military action. Charles could only beat another retreat. But he refused to sign his name to a legal abdication, and he determined to remain a king, even a king in exile. Nor would Switzerland now give refuge to the royal truant. On November 1, 1921, Charles and Zita left Hungary aboard a gunboat of the British Danube Flotilla. The Hungarian National Assembly passed a law permanently excluding the Hapsburg succession in Hungary. The monarchical form of the state was maintained, the Regent was still Regent, but "the election to the throne was adjourned." Charles was eventually taken to Madeira, where five months later he died. Zita continued to live abroad – for a time in Canada – but neither she nor her sons ever renounced the hope of an eventual Hapsburg restoration.

Count Bethlen became Hungarian Premier in April 1921, shortly after Charles's first attempt to regain the throne, and he remained in office for ten years. His administration was one of unrelieved reaction. Proposals for agrarian reform were whittled down almost to nothing. A new electoral law, depending upon intricate restrictions as to residence and education, eliminated all voters but the acceptable members of the squirearchy; the abolition of the secret ballot in the rural districts had the effect of disfranchising the peasants. In 1926 the National Assembly created a second chamber which was a virtual resurrection of the Table of Magnates, the upper house of the Magyars before 1918. The old Hungarian feudalism in all essentials had come back. Revolutionary activity was in the hands of the Fascist-like "Awakening Magyars" or "Defenders of the Race," led by men like Gömbös. Bethlen sufficiently indicated his own predilections when, in 1929, he appointed Gömbös his Minister of War.

It need hardly be said that Bethlen's domestic policies – combined with Charles's recent restorationist activities – were not calculated to appease the hatred and suspicion of Hungary's neighbors. The eventual Little Entente between Czechoslovakia, Yugoslavia, and Rumania blocked every hope of peaceful treaty revision and seemed to condemn the country to perpetual diplomatic isolation. Only in Fascist Italy could Bethlen find any signs of friendship; for Mussolini had his own good reasons for disliking the Little Entente. In 1927 Hungary and Italy entered into a treaty of amity and arbitration.

Czechoslovakia

The name "Czechoslovakia" has none of the euphony and romance of "Bohemia." Yet this graceless compound represented for many brave and promising years one of the more successful creations of the Peace Conference. It is a relief to come out of the gloom in which in this chapter we have been stumbling and look, if only for a moment, on this much brighter prospect.

The new state was first proclaimed in Paris on October 18, 1918, and established by a bloodless uprising in Prague on October 28. The two existing Czechoslovak "governments" – that of the Czechoslovak National Council in Paris under Masaryk and Beneš, and that of the patriot leaders at home under Kramář – were merged without friction. Masaryk became the first President, Kramář, Premier, and Beneš, Foreign Minister of a Provisional National Government in Prague. Some frontier fighting continued into 1919, especially to expel Hungarian detachments from Slovakia. There was no "Armistice Day" in the Middle Danube on which it could be said that the war had categorically ended.

The constitution of the state was eventually adopted by the National Assembly in February 1920. It provided for a President, Senate, and Chamber, and bore a marked resemblance to the Constitution of the United States. From the first, political parties were numerous, as might be expected in a country of diverse elements – thirty to forty distinct parties made their appearance in the four elections between 1920 and 1935. Nevertheless, Czechoslovakia showed a more hopeful "viability" and a more stable equilibrium than many a state of older and simpler composition. There were various steadying factors. One was doubtless the old Bohemian official class, which had survived from prewar days and which now became the cadre of a new civil service. A second steadying factor was the tendency of successive coalition governments to swing more and more toward conservatism. A third steadying factor was that the country possessed for so long one president and one foreign minister. Thomas Garrigue Masaryk, President in 1918, was re-elected in 1920, 1927, and 1934. He resigned in December 1935, and died in September 1937. Eduard Beneš, Foreign Minister in 1918, was reappointed through fourteen changes of government, till December 1935, when he succeeded Masaryk as President.

A fourth steadying factor was the country's unexpected economic strength. Almost alone of the succession states of Intermediate Europe, Czechoslovakia succeeded in putting her financial house in order. The new Czech crown, adopted in 1919, proved a stable currency from the first. Economically, the country was almost self-sufficient. Industrial Bohemia complemented agricultural Moravia, Slovakia, and Ruthenia. The Skoda, one of the great armament combines in Europe, lay in Czech territory. A fifth steadying factor was the very successful agrarian reform, the parceling out of the former crown lands and great estates, undertaken during 1919, within the first months of the nation's existence. Finally Czechoslovakia enjoyed respect, sympathy, and help from abroad, and she carefully fostered a "Western orientation." France was ready with diplomatic, financial, and military assistance. Thanks to Masaryk's former friendship with President Wilson, Czechoslovakia was one of the few states in Europe to be exempt from the general strictures of American isolationism. She always had a "good press" in the United States.

So much for the credit side of the ledger. But this happy example of progress and democracy in the midst of the European Continent had its debit side. Czechoslovakia had an unfortunate religious problem and, connected therewith, a minority problem. The religious problem arose indirectly from the current agrarian reforms. Anticlericalism in itself was no new thing in Czechoslovakia, or at least in Bohemia, albeit the majority of Czechs were good Catholics. Yet the memory of the medieval religious reformer, John Huss, was traditional to Czech nationalism. In the old imperial days Czechs had always thought that there had been too many German bishops in Bohemia, and in Czech eyes the evident alliance of Pope and Hapsburg had never reflected on the good name of either. Now in 1919 the ecclesiastical estates at long last were to fall to the ax of the law, and the Church was to be treated like any other swollen landowner.

In 1920 a "National" Czech Church seceded from the Roman Catholic Church. There were attempts to secularize education, and in 1924 members of the government participated in the anniversary celebration of Huss's martyrdom. The Vatican took affront, as indeed it was meant to do, and severed diplomatic relations. A compromise was reached in 1928, and Vatican-Czech relations were resumed. The old diocesan boundaries were redrawn to coincide with the new political frontiers, and it was agreed that in the future only Czechoslovak citizens should be nominated to Czechoslovak bishoprics. The religious controversy blew over, but not until considerable harm had been done, especially — as will be explained — in regard to Czech and Slovak good-fellowship.

The minority problem was the more serious and incurable. Czechoslovakia labored under an even heavier burden of divided nationality than lay on most succession states of the Middle Danube. In 1921 a population of 13,600,000 consisted of 6,570,000 Czechs, 2,190,000 Slovaks, 3,123,000 Germans, 747,000 Magyars, 459,000 Ruthenes, 76,000 Poles, 180,000 Jews, and 255,000 others defying ethnical definition. Yet, as the peacemakers of Paris had well realized, the alternative to a united Czechoslovak state would have been a monstrous and impossible fragmentation. Nationalism run wild could destroy what it was intended to create and inspire.

Czechoslovakia's minority legislation was liberal, well intentioned, and a good deal gentler in operation than that of other succession states. On the whole it conformed to the letter and the spirit of the Czechoslovak Minorities Treaty of 1919. By law all nationalities had the right to their own language for official and legal business in the areas in which they predominated, and they had the right to their own schools. But old hatreds died hard, and they were often kept alive by political incidents. For instance, the Magyars had had to be expelled from Slovakia by military action, and the campaign had done much to set the tone of Czech and Magyar relations thereafter. Then Czechs and Poles had hotly disputed their respective rights and claims in the border town and coal field of Teschen, and the division of the area in 1919 by the Allied Conference of Ambassadors had, of course, satisfied neither party.

The Germans in Czechoslovakia, especially the Sudeten Germans, so called after the Sudeten Mountains along the German-Bohemian frontier where numbers of them lived, were treated by the Czech Government with almost calculating favor. Never was a minorities treaty so scrupulously observed as in their case. But the hatred of Germans and Czechs was one of the oldest nationalist hatreds in Europe, long predating the nationalist movements of the nineteenth century, and it would have been surprising if, in their everyday unofficial relationships, friction between the two populations had not occurred. The Germans objected particularly to the constitution of 1920, which, so they claimed, relegated them to a minority status, and they objected to the Czech Government's foreign policy in the matter of the alignment with France and the formation of the Little Entente.

But in these early years no minority raised such serious difficulties as did that other component people of the republic, the Czech's own blood brothers and copartners, the Slovaks. Though so much alike in race and language, Czechs and Slovaks seemed to be at odds in almost every other attribute which makes for national unity. Their past histories had been separate, and with the best will in the world they could not suddenly be brought together. The Czechs had formerly lived under the relatively enlightened Austrian rule; they were men of the modern era; they needed no instruction in the liberal way of life; they assumed at once the rank of democratic people and of an international power. But the Slovaks had lived under the harsher Hungarian rule, they had become a backward and docile peasantry, and they now emerged for the first time from generations of servitude. The visions of the peacemakers of 1919 must have been sadly disappointed when it was discovered that there was not a sufficient number of educated Slovaks to staff a local civil service or officer a Slovak army contingent. Masaryk had Slovak interests much at heart — he himself was a Slovak from Moravia. But generally, in the prewar years, the few Slovaks of education and progressive spirit belonged to that very class that had been most readily Magyarized, and these Slovaks now, instead of wanting to collaborate in the work of a united Czechoslovak state, were clamoring for a return to their Hungarian allegiance. Their natural economic links were with the Hungarian plain, and formerly had always been so. Finally, the Czechs were Catholics, but with a strong trait of anticlericalism and free thought; the Slovaks were Catholics of simple, unquestioning, medieval faithfulness. The religious and agrarian controversy, just mentioned, had profoundly revolted Slovak sentiment. Mgr. Hlinka, leader of the Slovak People's party, at one time agitated for complete severance from Czech rule.

Masaryk and the Czech leaders, there is every good reason for believing, were genuinely grieved and embarrassed to have gone back on promises of regional autonomy which had been made to the Slovaks during the war. But they found themselves compelled increasingly to assume responsibility for local Slovak affairs and to send into Slovakia an increasing army of Czech officials, Czech police, Czech teachers, and Czech businessmen. The Slovaks watched the Czech "invasion" with growing resentment and, by the end of the 1920's, felt they had become subjects of a nationalist persecution as oppressive as any they had endured in the old Magyar era.

The Little Entente

The foreign policy of Czechoslovakia, as of all "victor" succession states, reduced itself to the preservation of the peace settlement which had called her into existence. From Austria, Czechoslovakia had little to fear as long as the *Anschluss* remained a moribund issue. Austria was as weak and ineffectual a unit as the map of the Middle Danube could show, and French and Italian vigilance could be depended on to keep her in that condition. But the proud, monarchical Magyar, who forgot nothing and learned nothing, presented a more serious problem, and Czechoslovakia was shortly concerting with Yugoslavia and Rumania for a very explicit alliance against Hungary and for the uncompromising maintenance of the Treaty of Trianon.

Conversations between Czechoslovakia, Yugoslavia, and Rumania – even then under the driving initiative of Beneš – were already taking place at the end of 1918, and continued thereafter during the Peace Conference at Paris. The first convention between Yugoslavia and Czechoslovakia was signed at Belgrade in August 1920, the Treaty of Trianon being at that time hardly two months old. Further conversations between the three states might well have been dilatory had they not been jolted into urgent activity by Charles's attempts to regain the Hungarian throne. A convention between Rumania and Czechoslovakia was signed at Bucharest in April 1921, and a convention between Yugoslavia and Rumania was signed in Belgrade in June 1921. All three conventions were alliances of mutual assistance, similarly worded, to go into effect in the event of an unprovoked attack upon a signatory on the part of Hungary. The completed system of alliances between Czechoslovakia, Yugoslavia, and Rumania came to be known as the Little Entente.

Czechoslovakia's relations with the greater powers are discussed in other chapters. But we may remark in passing the essential inclination of Czech policy at all times toward France. The United States, though always friendly, was averse to European entanglements; the British attitude was similar. France therefore remained the main author and guarantor of the young republic's existence. France, anxious to multiply her outposts about Germany, had reciprocated Czech advances; she had stood encouragingly in the background while the links in the Little Entente had been forged; and she had then entered separately into agreements with each of the three states in the system. In January 1924, she concluded an alliance with Czechoslovakia, in June 1926, with Rumania, and in November 1927, with Yugoslavia. She had already concluded an alliance with Poland. (See p. 155.) France, in a very true sense, was now the dominant external power in Intermediate Europe.

Yugoslavia

We pass now to the Balkans proper and take up the tale with Yugoslavia. In June 1917, during the war, representatives of Serbia, Montenegro, and the South Slav provinces of Austria-Hungary signed the Pact of Corfu, declaring their intention, upon the coming of peace, to erect a single, democratic nation under the Karageorgevich dynasty of Serbia. In October 1918, a Yugo-Slav (South Slav) National Council was established at Zagreb. In November the National Assembly of Montenegro deposed the Montenegrin King Nicholas and proclaimed the union of Montenegro with Serbia. Prince Alexander of Serbia accepted the regency of the new state. By the constitution of 1921, the kingdom of the Serbs, Croats, and Slovenes, later to be known as Yugoslavia, became a unitary, constitutional monarchy, with a unicameral parliament, the Skupshtina, based on manhood suffrage.

Yugoslavia was a composite state like Czechoslovakia. She was a compromise, once more, between the contradictory needs of viability and nationalism. Almost half the population were Orthodox Serbs, and rather more than a third were Catholic Croats and Slovenes. Orthodox and Catholic had had separate histories and were as temperamentally dissimilar as Czechs and Slovaks. They spoke much the same language, but typically the Serbs used the Cyrillic alphabet, and Croats and Slovenes used the Roman. Yet all were of the same blood, born and bred in the same hardy, mountainous country, and, though so often subject to conquest and despotism, they remained fiercely independent and intractable. Most of them were still illiterate and wanting in that political sophistication which the democratic system must assume, and they were all too easy a prey to corruption and crooked electioneering.

The new kingdom suffered under one grave geographical disability. It had no good outlet to the sea. The creation of Albania in 1913 had denied to Serbia a coastline on the Adriatic, and Albania had thereafter fallen under strong Italian influence. An essential part of the port of Fiume was ceded to Italy, under circumstances described elsewhere, and the subsequent Italo-Yugoslav agreement of 1920 had confirmed the arrangement. (See p. 236.) Salonika, Yugoslavia's "natural" commercial and strategic outlet to the Aegean Sea, was Greek. Between 1923 and 1925, Greece provided Yugoslavia with a "free zone" in Salonika, but there were persistent disputes over dock dues and railroad facilities. It was not until 1929 that the issues were ironed out and concord re-established between the two countries. But Yugoslavia continued to be a relatively landlocked state.

Yugoslavia's foremost domestic problem was the reconciliation of her diverse racial elements. It sufficiently indicates the true state of affairs to say that cabinets averaged three a year, and that, in the ten years after the constitution of 1921, only two cabinets survived in office as long as eleven months. The Croats always alleged that they had failed to secure in the new state even that degree of autonomy they had enjoyed under Hapsburg rule. During the early 1920's Pashich and Radich represented the two sides of the Serbo-Croat division. Nicholas Pashich, Serbian Premier in 1914, was a Serb imperialist who wanted Yugoslavia to be a Greater Serbia with a central capital at Belgrade. Stephen Radich, a Croat and leader of the Croat Peasant party, envisaged a loose federation with a separate Croat capital at Zagreb. For some years, Radich boycotted the Skupshtina and refused to participate in the nation's political life. But in 1925, he accepted the significant post of Minister of Education, and a temporary reconciliation was achieved. But in December 1926 Pashich died. On June 20, 1928, Radich was shot during a debate in the Skupshtina, and the Croat Deputies, withdrawing in a body, set up a separatist "parliament" at Zagreb. Radich died of his wounds two months later.

The defection of the Croats and the breakdown of parliamentary government led not unnaturally to a royal dictatorship. King Alexander progressively centralized the power in himself, and his rule was legalized by the new constitution of 1931. A single party, the Government party, was imposed upon the country. A new bicameral national assembly was set up; but nearly half the Senators of the upper house were royal appointees. The lower house was elected by direct manhood suffrage, though by open ballot. A final safeguard lay in the provision that the constitution could be suspended "whenever the public interest is generally menaced." The Serbo-Croat division for the time being lay under royal interdict.

King Alexander was one of those men whose stature increases with the passage of time. He was the second son of King Peter of Serbia. He was educated in Russia at the court of the Tsar and served in the Serbian Army in the wars of 1912, 1913, and 1914. He was a scholar by inclination, and, differently born, would doubtless have followed an academic career. He devoted his life quietly and unobtrusively to smoothing party and racial frictions. He was personally responsible for the reconciliation of Pashich and Radich in 1925. In happier circumstances he could have been a model constitutional monarch, rare in his or in any royal Balkan family, and Yugoslavia might have become a truly unified nation and gone forward to a great future. But on October 9, 1934, Alexander was assassinated by Croat terrorist exiles at Marseilles while on his way to a state visit to Paris. (See pp. 395 and 455.) He was succeeded by his son Peter, under the regency of his cousin, Prince Paul.

Rumania

Rumania had entered the First World War in 1916 on the Allied side under pledges of extensive acquisitions in the event of victory. At the Peace Conference the pledges were duly honored, and a new Rumania emerged more than double the area of the old. From Austria she received Bukovina; from Hungary she received territories including Transylvania; from Russia she received Bessarabia. Her frontier with Bulgaria reverted to its position in 1914 – which, in Bulgarian eyes, had the effect of giving her a part of the Bulgarian Dobruja. No other belligerent of the First World War had been so proportionately enriched. But her acquisitions brought her the enmity of the dispossessed nations, and they brought her the usual quota of minority problems. Some of these problems she herself had exacerbated – for example, by the entirely irresponsible and vindictive invasion of Hungary in 1919. (See p. 168.)

On the whole, despite these seeming disadvantages, Rumania was now to follow a progressive, prosperous course. She was fortunate in her leaders. One of them, just after the war, was the Transylvanian agrarian reformer Julius Maniu at the head of a National Peasant party. New agrarian laws broke up the old landed estates for the benefit of the peasants, and further decimated the landowning Conservative party, already much discredited by its former pro-German affiliations. The Liberal party, representing business and banking interests, was in office from 1922 to 1928, again under able leaders, this time the three Bratianu brothers – Ionel, Vintila, and Constantin Bratianu. The Liberal party was mainly responsible for Prince Carol's renunciation of his rights to the throne for the sake of his mistress, Magda Lupescu. The National Peasant party under Maniu was in office from 1928 to 1930. Carol returned in time to meet the economic depression of the 1930's, which in Rumania, as in many another country, was fatal to democratic government, and a royal dictatorship was eventually proclaimed in 1938.

Both National Peasant and Liberal parties were Francophile, and through the 1920's Rumania followed a foreign policy of friendship with France and of strong adherence to the Little Entente. Like Poland, she was ringed with potential enemies and occupied an international status far beyond her real strength. Significantly she was linked with Poland by a treaty in 1921.

Bulgaria

Bulgaria entered the postwar world with disabilities shared by no other Balkan state. She had been twice defeated – in the Second Balkan War and in the First World War. Under the Treaty of Neuilly she suffered the harshest of territorial and military settlements. Unredeemed Bulgarian populations were subject to Rumania in the Dobruja, and to Greece and Yugoslavia in Western Thrace and Macedonia. The port of Dedeagach (Alexandroupolis) was ceded to Greece.

The Bulgarian monarchy survived the war, though its former pro-German supporters were discredited. Boris III succeeded his exiled father, the Tsar Ferdinand, in October 1918. The new power in the country for the moment was the great international agrarian reformer, "the peasant dictator," Alexander Stambulisky, leader of the Agrarian party and now Premier of a purely Agrarian government. Stambulisky introduced sweeping land reforms. He conceived of the whole of the South Slav area as a federation of democratic governments, supported by peasant small holders. In 1920 he initiated the "Green International," which was to be neither capitalist nor Communist and which would incorporate all the peasant parties and cooperatives of Southeastern Europe. It was a great visionary scheme, but in promoting it Stambulisky antagonized other interests in Bulgarian politics, namely the professional classes and the army. He also antagonized the Internal Macedonian Revolutionary Organization (IMRO), a band of terrorists originally founded in the 1890's to conspire against the Turks and now revived to conspire against the new masters of Macedonia, the Yugoslavs. Bulgaria, indeed, followed the course of so many countries of these years, which, after the First World War, began their national life with Left-wing, often revolutionary regimes and were then forced, in part by their party factions and in part by their poverty, into reactionary, dictatorial forms of government.

In the furtherance of his projected South Slav federation, Stambulisky based his foreign policy on friendship and collaboration with his country's old Serbian foe, Yugoslavia. It was a policy that once more automatically provoked the IMRO. In June 1923, the professional classes, the army, and the IMRO seized control. Stambulisky was assassinated. Right-wing coalition governments followed — under Tsankov from 1923 to 1926, Liapchev from 1926 to 1931, and Malinov from 1931. But the IMRO was the real power in all these governments. In 1935 Boris, casting out one devil by means of another, was happy to suppress the IMRO with the army's help and to set up a military dictatorship.

Albania

As a modern state Albania dated from 1913. Her population included Orthodox and Catholic Christians, as well as Moslems. During the First World War she narrowly escaped partition. In 1917 she became an Italian protectorate. After the war, during Italy's pre-Fascist interim, the protectorate was withdrawn, but Italy never lost her semi-imperialist, semi-paternal interest in the country.

Albania's interwar history centers round the figure of Ahmed Bey Zogu, a national hero of the First World War and founder of a revolutionary dictatorship in the first years of peace. In 1924 he was driven into exile, but returned to become successively Commander in Chief, Premier, and President. On September 1, 1928, he assumed the title of Zog I, King of the Albanians. He introduced a Westernizing program — public works, public health, and a new legal code. But the financial backing throughout was Italian. In November 1927, an Italo-Albanian alliance was signed at the Albanian capital of Tirana, and by the 1930's, Albania, to all intents and purposes, was again becoming an Italian protectorate. Italian officials, Italian traders, and an Italian military mission were established in the country. In 1939, as we shall relate elsewhere, Albania yielded at last to outright Italian conquest and annexation. (See pp. 493-94.)

Greece

The pro-Ally government of Eleutherios Venizelos was installed in 1917, King Constantine was deposed in favor of his second son, Alexander, and, under Venizelos and Alexander, Greece came out of the war a victorious power. Venizelos attended the Peace Conference at Paris in 1919 to secure his country's territorial rewards. The Allied Supreme Council permitted Greek forces to occupy these prospective acquisitions in Thrace and around Smyrna (Izmir). But on October 25, 1920, King Alexander died as the result of blood poisoning from the bite of a pet monkey, and his death was the signal for a popular revulsion against Venizelos's extreme pro-Allied policies. Venizelos was defeated at the polls, and Constantine returned to his kingdom from exile.

Constantine was not to enjoy his restoration for long. France and Britain had supported Greece while Venizelos, their special protégé, had been in power; but both powers were now glad enough to wash their hands of a people so troublesome and inconstant. In 1920 Greek forces in occupation of the Smyrna area had been advancing into the interior of Anatolia and were engaging the resurgent Nationalist Turks in a campaign since known as the Turkish War of Independence. The Greeks were stopped just short of Angora (Ankara) and were heavily defeated. They retreated to their base at Smyrna, which in the course of hostilities was burned to the ground. Constantine abdicated a second time, and the army took control in the name of one more ephemeral Hellenic king, Constantine's eldest son, George, who reigned until the proclamation of a Greek republic in May 1924. Kondouriotis, a veteran Venizelist, became Provisional President. The drafting of a new constitution was interrupted by the one-day dictatorship of General Pangalos, and the constitution was not promulgated till September 1926. Venizelos was again Premier and held office through Greece's Locarno era, from 1928 to 1932. In 1935 King George returned. The country was then a sufferer of the world-wide economic depression, and it slipped by inevitable stages into the dictatorship of General Metaxas.

Democracy and Dictatorship in Intermediate Europe

One theme which recurs throughout the interwar history of the thirteen states of Intermediate Europe is the struggle between democracy and dictatorship. And generally, as we have seen, it was the latter which won. By the 1930's, in the Period of Crisis, all but one of these states — Finland — had become subject to some sort of centralized military or paramilitary rule, which was often supported in the country at large by terrorist "parties" — the Iron Wolf, the *Heimwehr,* the Awakening Magyars, and so forth. The circumstances differed in detail in each case — for these states were nothing if not various. But the final tally was strangely similar.

Hungary, it could be said, never made trial of democracy at all. Then in 1926 Poland and Lithuania fell away; in 1931 Yugoslavia; in 1933 Austria; in 1934 Estonia and Latvia; in 1935 Bulgaria and Greece; in

ing definite concessions from the Soviet Government, only to be "disowned" on his return. The whole episode, as we look back on it now, was a hapless combination of blunder, misinformation, and prejudice, for which no one in particular can be blamed.

Kolchak, Denikin, Yudenich

Three White Russian commanders contended against the Soviet during 1919. The first was Kolchak, operating from Omsk in Siberia; the second was Denikin, now in command of the "Volunteer Army" in the Crimea and the Don; and the third, a comparative newcomer in the field, was Yudenich in Estonia. Their three campaigns had very similar histories. They opened with sudden sorties from their base of operations, they gained rapid, initial successes, they seemed for a time to be on the high road to a decisive victory, but they gradually encountered difficulties, and they ended at last in humiliating retirement and "liquidation." In March 1919, Kolchak reached Ufa; in August and September, Denikin took Kiev and Orel; in October, Yudenich was in the very suburbs of Petrograd. The tides of White invasion into Red territory were deep and sweeping, yet they broke, one and all, and ebbed back to their points of origin.

All three commanders adopted a safe, democratic ideology. Their armies contained a goodly proportion of Tsarist officers, but any suspicion of monarchism was suppressed. No one attempted or suggested a Tsarist restoration. Kolchak, Denikin, and Yudenich each bore before him a standard declaring that he would recreate "a great, united, undivided Russia" on democratic lines. But they failed to coordinate their military efforts, or to enlist popular sympathy and support in the territories they occupied. Despite their professions, they brought back regimes that were essentially military and dictatorial. Under their protection the landlords returned to their estates, officials to their offices, manufacturers to their factories, and these, like all repatriated *émigrés,* had learned nothing and forgotten nothing. White grain requisitions were as ruinous as the Red; the executions without trial were as arbitrary and as numerous; the White soldiery behaved as brutally. There were sanguinary peasant revolts and uprisings along the tenuous lines of communication, and the Red Army began its education in those guerrilla tactics that it was to use with such deadly effect in the Second World War.

The Defeat of Counterrevolution

Soviet Russia in 1918 had fallen into such a state of atrophy and prostration that one is almost at a loss to explain how it ever survived. Early experiments in "workers' control" and "spontaneous nationalization" were abandoned in favor of centralized direction by the Supreme Economic Council (*Vesenkha*), a body originally set up just after the revolution in December 1917. But there was little enough to direct. Many factories were at a standstill, and their starving workers were in flight into the outlying country scavenging for food. Railways had deteriorated beyond pretense of usefulness, and the few trains that ran were seized by mobs of demobilized soldiers trying to get back to their homes. The Treaty of Brest Litovsk had taken away the Ukranian grain lands, 70 per cent of the former Russian iron and steel works, and 90 per cent of the former Russian sugar industries. The Austro-German evacuation after the armistice of November 1918, far from restoring these resources, left them in an advanced stage of devastation and decay.

It was in accordance with Marxist principles that the old order should be destroyed before the new should be created. Thus the old bureaucracy, the police, the law courts, the banks, had all been done away. Russia had lost the most elementary organs of civilized life. Class hatred, deliberately stirred up, assisted the process of destruction. Landowners, employers of labor, professional men, and officials were systematically "liquidated." Inflation enabled the government to pay for what it needed by the repeated issues of new paper money, but it seemed also designed to destroy everything which, under the former capitalist system, could be regarded as a saving or investment. In the absence of urban-manufactured consumer goods for which the peasant might be induced to exchange his produce, forcible methods of collecting grain shortly had to be used. During the summer of 1918, as the conditions in the cities declined to famine levels, the Food Commissar organized "Committees of the Poor," "unions of the hungry against the well fed," which were little better than foraging parties, whose function it was to "requisition" hidden stores, and whose services were paid for with a rake-off of the takings. Then, in the autumn of 1918, exasperated by the Social Revolutionary conspiracies, by the assassination of Uritsky and the attempted assassination of Lenin, the Cheka, the Bolshevik secret police, inaugurated a "Red Terror," and, at a conjecture, accounted for 50,000 lives.

And to all this was superadded the Civil War. At the height of the Kolchak-Denikin-Yudenich assault, when the White encirclement reached its narrowest circumference, the area which still paid allegiance to Bolshevism barely amounted to the provinces around Petrograd and Moscow, an area, as has been pointed out, about equal to the Muscovite principality of the fifteenth century. Well might Lenin predict that the defeat of Germany would result in "an offensive of world capital against us."

But revolutionary fanaticism is irrepressible and admits not defeat. Between 1918 and 1920, Soviet Russia, a country exhausted by war and revolution, threatened within by anarchy and economic collapse, threatened without by an advancing array of enemies, unrecognized and vilified by every other nation, not only survived but established itself as one of the powers of the world. Perhaps the Soviet Government had better tactical leadership and a more resilient organization than its adversaries. Or perhaps that convenient and irrefutable phantasm, "historic necessity," moved in its mysterious ways its wonders to perform and granted the victory to the seemingly weakest side in the conflict. Even the most violent detractors of Bolshevism cannot deny the facts of its triumph, or withhold some tribute of admiration for its amazing struggle for existence.

Trotsky (in light coat) addressing a demonstration in Red Square, Moscow

FREDERICK LEWIS

Leon Trotsky was the man of the moment. His extreme political doctrines had not always found favor among his colleagues, his workmanship at Brest Litovsk was much criticized, his Semitic origin never helped him to real popularity; yet he was a military organizer of undeniable genius. In April 1918, shortly after the signing of the Treaty of Brest Litovsk, he became Commissar for War and set about conscripting a new army, the Red Army, disciplined by political commissars and largely commanded by former Tsarist officers. By the end of 1918 he is said to have had 500,000 men, tolerably well armed and trained. He had begun to dream of the reconquest of Finland, Poland, and the Baltic, and of forging links with the future Soviets of Germany and the Middle Danube. One must surely turn to Hitler himself to find another man whose ambitions were most extravagant when his power seemed most ridiculously weak, and who achieved nevertheless most of what he set himself to do.

Trotsky's forces were supported and supplied by an economic system known as War Communism. It was the final *reductio* of Marxist theory, "the expropriation of the expropriators," the concentration of all the means of production and distribution in the hands of the Soviet bureaucracy, the militarization even of labor. From the founding of the Supreme Economic Council in December 1917 to the New Economic Policy (NEP) in 1921, to be described later, the state "nationalized" the banks, mines, and industries and staffed these enterprises, when necessary, with its own managers. It seized, as and when it desired, houses, libraries, gold, jewelry, and movable private property of any kind; it even broke open the deposit boxes in the banks. Gradually it abolished the little that was left of private trade and assumed a monopoly of the exchange of goods – except that exchange effected by a very flourishing black market. It increasingly substituted wage payments in kind for wage payments in the ever depreciating paper ruble. It levied taxes in kind. Later it instituted forced labor in the form of "labor armies," especially for mining, forestry, road-making, and repair work on the railroads. Finally, for food, it supported itself by means of grain requisitions. Under such a regime lived Moscow, Petrograd, and their districts in 1919, and the system gradually absorbed all Russia with the ebb of counterrevolution and civil war.

In 1920 the Russo-Polish War, the last act of the Civil War, broke out. In April of that year, Denikin in the Crimea resigned his command to General Wrangel, and, under French patronage, a joint invasion of Russia was launched by the Poles under Pilsudski, Wrangel, and Petlyura, leader of the Ukrainian Nationalists. In a couple of weeks the Poles had captured Kiev; Wrangel was advancing up the Dnieper; Petlyura ranged and pillaged like a nomad khan throughout the Ukraine. But, like every one of the counterrevolutionary campaigns, this one also opened with surprising initial successes and then developed into a halt and a reversal. (See p. 155.)

The Polish onslaught roused Russian fervor and indignation far more than all the rapacities of Kolchak and Denikin. Tortured and bled though she was, Russia experienced a tremendous upsurge of patriotism. A number of Tsarist generals, among them Brusilov, offered their services to the Red Army. By mid-June of 1920, the Red Army had retaken Kiev, and that hapless "Mother of Russian Cities," fought over by Germans, Austrians, Bolsheviks, Ukrainian Nationalists, Whites, and Poles, now changed hands again for the ninth time in three years of warfare. The Red Army crossed the Berezina and took Vilna, Kovno, and Brest Litovsk. A Polish Soviet government was set up at Bialystok. Danzig longshoremen struck and refused to unload Allied munitions for Poland.

The Poles appealed to the Allies. In July 1920, Grabski, the Polish Premier, hurried to Spa, where an Allied conference on reparations was being held. General Weygand, Foch's former Chief of Staff, at the head of a French military mission, was sent to organize the defense of Warsaw and was generously provided with French munitions. Lloyd George in Britain, though harried and hectored by Labor opposition against new interventionist schemes in Russia, was constrained, nevertheless, to threaten naval action in the Baltic if the Red Army's progress was not brought to a halt. And then occurred the "Miracle of the Vistula." On August 15, 1920, the Poles counterattacked, and the Red Army retreated as precipitately as it had advanced. A preliminary peace was signed at Riga in October 1920, followed by a definitive treaty, also signed at Riga, in March 1921.

The finale of the Russian Civil War was enacted in the picturesque peninsula of the Crimea, once the happy pleasance of grand dukes and tsars. Here, at the end of 1920, Wrangel was penned up with 30,000 men, and with them a motley host of fugitive nobles, governors, generals, bishops, and other ex-Tsarist officials, many with their wives and families. Only France still gave him aid. Britain, now winding up her Russian adventure, shunned him. British troops had evacuated Murmansk and Archangel; Krasin had been in London talking peace. In the end, White troops and refugees were evacuated from the Crimea in French warships, but thousands were left behind to be mercilessly butchered by the Red Army.

The Great Famine and the NEP

Once again, as after Brest Litovsk, the Soviet Government addressed itself to the work of reconstruction. The successful conclusion of the Civil War gave it at last that "breathing space" it had wanted so desperately in 1918. The country, as Lenin well knew, had borne the burden of War Communism only as long as the immediate military necessities demanded, but the people's murmurings would soon be more audible if the rigors of that regime were not lifted and the demobilization of the Red Army was not now accompanied by the promise of a brighter future. The indexes speak for themselves. By 1920 manufactured goods had declined to a mere 13 per cent of their figure in 1913; iron ore and cast iron to 1.6 and 2.4 per cent respectively; coal to 27 per cent. Peasant land seizures and the grain requisitions had reduced the area under cultivation to a third. In February 1921, the naval garrison at Kronstadt, once the stalwart supporters of the Bolshevik Revolution, mutinied, and almost simultaneously a peasant uprising occurred in Tambov, one of the central provinces, south of Moscow. For a moment it seemed as if the removal of the White peril was to be the signal for a general revolt of the impoverished, overburdened masses.

But still one more calamity was to visit Russia. Prolonged drought in 1920 caused a complete crop failure throughout the "black-earth" districts of the Volga, the Don, and over large parts of the Ukraine. War Communism, the requisitions, and the Allied blockade had exhausted the usual food reserves—even seed for sowing had been consumed. By the summer of 1921, famine gripped a population of 20,000,000 to 30,000,000, a fifth of European Russia. In the most stricken areas the inhabitants were in flight or were being evacuated by the government. Roughly 750,000 persons are said to have left their homes to be resettled, temporarily or permanently, elsewhere. Cholera and typhus broke out in the depleted towns and villages, and the epidemics were accompanied by those mental and moral phenomena of famine, the mass panics and suicides, and that terrible apathy that was perhaps the most obstinate and incurable of the effects of the whole weary tragedy.

The Soviet Government was in no position to provide relief on the requisite scale. Illustrated papers in Western countries published gruesome photographs of the cracked and barren Volga earth and the wretched, sunken-eyed, potbellied semiskeletons that then peopled it. Food and medicines were sent from abroad by charitable organizations in the United States, Britain, France, and even Germany. The American Relief Administration under Herbert Hoover for some months fed ten million persons daily.

Lenin already had a partial answer to Russia's economic predicament. "We are in a condition of such poverty, ruin, and exhaustion of the productive powers of the workers and peasants," he said in his speech at the Tenth Party Congress in March 1921, "that everything must be set aside to increase production," and he introduced a decree establishing a grain tax in the place of the former grain requisitions.[3] The NEP, the New Economic Policy as it was called, took its rise from this famous decree. In effect, a free market was opened to the peasant for his produce, and "normal" and uncontrolled trade between town and country was again encouraged. The individual tenure and exploitation of land was permitted. A state bank was founded. The new ruble was issued.

Many Bolshevik theorists, notably Trotsky, opposed the NEP on principle. War Communism, even with its compulsory features, they believed represented true Socialism in practice and was a system to be kept in perpetuity, whether for war or for peace. Trotsky declared that all his hard-won victories over the enemies of revolution would be betrayed if Soviet Russia was now to truck with capitalism and to reintroduce, even as a temporary measure, the old abuses of money, profit, and private enterprise. But the problem now was not one of preserving Marxist purism for its own sake, but of producing consumer goods. Lenin realized that the economic deterioration of Russia could go no further, and he decided to "beat a retreat." Lenin's grain decree of March 1921 was an outstanding example of his realism and of his disregard, when necessary, of Communist shibboleths.

Even if the NEP once more encouraged the kulak, the independent peasant, to hoard grain, even if in time it bred its own peculiar progeny, the new bourgeois or "Nepmen" as they were called, it was not too high a price to pay if the proletariat could once more get food to eat and clothes to wear. Furthermore, the NEP relieved the frantic bureaucratic congestion at Moscow, it brought about a welcome "decentralization" of the greater part of the monopolies vested in such bodies as the Supreme Economic Council, it repaired a little of the antagonism between town and country that the grain requisitions had engendered, and, above all, it abolished the forced labor that had been the most hateful feature of War Communism. The beneficial effects of the NEP were evident within a year of its introduction. Here again, as we so often see in this Age of Conflict, economic recovery, given a fair chance, even after appalling devastation, could be astonishingly rapid.

Soviet Foreign Relations After the Civil War

The defeat of their counterrevolutionary efforts induced the Allies to revise their Russian policy. Revolutions, it has been said, have a way of thriving on the resistance they offer to foreign intervention, and the Russian Revolution was no exception. During 1919 influential circles in Britain were already beginning to wonder whether the "Russian adventure" was not having the reverse of the intended effect. The British Labor party had always been opposed to intervention; Lloyd George had been persuaded to give it a trial only as long as it promised success; Lord Curzon's interest in Russia – he was then British Foreign Secretary – had been confined mainly to his fears of Russian aggression against his beloved India. Only Winston Churchill and a few extreme Tories persisted in their implacable Russophobia and demanded that something should be retrieved from the £100,000,000 of munitions that the British Government had thrown into Murmansk and the Don. Psychologically Britain was then entering upon her postwar retreat to isolationism and pacificism, and was looking to trade rather than to warfare as the norm of her relations with Europe. In January 1920, as a first indication of changed Anglo-Russian relations, the British Government raised the naval blockade. Between April and July 1920, British forces were withdrawn from northern Russia and Siberia. British forces were also withdrawn from the Caucasus, and British concession hunters tacitly renounced their quest for oil in the area. Soviet forces occupied Batum. Azerbaijan, Armenia, and later Georgia were organized as Soviet republics.

Leonid Krasin, the Soviet envoy, in the character of a "sober man of business," came to London to meet Lloyd George in May 1920 and, for the first time since the Bolshevik Revolution, ranking Western and Russian statesmen sat at the same conference table. Russia was "in the market" for trade agreements and diplomatic recognition, and it behooved Britain to make her bids while the bidding was good. But the conversations were anything but cordial. The press in both countries engaged in a malicious sniping campaign; the Russo-Polish War was still raging. Lloyd George, anxious though he was for Russian trade, was determined to quarantine Russia spiritually and to put a stop to Communist propaganda, especially in the East. After interminable conversations, breakdowns, and resumptions, an Anglo-Soviet trade agreement was signed on March 16, 1921. Nevertheless, Britain's full recognition of the Soviet Union waited until the MacDonald cabinet in 1924. (See p. 267.)

By 1920-21 Soviet Russia was busy making peace with all her neighbors. She signed treaties with Estonia, Latvia, Lithuania, and Finland during 1920; she signed treaties with Persia, Afghanistan, and Turkey in 1921. France faced the inevitable with greater reluctance. During 1920 she had still put her trust in Wrangel and had hoped that the Poles might triumph where Kolchak and Denikin had failed. French right-wing interests never recovered from their anti-Bolshevik complex; they never renounced their claims on the huge prewar indebtedness of Russia to France; they never gave the quietus to their fears of an eventual Russo-German *rapprochement*. France re-established relations with Russia at the time of the Herriot ministry in 1924.

The United States had withdrawn its forces from Siberia during 1920 but, despite this pacific gesture, it had continued in an attitude of official hostility toward the Soviet Government and refused formal recognition of a government "whose conceptions of international relations are so entirely alien to our own, so utterly repugnant to our moral sense." It did not recognize the Soviet Union till 1933. (See pp. 464-65.)

Japan withdrew her forces from Siberia in November 1922, after considerable pressure from the United States, but a small Japanese force continued to occupy the northern part of Sakhalin. A Japanese-Soviet settlement was signed in January 1925. Japan recognized the Soviet Union and agreed to evacuate the northern part of Sakhalin in return for certain oil concessions there.

During 1922, Lloyd George sought to secure Russian participation in his grandiose scheme for an economic "European Consortium." The NEP seemed to indicate a reformed attitude on the part of the Soviet Government, and reports then being received of the recent Volga famine were enough to convince any man with a drop of humanitarianism in his blood that whatever the politics of Russia's leaders, her people were in the direst need. We have elsewhere discussed the conference at Genoa in April 1922, convened to give effect to this Consortium. Poincaré from Paris was unhelpful, and the Russian delegates used the conference as a propaganda platform and then signed the Treaty of Rapallo with the German delegates. Lloyd George's Consortium was never heard of again. (See pp. 142-43.)

After Rapallo the Soviet and German Governments continued their somewhat incompatible but interesting flirtation. The Red Army and the *Reichswehr* established clandestine contacts. In April 1926, the two governments concluded a treaty of friendship and neutrality. The threat of a *rapprochement* between Russians and Germans indeed could always be used to blackmail the Western Powers. The final outcome was the Moscow Pact of 1939. (See pp. 148, 156, and 431.)

The Soviet System

The word *soviet* means "council" or "committee." In the revolts of 1905 the Russian Soviets had been committees of workers improvised for the occasion, and the Revolution of 1917 created them afresh. Each factory, each battalion, each ship, each village was soon electing its soviet of workers, soldiers, sailors, or peasants, as the case might be. As such there was nothing very novel or extraordinary in the idea. In moments of grave emergency, when civilized life breaks down, men will always form themselves into bands of one sort or another. We recall the well-known chapter on "Clubbism" in Carlyle's *French Revolution:*

> Are not such Societies [he might almost have said soviets] an incipient New Order of Society itself? The Aggregative Principle anew at work in a Society grown obsolete, cracked asunder, dissolving into rubbish and primary atoms?

But what was novel and extraordinary in the soviets of 1917 was their being employed, not only as "organs of rebellion," but also as the nuclei of a complete political system.

In the days before the First World War, in their party program of 1903, the Bolsheviks had demanded of their coming revolution nothing more than "a legislative assembly of the people's representatives," elected upon time-honored democratic lines. But Lenin, on his arrival in Russia in April 1917, soon sensed the importance of the soviets. The idea of a legislative assembly went into the discard, and in November 1917 the Bolsheviks seized control under their strange device, "All Power to the Soviets." When the long-promised Constituent Assembly met in Petrograd in January 1918, it was dissolved by decree of the Soviet Government. We paraphrase Lenin's words at the time:

> The Soviets are become the apparatus of government. They are a connection with the masses that is so intimate, so indissoluble, so readily verifiable and renewable, so informal and democratic, that nothing like it has ever been approached before. They exist without bureaucratic formalities and represent the most diverse occupations. They are the vanguard and the school of the whole gigantic mass of the oppressed classes which till now have stood outside all political life and all history. Compared with bourgeois parliamentarianism they are a development of democracy which is of world significance.

The Soviet system pyramided upward from a broad base of many thousands of smaller soviets. Thus the village (*selo*) soviets elected the territorial (*krai*) soviets; these elected the provincial (*oblast*) soviets; these elected the soviets of the constituent republics, and these finally elected the Congress of Soviets. The franchise at the base was of the greatest latitude. Every man and woman above the age of eighteen was qualified to vote and to be elected to any office. Only those employing labor for hire, those living on unearned incomes, and those mentally deranged or convicted of crime, as well as monks, priests, and members and officials of the former ruling dynasty, were "deprived." Voting took place at public meetings generally by a show of hands.

The Soviet system was regularized in a "Constitution or Fundamental Law," adopted by the Fifth (All-Russian) Congress of Soviets in July 1918, and at the same time the state was formally established under the title of the Russian Socialist Federated Soviet Republic, the R.S.F.S.R. The First All-Union Congress of Soviets, in December 1922, established the Soviet Union or Union of Soviet Socialist Republics, the U.S.S.R., of which the R.S.F.S.R. was thenceforth to be only one of a group of constituent republics. A new constitution was adopted by the Second All-Union Congress of Soviets in January 1924 to regularize this augmented state. The constituent republics were then seven in number: the R.S.F.S.R., the Ukraine, White Russia, the Transcaucasian Federation (itself a federation of three republics: Azerbaijan, Armenia, and Georgia), Turkmen, Uzbek, and Tajik.

In constitutional theory, the All-Union Congress of Soviets of some 2,000 or more Deputies, meeting once every two years, was the supreme repository of power. Each Deputy, in the roundabout way we have described, represented 25,000 town or city electors or 125,000 peasants, a disproportion greatly to the advantage of the urban proletariat, whose Communism was supposed to be more reliable and preponderant. But in practice the All-Union Congress of Soviets proved too unwieldy and intermittent for regular business. It became little more than a picturesque "biennial picnic" for distant provincial Deputies visiting the capital for the first time. It therefore elected, and delegated its authority to, the more permanent Central Executive Committee (TSIK), a bicameral body, which consisted of a Soviet of the Union of some 400 Deputies, representing the total population, and a Soviet of Nationalities of some 150 Deputies, representing the national subdivisions of the Soviet Union. The Presidium of the Central Executive Committee consisted of nine Deputies from the Soviet of the Union, nine from the Soviet of Nationalities, and nine elected by a joint session of those two bodies. The Presidium was a "collective presidency" of the Soviet Union, and it fulfilled the somewhat ceremonial and confirmatory functions exercised by the president or constitutional monarch of a democratic state. The greater part of the top-level executive work of the Soviet Government was formally entrusted by the Central Executive Committee to a Council of People's Commissars (*Sovnarkom*), which corresponded to the cabinet of ordinary democratic usages. At the time of which we are writing, Lenin was President of the Council of People's Commissars, and Trotsky was Commissar for War. Stalin was Commissar for Nationalities, and Chicherin Commissar for Foreign Affairs. The President of the Central Executive Committee and "President of the Soviet Union" was the former peasant and factory worker, Kalinin.

A second constitution, the so-called Stalin Constitution, to be mentioned later, was adopted in 1936. (See pp. 232-33.)

Communist Doctrine and the Communist Party

The new Russian state — the Communist, Bolshevik, Soviet State — sprang from a man and a doctrine. The man, it is true, was afterwards glorified beyond his deserts, and his doctrine was corrupted by the inevitable pragmatism of living politics. But he inspired the pristine fervors of the Revolution, and the Russia of our era is not to be understood without him. Karl Marx was the prophet of Communism. He was born in 1818 at Trier in Germany of a family of middle-class Christianized Jews. His extreme views — and his racial origins — debarred him from an academic career, and he lived in exile, supporting himself as best he might by journalism, but keeping in active touch with revolutionary movements around him. He spent the latter part of his life in London, where he wrote his great treatise on *Capital,* and where, in 1883, he died.

Like all social reformers Marx was obsessed by the sufferings and the inequality of man. For him the whole theme of history was the struggle between strong and weak, oppressor and oppressed, rich and poor, master and slave, capitalist and worker — between the class that controlled the means of production and the class that was thereby controlled. Under modern capitalism, Marx argued, by an inexorable logic, the rich became richer and the poor became poorer; wealth accumulated at one end of the scale and poverty at the other. The upper strata of society continually narrowed into luxurious isolation; the lower strata of society continually broadened into indigent proletarianism. Competition between capitalists was swallowed up in mergers and monopolies, and in the process capitalism lost its competitiveness, its only virtue and justification. Imperialistic wars and recurrent economic crises of increasing frequency and severity revealed the self-contradictory and self-destructive elements inherent in the system.

Capitalism, Marx argued further, required a coercive machinery for the advantage and protection of its beneficiaries. The State, with its law, police, and army, was that machinery. The State was not so much a device for maintaining peace and order as a product of the class struggle, and it exacerbated the class struggle. And the struggle would be brought to an end only when the proletariat, by violent revolution, set up its own dictatorship and created a free and equal classless society. The expropriators would then be expropriated; the State as such would no longer serve any political purpose and would wither away.[4]

For Marx, revolution was something necessary and infallible, like a law of nature. He belonged to an era when many regarded politics as an exact science. He believed that when the moment for revolution arrived, the course of events would work out as a sort of absolute causal series. Consequently, despite the detail of so much of his thought, and despite his close connection with the actual revolutionary movements of his day, he had little notion of the practical politics of revolutions. Nor did he ever fully realize that a revolution is a complicated undertaking, almost a military campaign, needing a trained cadre of men to direct it. Especially does a revolution need a trained cadre *after* it has succeeded and passed into the new political order.

We have become all too familiar today with the ways of revolutionary "parties." We have seen Fascists and Nazis, as well as Communists, at work. And — save the blasphemy — we can recall the history of the preaching friars, Jesuits, Puritans, and other *corps d'élite,* which from time to time have energized great human movements and given a new direction to the normally inert masses of mankind. It was precisely here that Marx's original teaching was so curiously deficient and needed to be supplemented by his Russian successors. Communism in practice required a Party. It had to be the concern of the so-called professional revolutionary, who belonged to a small conspirative band of men of hard training, fanatic courage, iron discipline, and, above all, tight and efficient organization. The ordinary democratic socialism of the West implied the usages of the ballot box and the representative parliamentary assembly; it implied the free participation of the whole people. Its parties were of loose and fluctuating membership, numerically unlimited. Communism, on the contrary, might look to an eventual dictatorship of the proletariat. But the proletariat, at least during and for some time after the critical revolutionary phase, called for the organization and leadership by a new exclusive, almost aristocratic clique, strictly limited in numbers.

The professional revolutionary was peculiarly the product of Tsarist Russia. The old Russian peasantry was backward, ignorant, and stupidly reactionary. Certainly it was unlikely material for a revolution. It might contribute much — as indeed it had done in times past, and did again in 1917 — to the destructive side of a popular mass revolt. But constructively it could contribute little to the permanent political form of a new state. Urban industrial labor was not to be despised, but it had never become the organized political force in Russia that it was in other industrialized countries. The old Russian middle class was numerically unimportant and without aggressive self-consciousness. If, then, revolution there was to be in

Russia, it would have to be the work of that curious, declassed, self-alienated, self-disinherited type of man – or woman – terroristic, fanatical, uniquely dedicated. He might be a peasant, a bourgeois, or even a "repentant" nobleman. More often he was of the urban intelligentsia; or he could be quite uneducated. But it was out of such stuff that the professional revolutionary – and thence the Party – was made.[5]

The Russian Social Democratic Workers' party was founded at Minsk in 1898. Already prominent in its counsels was Vladimir Ilich Ulianov, otherwise known as Lenin, though at that particular date he was in exile in Siberia. The party was burned and sharpened in the fires of the time as Lenin – again usually from places of exile in Germany, England, or Switzerland – forged out of it the hard metal he needed. At a congress held in London in 1903, the party split in two, the more radical Bolsheviks (literally "the majority") under Lenin and the more moderate Mensheviks (literally "the minority"). The issues were sharp and fundamental. Generally it may be said that the Bolsheviks represented the strict Party faction and the Mensheviks represented the wider democratic faction. The Bolsheviks wanted violent revolution led by themselves; the Mensheviks wanted gradual revolution by regular parliamentary methods. In February 1917, the Bolsheviks are said to have numbered 30,000, dispersed throughout the Tsarist empire. During the eight months of the Provisional Government in 1917, they grew to 200,000. In 1918, shortly after the conclusion of the Treaty of Brest Litovsk, they took the name of the Russian Communist Party (Bolsheviks). In 1921, after the first great purge, they numbered just under 500,000. In 1929 they numbered over 1,000,000; in 1939 they numbered over 1,500,000 and they boasted in addition some 5,000,000 young people under twenty-three years, known as Komsomols, Pioneers, and Octobrists. But never at any time before 1941 does it appear that the adult membership of the Party was more than 1 per cent of the total population of the Soviet Union.

The Party, accordingly, was never a political party in the Western democratic sense. We have called it a clique; it was a leadership corps, a blood brotherhood, even a religious order. Certainly no religious order demanded more of its initiates. Its membership was granted on the severest terms, and the member's credentials were checked and cross-checked and periodically purged by competent investigators. A man or woman once enrolled belonged to it body and soul, subscribed to an absolute belief in the Marxist creed, and rendered a blind, unquestioning obedience to his or her superior in the hierarchy. Stalin, in his funeral oration on Lenin, thus described the Party:

> Comrades! We Communists are people of a special mould. We are fashioned out of special stuff. We are they who form the army of the great proletarian general, the army of comrade Lenin. There is nothing higher than the honor of belonging to this army. There is nothing higher than the calling of a member of the party whose founder and leader is comrade Lenin. Not to every man is it given to be a member of such a party. Not to every man is it given to endure the tribulations and tempests which go with the membership of such a party. Sons of the working class, sons of need and strife, sons of unexampled

privations and heroic strivings — such are the men who, first and foremost, are fitted to be members of such a party . . .

In organization, the Party pyramided upward like the soviets. Any three or more members, wherever they were gathered together, constituted a "cell" or primary party organ. Cell members, in duty bound, assumed the leadership, whether in farm or factory or office or regiment, presented themselves as candidates for election to the local soviet, assisted at local meetings with advice and inspiration, showed themselves tireless, zealous, productive workers, and acted as transmitting agents of the orders and decisions of the higher powers. To them inevitably fell the greater part of the farm and factory managerships and the posts in the new bureaucracy. Above the cells, in due succession, in exact analogy to the soviet system, rose the "conferences," the urban, provincial, and republican conferences. Topping the pile was the Party Congress of some 3,000 delegates meeting in Moscow every three or four years.

The core of the Party Congress was the Central Committee (not to be confused with the Central Executive Committee of the Soviets); and within this committee were two further permanent, interlocking bodies, originally of five members each: the Politburo, whose origins we noted (see p. 76), and which gradually acquired the greatest effective concentration of power in the Soviet Union; and the Orgburo, the inspectorate of the Party's administration and personnel. A key member of both bodies was the Secretary General of the Central Committee — formerly Molotov, and then, after 1922, Stalin. In a book of this size we cannot describe the intricate inner history of the Party's organization, an organization moreover in constant development and change. But enough has been said to suggest that this huge devious pseudo-bureaucracy stretched downward from a central authority, mysteriously screened in the Kremlin in Moscow, and reached into every corner and cranny in the Russian state.

It is impossible to think of the Communist party or the Soviet Government without one organization, the secret police. "The Extraordinary Commission for Combating Counterrevolution and Sabotage," known from its initials as the Cheka, had been founded by Lenin in December 1917 under the presidency of Felix Dzerzhinsky. In these early genial days of the Russian Revolution, the Bolsheviks were theoretically opposed to the death penalty, and the Cheka was not a very powerful or sanguinary organization. But after the political assassinations of the summer of 1918, which, as we have said earlier, included Uritsky, one of the heads of the Cheka, and nearly included Lenin himself, the Cheka entered upon its first campaign of terrorism. In February 1922, about the time that the Soviet Government was trying to reconcile itself to foreign powers, the organization took the name of the General State Political Administration and was known, again from its initials, as the Ogpu; but apparently it changed neither its character nor much of its personnel. The old methods remained with it, the spying and delation, the secret arrests and interrogations, the forced labor camps, the "confessions," and "liquidations."

But in the eyes of the Bolsheviks there was no question that the existence of the organization was justified. Certainly their revolutionary sufferings had not been such as to dispose them toward charitable practices. Trotsky, who must bear much of the responsibility for the Cheka's work, in neither his writings nor his speeches showed the slightest compunction or misgiving, and Lenin, in a characteristic passage, asked if "our war" of the exploited against the exploiters, even at a cost of half a million lives, was less justified than the war of "international imperialism," which cost ten millions, "to decide whether British or German robbers should rule the whole world." [6]

Soviet Russia, it is impossible to deny, became a regular police state. Communism took the road to autocracy as once Tsardom had done. As has often been said, there was little difference between the ultimate development of Lenin's revolution and that of Peter the Great two centuries and a half before. Both initially were Western importations, both were violent ruptures with the native past, both introduced economic statism, both created a privileged bureaucracy, both were highly militarized, both became disproportionately interested in the preservation of power, both were permeated by terror, both exalted a supreme despot.

The Third International (Comintern)

In Communist doctrine the revolution is international. The worker knows no country. The world must be made safe for socialism. Marx himself founded the First International, or International Workingmen's Association, in 1864. It was an annual cosmopolitan gathering. The Paris Commune of 1871 and the secession of the Anarchists under Bakunin brought its troubled history to an end. The Second (Social Democratic) International was founded in 1889. It belonged to the era of parliamentary participation, and its chief ornaments were the parliamentary Socialists of the day, Jaurès, Bebel, Ebert, MacDonald, and the rest. It met for the last time in Brussels in July 1914, though the International Socialist conferences at Zimmerwald in 1915, at Kiental in 1916, and at Stockholm in 1917, were sometimes argued to be its successors. (See pp. 77-78.) The Third (Communist) International, or Comintern, was founded by Lenin in Moscow in March 1919, under the presidency of Zinoviev.

The Bolsheviks had once hopefully expected that their world revolution would follow automatically upon the end of the war in 1918. But, by the time the Peace Conference had assembled in Paris, it was being slowly borne in upon them that the victorious bourgeois-democratic Powers held the initiative in peacemaking and, if world revolution was now to be, a special agency must be established for its promotion. That agency, in Lenin's view, was not to be a loose association meeting intermittently, like the First and Second Internationals, but a permanent staff of professional revolutionaries, with expertly organized espionage and propaganda ramifying throughout the length and breadth of the inhabited world.

The Third International, or Comintern, was the agency for world Communist revolution. Its tactical method was to gain control, by propaganda and subsidies, over Communist parties in different countries, to plant "cells" in trade unions and workers' cooperatives, and thus to build up, openly or surreptitiously, a "united proletarian front." The central organ, or bureau, of the Comintern, "temporarily" established in Moscow, was in close contact with the Soviet Government — both indeed were dominated by the Party — but it was always careful to distinguish itself therefrom and to represent itself as an independent, supranational, supragovernmental body. It could therefore pursue its distinctively hostile campaign in foreign countries without compromising the Soviet Government, just as, at a later date, Germany and Japan could form an Anti-Comintern Pact without affecting their normal diplomatic relations with that government.

The Death and Glorification of Lenin

Early in 1922, it was plain that Lenin's health was failing. Unremitting study and hard work had gradually undermined a constitution which must once have been extraordinarily tough. In May of that year, he suffered a paralytic stroke and for a time lost the faculty of speech. He recovered sufficiently to take an advisory part in affairs, but he was never well again. He died on January 21, 1924.

Lenin was that rare combination, a theorist and a man of action. He gave his life to a doctrine and to its fulfillment. He had the qualities of a fanatic, but his fanaticism was tempered by clarity and calculation. He renounced theory without compunction if it proved to be unworkable. He bowed to circumstances he could not alter. Thus he accepted Brest Litovsk; he adopted the soviets; he introduced the NEP; he abandoned — perhaps temporarily — the ideal of world revolution. His instinct for men and situations — at least for men and situations in his native Russia — amounted to second sight. He knew just when to strike and when to retreat. He avoided terror if he could, but never hesitated to use terror if he thought it necessary. He had the defect of so many modern dictators and leaders of the people in that he was essentially cultureless. He had no sense of history, tradition, or romanticism. He read only for controversial purposes and for "technical" information. He had no spiritual gifts whatever. There was nothing in him that could be remotely described as otherworldly or religious.

In appearance he was short, stocky, and unprepossessing. He was of pure Russian blood — unlike so many great figures in Russian history. He was simple in manner, averse to theatricality, direct in all his dealings. He submitted to correction at the hands of his colleagues without a trace of false pride. He lived austerely, and, even in his days of power, he kept his old unaffected, familiar habits. He never wore a military uniform or decoration. Among European dictators, he must have been the least egotistic, the least histrionic, and the most normal. He was not ambitious for himself. He seized supreme power, but did not use it, or enjoy it, for its own sake. Indeed it could be said that the complete development of the Communist autocracy occurred after his death in the person of his successor, Stalin. His obsession was his revolution. He was the protagonist of a colossal social upheaval. He brought a people of many millions through revolution, civil war, famine, and economic collapse, and he founded a state whose influence the world will feel for all time. Whatever may be our judgment of his political philosophy, he was, by any standard of measurement, one of the mightiest figures of his generation.

The "Lenin Legend," as it developed after his death, was not untainted with propaganda and even with the grossest fetishism. His body was embalmed and laid in a glass-topped coffin in a mausoleum beneath the Kremlin walls, where it was visited by continuous lines of devotees. Every device was used to invest his written works with an aura of canonicity. Streets, factories, clubs, stadiums, towns, and cities were named after him. Petrograd became Leningrad. His portraits in photographs, in statuettes, medals, stamped on handkerchiefs, on ash trays, on cigarette cases, were treated almost like icons. Bolshevism, which had forsworn cults, adopted all the trappings of a cult of its own.

The Trotsky-Stalin Feud

Lenin's illness and death posed the dread question of his successor. Formerly his name had been linked with Trotsky's, so much so that, in Russia and abroad, the Lenin-Trotsky partnership had been looked upon as an indissoluble duumvirate. Lenin himself always had spoken as if Trotsky would succeed him as a matter of course. But it was soon seen that Trotsky had little strength alone. Despite Trotsky's services to the cause, despite his brilliance as organizer, executive, orator, and negotiator, he was not a real party man – he had not even been a party member before his return to Russia in 1917. His highhanded dealing with his colleagues – Stalin being one of them – especially during the Civil War, and his many disagreements on policy with Lenin himself, notably over Brest Litovsk and the NEP, could all be remembered to his discredit when the time was ripe.

The Russian people after years of war and revolution were physically and morally exhausted, and Trotsky's rhetorical, dynamic personality little matched their mood of prostration. The doctrine of permanent revolution that he preached and the exultant visions of a communized world that he was always seeing were jaded things to people who had almost forgotten what it was to be at peace. The devastated Russian homeland was tired of mirages which in the realization turned out to be yet more massacre and starvation. The Russian Revolution had passed beyond the stage of terrorism and was ready to weariness for the stabilization of an autocratic leader.

The struggle between Trotsky and Stalin for Lenin's vacant office is a long and complex story, and many of its details are not yet clear. But the struggle was virtually decided at the time of the NEP, a measure which, as we have said, Trotsky had strongly and unsuccessfully opposed. Then the failure of Bolshevism in Hungary, Germany, and China signalized the end of Trotsky's permanent revolution and encouraged that retreat to "Socialism in One Country" that Stalin made it his business to support. At the time of Lenin's death in 1924, Trotsky, sick and in disgrace, was on his way to the Caucasian Riviera. He might have staged a comeback at that moment; but he even failed to attend Lenin's funeral. He afterwards alleged that Stalin had misinformed him as to the date! Perhaps it is a point in his favor that Trotsky could sometimes be so curiously naïve in matters of political opportunity.

At the Eleventh Party Congress in 1922, Stalin succeeded Molotov as Secretary General, and between then and the Twelfth Party Congress in 1923 Stalin contrived to concentrate the real power in his own hands. His coadjutors in the process were Zinoviev and Kamenev, and their main strategy appears to have been to disperse possible rivals by appointing them to posts in remote districts. In 1925, with the support of Rykov and Bukharin, Stalin ousted Zinoviev and Kamenev, and then in 1929 he ousted Rykov and Bukharin. In the end, Stalin – and Kalinin – were the last survivors of the "Old Bolsheviks." Trotsky, in a long fight against the new despotism, was driven from one position after another. It was a marvel that he escaped with his life. He was expelled from the Politburo in 1926 and from the Party in 1927. In 1929 he was exiled from Russia. He lived in Turkey, in France, and in Mexico, nursing his wrath, writing his classic versions of the Russian Revolution, and continuing to evade the vengeance of his enemies – and of one enemy in particular. But his fate caught up with him at last. He was murdered in Mexico City on August 20, 1940.

The loss of Trotsky to Russia was a heavy moral one. He was at least an idealist, and ideals, even wrong ones, have a value. With Stalin, never overmuch possessed of such qualities, Russia reverted to "realism" and to a deepening isolation from the rest of the world. Yet the famous Trotsky-Stalin feud had something more fundamental in it than the antagonism of two men and two moralities. In the last analysis, the feud harked back to the old, old antithesis between East and West which has so often cleft the Russian character. Stalin, the essential party man, the untraveled, uncultured provincial, represented the East; Trotsky, the supreme individualist, the international Jew, the widely traveled master of foreign languages, represented the West. There could be no mean between men so diverse, and all Russia was the theater of their conflict.

Joseph Vissarionovich Dzhugashvily was born in 1879 of peasant stock in the small town of Gori near Tiflis in Georgia. His pious parents intended him for the priesthood, but he was expelled from his seminary at the age of nineteen and joined a local Social Democrat group. His career was then patterned after that of hundreds of other professional revolutionaries – agitation, intrigue, journalism, imprisonment, exile, escape. His physical constitution was above ordinary, and had need to be, for the life he led was never meant for weaklings. He changed his name several times, finally adopting the not unsuitable one of Stalin, from *stal* or "steel." In 1912 he was elected member of the Bolshevik Central Committee. He was already generally recognized to be a useful revolutionary handy man, an agent of commissions where tough nerves were wanted, although he seemed quite content to keep himself in the background. Lenin was afterwards to describe him as "too rude," but used him often enough. He spent the years of the First World War in exile in Siberia, but returned, as we have related, in 1917. He saw service in the Civil War; he fought against Kolchak,

Yudenich, and Pilsudski. His exploits at Tsaritsyn – though they have been much disputed – caused that city to be renamed Stalingrad after him.

Clearly Stalin had none of the intellectual finesse of men like Lenin or Trotsky, though, as his speeches and writings show, incondite and repetitive as they are, he had all the Communist's respect for theory. Trotsky once described him as "the outstanding mediocrity of the Party." Devoid of histrionic gifts, he early found his forte in the political machine, executing the ideas of others, without interest in original or creative thinking of his own. "Never a tribune, never a strategist or leader of rebellion, he has ever been only a bureaucrat of revolution." He had immense tenacity, an Asiatic patience, an infinite capacity for complicated intrigue, and a long, vindictive memory. But these very characteristics flourished best in concealment and obscurity. Stalin spoke in public and in committee only on rare occasions; otherwise he was of legendary reticence and, though living in a country of the most accomplished talkers in the world and at a time when talking was the highway to political advancement, he was always as blunt and as sparing of mere words as it was possible to be.

After 1922, and especially after 1924, he began to amass enormous personal power, but he still preferred the background. Public acclamation for him – though he came to receive a surfeit of it – seemed much more the part of a deliberate policy than a reward desired and striven for. By 1936 he had become the supreme autocrat. He spoke in public more often and gave frequent interviews to foreign visitors, but somehow contrived each time to convey the impression of a man emerging into unaccustomed publicity to give an ex-cathedra pronouncement on policy. Even now it is hard to say that Stalin was ever one *known* to his contemporaries, or to see in his early obscurity the qualities which afterward made him the taskmaster of the Five-Year Plans and Marshal of the Second World War.

The Five-Year Plans

Stalin's "Socialism in One Country" took shape in the Five-Year Plans. It was not all innovation. Historians have been at pains to point out that Peter the Great once projected a five-year plan and that Russia was already in process of accomplishing in 1914 much that Communism afterwards claimed to have done for her.[7] Under the later Tsars the canals, many of the railroads, the telegraphs, and certain banks were state enterprises bureaucratically managed. The state also owned great tracts of land, and vodka was a government monopoly. The winter of 1917-18 witnessed that hazardous experiment, the workers' control of the factories, an experiment that was followed by the drastic centralization of the Supreme Economic Council and then of War Communism. The first attempts at the collectivization of farms were made at this time. Then in 1920, in the midst of the Russo-Polish War, a special commission drew up plans for the electrification of the country, a vast scheme dear to the heart of Lenin himself. Communist literature was already being interlarded with those astronomical "control figures" (coordinated output targets), soon to become so familiar. Finally, in February 1921, the State Planning Commission (Gosplan) came into existence. The first of the Five-Year Plans was being publicly discussed in 1926 and was inaugurated on October 1, 1928. Simultaneously the NEP was officially discredited and revoked.

Communist doctrine had always dilated upon capitalism's "anarchy of production" and the inequalities of wealth that went therewith – the unpredictable business cycles, the recurrent and increasingly disastrous slumps, and all the evils of unemployment and poverty – and thence upon the need of devising some long-term policy sufficient to secure to the deserving inhabitants of the state the wherewithal of their physical and cultural sustenance. In a scientific era – and Communism was nothing if not scientific – the necessary reformation could be accomplished by scientific planning. In broad terms, accordingly, the Five-Year Plans had for their objectives: first, to transform a predominantly agrarian country into one of a greatly improved standard of living, possessing its own industries and capable of producing its own finished commodities from its own raw materials; second, to reorganize agriculture on the basis of the collective farm and thus to double or treble the productive capacity of the land; third, to reorganize the distributive system, to encourage the cooperatives as distributing agents, and to eliminate the middleman; fourth, to reorganize the transportation system; fifth, to create within the Soviet Union the technical and economic means for defense against foreign aggression; and sixth, to promote literacy and education.

All this was quite unexceptionable as far as it went. The backward Russian economy plainly cried out for modernization – even by drastic, autocratic methods. What dismayed outside observers was the frantic haste with which the great transformation was now to be rushed through. At the moment the rest of the world was entering upon the Locarno era; better times were in prospect. At least in Western bourgeois eyes there was no call to force the pace. But the Soviet Government did not always discern the signs in quite the same way. Communism had lately suffered world-wide reverses, and conservatism seemed never more strongly entrenched. The Ruhr crisis, for example, had installed the reactionary Stresemann in power, and the simultaneous Communist risings in Germany had all been suppressed. The Locarno Pact itself, hailed in the West as an instrument of peace, was received in Moscow with the greatest suspicion. Then, in 1928, the Soviet Union was pointedly not invited to sign the Pact of Paris – although arrangements were made for Soviet adhesion immediately afterwards. Meanwhile, on the other side of the world, Chiang Kai-shek had established an anti-Communist dictatorship in China. All in all, the Locarno era had brought the Soviet Union no lessening of traditional fears and recent alarms. (See pp. 125 and 338-39.)

In the event it was a minor domestic crisis in Russia which triggered off the so-called Second Revolution. There had lately been some complaint over the failure of the peasants to make the expected sales of their grain in the towns. The Soviet Government chose to interpret the default as a subversive affront, not to be tolerated, and magnified it into a general "wheat strike." Stalin resolved, not just on a reformatory collectivization of the farms, but on a nation-wide agrarian upheaval – and on an industrialization of corresponding scale and dispatch. It was as if the Russian Revolution, having safely survived the Civil War, had now to turn inward and spend itself in a sort of ferocious domestic debauch. Stalin himself, as observers have suggested, seemed to be driven by an irrational sixth sense, oblivious of the opposition he met and the suffering he caused. Like many another "man of destiny" he hardly knew what he was doing, but did it with blind demonic possession – and succeeded.

The Soviet Government had by now at its command a highly disciplined state and party machine and, let us not forget, a mass of younger men and women, educated in the Communist creed, growing up as a new class of intellectuals, all avid for responsibility. The Five-Year Plans were preeminently the work of the first post-Revolution generation of young technicians, largely recruited through the Party's youth organizations, such as the Komsomols. While their elders in the capital clawed each other for places in the hierarchy, these juniors in the Provinces, with ruthless disinterestedness and self-sacrifice, applied themselves to the tasks in hand. They made mistakes, they lived in a welter of chaos, but they did the job. Historians have never given sufficient credit to the anonymous rank-and-file of great movements.

When the exhilaration of enterprise faltered, there was always terror to fall back upon. Too many visitors to Russia at this time had described the extreme shortages of the barest necessities of life, even during the most productive years of the Plans – the midwinter bread lines, the overcrowded, underheated, dilapidated apartments, the patched and ragged clothes of all but the higher Party members. All this was sometimes admitted and publicly discussed. But the Soviet Government could not admit or discuss too much. If the target figures were not reached, if the machines were misused or overstrained, then the fault must be laid to "wreckers," or "foreign spies," or "imperialist agents," who must then be demonstratively uncovered and haled before the Soviet courts. Significantly most of the victims of the process were the older men.

Thus a series of deliberately staged sabotage trials was a necessary accompaniment of the Five-Year Plans. Visitors, bewildered and aghast, listened to these first performances of Communist "confessions." On one occasion in 1933 some British engineers working in Moscow were arrested and tried, and were released only under threats from London of a rupture of diplomatic relations and a British embargo on Russian trade. Soviet citizens were not so fortunate, and dozens of them disappeared into strange exiles in the outermost parts of the country. But somehow the trials fitted the collective mood of the Russian people and of their acknowledged Autocrat.

The Five-Year Plans were directed, as we have said, by a special government department, the State Planning Commission (Gosplan), a subcommittee of the Council of Commissars. This Commission superseded the Supreme Economic Council, although that body continued to exercise certain restricted functions till its abolition in 1932. The first Five-Year Plan for the Development of National Economy, to give its full name, inaugurated on October 1, 1928, was declared to have been completed under the time limit in December 1932. The second Five-Year Plan occupied the years from 1933 to 1937. The first Five-Year Plan was originally published in a three-volume text totaling some 1,600 pages, and the second in a two-volume text totaling over 1,300 pages. The volumes contained tables and statistics covering the entire national economy; machine-building, electric power, fuel, minerals, timber, chemicals, consumer goods, food industries, and cooperatives; agriculture, transportation, postal service, telegraph and telephone; labor, wages, standards of living, distribution and consumption; schools, literature, newspapers, housing, public health, and social insurance; and finance. Throughout, the emphasis was laid on "modes of production" and on the ultimate establishment of a classless Communist society. The text of the third Five-Year Plan was still in preparation when the Second World War broke out, although the Plan itself was officially inaugurated in 1938.

The material resources for the Plans presented no difficulty. They existed in abundance. The Soviet Union was 6,000 miles wide, east to west, at its greatest extent, and averaged 2,000 miles north to south. Its total area was 8,500,000 square miles, about the same area as the North American continent above Panama. Its mineral geology was rich and advantageously distributed. Upon such resources Soviet economic planning could erect industries that by the late 1930's were producing annually 130,000,000 tons of coal, 30,000,000 tons of oil, 15,000,000 tons of pig iron, 18,000,000 tons of steel, 350,000 tractors, 200,000 automobiles, and 40,000,000,000 kwh. of electricity.[8] The number of workers rose to 27,000,000. New industrial cities were laid out and built in virgin territory on a scale dwarfing even those of the boom days of the American West. The coal mines at Kuznetsk, the oil wells and refineries of the Caucasus and the Urals, the hydroelectric station of Dnepropetrovsk, the steel works at Magnitogorsk, the tractor factories at Chelyabinsk and Stalingrad, the airplane factories at Moscow, the Volga-Don Canal, the double-tracking of the Trans-Siberian Railway – all these, by any standard, represented stupendous achievements. It was not all planning for peace. We have said that one of the objectives of the Five-Year Plans was to create the means for defense, and the Red Army therefore was always a prior beneficiary of the country's productiveness. In 1935, when the European world was taking a renewed interest in armaments, foreign military experts were already speaking of the Red Army's 10,000 tanks, 150,000 tractors, 100,000 other transport vehicles, and probably 10,000 first-line planes. Foreign attachés, who attended the Red Army's maneuvers, came away with a healthy respect for its technical equipment and its technical personnel. The standing army probably numbered 1,500,000. All in all, the Soviet Union faced the Second World War as one of the greatest industrial and military powers.

Collectivization

Collectivization was the agricultural counterpart of industrialization. The one supported the other. In Tsarist Russia the average area of cultivated land per head of the agricultural population had amounted to three acres, often fragmented in the course of generations into multiple strips. The most primitive methods were still very general – plowing with the wooden plow, sowing by hand, reaping with the sickle, and threshing with the flail. The crop yield per acre was among the lowest in Europe. The amalgamation of all these scattered holdings into large collective farms (*kolkhozy*), each with skilled management and each with up-to-date mechanical equipment, had both an ideological and practical attractiveness. To make the peasant a sharecropper in a system of mass farming seemed to be the very quintessence of Communism. Moreover the peasant was a notoriously stubborn, intractable type, given to moods of passive resistance – as earlier regimes in Russia well knew. Collectivization would bring him under government controls and enable a proper supervision both of himself and his produce; this would be no small advantage in a centralized bureaucratic economy.

The Fifteenth Party Congress, in December 1927, adopted a resolution for collectivizing peasant farms, but on a voluntary basis. But then occurred the "wheat strike," which we mentioned above. The independent well-to-do peasants, or kulaks, under the NEP – so it was alleged – had grown arrogant with prosperity, and, crime of crimes, they had begun to show a class consciousness of their own. No Five-Year Plan could hope to succeed in the presence of such a danger. Collectivization must be enforced.

And enforced it was. By the outbreak of the Second World War, agriculture in the Soviet Union was 80 per cent collectivized; 15 per cent was operated by state farms (*sovkhozy*); perhaps a last 5 per cent remained as individual peasant holdings. But whether in fact the crop yields were appreciably increased would seem somewhat doubtful. Published statistics, massive though they were, do not suggest that the peasant's lot – or the lot of the townsman who bought his produce – had improved beyond the conditions of 1914. Then the bureaucracy often created its own confusion. In many districts draft animals were slaughtered wholesale because it was expected that the new tractors would take their place, but the tractors often enough did not come up to expectation either in quantity or quality. The countryside was littered with "cemeteries" of damaged, overworked, or otherwise defective machines. The Moscow planners nevertheless pushed through their programs and seemed to regard the human being as so much economic material. The death rate was part of the incidental and unregretted cost of an enterprise that must not be allowed to fail. The total casualties of collectivization have been estimated at 5,000,000.[9]

The Stalin Constitution

The Constitution of 1936 indicated a conscious need on the part of the Soviet Government periodically to define itself and take stock of its dynamic, developing estate. It was promulgated at a time inauspicious for new constitutions – the treason trials, which we shall describe later, were in progress – and it may therefore have been a demonstration of political solidarity at home. Abroad, Hitler had just brought off his Rhineland coup, the Italo-Ethiopian War had come to an end, and the Spanish Civil War had broken out. The constitution may also have been intended as a gesture towards the democratic West, whose friendship, in the newly breaking era of aggression, had become so suddenly and surprisingly desirable. (See pp. 431-32 and 454-55.)

In 1935 the Seventh All-Union Congress of Soviets had moved to revise the existing constitution (of 1924), and a Constitutional Commission was appointed under the chairmanship of Stalin. The Commission's draft was published in midsummer of 1936 and thrown open to public discussion, and we are given the impression that the Soviet Union for several months converted itself into a gigantic debating society upon the intricacies of the new *Lex Communista*. The 154,000 amendments voted and forwarded to Moscow by hundreds of local soviets do not appear to have exerted much influence on the Constitutional Commission, but there can be no question of the vitality of the discussions or of the education in political consciousness which they provided. The Eighth All-Union Congress of Soviets met in December 1936, amid the greatest enthusiasm, to vote with routine unanimity each of the 146 articles of the "Stalin Constitution."

The text of the constitution must rank high in the political philosophy of our time. But in the practical working of it we fail to discover that the essentials of Soviet rule were greatly changed. The personal directorship of Stalin remained; the omnipresence and the omnipotence of the Communist party and the Ogpu remained. The subsequent elections to the new Supreme Soviet yielded results conformable to the wishes of the Kremlin.

The constitution described the Soviet Union, the Union of Soviet Socialist Republics (U.S.S.R.), as "a Socialist state of workers and peasants," and invested the wealth of the land in the people. It named eleven constituent republics, the R.S.F.S.R., the Ukraine, White Russia (Byelorussia), Azerbaijan, Georgia, Armenia, Turkmen, Uzbek, Tajik, Kazak, and Kirghiz, all enjoying "equality of rights," even to the right of succession. In place of the old Central Executive Committee now appeared the Supreme Soviet, "the highest organ of state power," but composed as before of two chambers, the Soviet of the Union and the Soviet of Nationalities. The Soviet of the Union was to be elected directly on the basis of one Deputy for every 300,000 of the population, and the former cumbersome system of pyramidal election was abolished. The franchise was widened to include every citizen who had reached the age of eighteen, irrespective of sex, race, nationality, religion, education, residence, social origin, property status, or "past activity." Elections were to be conducted by secret ballot. The Presidium, a collective presidency of the Union, and the Council of People's Commissars (*Sovnarkom*) remained much as before. The Communist party was mentioned by name and thus given formal constitutional recognition for the first time.

13. ITALY: THE RISE AND ESTABLISHMENT OF FASCISM

The Decline of Italian Democracy

Postwar Italy was in the curious mental condition of a victor with a strong sense of defeat. The Italian Government under Antonio Salandra in 1915 had originally brought the country into the war, not so much out of necessity, but after protracted, almost sordid, negotiations with both belligerents. Throughout the war Italy had to contend with powerful groups who had not wanted the war and did not believe in it. To keep up the fighting spirit of the Italian people, and especially the fighting spirit of the forces at the front, wartime propaganda had been overlavish, and promises had been made which no mortal victory could have fulfilled. The returned soldier, having made his sacrifice, felt cheated of his deserts, and, to make matters worse, he became the butt of a despicable campaign at the hands of the stay-at-home Socialist on the general theme of "I told you so!" Instead of the prodigal banquet of peace and glory that he had been led to expect a grateful homeland would spread out before him, he found an ashen feast of riots, strikes, lockouts, and unemployment.

Italy was at best a halfhearted and inexperienced democratic state. In 1919 she had had only two generations of free institutions, and behind those generations her history stretched back through centuries of servitude and factional strife. Manhood suffrage had been granted only in 1912, and the election of 1913 was the first in which it had been exercised. The poverty of the average Italian worker left him with little time or inclination for interests outside the harsh necessities of his day-to-day existence. What politics he had were sharply attached to local jealousies. Meanwhile the parliament at Rome had long since become the seedbed of corruption. The multi-party system, as it had grown up in the 1860's and 1870's, in direct reflection of the fierce parochialism of the country, had lent itself, as multi-party systems invariably do, to intrigue and trickery. Italian politics had become tied to party machines under a series of party "bosses," who manipulated short-lived coalition blocs. In the election of November 1919, two popular parties rose sharply into prominence, both outside the old party machines – the Clerical party (*Popolari*) and the Socialists – and it was to a great extent the fear of these parties, representing the enfranchised masses, that turned the propertied classes against the entire democratic experiment. Much to the surprise of foreigners, who thought of Italy in terms of the liberal tradition of Cavour, the extension of the vote was in part responsible, if indirectly, for the eventual parliamentary breakdown.

The state of foreign politics was not much happier. Even Italians of insufficient education to appreciate the intricacies of world affairs had sensed the seeming anti-Italian bias of the Peace Conference at Paris, and they had been quick to take affront at the national humiliation that President Wilson seemed to be preparing there. The war was not the first one in which modern Italy had poured out her blood and treasure only to be contemptuously thrust aside by her allies when it was all over. President Wilson made his state visit to Rome early in January 1919; he was tumultuously entertained; he spoke in the Italian Chamber; he was received by the King and the Pope; and then, in return for all the homage and panegyric, he addressed his famous appeal from Paris to the Italian people and presumed to lecture them upon the wickedness of their dearest aspirations. The Peace Conference, instead of giving peace to Italy, only roused her to a frenzy of frustration and injured pride. All in all, the anticlimax of the army's homecoming, the parliamentary turmoil, the reactionism of the propertied classes, and now the supreme mortification at Paris combined to produce in Italy a very dangerous situation. (See p. 104.)

Fiume, the subject of President Wilson's moralizing strictures, became the test case and symbol of the whole postwar mood. Since November 1918, an Allied administration had been set up in the port, and a small Allied force was quartered there. In July 1919, the crisis over its affairs at the Peace Conference resulted in rioting in the town between bands of young Italian Fiumiani and local Croat inhabitants. Croat property was wrecked, and some French and Italian soldiers of the Allied force were killed. August was a calmer month. But on September 12, 1919, the Italian poet and aviator, Gabriele D'Annunzio, at the head of a corps of "legionaries," marched into Fiume and claimed possession of it in the name of Italy. The Allied force retired without fighting and attempted to form a cordon around the district.

D'Annunzio set up his own government in Fiume. He adopted the motto "*Me ne frego* (I don't give a damn)." He was joined by many hundreds of sympathizers. He had some twenty planes and a number of ships, and on one occasion he even captured an Italian destroyer. He sent a "delegate" to the Peace Conference, a gentleman who also opened a "legation" in Paris. There were daily parades and trooping of banners, edicts and ultimatums, and torrents of impassioned oratory. It was all a crazy, unreal sort of Ruritanian comic opera.

The Italian Government, of course, disavowed the coup, but took no immediate action. The Italian press was in ecstasies. Certainly the coup was audacious and spectacular, and there was about it just enough of sporting defiance of authority, just enough of dangerous living, to appeal to popular sentiment. Various solutions and compromises were proposed in Paris, only to be rejected by one or another of the parties concerned, and a settlement was not reached till November 1920, when the Treaty of Rapallo was negotiated between the Italian and Yugoslav governments. Even then D'Annunzio clung desperately to his conquest, and regular Italian troops had to be sent to eject him. In all, the poet maintained himself and his legionaries in Fiume for fifteen months.

Vittorio Orlando, Italian Premier since the Battle of Caporetto, resigned in June 1919, shortly after his withdrawal from the Peace Conference. His successor was Francesco Nitti, a man of liberal pacifist views, at the head of a moderate rightist coalition. During Nitti's term of office the elections of November 1919 took place and also the first serious postwar labor crisis. In that summer metalworkers in a factory at Dalmine near Bergamo hit upon the idea of "camping" in the factory. The idea seemed good, and in the ensuing months it spread through northern Italy. Sometimes the former clerks and foremen, who were indispensable to the running of the plant, were compelled to remain at work in the service of their new Socialist masters. Meanwhile the disturbances began to spill over into the open streets. Strikes led to rioting, looting, and bloodshed. There were several fatal bomb-throwing incidents. In the country the peasants attempted to seize the big private estates, killed or drove off the livestock, and set fire to the crops. Magistrates were afraid to give sentences for such "political" crimes. Bands of young men in colored shirts – blue shirts, gray shirts, and red shirts, each color representing some ardent political faction, but among whom Benito Mussolini's black-shirted Fascists seemed to be the best organized and most determined – terrorized the populace and wreaked vengeance on each other.

The government in Rome continued to decline in popular respect. Cabinets existed on a heterogeneity of supporters drawn from as many parties as possible. "Scenes" in the Chamber were frequent and exhausting. In June 1920, Giolitti, the old political manipulator, was prevailed upon to form a Cabinet and, by using all the methods that had already brought so much discredit on the Italian parliamentary system, he maintained himself in office for a full year. It was Giolitti who decided not to interfere in the factories, but instead to leave the "campers" in possession so that they might discover their own incompetence and exhaust themselves in sheer boredom – a successful strategy, as it often proved, but characteristically Giolittian and profoundly harmful to law and order. It was Giolitti also who decided to make no further resistance to the irregular warfare that had broken out in Italy's "Protectorate" across the Adriatic in Albania, to withdraw all Italian garrisons, and thereby to abdicate Italian influence in the Balkans. And it was Giolitti too whose Foreign Minister, Count Sforza, signed the "disgraceful" Treaty of Rapallo with Yugoslavia in November 1920, recognizing "the full liberty and independence" of the Free State of Fiume and surrendering to Yugoslavia the whole of the Dalmatian coast. The affairs of Italy, in the eyes of all patriotic Italians, could hardly have sunk lower.

Elections were held in May 1921, without much excitement, yet they

Mussolini and his Blackshirts: a Party occasion of 1930

WIDE WORLD

resulted in a landslide gain of 35 seats for the new Fascist movement. Giolitti resigned, to be followed by Ivanoe Bonomi, the Socialist, and then by Luigi Facta, a gentle, well-esteemed, but quite incapable old parliamentarian of the Giolittian school. In October 1922, the government was overthrown by Fascism.

The Rise and Establishment of Fascism

The Fascists, who in 1922 promised to bring order to Italy, in their own early days had not been easily distinguishable from the revolutionaries they so despised, and Mussolini and his Blackshirts had reveled in the melee of 1919 and 1920 as merrily as any wild extremist in it. In his tempestuous youth, before the First World War, the future Duce of Fascism had himself been an adherent of violent revolution and, though no serious political crimes had been successfully charged against him, his first flights in journalism had all been most laudatory of the anarchist bombings and assassinations of that time. After the war in 1919, his own paper, *Il Popolo d'Italia,* had always supported the strikes and seizures of the factories. Yet he marched to power in 1922 to a great extent by exploiting the antirevolutionary and anti-Bolshevik phobia that was then gripping all conservative Italians.

Mussolini's first *Fascio di Combattimento* was founded on March 23, 1919, at Milan, a brave nucleus of pioneers and missionaries, perhaps some hundred strong, mostly intellectuals and former soldiers. Its name was taken from the old fasces of the ancient Roman lictors, the symbol of unity and authority.[1] Similar Fasci were soon being formed in cities all over Italy. In every case their organization and doctrine were confused and frankly opportunist, but generally these early Fascists were antimonarchist, anticlerical, mainly antisocialist, and of course, vehemently anti-Communist. But they stood for certain tenets of socialist flavor such as proportional representation and a capital levy, and they adopted some syndicalist theories. They asserted that aggressive nationalism which D'Annunzio had lately illustrated so sensationally at Fiume. Finally, at a time when criticism of Italy's war effort was widespread, they preached that the recent war had been a good thing, that it had shown the nobility of the Italian soul, and that the country must return to the spirit inspired by it. Mussolini's eloquent glorification of war, addressed to a people humiliated by "defeat" – like Hitler's after him – was not the least of the causes of his rapid rise to popularity.

Fascism put forward two candidates at the elections in November 1919, Mussolini being one, but neither was successful. It put forward candidates at the elections in May 1921, Mussolini again being one, and 35 were successful. In those eighteen months the movement had waxed and thrived, it had grown into a national force of the first importance, but it had gradually lost its pure and pristine character. In May 1921 it probably counted 250,000 members, recruited largely from the "white youth" as they were called. Like Nazism after it, it was primarily a lower middle-class phenomenon. It incorporated D'Annunzio's legionnaries. It also incorporated various nationalists, liberals, conservatives, property owners, landlords, manufacturers; all of them, out of their genuine patriotism or for the better security of their worldly goods, put their high hopes in the movement. Its squadrists, garbed always in their black shirts, armed with cudgels and sometimes with more dangerous weapons, held their daily processions and fought their daily battles with the "Reds." They administered generous doses of castor oil. In their more outraged and primitive moods, they did not shrink from arson and murder. In November 1921, at its National Congress in Rome, Fascism reconstituted itself as a regular political party, the *Partito Nazionale Fascista*.

Fascism became more and more rightist in complexion, and it certainly derived the major part of its funds at this time from rightist sources. The idealistic, stoical, impecunious "Fascists of the first hour" evolved by sure, if imperceptible, stages into an army of fanatical squirearchs. It was indeed an odd concatenation of circumstances, material and moral, that converted that rabid Socialist, the Benito Mussolini of 1914 and 1919, into the antisocialist, antidemocratic Duce of 1922.

The last year before the assumption of power was a period of veritable civil war. Encouraged by their growing popularity and flushed with the assurance of triumph, the Blackshirts paraded and fought at will. They answered provocation with provocation; they visited reprisals with reprisals; they wrecked workingmen's clubs and cooperatives; they raided houses in working-class districts; they purged town offices of their Socialist mayors and Socialist officials. A general strike in August 1922, organized by the so-called Alliance of Labor, was the last serious challenge offered them. They were now an army of 300,000 men. They seized newspaper offices and strikers' headquarters; they broke up strikers' processions and meetings; for some days they ran the public services. The general strike collapsed miserably.

In September and October 1922, it was an open secret that Fascism was planning a supreme coup. Mussolini prepared the way by reconciling himself to the monarchy and the Church. He declared Fascism's unswerving loyalty to King Victor Emmanuel, and he assured the Vatican that, in the event of violence, Fascism would respect churches and church property everywhere. He relied on the regular army to preserve a benevolent neutrality. The police and the *Guardia Regia*,[2] he knew, would take the same attitude as the regular army. He held a meeting at Naples on October 24 to discuss a final plan of action. To direct the execution of the plan, he appointed a military "Quadrumvirate" composed of four prominent comrades in the cause — Michele Bianchi, Fascist Secretary; Italo Balbo, commander of the Blackshirts; Count Cesare De Vecchi, leader of the Fascist group in the Chamber; and General Emilio De Bono. He appointed Dino Grandi, then best known as the Fascist labor expert, as political chief of staff to the enterprise.

On October 27, 1922, the order for the mobilization of the Blackshirts went out, and the March on Rome began. Facta, the Premier, would probably have proclaimed martial law, but the King hesitated to sign the order. Mussolini himself did not lead, nor even accompany, the great March; he repaired rather unheroically to Milan, while Grandi and De Vecchi acted for him in Rome, in the capacity of a diplomatic mission, and persuaded the King to make him Premier. October 30 was a day of wild celebration in Rome. Fifty thousand Blackshirts demonstrated for hours. Mussolini arrived to receive his appointment at the hands of the King. "I bring Your Majesty," he said, "the Italy of Vittorio Veneto reconstructed by a new victory." He then addressed his Blackshirts from the Tomb of the Unknown Soldier in the National Monument, lauded their revolution, and pledged himself to a strong government at home and a strong foreign policy abroad.

Mussolini's first act in power was to dismiss his Blackshirts to their homes. It was a statesmanlike move; it prevented the demonstrations from degenerating into uncontrolled and needless violence; and it was an effective test of that discipline on which Mussolini had always insisted. Rome was evacuated by her invaders within twenty-four hours, and all over Italy Fascist concentrations were demobilized. The Fascist triumph, as it turned out, was orderly, bloodless, and decisive.

Mussolini did not at once disdain to use the usual machinery of parliamentary government. On the contrary, he now formed a "Ministry of Collaboration," composed, surprisingly, of only three Fascists and of nine members of other parties. In addition to the premiership, he himself took the portfolios of foreign and home affairs. On November 16, 1922, he addressed the Chamber – a Chamber in which only 6 per cent were Fascist Deputies:

> To the melancholy zealots of superconstitutionalism, I leave the task of making their more or less pitiful lamentations on recent events. I maintain that revolution has its rights. I add, in order that all may know it, that I am here to defend and enforce in the highest degree the revolution of the Black Shirts, injecting them intimately into the history of the nation as a force of development, progress, and equilibrium. I refused to overdo the victory, though I could have done so. . . . With 300,000 youths, fully armed, fully determined, and almost mystically ready to act at my command, I could have chastised all those who have defamed and tried to injure Fascism. I could have made of this sordid, gray assembly hall a bivouac for Squadrists, I could have kicked out parliament and constructed a government exclusively of Fascists. I could have done so, but I did not want to, at least not for the present.

On the next day, Mussolini laid the same arguments before the Senate, though this time in more respectful language. Eight days later the Chamber meekly voted a measure conferring upon him "full powers" for a year.

Fascist Foreign Politics

Mussolini had not long to wait to give the world an example of a "strong" foreign policy. On August 27, 1923, an Italian general and some aides who were engaged as representatives of the Conference of Ambassadors in demarcating the Greco-Albanian frontier were murdered near Ioannina on Greek soil. Mussolini at once instructed his minister at Athens to deliver to the Greek Government a note demanding an apology for the crime, a solemn funeral with military honors for the victims, an inquiry "with the assistance of the Italian military attaché," death sentences for the culprits, and an indemnity of 50,000,000 lire. The Greek Government agreed to the apology, the funeral, and the military honors, but rejected the other terms as "violating the sovereignty of the state." Thereupon an Italian naval squadron appeared off the Greek island of Corfu, bombarded its unarmed and obsolete citadel, killed fifteen Greek and Armenian refugees who had been quartered there, and landed a small occupying force.

The Greek Government appealed to the League of Nations, and at the same time declared its willingness to abide by any decision that might be reached in the matter by the Conference of Ambassadors. Public opinion, especially in the smaller nations of the League, was deeply outraged by the brutal and cowardly action of the Italian Navy, and it was clear that the League was face to face with a test case which it could not afford to handle weakly. The Fourth Assembly of the League met two days after the incident and at once became a forum of bitter denunciation of Italy. The Italian member on the League Council, who happened to be Salandra, the former Premier, in prophetic anticipation of Italy's attitude in another and greater crisis twelve years afterward (see p. 405), maintained throughout the discussions that the League was not competent to deal with the case. Mussolini threatened to resign League membership.

The League Council drew up a plan of settlement which it forwarded to the Conference of Ambassadors, and on that plan the dispute was eventually settled. Italy was awarded the total 50,000,000 lire she had originally demanded. The occupying force in Corfu was withdrawn. The smoke of wrath and rancor died away, but it was difficult to establish whether the League had won its first unqualified success or whether the Italian upstart had suffered his first decisive defeat. The Corfu incident served to awaken the postwar world to the presence of a new aggression in its midst and was an unhappy evidence of the fact that the spirit which had dictated the ultimatum to Serbia in 1914 was not yet destroyed.

From 1923 till 1934, when the Ethiopian crisis occurred, Mussolini committed no further overt breaches of the peace. But from time to time he fished for trouble wherever he could find it. He supported Fascistlike movements in other countries, notably in Spain, Austria, Hungary, and Germany. He picked in particular on France as Italy's chief rival in the Mediterranean. He championed the "revisionist" powers, which like Italy resented the Versailles settlement — one of these again being Hungary — and he thereby challenged the Little Entente and the French alliance system in Europe. In April 1927, Italy and Hungary entered into a treaty of amity and arbitration. In the 1930's Mussolini's demands for naval parity with France all but wrecked the naval disarmament conference. But these are events and episodes which are discussed on other pages. (See pp. 169-70 and 299-301.)

Fascist Domestic Politics

At home, Mussolini's first objects were to consolidate his power and to justify his many promises to the Italian people. He purged the public departments and offices, the police, the prefectures, and the municipalities of their surviving Socialist and Communist members, and substituted personnel of proven Fascist virtue. Stringent press regulations gave his government the right to suppress without appeal any extremist or anti-Fascist literature. A Fascist Militia was formed, in part for the purpose of reorganizing the old squads of Blackshirts, many of whom, in their original hasty and provisional recruitment, contained "unreliable elements," and in part in order that future squadrist activities might be carried out under the cloak of legality.

With the assistance of Alberto De Stefani, his very able Finance Minister, Mussolini made a vigorous attack on the economic distresses of the country. He cut expenditures in public departments and on the railroads, revised war pensions, abolished a vast accretion of official bonuses and perquisites, and levied the income tax on much wider income groups. At the same time he reduced legacy duties and certain taxes on real estate, thereby helping Italian family life. He caused several state concerns, such as the telephones, to be transferred to private companies, partly to save the endless government subsidies and partly in the hope that they might be more efficiently managed. Above all, social disturbances, strikes, and lockouts, which had been so constant a drain in the old days, were suppressed without mercy. It may have been the success of these drastic measures, or it may have been that Fascism's early years of power coincided with the general trade recovery of the Mediterranean countries; but Italian finances incontestably improved. The budget of 1921-22 showed a deficit of 17,000,000,000 lire; the budget of 1924-25 showed a surplus of 200,000,000 lire.

Mussolini's domestic policies also included the planning of public works, not only to stimulate employment, but to erect appropriate monuments to the glory of the Fascist regime. Mussolini's first interest, like that of all great autocrats, was architecture, and, in the course of the next few years, Italian cities were adorned with great blocks of offices, workers' tenements, stadiums, and other ceremonial buildings. Entirely new industrial townships were laid out. Marsh lands were drained and turned over to cultivation. New concrete highways, the famous *autostrade,* were constructed across the country.

Mussolini's parliamentary record was not so successful. Despite his undisguised contempt for the Chamber, he did at first make a sincere effort to work with and through it. But the Chamber, like the proverbial leopard, could not change its spots. The parties of the Ministry of Collaboration were anything but collaborative. Mussolini clearly was in no position to proceed with his program for the rejuvenation of Italy while a spiteful Opposition obstructed his every move. During 1923 a new electoral bill was introduced proposing that whatever party secured the plurality of votes in any election should automatically receive two-thirds of the seats in the Chamber. The old Chamber, Mussolini declared in so many words, was a nuisance and an anachronism, and he demanded, in effect, that it dissolve itself. And dissolve itself, after long and arduous debate, it did. The new electoral law was passed in July 1923.

Elections under the new law were held in April 1924. Mussolini was determined that Fascism should win a decisive victory. It is perhaps proof of the bankruptcy of the parliamentary system in Italy that, at this supremely critical moment, over twenty different parties appeared in various degrees of opposition to Fascism and to one another. Mussolini's "national list" won handsomely with 4,700,000 votes to the Opposition parties' 2,250,000. It would probably have won handsomely, even without the corruption and intimidation that were afterward alleged. But this rebuff still did not silence the Opposition. In the new Chamber the two Socialists, Giovanni Amendola and Giacomo Matteotti, were particularly fractious, and remained quite unconvinced when Mussolini patiently, but sternly, explained to them the true functions of a Fascist parliament. Then on the afternoon of June 10, 1924, Matteotti was kidnapped and killed.

Matteotti's was not the first of Fascism's murders. But he was an important Opposition leader, well respected and beloved, and usually Fascism had spilled the blood of lesser men. It was not then known, of course, to what extent the crime was "authorized," but Fascism was almost driven from its newly won power by the outburst of indignation which swept the country. Revelations made since 1943 have clearly implicated Mussolini himself. As it was, at the time, he had to face the full force of public suspicion. He stood contritely in the Chamber and swore to punish the guilty persons whoever they might be. "Only some enemy of mine," he said, "lying awake at night plotting something devilish against me, could have thought out this crime."

"Balcony Technique": Il Duce speaks

KEYSTONE

In later years he took the view that the case was "a practical joke which degenerated into a horrible tragedy against the will of its authors." He reformed his cabinet, and he dismissed General De Bono, who since the March on Rome had been Chief of Police. But he refused to touch his Fascist Militia or to call for new elections. Several members of the Opposition, after the manner of the ancient Roman plebs, withdrew in protest to the Aventine,[3] where, under the unofficial leadership of Amendola, they established headquarters and waged a bitter, wordy campaign against the Fascist government.

As seems always to happen in the history of revolutions, a reign of terror succeeded to an earlier reign of moderation. It was evident that many of the Aventine Opposition were motivated less by a genuine horror of the Matteotti crime than by a desire to make political capital out of it and, as soon as their diatribes showed signs of weakening, Mussolini decided on final repressive measures. He appointed to the post of Secretary of the Fascist party Roberto Farinacci, an uncompromising veteran of the movement, and the old campaign of bludgeon and castor oil was resumed with a new ferocity. A mass of legislation was passed during 1925 in general furtherance of the program, "all in the State, nothing outside the State, nothing against the State." Non-Fascist members of the Cabinet were dismissed. The old political parties were disbanded. The bureaucracy and local government throughout the country were "Fascistized." The censorship of the press was tightened, and only those journalists were allowed to exercise their profession who belonged to an authorized register. In 1926 under a Defense of the State Act, a special tribunal was set up which was a sort of court-martial, operating by means of secret denunciation, arrest, and custody without hearing, and a more or less secret trial; and appropriately enough the tribunal's magistrates were high officers of the army or the Fascist Militia, often directly appointed by the Duce himself. Finally there was organized that necessary appanage of all dictatorships, a secret police, the OVRA (*Organizzazione Vigilanza Reati Anti-Fascisti*).

Italy took on the aspect of a one-party totalitarian state. The Chamber became a mere rostrum for Fascist rhetoric, and its business was reduced more and more to the acclamatory approval of Fascist bills. In the words of

Mussolini, the Chamber was at last a legislative assembly which "really functioned." In January 1926, when a few straggling survivors from the Aventine Opposition tried to resume their seats in the Chamber, they were refused admittance. The Senate, be it said in parenthesis, behaved throughout the reformatory process in a most exemplary manner. It voted overwhelmingly Fascist on all occasions and basked happily and securely in the favors of the Duce. The King became a Merovingian cipher.

In March 1926, the Matteotti trial was held at last in the remote township of Chieti. Of those originally accused of the crime a number had escaped or were absolved, and only five remained to face a reduced charge of manslaughter. Two of the five were found not guilty; three were condemned to imprisonment, but were released after two months under an amnesty conveniently granted by the King in celebration of the twenty-fifth anniversary of his reign. Farinacci himself, the Party Secretary, acted as advocate for the principal defendant.

Amendola, Matteotti's colleague, himself repeatedly injured in squadrist affrays, died a few days after the trial.

Mussolini and the Fascist Party

Benito Mussolini's personality was a microcosm of Fascism. His combativeness, his opportunism, his showmanship, his vindictiveness – to say nothing of his physical appearance, the jerky, aggressive gait, the black, flashing eyes, and the jutting jaw – typified his cause and his party. "Not for nothing have I chosen for my motto in life 'Live dangerously,'" he declared, "and I say to you, like the old warrior, 'If I advance, follow me; if I retreat, kill me; if I die, avenge me!'" "Better a day like a lion than a hundred years like a sheep." "I am a cynic," he said again, "insensible to everything except adventure – mad adventure." These were characteristic utterances.

The facts of Mussolini's career are well known and quickly told. He was born in 1883. As a boy he suffered all the slings and arrows of the underprivileged. His father was a blacksmith and a Socialist in a Romagnese village where dreary, unrelieved want was the rule of life. He was cuffed and bullied and beaten. He got into barroom brawls and back-street stabbings. Only the greatest courage, perseverence, and hard work – and perhaps the influence of a devoted mother – could have raised him out of his environment and earned him his first success, a teacher's diploma.

He fled to Switzerland to escape military service, which at the time he professed to abhor. He supported himself, when he could, as a stonemason and a teacher. He attended lectures at the universities of Lausanne and Geneva. He was very much the center of that restaurant socialism which flourished in the Swiss border towns at the turn of the century. But his views were violent and subversive, and he was expelled from one canton after another. Once he was jailed for vagabondage. In 1905 he returned to Italy and to his military service. He already had some following as an agitator, a journalist, and a fomenter of strikes. In 1912 he became editor of the Socialist paper *Avanti!*

In August 1914, he was still violently pacifist. But in September 1914 he experienced "a miracle of conversion" – or perhaps, as has been creditably hinted, he was bought by French funds; – he acquired his own newspaper, *Il Popolo d'Italia,* and became violently pro-Ally and interventionist. In September 1915, he was called to the colors and saw some weeks of active service in the trenches. In February 1917, while at a training camp, he was wounded by the bursting of a mortar. He was invalided out of the army and went back to his *Popolo d'Italia.* Thence followed the turbulent years, the years of mad adventure, the strikes and lockouts, the seizures of the factories, the founding of the first Fascio, the party squabbles, the squadrism, the civil war of 1921-22, and the final meteoric rise to power.

Mussolini the Duce was perhaps not very different from Mussolini the journalist, the soldier, and the Blackshirt. But responsibility made room for the display of his more substantial capacities. The first impression he always gave was one of overpowering vitality. He is said to have worked sixteen hours a day and to have given eight thousand audiences in a single year. At one time he held the portfolios of eight state departments. Yet his many administrative duties never seemed to reduce the frequency of his public appearances, his speechmaking, or his attendance at meetings of Grand Council, Cabinet, or Chamber. His intellectual interests were wide and varied. He kept himself well informed and read voraciously. As one writer put it, no statesman since Gladstone was so concentratedly studious. His habits were frugal and abstemious. He made a cult of athletics. He had rare personal fascination, an intuitive judgment of men, and a demagogic genius of the first order. And yet, for all his many qualities, it is hard to think of another man of his time who before his career was run succeeded in making himself so contemptible.

The Fascist party in 1922 was said to have numbered 300,000, and in 1934 over 1,500,000. It was organized into some 9,500 local Fasci which then pyramided upward, through the provincial federations, to a National Party Directorate, administered by that exalted official – after the Duce perhaps the most powerful man in Fascist Italy – the Secretary of the Party. The Fascist Grand Council of some twenty members, the Duce's own privy council, crowned the edifice, and was to all intents and purposes the real governing body of Italy.

The Fascist Militia or, to give it its full name, the Voluntary Militia for National Security, was the legalized form which the more reliable elements of the old squadrists were given in 1923. Its members used to regard themselves as the elite of the party, but in course of time they lost a good deal of their original function and importance. Like the SA in Nazi Germany, they were the front fighters in the early days of the movement, but it was afterward hard to find other than a ceremonial use for them, and their internal struggles are often reminiscent of the struggles of Roehm with the Nazi party and the *Reichswehr.* But they were privileged to count as an army reserve, they were subject to the army's code of discipline, and they were always regarded as standing ready for immediate mobilization in moments of national emergency. The youth organizations, always so important to the Fascist movement, were progressively graded according to age group –

for boys, the *Balilla,* the *Avanguardia,* and the *Giovani Fascisti;* and for girls, the *Piccole Italiane* and the *Giovani Italiane* — all devoted to Fascist "education," sports, and ceremonies.

During the later 1920's and early 1930's, labor laws, notably the Labor Charter of 1927, entirely reconstituted the labor syndicates, trade unions, and other occupational associations that characterized the labor movement in Italy. The laws were extended to include, not only labor, but all trades and professions, employers and employees alike. At the same time "After Work" organizations (*"Dopolavoro"*), were formed to provide social and cultural facilities for workers and their families. Eventually, in 1939, the whole structure was completed by the creation of a Corporative Chamber, which then superseded the former Chamber of Deputies. The Senate however, be it noted, remained the upper legislative body with its powers and dignities theoretically unaltered.

The so-called Corporative State, which resulted, was regarded by Mussolini as Fascism's greatest contribution to political science. Under ordinary democratic usages the deputies, elected to a legislature, represent geographical "constituencies" and organize themselves into "parties." The new Corporative Chamber was composed of deputies representing trades and professions; it was in fact a sort of grandiose Trades Union Congress embodying the whole industrial life of the nation. To unsympathetic observers the Corporative State was an ingenious, high-sounding contrivance which gave the dictatorship absolute powers over industry, while seeming to respect the rights of both capital and labor, and allowing Fascism to describe itself as a benevolent, classless, non-party political system. But undeniably there were interesting features in it. Corporative ideas were creeping into other contemporary constitutions, and, but for the outbreak of the Second World War, the Italian experiment might have had a chance to work out an institution of more permanent value.

Fascist Ideology

On the superficial view, Fascism was indebted to certain literary and intellectual sources. Its leaders, like the leaders of the American and French revolutions, were strongly and consciously influenced by the political speculation of their day. The Duce, once a schoolmaster, had belonged to the intelligentsia, and, especially during his Swiss period, he lived on the fringes of the academic world. In an arduous self-education, Machiavelli, Nietzsche, Sorel, Pareto and, to a less extent, Schopenhauer, Hegel, Blanqui, William James, Bergson, and even Marx all made traceable contributions to that scholastic complex that was Mussolini's mind. The Fascist movement subsequently produced its own philosophers, like Giovanni Gentile and Alfredo Rocco, who composed their evangels and drew upon political prophets from Plato onward to authenticate and dignify their faith. There was a side to Fascism that had a decidedly intellectual and doctrinaire flavor.

At the same time Fascism was indebted less consciously to various contemporary influences. Its founder might indeed pick and choose the articles of his creed as best suited him, but he was also guided in his choice by an environment which was none of his devising. His very lack of principles made him more susceptible to the ideas which he found around him. Fascism, in fact, was a mass of "historical residues." It existed in an age of progress in science and material welfare, of romanticism in art and literature, of pragmatism in philosophy, of nationalism in politics, of doubt and indifference in religion; and every one of these things was observable in it. Its materialism, its irrationalism, its pseudo-mysticism are plain and evident to any student of the history of contemporary "isms."

A favorite Fascist myth was Imperial Rome. It had the greatest theatrical and propagandist possibilities. It had a grand emblematic heraldry, easy to revive; it had at hand in Italy the ancient classic monuments, themselves relics of an architecture not altogether alien to the Fascist spirit; it provided the Head of the State with the title of Caesar himself, the most coveted title in the history of Europe. It was both nationalist and totalitarian. It was lavish and obvious, and it appealed to the festive, carnival gifts which the Italian people had always possessed so abundantly. Said Mussolini on one occasion:

> We dream of a Roman Italy, wise and strong, disciplined and imperial. The immortal spirit of Rome resurges in Fascism. Roman are the lictor's rods; Roman our fighting organization; Roman our pride and our courage; *Civis romanus sum*.[4]

Yet there is surely another, less superficial view of Fascism — a view not reducible to literary sources. Fascism, if anything, invested itself with literary dignity after, and not before, it became a driving force in the world. It created its own dynamic first, and then borrowed its scholastic plumes as expediency seemed to direct. It borrowed not to enrich a creed or system, but to mobilize practical support for practical needs. Indeed, to look for a logical doctrinal basis in Fascism is to misunderstand it entirely. Such programs and slogans and constitutional enactments as it put forward from time to time were always makeshift and strategic. The Fascists themselves constantly vaunted their "realism." They disdained abstractions and principles. They expressed the faith that was in them by works. "I never think," exclaimed the young Fascist; "therefore I am!"

As he avowed, when he founded his first Fascio in 1919, Mussolini had "no specific doctrinal plan." He was always an extemporizer. "He had none of the scruples of those who, being convinced of an idea, fear to be false to it. He passed from theory to theory, from position to position, rapidly and inconsistently, without remorse or regret." Mussolini always had an advantage over other political leaders who had to be coherent and preserve a stated policy. In his rise to power he offered every party what it wanted and convinced each of his sincerity. Worker and magnate, peasant and landowner, layman and priest, commoner and king, at one time or another were all cajoled by his promises.

But a philosophy consistent only in inconsistency is no philosophy. The significance of Fascism for our generation lies not in its special dictatorial, or even in its aggressive, features. Other regimes have been dictatorial and aggressive, and have not been Fascist. The significance of Fascism lies in its profound spiritual negativity. Like Nazism after it, Fascism expended a terrific energy, but expended it for essentially destructive ends. So interpreted, the texts and doctrines, the sources and authorities fall away to reveal a total and abysmal nihilism.

We may say that there are three main streams whose confluence has given us the broad river of Western civilization: the law and peace of Rome; the love and salvation of Christianity; and the humanism and science of the Renaissance. All three streams found their historic source to an extraordinary degree in the Italian peninsula. But all three Fascism denied. Fascism was lawless and peaceless; it neither knew love on earth nor asked for salvation in heaven; it made use of the techniques of humanism and science with a total distortion of their spirit.

Communism and Fascism, it has often been argued, had many things in common. Both were "latter-day" phenomena; both were party-led mass movements; both lent themselves to dictatorships. But they had one insuperable difference. Communism at least had some positive features. It at least believed in an earthly paradise and tried to achieve it. But Fascism was all negation. Fascism denied even the earthly paradise. As Mussolini put it, "We do not believe in the materialistic concept of an economic happiness." Fascism was not just a parochial Italian aberration, induced by war weariness and an impatience with parliamentary methods. The most sinister feature of Fascism was its potential universality. It was a fate that could overtake any people, even a highly gifted and sophisticated people, and a people of the richest cultural heritage, who likewise renounced hitherto accepted civilized values.

To such a creed there was nothing left to glorify but its own destructiveness. For Fascism the end was war — it was the only end it permitted. Fascism exulted in the warlike virtues. Fascist rhetoric was interlarded with such words as "audacity," "will," "conflict," "decision," "discipline" — and an abundant and sonorous rhetoric it was. Fascist squads bore characteristic names: "Savages," "Damned," "Desperadoes." Thus wrote Mussolini in a classic passage:

> Fascism above all does not believe in either the possibility or the utility of universal peace. It rejects the pacifism which masks surrender and cowardice. War alone brings all human energies to their highest tension and imprints a seal of nobility on the peoples who have the virtue to face it.[5]

Sometimes Mussolini played with the notion of a special caste of warriors, a heroic breed, after the manner of the Nazi master race, who would forever do battle for the glory of Italy:

> To be sure this is a lofty dream, but I see it being realized little by little . . . The goal is always Empire! To build a city, to found a colony, to establish an empire, these are the prodigies of the human spirit. An empire is not merely territorial; it may be political, economic, spiritual . . . And toward this must we ever be moving. We must resolutely abandon the whole liberal phraseology and way of thinking. The word of command can be none but this . . . Discipline, discipline at home, in order that abroad we may present the granite block of a single national will.[6]

Time was when Mussolini's militarism was looked upon as mere Italian flamboyance and was dismissed as the defensiveness of a man who was too painfully aware of the absence of those qualities he lauded in the modern Italian people. To Anglo-Saxons especially, who wanted nothing so much as peace, it was nausea to see this idolatry of war in a nation whose military exploits had not always been too glittering. Yet Mussolini's militarism was no mere pathology or megalomania. Fascism might contain no other logic or doctrine, but this at least proceeded logically—all too logically—from Fascist premises. Its categorical imperative left Italian people, for all their unmilitary temperament, with no alternative but to become a military, militant state.

Fascist government therefore was a military government. Fascist organizations were military organizations. The Fascist hierarchy was an officer corps. The Fascist party was an army cadre. The Fascist economy was autarkic and ordered for war. The resources of the country, human and material, were trained and dedicated to the supreme inevitability:

> The plan of control for Italian economic policy in the coming Fascist era is determined by a single consideration: that our nation will be called to war. When? How? Nobody can say. But the wheel of fate is turning fast.

In such a state, tyranny and intolerance are reasonable and necessary. The dictator demands discipline from his people as a commander demands discipline from his army. In a democracy, where peace is regarded as a normal and perpetual condition, broken only by unnatural lapses into war, freedom of speech, freedom of conscience, political opposition, parliamentary debate, and liberal individualism are permissible luxuries. But in a Fascist state, where war is regarded as the normal and perpetual condition, broken only by unnatural lapses into peace, these things are tantamount to insubordination. Political opposition and parliamentary debate are no better than the discussion of orders; freedom of speech and freedom of conscience are subversive of the fighting morale and efficiency of the nation. Thus Mussolini could boast of "trampling upon the more or less decomposed body of the Goddess of Liberty":

> There is no longer any room for many things which were excellent in other times. Today, among the things for which there is no room, must be included the Opposition . . . All parties must end, must fall. I want to see a panorama of ruins about me, the ruins of the other political forces, so that Fascism may stand alone, gigantic and dominant.
>
> The plain truth that must stare into the eyes of anyone not blinded by dogmatism, is that men are perhaps tired of liberty. They have had an orgy of it. Today liberty is no longer the chaste, stern virgin for whom the generations of the first half of the last century fought and died. For the youth that is intrepid, restless, and hard, that faces the dawn of the new history, there are other words of much greater power, and they are: Order, Hierarchy, Discipline.[7]

The Vatican

In 1870 the Italian troops of Victor Emmanuel II had occupied the city of Rome, and the papal capital had been proclaimed the capital of united Italy. The Pope denounced the "usurping Power" and retired into voluntary imprisonment in the Vatican. He refused to recognize the Law of Papal Guarantees of 1871, by which the Italian Government tried to heal the estrangement. The Roman Question, as it was called, continued from that day to vex the conscience and ingenuity of Italian statesmanship, and ironic was the fate that decreed that the Fascist Government, the most secular of all Italian governments, should at long last be the one to find a solution of it.

Italy had her skeptics and her anticlericals, and the Vatican was traditionally opposed to Italian unity. But the Italian people, as a whole, especially in the rural districts, were a Catholic people, loyal and faithful as the people of Poland, Mexico, or Quebec. Mussolini himself had once been anticlerical, even as he had been antimonarchical, and in all fundamentals Fascism stood in opposition to the Catholic Church. But in 1922, before the March on Rome, Mussolini had made his peace with the Church and the monarchy. Like Napoleon perhaps, he found it politic to be on good diplomatic terms with the Vatican. During his first years in power, he made valiant efforts not to injure Catholic sensibilities. He was careful never to seem to interfere with religious instruction in the schools. Some of his more anticlerical Fascists even found they could stomach Catholicism more easily by regarding it as a "national" religion! His suppression of Freemasonry and secret societies in Italy was evidently intended to establish himself in the eyes of the Church as a worthy friend and ally. The Corporative State was supposed to be consonant with Catholic social doctrine. Even so, there were occasional incidents, and the Vatican had sometimes to deplore Fascist acts of violence against Catholic persons and property. In January 1927, Mussolini had the great temerity to disband the Catholic youth organization, the *Esploratori Cattolici,* which he felt to be a rival of his own *Balilla.*

However, despite the incidents, Mussolini's negotiations with the Vatican upon the Roman Question began quietly and informally in 1926 and lasted a difficult three years. Both sides clearly desired a final settlement; both were realistic enough to moderate their extreme demands. On February 11, 1929, at the Lateran Palace, Cardinal Gasparri, the Papal Secretary of State, and Mussolini signed a series of agreements.

The Lateran agreements comprised a treaty, a concordat, and a financial convention. Under the treaty, Italy recognized the sovereignty of the Holy See over "Vatican City," a neutral, inviolable territory – actually of less than a square mile in area with about 400 permanent inhabitants. Italy also granted extraterritorial rights to certain churches and other ecclesiastical property outside the Vatican. She accredited an ambassador to the Holy See and accepted an apostolic nuncio to herself. Under the concordat, she recognized Catholicism as the state religion, secured to the Church the performance of its rites and sacraments, bound herself to enforce canon law in regard to marriage, recognized the validity of ecclesiastical marriage without the necessity of a subsequent civil ceremony, and permitted compulsory religious instruction in both elementary and secondary schools. Under the financial convention, she paid the Vatican 1,750,000,000 lire (about $90,000,000) in cash and bonds "as a definite settlement of all its financial relations with Italy in consequence of the fall of the temporal power." Finally, the Holy See declared the Roman Question to be ended and eliminated, and recognized the Kingdom of Italy under the House of Savoy, with Rome as the capital of the Italian state. The ratifications were exchanged on June 7, 1929.

The Roman Catholic Church, in an age of spiritual agony, had become a powerful and growing influence. The extreme anticlericalism that had flourished in the nineteenth century had conspicuously declined. The twentieth century had no counterpart to Zola and Anatole France. Republican Spain and Nazi Germany were among exceptions to the rule but, generally speaking, at the time of which we are writing, the Church was treated with little hatred and considerable respect even by those who were farthest from it in their sympathies. Derogatory references to Catholics and their institutions were scrupulously avoided in the press, stage, and film in all democratic countries.

The Church enjoyed increasing international recognition. One country after another appreciated the importance of establishing diplomatic relations with it, and the Vatican became a unique cosmopolitan center, a "listening post" sensitive to every breath and breeze of political activity throughout the world. At Benedict XV's accession in 1914, fourteen states were represented at the Vatican; at his death in 1922, the number was twenty-five. In 1939 the number was thirty-seven. Myron Taylor went on his mission as President Roosevelt's "personal representative" to the Pope in 1940. During the interwar period, the Vatican renewed its practice of negotiating concordats with foreign Powers. In 1914 there were very few concordats in existence, and Pius X, in his pontificate from 1903 to 1914, negotiated only one, a concordat with Serbia which, because of the outbreak of the First World War, was never ratified. Pius XI negotiated concordats with all the leading governments of Europe except Britain and the Soviet Union. Furthermore, the Church showed its realization of its international responsibilities in its extended missionary activity and in its encouragement of new monastic and university foundations abroad. Of eighteen encyclicals issued between 1920 and 1939, eight concerned current international and economic questions. Pope Pius XII created twenty-six non-Italian cardinals at a single consistory in 1946, including a Chinese, an Armenian, an Australian, a Canadian, four Americans, and six Latin Americans.

Both recent popes were international figures of international experience. Achille Ratti was papal nuncio at Warsaw during the Russo-Polish War and Archbishop of Milan during the early years of the Fascist struggle for power. He succeeded Benedict XV as Pius XI in 1922, and his pontificate almost exactly coincided with the interwar period. Eugenio Pacelli, a master of eight languages, was papal nuncio at Munich and Berlin, and then papal Secretary of State. He knew Brazil, the United States, England, and most European countries. He succeeded Pius XI as Pius XII in 1939.[8]

14. FRANCE: THE THIRD REPUBLIC, FINANCE, AND SECURITY

Political Instability

It has often been argued that the game of politics counted for less in France than in many another country, that the continued ministerial changes were of no great moment, and that the main strength of the country was not to be judged by the irresponsible behavior of its parliamentary assemblies. Be that as it may, the political failure of France in modern times has appalled and surprised her many friends the more because it has seemed so utterly at variance with her rich intellectual gifts and with her superlative contributions to all the other arts of civilization. By 1914 the government of the Third Republic had fallen into the hands of a class of professional politicians. The best brains in France were not being drawn to public life. Little social prestige attached to membership of the Senate, and less to membership of the Chamber. A man had to be of tough fiber to be willing to submit to the vulgarity and coarseness of French electioneering. For those in power, patronage and graft were part of the normal way of things. Periodic financial scandals were relished by a scurrilous and sensational press. The electorate, grown old in cynicism, accepted the situation as a matter of course although, now and again, insulted and goaded beyond endurance, it would resort to acts of violence, or to dictatorial remedies, or both.

Modern France began with the Revolution of 1789. But the Revolution was not the wholesale upheaval that it is sometimes represented to have been. Catastrophic though it was, it was not the final liquidation of the old order. Powerful conservative elements survived, and the subsequent history of France from 1815 to 1940 is interpretable as the constant re-enactment of the selfsame revolutionary conflict. The Third Republic itself had come into being in the face of strong opposition; the adoption of the republican constitution by the Chamber of Deputies in 1875 had been carried by a majority of only one vote. As Thiers had said at the time, "The Republic divides us least" — an uncertain, almost negative motto for the new state.

The political parties, at the time of which we are writing, graded through the full semicircle from Left to Right. On the extreme Left were the Communist and Socialist parties, the parties in the main of the urban and rural workers. Theoretically their aims were identical, namely the establishment of the socialist state. The old watchwords of the Revolution – "Liberty, Equality, Fraternity" – no longer sufficed for the economic and spiritual needs of the new industrialized masses. Something stronger was more in keeping with the time, but there was no broad agreement as to what that something should be. Thus the Communist party preached the class struggle and the seizure of power by violence, and, in the interwar years, it was in close liaison with the Comintern in Moscow. The Socialist party shaded off into the Radical party. It favored a gradual, nonviolent process of reform, respected majority decisions, and was willing to use legal and constitutional means to gain its ends. Patriotic to a fault, it abhorred the Moscow connection. The domestic history of the Communist and Socialist parties centered round the burning question of collaboration with "bourgeois" governments.

On the moderate Left, perhaps halfway to the Right, and usually the largest of all the parties of the Third Republic, was the Radical party – or, to give it its full name, the Radical Socialist party (*le parti radical socialiste*).[1] It was the heir of the French Revolution, much as the Republican party in the United States was the heir of the Civil War. It was the "normal" party, holding power in "normal" times, the party of the *petit bourgeois,* a sort of coalition of all the innumerable individualities that made up the strength of post-Revolutionary France. Its creed was private enterprise and private property, and patriotism in foreign affairs; yet it was pacific at heart, the quintessence of French insularity. Compared with it, the other parties, in their various degrees, were parties of protest or of special interests.

The Right clung to the old authoritarian tradition, though, out of respect for the Revolution – and for electoral requirements – many of its parties adopted safe democratic labels, such as the Republican Democratic Union or the Democratic Alliance. Generally these parties were reactionary and represented big business and high finance; they were usually – but not always – staunchly Catholic; and more recently – though again not always – they were inclined to Fascism. There were also strong rightist parties which, like the antidemocratic and monarchist *Action Française,* declined to be represented in the Chamber, and operated from "outside." Such parties were served by brilliant writers and exerted a considerable literary influence.

The groups from Left to Right stood in varying degrees of opposition to one another, but the resultant all too often was a mutual canceling-out of voting strengths. Hence arose the jockeying for position, the forming of temporary blocs and coalitions, the cabinet reshufflings, and all the changeableness and indiscipline of the Republic's parliamentary life. Between 1875 and 1920 there were 59 ministries, and in the interwar period, from 1920 to 1939, there were 41. Occasionally a minister survived through several changes, but few were long enough in office to carry out a consistent, long-term policy.

Financial Instability

Then came the question of money. French politics were overshadowed by it. There was always something of the tightfisted peasant in the French character, and the preoccupation with money was a national trait. In the eyes of foreign observers the perpetual financial instability — the unbalanced budgets, evasion of taxes, mounting national debt and, after 1919, reparations and the fluctuation of exchange — was as typical of modern France as the perpetual political instability.

France had a tradition of unbalanced budgets going back for centuries. Colbert, the patron saint of French ministers of finance, balanced only eight of his twenty-four budgets. There was one short interim of surpluses, oddly enough in the middle of the Revolution, and another for a few years just before 1914. But generally the old tradition was resumed throughout the post-Revolutionary era. Not only were budgets unbalanced, but they were often passed months in arrears, and the sums were sometimes increased by various euphemistic "special" and "extraordinary" accounts. The system of taxation was complicated, by 1914 it was hopelessly out of date, and the evasion of taxes was a national scandal. But none of the political parties — except perhaps the Socialists — wanted to incur the odium of introducing reforms. It was a familiar saying that the average Frenchman would sooner die for France than pay her a franc of his savings. In any event, the reactionary "two hundred families," who were alleged to control the country's financial houses and the Senate, always formed an obstacle to progressive legislation. Between 1907 and 1914, Joseph Caillaux, the brilliant Minister of Finance, had tried to introduce an income tax, and an emasculated income tax bill did in fact become law in 1914, a few days before the outbreak of the First World War; but then, of course, it had to be postponed.

During the First World War, France spent money with little thought for the morrow. She had "muddled through" for so long, and wartime was no time to change the hallowed system. Victory could not be too dearly or too recklessly bought, and victory might pay for itself in the shape of German reparations. Except for an Excess War Profits Tax, which did not bring in a yield till 1918, and a luxury tax, no new taxes were imposed. On paper revenue remained about the same throughout the war; but, whereas revenue in 1914 met 40 per cent of the total state expenditure, in 1918 it met only 12 per cent. Meanwhile "invisible" sources of income, notably interest on foreign investments which had formerly taken up some of the deficit, disappeared. In 1914 these investments had reached the huge total of 45,000,000,000 francs ($9,000,000,000). But political motives had largely dictated French investment policy abroad, and the chief debtors of France were countries like Russia and Rumania, whose paying capacities the First World War had most disastrously interrupted.

A fiscal policy such as has been described could be carried on only by borrowing. In 1914 the French national debt was estimated at 34,000,000,000 francs ($6,600,000,000), a figure only slightly less than the national income at the time, and the service of the debt absorbed a third of the revenue. In 1918 the debt was over 150,000,000,000 francs, and in 1924 it was probably over 300,000,000,000 francs; in that year the service of the debt, plus war pensions of various kinds, absorbed over three-quarters of the revenue. The result, of course, was inflation. From 1914 to 1924 the gold reserve declined only slightly, but the note issue multiplied six times, and the percentage of gold to notes dropped from 70 to 10. In 1924, after the Ruhr episode, the value of the franc broke altogether.

Finance, therefore, in one way or another, was bound to be a major concern of interwar France, and no other country of the same size and potential wealth was so completely dominated by it. Throughout the 1920's, France's affairs, domestic and foreign, revolved around the everlasting franc. Ministries, Right and Left, rose and fell in the ceaseless Battle of the Budget. France's insistence on German reparations was no wanton revengefulness or political cunning, but absolute necessity.[2] Traditional indebtedness, complex and outmoded taxation, the loss of foreign investments, four years of unparalleled economic effort, the material and human devastations of the war, the substantial failure of reparations – all these made an accumulation of burdens which the exhausted country could no longer support.

France had been steadily losing her man power in foreign wars since Louis XIV, and now, as the woeful climax of centuries of wastage, she had borne the brunt of the First World War. It was commonly said that of every three Germans killed between 1914 and 1918, two died by the hand of a French soldier.[3] Her own casualties had been 1,400,000 killed, or 10 per cent of her active male population – the heaviest percentage of any major belligerent – and 1,500,000 disabled, or 11 per cent, again the heaviest of any major belligerent; and, in view of her declining birth rate, the loss was not likely to be made good. The German invasion and occupation had devastated ten of the French departments, and they were the ten that contained her most populous and most highly industrialized districts. In this area 2,500,000 of the inhabitants had been displaced, either by flight in 1914 or by forcible deportation afterward. Houses, farms, railroads, bridges, and canals had been destroyed, and most of the coal mines had been flooded. Manufacturing equipment had been systematically dismantled and removed. With whatever momentary feelings of triumph France may have ended the war in 1918, the reasons for her deeper, more persistent malaise in the interwar years were assuredly not far to seek.

De Poincaré à Poincaré

During 1919 the attention of France – and of the world – was centered on the Peace Conference of Paris. The French people were understandably gratified that their capital should have been chosen for this historic congress of nations. The occasion was no more than a just tribute to their sacrifices and their contribution to the great victory. But the disappointments and disillusionments were to begin in the first year of peace. All the usual economic indices, as the budget of May 1919 showed, were already unfavorable. The treaty with Germany was signed at Versailles in modest pomp on June 28, 1919, and after acrimonious debates was ratified by the Chambers between July and October. Evidently Clemenceau, despite his tigerish implacability, had been cajoled into too lenient measures against the enemy, and the Rhine frontier had not been secured. (See p. 104.) His defeat a year later in elections to the presidency of the Republic was due in part to old personal animosities and in part to the fear that he would not be content with a merely formal and decorative presidency. But the defeat also doubtless represented a national vote of censure on his work at the Conference. Clemenceau was like many another protagonist of the war years who suffered a revulsion of popularity at the coming of peace. He retired from public life. He was now eighty-one years of age, and perhaps he had some claim to spend "the evening of his thought" in leisure and quiet.

The first postwar phase was a rightist phase. Elections in November 1919 returned the "victors" of the war – in this case, a coalition of rightist parties under Alexandre Millerand which was to go by the name of the National Bloc. If there is a single word to epitomize the new government's state of mind, that word would be "anti-Sovietism." France in the early 1920's went through the worst agonies of her Bolshevik phobia. She supported the White and Polish armies in the Russian Civil War. She also reopened all those doctrinal disputes which traditionally characterized the Right, notably the clerical question, and the Chamber approved the establishment of formal relations with the Vatican for the first time since 1870. Millerand was elected President of the Republic in September 1920. He immediately set out to prove himself a strong executive, and proposed reforms in the presidential prerogatives, proposals which, mild though they were, his political opponents at once represented as the foretaste of a rightist dictatorship in France. In short – what with the Soviet question, the clerical question, and the presidential question – enough material was being collected to make the French parliament a very combustible institution.[4]

The National Bloc, however, was not as popular as it seemed. Accidents in the electoral system had added misleadingly to its numbers in the Chamber. What was more important, the wave of wartime enthusiasm which had originally carried it to power subsided gradually in proportion as the nation became conscious of its real weariness. Aristide Briand was Premier in 1921 and was followed by Poincaré in January 1922. Poincaré, largely responsible for the French occupation of the Ruhr in 1923, began to lose support when it became apparent that the occupation was not yielding its expected results (see p. 146). But, as was always the way in France, it was finance that completed the overthrow of the National Bloc. Early in 1924, at the time of the Dawes reparations conference, the franc dropped to 130 to the pound and to nearly 30 to the dollar. Elections in May 1924 returned to power a coalition of leftist parties, Radicals and Socialists, under the Radical Édouard Herriot, which took the name of the *Cartel des Gauches.*

The victory of the Cartel was as decisive as the former victory of the National Bloc. Herriot was now in control much as Millerand had once been, and he proceeded to reverse all the National Bloc's policies. For a start, he challenged Millerand's conception of the presidential prerogatives and demanded Millerand's resignation from the presidency. And resign Millerand did. Gaston Doumergue, a mild partisan of Millerand and at that time president of the Senate, was elected President. Herriot then took up the old clerical question. He played it for what it was worth, for anticlericalism was the single common denominator in all the variegated affinities of the parties of the Cartel, and he prepared to break off the newly restored relations with the Vatican. He tried to secularize the schools in Alsace, which had always been faithfully Catholic. Herriot's anticlericalism was symptomatic of the still unhealed revolutionary schisms in French society, and it stirred up an unfortunate "separatism" in Alsace, a province newly returned to French allegiance, where throughout all the years of the former German rule the Catholic Church had been the symbol of French nationality. Finally he revised the National Bloc's aggressive foreign policy. With Ramsay MacDonald, then Prime Minister in Britain, he liquidated the Ruhr invasion and agreed to the Dawes Plan. (See p. 146.) In October 1924, France formally recognized the Soviet Union.

As usual it was the wicked old serpent of finance that brought about the fall of the leftist paradise. Herriot, very much at home with doctrinal politics, was not the man to deal with so drab and sordid a thing as money. The Socialist party was unwise enough to raise the cry of a capital levy and, though Herriot personally showed no sympathy, the party could hardly have picked an issue better calculated to split the Cartel. In April 1925, Herriot and his ministry fell. The franc immediately weakened. Six short-lived ministries in a year wrestled with the problem. Even Caillaux, lately condemned for treasonable correspondence with the enemy during the First World War, was called out of his rustication for a few months to become Minister of Finance. In Paris, they called him the "Wizard," but he was a desperate and humiliating choice for the savior of financial France. A Herriot ministry enjoyed a single day of office during July 1926. The franc then stood at over 50 to the dollar. The press predicted national bankruptcy on a par with Germany's in 1923. The Paris mob, which always appeared at times like these, was already demonstrating noisily in the streets. Meanwhile it was creditably rumored that the Bank of France and the "two hundred families" had deliberately engineered the whole debacle to throw discredit onto the Socialist Left. The *crise du franc* had become a *crise de régime.*

On July 23, 1926, after the demise of Herriot's one-day ministry, Poincaré formed a ministry of all parties except the Socialists and Communists, and as a measure of the seriousness of the situation, the ministry included, besides himself, five past premiers, among whom was Herriot. Poincaré was his own Finance Minister. The Chamber, now thoroughly alarmed, would have done the bidding even of a Caillaux. It worked for Poincaré with unprecedented dispatch, and in a month it had voted that marvel of marvels in France, a balanced budget, this time moreover not in arrears, but actually in advance of the regular financial year. Yet all Poincaré's measures were perfectly orthodox. He increased taxation, tightened up the methods of collection, made drastic cuts in administrative expenses, and sheared off the French budget its all too numerous "special" and "extraordinary" appendages. The medicine was bitter, but it was effective. At the end of 1926 the franc stood at 25 to the dollar and was pegged at that level. In June 1928, France restored the gold standard.

Poincaré remained in office from July 1926 to July 1929. His three years coincided with the Locarno era, and they were years during which the whole of Europe was returning to something like prosperity. They were the most stable years, politically and financially, which France enjoyed in the interwar period. They showed, as had been shown already in other countries, how quickly a "technical" national bankruptcy could be relieved. But, by now, it seemed that at least some of the more superficial scars of war had been effaced. The building, automobile, silk, and luxury trades were almost flourishing. Paris was once more the leader of women's fashions. Every historic city and holiday resort in France was full of tourists.

Poincaré resigned at length, partly on grounds of ill-health, and was followed by a short-lived ministry under Briand and then by a ministry under his "political heir," André Tardieu. The ministries were reminiscent of the National Bloc and of the rightist tendencies of the early 1920's. But the withdrawal of Poincaré's strong hand brought back all the old instability. Sessions in the Chamber were uniformly stormy, and the harassed Tardieu sometimes had to put the question of confidence three times a day. The Young Plan for the final settlement of Germany's reparations, signed in January 1930, was far from popular in France. Then, in November 1930, occurred the Oustric bank failure, the first of a new round of financial scandals in France.

The French Alliance System

The great, central problem of peace in post-Versailles Europe was France's fear for her security. Three times in a century and twice in living memory had she been invaded — always by the same enemy and always from the same direction. In 1918, after terrible losses, she was at last victorious. She could have only one policy for the future — the permanent enfeeblement of her hereditary enemy and the permanent security of her thrice-violated soil. On this point at least her political parties were not divided.

France did not believe, as many in Britain seemed to want to believe, that Germany had learned the lesson of defeat and was militarily and morally broken. She saw on her eastern frontier only a great nation, the blood descendants of barbarian tribes which had already extinguished one historic civilization, a nation with a growing population, half again as numerous as hers, with industrial resources that had survived the recent war intact, a nation which, though momentarily reduced in the means of offense, had the potential of recuperation and was doubtless full of ideas of sweet revenge as soon as opportunity should beckon. Meanwhile France had no assurance — rather the contrary — that the fortunate combination of alliances of 1914-18, which had put Russia, Britain, and the United States on her side, would necessarily be repeated on a future occasion, and it did not seem that the League of Nations offered a compensating defense.

In her own view, France had not obtained at the Peace Conference even the minimum requirements of her security. She was, of course, confirmed in the repossession of Alsace-Lorraine. She obtained the coal mines of the Saar for a period of fifteen years as reparation for German damage to her own coal mines. But she did not secure the Rhine frontier. Clemenceau was persuaded to abandon his claims thereto for treaties of assistance by which the United States and Britain pledged immediate aid to France in the event of another German aggression, and the treaties were signed concurrently with the Treaty of Versailles. But the United States subsequently failed to ratify the Treaty of Versailles, and the entire arrangement had lapsed. (See pp. 104 and 295-95.) France found herself, therefore, on the morrow of the peace without her Rhine frontier, without her treaties of assistance, and with only the League of Nations — morally imposing but militarily powerless — to fill the strategic void.

Nor did frustration end there. France persuaded herself that she could recoup some of her huge material losses in the war from German reparations; but German reparations became a sorry comedy. And it was soon clear, into the bargain, that Germany was evading the disarmament clauses of the Treaty of Versailles.

Under these circumstances, France could try to make the most of whatever powers the League of Nations represented and she could try to develop out of them universal safeguards that might be more sufficient and dependent. From this policy resulted the Locarno Pact, which we described in an earlier chapter. (See pp. 121-24.) In the same category was the French-initiated Pact of Paris. But France could also construct across Europe a system of bilateral alliances. Such a policy perhaps better suited the French historical tradition. It harked back to Napoleon and to Louis XIV — if not to Charlemagne — when once before France had been the premier civilizing power in the West and had borne the standard of Latin culture for the world.

Militarily speaking, Belgium in 1919 was already a part of France, and that condition was expected to continue indefinitely. Since 1914 the ghost of Schlieffen had been added to the other fearful preoccupations of France, and only a clear military understanding with her northern neighbor could protect her should that menace ever arise again. During 1920 Marshal Foch and the Belgian General Staff concluded a defensive convention against Germany. Meanwhile the new Poland, from the day of her foundation, became a client state of France. Both nations recalled historic links which went back to Henry of Valois, successively king of Poland and France, in the sixteenth century. A French mission under Weygand materially assisted the Poles in the campaign for the defense of Warsaw in 1920, and a French mission was entrusted with the reorganization of the Polish Army. In February 1921, a Franco-Polish treaty was signed in Paris, concerting the foreign policies of the two countries and binding them to a common defense against unprovoked aggression. A commercial treaty and French loans to Poland followed. (See p. 155.)

The Little Entente between Czechoslovakia, Yugoslavia, and Rumania, if not actually wrought under French encouragement and initiative, was in perfect harmony with French ambitions. In January 1924, France and Czechoslovakia entered into a treaty of friendship and alliance, and undertook "to act together in respect of all external questions calculated to endanger their security, or to disturb the order of things established by the peace treaties to which both have set their hand." Finally France entered into similar treaties with Rumania in June 1926, and with Yugoslavia in November 1927. The several agreements were cemented from time to time by French loans to the three states. The Franco-Polish and the Franco Little Entente systems were unhappily prevented from achieving a further unity by the rift between Poland and Czechoslovakia, but they were linked to some extent by the treaty of 1921 between Poland and Rumania. (See pp. 155, 173-74, and 176.)

Throughout the 1920's the dominating figure in France's foreign policy was Aristide Briand. His political longevity compares with that of Stresemann, his contemporary and associate in the Locarno Pact in 1925 and in many another international transaction of the decade. A onetime Socialist, he first entered the Chamber in 1902, and from that date, with occasional intervals, there was hardly an important issue in French politics in which he did not take part. He was a brilliant orator and a shrewd parliamentary tactician. He was eleven times Premier – the first time in 1909 and the last in 1929. He became Foreign Minister in 1921 and again continuously from April 1925, through seven ministries – four his own – till January 1932, a few months before his death. In 1926 he was awarded the Nobel Peace Prize. In 1928, on behalf of France, he signed the Pact of Paris, often named after him and his American opposite, the Briand-Kellogg Pact. (See pp. 124-25.)

But it is sometimes to be wondered whether Briand – perhaps like Stresemann – did not combine in himself the character of the earnest, cosmopolitan ambassador of peace that he displayed to the world, and the character of the egotistic, astute patriot that he reserved for his own colleagues. In October 1926, he and Stresemann met over an informal lunch in the village of Thoiry on the French side of the Franco-Swiss border to discuss matters of general interest to their two countries. It was a sort of miniature Locarno, and in after years journalists still referred to it as "the idyll of Thoiry." Perhaps it was a case of Greek meeting Greek. At all events nothing resulted from it. In September 1929, Briand began his famous discussions in Geneva on the "United States of Europe." His plans were much publicized on both sides of the Atlantic. But in all the fine phraseology – and Briand was a master of fine phraseology – the anxious lover of peace among nations could look in vain for anything beyond a rhetorical affirmation of the Versailles *status quo*. At least there was a certain negative consistency in Briand's foreign policy.

In May 1931, Gaston Doumergue's term as President of the Republic came to its appointed end. Briand, believing that he deserved well of France, stood for election. All his friends expected him to win, but the National Assembly elected not Briand, but Paul Doumer, then president of the Senate. Briand swallowed his defeat, a defeat more to his vanity than to his real ambition, and returned to his congenial duties at the Foreign Ministry.

The Maginot Line

One other matter should be mentioned in this chapter – the fortification of the northeastern frontier of France. The so-called Maginot Line was not the first fortification of that frontier, nor was it necessarily a sign of special doubts and anxieties. Every shift of frontier in the past had always entailed an appropriate revision of the defensive system. Earlier military engineers, Vauban under Louis XIV, and Sère de Rivière after 1871, had built fortifications in their day, and their work had not been regarded as inconsistent with a courageous military spirit or with the simultaneous formation of alliances with foreign powers. During the early 1920's a Commission of Frontier Defense prepared the blueprint of a new "Wall of France," and Painlevé, as Minister of War, approved it in 1927. André Maginot was Minister of War under Tardieu in 1929, and to him fell the task of securing the necessary credits and of carrying out the first stages of the plan. The "Line" thereafter was always associated with his name. In the course of the next ten years, Alsace-Lorraine became a huge concrete molehill, studded with gun-turrets, tank traps, dragon's teeth, and all the paraphernalia of defensive warfare as then understood. The gun emplacements often weighed more than 120 tons apiece; 26,000,000 cubic feet of cement were used and more armor plate than would have built a battle fleet. The cost was over $500,000,000.

The Maginot Line was not without its critics, even in 1929. One school of thought, albeit a one-man school, was represented by a young staff colonel, Charles de Gaulle, evidently a man of large and supple imagination, whose book, *Vers L'Armée de Métier*, published in 1934, pleaded for a highly trained, highly specialized, professional, long-service, mechanized army of six divisions – 100,000 men in all – an army "moving entirely on caterpillar tractors," an army of great mobility and striking power, attacking by surprise with echelons of tanks under a curtain of aircraft, operating independently of any base, hauling its own artillery and supplies, penetrating deep into hostile territory, rupturing the enemy's vital communications. De Gaulle, in a word, predicted with astonishing accuracy the blitzkrieg of the Second World War. Both his tactics and his state of mind were diametrically opposed to the "Maginot complex."

But the full story of the Maginot Line was not so simple. The fault, as we know now, was twofold. First, the Maginot Line was not intended to be more than a partial defense; but second, public opinion in France was lulled into thinking, on the contrary, that it was an absolute and total defense. The flat Franco-Belgian frontier was not suited to heavy fortification, and the main mass of the Maginot Line therefore came to an end at Sedan. The French High Command, at all events after 1927 when Pétain was Commander in Chief, conceived of the Belgian defensive system, anchored on Liége, Eben Emael, and the Albert Canal, as the proper extension of the Maginot Line, and planned to reinforce the Belgian Army with four French armies. The entire strategic conception presumed and was based on the Franco-Belgian convention of 1920. Unfortunately, when the time came, Belgium had reverted to "neutrality," and the political premises of the French plan was falsified. (See p. 395.) The French High

Command also committed errors of detail, the most serious being its assumption that the hilly and forested Ardennes would be impassable terrain for mechanized forces. But, far worse than all this was the belief, a belief widespread not only in France but among France's allies, that the Maginot Line stretched north of Sedan to the coast of Flanders and was, in fact, impregnable along its entire length of four hundred miles. Here, in concrete and steel, so French public opinion was confidently given to think, had modern military science at last discovered the means to dam the fatal gap which, since the days of the Huns, had opened the fair country to more than thirty invasions. This vicious confusion of politics and psychology, as we shall tell anon, issued in the tragedy of 1940.

15. BRITAIN: LABOR, TRADE, AND THE NEW IMPERIALISM

Postwar Depression

The First World War raised the British people to one of the high pinnacles of their history. Once more, at the head of a Grand Alliance, they had fought and overthrown a military despotism which, but for them, might have dominated the world. Hohenzollern Germany had gone the way of the French Empire, the French Monarchy, and Spain. But the costs had been very heavy, and never before had the British people greeted a peace in so exhausted a condition. Nor did they, like many defeated belligerents, renew themselves by revolution. Victory seemed to be a justification of the old order of 1914. But the old order, the Victorian and Edwardian ascendancy, with its traditions and accustomed ways of life, had passed away never to return, and the British people had now to spend many years of wasted pride and prestige before they were brought to a realization of that unwelcome fact.

The nation had not suffered actually or relatively the losses of France. There were no devastated areas, and damage by air raid had been negligible. Casualties in the four years of the war amounted to 702,000 killed and 1,660,000 wounded. But the losses were more serious than the numbers signified. It is sometimes forgotten how the voluntary service army, Kitchener's Army of 1914-16, superb achievement though it was, had skimmed off the best of the race. Whereas other nations, which had conscript armies from the beginning of the war, lost a general cross section of their male populations, Britain lost the very flower of her manhood. She faced the problems of peace and reconstruction, therefore, most wanting in that irreplaceable "lost generation" of men of education, responsibility, and leadership.

Political Britain came out of the delirium of Armistice Day to find herself preparing for a general election. Lloyd George, Prime Minister since December 1916 and the great architect of Britain's war effort, had resolved to ask for a new mandate for his wartime Coalition government with which to face the Peace Conference at Paris. On constitutional grounds his attitude was entirely correct. The old Parliament, originally elected for five years, lasted eight. Under the Representation of the People Act of 1918, millions of new voters, including women, for the first time, had been added to the electorate. (See p. 43.) But the Khaki Election, as it was called, unleashed the hurt and hate of the past four years, and the British people, who had borne the great struggle with such unexampled fortitude, allowed themselves a most deplorable and uncharacteristic lapse of mass passion. Lloyd George himself was never party to the extremes which even cabinet ministers indulged, but the voters went to the polls nevertheless whipped to frenzy with the raucous electioneering slogans of "Hang the Kaiser!" and "Squeeze the German orange till the pips squeak!" As a result, Lloyd George's Coalition parties swept the board and won 484 seats. The independent Liberals, still under their old Liberal leader Asquith, won only 26 seats, a figure that signified the virtual demise of the Liberal party as such.[1] Lloyd George did indeed go to Paris with his mandate, but the hectoring, chauvinistic House he left behind was a sore trial to him.

The return to civil life was accomplished more easily than had been expected. A special Ministry of Reconstruction, prospectively created in 1917, had drafted a plan for the gradual demobilization of the fighting forces and munition workers. But now nothing so leisurely satisfied the popular mood. Soldiers and workers wanted only to get home, and the quicker the better. At several camps in the winter of 1918-19, in both England and France, British troops were mutinying because they considered that their exodus from military life was not fast enough. Nor had the government foreseen the boom that followed the Armistice. The country in 1919, instead of being forced to retrench and reorganize, found itself enjoying an artificial flurry of high prices. The government hurried to drop the various controls it had so rigidly maintained during the war. Mines, railroads, agriculture, indeed all industry, were allowed to return to "normal" at the earliest possible moment. The psychological release from war encouraged spending; peace brought demands for luxuries long denied; war savings and gratuities were flung on the market. Soldiers and workers not only were welcomed home, but the very condition of the country seemed to encourage their return, and 4,000,000 were absorbed into civilian industry in the course of the first postwar year.

The bubble burst in 1920. All the measures which a wary government had prepared and found unwanted now had to be put hurriedly into operation. The old workers' insurance of 1911 was converted into an Unemployment Insurance Act so as to provide a "dole" – in the unfortunate and misleading slang of the time – available to a much wider category of workers. A Relief Act was passed to empower government departments and local authorities to carry out public works, roads, and housing. But at the end of 1920 nearly 700,000 were registered as unemployed. The number doubled in the early weeks of 1921, and by March 1921, just before the great miners' strike, it stood at over 2,000,000.

In our usual historical phraseology the Depression, so-called, belongs to the early 1930's and began with the stock-market crash in New York in 1929. But depression in Britain began in the first postwar years. Parliament seemed to be debating nothing other than unemployment. The air was thick with schemes for housing, schemes for imperial preference, schemes for emigration. Two concrete measures resulted. First, an agreement was signed with the Soviet Government in March 1921 re-establishing commercial relations, and second, a Safeguarding of Industries Bill was passed in June to prevent foreign dumping and to protect, in particular, certain key industries essential to the country in time of war. The first was a clear departure from the anti-Soviet policy Britain had pursued in 1919, and the second was a clear departure from the old free-trade principles. But the British Government was desperate enough to revise policies and principles, however hallowed, if it could relieve in any possible way the country's economic distress.

Naturally enough these postwar years were full of labor unrest. Socialist ideas had penetrated Britain even as they had penetrated every part of the world. The war had postponed, and while postponing had aggravated, the old social problems. Recent accessions of high wages and of bargaining power put organized labor in a recalcitrant mood, and there was a widespread – and not unjustified – belief that the employers had made huge profits out of the war. Hardly a month passed but some strike or threat of strike, some lockout or threat of lockout, some acrimonious meeting of employers, workers, and government representatives did not occur in some part of industrial Britain. In August 1919, there had even been a strike of London's policemen. From time to time trade-union extremists talked dangerously of a general strike of all their members, "direct action," as they called it.

The most serious and persistent unrest was among the miners. The coal-mining industry was in a parlous state. It was technically conservative and inefficient, and it needed thorough rationalization. New fuels, notably oil, competed in the old markets, and German reparation deliveries of coal restricted the usual British sales abroad. Several coal mines that had operated under wartime prices could not be maintained at economic levels now that peace was restored, and it seemed that without continued government subsidies large coal fields would shortly be forced to go derelict. Meanwhile the squalid conditions under which the average miner was expected to live were a slur upon any self-respecting civilized state. Coal somehow symbolized the prosperity of England, and, if coal was at fault, the entire pride and prestige of the country's industry were affected.

The government made valiant efforts to bring employer and employee together in joint committees or before boards of arbitration, and in these postwar years we have the significant and often entertaining spectacle of mineowners, perhaps titled millionaires, seated at the same conference table with, and being cross-examined by, miners' delegates who kept themselves and their families on wages of 50 shillings ($12.50) a week. But the government rejected the report of a royal commission under Sir John Sankey, condemning the existing system of mineownership and recommending a measure of amalgamation and nationalization. The first miners' strike occurred in October and November 1920. The second, much more serious, strike lasted nearly three months from March to May 1921. In the second strike, even the pumpmen, who kept the pits free from flooding, were withdrawn. The government proclaimed an emergency. Troops occupied the supply depots, and armored cars patrolled the streets in the strike areas. In the end the miners were forced to accept wage settlements on the mine-owners' terms.

Conservative — Labor — Conservative — Labor

We have dwelled at length on Britain's domestic affairs at this time because it was here that the real history of the country — then and throughout the interwar period as a whole — was played out. Foreign affairs, at least in the public mind, were of lesser importance. The Treaty of Versailles was received with mixed feelings. Some people were grimly satisfied; a few were shocked and alarmed; the vast majority was uninterested. Yet, at the deeper levels of the public mind — if we may so describe it — there developed something of a "guilt complex" over the treaty, and the further news from Genoa and Chanaq — to say nothing of Ireland and India — induced a general feeling that "something had gone wrong." (See pp. 186 and 278.) The inevitable scapegoat was Lloyd George and his Coalition. He resigned at last in October 1922, and the British people reverted with an almost audible sigh of relief to the good old parliamentary struggles they had known before.

The defeat of Lloyd George in Britain in many ways resembled the defeat of President Wilson in the United States and of Clemenceau in France. All three countries were working back to what they imagined to be "normalcy"; all three were trying to forget the war and, within their respective circumstances, to be as isolationist as they could. Conservative, Labor, Conservative, Labor governments now followed one another in alternation during the remaining years of the decade. Unemployment and trade continued to be the main domestic problems, and each party, of course, regarded its particular doctrine as the sovereign panacea for the country's ills. The Conservatives argued for protection, the Liberals for free trade, and Labor for a capital levy and for the nationalization of key industries.

In October 1922, Andrew Bonar Law succeeded Lloyd George as Prime Minister of an all-Conservative government, with Lord Curzon as Foreign Secretary and Stanley Baldwin, a Midland iron and steel manufacturer, a comparative newcomer to politics, as Chancellor of the Exchequer. The French invasion of the Ruhr began in January 1923, an incident that disturbed British public opinion hardly at all, except insofar as it added one more exasperation to the increasing suspicion and impatience toward France. In the same month, Baldwin crossed to the United States and reached a settlement in Washington for funding the Anglo-American war debt. The settlement was long overdue and had a stabilizing effect politically, but it gave no economic relief. In May 1923, Bonar Law retired from the prime ministership on grounds of ill-health, to be succeeded, not by Curzon, whose seniority gave him some title to the office, but by Baldwin. In November Baldwin decided he must ask for a dissolution of Parliament and a general election on the issue of protection.

The result of the election was a stalemate. No party — Conservative, Liberal, or Labor — had a majority over the other two. Baldwin declined to form a new government. But it seemed that Labor might be able to govern – with Liberal support. At all events Labor was willing to try, and in January 1924, Ramsay MacDonald became Prime Minister and Foreign Secretary of Britain's first Labor cabinet. With him came an array of party colleagues, including Philip Snowden as Chancellor of the Exchequer and Arthur Henderson as Home Secretary.

The necessity of keeping Liberal support put a brake on Labor's policy, and, for all Labor's electioneering manifestos, MacDonald's government had now to make a very harmless display of Liberalism. Snowden, himself a zealous free trader, found no difficulty in introducing a Liberal budget. He even abolished Lloyd George's Safeguarding of Industries Act. Evidently the great Socialist revolution in Britain was not yet to be. MacDonald meanwhile occupied himself more promisingly in foreign affairs. He had been Britain's wartime pacifist and martyr, and he now took to the Foreign Office as if called to a mission. To heal the scars of war and of a peace-that-was-no-peace was a task worthy of a Socialist and a man. By a happy conjunction Herriot, a believer in the same philosophy, was then Premier in France. The Geneva Protocol and the Dawes Plan, characteristic monuments, were built from their collaboration. (See pp. 121 and 146.) On February 1, 1924, MacDonald telegraphed Moscow an unconditional recognition of the Soviet Union and invited Soviet representatives to London "to draw up the preliminary basis of a complete treaty to settle all questions outstanding between the two countries." And with Soviet representatives MacDonald proceeded to negotiate a commercial treaty – and a British loan.

Perhaps it was over the loan that MacDonald went too far. In Tory eyes such a transaction with a revolutionary government that regarded repudiation as an article of faith was indefensible folly, even if it were hedged about with "conditions" and "guarantees." The commercial treaty was concluded nevertheless in August 1924, but MacDonald, chafing under the opposition he had stirred up, resigned soon afterwards. In October new elections were called.

The election was the second within a year. It was exciting and unusual. It was one of those rare domestic occasions when foreign policy was a major issue. A strange document, afterward popularly known as the "Red Letter," had fallen into the hands of the Foreign Office just before MacDonald's resignation. It bore the signature of Zinoviev and purported to be addressed by the Comintern in Moscow to the British Communist party urging violent revolution in England. It made some references to "agitation propaganda" in the British Army and Navy and complained about "bourgeois opposition" to the proposed mooted loan to Russia. The Foreign Office, at the time apparently satisfied as to the authenticity of the document, published it. MacDonald himself would neither acknowledge nor deny it.[2] But an unscrupulous Conservative press played it for all it was worth as proof positive that Labor had been suborned by Moscow, and thousands of laggard voters, who normally showed no spark of interest in anything beyond their insular horizons, now surged to the polls with but one idea, that MacDonald and his traitorous cabal must go. The Conservatives won the election with a handsome majority over both Labor and Liberals. Baldwin resumed the prime ministership, with Winston Churchill as Chancellor of the Exchequer and Austen Chamberlain[3] as Foreign Secretary. Britain entered upon five years of Conservative rule.

Except toward the Soviet Union, the new government carried on the conciliatory foreign policy of its predecessor. The Locarno Pact of 1925, Austen Chamberlain's crowning achievement, appeared at last to give Western Europe a fair and stable peace. At home the government followed traditional Conservative policies. All Churchill's budgets were reactionary and protectionist in spirit. In May 1925, perhaps more in the interests of national prestige than of commercial interest, Britain returned to the gold standard.

But depression and unrest continued. The "Red Letter," authentic or not, had dropped a little too conveniently out of the blue on the eve of a general election. Labor leaders felt they had been victims of a sordid swindle and, in an angry mood, they began to gird themselves to renew the unfinished battles of 1920-21. The coal miners were discussing "direct action." A new royal commission under Sir Herbert Samuel reported early in 1926 and recommended some amalgamation and nationalization of the mines – though not as sweepingly as Sankey in 1919. But the report was again rejected by the government. The report also proposed drastic wage reductions. The miners replied with their slogan, "Not a penny off the pay, not a minute on the day," and after some weeks of futile negotiation, in which all sides showed all the obstinacy and blindness of their respective class, the dispute reached a complete deadlock.

On May 4, 1926, the General Strike began. Miners, railroadmen, transport workers, iron and steel workers, builders, and printers – 2,500,000 laboring men – quit work. The nation's industries were at a standstill. In reply, the government declared a virtual state of siege. Sir John Simon in the House of Commons pronounced the strike "unlawful." Troops guarded the depots and docks. Naval ratings occupied and operated the power stations and reservoirs. Warships were stationed off the Mersey, Tyne, and South Wales. Hundreds of strikers were jailed. Supply organizations were quickly improvised throughout the country and staffed by volunteers. Army trucks, rusting in their dumps since 1919, were brought out, furbished up, and put to use. A huge "milk pool" was stationed in Hyde Park in London. Young men of college type drove the busses, the streetcars, the subways, and even the railroad trains, unloaded the food ships in the docks, or patrolled the streets as special constables, hugely enjoying the excitement and novelty of the situation, and on the whole not doing their jobs too badly. Meanwhile, as the printers had gone on strike, the nation was without newspapers, and the government issued its own propaganda sheet, the *British Gazette,* under the editorship of Churchill. Baldwin himself, as somehow he always managed to do in a crisis, maintained an attitude of masterly inactivity.

The strikers had expected the government to collapse like the walls of Jericho. When the government did not collapse, the strikers were in a serious quandary. There were no Lenins among them, and they had prepared no revolutionary organs for the seizure of control. They kept insisting that the dispute was "industrial," not "political." J. H. Thomas, the

The General Strike, 1926: Arthur Henderson, Ramsay MacDonald, and J. H. Thomas leaving a conference at Memorial Hall in London

RADIO TIMES HULTON

railroadmen's leader, one of the few men in the strikers' camp who saw the contradictions of the situation, had been strongly opposed to the General Strike from the beginning. The country as a whole, while sympathizing with the miners, would not brook "rebellion" on the part of the trade unions as a class. The Trades Union General Council, greatly to its credit, called off the strike as soon as it saw that the strike had no chance of success and prevented the situation from degenerating into useless chaos and bloodshed. On May 12, 1926, the General Strike ended. But the miners, "betrayed" by their fellow workers, continued their struggle independently and did not return to work for another six months. In the end they accepted terms worse than those of 1921. As if to add insult to injury, the government early in 1927 passed a Trades Disputes Act which declared to be illegal all "sympathetic" strikes or any strikes calculated to coerce the government and intimidate the community.

The strike settlement, as it happened, synchronized with an improvement in the country's economic condition. The world was entering the Locarno era of the later 1920's. Baldwin, at the head of a safe Conservative government, was content to let events take their course. Lloyd George dubbed Baldwin's policy "torpid, sleepy, and barren"; but calculated inertia was probably not a bad tactic in the circumstances. Unemployment remained at just over the million mark; but, whether or not the government had done anything to help it, the future was undeniably a little rosier. Once more, presumably, peace was producing its own cure.

There was one lively incident in May 1927. The police made a raid on Soviet House, the London offices of the Soviet Trade Agency and of Arcos Ltd.[4] These twin organizations had continued to exist and do business despite the virtual lapsing of Lloyd George's Russian treaty of 1921 and of MacDonald's more recent treaty of 1924, and had become the particular bugaboo of the then Home Secretary, Joynson-Hicks. Whether Soviet House was a center of Soviet propaganda and military espionage or not was never definitely proved. But the police searched the premises from cellar to roof, and the Soviet agents were sent packing. The Labor Party, with that geniality which is British politics, entertained the indignant agents at lunch in the House of Commons before their departure. Diplomatic relations were broken off between the two countries. In general British public opinion was indifferent or mildly amused; but, to judge by current articles in *Pravda* and by subsequent events in Russia, the incident was taken far more seriously by the Soviet leaders. (See p. 430.)

In February 1928, Asquith, the old Liberal leader, died, and it almost seemed as if an age died with him. He had resigned from the Liberal party and from public life in 1926. Lloyd George remained leader of his own faction of the Liberal party. But Liberalism as a whole, divided and discredited despite the high caliber of many of its supporters, was no longer a force in Britain.

The life of Parliament came to its statutory end, and general elections were held in May 1929. Baldwin and the Conservative party went to the country with the characteristic slogan "Safety First," a tame acquiescence, the Opposition said, in all the evils from which, despite the evident economic recovery in the world at large, the country was still acknowledged to be suffering. The election resulted in a Conservative defeat. Ramsay MacDonald formed his second Labor government. But this time he did not combine the offices of Prime Minister and Foreign Secretary. Arthur Henderson was his Foreign Secretary. Philip Snowden again was his Chancellor of the Exchequer.

Ireland

Since the Irish Easter Rebellion of 1916, Sinn Fein had become the most important party in southern Ireland. (See p. 46.) In the general election of December 1918, it had returned 73 members out of a total Irish representation — including Ulster (Northern Ireland) — of 106. But the 73 declined to go to Westminster. They preferred instead to set up an independent parliament of their own, the Dail Eireann, and they held their first session in the Dublin Mansion House on January 21, 1919. The proceedings were prefaced by the reading of an Irish "Declaration of Independence." On his return to Ireland, after his escape from an English jail, Eamon de Valera, hero of the Easter Rebellion, was elected "President of the Irish Republic." The Dail, legally, was a rebel body, but the British authorities took no immediate steps to suppress it, even after the murder of two policemen — the first on the first day of its sessions. The British

The Irish Civil War, 1919-21: one of the "Black and Tans" making an arrest

EUROPEAN

Government evidently was reverting to its age-old Irish policy of blind leniency to be followed by equally blind violence.

Dan Breen, as is usually supposed, initiated the campaign of assassinating policemen, a campaign which, in the course of 1919, developed into the Irish Civil War. The Royal Irish Constabulary in the old days had always been a popular and highly respected force, recruited entirely from Irishmen, but its members now became the victims of systematic murder at the hands of their own countrymen. The crimes were normally credited to the self-styled Irish Republican Army, the IRA. They were carefully and skillfully planned; and were committed with virtual impunity, as no witness could be found who wished, or dared, to give evidence against an arrested suspect, and no jury could be empaneled which wished, or dared, to convict. If, as indeed did happen sometimes, a conviction was obtained, the prisoner went on a hunger strike and shortly had to be released.

The campaign soon turned against the military garrisons. Soldiers, as well as police, went in fear of their lives. They were fired on from passing cars, ambushed in the streets and country lanes, even shot down at the doors of their own lodgings by apparently innocent callers; and these activities were varied on occasion by raids on their barracks for the capture of arms. Soldiers and police, finding to their cost that the ordinary usages of the law were powerless to protect them, resorted to reprisals on their own account, and shot, wrecked, and burned with all the license of their assailants. Parish priests and bishops denounced the campaign from their pulpits, but with little effect. The majority of the Irish people seemed to have little sympathy with it, though there were many who could not but admire the courage and sheer persistence of the outrages. De Valera at the moment was in America enlisting sympathy and raising funds.

A curfew and other repressive measures went into force in September 1919. The Dail was proclaimed a dangerous association and forbidden to meet, and several Sinn Fein leaders were arrested. Search parties were sent out after hidden arms. Armored cars and cavalry swept the country. Dublin Castle looked like a besieged fortress. The British Government announced that hunger strikers would not be released. Terence MacSwiney, Mayor of Cork, died in Brixton Gaol on the seventy-fourth day of his hunger strike.

The Irish Civil War raged all through 1920. The British courts in several parts of Ireland ceased to function, and the Irish set up courts of their own. During the year strong reinforcements of troops arrived from England. An auxiliary police was formed largely of ex-army officers who, because there were insufficient police uniforms available, wore dark Glengarry caps and khaki, and came to be known as the "Black and Tans." On New Year's Day, 1921, "authorized reprisals" went into force. Districts where outrages had occurred were held collectively responsible on the general ground that the outrages could only have been possible with the assistance or connivance of the inhabitants — as indeed was usually the case — and they were collectively punished by burnings and demolitions. It could not be said that Southern Ireland was pacified by these measures. Murder and arson, countermurder and counterarson continued to run their ruinous course. Probably the Irish Republican Army had many more native sympathizers in 1921 than it had in 1919. But the measures did prove that the British Government possessed the means, whenever it had the will, to crush the Sinn Fein movement utterly.

Early in 1920, a new Government of Ireland Bill, to replace the long-since inoperative Home Rule Act of 1914, was being debated in the House of Commons in London and was eventually passed at the end of the year. The new act provided for two legislatures, one for Northern Ireland and one for Southern Ireland, and also for a joint Council of Ireland, where the discussion of matters common to both might take place. The British Government reserved to itself substantial control over the armed forces and over foreign relations. Ulster (Northern Ireland) accepted the Act without enthusiasm but proceeded to set up its separate legislature. In June 1921, the Northern Parliament accordingly assembled in Belfast; King George V attended the inauguration ceremonies in person and in his speech appealed to all Irishmen to bring their unhappy fratricidal feud to an end; Sir James Craig (later Lord Craigavon), leader of the old Ulster Unionists, became Prime Minister of the first Ulster Government. The Southern Parliament was declared open in Dublin later in the same month; but, out of 128 possible members, only four put in an appearance. The Southern Parliament did not meet again. So ended the century-old status of Ireland, as originally established under the Act of Union of 1800.

Throughout 1921, Ireland continued to be the first preoccupation of the British Government. The attitude of Lloyd George, then Prime Minister, was clear and logical. With one hand he offered peace within the Empire, and with the other he offered war to the finish. Ireland could have either. He and Churchill, who had just been made chairman of a Cabinet Committee on Irish Affairs, tried again and again to bring the protagonists in the struggle together in the quiet and dispassionate atmosphere of a round-table conference. De Valera had now returned from America and was living the life of a hunted outlaw with a price on his head. In July 1921, after many mysterious and secret exchanges, Lloyd George prevailed upon him to come to London, and for the moment a truce was proclaimed in Ireland.

Lloyd George received de Valera at No. 10 Downing Street on July 14, 1921. It was a moment of high drama. The head of a great, victorious empire confronted a man, technically a rebel, who determinedly posed throughout the meeting as the envoy of an independent state. Lloyd George, rising, as he always did, to an artistic opportunity, greeted his visitor as a brother Celt and replied to de Valera's opening speech in Irish with one in Welsh. Agreement, as was soon obvious, was going to be impossible, yet both sides were averse to allowing the parleys to break down. In October, in London, Lloyd George again met Sinn Fein delegates, this time headed by Arthur Griffith and Michael Collins. But two months of futile discussion exhausted what little was left of humor and patience. De Valera from his stronghold in Dublin kept issuing inflammatory proclamations on the general theme of "No Surrender." At last, on December 5, Lloyd George made his final offer of peace or war. He may have been bluffing, but apparently he convinced the Sinn Fein delegates that he was prepared, if need be, to go the lengths of a military reconquest of Ireland. On December 6, 1921, Arthur Griffith and Michael Collins capitulated and signed a treaty for the establishment of an Irish Free State.

The news of this wholly unexpected agreement raised a violent outcry, alike from English Conservatives, Ulster Unionists, and extreme Sinn Feiners. Each party, for its own good reasons, declared itself basely betrayed. Lloyd George and his colleague, Churchill, were the most reviled men in Britain. Griffith and Collins returned to Ireland to face an angry de Valera, who would not move an inch from his demands for the complete independence of a united Ireland. But on January 7, 1922, after three weeks' bitter debate, the Dail accepted the treaty by 64 votes to 57. De Valera promptly resigned his Presidency, and Griffith was elected in his place. A Provisional Irish Government was set up under Collins, and a committee appointed to draft a Southern Irish constitution. A subsequent general election in Ireland in June 1922 more than upheld the decision of the Dail.

The treaty gave the Irish Free State the status of a British Dominion. The members of its Parliament would be required to take an oath of "true faith and allegiance" to its constitution and of faithfulness to the King. The office of Lord Lieutenant was abolished, and a new representative of the Crown would be appointed by the British Government and entitled Governor General. The Free State would assume a share of the British national debt. It would maintain its own forces, but it would depend on the British Navy for the defense of its seas, and it would also concede certain naval and harbor facilities, notably at Berehaven and Queenstown, to the British Admiralty. These defensive provisions were held to be enough to allay the strategic fears which always lay at the bottom of England's attitude to Ireland.

The treaty also provided that Ulster (Northern Ireland) could elect either to come into the Free State or to retain her independence and separation. Northern Ireland preferred the latter option, and her Parliament and government, as already set up under the act of 1920, continued in being. A commission was appointed to determine the boundary between Northern and Southern Ireland.

But whatever England does in Ireland is always wrong. If, now that the treaty had been signed, British troops had not left the country, the sincerity of the British Government would have been in serious question. So the British troops did leave the country. Barracks and armories were evacuated; Dublin Castle was "surrendered"; hundreds of Irish prisoners were released from jail. Perhaps the British Government found an ironic satisfaction in transferring the burden of law and order to the Irish themselves. Actually they transferred Ireland to the mercies of the Irish Republican Army. Irishmen who had been loyal to the Crown, especially farming landowners, found themselves without protection. Even Communism enjoyed a short, mad frolic. "Soviets" sprang up and landless laborers sought to solve the "agrarian question" on Russian lines by seizing farmers' property. In April 1922, Rory O'Connor, at the head of a band of Republican "irregulars," occupied the Four Courts in Dublin and proclaimed himself head of a Republican Government of all Ireland, and he was only ejected two months later with the loan of two British field guns. There were border affrays in Armagh and Tyrone, the disputed counties between Northern and Southern Ireland, and there were anti-Catholic riots in Belfast. Without any doubt the year 1922 was the wickedest of the entire Irish Civil War.

Collins was determined to exterminate lawlessness in Ireland. Unlike the old "Black and Tans," he knew his men and their tactics. But on August 12, 1922, Griffith died suddenly of heart disease, and ten days later Collins himself was shot down in an ambush. The Irish Free State was left to begin its uncertain career under William Cosgrave.

The inevitable reaction set in. No people – not even the Irish – could have lived at this crisis tension indefinitely. By contrast with what had gone before, Cosgrave's era was almost pedestrian. He made an able President. He was committed to the treaty of 1921 and determined to see it carried out. A Tripartite Pact, in December 1925, at last settled the vexed boundary question between Northern and Southern Ireland, though the settlement was fiercely contested by de Valera's party. Ireland as a whole entered the later 1920's in more peaceful circumstances than she had known for years. Many a wishful observer at the time believed that the Irish Question had been solved.

It was not solved. It was only in abeyance till the Depression which struck the economic world in the early 1930's; and, in Ireland, as elsewhere, the Depression was the great tester of solutions. De Valera emerged from "underground," as we would say today, broke with Sinn Fein, and founded a new party, the Fianna Fail, the "Soldiers of Destiny." In the elections of February 1932, he won his first majority, became President, and put in hand a typical, if not unexpected, program of reforms. He rescinded the ban that had stopped the Irish Republican Army from holding parades and released such of its members as were then in jail. He imposed tariffs on a wide range of manufactured goods from Britain. He withheld the land annuities paid by Irish tenant farmers to the British Government as interest on bonds formerly issued to help them purchase their land.[5] He replaced James MacNeill, then Governor General, by one Donal Buckley, a Republican of pointed mediocrity, who took up his residence, not at the Viceregal Lodge, but in a house in a Dublin suburb. He finally abolished the oath of allegiance. One by one the clauses of the hated treaty of 1921 were repudiated.

Yet de Valera hesitated to make a final and irrevocable break with the British Commonwealth and for a time pursued oddly contradictory policies. Thus a Free State delegation attended the Ottawa Conference in 1932; but in December 1936, the Dail used the crisis over the abdication of Edward VIII to abolish the office of Governor General altogether, and the accession of George VI was not proclaimed in the Free State. At the same time, however, the Dail passed an External Relations Act, by which the King would act on behalf of the Free State "for the purposes of the appointment of diplomatic and consular representatives and the conclusion of international agreements."

In May 1937, de Valera introduced a new constitution and secured its approval in the Dail on June 14. The constitution ignored, and by inference replaced, the treaty of 1921. It provided for a President with powers somewhat analogous to those of the President of the United States and a Dail and a Senate of decidedly corporative flavor. It restored for Ireland the Gaelic name of "Eire." It mentioned neither King nor Commonwealth. A year later, after extended negotiations, a financial agreement was signed in London ending the dispute over the land annuities. The British Government handed over to Eire the port and harbor facilities which had been reserved for it under the treaty of 1921, notably Berehaven and Queenstown (Cóbh). Douglas Hyde, founder of the Gaelic League, a well-known scholar and a Protestant, was elected the first President of Eire in June 1938.

Meanwhile, it is to be noted parenthetically, Northern Ireland continued overwhelmingly in its British allegiance. In the Northern Ireland elections of November 1933, Lord Craigavon's Unionist party won 36 seats, an absolute majority of 20 over all other parties combined. De Valera, whom one constituency elected as its Member in that election, thus became the one man in Ireland with the right to sit in both parliaments. But he did not take his seat in Belfast.

The New Imperialism

The British Empire in 1914 was a vast, widely dispersed aggregation of territories, covering 13,000,000 square miles, one-quarter of the earth's land surface, and inhabited by a population of 450,000,000, one-quarter of the human race. Its white population was about 70,000,000, mainly Anglo-Saxon, but also in part French, Dutch, and Spanish. Its political structure was complex in the extreme, and the particular status or administration of the different parts of it was perhaps explainable only in terms of their histories. Its main constituents were the United Kingdom of Great Britain (England, Scotland, and Wales) and Ireland; the Dominions of Canada, Newfoundland, Australia, New Zealand, and South Africa;

the Indian Empire and the crown colonies and protectorates. The Dominions were self-governing, and their political heads were responsible to popularly elected legislatures; but their laws were theoretically subject to the assent of a governor general or governor, representing the King. The Indian Empire was ultimately administered, through a Viceroy, by the India Office in London. The crown colonies and protectorates were administered in whole or in part from the Colonial Office in London. There was also a class of territory ruled by native chiefs with the assistance of British "residents"; and there were certain "spheres of influence," defined by international treaties. There was finally the special position of Egypt, nominally independent but under British military occupation. To this aggregation the peace settlement of 1919-20 added 1,000,000 square miles of territory and native populations of 7,000,000 governable under the new mandates system.

The heterogeneity of the Empire was bewildering even to the best-informed of Britons. Nothing in French precision, German system, or American legal literalness could have conceived so unique an organization. The Empire had originally grown by no law but its own vitality; its ultimate governance was a code of conventions rather than a constitution. Time was when it represented no more than the military and economic ambition of a small class in Great Britain; but it had since become the repository of great political power, the field of a migration of peoples, and a vehicle of culture; and, like Rome itself, its culture was likely to survive, and to justify it in history, in long centuries after its power had gone and its people had lost their identity.

The British Empire began as one of the maritime and colonial enterprises of the seventeenth century. It expanded under eighteenth-century capitalism and the Industrial Revolution. It produced two classes of territory: first, the purely European settlements such as the original thirteen American States or the eventual Dominions; and second, the trading and bureaucratic dependencies such as India or the Crown Colonies. The first was the territory of permanent white immigrants, who regarded themselves as citizens of a new country; the second was the territory of impermanent white traders, soldiers, and officials, who went there for a career and then retired to England to live on their investments or their pensions. But, whatever form it took, the Empire was imbued with distinctive British ideas of government and bureaucratic integrity. Its white subjects enjoyed their degrees of democracy and representative institutions; its "dependent" subjects enjoyed the protection of a scrupulously administered law and medical, educational, and other paternalistic services, and they were invariably secured in their local creeds and customs. Nor was the Empire monopolistically British; it granted – at least in the nineteenth century – the same commercial opportunities to all nationalities, often including the native races themselves, as were enjoyed by the subjects of the Paramount Power.

Certainly the British Empire had sometimes exhibited the unpleasant aspects of all empires. In its time it had reared its freebooters, its slavers, and its nabobs. If it was a "white man's burden," it was a lucrative one. But freedom grew beside force, and trusteeship beside exploitation. Peace and law were established over areas of the world where they had been unknown before. The Empire's statesmen looked forward to the eventual independence of all its peoples. The truth is that British imperial ideology was a changing, growing thing. Each crisis of imperial history taught an appropriate lesson, learned and not forgotten. It might be said that in the past four centuries the British had had four empires. The first began with Cromwell, the second with the American Revolution, the third with the Indian Mutiny, and the fourth with the First World War. It was the third, the later Victorian Empire, which it became the fashion to decry, the Jingo Empire of Kipling's verses and the Diamond Jubilee. Yet that Empire too had its greatness. It was served by the best and finest Britain could give, men of the type of Grey, Dilke, Ripon, Lytton, Lansdowne, Cromer, Milner, Sandeman, Morley, Minto, Crewe, Lugard, Zetland, Curzon, and any number of others, products usually of the public schools and older universities, patricians every one of them. But by 1919 even those of them who still lived were already figures of the past, fit to spend their latter days in retirement, perhaps writing memoirs of exquisite classical polish about the good old days when the word of a British official from the Nile to the Yangtze was absolute and undisputed law. Lord Lloyd, the last of the line, was dismissed from his post by Arthur Henderson, Foreign Secretary of the Labor government of 1929.

The fourth Empire was the Empire of the Fourteen Points, of self-determination and the sovereignty of small states. Its main contribution to the doctrine of imperialism was the mandate. The ideology that made the new Europe also unmade the old Victorian Empire. The history of Ireland, Egypt, or India during the 1920's should have been well understood by the statesmen who contrived the revolts in Arabia or in the Middle Danube. The same ideology had already made new nations of the self-governing Dominions. In 1914 those Dominions had all entered the war of their own free will; in 1917 their representatives had met together as coequals of British statesmen at the Imperial War Conference in London; in 1919 their delegates had separately attended the Peace Conference in Paris and separately signed the Treaty of Versailles; they had become separate member states of the League of Nations. The very name "British Empire" at this time was being superseded by the more liberal and sonorous "British Commonwealth of Nations."

It was a thousand pities that the fourth Empire should have coincided with a period of grave national lassitude in Britain and a correspondingly weak foreign policy. The period may be said to have begun in October 1919, when Lord Curzon became Foreign Secretary, and it was a period of one bitter defeat after the other. The British people after the war had no heart for the old idols, and were content to suffer disastrous losses of prestige in the interest of "peace." The Labor left wing was doctrinally anti-imperialist. The strength of the British Navy was allowed to fall below the relative level of security. In Britain the decline of the birth rate gradually dried up the principal tributary of Empire emigration. Curious and extraordinary must it have seemed, nevertheless, that a nation whose armies had just fought at Baghdad, Megiddo, and Salonika should now suddenly be accepting such deep and repeated humiliation at the hands of men like Zaghlul, Amanullah, Riza Khan, and Kemal. And curious, too, and tragic that it should have been Curzon who had to initiate this period, Curzon with all his associations with the East, a former Viceroy of India, a very incarnation of the imperialism that had gone. Some of this story is told in these pages. But the general result was that transactions of policy, even though they were perfectly in line with the spirit of the times, instead of appearing to have been granted by a power in the full consciousness of its strength and rightness, appeared rather to have been extorted from a sort of moral impotence. Yet never was there a time in history when the guidance and stability of the Empire with its massive traditions were so urgently needed.

One matter that deserves more than a passing mention is the Statute of Westminster of 1931. The British people might be satisfied with the heterogeneity of their Empire, but one or two events since the First World War had called attention to the desirability of a greater legal precision, especially in the relations between Britain and the self-governing Dominions. In 1922, for instance, occurred the Chanaq crisis, one of the now forgotten crises, but one which at its time seemed serious enough. Kemal was then marching to victory over the Greeks in the Turkish War of Independence, and he narrowly avoided a clash with a small British force occupying the demilitarized zone of the Dardanelles at Chanaq. (See pp. 186 and 266.) For a few anxious days, Britain was on the point of war with the new Nationalist Turkey. The British Government was in immediate consultation with the Dominions in regard to their attitude in the event of such a war breaking out. Australia and New Zealand, both interested in Mediterranean communications and both participants in the Dardanelles campaign of 1915, at once "associated" themselves with Britain and promised, if necessary, to send contingents of troops. South Africa's decision was delayed – General Smuts, then Prime Minister, was absent on a hunting expedition in the bush and could not be reached – and when her reply was ready, the crisis had already passed. Canada temporized and avoided making any commitment. But Mackenzie King, the Canadian Prime Minister, subsequently stated his position on the occasion of the Treaty of Lausanne with Turkey in 1923. While he could not take exception to any course the British Government deemed it advisable to take, he said, he could not regard Canada as being bound by any obligations beyond those that the Canadian Parliament of its own volition decided to recognize.

Through the early 1920's the Dominions were all displaying considerable diplomatic independence. From the first sessions of the League Assembly, the Canadian delegate constantly struck out on a line of his own. In 1923, Canada created a precedent by signing a fisheries treaty with the United States, the first international treaty to be signed by a Dominion without the participation of a British representative. In 1925 a clause in the Locarno Pact specifically exempted the Dominions and India from any of its obligations unless and until they voluntarily adhered. In 1927 Canada took a seat on the Council of the League of Nations. It must be allowed that British foreign policy in the interwar years, weak as it sometimes was, was still weaker and more indecisive because of the necessity of consultation with the Dominions, none of whom felt much inclination to support far-flung commitments, often of no immediate concern to themselves, which might easily lead to their own involvement.

Imperial Conferences had been held in London more or less quadrennially since the Colonial Conference in the year of Queen Victoria's Jubilee, and it fell to the Imperial Conference of 1926 to try to regulate what could be regulated in the legalistic chaos of interimperial relations. A Committee on Interimperial Relations at that Conference, under the chairmanship of Balfour, reported that "the Empire, considered as a whole, defies classification and bears no real resemblance to any other political organization which now exists or has yet been tried," and then propounded a definition which, as one commentator put it, read like a clause from the Athanasian Creed:

> [Great Britain and the Dominions] are autonomous communities within the British Empire, equal in status, in no way subordinate one to another in any aspect of their domestic or external affairs, though united by a common allegiance to the Crown, and freely associated as members of the British Commonwealth of Nations.

The discussions were resumed at the Imperial Conference of 1930, and in December 1931, the British Parliament passed the Statute of Westminster, by which political power was formally transferred to the Dominions under their several constitutions. In the legal language of the Statute, no law made by a Dominion parliament should be void or inoperative on the ground that it was repugnant to the law of England, and no act passed by the British Parliament should extend to a Dominion otherwise than at the request, and with the consent, of that Dominion. Henceforth the self-governing Dominions of the British Commonwealth would bear themselves before the world as sovereign states.

Canada

This book in the main is a history of international relations. But a good deal of space in it has been given to the domestic politics of different states. A peculiarity of Europe, especially, has always been the constant interplay of foreign and home affairs, and the one is sometimes not intelligible without the other. And to some extent the same is true of the British Commonwealth. Canada, Australia, New Zealand, South Africa, India – and, of course, Ireland – all illustrate degrees of the selfsame interplay. We have already considered Ireland; and we shall further include in this chapter sections on such local problems in the other Commonwealth countries as may fairly be said to have had an international bearing at this time. Most remarkable in these countries was their great variation of historical circumstance and social character, despite the fact that their colonization took place in the main within a single century and was effected by a people of a single European, mostly British, culture. We begin with the oldest Dominion — Canada.

Canada was settled by European colonists about the same time and in much the same way as the United States. But whereas the United States, though originally of greater national admixture, came to form a single English-speaking amalgam, Canada remained divided between her two main French-speaking and English-speaking communities. The French originally possessed themselves of the St. Lawrence region or "Lower Canada," now coterminous with the Province of Quebec, but in course of time they migrated in considerable numbers into the Maritime Provinces and to the West. The English originally possessed themselves of Acadia (Nova Scotia). During the American Revolution the United Empire Loyalists founded the English-speaking provinces of Ontario and New Brunswick. In 1763 Canada passed under British rule, and further immigration from France almost wholly ceased. The British and European immigrations of the later nineteenth century were accompanied, as they were in the United States, by the opening of the West and the building of the great trans-Continental railroads. In 1921 the population of Canada was about 10,000,000, of whom 30 per cent were French speaking. Meanwhile there was little in the way of an Indian question and no Negro question at all.

In their Province of Quebec the French Canadians built up a civilization unique in the Western Hemisphere. Their language was French, but a French surviving from the eighteenth century; even their arts and architecture retained an eighteenth-century flavor. Their economy was almost entirely that of the small farmer, or *habitant* as he was called. Their religion was Roman Catholic. They were a people of charm and hardihood; but they were a people also of quite extraordinary exclusiveness. They never entirely lost a nostalgia — like the peasants of Spain, for instance — for the paternalist Catholic monarchy that had once ruled over them and, though they respected the British, and though they appreciated the equal status they were given, the British Empire as such lay outside their normal vision. In all the politics of Canada, domestic or foreign, therefore, the Canadian Government had always to reckon on the existence of a tight, self-regarding community, already one-third of the electorate and, by reason of its higher birth rate, of growing importance, a community that could be depended on to take a separatist attitude towards any and every national problem that arose. English-speaking Canadians — like some of their American cousins — were sometimes isolationist; but no people were ever so innately and obdurately isolationist as the French-speaking Canadians.

Nationalism in Canada was therefore a matter of some complexity. From time to time vague threats of secession, away from the Empire and away from one another, characterized both the English- and French-speaking communities. From 1914 a nationalist movement grew up among French Canadians and, in the 1930's, it became crystallized in a new provincial political party, the *Union Nationale*. The party agitated for local social reforms and against English-speaking and American ownership of Quebec's industries and resources, and it agitated with greater vehemence during the Depression years, but it did not otherwise develop much of a program. Just before the Second World War, more extreme French Canadian nationalism was taking almost a Fascist and corporative form. Nationalism of a sort was also common among Canadians of Irish origin, especially in Ontario. Britain and the United States each exerted its characteristic influence upon English-speaking Canadians; so much so that two types of English-speaking Canadians, the Anglophile and the Americophile, were often recognizable. All these are matters to be remembered in unraveling the mysteries of Canada's attitudes toward the British Commonwealth, toward the United States, toward the League of Nations, toward collective security, and toward the two World Wars.

Australia

Canada's characteristic domestic problem was that of nationality; Australia's was that of party. The Anglo-Saxon dominated the country from the start of white settlement, and the only minority — and that a small one — was the Irish. All classes, furthermore, were early resolved to keep Australia white. The aborigines were relatively few in numbers and of no political importance. But the eventual economy of Australia, based on wheat and wool and the great distance of the country from the sources of immigration as well as from natural markets, indirectly conspired to produce a population sharply divided between haves and have-nots. Agriculture and industry of whatever kind — even the later gold mining — required large-scale capital for its equipment; but its labor could be cheaply recruited from the indigent immigrant masses, and these masses all too often were the refugees of European economic depressions or of other revolutionary upheavals. Thus it used to be said that every European crisis — the Hungry Forties, the Irish Famine, the Revolution of 1848 — all generated population overspills into Australia. Even the original, unforgotten convict era — and for "convict" in our modern parlance we should read "political prisoner," usually again a revolutionary product — seemed to have decided the pattern of exploiter and exploited for the succeeding history of this remote and harshly inhospitable land.

Thus we note in Australia the emergence of two antagonistic social and political groups — later represented by the Conservative or Liberal and Country parties, and by the Labor party — and the two sharing a political life of extreme bitterness. The former was capitalist and friendly to the British imperial connection; the latter was anticapitalist and generally hostile to the British imperial connection. No eighteenth-century American rebel so abhorred the name of England as the nineteenth-century Australian Labor partisan. In the 1920's, as would be expected, Australia had the strongest Communist party of any British Dominion.

While Australia's characteristic domestic problem existed from her beginnings, her characteristic foreign problem arose only in the twentieth century. Australia, like the United States, Canada, and South Africa, long enjoyed generations of immunity from external danger. In 1901 the "Commonwealth of Australia" was formed, largely in response to German and French rivalry in the Pacific. But then, suddenly in 1905, the Australian people awoke to the portent of Tsushima, and thereafter, till 1945, the fear of Japan dominated the whole of Australia's international relations. In 1909, the Australian Government adopted conscription for home defense and began building an Australian Navy.

But already there were signs that Australia's foreign policy would be conducted along party lines. In 1901 the Conservatives had supported the formation of the Commonwealth of Australia; Labor had agreed to it with great reluctance. In 1909 the Conservatives had supported conscription; Labor had supported it, but only for home defense. In 1914 Australia found herself at war, indeed enthusiastically at war — but, in the Labor view, it was an imperialist war, in which for good measure Australia was the ally of Japan. In 1917 the country was split from top to bottom, along party lines, when William M. Hughes, the Labor Prime Minister, proposed to extend conscription to overseas service.[6] Yet both parties approved of Hughes's uncompromising stand during the Peace Conference of Paris in rejecting the Japanese demand for racial equality and in insisting on Australian or New Zealand mandates over former German islands in the southern Pacific. (See pp. 104-05.) In the 1920's, Australian anxieties were temporarily allayed by the Washington Conference and by the construction of the British naval base at Singapore. But then all the old issues were revived in the decade of crisis which followed the Japanese seizure of Manchuria in 1931.

On all counts Australia was then in a very weak position. The Depression bore heavily on her wool trade, her principal source of foreign currency, at a time when she needed to import war materials and to build up war industries. The naval base at Singapore was still far from complete, and the great British fleet that was to use it did not exist. The United States seemed only to emerge from its neutrality to promulgate high moral doctrine. More basically, Australia, though a vast territory, possessed a small population, and, despite a healthy birth rate and years of assisted immigration, she could put only a puny 7,000,000 into the scales against a fully armed, potential aggressor state in the North of more than ten times that figure.

It was inevitable that Australia's defense strategy should once more be bound up with party differences. Joseph A. Lyons, the Conservative Prime Minister at this time, argued for a big Australian Navy which, in cooperation with the British Navy, would intercept the foe far out to sea. John Curtin, the Leader of the Labor Opposition, argued for a more adaptable and rapid interceptor in the shape of a big air force. The Australian public in general favored either course so long as it kept the enemy out of range of home shores. In the end military expenditures, which were doubled between 1933 and 1936, were devoted chiefly to the navy and air force in roughly equal proportions. But in 1938, Australia still had no more than five cruisers, five destroyers, one seaplane carrier, and 150 first-line planes — and ground forces totaling 45,000 men.

New Zealand

Twelve hundred miles from Australia, across the Tasman Sea, lie the two major islands "capped by snow-clad peaks and protected by the thundering surf" which the Dutch explorers, in Abel Tasman's wake, loyally christened New Zealand. The ubiquitous Captain Cook declared the territory annexed to the British Crown in 1770; but the action was hastily disavowed by his government, which already had a plenitude of colonial problems in North America and had no inclination to add to them. In 1840, by treaty, British sovereignty was established, and the native Maoris were confirmed in the possession of their tribal lands; but the treaty was ill-observed in the intermittent Maori wars of the next thirty years. The discovery of gold brought an influx of white adventurers, many of whom, failing to strike it rich, settled down to the less romantic but steadier occupation of sheep-farming. In course of time an almost exclusively British immigration into a well-favored country of about the same size and temperate climate as the British Isles bred a population of extraordinary homogeneity, free from class and free from minorities, and living on terms of mutual respect with the fine Maori aborigines. It was also a population left wing in its political outlook, like the Australian, but entirely nondoctrinaire and without the embittered two-fold economic stratification of Australian society. The domestic history of New Zealand was one of progress and reform, embodied in advanced labor legislation and suffrage laws — including women's suffrage as early as 1894. Altogether New Zealand was a happy land, the product of a series of happy accidents, a veritable Welfare State before its time.

But with the coming of the twentieth century this earthly elysium too had to be disturbed by external pressures. In 1907 New Zealand was raised to Dominion status. In 1910 she introduced conscription for home defense, and in 1913 she set about the building of a navy. In the First World War her population of 1,500,000 yielded 124,000 men for active service, of whom 19,000 were killed in action. A hectic domestic prosperity at that time resulted from the British bulk purchase of New Zealand meat, wool, and dairy produce at guaranteed prices; but the continued militant temper of the country's labor force was shown in the widespread coal strike of 1917, the worst year of the war.

During the 1920's the normal life of the Dominion seemed to have been resumed. But the country's economy, based on the export of a narrow range of foodstuffs, suffered under the Depression of the 1930's. A Labor majority was returned in the elections of November 1935, and a spate of legislation followed, somewhat reminiscent of the Roosevelt program across the Pacific. But the experiment in the planned Good Life was increasingly vitiated by the feeling of military weakness. Faced with the Japanese menace, New Zealand shared all Australia's fears and reactions. One great war had lately shown, and another was soon to show again, that she could produce the best soldiers in the world; but in 1938 there were still less than 15,000 of them.

South Africa

The Union of South Africa covered rather less than 500,000 square miles at the southern extremity of the African continent. It was a rough, elevated land, the larger part a broad treeless veld, with warm temperatures and spasmodic rains, and an atmosphere as clear and as sunny as a mild summer's day in Canada. The southwestern part of Cape Colony enjoyed "Mediterranean" conditions, grew fruits, and made wines; but the Union's main agricultural wealth was pastoral, and its chief agricultural exports were wool and hides. There were rich gold fields around Johannesburg, producing nearly half the world's gold supply, and rich diamond fields around Kimberley.

The Dutch East India Company ruled and developed the original Cape Colony from 1652 to 1795. It drew its settlers largely from the Netherlands and to a lesser extent from Rhineland Germany and Huguenot France. The three national strains gradually fused into a single Boer, or Afrikaner, people speaking their distinctive Afrikaans language. The British occupied the territory in 1795, at first in order to deny it to the French, with whom they were at war; but from 1820 onward, British settlers began to make their way especially into the so-called Eastern Province. A considerable infiltration of Jews from the Baltic countries took place in the 1890's, and more recently Jews amounted to about 5 per cent of the white population. East Indians, mainly low-caste Hindus originally imported as coolie labor, were found in parts of Natal and the Transvaal. The native races of South Africa consisted of the primitive Bushmen, the less primitive Hottentots, and the incomparably finer and more warlike Bantu. In addition there should be mentioned the very numerous poor whites and half-castes, or "coloreds," mainly in and around the Cape. All told, from about 1910 to 1920, the total population consisted of 2,000,000 whites and 8,000,000 others. It used to be said that South Africa combined in a small compass the problems of Canada, India, Palestine, and the southern United States.

The recent political history of the country centered around reconciliation of Boer and British rights, and of both with those of the domiciled native and East Indian populations. The Boer was independent, intolerant of strangers, religious in his way, wedded to his lands and herds, a mixture – if we may stretch our imagination so far – of Magyar and Mormon. The British were enterprising and aggressive; they prospected and explored; their native policy was usually more liberal than that of the Boer; and ultimately the great mineral wealth of the country passed into their hands. Confederation of Boer and Briton along Canadian lines had been tried without success in 1877, and then South Africa had become involved in the general imperialist scramble for African territory which characterized the 1880's and 1890's. Out of that scramble emerged German Southwest Africa, the British Protectorate of Bechuanaland, and the British colonies of Southern and Northern Rhodesia, named after the great imperial pioneer and their virtual founder, Cecil Rhodes. The opening of the diamond fields and the gold fields and the building of the railroads created new rivalries. The entire accumulation of combustibles flared up in the South African War of

1899-1902, a wasteful, senseless struggle which ended in the British annexation of the two Boer republics, the Transvaal and the Orange Free State.

The settlement in 1902 so far as it affected the Boer and the British was rapid and gratifying, and was doubtless due to the common good sense of the leadership on both sides. The liberal policies of men like Louis Botha and Jan Christiaan Smuts, Boer generals in the recent war, prevailed over the narrow, embittered nationalism of men like the former Boer "President" Kruger. The Union of South Africa was founded in May 1910 with full Dominion status. Afrikaans and English were both made legal languages; each colony was allowed to retain its own franchise laws and native laws; and, by an ingenious compromise, Pretoria became the Union capital and the seat of the executive, Capetown the seat of Parliament, and Bloemfontein the seat of the Supreme Court.[7] Botha was Union Prime Minister from 1910 to his death in August 1919.

But the main problems, though quieted, were not wholly laid to rest. The problem of nonwhite labor, the problems of franchise and education, were always latent. The Union was the only one of the British Dominions in which secession was ever a serious practical issue. During the First World War, General James Hertzog formed a Nationalist party with a frankly antiwar, anti-imperialist platform. A short-lived rebellion broke out in the former Boer republics. But Union troops, Boer and British fighting side by side, afterward conquered German Southwest Africa, and Union expeditionary forces were sent to German East Africa and to the Western front. Smuts attended the Imperial Conference in London in 1917, and Botha and he represented South Africa in Paris in 1919. Smuts emerged from his European sojourn as one of the architects of the League of Nations and one of the foremost international statesmen of his day. Under the peace terms German Southwest Africa was assigned to the Union as a Class C mandate. (See p. 117.)

Smuts succeeded Botha as Prime Minister of the Union on Botha's death in 1919, but in 1924 his government was defeated in the face of a new upsurge of Boer nationalism and of Indian and labor unrest. Elections, fought with animus and violence, returned a Labor-Nationalist majority, and Hertzog became Prime Minister. During the remaining 1920's, public controversy centered around legislation introduced by the new government – a bill to segregate Indian settlements, limit Indian landownership, and halt Indian immigration; a Color Bar Bill to legalize the color line, especially in the mines; a Flag and Nationality Bill for the design of a new flag for the Union expressing "our independent nationhood . . . and our accepted national status" – all of which sufficiently illustrated the direction of Boer sentiment. In 1930 a section of Hertzog's followers founded a Republican League, the object of which was complete severance from Britain and the British Commonwealth. Hertzog himself denounced extremism of this sort, the Statute of Westminster in 1931 effected a certain mollification, and then South Africa passed into the new problems of the Depression.

At first South Africa had escaped the worst rigors of the Depression. As one of the premier gold producers of the world, she was in a fortunate position, and remained after 1931 a gold-standard country. But the Depression overtook the Dominion's economy in the end. In March 1933, in order to meet the crisis, Hertzog and Smuts formed a coalition with Hertzog as Prime Minister and Smuts as Deputy Prime Minister, and their two parties were fused under the name of the United party. In the subsequent election, the United party won an overwhelming success. Evidently economic adversity was having its effect and moderating the extremism of South African politics. Dr. Daniel F. Malan, a former supporter of Hertzog, broke away, however, and organized a new Nationalist party. The Hertzog-Smuts coalition was confirmed in elections in March 1938, "a decisive victory in the interest of national unity," although it was reported that there was considerable personal friction between the two leaders themselves. The proximity of war in Europe found Hertzog on the side of "neutrality," as he had been in 1914, and Smuts on the side of Britain.

India

The subcontinent of India measures 1,700,000 square miles, about three-fourths the area of Europe without Russia, or one-half the United States, or seventeen times Great Britain. Through the ages it has been subject to a succession of conquerors, coming mostly by way of the mountain passes in the northwest, and its population, as each wave of invaders overlaid the last, still gives a curious impression of stratification. The Aryan Hindus arrived supposedly between 2000 and 1000 B.C., and the Moslems from 1001 A.D. onward. According to the census of 1931, India had over 350,000,000 inhabitants, a fifth of the human race, speaking over two hundred languages and professing eight religions.[8] But, even apart from size and the extent and complexity of population, India at this time was perhaps the most interesting and significant of British overseas territories. The independence of Southern Ireland was the last act of nineteenth-century European nationalism; the independence of India was part of a far greater world-wide nationalist episode which, as we write, is not yet completed.

The first European contact with India was by sea in 1498, when the Portuguese explorer Vasco da Gama cast anchor off Malabar. Thereafter the Portuguese, Dutch, French, and British disputed the trade of the country till, by the middle of the eighteenth century, the British had firmly established themselves, not only in the "factories" of Bombay, Madras, and Calcutta, but in considerable areas of the hinterland. Wars, annexations, and treaties extended their sway, and they eventually ruled rather more than half of India, and exercised an indirect, but effective, "suzerainty" over the native Indian States in the remainder. The British Indian Empire was as crazed and patched as a map of medieval Germany, with an all-inclusive monarchy ringing an agglomeration of lesser principalities.

India is an object lesson to those anthropologists who claim that social character is a function of physical environment. For the two principal Indian communities, the Hindu and the Moslem, could hardly have been more dissimilar. Yet the land they lived in was the same land, burned by the same sun, watered by the same rains. The Hindus comprised about two-thirds of the population. Their religion was contained in no one doctrine and no one sacred text, and consisted rather of a multiplicity of rites and customs, often reaching back to a pagan antiquity, varying from locality to locality and, with easy tolerance, allowing the coexistence of the crudest idol worship, a luxuriant mythology, and a deep philosophical pantheism. Generally the Hindus cremated their dead and believed in the transmigration of souls and in the ultimate extinction of the individual self. Their religion was static and confined to India. They never proselytized and rarely admitted a convert.

The Hindu castes formed the most elaborate system of color lines in the world. The priestly Brahmans, the highest of the castes, were guardians of the shrines and temples, and teachers in the village schools; yet more recently they did not eschew, under necessity, the humbler professions of modern civilization as lawyers, newspapermen, clerks — and cooks. Beneath them the castes descended through the gamut of the trades and industries, the warrior, the merchant, the peasant, the moneylender, the cobbler, the barber — amounting to some 2,300 different castes in all. A man was born into his caste and never married outside it; a father passed on his calling and his property to his sons. The higher castes were strictly vegetarian, and all Hinduism regarded the slaughter of a cow as almost a greater crime than homicide. For Hindu women, marriage and childbearing were the be-all and end-all of existence, and both often took place before maturity. At the bottom of the caste system came the outcastes or "untouchables" — the Depressed Classes or Scheduled Castes, as official euphemism preferred to call them — who were supposed to number 50,000,000; they followed menial or "unclean" occupations and lived on the edge of starvation, segregated in their villages, forbidden the temples and schools, forbidden water from the communal well, sometimes even forbidden the very roads and highways, and hopeless of improving their degraded state so long as they remained within the Hindu community. The whole caste system was crossed and recrossed by sects and cults and also by more recent professional and political vocations derived from Europe. Yet, despite its rigidity and anachronism, the caste system did provide a stable way of life, a division of labor, and an apparatus for social security.

The Moslems, or Mohammedans, comprised nearly a quarter of the population. They were most numerous in districts nearest the invasion passes, in the Punjab and Kashmir, but also in Bengal. A proportion was descended from the original Pathan and Mogul conquerors, but the great majority were native converts. In contrast to the Hindus, the Moslems professed a simple monotheistic faith, founded by one Prophet, Mohammed, expressed in one sacred text, the Koran. They abominated idolatry and were generally disinclined to philosophical speculation. They had no priesthood and no caste system, and they preached and practiced the equality of man before God. They ate meat — but never the meat of the pig — and they abstained from alcohol and usury. They buried their dead and believed in the resurrection, the Last Judgment, paradise, and hell. They had a long history of proselytism and conquest. When roused — and it was never difficult to rouse them — they were capable of the most savage fanaticism. Their womenfolk lived in purdah,[9] saw no men and were seen by none outside their own households, and went out veiled or in closed conveyances.

Hindu-Moslem relations constituted the principal domestic problem of

British India. Members of the two communities might live side by side in formal peace in the same town or village for years, and then some provocation, when least expected – perhaps the killing of a cow by Moslems or the playing of a band by a Hindu marriage or funeral procession passing a mosque at prayer time – could start a riot. As a community the Moslems keenly felt their inferior numbers, but at the same time were conscious of belonging to a great international Moslem world outside India, a world which looked not to Delhi or Benares but to Mecca, a world which the more parochial Hindu could never know. The Moslems, with their conservative Koranic traditions, also keenly felt their failure to keep abreast of modern education, and they, once the lords of India and still the main strength of the Indian fighting forces, found themselves constantly ousted from the professions and from government service by the sharper-witted and more fluent-tongued Hindus. Indian nationalism, when it emerged, like so many nationalisms at this time, was vitiated by a chronic division within itself.

The remaining communities of India were relatively small in numbers, but often strong in influence – Sikhs, Jains, Parsis, Indian Christians. Europeans numbered 135,000 and represented a fraction of the population, self-conscious and self-contained, virtually a separate caste, economically and politically powerful, and perhaps spoiled by power. Thanks to the steamship and the Suez Canal, they did not settle in India like former conquerors of India, nor become part of Indian life. The Indian Civil Service, the "steel frame" of British rule, numbered a mere 1,200, about half (in 1939) being British whites and the rest, a growing proportion, being Indians. White British troops to the strength of 60,000 were quartered mostly within striking distance of the old invasion passes in the Northwest Frontier Province.

Politically, India wore two faces – British India and the Indian States. After the Mutiny of 1857, Britain abandoned her former annexationist policy in India and froze the map of the country in its configuration at that time. Thenceforward British India, rather more than half the area of the country and consisting of seventeen Provinces, was ruled "colonially"; and the Indian States, under their nearly six hundred reigning Rajahs or Princes, remained "independent," usually in treaty relations with the "Paramount Power." At the Center stood the Viceroy, appointed from London for a five-year term, governing with the assistance of an Executive Council, chosen by himself, and later with the assistance also of a Legislative Council, partly of nominated and partly of elected members, all responsible to the Secretary of State for India in London. After 1877 the British monarch bore the title of Emperor – or Empress – of India.

Economically, India was privileged to be the first and greatest example in the modern era of an "underdeveloped" country under Western impact. Some three-quarters of her population – Hindu and Moslem alike – lived in traditional poverty in small villages, which were often no more than clusters of thatched, mud-walled huts, and cultivated lots of five acres – sometimes of only one acre – per family, lots usually fragmented by generations of subdivision among heirs and under perpetual mortgage to professional native moneylenders. And this ancient system, miserable but stable, was now confounded by imported capital and industry and was converted in part to the production of cash crops and goods manufactured for export. Meanwhile relative freedom from war, famine, and plague under a beneficent alien domination permitted a growth of population in Malthusian progression, housed largely in new urban concentrations. But, as we have already seen in this book and as we shall see again, India's predicament in this respect, though vast, was not unique. India indeed was to become the modern world's greatest laboratory for perhaps the modern world's greatest political and economic problem.

At no time, and certainly not after the Mutiny of 1857, did the British regard their administration in India as a static and perfect instrument. Even Conservative Victorian statesmen believed in the eventual self-government of India and the eventual withdrawal of British power, though they might reserve their doubts as to when that self-government should be granted and as to whether that self-government should ever take the form of British parliamentary institutions. The Indian National Congress,[10] an unofficial association of Indians of all creeds and communities from all parts of British India, was founded in 1885, with the tacit approval and encouragement of the British Government of the time. Its resolutions at first were discreet and deferential, but it was soon regarding itself, if not as the germ of a native parliament, at least as a sort of *durbar* for the voicing of Indian aspirations. The All-India Moslem League, a similar association, but of exclusively Moslem membership, was founded in 1906. It must be emphasized that the nationalism that grew up in India was confined, at first, to British India. The Indian States, secure in their autocracy, would have none of it and made short shift of any "agitators" found within their borders. The Indian States remained somewhat aside and apart from India's political development.

The Morley-Minto reforms, so called after Lord Morley, Secretary of State for India, and Lord Minto, the Viceroy, were introduced in 1909, and – whatever their authors may have intended – they were regarded by Indians as a first installment of responsible government in India. The Indian Army played a gallant part in the First World War. In the four years of 1914-18, India enrolled 877,000 combatants by voluntary enlistment, of whom 620,000 served overseas and 62,000 were killed. The Indian Princes were loyal and made lavish contributions to the war effort. It was no more than a recognition of these many services which, in 1917, prompted Edwin S. Montagu, then Secretary of State for India, to announce "the increasing association of Indians in every branch of the administration and the gradual development of self-governing institutions with a view to the progressive realization of responsible government in India as an integral part of the British Empire." At the end of 1917, after conferences with Lord Chelmsford, the Viceroy, Montagu issued his recommendations in the form of the Montagu-Chelmsford Report.

The First World War was the release of many oppressions, and for India the First World War was consummated, not in the defeat of Germany or even of Turkey, but in the Irish East Rebellion, the Russian Revolution, and the Wilsonian pronouncements. By 1918 Indian National Congress and the Moslem League had grown into regular political parties, openly and violently agitating for *Swaraj*, or Home Rule. Moslems in particular were fearful that the Allies would dismember the Ottoman Empire and abolish the Caliphate. During the early months of 1919, serious rioting broke out, particularly in the Punjab, and several districts were put under martial law. Gandhi, the Hindu leader, began the first of his non-cooperation movements. At Amritsar buildings were fired by the rioters, some Europeans were murdered, and an Englishwoman was said to have been assaulted. On April 13, 1919, in the Jalianwala Bagh, a public enclosure in Amritsar, General Dyer, firmly believing that only an "example" could now prevent widespread revolution in India, ordered his troops to fire without warning on a crowded political meeting. Nearly 400 persons were killed and 1,000 wounded, and the dead and wounded were callously left unattended where they lay. Meanwhile fighting had broken out with the Emir Amanullah of Afghanistan, and some 300,000 British and Indian troops were engaged in the most formidable of frontier wars in British-Indian history.

Yet, undaunted, the British Government gave effect to the Montagu-Chelmsford Report in the India Act of 1919. The Viceroy and his Executive Council were to remain much as before, but the Legislative Council would be replaced by a bicameral parliamentary assembly of the Indian people. Complicated electoral groupings and classifications were designed to overcome the massive complexity and illiteracy of the country. Meanwhile the local powers over education, public health, and agriculture were "transferred" to new Provincial legislatures. The powers over the police, taxation, and famine relief were "reserved" to the Crown. But the Act was ill-received. Extremists in Congress wanted no truck with the dual division of authority into "transferred" and "reserved" subjects. They wanted *Swaraj* in all subjects — and at once. In November 1920, Congress, now under the leadership of Gandhi, refused to take part in the elections under the new Act, put forward no candidates, and registered no votes.

The political history of India thereafter resembled the political history of Palestine at the same time, though on a much more formidable scale. Conferences and reports followed one another at intervals and represented the successive efforts of British statesmanship to play fair with all sides in a situation which was steadily growing more contradictory and uncontrollable. Indianization of the Civil Service went forward smoothly and unobtrusively. Higher education, notably in law and medicine, was widespread. There was no question but that if and when the British left India, an Indian professional class would exist ready to take over. But this was a small part of India's real predicament. The mere change of administration by itself would work no miracles with the country's basic poverty and backwardness. So many of the malcontents in India, themselves products of Western professional education and beneficiaries of the imported capitalist system, were men who seemed to show little social conscience, and some of them all too obviously were using the nationalist movement for their own preferment. Nor did it look as if the communal question [11] would be settled at their hands — rather the contrary. Indeed, the Hindu-Moslem feud had become worse, not better, with the extension of political consciousness and concession. Finally, the British authorities in India were not only nonplused by the characteristically Indian techniques of agitation – Gandhi's campaigns of non-violence and his protest fasts – but they looked askance at the curious pacifist and isolationist trend in a country which had always been highly vulnerable to invasion and which, in a new era of international insecurity, had never been so much in need of strong defensive forces.

In 1921 Chelmsford was succeeded in the viceroyship by Lord Reading; in 1926 Reading by Lord Irwin (later Lord Halifax); in 1931 Irwin by Lord Willingdon; in 1936 Willingdon by Lord Linlithgow. In 1928 the Simon Commission arrived in India to review the working of the India Act of 1919. Round-table conferences of representatives of the British Government and the Indian parties met in London in 1930, 1931, and 1932. Meanwhile, despite the Gandhian non-violence, there were incessant boycotts, strikes, and riots in different parts of India, followed by terms of detention – but by very few death sentences. The majority in the National Congress was no longer satisfied with promises of "Dominion status." The National Congress was now passing under the control of extremists like Jawaharlal Nehru, whose object was absolute severance from the British connection. The Moslem League, officially supporting Dominion status, was now passing under the control of Jinnah, who in his own way could be as extremist as any Nehru and who was shortly to make himself the spokesman for a separate Moslem state in India – Pakistan. The gentle ascetic, Gandhi, though still revered by the Indian masses, seemed almost to have been passed over and left behind by the very forces that he had originally let loose.

In 1935 the British Parliament passed a new India Act, a voluminous document describing a federal constitution under a Viceroy, governing with the assistance of a bicameral legislature to be elected through a complicated adjustment between general and communal electorates. Part of the Act went into force in the Provinces almost at once, but its full operation at the Center was delayed by last-minute procrastination on the part of the Princes, and the difficulties were still not straightened out in 1939, when India was swept into the Second World War. Burma was created a separate Dominion with a separate constitution under a British Governor, and she too was then swept into the Second World War.

16. THE UNITED STATES: NORMALCY AND ISOLATIONISM

The Shift of Power

In 1914, when the history of this Age of Conflict begins, Europe was the power center of the world. In 1914, because of a provincial European quarrel, a war broke out, directly or indirectly involving fourteen non-European states. After the war, during the decade from 1919 to 1929 – during the Period of Settlement, as we have called it – the world still seemed to be a European world; "international relations" still meant the relations of some half-dozen Western European states. But, as we know now, Europe's predominance was already passing and was only being artificially maintained by the withdrawal of the United States into its former isolation – and by the temporary prostration of Russia. The essential shift of power away from Europe in fact had taken place. Significantly the United States was a sponsor and leading signatory of the Pact of Paris in 1928. In 1929 occurred the New York stock-market crash, a local event in itself, but one which was to spread its effects throughout the world.

The year 1929 saw the beginnings of the dissolution of the settlement in Europe, which had been largely inspired by the Wilsonian philosophy of 1918 and 1919. From now onward the United States was to be thrust more and more into world affairs – and there would be no second withdrawal. Appropriately, the Manchurian Crisis of 1931, the first great international crisis of the Period of Crisis, as we have called it, happened in a non-European, indeed in an American, "sphere of interest."

It is fitting therefore that we should conclude this Part of the book with a chapter on the United States. We shall return for a moment to 1919 and describe the immediate aftereffects of the war in the United States, namely the repudiation of President Wilson and the non-ratification of the Treaty of Versailles – in brief, the withdrawal into isolation. We shall then pass on to describe the four main international questions with which, in this decade from 1919 to 1929, the United States, despite its isolationism, was concerned: membership in the World Court, naval disarmament, relations with the Soviet Union, and the payment of the Allied debts. We shall conclude the chapter with a brief account of the New York stock-market crash and the onset of the Depression.

Postwar Isolationism – the Rejection of Versailles

In 1919 the American people, like many other belligerents after the First World War, hastened to revert to their old familiar ways of life which, so it seemed to them, the war had temporarily interrupted. But in their case perhaps the process was relatively easier. As their Allies ruefully, if not too gratefully, were fond of pointing out, the United States had not been long enough in the war – only nineteen months to be exact – and, despite the magnitude and decisiveness of its effort, the real iron of the great conflict had never deeply entered the national soul. The Meuse-Argonne, fantastic nightmare though it was, was a minor operation beside the Marnes and the Passchendaeles that the French and British armies had been fighting for four years. If other belligerents in 1919 could regard the war as a breach in the normal course of domestic peace, so could the United States – indeed more so. Once the stimulus of actual war had been removed the "slump in idealism," even President Wilson's idealism, could set in. The old well-tried watchword of American foreign policy – "no entangling alliances" – could then automatically reassert itself, and it needed only the first reported hints of the cynicism and egotism at the Peace Conference to complete the nation's psychological reversal. Significantly, the all-absorbing popular issues of American politics in 1919 were not war and peace, but the Eighteenth and Nineteenth Amendments – Prohibition and women's suffrage.

A somewhat similar revulsion of public opinion occurred in Britain and France. In the United States it was more decisive, and to some extent President Wilson himself contributed to it. Magnanimous pretensions and narrow political partisanship never look well together, and they did not look well in October 1918, when the high-minded President appealed for a Democratic victory in the forthcoming Congressional elections. The President was very well aware of the growing opposition to his war policy, and to himself personally, and he hoped he could come to terms with that opposition in time to allow him to go to the Peace Conference with a more united country behind him. All through 1918, former Presidents Roosevelt and Taft and Senators Borah, Lodge, Johnson, Knox, Harding, and others, had been mobilizing disaffected Republicans – "isolationists," "irreconcilables," and "nationalists" – into a fierce and highly personal anti-Wilson opposition.

The Congressional elections in November 1918 resulted in Republican majorities in both the Senate and the House, and President Wilson found himself three months later at the Peace Conference at Paris in the anomalous position of a national leader – and withal the great leader of world democracy – who had just been decisively repudiated at the polls. In his weakness he resorted to defiance. Largely at his behest, the Peace Conference had agreed to include the Covenant of the League of Nations as Part I of the text of the Treaty of Versailles, so that the rejection of the one meant the rejection of the other. In July 1919, President Wilson returned to the United States bringing the treaty with him for ratification, and he virtually challenged the Senate to do its worst with the inviolable document. He also brought with him the French treaty of assistance, by which the

United States would go immediately to the assistance of France in the event of unprovoked German aggression. (See p. 104.) By then President Wilson was an ailing man, borne on the strength of his own fervors, but no longer capable of the great physical strain which the struggle for ratification was now to put upon him. He was also a very lonely man. Colleagues and aides found him increasingly difficult to approach. He had long since quarreled with his Secretary of State, Robert Lansing; more recently he was estranged even from his great friend and counselor, Colonel House.

Senator Henry Cabot Lodge was now in the key position of Chairman of the Senate Foreign Relations Committee, and between him and President Wilson there developed one of those almost irrational personal animosities. Already, by his notorious "Round Robin," Lodge had served notice on the delegates at Paris that he and his supporters in Congress would not brook a Covenant integrated with the treaty of peace.[1] The Foreign Relations Committee, under his direction, began its hearings on the treaty at the end of July 1919, and for two exhausting months, subjected every article and clause to "pitiless publicity." The treaty was reported from committee with amendments and reservations amounting, as Wilson said, to "nullification." In particular, Article 10 of the League Covenant was argued to be a palpable, almost insulting infringement of American sovereignty and freedom of action.

Most of these discussions in Washington, it may be said, were lost on the country at large — as indeed Lodge and his committee perhaps hoped and intended. Lodge was honest enough to admit on one occasion that the great mass of the people did not understand the treaty. "All they want is peace," he said. "Only the vocal classes are friendly to the League and advocate it." But there were organized interests and groups in the country whose aggregate pressure was formidable. Lobbies of "hyphenated" communities — such as the German-American — which had watched the carving up of their ancestral homelands in Europe, were very ready to express their opposition and were encouraged to do so. The Irish groups launched a campaign especially directed against granting six votes to Britain and the British Dominions in the League Assembly as against the one vote to be granted to the United States. In September 1919, resolved to defend his Covenant and his treaty at all costs, President Wilson set out on a nationwide speaking tour, stumping in particular those areas where group criticisms had been sharpest. His health was causing the greatest anxiety; his own physician had warned him against the tour. At Wichita, Kansas, after delivering the fortieth speech of the tour, the President suffered a nervous collapse. He was never properly to recover. Nor was he ever again able to take an active part in his administration. In October the Senate began its formal voting on the Treaty of Versailles. Wilson's cabinet meanwhile tried to carry on without him. In February 1920, in a sick man's moment of petulance, Wilson dismissed Lansing for seeking "to assume presidential authority" and appointed Bainbridge Colby as his Secretary of State. The Senate's final rejection of the treaty came on March 19, 1920, by 49 votes to 35. A shift of seven votes would have met the constitutional requirement of approval by two-thirds of the senators present, and would have secured the ratification. The French treaty of assistance was rejected at the same time.

President Wilson lived thereafter in retirement and seclusion. He died on February 3, 1924.

In the Presidential elections of 1920, the convivial, easygoing, "one-hundred-per-cent-American" Warren G. Harding, Republican senator from Ohio, was elected by a landslide vote on the appropriate slogan "Back to Normalcy." In August 1921, the United States formally concluded peace with Germany, Austria, and Hungary. The American people, it seemed, had finished with the Wilsonian experiment in internationalism and had turned their backs on Europe. The Fordney-McCumber Tariff Act, passed in September 1922, generally embodying the traditional high-tariff policies of the Republican party, was the economic counterpart of political isolationism.

Harding gathered about him a strong cabinet – Charles Evans Hughes, Secretary of State; Andrew Mellon, Secretary of the Treasury; Herbert Hoover, Secretary of Commerce. But some of his lesser associates were incompetent and corrupt, and his domestic administration was soon to earn him about as disreputable a name as any President ever bore. But, in the prosperity which the country was now beginning to enjoy, few were troubled by such shortcomings. Harding died suddenly on August 2, 1923, in San Francisco, while on a speaking tour. Calvin Coolidge, Vice-President, succeeded and was re-elected in 1924. Mellon and Hoover remained in office; Frank B. Kellogg became Secretary of State early in 1925. Coolidge gave the country a conservative, but honest, administration – and let the rising prosperity take its course.

One piece of legislation of this time should be mentioned. In 1921 and again in 1924, in order that the American homeland in its present good fortune should be protected against abuse and subversion from undesirable elements from abroad, the former Immigration Act of 1917 was replaced by Quota Acts, which limited immigration from any one foreign country to an annual maximum of 2 per cent of its nationals resident in the United States in 1890 – a date when the "American" proportion of the population was high and the "alien" proportion was low. Further the Quota Acts totally excluded certain nationalities, notably all Orientals. The Acts thereby gave deep offense to Japan, already injured by the curtailment of naval armaments by the recent Washington Conference. The Japanese ambassador in Washington protested. A humiliated Japanese committed hara-kiri on the steps of the American Embassy in Tokyo. But Congress was unmoved. From 1924 the land of opportunity was to be closed to all but those who could be easily assimilated into Americanism.

The World Court Controversy

Despite the all-prevailing isolationism, it seemed at one time that the United States, while remaining outside the League of Nations, might adhere to some of the League's organizations. The United States, for example, was a member of the Committee on Intellectual Cooperation. Could it not also become a member of the World Court? Americans hitherto had taken an important part in international jurisprudence, and Elihu Root, a former Secretary of State, was one of the committee of jurists in 1920 which had drawn up the World Court's Statute.

In February 1923, President Harding submitted to the Senate a proposal for American adherence to the World Court. He was at pains to point out that no obligations under the League Covenant would be assumed. But the "bitter-enders" who had defeated the ratification of the Treaty of Versailles were still powerful. They condemned the World Court as a "League Court" and affirmed that membership would soon be opening a backdoor entry into the League itself. However, in spite of senatorial reluctance, both party platforms in the presidential election of 1924 favored adherence. President Coolidge himself had always been favorably predisposed thereto. In March 1925, the House voted overwhelmingly for adherence. The Senate then followed suit, but with five reservations, the last of which precluded the World Court from giving an advisory opinion on any matter affecting American interests without the prior consent of the United States. Since the proviso was not immediately accepted by the constituent nations of the World Court, President Coolidge took the stand that the question of American membership had lapsed.

Two years later, in 1928, the enthusiastic public reception of the Pact of Paris encouraged Secretary Kellogg to reopen the issue. A compromise formula, submitted by Elihu Root in 1929, was permitted to slumber in the pigeonholes of the Senate Foreign Relations Committee till 1935. The press, though at the time irritated by the nonpayment of Allied war debts and consequently more isolationist than ever, generally favored membership. But the Senate rejected the "Root formula" by 52 votes to 36 — again, as in the case of the rejection of the Treaty of Versailles, just seven votes short of the necessary two-thirds majority.

The Washington Naval Conference

It is easy to forget, but necessary to remember, that American isolationism meant isolation from Europe. Historically the overwhelming majority of the American people were descendants of, and often rebels against, their several European fatherlands. The Monroe Doctrine of 1823 was essentially an anti-European declaration. But the same detachment never marked the feelings or policies of the American people toward Latin America or the Far East. Certainly since 1853 China, Japan, and the Pacific were felt to be very much within the American international sphere. The Philippines had been annexed in 1898 — after some opposition in Congress, but annexed notwithstanding — and the annexation seemed more and more natural with the passing of time. The Open Door in China had been established in 1899, largely by American initiative. Finally, the United States was greatly concerned over the Anglo-Japanese Alliance of 1902 and made no secret of a strong aversion to it. American opinion saw nothing illogical therefore in an uncompromising disinterest in the affairs of Europe and an equally uncompromising interest in the affairs of the Far East.

With some anxiety the United States had watched Japan's belligerency in the First World War and her seizures of the German port of Tsingtao in Shantung and the German islands in the North Pacific. Early in 1915, when Japan attempted to establish a virtual protectorate over China by means of the Twenty-one Demands, Secretary of State William Jennings Bryan hastened to declare that the United States would recognize no treaty affecting the integrity of China or infringing the principle of the Open Door. In 1916 Congressional naval appropriations for the huge sum of $300,000,000, though motivated by resentment against the Allied blockade, could also be taken as a pointed warning to Japan. The Lansing-Ishii Agreement of 1917, signed after the entry of the United States into the war, reaffirmed the Open Door policy while recognizing Japan's "special interests" in China; but the agreement left both sides dissatisfied and suspicious.

The relations between the two Pacific Powers consequently were not improved by their participation on the Allied side in the war – nor, afterward, by their participation in the Peace Conference. Japan secured none of her three main objectives at Paris. She did not secure the outright cession to herself of the German islands in the North Pacific; she did not secure the outright cession to herself of Shantung; and she did not secure the inclusion of an article in the League Covenant recognizing racial equality. (See pp. 104-05.) Meanwhile Japanese and American forces had landed in eastern Siberia and were in competitive occupation of strategic points in the territory.

The tense situation that had thus developed in the Pacific seemed to justify the continuation of naval building by the United States, Japan, and Britain. Each country was left with incompleted programs from the war, and each feared to call a halt until its other two competitors did likewise. Public opinion in the United States, dismayed at the spectacle of these huge armaments so soon after "the war to end wars," was getting restive. In May and June 1921, Senator William E. Borah's resolution in favor of reducing naval expenditure was passed by Congress with large majorities. Elsewhere the time was opportune. The Anglo-Japanese Alliance of 1902 was about to lapse – or to be renewed – and it seemed that this unpopular treaty could now be superseded by a wider, more generally acceptable agreement. As for Britain, alliance with Japan had lost its purpose now that former fears of Russian aggression against India were removed. Meanwhile Canada, Australia, and New Zealand had been taking much the same attitude toward the alliance as the United States. Accordingly President Harding issued invitations to a conference on naval limitation, "in connection with which Pacific and Far Eastern questions could also be discussed." The conference would be held in Washington and would be attended by the nine powers – Soviet Russia alone excepted – that had interests in the area, namely the United States, Britain, France, Italy, Belgium, the Netherlands, Portugal, China, and Japan.

Secretary of State Hughes, presiding over the opening session on November 12, 1921, proposed with impassive countenance the most sweeping and spectacular reductions, a ten-year naval holiday, and the all-around scrapping of nearly 2,000,000 tons of shipping. The Japanese delegates had come to Washington in a disgruntled and suspicious mood. They had expressed their willingness to consider naval reductions, and had probably resigned themselves to the discontinuance of the Anglo-Japanese Alliance. But they were resolved, should the Anglo-American combination at the Conference compel them to pare their claws and to modify their recent aggressiveness in East Asia, to exact the maximum price for their complaisance. Even so, unless they confessed unfriendly designs, they could hardly do otherwise than accede to the general spirit of Hughes's policy. The bargaining was keen, but the substantial success of the Conference was never in doubt. In February 1922, the United States, Britain, Japan, France, and Italy put their signatures to a Five-Power Treaty establishing the ratio of 5 : 5 : 3 : 1.67 : 1.67 respectively for the replacement tonnage of their capital ships, the totals being:

NAVAL TONNAGES SANCTIONED BY THE WASHINGTON CONFERENCE, 1921-22

	United States	*Britain*	*Japan*	*France*	*Italy*
Capital ships	525,000	525,000	315,000	175,000	175,000
Aircraft carriers	135,000	135,000	81,000	60,000	60,000

Roughly 40 per cent of the capital ships of the signatories, in commission or under construction, was to be scrapped; no new capital ship was to be constructed for another ten years; none might be replaced till twenty years old; capital ships constructed after the ten-year holiday were to be limited to 35,000 tons and 16-inch guns, and aircraft carriers to 27,000 tons. The United States, Britain, and Japan agreed to maintain the *status quo* with regard to their Pacific fortifications, with the exception of Hawaii and Singapore. The treaty was to remain in force till December 31, 1936, and a signatory was to give two years' notice of intention to terminate the agreement.

In addition, the nine powers at the conference signed a Nine-Power Treaty reaffirming the Open Door in China. The United States, Britain, Japan, and France signed a Four-Power Treaty by which they agreed to respect one another's rights relating to their "insular possessions and insular Dominions in the Pacific Ocean" and to adjust any future differences there by mutual consultation. The last treaty was considered to have superseded and abrogated the old Anglo-Japanese Alliance.

The United States and Japan signed a treaty regarding the island of Yap in the midst of the Japanese mandated area, under the terms of which the United States was given access to that speck of territory and to the cable and radio installations upon it. Japan, after industrious American mediation, agreed to restore the province of Shantung to China. The Conference also passed resolutions prohibiting the use of poison gas and restricting the use of submarines to the rules of international law.

France played a characteristic role in this first of international conferences on the limitation of armaments. She had originally been willing to support the United States in return for a revival of the abortive treaty of assistance against Germany. She doubtless feared that a successful limitation of naval armaments at Washington would pave the way for future discussions on the limitation of land armaments, a limitation which, without some compensatory concession, she was not in any mood to accept. Secretary Hughes showed no inclination to humor the French delegates, who then took up an attitude of obstruction toward the entire Conference, and he was compelled to cable a direct appeal to the French Premier, Briand, before they would fall in with the allotted ratio in capital ships. But even the incisive diplomacy of Hughes could not bring the French to agree to any limitation on cruisers, destroyers, and submarines.

In the aggregate, however, the agreements reached at Washington appeared to be positive and encouraging. It was only gradually, in retrospect, that weaknesses were perceived. The treaties depended entirely on the good will of the signatories, and, as was soon to be reported, the Japanese were fortifying several islands in the North Pacific in contravention of the Five-Power Treaty. The limitation in capital-ship construction, if nothing else, would mean a welcome economy in national budgets. But many naval experts were pointing out that the capital ship as a weapon already might be becoming obsolete, and that the Conference had not extended any limitation to the lesser naval craft which were now so much more important. Britain was chagrined by the failure, largely because of French obstruction, to abolish the submarine. Finally the old bond between Japan and her European ally, Britain, had been severed, and when Japan emerged once more from her uncomfortable isolation, it was to associate herself with the new forces of aggression in the world.

The Geneva Naval Conference

The Washington Conference, ostensibly called to consider the limitation of all types of naval armament, had confined itself, as we have seen, to reducing the tonnages of capital ships and aircraft carriers. But from time to time American diplomats and publicists had returned to the charge in the hope that the reductions might be extended to cruisers, destroyers, and submarines, and that thereby the gap in the Washington agreements might be filled. Meanwhile the United States had not only failed to build up to the battleship strength allotted under the agreements, but was being outstripped by Britain and Japan in cruiser construction. The happier middle 1920's seemed to offer a new opportunity for reopening discussions. Locarno in 1925, though a European pact, had created a propitious atmosphere throughout the world. The British Admiralty was known to be working on a disarmament plan of its own. On the initiative of President Coolidge and Secretary of State Kellogg, invitations to the powers for a new naval disarmament conference were duly issued early in 1927.

Unhappily, sanguine expectations were disappointed. France and Italy, whose rivalry, since the rise of Mussolini, was becoming one of the factors of the international complex, were scowling at one another across the placid expanses of the Mediterranean. Both declined President Coolidge's invitation. In their absence, therefore, a Three-Power Naval Conference, attended by the United States, Britain, and Japan, opened in Geneva in June 1927. Hugh Gibson, American ambassador to Belgium, was the chief American delegate; Bridgeman, First Lord of the Admiralty, and Lord Cecil represented Britain; Viscount Saito and Viscount Ishii represented Japan. After the first plenary session, the work of the conference devolved upon a Technical Committee, where the divergencies between the British and American draft submissions gradually and surprisingly widened into a serious disagreement.

The British had been unwise enough to reopen the question of capital ships, which the American and Japanese delegations had come to Geneva unprepared to discuss and considered to have been settled at Washington in 1922. The issue was finally shelved, but only after it had created the impression in the minds of the American delegates that Britain was maneuvering to evade her Washington commitments. The Technical Committee was already in an irritated, suspicious mood when it turned to consider the question of cruisers. The United States wanted a small number of large cruisers; Britain wanted a large number of small cruisers. Both powers were consulting their strategic requirements, and clearly the United States with two concentrated fleets in two oceans, was differently situated from Britain, whose fleets had to patrol 80,000 miles of imperial communications in five. Admiral Jellicoe, who was attending the conference as the special delegate of New Zealand, explained that the 114 cruisers possessed by Britain in 1914 had been insufficient for the security of her sea lanes, and he fixed the absolute minimum of Britain's cruiser requirements at 70 ships. His rejection of cruiser parity between America and Britain was strongly supported by Churchill and the "Big Navy" wing of the British Cabinet in the fear that such cruiser parity would force Britain to abandon her blockade tactics of 1914-17 – tactics which, of course, the United States wished to be able to defy in the future. Japan, ironically enough, having forsaken the role of the "bad boy," which she had played with such damaging effect before 1922, was now acting as the anxious and indefatigable mediator between the other two exasperated powers.

It was common knowledge that in the course of the discussions Gibson and Bridgeman were both short-tempered. Voices were raised, and tables were banged. The conference moreover labored under deplorable misrepresentation in the press. References to 1812 were all too common at American public meetings at this time; Conservatives in Britain, for their part, were discussing a renewal of the old Anglo-Japanese Alliance. There was flagrant lobbying on the part of American shipping and armament manufacturers to wreck the conference. Altogether Anglo-American relations had not been so strained for years. On August 4, 1927, significantly the anniversary of the outbreak of war in 1914, the conference held its final plenary session; the delegates recapitulated their several points of view and separated. In February 1929, as a pointed postscript, President Coolidge approved naval appropriations totaling $274,000,000 for the construction of an aircraft carrier and of fifteen cruisers of the very type Gibson had asked for and had been refused at Geneva.

The London Naval Conference

The story of naval disarmament between the wars concludes with the London Conference of 1930. Herbert Hoover was President of the United States. He had come to office well known for his Quaker background and his distinguished record of international philanthropy. His feeding of Europe's hungry millions and his successful tenure at the Department of Commerce under the Harding and Coolidge administrations inspired the highest hopes in his ability to promote peace "by the limitation of arms and by the creation of the instrumentalities for the peaceful settlement of controversies." The advent of a Labor government in Britain in 1929 under the great pacifist Ramsay MacDonald opened the prospect of an offensive against heavy armaments from that quarter. The British Government was fully aware of the uneasiness created in the Dominions, particularly in Canada, by the recent deterioration of Anglo-American relations. Both the United States and Britain could not but appreciate the contradiction between the resounding protestations of the lately concluded Pact of Paris and the continued piling-up of naval armaments. MacDonald himself visited the United States in October 1929 and helped to make straight the way for a new naval disarmament conference. The New York stock-market crash of the same month, like every ill wind, had its compensations. It doubtless created that more chastened frame of mind in which the United States was now to approach the international problems of the hour.

The Five-Power Naval Conference met in London between January and April 1930 and was attended by delegates from the United States, Britain, Japan, France, and Italy. The delegates recognized the principle of Anglo American parity in all classes of ships, though the concurrence of the Japanese delegates was only obtained after the British Prime Minister, MacDonald, had appealed over their heads to the Japanese Premier, Hamaguchi, in Tokyo. Then the French began to balk. It was not in their nature to miss a chance for extending the French security system. They now desired a revision of Article 16 of the League Covenant so as to render mandatory an economic boycott against a declared aggressor. A British blockade in pursuance of such a boycott might have led to a head-on collision with the United States, jealous as always of its rights upon the seas. The British, inquiring what the attitude of the United States would be in that contingency, were given to understand by the American delegates that no commitment could be made. Accordingly France — and consequently Italy — refused to become party to any naval agreement that might emerge from the conference. The American policy of no entanglements and the French policy of total entanglements were in open conflict.

The remaining three powers, the United States, Britain, and Japan, came to an agreement among themselves in all their classes of ships on the main lines of the old Washington ratios. At the behest of Britain, an "Escalator Clause" was inserted in the agreement permitting construction above the maximum tonnages if any signatory considered itself to be threatened by the construction of a nonsignatory power — notably by France or Italy. The results of the conference were undeniably meager. Somehow the conviction was in the air that the very conference method in international relations was wearing a little thin, and that new forces were abroad in the world which had little use for conferences. (See pp. 390-92.)

The United States and the Soviet Union

The United States had been the first power to recognize the Provisional Government in Russia in March 1917. The Russian Revolution had removed the last obstacle to American participation in the war. The United States, the European Allies — and now Russia — were all democracies fighting for democracy. But in November 1917, when the Bolsheviks seized power in Petrograd, cordial relations abruptly ceased. There could be no community of ideas or of interest between the United States and the Russia of Lenin and Trotsky. In 1918 an American force occupied strategic points in eastern Siberia.

The withdrawal of the American force from Siberia in 1920 effected no improvement in relations. The founding of an American Communist party in the same year and the simultaneous wave of industrial strikes and mysterious bomb explosions were all very disturbing. In reply the police carried out widespread raids — later known as "Palmer Raids," after the Attorney General A. Mitchell Palmer, who directed them — and arrested a mixed assortment of 6,000 "dangerous radicals." During the Russo-Polish War, when the Red Army was advancing on Warsaw, the State Department hastened to approve of a loan of $50,000,000 to Poland. The Soviet Government was not invited to the Washington Conference in 1921, nor to Paris in 1928 for the signing of the Pact of Paris. Successive Secretaries of State — Colby, Hughes, and Kellogg — were all united in their opposition to recognizing the Soviet Government in Russia or to granting American aid to a regime that regarded expropriation as an instrument of national policy. Nonetheless, through the 1920's a certain amount of trade between the United States and the Soviet Union, particularly in agricultural equipment and agricultural products, was carried on in spite of various arbitrary embargoes and the lack of long-term credits.

In 1931 the Depression had become the prime fact in international relations. In that year the Japanese invaded Manchuria, and the United States and the Soviet Union began to draw together against the common threat to their Pacific interests. In 1933, in President Franklin D. Roosevelt's first year of office, the United States at last recognized the Soviet Union. (See pp. 464-65.)

The Allied Debt Question

The Allies after the First World War were all enmeshed in a network of debt. The greater part of the costs of the war had been met by loans; the new succession states were often established on loans; new minor wars in Intermediate Europe were fought on loans. Most of the obligations had been contracted under conditions of haste and emergency, the terms varied from one obligation to another and, in many cases, were still to be negotiated, and generally no interest had as yet been paid. The Allies had borrowed to some extent from one another, particularly from Britain; but on balance the one outstanding creditor was the United States, and the total debt owing to the United States amounted to the sum – enormous in those days – of $10,350,000,000.

Andrew Mellon, when he became Secretary of the Treasury in March 1921, would have preferred his Department to have had plenary powers to deal with the entire problem. But Congress resolved to set up a World War Foreign Debt Commission, responsible to itself. The new body began its meetings in April 1922 and eventually negotiated all the most important funding agreements. But it did not negotiate them without some show of protest from the debtors. In August 1922, over the name of Balfour, the British Government boldly proposed the cancellation of all wartime indebtedness. From a purely bookkeeping point of view Britain herself stood to lose thereby. But she had adopted a policy of general cancellation after the Napoleonic Wars and, in the long-term view, had had no subsequent cause for regret. Presumably the United States was now in an analogous position. Thus ran the Balfour note of 1922:

> His Majesty's Government content themselves with saying once again that so deeply are they convinced of the economic injury inflicted on the world by the existing state of things that this country would be prepared (subject to the just claims of other parts of the Empire) to abandon all further rights to German Reparation and all claims to repayment by Allies, provided that this renunciation formed part of a general plan by which this great problem could be dealt with as a whole and find a satisfactory solution.

But in the United States these pleas fell on deaf ears. On the contrary, American opinion sharply resented the triangular connection between debts and debts, and reparations and debts, which European statesmen were always trying to establish, and insisted that there must be no confusing of obligations separately contracted. As President Coolidge tartly asked, "They hired the money, didn't they?" and presumably, so long as the incorrigible peoples who inhabited the European Continent wanted to fight wars, they must not be released from the consequences thereof.

The debt question, in short, was soon rousing all the political passions of the moment. The Allies might well point to their own vast expenditure of blood and treasure before the American entry into the war; the Americans, now lapsed into isolationism, with all their traditional anti-European repugnance, could retort that the war was originally a European war, for which the Allies' own political and military systems were in great part responsible. And they could retort furthermore that the Allies seemed not to have taken to heart the real lesson of their misfortunes; for, while complaining of harsh treatment at the hands of their common creditor, the Allies were still unconvinced of the necessity of disarmament and were as busily engaged as ever in piling up the implements of war. Indebtedness to the United States was in fact about the only available restraint that the unrepentant warmongers of Europe could understand.

Thus were the arguments bandied to and fro; but the financial dilemma came no nearer a solution. It is generally acknowledged today that full and punctual liquidation of the debt was a technical impossibility from the first. The sums involved were too big, and the problems of repayment were too intricate. The debtor nations, perhaps with the exception of France, had not enough gold for any substantial and direct reduction of the principal. Repayment in the main could only take the form of goods and services, and these at once competed in the domestic and world market with American products. The American domestic market was stringently protected by the Fordney-McCumber Tariff Act, in part devised to guard it against any Allied debtor who resorted to dumping to liquidate his obligations.

Accordingly the World War Foreign Debt Commission addressed itself to its labors. Its first settlements were made with Finland in May 1923, and with Britain and Czechoslovakia in June 1923 – all at the rate of 3.3 per cent over 60 years. France and Italy proved recalcitrant until the State Department adopted a policy of discouraging private loans to these evasive debtors. Italy came to terms in 1925, paying a meager interest of 0.4 per cent, and France came to terms in 1926 at 1.6 per cent. The reduction of the rates of interest was an important relief, since the accumulated interest constituted a very high proportion of the debts. The reduction contributed to the cancellation of 30 per cent of the British debt, 80 per cent of the Italian, and 60 per cent of the French. The total funded debt would have more than doubled the original loans.

However, official Washington relented from its extreme aloofness from Europe, when it consented in 1924 to participate in a conference of "impartial" experts on Germany's capacity to pay reparations. Whether or not reparations were linked with debts, it still could not be denied that reparations, for good or ill, had become part of the interwar economic nexus in Europe. A few days before the French occupation of the Ruhr, Secretary of State Hughes had observed:

> The economic condition of Europe gives us the greatest concern . . . It is idle to say that we are not interested in these problems, for we are deeply interested from an economic standpoint, as our credit and markets are involved, and also from a humanitarian standpoint.

As we have noted elsewhere, American participation on this occasion resulted in the Dawes Plan. American interests subsequently contributed $105,000,000, or 55 per cent of the Dawes international loan. (See pp. 146-47.)

Thereafter, over the next few years, the American private investor was encouraged to buy $1,210,000,000 worth of German securities – at an average interest of 7 per cent, compared with the 3 per cent that he could generally obtain at home. Other advances to European countries, beginning with Austria and Hungary, raised the total of American loans to Europe between 1924 and 1929 to over $3,500,000,000. The consequences of this curious and entirely unpremeditated involvement of American finance in Europe we shall note in due course.

The Pact of Paris

The Pact of Paris, often called the Briand-Kellogg Pact, has already been described. It was signed ceremonially on August 27, 1928, by Briand for France, Kellogg for the United States, Stresemann for Germany, and the representatives of twelve other nations. (See pp. 124-25.) By the end of 1931, forty-five more nations had adhered, including the Soviet Union, and all together sixty sovereign states solemnly agreed to this sanguine instrument for the "outlawry of war" among themselves. Today the episode is mainly to be remembered for the spontaneous popular enthusiasm which it aroused, and suggests that, despite the isolationism and the persistent voting in Congress against European entanglements, there existed in the United States a tremendous reserve of good will which the statesmanship of the day left largely untapped. Doubtless that good will may have been naïve and capricious, but there was no question of its force and volume. For weeks during 1928, Kellogg and the Department of State were deluged by mail, by petitions, and by deputations, all pressing for the conclusion of the Pact. By all diplomatic usages the Pact was unorthodox, and it was entirely lacking in coercive machinery. But then, arguably, other international commitments were also lacking in coercive machinery and depended on the enlightened mutual interest of their signatories.

Yet the Pact had never been meant by its first sponsors to be much more than a *coup de théâtre*. For Briand in France, and for Stresemann in Germany – the two hardened old cynics that they were – it was an occasion for courtesies that could do no harm and might even do some good. The British Government disliked it, and the representative which it sent to Paris for the eventual signing of the Pact was pointedly an official of the second rank. Kellogg and his Department no doubt felt much as did the British Government. But the huge, confused, goodhearted public in the United States – and in Britain – were hardly to understand that they were being indulgently "babied along" by their political elders. The Pact, and particularly the fact of American participation in it, undoubtedly contributed to the financial boom in the United States. It remains the last monument of a better era when innocence was not a vice.

Latin-American Relations

Long before the days of the Fourteen Points of the Peace Conference of Paris, President Wilson had found nearer home, in Latin America, a field for the application of his political principles. He had also found there a confusion of strategic and commercial interests – often involving the United States – and an old, unyielding historical situation. But he had not found there very much of that "constitutionalism," the pride of his academic and public careers, the precious quality without which responsible government, as he conceived it, could not exist. In the end, President Wilson, in the first two years of his administration, intervened in Latin-American affairs no less frequently or forcefully than any of his less altruistically minded predecessors.

Mexico, for example, the nearest Latin-American neighbor, had relapsed into anarchy since the popular rising against the dictator Porfirio Diaz in 1910. General Huerta, whom Wilson himself stigmatized as a "desperate brute," had disposed of his rival by assassination in 1913, and had installed himself as ruler *de facto* in Mexico City. President Wilson refused to extend him diplomatic recognition or to sell arms to his supporters. When, in April 1914, a German merchantman put in at Veracruz with a cargo of arms, President Wilson authorized the bombardment and occupation of the port. The subsequent exile of Huerta and the election of a Mexican President acceptable to Wilson did not close the incident. The colorful bandit Francisco Villa, at the head of a force of peasant irregulars dissatisfied with the slow pace of land reform, was raiding the properties of the large landowners. A border affray in New Mexico, deliberately provoked, was designed to incite armed intervention and to carry Villa into the presidency in Mexico City on a wave of nationalist hatred of the "gringo." President Wilson promptly ordered General Pershing into Mexico with a force of cavalry. But Villa proved elusive, and in February 1917 President Wilson, foreseeing American involvement in Europe, recalled the expedition.

The entry of the United States into the First World War in 1917 met with a mixed reception in Latin America. Mexico, Argentina, and Chile, together with four other republics, remained neutral. Five, including Bolivia, severed diplomatic relations with Germany. Eight, including Brazil, declared war. (See pp. 79-80.) The actual contribution by the belligerent states to the Allied war effort in terms of front-line personnel – Brazil perhaps excepted – was little enough.[2] Vast supplies of grain and meat were shipped to Europe, and a war boom of considerable proportions supervened. The consequent accumulation of capital, and the difficulty of obtaining manufactured goods from embattled Europe, gave some impetus to industrialization.

Nor was the restoration of peace in 1918 a unanimously happy event. The "Colossus of the North" had emerged from the conflict more powerful and self-confident than ever. Its failure to join the League of Nations seemed clear proof that it would accept no external restraints upon its restless imperialist drive to the south. In 1914 there was not one United States bank in Latin America; by 1921 there were fifty-four. Bolivian tin, Chilean nitrate, and Brazilian coffee flowed northward in profusion, in return for automobiles from Detroit and machinery from Pittsburgh. By 1931, American investments in Latin America reached a total of over $5,000,000,000, an increase of 1,700 per cent since 1914. The impoverished politicos and opportunist generals who rose to the surface of Latin-American politics accepted the largesse readily. Their armies and police had to be paid, and their supporters rewarded. The problem of liquidating the loans could be bequeathed to succeeding administrations.

The Pan-American movement, it was hoped, would mollify the growing fear of *"el peligro Yanqui* (the Yankee peril)," promote closer political and cultural relations among the republics of the Western Hemisphere, and form a complement to the Monroe Doctrine. The first International Conference of American States had been held at Washington in 1889, but the ambitious projects for a customs union, a common silver currency, and an arbitral system for inter-American disputes that had been presented there were all voted down with scant ceremony. The Latin-American delegates suspected that the chief motive in calling the conference had been to woo Latin Americans from their liking for British sewing machines and textiles. The same unsleeping distrust had severely limited the usefulness of the three subsequent conferences held before 1914 and, as we have seen, the distrust increased rather than diminished after the restoration of peace in 1918. A most unfortunate impression was created, for example, at the Santiago Conference in 1923, when the United States delegation blocked a Uruguayan proposal for an American League of Nations based on the absolute equality of its members. It was concluded therefore that the United States still regarded the Monroe Doctrine as a right of protectorship over the southern republics and not as a guiding principle of policy freely accepted by equals.

Renewed intervention by the United States in the mid-1920's brought the whole problem of inter-American relations to a head. The firm grip on the economic life of Nicaragua, guaranteed since 1912 by the presence of American marines, had seemingly been relaxed by 1925, and the marines were withdrawn. But within a year there were fresh revolutionary commotions, and the marines were back again. The Democratic opposition in Congress kept up a steady drumfire of criticism, especially as the military operations in Nicaragua lacked Congressional sanction. President Coolidge, stressing the "moral responsibility" of the United States toward the governments north of Panama, sent Henry L. Stimson to Nicaragua in 1927 to mediate between the rebels and the regime in power. Stimson was able to arrange a fair election under United States auspices, the results of which were accepted by both parties. Clearly, as an alternative to military intervention and resulting ill will, mediation was full of interesting possibilities.

The role of "honest broker" was put to a more severe test in Mexico. The celebrated Article 27 of the Mexican constitution of 1917 had declared all lands, waters, and mineral deposits to be the property of the nation, which could expropriate them in the public interest. Oil lands were to be controlled by the government, which was empowered to lease them to private individuals for a period not exceeding fifty years. Foreign concessionaires were required not to invoke the protection of their government in the event of dispute. In 1925 President Calles of Mexico began not only to apply the law to foreign-held oil concessions, but to make it retroactive. The agent of United States mediation in this delicate situation was Dwight Morrow, the newly appointed ambassador to Mexico and a member of the firm of J. P. Morgan. By laying the "big stick" on the shelf, by displaying a maximum of good will, and by granting the Calles regime the American loan of which it was in dire need, Morrow was able to arrange a temporary settlement. He also recognized the competence of the Mexican Supreme Court to pronounce on the rights of the oil companies held by United States interests. In return, oil concessions granted before 1917 were confirmed, and the fifty-year limitation on foreign-held concessions was dropped.

In spite of this progress, a powerful undercurrent of resentment against the United States persisted in the debates of the Sixth Pan-American Conference at Havana in January 1928. Indeed, the future President Roosevelt wrote that feeling was "so bitter against the United States that it threatened to bring out not only hostile speeches, but definitely hostile action toward the United States." The high tariffs of the United States – a familiar topic – and the interventionist policy in Nicaragua were assailed in turn. A provocative resolution to the effect that no American state should intervene in the internal affairs of another received thirteen votes, and the eloquence of Charles Evans Hughes, at the head of the United States delegation, barely blocked its adoption. Hughes developed the familiar argument that if there was a breakdown of government, if "sovereignty faltered" in a Latin-American state, intervention to protect the lives and property of citizens of the United States was justified.

Hoover brought with him, as he brought to Anglo-American relations, a new expectation of peace. His good-will tour of Latin America at the end of 1928, while he was President-elect, suggested that his administration would persevere in the policy of mediation and nonintervention. It was not to be long before his conciliatory gifts were exercised to the full. The stock-market crash of 1929 reacted on Latin America as it had reacted on Europe, short-term loans were called in, unsold surpluses of Latin-American grain, meat, cotton, and coffee accumulated, exports sank, by 1933, to one-third of their value in 1929 and, as must always happen in Latin America, economic distress gave rise to a new wave of revolutions.

But, this time, the subversive mutterings in Haiti – occupied by United States marines since 1915 – were stilled, not by the intrusion of more marines, but by the appointment of the Forbes Commission, which recommended withdrawal. Harry F. Guggenheim, the American ambassador in Cuba, took an early opportunity to condemn the Platt Amendment,[3] and added: "Our relationship with Cuba, insofar as the special protection of American citizens is concerned, is, and should be clearly understood to be, suicidal to our relations with other American republics under international law." When, in October 1931, the Dominican Republic and Brazil announced the suspension of interest payments on their foreign debts, Washington made no move to put in the receivers, and it was slowly borne in upon the defaulting states that their insolvency would not be used as an excuse for intervention in their national affairs. The new regimes thrown up by revolution in Argentina, Brazil, Chile, Bolivia, and Peru were unhesitatingly recognized by the United States. In the words of the Clark Memorandum,[4] the Monroe Doctrine was no longer to be regarded as "an instrument of violence and oppression" against Latin America, but was what President Monroe had doubtless originally intended it to be, a guarantee of freedom and territorial integrity.

The New York Stock-Market Crash of 1929

In 1928 President Coolidge announced that he would not run for a second term. Herbert Hoover won the Presidential elections of the year by a handsome majority. In the course of his Inaugural Address on March 4, 1929, the new President delivered himself as follows:

> In the larger view, we have reached a higher degree of comfort and security than has ever existed before in the history of the world. Through liberation from widespread poverty we have reached a higher degree of individual freedom than ever before. The devotion to, and concern for, our institutions are deep and sincere. We are steadily building up a new race, and new civilization, great in its own attainments . . . Ours is a land rich with resources, stimulating in its glorious beauty, filled with millions of happy homes, blessed with comfort and opportunity . . . I have no fears for the future of our country. It is bright with hope.

The American people were then at the height of unprecedented prosperity. Wall Street had become the very symbol of easy money; fortunes, it seemed, were for anybody's asking. Technically, it has been said, the great boom had resulted from a deliberate policy of credit inflation on the part of the Federal Reserve Board and represented all the usual phenomena of an ascending "business cycle." But, far more than this, it was a psychological reaction to the successful part the United States had played in the war. The United States had become after 1918, on a magnified scale, what England had become after 1815. It was a young, expanding country whose resources, military and ideological, had contributed decisively to a great victory. Broken empires had adopted its political forms and begged for its largesse. It seemed to hold a lien on the wealth and welfare of all the world. European debts and reparations, by whatever circuit they flowed, found their eventual destination in its capacious lap. These were the grand, robust "roaring twenties," the days of an automobile to every four persons and a refrigerator to every second home. Architecture, always the symbol of economic and social conditions, was entering upon one of the great periods of its history. The problems of skyscraper design were being solved, and these graceful new monsters were rising in every city of the continent.

But prosperity, as was so soon to appear, was no single nation's absolute or inevitable birthright. For the few who could read the signs, the United States had been suffering a general retardation of business for some time before the critical year 1929 was reached. The usual economic indices – industrial production, house-building, carloadings, export surpluses, employment, and so forth – if they were still increasing, were increasing by relatively small fractions. Commodity prices rose to their peak in 1925 and, with some variations, had then begun to run into a decline. Most noticeable of all was the fall in agricultural prices in the United States and in Canada. The increase in crops, required during the war years, was no longer needed now that European harvests were returning to more normal figures; hence while the American farmer strove to adjust himself to a reduced economic level, he bought less and less from industry.

Yet speculation on Wall Street continued. Prices of stocks were out of all relation to possible dividends or future expansion. It was later estimated that of the population of the United States nearly a million had become amateurs in an art formerly confined to a small class of professional operators. New investment trusts were floated almost daily. In midsummer of 1929, some $11,000,000,000 was being carried by brokers' loans and bank loans to uphold a nationwide structure of borrowing on margin, to uphold in turn a pyramiding speculation of apparently illimitable altitudes. Call money — a significant index — at one time went as high as 20 per cent.[5] The Federal Reserve Board, whose easy-money policy had originally contributed so much to the boom, tried belatedly to apply the brakes. In July 1928, it had raised the discount rate to 5 per cent, and in August 1929, raised it to 6 per cent. During 1929 it continually sounded its warnings, though perhaps never very loudly or very forcibly. Plainly no one wanted to play the unpopular role of kill-joy and spoilsport. The government gave no help, and the private banks, which might have encouraged a little remedial liquidation before it was too late, had generally entered recklessly into the national revel themselves.

The first indisputable declines in the stock market began in the second week of September 1929, and the general lowering trend was then stimulated by events abroad. On September 20, 1929, in London, occurred the failure of Clarence Hatry and his bogus companies, a failure not unlike those of Oustric, Stavisky, Kreuger, and other famous "bubbles" of these years. Withdrawals of gold from the Bank of England at the same time were causing some anxiety. On September 26 the bank rate in England, already at 5½ per cent, was raised to 6½ per cent. For the first three weeks of October, Wall Street was in a very nervous mood, but even experienced operators declared that the sharp twinges that the market had been feeling were no more than passing "indigestion." But once the selling had begun and had become general, it was accelerated by the huge margin calls which it automatically developed. On October 23, almost in the last hour of the day's trading, the market suddenly collapsed. On October 24, "Black Thursday," the record number of 12,800,000 shares were sold, and 6,300,000 shares, another record, were sold on the curb market. Key stocks declined 50 to 75 points. The losses to American investors during October were put at $40,000,000,000. Early in November, under a general conspiracy of "returning confidence," the market seemed to recover, but selling developed again on November 6 and, with some fluctuations, prices continued to fall thereafter.

The refusal of leading bankers, of the public — and of the government — to believe the evidence of their senses acted momentarily as a "psychological brake." A conference of bankers, meeting at the offices of J. P. Morgan and Co., as early as October 24 was said to have put up perhaps as much as $240,000,000 in "organized support" of the market, and had tried in particular to rally despondent newspapermen to their own cheerful views of the crisis. On October 30 John D. Rockefeller announced that he and his son were steadily buying large blocks of common stock. Government spokesmen at Washington, including President Hoover himself, sent out almost routine messages emphasizing their belief in the fundamental soundness of American business. Professors and economists, branching out into popular journalism, learnedly recalled other crashes in the country's checkered past — and, by inference, other recoveries.

But a mere artificial optimism could not dissipate the obdurate facts. The American investor felt like a man in boastful good health who has been suddenly laid low by a mysterious ailment, and whose doctor persists in assuring him that there is nothing really the matter. Throughout 1930 the contagion kept spreading. Markets, profits, wages, production, and prices steadily and inexorably continued to drop. Business seemed to be seized with a sort of catalepsy. To give one good index of the situation, General Motors turned out 5,500,000 automobiles in 1929 and 2,500,000 in 1931. In 1931 the Treasury reported the first deficit in recent American budgetary history. By 1933 wholesale prices had fallen by almost one-third, industrial production by more than one-half, the national income by more than one-half, and the value of merchandise trade by more than two-thirds. That most fearful and intractable of all economic indices, unemployment, had become the big factor in American social life. In March 1933, the number of unemployed in the United States was conservatively estimated at over 14,000,000.

Many social scientists in the United States are of the belief that, certainly in so far as the American people are concerned, the Depression was a far more shattering national experience than the two World Wars themselves, because of the mystery of its origin and the bleakness of its prospects, and also because of its uncontrollable, almost fatalistic operation among a people traditionally accustomed to commanding their own destinies by their own free will. For the first time in the history of the Western Hemisphere, man in all his rugged individuality seemed not the master of his fate.

The passage thereafter from these events to the Depression belongs rather to world affairs than to American, and we shall resume the narrative in the next chapter.

Part Three

THE PERIOD OF CRISIS

In the future days, which we seek to make secure, we look forward to a world founded upon four essential human freedoms.

The first is freedom of speech and expression — everywhere in the world.

The second is freedom of every person to worship God in his own way — everywhere in the world.

The third is freedom from want — which, translated into world terms, means economic understandings which will secure to every nation a healthy peacetime life for its inhabitants — everywhere in the world.

UNITED PRESS INTERNATIONAL

The fourth is freedom from fear — which, translated into world terms, means a world-wide reduction of armaments to such a point and in such a thorough fashion that no nation will be in a position to commit an act of physical aggression against any neighbor — anywhere in the world.

That is no vision of a distant millennium. It is a definite basis for a kind of world attainable in our time and generation. That kind of world is the very antithesis of the so-called new order of tyranny which the dictators seek to create with the crash of a bomb.

— FRANKLIN D. ROOSEVELT

17. THE DEPRESSION AND THE BREAKDOWN OF THE SETTLEMENT

The Locarno Era

The interwar period lasted twenty years—from the Peace Conference of Paris in 1919 to the outbreak of the Second World War in 1939. It fell into two phases, the first of which this book has called the Period of Settlement, and the second the Period of Crisis. Though there is no easy dividing line in time between the two periods, the main watershed of events, so to speak, was provided by the stock-market crash in the United States in 1929 and the Depression which followed thereafter.

To its own contemporaries the Period of Settlement gave a convincing impression of mankind in convalescence, progressively achieving peace. A stability was returning to the world such as had not been known since 1914. The nations of Europe in particular were growing conscious of an intense weariness, and felt perhaps that a pause in their overmastering anxieties was no more than their due. The Locarno Pact in 1925 expressed and emblemized a universal desire. It is curious—curious to the point of tedium—how it has been possible in this book to write of each nation, with very few exceptions, as it entered these relatively passive years of the later 1920's, as having achieved its peace, tranquilized its frontiers, established an apparently stable constitution, and recovered something of its "normal" prosperity and well-being—even if at times it had to do so under an authoritarian regime. The difficult transition from wartime to peacetime economy seemed to have been made; reconstruction was going forward; the immediate monetary chaos had passed; the gold standard was generally restored; the vexatious problems of reparations and international debts appeared settled; production indices everywhere were healthily rising. Even so realistic an observer as Winston Churchill described the year 1928 as "The End of the World Crisis." [1] Not often does history, in its relentless continuity, so decelerate the onrush of events and provide so positive an interregnum.

France, for example, in the Locarno era, under Poincaré, was making her way from financial weakness to financial strength. The franc was stabilized, industries were humming, and Paris was full of tourists. Britain, under a safe Conservative government, was trying to forget her General Strike and her million unemployed. A strange quiet had descended upon her, and in all her recent history it is doubtful that she had gone through — we had almost said enjoyed — three years quite so uneventful as 1927, 1928, and 1929. Germany, under Stresemann, was on the highroad to economic recovery. Foreign loans were flowing, industry was being rationalized, the Dawes Plan no longer seemed so humiliating or so burdensome. Poland, under Pilsudski, looked as if she too had learned the lessons of stability. The Middle Danube — Austria perhaps excepted — was generally content and confident. Even Hungary, unhappy, truncated Hungary, could almost be said to have prospered for a time. Italy was busy building up her Corporative State. The Soviet Union was in the initial stages of its first Five-Year Plan.

The Balkan countries, mostly under various dictatorships, were quiescent. Turkey had become virtually identified with Kemal's benign rule. Palestine seemed to have overcome her many intricate problems. Iraq was fast attaining independent nationhood. Arabia was firmly in the hands of Ibn Saud. Egypt for the moment was less fractious. Across the Atlantic, the Americas in general, and the United States in particular, were in the midst of the boom we described in the last chapter. Across the Pacific, China was still full of discords; but Chiang Kai-shek had established his government at Nanking, and for the first time in years the country showed some promise of a unified and public-spirited administration. Only Japan was uneasy and was, in fact, approaching the end of her period of watchful waiting.

But the peace, we know, was not to be. The freedom from want and fear, however much it was becoming an established reality, however passionately it was desired by the people of all nations, lasted less than a decade. Yet here was a world that could have ranked beside the great Trajanic phases of history, when a sense of assured well-being had settled upon its citizens and was beginning to allow them once more the luxuries of security and permanence. It was a world of highly diffused science and humanitarianism. It was still hitched to the star of Progress. Its defects were many, but they could be regarded as defects of detail, each full of remedial possibilities, each a challenge to enterprise. To the contemporaries of the Locarno era there seemed to be nothing that normal intelligence, good will, and the lapse of time would not somehow heal. Yet in the space of a few years this world broke down into depression, terror, disbelief, and war.

Approach to the Crisis

Into the high metaphysics of the breakdown we cannot enter here. This book is not a philosophy of history. But of the more specific "causes" of the breakdown, particularly as they appeared to contemporaries, perhaps we can speak more freely. For these we may begin by going back to the errors of 1919, errors which the Locarno era temporarily hid from view. It was then, presumably, at the Peace Conference of Paris that the festering germs were injected into the world's body politic, and, however long or deceptive the delay, the infection would ultimately come to the surface. One fact which stood out at Paris was that few national statesmen – perhaps one only – who signed the peace treaties wholeheartedly subscribed to the avowed principles thereof, and that they committed a perjury which, in the fullness of time, was to exact its retribution. The ideology of the treaties, for good or ill, derived from President Wilson. But the victor states, forgathering in Paris, were already in process of "psychological retreat." France paid the Wilsonian philosophy no more than an expedient lip service. The United States and the British Dominions, and to some extent Britain herself, were withdrawing into isolationism. Japan, Italy, Poland, and the host of lesser powers came, negotiated, and signed with mental reservations of one kind or another. As one statesman at Paris put it, "President Wilson is the only Wilsonian here, and sometimes not even he!" There has perhaps never been a peace in the long history of war and peace which wholly adhered to its principles, and, in the strict, literal view, the peace treaties had interpreted the Fourteen Points with remarkable accuracy. But the moral contradiction was undeniable.

Nor has there ever been a treaty of comparable importance that was a finished and perfect document. But Paris, in 1919, was obsessed with finality. So unique an opportunity to legislate for the millennium was unlikely to recur, and the most had to be made of it. The British plea for a frankly temporary treaty was overridden. The Americans, with their eighteenth-century Constitution at the back of their minds, thought in terms of inflexible written documents. Despite its vagueness and despite Article 19, there was, for instance, an extraordinary rigidity in the League Covenant. President Wilson himself regarded the Covenant as the culmination of all democratic history, a sacred and inviolable testament. The subsequent treaties of Trianon and Neuilly, if anything, were more rigid than Versailles. We do not need great sagacity to anticipate the fortunes of a series of treaties in whose principles the signatories had so little faith and which contained so little provision for peaceful, legal change.

The treaties left Europe with a string of "danger spots," not quantitatively considerable in themselves, but likely to demand revision and, as it afterward turned out, likely to provide aggressor powers with a handle for troublemaking in the future. Danzig in itself, for example, was no more of a danger spot than Tangier, nor the Sudetenland than many a canton in Switzerland; but Danzig and the Sudetenland were very gifts for diplomatic exploitation at an inconvenient time. The new smaller nationalities would also doubtless demand revision, and would demand it periodically. Europe, it was said, had been "Balkanized"; exaggerated nationalism had reached its *reductio ad absurdum.* An empire such as Austria-Hungary, hitherto a viable economic unit, had been broken into fragments. In Intermediate Europe, in that band of territories running from Finland to Greece, there were thirteen minor independent states, created on the assumption of the permanent weakness or the political good faith of the two powers, Germany and Russia, which stood on either side of them, an assumption which needed only a few years to falsify. The Versailles system, in its pretended finality, expected an unalterable territorial configuration in Europe. The

Locarno Pact, the French alliances, the League of Nations itself, all were custodians of a new *status quo,* resistant to changes which consequently could only be made in defiance of the settlement.

Then the breakdown was ascribed to a great extent to the isolationism of the United States. But this is only another way of saying that the United States cast aside the whole psychosis of the war as quickly as possible and tried to re-create the familiar conditions of its former peace and domesticity. In this case, however, the defection was more serious than in other nations that tried to do the same. It was not merely that the United States was so powerful and could have enforced, if it had wished, a greater practical observance of the Wilsonian philosophy, but rather that in repudiating that philosophy it repudiated the entire Allied cause. By its participation in the war in 1917 the United States had given the Allies the assurance of victory, it had inspired their last year of fighting, it had received the enemy's surrender, it had dominated the Peace Conference, it had provided the only responsible ideology that the Allies had ever really had; and then, as a superb anticlimax, it had withdrawn. The higher the hope and the promise, the deeper the emptiness when the hope and the promise were gone.

Britain's isolationism was never so complete, and from the ideological point of view was never so serious. But the result of the combined isolationism of the United States and Britain was to leave France with the hegemony of Europe, and France was not a strong enough protector. France always regarded the international scene with military eyes, and unhappily, as time was to show, she no longer had the moral power to make her military power effective. The First World War had been won for her with British, American, and Russian help, and the peace, as she conceived the peace to be, could be secured only with a continuance of that help. Yet she pursued a foreign policy out of all proportion to her own unaided strength. She tried to create a Europe which could be instantly quelled at her discretion by the mere threat of a preventive war, and when, in 1936, the last chance for that war arose, she failed to act. She multiplied alliances with states whom she was to forsake or who were to forsake her. Admittedly, she was not altogether to blame. She was the victim of her inheritance. But hers was a tragic story nonetheless.

British and French policies in the postwar years were constantly at variance. In general, British policy aimed to remove the causes of unsettlement by means of judicious concession, the French to hold everything rigidly and uncompromisingly in check. Arguably either policy, British or French, might have succeeded if it had been followed exclusively. The simultaneous and vacillating prosecution of both together was disastrous. If nothing else, France should surely have been counseled by expedience. She needed Britain as a powerful friend; yet time and again she prevented the necessary friendship from forming. In every international conference, from the Peace Conference onward, she seemed to stand in determined opposition to her former ally. After 1936 she and Britain did reach an understanding. At that time, it could be said, she had proved her case, and her implacable attitude toward Germany had been more than justified. But at that time, it could also be said, a Franco-British understanding was already too late.

Germany's state of mind was an integral part of the postwar complex. Doubtless she greeted the coming of peace in 1918 with the same hysterical relief as her enemies; doubtless large sections of her people experienced the same retreat to pacifism; doubtless she had suffered, and doubtless she felt humiliated and abased. But it is difficult to believe that Germany, in her heart of hearts, ever accepted military defeat in the sense that Russia accepted military defeat in 1917 or France in 1940. Germany ascribed her collapse in November 1918 to the Allied blockade, to Allied propaganda, and to her own political disunity at home – in other words, to causes that were temporary and reparable. She denied that she had ever met decisive defeat in the field. She showed not the least contrition over her role in the events that had led to the outbreak of the war. The Allies stopped their propaganda at the Armistice and made no attempt to create in Germany a mood receptive to the peace conditions they intended to impose, conditions to which Germany therefore reacted in anger and, above all, in sheer astonishment. In later years, German military theorists and historians became more and more convinced of the real concatenation of trickery and blundering by which an uninvaded country and an "undefeated" army and navy had so unbelievably surrendered. The myth of the "stab in the back" was already current in Germany in 1919. We have said that the Peace Conference of Paris was obsessed with finality; for Germany, on the contrary, it was but a passing humiliation. Here too was a situation loaded with mischief.

Then it could be argued that the disequilibrium which had originally precipitated the First World War had not been removed. Many of the problems of 1914, far from being solved, were more serious than before. The interwar world was like a man who had just undergone a critical operation, an operation which had preserved his life, but not properly restored his health. Moreover he had afterward committed the crowning folly of thinking he was his old self again and could pick up the threads of his former ways just where he had dropped them. With the exception of Russia, and perhaps Turkey and China, the nations – out of pride in their pasts, or more often out of sheer habit and inertia – did everything in their power to return to the conditions of 1914. The vanquished were often more forward-looking than the victors; but all tried to treat the war, not as a painful process of transformation, which was its only historical justification, but as an unfortunate, mistaken lapse, itself to be forgotten and its results to be reversed. We might well believe that the Great Peace of 1914 in retrospect bade fair to become a sort of golden age, much as the memory of Imperial Rome was to the Middle Ages, a legendary norm which subsequent generations would always envy and futilely aspire to restore.

In Chapter 1 we drew a rough picture of the world of 1914. In 1929, at the point of the second collapse, the picture was not very different, except for the sharpening of some of its outlines. Science and industry were still producing their peculiar social and economic maladjustments. Peoples were more closely knit together, but civilized life was everywhere becoming more complicated and expensive. Breakdowns in the system, if and when they occurred, were correspondingly more dangerous and irreparable; weapons, war, and the consequences of war were becoming incomparably more frightful. Mass politics was a phenomenon of tremendous, scarcely comprehended potentiality. Nationality was still a powerful force, both for culture and anarchy. The eight "problem" nations which we singled out in Chapter 1 were still in the forefront of international affairs, and none could say in what combination they might clash once more. (See p. 8.) The wheel of causation that set the First World War in motion was still grinding itself out to a finish.

Among the larger, less specific "causes" of the breakdown in 1929 we may surely name the failure of democracy. To many of its participants the First World War was interpretable as the conquest of the last remaining strongholds of feudal and aristocratic tyranny. The whole course of history, from the Anglo-Saxon moot to the League of Nations, could be written as the progressive liberation of man, culminating in a grand, cataclysmic "war to end wars." By 1918 all the great autocracies had gone down in defeat – Tsarist Russia, Ottoman Turkey, Imperial Austria, Prussian Germany – not to forget Manchu China. Their oppressed peoples were set free; other oppressed peoples, from Ireland to the Philippines, were on their way to freedom; new units were being admitted to the family of independent nations. By 1919, it seemed, the world had been made safe for democracy.

Yet, in ten years, the gains of centuries of blood, toil, and tears were lost. Democracy at the moment of its greatest triumph seemed to be a spent and sinking force. The Russian Revolution quickly forsook its once high ideals and issued in a political system no less tyrannous than the one it had overthrown. Dictatorships of one form or another appeared in Turkey, Italy, Intermediate Europe, and Spain. National Socialism was shortly to appear in Germany. Even France, the classic home of revolution, was soon to be at grips with Fascist "Leagues." And all this happened, not only in so short a time, but often – and herein was the most frightening feature – as a voluntary renunciation. It happened not from reasoned argument, but in obedience to some blind upsurge of primitive passions. Men sold themselves to new masters not in horror and detestation, but of their free and almost fanatic choice, and they exulted in their slavery.

The new dictators had confidence, adventurousness, and extraordinary dynamism. They had, in fact, everything that current democracy lacked. Far from holding its accustomed place in the van of progress, democracy seemed to have become conservative, nostalgic, and outdated. Older democratic states, which had known a vigorous parliamentary life and vigorous liberal institutions, stood on the defensive, jealously misering the remnants of their riches, and encumbering themselves with bureaucratism and petty party corruption. Moreover, as events were to show so painfully, democracy also lost its accustomed tactical advantage in the great struggle of international politics. By a curious inversion its old strength was now its weakness. The liberal methods of open debate, free speech, tolerance of opposition, frank and honest dealing even with enemies, even the lesser courtesies and conventions of human intercourse – however much they might still withstand a long-term trial of strength – were at an initial loss against totalitarian regimentation, propaganda, abusive speech, secrecy, deception, and surprise decisions. If it was to be a matter of the survival of the fittest, the prospects for democracy were uncertain indeed. The very values of civilization seemed suddenly to have become the instruments of defeat and disaster.

The Economic Breakdown

But the most immediate and spectacular of the "causes" of the breakdown, which so to speak detonated all the rest, was not political and not European, but economic and American. It was the stock-market crash in New York in 1929. Here, as was at once dimly felt, if not at once consciously acknowledged, was no routine business recession, no mere provincial upset. Here was something, in magnitude alone, quite outside normal experience hitherto, something which was to involve the entire world. It was something which was to call in question, not only an economic system long taken for granted, but the way of life which that system supported. Worst of all, it was something that was oddly irrelevant. While statesmanship had been engaged in the familiar politics of alliances, armaments, frontiers, nationalisms, and other "danger spots," this new eruption burst out from quite unknown depths. Universal collapse in 1929, of the kind which actually occurred, was never farther from men's minds; but, when it came, it was so much the more subversive of all normal confidence because it came from the least expected and least explicable direction. It was like some diabolic quirk of fate beyond human understanding and free choice.

In the previous chapter – the chapter with which we concluded Part II of the work – we described the stock-market crash in New York in 1929. We must now turn from the general speculation, which has so far occupied us in the present chapter, to consider the European repercussions of the stock-market crash and the world-wide Depression which followed. We shall discuss the economic situation in Europe before and after 1929, and then, in successive chapters of this Part of the book, we shall pass on to the several crises of the Period of Crisis for which the Depression was the undoubted preparation.

Debts and Reparations

The Allied debt question was part of the general economic situation, and it was mentioned in the last chapter in its American context. We need add here only that the indebtedness was not all one way. The United States was not the sole creditor. Britain and France had been lenders to their allies as well as borrowers from the United States and from each other. Balfour's proposal in 1922 of a clean sweep of all debts and reparations would have involved the British Treasury in heavy loss. (See p. 303.) But, when the United States declined Balfour's proposal, the British Government felt obliged, "with the most perfect courtesy and in the exercise of its undoubted rights," to invite its debtors to conclude funding agreements.

The first of Britain's funding agreements was with Rumania in October 1925, and those with Italy, France, Portugal, Greece, and Yugoslavia followed in 1926 and 1927. Rates of interest were charged proportionately to the presumed paying capacity of the debtors and averaged 1½ per cent. At such rates, only about a third of the original obligations would have been paid off. Meanwhile the American funding agreements with thirteen debtor states were negotiated between 1922 and 1926. If now reparations are included, the following totals result: Germany had eleven creditors; the United States had sixteen debtors, Britain seventeen, and France ten. Twenty-eight states in all were involved as either creditors or debtors or both. In the year of the Hoover Moratorium, 1931-32, the aggregate transfers would have amounted to $750,000,000.[2]

We also mentioned that, under the Dawes Plan in 1924 in settlement of German reparations, Americans contributed more than half of the Dawes international loan. (See pp. 146-47.) From this point onward Americans invested heavily in German securities, largely issued by German municipalities and other public corporations. Interest rates were high, and at the time, in the good years of Germany's economic recovery, no securities seemed safer or more attractive. And doubtless, for their part, the German borrowers found it an easy and stimulating game to pay their private and their national obligations with loans, and the loans with more loans, *ad infinitum*. In later years the United States used to be accused of "paying for" German rearmament; and, indirectly, a case could be made out for such an accusation. An interesting cycle was in fact set up. American funds poured into Germany; Germany paid reparations; the recipients of the reparations, mainly Britain and France, paid their war debts to the United States. The situation might seem ridiculous if, by the standards of the day, it had not been perfectly in order. But it was certainly very dangerous. American speculators, despite the extent to which they had been playing the international market, traditionally regarded foreign lending as a sideline to be exploited for a time and then dropped if and when more attractive opportunities arose at home. By 1928 those opportunities were present, and idle funds found better use in Wall Street than in Europe. Money for Germany was becoming tight; the old loans were harder to come by. Then, in 1929, Wall Street collapsed. Germany, and the nations of the Middle Danube, which had been refloating their ships of state on the assumption that the American tidewater would flow indefinitely, suddenly found the precious element ebbing away from under them. Thereafter, as we shall see, the whole complex of debts, reparations, and loans was stranded beyond hope of saving.

Economic Nationalism

The European nations in the interwar period, both big nations and small, were bedeviled by high tariffs. They could always give the best of reasons for their respective policies, but the net result was an anarchy of economic nationalism. Even among former Allies tariffs were little changed, or were changed in an upward direction. Financial stringencies were always demanding new sources of revenue. A nation's trade needed to be defended against depreciated currencies abroad. Tariffs made a good bargaining point in negotiations between one government and another. The new succession states particularly, now building up their national economies from scratch, often from shattered foundations, were overvulnerable to competition. But, more than all these things, a sort of ardent national egotism, partly idealistic, partly military, required that a nation protect itself against imports which could endanger its own "key" industries. National self-sufficiency appeared to confer strength and immunity; for the smaller nations it was almost a part of the very regalia of sovereignty.

France and Italy made energetic tariff increases. Germany followed suit from 1925 onward, as soon as she was released from commercial restrictions under Versailles. The succession states of the Middle Danube walled themselves about with tariffs and dismembered an area which the elementary facts of history and geography had marked out as one for close economic union. Even Britain forsook her traditional free-trade principles. The United States introduced the Fordney-McCumber tariff of 1922 and the Smoot-Hawley tariff of 1929-30, which represented perhaps the two most exaggerated and indefensible tariff increases in the history of any nation.

President Wilson had once proclaimed the need for "the removal, so far as possible, of all economic barriers and the establishment of an equality of trade conditions among the nations consenting to the peace and associating themselves for its maintenance." But in practice, the achievement of economic disarmament, like military disarmament, was beyond the will of the nations.

Attempted Stabilization

Any program of normalcy demanded stabilization. International trade could make no headway with fluctuating currencies. The anarchy of economic nationalism often meant an anarchy of exchanges. Early in 1919, reputedly at the behest of London, the Allies unpegged their currencies which, during the war, they had so carefully stabilized each in terms of the other. Thereafter, from 1919 to 1925, we find one group of nations resorting to deflation, and another group allowing inflation to take its own sweet way with the value of their money. Britain was the foremost of the deflationary group, and in 1925, after a long struggle, when Winston Churchill was Chancellor of the Exchequer, she restored the gold standard.

Britain's action was all very honest and proper for the greatest of trading nations. But it put her at an "unfair" disadvantage with less generous rivals. Every debased currency could undersell her in foreign markets, and sometimes even at home. Nor could she, on account of her intricate and menacing labor situation, reduce wages, extend hours, or take other orthodox means to meet the competition. Old-fashioned methods of ownership and operation, especially in the coal industry, prevented any thoroughgoing rationalization or over-all "planning." As we have seen, Britain patiently bore her burden of unemployment even into the relatively better Locarno years rather than break with her financial traditions and prestige. (See p. 268.) Others of the deflationary group of nations, notably Australia and Japan, had much the same distressing experiences.

The inflationary group, provided the inflation was not allowed to get out of hand, and provided it was not accompanied by speculation, appeared at first to have the best of the bargain. For example, the French franc after many vagaries was stabilized in 1927 at about 25 to the dollar, a fifth of its prewar value. France was evidently content to accept a scaling-down of the value of domestic savings and capital, and a scaling-up of the cost in francs of her foreign obligations. Inflation enabled her to write off a goodly slice of her internal debt, to compete on favorable terms in foreign markets, to encourage the repatriation of capital which had escaped abroad, and eventually to buy gold in enormous quantities to replenish her gold reserve. Meanwhile her unemployment was negligible. To what extent France was motivated in all this, as in all her postwar policies, by ulterior political ends is not always easy to say. Perhaps it is fairest to give French statesmen and bankers the benefit of the doubt and to say that, in the beginning at least, they, like all the other experts of the day, were only imperfectly aware of the distant and indirect consequences of their acts.

Germany, another inflationary country, went too far and suffered the collapse of 1923 at the time of the Ruhr crisis. She subsequently restored her currency in the form of the new gold unit, the reichsmark, and, backed by foreign loans, she shared the relative prosperity of the Locarno era. The case of Soviet Russia was perhaps different; for there inflation was part of a deliberate policy to exterminate capital and pauperize the capitalist.

Yet however desirable stabilization might be, it was mechanically impossible if the point of reference was unsteady or shifting. The maldistribution of gold – or, more correctly, the change in the "normal" distribution of gold as it had been in 1914 – was perhaps the one "technical" cause of the failure to stabilize postwar exchanges and keep them stable. The maldistribution had already begun in the first year of the war, when so many currencies had gone off gold and when belligerents resorted more and more to gold as the most acceptable way of meeting the huge war bills abroad that they could not meet with loans. By 1919 the Scandinavian countries, the Netherlands, Switzerland, Argentina, Brazil, Japan, and above all the United States measured their wartime profits in their enormously increased gold reserves. After 1919 reparation payments and debts continued in much the same way to fleece certain powers for the apparent benefit of others.

In the network of international indebtedness the principal creditor country, as we have said, was the United States, and the United States was entrenched behind a dollar value of forbidding height. But the great problem of transfer, in respect of both reparations and debts, was at first hardly understood. Before 1914 the transfer of funds had been a commonplace of international banking, and in 1919, although the sums were enormously greater, the creditor countries vaguely expected that the same processes of transfer would continue to operate. It was not easy for the creditor countries to realize that the only way a debtor could pay his debts was by maintaining an export surplus, which in turn prejudiced the creditor countries' employment situation at home. When, moreover, the creditor countries, and in particular the United States, began of set purpose to "protect" themselves against a too inconvenient influx of foreign goods – the Fordney-McCumber tariff of 1922 was a case in point – the export surplus became correspondingly more difficult to dispose of. The net result could only be a flow of gold to the creditor countries and ultimately to the United States. And the net result of the flow of gold was a fall of prices in Europe, the further reduction of purchasing power, and the further reduction of the capacity of the debtors to find more gold with which to make their payments.

The United States tried to disembarrass itself of the unwelcome pile of treasure and lent generously – too generously, as it proved – to Germany and other European countries. But an irreducible residue of gold became sterilized. The situation was aggravated by France's policy of using her devalued franc for the purpose of buying gold, which she immediately consigned to a "war chest" and so sterilized also.[3] Gold-hoarding, whether in ancient Persia, sixteenth-century Spain, or eighteenth-century India, or in any other of the classic examples, never yet redounded to the benefit of the hoarder. But by 1929 half the world's gold supply lay in two countries, the United States and France, and the rest were going dangerously short. Meanwhile countries, deflationary or inflationary, were seeking to return to a gold standard and defeating their very object by thus creating an abnormal demand for gold. Visiting American financial experts, invited to reorganize some derelict national currency, invariably laid down three absolute desiderata: stability, a new central bank, and a gold reserve.

In the 1920's every struggling country wanted gold. Mining centers, such as South Africa or Canada, stimulated their gold production but could not satisfy the universal hunger. Several countries, notably Germany, Austria, Czechoslovakia, Yugoslavia, Rumania, Italy, and Finland, adopted the practice of backing their currencies with *Devisen,* that is, with paper funds payable in foreign currencies that were themselves convertible into gold. The practice economized gold, and it may have been unavoidable, but it made a number of "poorer" currencies dependent on the "richer," with disastrous results if the "richer" should ever prove unstable.

Debts and reparations, economic nationalism, and unstable currencies notwithstanding, the later 1920's did give the impression of a world in process of recovery. We have called this interval of relative peace and prosperity the Locarno era after the pact that initiated it. The recovery was not uniform – notably in countries, like Britain, of the deflationary group. But generally the European Continent – and, above all, the United States – enjoyed a productiveness and well-being that recalled, and often surpassed, the good old days before 1914. The standardization of manufactured goods, new and original advertising and salesmanship, new capital construction, housing and commercial building, the development of the automobile, motion picture, radio, civilian flying, and domestc laborsaving devices, all represented a solid body of achievement. A World Economic Conference met in Geneva in May 1927 with the express idea of consolidating the evident progress. The conference discussed the further standardization of manufactured goods and the possible all-around reduction of tariffs. It listened to speeches and it passed resolutions, of restrained optimism. In the words of its president:

> The Conference marks the beginning of a new era, during which international commerce will successively overcome all obstacles in its path that unduly hamper it and resume that general upward movement which is at once a sign of the world's economic health and the necessary condition for the development of civilization.

The Geneva Conference of 1927 remains today almost a curiosity among international conferences. Within a few years, far from resuming a general upward movement, international commerce was to lose one-quarter of its physical volume and two-thirds of its monetary value!

The Young Plan

The Young Plan is a convenient starting point in the history of the Depression. It was a contradictory transaction, and its mood, so to speak, showed both the confidence and the anxiety of the time. It was clearly predicated on the continuance of the progressive conditions lately obtaining in Germany and in Europe, and yet at the same time it somehow contrived to insinuate more than one doubt as to the ultimate permanence of those conditions. It was negotiated in the noonday glow of the 1920's; it was finally signed in January 1930, when the United States had already passed into the stock-market crash, and Germany was beginning to feel the first chills of the "economic blizzard."

The Dawes Plan was described in an earlier chapter. (See p. 146.) Since its signature in 1924 it had functioned fairly smoothly. Germany's annuities under the Plan had been paid on the dot and in full, albeit, as everyone knew, they had been paid with the help of foreign loans. But the Dawes Plan had never been intended as much more than a temporary settlement to tide over a crisis and, in particular, it had still left undetermined the total sum of Germany's reparations. The Germans themselves were not averse to reopening the whole reparations question, if the evacuation of the Rhineland could be expedited thereby and if a new settlement could be reached before the "standard" annuity of 2,500,000,000 gold marks ($595,000,000) for 1928-29 seemed to put their liability at an unalterably high level. Accordingly, in September 1928, at the time of the Ninth Assembly of the League, representatives of the interested powers, meeting privately at Geneva, decided to call "a committee of financial experts" with a view to reaching "a complete and final settlement of the reparations problem." The committee, under the chairmanship of the American Owen D. Young, sat in Paris in the earlier months of 1929 and formulated a series of recommendations which came to be known as the Young Plan.

The Young Plan was adopted after stormy sessions at a conference of the powers – France, Italy, Japan, Britain, the British Dominions, and Germany – at The Hague in August 1929. Philip Snowden, the British delegate, Chancellor of the Exchequer of the Labor government of that year, roundly accused France of repudiating her debts — "bilking," as he picturesquely put it — and he took very serious exception to a proposed new apportionment of the reparations receipts far less favorable to Britain than were the former Spa percentages of 1920. (See p. 142.) For a few delicious days a surprised and delighted Britain watched her Socialist Chancellor of the Exchequer doing doughty battle with French intransigence and egotism, and winning all but a complete victory. Most of the international conferences of this time seemed to hover on the brink of deadlock or collapse, but this one, for once, ended in a compromise greatly to the credit of Britain. The Young Plan was signed at last at a second conference at The Hague on January 20, 1930.

The Young Plan abolished the old Dawes Transfer Committee and thus placed squarely on Germany herself the burden not only of collecting the reparations payments but of transferring them to the recipients. Germany's exchange was to be protected by dividing the reparations into unconditional and conditional payments, the conditional being postponable whenever, in the opinion of a Special Advisory Committee, "Germany's economic life may be seriously endangered." The reparations figure was fixed at fifty-nine graduated annuities, derived from the Reich budget and railroads, and totaling 37,000,000,000 marks ($8,000,000,000 or £1,600,000,000). At the behest of France a new "sanction clause" was written into the agreements, providing for "full liberty of action" on the part of any creditor power if the World Court should find Germany in voluntary default. Finally, there was created a new institution, the Bank for International Settlements, which was to act as trustee for the creditor powers, as distributor of the reparations payments, as a link between the national central banks, and generally as "an organization, not simply concerned with the handling of reparations, but also with furnishing the world of international commerce and finance with important facilities hitherto lacking."

The Young Plan was well received everywhere but in Germany. The referendum upon it, instigated by the growing Nazi party, will be described in a later chapter. (See p. 354.) The fixing of the total reparations made little impression — there would have been protest in Germany however big or little the sum — and, in any case, high finance at this scale never meant much to the ordinary man. But the grim prospect of the payments continuing for fifty-nine years to 1988 was more readily appreciable and, war guilt or no war guilt, the transaction was an intolerable visitation of the iniquities of Versailles on guiltless generations yet unborn.

However, the Young Plan was ratified in Germany, and the necessary laws to give it effect were duly promulgated in March 1930. The Bank for International Settlements was declared open at offices in Basel. The final stages of the evacuation of the Rhineland were begun. For a moment all was quiet on the European front.

The Proposed Austro-German Customs Union

The European stock exchanges in 1929 and 1930 sagged in sympathy with Wall Street, and a tendency to liquidate set in everywhere. But there was no crash on the same quantitative scale or of the same dramatic intensity. The European "retreat from Locarno" was a far more gradual and drawn-out process. American lending in Europe, of course, came to an abrupt stop, and American loans were called in, to the special disadvantage of those states in Europe which, like Germany, had been financing themselves for so long on foreign loans and on the anticipation of more foreign loans to come. Throughout 1929 and 1930, the international trade of Europe had been declining, and all the indices – prices, production, and employment – had been declining in unison. But it was not till March and May 1931 that the European recession produced, first in the proposed Austro-German Customs Union and then in the failure of the Austrian Credit-Anstalt, crises on a par with the American stock-market crash of a year and a half previously.

The vexed question of the Austrian *Anschluss* with Germany has been discussed elsewhere, and it is a question which we must meet again in a much aggravated form. (See pp. 163-65 and 383-87.) But an Austro-German Customs Union might have been regarded as a more innocent transaction, especially in view of the fact that other bilateral trade pacts at this time between Germany and her neighbors had raised no suspicions or alarms. Certainly Austria by herself was too small a unit to resist the economic tensions of 1930 and 1931. She had owed her very preservation as a state to foreign financial intervention, and it was obvious that some such help must be forthcoming a second time if she was to continue in independent existence. But the announcement in March 1931 by Dr. Julius Curtius, the German Foreign Minister, that an Austro-German "technical customs union" was under discussion was immediately met with storms of protest from Italy, from the Little Entente, and of course from France. Britain was noncommittal, but characteristically she evinced some interest in the legalities of the case.

France was already profoundly agitated over the alleged rearmament of Germany and the rise of the Nazi party. The new commercial *Anschluss* merely added fuel to her fears. The kaleidoscopic fortunes of the year had thrown enormous financial power into her hands, a power which she was now beginning to use to impose her own terms on European suppliants for aid. Since Poincaré's stabilization of the franc, she had found herself able to make increasing purchases of gold abroad and, in the present state of Europe, gold was as effective a weapon as powder and steel. After months of bickering, which exacerbated all the old antagonisms between herself and Germany, France forced Austria and Germany to withdraw the proposals for their Customs Union. Curtius did not survive the defeat of his cherished scheme, and resigned. The legalities of the case meanwhile had been referred to the World Court at The Hague, and a judgment delivered in general support of the French objections. Austria was left to struggle with her difficulties, for a time, alone.

How serious those difficulties were had become apparent in May 1931, when the largest and most reputable banking concern in Vienna was discovered to be insolvent. The Credit-Anstalt für Handel und Gewerbe had been founded by the Rothschilds in the 1850's, and its many interests had since become woven into the financial fabric, not only of Austria, but of the whole Middle Danube. Since 1919 it had continued to share a somewhat precarious life with the reduced city and state it principally served. Possibly there had been extravagances in its management; probably the long arm of French finance, at the time of the recently projected Customs Union, had been exercised against it.

The House of Rothschild, the Austrian National Bank, the Austrian Government, and the Bank of England came forward with funds and guarantees. The Austrian Government announced that the Credit-Anstalt would be entirely reorganized. But the saving of one ship did not abate the storm, and other ships with sprung sides and leaky bottoms were now heaving to their destruction. At the end of May 1931, Germany hoisted distress signals. There was talk of a default on reparations. Several German business and insurance houses declared bankruptcies. Brüning, the German Chancellor, went to confer with MacDonald, the British Prime Minister, and tried to impress upon him the extreme gravity of Germany's – and Europe's – condition, but MacDonald could give him small comfort. President von Hindenburg issued emergency decrees imposing drastic new taxation and cuts in public salaries and relief. Meanwhile German Nazis, Nationalists, and Communists were busy rousing trouble each in his own way.

Finally Hindenburg telegraphed President Hoover an appeal for his good offices on behalf of the desperately foundering Reich.

The Hoover Moratorium

On June 20, 1931, President Hoover made his proposal for "the postponement during one year of all payments on intergovernmental debts." The proposal, added the President, "represents our willingness to make a contribution to the early restoration of world prosperity, in which our own people have so deep an interest."

The proposal not only carried the signature of the President of the United States, and therewith the evident endorsement of American opinion but, as everyone knew, it had also had the prior concurrence of London. It was received by the whole world – or almost the whole world – with sighs of relief. Only in France were there objections. France had not yet felt the full impact of the Depression. She had suffered some unemployment, but the figures had not been alarming. Her budget deficits had been no worse than usual. Gold poured steadily into her coffers, to the extreme puzzlement and concern of both London and New York. Opinion in France deeply resented the fact that, although President Hoover had seen fit to consult London before publishing his moratorium, he had not extended the same courtesy to Paris. Opinion in France resented no less the seeming world-wide conspiracy of condolence for a Germany who, for all her alleged inability to pay reparations, was finding money enough to lift herself surreptitiously out of her military impotence. The entire Hoover transaction could be read as a panic attempt to save recent American credits to Germany. Nor would it be a temporary measure, but a first step in the cancellation of all reparations payments.

A Depression bread line at New York's Water Street Mission

EWING GALLOWAY

Telegrams shuttled back and forth between Washington and Paris. In the upshot, the moratorium was agreed, but only after it had lost its "full tonic value." Meanwhile the spate of bankruptcies in Germany continued. On July 13 the Darmstädter und Nationalbank, the Danatbank as it was called, one of the four big German joint-stock banks, declared itself insolvent. All the circumstances of the Credit-Anstalt episode were repeated on a magnified scale. For the next two days all German banks were decreed on holiday. The Berlin Stock Exchange, the Boerse, closed for two months.

A feature of these critical weeks was the constant traveling of ministers and experts from conference to conference and from capital to capital. Stimson, American Secretary of State, and Mellon, American Secretary of the Treasury, were then in Europe and took part in the same migratory process. Hans Luther, then President of the Reichsbank, lived for days on end in airplanes and railroad coaches. In July ministers and experts alighted in London to hold one of the most impressive international conferences of the interwar period. Seven powers were represented in the persons of threc premiers, six foreign ministers, and four finance ministers,[5] but they did little more than recommend that nothing should be done to aggravate the situation, a recommendation that meant, in practice, that existing foreign credits to Germany should not be withdrawn. One writer of the time has compared the London Seven-Power Conference of 1931 to a consultation of fashionable doctors, anxious to protect their professional reputations, at the bedside of a patient whose case they know to be hopeless but whose relatives they know they will have to console. In August a further meeting of bankers at Basel, convened by the Bank for International Settlements, initialed a "Standstill Agreement" on similar lines. In October, Laval, then French Premier, crossed over to Washington for conversations with President Hoover and drew up what was tantamount to yet another standstill agreement. Laval undertook to halt French gold withdrawals from the United States, and Hoover to spring no more moratoriums on the world without first consulting France. Evidently the policy of the moment was for a breathing spell.

The Fall of the Pound

But while governments and banks might agree to "stand still," European John Citizen, nervous and grasping, did not. Any financial center that appeared to be vulnerable became subject to his panic withdrawals, and between July and September 1931 it was London's turn to be vulnerable. A good proportion of the credits to Germany, frozen under the Basel Standstill Agreement, had been granted by London. But, in addition to this, three important committees lately appointed by the British Government to inquire into public finance, one being the Royal Commission on Unemployment Insurance, reported during the summer of 1931. Their findings were both candid and disquieting. The Unemployment Insurance Fund was found to be running into debt at the rate of £1,000,000 a week; Britain's national expenditure was exceeding her national income; the next budget would show a deficit; in short, the island kingdom was living far beyond its means. Small blame on John Citizen for thinking that London, for two hundred years the money market of the world, was irrevocably shaken, and for wondering whether perhaps the predatory public finance of the new Labor government was not corrupting the once sound and blameless economy of the country. At the end of July, the Bank of England was losing gold at the rate of £2,500,000 a day, and restrictive measures were not appreciably stemming the outflow.

On August 24, 1931, Ramsay MacDonald and his Labor government resigned, and he at once formed an all-party National government expressly to deal with the economic crisis. A supplementary budget was passed on September 15 and generally created a good impression. But the same day the Admiralty reported that the announcement of pay cuts had led to "unrest" among naval ratings (enlisted men) at Invergordon. The British press played the incident down, but Continental papers magnified it into a serious mutiny. London's finance might well be shaky, but mutiny in the British Navy seemed to hint at new and unsuspected ramifications of the universal disorder. There were renewed losses of gold, and on one day, September 18, £18,000,000 were withdrawn from London.

On September 21, 1931, the British Government suspended the gold standard. The pound at once dropped in value and, after some fluctuations, settled at about 30 per cent below parity.

On receipt of the news from London, the European stock exchanges, with one or two exceptions, closed, and when they began to reopen a few days later, all their lists had substantially depreciated. Bank rates everywhere were protectively raised. Norway, Sweden, Denmark, Finland, all the nations and dependencies of the British Commonwealth – except South Africa, but including Ireland, India, Iraq, and Egypt – and a number of South American republics, all in quick succession went off gold. Japan went off gold three months later. Those countries with sterling reserves, the *Devisen* of which we have spoken, which did not follow suit suffered heavily. By April 1932 the only important financial powers to remain on the gold standard were France, Italy, Belgium, the Netherlands, Poland, Rumania, Switzerland, and the United States. Germany kept up the fiction of a gold standard, but she was already trying out complicated experiments in exchange control.

France, so far freakishly immune, began to feel the pinch of the crisis. A week after the fall of the pound, the Banque Nationale de Credit was found to be in difficulties and was saved only by government action. In October the Comptoir Lyon-Allemand failed. Returns for the year showed sharp decreases in the nation's exports and imports, and in December the Minister of Labor at last made an official admission of the fact that France had an unemployment problem.

No one had escaped it, not even France.

The End of Reparations and Debts

The Young Plan, by general consent, was already defunct. The German press was not only talking openly of repudiating reparations, but assumed the tone that repudiation was now only a matter of course. President von Hindenburg issued his emergency decrees, which had almost become a routine, and each time Germany was declared to be at the nether end of her resources. Just before Christmas 1931, the Advisory Committee, for whose meetings in special emergencies the Young Plan had provided, reported pessimistically both upon Germany's capacity to pay the conditional annuity in 1932 and upon the economic prospects for that year throughout the world. On January 9, 1932, Brüning, the German Chancellor, issued a categorical statement: "The situation in Germany makes the continuation of political payments impossible, and any attempt to uphold the political debt system would lead Germany and the world to disaster."

But a conference to legalize the inevitable was slow in meeting. Weeks and months went by while Britain and France approached "a common point of view." Mussolini lent the weight of his very considerable influence in favor of wiping the slate clean. "Only a stroke of the sponge will end the tragic bookkeeping of the war." Yet Laval in France, it seemed, was of set purpose, continually postponing the date of the conference, no doubt hoping that the suspense would cause a further deterioration of Germany's position. But the conference met at last, at Lausanne, in June 1932. Herriot had now succeeded Laval as French Premier and represented France; Papen was German Chancellor and represented Germany; MacDonald represented Britain. Under the Lausanne Convention, signed on July 9, the long and tortuous story of reparations ended in their complete abolition. Certain compensatory bonds, amounting to 3 per cent of the Young Plan total, were to be deposited by Germany with the Bank for International Settlements, but they were hedged about with so many protective conditions that it was morally certain not a pfennig of them would ever reach their creditors.

Lausanne had a sting in its tail of quite another kind. The "Allies" at the conference separately concluded among themselves a "gentlemen's agreement" not to ratify the Lausanne Convention "until a satisfactory settlement had been reached between them and their own creditors." In other words, the Allies intended to make quite sure that, if they granted Germany concessions with respect to reparations, their generosity would not go unrewarded by the United States in respect of their liabilities also. The Hoover Moratorium was drawing inexorably to its end and, unless some action were taken, the next installments on their American debts from the European debtors would fall due in December 1932. But the American Congress was in an unyielding mood. By no pleas or arguments would it admit the European thesis that reparations and debts were all a part of the same indissoluble complex. In American eyes, reparations were reparations, and debts were debts, and never the twain should meet; and Europe was Europe, the same old, incurable quarrelsome, militaristic Europe, which could always find money for its armaments but none for its solemnly contracted obligations. The Lausanne "gentlemen's agreement" seemed to be barefaced blackmail, typical of all European diplomacy. In the event, when December came round, Britain paid her American debt installment in full and in gold, but under formal protest; Italy, Czechoslovakia, Lithuania, and Finland also paid; France, Belgium, Hungary, Poland, Estonia, and Yugoslavia defaulted.

Meanwhile more positive efforts than cancellation were being made. In the general spirit of *sauve qui peut,* self-protective measures by individual nations usually took the form of still higher tariffs and more rigid import quotas. At the same time there was a good crop of bilateral trade agreements and clearing agreements. Then groups of nations met to discuss the mutual removal of trade barriers, for instance, the "Oslo" group of Scandinavian countries or the agrarian group of Eastern Europe. In July 1932, at Ottawa, the nations of the British Commonwealth met in an attempt to negotiate a sort of customs union. But generally these efforts were parochial, and they were not notably successful. Something more comprehensive was clearly indicated.

Accordingly in 1933 the World Economic Conference was held in London. It was called mainly on the initiative of the British Government and, more particularly, on the initiative of the British Prime Minister, Ramsay Mac-

Donald. That man of sublime faith, perhaps out of his Socialist inheritance, was unconquerable in his belief that the conference system was the norm of international relations, and that men of good will of whatever creed or color, freely assembled together, had it in them to melt the stoniest of problems. But Roosevelt was now President of the United States, and he was clearly averse to being drawn into an international discussion while the American situation itself was so confused. MacDonald visited Washington for exploratory conversations, but he failed to secure Roosevelt's interest in the debt question. It would be like playing *Hamlet* without the Prince of Denmark, but at all events the participation of the United States in the projected Conference was made contingent on the assurance that the debt question, the most vital of all questions, would be rigidly excluded from the agenda.

The World Economic Conference met in London in mid-June of 1933 under MacDonald's presidency. All the well-worn resources of staging and publicity were exhausted to magnify the supreme gravity of the occasion. King George welcomed the delegates of sixty-six states and commended them to their labors. If the Conference was prevented from discussing debts, it could at least discuss currency stabilization. Raymond Moley, an American economist whom President Roosevelt had sent over as an observer at the conference, went beyond his instructions and proceeded to negotiate a regular currency agreement. President Roosevelt replied by repudiating his overzealous subordinate and, in a somewhat hasty, hectoring statement, he berated the Conference on

> the specious fallacy of achieving a temporary and probably an artificial stability in foreign exchanges on the part of a few large countries only. The sound internal economic system of a nation is a greater factor in its well-being than the price of its currency in changing terms of other nations. . . .

The President's statement may have been a frank exposition of isolationist economics, but it finished the prospects of the Conference. One or two groups of delegates made use of their attendance to come to special agreements among themselves, but these minor and incidental successes hardly redeemed the major failure. The World Economic Conference "adjourned" at last at the end of July 1933.

The epilogue of the World Economic Conference was a general debt default. In June 1933, Britain made a "token" payment of $10,000,000 – in silver. Italy, Czechoslovakia, Rumania, Lithuania, and Latvia made similar "token" payments. Finland paid in full, in silver. France and the remaining debtor states defaulted. In December 1933, the same proceeding was repeated. In April 1934, Congress passed the Johnson Act closing American security markets to any foreign government which had defaulted on its debts. In June 1934, all the debtor states, except Finland, defaulted.

World Depression

In his Inaugural Address in March 1933, President Roosevelt had delivered himself as follows:

> Values have sunk to fantastic levels; our factories are without orders; taxes have risen; our ability to pay has fallen; government of all kinds is faced by a serious curtailment of income; the means of exchange are frozen; the withered leaves of our industrial enterprise lie on every side; farmers find no markets for their produce; and the savings of many years in thousands of families are gone. More important, a host of unemployed citizens face the grim problem of existence, and an equally great number toil with little return.

The picture he drew of America at that moment was the same for all the world. Some figures are striking. In 1933, in terms of gold, world commodity prices, as compared with 1928, had declined by a third, and raw-material prices by a half. Production indices had declined proportionately. The steel industry in the United States was operating at 10 per cent of capacity; the price of wheat at Winnipeg stood at the lowest level recorded in any primary market since the time of Queen Elizabeth I. Huge stocks of goods remained unsold, and the world made discovery of that queerest of all paradoxes, "poverty in the midst of plenty." National incomes in many countries had dropped by over 40 per cent. Government revenues had declined, but government expenditures, especially for social services and relief, were higher than ever. Thirty million workers all over the world were estimated to be unemployed.

The immediate reactions of the Depression, however, were not alone on the home fronts. In 1931 the Japanese invaded Manchuria, and the crisis passed onto the international plane. It is to this phase that we must now turn.

18. THE FAR EAST: MANCHURIA AND THE "CHINA INCIDENT"

Modern China and Japan

The First World War broke out in a Europe which, seemingly, was then enjoying profound political and economic stability. But the Far East at the time was already in revolution. The modern history of Europe, it may be said, began in 1914 – and that of the United States in 1917. The modern history of Japan began in 1905 – if not in 1853 – and of China in 1911. In this chapter we shall first make a rapid review of Japanese and Chinese affairs from these dates up to 1931. We shall discuss the Manchurian Crisis of that year, and then continue with the "China Incident" of 1937.

In 1853 when Commodore Perry sailed into Yeddo Bay with his four smoke-belching "black ships" on a mission to open up the Japanese Empire to diplomatic and commercial relations, he arrived most opportunely at the moment when domestic pressures in the country itself were working towards extensive and sudden changes. The modernization of Japan in the second half of the nineteenth century must have come inevitably, with or without American initiative, and the only questions were, How soon? and How fast? In 1868 a brief palace revolution in Kyoto "restored" the former authority of the Emperor and set in motion the reforms, political, judicial, industrial, and military, which within a generation were to convert the old feudal kingdom into a modern Great Power.

The conversion was effected with surprising little opposition. The old Japanese warrior aristocracy, professionally predisposed to respecting armed power, was quick to perceive the necessity for adopting Western weapons, and indeed, by its ready compliance and collaboration, it assured itself a place in the reformed state as the new class of militarists. A rapid and ruthless industrial expansion devolved upon a few wealthy, enterprising family trusts and became the basis of the country's economy. The Japanese Constitution of 1889 was modeled on that of the recently victorious German

Empire and was imposed from above as the free gift of the Japanese Emperor. Under its provisions the Emperor himself, the Son of Heaven, stood beyond politics and above criticism. His ministers were responsible to him alone. The Ministers for War and for the Navy enjoyed the right of direct access to himself, thus by-passing the other ministers who enjoyed only the right of indirect access through the Premier; and, by an ordinance of 1900, these two ministers had further to be active generals or admirals. By refusing to recommend appointments to these key posts the militarists could obstruct the formation of cabinets obnoxious to them. Meanwhile the popularly elected Diet was little more than a sounding board for public grievances. Its oratory was brave and vigorous; but its effect on policy negligible. The militarists, the Elder Statesmen, Big Business, and the Throne held the monopoly of power. The official ideology was Shintoism, the "Way of the Gods," inculcating a fiery patriotism, derived from ancestor worship and from a faith in the divine origin of the imperial house. It is hard to imagine a state more perfectly adapted to militant aggression.

Japan's first open international conflict was the war of 1894, directly against China but indirectly against Russian expansion in the Far East. In anticipation of a threatened Russian descent on Korea, the Japanese took over complete control of that territory, then nominally under Chinese suzerainty. In 1902 the Anglo-Japanese Alliance was signed, a treaty of mutual assistance if either party were attacked by more than one power. In 1904 the Russo-Japanese War broke out. In a series of victories the Japanese captured Port Arthur and, early in 1905, Mukden. At the Battle of Tsushima the Japanese annihilated the Russian fleet. The Treaty of Portsmouth in 1905, negotiated through the mediation of President Theodore Roosevelt, recognized Japan's paramount interests in Korea, ceded to her the southern half of Sakhalin and the Russian lease of the Kwantung Peninsula, together with the control of the South Manchuria Railway. The effect of these events throughout the Far East was extraordinary. By the Anglo-Japanese Alliance of 1902 Japan had achieved recognition as a Great Power; now in 1905 she had destroyed the myth of European military and naval superiority. The twentieth-century retreat of the West from the East had begun.

In 1908, in China, the Emperor and the Dowager Empress died, and with them passed what was left of the Manchu power, long since undermined by corruption, local rebellion — and European intervention. In 1911, amid general rioting, the old order finally collapsed. Out of the resulting turmoil two figures emerged — in the north, General Yuan Shih-kai, a former minister of the Empress and commander of an army of 80,000 men; and, in the south, Sun Yat-sen, the revolutionary leader, founder of the National Democratic party, or Kuomintang,[1] and momentarily the self-styled president of the provisional government in Nanking. Efforts to bring the two men together failed. Any sort of working compromise between the right-wing general and the left-wing president could hardly be expected. By 1914, when the European war broke out, Yuan was firmly established in power in the old Manchu capital of Peking — and in the good graces of the Western Allies — and Sun had fled into exile.

CHINA AND JAPAN, 1938

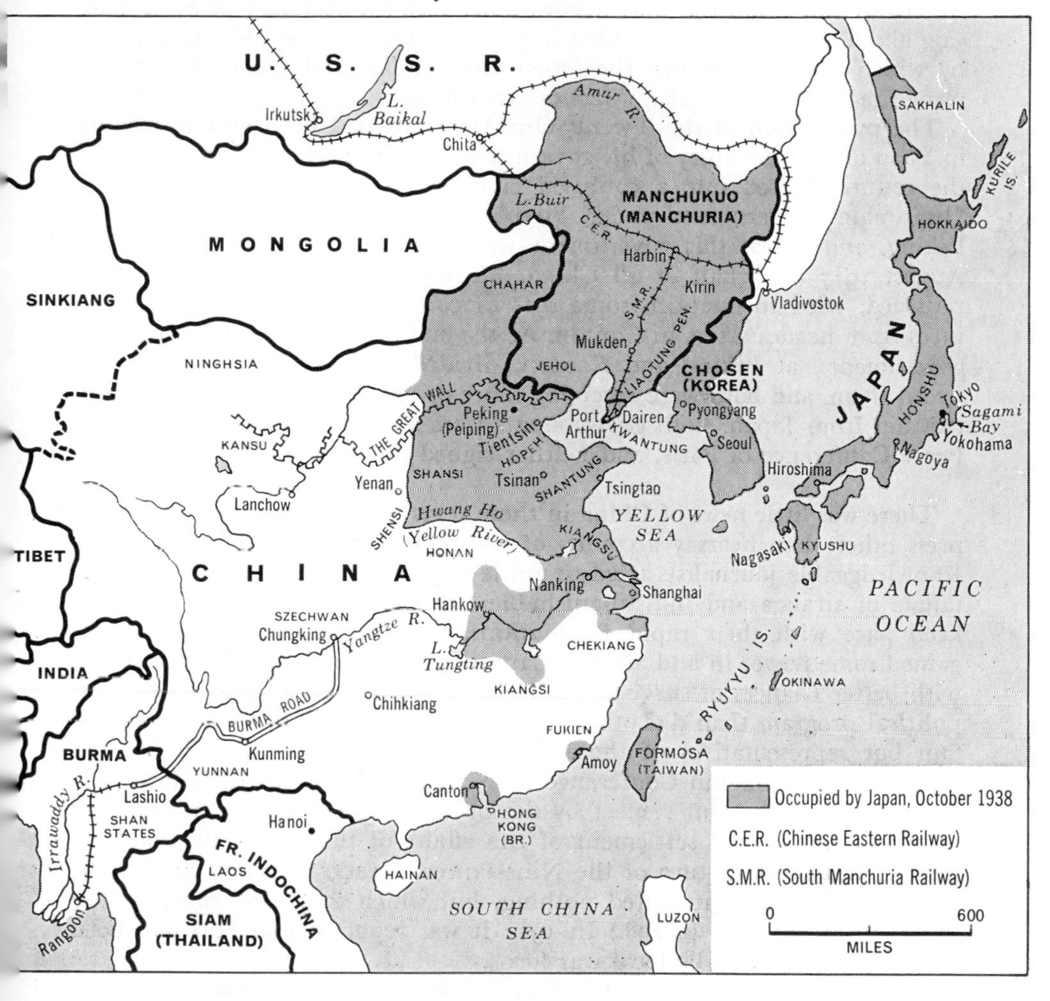

In 1914, in accordance with the Anglo-Japanese Alliance, Japan declared war on Germany. She captured the German port of Tsingtao and occupied the German islands in the North Pacific. In 1917, at the height of Germany's unrestricted submarine campaign, Japan sent a destroyer flotilla to the Mediterranean, an action which was afterwards acutely to embarrass the Peace Conference at Paris. (See pp. 67 and 104-05.) Certainly Japan's position in the First World War was most delicate. Officially an ally of Britain, she was held in unconcealed suspicion by the United States, no less than by Australia and New Zealand. Nevertheless her attitude remained entirely correct throughout, and only towards China did she attempt to exploit the situation to her advantage. Early in 1915, at first secretly, she handed General Yuan at Peking the notorious Twenty-One Demands, a virtual ultimatum, which would have reduced China to the status of a Japanese protectorate and Yuan to a Japanese puppet governor.[2] In 1917, after the American entry into the war, negotiations between Secretary of State Lansing and Viscount Ishii concluded in the so-called Lansing-Ishii Agreement, by which Japan reaffirmed the Open Door policy and the United States recognized Japan's "special interests" in China.[3]

The publication of the Twenty-One Demands had been very damaging to Yuan and to the unity of his government in China. He died in 1916, and the country lapsed into a confused civil war of provincial chieftains. A "legitimate" government under Yuan's successors continued to exist in Peking, and it was this government which declared war on Germany in August 1917 on behalf of all China. Meanwhile Sun Yat-sen, once more returned, tried to establish some sort of control over the southern provinces from headquarters in Canton. At the end of the war in 1918, the two governments, at Peking and Canton, divided the nominal authority between them, and both were receiving more or less covert financial and military aid from Japan. Both governments were afterwards represented at the Peace Conference of Paris, and neither signed the Treaty of Versailles.

There was little news of China in these years in the American and British press other than hearsay accounts of the rivalries of successive war lords. Knowledgeable journalists tried to guide their readers through the shifting tangle of strange and indistinguishable Chinese names, but could hardly keep pace with their rapid fluctuations. Sun Yat-sen appeared to have gained some power in and around Canton, and, for a time, he was credited with better chances of survival. At least he announced a more respectable political program than did other aspiring contestants. However, it was not Sun but representatives of the Peking government who were invited to attend the Washington Conference in November 1921, where indeed they were treated with scant respect by the other delegates. We have elsewhere described the general settlement of the affairs of the Pacific by that conference and the signature of the Nine-Power Treaty, to which in fact the Chinese delegates contributed nothing, but which they were more or less forced to accept. (See p. 298.) In 1922 it was reported that Sun had been driven out of Canton by local war lords.

It was perhaps inevitable that Sun Yat-sen, in his weakness, should approach, or be approached by, Soviet Russia. Early in 1923, at Shanghai, he received the Soviet emissary, Adolf Joffe, and a Sino-Soviet convention was drawn up. Under Soviet support, Sun and his Nationalist party, the Kuomintang, were re-established in Canton – with a certain Michael Borodin in attendance as the chief Soviet political agent in China, once a teacher in a Chicago commercial college and Communist agitator in Scotland. The first task of Sun's restored Nationalist government was the founding in 1924 of a military college at Whampoa near Canton. The forty instructors were headed by the Russian General Bluecher, who had recently been campaigning against the Japanese in Siberia; and the principal of the college was Sun's ardent young protégé, Chiang Kai-shek, lately returned from a three months' tour of Soviet Russia.

The second task of the Nationalist government was once more to attempt the unification of China – again with Soviet support and with the very efficient officers graduating from Whampoa. In December 1924, Sun arrived in Peking to conduct the necessary negotiations with the rival leaders there. But he was already in the grip of a mortal illness, and three months later he died, seemingly at the moment of achieving his life's ambition. His obvious successor was Chiang Kai-shek, now campaigning against the war lords of the Yangtze Valley. At the time, Chiang was being mentioned in the American and British press as just another in the series of indistinguishable Chinese names. But his forces were consistently successful everywhere, and it was evident that here was at last a war lord of genuinely enduring caliber. In March 1927, Chiang's forces took and sacked Nanking, which Chiang then proceeded to make into the capital of Nationalist China. He brought his campaign in the Yangtze Valley to a fitting close with the occupation of the native quarters of Shanghai.

Then, suddenly, Chiang turned against his Soviet benefactors. Borodin, Bluecher, and their staffs were sent packing back to Moscow; the Communist elements in the Kuomintang were purged; an attempted "Red Commune" in Canton was ruthlessly suppressed. In December 1927, Chiang symbolized his new allegiances by his marriage to Soong Mei-ling (a member of the class of 1917 at Wellesley), a family connection of the Soong banking interests. Chiang captured Peking in June 1928, renamed it Peiping, or "Northern Peace," and installed a Nationalist administration in the city. Chiang was roundly accused of having "betrayed the revolution" – and incidentally of having betrayed his former patron, Sun; – but he was now, or seemed to be, the master of all China. Happy in the recognition of foreign powers, Chiang was negotiating the revocation of the old "unequal" commercial treaties and the abolition of extra-territoriality, and he was shortly approaching the German Government for the services of new military advisers – General von Falkenhausen, and then later no less a person than General von Seeckt, former chief of the German *Reichswehr.*

The only surviving opposition to Chiang's authority was a band of Communist peasant guerrillas, operating in the hilly country between Hankow and Canton under the leadership of Mao Tse-tung and Chu Teh. In November 1931, a Chinese Soviet Republic under Mao Tse-tung was proclaimed in Kiangsi province. Chiang, stung to action, launched one punitive expedition after another against "this wretched and contemptible rebellion." Then, in 1934, Mao Tse-tung and Chu Teh led their Chinese Red Army out of Kiangsi, and, after an incredible "Long March," virtually a mass migration through the central provinces of China, they found a refuge at last at Yenan in Shensi province, on the borderlands of Mongolia where they stood within easier reach of Soviet supplies.

Aggression in Manchuria

Chiang Kai-shek was thus settling the affairs of China to his satisfaction. After years of civil war the country was enjoying an unwonted peace. The Communist opposition had not been extirpated, but it had gone into virtual self-exile. But, for Japan, the same period had been one of mounting frustration. She had been disappointed and discomfited at the

Peace Conference of Paris, and at the Washington Conference, and in Siberia. She had been forced to give undertakings to restore Tsingtao and Shantung to China; she was to occupy the former German islands in the Pacific, but under obstructive conditions. (See pp. 104-05 and 297-99.) In these reverses her principal opponent had been the United States. For a time she could concentrate upon her domestic affairs, and of these there were enough and to spare – the suffrage question, the trade unions, and peasant poverty. On September 1, 1923, an earthquake destroyed three quarters of Tokyo and a large part of the naval base of Yokosuka, to a total loss of life of 160,000 and $2,000,000,000 of property.

By 1930 there were signs that Japan was coming to the end of her enforced quiescence. Recent events in the United States, notably the New York stock-market crash, gave promise that American interest in the Far East might be very much reduced. In 1930 Japanese delegates attended the Five-Power Naval Conference in London and they had been humiliated by the British Prime Minister, Ramsay MacDonald, extorting their compliance to the proposed naval ratios by appealing over their heads to the Japanese Premier, Hamaguchi, in Tokyo. Within two weeks of his courageous defiance of the Japanese Navy, Hamaguchi was shot and mortally wounded by an outraged "patriot." Evidently the militarists in Japan were growing restive and were resorting to violence against "flabby politicians" who dared challenge them.

Meanwhile Japan's economy, closely tied to the American market, was struck by the Depression. A large proportion of her foreign trade was in luxury goods, and was therefore very vulnerable. Silk, for example, accounted for two-fifths of the total value of her exports, and 90 per cent of this silk went to the United States. Further, silk cultivation was an important supplementary item in the meager income of the Japanese peasant. Rice prices had fallen steadily since 1921 along with the world-wide decline in raw-commodity values. The Chinese were currently trying to impose a boycott of Japanese goods. In these conditions the big banks in Japan were following an orthodox deflationary policy. Japanese trade fell by a third between 1929 and 1930; and unemployment rose by official admission to 360,000, though the actual figure was variously estimated at from 1,000,000 to 3,000,000.

Fighting had already broken out during 1928 in Shantung between Chinese Nationalists and Japanese troops sent there to protect Japanese persons and property, and a Japanese force had temporarily occupied Tsinan, the capital of the province. North of the Great Wall, in Manchuria, in 1928, the Manchurian war lord, Chang Tso-lin, who was pro-Nationalist and anti-Japanese, and also anti-Russian, was killed in an explosion for which Japanese conspirators were held responsible. His son and successor, the so-called "Young Marshal," Chang Hsueh-liang, persisted in his father's policies. He organized "bandit raids" on Japanese settlers in Manchuria, and, more seriously, he began to build a railroad in competition with the Japanese-controlled South Manchuria Railway. In the far north, on the Soviet borders, bodies of Chang's troops engaged in affrays with units of the Soviet Far Eastern Army. The Soviet Government was evidently reluctant to get involved in irregular fighting in Manchuria, and Japanese observers were persuaded that they could count on its nonintervention even if more serious hostilities should break out in the area.

The year 1931 was the worst year of the Depression. Europe was struggling with the aftereffects of the Credit-Anstalt failure, and the United States with the Hoover Moratorium. In Britain, in August of that year, the Labor government resigned, and the National Coalition took office. On September 15, reports of insubordination over pay cuts among the naval ratings (enlisted men) at the Scottish port of Invergordon were magnified by several newspapers into a mutiny, the first mutiny in more than a century in that ancient arm of the sea, the British Navy. To the Japanese, from their Manchurian vantage point, the stormier these distant skies, the clearer were their own prospects nearer home. During the same September a certain Japanese captain, by name Nakamura, posing as a civilian agricultural expert, had been detained by the local Chinese authorities in the far interior of Manchuria, pending an investigation of his credentials, and he had then been shot "while trying to escape," a proceeding which, in view of his actual military rank, "showed arrogant disrespect for the Japanese Army and nation." On September 17, highly colored accounts of the affair were published in Japan. Then, on the night of September 18-19, while public indignation in Japan was seething, some three to four hundred Chinese of the forces of Chang Hsueh-liang near the Manchurian capital of Mukden were reported to have blown up a short stretch of the track of the South Manchuria Railway – some purists afterward estimated the length at thirty-one inches – and to have been resisted by Japanese patrols.

The next morning, September 19, 1931, the Japanese army quartered in the Kwantung Peninsula, the Kwantung Army as it was called, without declaration of war but obviously prepared for any incident, invaded Manchuria. The campaign was sharp and short. In five months the important strategic points in Manchuria were in Japanese hands. Chang's forces were scattered, and Chang himself was in flight to the south of the Great Wall. With the capture of Chinchow in the first week of January and of Harbin in the last week of January 1932, all organized resistance in Manchuria was at an end. In March 1932, the victors renamed their conquest Manchukuo, the "State of Manchu," and haled out of his retirement Henry Pu Yi, the surviving head of the old Manchu dynasty that had collapsed in 1911, and solemnly installed him as Regent.

The League and the Stimson Doctrine

It was now for politics and diplomacy to make what could be made out of the Manchurian Crisis. First reactions had been prompt. On September 19, 1931, China had appealed to the Council of the League of Nations under Article 11 of the Covenant and to the United States under the Pact of Paris. But politics and diplomacy had then to take their proper courses, and, as the generals of the Kwantung Army had doubtless calculated, their conquest would be an accomplished fact before any extraneous opposition could be mobilized against them. It had even been said that they had acted without the full knowledge of the Japanese Cabinet ministers in Tokyo – other than their own colleague and partisan, the Minister of War.

The League Council began its deliberations later on that same September 19, and almost at once Sze, the Chinese delegate, was at odds with Yoshizawa, the Japanese delegate, the former proposing an impartial commission of enquiry into the dispute and the latter proposing direct negotiations between the parties. Lord Cecil, the British delegate, put what might be called the "League" point of view and appealed to both sides "not to do anything to aggravate the position," to withdraw their troops "from the territory of the other party," and in particular not to misuse "the pretext of defense" to create a situation that could no longer be controlled. He also proposed that the United States should be kept informed "of what we are doing." Secretary of State Henry L. Stimson from Washington sent a note to the President of the League Council expressing "whole-hearted sympathy"; but he seemed to support the Japanese thesis for direct negotiations, presumably so as not to embarrass moderate elements in Japan, and he declined to invoke the Pact of Paris. On September 30, the Council unanimously adopted a resolution accepting the Japanese Government's assurance that it had no territorial designs in Manchuria and taking note of the fact that Japanese troops were reported – quite untruly – to have begun their withdrawal. The Council then adjourned.

The League Council reconvened on October 13, 1931, now under the presidency of Briand. By its invitation, an American representative, the American consul at Geneva, Prentiss Gilbert, took a seat at its table – a development which was somewhat robbed of its force when Gilbert made it quite plain that he intended to exercise only a watching brief. The sessions were marked by compliments and courtesies, no less than by confusion and delay, and concluded on October 24 with a resolution calling upon Japan to withdraw her troops in Manchuria to her legitimate railway zone. The Japanese delegate, Yoshizawa, referred obscurely to certain "fundamental points," which he claimed should be the basis of direct negotiations with China, but which he refused to divulge, and then asked for time to consult his government. The Council again adjourned.

The Council reconvened on November 16, 1931, on this occasion in Paris, in deference to the wishes of its president, Briand. Sir John Simon, recently appointed British Foreign Secretary, attended for the first time. Discussions were more forthright. Articles 15 and 16 of the Covenant – with their implication of sanctions – were freely mentioned. On November 21, Yoshizawa at last gracefully conceded the original Chinese proposal for an impartial commission of enquiry. But his apparent gesture of conciliation still left room for further obstruction, and the much-discussed proposal was adopted in an amended form on December 10. But by that date the Japanese military campaign in Manchuria had substantially achieved its objectives.

On January 7, 1932, as a sort of rider to his "parallel and incessant activities," Stimson handed to the Chinese and Japanese ambassadors in Washington the identical notes, since known after him as the Stimson Doctrine, giving notice that the American Government would not recognize any treaty or agreement which impaired the sovereignty, independence, or territorial integrity of China or infringed the Open Door policy, nor would recognize any situation, treaty, or agreement which was brought about by means contrary to the Pact of Paris. Stimson doubtless hoped that he would receive warm support for his declaration from the British Government and especially from his opposite number, Simon, the British Foreign Secretary. Instead, "he sustained one of the coldest public rebuffs it has ever been the lot of an American Secretary of State to receive at the hands of a friendly power." On January 11, it was curtly announced in London that, since Japan had given assurances in regard to the Open Door policy in Manchuria, "his Majesty's Government have not considered it necessary to address any formal note to the Japanese Government on the lines of the American Government's note." [4]

The Stimson-Simon incident has since aroused considerable controversy. Certainly the British Government's announcement of January 11 was gauche in the extreme – we are told that it was worded and issued by permanent officials of the Foreign Office and that Simon was not consulted. But there is also this to be said. Since September 1931 Stimson had been giving out formal protests against the Japanese aggression in Manchuria almost once a week with little practical effect. His belated reference on January 7 to the Pact of Paris was particularly lame. He had made no such reference at the height of the crisis, though pressed to do so by the Chinese Government. All through the long discussions in the League Council he had offered nothing but "whole-hearted sympathy." The American representative, Prentiss Gilbert, had confined himself to a watching brief. It is therefore easy to imagine the reaction of a less than senior official in the British Foreign Office to a declaration which, on the surface, was no more important than the several earlier ones, published at a moment when the fighting in Manchuria was all but over. Nevertheless, in March 1932, Simon made some amends, when the League Assembly unanimously adopted a resolution, introduced by himself, almost in Stimson's words, to follow the Stimson Doctrine.

The Japanese Government in 1931 was under the control of a group of men who wielded force and who would respond to nothing but force. The United States had not the least intention of applying force. The American people and Congress were distracted by their domestic anxieties, and, at no time during the Manchurian Crisis, did Stimson or the State Department suggest that recourse to force – that is, to outright war – was remotely contemplated. It is very doubtful whether the Navy Department at that time would have readily accepted a major challenge on the opposite side of the Pacific Ocean. Britain was in a far weaker position than the United States. The naval base at Singapore, begun in 1923, was far from complete, and the recent Labor government, in the interests of conciliation, had suspended construction. The fleet, which was to use it, existed as yet only on paper. In the event of hostilities the British Navy would have had to conduct operations from Malta in the Mediterranean – with every likelihood of repeating the Russian fiasco of Tsushima on a larger scale.

As for the League of Nations in the crisis, it hardly deserved the abuse that afterwards was heaped upon it. The League was effective within its constitutional powers. It was not organized for force and was hardly to be blamed for not exerting force. Its sanctions, under Article 15 and 16 of its Covenant, could only be imposed by the will of its members, and, even if its members had the will, perhaps only two of them really had the capacity. It became very clear in the course of the discussions in the League Council how easily the League machinery would lend itself to the kind of delaying tactics which the Japanese delegate adopted. The one "force," public morality and obligations on which the original founders of the League had so greatly relied, was seen to carry no weight at all. The rulers of Japan in 1931 were not impressed by moral strictures on their policy. Two hardy popular myths have survived from the Manchurian Crisis. The first is that Japanese aggression would have been stopped if Britain had supported the Stimson Doctrine; the second is that Japanese aggression would have been stopped if the League of Nations had taken "firm action." The first myth does not stand up to scrutiny of fact; the second myth depends entirely on the interpretation of "firm action."

Under the resolution of December 10, 1931, the League Council appointed its impartial commission of enquiry, the Lytton Commission, so called after the chairman, Lord Lytton, one time Viceroy of India. The commission visited China and Japan – and Manchuria – and was nowhere seriously obstructed in its collection of evidence. Its report, submitted in October 1932, denied that the Manchurian campaign could be justified as a defensive measure on the part of Japan, described the new Manchukuo as a puppet creation, and proposed its replacement by an autonomous regime under nominal Chinese suzerainty. In September 1932, on the eve of the publication of the report, Japan made a defiant gesture and formally recognized Manchukuo. In February 1933, the League at last adopted the report, and in the following month Japan gave notice of her withdrawal from League membership.

There was one postscript to the Manchurian Crisis which should be mentioned. In 1932 hostilities had flared up further south. The Chinese, in their military impotence, had been boycotting Japanese goods. Their action was unofficial and unorganized, but here and there it had led to disturbances, to riots and lynchings. On January 18, 1932, a Shanghai mob attacked five Japanese Buddhist monks, one of whom was killed. In retaliation a Japanese flotilla appeared off Shanghai; Japanese marines were landed, and they fought a pitched battle with the Chinese Nineteenth Route Army in the native quarter of the city. The Chinese retired after a five-week defense of great heroism and unexpected tenacity. American marines were sent from Manila to protect American lives and property, and an American fleet was reported to be concentrating in the China Sea. A truce was patched up in May 1932, and the Japanese marines were withdrawn.

The "China Incident"

The Shanghai affray showed that Japan was not yet ready to extend her military commitments to Southern China, but aggression in the north continued as opportunity offered. In February 1933, while the League Council was in process of adopting the Lytton Report, Japanese forces invaded Jehol province, brushed aside a feeble resistance by irregular Chinese forces and halted at the Great Wall on the very threshold of China proper. In December 1934, Japan formally announced her intention to abrogate the Washington naval ratios of 1922 and to tear up the agreements reached at the naval conferences of 1930. (See pp. 298, 301, and 392.) In 1935 Japanese forces in China pushed beyond the Great Wall and resumed their advance westward and southward into Chahar and Hopei. Europe meanwhile was fully preoccupied with the tremendous spectacle of German rearmament. In the League Assembly the crisis in Ethiopia took exclusive priority over all other business. Then in November 1936, the two great aggressive Powers of the world, Germany and Japan, came together and signed the so-called Anti-Comintern Pact. The signatories agreed to keep each other informed concerning the activities of the Comintern in their respective spheres, and, in a secret protocol, they agreed also to consult on measures of mutual assistance in the event of Soviet aggression. The pact was clearly designed to embarrass the Soviet's freedom of action both in Europe and Asia, and, in the Japanese view, it would give a pointed warning to the Soviet Union against possible intervention if more extensive fighting in China should again break out.

Chiang Kai-shek in China, meanwhile, could only persevere in delaying tactics and build up his defenses in the south as best he might. He was at last induced to swallow his pride and to come to terms with Mao Tse-tung's Communist regime at Yenan in Shensi, and thus to present a united front to the Japanese invader. He was receiving aid from the United States and Britain, aid which amounted to the small but not despicable total of $50,000,000. His armed forces were being reorganized by his new German military adviser, General von Seeckt. Chiang now had the men and the political unity — and even the martial fervor. But time was to show how far and how soon these precious assets could be converted into the realities of military power.

The internal situation in Japan simultaneously was deteriorating politically and economically. There had been some industrial recovery. By the end of 1935 Japanese exports had generally regained the levels of 1929. But, in a world of boycotts, quotas, and tariffs — all, it seemed, directed against Japan — even moderate Japanese opinion was now conceding that the Depression would be permanently beaten only by means of conquests in East Asia. The militarists, and especially the younger elements among them, were resorting to their own characteristic methods for urging the renewal of war in China. On February 26, 1936, their discontents exploded in an incident popularly known, from its date, as the "Two Twenty-Six." It was all very similar to one of the contemporaneous Nazi purges in Germany and Austria, which indeed may have inspired it. Fourteen hundred men, mainly of the Imperial Guard, under their captains and lieutenants, started out on a systematic assassination of their political opponents. Old Viscount Saito was disposed of at dawn in his own house. Finance Minister Takahashi Korekiyo, who had once scrutinized defense estimates so carefully and pruned them so rigorously, was shot as he lay in bed. Admiral Okada Keisuke, the Premier, warned in the nick of time by a system of alarm bells recently installed, took refuge in the large steel vault in his house which served as an earthquake shelter. The mutineers shot his brother-in-law, who markedly resembled him, and withdrew under the impression that their work was done. The next day, the Admiral suffered the indignity of being smuggled out of the house by his servants, disguised as a mourner at his own funeral. Another body of mutineers meanwhile occupied key points in central Tokyo. The summoning of the fleet into Tokyo Bay and a formal injunction from the Emperor were necessary before the mutineers consented to lay down their arms on the fourth day of the revolt. The rank and file were pardoned on the ground that they had acted under the orders of their military superiors, but fifteen of the ringleaders were tried by secret court-martial and shot. The city remained deathly silent throughout the incident, the civil population contemplating the sanguinary drama with a calm expressive of their stunted political instincts.

A brief reaction prevented the militarists from securing the cabinet they desired until June 1937. But in that month the "National" government of Prince Konoe Fumimato took office with an ambitious Pan-Asian program. The militarists had not long to wait for their war in China.

On the night of July 7, 1937, a small detachment of Japanese on night maneuvers exchanged some wild shots in the darkness with Chinese troops at the Marco Polo Bridge near Peiping. Neither side suffered casualties. But the situation was tense, and, not surprisingly, sporadic clashes – this time with casualties – occurred during the next few days. Japanese and Chinese officers on the spot went through the form of setting up a committee to fix the responsibility for the original shooting. But then suddenly, on July 26, the Japanese launched an attack in force and occupied the city of Peiping. No formal declaration of war was made by either side. The Japanese afterward used to refer to the hostilities which developed as the "China Incident."

Chiang Kai-shek was now Generalissimo of a Chinese Army of formidable size. The core of this army consisted of the crack divisions of the "Generalissimo's Own," numbering some 300,000 men, organized and trained by General von Seeckt. But even these elite troops were sadly inferior, judged by European – and Japanese – standards, especially in heavy equipment, aircraft, and road transport. Moreover they were almost entirely concentrated in the lower Yangtze Valley, the heart of Nationalist China. They were not heavily committed in the areas around Peiping which the Japanese were now attacking. With the single exception of Shensi, remote and mountainous, under the control of the Chinese Red Army, all five provinces north of the Yellow River were virtually abandoned to the Japanese by December 1937.

Chiang elected to make his main stand at Shanghai, the theater of the

Nineteenth Route Army's battle in 1932, and it was here that he engaged the best of his men and material. The Japanese effected their first landing at Shanghai on August 13, 1937, and it took them three months to reduce the city and district at a cost to themselves of over 40,000 casualties. The Japanese then pushed up the Yangtze Valley. The capture of the capital at Nanking, they hoped, might cause the collapse of the Chinese Nationalist Government and bring the entire "Chinese Incident" to a conclusion. Nanking was taken and sacked in December 1937. But, far from collapsing, the Chinese Nationalist Government moved to Hankow and thence to Chungking, well protected by the difficult gorges of the upper Yangtze and by the precipitous terrain that flanked them, and from there Chiang Kai-shek issued a national manifesto declaring that the struggle would continue till the ultimate victory of China.

Fighting proceeded during 1938. The Japanese gradually effected the junction of their armies in the northern provinces and in the Yangtze Valley. Chenchow, Hankow, and the Shantung Peninsula were captured after stiff Chinese delaying actions. Meanwhile a naval blockade of the Chinese coastline was established, and offshore islands were occupied. Independent Japanese expeditionary forces took Amoy in May and Canton in October 1938.

In the one-and-a-half years of the new Sino-Japanese War the Chinese lost the greater part of their original military effectives, all their main seaports and their most important centers of commerce, industry, and culture. Some 60,000,000 civilians were driven from their homes and were in flight. Extensive areas of the country were flooded or "scorched." Japanese casualties were estimated optimistically at 500,000.

By ordinary military standards the balance sheet of death and devastation added up to a total defeat. In all the technical aspects of the fighting the Chinese had been hopelessly outclassed. But there was another side to the picture. Chiang Kai-shek had taken every possible advantage of terrain and geography, and he had calculated to a nicety the maximum depth which the Japanese penetration could effect without obtaining the political conversion of the country. Useful materials, such as factory machinery in Hankow, were evacuated to Chungking under incredible difficulties, inadequate though these materials were for Chiang's military and civilian needs. Systematic demolition robbed the invader of much of what was left. Then some 50,000 Chinese were sent to operate behind the Japanese lines and wage guerrilla war on the tenuous Japanese communications. The Chinese Red Army in Shensi, now in full alliance with Chiang Kai-shek, harried the northern flanks of the common Japanese enemy. At the end of 1938, although the area under nominal Japanese occupation was writ large on the map of China, the area under effective military control was confined to the coasts, the railroads, and the main northern and central cities.

Meanwhile the reaction of the League of Nations toward the new crisis in China had followed, with ironical and depressing fidelity, the pattern of the Manchurian crisis of six years before. China appealed to Articles 10, 11, and 17 of the Covenant. In October 1937 the League duly declared that Japanese operations by land, sea, and air against China were not legitimate measures of self-defense, and that "such action cannot possibly facilitate or promote the friendly cooperation between the two nations that Japanese statesmen have affirmed to be the aim of their policy." But verbal admonitions made no impression on the offender, who in any case was no longer a member of the League. The Far Eastern Advisory Committee of the League further proposed a conference of the signatories of the Nine-Power Treaty of 1922 in the hope that Japan would accept friendly mediation of the conflict outside the framework of the League. The ensuing conference met in Brussels in November 1937. But Japan declined pointblank to attend, alleging that measures taken in self-defense fell outside the scope of the treaty in question. The conference drafted a resolution condemning Japan's attempt "to change by armed force the policy of China," and dissolved. The issue accordingly was thrown back into the lap of the League; but the League – or at least the European members of it – had other pressing concerns in Spain, Austria, and Czechoslovakia. Evidently crisis in the East was being timed to coincide with crisis in the West with evident advantages to the aggressor.

The United States was showing no greater strength of purpose than the League. Secretary Cordell Hull's protests to Japan were as positive in words and as negative in action as Stimson's formerly. President Roosevelt refrained from applying the neutrality legislation of 1935-37 on the ostensible ground that war had not been formally declared and that the parties were not belligerents. The continued sale of American gasoline, scrap metal, and machinery, to Japan were judged in Tokyo to be some assurance that the United States intended no drastic departures. The bombing by Japanese aircraft of the U.S. gunboat *Panay* on the Yangtze in December 1937, was settled by an indemnity of $2,214,000, which the Japanese Government, wanting no further complications, paid promptly and in full. (See p. 471.) It was not till July 1939 that Washington at last made more than a verbal remonstrance and denounced the American-Japanese Commercial Treaty of 1911.

From Chiang Kai-shek's point of view the situation was now becoming increasingly a problem of supplies. His fastness at Chungking may have been inaccessible to his enemies, but it was also isolated from his friends, and his defense could not continue indefinitely without material aid. Loans and credits were of little use if the goods they bought could not be delivered. A partial answer to the problem was found in the soon-to-be-famous Burma Road. From Rangoon a railroad threaded its way northwards past Mandalay, across the Gokteik Gorge – where American engineers in 1900 had constructed a "temporary" viaduct – and reached its terminus at Lashio at the foot of mountainous Yunnan province. From Lashio a soft-surface road through rugged country to Kunming was completed in 1937-38 at considerable cost in lives by a force of 100,000 coolies working under American-trained engineers. The last section of the road, from Kunming to Chungking, had already been constructed in 1935. Bad surfacing and landslides caused casualties and delays. In the rainy season, from July to September, traffic was brought to a complete standstill. Nevertheless the Burma Road circumvented the areas held by Japan and opened a back door, however steep and narrow, to the Chinese refuge.

We may leave the war in China at this point and resume our narrative of events in Europe. But it is perhaps worth remarking upon the chaotic situation which now obtained. If ever there was an international anarchy it was in East Asia at this time. Japan had pitted strength against weakness, but with every fresh success she seemed only to have widened the area of instability. Her friends were friends of convenience, and every other neighbor was an enemy, potential or actual. The Moscow Pact of 1939 was to show the real value of the Anti-Comintern Pact of 1936. Yet in 1939 it was characteristic of Japan, as we shall see, once again to try and snatch an advantage even from this reversal of fidelity. The Japanese, by repute, was always a gambler. If that is so, he was certainly making a fine display of his national vice.

19. GERMANY: THE RISE AND ESTABLISHMENT OF NAZISM

The Rise of Hitler and Nazism

Adolf Hitler, Führer of National Socialism and Chancellor of the Third Reich, was born on April 20, 1889, at Braunau, across from Bavaria, on the Austrian side of the river Inn. He was the son of a village cobbler who had become a minor customs official. He was a morose, unsociable boy, in sullen rebellion against his father and his schoolmasters. His one strong affection was for his mother, who probably pampered him to excess.

His early life was drab and aimless. He wanted to be a painter and, to judge by some of his surviving water colors, he had undeniably a conventional talent. But success smiled not upon his fitful efforts, and he appears to have spent his twentieth to his twenty-seventh years in utter poverty, wandering through Vienna and Munich, despising and avoiding manual work, but plying his uncertain craft and generally educating himself in the struggle for survival. He picked up some skill as an architectural draftsman, and he colored post cards which a friend peddled in the streets. Incidentally he talked politics, listened to Wagnerian opera, and developed a rabid German nationalism and a no less rabid anti-Socialism and anti-Semitism. The First World War was his road to Damascus. As he afterwards described it:

> To myself that hour brought redemption from all the vexations of my youth. I am not ashamed to say that, in a transport of rapture, I sank down on my knees and I thanked Heaven from an overflowing heart for having given me the good fortune to be alive at such a time.

He served as a volunteer in a Bavarian infantry regiment and, though this part of his history is also indefinite and since corrupted by legend, there is no reason to doubt that he made a brave and efficient soldier. He saw some of the heaviest fighting on the Western front, won the Iron Cross, First and Second Class, and was promoted to the rank of lance corporal.

Hindenburg, Hitler, and Göring attending the anniversary celebrations of the battle of Tannenberg at the Tannenberg War Memorial, August 27, 1933

BROWN BROTHERS

At the time of the Armistice, in November 1918, he was lying in hospital, gassed and almost blinded.

The next five years he spent in Munich, living the life of a political waif in that fermenting, disillusioned world that was postwar Germany. He became a member of the so-called German Workers' party, one of the dozens of organizations or quasi organizations that were then trying to eke out a little dignity and fellowship and a little vicarious revenge for their country's humiliation. Meanwhile, the *Reichswehr* was using him as a spy at Communist meetings, and this somewhat casual employment brought him into touch with Ernst Roehm, a stalwart of the Bavarian *Reichswehr.*

The five years were years of development both for himself and for his movement. He discovered a talent for oratory; he spoke tirelessly at public meetings; he wrangled with all comers in cafés and beer cellars. In 1920 the German Workers' party changed its name to the National Socialist German Workers' party (*National-Sozialistische Deutsche Arbeiterpartei,* NSDAP), drafted a program of twenty-five points, acquired a newspaper of its own, the *Völkischer Beobachter,* and established its permanent headquarters in Munich. It boasted some 3,000 members and it grew rapidly. The first units of the Brownshirts, the SA (*Sturmabteilung*), were formed in 1921 as a sort of Free Corps which provided ushers and "bouncers" at party meetings and terrorized the meetings of the opposition parties. The Fascist salute with the outstretched right arm, the *"Heil Hitler!,"* the swastika, the popular abbreviation "Nazi," and the entire technique of the public meeting with its flags and placards, marching and songs and mass effects all came into use at this time.

The party gained an important accession of power and notoriety during the Ruhr crisis, and especially after the "Beer Hall Putsch" of 1923, mentioned in an earlier chapter. (See p. 145.) For his part in the putsch Hitler was condemned to five years in the fortress of Landsberg-on-the-Lech. It was a reflection on the administration of justice in Germany at the time that the court violated the clear letter of the law in dealing with him so lightly that he, an Austrian and therefore an alien, was not deported, and that finally he was released on probation after serving less than nine months of his sentence. And he made good use of those months. Friends and helpers were allowed to visit him; he had time to study, to think, and to plan; and he dictated the greater part of *Mein Kampf,* the text and canon-to-be of National Socialism.

The years from 1923 to 1929 were the lean years of the Nazi movement, a hard, unrelenting interim occupied with underground politics and individual trials of strength not always of the most savory kind. The party organization was consolidated and developed, and its bigger personalities emerged. The SS (*Schutzstaffel*), or Blackshirts, the *corps d'élite* of the party and the personal entourage of the Führer, were formed in 1925. The struggle for power in the party, nerve-racking and soul-destroying as it was, was essential schooling for the larger struggle for power in the Reich which was to come. Advancement fell as much to ruthlessness and craft as to ability, and ruthlessness and craft were to be very useful qualifications in Nazi Germany.

Thus there was Ernst Roehm, already mentioned, a professional soldier, a Free Corps fighter and brawler at Communist demonstrations, an early member of the German Workers' party. He held a command in the SA, and planned to organize it as a secret army, an adjunct of the *Reichswehr.* There was Rudolf Hess, airman and university student, later to be the deputy and heir apparent of the Führer, general organizer at party headquarters, a mediocre, unbalanced, far from glittering personality, though at first a patient, faithful, industrious lieutenant. There was Gottfried Feder, participant in the putsch of 1923, an economic theorist, and one of the authors of the original twenty-five point program. There was Dietrich Eckart, journalist, formerly playwright and philosopher, sometime editor of the *Völkischer Beobachter.* There was Hermann Göring, ace airman of the war, participant in the putsch of 1923, and one of the first Nazis in the *Reichstag.* He survived the ravages of a vicious private life to become the mighty man of valor, "Iron Hermann" as he liked to be called, an immensely popular, swashbuckling hero — loud, genial, and obese, fond of his decorations, medals, and uniforms; a voracious collector of works of art, but credited with fiendish cruelties; first organizer of the Gestapo and the concentration camps, the future Premier of Prussia, Chief Forester and Huntsman, Plenipotentiary of the Four-Year Plan, Commander in Chief of the Luftwaffe, and *Reichsmarschall.* There was Joseph Goebbels, product of seven universities, a journalist, also one of the first Nazis in the *Reichstag,* of silvern but venomous tongue, lame in body and halt in mind, the future Minister of Propaganda, unpopular even with his colleagues but indispensable to the movement for his peculiar arts. There was Wilhelm Frick, police official, jurist, and zealous administrator. There was Martin Bormann, the Führer's secretary and chief of the party chancellery. There was Alfred Rosenberg, a Baltic German by birth, formerly an architectural student in Russia, then editor of the *Völkischer Beobachter,* at one time the principal theorist and philosopher of the movement, adviser on Russian affairs. There was Robert Ley, gross, debauched, but able organizer of the Labor Front. There was Baldur von Schirach, poet, youth leader, and educator. There was Hans Frank, Nazi lawmaker and future Governor General of Poland. There was Julius Streicher, Jew-baiter and editor of *Der Stürmer,* the notorious anti-Semitic weekly. There was Heinrich Himmler, Chief of the SS and later of the Gestapo, meticulous investigator of crime, perhaps the most sinister man of them all. There were the Strasser brothers, Gregor and Otto, Catholics and Socialists, and at one time storm centers of an anti-Hitlerite secession in northern Germany. At a later date there were Walther Darré, agricultural expert; Otto Dietrich, press chief; Walter Funk, journalist and economist; Joachim von Ribbentrop, former wine salesman, adviser on foreign affairs, future ambassador to Britain and Foreign Minister; Albert Speer, architect and future Minister of Armaments; Hans Fritzsche, news editor and broadcaster; Artur Seyss-Inquart, of Austrian extraction, future Chancellor of Austria and Commissioner of the Occupied Netherlands; Ernst Kaltenbrunner, Himmler's ambitious lieutenant in the SD (*Sicherheitsdienst*), the Nazi special security service. Strange and abnormal men they all were, riven by jealousies and self-seeking, but assuredly in their several ways as extraordinary a company as ever bid for a place in history.

The Nazi party continued to grow, but it cannot be said that it flourished. Its membership was 27,000 in 1925 and 178,000 in 1929. But its representation in the *Reichstag* consistently fell. In three elections between 1924 and 1928, it returned 32, 14, and 12 Deputies successively. The years from 1924 to 1929 covered the single interval of stability enjoyed by the interwar Reich, and they were years marked by a recession, certainly a slackening in the popularity of all the "parties of discontent." The argument that Nazism, like the kindred cult of Fascism, derived the greater part of its strength from economic rather than from moral forces seems to be borne out by the facts of the case, and, but for the grim resolution of the Führer and his aides, the movement might well have withered and disappeared under the benign fortunes of the Locarno era.

The financing of the party, the endless, heartless, heartbreaking scrounging for dues, subscriptions, gifts, and loans, makes no small part of the secret history of Nazism at this time. The *Völkischer Beobachter* paid well, but the party's other literature was an always expanding item, voracious of funds. Meetings, as ever, were extravagantly advertised and staged. Numberless rentals, stipends, pensions, and perquisites had to be met. It is hardly surprising that Hitler, like Mussolini in 1921, turned for help more and more to the big industrialists, the *Junkers,* and princes of the blood, who were inclined to support an anti-Communist, nationalist movement. Thus Fritz Thyssen, steel manufacturer; Alfred Hugenberg, newspaper magnate; Emil Kirdorf, coal owner; Baron Kurt von Schroeder, banker; Wilhelm Cuno, director of the Hamburg-Amerika Line and former Chancellor; several of the directors of the Farben Industries and of the potash industry, and many others were all subscribers to the cause. Oddly enough Gustav Krupp, titular head of the great armaments combine, was not one of the number – at least not at first – though at a later date he was converted and became a "super Nazi." Old radicals in the party, like the Strasser brothers, were deeply apprehensive of the capitalist-monarchist influences which thence seeped into the movement and sullied its pure and pristine socialism, but they were to learn as the world was to learn, that Hitler never hesitated to sacrifice a principle if the needs of the moment were better served thereby.

The Chancellorships of Müller and Brüning

In 1929 National Socialism was still a sect of unruly fanatics, a curiosity among political parties, the product of abnormal conditions, and expected soon to become a forgotten freak of German history. Its membership still seemed to be drawn from the disgruntled and the unbalanced. Men of responsibility and common sense, men of education and property, might perhaps play politics with it, but they would hardly fall victim to its power or influence themselves. The brutalities, the jealousies, and the known viciousness of the SA, the SS, and many of the party leaders were surely repellent to "decent" Germans. Abroad, Nazism was regarded as a reaction to the war, a painful stage which a people must go through in the quest for true democracy.

But 1929 was Germany's last year of economic stability. Hermann Müller, then Chancellor, found himself and his government in increasing difficulties. The fifth reparation annuity under the Dawes Plan had been paid punctually and in full, but the Reich budget, despite admitted manipulation of the figures, remained unbalanced. (See p. 146.) Some 15,000 businesses went bankrupt during the year. Fierce outbreaks of party squadrism were sure signs of deteriorating conditions. The May Day celebrations of 1929 cost over 200 casualties. On October 3, 1929, occurred the death of Stresemann, six years Minister of Foreign Affairs, the very symbol of the peace and progress of the Locarno era. The Young Plan was negotiated in December of that year. (See p. 326.) Nationalists and Nazis drummed up the four million signatures legally required to petition the government for a referendum against the Plan and, a few days before Christmas 1929, the German voters flocked excitedly to the polls to register their views on whether or not "further financial burdens based on the war-guilt acknowledgment shall be assumed." The referendum failed to repudiate the Plan, which was eventually ratified by the *Reichstag* by just 226 votes to 224, but it was a disturbing pointer of the Nazi growth.

In March 1930, Müller, the Chancellor, requested President von Hindenburg for emergency powers under Article 48 of the Constitution. (See p. 135.) Hindenburg refused, reputedly on the advice of General Kurt von Schleicher, the *Reichswehr*'s political mentor, who was now well entrenched in the good graces of Hindenburg himself; whereupon Müller resigned. A new, supposedly nonpartisan government, which was frankly a government of crisis, was formed under the Center leader, Dr. Heinrich Brüning, and it was clear before he took office that Brüning might have to rule by virtue of Article 48. Brüning did his best against six months' consistent obstructionism from parties of the extreme Left and Right in the *Reichstag,* and then called for new elections. If, however, he expected a popular reaction against extremism, he fatally miscalculated. Hitler and his Nazi troopers threw themselves into a whirlwind campaign of meetings and parades, oratory and terrorism in every town and hamlet of the Reich. The election took place on September 14, 1930, and the result was a Nazi landslide. Hitler won one-sixth of the total vote and 107 seats. The new *Reichstag* was little more than a drop screen for Nazi demonstrations. The 107 marched into the chamber in a body and in uniform and at once turned the sessions into a bedlam.

Brüning tried to combat the Nazis by stealing their thunder. He was *plus royaliste que le roi.* He never allowed it to be forgotten that his cabinet was composed of veterans of the First World War; he stood for the "active revision" of Versailles; he condoned a violent new phase of agitation against the Polish Corridor; in the matter of disarmament, he went to Geneva demanding the pledged disarmament of other nations; his Foreign Minister, Dr. Julius Curtius, proposed the Austro-German Customs Union, with results that we have elsewhere described. (See pp. 326-28.) For himself Brüning would probably have best liked a restoration of the monarchy. But, for all his efforts, Nazi influence was in the ascendant. Brüning could have been saved only by some striking economic concession from the Versailles Powers, but this he was never able to obtain. Hitler was now working hand in glove with Alfred Hugenberg, leader of the Nationalist party, a man who used his powerful newspaper interests for the promotion of extreme chauvinist and reactionary politics, and by whose munificence the Nazi party acquired the Brown House in Munich for its headquarters. On October 10, 1931, Hitler was received for the first time by President von Hindenburg. The confrontation of the two men was inconclusive, although the fact that it took place was significant of Hitler's rising prestige.

The presidential election fell due in March and April 1932. It was preceded by weeks of political jockeying, and it brought to a head the deep struggle of the German electorate between its loyalty to Hindenburg, and all he stood for, and the new idols of Nazism. After much weighing of the chances, Hitler put himself forward as the Nazi candidate. Ernst Thälmann was the Communist candidate; Theodor Düsterberg, a leader of the veterans' organization, the Stahlhelm, was the Nationalist candidate. Hindenburg was supported by Brüning and by the surviving moderate elements in the electorate. The campaign was hard fought and tumultuous. As there was no clear majority on the first ballot, the Constitution required a second. This time Düsterberg withdrew, and Hindenburg won 19,400,000 votes, Hitler 13,400,000, and Thälmann 3,700,000. Field Marshal Paul von Hindenburg, now aged eighty-four and almost senile, thus entered upon his second term as President of the Reich.

A few days after the election, Hindenburg signed a decree dissolving the Nazi SA and SS. The action appeared as a gallant, if belated and desperate attempt on the part of Brüning to assert law and order. During his last month of office, Brüning was ruling virtually by decree, appealing without compunction to Article 48 of the Constitution. The Depression was at its depths. Since 1929 industrial production had fallen by nearly a half, and prices by nearly a quarter. Unemployment had risen from 2,000,000 to 6,000,000. Probably Brüning would not have lasted much longer in any event, but he hastened his end by introducing a scheme for settling batches of unemployed ex-soldiers on derelict *Junker* estates in East Prussia – much to the alarm of his own *Junker* President, Hindenburg, and of Hindenburg's *Junker* friends and favorites. The first victim of the consequent purge was General Groener, Minister of Defense, who had supported the ban on the SS and SA and was being spitefully heckled in the *Reichstag*. On May 13, he resigned. Some days later, on May 30, Brüning, weary and sick at heart, resigned also.

Meanwhile, during April, elections for several of the State Diets had given another reflection of the growing extremism. In the Prussian *Landtag*, the Nazis won 162 seats and the Communists 56, and the two parties were soon brawling on the floor of the Chamber. Weimar and the Weimar era were dead, and Nazism everywhere was set and girded to profit by their going. A movement recruited hitherto from idealists, reactionaries, political wirepullers, placemen, and adventurers was now swelled by the broad masses of the lower middle class, "the uprooted and disinherited," the chief sufferers of the Depression. It was this part of the population, living in the vast social "no man's land," that most vividly remembered the inflation of 1923 and was sickened at the thought of a new pauperization, and that now felt so frustrated and misused and hopeless of a future except under the *ultima ratio* of violent leadership. In January 1930, the Nazi party membership was 200,000; in January 1931, it was 400,000; in January 1933, it was nearly 1,000,000.

The Left offered no comparable attraction. The Communists could still point to a slowly growing suffrage; every *Reichstag* election had increased their votes; they had earnest, able leaders like Ernst Thälmann and Ernst Torgler – Torgler, it used to be said, was the only man in the *Reichstag* who could stand up to Goebbels in debate. They were regarded by the Nazis, to judge by Nazi propaganda and conduct, as Germany's real enemy. But their organizations were scattered, mainly in the urban centers and over widely separated localities; their leaders were usually at odds over fine points of doctrine and party tactics; and Moscow, less internationally aggressive than of yore, had been stinting on its former assistance. The Social Democrats, once the largest of the parties numerically, had been long since too much identified with Weimar. They were fundamentally moderate at a time when extremism was the order of the day. Their pacifist tradition put them at a disadvantage in a contest in which rubber truncheons were more effective than votes. As for the extreme Right, the monarchists, the veterans' organization, the Stahlhelm, and the *Reichswehr*, though they had many of Hitler's aims and envied him his success, they lacked his perfervid demagogy, they had none of his mass following, and they still had enough of the decencies to be incapable of stooping to his methods.

The Chancellorships of Papen and Schleicher

President von Hindenburg's intimate circle at this time consisted of General Kurt von Schleicher, Franz von Papen, and the President's son, Oskar von Hindenburg. In constant attendance was the indispensable retainer, Dr. Otto von Meissner, Secretary of the Chancellery, who had held that office since Weimar days. Schleicher was the "strong man" of the circle, a born climber and schemer. He had been a fellow subaltern and friend of Oskar in the President's old regiment, the Third Foot Guards. He and Papen had been attached to the General Staff, and latterly he had served under General Groener in the *Reichswehr* Ministry. Papen had been an officer in the crack cavalry regiment, the Fifth Uhlans. He was an elegant child of fortune with a flair for adventure. By extraction he was not a Prussian, but Westphalian and Catholic, and through his wife he had connections with big industry in the Saar. He was remembered by Americans as the German military attaché in Washington in 1915, expelled for espionage. (See p. 33.) Former comradeships and the pressure of present interests welded this circle into a virtual inner cabinet. The upshot was President von Hindenburg's appointment of Papen on June 1, 1932, to succeed Brüning as Chancellor, with Schleicher as *Reichswehr* Minister. Baron Konstantin von Neurath, a career official and former ambassador in London, became Foreign Minister; and Count Lutz Schwerin von Krosigk, another career official, became Finance Minister.

Schleicher may have been genuinely interested in creating under Papen a hand-picked, reactionary government, a coalition of right-wing elements, a government which later might safely include one or two of Hitler's nominees — if not Hitler himself. The new cabinet indeed was so replete with *Junker* aristocracy that it was called a "Barons' Cabinet." Schleicher had assured himself that Hitler would give Papen the Nazi party's support — at least for the time being. Accordingly Papen's first act in office was to rescind Brüning's recent ban on the SA and the SS and once more to allow them their activities, their meetings, their parades, their broadcasts, and their terrorism. He broke up the democratic opposition in the Prussian *Landtag* by arbitrarily dismissing the Prussian Premier, the Social Democrat Otto Braun, and took the office himself. The Communists proclaimed a general strike in protest, but the workers, largely Social Democrat in sympathy and decimated by unemployment, made no response. The day was past when a general strike could break a putsch. (See pp. 134 and 138.)

In the streets the struggle for the "soul of Germany" was in full swing. Two *Reichstag* elections were held during Papen's term. In the first, in July 1932, the Nazis won 230 seats and became the strongest party in Germany. In the second, in November — incredible to relate — they dropped to 196, a loss of 34, though they still remained the strongest party. The sudden recession in their strength led many a wishful observer to believe that the Nazis were at last reaping the consequences of their tactics and that their power had passed its peak. An incident at Potempa in Upper Silesia, not many days before, when five drunken Nazi troopers had dragged a Communist worker out of bed and kicked him to death in the presence of his mother, had not smelled too sweetly in the nostrils of the German voter — and Hitler had since sent the five troopers, upon their conviction for murder, a telegram of "loyalty and consolation." For a short, fleeting moment it seemed as if the Nazi party was on the point of dissolution. Party comrades wavered in their allegiance; Gregor Strasser quarreled with Hitler and threw in his lot with Schleicher. Worse still, the elections had emptied the Nazi coffers, and the party was desperately in need of funds. Disconsolate Brownshirts could be seen at street corners tinkling their collecting boxes in the faces of indifferent passers-by. Hitler, who had expected to ride to power on the late elections, was crazed with surprise and dejection. Some even said he was meditating flight.

In December 1932, Schleicher, playing his own game, replaced Papen in the chancellorship. Schleicher evidently thought he could make and unmake Papens at will. But Schleicher's problem was the same as the man he had ousted. He had to find support either from Hindenburg and the *Junkers,* or else from the Nazis. As it turned out he was very neatly caught between two fires. He tried to cow the *Junkers* by threatening to publish a secret report on the *Osthilfe,* a fund for agrarian relief, originally instituted under Brüning and since allegedly misappropriated in the interests of the big East Prussian landowners. Naturally enough he succeeded in antagonizing the *Junkers* — and incidentally Hindenburg, himself a *Junker.* Meanwhile Papen was bargaining with Hitler — their intermediary was Joachim von Ribbentrop, the first appearance of that gentleman — and Hitler, still floundering in uncertainty, was glad to clutch even at the straws that Papen threw out to him. Cleverly, all too cleverly, Papen resolved the fears and doubts of the *Junker* clique and built up a formidable anti-Schleicher coalition. It only remained to persuade Hindenburg that the coalition, even under the nominal headship of the upstart "Bohemian corporal," would be a safe and workable proposition. Thus, on January 30, 1933, Hindenburg appointed Hitler Chancellor of the Reich.

The affair of January 30 was nothing better than a deal, an insolent, disingenuous, Machiavellian deal. Every party to it got something and believed he would soon get more. The cabinet again was a "Barons' Cabinet." Papen became Vice-Chancellor and was deliciously revenged on Schleicher. Of the Nazis, Göring became Minister without portfolio, and Frick Minister of the Interior. The other offices were equitably distributed among potentates of the Nationalist party, the Stahlhelm, and the *Reichswehr.* Alfred Hugenberg was Economic Minister; Franz Seldte, the Stahlhelm leader, was Labor Minister, and General Werner von Blomberg was *Reichswehr* Minister. Neurath remained Foreign Minister and Krosigk Finance Minister. In the end, three Nazis — Hitler, Göring, and Frick — in the cabinet of twelve did not seem a very serious proportion. Papen and his *Junker* aides might be pardoned for thinking they could hold the Nazis in check or for hoping that Hitler, for once in a position of high responsibility, might blunder himself into a spectacular fall. Yet Papen should also have remembered that Mussolini in 1922 had made just three Fascist appointments in a cabinet of twelve!

But Hitler had the chancellorship. His triumph put new heart into his declining cause. The Nazi rank and file gave themselves over to an orgy of celebration. Göring, on the radio, proclaimed the rebirth of the Reich, the obliteration of fourteen years of shame, and the founding of a new German state in freedom and honor. In Berlin, on the night of January 30, a gigantic torchlight procession of 250,000 marched past the Führer, while Hindenburg, woodenly expressionless in another window of the Chancellery, stood watching the phenomenon to which he had now given his official consecration. And the people of Germany watched too, some in fear, some in hope, and all in amazement.

The Chancellorship of Hitler

Hitler immediately put into effect his *Gleichschaltung,* a "leveling," "equalizing," or "coordinating" of the German body politic. Communism, the Nazi party's particular foe and scapegoat, was the first to feel the destructive wrath of the process. Communist meetings and papers were prohibited, and Communist leaders arrested. On the night of February 27, 1933, the *Reichstag* building caught fire and was completely gutted. Göring, by "a flash of intuition," recognized the outrage as "Communist arson," the first incident in a nefarious counterrevolutionary campaign directed at government property throughout Germany. A certain Marinus van der Lubbe, a Dutchman and reputedly a Communist, was arrested in the burning building. Also arrested were Torgler, chairman of the Communist fraction in the *Reichstag,* who had chanced to be in the building shortly before the fire broke out, and three Bulgarian Communist exiles, alleged to have been seen earlier in Lubbe's company, one of whom was Georgi Dimitrov, a veteran worker for the Comintern and in after years to become the Communist Premier of Bulgaria.[1]

Göring promised to substantiate his flash of intuition with incontrovertible proofs. Lubbe and the other arrested persons were afterward given a flamboyant trial at Leipzig. Lubbe appeared to be mentally subnormal and was quite useless under examination. He was eventually executed, and the others were acquitted. Meanwhile the Nazis made welcome use of the *Reichstag* fire as an electioneering cry and as their warrant for the extermination of Communism in Germany. On March 5, 1933, in a frenzy of hatred and fear of the "Red peril," the German electorate once more went to the polls. The Nazis turned on their terrorist machine; the SA were given the "freedom of the streets" to assault, torture, and kill as they pleased. Hitler wrung his hands over the reported atrocities, but did nothing to stop them. For all their efforts, the Nazis did not yet secure a clear majority. It is of interest that in this last "constitutional" election in Germany, when it may be presumed that all the advantages of coercion and publicity lay with Hitler, the Nazi party commanded no more than 44 per cent of the German vote.

The new *Reichstag* met ceremonially on March 21 in the Potsdam Garrison Church with President von Hindenburg in the chair, thus symbolizing the link between the new government and the Prussian military tradition. It reassembled for business two days later in the Kroll Opera House in Berlin; and, under the very pistols of the SA and SS and in the absence of all the Communist Deputies and many of the Social Democrats, who were under arrest, it passed an Enabling Act and thereby vested Hitler and his government with dictatorial powers for four years. On this critical occasion the Center Deputies voted with the Nazis; the Social Democrats present, with sublime but belated courage, voted against the Nazis. The Cabinet was "coordinated"; Goebbels became Minister of Propaganda, and Hess Minister without portfolio; Göring held, in addition to his cabinet office, the key post of Prussian Minister of the Interior, which gave him control of the Prussian police and Prussian state administration. Papen, Hugenberg and the *Junkers,* a sorry crew, were soon edged out of power and eventually out of office. The *Reichstag,* under the presidency of Göring, became a mere platform for the Führer's pronouncements. On paper everything had been correct and in proper legal order. The Weimar Constitution, it is to be remembered, was never formally abrogated, at that time or later.

From this moment coordination, the *"coup d'état* by installments," touched every part of the nation's life. The Nazi party was the one and only party permitted, and all the other parties were dissolved. The Stahlhelm and the remnants of the Free Corps either joined the SA or were dissolved. All the national symbols were stamped with the Nazi stamp; the black-red-gold flag of the Weimar Republic was replaced by the monarchist black-white-red, with the Nazi swastika in its center. In the civil services, all politically unreliable officials were dismissed. The separate state constitutions were superseded, and the States, or *Länder,* were put under the authority of regents (*Statthälter*), who often enough were also the local Nazi district leaders (*Gauleiter*). In Bavaria, where some resistance was expected, the ministers were intimidated into compliance, but not before two of them had been beaten to death.

The police and legal system were coordinated. The SA was tantamount to a state police, with no inconvenient restrictions. Göring, as Prussian Minister of the Interior, had more real power than an oriental satrap. By degrees the law became a pragmatic means to an end, arbitrary and changeable, wielding retribution for a great number of newly defined political crimes. The Führer, of course, was the supreme law lord with absolute powers. The fundamental rights and liberties of the individual citizen disappeared. Several new courts were set up, such as the People's Court for trying cases of "high treason and treason against the state," and their judgments were wholly political. In the criminal courts, the judge or public prosecutor was empowered to hear or reject evidence, lodge an appeal, or order a retrial at his discretion. A Secret State Police or Gestapo (*Geheime Staatspolizei*) was created, originally under Göring's control, to be reorganized and greatly extended by Heinrich Himmler. Concentration camps were established, the first of a system which in due time was to number three hundred centers. The SD (*Sicherheitsdienst*), an SS within the SS, virtually a private espionage force, was set up in June 1934 under Himmler's favorite lieutenant, Reinhard Heydrich.

Trade, industry, and labor were coordinated. Dr. Hjalmar Schacht was appointed president of the Reichsbank and Minister of Economics, and embarked on his ingenious career as financier of the Nazi economy. Nazi supervisors sat on boards of directors. The trade unions were destroyed and expropriated, and a new Labor Front under Ley provided for the workers' welfare, insurance, savings, and a certain amount of occupational training. Even the workers' leisure was coordinated in recreational organizations which bore the euphemistic name of "Strength through Joy" (*Kraft durch Freude*). The basic problem of the unemployed was attacked with vigor. Firms were required to increase their personnel; Jews, Communists, and women were replaced by the hundreds; road-building projects, notably the *Autobahnen,* and, above all, a huge rearmament program, were initiated. Labor Service for young men and women was made compulsory and militarized.

Schools and universities were coordinated. Education, from the cradle to the grave, subserved the New Order. Teaching staffs and student bodies were purged of non-Aryan elements; it is said that between 1933 and 1938 one-third of the official university posts changed hands. Textbooks were rewritten. New courses were introduced, such as "defense science" and geopolitics; history and biology took a "racial" slant. Special schools were founded, like the Adolf Hitler Schools, somewhat on the lines of the Prussian cadet schools, to train selected boys for party leadership. The whole of the country's youth in all its extraschool activities was regimented in semimilitary organizations known as the Hitler Youth (*Hitlerjugend*), nominally under the leadership of that "perfect Nordic," the poet Baldur von Schirach, and into them were forcibly absorbed the old German Youth Movement, the various German adaptations of the Boy Scouts and Y.M.C.A., and the Catholic and other confessional youth societies. The *Bund Deutscher Mädel* was the corresponding organization for girls.

Culture and the arts were coordinated. A Reich Culture Chamber controlled the seven fields of literature, journalism, radio, film, drama, music, and painting and sculpture, and over this far-flung province Goebbels was ruler. The results, judged by aesthetic standards, might not always have been of the highest, but a vast productive activity was brought into the service of the Nazi state, and a hungry army of mediocre talent but of acceptable political leanings — novelists, journalists, dramatists — were enabled to enjoy the sweets of success and popularity. Architecture, characteristically "German," yet often classical and traditional in style and in surprisingly good taste, was the personal monopoly of the Führer and his chosen master builders.

One year sufficed for Hitler to accomplish his revolution and transform the face of Germany. The German people may have been politically immature, and their social structure less surely laid than those of other Western lands. Yet their institutions one and all were overthrown with astonishing ease by a party whose beginnings were none too reputable and whose following in the electorate had at all times been doubtful. No other party or power in the field, it seemed, except the Nazi, was willing to face a fight for what it wanted or believed. At the last, Communists, Social Democrats, trade unions, Center, *Junkers,* Stahlhelm, *Reichswehr, Länder,* civil service, Supreme Court, and universities, all shrank from action, defeatist and defeated before a force which had become clothed in the very armor of historic necessity. "It was no victory," said Spengler, "for the enemies were lacking."

The churches alone offered some resistance, mainly through the courageous action of individuals, a resistance which was therefore ill-concerted and was of a declining effectiveness. And, of course, there was always the *Reichswehr;* and, connected therewith, there was the one and only important opposition which arose within the Party itself. For, in the midst of joys and celebrations, there had been grumbling. The long-standing rivalry between the two corps of troopers, the SA and the SS, broke out afresh, especially after Himmler's appointment to the SS leadership. The "old fighters" of the SA (*Altkämpfer*) in many ways represented the left wing of the Nazi party, and they were disappointed that their revolution had not always realized the Socialist pretensions of the party in its earlier times. Nor had their revolution brought them the expected personal rewards. Party organizations had swelled beyond all reason; appointments and commissions had been cast in all directions; yet the choicer plums had gone to the Nazi elite, the SS. The zealous wearers of the Brownshirt had been left unsatisfied. Even the hope that they might be incorporated into the *Reichswehr* on privileged terms, as Ernst Roehm, their leader, had urged so often, was disappointed. The *Reichswehr* was determined to pick and train its own recruits and looked askance at the rowdy, inchoate mass of 2,500,000 men which the SA had become. In sober truth Nazism had outgrown the SA. Power had made the party respectable and more exclusive. The earlier dynamism of the movement, of which the SA had been the vehicle, was clearly running down. As has happened in the history of revolutions before, the group of men which started the revolution was not always the group of men best fitted to carry it on. As for the Führer, he now liked to consort with magnates and generals, and perhaps was a little embarrassed by the plebeian horde that clamored for donatives and reminded him too forcibly of the base degrees of his ascent.

It seems likely that Hitler was forced into some sort of pact with the *Reichswehr.* In April 1934, he was present at naval maneuvers, aboard the pocket battleship *Deutschland,* in company with the highest army and navy chiefs, Generals Blomberg and Fritsch and Admiral Raeder. Probably terms for future cooperation between Führer and *Reichswehr* were then agreed: first, the inviolability of the *Reichswehr* as the sole armed force in Germany and the consequent cutting down of the SA; second, the succession of Hitler on the death of President von Hindenburg. On May Day 1934, the Nazi insignia, the swastika and the eagle, appeared on all *Reichswehr* uniforms.

The late spring of the year was outwardly quiet but full of rumors. Roehm was said to be plotting treason and to have found an aide in Gregor Strasser. But early in June, the SA were sent on furlough, and, on the 14th of that month, Hitler flew to Venice for the first of his meetings with

Mussolini. Crises surely were impossible with the SA off the streets and the Führer out of the country. But then, on the 17th, that accomplished gambler and troublemaker, Papen, in an address to students of the University of Marburg, delivered himself of some pointed criticisms of the Nazi regime and referred in particular to threats of a "second revolution." Goebbels tried to ban the publication of the address, but copies were printed abroad and smuggled back into Germany. Goebbels and Hess, in speeches at this time, were excoriating "reaction" and "reactionaries." At the end of June, units of the *Reichswehr* were alerted for emergencies, and an article by Blomberg appeared in the *Völkischer Beobachter* supporting the National Socialist State and its leaders, Hindenburg and Hitler.

Hitler's blow fell on June 30, 1934, "the night of the long knives." In a short, savage week-end, during which he acted, in his own words, as "the Supreme Justiciar of the German people," he, Göring, Himmler and the SS "exterminated without mercy the undisciplined and disobedient, the unsocial and sickly elements" of the Party and the SA. Hitler himself afterward admitted to 77 deaths, but the real number was more likely to have been nearer 1,000. Among the victims were Ernst Roehm, Gregor Strasser, and General von Schleicher and his wife. Several old scores were settled; the long arm of Hitler's vengeance even picked off the former Munich trio, Kahr, Lossow, and Seisser. (See p. 145.) Papen was saved at the last minute only, it was said, because of his personal relations with Hindenburg; but Papen's two secretaries were shot. Hindenburg congratulated the Führer "for his determined action and gallant personal intervention"; Blomberg apostrophized "the common ideals" of the Army and the "new SA." Said Göring:

> The Führer has accomplished great deeds out of the greatness of his heart, the passion of his will, and the goodness of his soul. Faith in him is alone the basis of our life. Who dares touch that faith has ceased to be a German and must be destroyed.

The first part of the *Deutschland* pact had been honored.

On August 2, 1934, Hindenburg died. He had been ailing for some time, and it is a pertinent question whether, since 1932, when he was reelected President, he had been in full possession of his faculties. The same day the second part of the *Deutschland* pact was honored. Hitler declined to succeed to the actual title of President, a title which he declared the late Field Marshal had invested with "unique and non-recurrent significance," and intimated that he would continue to be called Führer and Chancellor. But he succeeded none the less to the realities of the presidential power. Officers and men of the *Reichswehr* took their oath of allegiance to him personally as "Supreme Commander of the Armed Forces." Hindenburg was buried with impressive military pomp in the great war memorial at Tannenberg. On August 19, Hitler submitted himself in his new authority to the approval of the German people by means of one of the many national plebiscites at this time; over 95 per cent of the electorate went to the polls, and of these about 90 per cent voted *"Ja."*

The Churches and Jewry

The churches, we have said, offered some resistance to Nazism, though it was of declining effectiveness. Certain Nazis tried to found a German "National" Church with an Aryan clergy and an "Aryan ethic." Nazi propaganda represented Christ as a Nordic martyr done to death by Jews. The movement had some success in the excitement of the first year of Nazi rule, and many Protestant pastors and their congregations were swept into it. But opposition by men like Pastor Martin Niemöller made it clear to the Nazi leaders that more severe and subtle methods of repression would have to be adopted. In 1935 Dr. Hans Kerrl was appointed Minister for Church Affairs and, under his direction, the coordination of the Protestant churches in Germany became a long-drawn, relentless persecution in the form of dismissals from churches, detentions in concentration camps, confiscations of stipends and properties, suppression of periodicals, and closing of schools and seminaries.

In their dealings with the Roman Catholic Church the Nazis appeared again to meet at first with some success. Hitler himself was a Catholic born – though an ostentatiously nonpracticing one – and the reigning Pope, Pius XI, was believed by some to be inclined to Fascism. All Hitler's earliest pronouncements on religious questions had been studiedly conciliatory. In July 1933, a concordat with the Vatican regulating Catholic affairs in Germany was negotiated by Papen. It granted freedom of faith and of worship, recognized the secrecy of the confessional, guaranteed the maintenance and inviolability of Catholic organizations, orders, charities, and schools, and gave bishops the right to publish pastoral letters. But thereafter Catholics were subject to the same kind of persecution as Protestants, the same kind of *"coup d'état* by installments," and the terms of the concordat, one by one, were violated. Catholic priests had to face trumped-up charges in the Nazi courts, such as charges of evading the currency regulations or of committing sexual offenses. In March 1937, the papal encyclical, *Mit brennender Sorge,* was read from all Catholic pulpits in Germany, condemning the Nazi doctrines of the state and race. But, by the outbreak of the Second World War, the German churches, Catholic and Protestant, were in a sorry plight.

Toward the Jews the Nazis had no formal policy at first, though lootings, boycotts, expropriations, and the excesses of the prison and the concentration camp were their normal anti-Semitic ritual from the moment they came to power. Attempts to systematize and legalize the persecution followed in due course. Jews were debarred from civil service, professions, universities, learned societies, armed forces, and from membership in the Labor Front, without which it was almost impossible to conduct a business. More and more disabilities and humiliations were heaped on the unhappy community. In 1935, by the so-called Nuremberg "Racial Laws," Jews were deprived of German citizenship, prohibited from contracting marriages with "citizens of German or kindred blood," and prohibited also from employing as domestic servants "female citizens of German or kindred blood under 45 years of age." After the pogrom of November 1938, there was a general "Aryanization" of Jewish property, destruction of synagogues, and a collective "fine" of a billion marks. As a distinguishing sign, Jews were forced to wear the yellow Star of David.

Full Employment, Autarky, and Rearmament

Economically, the Nazis inherited both liabilities and assets. In 1932 Germany had 6,000,000 unemployed – some authorities have put the figure at 8,000,000 – and, by all standards of the day, she was bankrupt. But she still had her basic natural resources, and her people their high technical skills. The losses and deterioration of the First World War had long since been made good. The inflation of 1923 had wiped out the internal debt, and in 1932 Germany was free from reparations. In the chemical and optical industries she once more led the world, and she was making strides in shipbuilding and civil aviation. The "rationalization" and foreign loans of the Stresemann era had modernized her manufacturing equipment. Intensive cartelization was preparing her for a regimented national economy. Existing trusts, like Krupps and the Farben Industries, were all too ready to collaborate in the promised expansion. Brüning and Papen had anticipated something of the new regime's methods with their price controls and relief works and, in Papen's time, business indices were already showing unmistakable signs of a "normal" upswing.

It is interesting to note, in passing, that few of the Nazi economists were economists by training, and that Hitler and Göring never had to listen to "experts" who advised against their projects as "impossible." Walther Funk was a journalist; Joseph Wagner a schoolteacher; Göring's aides, when he became a director of the Four-Year Plan, were army generals. Hjalmar Schacht, a banker, was almost a stranger in this company; but then no one could have described Schacht as orthodox. But the Nazis, for all their methods, clung obstinately to old forms. There was no outright nationalization, and confiscation only touched the properties of Jews and of other political undesirables. The illusion of private ownership was maintained and even encouraged. If the Nazis needed a new commodity, they created a company, not a government department, to produce it. The DEA (*Deutsche Erdöl A.G.*), to which was entrusted the production of oil and petroleum from home sources, was such a company, and so also was the prodigious Hermann Göring Works, originally founded for the mining of iron ore. The parallel with the "war companies" of 1914 is obvious. (See p. 36.)

Nor was Nazi economics comprehensively "planned" in the way that Soviet economics was planned. In April 1933, Hitler created a Reich Defense Council (*Ministerrat für die Reichsverteidigung*), an inner circle of the highest ranking Nazis, which might have become a central planning office corresponding to the Soviet Gosplan. But its membership appears to have been very fluid, and Hitler doubtless invited to such meetings as it held whomsoever he desired at any particular moment. Göring's famous Four-Year Plan was a plan only in name. In general, Nazi controls were *ad hoc* transactions, typical mixtures of propaganda and coercion, with immediate returns as the standard of success. Coordination of effort derived rather from the men than the organizations in which they worked. The chain of command through the various government and party levels was tangled in the extreme. The ultimate decisions rested with the Führer, but his power of attorney, so to speak, was distributed over every lesser Führer in the hierarchy. There were few of these lesser Führers who did not hold office in more than one department, and the multiplication of their offices, like the multiplication of commercial directorships, enabled them to exercise authority, or at least to hold a watching brief, over several fields of activity at once. Thus Schacht, and after him Funk, was President of the Reichsbank as well as Minister of Economics; Göring was Prussian Premier, president of the *Reichstag,* Plenipotentiary of the Four-Year Plan, and Commander in Chief of the Luftwaffe. But at no point does it appear that jurisdictions were ever precisely defined. On the contrary, jurisdictions tended to grow and overlap in response to personal rivalries. Often indeed it seemed as if confusion and inefficiency were regarded by the Nazis themselves as desirable qualities befitting the spirit of their rule. And many an indigent party man who, in a different system, might have been redundant, found a job at some dead end of the bureaucratic labyrinth.

Yet, however indirect and capricious the authority might be, in total effect every stage of the economic process was under the most rigid control. Businesses could not be conducted without licenses; firms were forcibly created or closed according to the policy of the moment. The import and distribution of materials were controlled. Contracts were graded according to priorities. Distribution to the consumer was rationed. Wage rates were stabilized at their 1933 levels – which were usually minimum levels – and thereby the entire price structure was also stabilized. The old free mobility of labor was gradually halted; workers were allocated to jobs like materials or capital. Profits were controlled by special taxes and levies. Businesses paid each other subsidies as appeared to be necessary. Dividends and interest rates were limited, and any excess was plowed back into the business or invested in government bonds. A huge flow of funds was thus diverted, by one channel or another, into the Reich Treasury. The result was a "closed" economy resembling at many points the total wartime economy of 1914-18.

Within the citadel of such an economy Germany could order her life at will. She could develop in isolation any "uneconomic" process. She could make up her shortages of raw materials with substitutes. She could plunder Jews and occupied countries. The public debt might rise; but – here was the real secret of totalitarian bookkeeping – the public debt could rise to any ceiling so long as the interest was a "safe" percentage of the national income. Foreign trade alone was beyond Germany's absolute control, but foreign trade could be reduced to the unavoidable minimum. Foreign trade became organized barter, sometimes the crude interchange of goods for goods by individual contracts, sometimes a sort of deferred barter by means of clearing agreements. Under cover of a nominal gold standard, rates of exchange might be made to vary almost *ad hoc* so as to squeeze the most out of every transaction. Money owed to foreign creditors was put into blocked accounts which could be bought by the government at a heavy discount or else paid off with goods which the anxious creditor did not really want. Foreign balances could be used to purchase raw materials for armaments or to further economic penetration in politically desirable directions. Southeastern Europe was the classic example of the use of these techniques in all their variety to bring about an economic vassalage in the interests of Nazi *Grossraumwirtschaft.* And the manipulator-in-chief was Hitler's "wizard," Hjalmar Schacht.

The human costs of such a system were prodigious. Wages and prices might remain stable, but the purchasing power of those wages was reduced. The workers' pay was continually whittled away by various compulsory dues, savings, and other incidental levies—such as Winter Relief and "Strength through Joy." Mere money indeed lost its traditional meaning. The economic unit of measurement was not the mark but the amount of work a man could do. Yet evaluated in cold statistics the standard of living of the mass of the German people under Nazism, that is from 1933 to 1939, markedly improved. Unemployment, once so terrible a scourge, by 1936 was passing into a labor shortage. In addition, Germany succeeded in making herself, if not absolutely autarkic—Hitler himself always recognized that Germany could never be wholly independent of foreign trade—at least sufficiently self-contained to be free of the fear of another blockade like that of 1914-18. And she built herself the most powerful military machine in the world. In short, the balance sheet of the Nazi economics, from the Nazi point of view, could be acclaimed a formidable success. A well-knit, hard-working population of 70,000,000 stood ideologically inspired, physically trained, and materially equipped for the supreme business of making war.

The Nazi Führer and the Nazi Ideology

The man, Adolf Hitler, was unimpressive and unprepossessing in appearance. Short, spare, slightly mustached, with a strand of dark, lank hair across one brow, he had, at first sight, none of the lineaments of a world-shaking dictator. He was certainly not normal. His fantasies and hysterical storms, his claustrophobia, his persecution mania, his infinite capacity for hatred, his sudden alternations of mystic elation and suicidal dejection, were all symptoms familiar to the psychologist. He was a man without roots or personal loyalties, without home or family, hence wary, secretive, and pathologically distrustful, both fearing and despising his fellows. His private habits of life were simple and ascetic. He was a total abstainer and vegetarian. He played no games and took no recreation beyond an occasional Wagnerian opera, an occasional motion picture and, of course, an occasional retreat to his mountain haunt, the famous Berghof on the Obersalzberg in Bavaria—though some biographers, on the flimsiest evidence, have hinted at other, less reputable amusements.

Yet there was demoniac power in him. His followers have sworn to the extraordinary effect which his very look or word produced upon them, and even men unsympathetically disposed toward him would come away from his presence curiously shaken. His voice was rasping, but could throb with power. In action, in the heat of declamation, upon his rostrum, surrounded by his aides, facing a rapt and responding multitude, he was a being transfigured, "an unknown soldier uttering the thoughts of millions." At his greatest moments – and such moments no one can deny he had – he became the very symbol and embodiment of the Germany that worshipped him.

His mental caliber was not of a high order. He showed no trace of that seasoned moderation which is the mark of the philosopher and the intellectual. He had no use for learning. He disliked "experts." He never understood figures. He is supposed to have read extensively, not for education, but to provide materials for convictions already formed. His reading consisted of newspapers and political tracts, but his memory for sheer matters of fact thus obtained was astonishing. He never quoted a classic author, ancient or modern. He swept away impatiently all the toilsome apparatus that had formerly made Germany so famous in scholarship and research. The only argument he ever knew was reiteration. Action, emotion, and will ruled his life, intelligence *per se,* never. Yet he passes as an example of the wisdom of the unwise. He had that species of revelation "that often madness hits on, which reason and sanity could not so prosperously be believed of." His decisions seemed to be protected by a "sleepwalker's immunity."

A great deal has been written about Hitler's laziness. Rather we should say he was a man with an extraordinary genius for procrastination. He could always wait for the right moment to act, and in that waiting so often showed his almost superhuman political judgment. But, when he acted, he acted with compulsive force, and no difficulty was permitted to hold him. He had a way of cutting through the most complicated problems to solutions of extreme simplicity. Above all, he possessed the gift of prophetic self-assurance. His own *Mein Kampf,* with its vulgar but pseudoapocalyptic style, conveys throughout that compelling, infectious force of one who taught with authority, and the same impression is given by reports we have of his intimate conversations. Incredible it is that such powers should have been lodged in a man whose beginnings had been so unpromising and mean, and who had failed in all the normal pursuits of life. Heiden has described him as "an overpowering nonentity . . . as a human figure lamentable, as a political mind one of the tremendous phenomena of history . . . in a world of normalcy a Nothing, in chaos a Titan." [2]

He had no scruples whatever. His political principles, like those of his spiritual kinsman Mussolini, were extemporized as the occasion arose and were afterward dropped with as little compunction as they had been taken up. He could slough off into forgetfulness promises and assertions made only a moment before. In so far as he was himself conscious of his deceptions, he could be disarmingly candid about them. Yet he deceived everyone continually and consistently and with amazing success. As he said on one occasion:

> I am willing to sign anything. I will do anything to facilitate the success of my policy. I am prepared to guarantee all frontiers and to make non-aggression pacts and friendly alliances with anybody. It would be sheer stupidity to refuse to make use of such measures merely because one might possibly be driven into a position where a solemn promise would have to be broken. There has never been a sworn treaty which has not sooner or later been broken or become untenable. There is no such thing as an everlasting treaty . . . Why should I not

Parteitag, *Nuremberg, 1935: The Führer mounting the rostrum*

RADIO TIMES HULTON

make an agreement in good faith today and unhesitatingly break it tomorrow if the future of the German people demands it? [3]

He was the supreme master of all the devices of mass display and mass delusion. The great Nazi party rallies, especially the annual *Parteitag* at Nuremberg, in their overwhelming magnificence – no less than the concentration camps in their overwhelming horror – were minutely designed for maximum psychological effect. Yet, while Hitler could flatter the German people, he could also despise them and revile them in private. He had been one of them himself; he never ceased to study them; he knew the springs of their weakness and emotionalism. Whenever the author of *Mein Kampf* writes of "the psyche of the broad masses," he writes at once with the unmistakable touch of an artist describing his art. The curious reader may still ponder in his pages some of his technical precepts:

> . . . In the size of the lie there is always contained a certain factor of credibility; since the great masses of a people may be more corrupt in the bottom of their hearts than they will be consciously and intentionally bad, therefore with the primitive simplicity of their minds they will more easily fall victims to a great lie than to a small one, since they themselves perhaps also lie sometimes in little things, but would certainly still be too much ashamed of too great lies. Thus such an untruth will not at all enter their heads, and therefore they will be unable to believe in the possibility of the enormous impudence of the most

infamous distortion in others; indeed, they may doubt and hesitate even when being enlightened, and they will accept any cause at least as nevertheless being true; therefore, just for this reason some part of the most impudent lie will remain and stick; a fact which all great lying artists and societies of this world know only too well and therefore also villainously employ.[4]

Nazism always gave the appearance of pursuing long-range purposes. It was famous for its "blueprints," prepared months and years in advance, for every stage of its progress. *Mein Kampf* is supposed to have laid down the Führer's objectives, all of which he subsequently achieved one after another with clockwork precision.[5] Yet it is also true that the Nazi doctrine was changeable, opportunist, and contradictory. Its programs were hit-and-miss, hand-to-mouth affairs; its leaders fickle and unprincipled. If anything, Nazism was like its cognate Fascism, a philosophy without a philosophy. It is not easy to find a way through its confusion of purpose and purposelessness, of the ultimate and the provisional.

The first and only Nazi manifesto was the twenty-five point program written in Munich in 1920. (See p. 351.) It contained several articles with a more mature Nazi ring, such as the union of all German-speaking peoples in a Greater Germany, the repudiation of Versailles, the disfranchisement of Jews and aliens, the submergence of the individual in the state, the control of the press, and social and agrarian reforms. But it was the only document of its kind in Nazi history. It cannot be regarded as important; the experiment of an explicit creed was not tried again.

Nazism began as a movement of revolt against the defeat of 1918 and against the national miseries which were alleged to stem therefrom. Its own propagandized aims during its early "period of struggle" included the restoration of national pride and dignity, the repair of the bankrupt economic order, the replacement of the weak democratic Republic by a strong authoritarian leadership, and the punishment of Jews and Communists and other "aliens" whose special vices and disloyalty were supposed to have led to the military collapse. But Nazism, like Fascism, soon found that it wanted something more positive to feed on than disillusionment and revenge, and it found it in the doctrines of racism and the supremacy of the state and also in the so-called Führer principle.

Racism certainly defied the observable facts. It was the exaggeration of contemporary nationalism to the point of absurdity. The Celestials, the Chosen People, the Children of the Sun, and their numerous brethren belonged to a world of fable which no one with a smattering of modern science could be expected to take seriously. The pure race, like the pure language, never existed in any recorded time, and the Nazi leaders themselves, for that matter, made an oddly assorted anthropological gallery. The perfect Aryan, as the German humor of the day had it, was "as blond as Hitler, slim as Göring, and as manly as Goebbels." Yet this did not prevent the Nazis, ascientific as they essentially were, from believing in a sort of archetypal "Germanity" to which all the Aryan inhabitants of the Third Reich might rightfully claim kinship.

The Nazi version of racism was elaborated by the party philosopher, Alfred Rosenberg. Race, so ran his argument, is the primordial force of human society. Politics, law, government, history are without meaning except in relation to the race that vitalizes them. Race generates all beauty, progress, and grandeur. The *Herrenvolk,* the sovereign race of races is the Aryan or Nordic, a race born to rule, even as other races – the Latin, the Slav, the Semite, the Negro – are born to be ruled. The Nazi revolution must secure to this sovereign race its primacy and its deserts in the world, encourage its growth, and above all preserve its purity. Particularly the Jewish race, because unassimilable and parasitic, because a corruption and an adulteration of the pure strain, must be destroyed. Spurious internationalism, whether it be found in the Roman Catholic Church, Jewry, Freemasonry, the League of Nations, or Communism, to mention but a few of its most dangerous expressions, are all antithetic to the supreme "folk myth."

The soil that nurtures the race is sacred to it. Blood and soil are the twin ingredients of the world's elect. The great, sprawling, amorphous cities of the modern age, however necessary to industrialism, are centers of deracialization, dung heaps of cosmopolitan Jewry, which depopulate the land and contaminate the sound health of the nation. The myth of a master race, a caste of supermen, living upon the ancient soil of its fathers, conquerors of a world of lesser breeds – this is the very apotheosis of nationalism, an ideal fit to fire the true Nordic heart, an object worthy to be won by true Nordic valor.

The race must increase and multiply. Its quantity and quality must be nurtured by organized eugenics, by a high birth rate, and by unlimited provision for physical education and public health. The highest morality is biological morality. The race must draw to itself its scattered colonies throughout the world. The race must also be in process of steady geographical expansion. It must have its living space (*Lebensraum*). Imperialism is the proper mark of its health and vitality. Thus the Third Reich was a "rising power" doing battle with a host of "declining powers" such as France and Britain. The hegemony of Europe belonged to it by right, and the leadership of the rest of the world would also fall to it in proportion as the declining powers let go their weakening grip on their swollen possessions. "Today we count only 80,000,000 Germans in Europe," wrote Hitler in *Mein Kampf*. "We can only consider our foreign policy a success if, in less than 100 years, 250,000,000 Germans come to live on this continent. . . ."

The state is the race in being. It is much more than a political or geographical expression. The individual is part of the state, happiest in his complete integration with the state. Freedom, as understood by liberal democracy, is an effete and outworn code. The race, the folk, the state, is weakened by the nonconformity of its elements. The whole Nazi domestic program is contained in the word *Gleichschaltung,* conformity, leveling, equalization, coordination. Independence is hostility to one's fellows, treason to the state, and insubordination to the Führer. There should be no such thing as private life. The citizen's privilege is to live and work for the state. All his institutions, his politics, economics, law, science, religion, his house and family, even his leisure and recreation, have no other function than to serve the state. What benefits the state is right; what injures the state is wrong. Such was the true notion and informing spirit of the Third Reich, the "Reich of a thousand years."

The Führer principle (*Führerprinzip*) was the official philosophical sanction of the Führer's own office and person. The Führer is much more than a democratic representative, and the popular "consent," which has elevated him to the supreme responsibility, is not to be measured by so crude a method as counting votes. The Führer is the very symbol of the race, as is a king of his kingdom or a chieftain of his tribe. The Führer embodies his people in himself and expresses their collective will. He is the administrative head of the government, chief legislator and executive, supreme judge, party boss, and commander of the armed forces. His authority is unlimited; his decisions are infallible; obedience to him is an unquestioned and sacred duty.

The Führer governs through a hierarchy of lesser Führers, radiating downward from himself. And the same Führer principle operates at all levels. Every lesser Führer, be he Gauleiter or Blockwart, is the Führer of all he surveys. The Führers in the aggregate constitute the Leadership Corps, the new aristocracy, "the class of politically creative personalities," the concentration of all that is best in the race. It is not so much that the Führer and his Führers rule and command, as that they give organic form to the otherwise formless state. They are the elite of Germany, even as the Germans are the elite of the world.

Thus did Nazism interpret itself. But they who, in its time, stood outside it — and against it — saw it very differently. Several contemporary writers tried to trace the origins of the movement in the political and literary history of Germany — in Fichte, Hegel, and Schopenhauer, in Treitschke, Nietzsche, and Wagner, in the French Count de Gobineau and the English Houston Stewart Chamberlain, and since 1918 in Spengler, Moeller van den Bruck, and Keyserling. Some searched back to the pre-Jena Prussians, to Frederick the Great, to that favorite storm of modern historians, Martin Luther — even to the mythical Siegfried, especially Wagner's version of Siegfried. From such names these writers constructed a ramifying pedigree wherein the features of Nazism have recurred again and again. The Germans, on this interpretation, became a people who in all ages have been given to violence and treachery, sentimental but cruel, inwardly unsure but outwardly arrogant, self-pitying but incapable of pity, hating freedom and craving compulsion. Hitler was thus no sudden and wayward freak, but a more than usually repellant example of a constant type.

There is not a people in Europe whose history has not been drenched with war; but war seemed to have entered into the German soul to a degree beyond all others. The country stood in the center of the Continent, had no natural frontiers east or west, and suffered repeated invasion. Everything it ever had it had to fight for. The sense of insecurity was never absent. National unity developed painfully stage by stage, in the teeth of foreign opposition, and each stage was marked by war — 1813, 1864, 1866, 1870, 1914. Others might sometimes forget or minimize their wars: the Frenchman might look back to a revolution, the Englishman to a parliamentary enactment; but the German always looked back to a battle. In such an atmosphere, the political luxuries permitted to more fortunately placed peoples, the free institutions, free speech, and free education, had had to be denied to an ever struggling, once disunited Reich.

Unhappily for the world these trends and proclivities were once more translated into action at an epochal moment of German development. The Germans of 1914 were a people possessed – possessed by that spirit which, from century to century, has roused peoples out of their inertia and given them their great periods of creativity and expansion. What starry configuration produces these moments we do not know; but Greeks, Romans, Goths, Franks, Arabs, Spaniards, French, British, in their grand procession through history have all felt the influence. In our day, the Germans certainly exhibited all the usual signs of it. Especially since 1871, their national growth had been stupendous. No other nation – the United States perhaps excepted – so brilliantly exhibited the prizes of progress or made such formidable acquisitions of wealth and power. German historians and philosophers never wearied of marveling at their country's achievements and of predicting illimitable futures for it.

> In the sphere of force human records contain no manifestation like the eruption of the German volcano. For four years Germany fought and defied the five continents of the world by land and sea and air. The German armies upheld her tottering confederates, intervened in every theater with success, stood everywhere on conquered territory, and inflicted on their enemies twice the bloodshed they suffered themselves. To break their strength and science and curb their fury it was necessary to bring all the greatest nations of mankind into the field against them. Overwhelming populations, unlimited resources, measureless sacrifice, the Sea Blockade, could not prevail for fifty months. Small states were trampled down in the struggle; a mighty Empire was battered into unrecognizable fragments; and nearly twenty million men perished or shed their blood before the sword was wrested from that terrible hand. Surely, Germans, for history it is enough! [6]

Yet surely for history it was not enough. German dynamism was far from exhaustion point. Some residue of energy still remained to be drawn upon, and, in 1939, Germany was once more ready to defy the world.

Other contemporary writers took a psychological approach. Press and periodicals of the time used to carry articles on the defeat complex of the German people and on the mental reaction especially of the German middle classes to the miseries of the war, the blockade, the inflation, and the Depression. We used to read earnest, learned disquisitions on that morbid, gesticulating little man from Upper Austria, who symbolized the nation's revolt against its degradation. On this showing, Nazism became a technique for the restoration of national self-respect. The very race theory was an overcompensation for a race that had lost faith in itself. Nazi lust and violence were the natural reactions of a people who had not only borne intolerable suffering but believed that suffering to have been undeserved. Any ordinary man who has failed in the struggle for life may bear a grudge against the world, discredit the values he once accepted, give up the decencies of his breeding and education, and feel himself driven to antisocial courses. "The Germans," wrote one who knew them well, "have the peculiarity of believing, under all circumstances, that they have been wronged." [7] There was always something of the frustrate and habitual criminal in the Nazi state of mind.

Other writers – notably the French – attributed the failings of the German character to its lack of classical culture. Germany missed the two great historical waves of classicism which have swept across Europe. Rome never conquered her – Caesar's legions only set foot across the Rhine on punitive forays – and the Renaissance in Germany took uncouth, barbaric forms and then ran to waste in the Thirty Years' War. And by classicism is to be understood not merely a conventional devotion to Greek and Latin idols, but the whole tradition of intellectual self-discipline, sweet reasonableness, and good taste, with which the centuries of ancient learning have infused our Western civilization. In the nineteenth century Europe was shaken to its depths by the Romantic movement. Literature and the arts assumed new emotional forms, highly intense and individualistic. The Western nations, like France and Britain, safely grounded in their classicism – almost to the extent of no longer being conscious of the fact – survived the ordeal, and indeed were enriched and stimulated by it. Germany, never so grounded and "notoriously addicted to intoxicants," seemed to fall back into a half-forgotten but always lurking primitiveness. Nazism in many ways was the final *reductio* of the Romantic movement in Germany. Its apostles were all romantics. Its literature was excitable, lawless, catastrophic, distraught with a sort of ecstatic pseudoprofundity. It was almost comically the reverse of classic moderation.

Yet all the various "explanations" of the Nazi phenomenon never seemed to get to the root of the problem. Perhaps the profounder interpretation was offered by the German writer Rauschning in his *Revolution of Nihilism*. Nazism, like Fascism, of which it was a close variant, thus came among us as a force subversive of the hitherto acknowledged values of our civilization. It was an assault on European culture and part of a phase of history that affected the entire West. We live at a time of change and transformation. As we are so often told, an old epoch is dying, and a new is struggling to be born. That a destructive agent, like Nazism, should have appeared at such a time perhaps belongs to the logic of the situation. Nazism was always hung about with the odor of decomposition.

To be sure, Nazism used civilization. But it used it not as an ethos but as a technique. It used all the arts and sciences of civilization and used them with consummate German thoroughness. For instance, it used the forms of law. The "Beer Hall Putsch" of 1923 was Hitler's first and last attempt to bring off an illegal revolt. Thereafter he was always "Legality Adolf," as his more impatient henchmen nicknamed him. But the letter of the law was the instrument for corrupting its spirit. "Nazism was a combination of legality and terrorism in which terrorism was made legal and legality made terrible." [8] Lawful crime was one of the most frightening features of the system because, in the nature of things, it was one that the law-abiding world, so long as it remained lawful, was helpless to combat. By the inversion of accepted values Nazism could seize all the tactical advantages: it could appeal to the arguments of its opponents and blackmail their integrity; it could exploit justifiable grievances for quite other ends; it could represent aggression as "self-defense" and conquest as "self-determination." Appropriately the very first measures of Hitler's dictatorship in 1933 were introduced under an Enabling Act, "constitutionally" passed. After the slaughter of June 1934, Hitler could come before the German people as their "Supreme Justiciar." It was perfectly in keeping that even the concentration-camp commandant was covered by "law" — his powers were defined, and his every foulness was regularized on paper.

In the same way Nazism used the forms of religion — it has, in fact, sometimes been described as a religion. It had fanaticism, missionary zeal, self-sacrifice, and a sort of redemption. It lent itself to inspired ceremonies. But everything was in reverse. It was like a Black Mass in borrowed vestments. "[It] emptied religious ideas of their content and transformed them into a profane meaning . . . [It] enriched the vocabulary of unbelief with the heritage of Christian ideas." In the midst of a civilized world Nazism harked back to precivilization. Its Führer was a magnified tribal chief. Its swastika, like the Fascist fasces, was a sort of totem. It sacrificed a scapegoat to cleanse the tribe of its misfortunes. Its blood rites and initiations, its nocturnal festivals, its Wagnerian mysticism recalled a pagan ancestry. Its party rallies resembled nothing so much as a gathering of the tribes to drum up the warlike passions. "I know now what Gibbon meant," said an English visitor to a Nuremberg *Parteitag,* "when he wrote of 'the licentious clamors of the barbarians.' "

Beneath all the diatribes against Versailles, beneath the theories of blood and soil, beneath the racism and the Führer principle, beneath all the forms and guises Nazism took, there existed a crude, irreducible atavism. Nazism was like a psychoanalysis exploring "the nightside of the soul." It was surrealism in politics and demagogy. It had a sure instinct for discovering, *dis*-covering, and playing upon the aboriginal, the elemental, and the degenerate in the German masses.[9] If the Nazis had won, if they had emerged from the Second World War successful in their enterprises, political and military, it is a fair guess that the destruction of Europe as a civilization would have been hastened, not averted by them.

20. GERMANY: NAZI FOREIGN POLICY

The Disarmament Conference

After 1932 the foreign policy of Germany – and, it might be said, the foreign policies of her neighbors in Europe – was already revolving about the question of armaments. The Disarmament Conference, whose origins have been described in a previous chapter (see p. 127), had assembled at last in Geneva on February 2, 1932, four months before Brüning's dismissal and twelve months before Hitler's seizure of power. Of the sixty-four states invited, fifty-nine had sent delegates, including the United States and the Soviet Union. The omens had not been good. Arthur Henderson, the British Labor leader and former British Foreign Secretary, already elected president of the Conference, had lately lost his place in the British government and his seat in the House of Commons. He continued to preside over the Conference, however, but he presided as a private individual and without the more powerful position which an official status would have conferred upon him. Then, on that very February 2, Japanese marines were reported to be landing in Shanghai. (See p. 344.) On February 18, Brüning, the German Chancellor, uttered his demand for "equality," and reminded the Conference that German disarmament, under Versailles, was originally intended to be a "first step" toward general world-wide disarmament:

> This is Germany's legal and moral right, which no one can contest. The German people are counting on the present conference to find a solution of the problem of general disarmament on the basis of equal rights and equal security for all peoples.

The life of the Disarmament Conference was as painful and protracted as its preparation, and the reader may be spared any too detailed discussion of it. The French delegate, Paul-Boncour, came with a proposal for the setting-up of an international force, a proposal that revived in a different form Léon Bourgeois's militarized League of 1919. (See p. 115.) When this proposal failed of acceptance, Paul-Boncour produced another, which amounted to a series of concentric Locarno Pacts embracing the world. The British delegate, Sir John Simon, came with a proposal for "qualitative disarmament"; namely, for the prohibition of all types of offensive weapons. This proposal was more sympathetically received, but the military experts, to whom it was eventually referred, could discover no distinguishing criterion between offensive and defensive weapons. The British and American experts, for instance, regarded the submarine as offensive and the battleship as defensive; the French experts thought precisely the opposite. The Germans had already a clearcut test: offensive weapons were those which had been forbidden them by the Treaty of Versailles.

The Lausanne Conference on reparations, in June 1932 (see p. 332), created a diversion of interest, and when the Disarmament Conference was resumed, a fourth proposal was laid before it, this time from President Hoover, a proposal for a general slicing of all existing armaments by one-third – although with necessary allowance for "powers having colonial possessions." But none of the European delegates could be persuaded that armament was merely a problem of ratios. The German Government continued to demand that its claim to "equality" be recognized and implemented. From the French point of view, of course, the admission of such an "equality" would instantly grant an effective preponderance to the potentially stronger power, Germany. Between July and September 1932, the German delegates withdrew from the Conference and returned only after the French had been induced to agree to a formula which accorded the Reich "an equality of rights in a system of security for all nations."

The Disarmament Conference again resumed its sessions in February 1933. Its progress to date had been negligible, and the prospects for its future were gloomy enough. Hitler was now Chancellor of the Reich, and Japan was about to announce her withdrawal from the League. The famous Draft Convention, so carefully drawn during the earlier preparatory discussions, had hardly figured in the present Conference's discussions at all, and it was evidence of the prevailing desperation that Ramsay MacDonald, the British Prime Minister, should now have come to Geneva with a proposal which resembled that neglected document. (See p. 129.) The so-called MacDonald Plan was, in fact, the text of a disarmament treaty containing precise figures of men and matériel, and for the first time in its history the Disarmament Conference met in an atmosphere of definition and practicality.

Hitler, in these early days of his power, was advertising his pacific intentions and denying before the world the very evidence of his acts. In a speech in the *Reichstag* in May 1933, he said:

> Germany is ready at any time to assume further international obligations, if all nations are prepared to do so . . . Germany is ready to dissolve her entire military forces and destroy the weapons left to her, if other nations will do the same . . . Germany is ready to accept a general international control of armaments if other nations will do the same . . . The German Government is convinced that today there can be only one great task, and that is to assure the peace of the world.

During the summer months of 1933, the Disarmament Conference adjourned, and the World Economic Conference was held in the interim. (See p. 333.) But on October 14, a few days before it was due to reconvene,

Germany announced her final and irrevocable withdrawal. In the statement of Neurath, then German delegate:

> The Conference will not fulfill its object, namely, a general disarmament. Its failure is due solely to the unwillingness on the part of highly armed states to carry out their contractual obligations to disarm . . . and their attitude has made impossible the satisfaction of Germany's claim to equality of rights . . .

On October 21 Germany also gave notice of her withdrawal from the League of Nations. The Disarmament Conference was virtually at an end, but it was permitted to keep up the fiction of existence for two more years. On October 20, 1935, came the death of Henderson, the president of the conference, after four years' labor in vain.

Rearmament

The grim reality, as the world was soon to know, was not what Hitler's pacific protestations had made them out to be. At a later date, in 1939, when he could make his admission with impunity, Hitler thus delivered himself:

> I had to reorganize everything, beginning with the mass of the people and extending to the armed forces. First, internal reorganization, eradication of appearances of decay and of defeatist ideas, education for heroism. While reorganizing internally, I undertook the second task—to release Germany from her international ties . . . secession from the League of Nations and denunciation of the Disarmament Conference. . . . After that, the order for rearmament; after that, the introduction of conscription; after that, the militarization of the Rhineland.
>
> For more than six years now I have been engaged in building up the German armed forces. During this period more than ninety billion Reichsmarks have been spent . . . Today, ours are the best-equipped armed forces in the world, and they are superior to those of 1914 . . .

In 1933 the German Army consisted of 7 infantry divisions and 3 cavalry divisions; in 1939 it consisted of 39 divisions, of which 5 were armored and 4 fully motorized. In 1933 the German Navy consisted of 1 cruiser and 6 light cruisers; in 1939 it consisted of 2 battle cruisers, 3 pocket battleships, 8 light cruisers, 22 destroyers, and 60 submarines, of which 30 were coastwise and 30 ocean-going – and the battleships that were to be the *Bismarck* and the *Tirpitz* were under construction. In 1933 there was no German air force; in 1939 it consisted of 2,600 first-line planes.

The industrial foundation had developed concurrently. Out of the few factories permitted by the Treaty of Versailles or overlooked by the Control Commission there arose in Hitler's words "the mightiest armament industry in the world." Preparation for war was the supreme object of the nation's economy. On February 20, 1933, Dr. Hjalmar Schacht, the banker, was host to Hitler and Göring at a gathering of some twenty industrial magnates – including Gustav Krupp, who, no longer hesitant, was now an ardent Nazi – and we are given to understand that the assembled company enthusiastically greeted "the great intentions of the Führer for the rearmament period of 1933-39." Krupp was then boasting of his success in keeping Germany's war industries in being and in readiness in spite of the disarmament clauses of Versailles. Rearmament thereafter was a continuous and accelerating process limited only by the need for security. In May 1935, a few months after Hitler's conscription decree, a Law for the Defense of the Reich was passed, and Schacht was appointed Plenipotentiary for War Economy. The law, originally kept secret, was published only at the outbreak of war in 1939. It was a general sanction of total economic mobilization of the country and was described by one of the *Reichswehr* generals as "the cornerstone of our preparations for war." The name *Reichswehr* was changed to *Wehrmacht,* "the armed force and school of military education of the German people." In October 1936, Göring became Plenipotentiary of the Four-Year Plan with the main objective of putting the country on a war footing in four years. By 1937 Germany's armament program was sufficiently advanced for Hitler to be meditating military action against Czechoslovakia and Austria.

One of the most remarkable and revealing of Nazi documents to have survived is the record of a secret conference at the Chancellery in Berlin on November 5, 1937, between Hitler, Blomberg, Fritsch, Raeder, Göring, and Neurath. Hitler asked that his statements on this occasion "should be looked upon, in the case of his death, as his last will and testament." Germany could never be absolutely autarkic in raw materials and food, argued Hitler, nor could she adequately participate in the world economy overseas. The question for Germany, therefore, was the securing of greater living space, "an endeavor which at all times has been the cause of the formation of states and of the movements of nations." The question for Germany was "the greatest possible conquest at the least possible cost," and it was a question which could only be solved by way of force, whatever the risks thereof. Germany's rearmament was now virtually complete, her equipment was new, and further delay would incur the danger of obsolescence. "The aging of the Nazi movement and of its leaders," said Hitler, "the prospect of a lowering of the standard of living and a drop in the birth rate, leaves us no choice but to act. If the Führer is still living, then it will be his irrevocable decision to solve the German space problem not later than 1943-45." All considerations, argued Hitler further, pointed to the desirability of an early conquest of Czechoslovakia and Austria. The aggravation of recent tensions in the Mediterranean and the continuance of the Civil War in Spain would sufficiently distract Britain and France from intervention, and the intervention of the Soviet Union would be forestalled by the rapidity of operations – for the attack on Czechoslovakia would take place "with lightning speed" (*blitzartig schnell*). The prospects of the conquest of food for Germany, added Hitler, would be improved "if a compulsory emigration of two millions from Czechoslovakia and of one million from Austria could be carried out."

The Reactions of the Little Entente and Hungary

As might be expected, the first states to react to these events were those states of Intermediate Europe which were small and vulnerable:

Czechoslovakia, Austria, Poland, and further south, Yugoslavia and Rumania. These were the nations that would lose most and most quickly from the revival of a militant Germany bent on reversing the provisions of Versailles. Czechoslovakia and Austria had been specifically mentioned by Hitler in his conference of November 5, 1937, and no doubt they had been singled out for his prospective attentions long before that date. In Czechoslovakia, at one end of her territory, lived 3,000,000 Sudeten Germans — a full 20 per cent of her population — not in themselves a normally discontented community, but perhaps liable to become so, and presumably to be counted into Hitler's dream of a Greater Reich. At the other end of Czechoslovak territory lived 2,000,000 Slovaks who had never fully acquiesced in their somewhat unequal partnership in the Czech Republic. Czechoslovakia's position in the event of an Austro-German *Anschluss* would have amounted to encirclement and isolation. And every neighboring succession state had problems of a kind which would similarly become acute under German pressure.

As early as February 16, 1933, while Hitler had still not shown himself in his harshest colors, the Foreign Ministers of the Little Entente — Beneš of Czechoslovakia, Jevtich of Yugoslavia, and Titulescu of Rumania — then attending the Disarmament Conference at Geneva, concluded a "Pact of Organization." The three contracting parties agreed upon "the complete unification of their general policy," renewed the Little Entente in perpetuity, and set up a council of their Foreign Ministers to meet for consultation at regular intervals.

By the curious mechanics of international politics, one of Czechoslovakia's neighbors, Hungary, that perpetual waif of Europe, might almost stand to gain — at first — from a German recovery. Hungary and Germany had at least one common ground between them, a hatred of the peace treaties; and Hungary's enemies, like Germany's, were those powers that had once made, and now maintained, the "Versailles system." Hungarians had the deepest contempt for the nations of the Little Entente, some of whose peoples had once borne the Magyar yoke, and neither were the Hungarians too well disposed towards the ally of the Little Entente, France. In the circumstances it was perhaps not very surprising that Hungary and Germany should now be drawn together in a tentative *rapprochement.*

The Depression and the growth of Fascism in Hungary during the early 1930's injected another factor into the situation. The Depression had shaken the long-enjoyed security of Count Bethlen's government and, in August 1931, in the face of a failure of the harvest and a run on the banks, Bethlen had at last resigned. General Julius Gömbös, who succeeded him after a short interval, was one of the few commoners to achieve prominence in Hungarian politics. He was a bit of a fire-eater and well known for his Fascist and anti-Semitic views. He was now to show that he was an adept in all the techniques of mass politics. There was no formal German-Hungarian pact, but the interchange of state visits was significant. Gömbös visited Berlin in June 1933, at the height of Nazi disturbances then taking place in Austria. Göring and Papen visited Budapest at different times in 1934. Gömbös visited Warsaw in October 1934, an occasion of some importance in view of the German-Polish Nonaggression Pact signed earlier in that year. Thereafter it may be said that Hungary tended to revolve, though always uncomfortably, in the German orbit. In 1936 Gömbös retired on grounds of ill health, and the Hungarian premiership passed to the more moderate, but still Nazi-inclined Daranyi.

The relations of the Little Entente and Hungary represented a microcosm of European diplomacy in these years and exhibited the analogous alignments, for or against the new German Power, now to be worked out in the larger international world.

The Reaction of Poland

Poland's domestic affairs tossed and plunged along the stormy course we described in Chapter 9, but her foreign policy had managed for a time to keep a surprisingly even keel and, in more than a decade made only one important change of direction. Polish premiers came and went, but two men conducted the country's relations abroad. August Zaleski was appointed Foreign Minister after Pilsudski's coup of May 1926, and he resigned in November 1932. Joseph Beck, one of Pilsudski's "Colonels," a former fighter in his Legion, and subsequently his private secretary, succeeded Zaleski and showed an equally tenacious longevity in office. Altogether Beck survived six changes of ministry and fell at last only with the fall of Poland in 1939. We may roughly designate Zaleski's term by calling it the "French period," and the earlier part of Beck's term by calling it the "German period," of Polish foreign policy.

One of the primary assumptions of the Treaty of Versailles and of the Franco-Polish alliance of 1921 had been the permanent antagonism of the new Poland and Germany, and throughout the "French period," Polish-German relations were under a continual strain. Incidents on either side of the Polish-German frontier, incidents often puerile to anyone who did not share the passions of the participants, were constantly magnified by mutual provocation into serious crises. Patriotic associations had a way of holding demonstrations in border districts; prominent public men would make inflammatory speeches in border towns; "atrocities" would be mutually charged against German minorities in Poland or against Polish minorities in Germany. Schools attended by children of minority groups could always be depended on to provide excuses for disturbance. Zaleski and Stresemann in their meetings at Geneva were invariably at loggerheads. On every international problem Poland and Germany, as if in obedience to some blind mechanical law, would always be ranged on opposite sides. The Locarno Conference, the Allied evacuation of the Rhineland, Germany's admission to the League, the launching of Germany's first pocket battleship—these and every other imaginable question raised a stir of suspicion and animus along the bristling frontiers of the two nations. Meanwhile the essential contention between Poland and Germany in Danzig, in the Corridor, and in Upper Silesia remained unsolved and insoluble, and meanwhile the Franco-Polish alliance of 1921 formed the basis of Polish military security and the only support of Poland's unstable equilibrium.

Poland's position was certainly not enviable. She lay between Germany and the Soviet Union, who were now becoming first-class powers, and any prospective war in which they might be engaged — whether they fought against each other or as allies against a third party — must inevitably result in suffering, if not extinction, for the unhappy Polish fatherland. She had German and Russian minorities in great numbers within her territory. In the early 1930's, the Soviet Union was beginning to re-enter European diplomacy and to adopt an anti-German stand. If indeed Poland were forced to make a choice between Germany and the Soviet Union, many Poles thought she might do worse than choose Germany. At all events, Poland had a long history of Russian aggression and Russian oppression. Pilsudski, and presumably Beck, were typical and bitter Russophobes.

Hitler's seizure of power in Germany in 1933 was expected to create new stresses and strains in all the "danger spots" of Europe, and especially in Danzig, the Corridor, and Upper Silesia. The blindest optimist could not minimize the actual record of German-Polish relations since the First World War. It was true that political agitators had often been sobered by responsibility, and Hitler in power might not be the same Hitler as Hitler "in the wilderness." But that Hitler in power would reverse the entire policy of Germany toward Poland was a prodigy beyond belief. Yet reverse it he did. In 1933, after a decade of strife, Poland and Germany not only accommodated their differences, but regarded one another almost with cordiality.

Early in 1933, so the story goes, Pilsudski had invited his French allies to join him in a preventive war against Hitler — "to kill the adder in the egg." Pilsudski had taken the measure of his man. But Daladier, who was then French Premier, not only declined Pilsudski's proposals, but he went over Poland's head and enrolled France with Britain, Italy, and Germany in the Four-Power Pact of June 1933, a pact originated by Mussolini with the ostensible object of effecting a peaceful revision of the more disputable Versailles frontiers. As we shall relate in the next chapter, the pact was little more than a diplomatic gesture on the part of Mussolini in the interests of his prestige, and its eventual text was about as vague and harmless as could be. (See pp. 398-99.) But it was highly disturbing, nevertheless, to all those states in Europe, notably Poland, who owed their very existence to the Versailles settlement. To Pilsudski the offense was unpardonable. He therefore consulted his independent interests and resolved to agree with his German adversary as quickly as possible.

Hitler, for his part, was quite willing to postpone his final Polish settlement while he concentrated his main attentions elsewhere. In May 1933, he received the Polish minister in Berlin, and Beck simultaneously received the German minister in Warsaw, and both meetings were followed by pointedly pacific announcements. The improvement in German-Polish relations was immediate. Conversations between Berlin and Warsaw proceeded during the remainder of the year and a German-Polish ten-year nonaggression pact was finally signed on January 26, 1934.

The pact, when it was announced, made as much of a sensation as the Treaty of Rapallo in 1922 or the Moscow Pact of 1939. Nonaggression pacts were not uncommon, but this one represented Germany's first breach in the "Versailles Front," and it was a demonstrative revolt on the part of Poland against her "vassalage" to France. Poland, seemingly, was running with the hare and hunting with the hounds, and if Poland, a near-great power, was thus consulting her security, the weaker members of the French alliance system might find it necessary to do likewise. In the course of his speech in the *Reichstag* on January 30, 1934, the first anniversary of his chancellorship, Hitler greeted the better relationship with Poland. When he had come to power, he said, there was every prospect that Polish-German hostility would harden into a menacing political heritage, and it was his happiness to have been able to show that two nations so disposed could always find a settlement. The new nonaggression pact, by implication, was an object lesson to all the world of enlightened, peace-loving statesmanship.

The Reaction of Austria

After the settlement of her earlier revolutionary and financial troubles, Austria, it had been hoped, would settle down to a decent obscurity. Her *Anschluss* with Germany, like the Hapsburg succession, would remain only a distant possibility, unlikely ever to be realized. She would cease to be counted among the "danger spots" and "powder kegs" so beloved of scaremongering correspondents. She would even become a popular tourist resort and a center for medical and psychological research. Granted normal prosperity and normal good will she would enjoy a status as safe and as honorable as that of Denmark or Switzerland or any other of the old-established smaller nations of Europe.

But, beneath the surface, Austria's moral and economic disabilities had never been repaired. She was a small country by any standard. Yet she indulged herself in the luxury of nine provincial Diets and at least four political parties, and she was gradually relapsing into the factional obstructionism that had made havoc of her parliamentary experiment before 1914. In particular the Social Democratic *Schutzbund* and the reactionary *Heimwehr,* at one time no better than irregular bands of squadrists of the Italian pattern, had grown into veritable private armies and were dividing the country into opposing camps. (See p. 167.) Their parades – sometimes held provocatively on the same days and in the same towns – numbered as many as 15,000 to 20,000 demonstrators, and ended often enough in bloodshed. Prince von Starhemberg, that handsome gallant, was leader of the *Heimwehr,* converting his castles into secret armories and running arms with complete immunity from police interference.

Ignaz Seipel resigned from the Austrian chancellorship in April 1929, and was followed by a succession of chancellors, all of whom, rather by force of circumstances than personal inclination, supported the *Heimwehr* and gave an unmistakable Fascist tinge to Austrian politics. The Depression broke on Austria in the early 1930's. Curtius, the German Foreign Minister, proposed his ill-starred Austro-German Customs Union in 1931, and the bankruptcy of the Credit-Anstalt followed shortly afterward. (See pp.

326-28.) In 1931, in fact, not only did Austria sink into her former needy estate, but she enjoyed the doubtful distinction of being the precipitating cause of the general economic crisis in Europe. In May 1932, Dr. Engelbert Dollfuss, a Christian Social,[1] became Chancellor at the head of a cabinet strongly representative of the *Heimwehr*. Dr. Kurt von Schuschnigg was his Minister of Justice, a man who was to be his constant associate and companion in his short term of office. Seipel, in retirement, died in August of the same year.

All in all, Austria was in no condition to resist the uncompromising and subversive forces of Nazism now in full development across her border. She already had her own Nazi party and, as in Germany, it had flourished almost barometrically in accordance with the country's economic distress. In 1928 the Austrian Nazis numbered a modest 7,000; in 1930 they were already 100,000. They maintained the closest connection with their spiritual brethren in Germany. They used German propaganda, German funds, and German tactics. Hitler himself regarded them as a branch of his own party, natives of his own native land, destined eventually to return to the Greater Reich. In July 1931, Hitler appointed a loyal henchman, Theo Habicht, special "Inspector of Austria."

The pace quickened in 1932. Nazi leaders of the eminence of Göring, Goebbels, Gregor Strasser, and Hans Frank visited Austria to address meetings. An armed clash in these days between the *Schutzbund* and *Heimwehr* was no novelty, but Austrian towns and cities were now being treated to types of street demonstrations, accompanied by outrages on Social Democrats and Jews, more savage and uncontrollable than anything they had known before. In October 1932, Dollfuss appointed a Major Emil Fey Minister for Public Security. Fey was one of the original founders of the *Heimwehr,* a man who had good reasons of his own for being well acquainted with terrorist methods. In January 1933, when Hitler seized power in Germany, Nazism in Austria at once acquired the stature of a grave international issue. But the Nazis did not moderate their campaign — rather the reverse. Habicht, Inspector of Austria, gave insulting anti-Austrian broadcasts from Munich; there were propagandist leaflet raids by German aircraft over the Austrian frontier. Dollfuss's protests to Berlin were entirely ineffectual.

In March 1933, the president of the Austrian National Assembly resigned. A constitutional technicality regarding the election of a successor automatically brought the sessions of the Assembly to an end. Wilhelm Miklas, then the Austrian President, refused Dollfuss's offer of resignation, but he allowed Dollfuss to take advantage of the absence of the Assembly to govern by means of emergency decrees. As a counterblast to the Nazis, an Austrian patriotic association, the Fatherland Front, recruited mainly from the *Heimwehr,* was now formed and given the tacit blessings of the Austrian Government. Public meetings and street demonstrations by any party but the new association were forbidden. The Social Democratic *Schutzbund* was dissolved, but it continued to operate underground. The Austrian Army was raised to the full strength permitted under the peace treaty. In June 1933, Fey ordered the dissolution of the Nazi party in Austria and began to eject Nazi deputies from the provincial Diets.

In that June, Dollfuss had been in London for the World Economic Conference and had there scored a great personal triumph. The English newspapers had featured this diminutive little man — he was only four feet, eleven inches in height — as a modern St. George battling the Nazi dragon. He was called the "Pocket Chancellor" or "Millimetternich." But it cannot be said that Dollfuss's program on his return home, even under the plea of necessity, would have won him the same sympathy. Dollfuss determined to fight dictatorship with dictatorship, to cast out one devil by invoking another, and the role of Fascist sat upon him far better than the role of St. George. He was already ruling without a parliament, and he now proceeded to destroy the last vestiges of democracy in the Austrian Republic. In September 1933 a great Catholic Congress met in Vienna, and the Fatherland Front held an impressive rally simultaneously. It was a gala month, packed with historic centenaries. From the Austrian provinces 200,000 people came to attend the festivities. Dollfuss spoke in favor of a new constitution for a "German Christian Austria" on corporative lines. A few days later he reconstituted his cabinet and, Mussolini-like, he took most of the portfolios himself. Fey became his Vice-Chancellor. The *Heimwehr* under its leader, Prince von Starhemberg, joined the Fatherland Front en masse. Dollfuss tried to avoid the appearance of dependence on any one faction or party, but the ascendancy of the *Heimwehr* and of these new mayors of the palace, Fey and Starhemberg, was evident to anyone who had eyes to see.

Dollfuss was happy in diplomatic support from abroad. The powers of Europe and the Little Entente had good reasons for fearing the spread of the Nazi contagion in the Middle Danube. With the Vatican, Dollfuss, a good Catholic and a Christian Social, preserved the most filial relations. In particular, Dollfuss and the *Heimwehr* had always been cordially disposed toward Italy, in spite of Mussolini's supposed partiality for Nazism at this time. Dollfuss's visits to Rome in 1933 and his somewhat ostentatious consultations with the Duce had become a regular feature of the diplomatic scene. Starhemberg frankly modeled his squads on the Fascist Militia. Mussolini, for his part, never missed an opportunity to exert a protectorate over as much of the Middle Danube as would accept his advances. A series of agreements in March 1934, the so-called Rome Protocols, between Italy, Austria, and Hungary, was the formal recognition of his Danubian interests.

Dollfuss felt himself strong enough to try conclusions with his old foemen of the *Schutzbund* and the Social Democratic party. Fey and Starhemberg talked threateningly of "cleaning up" Austria, and dispatched their squads to hunt for caches of *Schutzbund* arms. The *Heimwehr* quietly but efficiently "suppressed" unsympathetic local governments in the provinces and climaxed its operations by hauling off into custody the Social Democratic Burgomaster of Vienna. Toward mid-February 1934, sniping and skirmishing between the *Heimwehr* and *Schutzbund* broke out in provincial capitals and towns. A veritable civil war raged in the working-class districts of Vienna. In four days' fighting, casualties amounted to some 300 dead. A great block of workers' tenements, the Karl Marx-Hof, a fine piece of modern architecture which the Social Democrats were supposed to have converted into a "fortress," was mercilessly shelled by government artillery and left in a badly damaged condition. Miklas and Dollfuss both promised clemency to the rebel Social Democrats, but the Fascistization of Austria under the strong arm of the Fatherland Front proceeded apace. On April 30, 1934, the new corporative constitution of Austria was promulgated, and the old National Assembly met for the last time to vote itself out of existence. Dollfuss's dictatorship was complete. But, in destroying Social Democracy in Austria, Dollfuss had destroyed his best ally against a Nazi invasion of his country – and a Nazi assault upon himself.

In July 1934, the Nazis plotted to dispose of Dollfuss and to set up a government in Vienna under their own leaders, Dr. Anton Rintelen and Theo Habicht. An "Austrian Legion," mostly of Austrian Nazis who had escaped into Germany – their numbers were said to be between 30,000 and 50,000 – was mobilized behind the German frontier, ready to march into Austria. The Austrian Cabinet and police had some information of the coming putsch, but in Vienna precautions were not taken at once. The fact is that the Vienna police were much infected with Nazism, several police officers were doubtless privy to the putsch, and even in Dollfuss's own entourage it had become impossible to say who were friends or foes, partisans or traitors. On the afternoon of July 25, a party of Nazis wearing the uniforms of the Austrian police and of the regular Austrian Army drove up in trucks, entered the Chancellery building, overpowered the guard, forced their way into Dollfuss's room, and shot and wounded him. Fey was "arrested," but was afterward released unhurt. Perhaps from fear of establishing communications outside the building, perhaps from outright cruelty, the Nazis refused to send for either doctor or priest to attend the stricken Dollfuss, and he died at last from loss of blood, after three hours of agony. Simultaneously another party of Nazis seized the Vienna radio station and broadcast the resignation of the government in favor of Rintelen.

By the evening of the 25th, it was clear that the putsch had failed. Schuschnigg succeeded to the chancellorship unopposed. Loyal police were busy making arrests. Martial law was proclaimed in Vienna. In Germany, at three o'clock the next morning, Hitler called Papen out of bed and bundled him off to Vienna as his special envoy "to bring about an easing of the general situation." Rintelen tried to commit suicide, but he afterwards recovered from his self-inflicted wounds and was sentenced to life imprisonment. Otto Planetta, the Nazi who had fired the actual shots at Dollfuss, was tried and condemned to death, and went to the scaffold shouting *"Heil Hitler!"* Habicht disappeared into well-deserved obscurity.

The Nazis had fully expected the putsch of July 1934 in Vienna to be one of their bloodless victories. But blood had been shed, and the putsch had not been a victory. Mussolini telegraphed the Austrian Government his condolences upon the death of a man to whom he was bound "by ties of personal friendship and common political views . . . The independence of Austria is a principle which Italy also will strenuously defend in these times of exceptional difficulty." At the end of July an Italian force of some 200,000 men was mobilized at the Brenner Pass, ready to meet an attempted German invasion of Austria. Czechs and Yugoslavs would probably have descended on Vienna in the wake of Mussolini's army.

World-wide repugnance of Nazi tactics in Austria and the military demonstration on the part of Italy had their effect. The Austrian Nazi movement suffered a sharp setback, and it was three full years before Hitler openly resumed his offensive against the land of his birth. In May 1935, in a speech in the *Reichstag,* Hitler denied that he had ever intended to interfere in Austria's internal affairs, or to bring about an annexation or *Anschluss.* In July 1936, after lengthy negotiations in which Papen was the intermediary, Austria and Germany concluded an agreement in "permanent settlement" of their mutual problems. Germany and Austria acknowledged their respective Nazi movements as the private affair of each state, an affair which neither would seek to influence, directly or indirectly. Hitler, Schuschnigg, Mussolini, and Gömbös simultaneously, in a flutter of telegraphic communiqués, advertised their full recognition of Austria's independence and the continuance of their own peaceful relations in the Middle Danube.

The Saar Plebiscite

The reactions of the Great Powers to the emerging pattern of Nazi foreign policy will occupy us for the remainder of this Part of the book. The Period of Crisis, which began in the Far East, now runs its course in the West — and in the United States. In the succeeding chapters accordingly we shall describe the affairs of the Soviet Union, Italy, Britain, France, and the United States; and the theme throughout is German rearmament. It was a time of intense diplomatic activity. Treaties and counter-treaties were signed and revoked. Barthou, the French Foreign Minister, toured Europe in 1934 in an attempt to bind an iron ring round Germany. The Soviet Union became a member of the League of Nations. The crises in Ethiopia and Spain were essentially parts of the same picture.

But, before we take up these episodes, we should describe certain events in 1935, best seen perhaps from the German point of view and most appropriately included in this chapter, namely the Saar plebiscite, the German conscription decree, the Stresa Front, and the Anglo-German Naval Agreement. All these events may have increased the existing international tensions, but none broke into actual war. The year 1935 in fact was afterwards called the "last year of peace." After 1935, the deluge! Towards the end of 1935 the Italo-Ethiopian War began, and in 1936 came the Rhineland Crisis and the Spanish Civil War. We proceed thence, step by step, to the Austrian *Anschluss,* Munich, Aibania, the Moscow Pact — and the Second World War.

The Saar plebiscite was a corollary of the Treaty of Versailles, under the terms of which the inhabitants of the territory were now due to voice their own destiny. (See p. 107.) The Saar had felt the usual repercussions of the Nazi revolution, but it had been spared the extreme war of nerves of Danzig or the Corridor. No doubt Hitler expected the plebiscite to result in a clear German victory, and he was not one to force a cheap success in a cause which mere legalities would inevitably win for him. The Saar was primarily Catholic and Social Democrat in affiliation, and Nazi proselytism had not made much headway there, but French hopes of the emergence of a decisive anti-Nazi bloc never materialized. Despite mounting excitement as the date approached and despite the Nazi campaign of open propaganda and underground terrorism, the plebiscite took place on January 13, 1935, in an orderly manner and according to plan.

The League Council delegated the arrangements for the plebiscite to a special committee, which in turn appointed executive organs in the territory itself. The local police were reinforced with some 3,300 troops – British, Italian, Dutch, and Swedish – under the command of a British general. The result of the plebiscite was an overwhelming majority for reunion with Germany. On March 1, 1935, amid hysterical rejoicing, the Saar returned to the Fatherland. Hitler paid a surprise visit the same day and toured the length of the territory. He declared afterward that he could now give his solemn pledge that Germany would make no further territorial claims on France; the frontier that had fluctuated for a thousand years had come to rest.

The German Conscription Decree

The German conscription decree of March 16, 1935, was the first overt breach with the Treaty of Versailles. Earlier moves of Nazi foreign policy, such as the German-Polish Nonaggression Pact of 1934, however disturbing, had been proper and correct. The Austrian putsch had failed, and Hitler had been able to shelve the responsibility for it on internal party quarreling in Austria in which he, in Germany, could profess no interest. The Saar plebiscite had taken place in fulfillment of the actual Versailles terms. But the conscription decree was something of an entirely different political level – though represented by Germany, of course, as an act of self-defense.

The initiative, indirectly, had been Britain's. The British people were then isolationist in mood, almost anti-French, preoccupied with their economic problems. Official Britain nevertheless was becoming much exercised by reports of German rearmament and, in particular, was awakening to the dangers and horrors of modern aerial warfare. Early in March 1935, over MacDonald's initials, the British Government issued a *Statement Relating to Defense,* which reviewed the whole position of British armaments. The paper made mention of Germany by name. Hitler affected deep offense, contracted a "diplomatic" cold, and for some days absented himself from active business. In consequence, Sir John Simon, British Foreign Secretary, postponed a prospective visit to Berlin, a visit that he was to have made in company with Anthony Eden, then Lord Privy Seal and now coming to the fore in British foreign politics. Yet the defense paper was fully confirmed a few days later by Germany's public admission that she had an air force in being and that, in fact, it had been "officially" in being since March 1, 1935. Göring himself gave an interview to that effect to a correspondent of the *Daily Mail*.

The storm now switched to France. As the result of France's reduced birth rate during the years of the First World War, the classes of young men currently due to be called up for service in the French Army were much under strength. On March 15, after a lengthy debate, the French Chamber approved a measure for prolonging the period of military service. Germany at once seized upon the measure as her cue. The following day, the German Government decreed universal compulsory military service in Germany and defined the peace footing of the German Army at 12 corps and 36 divisions or, as Hitler subsequently estimated it, at about 550,000 men. Germany, so said the accompanying proclamation of the German Government, had once disarmed herself in fulfillment of the Treaty of Versailles, but the victor nations had defaulted in their complementary obligations, and she could no longer endure a situation by which she remained a military vacuum in the midst of other heavily armed states, open to every threat and menace.

The Stresa Front

The German conscription decree did not lack for drama and positiveness and, like so many of Hitler's acts, it came at a moment which exploited to the full the disunity and preoccupation of its possible opponents. A new Franco-Soviet pact was under discussion; Italy was engaged in her Ethiopian preparations; Britain, still in an anti-French mood, almost derived satisfaction from Germany's revolt against fifteen years of French egotism and obstruction in Europe. But something had to be done. The German conscription decree could not be allowed to pass without at least some diplomatic protest. From April 11 to 14, 1935, representatives of France, Italy, and Britain — respectively Flandin and Laval, Mussolini, and MacDonald and Simon — met at the small Piedmontese village of Stresa to concert what was afterwards called the Stresa Front. Count Galeazzo Ciano, Mussolini's son-in-law and then Italian Minister of Propaganda, made his international debut. The assembled statesmen discussed Austria, they discussed an air pact, they reaffirmed their loyalty to Locarno and the League, and they "regretfully recognized that the method of unilateral repudiation adopted by the German Government had undermined public confidence in the security of a peaceful order." But what was not mentioned, though it was well known to all, was the fact that one of the parties at the Stresa Conference at that very moment was meditating in Ethiopia further unilateral breaches of his solemn covenants. The Stresa Front was soon relegated to the limbo of many another attempt to build up a united resistance to Nazi Germany.

The conscription decree, however, hastened the formation of two new alliances. On May 2, 1935, France and the Soviet Union entered into a mutual assistance pact, providing for common consultation and immediate and automatic assistance in the event of unprovoked aggression against one of themselves on the part of a third power. A fortnight later the pact was followed by a complementary and similarly worded Czech-Soviet Mutual Assistance Pact. But this time, the pact was to go into force only if France had already gone to the help of the attacked country in accordance with the Franco-Czech and the Franco-Soviet treaties. (See pp. 432 and 455.)

The Anglo-German Naval Agreement

Naval armaments since 1931, throughout the world, had been reflecting the general political deterioration. The Japanese invasion of Manchuria had been the immediate cause of President Roosevelt's decision in 1933 to build the American Navy up to the full limits allowed under the Washington Treaty of 1922. In December 1934, the Japanese Government availed itself of the privilege to denounce the Washington Treaty. In Europe, Germany's new fleet of pocket battleships had been the object of the greatest curiosity and uneasiness. The *Deutschland* had been launched in March 1931, and two similar ships had been laid down in the two following years. All three were armored cruisers of 10,000 tons each and conformed to the stipulations of the Treaty of Versailles, but they were faster and more heavily armed than any other ship of the same class in the world. The British Admiralty feared that these ingenuities of naval architecture were intended as commerce raiders. The Soviet Union, meanwhile, was said to be engaged on a vast submarine program. France and Italy were in the incipient stages of a battleship-building race between themselves.

Such were the antecedents of a new naval conference shortly to be called. Preliminary talks *à deux* were already taking place in London between representatives of the naval powers in the latter part of 1934 and early 1935. But little appeared to be transpiring beyond the ventilation of irreconciliable points of view. The Japanese wanted parity; the Americans wanted the old ratios; the British wanted more cruisers; Italy wanted to outclass France; and France wanted to outclass Italy and Germany together. In April 1935, the Germans suddenly assembled twelve submarines from parts that they had been secretly manufacturing, and in July they announced that they had already under way a naval building program which included two battle cruisers, afterward named the *Scharnhorst* and *Gneisenau,* of 26,000 tons each. Both the submarines and the battle cruisers were in flagrant violation of Versailles. It was in the midst of these talks and preparations that the Anglo-German Naval Agreement of June 18, 1935, was ineptly sprung upon the world.

Today that transaction has a noisome odor. But before we condemn it, we should in justice think ourselves back into the attitudes of mind of the time. British statesmanship in 1935 was already chasing the will-o'-the-wisp of appeasement. Hitler was Chancellor of the German Reich, but he had not yet shown himself for what he was. Political courtesies, if nothing else, demanded that his professions should be taken at their face value, especially when, by repeated assurances, he had given out that he wanted nothing so much as the trust and friendship of England and that he would never allow Germany to repeat the former naval follies of Kaiser William II. In the

British view it was impossible to expect a proud and vigorous nation like Germany to remain in a state of perpetual inferiority, and it was better to meet her inferiority halfway – or, in this case, one-third of the way – than to goad her, as France had always done, by exasperating and ineffective opposition. There also seemed to be good reasons at this time for expecting some kind of Western air pact. Of all the powers, a Germany in the very midst of Europe stood to lose most from the depredations of modern bomber warfare and could surely be counted upon to show an even greater interest in air limitation than a Britain situated in the comparative immunity of her island. In 1935 the British and German peoples were enjoying better relations than at any other time during the Nazi regime. British tourists to Germany in that year and especially in 1936, the year of the Olympic Games in Berlin, were returning home with appreciative stories of the kindness and hospitality they had met. Organizations of veterans and students, youth groups, and football teams in the two countries were exchanging visits, and even the Germans must sometimes have been deceived by the signs.

Joachim von Ribbentrop had come to England in midsummer of 1935. He was then German Minister Plenipotentiary-at-Large and perhaps one of the least attractive members of Hitler's entourage. He had been a wine merchant, enjoyed good social connections in his own country, and was well traveled abroad, notably in Canada. He had entered Nazi politics as an intermediary between Papen and Hitler in the critical days of 1932, and he had subsequently gained Hitler's confidence as an international expert and interpreter of the British point of view. In this last capacity he had built up in Berlin a virtual foreign ministry of his own. As a man pretending to gentlemanly attainments and displaying a veneer of cosmopolitanism, Ribbentrop, for all the rudeness incumbent on him as a good Nazi, scored a great personal success in the London of 1935. He was lavishly entertained, and entertained lavishly in return. He moved freely in certain rather "pro-German" and extreme Tory circles in England, and quite misunderstood their mood. Finally he persuaded the British Government to conclude a naval agreement permitting Germany a surface tonnage of 35 per cent of the British and a submarine tonnage of 100 per cent.

The Anglo-German Naval Agreement, as we now know, merely legalized Germany's naval program as already projected at the time, and doubtless she intended to observe it only until that program was completed. But far worse was the effect of the agreement on the Continent. France was, if anything, more shocked by the publication of its terms than by the German conscription decree itself. Perfidious Albion, it would appear, was condoning Germany's rearmament and aiding and abetting her in new breaches of Versailles. The Stresa Front, which France, Italy, and Britain had only just established, was shattered utterly. How indeed was the concert of security to be built up, how indeed was the harmony of Locarno and the League to be preserved, if Britain, one of the chief supporters thereof, went behind the backs of her companions to negotiate treaties with the common enemy?

Even this was not the end. In the design of any of her new battleships under the agreement, Germany would have the further advantage of not being bound by the former 35,000-ton limit of the Washington Conference, to which, of course, she had never been a party. The two battleships, the *Bismarck* and the *Tirpitz,* which she now proceeded to lay down, were designed with a displacement of over 45,000 tons and, when completed, they would outclass any other vessel afloat. In other words, Germany, by the innocent ruse of building up to a third of the British tonnage, would set the entire naval world by the ears and start off a new armament race in superbattleships.

In the resulting outcry, the proposed Western air pact, on which Britain had so much set her heart, failed. Conversations upon such a pact were largely kept from the public ear, but there appears to have been no want of pressure or persistence about them. Chancelleries and embassies in London, Paris, and Berlin fairly hummed with proposals. Baldwin and Simon, then British Prime Minister and Foreign Secretary, were deeply engaged in the conversations. But Germany and France as usual were at odds. Germany claimed that the new Franco-Soviet Mutual Assistance Pact forced her to take into account the eventuality of an aerial war on two fronts. France claimed that no air pact would be of the slightest military value unless it could be reinforced by a new automatic assistance pact between herself and Britain. The prospects of the aerial terror were perhaps much exaggerated beyond what did actually happen in 1940. Aerial warfare, as then imagined, could burst open in the hour, and Göring's Luftwaffe could lay all Paris in ashes, while France's own delegates at Geneva sat round a table defining the aggressor. But Britain claimed that France had pacts enough – that she was veritably buried in pacts – and that she still seemed neither satisfied nor grateful.

The naval conference, for which the foregoing exchanges were the preparation, met in London in 1935. It was the last of the series of naval conferences that had begun so hopefully at Washington in 1921. It was attended by delegates of the United States, Britain, Japan, France, and Italy. The United States and Britain refused to accept the Japanese proposals for a "common upper limit," and the Japanese delegates withdrew from the Conference. At the end of February 1936, the conference was still sitting, but the Italian delegates, citing the Mediterranean repercussions of the Italo-Ethiopian War, now also withdrew. The United States, Britain, and France were therefore left to salvage what they could from the wreckage of the discussions. On March 25, 1936, they signed a Three-Power Naval Treaty which, having defined certain qualitative limitations, permitted any signatory to exceed these limitations if it felt itself being outclassed or outbuilt by a nonsignatory power.

The Rhineland Crisis

At the beginning of 1936, rumors were circulating that Germany would soon seek to alter by force of arms the demilitarized status that Versailles and Locarno had imposed upon the Rhineland, and the rumors were persistent enough to call for emphatic denials from the Führer himself. (See pp. 107 and 123.)

The Franco-Soviet Mutual Assistance Pact, as we noted above, had been signed the previous May but, curiously enough, Pierre Laval, now French Premier, had shown no great anxiety to complete its ratification. Laval may have been delaying final action in deference to anti-Communist feeling in France, or perhaps he was already showing signs of his subsequent pro-Nazi predilections. He was apt at this time to keep Litvinov fretting in his antechambers while he dallied with Mussolini and Hitler. In January 1936, however, Sarraut succeeded Laval, and Flandin, the new Foreign Minister, laid the much abused treaty before the Chamber. On February 27, after an unhurried but not too acrimonious debate, it was duly passed by the Chamber by a large majority and passed to the Senate.

But Germany did not wait for the outcome of this leisurely legislation. If it was the part of a parliament to deliberate, it was the part of a dictatorship to act. In Hitler's professed view the entire Franco-Soviet *rapprochement* violated the Locarno Pact and introduced into Europe a new alignment of power, against which her elementary rights demanded that Germany protect herself. On March 1, 1936, Hitler resolved on the seizure of the Rhineland, and the necessary orders were prepared by General von Blomberg next day. The chiefs of the *Wehrmacht* to a man were apprehensive of the impending adventure. Of the 36 divisions planned under the recent conscription decree only 20 were so far organized; France, Poland, and Czechoslovakia had 90 and could mobilize another 100 in the event of war – to say nothing of their new ally, the Soviet Union. But Hitler derided his generals' pusillanimity, and the orders went out. On the morning of March 7, 1936, at dawn, units of the German Army to the probable strength of 35,000 men began their march into the Rhineland and up to the French borders beyond. Everywhere they were received by the populace with flags, flowers, and jubilation. Yet it is fairly certain that German officers in the operation would have given orders to retire at once had they encountered French resistance.

On the same March 7, Hitler announced in the *Reichstag* that he had restored "the full and unrestricted sovereignty of Germany in the demilitarized zone of the Rhineland." He also announced new *Reichstag* elections in order that the German people might confirm "all that he and his colleagues had done." Simultaneously, the German Foreign Minister, Neurath, summoned a meeting in Berlin of the ambassadors of the Locarno Powers – France, Belgium, Italy, and Britain – announced the "symbolic" occupation of the Rhineland by "token" forces, proposed twenty-five-year nonaggression pacts both in the West and in the East, proposed an air pact, and even expressed Germany's willingness to re-enter the League of Nations.

The French Government spent these days of the Rhineland crisis in an agony of impotence and humiliation. Sarraut's ministry was then in office. It was admittedly a stopgap till impending elections. Sarraut's first bold impulse, nevertheless, had been to order partial mobilization, and some specialized units of the French Army were moved up to the Maginot Line.

The general staffs of the French Army, Navy, and Air Force waited expectantly for their orders. Representatives of the Soviet Union, Czechoslovakia, and Yugoslavia assured Sarraut of their fullest support under the terms of their several treaties. On March 8, the French Government dispatched to Geneva a veritable catalogue of breaches of her obligations which Germany by her action in the Rhineland had committed and called for an early meeting of the League Council. Sarraut broadcast to the French nation in bitter condemnation of Hitler's *"coup brutal."*

France, however, could hardly have acted without the other Locarno Powers, particularly Britain and Italy. But Italy, at the moment, was triumphantly winding up her Ethiopian campaign and was glad of a crisis that embarrassed the powers that recently had dared to pass sanctions upon her. The British attitude was no more than "correct." Anthony Eden, who had recently become British Foreign Secretary, made it plain to the German ambassador in London that the effect of Germany's repudiation of the Locarno Pact, a treaty "freely negotiated and freely signed," must inevitably be "deplorable." But the British people as a whole lost no sleep and shed no tears over the Rhineland. Hitler had some "right" on his side — after all, he was only going "into his own back garden." Loungers in the clubs and bars of London talked with evident relish at the discomfiture of France and at the retribution she was now reaping for her shortsighted and egotistical policies in Europe.

The four Locarno Powers, France, Belgium, Italy, and Britain, met in Paris on March 12, 1936. Flandin, the French Foreign Minister, demanded the withdrawal of the German troops from the Rhineland, he demanded sanctions, he demanded reparations, he demanded guarantees, he demanded that the question of the compatibility of the Franco-Soviet Mutual Assistance Pact with Locarno should be submitted to the World Court. He threatened France's resignation from the League; he hinted at an entire reorientation of France's foreign policy — presumably toward an accommodation with Germany. The meeting of the Locarno Powers was resumed in London. There too the League Council assembled and passed a resolution declaring Germany to be guilty of breaches of Versailles and Locarno. Under Eden's insistence, consultations were initiated between the French, Belgian, and British general staffs. But there still ensued no overt action against the culprit. Hitler, at a stroke, had transformed the military situation in Western Europe without so much as having a shot fired to oppose him.

On March 29, 1936, with prayers, songs, and the pealing of bells, the promised *Reichstag* elections took place. Ninety-nine per cent of the German electorate voted, and of that number nearly all voted for the Nazi party ticket. The crisis was over, and there were soon other distractions. On May 9, Mussolini, from his balcony in Rome, announced the victorious termination of the Italo-Ethiopian War; and in July the Spanish Civil War broke out. The Rhineland was already relegated to a second place in public interest. In November of the year, Hitler announced the resumption of German sovereignty over the Kiel Canal and over the German rivers internationalized under the Treaty of Versailles. (See p. 108.)

One consequence of the Rhineland crisis was the isolationism of Belgium. King Leopold had already been moving tentatively in that direction. In October 1936, he made a formal statement to his cabinet, pointed to the rearmament of the Great Powers and to the deterioration of international good faith, and argued that no defensive agreement would save Belgium in a modern war and that therefore she must follow an exclusively "Belgian policy." Leopold visited London in March 1937, when it was announced that the British and French Governments had released Belgium from her commitments under the Locarno Pact. The Belgian action may have been politically excusable, but, as we shall see, it entirely disjointed the French strategic plan. (See pp. 261-62 and 509-10.)

The Reactions in the Balkans and Turkey

Immediate reactions in the Balkans to events north of the Danube had been to mobilize sentiment for greater Balkan unity. Conferences between sympathetic Balkan personalities had already been held annually since 1930 and had been devoted to economic and cultural problems of common interest, and it had been hoped that these conferences might have led in time to closer political cooperation. The Little Entente's Pact of Organization in February 1933 offered an obvious example which the Balkan states might quickly reproduce to their advantage. In September 1933, a ten-year nonaggression pact was signed by the two hitherto irreconcilables, Greece and Turkey, and was shortly followed by a pact of friendship between Yugoslavia and Turkey. By the end of 1933, with these encouraging precedents, a Balkan Pact had become very much a possibility, and even that perpetual Balkan outcast, Bulgaria, was being drawn toward it.

On February 9, 1934, at Athens the Balkan Pact was duly signed by representatives of Greece, Yugoslavia, Rumania, and Turkey. The pact constituted a general undertaking "to contribute to the consolidation of peace" and to consult on measures to be taken in contingencies affecting Balkan security. At a better time the pact might have marked the beginnings of a genuine unification in an area of historic conflicts. But, by 1934, both internal and external developments in the Balkans had already made it ineffective. The Depression and Nazidom were making their presence felt.

By 1934, in fact, every one of the Balkan states was drifting deeper into dictatorship – usually a combination of rule by the legitimate monarch and a favorite premier – and the government party, often inclined to Fascism, if not to Nazism, found itself suppressing a liberal opposition of French or British sympathies. In Yugoslavia, for instance, after the assassination of King Alexander in October 1934, a regency under Prince Paul governed in the name of the young King Peter. (See p. 175.) But the real power behind the throne was the Premier, Dr. Milan Stoyadinovich and his Yugoslav Radical Union, originally a coalition of convenience between Orthodox Serb Radicals, Catholic Slovenes, and Bosnian Moslems. The nationalist Croat opposition was still active under the leadership of Dr. Vlasko

Machek and his Agrarian Democratic party. But Stoyadinovich was soon representing pro-Axis sentiment in the country, and Machek anti-Axis sentiment. Eventually the opposition proved too strong for Stoyadinovich, and, in February 1939, he resigned. In August 1939, after complicated negotiations, an agreement was reached by which "Croatia" under a governor of its own obtained a degree of cultural and economic autonomy, and Yugoslavia was reorganized on a federal basis. Dragisa Cvetkovich, a Serb, formerly Stoyadinovich's Minister of Social Affairs, was now Premier, and Machek Vice-Premier. Yugoslavia seemed to have achieved a long-desired ethnic unity, but she had done so at the cost of all her former freedoms.

In Bulgaria, in 1935, the army had voluntarily retired from the unequal fight against the country's political and economic difficulties, leaving King Boris to rule with George Kiosseivanov, a close friend, as premier. (See p. 177.) Meanwhile a Nazi type of movement grew up under the leadership of a certain Professor Tsankov, the original instigator of the right-wing revolt against Stambulisky and the Peasant party in 1923. King Boris himself was halfheartedly pro-German, or at least anti-Little Entente, while the great mass of the Bulgarian people clung inarticulately to their traditional and sentimental attachment to Slavic Russia.

In Rumania, the dictatorial process matured more slowly. In the early 1930's, the Liberals were still in power, and Carol was once more King. (See p. 176.) Rumania's foreign relations were in the hands of her distinguished Foreign Minister Nicholas Titulescu, one of the chief negotiators of the Balkan Pact of 1934. But Rumania at the time already had her version of Fascist squadrism in the Iron Guard, which had claimed its first victim in December 1933, when the Liberal Premier, Ion Duca, had been assassinated, and which was soon identified with such reactionary and anti-Semitic groups as Octavian Goga's National Christian party. At the end of 1937, King Carol unexpectedly appointed Goga Premier, and Goga in a forty-five day orgy of anti-Semitic legislation thoroughly discredited himself and his party, both at home and abroad. Goga's resulting unpopularity gave the King his chance. In spite of violent opposition from the Iron Guard, King Carol dissolved parliament, suspended the existing constitution, suppressed all political parties, and then, on February 10, 1938, proclaimed a royal dictatorship. He created a single party, the Front of National Rebirth, effectively supported by a National Guard.

In Greece, King George, upon his restoration to the throne in 1935, proclaimed a general amnesty and began ruling constitutionally. But he was far from fortunate. The "Brain Trust," or government of experts, which he had caused to be formed, was not popular in the country, and his efforts were further jeopardized by the sudden deaths of several public men in Greece on whose help and counsel he had counted, including General Kondylis — and the veteran Venizelos, then in Paris. Amid an epidemic of strikes and risings it was natural that he should look for the usual contemporary remedy — a strong man. In August 1936, General Metaxas, his Premier, alleging the danger of a Communist revolution, carried out a *coup d'état* and established a personal dictatorship. Metaxas was a distinguished staff officer and strategist who had received his military education in Germany. He now proceeded to organize Greece as a totalitarian, corporative state. He suppressed public liberties but embarked upon an extensive program of public works and social legislation, relying upon the army to support his every measure. He made an effort to retain the good will of Britain, France, and Turkey, but his growing economic and psychological dependence on Germany was soon too obvious to be denied.

By these events the Balkans were conveniently softened up for the Nazi economic assault. The process was started in 1936, when Schacht toured the Balkan capitals and, in a series of barter agreements, put in hand all those exchange techniques we have described. (See pp. 366-67.) In the midst of the Depression, with their limited choice of markets, Balkan statesmen were helpless. Clearly the Balkans presented Germany with an area, quick of access, rich in raw materials, free from any future naval blockade, and, should the necessity arise, easy to dominate militarily. The Balkans in fact in these years served as the experimental ground for Nazi economic exploitation and anticipated many of the features that were later to distinguish Hitler's New Order in Europe.

Turkey turned instinctively to Britain and France as soon as she too began to feel Nazi pressures in the Balkans. When she "requested" the signatories of the Treaty of Lausanne to consider a revision of the status of the Straits, both Britain and France responded favorably. By the Montreux Convention of July 1936, Turkey once again became "Guardian of the Straits" and was allowed to refortify them. Thereafter British influence increased rapidly at Ankara. On May 12, 1939, an Anglo-Turkish mutual assistance pact was signed against possible aggression in the Eastern Mediterranean.

A similar Turkish agreement with France was delayed until the settlement of the old dispute over the Alexandretta zone, otherwise known as the Sanjak of Antioch and Alexandretta. This territory was part of France's Syrian mandate, but had been administered separately in deference to its considerable Turkish population. During 1937 and 1938, Turkey and France entered into negotiations for the removal of this potential Alsace-Lorraine of the Near East. By successive steps, the Sanjak of Antioch and Alexandretta became first the autonomous Republic of Hatay, and then, in July 1939, it was finally annexed by Turkey and metamorphosed into the sixty-third vilayet of the Turkish Republic. On June 23, 1939, the conclusion of the process had already been anticipated by the signature of a special Franco-Turkish agreement, and the Hatay agreement was supplemented by specific Turkish guarantees to Syria and by a general Franco-Turkish mutual assistance pact. (See pp. 494-95.)

21. ITALY: FASCIST FOREIGN POLICY AND THE ITALO-ETHIOPIAN WAR

The Four-Power Pact of 1933

The immediate reaction in Italy to German Nazism had been one of pronounced sympathy. She could not but patronize a movement that appeared to have so decided an affinity with Fascism. Moreover, memories of Fiume and Corfu predisposed her against the Western Powers and especially against her rival in the Mediterranean, France. Italy's first diplomatic move, the Four-Power Pact of 1933, however, seemed innocuous enough.

The pact is almost forgotten now. In its day it purported to find a new basis for stability in a Europe that was being suddenly thrown into flux and confusion. It started as a characteristically Mussolinian maneuver to assert Italian prestige, and it was also a good example of that mildly avuncular relationship which the Fascist Duce at this time bore toward the Nazi Führer. Even before 1933, Mussolini had often expressed his belief that if only the Great Powers of Europe — France, Italy, Germany, and Britain — could be induced to "collaborate," their peace would be secure. These Powers acting together could effect with safety all those treaty revisions and those frontier and colonial rectifications which justice and common sense demanded. So stated and so aimed, a Four-Power Pact would be a simple and commendable transaction. It would grant Italy a cherished status within the Big Four of her world, and it would recognize the "equality" of Germany. But correspondingly it offered a covert challenge to France's hegemony in Europe and to the status of France's allies. Poland and the Little Entente were quick to realize that the new Concert of Mussolini would put them outside the Great-Power pale and that they would probably be the first victims of any treaty revisions which the pact meditated. Under pressure from France, therefore, the pact's terms were so diluted that in the end the whole affair amounted to little more than a pious diplomatic gesture. But the original offense to France's allies still rankled nevertheless. Pilsudski in high dudgeon, as we saw in the last chapter, went so far as to compound his nonaggression pact of January 1934 with Germany. (See pp. 382-83.)

For MacDonald, the British Prime Minister, the pact was a genuine attempt to relieve some of the acknowledged harshnesses of Versailles, and, as such, it could be interpreted as the first act in Britain's policy of "appeasement." Accordingly, on June 7, 1933, the Four-Power Pact between France, Italy, Germany, and Britain was initialed in Rome.

Meanwhile Mussolini continued to cultivate his German friendship. Almost a year to a day after the conclusion of the Four-Power Pact, between June 14 and 16, 1934, in carnival atmosphere in Venice, he and Hitler met for the first time. "In these hours which we spent together," Mussolini announced afterward, "our spirits were in intimate communion." But the Venetian idyl was the end of the first phase of Mussolini's pro-Nazi policy. June 30, 1934, was the "Night of the Long Knives" in Germany, and on July 25 Dollfuss was killed in Vienna by Nazi troopers. These events were violent enough to cure any hope or wish Mussolini might till then have cherished that Nazism would develop in filial imitation of Italian Fascism. At the end of July he mobilized his divisions on the Brenner Pass, and the world was treated to the spectacle of militant, filibustering Italy belatedly facing up to the new Ghibelline menace from the North and joining in the common scramble to revise her former enmities and friendships. One result was the Franco-Italian Agreement of January 1935, which will be described later in this chapter.

Then on December 5, 1934, an incident occurred at Walwal, an obscure native settlement on the frontier between Italian Somaliland and Ethiopia, and the first shots were exchanged in the Italo-Ethiopian War.

Ethiopia

Ethiopia, or Abyssinia, was an inland empire of northeastern Africa consisting of some 350,000 square miles of mountainous plateau, riven by deep gorges and gullies, generally covered with thick and scrubby forest, and relieved here and there by sparse grasslands. Its inhabitants were an ancient people, numbering perhaps 6,000,000, of Semitic and Negroid extraction. A few were Moslems, but most of them were Christians of the Coptic Church, and they supported themselves by agriculture and stock raising. Their political structure was primitively feudal. Their territory was divided among a number of provincial chiefs, or rases, who enjoyed varying degrees of independence of, or dependence on, whatever central government claimed the hegemony at the moment, and such political history as Ethiopia may be said to have had consisted of the almost perpetual warfare of these rases with one another.

The extreme inaccessibility of the country had long preserved it, like another Tibet, in isolation from the outside world, an isolation disturbed only by an occasional explorer, trader, or missionary. The main currents of Moslem conquest and European imperialism alike had passed it by, and until the Italian campaign of 1935 and the British campaign of 1940-41, it had generally been regarded as impracticable terrain for large-scale military operations. The construction of the Suez Canal in 1869, however, began indirectly to draw the country into the vortex of contending powers. In 1889 Italian aid enabled Menelik, Negus of Shoa, to usurp the Ethiopian throne, and Ethiopia virtually passed into Italy's "sphere of influence." In 1896, on the famous field of Adua, the same Menelik decisively repulsed an attempted invasion of his territories by an Italian army from Eritrea. During the first decade of the new century, the French built a railroad from their Red Sea colony at Jibuti and opened up the central areas of the country to commercial enterprise. Thereafter, French, British, Italians, Germans, Dutch, and Americans – and even Japanese – began to creep in. Foreign consulates and business houses were established. But it may still be said that, till 1918, Ethiopia continued to be a mysterious semimedieval fastness, a rugged, rocky highland beyond the swirl and eddy of world events.

Revolutionary changes in Ethiopia's ancient isolation were introduced by a new monarch, Ras Tafari Makonnen, son of a nephew of Menelik, and a protégé of France and Britain. He became regent in 1916 and soon proved to be a model "Westernizing" ruler. He was crowned Emperor Haile Selassie I in 1930. He styled himself the Lion of Judah and the King of the Kings, and he claimed descent from Solomon and the Queen of Sheba. In a series of sanguinary struggles he disciplined the feudal rases and established an unchallenged authority throughout his Empire. He built roads and schools and hospitals. He sent promising Ethiopian youths to complete their education in Europe and America. He granted concessions likely to promote trade and intercourse. He invited foreign advisers, experts, and technicians to his court. He gave his capital at Addis Ababa more and more the aspect of a modern commercial city. He introduced new laws for the abolition of Ethiopia's national vice, the slave trade. He even called together a parliament. The Powers of Europe at an early date recognized him for what he was when, in 1923, Ethiopia became a member state of the League of Nations. In 1928 Ethiopia and Italy signed a Treaty of Friendship and Arbitration.

In the military sphere alone the Emperor's revolutionary enterprises lagged. The Ethiopian was good fighting material, could he have been given modern weapons and training. But the imperial finances discouraged any too thoroughgoing military program, and various international treaties – though they were not always observed – restricted the importation of arms. More serious still, the old feudal constitution of the Empire put insuperable obstacles in the way of a unified command. When therefore, in 1935, the test of war came, there existed an "Imperial Guard," armed with old German rifles, some machine guns, and some pieces of light artillery, but the vast mass of the Emperor's dusky warriors were still led by semi-independent rases, were arrayed in light cotton *shammas,* were armed with little better than matchlock rifles, and employed tactics little more advanced than that of Dervishes.

NORTHEAST AFRICA, 1934

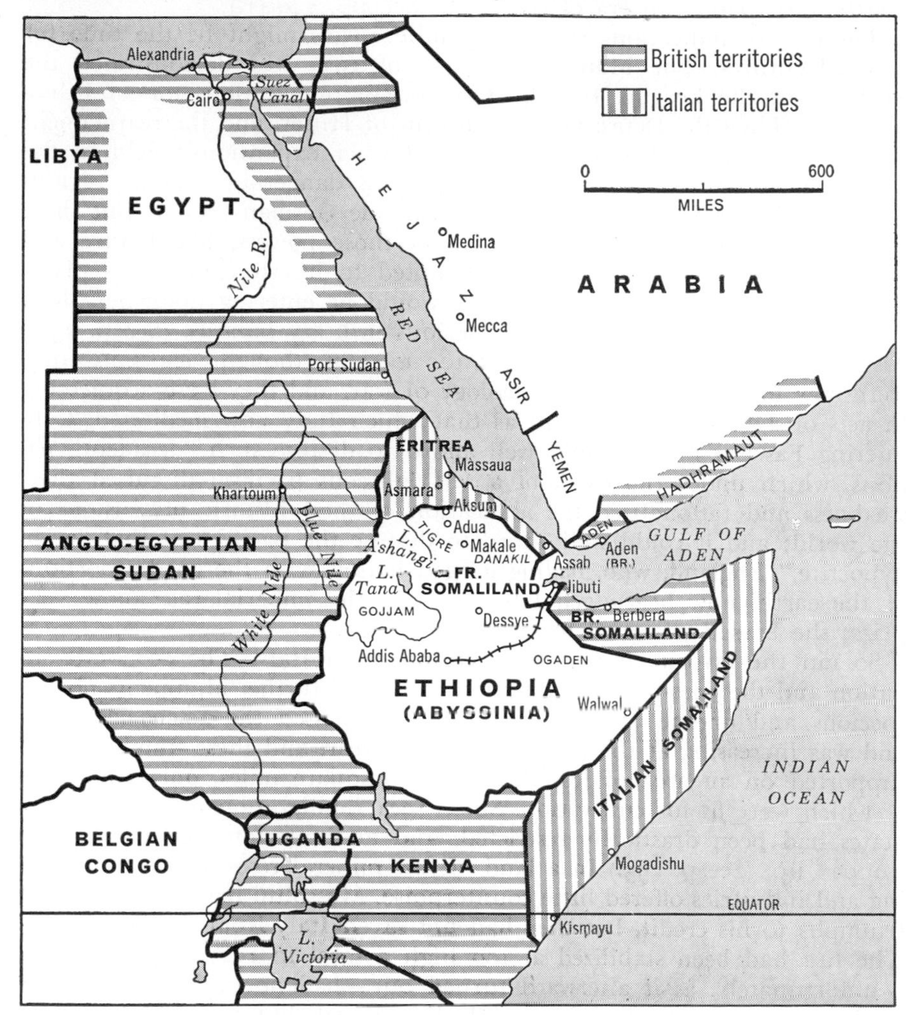

Fascist Imperialism

Italy now regarded herself as an expanding power. Her seizures and penetrations in Eritrea, Somaliland, and Libya between 1885 and 1912 had given her the beginnings of a colonial empire overseas. The First World War had been for her another step, a mightier effort, a severer trial – and a painful setback – in the same process. The Peace Conference in 1919 had mulcted her perfidiously – so she believed, and so later Fascist propaganda claimed – of the acquisitions in Africa which her Allies had led her to expect. But, under the guise of Fascism, she had resumed the old imperial drive thereafter. She had put behind her the shoddy, sordid relapse of her postwar socialism. The Corfu episode in 1923 had represented, in her eyes, the restless striving and straining of a people impatiently anticipating an era of conquest. (See pp. 240-41.)

There were indications that the middle 1930's might be the time for new adventures. The Manchurian crisis of 1931 had demonstrated the weakness of the League. In 1932 Italy began preparations for an Ethiopian war. Then the Depression, the advent of Hitler, and the rearmament of Germany turned her away from her former expansionist field in the Middle Danube and the Balkans toward less dangerous colonial regions which would be free from the risk of possible German rivalry. But these same events would also serve to distract those powers, like France and Britain, which otherwise might be tempted to interfere in Italy's plans. France in the middle 1930's moreover would be entering upon her "lean years" and must at all costs avoid serious military hazards. (See p. 456.) Also France and Britain, it was all too evident, though victors in 1918, were now forsaking the heroic ideology of war, and they were acquiescing in acts of aggression as flagrant as that which Italy now meditated. Conquering Fascism indeed could well afford to despise such "decadent" nations, which under the cloak of a self-righteous pacifism disguised their weakness and rationalized the abdication of their historic pretensions in the world; and it could well afford to despise the pacifism of that "arch-hypocrite," England, who, having gorged herself with the goodly portions of the earth, now begrudged latecomers in the imperial race those very prizes she herself possessed to satiety.

So ran the favorite imperialistic argument in Italy. The economic situation and the pressure of population presented further arguments no less specious and urgent. Italy's population had passed the 40,000,000 mark and was increasing at the rate of 400,000 a year, and these numbers were supported on an area of less than 120,000 square miles, only two-thirds of which were fit for cultivation. Since 1921 immigration into the United States had been drastically restricted, and an important relief had been stopped up. (See p. 295.) In a land of few mineral resources, manufacturing and industries offered little counterpoise. Mussolini had many domestic triumphs to his credit, but they had not saved Italy from the Depression. The lira had been stabilized at too high a level in 1927, and Mussolini – unfortunately, as it afterward turned out – had not only sworn to defend its value to the last drop of Italian blood, but had had his awful oath engraved on stone for all the world to see. In the early 1930's the Italian budget showed a habitual deficit; the tourist trade, Peter's pence, and remittances from emigrants to the Americas had all been falling off. All the indices were pointing to an early economic collapse unless some extraneous cure or distraction could be found.

Ethiopia therefore promised the fulfillment of a high ambition and the solution of many present difficulties. It lay between Eritrea and Somaliland, territories already in Italian possession, territories which its conquest could link into a single, worthy empire. Moreover, war against Ethiopia would not be a war against a brother European state – albeit Ethiopia was a member of the League. It would be a war against a primitive country that had given ample proofs of its barbarism and its incompetence in self-government. Italian propaganda at this time was always ready with gruesome statistics of the slave trade in Ethiopia or of the bloody repressions of the rases. Italy, it was argued, was manifestly entitled to carry the lights of civilization, even by force of arms, into this last stronghold of African darkness, to wipe out those standing insults to the dominance of the white man, insults of which the Battle of Adua in 1896 still remained a painful memory, and to extend in any way possible the blessings of the new Fascist order.

The Reactions of Britain and France

But, for the Western Powers, especially Britain, the issues were not so convincing. There were two views in Britain, the official view and the popular view, and to that duality is attributable the tragic contradictions of the British attitude when the crisis broke. In the official view, an Italian conquest of Ethiopia would place a potentially hostile power athwart British communications with the East and might hand over to that power the control of the headwaters of the Blue Nile and therewith the irrigation system of Egypt. But, even so, the conquest was not of importance comparable to more dangerous developments in other parts of the world, notably in Germany and the Far East. In the official view, therefore, opposition to Mussolini in Ethiopia offered risks which, on balance, were not worth taking.

In the popular view in Britain, the impending war was not to be judged in colonial or territorial terms. It was a test case, more significant – and nearer home – than the recent crisis in Manchuria, of the whole ideology of the interwar era. As one of the victors of 1918, the British people felt that they were in a position to take stock of the poor moral and material profits of war, and, if Italians thought otherwise, then it only went to show, as the British people sometimes suspected, that Italy's participation in the First World War had never been a very serious national experience. Were all the ideals of peace, for which the British people had fought and bled, to be so crudely menaced by a nation which, for all its strutting and bragging, was so wanting in real fighting quality? Opinion in the British Dominions was similar. South Africa, particularly, regarded the crisis as an African affair. Far from sympathizing with their fellow whites in a war against barbarian blacks, South Africans sympathized with fellow Africans battling for their independence against this latest upsurge of European imperialism.

It was enough to note the breaches in her obligations, once freely and solemnly given, which Italy was about to commit – breaches notably of the Gas Protocol of 1925, the Italo-Ethiopian Treaty of 1928, the Pact of Paris of 1928, to say nothing of the Covenant of the League of Nations – an impressive catalogue of derelictions, however big or little, or near or far, the occasion.

France, for her part, was distracted by the return of the German menace. Since the German-Polish Nonaggression Pact, France's system of alliances across Europe, once built on the presupposition of her military superiority, had been badly shaken. A strong Foreign Minister, Barthou, had been assassinated in 1934 and had been succeeded by that somewhat unknown quantity, Laval. Britain had lately struck out on a policy of her own, a policy that had reached its most deplorable expression in the recent Anglo-German Naval Agreement. The growth of the Fascist "Leagues" in France also helped to tie the hands of any French government in its attitude towards Italy.

Pierre Laval had become French Foreign Minister in October 1934 and Premier in June 1935. His policy was to respond to the pro-Gallic advances, which, since the death of Dollfuss in Austria, Mussolini had been making. Laval was consistently anti-British, anti-Soviet, and pro-Italian; his purpose presumably was to draw Italy into the French alliance system. He was one of the most artistic negotiators of the day, a man of infinite resource – and surprisingly, of very real charm – and, it must be said, he enjoyed from the first a strong personal liking for Mussolini, which Mussolini evidently reciprocated.

In the early days of 1935, Laval visited Rome and there negotiated a thoroughgoing Franco-Italian Agreement. The whole field of French and Italian relations was covered, it would seem, greatly to the advantage of France. Italy's territorial acquisitions, under which she renounced all further claims on France in respect to African colonies, comprised large slices of about as arid a stretch of sand and rock as is to be found in North Africa, plus some thirteen miles of strategically useful coast line along the Strait of Bab el Mandeb, opposite the British base at Aden. In addition, Italy undertook progressively to liquidate her interests in Tunisia, which hitherto she had always eyed so jealously. And all this for what? The Franco-Italian Agreement, as far as we know, contained no secret clauses. But Mussolini's preparations for his Ethiopian war were then well advanced, and there must have been a tacit understanding between himself and Laval that, if and when the war broke out, France would remain a disinterested spectator.

The Walwal Incident and the League of Nations

Italo-Ethiopian relations had been deteriorating ever since the signing of the Treaty of Friendship of 1928 – and deteriorating, it seemed, of set purpose. Italy piled up a formidable list of grievances. Italian commercial agents and consular officials had suffered various "affronts"; Ethiopia was being infiltrated by foreign experts and technicians, among whom Italians were conspicuous by their absence. Meanwhile disaffected rases were rumored to have been generously plied with Italian promises and money. Mussolini was evidently trying to provoke a rebellion in the country as a pretext for armed intervention. Political and military preparation on the part of Italy was well advanced when, on December 5, 1934, at Walwal, 500 native Italian troops clashed with 1,500 Ethiopian warriors with some loss of life to both sides.

Certainly Walwal might seem a poor enough excuse for a war. It lay within a no man's land of dreary, barren "camel-scrub desert" at a point where the border between Ethiopia and Italian Somaliland had never been properly demarcated. But the incident led to a brisk exchange of notes between the Italian and Ethiopian governments which discovered considerable indignation and obstinacy on both sides, and when, at the turn of the year, the two governments reported their respective versions to the League of Nations, the chances of a peaceful settlement were already remote.

From Mussolini's point of view, the incident had been well timed. The early weeks of the crisis had coincided with Laval's visit to Rome and the negotiation of the Franco-Italian Agreement. Its subsequent repercussions chimed with the German conscription decree and the formation of the Stresa Front. (See pp. 388-90.) The League Council postponed action while Italy and Ethiopia went through the form of negotiations "out of court." But Mussolini, far from meditating a pacific settlement, was busy reviewing his troops, speeding them on their departure for East Africa, and assuring them that they were about to embark on a war for the greater glory of the Italian Empire.

The crisis was discussed at last in the League Council in September 1935. Baron Aloisi, for Italy, presented a voluminous memorandum arraigning the backwardness and barbarity of the Ethiopians and justifying Italy in anticipation for any measures which she might deem it necessary to take "to defend her own security, rights, and dignity." He also argued with considerable skill that the dispute lay outside the League's competence altogether – a type of argument that in the years to come was to be so painfully familiar. Efforts at appeasement outside the League, offers of economic concessions and of exchanges of territory, were roundly characterized by Mussolini as "not only unacceptable, but derisory":

> Italy's need for expansion in East Africa is not to be satisfied by the cession of a couple of deserts, one of salt and one of stone. The League Council seems to think I am a collector of deserts.

Then on September 11, 1935, in the League Assembly, came the famous speech of Sir Samuel Hoare, British Foreign Secretary:

> The British people are deeply and genuinely moved by a great ideal . . . In spite of the grim experiences of the past, in spite of the worship of force in the present, the British people have clung to that ideal, and they are not prepared to abandon it . . . The ideals enshrined in the Covenant and in particular the aspiration to establish the rule of law in international affairs, have appealed with growing force to the strain of idealism which has its place in our national character, and have become a part of our national conscience.

Hoare's speech, as a delegate who heard it said afterward, was "one of the great electrifying moments in the history of the League." The Assembly and the world at large – and the British electorate, to whom, as we believe, the speech was mainly addressed – were not to know that it was other than an open and passionate avowal of the British Government's attitude. Negotiations were already in train that afterward betrayed and falsified every hope that the speech inspired. But for the moment the League seemed to be taking a powerful, even heroic, stand. Meanwhile the British Government ordered the Mediterranean Fleet to Alexandria and reinforced it with units from the Home Fleet and even from the China Squadron. The garrisons at Malta and Aden were brought up to strength.

The British Government also sought to enlist the support of those Mediterranean states that it had reason to hope were sincere and responsible members of the League. In December 1935, Yugoslavia, Greece, and Turkey gave positive assurances of assistance in the event of an Italian attack on the British fleet, and they were promptly seconded by Czechoslovakia and Rumania. France, under Laval, bargained and evaded, but eventually promised support "fully and in advance" within her obligations under the Covenant. Yet, for all these verbal protestations by the Mediterranean Powers, it was clear enough to the British Government that Britain herself would have to bear the brunt of any extension of Italy's war. As Hoare afterward declared, except for the dispositions of the British fleet, "not a ship, not a machine, not a man" was moved by any other member of the League.

Sanctions and the Hoare-Laval Plan

On October 3, 1935, the Italian forces in Eritrea began the invasion of Ethiopia. At Geneva, between October 9 and 11, fifty out of fifty-four nations in the League Assembly concurred in the findings of the Council that the Italian Government had resorted to war in disregard of its covenants. The four dissenting states were Italy herself and Italy's "clients," Austria, Hungary, and Albania. Germany was about to withdraw from the League. A Coordination Committee was at once set up to examine the ways and means of imposing economic sanctions against the aggressor.

Article 16 of the Covenant obliged the states of the League to sever "all trade or financial relations" and "all intercourse" between themselves and the Covenant-breaking member. Mussolini threatened to meet the application of this article with dire reprisals, not excluding war. But even without his defiant thunders, the League's problem was not a simple one and, perhaps not surprisingly, the Coordination Committee finally recommended a rather more restricted program of sanctions than honest opinion wished or than strict legality should have required. No doubt cowardice and cupidity played their part, but it is also a fact that the thoroughgoing economic boycott of a first-class power, except by blockade and war, was soon found to be an almost insuperable task. However, a formidable array of nations accepted the proposals of the Coordination Committee, and on November 18, 1935, the League's first experiment in international sanctions went into force. Italy was deprived of arms, loans, and certain raw materials, and her own exports were denied by the signatory powers.

It is not easy to assess "leakages" in the scheme. Since the nonsignatory powers were few and small, the rift in the sanctionist front that they caused was unlikely to be vital. Germany was more important, but she had joined in the arms embargo, she had not yet developed her pro-Italian policies, and, in her present economic condition, large increases in her Italian trade were not to be expected. But it was at this point that the United States indirectly entered the fray. The United States was not a member of the League and was bound officially to ignore its proceedings. Recent neutrality legislation in the United States imposed an embargo on "arms, ammunition, or the implements of war," but covered raw materials, such as oil, only at the discretion of the President. However, President Roosevelt pleaded with American traders not to increase above the normal amount their business with Italy in these raw materials, and no doubt he might have mobilized greater support for the League had not American opinion been now revolted by the premature disclosure of the Hoare-Laval Plan.

It speaks volumes for the rapid development of military science that between 1918 and 1935, a short interval of seventeen years, a single commodity should have become so essential. In 1918 oil was important to warfare – important, but no more; in 1935 warfare was impossible without it. We can as well imagine the Cossacks without horses, or the Elizabethan seamen without oak, as the Fascist armies in Ethiopia without oil. When therefore the League Coordination Committee began to discuss the extension of its list of embargoes to "petroleum and the derivatives, by-products and residues of petroleum," it lighted at once upon what was fated to be the supreme test of its purpose and authority. There is no doubt but that France was now the immediate obstacle. Laval considered that he had already baited Italy more than was safe for the recent Franco-Italian Agreement and was resolved that oil sanctions should not go into force. He pleaded with the British Government to make one last effort at peace by negotiation before letting the League go too far along its present drastic course, and with this object he and Hoare now entered into direct discussions.

Sir Samuel Hoare, the British Foreign Secretary, was a man of broad attainments and ripe experience, as sincere in purpose and straight in action as any good servant of the Crown. He had been Secretary for Air and Secretary for India. In every field his record had been unexceptionable. We may at least say, in extenuation of his diplomacy at the present juncture, that he probably believed – his information probably led him to believe – that Ethiopia's military position was desperate, and that any serious defense by her against an Italian attack was out of the question. He was fearful that Britain might be induced to make Ethiopia promises of support which, even if forthcoming, would not avert her inevitable defeat. Mussolini on more than one occasion had declared that oil sanctions would lead to war, and he appeared to mean what he said. Hoare doubted whether the other powers who so clamorously demanded strong action would render effective military assistance in an extremity; and he was morally certain that France, for one, would not. Hoare did not doubt that Britain would be the victor in a conflict with Italy. But he considered that the losses the conflict might entail were not legitimate losses at a time when other potential enemies of Britain, of far greater strength than Italy, were engaged on heavy naval construction programs. The loss of half a dozen battleships, which was the British Admiralty's estimate of the probable cost of a naval war in the Mediterranean, would have resulted in a decisive unbalancing of British naval tonnage vis-à-vis Japan. British ships in 1935 were not yet provided with the antiaircraft devices they afterward had, and the Italian Air Force of that date, even discounting the exaggerations of Fascist propaganda, was believed to have superior first-line planes for Mediterranean warfare.

In other words, Hoare's view in all essentials was Laval's view: Italy might be in the wrong, but Ethiopia was not worth a war. And to that view he now committed his government and his country.

The Hoare-Laval Plan, as it was called, was drawn up early in December 1935. Its details are now of little importance. Extensive Ethiopian territories were to be ceded to Italy outright, and other Ethiopian territories were to be assigned to Italy as a "zone of economic expansion and settlement." In exchange, the Italian port of Assab in Eritrea was to be ceded to Ethiopia. The two negotiators, Hoare and Laval, pledged one another to secrecy until the plan should have been submitted to the interested parties: Italy, Ethiopia, and the League. But Laval gave the plan immediate publicity in the French press. The British Government was placed in a terrible position. Baldwin, the Prime Minister, took refuge in denials and evasions. "My lips are not yet unsealed," he said in the House of Commons. "Were these troubles over I would make a case, and I guarantee that not a man would go into the lobby against me."

The British Parliament, press, and people, after a day or two of dumb astonishment, broke out into a chorus of expostulation. The aggressor in Africa, it seemed, had been virtually handed the spoils of a victory which he had not yet won, by a man who not long since, in the League Assembly, had categorically denounced his crime. Hoare returned from vacation in Switzerland, where, already somewhat exhausted, he had further impaired his health by injuring himself in a skating accident. At first he gave out that he would give the country a full account of himself, but he bowed to the storm and resigned. He was succeeded as Foreign Secretary by Anthony Eden. Laval in France meanwhile was given a drubbing at the hands of the Chamber but survived in office for another few weeks.

Mussolini, for his part, preserved a discreet silence and then, when the furor was safely abating, declared his rejection of the plan. For the League there was nothing left to do but perform the obsequies on oil sanctions as decently as possible, and it was decided to defer further consideration of the matter sine die. But the League, not long since defeated over the Manchurian crisis, had now suffered another humiliating setback.

The Course of the War

"Colonial" wars have usually been small affairs in which European arms and discipline made up for lack of numbers. But in Ethiopia, Mussolini took no chances. He wanted not only victory but a quick victory. By the end of the war the Italian command disposed of ten divisions, or 250,000 white combatants, a number which with Africans and labor battalions amounted to 400,000 men; and this force was supported by a formidable array of tanks, motorized units, and aircraft. Barracks, hospitals, and, above all, roads, were commensurate. The Red Sea port of Massaua and the Eritrean capital, Asmara, were virtually rebuilt. The conditions of climate and topography were as difficult as it is possible to imagine, but these huge masses of men and material moved with extraordinary smoothness, to the great chagrin of critics who always derided the Italian ability for organization. If we may judge by the Italian casualty lists, Mussolini's calculations were eminently justified. In seven months of war Italy lost only 3,000 men. Well might Mussolini say that he preferred "to err by excess than by deficiency."

Against the huge armament that Italy thus brought into the field, the Ethiopians could oppose only their primitive man power, estimated at less than 300,000. They had no heavy artillery, no tanks, and no air force. They are reported to have had 200 pieces of light artillery of antique pattern, 1,000 machine guns, and a scattering of antiaircraft guns. Their rifle ration for the campaign worked out at about 150 rounds per man. It was well said that the majority of the Emperor's army were more poorly armed than Italian noncombatants. Nor did tactics and leadership compensate for material deficiencies. Each one of the Ethiopian contingents was independently led by its own ras, and any sort of unified action was lost in personal and tribal jealousies. European officers in the Emperor's train were treated with traditional suspicion, and such advice as they gave was wasted on the desert air. The obvious type of fighting should have been guerrilla fighting. Afghan and Riffian tactics could make the country impregnable. Yet the rases disdained to behave like "bandits" and, in their suicidal pride and ignorance, they persisted in maneuvering and fighting in compact masses.

In the course of the war both sides charged one another with barbarities in contravention of international treaties, and in 1936 Geneva fairly rang with mutual accusations. Both sides were believed to have used dumdum bullets. In particular, the Italians paid little respect to the Ethiopian Red Cross. On one memorable occasion an Italian airman, forced down behind the Ethiopian lines, was beheaded. But the gravest of all such accusations was in regard to chemical warfare on the part of Italy. De Bono, the first Italian Commander, was guiltless in this respect, but his successor, Badoglio, afterward used gas as part of his more aggressive tactics. At the height of the campaign, especially in March 1936, the Ethiopian forces in retreat were constantly sprayed with mustard gas from the air, and whole areas which were likely to be used for the concentration of reserves were sometimes saturated with it. The Ethiopians had the means neither of protection nor of retaliation, and their appeals to the League brought them no redress. Italy's action was a clear breach of the Gas Protocol of 1925, to which both she and Ethiopia were adherents (see p. 127).

The Italian campaign lasted seven months, from October 3, 1935, to May 9, 1936, and occupied the interval between one rainy season and the next. The campaign fell into two main phases, the first under General Emilio De Bono up to the end of November 1935, and the second under Marshal Pietro Badoglio. The main blow was struck from the north, that is, from the Eritrean front, and here the Italian command concentrated nine out of the total ten divisions of the expeditionary force. A secondary blow was struck from the south, that is, from the Somaliland front, by the tenth division, under General Rodolfo Graziani.

During October 1935, De Bono's forces quickly occupied Adua. Nowhere did they meet with serious opposition; but the fall of Adua nonetheless was celebrated in Italy as a great victory, a revenge long overdue for the shameful defeat of 1896. The priests of the Holy City of Aksum and Haile Selassie

Gugsa, the dissolute ras of Tigré, a son-in-law of the Emperor, went over to the Italians without resistance. Thereafter De Bono halted while his engineers and labor battalions worked on his lines of communication. Perhaps he was waiting for other rases to follow Gugsa's treacherous example and save the Italian forces from the necessity of fighting. Graziani, operating in the south, penetrated the Ogaden, but also moved with remarkable caution. Mussolini, in Rome, prodded his commanders with telegrams urging a more expeditious campaign, and then, losing patience, dismissed De Bono from his post.

Evidently De Bono was a better Fascist than soldier. But he was an able organizer, and he had laid the groundwork for the subsequent Italian operations. Badoglio, was a better soldier than Fascist – in fact, his party leanings had always been highly suspect. His appointment signified a bolder phase of the Ethiopian War. The greater battles of the campaign were fought under him in January, February, and March 1936, and ended everywhere in decisive victories for the Italians. The Emperor Haile Selassie himself was defeated at Lake Ashangi at the beginning of April. Thereafter the important strongholds fell quickly and easily into Italian hands. The final Italian spurt from Dessye to Addis Ababa was a triumphal promenade conducted by two of the longest columns of mechanized vehicles ever yet assembled in a modern war. On May 2, 1936, the Emperor left his stricken realm from Jibuti aboard a British warship. The Italian forces entered Addis Ababa three days later. Graziani's columns moving up from the south made contact with the northern columns. The campaign was at an end.

On May 9, 1936, Mussolini proclaimed the annexation of Ethiopia to Italy and the King of Italy's assumption of the title of Emperor of Ethiopia.

The Liquidation of Sanctions

In Britain the news of the Italian victory produced the profoundest depression. Enthusiasts of the League, the Labor party to a man, and several public figures continued to demand effective action against the aggressor. A throng of sympathizers welcomed the fugitive Emperor Haile Selassie to London, and the police had some difficulty in preventing the Ethiopian Legation from becoming a place of pilgrimage. But the British Government and the growing mass of "realists" in the country, once they had digested the shock and humiliation, were secretly relieved that the Italo-Ethiopian War had ended so soon and without more serious complications. Neville Chamberlain, Chancellor of the Exchequer, speaking presumably in a private capacity at a dinner of the Nineteen Hundred Club, averred that the continuation or intensification of sanctions would be "the very midsummer of madness." The government was grateful for his lead and, one after another, members of the Cabinet expressed themselves with increasing emphasis in favor of the liquidation of sanctions and the return to normal relations with Italy. "It cannot be expected by anyone," said Eden in the House of Commons, "that the continuance of existing sanctions will restore in Abyssinia the position which has been destroyed. That position can only be restored

The Italo-Ethiopian War, 1935-36: Ethiopian chiefs mustering at Addis Ababa

FREDERICK LEWIS

by military action. So far as I am aware no other government, certainly not this government, is prepared to take such military action."

In France, on June 4, 1936, Blum entered office at the head of the Popular Front, and it seemed as if France, at the very moment that Britain was bethinking herself of liquidating sanctions, was to suffer a prick of conscience in favor of a strong League policy. However Blum, for all his Socialist principles, gave out that he would acquiesce in whatever decision the League might make, and he hinted that practical considerations pointed to an end of sanctions. The British Dominions and the remaining states of Europe signified the same views. On June 20, President Roosevelt raised the American arms embargo on Italy and Ethiopia. The League Assembly met at the end of the same month. The Emperor Haile Selassie, a pathetic but dignified figure, came to Geneva to plead his cause in person. He spoke eloquently, but it was clear that he could expect nothing. A single lonely voice in favor of maintaining sanctions in full vigor was raised by the South African delegate. Sanctions against Italy ceased as of July 15, 1936.

The Rome-Berlin Axis

In the early part of the Italo-Ethiopian War, Germany had maintained a scrupulously "correct" attitude. The results of the war and of the accompanying sanctionist struggle were both uncertain. But Germany was in a position to wait and to gain some advantage whatever the end might turn out to be. In March 1936, Hitler made use of the preoccupation of the various powers concerned to achieve his Rhineland coup, and the first signs of Italo-German collaboration in Europe were increasingly in evidence thereafter. The Rhineland, in short, was the end of the Stresa Front of 1935 and the beginning of the Rome-Berlin Axis. (See pp. 389-90.)

On June 9, 1936, the young Fascist Count Galeazzo Ciano, Mussolini's son-in-law, formerly Italian Propaganda Minister and lately commander of a bomber squadron in Ethiopia, became Italian Foreign Minister. Thereafter the *rapprochement* of Italy and Germany developed rapidly, and by July 1936, when the Spanish Civil War broke out, it was sufficiently advanced for the two powers to act in all but open concert in their affairs in Spain. A series of state visits signified the fast-maturing political realities. Edda, Countess Ciano, Mussolini's daughter, enjoyed a month of social festivities in Berlin. The Prince of Piedmont attended the Olympic Games in Berlin. Goebbels visited Venice. Himmler and Hans Frank visited Rome. The series culminated at the end of October when Ciano spent some days in Berlin, Munich, and Berchestgaden "to coordinate the policies of the Italian and German Governments" and concluded with Hitler the so-called October Protocols, a secret agreement, tantamount to an integration of Italian and German foreign policies. At the same time Hitler recognized the Italian Empire of Ethiopia. Finally, in November 1937, Italy adhered to the German-Japanese Anti-Comintern Pact. (See p. 345.)

At Milan on November 1, 1936, Mussolini spoke as follows:

> The meetings at Berlin have resulted in an agreement between our two countries on certain questions, some of which are particularly interesting in these days. But these agreements that have been included in special statements and duly signed, this vertical line between Rome and Berlin, is not a partition but rather an axis round which all European states animated by the will to collaboration and peace can also collaborate.

In 1936 a new balance of the European powers emerged. Italy and Germany in virtual alliance confronted the somewhat vague alignment of Britain, France, the Soviet Union, and a battered, shaken League of Nations.

22. SPAIN: REPUBLIC AND CIVIL WAR

Spanish Localities and Peoples

Spain, a country that flared up into a civil war in 1936 and all but drew the rest of Europe into its fires, had lain for generations at a distance from the fiercer conflagrations of international politics. She had known civil wars before; hers was a people of passionate and recurrent violence, but of a violence that usually bred and spent itself within her own parochial limits. She had sometimes been the indirect occasion of international war – France and Prussia had clashed over the "Spanish succession" in 1870 – and she had herself fought a sordid and undistinguished war with the United States in 1898. But none of these wars within or wars without compared in significance with the Civil War of 1936. In that vicious, fratricidal year Spain became in miniature the battlefield of all the wider rivalries of Europe.

The map of Spain is square and blocky. But her social geography was as diverse and incoherent as that of medieval France or Italy. In a long history, Iberians, Basques, Celts, Phoenicians, Greeks, Carthaginians, Romans, Goths, Arabs, and French had left their seed and culture to fructify into an extraordinarily variegated nation. Four languages were spoken in the peninsula. Mountainous territory made for surprising alternations of climate and produce, and intensified the divisions and particularisms of the people. The Spaniard had always been proud and egotistical, fiercely independent, owing his first allegiance to his town or village, and in many ways he had never outgrown his ancient tribalism. Ortega y Gasset, in a well-known book, called the country "invertebrate." Time was when the Catholic Church and the Crown imposed their bond of unity, but of recent years the authority of both had been grievously declining.

Economically the country showed the same contrasts and contrariness. In some parts there existed a system of large landed estates – notably in Andalusia and Estremadura; in some parts there existed a system of small agricultural holdings; in the Basque country and in Catalonia was an advanced industrialism. Generally peasants and workers were very poor. But poverty was never a disgrace in Spain. It was in the nature of the people to show an almost Irish contempt for economic betterment. Two of the twenty-two millions of the population lived in the two great cities, Madrid and Barcelona. Political partisanship ran the gamut between a feudal, clerical conservatism and the extremest forms of Communism and anarchism.

The Basques and the Catalans formed two separate nationalist groups in Spain, each with a distinctive history, language, and economic life. The Basques were one of the great anthropological puzzles of Europe. They inhabited the three provinces, the "Three-One" of Vizcaya, Guipúzcoa, and Álava. Throughout their history they had preserved certain regional rights, and their land was deservedly known as a "land apart." Their iron mines near Bilbao had been worked since prehistoric times. Latterly the Basques had adopted modern industries, and the great hydroelectric potentialities of their mountainous districts had been developed. They were devout Catholics and, like so many industrialized peoples, were often Socialists. Apparently their religious and political creeds were each faithfully observed without prejudice to the other.

Catalonia could almost be described as another "land apart." Ever since Charlemagne had established it as a frontier march, it had been more closely linked with trans-Pyrenean Europe than with the rest of Spain. Barcelona, its capital city and chief port, shared the life of Mediterranean France and Italy. Catalonia had fallen under the dominion of Aragon, but it had never lost its original centrifugalism, and its people were among the first "submerged nationalities" in more recent times to heed the call of independence and self-rule. Barcelona meanwhile had grown into a great commercial center, like another Belfast, separated both in political sentiment and in economic interest from a more slowly moving agricultural hinterland.

The Directorate of Primo de Rivera and the Republican Revolution

Alfonso XIII ascended the throne of his fathers in 1902, on his sixteenth birthday, in mind and heart a Bourbon, devoted to family and Church, fond of authority, proud of his kingly office, enjoying excitement and intrigue, yet shrewd beyond the ordinary, and willing perhaps to give constitutionalism an honest trial. But the best intentions could not mold events in Spain. Ministers and ministries were constant in nothing but change. Between 1902 and 1923 there were thirty-three different governments. Not a year passed but had its strikes and mutinies. The First World War brought a lull, and trade with the Allies greatly benefited the Spanish exchequer; but it was only a lull. The Spanish Army meanwhile carried on exhausting operations against Abd el-Krim and the rebel Riff tribesmen in Morocco, and on one dreadful occasion it seemed that foolhardy orders from the King himself had involved the Spaniards in a major defeat. In September 1923, the Captain General of Catalonia, Don Miguel Primo de Rivera, the Marqués de Estella, headed a monarchist-military revolt against the government. In a long proclamation the General accused the professional politicians of bringing ruin on the country and declared that he and the army were acting only in honest indignation and with real support of public opinion.

It was not the first time a general had ruled in Spain, but the directorate of Primo de Rivera was significant by reason of the existence of other autocratic figures in the contemporary European scene. Mussolini had enjoyed power for a year; Kemal was about to become the first President of the Turkish Republic. Indeed, on a visit to Italy in November 1923, Alfonso XIII and his General were indiscreet enough to express public approval of Fascist ways and works and, once returned to Spain, Primo de Rivera proceeded Fascist-like to destroy the remnants of constitutional rule, to suppress hostile political parties, to censor the press, to control public assembly and the universities, and to reorganize the country's economy upon what has since come to be called totalitarian lines. In 1926 the war against the Riffs in Morocco was at last brought to a favorable conclusion, albeit with essential assistance from France, and Primo de Rivera – again Fascist-like – was able to reinforce his position and popularity at home with the help of a military success abroad. Meanwhile new arterial roads, new irrigation schemes, and international exhibitions at Barcelona and Seville were among his directorate's more meritorious domestic monuments, all built with the assistance of his brilliant young Minister of Finance, José Calvo Sotelo.

Primo de Rivera was a man of high, if limited, principles, but he had all the quixotry of the legendary Spaniard, and he was certainly not of the stuff of which modern Caesars are made. He was the mayor of a palace revolution rather than the leader of a popular national revival. He was garrulous, gallant, and sometimes slightly foolish, a habitué of cafés, fond of his pleasures. He governed for six and a half years, but brought no interval of real peace or real pacification. If anything, the Right became more violently rightist, and the Left more violently leftist, and the moderate groups that might have kept the balance became steadily weaker. Primo de Rivera's worst mistake was his repressive policy in Catalonia. He finally lost even the support of the army. In January 1930 he resigned.

It was clear that events were moving toward one of those political upheavals which had so often punctuated the history of Spain. In midsummer of 1930, leading Republicans openly formed themselves into a Revolutionary Committee, and they were shortly joined by leading Catalans. In April 1931, mainly to test public opinion, municipal elections were held and showed overwhelming Republican sympathies in the towns. A calamitous fall of the peseta heralded a change of regime. General José Sanjurjo declined to be responsible for the loyalty of the Civil Guards,[1] and King Alfonso, without actually abdicating, deemed it the better part of valor to flee the country. The Revolutionary Committee proclaimed a Provisional Government in Madrid, and the Catalans proclaimed an autonomous Republic in Barcelona. Elections in June 1931 for a Constituent Cortes resulted in a decisive victory for the parties of the Left.

For the next five years Spain was a republic. In December 1931, the Cortes voted a constitution. Niceto Alcalá Zamora, a Catholic Progressive, became President; and Manuel Azaña, a Republican, became Premier. The new legislators addressed themselves to the perennial problems of Spain – the Church, Catalonia, and the land. The Jesuit Order was dissolved; Church schools were closed; the state support of the clergy was abolished. A Catalan autonomy bill was passed. An agrarian law sought to amend the unequal and necessitous condition of the peasants; but it was slow in operation, and the peasants were soon resorting to the seizure of land by the quicker and more intelligible method of force. The result was rioting in many parts of the country, the burning of churches and convents, and the murder of Civil Guards. Meanwhile the Depression laid its wasting hand on Spain's industry and trade, and the attendant hardships of course were blamed on the government. General Sanjurjo, in a mood of reactionary despair, attempted unsuccessfully to set up a military directorate in Seville. In elections in November 1933, the Left suffered heavy defeats everywhere. The monarchists emerged from hiding to agitate openly for the restoration of King Alfonso. A Spanish Fascist party, called the Falange, made its appearance under the leadership of José Antonio Primo de Rivera, a son of the former dictator. A weak, reactionary government took office under the Catalan Radical Alejandro Lerroux in coalition with the Catholic Popular Action party of José María Gil Robles.

It is not necessary to guide the reader through all the ups and downs of modern Spanish politics. The story would be tedious if it were not so tragic. Perhaps enough has been said to convey the impression that Spain was no country of sunny orange groves, colorful religious festivals, and laughing, dancing senoritas, but a country of blood and tears and of violent extremes. The etchings of Goya are more illustrative of the real Spain than the music of Bizet and Rossini. For the moment exhaustion seemed to induce a slackening in the tempo of events, but Lerroux's term of office was still marked by four strikes which could be designated as "general," as well as several lesser strikes and local military coups. In October 1934, a rebellion broke out among the miners of Asturias. It was a very considerable affair, and used afterward to be called the "rehearsal of the Civil War." It devastated the city of Oviedo, caused over 1,500 deaths, and was accompanied by more than usually savage mutilations and torturings. The government called in General Francisco Franco and the Foreign Legion from Morocco to suppress the rebellion.

The elections of February 1936 swung back to the Left once more, and a combination of parties of the Left took office under Azaña and Santiago Casares Quiroga, the liberal-minded leader of the local autonomist movement in Galicia. The combination took the name of the Popular Front (*Frente Popular*) after the similar and contemporary improvisation in France. The new government at once amnestied political prisoners jailed under the former governments and set about filling the cells thus emptied with as many of the prominent representatives of the Right as it could lay its hands on. The vindictive swing of opinion even fastened itself on Alcalá Zamora, the President of the Republic, and the Cortes suddenly voted his impeachment, dangerously stretching a point of the constitution to do so. Azaña was then elected President, and Casares Quiroga became Premier. The revolutionary program of 1931 – especially the land seizures – was resumed.

The situation in 1936 had certainly worsened since 1931. The Popular

Front, thanks to the electoral system, held a majority of seats in the Cortes upon a minority of votes in the country – a none too happy position. Nevertheless, the domestic affairs of Spain might have continued to boil and bubble, as for years they had already done, without spilling over into civil war. Strikes, robberies, murders, the raiding of political clubs and newspaper offices, the burning of churches and convents, the assaults on priests and nuns – all these things had happened in Spain before. There was, of course, the threat of a military plot. General Franco, lately promoted Chief of the General Staff, who was implicated, was safely degraded to the governorship of the Canaries, and several other "politically active" officers were retired on pension. The mildness of these precautions was significant of the government's weakness. But it was not the first time in Spain, in these early months of 1936, that men had sat nervously in the cafés of Madrid and Barcelona with the air about them thick with potential calamity, and nothing had happened beyond what was already normal to the restless disposition of Spain.

There was, however, one further factor in the situation in 1936 that was unusual and dangerous. The moderate Center parties of the electorate had fallen in strength to the point of ineffectiveness, and at the same time, at either end of the scale, extremes of the Left and Right had become more sharply defined and united – the Popular Front itself was a case in point. And, if now these extremes are dubbed Fascist and Communist, or Nationalist and Republican, the situation becomes very much simplified, and a new and very formidable hostility emerges. The words "Fascist" and "Communist" as applied to Spanish affairs may be inaccurate and misleading, and for that reason "Nationalist" and "Republican" are less objectionable, but the words do signify what was indeed the important fact of the moment, that in 1936 the chaos of the Spanish political parties was beginning to crystallize into two rival coalitions and that each was forming a connection with powerful sympathizers outside the country.

On July 12-13, 1936, the prologue to the final tragedy was enacted in the form of two murders, the first of a certain José Castillo, and the second of Calvo Sotelo. Castillo was a lieutenant of the Assault Guards [2] and a partisan of the Left; perhaps he was not a particularly important personage. Calvo Sotelo, however, was the former Finance Minister of Primo de Rivera, a prominent Conservative and monarchist, and many regarded him as the next in Spain's long history of dictators. His assassins were Assault Guards revenging themselves for the death of their comrade, Castillo.

The Outbreak of the Civil War

The simultaneity of the army risings throughout Spain showed them to be no sudden coup, but a long and ably planned affair. The army in Morocco revolted on July 17, 1936, and during the following days the areas round Cordoba, Cadiz, and Seville in the south and round Saragossa, Burgos, Valladolid, and Galicia in the north went over to the insurgent side. General Sanjurjo, who expected to become Chief of the new Spanish State, was killed in an air crash on his way to Burgos to assume command. The leadership thus devolved undisputed onto General Franco.

On the side of the insurgents, or Nationalists as they were now to be called, stood the traditional, monarchist, clerical, and other conservative elements which we have described. In military effectives this included most of the officers of the regular army, the Moorish Regulares, the Foreign Legion, the Civil Guards, and privately recruited bodies such as the Carlists [3] and the Falangists—at the beginning, a total of some 27,000 men. A good proportion of them had seen active service in Morocco, and some of them in Cuba. They had also had experience in quelling civil disturbances in Spain. The Nationalists also seized one of the two battleships of the Spanish Navy and some lesser ships. By the end of 1936, the Nationalists controlled about three-fifths of Spain. A Nationalist Government was set up in Burgos with General Franco as *Caudillo* or Leader.

On the side of the Republicans stood large sections of the peasantry and the urban workers, arrayed in their various unions and political groups—Socialists, Anarcho-Syndicalists, the POUM, Communists, and others—and also the majority of the Basques and Catalans.[4] In military effectives this included whole regiments of unofficered conscripts and a few isolated army officers, among whom was General José Miaja. The 6,500 Assault Guards were about the only body of men with a corporate identity and a professional leadership. The trade unions recruited many thousands of "militia men" and armed them by the simple expedient of throwing open available military stores and armories. Such troops were adept at tearing noisily up and down the streets of the bigger cities in motor trucks, which appears at first to have been their favorite occupation; they might have been well suited for guerrilla fighting in the mountainous country, especially in defense of their own localities. But they had high courage and revolutionary zeal, they had more than one spiritual link with other historic eruptions of the Spanish people. Time would show what they were worth in sustained and regular warfare. At sea, the Republicans had the second, the newer and more powerful, battleship of the Spanish Navy and three cruisers. But, generally speaking, naval forces on either side played a far smaller part in the Civil War than their original paper strength, their strategic opportunities, or the Spanish maritime traditions gave reason to expect.

The Republicans commanded important economic resources which, given a chance, should have put them in a very favorable position. They had seized the gold reserves of the Bank of Spain. Their territories included the industrial districts of Madrid, Barcelona, and Bilbao and the Asturias coal mines. They held the Levante, Spain's richest agricultural area. But the Republicans were desperately in need of organization and training. First loyalties, for every Spaniard, were always to locality or party. The Civil War, as some said at the time, was the "trumphant assertion of regionalism." The early Republican "committees of defense" were half juntas, half soviets, hastily improvised, with all the character and affiliation of their multiform origins. The Communists, who had links with Moscow, would consult political commissars or hold meetings before acting on their orders. There was nothing in these groups to predispose them towards military discipline, and the political history of the war, behind the scenes, on the Republican side,

SPAIN, 1936-39

largely consists of their constant feuds. Then, as a further complicating factor, there were wholesale experiments in the collectivization of industries and farms, experiments which were more successful perhaps than similar experiments of the Italian Socialists in 1920, but the methods of expropriation varied with the political views of the expropriators, and the results were not exactly uniform. The Republican government, eventually established at Valencia, under Francisco Largo Caballero, leader of the extreme Socialist wing, was fated to go through some very rough passages.

To the world at large, the outbreak of the Spanish Civil War came as a shock. Normally Spain had had a poor press. She was one of the "faraway" countries; since 1898 she had hardly figured as front-page news anywhere; she had been neutral in the First World War. Alfonso XIII was known as a man of shrewd and picturesque character; with his English Queen, he was always much photographed in society magazines; but Spain herself had never shared the familiarity with which her monarch was regarded abroad. Like the "turbulent Balkans," or like her own neighbor Portugal, Spain's internal troubles and crises belonged to a normal, unchanging condition, to which the world had formerly paid but little heed. But this time it was clear that she had become the theater of a conflict bigger than herself and supremely important to the entire European family.

But even while at first the objects and alignments of the Civil War were still obscure, newspaper readers abroad were startled and appalled by reports of the savagery with which it was being conducted. Granted that civil wars are the bitterest of all wars, granted that the Spaniard is passionate and cruel, granted that the war had released overcharged and pent-up hatreds, granted too, as was soon quite obvious, that the reports of atrocities were exaggerated in one way or another by propaganda, granted many reasons and extenuations, the grim facts were shocking beyond the credence of contemporaries who, in 1936, had only begun their modern education in insensitiveness to horror.

Presumably the Nationalists had the greater opportunity for terrorism. Their forces made their biggest advances between August and October 1936, at a time when the taking of prisoners alive was accounted an uncommon clemency and when there were hostile towns and territories to pacify. But among the Republicans were men indoctrinated in political crime, and it was these who most indulged in class murders, in murders of priests, grandees, capitalists, factory managers, landlords, and army officers. The Anarcho-Syndicalists, who were strong in Barcelona, regarded class murder, "killing without hatred," as an ethical principle. Both Nationalist and Republicans seem to have been equally guilty of executing suspects on the flimsiest evidence or on no evidence at all. Courts and investigating committees were a farce. Murders from private grudges were common; murders of hostages were common.

The Reactions of the Powers

Unofficial aid in fighting personnel, preponderantly on the Republican side, was immediately forthcoming. Volunteers flocked to the recruiting stations in Paris or made their own independent ways to Spain. The war appealed to idealists and adventurers who otherwise had little or no interest in the country's affairs. A host of young poets, novelists, and university teachers of several nationalities joined the International Brigades, and many died in action. To this day the Spanish Civil War inspires arts and letters as no other war in recent times.[5]

Official aid – if we may so call it – came in the main from the Soviet Union, Italy, and Germany. All three states were probably making use of Spanish funds and factions for their own ends long before 1936. The Soviet Union had maintained a loose affiliation with the Spanish Communists for years, and it had supplied funds and "ideological assistance" to interested groups. The Communist revolution had failed lamentably in Central Europe during the 1920's, and perhaps the strategists of the Moscow Comintern found some consolation in a prospective, if belated, success in the Iberian Peninsula during the 1930's. Spain, in fact, exhibited all those characteristics – a pauperized and embittered peasantry and proletariat, a privileged and oppressive aristocracy and Church — that should have made her ripe material for social subversion.

The Civil War in Spain, however, had broken out at one of those difficult transitional moments in Soviet affairs. The old Trotskyite crusade for "permanent world revolution" had receded into the background, and the Soviet Government was now in the midst of domestic preoccupations — the second Five-Year Plan and preparations for the treason trials. The recent setbacks of the League, just when the Soviet Union had become a member of it, had thrown another element of uncertainty into the situation. The Soviet's oral pronouncements were categorical enough, the Civil War was officially welcomed in Russia, and the usual greetings were showered, as only totalitarians know how, on the comrades fighting for the Republican cause in Spain. During August 1936, there were pro-Republican demonstrations and pageants all over the Soviet Union. The Soviet's political and ideological aid to the Republican government was considerable. The Soviet, through its Spanish embassy and consular officials, gave advice, direction, and eventually dictation. It largely inspired the International Brigades. Soviet material aid to the Republican side was hesitantly begun in September 1936 and came at first from very devious origins. In October and November heavy shipments were made through the Dardanelles direct from Russia. But Soviet aid was always of a kind which could be easily discontinued and never amounted, as did Italian aid, to an irrevocable commitment. It consisted of arms, aircraft, transport, fuel oil, machinery, and food, and much of it was paid for in Spanish gold. Soviet personnel in Spain was limited to technicians, pilot instructors, and the like, none of whom saw active service in the line.[6]

Italy's intervention on the Nationalist side was more direct, more extensive, and more brazen. Fascism, of course, was anti-Communist and wholeheartedly at one with the ideological professions of Franco and his partisans. Fascism was also in an expansionist mood and hankering after military glory. An extension of Italian power in the Mediterranean would automatically weaken that of Britain and France. An Italian Majorca, an Italian Ceuta, even an Italian Gibraltar were possibilities most pleasant to contemplate, possibilities which a good war in Spain might well convert into realities. Mussolini was ambitious to secure and eventually to annex Tunisia — and, as some said, Algeria also. Then in May 1936, the fighting in Ethiopia had come to an end, and Mussolini might conceivably have need of another diversion for his heroic veterans. Italian forces in Spain, at their maximum in 1937, numbered about 50,000; their death roll in the course of the war was about 6,000. Italian aid included over 750 aircraft and their pilots; and Italian warships and submarines participated in the blockade of Republican ports.[7]

Germany, like Italy, had an obvious ideological and strategic stake in the Spanish Civil War. Hitler had received a personal letter from Franco inviting his aid just after the first hostilities had broken out. The Nazi press and radio at once played up the wicked machinations of the Soviet Union and described unhappy Spain as the arena where the anarchy and destructiveness of Bolshevism were being pitted against the law and order of authoritarianism. Germany had need of Spanish raw materials, such as iron and tin. Spanish ports, like El Ferrol, Vigo, and Cadiz, were convertible into useful submarine bases. The creation of a Fascist-minded state on the southwestern border of France would complement the recent German march into the Rhineland. Hitler eventually sent men and supplies to Spain – including the famous Condor Legion under General von Sperrle and a tank corps under Colonel von Thoma. Probably some 16,000 Germans served in Spain in one capacity or another.[8]

It is well attested that the *Reichswehr* chiefs made good use of the Spanish Civil War to try out their newly forged weapons. In 1914, apart from an occasional military attaché sent to Manchuria or the Balkans, there was hardly a German soldier who had seen active service, and an entire generation of the German officer corps was wanting in experience in the field. In a war of the future, thanks to the Spanish laboratory, that deficiency could be remedied. Weapons would be available that had been tried, and instructors would be available that had used them. For example, the ferocious attack that German aircraft made on the Basque city of Guernica on April 26, 1937, if it was not useless brutality, was explainable as a "vivisectional experiment" in modern bombing tactics. Combined operations of tanks and planes were tried constantly and at no time more successfully than in the final Nationalist drive down the Ebro in 1938.

The British and French attitudes to the Spanish Civil War reflected all the "weakness" to which the democracies in these years were so painfully subject. Neither country was united in opinion or in will. As in the Italo-Ethiopian War, official Britain – that is, the Foreign Office and the Conservative government – in the interests of caution and "peace," seemed to condone the Fascist aggression. It ignored Fascist threats to British imperial life lines and Fascist expropriations of British properties and investments. If anything, it gave its sympathy, though not a very hearty or convinced sympathy, to the Nationalists. English Catholicism was believed to be pro-Nationalist or, at any rate, anti-Republican. British Labor gave its sympathy to the Republicans and often clamored for action which British morale and British armaments were then in no position to undertake.

The British people generally were indifferent and could find little to choose between the "gangsters of Valencia" and the "gangsters of Burgos." They were discouraged by the recent outcome in Ethiopia, and they made no such outbursts of enthusiasm as had attended Sir Samuel Hoare's famous speech in the League Assembly in September 1935. Appeasement was the new watchword, and neither Italian troublemaking in the Mediterranean nor German troublemaking in Central Europe could rouse them from the pacifist lethargy into which they had sunk. Perhaps they derived some consolation from the thought that intervention in the civil wars of the past – as witness the miserable episode in Russia in 1919 – had invariably defeated its objects in the end. Furthermore, after the present Civil War, a people of the fierce pride of the Spaniards would be more likely to extend the hand of friendship to those nations that had had the good sense to leave them to fight their battles by themselves. Surprisingly the exploits of the International Brigades made little impact on public opinion; the British participants were generally regarded as cranks or Communists who had found suitable expression for their fanaticisms at a safe distance from home.

In 1937 and subsequently, as we shall describe more fully elsewhere, Neville Chamberlain became pre-eminently responsible for British foreign policy, and he was particularly concerned with conciliating Italy and with trying to tempt her out of her newly formed Axis with Germany and back into the Western fold. (See pp. 474-75.) In January 1937, while he was still Chancellor of the Exchequer, Britain and Italy signed a "Gentleman's Agreement," mutually regulating their Mediterranean affairs. He became Prime Minister in May 1937 and initiated further discussions which came to a conclusion in the Anglo-Italian Agreement of April 1938. Meanwhile he was in constant friction with his anti-Italian Foreign Secretary, Anthony Eden. In July 1937, a further diversion appeared in the outbreak of the renewed Japanese war in China.

In 1936 France was administered by Léon Blum's Popular Front, a government which ought to have had an ideological affiliation with its Spanish namesake. Then, for centuries, a first dictum of French foreign policy had been to prevent the growth of an understanding between Spain and any Central European power. The parties of the Left in France, that is to say the parties of Blum's Popular Front, clamored like British Labor for action on the Republican side. But France had extraordinary need for caution. One of her frontiers marched with Spain, and the danger of immediate proximity was added to her other anxieties. She obtained little encouragement from the appeasing statesmen of Britain. Shortly after the outbreak of the war, two hundred French aircraft were dispatched to the Republicans. But thereafter France adhered to the restrictions of the Nonintervention Committee, and all but the merest trickle of supplies was stopped. France in these years, even more than Britain, had the pathetic aspect of a great nation buying peace at the price of its vital interests.

The Nonintervention Committee

On July 30, 1936, three Italian military planes had made a forced landing in Algeria. Their crews were Italian but were wearing Spanish uniforms, and they were presumed to be bound for Franco's headquarters in Morocco. Evidently they were the first installment of a prearranged program of Italian aid. On August 1, the French Government submitted a proposal to the Italian and British Governments to the effect that all three powers should refrain from sending supplies of war matériel to either belligerent in the Spanish war. The British Government suggested the extension of the proposal to all interested powers and, by the end of August, France, Italy, Britain, Germany, the Soviet Union, and Portugal had adhered to a Nonintervention Agreement. In September a Nonintervention Committee, representing these and fifteen other states, began to hold regular meetings in London.

The Nonintervention Committee had the contradictory effect of so many well intentioned measures at this time. All it did was to restrict the flow of arms to the Republican forces, while the aggressor, not averse to breaking his plighted word, could obtain all the military aid he wanted. The international volunteers, for example, posed a typical problem – especially those who joined the Republican forces and fought in the International Brigades. These men were genuine volunteers, moved by their own initiative, in response to the call of sentiment and propaganda. But the organized units of Italian troops – and of German troops to a less extent – complete with their uniforms, arms, and equipment, under their own officers, which fought on the Nationalist side, belonged to another category altogether. They were "Expeditionary Forces," and so indeed they were often described at the time in official Italian reports. The Nonintervention Committee spent weary weeks discussing the withdrawal of all non-Spanish nationals who were known already to have arrived and to be serving in one or the other of the contending Spanish armies. But the task was an idle one, especially while the Italian press was exulting in the deeds of valor performed by the Fascist youth in Franco's army, and while Mussolini continued to entangle his prestige ever more irretrievably in the prospects of a Nationalist triumph.

The problem of the naval patrol was also typical. Obviously, in order to prevent the arrival of foreign men and munitions in Spain, the country would have to be circled by some kind of inspection system. Thus, in the face of continuous Fascist obstruction, the Nonintervention Committee drew up a plan for the patrol of Spanish waters, divided the coast into zones, and assigned the zones to naval units of France, Britain, Germany, and Italy. A separate agreement was reached for the supervision of the land frontiers of Spain by a corps of neutral observers. The plan went into force at the end of April 1937. But the Republicans, meanwhile, had begun to retaliate against Franco's attempt to establish an independent naval blockade, and in May 1937, Republican aircraft bombed a battleship which was afterward discovered to be the German *Deutschland*. A German squadron replied by bombarding the undefended Republican seaside resort of Almería. In June, Germany and Italy withdrew from the patrol plan, and the entire Nonintervention Committee reached a virtual breakdown.

In the late summer of 1937, there was a mysterious outbreak of submarine piracy against French, British, and Soviet shipping in the Western Mediterranean. Italian submarines were suspected. This new development was considered in September at a conference at Nyon, near Geneva, attended by France, Britain, and the Soviet Union, in the persons of Delbos, Eden, and Litvinov, and by other affected Mediterranean countries. Germany and Italy declined to be represented in consequence of a Soviet imputation that Italy had been responsible for certain of the acts of piracy in question. The conference was one of the few occasions in the 1930's when the Western Powers made a resolute stand against totalitarian lawlessness and aggression. It was a personal triumph for the British Foreign Secretary, Anthony Eden. The conference agreed that submarines attacking any non-Spanish merchant ships would be counterattacked and destroyed and that the British and French fleets would give "practical effect" to that agreement. Italy was afterward persuaded to adhere. No further acts of submarine piracy were reported.

The Spanish Civil War, 1936-39: defeated Spanish Republican troops retreating into France behind a French frontier guard

ROBERT CAPA-MAGNUM

The Course of the War

The first month of the war had been very confused. The fighting had broken out in several places at once and consisted for the most part of mutual mopping-up operations, the consolidation of sympathetic areas, and the strengthening of communications. The important engagements of these days, if engagements they can be called, were the seizures of Madrid and Barcelona by the Republicans and the seizures of Teruel, Saragossa, and the Balearic islands of Majorca and Iviza by the Nationalists.

Thereafter the war entered upon its campaigning phase. The two groups of Nationalist forces in the north and south of Spain converged upon the Tagus, and by early November 1936 were investing the suburbs of Madrid. The Basque Provinces and Asturias were separated from the main Republican areas to the south and east. Simultaneously the Nationalists took Irun and San Sebastian, thus cutting off the Republicans from an important road link with France. The Nationalists — and their German and Italian allies — clearly expected the war would be finished in a matter of weeks. On November 18, 1936, Germany and Italy recognized the Nationalist government. But at this point the Nationalists were stopped in their tracks. The Republican government retired to Valencia. General Miaja, a professional soldier, organized the defense of Madrid, and he was reinforced by strong contingents, notably the first of the International Brigades. Foreign munitions were beginning to have their effect. Snub-nosed Russian fighter planes were being pitted against Junkers, Heinkels, and Capronis. The defenders of Madrid were going into battle chanting the refrain, "They shall not pass!" (*No pasarán*), a reminiscence of Verdun in 1916. The city held fast, and the Spanish Civil War developed into a long, tedious, and expensive struggle.

In the early spring of 1937, Franco again tried and failed to take Madrid. Mussolini's legionaries were routed by a detachment of the International Brigades at the Battle of Guadalajara. Franco then turned his attention to Basque Provinces and Asturias. His slow, bitterly contested advance ended in the capture of Bilbao in midsummer, but organized resistance in the north persisted into the autumn months. Meanwhile the Republican Government had been reconstituted. In May 1937, Juan Negrín, a right-wing Socialist, had succeeded Largo Caballero as Premier at the head of a leftist, largely Communist-dominated coalition. Conscription was introduced throughout the Republican territories, and it is said that by the end of 1937, the Republicans had an army of 800,000 men in the field. In October 1937, the Republican government moved to Barcelona. The assault and capture of Teruel by Republican forces in December 1937 were the first fruits of the military and political reorganization that had been effected.

In February 1938, Franco launched a series of actions designed to bring him his long-deferred victory. The Nationalists recaptured Teruel and thereafter developed a steady, irresistible offensive down the Ebro. In April they captured Vinaroz, and Franco felt himself justified in broadcasting the end of the war. But the Republicans, with sheer Iberian tenacity, continued to fight back. Barcelona resisted till February 20, and Madrid till March 28, 1939.

On April 20, 1939, three weeks after the fall of Madrid, the Nonintervention Committee in London wound up its work and dissolved. But the final departure of the volunteers in the Nationalist Army was postponed till after they had had a chance to appear in Franco's victory parade in Madrid. The date was altered for one reason or another, and the parade did not take place till May 19, actually in pouring rain and in an atmosphere of intense depression.

The Spanish Civil War lasted nearly three years and cost the country 600,000 lives. Of these some 100,000 died by murder or summary execution, 200,000 by disease or malnutrition, and 300,000 on the battle field. Spain had peace at last, but it was the peace of the desert.

Portugal

We should not leave this chapter without a glance at Spain's partner in the Iberian Peninsula — Portugal.

It is again one of the puzzles of anthropology that despite the similar physical environment the Spanish and Portuguese peoples should differ so markedly from one another. In Portugal the whole social atmosphere was milder, and, as travelers have said, the country often recalled the happier disposition of pre-1914 Austria. Here, as in Spain, were a largely peasant economy and the beginnings of industrial development, and here too were devout Catholicism and various brands of revolution; but the consequent political conflict somehow avoided the excesses so characteristic of Spain.

In one respect, however, Portugal resembled Spain – in her political instability. Between 1910, when King Manuel II was deposed, and 1932, when Salazar became Premier, the country had more than forty "democratic" governments. In 1926, when it may be said that Portugal enters our period of history, the government was in the hands of a triumvirate consisting of two generals and an admiral. The most urgent problem of the moment was the national insolvency. General Carmona, one of the triumvirate, hit upon the idea of inviting the professor of economics from the Portuguese University of Coimbra, a certain Dr. Antonio de Oliveira Salazar, to become Minister of Finance, and Salazar eventually agreed to take the appointment – on condition that he should have absolute control over the budget. The experiment turned out a great success. Carmona became sole President of Portugal in 1928, and he remained President till his death in 1951. But Salazar was the real force in the administration and from time to time held the major portfolios of office in it. He became Premier in 1932, and as we write, he is Premier still.

Salazar has been called the "quiet dictator." He is a man of retiring disposition – and here we must drop into the present tense – of scholarly tastes, simple and modest in his way of life, detesting the histrionics of others of his dictatorial fellowship in Europe. He has governed autocratically for thirty years without recourse to the death penalty for political offences. He has given Portugal a regime of strict economic orthodoxy. He has balanced his budgets, increased exports, and reduced unemployment almost to nothing. He has prohibited both strikes and lockouts; by legislation, he has precisely defined the limits of private property and public utilities. His administration is corporative in spirit – he would like to call it "Catholic" – although there is no question but that it protects the landlord and employer. He has done little in the way of land reform, and the condition of the Portuguese peasant remains today very much as it was a generation ago. Communism is suppressed.

In foreign policy he has followed a neutral line. As Foreign Minister from 1936 to 1947, he guided Portugal through the difficult phases of the Spanish Civil War and the Second World War, and, moreover, kept her free from involvement in the concurrent ideological conflicts.

23. RUSSIA: SOVIET FOREIGN POLICY

Defensive Aspects

The commentator on our contemporary affairs, trying to be impartial, must find the appraisal of the Soviet experiment in Russia the most difficult of all the tasks that this Age of Conflict sets him. He may read every book and article; he may hear every lecture and broadcast; he may even go to Russia himself. Yet, as he increaseth knowledge, he increaseth confusion; and his confusion will be aggravated by the feeling of the paramount importance of his subject and the paramount need for coming to conclusions with it. In this Part of our narrative Nazi Germany has loomed larger – indeed in the Period of Crisis, Nazi Germany has been the main theme. But Nazi Germany has since gone; and the Soviet experiment is still with us and, as it has turned out, has in greater measure the "gift of destiny." In his appraisal of Russia the commentator is not only being asked to judge the past and the present, but to see into the future; for Russia, as no other country today, is the great hope or the great fear of every man.

Yet Soviet foreign policy in these years need not be an entirely impenetrable mystery. Soviet foreign policy, like the foreign policy of any other power, was a mixture – even a contradictory mixture – of defense and offense. In this chapter we shall try to examine these two aspects of it – or at least we shall reproduce, much as we did in the case of Nazism in an earlier chapter, some of the arguments commonly put forward – especially during the 1930's, at the time of which we are now writing – to explain them. It will be for the reader, as he follows our discussion, to decide what light we have been able to throw upon the Russian question.

The English-speaking peoples, in their long freedom from invasion – and even from the fear of it – have been spared the characteristic psychosis of those less fortunate nations of the world for whom invasion has been a repeated historical experience. Since the dawn of history the Russian steppe has been swept by great migrations. East and west it has been beset with raid and conquest. Latterly the Russian people fought the Napoleonic War of 1812, the Crimean War of 1854-56, the Japanese War of 1904-05, the Austro-German War of 1914-18, and the Civil War of 1918-20, every one of which followed the familiar ancient pattern. Furthermore, all these wars were a repeated revelation of the technological "backwardness" of the Russian people. Again and again they were in the curious predicament of having to purchase protection by learning the more "advanced" arts and sciences of their enemies. Thus Stalin in an address in 1931, in the midst of the first Five-Year Plan:

> Those who fall behind are beaten. Old Russia was beaten by the Mongol Khans; she was beaten by the Turkish beys; she was beaten by the Swedish feudal lords; she was beaten by the Polish and Lithuanian gentry; she was beaten by the British and French capitalists; she was beaten by the Japanese barons. All beat her — for her backwardness, for her military, cultural, political, industrial and agricultural backwardness. She was beaten because it was profitable to beat her and because she could be beaten with impunity. Do you remember the words of the poet "Thou art poor and abundant, mighty and impotent, Mother Russia"? That is why we must no longer lag behind; that is why we must build up the socialist system of economy in the shortest possible time. There is no other way. Either we do so, or we shall be crushed.

Traditional fears were aggravated by Marxist doctrine, and by the warnings of Lenin, that the capitalist powers would surely assault the young Communist state in its moments of weakness. The Civil War and its tale of "intervention" eventually came to an end in 1920, but, in Russian eyes, the basic conflict had not been resolved. The basic conflict had been renewed with other weapons in the subsequent campaign of misunderstanding and misrepresentation in the capitalist world. For example, Soviet Russia had been pointedly excluded from the Washington Conference at the end of 1921, though an interested Pacific power, and her reception at the Genoa Conference in 1922 had been far from cordial. (See pp. 142-43 and 297.) Throughout the interwar years, the Soviet Union remained almost paranoiac in her apprehensiveness toward her neighbors, and the seeming reversals of principle, the seeming absence of principle in all Soviet diplomacy are arguably attributable to a sort of frenzied defense complex against capitalist imperialist aggression. This attitude of mind, we might add, came all too easily to the average Communist leader, a man of revolutionary background — whether he were an old Bolshevik brought up in the lurking shadows of Tsarist conspiracy or a young son of the Soviet Union brought up in the lurking shadows of the party purge — a man whose normal emotions, from very childhood, were compounded of suspicion and betrayal.

It would be hard to imagine governments less desirous of war than those of Britain and France in the Locarno era. Yet the Soviet Union passed these halcyon years in a state of mortal panic over their fell designs against itself. Soviet opinion, for instance, regarded the League of Nations as a capitalist junta for the maintenance of the imperialist Versailles order. Locarno itself, because it excluded the Soviet Union and because it was concerned only with the Western European frontiers, could be read by inference as an acknowledgment that the Eastern European frontiers might still fluctuate, and perhaps be encouraged to fluctuate under the impact of new wars, at the expense of the Soviet Union. The carefree citizen of Britain or France would have been much surprised to learn that 1927 — of all years — was one in which the Soviet Union expected a treacherous military assault. Conservative governments had been established at that time in Britain and France, Germany and Austria; Italy, Hungary, Poland and Lithuania, as well as Turkey and other states of the Near East had passed under reactionary anti-Soviet dictatorships; the Kuomintang had triumphed in China, and a military party in Japan; within the Soviet Union, the struggle between Stalinists and Trotskyists was at its height; and all these events, in Soviet eyes, had a sinister concurrence. The raid of the London police on Arcos, the Russian trade agency, in May 1927, a raid regarded by the British press with half-amused and cynical indifference, was interpreted in Russia as the climax of a long campaign all pointing in one direction. (See p. 270.) "Be on your guard!" cried Voroshilov, Commissar for War, in his speech to the Congress of Soviets in 1927. "You are surrounded by enemies." Chicherin even dubbed the Pact of Paris in 1928 as "an instrument for the isolation of, and the struggle with, the Soviet Union." Stalin himself predicted that the year 1928 would be a period "of imperialist attacks and intervention against the Soviet Union."

The theme of defense therefore runs through and seems to explain many of the phases of Soviet diplomacy in the interwar years. To allay the omnipresent fear, Soviet diplomacy sought to enter into bilateral security pacts with the Soviet Union's territorial neighbors and near neighbors. It was the standard policy of the Soviet Union to entrench itself behind security pacts, much as France entrenched herself behind alliances. The first of the pacts, and the model for the rest, was the Turkish-Soviet Treaty of December 1925. The signatories agreed to remain neutral in any war involving the other, never to attack each other, nor to enter into blocs or coalitions hostile to each other. During 1926 and 1927, the Soviet Union signed similar pacts with Afghanistan, Persia (Iran), the Baltic States — and, as will be mentioned again, with Germany. At the same time, under Soviet influence, a series of analogous, interlocking bilateral pacts were signed by Turkey, Afghanistan, and Persia.

Maxim Litvinov succeeded Chicherin as Soviet Foreign Commissar early in 1929 to become for the next ten years a familiar figure at Geneva and at every international conference of importance. He had already made a dramatic appearance in 1927 at the Preparatory Commission for the Disarmament Conference and had appealed there for universal and total disarmament. For a few years Litvinov seemed to be forsaking the traditional pattern of Russian foreign policy and to be making trial of collective security as understood in the West. In 1928 the Soviet Union adhered to the Pact of Paris, and Litvinov set about constructing a similar pact applicable more particularly to the States within the Soviet Union. On February 9, 1929, the Litvinov Protocol, as it was called, was signed in Moscow, and six states — Poland, Rumania, Lithuania, Danzig, Turkey, and Persia — solemnly affirmed the Pact of Paris as binding on themselves. (See p. 125.)

The Soviet Union's relations with Germany are of particular interest, especially in view of the events of 1939. There was little in the way of common ideological ground between the two countries, even in the Weimar period. The German Communist party had met with defeat in the early 1920's, and the Comintern in Moscow had since evinced no great interest in it. But, for a time, the two countries had a diplomatic and an economic need for each other. It had been so in Bismarck's day; it was so in Stresemann's. As Stalin said, "solidarity is necessary between the countries defeated in the World War, the countries most hurt and robbed," which must consequently stand together in opposition to "the dominating concert of the Great Powers."

The Soviet Union was a field for unlimited economic development, and Germany could contribute the necessary machinery and technical skills therefor. Germany herself, afflicted with the claustrophobia of Versailles, was hungry to take a share in the exploitation of any *Lebensraum* as vastly unrestricted as the plains of Russia. The *Reichswehr* chiefs and the Red Army chiefs enjoyed very close relations. Thus, whenever Germany felt weak, she turned to Russia and invariably found there some solace from the pressure of the Western Powers. Throughout the Peace Conference of Paris in 1919, a Soviet-German *rapprochement* had been a very real threat. In 1922, at Rapallo, that *rapprochement* had become a fact. In 1926, just after Locarno, when the League of Nations had failed immediately to implement the Powers' promises of Germany's membership, Germany once more had turned eastward and signed with the Soviet Union a treaty of friendship, the Treaty of Berlin of April 24, 1926. The pact was extended by a Protocol signed in Moscow in June 1931. The Moscow Pact of 1939, which so astonished the world, had its precedents indeed. (See pp. 148, 156, and 218.)

But in the early 1930's it was Germany that was the menace, not Britain or France. In 1931 the Soviet Union put in train a new series of nonaggression pacts with Afghanistan, Turkey, and Lithuania, and these were extended in 1932 by similar pacts with Finland, Latvia, Estonia, and Poland. All these agreements signified by implication the renunciation of Russia's former expansionism in the Baltic, the Balkans, and the Near East. The Soviet Union signed no pact with Rumania, but it formally reaffirmed the Pact of Paris and the Litvinov Protocol with respect to Rumania, and thus assured the Rumanian Government that it had no designs on Bessarabia. The Soviet security structure was crowned in November 1932 by a nonaggression pact with France, and in 1933 by a similar convention with Italy. In 1933 at the World Economic Conference in London, Litvinov, who never missed an opportunity to press his policy of peace, proposed to the delegates from the signatory countries of the Litvinov Protocol that they should sign a multilateral convention defining aggression. The proposal was accepted and during July 1933 conventions to that effect were signed by the Soviet Union, Afghanistan, Estonia, Latvia, Persia, Poland, Rumania, Turkey, Czechoslovakia, Yugoslavia, and Finland. In November 1933, Litvinov was in Washington to exchange recognitions with President Roosevelt.

In 1934 the Soviet Union became a member of the League of Nations.

Here too was a reversal of attitude unthinkable a year or two previously. But at the same time Germany – and Japan – potential enemies of the Soviet Union, were both on the point of withdrawing from the League. Early in 1934, Barthou had become Foreign Minister of France. He had roughly broken off negotiations for inducing Germany to return to the Disarmament Conference and had applied himself to the construction of a Grand Alliance for the containment of the Nazi Reich. (See p. 454.) Litvinov shared all Barthou's vigorous realism, and, as a first step to alignment in Barthou's plan, the Soviet Union moved to join the League. Under Barthou's driving guidance, the soundings made of individual member states discovered a remarkable unanimity in favor of the Soviet Union's admission. The only obvious objector was Poland, who, since her nonaggression pact of January 1934 with Germany, had already seemed to have deserted to the "other camp." Eventually, in September 1934, at the Fifteenth Assembly of the League, the Soviet Union was admitted to membership of the League, and to a permanent seat on the League Council.

Thereafter, till 1939, the Soviet Union acted as a loyal and enthusiastic member of the League. Litvinov bore himself as the complete League statesman. Barthou was assassinated in October 1934 in circumstances which we shall elsewhere describe, and his Grand Alliance, in the form in which he had envisaged it, was never realized. But a reduced version survived in the two mutual assistance pacts in May 1935 between the Soviet Union and France, and the Soviet Union and Czechoslovakia. (See pp. 389-90 and 455.)

The Soviet Union sought to repeat in the Far East the policy it pursued in the Near East and West though without the same success. The Soviet Union had accepted the Japanese aggression in Manchuria with remarkable passivity. It was perhaps in no position to do otherwise. Chiang Kai-shek in China was virulently anti-Soviet, his military advisors were German, and, except for the small struggling group of Chinese Communists in Kiangsi and Fukien, Soviet influence in the Far East at this time was at a minimum. Litvinov, striving for a Chinese-Soviet nonaggression pact of the usual pattern, met with nothing but continual rebuffs. In March 1936, the Soviet Union signed a protocol, virtually a nonaggression pact, with the Mongolian People's Republic. In November of the same year, Japan and Germany concluded their Anti-Comintern Pact. In August 1937, the month after the outbreak of the "China incident," the Soviet Union and China at long last signed a nonaggression pact.

Purges and Trials

In Chapter 12 we mentioned the sabotage trials in the Soviet Union which, in the early 1930's, accompanied the Five-Year Plans. The so-called treason trials took place in the middle 1930's. The two series of trials are not to be confused, though their forensic techniques were similar and though the theme in both was again defense.

Russia's unending political problem has always been the founding of a unitary state out of an amorphous people in an amorphous land, a people with a perpetual streak of primitive nomadism in their blood, subject as much to destructive revolts from within as to invasions from without. In the wide Euro-Asiatic Plain a strong central authority must always have been, and still must be, the prior condition for the survival of any polity other than the tribal. If then the Russian people traditionally feared external aggression, they – and their rulers – feared "internal aggression" no less. English-speaking peoples have been spared both these fears, and the traitor has been a relatively rare figure in their histories. But in recent years the rise of ideological loyalties at the expense of national loyalties introduced these strange new phenomena into the contemporary scene, and we have known them under such names as the "Trojan Horse" or the "Fifth Column." But to Russians, past or present, these things were never new or strange.

Interestingly enough, however, in the early 1930's, as part of its general "Western orientation" of the time, the Soviet Union was feeling its way very cautiously and tentatively to greater domestic liberalism. Russian intellectuals and scientific workers were receiving back some of their old freedoms and privileges. Schools throughout the Soviet Union were adopting less Russocentric curricula, especially in the teaching of history. Younger folk began to borrow some of the trappings of Western culture; many of the men shaved and wore white collars; the women took to lipstick. There were rumors of an impending amnesty for many thousands of kulaks and other "deviators" in exile in Siberia. The Ogpu became part of a specially created Commissariat of the Interior, thereafter called by the initials of this Commissariat, the NKVD. Several kinds of political crime were removed from Ogpu jurisdiction although, as once before in the reorganization of the political police in Russia, the changes were not always immediately apparent.

But suddenly this promising process stopped. In 1933 Hitler came to power in Germany with his ferocious philippics against Communism and the "subhuman monsters of the Kremlin." Then, as often happens, liberal concessions, instead of being accepted in gratitude, tended to release pent-up criticism. On December 1, 1934, Sergei Kirov, one of Stalin's junior intimates and latterly party chief in Leningrad – and incidentally one of the "liberals" – was assassinated. Since the murder of Uritsky in 1918, also the party chief of his day in Leningrad, no political crime of equal magnitude had been committed in Russia. Other assassinations had lately rent the peace of Europe – Dollfuss in Austria, and King Alexander of Yugoslavia, and Barthou in France – events that were quite enough to stir up the old psychosis in Russia. Stalin and the inner party circle resolved on a veritable reign of extermination. Andrei Zhdanov, a capable young apprentice in terrorism, succeeded Kirov in Leningrad.[1]

During December 1934, secret trials took place of dozens of "counter-revolutionary conspirators," many of them foreign nationals and illegal entrants into Russia, and the greater number were summarily executed. In January 1935, Zinoviev and Kamenev were arrested and accused of having planned the murder of Kirov and of planning to murder Stalin with the aid, not only of Trotsky, but of the Nazi Gestapo. A plot was said to have been unearthed to detach the Ukraine from the Soviet Union. It was reported that the Nazis were holding Skoropadsky in Berlin – the same

Skoropadsky who had been puppet ruler of the Ukraine under the Austro-German occupation in 1918 and who was now allegedly being groomed as the Nazi governor of a future Ukrainian "Manchukuo." Zinoviev was sentenced to ten years' imprisonment, and Kamenev to five. (See p. 208.)

For more than three years, in an atmosphere of mounting hysteria, the sanguinary inquisition continued. In August 1936, Zinoviev and Kamenev, together with other "Trotskyite" survivors, stood for retrial before the Supreme Military Tribunal, with Vyshinsky, Commissar for Justice, as state prosecutor. The defendants bore eloquent witness against each other, made fluent and highly dramatic confessions of their sins, and in general produced that picture of exaggerated self-immolation that was to become associated with all Soviet trials. In the end, all the defendants were sentenced to be shot, and their personal property confiscated.

The trials did not interrupt the discussions that attended the drafting of the new Soviet constitution, eventually adopted in December 1936 – the Stalin Constitution, which we have described in Chapter 12. (See pp. 232-33.) On the contrary it was argued that the revelation of such widespread treachery in the Soviet Union was an additional reason, in Stalin's eyes, for the solidification of his system in unassailable documentary form. In that December the pogrom in Russia was more ruthless and extensive than ever. The Anti-Comintern Pact between Germany and Japan had just been signed with all its sinister implications for the Soviet state. Karl Radek, once a leading light in the Comintern, was now under arrest, together with Sokolnikov, former Soviet Ambassador in London, and Pyatakov, Vice-Commissar for Heavy Industry. Tomsky, President of the Council of Trade Unions, committed suicide. Alexei Rykov, Lenin's successor as President of the Council of Commissars, was able for the moment to absolve himself from all charges. In January 1937, Radek, Sokolnikov, and Pyatakov were brought to trial for organizing a conspiracy "to expedite an armed attack on the Soviet Union, and to assist foreign aggressors to seize its territory." Radek and Sokolnikov were sentenced to ten years' imprisonment, and Pyatakov was shot. In April 1937, Yagoda, chief of the Ogpu, and self-styled "Sword-bearer of the Revolution," was himself arrested for crimes committed during his term of office and was succeeded by Yezhov, afterward entitled General Commissar for Public Security.

During 1937 tens of thousands were taken into custody, tried for alleged sabotage or conspiracy, and executed or exiled to remote parts of the Soviet Union. Separatist movements among the national minorities, notably in the Ukraine, suffered special persecution. There were wholesale administrative changes in the individual republics. Ten government heads, fifty commissars, and seven ranking party secretaries were removed from their offices. Priests, both Orthodox and Catholic, and even Moslem mullahs, were charged with espionage on behalf of Fascist Powers. Soviet ambassadors and diplomatic officials abroad were ordered home "to report." Karakhan, Vice-Commissar for Foreign Affairs and former ambassador to China, was executed. Krylenko, Borodin, and other famous Bolsheviks in one way or another vanished from the scenes. Krivitsky escaped abroad. Even foreign residents, many of them Communist refugees in Russia – Béla Kun of Hungary was one – were imprisoned or deported.

Stalin and Khrushchev at the time of the Spanish Civil War, 1936

SOVFOTO

In May 1937, Gamarnik, Chief of the Red Army Political Department, Vice-Commissar for War, and alleged associate of the late Pyatakov, committed suicide. In June, a Supreme Military Tribunal, composed of Voroshilov, Budenny and Bluecher, sentenced to death Marshal Tukhachevsky and seven other ranking generals of the Red Army, all former heroes of the Civil War, on charges of military conspiracy "with an unfriendly state" – presumably Germany. Relations between the Red Army chiefs and the *Reichswehr* chiefs, as we have said, had been very close – close enough perhaps for conspiracy. One story has it that Beneš, the Czechoslovak Foreign Minister, discovered that the Soviet Embassy in Prague was being secretly used for communication between the Red Army and the *Reichswehr* and that he reported the discovery to Stalin. Another story has it that Tukhachevsky and Blomberg, both attending the funeral of King George V in London in January 1936, had met and concocted a coup in Moscow. It seems unlikely that the full facts will ever be known. At all events the generals were tried in camera by their own peers in the presence of a hundred or more Red Army officers summoned from all over the Union; they confessed their guilt, and they were shot within twenty-four hours of receiving sentence. It is significant of the extraordinary conditions of the Soviet Union at this time that of the eight military judges at the trial, six were disgraced, degraded, or otherwise removed by the end of 1938, and only Voroshilov and Budenny remained in possession of their rank and position.

The last of the trials, in many ways the most important and most theatrical of them all, took place in March 1938. There were twenty-one defendants, among whom were Rykov, President of the Council of Commissars; Bukharin, editor of *Pravda,* and one of the philosophers of Communism; Krestinsky, former ambassador in Berlin; Rakovsky, former ambassador in London and Paris; and Yagoda, former chief of the Ogpu. They were charged with conspiring with Trotsky and with the intelligence services of Germany and Japan to overthrow the Soviet Government. All confessed their guilt. Rykov, Bukharin, Krestinsky, and Yagoda were sentenced to death, and Rakovsky – then in his seventieth year – to penal servitude for twenty years. The last major victim of the Great Purge was its main organizer, Yezhov. He was succeeded by Lavrenty Beria.

The effect of the trials abroad was a mixture of mystification and horror. The year 1938 was the year of Hitler's Austrian coup and the year of Munich, the year of all years for a nation to appear sure, strong, and well respected. But when, in 1938, the indefatigable Litvinov reaffirmed Soviet pledges to Czechoslovakia and France, and preached his jeremiads against the saboteurs of collective security, not a chancellery or general staff in Western Europe believed for a moment that the Soviet Government and Red Army, decimated in its leadership, shaken and demoralized, was in any position to support so bold a policy. The French in particular again and again avoided staff talks with the Red Army chiefs, any one of whom, it seemed, might suddenly be moved to confess to the most heinous treacheries and divulge vital military secrets. When Colonel Charles Lindbergh, for instance, reported unfavorably upon the Soviet Air Force, his words fell upon already well-seeded soil; and when the Soviet forces in 1940 took so long to crack the defenses of the little republic of Finland, military authorities throughout the world merely felt that they had been confirmed in their low estimate of Soviet military prowess. Small wonder that Hitler was so confident that he could overthrow the Soviet state.

Offensive Aspects

But defense explains only a part of Soviet foreign policy, and it is the other part in which we are perhaps more interested. The heirs of mediaeval Muscovy today would not be occupying one-sixth of the surface of the Earth if defense had been the sole and only motive of their statecraft. The age-long pressure towards Intermediate Europe, the Dardanelles, the Levant, Persia, Afghanistan, Mongolia, and Manchuria characterized both the Tsarist and Soviet empires. Soviet territory shrank during the Civil War only to expand once more at the expense of the border nationalities. In 1920 the Red Army carried the Soviet advance to Warsaw, and, for a moment, all Europe east of the Rhine was under threat. Again, after the contraction and expansion of the Second World War, the Soviet Union came to incorporate or dominate territories beyond its frontiers of 1939 and indeed beyond the Russian frontiers of 1914. Meanwhile the Comintern and Cominform carried on their subversive mission throughout the world. (See pp. 224-25 and 659.)

All this is so obvious and well known as hardly to call for comment. But there was one distinctive feature of the Soviet offensive that marked it as unique among other offensive movements in Russian history, namely the Communist doctrine which it now purported to express. Something of this doctrine was discussed in Chapter 12, but mainly insofar as it affected the Communist party and the Soviet governmental structure. It remains to discuss here the consequences of that doctrine on Soviet foreign policy.

Many a student of modern politics has felt how elusive, in the superficial view, were the differences between democracy and Communism. In practice, certainly, they might seem poles apart. The free institutions of the one had little in common with the totalitarian institutions of the other. The popular representative assemblies of a democracy – even with their party "machines" and occasional disciplines – were not comparable with a one-party dictatorship. But, beyond this, the essential antagonism of the two political forms is not so easy to point out. Historically, both democracy and Communism grew out of popular revolts against tyranny and want. Both sought to order this earthly scheme of things for the betterment of the "under-privileged and disinherited." Both were kinds of "welfare politics." Both were profoundly "Antinomian."[2] And, if democracy set a high value on the individual human creature and made the State his servant, no less did Communism work for the eventual disappearance of the State, so as to leave the individual in the unmolested enjoyment of his rights and freedoms.

But democracy was never a finished theoretic system. Freedoms of speech and of assembly, representative government and majority decisions were its means, not its ends. They were the technical, administrative, empirically tested means of securing a way of life, sometimes called the Good Life. If the Rights of Man or the Four Freedoms could have been better secured under absolute monarchy, then doubtless under absolute monarchy would Western democratic man have chosen to flourish and grow. But it was his experience through the centuries that absolutism, however benevolent, corrupted the monarch and eventually destroyed those things that seemed most desirable. Democracy was never perfectionist. Democracy sought to give as practical an approximation to the basic human rights and freedoms as may reasonably be expected in an imperfect world. It did not look forward to a day when man would cease to be evil, and all crime and corruption should be done away. It only knew what was better, not what was best. It put its heaven in a problematic future, for which the art of politics was the never-ending quest. Democracy, for all its essential secularism, never committed the offense of the builders of the Tower of Babel.

Democracy then was a practical, pragmatic, evolutionary, inconclusive process. Its history was the history of experiment, a series of New Deals, judged by their limited success, none a final solution. Communism, by contrast, was a theoretical system, a rigid inalterable creed, once enunciated by a prophet, never questioned in its mental processes, but sacrosanct and applicable in its totality to the entire historic situation. It had a revolutionary, catastrophic ideal, a sort of earthly apocalypse. Its series of Five-Year Plans, for example, were forced through to completion irrespective, even contemptuous of, "success." The Communist did not proceed by trial and error. He made no concessions to human frailty. He had no counterpart in his creed for original sin. Dialectical materialism and historic necessity were on his side, and all he needed was the correct tactic for the moment to hasten the inevitable, inexorable march of events. Success or failure neither proved nor disproved his thesis. Communism was true, not because it *worked,* but because it was *the* doctrine.

In the West the criterion of truth was verifiability, and it had been so since the Renaissance. The Russian who stood on the periphery of the Renaissance and never wholly participated in it, equated truth quasi-scholastically with conformity to dogma. Democratic "truth" operated through compromise, toleration, the cross-fertilization of opposing views, incessant criticism and revision. Communist "truth" was vested in an uncompromising, intolerant, oracular, literal, final orthodoxy. Democracy thrived in a philosophical era, when it was the main intellectual tradition to analyze fundamental assumptions, an era in which doctrine *qua* doctrine was subject, almost as a matter of mental habit, to intensive, often destructive, interrogation. The Russian world never had its Lockes and Kants who, whatever else may have been the value of their work, at least set limits to the arrogance of human thought. Significantly the post-Kantian philosopher of the West, who most influenced the Russian world, was Hegel, the bearer of new certitudes.

Communism was devoted to what often seemed to be no more than verbal subtleties. Stalin himself, in his writings, was infinitely painstaking with the minutiae of doctrine. And this was not an amiable eccentricity, a pedantic weakness, permitted to an otherwise busy and hard-headed man, but was fundamental to his faith and training as a Communist. "The Party," he wrote, "must be armed with revolutionary theory, with a knowledge of the laws of revolution." Otherwise it would be incapable of directing the struggle of the proletariat. Stalin believed that in Marxism-Leninism he possessed a view of human history and society, an exact science, a detailed and infallible instrument, with which "to grasp the internal connection of surrounding events, to foresee the course of events and to discern not only how and when these events are developing in the present but also how and when they must develop in the future."

The notorious opportunism of Communist politics was no derogation of the ultimate theoretical objective. The Party "line" was a tactical stratagem accepted and encouraged when felt to be necessary. Thus Stalin, quoting Lenin, could say:

> To carry on a war for the overthrow of the international bourgeoisie, a war which is a hundred times more difficult, protracted and complicated than the most stubborn of ordinary wars between states, and to refuse beforehand to maneuver, to utilize the conflict of interests (even though temporary) among one's enemies, to refuse to temporize and compromise with possible (even though transient, unstable, vacillating and conditional) allies — is not this ridiculous in the extreme? Is it not the same as if in the difficult ascent of an unexplored and heretofore inaccessible mountain we were to renounce beforehand the idea that at times we might have to go in zigzags, sometimes retracting our steps, sometimes giving up the course once selected and trying various others?

But, be it noted, in these zigzags and maneuverings the mountain summit did not shift or change. Thus Brest Litovsk, the NEP, "Socialism in one country," the Moscow Pact, the dissolution of the Comintern, the various *rapprochements* with Western diplomacy, the pliant methods of Communist parties abroad, the occasional participation in parliamentary socialism, the very Soviet system itself, all these were temporary accommodations to be used only so long as were tactically advantageous.

At the Fourteenth Party Congress in 1925, which adopted the policy of "Socialism in one country," Stalin justified himself with quotations from Lenin:

> There is not the slightest doubt that a final victory of our revolution, if it remained isolated, if there were no revolutionary movements in other countries, would be hopeless. . . . The existence of the Soviet republic side by side with imperialist states for a prolonged period is unthinkable. In the end either one or the other will conquer. . . . In order to achieve a solid victory, we must achieve the victory of the proletarian revolution in all, or at any rate, in several, of the chief capitalist countries.

Or further, from Stalin's lectures on "The Foundations of Leninism":

> The dictatorship of the proletariat, the transition from capitalism to Communism, must not be regarded as a fleeting period of "super-revolutionary" acts and decrees, but as an entire historical era, replete with civil wars and external conflicts, with persistent organizational work and economic construction, with advances and retreats, victories and defeats.
>
> The law of violent proletarian revolution, the law of the smashing of the bourgeois state machine as a preliminary condition for such a revolution, is an inevitable law of the revolutionary movement in the imperialist countries of the world.
>
> Without a stubborn, continuous and determined struggle against the imperialist chauvinism of the Socialists of the ruling nations — Britain, France, the United States, Italy, Japan, etc. — without such a struggle the education of the working class of the ruling nations in the spirit of true internationalism, in the spirit of *rapprochement* with the toiling masses of the dependent countries and colonies, in the spirit of real preparation for the proletarian revolution, is inconceivable. . . . Without this it would have been impossible to consolidate the Soviet power, to implant true internationalism and to create that remarkable organization for the collaboration of nations which is called the Union of Soviet Socialist Republics — the living prototype of the future union of nations in a single world economic system.
>
> The victorious proletariat of one country having expropriated the capitalists and organized its own Socialist production, would stand up against the rest of the capitalist world, attracting to its cause the oppressed classes of other countries, raising revolt among them against the capitalists, and, in the event of necessity, come out even with armed force against the exploiting classes and their states.[3]

Nor let it be thought that the successors of Stalin permitted any relaxation from this extreme ideological attitude. Khrushchev, for example, a "practical" politician if ever there was one, temperamentally an extrovert, at first sight might have seemed to have no theoretical interests. His many speeches, especially those delivered during his tours abroad and in the United Nations, show a lively concern for the tactics of the moment. But doctrine was in him too. He did not talk about world revolution and war as Stalin did; he preferred "peaceful coexistence." But, whatever he talked about, the language was unmistakably the same. We may cite his famous report at the Twentieth Party Congress and note, in this report, how again and again in the midst of burning humanitarian indignation against the crimes of the "cult of the individual," the unpardonable sin of his code was deviation from Communist orthodoxy. It is enough to quote the peroration of the report:

> Comrades! We must abolish the cult of the individual decisively, once and for all; we must draw the proper conclusions concerning both ideological-theoretical and practical work.
>
> It is necessary for this purpose:
>
> First, in a Bolshevik manner to condemn and to eradicate the cult of the individual as alien to Marxism-Leninism and not consonant with the principles of party leadership and the norms of party life, and to fight inexorably all attempts at bringing back this practice in one form or another.
>
> To return to and actually to practice in all our ideological work the most important theses of Marxist-Leninist science about the people as the creator of history and as the creator of all the material and spiritual good of humanity, about the decisive role of the Party in the revolutionary fight for the transformation of society, about the victory of Communism.
>
> In this connection we will be forced to do much work in order to examine critically from the Marxist-Leninist viewpoint and to correct the widespread erroneous views connected with the cult of the individual in the sphere of history, philosophy, economics, and of other sciences, as well as in literature and the fine arts. It is especially necessary that in the immediate future we compile a serious textbook of the history of our Party which will be edited in accordance with scientific Marxist objectivism, a textbook of the history of Soviet society, a book pertaining to the events of the Civil War and the great patriotic war.
>
> Secondly, to continue systematically and consistently the work done by the Party's Central Committee during the last years, a work characterized by minute observation in all party organizations, from the bottom to the top, of the Leninist principles of party leadership, characterized, above all, by the main principle of collective leadership, characterized by the observation of the norms of party life, described in the statutes of our Party, and finally characterized by the wide practice of criticism and self-criticism.
>
> Thirdly, to restore completely the Leninist principles of Soviet Socialist democracy, expressed in the Constitution of the Soviet Union, to fight the wilfulness of individuals abusing their power. The evil caused by acts violating revolutionary Socialist legality, which have accumulated during a long time as a result of the negative influence of the cult of the individual, has to be completely corrected.
>
> Comrades! The Twentieth Congress of the Communist Party of the Soviet Union has manifested with a new strength the unshakable unity of our Party, its cohesiveness round the Central Committee, its resolute will to accomplish the great task of building Communism . . .[4]

If this was the authentic voice of the Soviet Union, our former question regarding the defensiveness or aggressiveness of Soviet foreign policy takes on an almost irrelevant, unreal, and outmoded air. The above quotation would seem to represent not a democratic debater's modest statement of opinion, but a dogma, an affirmation of faith. They reveal a world picture, a historical *reality,* which the Communist assumed to be literally and absolutely true. All other world pictures were heresy or fraud. There could be no meeting between such a mind and other minds elsewhere. If such a mind believed in the necessity of war, counterargument would be useless against it. The processes of rational discourse and cooperation, as developed and practiced in the West, belonged to an altogether different mental idiom.

24. BRITAIN: COALITION AND APPEASEMENT

The National Governments

Britain consumed the early 1930's in a grim struggle with the Depression. Ramsay MacDonald and his Labor government resigned in August 1931, but returned with an all-party National government expressly to deal with the crisis. (See pp. 330-31.) It was not the first time in British history that a moment of emergency seemed to call for a coalition. Both the Liberal and Labor parties split over the issue, and the orthodox remnant in each carefully distinguished itself from the "National Liberals" and "National Labor" who now "deserted" them to support the new government. George Lansbury, the extreme pacifist, succeeded to the leadership of the rump of the Labor party. On September 21, 1931, Britain abandoned the gold standard.

The position of the National government was uncomfortable and anomalous. It had been more or less self-constituted and, beyond the solution of the financial crisis, it had neither object nor policy. The Conservatives revived all their old protectionist cries, with which of course Philip Snowden, the Chancellor of the Exchequer, a Labor man and an austere free trader, would have nothing to do. In the end MacDonald advised the King to dissolve Parliament. Elections were held at the end of October 1931. Conservative, National Liberal and National Labor members of the government appealed to the country for a "doctor's mandate" – such was their not very imaginative slogan – to carry on the good work of financial recovery they claimed to have begun. The election was fought without much excitement, and experienced campaigners averred afterward that there was far less rowdyism than they had expected. The result was a general Conservative victory. The nation, in the way that is peculiar to the Anglo-Saxon democracy, had made up its collective mind that, for the moment, orthodox Conservatism would probably serve its interests best. The Communists and a new "Fascist party," led by Sir Oswald Mosley, both failed to win a single seat.

The government still called itself the National government and regarded itself as a continuation of its predecessor, but it was essentially Conservative in composition. Ramsay MacDonald remained Prime Minister, although he was increasingly out of sympathy with his new colleagues. Neville Chamberlain, a leading Conservative and avowed protectionist, was Chancellor of the Exchequer. Sir John Simon was Foreign Secretary, and Anthony Eden Foreign Under-Secretary. Snowden afterward went to the House of Lords, but for the time being retained a minor Cabinet post. Parliament at once joined battle over protectionism. Debates on a general tariff were opened by Neville Chamberlain early in February 1932, and were continued throughout the month. Chamberlain adduced all the classic arguments. Protection would rectify the balance of trade, stabilize the currency, produce revenue, encourage home industries and imperial reciprocity, and furnish a useful bargaining point in trade negotiations with other countries. An Import Duties Bill became law in February 29, 1932, and provided for a duty of 10 per cent on a long list of goods. Thus did Britain again become a protectionist country.

The fall of the pound, and the psychological reaction thereto, had given an indirect stimulus to trade, and it was undeniable that the country was showing the first faint gleams of economic recovery. Neville Chamberlain presented a balanced budget, the first of five which he was now to present in successive years. He sliced expenditures by a tenth, and he made full use of the new tariffs. An Exchange Equalization Fund of £150,000,000 was established to offset sudden withdrawals of gold and to absorb exceptional speculative movements. In July 1932, the Lausanne Conference made an end of German reparations, and later in the same month the Imperial Economic Conference met in Ottawa. The year 1933 was the year of the World Economic Conference in London and its attendant disappointments, but Britain's slow recovery seemed to continue. Trade agreements were signed with Denmark, Germany, and Argentina and, in spite of the current "sabotage trials" in Moscow, trade negotiations were even reopened with the Soviet Union. Britain defaulted on her debt installments to the United States in circumstances described elsewhere, and the relief therefrom contributed to Chamberlain's budget surpluses. (See p. 333.) The unemployed still cried out for succor, but there were now fewer to take care of. At the end of 1934, the figure stood at 2,000,000, and by the end of 1936, at 1,600,000. Trade indices at home and abroad were more encouraging. The building trades and armaments, for instance, were showing a strong spurt of activity. In all this the government followed no "plan." Essentially a Conservative government, it was opposed to plans on principle. Economists described the evident recovery as a "normal upswing."

Early in June 1935, the government was reconstructed. Ramsay MacDonald had been Prime Minister since June 1929 and Prime Minister of the National governments since August 1931. Six years of heavy responsibility had told upon his health, and his colleagues were said to be finding him increasingly short of temper and difficult to approach. His oratory wandered and lost itself in outworn grandiloquence. His foreign policy in previous years, to judge by the present state of Europe, had not been a success, and his long "titular" leadership of an all but Conservative cabinet, years after the crisis was past which had once justified it, was becoming faintly ridiculous. He was succeeded by his old rival, Stanley Baldwin, who thus became Prime Minister for the third time. Sir Samuel Hoare, formerly Secretary for India, became Secretary for Foreign Affairs. Anthony Eden was appointed to a new office, Minister for League of Nations Affairs.

Baldwin, hoping to remedy some of the anomalies of the National government, had already decided on an appeal to the country. Elections were fought in November 1935 in the electric atmosphere of the Italo-Ethiopian crisis. Hoare had just made his crusading speech in the League Assembly in condemnation of Italy's attitude, and it seemed as if the National government was asking for the support of the British people to deal sternly with the Roman aggressor. (See p. 405.) Baldwin himself, in his guise of a bluff, comfortable, yeomanly type of Englishman – always with his pipe – was well liked and well trusted, and to the great majority of voters his continuance as Prime Minister seemed as inevitable as it was satisfactory. The election figures showed a slight recession in the strength of the National government, but the overriding Conservative majority was safely retained. Labor trebled its representation, and the number of votes cast in its favor was far more formidable than the proportion of seats in the House it was actually able to secure. MacDonald, in a "tremendously keen, but filthy" contest, was heavily defeated in his old constituency at Seaham Harbour, Durham, though another constituency was afterward found for him.

The government still called itself the National government. Baldwin remained Prime Minister. He was Prime Minister during the London Naval Conference, the Italo-Ethiopian War, Hitler's march into the Rhineland, the outbreak of the Spanish Civil War – and during the reign and abdication of Edward VIII. But the real force in the government, it was coming to be recognized, was the Chancellor of the Exchequer, Neville Chamberlain. Baldwin resigned office in May 1937, after the coronation of George VI, and Chamberlain was his logical successor.

The Ottawa Conference

Chamberlain's protectionist policy was tied up with trade within the British Commonwealth. In July 1932, less than six months after the passing of the Import Duties Act, a conference convened at Ottawa, at the invitation of the Canadian Government, attended by representatives of all the Dominions and of India and Ireland. At the time, the conference was publicized as the British Commonwealth's own answer to the Depression; but it was soon encountering wider political, if not international, problems. The Dominions, notably Canada, were rapidly developing industries, and they were no longer what they had been before 1914, "colonial" producers of food and raw materials for the British market. Also, like Britain, they were building up substantial trade with non-Commonwealth customers. The march of facts had outdated both the older slogan, "Empire free trade," and the newer, "Complementary industrial production."

The delegates at Ottawa discovered, therefore, as soon as they descended from their rhetorical clouds to the firm earth of statistics, that the existing commerce of their respective countries often cut across, and indeed was often antagonistic to, the imperial connection. The British delegates were made sharply aware of the fact that, from the crude economic point of view, Argentina or Brazil was more closely knit to Britain than were any of her Dominions. Australia wanted to eat her Japanese cake and have her British cake as well. Canada declared she was selling less lumber in the British market than the Soviet Union was selling. All the Dominions were highly protectionist, and, though they were quite willing to cooperate in raising tariffs against non-Empire goods, they were all averse to lowering a single existing duty to their mutual advantage.

The Ottawa Agreement was eventually signed in August 1932. In essence it was just another *ad hoc* palliative in the style of orthodox Conservative economics. The Depression had plowed its wake through Dominion and colony alike. Australia and New Zealand afterward, both under Labor governments, conducted extremely interesting and instructive experiments in recovery. But economic planning on a Commonwealth scale was not a solution within the compass of practical politics. Under the Ottawa Agreement the Dominions did no more than undertake to keep their protective duties at a level that would give British producers "full opportunity of reasonable competition." Britain agreed to impose higher duties and quotas on primary products from non-Commonwealth sources that competed with any of the Dominions, notably dairy and other agricultural products. It is possible that, on the whole, Britain sacrificed a good deal for the benefit of the Commonwealth; but, more serious perhaps, the Ottawa Agreement caused severe losses to the old customers of Britain, losses only partially retrieved by subsequent separate trade agreements with Denmark, Germany, and Argentina. Continental economists argued that Ottawa aggravated the economic strains in Europe and gave a sharp fillip to the Nazi movement. The British Commonwealth, like the world at large, was still learning the very hard way that its various domestic problems were curiously and unpreventably entangled with its foreign relations.

The Silver Jubilee and the Death of George V; The Reign and Abdication of Edward VIII

King George V had ascended the throne on May 6, 1910, to reign over a people during a generation of violent changes – and of changes also in the ancient institution of monarchy. But he and Queen Mary had performed their many duties with unfailing tact and devotion. Everywhere he identified himself with the life of Britain and the Empire. Everywhere he appeared as the necessary symbol of tradition and authority. Whether at an investiture at the Palace, a state welcome to a foreign potentate, an opening of Parliament, the launching of a battleship, a thanksgiving service at St. Paul's, or the unveiling of a national monument, the ceremonial perforce centered about the person of the monarch. When in many other countries thrones were toppling into dust and ignominy, Britain's never stood higher in the esteem and affection of her people.

At the end of 1928, King George was stricken with pleurisy. Immense crowds gathered daily to wait for the medical bulletins posted outside Buckingham Palace, and many Britons were surprised, and rather awed, by the demonstrations of anxiety that the King's illness aroused. In May 1935, with Queen Mary, he celebrated the Silver Jubilee of his accession. He died on January 20, 1936, at the age of seventy, in the twenty-fifth year of his reign.

The new King came to the throne as Edward VIII. As Prince of Wales he had been widely traveled, widely known, and widely adulated. He was youthful, almost immature, in appearance – though he was forty years of age at the time of his accession. The persistent bachelorhood of this most eligible of all Prince Charmings had always evoked much intriguing speculation. He was a man of independence of mind, not an uncommon quality in his family, but a quality that in his case he was quite prepared to assert.

The reign began uneventfully. The King supported the government's drive to reduce expenditure by waiving a substantial portion of his income. He unveiled the Canadian War Memorial at Vimy Ridge. During the late summer of 1936, he went on a cruise in the Eastern Mediterranean aboard the luxury yacht *Nahlin,* touching at points in Dalmatia, Greece, and Turkey and, but for the unhappy sequel, the tour would have had considerable diplomatic value. In November, after his return home, he visited some of the "distressed" areas in South Wales; [1] he showed a decided disinclination to follow routes prescribed for him, and, much to the embarrassment of the ministers in attendance, he sometimes expressed very outspoken views on the conditions he found.

It was at this juncture that the first rumblings of the so-called Constitutional Crisis began to be heard. For some months past the yellow press in the United States – and not always the yellow press – had been reveling in accounts of the King's familiarity with a certain Mrs. Wallis W. Simpson, an American who had been divorced from her first husband ten years before and who was about to be divorced from her second. The British press, by tacit agreement, had been preserving a discreet silence in regard to the affair. But on December 1, 1936, the Bishop of Bradford, in the course of an address to the Bradford Diocesan Conference, let fall some remarks which appeared to be directed at His Majesty's more questionable friendships. Whereupon the British press broke its self-denying ordinance and published the entire story. The biography of the unfortunate lady was exposed to the British public's gaze, together with photographs of the King's party on the recent *Nahlin* cruise, of which, it was now revealed, she had been a member. The Spanish Civil War, Egypt, Palestine, the unemployed, and the new rearmament program were all dropped from the headlines to give place to this new sensation.

Once the initial stir and confusion had passed, sentiment in the country and in the Dominions to an overwhelming extent was profoundly outraged at the course of action the King was evidently proposing to take. The churches, in particular, proved to be a very powerful influence. It was not that the lady in question was the citizen of a nonmonarchical state or that in marrying her the King would contract a morganatic union by which neither wife nor children acquire titles. An American marriage of the right kind would have been immensely popular. But neither homeland nor Dominions could countenance a double divorcee as Queen. Baldwin, the Prime Minister, meanwhile gave a full account in Parliament of his pleadings with the King. Mrs. Simpson, to do her justice, offered to part from the King if he so wished. But, on December 10, he formally abdicated the throne.

On December 12, 1936, Prince Albert, Duke of York, succeeded to the throne as George VI. One of his first acts was to create his brother, the former King, Duke of Windsor. His coronation took place with all its historic color and ceremony in Westminster Abbey on May 12, 1937.

The Appeasement Policy

Baldwin, we have said, resigned from office shortly after the coronation of George VI and was succeeded by Chamberlain. Baldwin had handled the Constitutional Crisis and abdication with consummate tact and skill, and he retired from his long period of public service in an aura of public esteem, with an earldom and the supreme honor of the Order of the Garter. "He laid down the wide authority he had gathered and carefully maintained," wrote Churchill, "but had used as little as possible . . ." He had been "a profoundly astute party manager, thinking in majorities and aiming at a quiet life between elections." [2] He belonged perhaps to that school of Conservative statesmen — Walpole was his spiritual ancestor — who wait upon events, leave well enough alone, and expect all things to work out for the best in the end. Yet, surprisingly, he was also a man with a profound sense of mission and belief in his own fitness for office.

Neville Chamberlain became Prime Minister in May 1937. Like Baldwin he too was of the propertied class and had inherited a family business. He was the half brother of Austen Chamberlain, Foreign Secretary in 1924-29. His critics alleged that he was provincial and insular, but he was a man of unexceptional directness and honesty. He was simple, almost conversational in his public speeches, but sometimes chill and precise. He was certainly oversure in his methods of conducting business. But, whereas Baldwin had been passive, Chamberlain was active; whereas Baldwin was lazy, Chamberlain was for all his years a man of passionate driving force. His opinions and decisions, unfortunate though they often were, were always positive and masterful. He took great pride in being "practical" and "sensible." We can well imagine him, conscious of his own capacities, watching with growing concern a Europe in process of deterioration, pleading for a candid re-examination and redress of the evils that were admitted to exist. Then we can see him urging himself at last to take a position of public responsibility that would entitle him to demand, "Can't we practical, sensible men get together and settle this thing in a practical, sensible way?"

In a speech in the early part of 1938 he said:

> The peace of Europe must depend on the attitude of the four major Powers — Germany, Italy, France, and ourselves. For ourselves, we are linked to France by common ideals of democracy, of liberty, and of parliamentary government . . . On the other side we find Germany and Italy are also linked by affinities of outlook and in the form of their government. The question that we have to think of is this. Are we to allow these two pairs of nations to go on glowering at one another across their frontiers, allowing the feeling between the two sides to become more and more embittered, until at last the barriers are broken down and the conflict begins which many think would mark the end of civilization? Or can we bring them to an understanding of one another's aims and objects and to such discussion as may lead to a final settlement? If we can do that, if we can bring these four nations into friendly discussion, into a settling of their differences, we shall have saved the peace of Europe for a generation.

Those were not the words of an idealist or even of a trained diplomat — they were in fact a somewhat tactless reminder of the Four-Power Pact of 1933. (See pp. 398-99.) They were the words of a company director recommending a merger to fend off a mutually ruinous competition. They were also the words of a man of perfect sincerity and enlightened self-interest, a man who expected, as a matter of course, that others would meet him in the same spirit. And herein too was the essence of "appeasement."

Chamberlain well realized, again as a businessman, that his friendly discussions must be entered into from strength and not from weakness, and that, as he put it, "the effort to remove the causes which are delaying the return of confidence in Europe" must be combined with "our programme for the re-establishment of our defence forces." But he seemed to believe that the sheer weight of rearmament might of itself act as a deterrent to aggressor powers, and that designing enemies could be frightened into submission by huge budget figures. His was a typical financial rendering of the French colonial maxim — "Make a show of force, but do not use it," a maxim that proved effective enough against the tribesmen of Morocco, but was not to prove so effective against the tribesmen of Europe. Chamberlain's faith in money was tragically characteristic. "The richer country must win in the end," he used to say, and by inference the poverty of Germany, if strained beyond a certain point, must eventually bring about her destruction. He entered into the great European rearmament race as if it were some fantastic auction in which victory went to the highest bidder and defeat to the struggling bankrupt. But as Macaulay wrote of one of Chamberlain's predecessors on a similar occasion:

> It was pitiable to hear him [William Pitt] proving to an admiring audience that the wicked Republic was exhausted, that she could not hold out, that her credit was gone, and her assignats were not worth more than the paper of which they were made; as if credit was necessary to a government of which the principle was rapine, as if Alboin could not turn Italy into a desert till he had negotiated a loan at 5 per cent, as if the exchequer bills of Attila had been at par.

Unfortunately, in the present case, the richer country's expenditure on armaments per annum was one third that of the poorer aggressor.

But in all discussions, friendly and otherwise, there must be conventions. There may be honor among businessmen, as there is honor among thieves. Businessmen can deal with businessmen, and thieves with thieves. But businessmen and thieves cannot deal one with another. Democracy and Nazism each obeyed a mutually contradictory scale of values. To bring them together on the basis of contract was impossible. To Chamberlain contract was the very fabric of the life he knew; to Hitler contract was a *ruse de guerre*. The *Ehre* of the German had never become associated, as "honor" in Chamberlain's bourgeois mind had become associated, with scraps of paper. Appeasement therefore was not so much a forlorn hope, tried too late. Appeasement subsumed a technique and a code – conference, compromise, concession, contract – which were as natural to Chamberlain as the very English he spoke, but wholly beyond the custom or comprehension of his opposite. Throughout the Chamberlain-Hitler episode, as it afterward developed, the impression is borne in upon us again and again that neither understood the other – and that Chamberlain only half-realized the fact.[3]

It was unfortunate that appeasement thereafter should have become associated with the Conservative party. Appeasement as such was supposed to be in line with the near-Nazi proclivities of other reactionary groups in Europe at the time. Especially scandalous was the reputation of the extreme Conservatives of the "Cliveden set," so called after the country house where their week-end parties were supposed to have been held – parties to which Ribbentrop and other sympathetic Germans were allegedly invited, and whose discussions were faithfully reported back to the Führer in Germany.

The fact is that the Cliveden set never existed except in the imaginations of certain journalists. But it is also the fact that the British people as a whole, of whatever political color, passionately desired that the great experiment of appeasement be tried, and they were themselves culpable, if ever a people was culpable, for the kind of leadership which Chamberlain gave them. What faults he had and what mistakes he made were their faults and their mistakes. The minority, largely a Labor minority, which opposed Chamberlain in his day and clamored for a "strong" foreign policy, was often made of those elements who were once most pacific and most belligerently insistent on their country's unilateral disarmament. To the very end, in 1939, when the country was on the brink of war, Labor Members in the House of Commons were still steadily opposing the government's rearmament and conscription measures. Churchill's lone warnings on the growing strength of Germany, notably her growing strength in the air, were regarded as the dangerous troublemaking of an incorrigible and irresponsible warmonger.

Moreover, as is too often forgotten by adverse commentators, Chamberlain had continually to consider the British Dominions. Never at any time had the hands of British statesmen been so tied as now by the affairs of the Commonwealth. New liberties, however desirable, had converted the far-flung British family into a group of independent nations, each with an internal and external policy of its own. Canada was as isolationist as the United States and had to accommodate her attitude to a strong French-

Canadian minority which was largely indifferent to the British connection. South Africa was absorbed in the triangular contest between Smuts, Hertzog, and Malan and had to accommodate her attitude to a strong Boer majority that was largely hostile to the British connection. Australia and New Zealand were more concerned over the Japanese menace than the German. India had her own particular distractions. The possibility therefore that the Commonwealth, like the Empire of 1914, would once more participate wholeheartedly and collectively in the mother country's conflicts clearly had to wait upon the event and, in any case, was not a matter of perfunctory calculation in advance.

If an example is wanted of the extreme pacifism which consumed the British people during the interwar years, it is surely to be found in the National Peace Ballot of 1934. This huge referendum of British public opinion, a sort of magnified Gallup Poll, was organized by a committee representing the League of Nations Union [4] and a number of other political and religious bodies. The voter was invited to answer "Yes" or "No" to a series of questions:

> Should Great Britain remain a member of the League of Nations? Are you in favor of an all-round reduction in armaments by international agreement? . . . Do you consider that, if one nation insists on attacking another, the other nations should combine to compel it to stop by, (a) economic sanctions, (b) if necessary, military measures?

The *Times* complained that the Peace Ballot was a "deplorable waste of time and effort." Simon pointed out in the House of Commons that its questions were hardly fair. Chamberlain himself dubbed it "terribly mischievous." But the Ballot evoked an extraordinary response, and the 11,559,165 votes which were cast represented nearly 40 per cent of the British electorate. The result, announced at a monster meeting in the Albert Hall on June 27, 1935, was taken to be an overwhelming endorsement of the principle of collective security and peace.

The general election of November 1935, which returned Baldwin's National government to power, was fought in the shadow of the Italo-Ethiopian crisis and under the afterglow of the National Peace Ballot. Baldwin was severely censured for having admitted subsequently, in a speech of "appalling frankness" that, if at that time he had divulged what he knew of the progress of Germany's rearmament, his party might have lost the election. But Baldwin's "appalling frankness" cut two ways, and his censure surely was also to be shared by the British electorate, which in its obstinate pacifism was in no fit state to be told the truth.[5]

If this then was the precedent, appeasement was not so blameworthy. Never did a statesman give a more democratic and more accurate interpretation of a people's will than did Chamberlain in 1937 and 1938. But the day of disillusion, for both statesman and people, was at hand.

25. FRANCE: LEAGUES, POPULAR FRONT, AND GRAND ALLIANCE

The End of Prosperity

France had withstood the first onset of the Depression with extraordinary resilience, and she was for a time an almost freakish oasis of prosperity and financial power in the midst of a desolate world. During 1930 the gold reserve of the Bank of France rose from 40,000,000,000 to 80,000,000,000 francs, the budget showed a surplus, and on one occasion the Premier, André Tardieu, was so guilty of misjudgment — and of bad taste — as to declare his belief that France would continue to escape the economic ills that were then afflicting every other nation in the world. France's position was in strange contrast to her unhappy state of five years before. (See pp. 328 and 331.)

In January 1931, Pierre Laval became Premier of France. He was a comparative newcomer. He was provincial born — his father had kept a café and butcher shop at Châteldon in Auvergne. He was always proud to call himself a "man of the people." He spent his early life in Paris as a "poor man's lawyer" and legal adviser to trade unions. At that time he was regarded as a dangerous Socialist and revolutionary, and he was certainly one of the defeatists of the First World War. But he gradually matured into an exponent of thrifty conservative administration, a successful negotiator of workers' strikes, and he entered high politics, appropriately, as Minister of Labor, first under Poincaré in 1926 and then under Tardieu in 1930. He was Premier throughout 1931, at the heyday of France's financial supremacy, and he rode roughshod over all Europe. He may be said to have been responsible for those triumphs of French policy in that year, namely, the failure of the Austro-German Customs Union and the comparative failure of the Hoover Moratorium. Brüning, the German Chancellor, came to Paris like a humble suppliant at the table of the international Dives. In October 1931, Laval visited Washington and all but dictated to President Hoover of the United States. (See pp. 326-30.)

But France's financial supremacy was not to last. Laval resigned in February 1932. The budget of that year was very different from the surplus budget of 1930. France too had now become a resentful, bewildered, and very frightened victim of the universal Depression. The Lausanne reparations settlement was a catastrophe, and so also – but in a different way – was the repudiation of the French war debt to the United States. (See pp. 331-33.) General elections swung back to the Left, and through 1932 and 1933 there was a succession of Radical premiers, such as Daladier, Sarraut, and Chautemps. The slaughter of governments was a sure sign of the resumption of France's chronic Battle of the Budget. Extreme rightist interests were already launching an antiparliamentary campaign, and the Fascist "Leagues" began to appear in France in evident imitation of Italian and German prototypes. During the elections of May 1932, President Doumer was assassinated by a Russian *émigré* in Paris. The crime had no political implications, though, at the time, the Right tried to exploit it much as the British Conservatives had tried to exploit the "Red Letter" of evil memory. (See p. 267.) Albert Lebrun, then president of the Senate, was unanimously elected President of the Republic in succession to Doumer. In January 1934, the Stavisky affair burst upon the country.

The Stavisky Affair and the Sixth of February

Serge Alexandre Stavisky was an unsavory scoundrel. Born in Kiev in the 1890's, the son of a Jewish dentist, he emigrated with his parents to Paris. He was given a good education, and at one time was intended for medicine. But he drifted into petty crime, blackmail, forgery, and the drug traffic, and became a confirmed hanger-on of the Parisian underworld. He essayed the first of his bigger frauds in 1926, when he swindled 7,500,000 francs out of a stockbroker. He was arrested, but then "provisionally" released, and his trial was postponed. The transaction, however, whetted his appetite, and he now went on from strength to strength. He posed as a great financier, frequented fashionable vacation resorts, and cultivated an extraordinary variety of political contacts. He promoted bogus companies, backed a vaudeville theater, and bought up one or two boulevard journals. In December 1933, the authorities began to make inconvenient inquiries into his management of the Bayonne municipal pawnshop.[1] On January 8, 1934, at a villa near Chamonix, he was found by the police with a bullet through his head, apparently a suicide. It was suggested that the police themselves had shot him to prevent his revealing damaging information.

At any other time the Stavisky affair would have stirred no more than a muddy ripple. France had had financial scandals before, and mass hysteria was something of a periodical phenomenon. But in 1934 France was more than ordinarily depressed, and the affair seemed to point unanswerably to the incompetence and corruption not only of recent governments in France, but of the entire principle of liberal democracy. Camille Chautemps, now Premier, drew considerable suspicion on himself by refusing to appoint a parliamentary committee of inquiry into Stavisky's past immunity from arrest, presumably because Chautemps' brother-in-law was head of the Paris Parquet, a body that initiated official prosecutions. It was easy enough for the Royalist paper, *L'Action Française,* to link Stavisky with Chautemps and with the Radical party, and hint, with great parade of circumstantial evidence, that the archswindler in the course of his career had enjoyed considerable protection from persons highly placed. At the end of January 1934, Chautemps resigned office.

Édouard Daladier returned to the premiership determined to form an "above-party government of strong men." He dismissed Jean Chiappe, the Prefect of Police, who had been showing too much indulgence toward recent rightist demonstrations in the streets of Paris. But, however justified Chiappe's dismissal might have been, it weakened and demoralized the police force at a critical moment, the more so as Chiappe's second-in-command was then in the hospital undergoing an operation. On the afternoon of February 6, 1934, Daladier and his new government confronted the Chamber, and he was virtually howled down in the middle of his Ministerial Declaration. Meanwhile, across the Seine from the Chamber of Deputies, in the Place de la Concorde, various patriotic and League organizations had begun to assemble and were shortly battling the police. By nightfall, outright fighting had developed. In so far as they had any objective at all, the rioters tried to force the police cordon on the Pont de la Concorde and, had they succeeded, they would probably have made fire and havoc of the Chamber of Deputies. They tore up the street paving for ammunition and made very effective use of pieces of iron railing from the nearby Tuileries Gardens. They slashed at the horses of the mounted police with razors tied onto the ends of walking sticks. Automobiles and busses were overturned and set on fire. In the end 20 rioters and a policeman were killed, and well over 1,000 rioters, police, and spectators were more or less seriously injured. Nothing like it had been seen in Paris since the Commune. Nevertheless, despite riots without and hubbub within, the Chamber passed a vote of confidence in Daladier by a fair majority. But the next day, faced with the prospect of more disorders and bloodshed, Daladier resigned. It was particularly ominous that a government which had just won the confidence of the Chamber should be frightened out of office by the "blackmail of the street."

On February 8, 1934, Gaston Doumergue, onetime President of the Republic, came out of his retirement, like Poincaré in 1926, to form an emergency cabinet of all parties but the Socialists and Communists, and like Poincaré's cabinet in 1926, Doumergue's seemed to be a veritable galaxy of former premiers. Jean-Louis Barthou was his Foreign Minister and Marshal Pétain his Minister of War. He appointed two committees, one to investigate the Stavisky affair and another to investigate the riots of "the Sixth of February." But the streets were still in ferment. Socialist and Communist trade unions, on February 12, combined to organize a general strike — the germ, as it afterward proved, of the Popular Front — in protest against Fascism. On February 21, the truncated body of Albert Prince, a magistrate who might have been one of the principal witnesses in Doumergue's investigating committees, was found on the railroad tracks near Dijon in circumstances which pointed to an elaborate and particularly horrible suicide. Other suicides and attempted suicides followed. For weeks Paris lived in a daze of arrests, grillings, confessions, and deepening suspicion. Prominent names were recklessly bandied about. The press made jubilee, and with that unscrupulous license which French journalism enjoyed, and supported no doubt by that underground political bribery which French journalism also enjoyed, it revealed — or invented — the most intricate ramifications of public corruption.

The Fascist "Leagues" in France had a flashy dangerousness, which in retrospect seems rather to recede in importance. But they were a symptom of the time, and they showed that Fascist ways and works could be attractive even to men of the independent fiber of the normal Frenchman. There were several kinds of these "Leagues," such as the Royalist *Camelots du Roi,* who were the storm troopers of the *Action Française;* the chauvinistic *Jeunesse Patriote;* and the pseudo-Bonapartist *Solidarité Française,* founded by the perfumer François Coty. Of them all, the *Croix de Feu* was the best known and most influential. It had been founded in 1927 as an exclusive veterans' organization and had originally admitted to membership only front-line men who had been decorated for bravery. But it had gradually become involved in politics and identified its interests with the upper middle class. Its program, Fascist-like, was opportunist but always fiercely patriotic, antiparliamentarian and, of course, anti-Communist. By 1933-34, it had over 30,000 members and various affiliated youth groups. It was highly organized, possessed a certain quantity of firearms and even one or two airplanes, and specialized in sudden and ubiquitous mobilizations. Its members always wore a characteristic beret. Its leader was a Colonel de la Rocque, a professional soldier, not a scintillating personality, but able to create a *mystique* of his own. He maintained an unofficial connection with the army — herein lay the real menace of his movement — and any revolutionary action he might have essayed would probably have taken the form of a military coup in the regular Napoleonic tradition.

De la Rocque described Doumergue's government as "a poultice on a gangrenous leg," but his actual relations with Doumergue were closer than he allowed to be known. Doumergue, it was said, was trying to use de la Rocque much as Papen had once tried to use Hitler. But Doumergue was already digging his own political grave. A vain, pompous old man, at the head of an emergency cabinet, he had come to regard himself as indispensable, and took to making patronizing broadcasts to the nation almost in the style of royalty. He revived Millerand's former attempted reforms of the presidential office, and was at once accused by the Left of brazenly maneuvering to smuggle dictatorship into France. (See p. 256.) On October 9, 1934, his Foreign Minister, Barthou, and King Alexander of Yugoslavia were assassinated at Marseilles. But even without this blow, Doumergue's popularity was very shaken. In November 1934, he and his emergency cabinet resigned. At the last he allowed himself to be seen in public, in company with de la Rocque, a decrepit, half-senile figure, crowned with the Rocquian beret. Doumergue, after all, was far from indispensable, and his departure did not result in a revival of the street riots which had originally brought him into office.

Barthou's Grand Alliance

Distracted though she might be at home, France in 1934 followed a vigorous foreign policy. She bestirred herself to make a last effort to stop the rot in the international situation. Barthou, Doumergue's Foreign Minister, was a former chairman of the Reparation Commission, one of the instigators of the Ruhr invasion, and the close associate of Poincaré in the long struggle for the absolute and literal fulfillment of the Treaty of Versailles. He arrived at the Quai D'Orsay in February 1934 to find negotiations in train to induce Germany to return to the Disarmament Conference, and these negotiations he categorically broke off. German rearmament was now a fact well known to the chancelleries of Europe, a fact over which Barthou was resolved to shed no more tears. Instead he set about with consuming energy to overhaul France's alliance system, to furbish old links, to forge new ones, and, in short, to build a prison house so formidable that its German inmate, however powerful he grew, would not dare to try his strength against it. Short of a preventive war against Hitler, an alternative that France had already declined, Barthou could see no other policy.

Barthou began by trying to mend the unfortunate effects of the recent German-Polish Nonaggression Pact and Poland's virtual desertion from the "Versailles Front." Toward the end of April 1934, he visited Warsaw for conversations with Pilsudski and Beck. It cannot be said that Barthou succeeded too well in thawing the chill that then characterized official Polish sentiments toward France. But Barthou's visits to Prague a few days later, and then to Bucharest and Belgrade, were in the nature of a triumphal progress. If Poland was now determined to follow her own devices, the Little Entente at least remained in stanch association with France. The Balkan Pact had been concluded in the previous February, and Barthou might be excused a brief ecstasy of optimism over the "zone of peace" which, in his words, "stretched from Prague to Ankara."

Toward the Soviet Union Barthou was conspicuously friendly. The Soviet Union itself in recent years had been revising its foreign policy. Litvinov had succeeded Chicherin as Foreign Commissar in 1929; he had been prime mover of the Litvinov Protocol and had come to identify his name, more and more, with the Western democratic ideal of collective security. In November 1932, the Soviet Union and France signed a nonaggression pact, one of the type of bilateral pacts so favored by Soviet diplomacy. The Soviet Union was evidently anticipating, and preparing for, the approaching Nazi threat. And even toward the League of Nations Litvinov was now being permitted to take a more tolerant attitude. Accordingly, in the early months of 1934, Barthou and Litvinov were in negotiation for the Soviet Union's admission to the League. Powers, great and small, beginning with Spain – at that time a Left-wing republic – the Little Entente, and Britain, one by one withdrew their objections to, or intimated their support of, Soviet membership. On September 15, 1934, a letter of invitation bearing thirty signatures was sent to Litvinov and was formally accepted by him. Three days later the Fifteenth Assembly of the League admitted the Soviet Union to membership and to a permanent seat on the League Council.

Right-wing opinion in France was anything but happy over Barthou's

Soviet *rapprochement*. But it was pointed out that Francis I had once found an ally in the Grand Turk, and Richelieu in the German Protestants, and it was not for modern France in her present extremity to be too fastidious in her friendships. Barthou was conceiving a wide scheme, a Grand Alliance in complete encirclement of Germany. With the Soviet Union safely in the League, he now proposed an East European Pact of Mutual Assistance, which would tie up with the Little Entente and put the Soviet Union on guard on the eastern frontiers of Germany, much as the Locarno Pact had put France on guard on the western frontiers. How Barthou's ambitious diplomacy would have ended we cannot tell. For, on October 9, 1934, when he was at Marseilles to welcome King Alexander of Yugoslavia on a state visit to France, both he and the King were struck down by the bullets of a Croat assassin.[2]

The prophets and pessimists of Europe compared Marseilles with that other assassination at Sarajevo which had once had such dire consequences. Some of the more prophetic and pessimistic ones thought they could detect the hand of the Nazi in the crime. Certainly a drama of blood and treachery, such as this, would have been in keeping with the Nazi character, and nothing could have been so diabolically well calculated to disrupt the entire anti-German coalition that Barthou had been so industriously building up. It would set France and Yugoslavia against each other, and thence disorganize the Little Entente. Furthermore, as soon seemed evident, the assassin of Marseilles was one of a band of Croat revolutionaries who had established themselves in Hungary under the Croat traitor Ante Pavelich. Mussolini, who was already scheming to extend his influence in "Croatia," was probably well acquainted with their activities. The assassination therefore implicated Italy and indirectly jeopardized the *rapprochement*, now fast maturing, between Italy and France. (See pp. 175 and 432.)

The French Government exerted itself in every possible way to express its sorrow and concern to the Yugoslav Government and to compensate for its lack of proper precautions at Marseilles. Several French police officials were dismissed. Some days later, at Belgrade, a distinguished cortege followed in the dead monarch's funeral procession – President Lebrun and Marshal Pétain, King Carol, the Duke of Kent, Göring, Beneš, Titulescu, and other international notables – and perhaps the Yugoslavs were a little surprised and comforted by this evidence of the importance that their king and country had suddenly assumed in the estimation of an anxious Europe.

The failure of Barthou's East European Pact, however, was not all loss. The logic of it was too convincing. Mutual assistance pacts between France and the Soviet Union, and between Czechoslovakia and the Soviet Union were signed in May 1935. (See pp. 389-90 and 432.)

The Popular Front

Pierre-Étienne Flandin, who had been appearing in ministerial posts since the Laval government in 1931, succeeded Doumergue in the premiership, and brought back to office with him most of Doumergue's outgoing cabinet. Laval, his former patron, was his Foreign Minister who now proceeded to negotiate the Franco-Italian Agreement of January 1935, described elsewhere. (See p. 404.) Indeed international events in Flandin's term were disturbing enough to take the minds of most Frenchmen off their domestic affairs. Doumergue's controversy over the presidential prerogatives lapsed, and even the ardor of the Leagues was chilled for a time. In February 1935, Flandin introduced a bill to prolong the military service of certain classes in order to tide over the "lean years" when, as the result of the lowered birth rate during the First World War, there would now be a heavy decrease in France's man power. It was this bill that Germany used as a pretext for her conscription decree. Thereafter followed the Stresa Front and the beginnings of the Italo-Ethiopian crisis. (See pp. 388-90.)

One domestic problem, however, could not be evaded, namely finance. The Depression was becoming unendurably heavy. But the gold standard was still retained, and in the Chamber, in the intervals between the current international crises, the deflationists and the inflationists disputed the merits of their respective philosophies. In the spring months of 1935, there was a run on the franc of almost panic proportions. Bouisson followed Flandin in May 1935, in a government that lasted one day; Laval followed Bouisson till he was ousted in January 1936, shortly after the collapse of the Hoare-Laval Plan; Albert Sarraut was in office at the time of Hitler's Rhineland coup of March 1936.

Meanwhile a new oscillation to the Left was in preparation. It was partly the inevitable reaction to the series of rightist governments which had begun with Doumergue. But the new movement had novel and interesting features. It was to be a more ambitious and spectacular cartel than the Cartel of 1924, and more than a mere accommodation for election purposes. This time it was to be a Popular Front which combined all three parties of the Left — Radicals, Socialists, and Communists. Doubtless "the Sixth of February," the general strike of February 12, 1934, and the subsequent provocations of the Fascist "Leagues" had contributed to its formation. More particularly, France and the Soviet Union were enjoying a moment of *rapprochement;* the Franco-Soviet Mutual Assistance Pact was signed in May 1935 (see p. 432) and the Comintern in Moscow had lately been instructing the French Communists to act collaboratively. In June, all France suffered the intense chagrin of the Anglo-German Naval Agreement. (See p. 391.) On Bastille Day, July 14, 1935, Radicals, Socialists, and Communists held a monster demonstration in Paris, and Édouard Daladier the Radical, Léon Blum the Socialist, and Maurice Thorez the Communist were seen marching arm in arm at the head of one of the processions. At the elections in the spring of 1936, the Popular Front won a convincing victory. Léon Blum eventually formed a Socialist and Radical government on June 4, 1936. The Communists did not appear in the ministerial list, but Thorez, the Communist leader, reaffirmed his loyalty to the Popular Front and pledged his stanch support in the Chamber. Yvon Delbos was Foreign Minister. Three undersecretaries in the new government were women — a startling innovation.

Five times since the First World War had France tried a fresh political experiment. Millerand's National Bloc, Herriot's Cartel, Poincaré's National

Government, Doumergue's National Government, and now Blum's Popular Front had each been hailed in its day as the definitive cure of the country's chronic ills. Five times had France had a new "savior"; five times was it predicted that she would stabilize herself at last under a regime of enduring beneficence; five times had great hopes disappeared in failure and anticlimax. In 1936 Blum came to office with even more than the usual blaze of expectancy. Contemporary historians compared his advent with 1789; the foreign press glowed with sympathetic anticipation.

Blum introduced sweeping reforms. He dissolved the Leagues. He "democratized" the Bank of France, that stronghold of reaction, and gave its oligarchy of 200 largest shareholders a vote apiece along with its 40,000 lesser shareholders, with the result that a majority of the Bank's Board of Regents would henceforth be appointed by the Government. He took steps to nationalize the armament and aircraft industries. For the workers he brought in a long-cherished program, a forty-hour week, vacations with pay, collective labor contracts, and a scale of minimum wages.

But Blum never had a chance. If he had come, as Herriot had come, in the comparative peace of 1924, he might have fulfilled his mission, and France and the world would have been the better and happier for it. Clearly he tried to give France a New Deal, but circumstances over which he had no control harried him like an evil genius. The famous "sit-down strikes" were already in full swing when his government was formed and, according to one estimate, a million workers were "in occupation" of their factories in midsummer 1936. The flight of capital, which had begun under Flandin, continued. In September 1936, the franc was devalued 30 per cent, and a tripartite agreement was entered into with Britain and the United States for the control of the three exchanges. But the devaluation of the franc, while beneficial to foreign exchange, had the effect of raising prices in France and more than offset the wage increases that the workers had been gaining. The Fascist Leagues had been officially dissolved, but that did not prevent their reappearing under altered names. Nor did it prevent the emergence of other political eccentricities like the "Popular party" of the former Communist, Jacques Doriot, or the grotesque Fascist secret society, the *Cagoulards,* or Hooded Men. A new "European Order" was being preached by the Neo-Socialist, Marcel Déat, and closer Franco-German "cultural understanding" by Ferdinand de Brinon. Meanwhile civil war had broken out in Spain, where a legitimate Republican government, also bearing the name of a Popular Front, was battling for its existence against Fascist reaction and against the intervention of Germany and Italy, the potential enemies of France. Blum, in short, was continually distracted by matters extraneous but indirectly damaging to his program. He was like a man trying to preach a sermon in an air raid. It might have been a good sermon, but somehow it was beside the point, and the congregation, through no fault of the preacher, was not very attentive.

Superficially the year 1937 was not one of striking events. It was the year in which Hitler promised "no surprises," and France reflected the uneasy calm of her eastern neighbor. (See p. 474.) It was also the year of the Paris Exposition with its eccentric architecture along the banks of the Seine and deceptive display of returning prosperity and universal brotherhood. Blum meanwhile made less and less headway against his difficulties. He appealed for "a pause, so that we may consolidate the ground we have conquered," which meant that his government was to be absolved from initiating further reforms, especially if they involved increased expenditure. In June 1937, Blum resigned. Chautemps formed a cabinet, ostensibly a continuation of Blum's, and several of the outgoing ministers reappeared in his "Republican Combination," as he called it. But he relied increasingly on Radical support, and the Communists were no longer being instructed to act collaboratively. Blum remained Vice-President; Delbos remained Foreign Minister; Georges Bonnet was specially brought over from his ambassadorship in Washington to be Finance Minister and the new wizard that was to save the franc.

In December 1937, Delbos made his grand tour of France's allied capitals – Warsaw, Bucharest, Belgrade, and Prague. It seemed like the triumphal progress of Barthou's similar tour of three years before. At Warsaw, Colonel Beck declared that the time was ripe for demonstrating the "vitality, strength, and permanence" of the Franco-Polish alliance. At Bucharest, Tatarescu and Antonescu were still in power and anxious to be cordial. At Prague, Beneš responded with enthusiasm when he described his country as "a very extension (*un prolongement*) of France." Only in Belgrade did Stoyadinovich – then flirting with the Axis – give him an inhospitable reception; but, as if in compensation, the pro-French demonstrations which greeted him in the streets of Belgrade were spontaneous and convincing.

But there was something, something not quite satisfying. In 1936 France had failed to prevent Hitler's remilitarization of the Rhineland, and France's entire strategic situation vis-à-vis her Eastern and Central European allies had been fundamentally changed. The Spanish Civil War, it is true, caused less agony of conscience in France than might have been expected. Public opinion in France, as in Britain, was refusing to face up to the facts in Spain. But France's weak Spanish policy was also torturing to her European allies. While the Popular Front in France had been trying to pursue its social revolution in its own artificial vacuum – and that none too successfully – its Spanish namesake and spiritual affiliate was being denied legitimate and desperately needed assistance, and the Fascist Powers were driving forward to yet another of their undeserved victories. Delbos, in fact, returned from his grand tour far from sure of himself. Somehow, the glory was departed.

In April 1938, Daladier again became Premier. He was Premier during the Munich crisis and at the outbreak of the Second World War.

26. THE UNITED STATES: NEW DEAL AND NEUTRALITY

The New Deal

The Roosevelt era falls into three phases, roughly of four years each. In the first, from 1933 to 1937, the United States was almost wholly preoccupied with the New Deal; in the second, from 1937 to 1941, it was being gradually and inexorably involved in the affairs of the world outside; in the third, from 1941 to 1945, it was a belligerent in the Second World War. In this chapter we shall be concerned with the first and second of these phases.

The President, Franklin Delano Roosevelt, by tradition, training, and personal inclination, no less than by the immediate political occasion, was drawn primarily to domestic affairs. In this respect he was not unlike Woodrow Wilson, his Democratic predecessor of twenty years before. But, also like that predecessor, Roosevelt was fated to lead his country into a great war. Between the crash of October 1929 and Inauguration Day, March 4, 1933, there had lain three years of deepening national bewilderment and distress. It was estimated that, on that day, 15,000,000 Americans were out of work, a fourth of the country's labor force. The national income was less than half the pre-Depression figure. On the very morning of Inauguration Day, every bank in the forty-eight states had closed its doors.[1] Yet the new President seemed entirely undismayed. From the first accents of his Inaugural Address it was evident that a new leadership had arisen in America, a leadership of initiative, authority, and buoyant good hope. His every word conveyed an infectious confidence which the nation had almost forgotten how to feel.

> . . . This great Nation will endure as it has endured, will revive and will prosper. So, first of all, let me assert my firm belief that the only thing we have to fear is fear itself — nameless, unreasoning, unjustified terror which paralyzes needed efforts to convert retreat into advance . . . Rulers of the exchange of mankind's goods have failed through their own stubbornness and their own incompetence, have admitted their failure, and have abdicated . . . There must

> be an end to a conduct in banking and in business which too often has given to a sacred trust the likeness of callous and selfish wrongdoing . . .

And the President proceeded to outline schemes for stimulating employment, reorganizing industry and agriculture, protecting mortgagees, planning relief works on a national scale, supervising investment. "These are the lines of attack. I shall presently urge upon a new Congress, in special session, detailed measures for their fulfilment" – even to the extent, the President added, "in the event that the national emergency is still critical," of asking Congress to grant "broad executive power . . . as great as the power that would be given to me if we were in fact invaded by a foreign foe." The President concluded:

> . . . In their need [the people of the United States] have registered a mandate that they want direct, vigorous action. They have asked for discipline and direction under leadership. They have made me the present instrument of their wishes. In the spirit of the gift I take it.

On March 6, two days after the Inauguration, Roosevelt proclaimed a Bank Holiday. The banks were closed anyway; but, under the proclamation, the closure was legalized and, except for essential business connected with wages and the purchase of the necessities of life, was compulsorily extended for four days. Congress met in special session on March 9, and thereafter, until its adjournment on June 15 – the celebrated "Hundred Days" – it passed the series of enactments that came collectively to be called the "New Deal," a phrase attributed to Stuart Chase, but inspired perhaps by lingering recollections of Theodore Roosevelt's "Square Deal." We may conveniently list the most important of these enactments and their dates in tabular form:

Emergency Banking Act, March 9, the first day of the Session, passed without debate and even without roll call of the House. It confirmed the emergency measures under the Bank Holiday and gave the Administration further powers over dealings in foreign exchange.

Economy Act, March 20, empowering the Administration to reduce pensions (including Veterans' pensions) and Federal salaries.

An act establishing the Civilian Conservation Corps (CCC), March 31, to provide work in forestry, soil conservation, and flood control for 250,000 young men.

Abandonment of the gold standard, April 19.

An act establishing the Federal Emergency Relief Administration (FERA), May 12, to administer a national relief system. Harry L. Hopkins, formerly chairman of the Emergency Relief Administration in New York State, was appointed Administrator.

An act establishing the Agricultural Adjustment Administration (AAA), May 12, to restore farm prices and farmers' purchasing power. George N. Peek was appointed Administrator.

Emergency Farm Mortgage Act, May 12, providing for the refinancing of farm mortgages.

An act establishing the Tennessee Valley Authority (TVA), May 18, to secure the unified development and control of the Tennessee Valley.

Securities Act, May 27, requiring full and fair disclosure of new security issues.

Home Owners Loan Corporation Act (HOLC), June 13, providing for the refinancing of home mortgages.

National Industrial Recovery Act (NIRA), June 16. It established (i) the National Recovery Administration (NRA) to secure cooperation and "fair competition" in business, according to agreed codes of conduct, under government supervision. General Hugh S. Johnson was appointed Administrator. The Act also established (ii) the Public Works Administration (PWA), which disbursed $3,300,000,000 on buildings, reclamation, dams, roads, bridges, airfields, and similar projects.

Banking Act, June 16, insuring bank deposits.

Emergency Railroad Transportation Act, June 16, financing and reorganizing the national railroads.

Roosevelt also urged the repeal of prohibition (the Eighteenth Amendment). But it was not repealed till December 5, 1933.

In this huge legislative program Roosevelt enjoyed the support of a devoted band of aides. We have already mentioned Hopkins, Peek, and Johnson, administrators of the three principal offices (FERA, AAA, and NRA) of the entire recovery structure. A "brain trust," as it was somewhat derogatively called, had assisted Roosevelt during his election campaign and continued to assist him during his first term. It included Raymond Moley, Rexford G. Tugwell, and Adolf A. Berle, all professors from Columbia University, all of whom had a taste of office as Assistant Secretaries. And to these names may be added that of the brain trust's reputed creator, Samuel Rosenman, New York lawyer and judge, Roosevelt's constant counselor. The Cabinet included Cordell Hull, Secretary of State; William H. Woodin, Secretary of the Treasury, shortly to be succeeded by Henry Morgenthau; Harold L. Ickes, Secretary of the Interior; Henry A. Wallace, Secretary of Agriculture; Frances Perkins, Secretary for Labor; and James Farley, the old political campaigner and chairman of the Democratic National Committee, Postmaster General. Lewis Douglas was Director of the Budget. Louis Howe, though now an invalid seldom moving from his rooms in the White House, carried on his curious, indispensable role as a sort of Presidential manager and chamberlain.

The New Deal was frankly experimental. It was a series of empirical measures designed to meet an extraordinary situation. The President himself had little use for theories, economic or otherwise, and, least of all, had he any intention of overthrowing the existing order of things. The huge expenditures for relief works subserved, in his own words, a policy of "priming the pump" till normal business should once more be resumed. Even so, the New Deal was something more than a collection of *ad hoc* regulations. It had a tacit philosophy of sorts predicated on the cooperation of capital and labor under the benevolent despotism of government controls. And it worked so long as capital and labor were too frightened or too desperate to obstruct it. Its early, short-term recoveries were decidedly encouraging. But this very recovery raised up an opposition. Neither partner in the New Deal, it seemed, had learned enough or forgotten enough to profit permanently from his experience, and the program was soon being menaced by clashes between capital and labor, and between both and the government. A succession of strikes in the automobile and textile industries was touched off in particular by Section 7A of the NIRA, which conceded the right of unionization and collective bargaining. The newly established National Labor Relations Board (NLRB) was besieged with disputes.

The New Deal was also threatened by popular idiosyncrasy in many forms and guises. It was a time for cranks, rogues, and honest men who championed or challenged the program according to their lights or who just crudely exploited the national predicament for publicity and power. Such were Father Coughlin, a Roman Catholic priest; Seward Collins, a young literary editor; Lawrence Dennis; William Dudley Pelley, and others – names once famous or infamous, often curiously reflecting the contemporary demagogism in Europe. Ezra Pound, the poet, could be numbered among them. Undoubtedly the most sinister was Huey Long, Senator from Louisiana, who reduced his state to a personal dictatorship and tried to browbeat the Senate itself. More serious-minded and genuine perhaps were Francis E. Townsend, a country doctor who produced a plan for old-age pensions; Upton Sinclair, who produced a plan to End Poverty in California (EPIC); Floyd B. Olson, Governor of Minnesota, who produced a plan for the public ownership of industry. Naturally enough the Communist Party was active. Many acknowledged intellectuals were openly expressing Communist or near-Communist views. During 1934, Congress, alarmed by some of these developments, set up a Committee to investigate Un-American Activities.

But the President was not to be deterred or deflected. In January 1935, he submitted to Congress a Work Relief Program (WRP) to put 3,500,000 unemployed to work at a cost of $5,000,000,000, a program that was eventually entrusted to a new body, the Works Progress Administration (WPA), with Hopkins as its Administrator. During the same summer, 1935, after protracted debate, Congress passed two other highly revolutionary measures, the National Labor Relations Act, or Wagner Act as it came to be known, providing again for collective bargaining and defining unfair labor practices on the part of employers, and the Social Security Act, providing for old-age and unemployment insurance, financed in part by compulsory contributions from employer and employee.

The "Second New Deal"

The decisive obstruction to the New Deal came at last from the Supreme Court. It was not entirely unexpected. Federal courts had already been issuing adverse injunctions when, on May 27, 1935, "Black Monday," the Supreme Court returned a unanimous verdict for the plaintiff in the Schechter case and, in effect, declared the NIRA to be unconstitutional. In January 1936, the Agricultural Adjustment Act was similarly declared to be unconstitutional. Beneath these sudden strokes the New Deal, in its existing form, was all but killed. In the Presidential elections in November 1936,

Roosevelt won an overwhelming victory. The Supreme Court was not a direct issue in the election, but the country was obviously incensed by its conduct, and it was an angry electorate that went to the polls. Roosevelt gained the largest electoral vote on record; he lost only two states, Maine and Vermont.

Roosevelt returned to office immeasurably strengthened in his personal prestige and confirmed in his domestic policies. He retained most of his former Cabinet; Hull, Morgenthau, Ickes, Wallace, Frances Perkins, and Farley, all continued at their posts. He began his second term by submitting a bill to Congress for the purge of the refractory Supreme Court – and, ironically enough, for all his recent victory at the polls, he now suffered one of the sharpest setbacks of his presidency. The bill would have appointed a new Justice to the Court whenever any present member reached the age of seventy without retiring or resigning. It was a devious, unworthy maneuver to humble an otherwise revered body of men, of whom six out of nine were already past the critical seventy years. The bill failed of passage before Congress adjourned in August 1937.

However, Roosevelt gained his objective in the end. He had not long to wait. In a couple of years the six Justices had retired or resigned, and Roosevelt had put his own appointees in their place. But, in any case, it could be said that by 1937 the original New Deal had largely fulfilled its function. A fresh stage of thinking and a fresh complex of circumstances were on the way. The former brain trust had long since dispersed. Lewis Douglas, who latterly had found himself in strong disagreement with the Administration's spending policy, had returned to private business and was shortly to have a spell as principal of a Canadian university. Lawyers like Thomas G. Corcoran and Benjamin V. Cohen, products of the Harvard Law School, less reformist and more bureaucratic in spirit, were now the new types of men behind the scenes in Washington. In economics they were inclined to Keynesian doctrines and advocated government spending, not merely for "priming the pump," but as a deliberate and permanent national policy; and their chosen instruments were, not so much the NRA and AAA, invalidated by the Supreme Court's decisions, as the Federal Reserve System. Hopkins' WPA at this time was increasingly the main agent for federal relief. The general trend was less toward *ad hoc* palliatives and more toward long-term plans, for instance, for soil conservation and forest land development. The Administration was giving considerable attention to the nation's potential resources, notably in oil and in hydroelectric power. Some writers have referred to this stage as the "Second New Deal."

But 1937 was not only the year of the Second New Deal. It was the end of the phase which we earlier described as the first phase of the Roosevelt era and the beginning of the second. The year 1937 marks the passage from domestic to foreign preoccupation. Early in 1938, the President, as if by routine, was recommending to Congress appropriations of $4,000,000,000 for relief and public works. But rearmament was in the air, and the military budget was about to effect an expansion of government spending sufficient to satisfy the most adventurous of economic planners. The year 1938 was in fact a "recession" year; unemployment, still estimated at 10,000,000, continued to worsen. But, in the end, by 1940, the trend was evidently in reverse. The threat of general war, it seemed, was to be the most effective and lasting of the Depression's remedies.

At this point we should return to 1933 and survey the whole of United States international relations from that date.

The Recognition of the Soviet Union

If the United States was isolationist before the Depression, it was certainly even more so afterward. We have elsewhere mentioned the Manchurian Crisis of 1931, a crisis born of the Depression. (See pp. 339ff.) Secretary Stimson had done his diplomatic best in that situation, but he had known – as no doubt the Japanese Government had known – what little support or even interest he commanded in his own distracted homeland. Nonetheless, despite the profound indifference of public opinion, official Washington had perforce to take note of world affairs, and Roosevelt himself had a lively and growing, if unshared, concern over what was going on in the continents across the oceans.

The recognition of the Soviet Union was the first important international event of Roosevelt's presidency. No doubt it was primarily dictated by the domestic situation and was part of the general policy of amelioration to which the new Administration was committed. In the gray days of the Depression any opportunity for increasing foreign trade could not be passed by lightly. The Soviet Union in 1933 was no longer, as Secretary Hughes had once put it, "a gigantic economic vacuum." The Soviet Five-Year Plan of 1928 had greatly increased Soviet demands for American locomotives, agricultural machinery, and electrical equipment. At the World Economic Conference in London in 1933, the Soviet delegate Litvinov, shrewdly baiting the hook, had expressed the willingness of his government to place orders abroad totaling $1,000,000,000.

The recognition, of course, would be a complete reversal of policy from the Coolidge and Hoover days, when the official attitude of the United States toward the Soviet Union had been one of uncompromising abhorrence. American property to the estimated value of $440,000,000 had been destroyed or confiscated in the turmoil of the Bolshevik Revolution. An American loan of $332,000,000 to the Kerensky government had not been honored by the Soviets, which had preferred counterclaims of their own for damages inflicted by American forces during the Siberian expedition of 1918-20. These were no small obstacles to be overcome before normal diplomatic relations could be restored. But perhaps the threatened debt defaults on the part of the European nations in 1933 suggested that the Soviet Union was no longer to be singled out as the only black sheep in the flock of America's debtors.

The recent Japanese aggression in Manchuria had induced a no less unwonted readiness on the part of the Soviet Union toward a general Soviet-American *rapprochement*. Accordingly, in October 1933, President Roosevelt sent a personal note to President Kalinin regretting past differences and adding that he would gladly receive any representatives that the Soviet Union might designate "to explore with me personally all questions outstanding between our two countries." Kalinin replied in equally cordial terms. During November, Litvinov arrived in Washington as special Soviet envoy. Between his hours of business at the White House and the State Department, he was dined and feted, and he used every occasion to declare his belief in the enduring peace and cooperation that must henceforth distinguish Soviet-American relations. Eight days of discussion sufficed for an agreement, and formal diplomatic relations were established by an exchange of notes between Roosevelt and Litvinov. Litvinov dropped all claims for damages against the United States on account of the Siberian expedition and pledged his government to give protection to American citizens in the Soviet Union and to abstain from revolutionary propaganda in the United States. William C. Bullitt was appointed American ambassador in Moscow.

The Good Neighbor Policy and Latin America

The intense isolationism of the United States toward countries in Europe and Asia was evidently not felt so strongly toward those within its own hemisphere. Here, especially to the south, lay the old area of operation of the Monroe Doctrine and the special preserve of American enterprise and interest. "In the field of foreign policy," said Roosevelt in his first Inaugural, "I would dedicate this nation to the policy of the Good Neighbor." And, under Secretary Hull's guidance, that policy, in particular, was to be applied to the Latin-American republics. In June 1934, Congress passed a Trade Agreements Act, which empowered the government to negotiate reciprocal trade agreements with foreign states and to raise or lower tariffs by a maximum of 50 per cent. Thus armed, Secretary Hull proceeded to negotiate a series of such agreements – sixteen in all between 1934 and 1937. The most significant of them were with Cuba, Brazil, Venezuela – and with Canada and several European countries. The Hull program quickly enough gained further powerful impetus when, in Roosevelt's second term, the United States began "stockpiling" strategic raw materials.

Meanwhile the final phase of the independence of the Philippines in March 1934 made a happy impression, although some would-be critics questioned the wisdom of abandoning the Philippines at the precise moment of Japan's eruption in the East. The Good Neighbor policy toward Latin America was confirmed in a series of conferences: at Montevideo in December 1933, at Buenos Aires in December 1936 – attended in this instance by President Roosevelt in person, "a traveling salesman for peace" – and finally at Lima in December 1938. But it was still far from plain sailing. Suspicion of the United States was endemic, especially in Cuba, Mexico, and Argentina, and was not noticeably dispelled by the treaty with Cuba in May 1934, by which the United States renounced its former rights of intervention in the island's affairs.

The situation was soon to be complicated by the mixed allegiances arising in the Latin-American republics toward the factions in the Spanish Civil War and toward the Nazis and Communists. Italian, German, and Japanese settlers in Latin America – 6,000,000, 1,300,000, and 200,000 respectively – tended to be restless in these years as their former homelands reported military and diplomatic victories and as the prestige of Western democracies correspondingly declined. Both Nazi and Communist penetration was said to be rife, the Nazi especially in Argentina, and the Communist especially in Mexico. During the late 1930's in Mexico, the revolutionary President Cardenas nationalized a number of American- and British-owned railroad and oil properties. His action was arguably legal, but the occasion and the manner of it were highly disturbing. The Pan-American Conference at Lima in December 1938 eventually succeeded in drafting a sort of standstill declaration that provided for consultation by the respective foreign ministers of the twenty-one American republics in the event of a threat to the peace and security of an American nation. Any such threat was declared to be a common concern, and was to be met by the measures which each government deemed appropriate. Thus, while the declaration paid verbal homage to the United States thesis of "continental solidarity," none of the Latin-American republics sacrificed one iota of its independence or freedom of action.

The Neutrality Acts

The neutrality legislation of the later 1930's was inspired by the same isolationism, now in reluctant conflict with evidences of the growing crisis in Europe. Public opinion, always prone to seeking scapegoats, and ascribing the Depression in great part to the wickedness of bankers and financiers, found a further congenial enemy in the armament manufacturers. During 1934 and 1935 an investigating committee under Senator Gerald Nye, an extreme isolationist and a Republican, had made startling disclosures as to the enormous profits made by American armament manufacturers in the First World War, and it was a simple matter to deduce that these "merchants of death," who had prodded an honest and simple-minded country into one war, clearly must be prevented from prodding it into another. Isolationism therefore meant clipping the claws of the armament manufacturers at home as well as showing an unqualified neutrality toward all disturbers of the peace abroad.[1]

We need not submit these views to detailed analysis. It is sufficient to observe that they were widely held and deeply felt. Consequently, the open announcement of German rearmament in March 1935, and Italian mobilization against Ethiopia in the summer of the same year, produced a tremendous upsurge of antiwar sentiment in the United States. (See pp. 388-89.) Under the threat of a filibuster, the strong neutrality bloc in Congress rushed through a hastily devised resolution prohibiting the sale and transport of "arms, ammunition, or implements of war" to belligerents after the President had recognized, by proclamation, a state of war in any area. This Neutrality Act, as it was called, received the presidential signature in August 1935. Under its provisions the President could decide at his own discretion what articles were to be embargoed. He could similarly prohibit travel by American citizens on belligerent ships, save at their own risk, and he could exclude belligerent submarines from American ports. Manifestly the Act sought to avoid the immediate circumstances of American involvement in the First World War, but it was full of technical difficulties which, in the passion of the moment, Congress had sublimely ignored.

Shortly after the presidential signature, the Neutrality Act, with all its imperfections on its head, was applied to the Italo-Ethiopian War. Hull strove to stop one loophole by imposing a "moral embargo" on the export of oil, copper, trucks, scrap iron, and similar articles. But his unofficial pressure produced little effect. Exports from the United States to Italy rocketed from a monthly average of $25,000 in 1934 to $583,000 in November 1935. Seemingly the armament manufacturers were at their old games again. It is possible that, had the League of Nations imposed oil sanctions against Italy, the Administration might have asked Congress for permission to follow suit. Hull himself was deeply disturbed by Mussolini's forthright application of military force to gain Italian ends in Ethiopia—ends which, Hull argued, Mussolini could have gained far more easily by peaceful means. But then came the premature publication of the Hoare-Laval Plan, and whatever American cooperation might or might not have been offered to the League was at once stultified by this sudden and barefaced reversion to the most abhorrent practices of the old secret diplomacy. (See pp. 406-07.)

Congress, more isolationist than ever, went on to build the Chinese Wall of neutrality still higher. When the embargo provisions of the Neutrality Act became due to expire, the act was prolonged till May 1937. A number of amendments were written into it, prohibiting, among other things, the granting of government loans and credits to belligerents. In January 1937, the Act, so amended, was applied to the Spanish Civil War. But the effect of the Act was to deny arms to the legitimate Spanish government at a time when Germany and Italy were free to aid the rebel Nationalists. The Act, in short, discriminated against the victim of aggression and the democratic party in the conflict.

A further act of "permanent neutrality" was accordingly drafted and passed by Congress in May 1937. The ban on the export of munitions, on the transportation of arms to belligerents on American ships, on travel by American citizens on belligerent ships, and on the granting of loans to warring powers was retained. Furthermore, no American ship engaged in routine commerce with belligerents was to be armed. But the President now had authority to permit the export of goods (other than arms and ammunition) to a belligerent if such goods were paid for on delivery, and if they were shipped from the United States in the purchaser's ships. This "cash-and-carry" clause obviously favored any power that controlled the seas and that possessed the necessary investments and credits in the United States, and it need hardly be added that, in the event of a war in Europe, the act would operate in favor of the Western democracies and against the Axis.

Isolation and Rearmament

The United States, in the later 1930's, bore more than one point of resemblance to Britain during the same period. A peace-hungry people, disillusioned over the course of events that they had sought in vain to mold to their own ways of thinking, were gradually made aware of the perils in which they lived and moved. There was one difference. Whereas the government in Britain seemed to be aiding and abetting the people in their ostrichlike pacifism, the government of the United States – and notably the President and his Secretary of State – were in advance of the people in appreciating the dangerous drift of world events. Sporadic anti-German demonstrations occurred; on one occasion, the swastika flag was torn down from the *Bremen* in New York Harbor. But such incidents were mere ripples on the surface of a deep national apathy. Popular radio commentators kept their listeners well informed – indeed sheer information was never a problem in these years – but their breathless, melodramatic manner of delivery bred a sort of immunity to news of crises from abroad. Isolationism could always cite its own more comfortable theses, for example, that Nazi energies were fully taken up by internal problems in Germany, or that Italy had just had one war and could not possibly want another, or that Japan was too weak economically to engage in a major Pacific showdown, or that the simple facts of geography made nonsense of so fantastic an idea as an Axis assault on the Western Hemisphere. The year 1937 closed with the curious and significant episode of the War Referendum. Representative Louis L. Ludlow had succeeded in introducing into the House a resolution for a Constitutional Amendment whereby the authority of Congress to declare war would require confirmation by a nation-wide referendum. Public opinion polls at the time showed that the idea was highly popular; and, when the resolution eventually came to a vote of the House early in 1938, it was only defeated by the narrow margin of 209 to 188.

Meanwhile Roosevelt, in his foreign diplomacy and his public appeals, persisted in every device permitted him to issue his double-pointed warnings to aggressors abroad and to isolationists at home. On October 5, 1937, he made his famous "quarantine" speech in Chicago:

> The peace, the freedom, and the security of ninety percent of the population of the world is being jeopardized by the remaining ten percent, who are threatening a breakdown of all international law and order. Surely the ninety percent, who want to live under law and in accordance with moral standards that have received almost universal acceptance through the centuries, can and must find some way to make their will prevail. The situation is definitely of universal concern . . .
>
> It seems to be unfortunately true that the epidemic of world lawlessness is spreading. When an epidemic of physical disease starts to spread, the community approves and joins in a quarantine of the patients in order to protect the health of the community against the spread of disease . . .

Public reaction to the speech was instant and uncompromising. Peace organizations, the labor unions, and the embattled pacifists in Congress, all united in a campaign "to keep America out of war." Two Representatives sought to have the President impeached. However, early in 1938, in a special message to Congress, the President recommended immediate, increased appropriations for defense; and, with supplementaries, the total appropriations for defense for the fiscal year 1938-39 passed the billion-dollar mark at $1,042,000,000.

The effect of the Czechoslovak crisis of May and September 1938 was more confused and uncertain, but it inspired in the United States the first unmistakable signs of fear. In August, while the second phase of the crisis was still mounting, Roosevelt, speaking at Kingston, Ontario, in Canada, gave out the explicit assurance "that the people of the United States will not stand idly by if domination of Canadian soil is threatened by any other Empire." In this instance, public and Congressional reaction was more favorable, since "hemisphere defense" was one of the accepted policies of the day. In September, after Munich, the immediate reaction in the United States, as elsewhere, was one of heartfelt relief that war had been avoided, but—again, as elsewhere, only a few days were to elapse before the damaging items in the balance sheet were better realized, and a storm of protest was then raised against this "peace that passeth understanding." The mood thereafter settled down to what has been described as "an isolation of disgust"; but it was still an isolationism. (See pp. 488-89.)

In January 1939, in his Annual Message, the President put up another trial balloon: "There are many methods short of war, but stronger and more effective than mere words, of bringing home to aggressor governments the aggregate sentiments of our people"; and he made proposals in particular for the revision of the Neutrality Act, which, in its present form, "may actually give aid to an aggressor and deny it to the victim," and for "adequate defense." Appropriations for defense were shortly passed to the tune of $1,300,000,000; but the Neutrality Act, notably its crucial cash-and-carry clause, was left untouched. Indeed, the accidental revelation that the Administration had allowed a French military observer to fly in one of the latest Douglas bombers aroused such a revulsion of criticism that the President, at his next news conference, felt obliged once more to reaffirm the orthodox policy of "no commitments."

On April 14, 1939, in a speech at the Pan-American Union in Washington, Roosevelt gave unconditional pledges of economic and military support to any American nation threatened with economic or military aggression. Then the same evening he addressed a joint appeal for peace to Hitler and Mussolini, and in the course of it he asked for their assurance that they had no intention of attacking thirty independent nations, which he mentioned by name. (See pp. 494-95.) Roosevelt was mistaken if he thought he could put two such wily controversialists as Hitler and Mussolini "on the spot" in this way, but the replies which the two dictators eventually vouchsafed probably did more to rouse the American public than all the President's messages, conferences, and "fireside chats." The best propaganda for the Western democracies in these years often came from the enemy!

"The New Order in East Asia"

In the East, vis-à-vis Japan, much the same story unfolded as in the West, vis-à-vis Germany and Italy. The administration's first year was sufficient to establish its general policy. In November 1933, as we have noted, the United States recognized the Soviet Union, an action at once regarded in Tokyo as an open, flagrant attempt to create counterpoises to Japanese power in the Pacific. In May 1934, the United States made available a total credit of $50,000,000 to the Chinese Government; [2] American sales of airplanes to China doubled, though the total was still inconsiderable. The State Department was not very surprised, therefore, when in 1934 Japan demanded naval parity with the United States and Britain and denounced the Washington Treaty of 1922. As we have elsewhere described, the London Naval Conference at the end of 1935 failed in a last-minute attempt to patch up an agreement on naval ratios between the major naval powers. (See p. 392.) But at least it could be said in consolation that Japan by now had engineered her own isolation in the Far East. From this moment onward, in whatever direction she looked – toward China, toward the Soviet Union, toward the United States – Japan saw only enemies, actual or potential. In 1936 she sought a way of escape from this unwelcome, if well-merited, predicament by entering into the Anti-Comintern Pact with Germany – and in 1937 with Italy. By an irresistible logic, the aggressor of the East became linked with the aggressors of the West.

Hull tried to reinforce his policy by "parallel action" with Britain and with the League of Nations – at least he could avoid the fiasco of the Stimson Doctrine in 1932 – and as far as possible he worked in collaboration with Neville Chamberlain, who became British Prime Minister in 1937. Speeches and protests were sometimes synchronized and even couched in similar phraseologies. But Hull's extreme weakness was all too evident. With neither the material force in his right hand nor the moral support of the American people in his left, his policy could be little more than a series of frustrations which, only by his own high principles, was preserved from indignity. He would even resort to lecturing the Japanese ambassador in Washington, and periodically that plausible gentleman would appear at his office in the State Department with apparent shamefacedness to hear out his strictures upon the Japanese Government's or the Japanese Army's latest outrage in China.

Large-scale fighting was renewed in China after the Marco Polo Bridge incident in July 1937. Public opinion in the United States was little disturbed. After all, war in China was not precisely a novelty. The administration, aware that the cash-and-carry principle operated to the advantage of the power holding command of the seas – in this case, Japan – did not invoke the Neutrality Act, on the ostensible ground that neither belligerent had formally declared war. The sale of munitions by American firms to both China and Japan was therefore permissible, but, under the terms of the Act, it would have to be carried on at the risk of the exporter. Of more immediate concern, however, was the safety of American lives and property in China. Wild marksmanship on the part of Chinese airmen had resulted in casualties to Americans in the International Settlement in Shanghai and on American ships in Shanghai Harbor. Hull gave out the information that the United States Government would protect its citizens to the best of its ability, but, at the same time, strongly advised those who could to leave the country. During August, 1,200 United States marines were landed in Shanghai.

The sinking by Japanese aircraft of the United States gunboat *Panay* on December 12, 1937, together with three oil tankers that it was escorting up the River Yangtze, again showed the depth of popular aversion to involvement in war. Even a motion picture of the episode, which a resourceful American journalist had been able to smuggle out of China, failed to arouse any serious demand for retaliation. The Japanese made a prompt apology for their carelessness, paid an indemnity, and the affair was closed. The general conviction was that American material stakes in China were not sufficient to justify strong action; extreme isolationists urged early withdrawal from the Far East lest another such incident might start the landslide toward war; cautious strategists pointed out that American bases and naval strength in the Pacific were still far from adequate. Nevertheless, the *Panay* incident and accumulating reports of ruthless Japanese bombing of civilians in China roused demands for an embargo on the sale of war materials to Japan. In July 1938, the Administration responded to the extent of imposing a moral embargo on the export of aircraft to Japan. In a letter addressed to 148 aircraft manufacturers, the Department of State affirmed that licenses would be issued only "with great regret" to any firm exporting aircraft or aircraft parts to countries the armed forces of which bombed civilians from the air. However, embargo or no embargo, the Japanese conquests in China proceeded. In October 1938, the current phase of the campaign was brought to an end with the capture of Canton. (See p. 347.)

All through these months, the Japanese Government, through the mouths of the Premier, Konoye, and the Foreign Minister, Hirota, argued that Japan had no territorial ambitions in China and desired no annexation of Chinese soil; but, at the same time, it could hardly be denied that the Japanese armed forces in China were busy establishing the crude realities of military and economic control. Whatever statesmanlike language might assert, the fact was that the old "Open Door" was now most effectively shut, bolted, and barred. The United States Government's protests against the destruction of American property, the molestation of American citizens, or the closing of American schools and missions, all met with that polite evasiveness of which Japanese diplomacy was so accomplished a master. However, on November 3, 1938, the mask was partly raised when the Japanese Government formally proclaimed that its long-term objective was the creation of a "New Order in East Asia" and invited other powers "to adapt their attitude to the new situation."

In July 1937, a few days after the Marco Polo Bridge incident, Hull made a major statement of policy – and of his political creed:

> [We advocate] national and international self-restraint; abstinence by all nations from use of force in pursuit of policy and from interference in the internal affairs of other nations; adjustment of international problems by peaceful negotiation and agreement; faithful observance of international agreements; modi-

fication of treaties, when necessary, by orderly processes in a spirit of mutual helpfulness and accommodation; respect by all nations for the rights of others and performance of established obligations; revitalizing and strengthening of international law; economic security and stability the world over; lowering or removing excessive trade barriers; effective equality of commercial opportunity and treatment; limitation and reduction of armament . . .

> Realizing the necessity for maintaining armed forces adequate for national security, we are prepared to reduce or to increase our own armed forces in proportion to reductions or increases made by other countries. We avoid entering into alliances or entangling commitments, but we believe in cooperative effort by peaceful and practicable means in support of the principles hereinbefore stated.

These principles, said Hull further, were not "vague formulae." They were "as vital in international relations as the Ten Commandments in personal relations."

> I never lost an opportunity to state and restate these principles in public speeches, statements, diplomatic notes, and conversations with foreign diplomats and visiting statesmen. To me there was nothing vague about them. They were solid, living, all-essential rules. If the world followed them, the world could live at peace forever. If the world ignored them, war would be eternal.

But on another occasion, in a moment of truth, the Secretary of State admitted, "[Wars] are not likely to be brought to an end by manifestations of disapprobation on moral or legal grounds." [3]

"The New Order in Europe"

It has been pointed out that the Depression reversed the two basic tenets of the traditional American public philosophy. Before the Depression the rule in domestic affairs was competition, and in foreign affairs, cooperation. After the Depression the rule in domestic affairs was cooperation, and in foreign affairs, competition. Naturally enough beliefs once so deeply grounded were not abandoned willingly or wholly. Given a return to remotely "normal" circumstances, they would have been quickly taken up again. But the United States was not unique in its agony. The whole of Western civilization in these years — and never was the United States so unconvincingly and so integrally a part of that civilization — was being subjected to a profound revaluation of many of its hitherto most accepted and unquestioned values. The Roosevelt Administration might try to minimize the revolutionary nature of its program both at home and abroad, the President and his aides might talk in the older idioms in which they had been born and bred, but none the less the United States was making a rupture with the past which was decisive and irreversible. After 1929 and 1933, the American world could never be the same again.

The final testing time was soon to be at hand. On September 1, 1939, German forces invaded Poland, and the Second World War began.

We cannot leave this chapter without a glance at the man who dominated the period it describes. Franklin Delano Roosevelt was born in 1882 of a distinguished family that was partially of New York Dutch extraction. He was a distant cousin of Theodore Roosevelt, a predecessor in the presidency. He was educated at Groton and Harvard and then practiced law in New York. In 1910 he began his political career as Democratic state senator from that Republican stronghold, Dutchess County, and at once opened his long fight against Tammany Hall and the corrupt political machine of that day. During the First World War he was Assistant Secretary of the Navy. Shortly after his return to civil life he was struck down by infantile paralysis. He had once been a man of fine physique, fond of athletics. The illness left him crippled, but it did not break his spirit or put an end to his public life. He was one of those rare characters whom physical affliction makes stronger and finer.

He was Governor of New York for two terms. He was nominated as presidential candidate by the Democratic Convention of 1932, and he defeated the Republican candidate, Hoover, in the ensuing election. He was re-elected President of the United States in 1936, 1940, and 1944 for the unprecedented period of four terms. He died during his fourth term, on April 12, 1945, as the Second World War was approaching its finale, still in his early sixties, exhausted by work and responsibility.

Roosevelt was that combination, far too uncommon in modern democracy, of keen political acumen and long-term idealism. His maneuvering was unmatched, though it always served a larger purpose. Naturally he made enemies, but even the bitterest of them seldom questioned his essential integrity. He had infinite charm and the true leader's gift of inspiring confidence in desperate situations. He was master of an informal but impressive oratory; his voice of slightly minor timbre was peculiarly adapted to his favorite medium, the radio. He often saw further and more clearly than his closest advisers, especially in foreign affairs. It used to be said that he was always one move ahead of public opinion; but no one now would deny the consistent accuracy of his vision. To a stricken Europe he gave a hope as great as President Wilson had ever given, a hope, moreover, that was far more realistic and substantial. His death, at the moment of his supreme triumph and indispensability, was one of the greatest tragedies of the era.

27. THE APPROACH OF WAR

Arms and Appeasement

In the middle 1930's, Hitler and his generals had one anxiety – the preventive blow against Germany while her rearmament was half completed. Such a blow could have been struck in 1936 at the time of the Rhineland coup. It would have been justified by Germany's treaty violations alone. Thereafter the critical period passed rapidly beyond recall. By 1937 the blueprints were factories; the assembly lines were rolling out their fantastic products; the country was filling with uniformed, marching men. During 1937 Germany is believed to have spent $4,500,000,000 on armaments; by contrast, Britain and France together spent less than $2,000,000,000; and the two pairs of figures, though steadily increasing up to 1939, continued to bear much the same ratio to each other. Hitler himself estimated Germany's total expenditure on armaments up to the Second World War as 90,000,000,000 marks ($37,500,000,000). Even without the additional contributions of Italy and Japan against them, the Western democracies were being decisively outclassed and outrun in the great race.

In his anniversary speech of January 30, 1937, Hitler declared that "the period of so-called surprises is at an end," and, to be sure, the year turned out somewhat deceptively as one of no overt incidents – at least as far as Germany was concerned. The Civil War continued in Spain; the treason trials occupied the Soviet Union; Japan's undeclared war broke out in China. But Western Europe lay momentarily under a pall of uneventfulness. In France, Blum and Chautemps were sedulously humoring the national escapism; in Britain, Neville Chamberlain was inaugurating the classic phase of his appeasement policy. At the end of April 1937, Sir Nevile Henderson arrived in Berlin as British ambassador with instructions to work for Anglo-German conciliation, and he so far interpreted his mission as to form friendships with several of the Nazi leaders and publicly to express his admiration for several features of the Nazi order.

Chamberlain was exerting himself in particular on behalf of an understanding with Italy. In January 1937, the so-called Gentleman's Agreement between Britain and Italy had been signed in Rome, mutually recognizing the interests of the two powers in the Mediterranean, and this was now to be confirmed by a more explicit instrument. Chamberlain's Foreign Secretary was Anthony Eden, the stalwart representative of that wing of the Conservative party that still upheld the ideals of the League of Nations and of collective security. But it was already clear that the real direction of British foreign affairs had been assumed by Chamberlain himself and by his colleague, Lord Halifax.[1] Whatever may have been his private feelings, in public Chamberlain showed no dismay over Italy's and Germany's continued intervention in the Spanish Civil War, nor over Italy's adherence in November 1937 to the German-Japanese Anti-Comintern Pact and the consequent extension of the Axis into a formidable combination triangularly embracing the globe. (See p. 412.) In January 1938, Chamberlain received a personal letter from President Roosevelt suggesting a conference in Washington between interested powers to discuss the deteriorating international situation. "Here," wrote Winston Churchill, "was a formidable and measureless step."[2] But Chamberlain returned a chilling answer. He was then preparing to grant Britain's recognition of Mussolini's Ethiopian conquest, and doubtless the President's intervention would have cut across his efforts. Eden, it is worth mentioning, was away on vacation at the time and was not consulted. He resigned shortly afterward and was succeeded as Foreign Secretary by Halifax.

On April 16, 1938, the pending Anglo-Italian Agreement was signed in Rome by the British ambassador, Lord Perth, and the Italian Foreign Minister, Count Ciano. It was intended to be a general settlement of the whole field of Anglo-Italian affairs and a permanent reconciliation of the two powers after their recent unhappy differences over Ethiopia and Spain. Clearly it was Chamberlain's definitive attempt to detach Italy from her German connection and once more to bind her to the community of "peace-loving" nations. It mutually disallowed injurious propaganda, provided for the exchange of information regarding armed forces of the two powers in the Mediterranean and East Africa, regulated the waters of Lake Tana, the source of the Blue Nile, and reaffirmed the existing status of the Suez Canal. In particular, Italy agreed to the British formula for the proportional evacuation of foreign volunteers from Spain, and she disclaimed any territorial or political aims in regard to Spain or the Spanish possessions overseas. Britain agreed to take steps at Geneva to remove "such obstacles as may at present be held to impede the freedom of member states as regards recognition of Italian sovereignty over Ethiopia."

The Austrian Crisis

The Austrian *Anschluss* had always been a primary Nazi aim. It was mentioned on the first page of *Mein Kampf,* and no knowledgeable person, in or out of Germany, doubted that Hitler, Austrian born, was committed to its fulfillment. Yet, for three years after the assassination of Dollfuss, the Nazis in Austria looked as if they had forsworn their past. The Austro-German agreement of 1936 formally recognized the tranquillity that now outwardly mantled the country. (See p. 387.) Hitler almost overreached himself in protestations of good will. The Chancellor, Dr. Kurt von Schuschnigg – the modest, scholarly, self-effacing, pious Schuschnigg – seemed securely in power. For himself, Schuschnigg probably inclined toward a mildly nostalgic affection for the exiled Hapsburgs and fancied himself as a sort of regent. He had dropped both Major Fey and Prince von Starhemberg and was virtually governing Austria alone. He wanted no further support from the Fatherland Front or from the Italian Fascists — although he held one or two somewhat frigid meetings with Mussolini. In deference to Hitler he had appointed as his assistant Foreign Minister the pro-Nazi Guido Schmidt, who had assisted in the negotiations for the treaty of 1936. Wilhelm Miklas was still Austrian President, apparently sympathetic to his general policy. Diplomatic Europe on the whole looked forward complacently to the continuation of the Schuschnigg regime, despite its dictatorial and monarchial eccentricities, when early in 1938 it was painfully surprised by reports of new Nazi machinations in Austria.

In January 1938, the Austrian Government narrowly averted a Nazi putsch, a repetition of the Rintelen-Habicht incident of four years previously, this time under a certain Dr. Leopold Tavs and a certain Dr. Artur Seyss-Inquart. Presumably this new Nazi attempt "to liberate" Austria was timed to be completed by January 30 and to be announced by Hitler himself in his anniversary speech on that day. But the Vienna police got wind of the putsch and raided Tavs's offices. Hitler postponed his speech till February 20 and made use of the interval to prepare a more open assault on Austria than that which had just been frustrated and, incidentally, to turn to his own advantage a tangled scandal in the German *Reichswehr*.

On January 11, 1938, the *Reichswehr* Minister, Field Marshal Werner von Blomberg, had quietly married a certain Erna Gruhn. The date was Göring's birthday, and Hitler and Göring had themselves graced the wedding ceremony with their presence. But Erna Gruhn, even without the unsavory police record that she was discovered to have, was far from qualifying as socially eligible by the standards of the German officer caste. Hitler was incensed beyond measure to have to learn too late the real character of the lady in the case. Obviously he could no longer keep Blomberg as *Reichswehr* Minister, and Blomberg was not only dismissed but forbidden to set foot in the Chancellery or even to wear uniform.

Blomberg's logical successor was the Commander in Chief of the Army, General Frieherr Werner von Fritsch. But Himmler now produced a dossier from his inexhaustible secret files which seemed to show that Fritsch was guilty of homosexual offenses. The wrathful Fritsch of course denied the charges and demanded an inquiry by court martial. On February 3, after some days of the wildest rumors, Hitler decided matters after his own fashion. He himself took over the *Reichswehr* Ministry and the supreme command of the army. Fritsch and a dozen other ranking officers were retired. Göring, who had had some ambitions toward the *Reichswehr* Ministry, was consoled by being promoted to Field Marshal. A new body, the High Command of the Defense Forces, OKW (*Oberkommando der Wehrmacht*), made its appearance as the supreme military authority in Germany, with a new roster of names — Keitel, Jodl, Reichenau, and Brauchitsch — in the highest offices. Joachim von Ribbentrop, recently ambassador in London, succeeded Neurath as Foreign Minister; Walther Funk succeeded Schacht as Minister of Economics. Meanwhile the uxorious Blomberg had departed on his honeymoon to Capri. Fritsch was afterwards exonerated by a court martial, but he was not reinstated. He was eventually killed in action in the Polish campaign of 1939.

At a stroke Hitler had rid himself of a number of contumacious generals and had replaced them by officers more amenable to his policies. He had fought and won another round in his long struggle for the control of the armed forces of the Reich. But, as we shall see, strong opposition still remained.

On February 8, 1938, Papen, Hitler's envoy in Vienna, delivered an invitation to Schuschnigg to a meeting with Hitler at the Berghof at Berchtesgaden. On the face of it, the invitation was entirely innocuous. The heads of European states met constantly. All unsuspecting, Schuschnigg proceeded accordingly to Berchtesgaden by rail and road on the morning of February 12, accompanied by his assistant Foreign Minister, Guido Schmidt. Papen joined the party as courier at the German frontier.

The details of that agonizing interview in the Berghof are now known to us. Hitler received his guest significantly in the presence of Generals Keitel and Reichenau. In his private talks with Schuschnigg he delivered himself of a long harangue, the usual mixture of Hitlerian piety and menace, on the theme of his achievements for Germany:

> I am telling you once more that things cannot go on in this way. I have a historic mission; and this mission I will fulfill because Providence has destined me to do so. I thoroughly believe in this mission; it is my life. And I believe in God; I am a religious man . . . Consider the path I have chosen; consider what I have achieved . . . Look around you in Germany today, Herr Schuschnigg, and you will find that there is but one will. I was predestined to accomplish this task; I have chosen the most difficult road that any German ever took; I have made the greatest achievement in the history of Germany, greater than any other German. And not by force, mind you. I am carried along by the love of my people . . .[3]

Meanwhile Ribbentrop, Papen, the generals, and Schmidt conferred in an adjoining room. Lunch and further conversations followed. Ribbentrop then presented Schuschnigg with Hitler's ultimatum: The Nazi Seyss-Inquart was to be appointed Minister for Public Security, a key post that carried with it control over the police; any Austrian might profess the National Socialist creed; Austrian Nazis were allowed to engage in "legal activity" within the framework of the Fatherland Front, and all imprisoned members of the party, including the participants in the assassination of Dollfuss, were to be amnestied; a hundred officers of the German Army were to be detailed for duty with the Austrian Army. In default of immediate acceptance, Schuschnigg faced a German military invasion of his country. At one point in the conversations Hitler shouted for Keitel to be present. Toward evening Schuschnigg signed. As a magnanimous concession, Hitler allowed him three days to put the ultimatum into effect.

Schuschnigg spent the three days of grace in earnest discussions with President Miklas, with his cabinet, with leaders of the Fatherland Front, and even with the long-ostracized Social Democrats. Mussolini at first gave out that Italy's position in regard to the Austrian question was "unchanged" and then, eventually, that he could offer "no advice in the circumstances." London and Paris likewise gave Schuschnigg little word of comfort. At that moment, Chautemps' "Republican Combination" was rocking to its fall, and France was without a government. As usual, the fates everywhere seemed to be conspiring in the Führer's favor. Schuschnigg bowed to the inevitable. The Nazi terms were accepted; the Austrian Cabinet was reconstructed with Hitler's nominee, Seyss-Inquart, as Minister for Public Security. Schmidt was promoted from assistant to full Minister for Foreign Affairs.

On February 20, Hitler delivered his postponed anniversary speech in Berlin. He regaled the *Reichstag* with three hours of sustained truculence, denouncing in particular the League of Nations, Britain's colonial empire, and the unsympathetic democratic press. He made derogatory references to Eden, the British Foreign Secretary – who just then happened to be on the point of resigning office. He paid compliments to Japan and announced his recognition of Manchukuo. He disclaimed all territorial interests in the Far East and in Spain. He referred with special significance to the 10,000,000 Germans outside the Reich.

Hitler's immediate plans in Austria were still obscure. Perhaps he hoped that Austria, under the efficient manipulation of Seyss-Inquart or under a renewed outbreak of squadrism on the part of the amnestied Austrian Nazis, would now fall effortlessly into his hands. But that he was now determined to achieve the realities of political control in Austria, whatever the means thereto might be, there can be no possible doubt. Contingents of the German Army were drawn up along the Austrian frontier "shamming military action." Schuschnigg himself probably precipitated the more violent course, when on March 9 he announced that he would hold a national plebiscite on the question of Austria's independence. Hitler retorted in fury at his favorite device for appealing to public opinion being thus used against him. Göring in a series of telephone calls from Berlin to Vienna induced Schuschnigg to call off the plebiscite and then virtually ordered Seyss-Inquart to take over the government of Austria.

At midnight, March 11, President Miklas appointed Seyss-Inquart Chancellor. Units of the German Army by then had already crossed the Austrian frontier. By midday March 12, Vienna was in occupation. Himmler, Heydrich, and the Gestapo took up prepared quarters. German and Italian troops exchanged formal greetings at the summit of the Brenner Pass. Hitler himself drove into Braunau, his Austrian birthplace, the same afternoon and was officially welcomed by Seyss-Inquart at Linz. On the 13th he visited his parents' graves at the nearby village of Leonding. He reached Vienna on the morning of the 14th – after delays over the breakdown of the German tanks and motorized artillery. Throughout his route, buildings were hung with swastikas and the streets were thronged with masses of heiling, hysterical partisans. Cardinal Innitzer, Archbishop of Vienna, ordered the church bells to be rung. The swastika was flown from the spire of St. Stephen's Cathedral.

Reactions among the European powers were sharp and painful, but entirely negative. "Horrible, horrible!" cried Halifax afterward. "I never thought they would do it!" In general, British Conservatives, as at the time of the Rhineland coup in 1936, could not find it in their hearts to condemn an Austro-German *Anschluss,* however unpleasant the means thereof, so long as they believed it was desired by a majority of both parties concerned. France was still in the midst of a ministerial crisis, and incapable of affirming a definite policy. Chautemps resigned on March 10, to be followed by Blum at the head of a weak reconstruction of the old Popular Front. Italy was bound to her German ally and accepted the invasion with professions of satisfaction. "Mussolini, I shall never forget you for this!" Hitler had telegraphed from Linz on March 12, and Mussolini had made answer: "My attitude is determined by the friendship between our two countries, which is consecrated in the Axis."

Hitler's "coordination" of his Austrian conquest was rapid and thorough. President Miklas resigned. Austria was declared to be a *Land* of the Reich and named the Ostmark. Hitler referred to Seyss-Inquart as his "Regent." The Austrian National Bank was taken over by the Reichsbank, together with its gold reserve of $100,000,000. The Austrian Army was incorporated into the *Reichswehr.* Josef Bürckel, former Nazi Governor of the Saar, reorganized the Austrian Nazi party, and was later created Commissioner for the Ostmark. Himmler and Hess laid wreaths on the grave of Dollfuss's assassin, Otto Planetta. (See p. 386.)

In Vienna and in the country at large the usual Nazi *Gleichschaltung* went into force, and the leaders of the Fatherland Front, Social Democrats, and Jews bore the main brunt of its violence. Brutalities of which we have little ken and less understanding were loosed upon the defenseless country. Storm troopers systematically plundered houses, shops, and public premises. A common sight in Vienna in these days were "cleansing squads" of Jews, men and women, on their knees scrubbing off the sidewalks the propaganda signs that had been painted at the time of Schuschnigg's abortive plebiscite. Jews were dismissed from public offices, universities, and schools, and from professional appointments. Thousands fled to Czechoslovakia or Switzerland, but the frontiers were soon closed, and thousands more were stopped. The number of arrests of all types of Austrian citizens has been put at between 30,000 and 40,000, many of whom eventually found their way to the concentration camps at Dachau and Buchenwald. Suicides numbered a hundred a day. Major Fey, his family – and even his dog – were found shot. Dollfuss's family escaped. Starhemberg was already in Switzerland. Sigmund Freud, the psychologist, was allowed to accept an invitation from England. Cardinal Innitzer and the Catholic hierarchy in Austria, having once greeted the Nazi invasion with joy and blessings – for which they earned the remonstrances of the Vatican and indirectly of Cardinal Faulhaber of Munich – soon repented their impulsive loyalty. The Catholic Church in Austria was "coordinated" with more than the usual Nazi ruthlessness. Catholic organizations were dissolved, Catholic properties confiscated, Catholic monasteries and convents closed. Later in the year the Cardinal's palace in Vienna was raided and sacked by Nazi mobs, and the Cardinal himself escaped only by being put under protective arrest. Schuschnigg was confined in a room of the

Hotel Metropole, the Gestapo headquarters in Vienna, for some months, subject to the gross indignities since described in his book, and was afterward held at concentration camps.

The Czechoslovak Crisis

Czechoslovakia and her dangerous minority problems have been described elsewhere. (See p. 172.) The Republic was always considered by the Versailles Powers as one of the happier creations of their new order in Europe, and the success of its first years of statehood, the political maturity of its Czech population, the wealth of its resources and industries – and the skill of its propaganda abroad – had sometimes caused the heterogeneous and centrifugal elements in its composition to be forgotten. The Republic moreover occupied a position of the highest strategic importance in the heart of Central Europe. It lay behind mountain barriers whose natural strength had been improved by modern fortifications, and the output of its Skoda munition works was that of a first-class power. Czechoslovakia had become the keystone of the French and the Franco-Soviet alliance systems and the main bulwark against German expansion into the Middle Danube. Well might it be said in 1938, as in Bismarck's day, "He who controls the Bohemian bastion controls Europe."

The Depression had tested Czechoslovakia as it had tested every other country in the world. In 1931, for the first time since 1923, the Czech budget had showed a deficit, and the harvest had been the worst in years. The Czech government was in the hands of moderate coalitions that seemed incapable of initiative. Any sort of "plan" was difficult to devise without upsetting some party or interest essential to the government's support. The situation was ready-made for the provocation of latent racial and ideological discontents.

Of the Republic's 15,000,000 inhabitants, the Sudeten Germans numbered 3,000,000, and the question of their political destiny had been revived in an acute form since the rise of the Nazi party in Germany. (See p. 380.) In the early 1930's Sudeten extremists were already modeling themselves on Nazi prototypes. "Sports" organizations inculcated a distinctive German political mysticism, and their members wore semi-SA uniforms and drilled themselves on German lines. In October 1933, Sudeten Nazis anticipated an impending government ban by voluntarily dissolving themselves, but within a year they were flocking to the standard of Henlein, leader of the so-called *Heimatfront*. In December 1935, Masaryk resigned from the presidency of the Republic and was succeeded by the faithful Beneš. The continuity of foreign policy and the attitude toward Germany were maintained. Masaryk died almost two years later, aged eighty-seven, mercifully spared from seeing the destruction of the state he had done so much to build.

Konrad Henlein, who now appears as one of the protagonists of the Czechoslovak crisis, was a bank clerk and teacher of gymnastics. He was disarmingly mild of manner, not a scintillating character, though personable enough, and a persuasive pleader of his cause. He enjoyed reputable connections with non-German circles abroad, especially in Britain where, of course, he was careful to show himself as anything but the typical Nazi trooper. In 1935 his *Heimatfront* took the name of the Sudeten German party and won 44 seats in the Czech Chamber. He vehemently denied that it then had any Nazi or Pan-German aims or was otherwise than loyal to the existing democratic Czech state, although by then he was in regular receipt of German funds. Henlein met Hitler at the Olympic Games in Berlin in 1936, and it is clear that his party thereafter became secretly assimilated to Nazism and that the Sudetenland was regarded in Germany as a surreptitious Nazi *Gau*. After the Austrian *Anschluss,* Henlein intensified his activities. He founded a special terroristic Free Corps, known as the FS (*Freiwilliger Selbstschutz*), modeled and trained after the Nazi SS. Then suddenly, on April 24, 1938, speaking at a congress of his party at Karlsbad, Henlein threw off the mask and enunciated his Karlsbad Program, as it was called, demanding autonomy for the Sudeten areas, reparation for "injustices" inflicted on Sudeten Germans since 1918, and full liberty for Sudeten Germans to profess German political philosophy.

In May 1938, it seemed that Hitler might strike. He and Mussolini had just celebrated in Rome and Naples a more than usually flamboyant meeting. German troop movements were reported along the Czech frontier. On May 21, the Czech Government, believing that it had information of another of Hitler's "Rhineland marches" ordered partial mobilization. Half a million Czechs were under arms. The British, French, and Soviet governments added the weight of their solemn and repeated representations in Berlin.

The "May Crisis" passed. The democratic press in Europe was jubilant and made out that Czechoslovakia, by her timely mobilization, had won a great victory. Every newspaper outside Germany – and Italy – proclaimed that the courageous action of a small but determined people had at last called the bully's bluff and turned him from his fell purpose. The principle of collective security had been brilliantly and bloodlessly vindicated. But whatever Hitler's actual intention may have been, the effect upon him of this premature rejoicing is not difficult to imagine. Hitler resolved there and then that "Czechoslovakia must be wiped off the map!"

But at this time it was the great power, France, which was giving more reason for anxiety than the little power, Czechoslovakia. The Blum government, which had been formed at the time of Hitler's Austrian coup in March, had lasted exactly twenty-eight days. In April 1938, Daladier took office with Chautemps Vice-Premier and Bonnet Foreign Minister. Daladier indeed was to remain in office till March 1940, a commendably long period, but at no time during it could he have been described as the leader of a "strong" administration. Even in his original Ministerial Declaration his references to foreign affairs, the most important affairs of the hour, had been lamentably and ominously evasive.

Georges Bonnet was a confirmed proponent of appeasement. He made a pathetic attempt to come to terms with Italy on the lines of the recent Anglo-Italian Agreement, and earned nothing but insult and scorn for his pains. On May 14, 1938, at Genoa, Mussolini made one of his most bellicose speeches and singled out France for a particularly venomous attack. Yet in that May, at the League Council in Geneva, France had helped to read the obsequies over the dead body of Ethiopia; in June, France closed the Catalan frontier to further shipment of arms to the Spanish Republican government; and in July the Paris Court of Appeal rejected the Spanish Republican government's claim to the Spanish gold reserve which had been held by the Bank of France since 1931. Appeasement could hardly have stooped lower.

The possibility of direct mediation of the Sudeten problem in Czechoslovakia had been discussed during the spring of 1938 between the British and French Governments, and the appointment of Lord Runciman as "investigator and mediator" was discussed and confirmed during the early summer. Britain had no alliance or commitment in regard to Czechoslovakia as had France, and she was therefore in a position to propose an "independent" settlement of the Czech crisis. Chamberlain afterward gave out that the Czechs had themselves desired and asked for a British mediator, but it seems that Runciman was "wished" on them at the instance of the British Government. Runciman himself was a curious choice for so delicate and complicated a mission. He was a businessman and a shipowner, reputed to be wealthy, and he had been President of the Board of Trade; but he had no qualifications which suggested capacity or experience in Central European affairs.

Runciman's inquiries opened in early August, however, with much appearance of good will on all sides. He duly met the Czech leaders, but he spent the best part of his time with Henlein and the Sudeten German party. Beneš and the Czech Premier, Milan Hodza, with indefatigable resource, produced one plan after another, only to see each rejected by the inflexible Sudetens. The so-called Fourth Plan offered the Sudetens complete regional autonomy on a cantonal basis, a plan which, in Runciman's view, could have been made to cover the Karlsbad Program. But it was evident that the marionette Henlein was being worked from Germany, and that the purpose of himself and his party was not to allow negotiations to succeed. Runciman did not consider it within his terms of reference "to mediate between Czechoslovakia and Germany." Meanwhile the war of nerves on the Czech frontiers continued. The Nazi press, in a campaign of incredible vulgarity, magnified almost daily incidents — many of them provoked by Henlein's Free Corps, the FS — into the most frightful atrocities. To judge by Goebbels's headlines in those days, the Sudetenland, at the hands of its sadistic Czech overlords, had degenerated into an inferno of robbery, torture, murder, and Bolshevism.

On September 6, Hitler opened the Nazi *Parteitag* in Nuremberg. On all hands it was expected that he would use the occasion to bring the Sudeten crisis to explosion point. Göring, rising to an almost apoplectic rhetorical effort, boasted that Germany now had impregnable fortifications on the Rhine, foodstuffs and raw materials for an indefinite blockade, an invincible army, a great navy, and the mightiest air force in the world. On September 12, Hitler spoke:

> Three and a half million Germans are being oppressed in the Czech state. They too are the creatures of God. The Almighty did not create them that they should be surrendered by Versailles to a foreign Power which is hateful to them . . . I say that if these tortured souls cannot obtain rights and help by themselves, they can obtain them from us!

Hitler's speech was hailed with riots — apparently organized riots — in the Sudetenland. The Czech Government proclaimed martial law in several districts. Henlein broke off relations with the Czechs and with Runciman, declaring that Hitler's speech had now superseded the Karlsbad Program. He then fled to Germany and thence broadcast his determination to lead the Sudetens "home to the Reich." Runciman returned to London.

Berchtesgaden, Godesberg, Munich

On August 18, 1938, General Ludwig Beck, Chief of the German General Staff, had resigned. He had for some time represented the surviving resistance within the *Wehrmacht* to Hitler's adventurous foreign policy. His successor in office was General Franz Halder, a man no more enamoured of Hitler's policy than Beck. Beck, at the time, was the main inspirer and organizer of a conspiracy against Hitler on the part of a "military peace party," which included Generals Halder and Erwin von Witzleben and a number of civilians such as Schacht, the former mayor of Leipzig Carl Goerdeler, and the German ambassador in Rome Ulrich von Hassell. General Walther von Brauchitsch, lately appointed Commander in Chief of the Army, gave the conspirators his grudging support. Some accounts have it that, on the outbreak of war with Czechoslovakia, Hitler was to be arrested and deposed, and a military dictatorship would temporarily seize control. But the conspirators were never put to the test. The war with Czechoslovakia did not break out; the crisis issued in a "political settlement" — and in another convincing triumph for the Führer. On September 13, Neville Chamberlain, the British Prime Minister, telegraphed Hitler an offer, in almost abject terms, to intercede with him in person: "Please indicate earliest time at which you can see me and suggest a place for meeting." Hitler accepted at once. Perhaps in his curious vanity he could not resist the prospect of entertaining the head of the British Government in suppliant mood at his own hearth at Berchtesgaden.

Chamberlain arrived at Munich by plane on the morning of September 15, and proceeded thence to Berchtesgaden and the Berghof. He was alone with Hitler — except for an interpreter — for three hours. In a rambling conversation, in which Hitler apparently did most of the talking, there emerged the outlines of a proposal that the Sudeten question should be solved by means of "self-determination." Chamberlain undertook to submit the proposal to his cabinet and to the French and Czech governments. He returned to London the next morning, September 16. Cabinet meetings in London were attended by Runciman. Daladier and Bonnet crossed over from France. The result was the so-called Anglo-French Plan, urging the Czech Government to transfer to the Reich the Sudeten areas whose population was known to be more than 50 per cent German, and to accept an Anglo-French guarantee for the new Czech frontier. It was subsequently explained to the Czech Government that the transfer would be effected, where necessary, by plebiscite or would otherwise be regulated by "an international commission."

Chamberlain flew to his second meeting with Hitler at the picturesque Rhineland town of Godesberg on September 22, in the full belief that only the technical details for the transfer of the Sudeten areas remained to be settled. But self-determination now no longer satisfied the Führer. He wanted neither plebiscites nor commissions, but surrender, and surrender at once. In addition, since the former meeting at Berchtesgaden, Hungary and Poland, both friends of Germany, had preferred claims to Czechoslovak territories inhabited by their respective nationals, claims that Hitler now took it upon himself to support. Chamberlain, shocked and reproachful, declared that he could not keep returning to London with fresh proposals only to discover as soon as he had secured their acceptance from the interested parties that they had been outdistanced by new events. The conference was resumed the following evening after an interchange of letters. Hitler then presented his "last word" in the form of a "Memorandum" categorically demanding the evacuation of the Sudeten areas, as defined by him on an attached map, and their occupation by German forces between September 26 and 28. A moment of frank and angry talk from Chamberlain persuaded the Führer to change the operative date to October 1, and Chamberlain returned to London with the memorandum thus amended. The British press reported that the negotiations had failed.

The Czechs had acceded to the original Anglo-French Plan under virtual threat and blackmail. The British minister at Prague, on behalf of his government, had clearly intimated to Beneš that if Czechoslovakia rejected the plan she would be responsible for the ensuing war and that she would be the cause of her own destruction. The French minister, for his part, was under the painful necessity of adding that in that event, despite the Franco-Czech alliance and despite her repeated assurances, France would not fulfill her treaty obligations. Beneš was also warned that a German invasion of Czechoslovakia would certainly be followed by invasions from Hungary and Poland. Hodza, the Czech Premier, resigned on September 22, and a government of "national concentration" was immediately set up under General Syrovy, former commander of the Czech Legion in Siberia. On September 24, two days after Godesberg, the new Czech Government ordered general mobilization, and on the same day the French Government ordered the mobilization of two categories, representing a partial mobilization of about 600,000 reservists.

The post-Godesberg negotiations were carried on by Sir Nevile Henderson, the British ambassador in Berlin. There was a distinct hardening of hearts since the first amiable exchange of views at Berchtesgaden. The Syrovy government, with a return of courage and confidence characterized the new Godesberg Memorandum as "absolutely and unconditionally inacceptable." Meanwhile Litvinov stated in the League Assembly at Geneva that the Soviet commitments to Czechoslovakia held good, and the Soviet

Tea at Berchtesgaden; (left to right) Neville Chamberlain, Hitler, Ribbentrop, and Sir Nevile Henderson, the British ambassador

WIDE WORLD

Government simultaneously warned the Polish Government that it would denounce the Soviet-Polish Nonaggression Pact if Poland joined in an attack on Czechoslovakia. Mussolini added his appropriate contribution to the crisis in a series of belligerent speeches in different parts of Italy — almost one speech a day for more than a week — demanding a "totalitarian" solution of the Sudeten problem. "If a United Front comes into being, for or against Prague, let it be known that Italy's place is already chosen."

On September 26, Hitler spoke to his battle-crazed myrmidons in the Sportpalast in Berlin. The speech was punctuated with jeering, and with offensive references to Beneš. It also renewed the demand for the cession of the Sudetenland by October 1:

> This is the last territorial claim I shall make in Europe, but it is a claim from which I shall not recede and which I shall fulfil, God willing . . . Once the Czechs come to an understanding with their other minorities, I shall have no further interest in the Czech state; in fact I am prepared to guarantee it. We do not want Czechs any more. But so far as the Sudeten problem is concerned, I declare my patience at an end . . . We are resolved. Let Herr Beneš decide.

On September 28, the British Government acceded to the pressure of its First Lord of the Admiralty, that energetic rebel against appeasement, Duff Cooper, and ordered the mobilization of the navy. The same evening, Chamberlain broadcast to the British people. The voice that came over the air was that of an aged, weary, and broken man:

How horrible, fantastic, incredible it is that we should be digging trenches and trying on gas masks here because of a quarrel in a faraway country between people of whom we know nothing.

But it was Mussolini, the Italian Duce, who saved the situation. About midday September 28, through Attolico, the Italian ambassador in Berlin, he appealed to Hitler to postpone the march of the German Army for twenty-four hours. The result was the Four-Power Conference at Munich.

The meeting of the four statesmen – Hitler, Chamberlain, Daladier, and Mussolini – began on the afternoon of September 29 at the Brown House in Munich, and the final Munich Agreement was drafted and signed in the early hours of the next day. The terms incorporated the essentials of the Godesberg Memorandum, but without its more peremptory details. The Czechs were given from October 1 to October 10 to complete their evacuation of the Sudeten areas, "without any existing installations having been destroyed." The German occupation would take place in four stages, and the final frontiers would be fixed not by Hitler's map, but by an international commission consisting of representatives of the four Powers and Czechoslovakia. Plebiscites were stipulated for the questionable districts, and the right of option into or out of the transferred territory was secured to any of its inhabitants. At the same time Hitler and Chamberlain signed a separate Anglo-German Pact resolving to use "the method of consultation" in questions concerning their two countries. Britain and France declared a guarantee of the new Czechoslovak frontiers against unprovoked aggression, a guarantee in which Germany and Italy undertook to participate once the revisionist claims of Hungary and Poland had been met. Britain afterward granted Czechoslovakia a loan of £10,000,000, ostensibly to tide over the temporary disruptive effects of the Munich Agreement on her economic life.

Reactions of the Powers

The immediate reaction to Munich everywhere – except in Czechoslovakia – was one of joy and thankfulness. "No conqueror returning from a victory on the battlefield," said the London *Times* on October 1, "has come home adorned with nobler laurels than Mr. Chamberlain from Munich yesterday," and it would be hard to find an English – or French – paper of the date that did not express the same feelings. Yet the cold, gray morning-after brought the inevitable revulsion. Certainly Britain had no legal stake in, or alliance with, Czechoslovakia, and it is impossible to accuse her of evading obligations which she had never contracted. But Britain indirectly and undeniably breathed the atmosphere of dictation at Munich – and of dictation from a power that she had once defeated and whose present form of government she despised. Churchill's speech in the House of Commons had the ring of truth in it:

We have suffered a total and unmitigated defeat. All is over. Silent, mournful, abandoned, broken Czechoslovakia recedes into the darkness . . . I think you will find that in a period of time, which may be measured by years but may be

Chamberlain addressing the welcoming crowd at Heston Airport, London, September 30, 1938, on his return from Munich

RADIO TIMES HULTON

> measured by months, Czechoslovakia will be engulfed in the Nazi regime . . . We have passed an awful milestone in our history, when the whole equilibrium of Europe has been deranged, and the terrible words have for the time being been pronounced against the Western democracies: Thou are weighed in the balance and found wanting!

No one realized better than the British people themselves that they were morally and materially unready for war. The British rearmament program was but half begun. In September 1938, the German air force was numerically superior to those of Britain, France, and Czechoslovakia combined. Saying "No" to Mussolini in 1935 was very different from saying "No" to Hitler in 1938. The one meant a sedentary warfare of protests and sanctions; the other meant aerial warfare on a hitherto unimaginable scale.

For France, the moral predicament was never in doubt. The legal state was all too clear. The Franco-Czechoslovak alliance had been so often reiterated in the past than any casuistic dispute or evasion of it was impossible. The public mood of France can be described only as one of inertia, a refusal to think and a wish to forget. It was too far gone even for humiliation or shame. French foreign policy in 1938 received its final seal and confirmation on December 6, when Ribbentrop visited Paris and signed with Bonnet a Franco-German Declaration of Friendship, ostensibly guaranteeing the existing Franco-German frontier.

For Czechoslovakia, Munich was a cruel defeat and a crueler betrayal. She had remained loyal to the ideals of her founders; she had been unwavering in her democratic faith; she had not allowed herself to be suborned to Nazism as Poland had been. She had always been assiduously flattered by the high regard of Western democracy; but now she had been condemned without a hearing. She had not been invited to Godesberg or to Munich, and she, a democratic country, had afterward been forced to accept the decisions of others respecting her very existence as a nation, without even being permitted to consult her own parliament. In terms of acres and cents, she lost to Germany her entire system of fortifications in Bohemia, three-quarters of her heavy industries, and essential roads and railroads; in terms of morale, her losses were incalculable.

Munich was the surrender of democracy's once strongest and last surviving outpost in the Middle Danube. It transformed the entire political and strategic situation on the Continent of Europe. It was the total subversion of Versailles and of all that Versailles had stood for. It broke the French alliance system beyond repair. It threw into confusion all established allegiances and alignments. It destroyed the Little Entente. It left the Balkans open to Nazi penetration.

For the Soviet Union, reactions were not simple. Munich fell at the precise juncture when Moscow was bethinking itself of a new isolationist withdrawal. The Spanish Civil War and the treason trials complicated the process. But evidently Litvinov's excursion into collective security had not paid off. Both before and after Munich, Litvinov gave repeated and categorical assurances that the Soviet Government would stand by its treaty obligations with Czechoslovakia, notably the Czech-Soviet Mutual Assistance Pact of 1935, but his pleas had been ignored. The Czech crisis had not been discussed in the League Council, of which the Soviet Union had only recently become a member, nor had the Soviet Government been invited to send a representative to the Munich Conference. In Soviet eyes these omissions were not only a palpable diplomatic insult, but proof positive that Western imperialism was up to all its old tricks and was trying to divert Hitler's expansionist energies toward the East. The Soviet Government subsequently denounced the Czech-Soviet Mutual Assistance Pact. On March 10, 1939, at the Eighteenth Party Congress, Stalin roundly accused Britain and France of trying to provoke a war in which "Germany and the Soviet Union would weaken and exhaust each other" and then of hoping "to appear on the scene with fresh strength to dictate conditions to the enfeebled belligerents."

In the United States the first reaction to Munich was of profound relief that the peace had been preserved, and it was some days before the mood changed to one of undisguised disgust, not unmixed, for the first time in these critical years, with fear. Seven months previously the isolationists, however shocked, could still speak of the Austrian crisis, in the words of Senator Borah, as "a thing which is not of the slightest moment to the Government, as a Government, of the United States." At that time the Administration made some effort to alleviate the distress of individuals in Austria, notably Catholics and Jews, especially after the ensuing November pogrom in Germany. The issue of immigration visas from Austria was speeded up.

Secretary Hull, in a speech which presumably reflected the views of the State Department, appealed for a "cooperative effort" among nations for the sake of peace and argued emphatically that "aloofness" encouraged and virtually invited other lawlessly inclined nations.

But Munich was a decisive turning point of American public opinion. As the crisis had mounted, news commentators deplored the degeneration of European affairs to a state comparable to "the manners of a top sergeant, the veracity of a paid propagandist, and the methods of a college cheer-leader." The virtual destruction of Czechoslovakia, a democratic country, which had always enjoyed the high regard and affection of the American people, found hardly even an isolationist voice to rise and excuse it. "Czechoslovakia has been sold down the river, but no man yet knows at what cost of blood and tears."

The German press did not minimize the significance of Munich. A dangerous enemy had been neutralized, the monstrosity of Versailles had been removed, the power of the Third Reich had been demonstrated, important new resources of men and material had been added to the German military establishment, *Mitteleuropa* had once more been made a realizable dream, and all had been accomplished bloodlessly and with the maximum of drama by the divine genius of Adolf Hitler.

It is necessary to mention only one incident at this point, an incident that must have dissipated any last lingering illusions that might still have existed abroad regarding the true nature of the Third Reich and the emollient effects of Munich upon the Nazi heart. On November 7, 1938, Herschel Grynszpan, a seventeen-year-old Jewish refugee, thinking to avenge the mistreatment of his parents in Germany, forced his way into the German Embassy in Paris and shot the first German he could find. His victim, an official of the Embassy, Ernst vom Rath, died of his injuries some days later. Hardly six weeks after Munich, on November 10, the anniversary of Hitler's Munich putsch of 1923, the Nazis opened their worst Jewish pogrom to date. Wrecking squads of troopers tore through the streets of Berlin and other cities, including Vienna, setting fire to Jewish shops, houses, and synagogues, ejecting whole families into the streets, making indiscriminate arrests, and sometimes picking on a defenseless individual for the more exquisite forms of torment. It seemed as if half the population of Berlin had gone berserk. The police made no attempt to interfere. German mothers perched children on their shoulders to let them see the sport.

Clearly the pogrom had been no capricious outburst, and the probabilities point to Göring as its organizer. At the time he was concerned over the stresses and strains which rearmament was imposing on the German economy, and he was clutching at any relief that was ready to hand. Jewry offered him a goodly haul of wealth and labor. "I'm going to make barbaric use of the plenipotentiary powers given to me by the Führer," he said. On November 13, in a special decree, he ordered the Jews to make good at their own expense the damage that had been done during the pogrom, and in addition imposed a fine of 1,000,000,000 marks on the Jewish community in Germany for the murder of vom Rath.

The Extinction of Czechoslovakia

The international commission established under the Munich Agreement to devise the new Czechoslovak frontiers held its first meeting on October 1. As it happened, there were no plebiscites, and all important decisions were made by the German military members of the commission, Keitel and Brauchitsch. Britain and France evinced no further interest in the guarantees of the new frontiers which at Munich they had solemnly pledged themselves to give. The isolation of the Czech Republic was about as complete as it was possible to be. The Poles seized the Teschen area and coal fields on October 2. By the so-called Vienna Award on November 2, the "Second Munich," Germany and Italy, in the capacity of mediators, assigned a generous strip of Slovakia and Ruthenia to Hungary. On November 21, Czechoslovakia ceded to Germany a corridor through the heart of the country to be used for a new automobile highway connecting Vienna and Breslau, and to be regarded to all intents and purposes as German territory.

The "coordination" of the occupied Sudeten territory was quickly effected. Henlein reappeared in his old homeland as its Gauleiter. The remainder of the mutilated state fast broke into its elements. All its former centrifugal and disruptive forces, now abetted by German agency, were given full play. The Slovak People's party demanded autonomy and showed unmistakable Nazi tendencies. On October 7, an autonomous government was formed in Slovakia under Mgr. Tiso, successor to Mgr. Hlinka in the leadership of the Slovak People's party, and took up its quarters in Bratislava. (See p. 172.) An autonomous government was formed in Ruthenia a few days afterward. The very name "Czechoslovakia" was changed to "Czecho-Slovakia." Ruthenia took the name of "Carpatho-Ukraine."

On October 5, 1938, Beneš resigned the presidency and went into voluntary exile. Hitler maintained the fiction of good relations with his successors, Emil Hacha and František Chvalkovsky in Prague and Tiso in Bratislava, but, within a week of the Munich Conference, he was consulting Keitel in regard to the final military subjugation of the country. The finale came early in 1939. On March 13, Tiso and on March 14, Hacha and Chvalkovsky were summoned to Berlin, as Schuschnigg had once been summoned to Berchtesgaden, to hear from Hitler and Ribbentrop the dissolution of their respective states. Units of the German Army had already crossed the Czech borders. By midday of March 15, Prague was in occupation. The Skoda armament works at Pilsen fell intact into German hands. Hitler entered his new territory and from the Hradschin, the palace of the old Bohemian kings, proclaimed Bohemia and Moravia a Protectorate of the Reich. Neurath was appointed Protector with Konrad Henlein and Karl Hermann Frank as his aides in office. The Hungarians simultaneously invaded Carpatho-Ukraine and annexed it to Hungary.

So ended the First Republic of Czechoslovakia.

Simultaneously Memel returned to the Reich. The transaction was prefaced by the usual press campaign in Germany and the usual efforts at appeasement on the part of the Lithuanian Government. Juozas Urbšys, the

THE PARTITION OF CZECHOSLOVAKIA, 1938-39

Lithuanian Foreign Minister, visiting Berlin, was bluntly told by Ribbentrop that the port and territory of Memel must be surrendered without more ado, and the Lithuanian Government had no alternative but acquiescence. In return Germany promised Lithuania a free harbor in Memel, and gave her the inevitable guarantee of nonaggression. On March 23, 1939, Hitler and the German Baltic Fleet visited the surrendered port.

The Polish Crisis

Poland had made her choice in January 1934, when she concluded the German-Polish Nonaggression Pact and drove the first breach in the "Versailles Front." (See p. 382.) But her situation was highly artificial and all but acknowledged to be so. She felt all the shocks and repercussions of the Ethiopian crisis of 1935 and particularly the Rhineland crisis of 1936. A painful hesitancy began to govern her foreign policy, a hesitancy common to many another smaller – and bigger – power in the Europe of the day trying frantically to predict the future. Her incontinent conduct in the early days of her liberation and her irresponsible baiting of Lithuania and Czechoslovakia more recently looked as if they might be bringing home their appropriate reward. An attempt to thaw the frigid relations with France was a feature of the year 1936. General Gamelin, Chief of the French General Staff, visited Warsaw, and General Smigly-Ridz visited Paris. The respective receptions of both soldiers were significantly cordial, and technical staff talks appear to have taken place on the second occasion.

Danzig, always an infallible barometer of German-Polish relations, now had a Nazi party, which held a majority in the local Danzig legislative assembly, the *Volkstag,* and which was stirring up its characteristic "incidents" in the city and the port. Hermann Rauschning had resigned the presidency of the Danzig Senate in November 1934, shortly to go into exile and write his classic exposures of Nazism, and he had been succeeded by the Nazi, Arthur Karl Greiser. Greiser overrode the city's constitution as he pleased and went out of his way to insult the League of Nations' High Commissioner in Danzig. Albert Forster, the Nazi Gauleiter in Danzig, announced that he did not regard himself as responsible to the authorities in Danzig, but to his Führer in Germany. Forster had not the slightest legal status in Danzig. He was a German national and a Deputy of the German *Reichstag,* one of Hitler's intimate circle and a regular visitor at Berchtesgaden. But he conducted himself as if he were of higher rank – as in the Nazi hierarchy he was – than Greiser, the president of the Danzig Senate. In July 1936, Greiser, invited to Geneva to give an account of himself before the League Council, behaved as offensively as he could. He gave the Nazi salute in the Council chamber and thumbed his nose at journalists in the press gallery who laughed at him. He was making a display – as he thought – of Nazi temerity; he was making a display – as the League Council thought – of the kind of statesmanship that Nazism was now raising up to power and prominence in the world.

In 1938, after the Austrian and Czechoslovak crises, it was becoming evident that the heat would soon be turned on Poland. In October of that year, at a luncheon at a Berchtesgaden hotel, Ribbentrop had demanded of Joseph Lipski, the Polish ambassador to Germany, the return of Danzig to the Reich and the construction of an all-German automobile highway and railroad, extraterritorially controlled, across the Corridor. The demands were formally renewed in January 1939, when Ribbentrop visited Warsaw, and again in March 1939, after the incorporation of Memel. Ribbentrop also proposed that Poland should join the Anti-Comintern Pact. On each occasion the demands were firmly rejected by Poland. Meanwhile the German press suddenly discovered evidences of Polish terrorism against German minorities in Poland and let loose the usual campaign of vituperation. Yet on January 30, 1939, during his anniversary speech, Hitler had celebrated the fifth anniversary of the German-Polish Nonaggression Pact in reassuring and friendly words. The Hitlerian technique was following its regular pattern.

Chamberlain in Britain made little reference to the German occupation of Prague in March 1939. He countered questions in the Commons with all his "freezing gift of understatement." But opinion in the country was agitated and accusing, and Hitler's new demand for Danzig roused all parties to genuine anger and resolution. On March 31, Chamberlain announced in the Commons that the British Government had extended a guarantee to Poland and had committed itself, "in the event of any action which clearly threatened Polish independence, and which the Polish Government accordingly considered it vital to resist with their national forces . . . at once to lend the Polish Government all the support in their power." The guarantee was so worded that the Poles themselves would be the judges of the right cause and the right moment for resistance. It was an epochal departure for British foreign policy, which hitherto had shrunk from entanglements east of the Rhine. France at once associated herself with the British action. On April 6, the guarantee was verbally confirmed in conversations in London with Joseph Beck, the Polish Foreign Minister.

The German plan for military operations against Poland was ready in April 1939. On May 23, at the Chancellery in Berlin, Hitler held one of his briefing conferences with his high-ranking officers, including Göring, Brauchitsch, Keitel, and Admiral Raeder. The entire political and military situation was surveyed. Germany, Hitler argued, had re-emerged as a great power, but all her demands for the necessities of life were regarded abroad as "encroachments." The problems of ideology and national unity had been solved; the problem of living space remained:

> Danzig is not the subject of the dispute at all. It is a question of expanding our living space in the East and of securing our food supplies. The Polish problem is inseparable from conflict with the West . . . [We must] *attack Poland at the first suitable opportunity* [underscored in the original German text]. We cannot expect a repetition of the Czech affair. There will be fighting. Our task is to isolate Poland. The success of the isolation will be decisive . . . Economic relations with Russia are possible only if political relations have improved . . . If England intends to intervene in the Polish war, we must occupy Holland with lightning speed . . . The war with England and France will be a life-and-death struggle . . . The government must be prepared for a war of ten to fifteen years' duration . . .

And so forth. But the isolation of Poland was conditional upon the disinterest of the Soviet Union, and Hitler now vouchsafed for the first time his view that it might be necessary for him to come to a temporary *rapprochement* with the Soviet Union. A German-Soviet pact would be the prelude to a German-Polish war.

The Albanian Crisis

It had been hoped in Britain that the end of the Spanish Civil War would at least rid the world of one source of perpetual tension, that the recent Anglo-Italian Agreement might become infused with some of the reality it had always seemed to lack, and that there might even be a corresponding improvement in French and Italian relations. But the year 1938 had closed in Rome with violent anti-French demonstrations. François-Poncet, the new French ambassador in Rome, from his diplomatic seat in the Italian Chamber had himself been a witness of an offensive outcry—doubtless prearranged for his benefit—on the part of the Italian Deputies for "Corsica, Tunis, Savoy, Jibuti!" Some days later, on December 17, 1938, Mussolini denounced the Franco-Italian Agreement of 1935.

On March 26, 1939, speaking in Rome at a giant rally of his squadrists on the twentieth anniversary of the Fascist party, Mussolini made it very clear that the recent successes of his German ally in Central Europe had only hardened his heart the more against France:

[The French Government] must not complain if the furrow which now separates our two countries, becomes so wide that it cannot be filled. We do not want to hear any more about brotherly, sisterly, cousinly, or any other sort of bastard relationship, because relations between states depend on a balance of forces between them . . . The word "peace" has been rather overworked and has a nasty ring like bad memory. . . . The order of the day is more guns, more ships, more planes, even at the cost of dispensing with what is called civilian life. . . . As history teaches us, woe to them who cannot defend themselves!

Early in April 1939, Italian troop concentrations at Bari and Brindisi had been reaching suspicious proportions. Inquiries from Lord Perth, the British ambassador in Rome, elicited nothing beyond reassurances and evasions. But on April 7, Good Friday, Italian transports steamed across the Strait of Otranto and landed an Italian invading force in Albania. Evidently Mussolini in recent months had been feeling the need of some military demonstration to parallel the success of his Axis partner in Central Europe. Albania had always belonged to the Italian sphere of influence; it had been evacuated in "disgraceful" circumstances the year before the Fascist rise to power; but, of more recent years, it had been subject to increasing economic penetration on the part of Italy. Count Ciano in particular had constantly urged Mussolini to reoccupy it. The present Italian action plainly contravened a number of treaties, notably the recent Anglo-Italian Agreement. But that particular difficulty could always be swept aside. By April 8, Italian troops had entered the Albanian capital, Tirana. King Zog of Albania, Queen Geraldine, and their infant son fled to Greece. The crown of Albania was assumed by King Victor Emmanuel.

On April 13, the British and French Governments replied to this new Axis incursion into the Balkans by extending guarantees, on the lines of the recent Polish guarantee, to Greece and Rumania. A month later the British Government announced an Anglo-Turkish Mutual Assistance Pact, to go into immediate effect "in the event of aggression leading to war in the Mediterranean area." At the same time it became known that France and Turkey, preparatory to a similar pact, were negotiating the transfer to Turkish possession of their old bone of contention in Syria, the Sanjak of Antioch and Alexandretta. (See p. 397.)

At this moment the United States Government entered the lists. On April 14, 1939, in his Pan-American Day address in Washington, President Roosevelt used the following words:

The issue is really whether our civilization is to be dragged into the vortex of unending militarism, punctuated by periodic wars, or whether we shall be able to maintain the ideal of peace, individuality, and civilization as the fabric of our lives. We have the right to say that there shall not be an organization of world affairs which permits us no choice but to turn our countries into barracks, unless we be the vassals of some conquering empire.

The same evening, President Roosevelt sent a message to the two European dictators asking them, as "an immediate measure of relief," to give assurances that their armed forces would not attack or invade, for a period of ten years, thirty states whose names he listed. The message was hailed everywhere but in Germany and Italy, where the press denounced it as "an infamous trick," "a tactical maneuver," "a shabby propaganda pamphlet." For a moment America took the place of England as the favored object of totalitarian scorn and execration. (See p. 469.)

Mussolini answered President Roosevelt's message in a public speech on April 20. He reprobated "the unjust attempt to put the two Axis nations in the dock," and asked how Italy could be accused of trying to set the world on fire at the moment when the whole of her energies were concentrated on the preparations for the great Fascist Exhibition to be held in Rome in 1942. The speech was not one of the Duce's best efforts, but it was more conciliatory than his recent belligerent utterances. Hitler made his answer in a speech of two and a half hours in the *Reichstag* on April 28. It was a considerable, well-prepared and – for Hitler – closely reasoned review of the Nazi movement, running the whole gamut from the *"Diktat"* of Versailles to the Czech crisis. It was one of his greatest oratorical efforts. As usual he labored the villainies of the Jews, the impostures of the League of Nations, the pacific purposes of the Third Reich, and the favors of Providence. His mood switched deftly from declamation to pleading, from menace to injured innocence, from arrogance to defensiveness. He denounced the Anglo German Naval Agreement of 1935 and the German-Polish Pact of 1934, both of which, he claimed, had been superseded and destroyed by infringements of the other parties to them. To President Roosevelt he referred in terms of contempt and irony, suggesting a Monroe Doctrine for Europe, and hinting that the President would have rendered a nobler service to peace if he had redeemed the promises of Woodrow Wilson.

The Moscow Pact

The spring and summer of 1939 wore on in an atmosphere of gathering oppressiveness – and confusion. In Britain, against strenuous Labor and pacifist opposition, Parliament introduced conscription, as revolutionary an innovation in Britain's traditional domestic policy in peacetime as the recent Polish guarantee had been in her traditional foreign policy. After lengthy conversations between Göring and Mussolini, Ribbentrop and Ciano, Germany and Italy converted their Axis into a formal military alliance, a "Pact of Steel," as Mussolini called it. Germany and Denmark signed a nonaggression pact. France and Turkey, having settled the matter of Alexandretta to their satisfaction, entered into a mutual assistance pact in the Mediterranean. Several thousand German-speaking Tirolese, at the behest of Mussolini, were uprooted from their ancient homeland and transferred to the Reich. The British sovereigns, King George and Queen Elizabeth, went on a tour of Canada and visited the United States, a felicitous and heartening, if somewhat transparent, piece of diplomacy. Meanwhile Hitler, edging toward Danzig and Poland, was putting into motion all those tactical thrusts and feints which the world had now come to recognize as the preliminaries of a Nazi coup.

But the question of the hour was Russia. The Peace Front which Britain and France had been constructing against Germany and which now included Poland, Greece, Rumania, and Turkey, was essentially unreal and incomplete without the adherence of the great power in the East. Litvinov and Sir William Seeds, the British ambassador in Moscow, Halifax and Ivan Maisky, the Soviet ambassador in London, Bonnet and Jacob Suritz, the Soviet ambassador in Paris, were engaged in continual, cordial, but apparently fruitless conversations. Shortly after the fall of Prague on March 15, Litvinov himself had proposed a Six-Power Conference – of the Soviet Union, Britain, France, Poland, Rumania, and Turkey – to discuss the possibilities of common action. Chamberlain was then urging a Joint Declaration on the part of Britain, France, Poland, and the Soviet Union. But this phase of diplomacy, as we have seen, concluded with the British guarantee to Poland on March 31, a guarantee made without consulting the Soviet Union and much disliked by it.

It could not have escaped the acute observer that Hitler's speech of April 28 had omitted the usual references to "Jewish Marxism" and to the subhuman monsters who inhabited the Kremlin. On May 3, Litvinov, once the indefatigable supporter of the League of Nations, was suddenly relieved of his post as Soviet Foreign Commissar to be succeeded by the colorless, provincial, but grimly impassive President of the Council of People's Commissars, one-time Secretary-General of the Party, Vyacheslav M. Molotov. Moscow was seething with rumor. On May 20, Molotov had a "most friendly" talk with the German ambassador Count von der Schulenburg and, on his own initiative, hinted that the trade negotiations then in train between the German and Soviet governments would go more smoothly if the "necessary political bases" for them could be created. On May 23, as we have said above, Hitler divulged to his army chiefs his plans for a temporary *rapprochement* in the East. But, though a sudden superficial cordiality now marked German-Soviet ambassadorial meetings, the diplomatic process was slow and cautious, presumably to permit Molotov to overcome his intense distrust of his German opposites.

On May 31, in Moscow, Molotov delivered an important statement of policy. The Peace Front, he said, was faltering because the elementary principle of reciprocity and equal obligations had not been accepted by Britain and France. Moreover, guarantees must cover the border states of the Soviet Union; that is to say, Finland and the three Baltic states must clearly enjoy the same pledges as had been extended to Poland, Greece, Rumania, and Turkey. Finally Molotov hinted at a possible German-Soviet accommodation. In mid-June Chamberlain sent William Strang, his former aide at Godesberg, a high official of the Foreign Office, and an expert in Russian affairs, as a special emissary to Moscow to speed up the lagging discussions; but Strang found himself being treated to the since-famous Molotovian technique of obstruction. Meetings were interminably protracted over definitions of "direct aggression" and "indirect aggression." British and French army and navy officers sent to Moscow in July and August for staff talks, though they received every courtesy at first, were soon working against similar evasions and delays. Meanwhile the Baltic states, round which so much of the discussions was now revolving, clearly preferred to cling to their precarious neutrality and were averse to having guarantees thrust upon them whatever kind of aggression might be threat-

Parteitag, *Nuremberg, 1938: Hitler Youth saluting the Führer*

ASSOCIATED PRESS

The German invasion of Czechoslovakia, 1939: German Czechs saluting the Führer

RADIO TIMES HULTON

ening. Latvia and Estonia in fact were negotiating separate nonaggression pacts, not with the Anglo-French-Soviet Peace Front, but with Germany. Furthermore the Polish Government made no secret of its extreme repugnance to permitting Soviet forces, in the execution of a general mutual assistance pact, to enter Polish territory.

But, by now, Molotov had struck his bargain with the other side. On August 21, the imminent conclusion of a German-Soviet nonaggression pact was announced in Berlin, and Ribbentrop proceeded by air to Moscow two days later for the formal signing of it.

The published text of the Moscow Pact of 1939 was short and simple. The two contracting parties undertook to desist from any act of violence against each other, to give no support to any third power which should make either of them "an object of belligerent action," to consult on questions of common interest, and to settle any future disputes "through friendly exchange of opinion." The Pact contained no "escape clause." It was to be valid for ten years. But in addition there was appended to the Pact a secret protocol to the effect: first, that, in the event of a "territorial or political rearrangement" in the Baltic States, the northern boundary of Lithuania should represent the boundary between the German and Soviet spheres of influence, while both parties recognized Lithuania's interest in Vilna – that is to say, Finland, Estonia, and Latvia should be relegated to the Soviet sphere of influence, and Lithuania to the German; second, that, in the event of a similar rearrangement in Poland, the German and Soviet spheres of influence should be delimited approximately along the line of the Narew, Vistula, and San, and that the question of maintaining an independent Poland would be decided only "in the course of further political developments" and would, "in any case," be solved "by means of a friendly agreement"; and third, that the Soviet's interest – and Germany's disinterest – in Bessarabia was affirmed.

Even a world whose values were awry and whose experience of Hitler's blitz diplomacy was already long and bitter, could hardly credit so astonishing and so cynical an end to the war of ideologies between Nazism and Communism. The German and Soviet peoples themselves, no less than their respective sympathizers abroad, were profoundly shaken. Opinion in Britain and France was particularly revolted at the duplicity of the Soviet Government in negotiating the Pact at the very moment that British and French officers were engaged in staff talks in Moscow. But there was no time now for regrets or recriminations. On August 25, as if to show that she was not to be intimidated by the new development, Britain confirmed her Polish guarantee into a formal Anglo-Polish Alliance. Appeals to Hitler from Chamberlain and Daladier, President Roosevelt, and the Canadian Prime Minister Mackenzie King; secret meetings between Lord Halifax and a Swedish friend of Göring's, one Birger Dahlerus; the Pope's broadcast for peace; offers of mediation from Queen Wilhelmina of the Netherlands and King Leopold of Belgium; an eleventh-hour proposal for a second Munich from Mussolini, all these made no impression on the frenzied, infatuated Führer.

It seems almost comically irrelevant that, in the midst of these events, there were still generals of the "military peace party" in the German *Wehrmacht* — with Halder now at their head — opposed to the inevitable war. But there was no longer any conviction in them. The General Staff had become little more than the technical executant of Hitler's will. On August 22, 1939, at the Berghof, Hitler was giving his assembled retinue his own appreciation of the situation:

> . . . Everything depends on me, on my existence . . . No one will ever again have the confidence of the whole German people as I have. There will probably never again be a man in the future with more authority. My existence is, therefore, a factor of great value . . . For us it is easy to make decisions. We have nothing to lose . . . Our enemies have men who are below average, no personalities, no masters, no men of action . . . All these fortunate circumstances will no longer prevail in two or three years . . . Therefore conflict is better now. I am only afraid that at the last minute some *Schweinhund* will make a proposal for mediation . . . I shall give a propagandist cause for starting the war, never mind whether it be plausible or not. The victor will not be asked, later on, whether we told the truth or not. In starting and making a war, it is not the Right that matters, but Victory.

On August 29, Hitler demanded the dispatch to Berlin of a Polish emissary with full powers to negotiate the cession of Danzig and the Corridor to Germany. The demand was unmistakably redolent of the recent Schuschnigg and Hacha incidents, but this time no emissary was sent. Final German proposals for a Polish settlement were prepared and, at midnight on August 30, Ribbentrop received Henderson, the British ambassador, and read the text to him in German "at top speed" but refused to hand him a copy. Nor did official copies of the proposals ever reach — no doubt they were never intended to reach — either the Polish ambassador in Berlin or the Polish Government in Warsaw, and the Poles remained in ignorance of this last gracious and magnanimous offer of the Nazi Führer. Early in the morning of September 1, 1939, without declaration of war, German troops and planes crossed the Polish border. The Second World War had begun.

Part Four

THE SECOND WORLD WAR

A wonderful story is unfolding before our eyes. How it will end we are not allowed to know. We are sure that the character of human society will be shaped by the resolves we take and the deeds we do. We need not bewail the fact that we have been called upon to face such solemn responsibilities. We may be proud and even rejoice amid our tribulations that we have been born at this cardinal time for so great an age, so splendid an opportunity of service here below.

— WINSTON CHURCHILL

IMPERIAL WAR MUSEUM

28. THE OPENING PHASES—1939-41

The Conquest and Partition of Poland

The first waves of the German *Luftwaffe* crossed the Polish frontiers at dawn on September 1, 1939. The main German invasion forces were disposed in two army groups, a northern group of two armies commanded by General Fedor von Bock, and a southern group of three armies commanded by General Gerd von Rundstedt. The forces totaled 47 divisions and 9 armored divisions, with a first-line air strength of 1,500 planes – some 1,000,000 men in all. General Walther von Brauchitsch in Berlin was in supreme command of all operations of the German Army, with General Franz Halder as his Chief of Staff. The plan of campaign was a simple pincer movement by the northern and southern army groups converging on Warsaw.

The Polish Army, numbering 2,000,000 men on paper, was paralyzed by the bombing of its roads and railroads and was never fully mobilized. It met the impact of the German invasion with 30 divisions, a single armored brigade – and, incredible to relate, 12 cavalry brigades, fully horsed, booted, and spurred. In numbers concentrated for action, in position, armament, and transport, the Polish Army was hopelessly outmatched. The campaign was virtually decided in a week; organized Polish resistance collapsed in three weeks; Warsaw fell on September 27; a few isolated Polish units held out heroically and uselessly till the beginning of October. Several ships of the Polish Navy escaped and were ordered to England. President Moscicki, Marshal Smigly-Rydz, and the Foreign Minister Joseph Beck fled to Rumania – and thence to France. A power of 30,000,000 population had gone down to overwhelming defeat.

On September 17, without warning but in accordance with the secret protocol of the recent Moscow Pact, Soviet troops crossed the eastern frontiers of Poland and, meeting no resistance, proceeded to occupy the eastern Polish provinces. (See p. 497.) Under a new Frontier Agreement on September 29, the Soviet and German governments revised the terms of their original pact so that the greater part of Lithuania fell within the Soviet sphere of influence and Polish territories west of the river Bug fell within the German sphere of influence. In effect, the Soviet Union and Germany partitioned the conquered country along a line roughly coincident with the once famous Curzon Line. (See p. 154.) Germany reannexed the pre-Versailles German territories in Poland; she also annexed Lodz and Katowice. The remaining core of German-occupied Poland was then organized as a Government General with Cracow as its capital and Hans Frank as its Nazi administrator. The persecution of the Polish intelligentsia, clergy, nobility, and Jews and the economic exploitation of the country were put in hand with all dispatch. Hitler was already talking about "extermination" as the "final solution of the Polish problem."

The German conquest of Poland had been a perfect textbook demonstration of the new blitzkrieg tactics. The German Army attacked a selected and isolated enemy. The first phase of the assault was made by the *Luftwaffe.* The Polish air force of perhaps 500 first-line planes was destroyed in 48 hours by the concentrated bombing of its airfields. "Artillery preparation" was provided simultaneously by the dive bomber, or Stuka, designed to spread terror as much as to demolish rearward communications. The second phase of the assault was made by the armored divisions of tanks or *Panzers* with the lighter motorized divisions following. In this new warfare a battle consisted, not of two continuous "fronts" but of sudden and deep infiltrations. All the advantages went to the side that seized and held the initiative in attack. The tanks were conceived of as an independent arm, not as in 1918 as a protective screen for advancing infantry. Often enough the tanks raced ahead of the main body of infantry, from which they might become separated by several days' marching distance. They pressed home their attacks at weak points and bypassed strong points. Their primary objectives were the enemy's road and railroad junctions, bridges, airfields, telegraph stations, and headquarters. Infantry "mopped up" afterward with air and artillery support. Once a deep armored penetration had been effected and exploited to the full, the defense could have been restored only by an armored counterattack of equal strength, and this was exactly the type of counterattack that the enemies of Germany in the first two years of the war had not the material to deliver. The new warfare developed an extraordinary fluidity. Contact between armored forces could be maintained by wireless, and the whole battlefield, from the defender's point of view, became a ubiquitous, amorphous permeation, "like a migration of vermin across a garden." Meanwhile an efficient and well-briefed "fifth column," deep in the rear, aided and abetted the terror and disorganization.

Inaction in the West

Despite his "Pact of Steel" with Hitler and despite his own hankering after warlike glory, Mussolini had resolved for the time being on nonbelligerency. On September 1, 1939, the Fascist Grand Council declared that Italy "would take no initiative in military operations."

On September 3, Britain and — after some hesitation — France were formally at war with Germany. Australia and New Zealand declared war. The Viceroy declared war on behalf of India. In South Africa, Hertzog resigned the premiership, and Smuts formed a government that at once declared war. In Canada the declaration of war was delayed till September 10. Ireland remained neutral — thus denying the use of the Irish ports to the British Navy. (See pp. 273 and 275.)

The British Expeditionary Force of 158,000 men was dispatched to France under Field Marshal Lord Gort. The supreme direction of the Allied armies in France was given to General Maurice Gamelin. An Anglo-French army of 150,000 was grouped in the Near East. The Anzacs were once more on the banks of the Suez Canal. But these preparations did not immediately result in major actions. For all that the German invasion of Poland had automatically invoked the British and French guarantees, all parties realized that the original treaties could have acted only as deterrents to aggression. There was never any question of sending direct military aid to Poland, aid that could have reached her only through the Baltic. For the time being the French contented themselves with probing offensives in the Saar, and even these operations were curtailed after the Polish collapse.

Hitler celebrated the Nazi conquest of Poland in a speech in the *Reichstag* on October 6, in which he made somewhat devious peace overtures to Britain and France. He preferred no claims on France, he said, and, except for colonies, none on Britain. Why therefore should the war continue? — to restore the Poland of Versailles, "to recreate a system which only the Poles themselves did not regard as an abortion"? But Hitler's protestations after every crisis had a familiar ring. "We have taken up arms against aggression," said Daladier some days later. "We shall not lay them down until we have certain guarantees of security, a security which will not be called into question every six months." "The truth is," said Chamberlain, "that after our past experience it is no longer possible to rely upon the unsupported word of the present German Government."

And so the war in the West went on. But for the next six months it was a strange war, soon to be nicknamed the "Twilight War" — or, more popularly, the "Phony War" or "Sitzkrieg." The French were ensconced in their Maginot Line, and the Germans in their Siegfried Line, the so-called West Wall. Two defensive systems confronted one another, and it seemed as if scientific position warfare in 1939 had become more stationary and sterile than it had been in 1914-18. Even the war in the air failed to materialize. Britons, for whom for months past Air Raid Precautions (ARP) had become the uppermost preoccupation, were surprised that the sky above was not instantly filled with myriads of bombers nor the earth beneath rent with myriads of explosive fires. The densely populated centers of Britain and France did not share the fate of Warsaw — as yet. The rival air forces engaged in reconnaissance flights and in occasional raids on naval bases, all exploratory and usually ineffectual.

But appearances were deceptive. In October, upon the failure of his peace overtures, Hitler was already urging upon his cautious generals plans for "battles of annihilation" in the West, and, but for the severe weather conditions, the German Army might well have received orders that very November to try to repeat its Polish triumph in France and Flanders. The blitzkrieg would be loosed again as soon as conditions permitted.

While these military preparations were going forward, there was another flutteration among the Beck-Goerdeler band of conspirators planning the arrest and deposition of Hitler on the eve of the new offensive in the West. (See p. 483.) But, when the offensive was postponed, the Zossen Conspiracy — so called after Zossen, then the headquarters of the High Command — came to nothing. A much more exciting incident occurred, however, on November 8 in Munich during the anniversary celebrations of the "Beer Hall Putsch" of 1923, when an attempt was made on Hitler's life by one Georg Elser, a Communist, and a carpenter and electrician by trade, using a bomb of his own invention. But Hitler left the hall just before the explosion. It was afterwards very circumstantially hinted that the entire plot — and, of course, the "miraculous escape" — had been engineered by the Gestapo as a means of raising the Führer's popularity. The Gestapo tried afterward to implicate in the plot two British "agents" whom it kidnaped in Holland.

At sea, each side had at once resorted to the blockade strategy it had developed in the First World War. The Cunard liner *Athenia* was sunk by a German submarine on the first day of hostilities with a loss of 112 lives, including 28 Americans. The *Athenia* was hardly a test case either navally or diplomatically — doubtless British precautionary measures at sea had not yet been undertaken — although the incident served a warning on the world at large that the pirates of the *Lusitania* were ranging the seas again. But the German submarine continued to be active thereafter, and its depredations were more serious than had been expected. The *Courageous,* an aircraft carrier, was sunk on September 17, 1939, and the *Royal Oak,* a battleship, was sunk by a most daring action in Scapa Flow on October 14. About 550,000 tons of Allied merchant shipping were lost at sea by the end of the year. Meanwhile surface fighting — despite Germany's much vaunted pocket battleships — turned out to be less serious than expected. In December 1939, the *Graf Spee* was intercepted off the Uruguayan coast, skillfully outmaneuvered, and severely damaged by three British cruisers of shorter range and lighter gun caliber. She eventually found a neutral haven in Montevideo, and there, rather than renew the action, she was scuttled on orders from Berlin.

The first months of the war in 1939, as in 1914, established the blockade of the German surface fleet by the British and French navies. But the conditions, which had formerly made the blockade decisive, were no longer present. Hitler's economic strategy had been dedicated to preventing those conditions from occurring again. We recall the spate of books that issued from the press in 1939, proving by infallible statistics that for lack of resources Germany could not win the war. But Hitler was now fighting on one front at a time, and he had an intimidated Balkans and a friendly Italy — and a friendly Soviet Union — at his beck and call. Within Germany there was a heavy industry second only to that of the United States, and — except perhaps for iron ore and oil — it was amply stocked with raw materials.

For Britain and France these months provided a welcome respite for their own economic deployment. As between themselves they entered at once into the closest cooperation and again set up all the well-tried machinery of the Inter-Allied Councils of 1917-18. Their joint resources were impressive enough. We also recall that other spate of books in 1939 which regaled its readers with pictures of their limitless industrial power. They had overseas empires and most of the neutral world to draw upon. "Cash-and-carry" secured supplies from the United States, and, by an act of Congress in November 1939, these supplies were made to include arms and ammunition. (See pp. 467 and 533.)

On the home front emergency enactments extended all the administrative controls. In Britain, Neville Chamberlain created an inner War Cabinet consisting of himself and ten other ministers. Winston Churchill was First Lord of the Admiralty, the post he had held in 1914. In France, Daladier was not so happily placed. He began by reconstructing his cabinet, relegating Bonnet, the old champion of appeasement, to the Ministry of Justice. His attempt to include Socialists failed. The French Communist party was proscribed, and its leaders, including most of its representatives in the Chamber, were put under arrest. Daladier's compulsory unification of the government and the chambers was a far cry from the perfervid *Union Sacrée* of 1914. (See p. 34.) On March 20, 1940, after a stormy secret debate in a chamber that was already dissatisfied with the lethargic prosecution of the war, Daladier resigned, to be followed by Paul Reynaud, former Minister of Finance. On March 28, in London, Churchill and Reynaud made the formal declaration that the British and French governments would not separately conclude an armistice or treaty of peace.

The Soviet Union, the Baltic, and Finland

Soviet foreign policy at this time was dominated by the Moscow Pact. Official Soviet pronouncements, the speeches of Molotov, and articles in *Izvestia* harped on Anglo-French efforts to embroil the Soviet Union in a mutually destructive war with Germany. Communists in Britain, and especially in France, in evident liaison with Moscow, used their influence to obstruct the war effort of their respective countries.

But diplomatic loyalty did not prevent the Soviet Union from taking advantage of Germany's preoccupation in the West to strengthen its own territorial and strategic position. The secret protocol of the Moscow Pact and the subsequent Frontier Agreement had designated the Baltic States as a Soviet sphere of influence. (See p. 502.) In September and October 1939, Soviet treaties with Estonia, Latvia, and Lithuania entitled the Soviet Government to establish military, naval, and air bases in these territories, and the treaties, no one doubted, were only preliminary to outright political annexation. Lithuania, by way of compensation, received the long-desired district and city of Vilna. Finally, under a further German-Soviet agreement, Germans resident in the area, the old German landowning "Baltic Barons," were evacuated to Germany. Evidently the Soviet Union had no relish for a "Sudeten" problem in the Baltic. Intellectuals, property owners, and anti-Communist elements were deported.

Late in October 1939, the Soviet Government formally demanded of Finland territorial cessions in the Karelian Isthmus and round Petsamo and a naval base at Hangö. It offered substantial compensations elsewhere. But the cessions in the Karelian Isthmus would have deprived the Finns of their recently completed frontier fortifications, the Mannerheim Line, so called after their leader and national hero. Certainly it was unlikely that the Soviet Union would always tolerate the existence of such formidable military installations almost within artillery range of Leningrad. As one commentator remarked, one might have asked New York to rest contentedly beneath the guns of a foreign power on Staten Island. Negotiations between the Soviet and Finnish governments continued through November 1939 and seemed at one time to be nearing a successful conclusion. But on November 28, the Soviet Union denounced its nonaggression pact with Finland and two days later sent forward its troops to attack.

Finland appealed to the League of Nations and, on December 14, 1939, that body, with exceptional promptitude, declared the Soviet Union the aggressor and expelled it from League membership – the only state, we may note, ever to have been so expelled. The Soviet invasion of Finland aroused widespread indignation in Britain and France, in the Scandinavian countries, in the United States – and in Italy. The Finns had a long history of Russian oppression behind them, and the new Soviet-Finnish War seemed like the resumption of an age-old struggle. They now defended themselves with unexpected tenacity, and – for a time – the Mannerheim Line proved equal to any assault that the Soviet could make against it. Volunteers, especially from Sweden, were soon coming forward to join the Finns. Early in February 1940, the British and French governments were approaching the Norwegian and Swedish governments to permit the passage of an expeditionary force of 100,000 to Finland; but the Norwegian and Swedish governments refused. Britain and France, it is interesting to remember, were within an ace of war with the Soviet Union in 1940.

But, in that February, the Soviet Government had reorganized its command on the Finnish front, had brought up considerable reinforcements especially of heavy artillery, and had launched a major offensive against the Mannerheim Line. A fortnight's bombardment and piecemeal advances – tactics reminiscent of Verdun in 1916 – gradually wore away the Finnish positions. By March 1, 1940, the Soviet forces were investing the port of Viipuri. The Finnish capital, Helsinki, and Hangö were bombed constantly. On March 12, in the midst of renewed Allied negotiations with Sweden for the passage of an expeditionary force, news arrived that Finnish representatives in Moscow had agreed to peace.

The Soviet-Finnish Treaty of Moscow was severer than the original Soviet demands of October 1939, but not so severe as might have been expected. Finland ceded the Karelian Isthmus, the port of Viipuri, several islands in the Gulf of Finland, some territory north and west of Lake Ladoga, a tract of land near Salla, a tract of land near Petsamo, and granted the Soviet Government a thirty-year lease on the port of Hangö. The Soviet Government reorganized its Karelian acquisition as a new Soviet republic.

The Nazi plan for the invasion of Norway and Denmark originated during the winter of 1939 with Admiral Erich Raeder and the Nazi philosopher, Alfred Rosenberg – it is said, against the strongest advice of the generals of the High Command. The invasion was intended at first to anticipate an Allied occupation of Norway, an occupation which might well have followed an Allied involvement in the Russo-Finnish War. It was supported also by Admiral Karl Doenitz, commander of submarines, who badly wanted a Norwegian base. Furthermore, the possession of Norway would secure the important supplies of Swedish iron ore which could be shipped from the Norwegian port of Narvik in wintertime. Secret contacts were made with Major Vidkun Quisling, leader of the Norwegian Nazi party, who went to Berlin to confer with Hitler in person. The projected invasion, of course, would violate Nazi assurances, often from the mouth of Hitler himself, to respect the neutrality of the Scandinavian countries, and it would violate in particular the German-Danish Nonaggression Pact of May 1939. The invasion was launched on April 9, 1940, and was indeed the first of the lightning thrusts which were now to embroil the Western world in open war.

British naval units were already laying mines in Norwegian territorial waters, partly to force the German ore ships from Narvik into the open sea, where they might be intercepted, and partly in answer to reports of unusual German naval activity in the Skagerrak; but the British Government and its Intelligence had certainly not calculated on an operation of the suddenness and magnitude that actually developed. By early morning of April 9, 1940, German warships were in action from Narvik to Copenhagen, and German transports were discharging their cargoes of men and machines. The Danes could offer no serious resistance. In Norway, some 100,000 Norwegians were under arms, and here fighting was resolute, if confused, but all the main objectives appeared to have been taken by the enemy, as if by schedule, in the first days of the campaign. British and Norwegian destroyers and submarines struck back at the German forces in the Skagerrak. But the real decision was in the air. German fighter planes, from bases in Denmark, gained a complete mastery over the narrow seas, and gave a convincing demonstration of the effectiveness of air power in amphibious operations.

British advance detachments were landed on the coast of Norway as early as April 14, and were shortly followed by a sizable expeditionary force. Troops and supplies once designated for Finland were used in Norway. But again the advantages went to the side with the nearest fighter bases. The British landing points in Norway and the seaward approaches thereto were mercilessly attacked by German planes. On May 1-2, the expeditionary force was withdrawn. A British force afterward recaptured the port of Narvik and played havoc with the iron-ore shipments, but early in June, in response to developments in France, this force too had to be withdrawn. Heavy German naval units attacked the British ships sent to cover the evacuation, and, in the confused action that followed, the British carrier *Glorious,* two cruisers, and nine destroyers were sunk and several other ships damaged. It was a serious British naval reverse, but the Germans themselves sustained such losses that, as Churchill writes, "at the end of June 1940, a momentous date, the effective German Fleet consisted of no more than one eight-inch cruiser, two light cruisers, and four destroyers." Meanwhile King Haakon and the Norwegian Government escaped to England. The Germans set up their own administration in Norway under their collaborator, Quisling.

The Norwegian campaign had galvanized the British people and government. Complacence, like appeasement, had had its day, and Britain wanted – and needed – a more realistic and pugnacious leadership. Chamberlain resigned, and on May 10, 1940, Winston Churchill became Prime Minister. Churchill's inner War Cabinet consisted of himself, Lord Halifax, Chamberlain, and two Labor men, Clement Attlee and Arthur Greenwood. Halifax in addition was Foreign Secretary. Anthony Eden was Secretary for War, Ernest Bevin Minister of Labor, Duff Cooper Minister of Information, and Lord Beaverbrook Minister of Aircraft production. Churchill's statement of policy in the House had little of the usual Chamberlainian tone of aggrievement and self-righteousness:

> I have nothing to offer but blood, toil, tears, and sweat. We have before us an ordeal of the most grievous kind. We have before us many, many long months of struggle and of suffering. You ask, what is our policy? I will say: it is to wage war, by sea, by land, and air, with all our might and with all the strength that God can give us: to wage war against a monstrous tyranny, never surpassed in the dark, lamentable catalogue of human crime.

Germany's invasion of Holland, Belgium, Luxembourg – and France – had already begun on the night of May 9-10. It was accompanied by the usual diplomatic protestations that she was foiling an Allied aggression and that her only aim was to extend her protection to innocent peoples malignly threatened.

The German forces in the West totaled 136 divisions in three army groups, under the generals of the Polish campaign, Bock and Rundstedt, and Wilhelm Ritter von Leeb. They were disposed according to a plan of attack generally accredited to General Erich von Manstein, lately Chief of Staff to Rundstedt. The heaviest concentration was under Rundstedt in the center, facing the Ardennes, and included a shock corps of 8 armored and motorized divisions under General Ewald von Kleist. Opposing the German forces were 94 French, 22 Belgian, 10 Dutch, and 9 British divisions – 135 in all. The numbers on paper were equivalent. But at the precise point where the Germans were strongest the Allies were weakest. The Allied "Plan D," drawn up the previous November by General Gamelin, required that, at the moment of the German invasion of the Low Countries, the French and British armies on the Belgian frontier should advance and take up positions between Antwerp and Namur. The Maginot Line supposedly would hold the frontier further south. In the Ardennes the Maginot Line dwindled into a series of strong points. But the Ardennes, hilly and forested, and protected by the natural "tank ditch" of the River Meuse, it was believed, would be a sufficient obstacle to a mechanized force debouching from the East, and here, in what was expected to be a quiet, uneventful sector, was stationed a weak French army, the Ninth, under General Corap.

Military critics have argued that Plan D was fundamentally misconceived and have pointed to other famous battles in history where an army was enticed out of a favorable defensive position to meet with defeat in the open field. The plan was handicapped politically; in the interests of Belgian and Dutch neutrality, there had been little in the way of preparatory staff talks between the French and Belgians, and none at all between the Belgians and Dutch. (See p. 395.) With all its imperfections the plan was no match for the new warfare of dive bomber, *Panzer,* and parachutist, the terror bombing of towns, the deliberately induced exodus of the civil population, the chaos of communications and services, and organized treachery in the rear. Nor do we find it easy to credit the many persistent reports, which afterward came out of Germany, that this war, requiring such vision and preparation and fought by all ranks with such passion, could have been directed by generals who had originally opposed it and who even conspired among themselves to prevent its taking place.

The Dutch defense collapsed in five days. German paratroops seized the Dutch airfields. Bridges fell intact to troops wearing false uniforms and trained in detail for their tasks. Flooding of the Dutch terrain offered little obstacle. The central area of Rotterdam, after concentrated air attack, was left in flames. On May 15, 1940, the Dutch Army capitulated. Queen Wilhelmina and the Dutch Government escaped to England.

By May 12, the Belgians had already lost their fortifications at Eben Emael and Liége. Kleist's tanks were crashing through the Ardennes and through Corap's army, and driving a fifty-mile breach in the French lines at Sedan. In a single, cataclysmic week, Champagne and Picardy were overrun. The Artois and Flanders, containing twenty French divisions and the whole of the British and Belgian forces, were cut off. On May 28, King Leopold of the Belgians surrendered in person, and the Belgian Army capitulated.

On May 18, Reynaud, the French Premier, reconstituted his cabinet and appointed Marshal Pétain Vice-Premier. The next day he removed Gamelin from the supreme command and appointed General Weygand, former Chief of Staff to Foch in 1918. The resurrection of two heroes of the First World War, Pétain and Weygand, one now aged eighty-five and the other seventy-two, was a measure of the crisis, but public opinion in France was momentarily heartened. Weygand's obvious plan on paper was to cut the ribbonlike salient which the German tanks were rolling out across northern France. But the general stupefaction and confusion on the flanks of the salient were complete. German mechanized forces were already fanning out along the Channel coast. One French corps made a stand around Lille; another made a stand in the loop of Dutch territory south of the Scheldt; a British brigade held out for three days at Calais, and behind this screen the greater part of the British Expeditionary Force and remnants of French divisions retired on Dunkirk, the only port still free of the enemy.

The Germans conspicuously failed to press their overwhelming advantage at Dunkirk. But Rundstedt – and Hitler – preferred to regroup their

Withdrawal from Dunkirk, June 1940

RADIO-TIMES HULTON

Panzers for the further operations against France, and by all military standards their decision was "correct." German naval losses at Narvik sufficiently account for the absence of any attempt at interference on the part of the German Navy. Meanwhile, from the ports and piers of the southeast coast of England, the British Admiralty was assembling a motley, impromptu fleet of over 850 vessels for the evacuation of the stranded Allied forces. Destroyers backed into the Dunkirk beaches and packed their decks with hundreds of men a trip. Seaside paddle steamers, river tugs, lifeboats, motor launches, fishing craft shuttled back and forth across the Channel. The Royal Air Force (RAF), covering the evacuation, won its first victory over the *Luftwaffe*. Some 366,000 British, French, and Belgians were brought off to safety – but with the total loss of their equipment.

Weygand hurriedly organized new defenses along the southern banks of the Somme and Aisne. On June 5, 1940, the Germans resumed their attack. In two days' fighting the "Weygand Line" was pierced at either extremity. Weygand announced that the "Battle of France" had begun. Reynaud, as an indication of his spirit, took into his cabinet as Under-Secretary for Defense, General Charles de Gaulle, the soldier and military critic who had long since vainly advocated the proper mechanization of the French Army. (See p. 261.) But the French Government was already retiring to Tours and thence to Bordeaux. Several ministers and deputies planned to form a new center of resistance in North Africa. Paris was declared an "open city" and on June 14 surrendered. Reynaud appealed to President Roosevelt "to throw into the balance, this very day, the weight of American power."

But Reynaud, from the moment of his arrival at Bordeaux, was being dunned by the defeatists of his immediate circle to abandon the fight. Pétain and Weygand both regarded the situation as hopeless. The city of

Bordeaux, panic-stricken and overcrowded, was being intermittently bombed by German aircraft. On June 16, his nerve broken, Reynaud resigned. Pétain formed a new government with Chautemps as Vice-Premier, Weygand as Minister of Defense, and Admiral Jean Darlan as Minister of Marine. Pierre Laval, though not a member of this government, had been active in its formation and had already made himself the center of a group of politicians at Bordeaux anxious for understanding and collaboration with Germany.

Pétain at once sued the enemy for an armistice and "a soldier's peace." On June 22, 1940, at Compiègne, in the same railroad coach in which, in 1918, Foch had received the German Armistice Commission, the French delegates accepted Nazi Germany's terms.

"It is humiliating to sit with one's hands folded," Mussolini was once reported to say, "while others make history." On June 10, 1940, the day the Germans crossed the Seine, Italy declared war on France. Even then the Italian Army delayed its offensive against the French positions on the Alpine frontier till June 21, when the French delegates were already on their way to Compiègne. Mussolini's action was as derisory as any in his career. Whether or not it made history, it at least aroused the neutral world to a fine contempt and indignation, which President Roosevelt appropriately touched off in an address at the University of Virginia:

> On this tenth day of June 1940, the hand that held the dagger has struck it into the back of its neighbor. On this tenth day of June 1940, from this university, founded by the great American teacher of democracy, we send forward our prayers and our hopes to those beyond the seas who are maintaining with magnificent valor their battle for freedom.

The Franco-German armistice confirmed Germany in the occupation of two-thirds of France, including the chief industrial areas – except Lyons – and the whole of the Channel and French Atlantic coasts. The French armed forces were to be demobilized; all fortifications and military stores were to be surrendered; French merchant shipping was to be called home; French prisoners of war were to remain in German hands until the conclusion of peace. The French Government was to surrender on demand – presumably to the Gestapo – German political refugees in France. The French Navy was to be collected, demobilized, and laid up in ports, afterward to be designated, under German and Italian control. The German Government "solemnly declared that it does not intend to use the French Fleet for its purpose in war." The Franco-Italian armistice required the surrender of certain military stores, the demilitarization of certain zones, and the surrender of the Red Sea port of Jibuti. The Italians were also permitted to continue to occupy the strip of frontier territory which they had taken in their Alpine offensive. Corsica remained under the French government.

The shock – and relief – of Dunkirk had prepared the British people mentally for the collapse of France, and the final armistice was only the least terrible of the succession of terrors that the Nazi blitzkrieg had brought in its train. Up to six days before the armistice, Churchill had

THE WESTERN FRONT, 1940-45

still refused to release the French Government from its obligations, especially in respect of the recent declaration of March 28. He made France an offer of complete union with Britain – a common citizenship, administration, possessions, and resources. It was a fine, if despairing gesture; but he was compelled by events to acquiesce at last in a separate French capitulation. But his insistence, and French reassurances, that the French

Navy would be handed over to Britain, or at least interned in ports where it would be useless to the enemy were clearly not fulfilled in the armistice terms. Units of the French Navy which happened to be at British bases — for instance in Portsmouth, Plymouth, or Alexandria — were at once seized. On July 3, the French fleet at Oran in Algeria — after its commander had been given every offer consistent with military honor and with the ultimate interest of the Allied cause — was bombarded by a British squadron under Admiral Sir James F. Somerville, and of its four battleships, two were destroyed and two disabled. A few days later a fifth French battleship was attacked and badly damaged at Dakar.

It was a hard and sad necessity that turned one ally against another. But the British Government could not risk leaving the disposal of so formidable a weapon as the French Navy to the caprice of a group of defeated and potentially hostile men. The Pétain government in Unoccupied France afterward broke off relations with Britain. The British blockade was applied to the whole of the French coast; the RAF bombed French ports and military targets in Occupied France. From a comradeship of arms Britain and France seemed to be drifting inexorably toward antagonism and open war.

Germany's acquisitions in the seventy days of her blitzkrieg in the West were impressive indeed. The coasts of Europe from the Arctic to the Bay of Biscay were in her hands. From a chain of sea and air bases she invested the British Isles. She possessed the farms and pastures of Denmark and Holland, the fisheries and forests of Norway, the mines and industries of Belgium, and at least three-fourths of the wealth of France. She held at her absolute disposal 2,000,000 prisoners of war. The French Government under Pétain, established at Vichy in unoccupied territory, was her virtual client. Italy if anything was even more firmly tied to her than France.

The Fall of France upset the entire international balance of forces. In the Mediterranean, up to April 1940, the Anglo-French combination had dominated the scene; from July 1940, Britain was everywhere in vulnerable isolation. Greece and Turkey, once favored and eager partners in Allied alliances and guarantees, looked as if they would be abandoned to their own devices. The French commanders and governors of Syria — and then of Dakar and Madagascar — threw in their lot with Vichy. A pro-Vichy Governor General was appointed in Indochina.

For a moment it seemed that Spain would enter the conflict, that Gibraltar would be besieged, and that the German occupation would be extended to Morocco and even to the Canary Islands and the Azores. On June 12, 1940, two days after Mussolini's intervention, the Spanish dictator, Franco, suddenly renounced his former declared neutrality for the equivocal and ominous status of "nonbelligerency." Spanish forces occupied the international territory of Tangier. On October 23, Hitler and Franco met at Hendaye to bargain for an alliance. But by then the Battle of Britain had been fought, and the further threat of a British naval blockade and of the stoppage of essential imports from the Americas, no doubt decided Franco against "a change in foreign policy." Sir Samuel

Hoare was appointed British ambassador in Madrid, there to conduct a mission as difficult and delicate as any in the whole field of his country's harassed diplomacy.

In mid-June, while the Battle of France was yet at its height, the Soviet Union unobtrusively completed its occupation of the Baltic states of Lithuania, Latvia, and Estonia, and by the end of the month had also incorporated the Rumanian province of Bessarabia into the new Soviet republic of Moldavia. King Carol's government in Rumania purged itself of pro-Ally elements, denounced the Anglo-French guarantee of 1939, and declared for a "fundamental integration with the Axis system." But Carol's sycophancy did not protect him from further losses of his Rumanian provinces to Bulgaria and Hungary. On August 19, 1940, the southern Dobruja was transferred to Bulgaria; and on August 30, at a conference in Vienna, at the dictation of Ribbentrop and Ciano, about half of Transylvania was transferred to Hungary. The discredited Carol thereupon abdicated in favor of his son Michael, leaving the pro-Nazi General Ion Antonescu as the real ruler of the country. The nontotalitarian world may have been entertained by the spectacle of totalitarians carving up one of their fellow's property; but the further significance of the Vienna Award, as it was called, was the indirect check that it offered to Soviet expansion in the Balkans. Under the terms of the Moscow Pact, the two signatories had agreed "to consult on questions of common interest"; but no such consultation had taken place on this occasion. Germany and the Soviet Union were clearly entering on a mounting rivalry in that old tiltyard of power politics, the Balkans.

The Battle of Britain

Yet, for Britain, the German blitzkrieg in the West had not been all disaster. By far the greater part of the British Expeditionary Force had been evacuated from Dunkirk – with the total loss of its equipment, but at least it had been evacuated. The Channel Islands had been abandoned to the enemy. But there had been another side to the defeat. The sovereigns and governments of Norway and Holland were in England, and with them had come the bulk of their navies and merchant fleets. King Leopold of the Belgians was a prisoner of war, but the Belgian Government eventually reached London. A Free French Committee was set up in London under General de Gaulle, controlling important military and naval resources and territories in French Equatorial Africa and in the Pacific. A Czechoslovak Government in exile and the Polish Government in exile were formed and granted recognition. Danish territories, the Faeroe Islands and Iceland, were in British occupation; the United States and Canada were both showing interest in the security of Greenland. The Netherlands East Indies with their wealth in oil and minerals were pooled with the Allied military exchequer. The Governor of the Belgian Congo supported the Belgian Government in London. The Americas were awakened to an increasingly active sympathy for the cause against Nazism. President Roosevelt and Churchill were in regular correspondence. During

July, a consignment of rifles, machine guns, and artillery, not new but nevertheless invaluable, arrived in Britain from the United States.

The defeat wrought a new fellowship in the British Commonwealth. The Dominions and colonies were responding to the call upon their men and resources. In South Africa the decision had already been taken to send an expedition to East Africa, but the Nazi invasion of Holland converted the still wavering attitude of many Afrikaners. In Canada the Empire Air Training Scheme was started for air-force and radar personnel from all parts of the Commonwealth. The government in Britain was strong. Labor was represented in the British Cabinet by men of superparty caliber. Churchill was established in his leadership, and had begun to give his magnificent martial oratory to the world. The troops available in Britain were being reorganized under General Sir John Dill, newly appointed Chief of the Imperial General Staff, and General Sir Alan Brooke, newly appointed Commander in Chief Home Forces, lately one of the corps commanders of the British Expeditionary Force in France. Concrete strong points and earthworks were hurriedly constructed in the southeastern coastal areas. The Local Defense Volunteers – later renamed the Home Guard – absorbed a good deal of the nation's otherwise undirected man power and fighting spirit – but its units at this time often had to arm themselves with old rifles and shotguns. Yet the British people everywhere almost felt an exhilaration in knowing the worst, and knowing also that the worst was not without its compensations.

Hitler issued his operational directive "Sea Lion" for the invasion of Britain on July 16, 1940; the invasion date was originally fixed for mid-August. The last British ship had left the Dunkirk beaches on June 4, and the French armistice had been signed on June 22. In view of Hitler's usual rapidity of action, the delay needs explaining. It has been suggested that, after the Fall of France, Hitler had expected a British capitulation without his having to exert further military pressure; or that, in his curious tenderness for things British, he had hoped for a "deal" by which he would have "guaranteed" the British Empire in return for a recognition of his own military supremacy. On July 19, in a speech in the *Reichstag,* he made his "last appeal to common sense": "I see no reason why this war need go on . . ." But the delay was needed for preparation of an amphibious operation for which the German High Command had no proper equipment and – excepting Norway – no experience, and much precious time was consumed in acrimonious discussions of the German service chiefs over the technical problems of the Channel crossing. The mass of towed barges that it was proposed to use would be extraordinarily vulnerable to sea and air attack in a stretch of water notoriously stormy. Records show that Admiral Raeder could give no assurance of success. Recent German losses at Narvik had materially reduced the available escort forces. But Hitler's advisers were all agreed on one point. "Sea Lion" would be an imaginary dream without command of the air. An essential preliminary would be an assault by Göring's *Luftwaffe,* the assault which indeed developed into what we now know as the Battle of Britain.

But to Britain the delay was priceless. By a heroic industrial and organizational effort the Dunkirk army was completely refitted. Churchill strengthened his War Cabinet by including the two ministers, who were most responsible for that effort, Lord Beaverbrook and Ernest Bevin. Hitler eventually postponed the invasion date to September 15, by which time there were sixteen British divisions ready for action on the south coast of England; of these, three were armored. In the same month, under the "Destroyers for Bases Deal," the United States handed over to Britain fifty destroyers in exchange for the gift or lease of a string of naval bases from Newfoundland to British Guiana. The destroyers were overage – they had been built in 1918-20 – but they were a valuable reinforcement for the British Navy's antisubmarine forces in the Atlantic. (See p. 526.)

In August 1940, the *Luftwaffe*'s strength amounted to some 3,500 first-line planes, of which "Sea Lion's" portion was to be 2,670. The RAF had 1,475 first-line planes at home and some 500 overseas. But, to compensate for the disparity of numbers, the British had the use of radar, a new invention almost exclusively developed by British physicists and engineers, which enabled enemy aircraft to be "sighted" fifty, and often a hundred, miles before they approached their targets. German enticement and reconnaissance sorties were being intensified in the latter half of July. The main assault was ordered by Göring at a briefing conference of his *Luftwaffe* chiefs at his country house, Karin Hall, on August 6, and was launched two days later.

Göring's first targets were the southeast harbors and Channel shipping. On August 12, he extended his range to the RAF fighter airfields and factories, and particularly the radar stations. The heaviest action – and the heaviest German casualties of the entire battle – occurred on August 15, when the Germans lost 76 aircraft to the British 34. Fighting was then somewhat curtailed by bad weather, but it was resumed on August 24 with German attacks mainly on the airfields and on the RAF Fighter Sector Stations around London. This was the crucial period of the battle. But, on September 7, Göring turned on London. The shift of target was decisive. It was uncomfortable for London, but it was also Göring's admission that he had failed to destroy the RAF fighter strength. The Battle of Britain was then as good as won. London was bombed daily for a month. Heavy German losses continued, despite increased fighter protection. Sometimes German bombers were accompanied by as many as five fighters apiece. On September 15, the culminating date of this phase of the battle, the Germans lost 56 planes.

While RAF Fighter Command had thus been defending Britain, RAF Bomber Command had opened its counterattack on the invasion bases and on Germany herself, though its effort was slight enough by later standards. It raided the concentrations of the German invasion barges, railroads and canals, oil refineries and synthetic-oil plants. It raided the Ruhr and Rhineland, it raided as far as the Skoda works at Pilsen and the "industrial triangle" in northern Italy. On August 25, 1940, for the first time, it raided Berlin.

The Battle of Britain was a truly Elizabethan victory. A few hundred young British and Dominion fighter pilots, many of them not yet twenty years of age – and a few score Poles, Czechs, French, and Belgians – engaged and repulsed Germany's armada of bombers. "Never in the field of human conflict," said Churchill at the height of the battle, "was so much owed by so many to so few." In the words of the Air Ministry's account:

> The battle was fought three, four, five and sometimes more than six miles above the surface of the earth by some hundreds of aircraft flying at speeds often in excess of three hundred miles an hour . . . [It] was not shrouded in the majestic and terrible smoke of a land bombardment with its roar of guns, its flash of shells, its fountains of erupting earth. There was no sound of fury — only a pattern of white vapour trails, leisurely changing form and shape, traced by a number of tiny specks, scintillating like diamonds in the splendid sunlight.

On September 17, Hitler gave orders that "Sea Lion" must be postponed indefinitely. German attacks during October were made mainly at night, and by the end of October German interest had been diverted to Midland manufacturing towns, such as Coventry, which was "terror-raided" on the night of November 14 by 500 German bombers. The City of London had perhaps its worst raid on December 29.

One of the welcome surprises of the Battle of Britain was the small civilian loss of life. In London, for example, 20,000 were killed — but *it* took nearly 20,000 tons of bombs to do it. Industrial production, mainly concentrated in the Midlands and North, was not seriously affected, and the flow of overseas shipping, though temporarily diverted from London and the Channel, was maintained. The material damage to buildings in the bombed areas of course was enormous, especially in the East End boroughs and docks of London. It was difficult to believe, in the nightly furnace, that the number of casualties was not greater. But Air Raid Precautions (ARP), reorganized as the Civil Defense Service, had withstood the test of experience; "fire-watching" for incendiary bombs was now a compulsory routine imposed on all civilians; repair and demolition squads went about their work with the greatest efficiency; the mass hospitalization that had been so carefully prepared was found to be much in excess of need; the medical authorities afterward reported favorably on the good health of the population. Essential services — water, electricity, gas, sewerage, railroads, telephones — if interrupted, were interrupted for only short periods. Public morale, far from being broken, was infinitely fortified by the ordeal.

The Balkans, the Middle East, and East Africa

It has always been the part of Britain, a maritime power with interests and responsibilities all over the globe, whenever she has been engaged in a general war, to have to fight in many widely separated theaters. In particular she has tried to hold the great "strategic arc" represented by Gibraltar-Malta-Suez-Aden. But her position here, after the Fall of France in 1940, was precarious in the extreme. The use of the French naval bases was denied her; Syria had gone over to Vichy; Malta was constantly bombed and almost isolated. Italian planes raided as far afield as Alexandria and Suez. In the Red Sea, Italian forces took over the French port

St. Paul's in the London Blitz: the "incendiary classic" of December 29, 1940

UNITED PRESS INTERNATIONAL

Winston Churchill in May 1940, shortly after becoming Prime Minister

RADIO-TIMES HULTON

of Jibuti under the terms of the armistice with France. In August 1940 they invaded and occupied British Somaliland. They seized trading posts on the borders of Sudan and Kenya. In September 1940, the Italian army in Cyrenaica, under Marshal Graziani, crossed the Egyptian frontier on the first stage, as it then seemed, of an attempted conquest of Egypt.

Admiral Sir Andrew Cunningham, commanding the British Mediterranean Fleet, inferior in every respect, could only maintain himself by superb bluff. "However, because of the very fact of our weakness," he said, "our policy had obviously to be one of aggressiveness, and it paid handsome dividends." The Mediterranean was closed to British merchant shipping, but some military convoys, carefully coordinated with Cunningham's offensive sallies, got through to Malta and Alexandria. During all the critical months of 1940, when even her friends were expecting her to capitulate in her own homeland, Britain was depleting and dividing her overstrained resources and running the Mediterranean gauntlet to build up her Army of the Nile, as it was then called. In August 1940, Churchill had made the bold decision to send out to Egypt an armored division, complete with "Matildas," then one of the most formidable tank types in the world, badly though it was needed in England – and, on this occasion, the division sailed the long way round the Cape. To Egypt also came strong reinforcements from India, Australia, and New Zealand, and to Kenya from South Africa. By the winter of 1940, under General Sir Archibald Wavell, Commander in Chief Middle East, there was a tolerably well-equipped but widely dispersed British army of 80,000-90,000 men.

To Mussolini, the Italian Duce, as he surveyed the field at this time, the alternatives for diplomatic and military action must have looked numerous and enticing. He toyed for a while with the idea of creating a separate state of Croatia which he could carve out of Yugoslavia and take under Italian protection. He finally resolved on an attack on Greece, a country against which, ever since the Corfu incident of 1923, he had nourished a grievance. On October 28, 1940, without consulting his German ally and in spite of the warnings of his most responsible generals, who better knew the poor material and moral condition of the Italian forces, his army in Albania invaded the Greek Epirus.

But from this moment Mussolini's fortunes began to decline. In five months, despite his apparent relative strength, first in Greece, then in Cyrenaica, then in East Africa, his legions suffered one reverse after another. The Italian forces invading Greece were met by defenders with inferior equipment, but knowing their own terrain and employing their own tactics. The British implemented their treaty guarantee to Greece with naval and aerial aid – little enough, but at least quickly dispatched. A British force was landed in Crete. The Greeks were commanded by General Metaxas, one of the acknowledged strategists of his day. The Greeks themselves were shortly advancing into Albania. On November 11, Admiral Cunningham achieved his most audacious triumph. A squadron of British torpedo planes of obsolete pattern and, by any reasonable standard, of insufficient numbers for the operation, took off from the carrier *Illustrious* and raided the Italian naval base at Taranto, sank one battleship and seriously damaged two others, and by this single stroke put out of action half the capital strength of the Italian Navy. Then in the Western Desert, on December 9, with the new armored division as his spearhead, Wavell launched his "raid in force," and in two months' fighting of perfect co-operation between all arms, the Army of the Nile swept across Cyrenaica into Libya, defeated an enemy of greatly superior numbers, and took 113,000 prisoners – all at a cost to itself of 1,774 casualties, of whom 438 were killed. In February 1941, the British stood at Agheila on the border of Tripolitania.

The British campaign in East Africa was confined at first to minor raiding operations but developed into one of the most militarily and politically complex "side shows" of the war. The Emperor of Ethiopia, Haile Selassie, reappeared on the scene, and, before the end of 1940, guerrilla revolts with his collaboration and with British arms were being stirred up in Ethiopia and Eritrea. In February 1941, British and South Africans, moving up from Kenya, invaded Italian Somaliland. Difficult fighting in most difficult terrain followed, resembling on a smaller scale the Italian campaign of 1935. By early April, British Somaliland was reoccupied, and a combined British force entered Addis Ababa. Haile Selassie returned to his capital. Mussolini's East African empire was at an end.

The British Navy meanwhile was continuing its contribution to the general Italian rout. On February 9, 1941, in broad daylight, "Force H" under Admiral Somerville bombarded Genoa and destroyed power stations, railroad yards, and oil stores in the harbor. On the night of March 28, in a running engagement off Cape Matapan, two Italian fleets trying to intercept convoys bearing British aid to Greece suffered the loss of three cruisers and serious damage to one battleship. The British ships, using radar to direct their gunnery in the darkness, emerged from the action unscathed.

Preparations in the East

In the larger view, the Italo-Greek and Italo-British wars of 1940-41 were incidental to the greater war between Germany and the Soviet Union shortly to break out. The Moscow Pact of 1939 had served its two signatories well. Germany had secured herself against the complications of a second front while she overwhelmed the West; the Soviet Union had improved its frontiers in Intermediate Europe. The subsequent German-Soviet economic interchange had been mutually beneficial. But old fears and frictions had not been removed. The Kremlin, which had counted on Germany's long and exhausting preoccupation with the Western Powers, must have been profoundly alarmed at the ease and decisiveness of her victories over them. Both sides had been guilty of arbitrary acts inconsistent with the spirit of their pact. The Soviet Union had seized the Baltic territories and Bessarabia; Germany had contrived the Vienna Award – and each had done so without consultation with the other. In Berlin on September 27, 1940, Germany, Italy, and Japan entered into a Tripartite Pact by which they recognized one another's leadership in their respective spheres and undertook "to assist one another with all political, economic, and military means if one of the three contracting Powers is attacked by a Power not at present involved in the European War or in the Sino-Japanese War." Somewhat too obviously, a further clause hastened to deny that the pact was directed against the Soviet Union — the inference being that it was directed against the United States. And if this was not enough, the Battle of Britain at this time was not going well for Hitler, who, balked of his victory, might follow the Napoleonic precedent and turn eastward.

Indeed relations between Germany and the Soviet Union had by now become so strained that it was deemed advisable to try a sort of Bismarckian reinsurance. Accordingly Molotov was invited to Berlin in November 1940 to take part in the gaudy courtesies of a full-dress totalitarian conference, and for a couple of days he was guest at a program of speeches, dinners, and parades, all arranged by Hitler and Ribbentrop in his especial honor. But no positive decisions were reached. His hosts were preening themselves on their recent victories in France and could hardly avoid an attitude of patronage toward him. Hitler, in anticipation of Britain's surrender, which he made out he was then momentarily expecting, was congenially occupied in winding up "the gigantic world-wide estate in bankruptcy, the British Empire." He spoke expansively of "an Asiatic Area toward the South" as the Soviet's future sphere of influence; he invited the Soviet Union to enter into an agreement with the members of the Tripartite Pact. Molotov, less interested in the Führer's grand historic reconstructions, demanded quite precisely assurances for the independence of Bulgaria and Sweden, the establishment of a Soviet base on the Dardanelles, and the removal of German personnel from Finland. The conversations were interrupted by air raids and at one point had to be carried on in an underground shelter. Molotov could hardly have been entirely satisfied with his visit.

On the very day of Molotov's arrival in Berlin, Hitler had issued instructions to his army chiefs "for the continuation of preparations in the East." Hungary, Rumania, and Slovakia shortly joined the Tripartite Pact. Hitler's operational directive, "Barbarossa," "for crushing Russia in a quick campaign" to start not later than May 15, 1941, was ready on December 18, 1940. Nazi penetration and military preparations in the Balkans had reached a stage when they could no longer be disguised. In Rumania, in a three-day civil war, General Antonescu with Himmler's help purged the truculent opposition of the Iron Guard, once the favored agent of Nazi-provoked disturbances. Rumania, by then, was full of German soldiers; the Rumanian oil fields were taken under German management; the country was virtually a German base. Early in 1941, it was evident that Bulgaria was submitting to the same fate. Hitler and the Tsar Boris had already met in conference. On March 1, 1941, Bulgaria adhered to the Tripartite Pact.

Yugoslavia under the regency of Prince Paul had been drawing Axisward for some time. (See pp. 395-96.) In October 1940, a trade treaty with Germany seemed to signify her assimilation — in the economic sense if nothing else — into Hitler's rapidly developing Balkan system. But the trend was not popular in the country, and groups of Yugoslav patriots were already organizing a resistance. In February 1941, the Yugoslav Premier,

Cvetkovich, joined the lengthening procession of minor statesmen to Berchtesgaden and offered Hitler full cooperation short of an explicit military alliance. Count Ciano, the Italian Foreign Minister, meanwhile was plying his own independent oar and negotiating directly with the disaffected Croat leader Ante Pavelich. On March 25, 1941, the Yugoslav Government formally adhered to the Tripartite Pact.

But at this point Yugoslav patriots and army revolted. In a bloodless coup, General Simovich occupied Belgrade, installed the young King Peter on the throne, and himself assumed the premiership of an anti-Axis government. Prince Paul fled. Machek, the loyal Croat leader, consented to serve as Vice-Premier and thereby to demonstrate the solidarity of the Serb and Croat peoples. The mobilization of the Yugoslav Army, already begun, was rushed to completion. The revolt had been entirely spontaneous, but it was tantamount to a defiance of the Nazi Reich, and its reckless bravado could lead to only one result.

The Soviet Government threw off the last pretense of collaboration with Germany. It sent its warnings to the several Balkan governments and encouraged them to resist the widening Nazi encroachments, those, notably the governments of Yugoslavia and Turkey, which still had some freedom of action. On April 5, 1941, the Kremlin solemnly reaffirmed the ancient Russian comradeship with the South Slavs and concluded with the new government of Yugoslavia a pact of friendship. Commentators were quick to recall that the war in 1914 had been precipitated by Russia's decision to come to the aid of a Serbia threatened, then as now, by Teutonic aggression.

An interlude was provided at this time by the visit of Yosuke Matsuoka, then Japanese Foreign Minister, to Moscow, Berlin, Rome, and again Moscow. The Japanese had already agreed to the Tripartite Pact with some misgivings – they had never overcome their profound suspicion of their German ally ever since the Moscow Pact of 1939 – and they were now again sufficiently concerned over European developments to send a ranking Cabinet minister on a tour of investigation on the spot. Matsuoka accordingly arrived in Berlin at the end of March 1941. Hitler and Ribbentrop were even more condescending to their Oriental visitor than they had been to Molotov. The conversations were entirely unreal, and reading them today we cannot help asking the question, Who among these undoubtedly informed and disingenuous men thought he was deceiving whom? Hitler regarded a Japanese war with the United States as undesirable, but, should it occur, he said, Germany would promptly honor the Tripartite Pact and take her stand beside her Japanese ally. Matsuoka was confident that the Japanese Navy could destroy the American Navy "without trouble," and his only fear in this respect was that the American Navy would avoid giving battle. Hitler, for his part, would have preferred a Japanese attack on Singapore, and Ribbentrop added that the Führer, "who must be considered the greatest military expert of modern times," would advise Japan as to the best method for that attack. Ribbentrop hinted to Matsuoka that Germany could not much longer tolerate the growing unfriendliness of the Soviet Union and that she had at her disposal 240 "unemployed divisions," with which, if need be, she could totally crush the Soviet Army and the Soviet state. Matsuoka then went on to Rome where he was duly received by Mussolini and by the Pope.

Matsuoka, however, returned to Moscow, and there, on April 13, 1941, he signed a Soviet-Japanese Neutrality Pact. He acted seemingly on his own initiative without consulting his Government in Tokyo – although with his Emperor's authority. It was a moment of delicious poetic justice. Like the earlier Moscow Pact of 1939, this newer one was burst upon the world with the same sort of drama and surprise and, in its own area in the East, with the same sort of diplomatic effect. Two old and declared antagonists, in their own cynical self-interest, had suddenly composed their differences. Both stood to make a temporary gain from mutual peace; both wanted a free hand in their respective spheres; both wanted an assurance meanwhile of the other's neutrality; both seized the opportunity of making an unmistakable assertion of resistance to dictation from Berlin. The importance of the pact was underscored by unusual ceremonies in the Kremlin, and Stalin himself afterward paid his Japanese guest the unprecedented compliment of attending his departure in person at the Moscow railroad station.

Hitler's war in Russia now needed but one last preliminary. His "right shoulder" in the Balkans and Middle East must be freed for action. Mussolini's war in Greece must be finished, and British influence in the area eliminated. Early in 1941, German pilots and planes began to appear over the Mediterranean and to attack British convoys in the Sicilian Channel. In one famous engagement they damaged and almost sank the carrier *Illustrious*. A German elite force, the so-called Africa Corps, armed and trained for desert warfare, was built up in Libya under General Erwin Rommel, one of Kleist's intrepid subordinates in the Battle of France.

Britain had already sent aerial aid to Greece. A possible German invasion of Greece, however, would invoke the British guarantee of 1939 and entail a far heavier commitment. It was a hard choice. An expedition to Greece would mean depleting the forces already engaged in Wavell's highly successful offensive in the Western Desert. Political and military requirements were sharply at odds. On the one hand, it seemed imperative that in a world of crashing alliances one power at least should still show respect for its plighted word. On the other hand, to withdraw troops from a campaign that they were brilliantly winning to take part in a campaign that they were pretty certain to lose was hardly in the highest flight of military judgment. Nevertheless the offensive in Libya was called off, and, during March 1941, 53,000 men – British, Australians, New Zealanders, and a Polish contingent – under General Sir Henry Maitland Wilson were duly disembarked in Greece.

On April 6, 1941, the day after the Soviet-Yugoslav pact of friendship had been signed, a German army simultaneously invaded both Yugoslavia and Greece. The Yugoslav patriots under Simovich had concerted no joint defense with the Greek and British forces, and Hitler's legions found themselves as usual fighting against ill-prepared and ill-coordinated adversaries. The invasion was just another example of a Nazi blitzkrieg in all its virtuosity. Belgrade was bombed as Warsaw, Rotterdam, and London had been bombed. Yugoslavia was broken as a fighting entity in five days. The Greek defense was more stubborn, but its collapse was equally inevitable. The Greek Army capitulated on April 24. The Germans entered Athens and hoisted the swastika on the Acropolis. Of General Wilson's 53,000 men, 41,000 were evacuated by the British Navy, in the main to Crete.

From this moment disaster crowded in from everywhere. At the end of March 1941 Rommel's Africa Corps attacked the depleted British forces in Libya and in three weeks drove them back once more to the Egyptian frontier — although they left behind them a single key point at Tobruk. Then on May 2, an anti-British coup occurred in Iraq in evident collaboration with pro-Vichy Syria. On May 20, the German Airborne Corps made a mass descent on Crete and, in ten days' fighting, compelled the surviving British forces to withdraw with heavy losses to themselves and to their naval support. Early in June, a counteroffensive by Wavell to regain lost ground and relieve Tobruk was repulsed. The entire British position in the Middle East seemed to be crumbling. On June 18, the well-disposed but cautious Turks, reading the signs, entered into a treaty of friendship with Germany.

But Hitler was no longer interested in the Middle East. The area had been sufficiently neutralized for his immediate purposes. His "right shoulder" was free. The Balkans had been virtually converted into a German military base. The concentration of the German Army for the invasion of Russia was complete, and the invasion began at last on June 22, 1941.

The Battle of the Atlantic

In the Atlantic Ocean another battle was now being fought, less spectacular perhaps, but as decisive in its element. On its outcome depended the life of Britain and the possibility of an eventual assault on Germany from the West. American aid under cash-and-carry and Lend-Lease was all part of it. (See pp. 533-35.) In terms of grand strategy the British Isles were becoming the outpost, and the North American continent the base, of a great global effort against Nazi-dominated Europe. Between outpost and base lay the all-pervasive war at sea, the Battle of the Atlantic.

The battle had begun within hours of Britain's declaration of war on September 3, 1939, with the sinking of the *Athenia*. It ended only with the German surrender on May 7, 1945. Tactically, the battle was a protracted competition of scientific ingenuities. Detecting devices, "asdic," radar, and "degaussing," the use of aircraft for spotting and depth-charging, bombing attacks on submarine pens and assembly plants, and on factories in Germany manufacturing submarine parts, the whole parade of convoy and escort — all this was pitted against an offensive resourcefulness and invention that never flagged or tired.

The success of the convoy system in 1917-18 gave good reason for hoping at first that the submarine in the Second World War would not be the all-important weapon that it had been in the First, and that Germany's main effort at sea would be made by her surface ships. The fact that the German pocket battleships had been specifically designed as commerce raiders gave additional force to the prediction. We have already described the episode of the *Graf Spee*. For a time converted merchant ships were also used as raiders. The climax of this kind of fighting came in May 1941 with the hunting down of the *Bismarck,* 45,000 tons, the most powerful battleship afloat, "loose" in the North Atlantic on her maiden voyage at a moment when eleven British convoys were at sea. In a five-day chase she sank the British battle cruiser *Hood,* before she was herself brought to bay, disabled, and sunk at last, 400 miles off the coast of France, by a fleet gathered from both sides of the ocean and including four battleships, five cruisers, two carriers – and two more battleships on the way. The cruiser *Prinz Eugen,* which had accompanied the *Bismarck* in the earlier part of her voyage, escaped undamaged.

But, as it turned out, it was the submarine which was again the more deadly arm. The German U-boats of 1939-45 had a far greater range, speed, and destructive power than those of twenty-five years before, and they operated later not singly but in "wolf packs," with an occasional supply ship near by for refueling and minor repairs at sea. In 1914-18, Britain blockaded Germany across a narrow North Sea and Channel frontage, and, in addition to her own naval bases, including those in Ireland, she had the use of the French bases in the Mediterranean. In 1940, after the Fall of France, she faced a Germany which herself occupied bases from Norway to Spain and round to the Aegean, and she fought, moreover, without the bases in neutral Ireland and the French Mediterranean. In partial compensation, she had occupied Iceland and the Faeroe Islands, and she set about the naval development of Londonderry in Northern Ireland. At the same time, escort craft and patrol ships were in woefully short supply. Trawlers and other auxiliary ships had taken over to some extent, but the extra cruisers, destroyers, and corvettes had to be built, and built in shipyards that were already overworked and often bombed. Merchantmen could be armed both against submarine and aerial attack and, in three months of war, the Admiralty was able to announce that a thousand ships had been fitted with guns of some kind. Early in September 1940 came the grateful news of the transfer of the fifty American destroyers. (See pp. 517 and 534.)

The center of gravity of the Battle of the Atlantic moved constantly. No sooner had countermeasures been developed in one locality than the enemy withdrew and probed for another "soft spot" elsewhere. Official maps, since published, of "phases" of the battle show graphically the shifting of the main area of the sinkings, now toward Britain and France, then north toward Iceland, then south toward Dakar, and so forth. After Pearl Harbor, when the United States transferred almost its entire Atlantic Fleet to the Pacific, the area shifted to the Caribbean and North American coast. At the turning point, in the early summer of 1943, the maps become suddenly clear of sinkings and remain relatively clear to the final triumph in 1945. The total Allied and neutral losses (including American) of merchant (and fishing) ships by enemy action of all kinds in the six years of the Second World War are shown in the accompanying table.

TOTAL LOSSES OF MERCHANT SHIPS BY ENEMY ACTION, 1939-45 [1]

	British	Others	Total	Total Monthly Average
Phase I	*Sept. 3, 1939–Apr. 9, 1940*			
	339,000	349,000	688,000	95,500
Phase II	*Apr. 10, 1940–Mar. 17, 1941*			
	1,677,000	637,000	2,314,000	206,000
Phase III	*Mar. 18, 1941–Dec. 6, 1941*			
	1,134,000	430,000	1,564,000	178,000
Phase IV	*Dec. 7, 1941–July 31, 1942*			
	1,144,000	2,106,000	3,250,000	417,500
Phase V	*Aug. 1, 1942–May 21, 1943*			
	1,974,000	1,786,000	3,760,000	389,000
Phase VI	*May 22, 1943–Sept. 18, 1943*			
	46,000	161,000	207,000	54,000
Phase VII	*Sept. 19, 1943–May 15, 1944*			
	120,000	195,000	315,000	40,000
Phase VIII	*May 16, 1944–May 8, 1945*			
	208,000	268,000	476,000	41,000
	6,642,000	5,932,000	12,574,000	185,000

Of this total of 12,574,000 tons, 70 per cent was lost by U-boat and 30 per cent by mines, surface ships, and aircraft. Three quarters in all were lost in the Atlantic Ocean.

The dominating figure of the period we have been discussing in this chapter was Churchill.

Winston Leonard Spencer Churchill was born in 1874, the son of Lord Randolph Churchill, in the line of the Dukes of Marlborough, and of Jennie Jerome, daughter of a former proprietor and editor of the New York *Times.* He was educated at Harrow – without much distinction – for the Royal Military College at Sandhurst and was commissioned in a cavalry regiment. Before he was twenty-six years old he had already packed enough adventure and experience into his life to have fulfilled any lesser man. Wherever there was a war, he had to be in it. He saw action in Cuba, on the Northwest Indian frontier, and in the Sudan. He was a war correspondent in South Africa, was captured, and escaped. He returned home to be elected to Parliament in 1900 as a Conservative, but, as a convinced free trader, he joined the Liberals in 1905. Under Asquith he held office as President of the Board of Trade and Home Secretary. The year 1914 found him First Lord of the Admiralty and the colleague of Admiral Lord Fisher in the building up of the modern British Navy.

In the First World War his reputation was almost ruined by Gallipoli in 1915, an episode which – whether or not he was really responsible – took him all of the next twenty years to live down. During the interwar period he was in and out of Parliament and in and out of office – once more as a Conservative. In office, he had the misfortune again and again to back the unsuccessful policy — in the Irish and Palestine questions, in the restoration of the gold standard, in the "Constitutional Crisis" over the abdication of Edward VIII, and above all in the Indian question. Out of office, he devoted his leisure to literary works such as *The World Crisis* and *Marlborough* — and to painting and building. Then, for good measure, in the later 1930's, he took it upon himself, almost singlehanded, to warn the country on its disastrous weakness in armaments. Throughout all these varied issues he never courted popularity by means of compromise, he never used the soft answer to turn away wrath. Unlike so many of his contemporaries, there was no trace of the demagogue in him. Yet he was an odd mixture of tough- and tender-mindedness, of ruthlessness and sentimentality. He was a lover of action and even more a lover of words. In 1940, for all his faults — perhaps because of them — the people of Britain gave him their entire confidence, and he repaid them with six years of the greatest leadership in their history.

No doubt Churchill's policies in detail during the Second World War were sometimes ill judged. But he showed his qualities as much in his choice of advisers with whom he surrounded himself — Brooke, Ismay, Cockcroft, and many others — as in the generosity with which he heard and accepted their views. His real leadership was of another level. In 1940 he was a man inspired, the mouthpiece of a world cause. This one moment of incomparable achievement no one can ever take away.

29. THE MIDDLE PHASES—1941-43

The German Invasion of Russia

Preparations on both sides for the coming clash were under way in the autumn of 1940. The Russians constructed a belt of strong points, the so-called Stalin Line, along their western frontiers and through their recent territorial acquisitions in the Baltic, Poland, and Rumania. Hitler's directive, "Barbarossa," was ready, as we have said, in December. But the original invasion date, May 15, 1941, was postponed, in part because of bad weather and in part in order that the Greek and Yugoslav complications might be settled. (See pp. 524-25.) It is tempting to believe therefore that the British intervention in Greece delayed the start of the campaign in Russia by some four to five weeks, a margin of time which, in the event, proved to be of decisive importance. The huge German concentrations along the Soviet frontiers could hardly be kept secret, and by April, Moscow, London, and Washington were aware that a new phase of the war was about to begin. Meanwhile all alternative German plans were in abeyance. Even air raids over England in the early spring of 1941 were reduced. Sir Stafford Cripps, then British ambassador in Moscow, predicted June 22 as the invasion date.

In April 1941, Alfred Rosenberg, the philosopher of Nazism and "expert" on Russian affairs, and lately one of the instigators of the German attack on Norway, was secretly appointed by Hitler as Reich Commissioner for the Eastern Occupied Territories with a view to his assuming responsibility for the civil administration of the German Army's conquests. The final spur to action was President Roosevelt's proclamation on May 27, 1941, of an "Unlimited National Emergency" in the United States. (See p. 536.) The rising temper of the American people left Hitler with no alternative but to rush his New Order to completion. The new Lend-Lease Act, just then passed by Congress, would soon be yielding its products, and in another year the trans-Atlantic "arsenal of the democracies" might well become uncomfortably strong, unless he could counterbalance it with Russian acquisitions on a Continental scale. On May 6, it was announced from Moscow that Stalin had personally assumed the presidency of the Council of People's Commissars and had thus embodied in himself, actually and symbolically, the supreme executive power in the Soviet Union.

On May 10, 1941, the Nazi leader, Rudolf Hess, then commonly regarded as Hitler's deputy and successor designate, made a solo flight to Scotland and parachuted to earth near Glasgow. Many interpretations of this astonishing adventure were put out at the time; but according to his own account, Hess expected to contact influential persons in Britain who he imagined were in favor of a negotiated peace. With the air so thick with nonaggression pacts, the German attack on Russia might conceivably be prefaced with such a pact between Germany and Britain. But there were no such peace advocates in Britain, and the deluded aviator was interned as a prisoner of war.

On the early morning of June 22, 1941, Germany declared war on the Soviet Union, and the German invasion began along the entire Soviet frontier. The same evening Churchill broadcast on behalf of Britain:

> . . . No one has been a more consistent opponent of Communism than I have for the last twenty-five years. I will unsay no word that I have spoken about it. But all this fades away before the spectacle which is now unfolding. . . . Behind all this glare, behind all this storm, I see that small group of villainous men who plan, organize, and launch this cataract of horrors upon mankind . . . I have to declare the decision of His Majesty's Government, but can you doubt what our policy will be? We have but one aim and one single, irrevocable purpose. We are resolved to destroy Hitler and every vestige of the Nazi régime. From this nothing will turn us – nothing . . . Any man or state who fights on against Nazism will have our aid. Any man or state who marches with Hitler is our foe . . . That is our policy and that is our declaration. It follows therefore that we shall give whatever help we can to Russia and the Russian people. We shall appeal to our friends and allies in every part of the world to take the same course and pursue it, as we shall, faithfully and steadfastly to the end. . . .

Germany deployed against the Soviet Union 146 divisions, 19 armored divisions, and four-fifths of the *Luftwaffe*. This huge concentration was divided into three army groups under the three commanders who had conducted the invasion of France – a northern army group under Leeb, a central under Bock, and a southern under Rundstedt – all three commanders now being Field Marshals. The names of Kluge, Guderian, Reichenau, Stuelpnagel,[1] Manstein, and Kleist appear among the army commanders. On the extreme left, in Finland, a Finnish contingent under Marshal Mannerheim "resumed the Soviet-Finnish War"; Hungarian and Slovak contingents were incorporated in the southern army group; a Rumanian contingent under General Antonescu marched on the extreme right wing, clamoring to repossess the lost province of Bessarabia. The Red Army opposed with some 140 divisions and 45 tank brigades, divided into three army groups, a northern commanded by Marshal Voroshilov, a central by Marshal Timoshenko, and a southern by Marshal Budenny. In all 9,000,000 fighting men – Germans, Rumanians, Hungarians, Finns, and Russians – joined battle along a thousand-mile front. The so-called Battle of the Frontier lasted some three to four weeks. The Stalin Line was breached throughout its length.

The fighting was swift moving. Fronts lost themselves in vast areas whose limits were often unknown to the very commanders on the spot. Pincers became pockets, and pockets, pincers. Tank offensives were cut off from their supporting infantry; Russian guerrillas were left far behind in the rear. Roads and railroads, rather than towns, were the immediate objectives. Peasant and civilian populations were swallowed up in the flood of battle. The resources of the land were put to the torch by the retreating Russians before they passed into German hands. In five months followed the battles of Smolensk, Kiev, Odessa, Leningrad, Dnepropetrovsk, the Crimea, and Moscow. It is as easy to contemplate the clash of worlds in space as this stupendous warfare.

Hitler's strategy was not to be measured in conventional military terms. The East was not like the West; the East, as Hindenburg had once said, "had no heart against which a mortal blow could be struck." Hitler's strategy was not just to possess territory or to capture cities or to win battles or even, in the regular phraseology of German military liteature, "to break the war-will of the enemy." Hitler's strategy – if it can be called strategy – was to destroy Russia. In orders to his commanders before the invasion, he had thus clarified himself:

> The war against Russia will not be of a kind that can be conducted in knightly fashion. It will be a struggle of ideologies and racial differences and will have to be waged with unprecedented, unmerciful, and unrelenting harshness. All officers must rid themselves of old-fashioned and obsolete doctrines . . .

And the Soviet High Command retaliated in the same spirit. The Red Army accepted the initial superiority of the German armament and war-craft in the field, and thence the necessity for a general retirement, but it always exacted the maximum price in German life. It would give its territory and its cities, it would lose battles, but it would also permanently injure the aggressor nation's human resources. Russia so conducted her resistance that, even if she lost the war, the Teutonic race would never recover from its victory. German military theorists had formerly expatiated on the war of annihilation. Thanks to Adolf Hitler, they were now seeing their theories realized.

By the beginning of December 1941, the German armies and their allies had advanced 600 miles on their total front. In the north they closely invested Leningrad, and in the south they closely invested Sebastopol, but both cities remained in Soviet hands. In the center they were approaching Moscow; advance units were fighting in the suburbs and were in sight of the walls and towers of the Kremlin. The whole of western European Russia and the Ukraine had been substantially devastated in the course of the campaign, and now lay under German occupation. The Soviet Government had retired to Kuibyshev, though Stalin himself had stayed in Moscow. On October 3, 1941, Hitler had openly proclaimed that "the enemy is already broken and will never rise again." A few days later Hitler's press chief, Otto Dietrich, had uttered the sweeping assurance, "For all military purposes the Soviet Union is finished." On December 8, 1941, German operations for the year were officially declared to be at an end. The Russian winter had supervened.

Almost immediately the Red Army opened its counteroffensive, clearly aiming to relieve the pressure on Moscow and Leningrad. Russian guerrillas operated in the rear, harrying German lines of communication, destroying isolated garrisons. For six months, newspapers and radio gave out almost routine communiqués of a slow, plodding, and presumably expensive Russian advance over lost ground. The final gains were small compared with the areas under German occupation, but the watching world was infinitely surprised and heartened to see that the Red Army, in its first campaigning year of the war, had won the main "battle of calculation" and that, for all its losses and for all the hysterical announcements of its extermination that regularly proceeded from Nazi press headquarters, it was still a force in being, capable of offensive operations. German troops, short of winter equipment and clothing, which Hitler in his overconfidence had never expected to be needed, suffered appalling hardships. In a general shake-up of the High Command, just before Christmas 1941, Hitler dismissed the commanders who had failed in the great offensive – Field Marshal von Brauchitsch, the Commander in Chief in Berlin, and the three army group commanders, Leeb, Bock, and Rundstedt. Hitler then himself assumed the supreme command of the German Army in the field. Halder remained Chief of Staff in Berlin – for the time being.

The extension of the war to Russia for the moment brought relief to all British theaters – except at sea. The Nazi assault on Crete in May 1941, although it had forced a costly British withdrawal, had been the virtual massacre of the German Airborne Corps, and it was in fact the first and last of the type of operation to be attempted by the German High Command. The expected German attack on Cyprus did not materialize. In June 1941, British forces suppressed the pro-Axis coup in Iraq and occupied the principal strategic points and airfields in the country. (See p. 525.) Syria was occupied by British and Free French forces after a short but unexpectedly stiff resistance. During August and September, British and Soviet forces entered Persia, occupied the oil wells, compelled Riza Shah to resign, installed his more friendly son in his stead, and began to construct a new "Corridor" from the Persian Gulf to the Caspian Sea for the transit of Lend-Lease aid to the Soviet Union.

In June 1941, British commands in the Middle East had been reshuffled. General Sir Claude Auchinleck, then Commander in Chief in India, succeeded Wavell, and Wavell took Auchinleck's place in India. A Middle East Supply Center (MESC), lately established at Cairo under the auspices of the British Ministry of Shipping, was allocating shipping space, organizing transport, and encouraging local industries of wartime usefulness. A new force, known as the Eighth Army, was formed in the Western Desert, and, in November 1941, this force launched a successful, but hard-fought offensive against the combined German-Italian army in Cyrenaica, the Second Libyan Campaign, as it has somtimes been called. The Eighth Army defeated Rommel's Africa Corps, relieved Tobruk – which since the previous April had remained under siege – and drove forward, point by point, to Agheila, the old high-water mark of the First Libyan Campaign, Wavell's "raid in force." By the end of 1941, in the Middle East, that strange ding-dong theater of the war, the British position, which had almost crumbled earlier in the year, had been substantially restored.

"The Arsenal of Democracy"

We return for a moment to 1939 and consider the first impacts of the war on the United States.

On the evening of September 3, 1939, President Roosevelt gave one of his radio "fireside chats" — "to the whole of America." He reviewed the position of the United States and its foreign relations and added that, despite distance and detachment, "when peace has been broken anywhere, the peace of all countries everywhere is in danger." The nation, he said, would remain a neutral nation, but he did not ask, as President Wilson had asked on a similar occasion twenty-five years before, that every American remain neutral in thought as well.

> . . . Even a neutral cannot be asked to close his mind and his conscience. I have said not once, but many times, that I have seen war and that I hate war. I say that again and again. I hope that the United States will keep out of this war. I believe that it will. And I give you assurance and reassurance that every effort of your Government will be directed toward that end. As long as it remains within my power to prevent, there will be no black-out of peace in the United States.

On September 5, President Roosevelt formally proclaimed the neutrality of the United States and invoked the Neutrality Act of 1937 with its embargo on the shipment of arms to belligerents. On the 8th, he proclaimed a "Limited National Emergency." Further, at the end of September, in the interests of "hemisphere solidarity" and in accordance with the consultative machinery devised at the Pan-American Conference at Lima in 1938, the foreign ministers of the twenty-one American republics met at Panama and thence issued a declaration establishing a "neutrality zone" of coastal waters extending 300 miles offshore as far north as Canada, in which hostile acts by non-American belligerents would not be tolerated.

But on September 21, 1939, at a special session of Congress, the President called for a repeal of the arms embargo. The engulfment of Poland by Germany and the Soviet Union had exerted its effect on Congressional and public opinion alike. However anxious the nation might be to avoid involvement in the war, the majority was almost equally intent on providing an indeterminate degree of assistance to the European democracies. In November 1939, Congress accordingly passed a revised Neutrality Act, prohibiting loans to belligerents, travel on belligerent vessels, and the arming of American merchantmen, and prohibiting American citizens, ships, and planes from entering a combat zone covering the North Sea and eastern Atlantic. In return for this considerable reaffirmation of neutrality, isolationists in Congress agreed to the extension of the cash-and-carry principle in the new act to arms and ammunition. (See p. 467.)

As was to be expected, public interest and anxiety subsided during the months of the "Phony War." Early in 1940, so quiet was the situation that Sumner Welles, Under Secretary of State, went on a tour of Europe, much like Colonel House's tour in 1915, with a general commission to study the prospects of peace. But in April Germany invaded Denmark and Norway. President Roosevelt denounced this latest "unlawful exercise of force." He exerted himself, in personal appeals to Mussolini, to keep Italy out of the war. On June 10, he responded to Italy's intervention with his address at the University of Virginia. (See p. 512.) He took into his cabinet two Republicans, both firm advocates of increased aid to Britain – Henry L. Stimson, whom he made Secretary of War, and Frank Knox, whom he made Secretary of the Navy. He reorganized his own Executive Office with a view to the needs of industrial mobilization which he foresaw, and, although this part of his policy did not in fact prove very successful, he gave appointments to a number of industrial leaders, such as Donald M. Nelson of Sears, Roebuck, whom he made Coordinator of National Defense Purchases. In July, a consignment of rifles, machine guns, and artillery – old stocks of the First World War, but as such immediately available – was shipped to Britain in time to meet the threatened German invasion. Congress hurried through additional appropriations of $5,000,000,000 to be devoted in large part to a 70 per cent increase in naval tonnage. In conversations at Ogdensburg, Roosevelt and the Canadian Prime Minister, Mackenzie King, agreed to set up a Permanent Joint Board on Defense. During September, after weeks of debate, Congress passed the Selective Service Act. In the same month, by means of the "Destroyers-for-Bases Deal," the United States handed over to Britain fifty overage destroyers in exchange for the gift or lease of a string of naval bases from Newfoundland to British Guiana. (See pp. 517 and 526.)

The American people were manifestly girding themselves, physically and psychologically, to meet the situation created by Hitler's blitzkrieg in the West, the Fall of France, and the possible fall of Britain, and they were startled into a realization of the tacit, unacknowledged protection which had hitherto been afforded them by the existence of British power in the Atlantic. Particularly alarming was the ease with which the French Navy might have fallen as spoils to the aggressor. In July 1940, the foreign ministers of the twenty-one American republics met again in Havana and issued the so-called Act of Havana providing for a collective trusteeship by the American republics over the French and Dutch possessions in the Western Hemisphere, left orphaned by events in Europe. The ministers also adopted a resolution that aggression by a non-American state against any one of the American republics should be construed as aggression against all. But move and countermove were now piling up against each other. In September 1940, Germany, Italy, and Japan concluded their Tripartite Pact, which, by implication, was directed against the United States – if not against the entire Pan-American system – and faced the United States with the menace of a two-front war in the Atlantic and Pacific. The presidential election was then being fought, and isolationism was already an obsolescent issue. The American people, if unconvinced by speeches and suspicions of "propaganda," could not but respond to the force of events. Wendell Willkie, the Republican candidate, in the early stages of the election campaign cautiously balanced himself astride the fence on the isolationist issue, but he finally came down on the same side as his Democratic opponent: "All aid to Britain short of war." On November 5, 1940, Roosevelt was elected President of the United States for a third term.

Strengthened by his victory, President Roosevelt created an Office of Production Management under the directorship of William S. Knudsen of General Motors with the declared objective of a two-ocean navy, 50,000 planes a year, and a modernized army of 1,000,000 men. Almost daily, it seemed, reports appeared in the press of new billions for war services, while the national debt soared to further record heights. Secret Anglo-American staff talks were begun in Washington. In his "fireside chat" of December 29, 1940, Roosevelt voiced another of his warnings against present and growing perils:

> . . . There can be no appeasement with ruthlessness. . . . Certain facts are self-evident. In a military sense, Great Britain and the British Empire are today the spearhead of resistance to world conquest. . . . We are planning our own defense with the utmost urgency; and in its vast scale we must integrate the war needs of Britain and the other free nations which are resisting aggression. . . . We must be the great arsenal of democracy. For us this is an emergency as serious as war itself. . . .

In his Annual Message to Congress on January 6, 1941, Roosevelt described the "Four Freedoms" – freedom of speech, freedom of worship, freedom from want, and freedom from fear – "no vision of a distant millennium," he added, but "a definite basis for a kind of world attainable in our own time and generation, . . . the very antithesis of the so-called new order of tyranny which the dictators seek to create with the crash of a bomb."

Early in January 1941, Congress began discussions of a bill for greatly extended aid, mainly to Britain. In public hearings it was pointed out that Britain had already exhausted her available assets of $4,500,000,000 in the United States and could no longer resort to cash-and-carry for the sustenance of her war effort. Lawyers of the Treasury Department unearthed a partial solution in a statute of 1892 authorizing the Secretary of War to lease army property "not required for public use" for a period of five years. This germinal idea was elaborated in consultations between the President and his advisers and was introduced into Congress as H.R. 1776, otherwise known as Lend-Lease. The bill was speeded through the Senate by 60 votes to 31, and through the House by 317 votes to 71, and it received the presidential signature on March 11, 1941. In the most sweeping terms it enjoined that "any defense article" could be sold, transferred, exchanged, leased, or lent to any country "whose defense the President deems vital to the defense of the United States," and that in order to avoid the old tangle of the Allied debts of the First World War repayment was to be made "in kind or property, or any other direct or indirect benefit which the President deems satisfactory." An initial appropriation of $7,000,000,000 gave some indication of the extent of the aid envisaged. In the beginning the chief responsibility for this huge scheme was put in the hands of that frail, many-sided, devoted man, Harry Hopkins, former WPA Administrator, Roosevelt's constant companion and adviser. Edward R. Stettinius of the United States Steel Corporation succeeded him as Administrator in August. Meanwhile the Canadian Government was moving in the same direction by making its first billion-dollar gift to Britain. Henceforth the entire economy of Britain and North America would be integrated in a common war effort.

But, again, as in the First World War, the massive aid now being forged in the United States and Canada was nothing unless it could be delivered. Hitler's submarine wolf packs were roaming the Atlantic and inflicting losses to shipping that currently amounted to 175,000 tons a month. In April 1941, by agreement with the Danish Minister in Washington, and in evident preparation for convoy operations, the United States established bases for air patrols in Greenland. "Incidents" at sea were already beginning with the sinking of the *Robin Moor*, an American merchantman, on May 20. A few days later, President Roosevelt proclaimed an "Unlimited National Emergency," by which he reasserted "the ancient American doctrine of the freedom of the seas" and required "the strengthening of our defense to the extreme limit of our national power and authority." In July the United States took over another Danish territory, Iceland, then under British occupation. During the next few months American destroyers were escorting convoys of ships of all nationalities to Iceland, and later to South Africa. The first American destroyer to exchange shots with a German U-boat was the *Greer* on September 4. In the same week President Roosevelt at last ordered all United States ships and planes on patrol "to shoot at sight."

On August 9-12, 1941, Roosevelt and Churchill, their Chiefs of Staff and political advisers, met "at sea" in Placentia Bay, Newfoundland, to consider their cooperation in the problems of war and peace. Discussions covered in particular the Battle of the Atlantic, aid to the Soviet Union, and the problem of Japan. At the conclusion of the meeting the Atlantic Charter was published, a "Joint Declaration by the President and the Prime Minister . . . to make known certain common principles in the national policies of their respective countries on which they base their hopes for a better future for the world." It was an expression of ideals and of "war aims" by two powers, one belligerent, one technically neutral; it referred explicitly to "the final destruction of the Nazi tyranny." (See Appendix, p. 839.)

Pearl Harbor

The Japanese Government had declared its "non-involvement" in the war on September 4, 1939, but it had participated actively enough in the incidental diplomacy of the war – notably in the Tripartite Pact of 1940 and in the Soviet-Japanese Neutrality Pact of 1941. The "China Incident" continued. A Japanese-sponsored "National Government of China" had been set up in Nanking under the pliant and ingenious puppet, Wang Ching-wei, but Chiang Kai-shek in his stronghold at Chungking still held out and showed no more disposition to accept a Japanese peace in China than he had been in 1937.

Meanwhile, with the United States, Japanese relations were sadly deteriorating. Protests to Tokyo from the State Department, notably in respect of injury by Japanese bombing to American persons and property in China, were acquiring an almost routine and familiar sequence. Simultaneously American economic pressure on Japan steadily increased. The sale of American aircraft to Japan had already been virtually stopped at the end of 1938 by the President's "moral embargo." In July 1939, the United States formally terminated the old American-Japanese commercial treaty of 1911. Thereafter followed, step by step, curtailments or total prohibitions of the export of strategic materials, including metals, chemicals, machine tools, aircraft parts, and aviation gasoline. The process culminated in July 1941, when the President ordered the freezing of Japanese assets in the United States and, in the following month, by means of a final list of prohibitions, all but brought American trade with Japan to a complete standstill.

The fall of the Netherlands and France in 1940 left their respective possessions in the East Indies and in Indochina wide open to invasion. But the territories were protected for the time being by expressions of extreme concern from the United States over changes in the *status quo* – and, in respect of Indochina, by the unwillingness of the Japanese themselves to embarrass the Vichy Government. The French authorities in Indochina, however, agreed to halt the transit of war materials to Chiang Kai-shek by way of Indochinese ports and railroads. In July 1940, as a gesture to Japan, the British Government closed the Burma Road for a period of three months. The bulk of the British forces were withdrawn from China, including those in the International Settlement in Shanghai. Siam was then being incited to press for the restoration of portions of Laos and Cambodia, annexed to French Indochina some forty years before; clashes occurred along the Siamese frontiers, and Siamese forces eventually occupied some miles of the disputed areas. On September 22, 1940, Admiral Jean Decoux, the French Governor General of Indochina, was at last compelled to permit the Japanese to build air bases and virtually to occupy the whole of Tongking. It was five days later that the Tripartite Pact was signed in Berlin.

The Japanese homeland was now preparing for war without pretense of concealment. Political parties were merged into a single, monolithic "Imperial Rule Assistance Association." Government control of industry, bitterly contested by the Zaibatsu, the industrial combine, was progressively imposed by means of a National Mobilization Law, which had been passed in anticipation in 1938. The Premier, Prince Konoe, still exerted himself, though with weakening conviction, to reach a settlement with the United States, and, during 1941, he sought to invite President Roosevelt himself to what at a later date would have been called a Summit Conference. By a coincidence, Konoe's proposals were made at the very moment of Roosevelt's and Churchill's secret Atlantic meeting. But Roosevelt required substantial preparatory agreement, and Konoe's proposals lapsed. In October 1941, Konoe resigned the Premiership. He was succeeded by the former War Minister, General Hideki Tojo, "Razor Brain," at the head of a cabinet of army and navy officers – a cabinet, it was said, which "smelled of gunpowder." During November, in Washington, Admiral Nomura, the Japanese ambassador, and Saburo Kurusu, a special envoy sent over to assist him, held an eleventh-hour series of conversations with Secretary of State Cordell Hull. Each side made demands which appeared impossible, even insulting, to the other, and which only illustrated the gaping chasm between them. But Hull at this time was perfectly well informed as to the real situation in Japan. Thanks to "Magic," the Cryptanalytic Division of the United States Army and Navy, which had succeeded in breaking the Japanese radio code, the State Department had all the intelligence it needed as to the day-to-day decisions of the Japanese Government.

At the Japanese Imperial Conference of November 5, 1941, it was decided that Japan would go to war with the United States and Britain if the Washington conversations produced no successful results by November 25 – a date later extended to the 29th (28th in Washington, EST). The Japanese press and Diet were ringing with bellicose articles and speeches. On November 7, Hull warned his Cabinet colleagues in Washington that a Japanese military attack might come "anywhere at any time." On November 24, a first "alert" was sent to Pearl Harbor from Washington. On November 26, in a strongly worded note, Hull presented his final demands to the Japanese Government – namely for a nonaggression pact between the Pacific Powers, the withdrawal of Japanese forces from China and from Indochina, a guarantee of the territorial integrity of China, and Japanese recognition of the Nationalist government of Chiang Kai-shek – but Hull could hardly have expected much from so peremptory a catalogue. The next day Secretary of War Stimson warned General Douglas MacArthur, commander of the United States armed forces in the Far East, stationed in the Philippines, that negotiations appeared to be terminated "to all practical purposes." The Japanese task force for Pearl Harbor was by then at sea.

The final Japanese Imperial Conference of December 1 was little more than a formality. The date for hostilities was fixed for the 8th (7th, EST), and appropriate instructions were dispatched to the army and navy commands and to diplomatic representatives abroad. Japanese warships and transports were reported in the Gulf of Siam. On December 6, President Roosevelt sent a personal appeal to Emperor Hirohito "to give thought in this definite emergency to ways of dispelling the dark clouds" – to which His Majesty graciously replied that peace in the Pacific, and in the world, had always been his "cherished desire." Almost simultaneously "Magic" was intercepting Tokyo's reply to Hull's counterdemands of November 26, a reply which amounted to a categorical and truculent rejection. As soon as its tenor and timing could be fully appreciated, General George C. Marshall, Chief of Staff, prepared a further hurried "alert" to Pearl Harbor. Static difficulties prevented the use of the Army radio, and the message was ultimately sent by commercial channels. "The Honolulu office . . . confided the telegram to a messenger boy who set off on his bicycle. He was pedaling on his way when the first bombs fell, and not unnaturally spent the next couple of hours in a roadside ditch." [2]

At 6:45 A.M. on December 7, 1941, the American destroyer *Ward,* on routine patrol off Pearl Harbor, detected and sank a Japanese midget submarine. Two privates spotted approaching planes at a distance of 137 miles from their radar station, but the lieutenant to whom they reported judged the planes to be a flight of B-17's expected from the mainland and took no action. Thirty minutes later the first wave of 189 Japanese bombers appeared out of the morning haze, sweeping in low from the sea. Their marksmanship on a relatively concentrated target was devastatingly accurate. The battleship *Arizona,* struck in the forward magazine by an armor-piercing

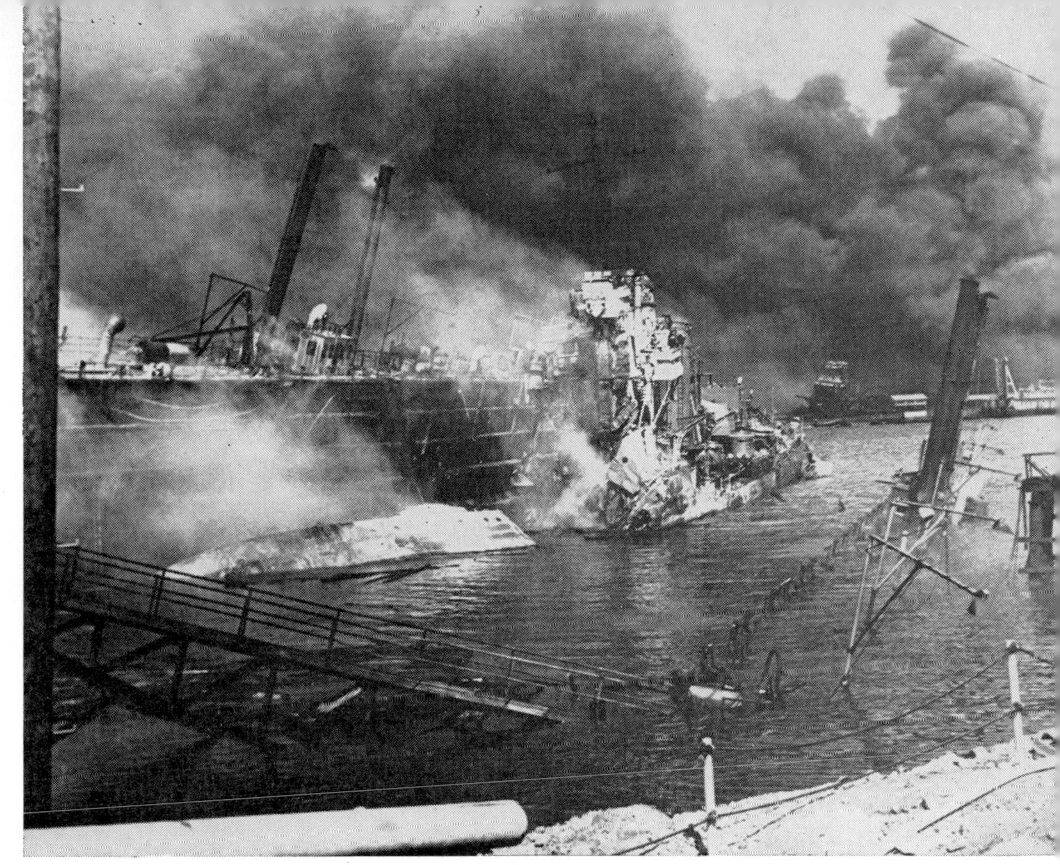

Pearl Harbor, December 7, 1941

FRANKLIN D. ROOSEVELT LIBRARY

bomb, was almost completely destroyed. The *Oklahoma* received repeated torpedo hits, and capsized in shallow water. Six other battleships, three cruisers, and three destroyers were damaged more or less seriously and put out of commission. Heavy destruction was wrought among grounded aircraft, which were prevented from raising an adequate defensive umbrella over the harbor. Total American casualties for both services amounted to 3,435. The attackers lost 29 aircraft, 5 midget submarines, and 1 fleet submarine.

The Japanese attack on Pearl Harbor completed the alignment of the major forces in the spreading global conflict. The United States and Britain declared war on Japan on December 8, 1941. The British Dominions, the Netherlands Government in exile, and Chiang Kai-shek's Nationalist government followed suit. Three days later, in accordance with their Tripartite Pact, Germany and Italy proclaimed a state of war with the United States.

The "Year of Agony," 1942

The entry of the United States into active belligerency righted the anomalous position it had occupied for some time. American material potential had been openly mobilized in the cause against Nazism since President Roosevelt's election to his third term in November 1940. American ideological potential had been mobilized as openly since the Atlantic Charter of August 1941. The growing breach with Japan was becoming evident at the same time. Pearl Harbor, for all its shock and surprise, was the climax of a maturing process.

During Christmas week 1941, Churchill and the British Chiefs of Staff visited Washington for the "Arcadia" conference. In a series of meetings with Roosevelt and the American Chiefs of Staffs, the total integration of the Anglo-American war effort was planned and programed. The Combined Chiefs of Staff Committee was set up under the chairmanship of General Marshall, Chief of the U.S. Army General Staff, eventually to be responsible for the "strategic conduct of the war." The all-important decision was made to regard Germany as the prime enemy, and thereafter—though many Americans, notably many American admirals, were opposed—"Hitler First" was the major premise of Allied strategy. Commands in the different theaters of the war were defined and allocated. Tentatively, North Africa was selected for the landing of an Anglo-American expeditionary force sometime in 1942. A legion of "combined boards," in particular the Combined Munitions Assignment Board, were organized at Washington. In the course of the visit, Churchill addressed a joint session of Congress. He afterward went on to Ottawa for a similar round of conferences with the Canadian leaders. He left in Washington Field Marshal Sir John Dill as his personal military representative with the President. General Sir Alan Brooke succeeded Dill as Chief of the Imperial General Staff to act throughout the remainder of the war as Churchill's virtual Chief of Staff.

On January 1 and 2, 1942, at Washington, representatives of twenty-six "United Nations" signed a declaration, subscribing to the principles of the Atlantic Charter and agreeing to apply their full resources to the common struggle.

It was to be expected that the entry of the United States into the war would produce a surge of optimism, entirely welcome and entirely justified. But that optimism was soon finding expression in talk of a Second Front in Europe in 1942, which, as was to turn out, was not so welcome and certainly not justified. Generals Marshall and Dwight D. Eisenhower, then Chief of the Operations Division, were both convinced of the possibilities of the Second Front. Molotov, visiting Washington in May 1942, was assured that it was intended, and the assurance was shortly published in the American, British, and Russian press. Molotov announced it on his return to Moscow along with the text of a new Anglo-Soviet mutual-aid treaty. In point of fact the greater part of 1942—indeed till Alamein in October—was a phase of almost unrelieved disaster, the veritable "Year of Agony" of the Second World War, and for the time being any sort of strategy other than defense was out of the question. Axis offensives developed in North Africa, in the Pacific, and in Russia, like a huge three-taloned claw closing in upon the Eurasian hemisphere. In 1942 the Battle of the Atlantic reached its highest average sinkings of 400,000 tons a month.

The phase had begun with heavy naval losses in the Mediterranean. Before Christmas 1941, the British aircraft carrier *Ark Royal* and the battleship *Barham* were sunk by German submarines; the battleships *Queen Elizabeth* and *Valiant,* lying at anchor in the harbor at Alexandria, were disabled by Italian "sticky mines," planted by underwater swimmers. By the turn of the year the British Eastern Mediterranean Fleet was reduced to three cruisers and a destroyer flotilla. Meanwhile the German *Luftwaffe* stepped up its raids on Malta, and though failing to subdue the heroic island, temporarily crippled it as an aerial and naval base. For a time there were just three serviceable fighter planes left in Malta – christened by their pilots "Faith," "Hope," and "Charity" – and British convoys in the Sicilian Channel were losing half their strength. During January and February 1942, Rommel in the Western Desert, greatly daring and determined to profit from the British reverses in the Mediterranean, struck back at the Eighth Army and advanced precipitately into Cyrenaica. In the second offensive in May and June, he prepared to launch the invasion and conquest of Egypt, took Tobruk, and thence advanced to Alamein, a scant fifty miles from Alexandria. A grateful Führer created him Field Marshal in anticipation of his early entry into Cairo and final subjugation of the Middle East.

Japan's offensive in the Pacific had begun, like an explosive discharge, in all directions. Within four days of Pearl Harbor, her air forces had attacked Singapore, Manila, Midway, Wake, and Guam, and her land forces had seized footholds in Malaya, Burma, Hong Kong, and Luzon. On December 10, 1941, in the absence of fighter protection, the British battleship *Prince of Wales* and the battle cruiser *Repulse,* operating against Japanese transports in the Gulf of Siam, were sunk by Japanese shore-based aircraft. Resistance in Hong Kong, Wake, and Guam was extinguished before Christmas. Midway remained in American possession.

Less than a couple of months sufficed for Japanese land forces – tanks and all – under the command of General Yamashita, to infiltrate the dense jungle country of the Malay Peninsula, which hitherto was believed to be impenetrable. At the beginning of February 1942, the Japanese stood at the Strait of Johore, a thread of water some five hundred yards wide separating the mainland from the island of Singapore. The defenders were pressed back to southern points on the island, while shattering air raids demoralized the population of the city of Singapore. The great naval base was blown up; stores and equipment were fired by the defenders. On the evening of February 15, 1942, a weary, disorganized, dispirited army of 80,000 British, Australian, and Indian troops surrendered to 50,000 Japanese. Churchill, who had consistently underestimated the Japanese, afterwards described the fall of Singapore as "the worst disaster and largest capitulation in British history." For the prestige of the European in the East it was a worse disaster than Tsushima, a generation before.

Japanese forces crossed the Burmese frontier on December 10, 1941, at the Isthmus of Kra. By March and April, Rangoon, Mandalay, and the town of Lashio at the terminus of the Burma Road, were all in Japanese hands. Two divisions of British and Indian troops, under General Sir Harold Alexander, preceded by a host of refugees, retreated by obscure jungle trails into Bengal. A Chinese force under General Joseph W. Stilwell, Chiang Kai-shek's recently appointed American Chief of Staff, struggled into Assam. Burma was substantially a Japanese conquest, and India was threatened with invasion.

The Japanese assault on the Philippines began on the day after Pearl Harbor. Destructive Japanese air raids on Clark Field near Manila and on the naval base at Cavite deprived General MacArthur, commanding the American-Filipino forces, of the bulk of his air support at the very outset of the campaign. The Japanese expeditionary force under General Homma was thus able to select its points of landing on Luzon and, by the end of December 1941, several columns of invaders were converging on Manila. A skeleton Japanese force entered the city on January 2, 1942, while the main Japanese force pursued the defenders in the direction of the mountainous and well-wooded Bataan Peninsula.

Prepared positions, extending across the narrow neck of the Bataan Peninsula and protected from sea attack by the heavy guns of Corregidor at the entrance to Manila Bay, offered a prospect of holding the Japanese advance. For three months, the American-Filipino lines under MacArthur stood firm against every tactical operation Japanese military ingenuity could devise — frontal attack, flank attack, sea-borne attack, and infiltration. Unrelenting bombardment, combined with the ravages of malaria, sapped the physical strength, if not the morale, of the garrison. Efforts to send reinforcements from Australia were initiated in January, but only one vessel in three reached its destination. On March 17, MacArthur relinquished his command in Bataan, on instructions from President Roosevelt, to assume command of new American concentrations to be built up in Australia, and left General Jonathan M. Wainwright to conduct the closing phases of the gallant defense. General Yamashita, fresh from his victory at Singapore, succeeding the now somewhat discomfited Homma, took Bataan at last on April 9 and Corregidor on May 6, 1942. Resistance continued mainly from Philippine guerrillas, at scattered points on the mainland, and provided the Japanese with opportunities for demonstrating their methods of "pacification."

The islands of the Netherlands East Indies fell to enemy offensives of a type that was now becoming so tragically familiar. Between January and March 1942, Sumatra, Borneo, the Celebes, Java, Bali, Timor, and the northern parts of New Guinea were overrun in rapid succession. On February 27, in the Java Sea, an attempt by a combined British, Australian, Dutch, and American fleet to intercept a superior Japanese force escorting a convoy was repulsed with the loss of five cruisers and seven destroyers. Japanese losses in the engagement and in the course of this part of the campaign are not known, but were probably considerable. A systematic "scorched-earth" policy and the destruction of oil fields robbed the conqueror of immediate material gain from his conquests, but the consolation was negative and mortifying. General ter Poorten, the Dutch Commander in Chief, capitulated with his army at Bandung on March 8.

The fall of Malaya, Burma, the Philippines, and the Netherlands East Indies brought the all-conquering Japanese armies into perilous proximity to Australia and India. The Andaman Islands in the Indian Ocean were already in Japanese hands. Japanese carrier-based planes raided Trincomalee in Ceylon. Japanese cruisers sank some 135,000 tons of British shipping in the Bay of Bengal. Far across the Pacific, small Japanese forces occupied Attu and Kiska in the Aleutians. An Anglo-South African seizure of Madagascar from Vichy forces – in the first sea-borne "invasion" of the war to be attempted on the Allied side – only barely anticipated a Japanese drive across the southern chord of the Indian Ocean. No one could yet say whether this phenomenal expansion of Japanese power had reached its limit or was still in the full momentum of its rage and energy.

In Britain, meanwhile, the mood was dismayed and critical. Yet public opinion, in its illogic, seemed far less galled by the disasters in the East than by an incident nearer home. On the night of February 11, 1942, the German battleships *Scharnhorst* and *Gneisenau,* lying for weeks at Brest under constant RAF attack, slipped out of harbor, up the Channel and through the Strait of Dover, under attack from shore-based aircraft on the way and, though damaged by mines, succeeded in reaching home ports in Germany.

Political reactions in Australia, New Zealand, and India were more serious. Australian and New Zealand troops prepared to withdraw from the Middle East for the defense of their own homelands. John Curtin, the Australian Prime Minister, arraigned Churchill for the "inexcusable betrayal" at Singapore. In March 1942, Churchill sent Sir Stafford Cripps out to India as bearer of an "offer" to the Indian leaders. He authorized Cripps to pledge the creation, after the war, of a self-governing "Indian Union" with Dominion status and with a constitution of its own making – and with the right, if it so desired, to secede from the British Commonwealth. Meanwhile, however, the defense of India must remain the responsibility of the existing British Government. After exhaustive discussions, the offer was rejected by Nehru and the Indian National Congress, mainly on the ground that it looked too much like a disguised scheme for some sort of political partition in India; but it was, for the same reason, more favorably received at first by Jinnah and the Moslem League. By the "Quit India" resolution, the Indian National Congress categorically demanded the independence of India, not after the war, but "here and now." Cripps' "offer" therefore signally failed to unite and mobolize Indian political opinion against Japan. The majority of the Indian leaders, defeatist and disillusioned, dubbed it as just another overdue attempt to purchase time by an imperial power under judgment of deserved downfall. The offer was, as Gandhi is reported to have said, a "postdated check on a bank that was obviously crashing."

In Britain, Churchill defended himself in a secret session of the House. He also made changes in his cabinet. Lord Beaverbrook left the Ministry of Supply to become head of the London Board of the Combined Munitions Assignment Board; Oliver Lyttelton became Minister of Production; Clement Attlee became Deputy Prime Minister and Secretary for the Dominions. In May and June 1942, American naval victories in the Pacific, the two battles of the Coral Sea and of Midway, indicated a strong and welcome recovery in one theater of the war at least. In that June, a Roosevelt-Churchill meeting took place in Washington and was shortly followed by a Combined Chiefs of Staff meeting in London. It was decided that a Second Front in Europe could not be put into effect "before late 1943 at the earliest . . . and might be postponed until the spring of 1944" and that the most promising area for Anglo-American operations in the near future would be North Africa. In August, a Churchill-Stalin meeting took place in Moscow, and it fell to Churchill to break the news to his Russian ally that the Second Front in Europe, so urgently demanded, was not yet to be.

Early in May 1942, as a preface to the German summer operations in Russia, an army under Field Marshal von Manstein attacked the Soviet naval base and fortress of Sevastopol and took it after a tremendous siege of seven weeks. But Manstein failed to trap the Soviet Black Sea fleet, which continued to deny the use of the Black Sea to German ships. In June, Field Marshal von Bock, in command of an army group of eight armies in the Ukraine, launched a general offensive. The rapid and sustained German advance of 1941 was momentarily resumed. Once more the Nazi press and radio announced the imminent destruction of the Red Army and the collapse of the Soviet Union. By September, the German Sixth Army had reached the Volga and was threatening Stalingrad; the First Panzer Army, under the veteran tank general, Kleist, was deep in the open country north of the Caucasus overrunning the Caucasian oil fields. Supply routes from Persia were cut. The German High Command was credited with planning a vast wheeling maneuver up the Volga toward Kuibyshev and Kazan, a maneuver worthy of Schlieffen, which would have enveloped the central Moscow area and rolled up the entire Eastern front.

The Turning Point

The Second World War lasted nearly six years and fell into two clearly marked phases of roughly equal length. The first was a confused phase. Nations were involved, fronts were started up, and great battles were joined in several parts of the world at once. There was little apparent connection in the welter of events except, on the one side, a general expanding offensive and, on the other side, a grim determination to hold on. We have called 1942 the "Year of Agony." The Africa Corps was striking for Cairo; the Japanese looked as if they were about to spring on India and Australia; the German Sixth Army was approaching Stalingrad. The Battle of the Atlantic at times seemed almost lost. Yet the year was also in Churchill's words "the end of the beginning." For the three great Allies, Britain, the United States, and the Soviet Union, the year saw the translation of their immense material potential into actuality. It was the period during which, despite their initial losses and defeats, they were at last overhauling the technical advantages that had formerly lain with their enemies. From then onward the war passed gradually but irresistibly into its second phase, and the whole scattered global melee seemed to resolve itself into a grand unified strategic plan that could have but one conclusion.

The disaster at Pearl Harbor had fallen most heavily on the older ships of the American battle fleet. The more modern ships, including the carriers, remained intact. In the first week of May 1942, two task forces, which included the carriers *Yorktown* and *Lexington* and three cruisers, intercepted a Japanese concentration in the Coral Sea making for Port Moresby in New Guinea. In a three-day action, hitherto unique in naval history, fought out entirely by carrier aircraft — an action in which surface ships were never in contact — the Japanese lost one carrier, four cruisers, and a number of troop transports and sustained serious damage to another carrier and three cruisers. The *Lexington,* hit by torpedoes and burning fiercely, was eventually abandoned and sunk. The Americans lost 33 aircraft, and the Japanese 43. A month later, the Japanese, under the command of Admiral Yamamoto, assembled fleets of some 80 warships and transports, their most powerful concentration to date, in an attempt to destroy the remnants of the American battle fleet and to capture the island of Midway. The possession of this important outpost of the American defense system in the Pacific would have threatened the Australian supply line and would have given Japan a forward base for raids against Hawaii and thence against the United States itself. The movements of the Japanese fleets, however, were precisely anticipated by "Magic," and on June 4, 1942, a general naval and aerial battle developed. Four Japanese carriers and two cruisers were sunk. The American carrier *Yorktown,* badly damaged, was abandoned and was later sunk by a Japanese submarine. The Americans lost 150 aircraft, and the Japanese 250.

The battles of the Coral Sea and Midway, within six months of Pearl Harbor, gave sufficient proof of the extraordinary recovery of the United States. In particular the loss to the Japanese of aircraft carriers, five in all — not to mention others disabled — irretrievably depleted their available aerial striking power. In August 1942, American marines seized beachheads on Guadalcanal in the Solomons. Japanese in northern New Guinea began to give ground under attacks by Australasian and American forces. The great Japanese expansion in the Pacific had reached its high-water mark.

North Africa

The first convoy of American troops had arrived in Northern Ireland as early as January 1942. But commitments in the Pacific delayed the massive build-up of American strength in Britain until well into the summer of the year. In June 1942, a European Theater of Operations was created with headquarters in London and with General Eisenhower as commanding general, Admiral Harold R. Stark as naval commander, and General Carl A. Spaatz commanding the United States Eighth Air Force. General Walter Bedell Smith shortly arrived as Chief of Staff. On July 4, 1942, Independence Day, American bombers raided German airfields in Holland, their first targets in Europe.

At the same time the reinforcement of the Eighth Army, now at Alamein, was given every possible priority. But it was a logistic task unprecedented even in the Pacific theater. An infantry division of this time required 3,000 motor vehicles and 400 tons of supplies a day; an armored division in action required 70,000 tons of gasoline, 350 tons of ammunition, and 50 tons of spare parts a day. Quantities of this magnitude had now to be transported to Egypt round the Cape and up the Red Sea. Yet, in the three months that followed the fall of Tobruk, the Eighth Army was virtually re-equipped and converted into a force ready to recover the initiative. The Sherman tank made its debut in the desert, a weapon that was soon proved to outclass its German equivalent of that date. Early in August 1942, Churchill appointed General Sir Harold Alexander Commander in Chief Middle East with headquarters at Cairo, and General Sir Bernard Montgomery commander of the Eighth Army.

On August 19, 1942, the Second Front found a momentary echo in a cross-Channel "diversionary assault" on Dieppe, carried out by a largely Canadian contingent. It was not a success, even if it could be justified as "experience." Thereafter, except for occasional commando raids, no further cross-Channel operations were attempted till the invasion of 1944. But all eyes were now turned to North Africa.

On the last day of August 1942, in an attempt to resume his long drive for Egypt, Rommel attacked the Eighth Army at Alamein. But the Eighth Army was already strong enough to inflict upon him a heavy repulse. Late in the evening of October 23, Montgomery launched his own offensive, which we now know as the Battle of Alamein, the opening round of what was to be the third and last of the British Libyan campaigns. Preliminary mine-lifting was done under moonlight by infantry. An artillery barrage from 1,000 guns, recalling in intensity the great bombardments on the Western front in the First World War, broke the crust of the enemy's resistance and opened up a way for the British armor. Twelve days' fighting ended in the total rout of the German and Italian armies. Rommel himself, on sick leave when the battle began, returned in time for its crisis. General von Thoma, commander of the Africa Corps, was taken prisoner. The pursuit was pressed closely. The enemy forces were harried by air and by naval bombardment along the coast road as they streamed back to Cyrenaica, and only a sudden turn of rainy weather held up the British armor and saved the Axis forces from complete destruction. German and Italian losses in the battle were put at 60,000 men, 1,000 guns, and 500 tanks.

The battle, Churchill wrote afterwards, "was the turning of the Hinge of Fate. . . . Before Alamein we never had a victory. After Alamein we never had a defeat." On November 7-8, 1942, Anglo-American forces effected landings in Morocco and Algeria. On Sunday, November 15, church bells were rung in England for the first time since 1939.

The Anglo-American sea-borne invasion of North Africa – "Torch," as it came to be called – had been decided, as we have said, at the conferences in Washington and London in June and July 1942. Political preparations had begun in earlier American conversations with anti-Vichy groups

British Crusader tanks in the Western Desert, November 1942

IMPERIAL WAR MUSEUM

in Algeria, conversations largely by Robert Murphy, American consul general in North Africa, which had been going on intermittently ever since the Fall of France in 1940. But any success these conversations might have had had always been stalled by the absence of a responsible French leader with a popular appeal able to rally not only the Free French forces of de Gaulle in Britain but the forces of French patriotism everywhere. Then, early in 1942, General Giraud escaped from his confinement in Germany and returned secretly to France. He had commanded a French army in Belgium in 1940, when he had been taken prisoner. His seniority and his irreproachable record of service – irreproachable both militarily and politically – marked him out as the man the Anglo-American Allies had been waiting for. Contacts were made with him at Marseilles and with his agents at Algiers. During the night of October 22-23, 1942, just as the Battle of Alamein was opening, a British submarine landed the American General Mark Clark and a party of officers at a rendezvous at a house on the Algerian coast where details of the impending Allied invasion of North Africa and of possible French collaboration were discussed with local representatives. Yet, despite the thick blanket of security, some hint of the invasion must have leaked out, for Admiral Darlan, Commander in Chief of the armed forces of the Vichy government, chose that moment to make a somewhat ostentatious visit to North Africa and Dakar to inspect the French defenses. These tense preinvasion weeks give a fine flavor of Hollywoodlike intrigue – light signals from darkened windows, hide-and-seek in underground cellars, and sudden swoops by secret police.

Gallipoli in 1915 was the classic reminder of the extraordinary hazards of sea-borne invasions. But the Japanese had lately shown themselves masters of the operation; the British had effected landings in Madagascar and at Dieppe, and the Americans on Gaudalcanal. But, even with these precedents, the invasion now contemplated had novel military and diplomatic features. The Anglo-American operations in North Africa were placed under the supreme command of Eisenhower, and all naval operations under the command of Admiral Cunningham. On the night of November 7, 1942, some 850 ships — warships, transports, and landing craft — in three great convoys, one from the United States and two from England, arrived respectively at Casablanca, Oran, and Algiers. Fighter cover was provided from Gibraltar. There was the minimum of interference by enemy submarines and aircraft. The landings encountered some French resistance, especially at Casablanca and Oran. In three weeks, 185,000 men, 20,000 vehicles, and 200,000 tons of supplies were safely put ashore. The German reaction was an immediate occupation of Vichy France. French warships, lying at Toulon, were scuttled by their crews before the Germans arrived. German forces, hurriedly flown into Bizerta and Tunis, prepared a stiff defense. Italians occupied Corsica and Nice.

The invasion of North Africa was not only tactically audacious. It was a prodigious strategic and political gamble. Its success and its bearing on subsequent operations in Europe have since endowed it with a logic and obviousness which, at the time, it could not have had. Certainly it did not amount to the Second Front for which the Soviet Government had been so desperately and insistently pleading. The Red Army appeared to be *in extremis;* its astonishing recovery at Stalingrad was not yet in sight. The invasion of North Africa might itself have failed. But, even had it succeeded, the possible defeat of the Red Army would have released German divisions for operations in Spain and Turkey to the consequent isolation and collapse of the entire position that the Anglo-American Allies were establishing. Throughout the operation, the Franco government in Spain was an unknown, unpredictable quantity.

In Algeria the political situation was involved and delicate. The local administrative officials were pro-Vichy, and the French businessmen and landowners were inclined to Fascism. The Arab population was tense and restless. General de Gaulle and his British sponsors were unpopular — memories of Oran in 1940 were still alive — and de Gaulle in addition was personally disliked by President Roosevelt and the American Government. The man of the moment — for the moment — as it now turned out, was not de Gaulle or Giraud, but Darlan. Admiral Darlan had returned to France from his tour of inspection in North Africa a few days before the invasion, but he now flew back, allegedly to visit the sickbed of an ailing son in Algiers. His record at Vichy had not been such as to recommend him to the Allies, but it seemed possible that he could now swing over the pro-Vichy elements in Algeria. Eisenhower and Clark, as soldiers, desired nothing so much as to bring off their invasion with as little bloodshed as possible and were willing to accept any help from any quarter if it would contribute to that result.

Darlan at least showed his value by officially ordering the cessation of

French resistance in North Africa forty-eight hours after the first landings and by securing the cooperation of the French governors of Algeria, Morocco, and Dakar. With Eisenhower's concurrence, he set himself up as French political chief in North Africa, with Giraud as military chief. Throughout he protested that he was faithful to Pétain, now helpless in German custody, and was carrying out Pétain's secret wishes. But on Christmas Eve, Darlan was assassinated in his office in Algiers by a young French patriot. Giraud was designated his successor. Final judgments on Darlan are still best deferred. The installation of a collaborator and turncoat in high office under the victorious Allies, however great his accidental usefulness might be, seemed a sordid enough deal at a moment when an oppressed and stifled world was gasping for a breath of idealism. It was one of the pathetic problems of the liberation that the fervid simplicities of popular patriotism should so often have had to be complicated by political and military "expedience."

The Anglo-American landings in North Africa had been made with surprising ease. The political situation had reached a partial but sufficiently practical solution in the way we have described. Meanwhile the Eighth Army was chasing and bombing the Africa Corps across Libya. It looked as if Axis power in North Africa would soon collapse. But then the real campaigning difficulties in the country began to develop. British and American troops in Algeria were not the hardened veterans of the Eighth Army, and both they and their officers had to learn the art of war in a new and unexpected terrain. Harbors, notably Algiers, needed to be cleared; roads and railroads were in disrepair and, in any case, inadequate. About Christmas, heavy rains soaked the airfields and made fighter support of advanced troops impossible. The Germans had all the logistic advantages, and their reinforcements were being ferried over the short lap from Europe by transport plane at the rate of 1,500 men a night. By December 1, they were counterattacking strongly. At the turn of the year, the Axis strength in Tunisia amounted to 150,000 men, still being reinforced, strongly entrenched in rough, easily defensible, semimountainous country, backed by first-class ports, all-weather airfields, and by a relatively fertile, well-roaded land. Evidently the battle for Tunisia was going to be no walkover, but would be one of the great campaigns of the war.

The Eighth Army under Montgomery had continued its career in Libya. It took Tripoli on January 23, 1943, and by the end of the month was approaching the southern borders of Tunisia and the fortified system known as the Mareth Line, where it seemed that Rommel might make a stand. Since the Battle of Alamein in October, the Eighth Army had covered 1,400 miles and, at the height of the pursuit, its pace had been as much as 40 miles a day. It had outfought at every point a wary and resourceful foe. The British Navy had served it well, protecting its seaward flank and its attendant coastwise shipping; essential ports along its route had been put into use in a matter of days. The terrain and the climate in Libya improved with the advance. After Tripoli there were flowering gardens and green grass to greet men, many of whom had seen nothing but the desert for three years. Meanwhile, a French column under General Leclerc traversed the Sahara from Lake Chad and joined the flank of the Eighth Army before the Mareth Line.

From January 14, 1943, for ten days, Roosevelt, Churchill, and their Chiefs of Staff held a conference at Casablanca. The North African campaign, as was now evident, was likely to be successful; news from Stalingrad had been changing from despair to hope. The main decisions of the conference were to launch an attack on Sicily in the course of the summer, to continue the massing in Britain of the army necessary for the eventual invasion of Western Europe, to step up the strategic bomber attack on Germany in preparation for that invasion, and finally to intensify the antisubmarine war. Afterward, to the press, Roosevelt announced that the objective of the war was "unconditional surrender" by Germany, Italy, and Japan. Stalin had been invited to the conference but had excused himself from attending "on account of the great offensive [in Russia] which he himself, as Commander-in-Chief, was directing," but he subsequently adhered to the formula of "unconditional surrender." One by-product of the conference was the formal meeting and agreement between the French leaders, Giraud and de Gaulle.

The battle for Tunisia continued indecisively during February and March 1943. We are still surprised that the Germans should have staked so much and fought so stubbornly in the area, but presumably they were satisfied that their campaign, even when it became clear that no success could come of it, was justified as a gigantic delaying action. The Eighth Army broke the Mareth Line during the last week of March, and the first links were made with American units on April 7. Gradually the Anglo-American forces took the offensive everywhere. Tactically the battles were often experimental combats between new types of tanks. In the air and at sea the Allies established undisputed superiority and steadily reduced the German resistance by the starvation of oil supplies.

The end, when it came, came quickly. For the moment the Italians, who had never greatly distinguished themselves in North Africa, in their singular capriciousness were now inspired by the hopelessness of their position to fight with conspicuous courage. Their commander, Field Marshal Messe, was the last general officer to surrender and, with a typical native gesture, insisted on giving his sword in person to Montgomery. Remaining Axis units were rounded up in their refuges on Cape Bon on May 13, 1943. In the final count, 250,000 Germans and Italians were killed or captured in Tunisia. The naval benefits to the Allies were immediate. The Mediterranean Sea throughout its length was opened for Allied shipping, and the long route round the Cape eliminated. Important material resources in Algeria, Tunis, and Libya were made available. A base was provided for Allied attack upon "the soft underbelly of the Axis." Above all, the Allies, after years of defeat, had the satisfaction of a great victory. Months of intricate preparation had been brilliantly vindicated. Anglo-American cooperation had been tested and tried in the field of action.

The postscript of these events in North Africa was further progress in the settlement of the French political situation. As we have said, the French leaders, de Gaulle and Giraud, had met at Casablanca in January 1943, at the time of the Churchill-Roosevelt conference, and were formally reconciled. A general unification and coordination of all French pro-Allied forces was in train. In May 1943, in Occupied France, an underground Council of Resistance was organized to include representatives from the main resistance groups and from de Gaulle's Free French in London. In June, in Algiers, a French Committee of National Liberation was set up, with de Gaulle and Giraud as joint Presidents, to reorganize the French Army, to receive the allegiance of all parts of the French Empire, except Indochina which was under Japanese occupation, and to institute a purge of former collaborationists. The reconciliation of de Gaulle and Giraud had served its purpose, even if it did not last. Giraud afterward retired, evidently wearied of the unending personal rivalry, leaving de Gaulle the undisputed master of the scene. In November 1943, also in Algiers, a Consultative Assembly began to hold meetings. It was composed of some hundred members, largely self-nominated on the initiative of Félix Gouin, a Socialist, who acted as its chairman, and it purported to be a sort of parliament in exile and custodian of the French democratic tradition. Subsequently, in May 1944, this Assembly passed a resolution inviting the Committee of National Liberation to become the "Provisional Government of the French Republic." Thus, by the time of the Allied invasion of Normandy, de Gaulle was firmly established in his leadership, and French political organs and a French Army were in being, waiting to move into metropolitan France.

Stalingrad

It may be that one day an authentic and credible account of the Eastern front in the Second World War will be available to English-speaking readers. The mere names of Dunkirk, Bataan, Gaudalcanal, Alamein, Normandy, Arnhem, Okinawa, or of any of the other great battles fought by the Western Allies conjure up pictures even to those who did not participate in them. But the best informed and most imaginative of us must find it hard mentally to reconstruct a battle like that of Stalingrad, between two anonymous masses of men, locked in continuous month-long combat, in a terrain almost empty of roads and railroads, in ruined streets and shattered buildings, in sub-zero weather, with a vast snow-covered steppe on the one side and a frozen river two miles wide on the other. Stalingrad has been compared with Verdun, though the tactical and strategic circumstances were different. More men were engaged at Verdun, more were killed and wounded, and the battle lasted longer. But there was the same sense of ultimate decision in both, the same disregard of cost, the same feats of that almost automatic heroism which lies beyond physical exhaustion, the same "death grapple between two fanaticisms."

The Battle of Stalingrad may be said to have begun at the end of August 1942, when armored units of the German Sixth Army crossed the great bend of the river Don less than fifty miles from Stalingrad. The time and season were already causing extreme anxiety to the German High Command, for hardly two months of campaigning weather were then left to complete the gigantic maneuver up the Volga to Kazan that the German High Command was credited to be planning, a maneuver that would have effected the final envelopment of the Red Army and brought the war in Russia to an end. Soviet communiqués made no attempt to minimize the peril of the situation. For the first time in the entire Russian campaign, the Red Army could no longer rely on indefinite retirement to relieve its plight. The moral, material, and strategic stakes at Stalingrad were acknowledged by both sides to be paramount.

We may well ask whether the Germans, flushed as they were with uninterrupted victories, expected or wanted a decisive battle to develop at this point. We may ask why they chose to direct their armored spearheads at Stalingrad when all their previous advances had been made by bypassing the great urban obstacles in their path, why indeed they permitted themselves to become entangled in a battle of attrition, above all at so critical a moment, when all their previous successes in Russia had been won in swift maneuver on open ground. Or we may ask why, if the Germans had really intended to take Stalingrad by assault, they had failed, when far stronger positions, from Eben Emael to Sevastopol, had all gone down before them. The Battle of Stalingrad continued through September and October into November 1942. The German Sixth Army was now under the command of General Friedrich von Paulus, with Hitler's personal orders not to retire. Then, as had happened the year before, the Red Army opened its own general winter offensive. Rzhev on the upper Volga and Leningrad for some weeks had already been the theater of major Soviet actions. Late in November, similar Soviet actions began in the Caucasus.

On November 19, 1942, under the command of General Zhukov, the Soviet forces in the Stalingrad sector went over to the offensive. One army under General Rokossovsky attacked to the north of the city, and another army under General Yeremenko attacked to the south, the two armies forming, as it were, the arms of a great pincers. At first the dimensions of the offensive were not realized by the outside world, and it was only gradually, as one terse Soviet communiqué followed another, that the immense resources, the strategic sweep and timing and, above all, the long and secret Soviet rearward reorganization could be appreciated. Within a week, the arms of the pincers had closed round the German Sixth Army. Manstein, now commanding the German army group in the theater, tried to relieve the encircled forces and lost half his armor in the attempt. He sent supplies by transport plane, but the supplies dwindled as the Russians progressively occupied the airfields remaining in the Stalingrad pocket. The final surrender of the German Sixth Army — 137,500 men out of an original 300,000 — together with its commander, Paulus, only recently created Field Marshal, and 15 general officers, was made on January 31, 1943. Simultaneous operations in the Caucasus and on the Don accounted for another 300,000 enemy casualties, largely Italian and Rumanian. Since September 1942, the Germans had lost a fifth of their total strength on the Eastern front. The entire German position in southern Russia was momentarily at the point of collapse.

The Battle of Stalingrad was soon merged into the general Soviet winter offensive. Early in the New Year 1943, the Soviet forces in sorties round

THE EASTERN FRONT, 1940-45

Leningrad rolled back the German investment lines and raised the siege of the city, a siege that had lasted sixteen months. Between January and March the headlines announced a succession of towns and cities liberated all along the front — Maikop, Krasnodar, Rostov, Voroshilovgrad, Kharkov, Rzhev, Vyazma. At the end of March, the Germans counterattacked and recaptured Kharkov. Operations came to an end with the spring thaw. Hitler's armies had lost, at enormous cost, all the ground they had gained in 1942.

The German army in Russia was now in "natural" decline. The farther it penetrated the Russian plains the thinner did it spread its numbers. Its reserves of man power were not inexhaustible and could not be expended as hitherto. In 1943 the strength of a high percentage of German divisions in Russia could only be maintained with foreign recruits. Even the newly formed *Waffen SS* divisions contained "ideological volunteers" from various parts of Nazi Europe. The German home front, as we shall relate in the next chapter, was unprepared and inadequate for the strains which developed at this time. Yet Hitler, in supreme command, ordered suicidal operations rather than cut his losses and match his ambitions to his remaining resources. In 1943 the Soviet Union, like its Western Allies, was at last converting its war potential into actuality, and the Russian soldier, for the first time in his history, was going into battle with equipment equal to his enemy's. Siberian and Asiatic man power was being drawn upon. Lend-Lease and the Anglo-American bombing of German munition centers were further favorable weights in the scales. The arrival of 200,000 American trucks and jeeps revolutionized the Soviet transport situation. But, with or without these aids, it was gradually becoming evident what a colossal military power had at last come to birth in the Soviet Union. For the Western Allies, months of doubt were being changed into something akin to a new apprehension.

The closing operations of the winter of 1942-43 had left a Soviet salient round Kursk and a German salient round Orel. Both invited attack. On July 5, 1943, some four German divisions under Kluge opened against the Soviet salient round Kursk what appeared to be the start of the regular German summer offensive. The maneuver was no surprise. Both sides had been concentrating for action; both sides, throughout that June, had been making local attacks in the area for the testing of their enemy's defenses and for the capture of information. In the event, two well-prepared armies met "in the most violent battle of machines of the war."

But the days of the Nazi blitzkrieg were over. In less than a fortnight the German offensive had exhausted itself. The Germans lost 70,000 officers and men and more than half the armor with which they had first attacked. On July 12, 1943, the Soviet forces attacked the German salient round Orel. Reports of the battle indicate a Soviet use of artillery that recalls Alamein; evidently the Red Army commanders had simultaneously made the same tactical discovery as Montgomery. On August 5, Orel was stormed and taken. The Soviet offensive spread along the Eastern front. Through September, October, and November, came reports of the liberation of Kharkov, Taganrog, Novorossiysk, Bryansk, Smolensk, Nevel,

Dnepropetrovsk, Perekop, Kiev, Zhitomir. The names of Red Army commanders were becoming known to the Anglo-American press — Zhukov, Sokolovsky, Rokossovsky, Vatutin, Koniev, Malinovsky, and Tolbukhin. On November 4, 1943, a special Soviet communiqué, reviewing the results of four months' fighting since the start of the German offensive around Kursk, announced the restoration of 140,000 square miles of territory in the most fertile and highly developed regions of the Soviet Union, the liberation of 38,000 "inhabited localities" — and the infliction on the enemy of 900,000 casualties. Of the Germans it could be said, however, that they conducted their withdrawals with traditional military skill. They were retreating, but they were retreating in good order and at their own pace. Manstein's "retirement according to plan" was no euphemism.

The Collapse of Italy

The battles in North Africa were the beginning of the elimination of Italy, the destruction of Fascism in its original homeland, and a deep breach in the southern glacis of the Nazi Fortress of Europe. Thereafter every Mediterranean country was a fair field for military and political exploitation by the Allies. In May 1943, at the "Trident" Conference in Washington between Roosevelt, Churchill, and their Combined Chiefs of Staff, the decision was taken "to extend Allied influence in the Mediterranean to a point where Italy should be forced to withdraw from the war." The conference also discussed the situation in Turkey, a country which it was then hoped might join the Allies, and the situation in Burma where the war continued to go badly. The strategy in the Pacific was generally confirmed.

Early in June 1943, Sicily and Sardinia were already being subjected to softening-up raids. Italy's "Helgoland," the small fortress of Pantelleria, was reduced by concentrated aerial and naval bombardment, and its Italian commander raised the white flag before a single Allied soldier was put ashore. The Allied force, the Fifteenth Army Group under the command of Alexander, made its first landings in Sicily early on July 10. General George S. Patton commanded the United States Seventh Army to the left, and Montgomery the British Eighth Army to the right. The enemy had expected the invasion, but tactical surprise as to exact date and position was as complete as in the invasion of North Africa. The Allied conquest of Sicily was completed in rather more than a month. The Seventh Army, after initial difficulties at Gela, swung across the center and west of the island, and took Palermo on July 22. The Eighth Army, now strongly reinforced by Canadians, made a more plodding progress in the east, against mainly German resistance, and took Catania on August 5. Crack Italian regiments laid down their arms after a token resistance. The civilian population greeted the invaders tumultuously. The Germans transported 60,000 men to the mainland, two-thirds of their total strength, in one of the most successful "Dunkirks" of the war. The first Allied units themselves crossed the Strait of Messina on August 17, to be followed by two divisions of the Eighth Army on September 3.

In Italy, successive military disasters were producing their logical effects on a dictatorship that needed perpetual victories for its sustenance. A nation which had been taught to regard itself as the veritable reincarnation of the Roman Empire had seen its overseas provinces lost, its armed forces scattered, its economy bankrupted, and its very soil occupied by its own ally. A forecast of the approaching political crisis had been given in February 1943, two weeks after the Eighth Army had captured Tripoli, when Mussolini had "purged" his cabinet, dismissed Ciano from the Foreign Ministry, and then appointed him Italian envoy to the Holy See. On July 19, Mussolini met Hitler in conference at Feltre – it was to be the last conference of the two dictators – but nothing transpired from the meeting. Neither Mussolini nor Hitler was then in a position to offer the other material aid or moral consolation. On the same day, the 19th, Rome was bombed for the first time. A panic-stricken crowd surged into the neutral sanctuary of Vatican City and converted the Piazza of St. Peter's into a huge refugee encampment.

Mussolini summoned the Fascist Grand Council on July 24, 1943 – its first meeting since 1939 – to face a revolt of his onetime supporters, led by Grandi, Ciano, and the former Minister of Education, Bottai. Nineteen out of twenty-six members of the Grand Council, after debates lasting far into the night, passed a resolution demanding that Mussolini immediately relinquish command of the armed forces of Italy. The next day, the 25th, Mussolini reported to the King, hoping and expecting to enlist the King's support, and was bluntly told that he was no longer Premier. He was arrested as he left the palace and driven off in a waiting ambulance. King Victor Emmanuel at once issued a proclamation announcing his own assumption of the command of the armed forces, the resignation of Mussolini, and the formation of a new government under Marshal Badoglio. Spontaneous popular demonstrations broke out all over Italy. Fascist symbols were torn down from buildings and street hoardings. The Fascist party, its functionaries, and police dissolved and disappeared. Forgotten leaders of Italian democracy emerged from hiding or incarceration to give impromptu gatherings of bemused listeners at street corners their first exhibition of free speech in more than twenty years.

Badoglio's immediate concern was to extricate his country from the dread verdict of "unconditional surrender" and more particularly from the vengeance of its former German ally. But on September 3, after weeks of parleys and secret comings and goings, an armistice was signed on the basis of the inevitable formula and on the 8th, by prearrangement, the terms were broadcast almost simultaneously by Eisenhower and Badoglio.

The Allies had expected a convenient chaos in Italy, a chaos which would itself deliver the country to them without the need of further military effort and permit them to transfer their forces elsewhere – notably to England for the invasion of France. But there was still one undefeated and resolute enemy in Italy, an enemy apt at taking rapid countermeasures. The Germans used to full advantage the "Forty-five Days" between July 25 and September 8, 1943. They gained control of the Po Valley, and they occupied Rome and Vatican City. They sent a parachute company to rescue

Cheering Sicilians greeting American troops in Monreale, July 1943

ROBERT CAPA-MAGNUM

Mussolini from his confinement in a hotel in the Abruzzi mountains and set him up as head of a "Republican Fascist State" in northern Italy, a rallying point for all such loyal Fascist elements as could still be found. Allied prisoners in Italian camps were handed over to German guards to be transported to the Reich. Rommel assumed the command of all the German forces in northern Italy. The Fifth Army, under General Clark, landed on the Salerno beaches on September 9 in an attempt to cut off the whole of southern Italy. But the military situation by then had stiffened. The Fifth Army found the Germans ready and waiting, and fought there one of the most critical actions of the war.

The King of Italy, the Crown Prince Umberto, and Marshal Badoglio escaped to Bari, where they set up their government. The greater part of the Italian Navy, under broadcast instructions from Badoglio and Cunningham, sailed under its own steam for Malta and other ports under Allied control. Its surrender released considerable Allied naval strength for service in the Atlantic and Pacific. The Germans made a halfhearted and unsuccessful effort to hold Sardinia. Their effort to hold the more strategically important island of Corsica was frustrated by a rising of local partisans and the prompt landing of Free French forces. Partisans in Yugoslavia were stimulated into new activity, and regular Allied liaison was established with them by air and parachute. The Germans remained for the time being in effective occupation of Crete, Rhodes, and the Aegean area. On September 15, the Fifth Army at Salerno made contact with the Eighth Army racing up from Calabria, and the two armies, now deployed abreast, began their slow and painful progress northward. Naples was taken on October 1.

The Italian Government of Badoglio declared war on Germany on October 13. Bad weather was an unexpected and serious obstacle and for long months sunny Italy was a land of torrential rains, flooded gorges, and mud-sodden roads. At the end of January 1944, an American corps with a British division landed at Anzio, in an attempt once more, as at Salerno, to turn the flank of the German positions from the sea. But thereafter the diversion of landing craft to England in preparation for the invasion of France prevented a repetition of these leapfrog landings up the coast of Italy, and the campaign was perforce relegated to a secondary place in Allied strategy. The great natural fortress of Cassino, topped by its ancient monastery, blocking the approaches to Rome, was bombed and stormed in a series of heavy actions between March and May. Rome was eventually entered on June 4, 1944.

Two days later, on June 6, on the Normandy beaches, on the other side of Europe, Anglo-American forces launched the invasion of France.

The Pacific and Southeast Asia

By mid-1942, in a campaign of six months, the Japanese had conquered an empire (not counting China) of 1,300,000 square miles, of a population of over 100,000,000, and of economic resources which included 95 per cent of the world's rubber, 70 per cent of its tin, and 60 per cent of its rice. This huge array of territories, peoples, and wealth they were now organizing as the "Co-Prosperity Sphere in East Asia," to some extent the imitation and complement of the contemporary creation, the Nazi New Order in Europe.

In their grand design the Japanese sought as far as possible to work through local collaborators, such as Pibul in Siam, Ba Maw in Burma, Soekarno in Indonesia – and, of course, Pu Yi in Manchukuo and Wang Ching-wei in China. Among these may be numbered Admiral Decoux, the French Governor General of Indochina. But the realities of control rested with their own Japanese governors and mayors, "ambassadors" and "advisers," who swarmed into the executive and lucrative jobs on the heels of their armies, and any sort of economic policy was then directed, through these representatives, in accordance with the overriding needs of the war. But, to give the Devil his due, it must be said at least that, unlike the Nazi New Order in Europe, terror as a deliberate and hallowed doctrine was no part of the plan. The Japanese associated their Asiatic friends as partners with themselves in an "Asia for the Asiatics" and kept the incidental terror in their system for their enemies, especially the white man and the Chinese. They showed what they were capable of in the way of organized cruelty, for example in the Bataan "Death March" or in the construction of the Burma-Siam railroad, but their worst atrocities were inflicted on white prisoners of war and native resistance fighters.

Unlike the Nazi New Order, the Co-Prosperity Sphere was not continental, but maritime, and it began to fall apart, not only when its outer perimeter was attacked, but when its interior communications were cut. Japan's principal industries were all in her home islands, her principal sources of raw materials were all overseas, and a more vulnerable situation it is difficult to imagine. A few hours after Pearl Harbor, the United States Navy was ordered to commence unrestricted submarine war on enemy shipping, and the long relentless offensive began against the 6,000,000 tons of the original Japanese merchant fleet — especially its oil tankers. Yet, oddly enough, the Japanese shipbuilding program was inadequately stepped up, and in the years of war (1942-44) only some 90 destroyers and escort craft were built. In consequence, a Japanese convoy system was very slowly developed and was not generally instituted till the autumn of 1943, by which time the Japanese had already lost about half their available tonnage. In the same years of war (1942-44), by contrast, over 200 American submarines were built to give the United States the strongest submarine force in the world, and the greater part of this huge armament operated in the Pacific, in the South and East China Seas. In the entire course of the war the Japanese lost 8,600,000 tons of merchant shipping, of which 90 per cent was sunk by submarines.

During 1943, American surface armament in the Pacific was also gaining the lead. The greater part of the losses at Pearl Harbor had been repaired. The battle of mobilization and production in the United States had been won. Heavy American ground forces had been built up under MacArthur in Australia. The bulk of the United States Navy, including all its aircraft carriers, was now operating west of Hawaii under Admiral Chester W. Nimitz. Correspondingly the Atlantic theater was assigned almost wholly to the British Navy.

The American counteroffensive in the Pacific was fought with an unstinted use of material and an extreme economy of personnel. True to character the Americans relied on their native inventiveness and their machines to bypass territory — and to save life. The campaign was spread over vast, largely empty areas. The Pacific Ocean, as we sometimes forget, covers half the surface of the globe. Panama and Singapore are at nearly antipodal points. From Manila to Honolulu measures 5,000 miles; the length of the Pacific coast from Skagway to Guatemala, or more than twice the length of the Mediterranean; the Solomons from tip to tip measure 1,000 miles, the distance from Baltimore to Miami, or twice the length of Great Britain. Only a highly specialized development of naval architecture and fleet organization could stretch the effective range of warships to meet these conditions. The basic operational unit was the aircraft carrier, the "movable airfield," which extended the navy's striking power and enabled an attack to be delivered on enemy ships and land bases far beyond the reach of normal gunfire. After the Battles of the Coral Sea and Midway, the American naval task force was always built around the aircraft carrier.

The immediate objectives of the offensive were airfields or places where airfields could be made. Naval or aerial bombardment, or both, prepared the way for a landing, a landing if possible at a point some distance from the main center of the enemy's resistance. As was said in the First World War "Artillery conquers, infantry occupies" (*L'artillerie conquiert, l'infanterie occupe*). Infantry stormed ashore from landing craft; bulldozers followed almost at their heels; airstrips were being prepared, and planes were landing, while fighting at the periphery of the bridgehead was still

THE PACIFIC FRONT, 1941-45

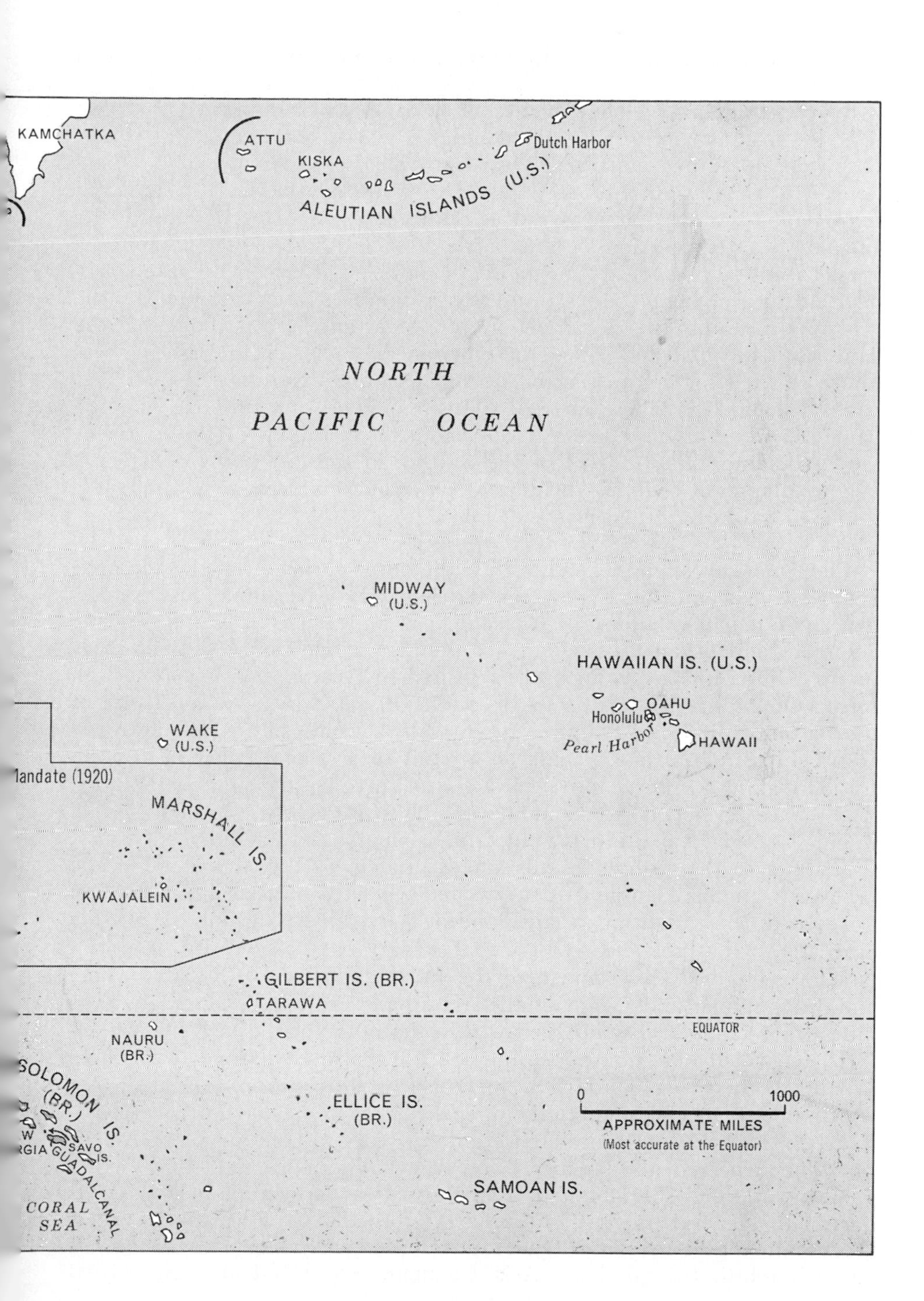
KAMCHATKA
ATTU
KISKA
Dutch Harbor
ALEUTIAN ISLANDS (U.S.)
NORTH
PACIFIC OCEAN
MIDWAY
(U.S.)
HAWAIIAN IS. (U.S.)
OAHU
Honolulu
Pearl Harbor
HAWAII
WAKE
(U.S.)
Mandate (1920)
MARSHALL IS.
KWAJALEIN
GILBERT IS. (BR.)
TARAWA
EQUATOR
NAURU
(BR.)
SOLOMON IS.
(BR.)
SAVO IS.
GUADALCANAL
ELLICE IS.
(BR.)
0
1000
APPROXIMATE MILES
(Most accurate at the Equator)
SAMOAN IS.
CORAL
SEA

continuing. Communications, throughout the action and afterward, were maintained by sea and air, and transport inland was maintained by the ubiquitous and never-failing jeep. The same process was carried on, from island to island, from airfield to airfield, ultimately from Guadalcanal to Okinawa.

By these operations large bodies of Japanese were bypassed and left stranded in their atolls or in inland jungles, where, in MacArthur's words, they were not worth destroying "by assault methods" and could be abandoned "to the various processes of attrition." The Americans were saved innumerable scattered actions. But at points where fighting developed, the Japanese resisted ferociously. One battle after another was remarkable, by Western military standards, for the small numbers of the enemy taken prisoner. In the Japanese code, capture was a disgrace, rarely accepted by the rank and file, and never by an officer. Word was also spread about that the Americans tortured and killed their prisoners. In result the fighting was unprecedented for fanaticism and horror, and often the only weapon that could dislodge a Japanese garrison from its bunkers and pillboxes was the flame thrower. "*Banzai* charges" by detachments of infantry refusing to surrender became almost a part of the routine in the last hours of defense. Whole colonies of civilians, including women and children, were afterwards found to have committed mass suicide.

The American offensive, first against the outer perimeter of the Japanese empire, had begun shortly after the Battle of Midway. On August 7, 1942, American marines landed on Guadalcanal and adjacent islands in the Solomons and began a desperate, six-month struggle for possession. Early in 1943, Buna in New Guinea was captured by Australasian and American forces. On March 1-2, in the Battle of the Bismarck Sea — a repetition of the Battle of the Coral Sea on a larger scale — American aircraft destroyed 10 warships, 12 transports, and 100 aircraft of a second Japanese concentration making for Port Moresby at a cost of three fighters and one bomber. And thence developed the island-hopping "blitz-in-reverse," through Munda in New Georgia, Rabaul in New Britain, Salamaua and Lae in New Guinea, to Tarawa in the Gilbert Islands and Kwajalein in the Marshalls. In the far North, in the Aleutians, Attu was retaken by American and Canadian forces after heavy fighting; a later landing party on Kiska found it already evacuated by its Japanese garrison. In February 1944, a powerful American task force bombed and bombarded the Japanese fortress of Truk. In June and July, Saipan and Guam in the Marianas were seized, less than 1,500 miles from Japan, a distance well within the range of the new B-29 superfortresses which were now appearing over the Pacific. On June 19-21, three Japanese carriers were sunk in the Battle of the Philippine Sea, during which, in a single eight-hour aerial operation, the "Marianas Turkey Shoot," more than 300 Japanese aircraft were destroyed — for the loss of 23 American. The air arm of the Japanese Navy was crippled for good.

Meanwhile the "forgotten front" in Burma was recovering and taking its part in the general progress in the Far Eastern theater. At a conference at Quebec in August 1943, the "Quadrant" Conference, attended by Roosevelt and Churchill, the Southeast Asia Command (SEAC) had been created under Admiral Lord Mountbatten with General Stilwell, Chief of Staff to Chiang Kai-shek as his deputy. The Fourteenth Army under General Sir William J. Slim was concentrated for the reconquest of Burma. During 1944, jungle fighters, trained and led by the British Brigadier Orde Wingate and the American General Frank D. Merrill — amounting in all to some 50,000 men — wholly dependent on air-borne supplies, were operating behind the Japanese lines on the upper Irrawaddy River and in the hill country to the north and west of Myitkyina, harrying Japanese outposts and communications, destroying bridges and ammunition dumps. SEAC never enjoyed generous treatment, and there were always more important fronts to warrant priorities in shipping, landing craft, and other supplies. Nevertheless the Fourteenth Army made a slow advance into the territory round Arakan. Myitkyina, the key town in northern Burma was taken on August 3, 1944, just as the first monsoon rains had begun to break. Shortly afterwards Stilwell returned home to the United States and was succeeded by General Daniel I. Sultan.

The Aerial Assault on Germany

On the night of May 30, 1942, RAF Bomber Command made its first 1,000-plane raid, with Cologne as its target, and followed up, during that summer, with raids of equivalent weight on Essen and other industrial cities of the Ruhr. The United States Eighth Air Force was then being organized in Britain. The air war was developing into an extensive, many-faceted campaign — the bombing of the enemy's naval bases and U-boat pens, participation in the Battle of the Atlantic, mine laying, the transportation of troops and supplies, parachutage to partisan forces in Europe, as well as the bombing of German industry and communications. It required an extensive establishment in ground crews, construction squads, medical services, meteorological services, photographic services, intelligence, and research. It required the constant development of new types of planes and new technical devices — precision sights, radar and other "blind" navigational aids, "pathfinder" tactics. It required a proportionate industrial foundation. In the spring of 1942, the American output was already 3,000 planes a month, and the Canadian aluminum industry was producing 80 per cent of the RAF's aluminum supplies.

Unlike the German raids in the Battle of Britain, the raid was now a sudden mass attack. "Concentrated" attack was defined as attack at the rate of 800 bombers an hour; the subsequent "superconcentrated" or "saturation" attack was defined as attack at the rate of 1,800 bombers an hour, the attack itself lasting 15 to 20 minutes. By 1943, when it was clear that the invasion of France was not yet to be attempted, the aerial assault represented the main part of the Anglo-American war effort in Europe, and "area" bombing for the obliteration of German industry was already the adopted policy. In March 1943, the Battle of the Ruhr began. In four months, over 7,000 tons of bombs were dropped on Essen in six raids, over 5,000 on Duisburg in five, 4,000 on Düsseldorf in two, and 3,500 on Wuppertal in one. At the end of July, over 7,000 tons were dropped on Hamburg in three of the most terrible raids to date. The Hamburg *"Katastrophe,"* as the Germans called it, was the greatest man-made inferno before Hiroshima.

In 1944 RAF Bomber Command's main interest was concentrated on the invasion of France, which we shall describe in Chapter 31. The United States Eighth Air Force in Britain was integrated with the United States Fifteenth Air Force in the Mediterranean to form the United States Strategic Air Force in Europe under General Spaatz. The Tactical Air Force, which had originally been an innovation of the Tunisian campaign, was assigned to immediate invasion targets, and the support of the invasion forces. Strategic targets were fighter-production factories, synthetic rubber and ball-bearing factories, oil refineries, railroad rolling stock and switch-yards, dams and dikes, coastal shipping, river and canal barges, research stations, and later the V-1 and V-2 depots and launching sites. This was also the year which saw so many missions by single fighter bombers, picking off, for example, a Gestapo headquarters in an occupied capital, planting a bomb at the mouth of a railroad tunnel, slicing the arches of a viaduct, or the lock gates of a canal. As the Red Army moved westward, an agreement was reached with the Soviet Government for the use of airfields behind the Soviet lines in Rumania and Poland, and Danubian and Balkan targets could then be bombed en route. But "shuttle bombing," as it was called, might have been more effective with greater Soviet cordiality and cooperation.

The Reich was encircled by Allied air power and it was a power that now seemed unlimited. The 10-ton bomb was first used in March 1945, and the 11-ton bomb was being developed. German cities could be subjected for an hour to an ordeal exceeding that which London had experienced in the whole of the Battle of Britain. Yet the total assessment of this campaign of devastation, both the physical extent and the military value, is still problematical. In the course of the war the RAF attacked some 70 German cities according to a comprehensive and carefully ordered strategic and economic plan. In 23 of these a third or more of the built-up area was destroyed and, in 46, about half of the built-up area was destroyed. In Berlin, nearly 6,500 acres, or 10 square miles, were destroyed. In London, we may note in passing, 600 acres were destroyed, in Plymouth, 400, in Coventry, 100. But it is impossible to estimate how far industrial output was directly or indirectly affected. Factories and railroads were often in full operation within days of a major raid. The output of munitions, according to German claims, reached its maximum in 1944, the year when the aerial assault was at its heaviest. Bombing had additional incidental effects — traffic hold-ups on damaged roads, railroads, and canals, the destruction of workers' housing, and especially the enforced dispersion of industries — without which the output of munitions must surely have been higher. Some million German workers were allocated to clearance and repair and were thus diverted from other occupations. At the same time the loss of civilian life, as in the Battle of Britain, was well below expectation. Total civilian deaths by air raid in Germany throughout the war have been estimated at 305,000.

30. GERMANY AND THE NEW ORDER IN EUROPE

"The War Behind the War"

In Part One of this book, on the First World War, we included a chapter on the belligerent home fronts and described the industrial mobilizations, the wartime controls, the allocations of man power, and the wartime administrations. We selected Britain, Russia, and Germany in particular for our examples. Most of the problems which we discussed were new, and the various national solutions of them – or attempted solutions of them – had to be highly experimental. There were a number of accompanying or consequent political crises, and these occupied a good deal of our attention. Our general theme, in short, was the belligerent world learning the lesson of total war.

In the Second World War these problems were no longer new. Social and industrial mobilization had often been planned, and sometimes accomplished, before the outbreak of war in 1939. Part of this story we have told. (See pp. 474ff.) Nor, except in France and later in Italy, were there decisive political crises. The early disasters, for instance at Dunkirk or Pearl Harbor, did not result in violent governmental changes. In Britain, Chamberlain had resigned in May 1940 after the fighting in Norway, and Churchill was already Prime Minister at the time of Dunkirk and remained Prime Minister till 1945. Roosevelt was President of the United States and was re-elected in 1940 and 1944. We have described the repeal of the arms embargo in September 1939, the "Destroyers-for-Bases" deal in September 1940, Lend-Lease in March 1941, and the concurrent beginnings of Anglo-American cooperation. (See pp. 533-35 and 540.) Pearl Harbor thereafter, we could almost say, became indeed the same sort of inverted triumph for the American people that Dunkirk had been for the British. We have also described the political crises following upon the Fall of France and the fall of the Fascist regime in Italy. Meanwhile, in the Soviet Union, Stalin rode out the four years of the German invasion and its repulse.

A chapter on the home fronts in the present Part Four of this book, therefore, would not seem to be so necessary – with the one outstanding exception perhaps of Germany. This time the controls, mobilizations, and administrations would lend themselves to little more than statistical accounts. But, if there was one episode in the Second World War which could be called the "War behind the War," it was the Nazi New Order in Europe. Here was a complex of events of the greatest historical significance, and we should surely be misconceiving our task not to devote some space to it. And within this complex would also come the collaboration and resistance in the occupied countries, and the governments in exile.

The German Home Front

The initiative at the outbreak of war, both in the military and domestic spheres, was pre-eminently Germany's. It had been so in 1914; it was so again in 1939. "Total war," once predicted by Clausewitz, brought into being by Ludendorff, reached its full development under Hitler. Of all the belligerents in 1939, Germany was the most completely prepared. Her leaders knew just what kind of war they wanted to fight, and they had forged just the kind of weapons with which to fight it. If nothing else, the German war plans of 1939 against Poland, of 1940 against France, and of 1941 against Russia represented a gigantic intellectual and technical achievement.

Years of propaganda and coercion had welded the German people into a cohesive instrument. All parties of dissent had been eliminated. This time there would be no "stab in the back." None the less it was a serious shock to the Nazi leaders that the war, when it came, the great event for which they had labored so incessantly, was so indifferently received by the German people at large. At the crucial test Nazi mysticism conspicuously failed to inspire the spontaneous, single-minded ecstasy of 1914. The popular mood in 1939 was rather of a sullen, nameless dread of the actualities of war. It was as if the German people, for the first time, had awakened to the full realization of the consequences of the regime they had hitherto so heedlessly and so vociferously supported.

The victories in Poland and in the West brought reactions of relief, pride, hopes of an early peace, but no wild elation, no public rejoicing. Casualties in the fighting had been extraordinarily light. Living conditions in Germany meanwhile had not deteriorated. So far the war had been all too easy. Civilian man power, already in short supply, had not been subjected to any special wartime remobilization; and woman power had not been touched at all. The dreaded bomber war had not developed. The first raids by the Royal Air Force – notably the bombing of Berlin on August 25, 1940 – had cast some reflection on Göring's boastful utterances regarding the inviolable defenses of the Reich, but in honesty they had not been very effective. The failure of the Battle of Britain had been easy for propaganda to minimize. The legend of the Führer's infallibility emerged unscathed. They might not rejoice, but the German people in 1940 could still give grateful credit for their many triumphs to the far-seeing and invincible genius of Adolf Hitler.

During the early months of 1941, the constant theme of Nazi propaganda was Germany's indissoluble friendship with the Soviet Union. The very force and reiteration of these protestations should perhaps have been their own warning. The invasion of Russia therefore took the German people by surprise. The Moscow Pact in 1939 had been one *volte-face;* and this was another, for all that it meant a resumption of the former familiar anti-Communist attitude. However, it was not doubted that the Russian campaign would repeat the pattern of the French, if indeed on a larger scale and with heavier casualties. Every military authority in Europe in fact had underestimated the Soviet Union – the British and French had lightheartedly run the risk of involvement in war with the Soviet Union over Finland – and there is evidence that Hitler did not originally deploy his full resources on the Eastern front, but was even directing that several of his war factories should be converted to the production of consumer goods for the benefit of a brave and deserving civilian population. The "brittle state edifice" in Russia would surely fall at the touch of a Nazi blitzkrieg, even as the Third Republic of France had fallen, that once-reputed first-class power and historic custodian of the military art. The German soldier went to battle in 1941 long nourished on the belief that the Red Army, lately purged of its top-ranking officers, was riddled with treachery and that its rank and file were a barbaric horde incapable of discipline and ignorant of modern arms.

Triumphant communiqués from the Eastern front reported, as if by routine, "the mightiest victories in the history of the world." "The enemy is already broken," cried Hitler in a speech on October 3, 1941, "and will never rise again." All that remained for the German Army to do in Russia, it seemed, was a police operation against disorganized enemy units which, in their perversity, refused to surrender. Yet, instead of victory and peace before Christmas, the German people found themselves committed to a conflict of indefinite duration and unlimited sacrifice. At the end of 1941, the German Army in Russia was strewn out across vast, amorphous territories, which had been deliberately "scorched," with its communications stretched to the limit, harried by guerrillas, and digging in for a winter that happened to be one of the earliest and severest on record. That all was not well was indicated by the hasty levy of warm clothing made throughout Germany shortly after Christmas – "Goebbels' jumble sale," as the British newspapers called it. The German home front that winter was full of harrowing rumors, and it was commonly whispered that more German soldiers in Russia were dying from exposure and frostbite than from enemy action.

The upshot was crisis in supply, production – and labor – on a par with that of 1916. (See pp. 38-39.) Generally speaking, preparations which were more than adequate for a short war – that is, for the kind of war in Poland or France – were entirely inadequate for the war now developing in Russia. Reserves of oil, in particular, had been seriously depleted. But it was also found that other essential materials, notably coal, had been allowed to decline. German coal mines in 1941, thanks to the loss of miners to the army, produced 15 per cent, and sometimes 25 per cent, less than in 1940.

But the demand for coal had risen steeply, mainly on account of the lengthened railroad distances on the Eastern front. The railroads were unequal to the emergency calls now made upon them. For some years past, the new motor roads, the *Autobahnen,* and the new commercial airlines had been an attractive diversion of public interest, and the railroads were suffering from serious neglect. There was less rolling stock in Germany in 1941 than in 1914. All the privations inflicted by the Nazis on the German people since 1933 had had a cumulative effect which, by some diabolic fate, suddenly touched bottom in the winter of 1941-42, and it was a winter whose exceptional severities we have mentioned. Plant and machinery had deteriorated from the wear and tear of eight years of intensive use. Maintenance and replacements had always been shelved in the supreme calculation on a successful blitzkrieg.

In January 1942, a national emergency program, recalling the Hindenburg Program of 1916, was initiated. (See p. 39.) Industries not considered important for war purposes were "silenced." Civilian transport was drastically cut, and automobiles began to appear on the roads ingeniously propelled by charcoal gas. But it was soon evident that exceptional measures would have to be taken in the country and that the driving force would have to be provided by the Nazi party itself. In February 1942, Fritz Todt, then Minister of Armaments and Chief of the so-called Organization Todt for the construction of fortifications, was killed in an air crash and was succeeded by Hitler's architect, Albert Speer. The new appointment in the field of home economy had much the same effect as Ludendorff's in 1916. Speer realized that the crisis at bottom was a labor crisis, and his first step was to demand of Hitler, and obtain, unconditional priority for himself over all civilian labor, German and non-German. His aide was the then relatively unknown Fritz Sauckel, former Gauleiter of Thuringia, whom Hitler made Plenipotentiary for Labor Allocation (*Arbeitseinsatz*). A series of almost panic labor decrees followed. The Labor Front threw in its support under the slogan, "Two must do the work of three" (*Zwei für drei*); non-Germans and prisoners of war were increasingly put to work to such an extent that their employment was eventually a major feature in the economy of Hitler's Europe. The Speer-Sauckel partnership was a virtual economic dictatorship.

During 1942, the Nazi authorities tried a variety of experiments to coax higher production out of the German workers, "those faithful and honest comrades on the home front." Medals were given "for outstanding achievements." Existing wage controls prevented any general interference with the basic pay, but piecework rates, overtime rates, and Sunday work were generously introduced. Often extra pay took the far more acceptable form of food. Meanwhile the Gestapo hung about the wings and contributed its own form of encouragement in the arrest and incarceration of grumblers, loafers, and other "promoters of disturbance." By a *Reichstag* resolution of April 26, 1942 – perhaps the most extraordinary of all the Nazi enactments – Hitler assumed the absolute right, "without being tied to existing laws . . . and by all means suitable," to force every German of whatever rank or degree "to fulfill his duties."

As for food, Germany escaped the harsh stringencies which she had suffered in the First World War. Hitler had seen to it that no blockade should afflict the Reich a second time. Rationing of most food stuffs was introduced from August 1939, and, except for consumers subject to deliberate discrimination, the German people enjoyed sufficiency for the entire six years of the war. To be sure there was a threatened change for the worse in the winter of 1941-42, and it seemed for a moment as if the old story of shortages, rising prices, secret hoarding, and ersatz would be repeated – not only in food, but also in clothing and footwear. The rationing, moreover, was largely party-managed, and the average Gauleiter was never the most efficient or honest of administrators. To the situation was now added an element from which the Germany of 1914-18 had been entirely free – a corrupt administration. But generally, in respect to food, the threats of 1941-42 were safely passed. The German conquests yielded their quota of produce. Non-Germans might lack the necessities of life; but as Göring put it: "If, through enemy action, difficulties of food supply arise, then all must know that if there is hunger anywhere it shall in no case be in Germany."

Meanwhile the general tone of Nazi propaganda was changing. Hitler, of course, had promised that the summer campaign of 1942 in Russia would bring the victory denied in 1941. The winter of 1941-42 had been "a hard test, a bitter trial . . . Worse things cannot and will not happen again . . . That we overcame that winter is proof that Providence is well pleased with the German people." But gone was the old exultant assurance. Ultimate peace would now be reached by no quick and simple road. The categorical alternative was no longer between war and peace, but between survival and annihilation. Despite "monster successes" in Russia, the global war was still spreading, and events seemed to have passed beyond human control. "We are being destroyed by our victories" (*Wir siegen uns zu Tode*). By 1942 the United States, the decisive victor of 1918, had once again been added to the foes of the Fatherland. Japan, by compensation, was a distant and incalculable ally. Germany herself had become one element in a widening conflict, in which she no longer held the initiative or was even the only focal point.

Then, at the end of 1942, came the Battle of Stalingrad. An irresistible whispering campaign, by a sort of mass telepathy, had already prepared the German people for the great tragedy before the German High Command published its official admission. The fateful communiqué was broadcast at last to the accompaniment of solemn strains from Wagner's *Götterdämmerung*. A three-day public mourning was proclaimed for the 300,000 heroes of the Sixth Army who, "obedient to the Führer's command", had defended themselves to the last man. The Führer himself, who had normally used every major occasion of the war to deliver a public exposition, was strangely silent. Goebbels was his chief spokesman, and Goebbels, from this moment onward, comes forward undeniably as the most courageous and resourceful of the Nazi leaders. Rumor had it that the Führer had suffered a nervous breakdown. When at last he did appear, on March 21, 1943, his speech lasted only a few minutes, and his voice sounded tired and monotonous. And, by that March, Stalingrad was not the only defeat to be explained away. The fighting in North Africa could hardly be dismissed as "an insignificant reverse" at "the periphery of events."

On January 27, 1943, Sauckel decreed the total mobilization of the home front. Compulsory labor was instituted for men from 16 to 65 years and for women from 17 to 45. Small shops and industries were merged, and employees thereby released were drafted into the army or into munition work. Cumulatively these measures raised 3,500,000 adult native Germans; and in addition some 6,000,000 children were mobilized for light work mainly in small local industries and on the farms. Prisons and concentration camps were converted into "production workshops." On July 25, 1944, just after the attempted assassination of Hitler, Goebbels was appointed "Plenipotentiary for Total War." It is difficult to imagine what more could by then have been squeezed out of the German people, but apparently there was still room for this last and most total of mobilizations; there were still men and women to be taken from schools, universities, domestic service, and the entertainment professions "who were not directly serving the war effort."

On Speer's own testimony the production of munitions increased by 55 per cent by midsummer 1942, in the first six months of his appointment as Minister of Armaments, and doubled by 1943. It reached its peak in the autumn months of 1944, when he claimed he had sufficient equipment in hand for 130 infantry divisions and 40 armored divisions, that is for 2,000,000 men.[1] And Speer achieved these remarkable figures in spite of constant political obstruction, administrative inefficiency, and the steady increase of Allied bombing. Thereafter production sharply declined and continued to decline at an accelerating rate till the surrender in May 1945. (See p. 564.)

"The New Order in Europe"

The ideological sanctions of the New Order in Europe went back to the earliest pronouncements of the Nazi movement. Concepts which belonged to the demented dreamworld of Hitler's *Mein Kampf* or Rosenberg's *Mythus,* incredible on paper, were translated into fact. But as usual there was considerable conflict—and even absence—of plan or doctrine. Here too the detail of Nazi politics, as we have had occasion to notice before, remained very hand-to-mouth; the traditional orderly, formalizing German mind was conspicuously wanting. As one critic tartly remarked, the New Order, in its welter of incongruities, would have been better suited to a British Empire than a German! Thus the map of Europe, as it developed under the expanding occupation, showed all the accidents of its history. Short-term objectives conflicted with long-term; the immediate needs of strategy and economics conflicted with the more permanent requirements of the New Order; deliberately incited national feuds and factions conflicted with the larger possibilities of a united, integrated Europe. Some of the new frontiers seemed to have been drawn to no reason or principle except in so far as they were demonstrative and vindictive reversals of Versailles. The propaganda of the occupation meanwhile, in so far as it was addressed both to Germans and to their vassels, varied with the varying fortunes of the war.

Nazism was always haunted by a sort of historical romanticism. The Third Reich, by its very name, implied a successorship to two other Reichs of ascendant Germandom in former times. There was an alleged coincidence between Nazi Europe and the Europe of the early Middle Ages when once before the Aryan *Herrenvolk* lorded their might over inferior breeds of men – Normans and Burgundians in France, Visigoths in Spain, Lombards in Italy, Scandinavians in the Baltic, and Teutonic Knights in Poland. The armistice of 1940 in France was not only a strategic instrument but a delimitation between "Frankish" and "Latin" France. The occupied territories often looked like medieval fiefs organized for the benefit of their new Teutonic barons. Italy was suitably relegated to her medieval role of leadership in the Mediterranean under the superior direction of a Transalpine Empire.

The treatment meted out to individual occupied territories varied according to race and, to a less extent, according to the degree of opposition they had offered to their conquerors. Thus Danes and Luxembourgers, who ranked as "Aryans" and had succumbed without resistance, were offered virtual German citizenship. The Danes were so favored indeed as to be obliged to join the Anti-Comintern Pact. The French – "the Latinized, Negroidized, Hebraicized French" – were only fit to fall into deserved decay. The worst treatment of all was reserved for peoples like the Poles, who were not only inferior in the "hierarchy of blood" but who had also dared defend themselves against their rightful masters. A policy of divide and rule revived the nationalistic differences between Flemings and Walloons, French and Bretons, Czechs and Slovaks, Serbs and Croats, Bulgars and Greeks.

Roughly, there were some seven categories of administration in the New Order:

First, there were the territories annexed and wholly incorporated into Germany: Austria, the Sudetenland, Memel, Danzig, and Teschen; "Wartheland," Bialystok, and extensions of East and West Prussia; part of Slovenia; Alsace and Lorraine (attached respectively to Baden and to Saar-Pfalz), Luxembourg (attached to Coblenz-Trier), and Eupen-Malmédy-Moresnet (attached to Aachen).

Second, there were territories, not incorporated into Germany, but regarded as parts of "Greater Germany" and designated for future German "colonization": the Protectorate of Bohemia-Moravia, administered by a Reich Protector (at first Neurath); and the Government General ("residual" Poland), administered by the Governor General (Hans Frank). In this category might also be included the two "Commissariats," Ostland and Ukraine, administered by German commissioners responsible to a Reich Minister for Eastern Occupied Territories (Alfred Rosenberg).

Third, there were the territories under military occupation, administered

AXIS-OCCUPIED TERRITORIES IN EUROPE

1 SUDETENLAND **2** WARTHELAND **3** BIALYSTOK **4** Extension of EAST PRUSSIA **5** Extension of WEST PRUSSIA **6** Part of SLOVENIA **7** ALSACE **8** LORRAINE **9** EUPEN-MALMÉDY-MORESNET **10** PROTECTORATE OF BOHEMIA-MORAVIA **11** MACEDONIA **12** TRANSYLVANIA **13** BESSARABIA **14** TRANSNISTRIA **15** THRACE **16** DOBRUJA **17** MONTENEGRO **18** ADRIADISCHES KÜSTENLAND **19** ALPENVORLAND

Territories incorporated into Germany: Austria, Sudetenland, Memel, Danzig, Teschen, Eupen-et-Malmédy, Luxembourg (LUX.), Alsace, Lorraine, part of Slovenia, Wartheland, and Bialystok. West Prussia and East Prussia were enlarged. Alpenvorland and Adriatrisches Küstenland were formed in 1943 after the collapse of Italy.

Territories not incorporated into Germany, but regarded as part of "Greater Germany." The Protectorate of Bohemia-Moravia, and the Government General of Poland.

by German military governors: Occupied France and the Channel Islands; Belgium; the Serbian "rump"; Greece (jointly administered with Italy), Macedonia, Crete and the Aegean Islands; and the Crimea.

Fourth, there were "autonomous" territories, favored with special administrations: the "model protectorate" of Denmark (at first under her own King and parliament); Norway, under a Reich Commissioner (Joseph Terboven), assisted by a Norwegian cabinet (under Vidkun Quisling); the Netherlands, under another Reich Commissioner (Seyss-Inquart), assisted by a Dutch cabinet; and Unoccupied France with its government at Vichy.

Fifth, there were the "legionnaire" or satellite states: Slovakia; Hungary, including part of Transylvania; Rumania, including Bessarabia and "Transnistria"; Bulgaria, including Thrace and parts of Serbia and the Dobruja; and Finland.

Sixth, there was the Italian portion of the New Order, the territories under Italian military governors: the French Alpine frontier, Albania, Greece (jointly administered with Germany); "Croatia" (under Pavelich); and a recreated Montenegro.

Seventh, there were two small military districts created by Germany after the fall of Italy in 1943: the Adriatic Littoral (*Adriatisches Küstenland*); and the Alpine Foreland (*Alpenvorland*).

Generally two lines of economic policy were followed. The first was the obvious short-term policy of spoliation. Raw materials, armaments, machinery, rolling stock, foodstuffs, anything in short which could be described as having an immediate military value, were seized, dispatched to Germany, or otherwise held at the disposal of the conqueror's commissariat. The second was the less obvious long-term policy of building up a united, integrated Europe. In this second policy, as we have said, there seemed to be no detailed plan or even consistent doctrine, though, in general, Greater Germany was expected to include the main industrial areas. She would be "the steely core, . . . a block of one hundred million people, indestructible, without flaw or alien element, the firm foundation of our power." Thence would radiate outer rings of vassal states, sources of raw materials, unfinished goods, and agricultural products natural to them. A centralized, balanced, self-sufficient economy would thus supersede the old liberal, national-

---

Territories under German military administration: Belgium and a part of northern France, Occupied France and Brittany, Serbia, Macedonia, the Aegean Islands, Crete, and the Russian Operational Base including the Crimea.

Territories under Italian military administration: Mentone and the French Alpine frontier territories, Corsica and Greece.

German-controlled territories under semicivilian administration: Denmark, Norway, Holland, Unoccupied France, Reich Commissariat Ostland, and Reich Commissariat Ukraine.

Italian-controlled territories: Albania, Dalmatia, Croatia, and Montenegro.

Satellite States: Slovakia, Hungary including Transylvania, Rumania including Bessarabia and Transnistria, Bulgaria including Thrace and part of the Dobruja, and Finland.

istic anarchy, and a universal, unassailable prosperity for all would be assured.

The official bodies entrusted with these policies were largely *ad hoc* affairs, much like the tasks they undertook. The Office of the Four-Year Plan and the Ministries of Armaments, Economics, and Food in Berlin exercised some sort of coordination; the lesser agencies and inspectorates in the occupied territories were various to the point of chaos. Local administrations, if they were prepared to be collaborative, were invariably retained – though, of course, under German supervision – and it was probably they more than any other single factor which kept the crazy, overburdened structure of the New Order from collapsing under its own weight. But the main instrument of control and enforcement available to the central power in Berlin was finance. In other words Germany evolved a huge system of "paying" for the goods she desired to seize at rates fixed by herself, and this strange procedure of "plunder by accountancy" had all the appearance of legality and good faith.

Financial controls, exercised by the so-called *Reichskreditkassen,* were imposed in all the occupied territories, and the imposition was made easier by the fact that, in most of the countries concerned, lately sufferers and participants themselves in the critical state of world economics, controls of one kind or another existed already. All the curious financial techniques, especially in respect of foreign exchange, which the Nazis had perfected in the years 1933-39, were extended throughout Europe. Often it was enough to reinstate the native personnel of the banks of a particular country or region and, with a few, but all-important instructions, permit them to carry on their business. Of course, gold reserves were seized when and where they could be found. Occupation costs were charged to every "hostile" country. In France, for example, the annual German occupation costs exactly equalled France's war budget of 1940. Clearly the Germans were guided by France's "capacity to pay" and probably relished the poetic justice of using France's war budget against herself. At the same time the Germans were legatees to a whole variety of "windfalls" as they called them – arising from the confiscation of Jewish, anti-Nazi, and Allied properties, from collective fines levied on municipalities for "acts of hostility," and from the reimbursement of German reparations paid between 1920 and 1932. All in all the Germans were able to accumulate huge credits with which to meet their requisitions in whatever industry or enterprise that took their insatiable fancy.

The shortage of labor, which developed on all home fronts in the First World War, was already in some evidence in Germany before 1939, and in 1942, as we have seen, had become the basic economic problem. At the same time one of the immediate effects of the war was to create serious unemployment in all the invaded countries. It was a similar situation in 1916 which had induced the German High Command of that day to resort to the Belgian deportations. As was so often the case, the First World War provided the precedent and education for the Second; but in the Second World War the wholesale deportations in occupied Europe were used not only as an economic, but also as a political weapon. Germany's conquests in 1940-42 delivered millions of native levies and prisoners of war into her hands, and all Europe was soon a laboratory in which *Herrenvolk* and *Hilfsvolk,* the master race and its modern helotry, worked out their appropriate relations to one another. The result was a forcible displacement of populations unprecedented since the time of ancient Assyria and Babylon.

The Government General of Poland was significantly termed an *Arbeitsreich.* Plans for the exploitation of Polish labor had been prepared several months in advance of the invasion in 1939 and were put into force by the Governor General, Hans Frank. In normal times there had always been a certain amount of seasonable Polish migration into East Prussia. Voluntary recruitment on similar lines was tried at first, but then abandoned, and the Poles were rounded up by SS raiding squads – in the streets, in their homes, in railroad stations, and in churches. These unfortunates in the thousands were herded together at assembly points resembling concentration camps, crowded onto trains, and transported to Germany often in open trucks without the elements of sanitation and often during zero and sub-zero weather. A high percentage, sometimes as much as a quarter, arrived at their destinations so incapacitated by their treatment that they often had to be sent back – under the same conditions as they had already suffered. Once in Germany, they were housed and fed on the general principle of "exploitation to the highest possible extent at the lowest conceivable degree of expenditure." Terror was the incentive of production; starvation, lack of medical care, excessive work, as well as the more positive forms of physical torture were the ordinary incidentals of existence. Violations of discipline, malingering, attempts to escape were punishable by transfer to a concentration camp or, "in especially severe cases," by "special treatment" – special treatment being the euphemism for hanging. In the words of Arthur Greiser, Gauleiter of Wartheland, "For us Polish nationality is only labor power and nothing more."

The policy begun in Poland was extended in the wake of military operations to the West and then to the Russian East. The deportees were put to all kinds of work – agriculture, road and railroad repair, coal mining, industries including armaments, and fortifications. Western deportees on the whole, as a tribute to their higher "civilization" and technical skills, usually received better treatment, but the general conditions of forced labor, especially after the labor crisis of 1942, applied to all races without discrimination. Puppet administrations lent their aid, and many a collaborator owed his job to his resourcefulness as procurer of the required human commodity. In Holland, appropriately, the deportations went by the name of "Operation Sauckel." On March 23, 1943, it was announced that the two-thousandth train carrying the millionth Polish worker had left the Government General. In September 1943, at the end of his first six months as Plenipotentiary for Labor Allocation, Sauckel reported to his Führer that 3,638,056 foreign workers had been fed into Germany's war economy. The total figure of this displacement of peoples has been put at 7,500,000, of which in Sauckel's own admission, "not even 200,000 came voluntarily."

"Germanization" was defined at Nuremberg as "the obliteration of the former national character of the conquered territories and the extermination of all elements which could not be reconciled with the Nazi ideology." The policy went hand in hand with the economic and demographic spoliation we have been describing. Its character and method were sufficiently indicated from the fact that it was put in charge of Himmler, whom Hitler, in October 1939, appointed Reich Commissioner for the Consolidation of Germandom (*Reichskommissar für die Festigung des deutschen Volkstums*). The peripheral areas of Greater Germany were designated for his operations, the ultimate objective being the creation of that "steely [German] core . . . without alien element, the firm foundation of our power."

Indigenous Germans or *Volksdeutsche,* already inhabitants in these peripheral areas, were usually former members of local Nazi parties. During preinvasion days, they had constituted a fifth column and, after the invasion, they received their reward in special positions and privileges. The fate of non-Germans in these areas was deportation, enslavement to the Nazi war machine, or eventual "extermination through work." The word *genocide* has been coined for "the destruction of a nation or of an ethnic group." Particularly must the intelligentsia be removed – for example, "the Polish intelligentsia and clergy, who have been politically active in the past" and who had provided the political, patriotic, and religious leadership of the state. "Thanks to the heroic courage of our soldiers," wrote Hans Frank in his diary, "[Poland] has become German, and the time will come when the valley of the Vistula, from its source to its mouth at the sea, will be as German as the valley of the Rhine."

Germanization was applied in varying degrees in the South and West. The Slovenes, for reasons which have never been clear, were marked out for the same destructive treatment as the Poles. General deportations occurred in the Sudetenland, in Memel, and in other hitherto "German" Baltic cities. In Alsace-Lorraine "racially alien elements" were expelled, at first to France, and then, after the labor crisis of 1942, to Germany. A small French minority which opted for German citizenship was sent to "re-education" camps. Probably some 500,000 Alsatians and Lorrainers were deported in all, and their properties confiscated for the benefit of "loyal elements" or German settlers.

Jews in the occupied territories suffered the fate of their brethren in the Reich. All the satellite countries, notably Hungary and Rumania, where the Jews had always been so important a part of the population, introduced anti-Semitic legislation. The detail and chronology of the Jewish liquidation in Europe may have varied from place to place and from time to time, but there is no doubt of its thoroughness and deliberation. Generally "usable" Jews would be screened from the "unusable," the "usable" being earmarked for deportation to factories or labor camps and the "unusable" being segregated into ghettos or other reservations for extermination.

The mass slaughter of human beings raises considerable mechanical, sanitary, and aesthetic problems. Some of the ghettos were reduced by starvation, some by military action, some by a combination of both. In April 1943, the ghetto in Warsaw, for example, with its remnant of 60,000 Jews, was systematically destroyed by SS and *Wehrmacht* units in an operation that lasted several days, and the "pluck, courage, and devotion to duty" displayed by these forces against a desperate and destitute people was afterward recorded in an ornate, illustrated, leather-bound volume, signed by SS Brigade-führer Jürgen Stroop, commander of the *Grossaktion,* as he called it, and presented by him to the Governor General Hans Frank. But the principal instrument of mass murder was the extermination camp (*Vernichtungslager*), such as at Auschwitz, Mauthausen, or Treblinka, with its gas chambers and crematoriums.

This part of the history of the New Order in Europe is now well enough known, often from the Nazis' own meticulous records of it, records which themselves remain so characteristic a feature of the Nazi mentality. We possess authentic accounts of the careers of Adolf Eichmann, chief of the Jewish Office of the Gestapo; Dr. Sigmund Rascher, the medical experimenter; Joseph Kramer, the "Beast of Belsen"; Rudolf Hoess, commandant at Auschwitz, who afterwards testified to his part in the taking of 3,000,000 human lives, and many others. The total death roll under the Third Reich at the thirty principal Nazi concentration camps has been estimated at over 7,000,000. The Jewish genocide amounted to 5,700,000. "A thousand years will pass," cried Hans Frank, Governor General of Poland, after his trial at Nuremberg, "and the guilt of Germany will not be erased!"

Collaboration

In most of the occupied countries the Germans were able to find native officials, industrialists, bankers, teachers, writers, and artists who took kindly to their rule. There were also leaders and members of local Nazi parties – Moravec in the Protectorate, Degrelle in Belgium, Mussert in Holland, Clausen in Denmark, Quisling in Norway – the last of whom gave his name to the entire tribe. The motives of these men were mixed and complex. Some loved their earthly possessions; some seized the opportunity for power; some believed they could best protect the interests of their country by remaining at their posts; some were sincere converts to Nazism; most were ordinary, frightened, bewildered mortals swept into situations beyond their control. As a general rule, whereas the resistance, as we shall relate, so often had a revolutionary left-wing tendency, genuine collaboration was invariably of the Right. But, again as a general rule, collaboration was mainly helpful to the Germans in the early period of the occupation. After the labor deportations and after the German military reverses of 1942 and 1943, the inevitable doubts, desertions, and revolts set in. We should note that, of all the occupied territories, in Poland alone there was no collaboration at any time during the war.

The classic home of collaboration was Vichy. On July 11, 1940, at Vichy in Unoccupied France, a National Assembly consisting of what was left of the French Chamber and Senate, overwhelmingly voted Marshal Pétain full powers to promulgate a new constitution for France. The next day Pétain assumed the title of Chief of State, repealed the constitution of 1875, and indefinitely adjourned the Chamber and Senate. He appointed Pierre Laval his Vice-Premier. On October 24, at Montoire, on the initiative of Laval, he met Hitler and Ribbentrop in conference and "formally and irrevocably entered upon the path of collaboration." Laval for his pains was made Foreign Minister. Vichy at once began to adopt the features of dictatorship. A new watchword, "Work, Family, Country" replaced the former "Liberty, Equality, Fraternity." "The French State" (*État français*) superseded the word "Republic." Familiar totalitarianisms were introduced, the usual censorships and controls, the usual anti-Communist and anti-Semitic enactments – and, of course, the cult of the new leader, Pétain. Meanwhile, beneath the show and the make-believe, the real government was carried on by the surviving civil service.

The personality, and indeed the personal appeal, of Pétain, find no simple, rational explanation. Certainly he was old, fatalistic, broken to the point of insensitiveness. Yet, in moments of self-assertion, he could still try to resist the harshest forms of Nazi pressure and intimidation. In December 1940, at the height of the expulsions of population from Alsace-Lorraine, he summarily dismissed Laval and sent a note to Hitler defining the extent of his willingness to collaborate. But, under threat from the Germans in Paris, Laval was succeeded by Flandin, and, some weeks later, Flandin in turn was succeeded by Admiral Jean Darlan. Flandin had been almost Germanophile; Darlan, ever since the destruction of the French fleet at Oran, was violently Anglophobe; and in their twin hands the path of collaboration could only become smoother, broader, and steeper. Laval, now under German protection in Paris, intrigued for his own return and advancement.

The United States remained in diplomatic relations with Vichy – and so also did Canada, Australia, and New Zealand. Vichy, after all, in the view of the State Department, was the legal successor of the Third Republic, and there might be something to be gained, and nothing lost, by maintaining a link therewith. At the end of 1940, Admiral William D. Leahy came to Vichy as ambassador and personal representative of President Roosevelt. He remained till April 1942, exerting himself to minimize the influence of Darlan, effecting some relief from the British blockade, and sending his President priceless information on the ever shifting situation in France and Europe. Meanwhile Vichy's breach with Britain seemed to be final, though there were several secret, if ineffective, contacts between them.

There is no need to follow the story of Vichy in all its detail. It was a long, dull battle of wits between Laval, Darlan, and Pétain, the last named gradually failing in energy and influence. The Germans held all the realities of power and, though they began by using that power with discretion, the political deterioration in France was an inevitable process. The people, both of Occupied and Unoccupied France, suffered great privations. The social and economic barrier between the two zones was rigidly maintained. Worst of all, nearly 2,000,000 Frenchmen were prisoners of war in the hands of an enemy who did not scruple to use them as a kind of blackmail. The mere absence of these men from their homes for six years disastrously depressed the nation's birth rate – as, no doubt, the Germans intended it should do. Former "Leaguers" Marcel Déat and Jacques Doriot, tried to form political parties with totalitarian principles, collaborating with Germany, the main difference between them apparently being that Déat opposed, and Doriot supported, Pétain's government. But they managed to recruit a contingent, the so-called Tricolor Legion, whose members wore a Nazi type of uniform, pledged fealty to Hitler, and served against the Soviet Union on the Eastern front.

The pace quickened during 1941. The French resistance movement, born at the time of the Battle of Britain, took increased encouragement from the war in Russia. Underground newspapers with appropriate titles, *Combat, Franc-Tireur, Libération, L'Humanité,* were circulated in their thousands. Attacks on German soldiers in Occupied France led the German Military Governor, General Otto von Stuelpnagel,[2] to retaliate by shooting hostages — fifty Frenchmen for every German killed. Terror bred terror, and the Germans began to lose confidence in Darlan's ability to cope with the spreading unrest. From Germany, Speer and Sauckel were casting avid eyes on the unemployed French masses.

In April 1942, a series of meetings between Pétain, Darlan, and Laval, under the watchful eyes of Otto Abetz, Hitler's ambassador to France, concluded with the formation of a new government at Vichy. Pétain entrusted Laval with the "effective direction of internal and foreign policy" and made him the virtual dictator of Unoccupied France. The discredited Darlan was not a member of the new government, but he remained Commander in Chief of the armed forces and successor designate of Pétain. Laval's term of office was punctuated with the derailing of trains, the blowing up of bridges, assassinations, and the inevitable executions of hostages. But he fulfilled to the best of his ability the object that the Germans had in mind when they supported his return to power. He opened an intensive propaganda campaign to induce French workers to volunteer for service in Germany, and he was promised a proportionate return of French prisoners of war in exchange. Even so, the campaign achieved so meager a result that, in February 1943, compulsory recruitment was decreed. But, by that date, the Anglo-American landings had taken place in North Africa, and Vichy was absorbed into Occupied France.

The "Free" Movements and the Governments in Exile

Meanwhile, official governments of countries overrun by the Nazis were often able to establish themselves in exile. They were joined by as much of their combatant and merchant navies as could evade capture, and their territorial possessions and assets abroad were pooled with the Allied war chest. They built up fighting contingents. They engaged in propaganda, notably broadcast appeals and news services to their homelands. They kept in touch with their national resistance movements. They were beneficiaries of American Lend-Lease.

In 1940 King Haakon of Norway and Queen Wilhelmina of the Netherlands with their respective families and governments made good their escape. King Christian of Denmark and his government remained in Denmark, but a Danish Council was organized in London late in 1940 and rallied all Free Danes to itself. King Leopold of the Belgians remained a voluntary prisoner of war in German hands, but the Belgian Government eventually reached London. A Czechoslovak National Committee was set up in London with Beneš as President and Jan Masaryk, the son of the late Thomas Masaryk and lately Czech minister in London, as Foreign Minister and, in 1941, after the German invasion of Russia, it was recognized by Britain and the Soviet Union. During 1941, King Peter of Yugoslavia and his government were established in London; and King George of the Hellenes and his government were established in part in London and in part in Cairo.

After the Fall of France, General de Gaulle was recognized by the British Government as the "leader of all Free Frenchmen wherever they may be, who rally to him in support of the Allied cause." But his French National Committee in London was not granted the recognition of a government in exile. The United States cold-shouldered him even after December 1942, when it broke off relations with Vichy. Certainly de Gaulle was not a man of sympathetic personal appeal, and his politics was an unknown quantity. Yet courage and dignity he did not lack, and he made himself the symbol of French patriotism and morale. The greater part of French Equatorial Africa – with the unhappy exception of Dakar – came over to his side. Free French forces took part in operations in Syria and in many forays by sea and air – and eventually in the invasion of 1944.

The most tangled and tragic of all the histories of the governments in exile was that of Poland. On September 30, 1939, with the authority of President Moscicki, then a refugee in Rumania, a Polish Government was formed in Paris with Ladislas Raczkiewicz, former Marshal of the Sejm, as President and General Ladislas Sikorski as Premier and Commander in Chief. Units of the Polish Navy and several Polish merchant ships had already escaped to English ports. Some hundreds of Poles fought in the Battle of France, and scores of Polish pilots in the Battle of Britain. In 1940, after the Fall of France, the Polish Government was transferred to London.

In exile, Polish affairs proceeded smoothly enough – at first. In December 1941, Sikorski visited Moscow and signed with Stalin a Soviet-Polish "Declaration of Friendship and Mutual Assistance." Sikorski twice visited the United States to negotiate Lend-Lease aid and to rally the support of Polish Americans. In London he was on the best of terms with Beneš and the Czechoslovak Committee. But Polish relations with the Soviet Union were already deteriorating in 1942. The Polish General Anders, organizing a Polish army in the Soviet Union, was soon finding difficulties over supplies and rations, and he eventually agreed to evacuate his force via Persia to the Middle East, where it was to see distinguished service. In Poland a fierce antagonism was developing between rival resistance groups, that is between the so-called People's Guard of Communist origins and the so-called Home Army of Socialist origins. The Soviet Government supported the People's Guard, whereas the Polish Government in London, largely composed of the old squirearchical elements, rather lukewarmly supported the Home Army and uncompromisingly abhorred the People's Guard. Then, after Stalingrad, when it appeared that the Red Army might recover the lost Soviet territories, the old problem of the Soviet-Polish frontier – a problem safely academic in 1940-41 – became of urgent and unavoidable practical importance. In April 1943, over Radio Berlin, the Germans announced the discovery of the bodies of 10,000 Polish officers buried in a common grave at Katyn, a village near Smolensk, prisoners of the Red Army's advance into Poland in 1939 and allegedly massacred by the NKVD in the spring of 1940. Polish-Soviet relations were at once broken off.

On July 4, 1943, at the height of the Katyn affair, General Sikorski was killed in an air crash and was succeeded as Premier by Stanislas Mikolajczyk of the Peasant party, hitherto Vice Premier. In the same month the Soviet Government recognized the so-called Lublin Administration, organized by the People's Guard – now the People's Army – as the future government of liberated Poland. In November 1943, at the Teheran Conference, Churchill and Stalin agreed that the Curzon Line should be the eastern frontier of Poland and that Poland should acquire compensation up to the Oder. The agreement was verbal, Roosevelt was not party to it, and it was not explicitly revealed; but Churchill afterward announced a virtual recognition of it in the House of Commons in the course of one of his periodic reviews of the war.

The Polish-Soviet dispute was a sore embarrassment to the Allied cause. It was the first indication of the eventual rift between East and West. The Kremlin was already resolved to impose its own political pattern on Intermediate Europe and to cure, by force or friendship, the historic anti-Russianism of its western neighbors. And to every protest it could always return the short answer of its own military predominance, present or prospective, in the territories in question. The final act was the German massacre of the Polish Home Army in Warsaw in August 1944 – apparently with the cynical connivance of the Soviet Government – at the very moment that Mikolajczyk was visiting Moscow. (See p. 594.)

In November 1944, Mikolajczyk resigned. It was clear that the Polish Government in London could have little further influence with its former Anglo-American allies. Early in 1945, the Lublin Administration transformed itself into a Provisional Government of the Polish Republic with Soviet recognition. At the Yalta Conference in that February, Allied diplomacy gave its seal of approval to the existing situation.

Resistance

The story of the resistance is not suited to a chronicle. The popular mythology which has grown up around it, however well deserved, has only dramatized certain of its exceptional incidents. Generally it was a story of day-to-day routines by unknown individuals, the story of a kind of valor that, in the nature of the case, had to be anonymous and unrecorded.

The resistance took many forms, from simple boycott to full-scale guerrilla warfare. It was not given to every patriot to kill an SS man, but the more peaceful ways of non-cooperation were as various as human ingenuity. In the long, dreary, nerve-racking siege it was something for a man to keep himself and his hopes alive. For the more active spirits there was the spreading of information, usually obtained from the BBC (British Broadcasting Corporation); there was an underground journalism of over a hundred regular resistance papers; there was the secret "grapevine" to assist the escape of Allied airmen and prisoners of war; there was unlimited espionage. Workers in the factories, especially in the factories producing war material, would "go slow" and depress output even in cases where the working week was extended to 100 hours. It was impossible to supervise every worker and every manual operation. The most precise and ruthless inspection could not prevent "dud" shells and bombs from being delivered to the depots. Workers removed essential parts of machines; they put powdered glass into lubricating oil and sugar into gasoline; they started fires and explosions. In the country at large, peasants and agricultural laborers hid or spoiled their crops. Saboteurs blew up roads, railroads, and bridges and wrecked telephone, telegraph, and electric power lines. The resistance was gradually organized; special personnel were trained in England and parachuted into occupied territories with radio sets, arms, and explosives. Toward the second half of the war, and especially just before the Allied invasion of Normandy, the resistance was being directed like a regular military operation.

But there were aspects of the resistance more apposite to our theme. In course of time, and especially as it became organized, the resistance became a political as much as a military movement, and it was linked with political parties. Thus the resistance not only fought the foreign enemy, but it fought to create a better state of things to fill the vacuum when that enemy was defeated and expelled; and there were many views as to what that better state of things should be. The inspiration and even the tactics of the resistance varied with the background of the resister. Many industrial workers already had a history of resistance behind them and a conscious class solidarity, and they had special opportunities for sabotage. The first cells of the resistance often grew out of the trade unions. The Communists were already acquainted with the cell system and with all the technique of underground activity. The churches, with their memories of persecution and martyrdom, provided another ready-made organization. Catholics found apt use for their doctrines of sanctuary, secrecy of the confessional, and inviolability of the priesthood. But political and ecclesiastical partisanship reflected too often the complexities of the former peacetime state. The situation varied from Denmark, Norway, or the Protectorate with their unified resistance to Yugoslavia or Greece, where the factions in the resistance fought one another as well as their common enemy and where, in addition, they became embroiled in the power politics of their greater allies. In addition, it often happened that the resistance in a country took an extreme revolutionary form, while that country's official government in exile was reactionary. The consequences were later in painful evidence if the resistance afterward arrogated to itself the functions of the first liberation government.

The Protectorate of Bohemia-Moravia was marked out from the first for special mistreatment, and the resistance in it was roused or cowed accordingly. In March 1939, Hitler had appointed Neurath Protector, directly responsible to himself. Neurath's Secretary of State and the real driving force in the earlier history of the occupation was the Sudeten German and former supporter of Konrad Henlein, Karl Hermann Frank (not to be confused with Hans Frank, the Governor General of Poland). Dr. Emil Hacha remained "President" of a "Committee of National Trusteeship" of fifty subservient Czech colleagues with entirely phantom prerogatives, and made periodic and ineffectual appeals to the Czech people "to realize their changed condition and to accept the advantages of their incorporation into Greater Germany." Henlein extended his party network over the territory, and all other parties ceased to exist. The Nuremberg anti-Semitic laws were introduced. Local Germans were granted special privileges and were regarded as the aristocracy of the Protectorate.

Hitler evidently purposed the total strategic and cultural destruction of the "Bohemian Bastion," and his campaign was made the more barbarous by his insane hatred of a people whom he had once injured. A long-term program of Germanization was directed especially against the cultural life of the Czech people. Czech universities were closed to Czechs; Czech learned and historical societies, as well as the *Sokol,* the famous physical-culture institution, were dissolved; Czech libraries and art galleries were rifled of their treasures. Great numbers of Czech schools were closed and, in the few that remained open, the children were subjected to Nazi educational methods on the general thesis that the "Masaryk-Beneš period" was a historical aberration which a benign Führer had now been sent to rectify. National holidays, national colors, national songs were prohibited; several national monuments and memorials were demolished. Former members of the Czech Legion were deprived of their pensions. Clergy were arrested, monastic orders dissolved, and ecclesiastical properties confiscated. Intellectuals in concentration camps in 1940 were estimated at 70,000.

But the Czechs with their long history of revolt were not ready to submit without a struggle. Student demonstrations, which ended all too tragically, were staged as early as October 1939. The war in Russia in 1941 was the signal for the first serious cases of sabotage on the part of Czech munition workers in the Skoda factories. In September 1941, Neurath, who did not seem to have the heart to deal with the situation, went on extended leave on grounds of ill health, and effective control passed to Reinhard Heydrich, head of the SD and one of the most savage of Himmler's lieutenants, who at once initiated a reign of terror. (See pp. 360-61.) In 1942 Heydrich became the instrument of the labor deportations in the Protectorate, but on May 27, a grenade was thrown at his car as he was driving through one of the less frequented suburbs of Prague, and he died of his wounds some days later. A state of emergency was declared, and a reward of 10,000,000 crowns ($250,000) was offered for information leading to the apprehension of his assailants. Executions took place daily of persons young and old, eminent and obscure, charged with complicity. The village of Lidice, where one of the assailants had allegedly hidden, was razed to the ground, and its inhabitants massacred. The Berlin radio afterward announced that the wanted men had been shot in a skirmish in an old disused church. Heydrich's successor as head of the SD was another of Himmler's creatures, Ernst Kaltenbrunner.

The resistance in Yugoslavia reared its head from the first days of the occupation. Colonel Draza Mihailovich organized his "Chetniks" on the model of the Serb bands which, in times past, had risen up to fight the invader. They were composed of independent, scattered guerrillas, largely drawn from regulars of the disbanded Yugoslav Army, many of whom were soon waging war on the Germans and Bulgars and on native nonconformists. Mihailovich attempted no large-scale fighting but chose rather to husband his few resources for eventual harrying operations on the flank of the future Allied liberation. Indiscriminate massacre by the Germans, after his every raid, was its own validation of his limited strategy. Furthermore he was an ardent Serb nationalist and monarchist, anti-Croat, an opponent of federalism in Yugoslavia, and, more important still, a bitter enemy of Communism.

The German invasion of Russia in 1941 was accompanied by new partisan activity and counter-terrorism in Yugoslavia, and there emerged therefrom the resistance group of Joseph Broz, afterward known as Tito. The new leader was a Croat by birth and a blacksmith by early occupation. He had deserted from the Austro-Hungarian Army in the First World War, had subsequently fought in the Russian Civil War, and had returned to his homeland a trained and disciplined agitator for the Communist cause. He had spent his term in prison and "underground." As soon as the war in 1941 had become meaningful to the Communists, his role was obvious, and he set out to capture the upsurging resistance in his country for his own purposes.

At a meeting in the early autumn of 1941, Tito and Mihailovich agreed on joint action against their mutual enemy, but not on the division of their commands. Divergent purposes engendered distrust and, before the end of the year, the two leaders and their respective forces were feuding openly. Mihailovich's influence thereafter began to fall away, and, during 1943, after circumstantial reports that he was collaborating with the Germans and sometimes with the Italians, Churchill took the initiative in transferring Anglo-American aid exclusively to his rival. Accordingly Tito organized an "Anti-Fascist Council for National Liberation," and this Council, purportedly gathered from the whole country and representing all the democratic parties, spread its hierarchy of committees into such villages and districts as the fortunes of the day allowed it to command. In November 1943, the Council assumed the status of a government with Tito, now styling himself Marshal, as its effective head, and it proceeded to pass resolutions forbidding King Peter and the members of the Yugoslav government in exile to return home till the people had decided for themselves their constitutional future.

The Yugoslav government in exile in London, meanwhile, was too torn by dissension to be able to offer constructive leadership to, or impose its authority on, the embittered factions in Yugoslavia. In June 1944, however, under British pressure, King Peter at last agreed not to return home until a plebiscite had been held, and he sent his latest Premier, Ivan Subasich, to negotiate with Tito. In July, a "cabinet" was formed representing the interests of both the King and Tito, and a joint subordinate body was charged with coordinating matters involving the war, foreign affairs, and reconstruction. In August 1944, pursuant to this policy of cooperation, King Peter designated Tito as sole leader of the Yugoslav forces of resistance. But the Red Army was now on the borders of Yugoslavia. Tito secretly flew to Moscow and made his own independent bargain with the prospective liberators of his country. In October 1944, Belgrade was free, and Tito was in complete control.

The Axis occupation of Greece brought untold hardships upon the Greek people. A succession of impotent puppet governments, continuous friction between the German and Italian occupation authorities, jackal operations by Bulgarians in Thrace and Macedonia, Gestapo reprisals, and, above all, crop failures of famine proportions, all helped to reduce the country to misery and chaos. Resistance groups were diverse and fiercely divided against each other. Chief among them were EAM (National Liberation Movement), with its military organization ELAS (National People's Liberation Army), and EDES (National Republican Greek League). EAM, by far the best organized and most tough-spirited of the groups, was an outgrowth of the prewar Greek Communists. Fighting broke out during 1943-44, between EAM and EDES at the time of the Soviet military successes. The whole future character and allegiance of the Greek state was called into question, and the old conflict of republicans and monarchists was reopened in sharpened form. The British Government was committed to the restoration of King George and was obviously concerned about its own strategic interests in Greece, a maritime country, close to the Soviet Union. These problems were increasingly urgent as the Allied occupation of North Africa brought within sight the possibilities of Allied landings in the Balkans. Moreover it was evident that EAM, the dominant resistance group, was becoming more and more pro-Communist than anti-Nazi, or even pro-Greek, and that it was entrenching itself firmly for the eventual seizure of power in Greece.

There was continual friction between the Greek resistance leaders and the Greek government in exile, particularly after that government had refused to include within itself representatives of the resistance or to undertake that the Greek King should not return to his country until a plebiscite had been held. Mutinies broke out in Greek army and naval units in Egypt in April 1944 and were quelled with difficulty. King George afterward issued a statement from Cairo pledging to submit freely to the judgment of his people when Greece was liberated. In May 1944, Greek leaders, including resistance delegates, held a conference in the Lebanon, presided over by Papandreou, the Greek Social Democrat, who had been appointed by King George to form a government. An agreement was drawn up, the "Lebanon Charter," which included resolutions to suppress terrorism in Greece and to "unify" and "discipline" the Greek resistance groups.

The Axis forces withdrew from Greece in October 1944, and Papandreou and his government entered Athens under British protection. But the situation was still uncertain as Greece passed into the postwar era.

Perhaps we should remark parenthetically at this point on the resistance in Germany. There appear to have been several resistance groups of fluctuating strength and conviction. One of them, which we have already noted from time to time, was the group comprising General Beck and his associates in the *Wehrmacht,* and to this group also belonged civilians like Schacht and Goerdeler, the treasury official Johannes Popitz, and the career diplomat Ulrich von Hassell. (See pp. 483 and 505.) Another group was the "Kreisau Circle," a salon of all parties, led in the main by Count Helmuth von Moltke. Yet another was the "Canaris Circle" of Admiral Wilhelm Canaris, head of the *Abwehr* or Counter-Espionage Service. The groups were dormant in the first two years of the war, but were roused into activity after the setbacks on the Russian front—and especially after the fall of Mussolini and the installation of a government under Badoglio, events which provided an obvious model for a like-minded incident in Germany. And, in addition, we might mention Field Marshal Paulus, commander of the German Sixth Army at Stalingrad, who broadcast to Germany from his captivity in Russia instigating revolt. (See p. 552.)

It was characteristic of all these groups that they consisted of men of the highest rank, and, unlike the resistance elsewhere, none, not even the Kreisau Circle, seems to have had any popular membership or support. They were essentially small conspirative cliques, which aimed to bring off a *coup d'état* or perhaps an appeal to the Allies, but never a national revolt. For that reason it is still difficult to assess their importance. From time to time they were intensely busy, so much so that we cannot believe their incessant comings and goings were always concealed from those against whom they were plotting. But, to all of them, the one overpowering problem was to select the moment for action. They could hardly strike when Hitler was riding upon success, and to strike when his fortunes were in reverse looked like treachery to the Reich. The war could not stand still in order to provide them with just the most suitable interval they needed. Moreover, for many, there always remained the paralyzing inhibition of their personal oath to the Führer, an oath which apparently no German could violate without the profoundest revulsion of conscience. Many essential recruits to a military putsch were lost from this single obstacle. The almost insuperable sanctity of the soldier's oath was indeed curious in this class of man for whom other forms of good faith were so lightly held.

In the end the putsch of July 20, 1944, which again had the Beck-Goerdeler group behind it, was a failure and, in any case it came too late. After January 1943, the Allies were committed to their formula of "unconditional surrender" and would hardly have consented to negotiate with any German government of whatever political coloration which represented itself as the successor to the Nazi rule. On July 20, 1944, after elaborate preparations extending over a year, a member of this dedicated band, Count Klaus von Stauffenberg, a staff colonel, recently wounded and crippled in the fighting in North Africa, planted a bomb at Hitler's headquarters at Rastenburg on the Eastern front. The bomb exploded, but

Hitler only sustained minor wounds and burns. The conspirators at the two key points, Berlin and Paris, failed to act, arguing among themselves while waiting for confirmation of Hitler's death. A quick-witted Major Otto Remer, acting under Goebbels' orders, with a single guards battalion, took control in Berlin. The same night Hitler was fit enough to broadcast to the German people assuring them of his miraculous escape from a plot laid by "an extremely small clique of ambitious, conscienceless, criminal, and stupid officers, who are now being mercilessly exterminated." Subsequently Goerdeler, Stauffenberg, Field Marshal von Witzleben, two generals, and four other ranking officers were tried for their part in the putsch and hanged. Probably there were over three hundred executions in all, and many others, variously implicated, such as Beck, Kluge, and Rommel, committed suicide or were put to death. The putsch of July 20, 1944, far from overthrowing the Nazi regime, resulted indeed in the final liquidation of the higher ranks of the Prussian officer corps.

31. THE CLOSING PHASES—1944-45

Normandy and the Rhine

The year 1943 was one of high-level Allied conferences. The series had begun in January with the meeting of Roosevelt, Churchill, and their Chiefs of Staff in Casablanca, and had continued in May with their meeting at the "Trident" Conference in Washington. In August 1943, Roosevelt, Churchill, the Canadian Prime Minister Mackenzie King, and their several Chiefs of Staff met at the "Quadrant" Conference in Quebec. In October 1943, the foreign ministers, Hull, Eden, and Molotov, met in Moscow. In November, Roosevelt, Churchill, and Chiang Kai-shek met at the "Sextant" Conference in Cairo, and later in November, Roosevelt, Churchill, and Stalin met at the "Eureka" Conference in Teheran. In December, Roosevelt and Churchill met in Cairo. It is not necessary for us to follow the involved and sometimes acrimonious stages through which these conferences passed. Well documented histories of them are now available; many of their protagonists have contributed comments. The fundamental problem of priorities—as between the European and Pacific theaters of war, or as between the Italian and a possible Balkan theater of war; the allocation of resources, above all of shipping, aircraft, and landing craft; the political impasse in respect to Poland; the possible entry into the war of Sweden and Turkey; the transfusion of more men and material into the "forgotten front" in Burma—all these matters were discussed and variously settled. It was decided to set up a European Advisory Commission in London, particularly to make plans for the Allied occupation of Germany. There was some exploration of a future system of international cooperation to replace the League of Nations. A strong section of American opinion, represented in the main by Admiral King of the United States Joint Chiefs of Staff, and to some extent by Admiral Leahy, personal Chief of Staff to the President, still argued implacably for the primacy of the Pacific theater. But President Roosevelt never wavered in his original strategy of "Hitler First," and usually he found good support in General Marshall.

At all events, 1943 had seen the steadily mounting preparation for operation "Overlord," the invasion of France. The year had brought the Allied victories in the Pacific, in North Africa, Sicily, and Italy; it had brought the fall of Mussolini; it had brought the aerial assault on Germany up to new levels of weight and power; it had brought the Red Army's advance beyond the Don and the Dnieper. Not least, the year 1943 had brought a virtual end to the German submarine menace at sea. March 1943 had been the climax of the enemy's naval effort in the North Atlantic. In the words of the British Admiralty's official account, "the months of April and May 1943 will probably be chosen by future historians as the critical period when the offensive at sea finally passed into the hands of the Allies." Antisubmarine devices were now very formidable. Convoys of Allied merchant ships were being escorted by ever larger numbers of destroyers and corvettes, many of them built in Canada and manned by Canadian crews, and later by a new class of vessel for which the old name of "frigate" was revived. The air umbrella was widened till there were only some 300 miles of the Atlantic gap, the "Black Pit" as it was called, not regularly patrolled by land-based planes, and, over this 300 miles, convoys were escorted by aircraft carriers and merchant aircraft carriers. The statistics of losses at sea, quoted at the end of Chapter 28, tell their own story. The war's turning point in every element and in every theater was well passed.

The build-up for "Overlord" was a stupendous logistic undertaking. A million and a half men were to be trained and equipped, and transported and maintained in Britain. By July 1943, the flow of material from the United States to Britain reached 753,000 tons a month – a figure which was to increase to 1,900,000 tons in the month preceding the landings – and the flow of men had then reached an average of 150,000 a month. The most serious problem was that of landing craft; sometimes it seemed as if the entire Allied command was completely absorbed and frustrated by it. Two artificial harbors, the famous "Mulberry" harbors, each as large as Dover Harbor, were built for emplacement along the invasion beaches.

For weeks before the invasion Nazi propaganda had been lauding the "Fortress of Europe" and the "Atlantic Wall." But the actual situation was sometimes less than the boast. In June 1944, there were some 60 German divisions in France, believed to be a quarter of the total German Army then in the field; but many of these divisions were weak in quantity and quality, and many contained non-German "volunteers." Obviously the European coastline from Norway to Spain – some 2,500 miles – could not have been defended in strength throughout, and only certain sectors, such as the Pas de Calais and the principal sea ports, were heavily fortified. In simple arithmetic a million men straddled out along such a distance would be the equivalent of one man in every four or five yards, an inadequate screen to offer an invading enemy, possessing, as did the Anglo-American forces, complete superiority by sea and air and therefore the freedom to strike wherever they wished. Even so, the Anglo-American forces, when they made their choice of Normandy, encountered a belt of strong points, concreted gun positions, mine fields both at sea and on land, underwater obstacles, wire entanglements, and tank traps. But much of this construction, formidable though it was, had been improvised in the month before the invasion.

Hitler had appointed Rundstedt to the supreme command in the West and placed under him two army groups of two armies each, a northern army group under Rommel and a southern army group under Field Marshal Blaskowitz. Rommel's sector included the Channel and the Low Countries – presumably the invasion area to be. Judicious concentration, especially of armor and reserves, was of the essence of any defensive plan, and, in the extreme uncertainties of the situation, it is not surprising that Rommel and Rundstedt, from the beginning of their association, should have discovered sharp divergencies between them. Rommel, more adventurous, would have taken his chance and fought his main battle on the beaches; Rundstedt, more cautious, would have let the invaders come ashore and then tried to defeat them in a pitched battle at some point selected by himself several miles inland. But the big question, "Concentration where?" remained the same for both commanders, and on this point at least they happened to be in agreement. Rommel and Rundstedt both expected that the main Allied attempt would be made at the Pas de Calais. Hitler, as usual relying on "intuition," expected it to be made in Normandy.

The problem of unified command on the Allied side, the problem that had caused so much resentment in the First World War, was not allowed to arise in the Second. The Supreme Commander at Supreme Headquarters Allied Expeditionary Force (SHAEF), was General Eisenhower. He had been supreme commander for the North African campaign. Hitherto he had held a rising series of staff appointments, notably in Washington and Manila, but had had no experience in the field. But he knew well the political aspects of his service, and he now proved to be as much a statesman as a soldier, a man of infinite tact, humor, and strength, the ideal coalition leader. His deputy commander of the ground assault forces was General Montgomery.

In England as invasion day, "D day," approached, the southern counties were sealed off as a security measure by police cordon. To the civilian inhabitants in the area, the rumble of trucks and tanks on the road, the roar of passing planes, and muffled spurts of firing from the artillery ranges were familiar sounds at all times of the day and night. Landing craft assembled at embarkation ports. Bombers attacked German airfields and communications. By the time the invasion was launched, the Allies had established an absolute aerial supremacy over the Channel. In the last few days before D day, 1,000-bomber waves were dropping 5,000 tons on German coastal defenses and targets inland. All the Seine and Loire bridges, except one, were demolished. Commandos wrecked the German radar installations. French resistance groups, now organized as the FFI (French Forces of the Interior), were regularly contacted, and sabotage materials were dropped to them. Meanwhile meteorologists studied the one unpredictable element, the weather. Suitable tides and a full moon would occur early in June, but early June, when it arrived, was unseasonably stormy. On June 5, taking advantage of a forecast of a fair interval, Eisenhower gave orders to move. On June 6, shortly after midnight, British and American airborne divisions were dropped over points at either end of the assault area so as to seal it off from immediate counterattack. Aerial bombardment of coastal defenses continued during the early hours, and naval bombardment began after sunrise. Minesweepers preceded the landing craft. A fleet of 4,000 vessels of all kinds converged on the Normandy beaches. Meanwhile a "diversionary" invasion towards Flanders was carried out with dummy paratroops.

The operation was a greater success than could have been hoped for. Initial surprise was complete. There was some loss at sea from rough weather; shore obstacles were fouled; amphibious tanks suffered particularly. But, on the first day, 130,000 men and 20,000 vehicles were landed; the "crust" of the German system was broken. By the sixth day, 326,000 men and 54,000 vehicles had been landed. The bridgehead was 50 miles wide and 8 to 12 miles deep. The "Mulberry" harbors had been towed into position. The most critical time came during the storm which raged throughout the four days from June 19 to 22 and virtually wrecked the "Mulberry" harbor in the American sector.

By July 2, 1944, less than a month after D Day, an Allied army of nearly a million men had been landed in Normandy, composed of 13 American, 11 British, and 1 Canadian divisions. The Allied plan of campaign, generally credited to Montgomery, was for the British forces on the left to contain the main German strength, especially the German armor, at Caen, and for the American forces on the right, trained and equipped for mobility, to effect a breakout into Brittany and Maine and thence to turn eastward in a wide enveloping movement to the Seine. All through July the Germans counterattacked around Caen, and were held there. The American breakout was launched on July 25. Heavy bombers to the number of 1,500 laid down a "carpet" of bombs on a narrow front. General Omar N. Bradley's forces, organized as the United States First Army under General Courtney H. Hodges and later the United States Third Army under General George S. Patton, deployed rapidly through the penetration thus effected into the open country. The subsequent enveloping movement trapped 100,000 of the enemy in the "Falaise pocket." On August 15, a new American army under General Alexander M. Patch, with strong French reinforcements, landed in southern France and began to advance inland up to the Rhone Valley. The Germans in northern France were now retiring under pressure to the Seine and making a general withdrawal toward their own frontiers. Since D Day, their losses had amounted to 400,000 men, killed, wounded, or missing. Rundstedt, opposed to the continuation of the war, had been superseded by Field Marshal von Kluge early in July; and Kluge was succeeded by Field Marshal Model, a "retreat specialist" from the Eastern front, at the end of August. Rommel, wounded in Normandy, and then allegedly implicated in the attempt on Hitler's life on July 20, died in mysterious circumstances.

By the end of August 1944, the Allied strength in France amounted to 2,000,000 men organized in three army groups – Montgomery in the north, Bradley in the center, and General Jacob L. Devers in the south. Eisenhower and SHAEF were at Versailles, and later at Reims.

There was one lively interlude at this time. Shortly after D day, the Germans, from launching sites in the Pas de Calais, began to fire over to

England their V-1's, or flying bombs – "buzz bombs" or "doodlebugs" as they were soon nicknamed. These were among Hitler's "secret weapons," with which he hoped to redress the Allied successes. They were small pilotless planes, jet-propelled. With proper time and opportunity for development, they might have amounted to a very serious menace. As it was, they gave the London area a decidedly uncomfortable two months. A great balloon barrage was prepared for them in Kent and Sussex, and thousands of them were destroyed in mid-passage. In the end they made no difference to the course of Allied strategy. Later, in August, the Germans sent over their V-2's or rocket bombs, flying at supersonic velocity, a much more terrible weapon, against which there was no defense and which wrought great devastation, especially in the East End of London, until the advancing Allies began to capture their launching sites. In the winter of 1944-45, the V-1's and V-2's were aimed at urban centers still within range, notably Brussels and Antwerp.

On August 19, 1944, units of the FFI and local partisans had risen in Paris. Six days later a French armored division under General Leclerc, together with an American infantry division, completed the liberation of the city. Allied forces were sweeping through France. During September they overran Dieppe, Verdun, Brussels, Mons, Lille, Namur, Ghent, Ypres, Ostend, Liége, Luxembourg, Le Havre, Maastricht. The destruction of the main German armies in France seemed in sight. Optimistic newspaper reporters were predicting an end to the war before Christmas. The Germans made their stubbornest stands at the ports, Brest, St. Nazaire, St. Malo, Lorient, Le Havre, Boulogne, Calais, and finally Antwerp, in order to deny to the Allies harbor facilities indispensable for the supply of their great deployment. Their resistance also stiffened as they neared their own frontier, their old West Wall, the Siegfried Line of 1939. Late in September, at the Battle of Arnhem, they successfully foiled Montgomery's attempt to "bounce" a crossing of the Rhine by air-borne attack.

The Battle of Arnhem was a heroic gamble to end the war quickly. Its failure meant another winter and more months of hard fighting. The headlong Allied advance through France had evidently overreached itself. Time was needed for the resting and refitting of divisions, many of whom had been in continuous action for four months, and especially for the reconstruction of ports and communications. Roosevelt and Churchill met for their second conference at Quebec, the "Octagon" Conference, a few days before Arnhem, for one of their periodic reviews of the military and political situation. It was at this conference that the so-called Morgenthau Plan for "pastoralizing" Germany and for destroying her industrial potential was mooted and presumably agreed. But Germany was still far from accepting so total a defeat. Eisenhower was then reporting that the breach of the West Wall might be a slow, plodding, expensive operation. Some of the hardest fighting of the campaign took place during that November and early December – the clearance of the Scheldt and the approaches to Antwerp by the Canadian First Army, the penetration of the flooded Roer area by the British Second Army and the United States Ninth Army, and

De Gaulle returning to Paris after the Liberation, August 1944

ROBERT CAPA-MAGNUM

the costly advance beyond Aachen through the Hurtgen Forest by the United States First Army.

Warsaw and Budapest

The Red Army now consisted of some 300 divisions of over 5,000,000 men, and against it stood 200 German divisions of perhaps 2,000,000 men. Lack of German reserve strength was manifest. All German units were under establishment, both in personnel and equipment. The once proud *Wehrmacht,* increasingly diluted with non-Germans – including Russians – recalled the polyglot hordes of the later stages of the Thirty Years' War.

In April 1944, forces of Marshal Tolbukhin's army group broke through the Perekop Isthmus, joined hands with General Yeremenko's army from Kerch, and cleared the Crimea at a cost to the enemy of 100,000 casualties. Sevastopol fell on May 9, and with its capture was restored the Soviet use of the Black Sea. In June, in the Karelian area in the far north, the Russians breached the old Mannerheim Line which had proved so tough an obstacle in 1940. In the center, the Russians resumed their assault on Vitebsk, and that stubborn stronghold, together with the German defensive system in White Russia, the Fatherland Line, which was anchored to it, was overrun. Through July the Soviet northern army groups invaded the Baltic States; the central army groups crossed the (Polish) Bug into the very heart of

Poland; the southern army groups crossed the (Ukrainian) Bug into Moldavia.

At the end of July 1944, Marshal Rokossovsky, in command of one of the central army groups, was approaching Warsaw. In Warsaw itself the Polish Home Army was in insurrection and had taken possession of several districts in the city. But on August 1, when Rokossovsky's forces failed to maintain their advance, the Germans turned savagely on the Home Army. The Soviet High Command refused Anglo-American planes the use of airfields behind the Soviet lines so as to enable a shuttle service to be organized for dropping arms and supplies to the beleaguered partisans. The insurrection was mercilessly crushed. We have elsewhere described the political background of this ghastly episode. (See p. 581.)

The Soviet advance continued in other sectors. In the north, Tartu, Tallinn, and Riga all fell in September and October. Remnants of the German Baltic Army were left stranded in the tip of Estonia. Finland was already preparing to withdraw from the unequal contest. Marshal Mannerheim appointed a new government, which shortly broke off relations with Germany and demanded the evacuation of German troops from Finnish soil. Finnish delegates proceeded to Moscow and signed an armistice there on September 19, 1944.

In the south Hitler's New Order was in dissolution, and its various satellite members were consulting the best means for their own survival. In Rumania, General Antonescu's opponents had already made secret contacts with the Allies. On August 23, 1944, the young King Michael, taking his courage and his prerogatives into his own hands, called Antonescu into his study, informed him he was dismissed and had him locked in a vault for safekeeping. Michael then announced the cessation of hostilities and appointed a pro-Soviet cabinet under General Sanatescu. The Germans replied with a savage bombing of Bucharest; whereupon the new cabinet declared war on Germany. By August 30, Soviet forces had occupied Bucharest and the oil fields at Ploesti. Rumanian delegates signed an armistice in Moscow on September 12, 1944.

Bulgaria, who had never been a full belligerent and had not even declared war on the Soviet Union, hastened to make her peace with the victors. Since the mysterious death of Tsar Boris in 1943, a series of regents for the young Prince Simeon kept up a show of collaboration with Germany. But changing of cabinets and arresting of ministers were now no longer expedients sufficient to keep Bulgaria in line. In August 1944, Bulgarian emissaries made secret contacts with the Allies in Cairo. On September 2, under Allied pressure, a new cabinet was installed, which broke off relations with Germany. On the 5th, amid feverish, last-minute efforts to avoid open hostilities, the Soviet Union made a surprise declaration of war on Bulgaria, and Soviet forces were shortly pouring into the country. The cabinet sued for an armistice and declared war on Germany. But on September 9 a strong-arm gang broke in on the cabinet meeting, and a new government and Regency Council, both acceptable to the Soviet, were ostensibly put in charge of Bulgarian affairs. Bulgarian delegates signed an armistice in Moscow on October 28, 1944.

By October the Red Army had crossed the borders of East Prussia and of Hungary. Marshal Malinovsky was driving toward Budapest. On October 15, in a broadcast, the Hungarian Regent, Horthy, bitterly reproached the Nazis for their infringements of Hungarian sovereignty and announced that he would sue for an armistice. Horthy found himself promptly deposed, and a new Hungarian government took control under the pro-Fascist Ferenc Szalasi. On October 20 Marshal Tolbukhin took Belgrade and effected a junction with Yugoslav resistance groups and with Tito.

The last act in Hungary was performed, not by the pro-Fascist Szalasi, but by the Hungarian General Miklos, commander of the Hungarian First Army, who went over to the Russians with offers to form a new government. In the latter part of December, elections for a provisional assembly were held in the liberated parts of Hungary; the assembly duly met at Debrecen on December 21 and set up a government under Miklos, which at once declared war on Germany. Hungarian delegates signed an armistice in Moscow on January 20, 1945. The Germans continued to hold out in the citadel of Buda even as they were still holding out in Warsaw.

During October 1944, Churchill and Eden were in conference in Moscow with Stalin and Molotov with a view to reaching some settlement, or at least mutual recognition, of Anglo-Soviet interests in Intermediate Europe. Averell Harriman was present, representing the United States. Churchill had been much concerned over the sweeping Soviet conquests in Intermediate Europe. He had repeatedly but unsuccessfully urged his American allies to support him in a more active policy, especially in the Balkans. But by this time there was little to be done except acquiesce in the accomplished military fact. Poland was discussed without further result; but it was agreed that, while the Soviet Union should have "predominance" in Rumania and Bulgaria, Britain should have "ninety per cent of the say in Greece." British commando units had already landed at Patras in the Gulf of Corinth on October 4, a week before the conference had begun, and, with Soviet abstention secured, the British occupation of Greece proceeded. On the 14th Athens was liberated. Papandreou and the Greek Government returned to their homeland. But, as was soon to appear, the British were to find complications enough in Greece, even without more direct Soviet intervention. (See pp. 585 and 685-87.)

The Collapse of Germany

At the end of 1944, on every front, west, south, and east, Allied armies were swarming toward Germany. In the West, their advance had reached points roughly coincident with the Belgian and French frontiers. They stood on German soil at Aachen and Trier. In the south in Italy, the Allied advance had reached Ravenna and Forli. British forces were operating in Greece and Dalmatia. In the East, the Red Army stood on German soil in East Prussia and had advanced to Warsaw and Budapest. Meanwhile, at sea, the German submarine had ceased to be a serious menace. The long five-year Battle of the Atlantic had been won. The German battle fleet was bombed and disabled in its dockyards. In November 1944, the great sister ship of the *Bismarck,* the *Tirpitz,* already damaged by British midget submarines as she lay in a Norwegian fiord, was sunk after two raids and three direct hits by 12,000-pound bombs.

On December 16, 1944, in the Ardennes, the Germans suddenly launched a "spoiling offensive," allegedly ordered by Hitler himself and recalling the Kursk offensive of the previous year. (See p. 554.) Rundstedt, restored to his command in the West, was directed to attack with 24 divisions, 10 of them armored, across the old Ardennes battlefield of 1940. Like all Hitler's projects, the "Battle of the Bulge" showed a flash of strategic insight. It caught the American Intelligence off guard, and was helped by foggy weather that prevented Allied aerial counteroperations. Fought with more material and perhaps more will on the part of its commander, it could have played havoc with the entire Allied position in Belgium. It was the *Wehrmacht's* last blow. Quick Allied recovery made up for early surprise. Eisenhower halted all offensive operations and hastened his reserves to the flanks of the German salient. Pockets of American resistance developed at St. Vith and Bastogne. On December 24, the weather cleared, and 5,000 Allied aircraft were loosed upon the German supply lines. Patton and the United States Third Army counterattacked from the south; and Montgomery, temporarily placed in command of the greater part of the United States First and Ninth Armies, attacked from the north. By the end of January 1945, the Germans had been forced back to their original positions. The battle had cost them 120,000 men, killed, wounded, and prisoners, 600 tanks, and 1,600 planes, a loss they could ill afford.

Thereafter the German armies in the West, under the Allies' unrelenting pressure, on the ground and in the air, were steadily driven back into the heart of the Fatherland. During February and March 1945, the Allies took Colmar, München-Gladbach, Cologne, Bonn, Kreuznach, Worms. On March 7, an American armored division crossed the Rhine at Remagen over a bridge that the enemy, by an extraordinary blunder, had failed to demolish. The First Army in the succeeding two weeks pushed across elements of three corps. On March 23, behind the most successful air drop of the campaign, units of the British Twenty-first Army Group crossed the Rhine above Wesel. By the last week in March, all territory on the west bank of the Rhine had been cleared of the enemy, and the bridgeheads on the east bank were being rapidly expanded.

The Rhine proved to be the last serious obstacle in the West. The Allied advance beyond it was made against a demoralized and broken enemy. Allied air operations were now virtually unopposed. The dread *Luftwaffe* that had once consumed Warsaw, Rotterdam, Belgrade, and London in flame and terror had ceased to exist as an effective weapon. The main Allied thrust on land was made north and south of the Ruhr by the British Second Army and the United States Ninth Army. The United States Third and Seventh Armies struck through Mainz and Frankfort. During March an average of 10,000 Germans a day were being taken prisoner on the Western front, and in April the figure rose to 50,000. There were several rumors of a last desperate suicidal stand to be made by a new Nazi guerrilla force, the "Werewolves" in a "Southern Redoubt" in the Bavarian uplands, presumably centered around Berchtesgaden, but Patton and the Third Army encountered little resistance when they penetrated the area.

Allied operations in Italy meanwhile had been somewhat curtailed by heavy withdrawals of effectives to France. But in April 1945, General Mark Clark's forces launched their final offensive of the campaign, took Bologna, and broke into the Po Valley. Mantua, Parma, Verona, and Milan fell in quick succession. Genoa was seized by Italian partisans, and Trieste by Yugoslavs. On April 28, Mussolini and twelve of his cabinet were recognized attempting to cross the frontier into Switzerland and "executed" by Italian partisans near Milan. On April 29, at Caserta, German officers, on behalf of the German armies in Italy, accepted unconditional surrender. Hostilities in Italy ceased at noon on May 2, 1945.

On the Eastern front, German counterattacks before Warsaw and Budapest had paralleled the Ardennes offensive. It took the whole of January 1945 for Marshal Malinovsky to invest and reduce Warsaw. Isolated German units were still holding out in the castle area of Buda up to mid-February. What was still left of these two handsome and historic cities was largely destroyed in these obstinate operations. Thereafter the Red Army swept irresistibly into Austria and Germany with Vienna and Berlin as its ultimate goals. The Polish winter had been exceptionally mild, and fighting had continued along the entire front without the usual seasonal interruption. The central army groups were now advancing toward Königsberg, Poznan, and Breslau. As in the West, the Germans clung to the seaports, and Memel, Königsberg and Danzig were holding out long after they had been bypassed by the main Soviet forces. Poznan and Breslau were taken during February and March, and Bratislava early in April. Vienna fell to a concentration of Malinovsky's and Tolbukhin's armies on April 13. At that moment Marshal Zhukov, now commanding one of the central army groups, was already pounding at the suburbs of Berlin.

Yalta, Reims, Berlin, and Potsdam

In November 1944, Roosevelt had been re-elected President of the United States for a fourth term. The next formal Allied conference between himself, Churchill, and Stalin, their foreign ministers and Chiefs of Staff, took place shortly after his inauguration, on February 4-11, 1945, at Yalta in the Crimea. The three statesmen discussed the surrender and dismemberment of Germany and their future policy in Europe. They agreed that the three Allied Powers should occupy separate zones in Germany and to establish a Control Commission with headquarters in Berlin, and that France should be invited to take over a fourth zone as a fourth member of the Control Commission. They reaffirmed the principle of "unconditional surrender" and their "inflexible purpose" to destroy German militarism and Nazism, to disarm and disband all German forces, to break up the German General Staff, to destroy or remove German military potential, to bring all war criminals to justice, and to eliminate the Nazi party, its organizations and influence, and to exact reparation "in kind to the greatest extent possible." They agreed to call a conference of the United Nations at San Francisco in April 1945 to prepare the charter of a new international organization, and they announced that they had been able to solve the question of its "voting procedure." They reaffirmed the Atlantic Charter. They agreed that the states of liberated Europe must solve "by democratic means their pressing political and economic problems," and pledged "the earliest possible establishment, through free elections, of governments responsive to the will of the people." They agreed to the formation of a Polish Provisional Government of National Unity, which should include "democratic leaders from Poland itself and from Poles abroad," and which should hold "free and unfettered elections as soon as possible." They agreed that the eastern frontier of Poland should generally follow the Curzon Line, but that she must receive "substantial accessions of territory," presumably at the expense of Germany, to the north and west. They recognized the Tito-Subasich agreement regarding Yugoslavia. (See pp. 584-85.) By a further secret agreement Stalin undertook that the Soviet Union would enter the war against Japan "two or three months after Germany has surrendered" on condition that the Soviet Union receive from Japan territories and rights she had "seized from the former Russian state in Sakhalin, Manchuria, and Port Arthur, and also the Kurile Islands." Superficially the Yalta Conference was a tremendous success. The three statesmen in their personal relations had never seemed more cordial. Roosevelt's mood afterward was one "of supreme exaltation." But there were items in the agreement, notably the arrangements for Intermediate Europe, which, as we shall see, were soon to be evaded by one of the parties. After Yalta the "strange alliance" began to falter and fail.

On his way back from Yalta, at stopping points aboard American warships, President Roosevelt conferred with King Farouk of Egypt, Emperor Haile Selassie of Ethiopia, and King Ibn Saud of Arabia. He met Churchill again at Alexandria. De Gaulle declined an invitation to a meeting at Algiers as a mark of protest against the exclusion of France from the Yalta Conference, thereby committing as grave a diplomatic discourtesy as any in his stubborn career. On March 1, at Washington, Roosevelt made a "personal report" to Congress on the Conference and broadcast to the American people. Rumors were then appearing in the press, and being denied, regarding Roosevelt's failing health. Such rumors had not been uncommon ever since his election to a fourth term. Those who knew him best had perhaps grown used to the evident marks of strain which twelve years as President had left on him. He had staged "comebacks" before, and his mental and physical resilience was extraordinary. His daily round and his public appearances continued as normally. But he died suddenly on April 12, 1945, struck down on the very eve of military victory.

Roosevelt was succeeded by Vice-President Harry S. Truman. The conference to draw up the Charter of the United Nations was duly opened at San Francisco with an address by the new President on April 25, the day that the American and Soviet forces made contact on the Elbe.

Churchill, Roosevelt, and Stalin at the Yalta Conference, February 1945

IMPERIAL WAR MUSEUM

The end of Hitler and his Reich now came quickly. He had spent some weeks on the Western front at the time of the Ardennes offensive and returned to Berlin in mid-January 1945. The attempted assassination of July 1944 left him partly deaf and had probably aggravated his former maladies. In the last phase, he is described as broken in health, a stooping, shambling figure, ashy pale, convulsed with stomach cramps, his hands in a perpetual tremor, with fits of depression alternating with his ever more frequent storms and rages. He took no exercise, worked round the clock, and slept three hours in the twenty-four. He suffered from the occupational disease of all tyrants, the phobia of treachery; betrayal and bad faith lurked in every shadow; every man's hand was raised against his sacred person. A quack physician is said to have been giving him constant drug injections. At this time, the Chancellery building in Berlin being badly damaged and burned, he and his immediate circle occupied somewhat restricted quarters in a concrete air-raid bunker in the Chancellery garden.

Hitler's fifty-sixth birthday, April 20, 1945, was a day of critical conferences. The Allied advance, east and west, was about to cut Germany in halves; Russian shells were already thudding round the bunker. The magnates of the regime, Göring, Goebbels, Himmler, Bormann, Ribbentrop, Speer, Doenitz, Keitel, Jodl — and Eva Braun — were all in attendance. The main problems before them were allocation of political authority under the fast deteriorating military situation, the successorship to the Führer in the now very probable event of his death, and diplomatic contact with the enemy for a cessation of hostilities. Yet in the bunker, in that "subterranean madhouse," in the midst of these understandable and legitimate problems, we still see the old party strifes and intrigues continuing, and the old personal hatreds, instead of being decently buried by the proximity of disaster, seeking out new opportunities for their gratification; we still see the fanatic rivalry of court favorites snatching at positions of command, however momentary, in a state and army both of which had largely ceased to exist.

In the upshot, Hitler appointed Admiral Doenitz to the command of the German forces in the northern half of Germany, and Doenitz shortly left for headquarters at Plön in Schleswig-Holstein. The remainder dispersed or stayed as their duties seemed to dictate – Keitel and Jodl to their headquarters at the front, Göring to Berchtesgaden, Himmler and Speer to their respective offices in Berlin. Göring attempted to open secret peace parleys with the enemy in the West. Himmler became immersed in similar parleys of great intricacy through Count Folke Bernadotte of the Swedish Red Cross. Himmler appears to have believed that he could found a new political party and survive the wreck of Germany with himself securely at his head. For Hitler, the revelation of these peace intrigues was the unkindest cut of all. The oldest and most trusted of his lieutenants, it seemed, were meditating desertion. Speer, Himmler, and Ribbentrop eventually joined Doenitz at Plön. Meanwhile Goebbels and Bormann remained with Hitler in the bunker – and with them Eva Braun, Hitler's mistress, and the Goebbels family.

On the night of April 28, Hitler gave orders for a last-ditch defense of the Chancellery – the Russians were now only a few streets away – and to that end he summoned to Berlin General Ritter von Greim, a high-ranking officer of the *Luftwaffe,* appointed him Commander in Chief of the *Luftwaffe* in succession to the traitorous Göring, and then sent him to find and collect what German pilots and aircraft were still available for operations. Greim, in the last plane to leave Berlin, with Hitler's desperate and impossible instructions in his pocket, made off for Doenitz's headquarters at Plön. Next Hitler married Eva Braun, and wrote his will and his political testament, in which he reviewed his career, protested his desire for peace, expelled Göring and Himmler from the Nazi party, and appointed Doenitz Reich President, Minister of War, and Commander in Chief of the *Wehrmacht.* Copies of the document were entrusted to envoys, who left the Chancellery on foot to penetrate the Soviet lines as best they could, with orders to proceed to Plön. On April 30, in the afternoon, after elaborate farewells among those present, Hitler and Eva Braun committed suicide. Their bodies were burned in gasoline. No traces were ever found. Goebbels and his family committed suicide. Bormann escaped alive and was never heard of again.

Doenitz broadcast his assumption of authority to the German armed forces and people on May 1 and called on them for further efforts in the struggle against Bolshevism. He formed a new government with Count Schwerin von Krosigk as Foreign Minister, a career official who had been Finance Minister

Russian soldiers raising their flag on the ruined Reichstag *building, Berlin, May 1, 1945*

SOVFOTO

since Papen's day in 1932. Ribbentrop was ignored. Admiral von Friedeburg was appointed Commander in Chief of the German Navy. On May 2, Doenitz moved his headquarters from Plön to Flensburg, near the Danish border. The same day he sent Friedeburg to Montgomery with proposals to capitulate in the West but to continue fighting in the East. Montgomery rejected the offer and demanded unconditional surrender on all fronts.

The final German capitulation was patchy and piecemeal. There was neither the need nor the opportunity for theater. Eisenhower issued instructions that subordinate commanders could accept surrenders on their respective fronts. On May 4 the unconditional surrender of the German forces in Holland, northwest Germany, and Denmark was signed at Montgomery's headquarters on Lüneburg Heath. On May 7, the general instrument of surrender was signed by Jodl at Eisenhower's headquarters at Reims and ratified by Keitel on May 9, at Zhukov's headquarters at Berlin. Surrenders of isolated German units, in Norway, the Aegean, and Bohemia were announced severally in the course of the next few days.

On July 16, 1945, at Alamogordo in the deserts of New Mexico, in great secrecy, the first nuclear explosion was carried out. The next day, from July 17 to August 2, the Potsdam Conference – or Berlin Conference to give it its official name, or "Terminal" Conference to give it its code name – was held at the Cecilienhof in Potsdam. The United States was represented by President Truman and Secretary of State James F. Byrnes; the Soviet Union

"Unconditional Surrender": (left to right) an aide, General Jodl, and Admiral von Friedeburg at Eisenhower Headquarters, Reims, May 7, 1945

IMPERIAL WAR MUSEUM

was represented by Stalin and Molotov. In Britain, Churchill's government had lately dissolved, and the results of the subsequent general election were not announced till July 26, while the Potsdam Conference was actually in session. Churchill and the Conservative party were defeated, and a Labor government took office under Attlee, with Bevin as Foreign Secretary. For the first part of the conference, therefore, Britain was represented by Churchill and Eden, with Attlee in attendance; and for the second part by Attlee and Bevin. No French representative was invited.

The Yalta Conference had been the high point of Allied unity and comradeship in arms. But some of the agreements, notably over Poland, had been less than frank or happy. During May, President Truman had sent Hopkins on a special mission to Moscow to see if, in personal conversation with Stalin, some means could not be found for repairing the sharp deterioration in American-Soviet relations. The United Nations Conference in San Francisco was then in session, and there too Poland had been an issue. But Hopkins' conversations in Moscow were further dogged by news of the recent Soviet arrest of sixteen Polish resistance leaders, who according to the Soviet report had engaged in "deviationist activities," if not in out-and-out espionage. There were few items on the agenda at Potsdam that did not become cues for wider and deeper disagreements between the Soviet and the Anglo-American Allies, not only over Poland, but over Intermediate Europe in general, over Italy and the Italian colonies, Austria, Spain, the Middle East — and finally over Germany and in particular over German reparations.

However, none of these disagreements was publicly divulged, though informed journalism was already aware of them and was discussing them. The Protocol on the Conference, the lengthiest and most comprehensive of these Allied pronouncements, was issued on August 2. It announced the for-

General Eisenhower and Field Marshal Montgomery, 1945

RADIO-TIMES HULTON

mation of a Council of Foreign Ministers of the five Allies – the United States, Britain, the Soviet Union, France, and China – charged to undertake the preparation of the peace treaties for Italy, Bulgaria, Finland, Hungary, and Rumania. It enunciated the political and economic principles which should govern the treatment of Germany in the initial control period, effect her total disarmament and denazification, bring home to her people at large the absolute conviction of their military defeat, and prepare for the eventual reconstruction of her political life on a democratic basis. It indicated, in sufficiently specific terms, the industrial levels to be permitted to Germany and the reparations to be exacted. It recognized the transfer of Königsberg to the Soviet Union. It reaffirmed former Allied declarations to bring war criminals to justice. It reserved the final delimitation of the western frontier of Poland to the future peace settlement, but assigned an area of Polish "Administration" up to the Oder and Neisse rivers and including Danzig. It expressed satisfaction over the formation of the Polish Provisional Government of National Unity. It urged the orderly and humane transfer of German populations from Poland, Czechoslovakia, and Hungary.

During the Conference, Stalin had still temporized on the question of an immediate Soviet declaration of war on Japan, though he was informed by Truman of a "new" secret weapon in the hands of the United States. On July 26, from Potsdam, Truman, Attlee, Stalin, and Chiang Kai-shek, in the names of their governments, issued an ultimatum to Japan warning her of the immeasurable armed forces now at their disposal and demanding her instant and unconditional surrender. "The alternative for Japan is complete and utter destruction."

The Collapse of Japan

We retrace our steps to consider the East in 1944. Burma had become, like Italy, a relatively forlorn theater of the war, bypassed by greater happenings elsewhere. But the situation there had very considerably improved since the hard battle for Myitkyina. (See p. 563.) By the end of 1944, Japanese forces in Burma were cut off by the developing naval blockade from their supply centers in their distant homeland, and, like the many isolated Japanese units in the Pacific, they were progressively suffering siege conditions. British submarines were roaming in the Strait of Malacca and the Java Sea, complementing the efforts of American submarines further east. British planes were raiding Rangoon, Bangkok, and Singapore without meeting serious opposition. Wingate's jungle fighters in the heart of Burma were now operating in freedom from Japanese aerial interference. Troops, equipment, guns, jeeps, even bullocks and mules were being set down on airstrips in the battle areas.

The monsoon of 1944 had restricted but not wholly stopped the fighting in Burma, and the Allied advance had continued beyond Myitkyina. Operations were intensified with the return of good weather. Three main Allied forces were then closing in on central Burma – the British Fourteenth Army under General Slim, pressing eastward from Arakan, the American-Chinese force under General Sultan pressing southward from Myitkyina, and the Chinese force pressing westward from Yunnan in China. The immediate objective, the reopening of the Burma Road, was declared to have been achieved on January 22, 1945. Mandalay was taken on March 20. Meanwhile British amphibious and air-borne forces were preparing for a descent on the extreme tip of Burma from the sea. They landed south of Rangoon on May 1, and the city fell, almost without loss, in the course of the next two days. Except for Japanese remnants still holding out in the northern and eastern jungles upcountry, the Burmese campaign had been completed

Plans for the closing phases of the war against metropolitan Japan had been made earlier in September 1944 at the "Octagon" Conference at Quebec. Reports at hand from MacArthur and Nimitz had been so favorable that the Chiefs of Staff approved an early assault on Leyte in the center of the Philippine archipelago. On September 17, the day after the conference ended, American forces landed on Anguar in the Palau Islands, 550 miles from the nearest point in the Philippines. A month later, on October 20, 1944, a huge armada of 750 ships, stretching from horizon to horizon, bore the four divisions of the United States Sixth Army, numbering 250,000 men, towards Leyte. The covering naval force, under Admiral Thomas C. Kinkaid, consisted of six battleships and their accompanying cruisers and destroyers. A carrier fleet, under Admiral William F. Halsey, stood out at sea.

The threat to the Philippines, to the East Indies, and to the entire Japanese empire was clear enough. The Japanese High Command made the decision to commit the heaviest units of the Japanese Navy in the greatest naval battle of the Second World War. Two Japanese Fleets would penetrate the straits on the north and south of Leyte and would close in upon the American transports in the midst of landing operations, while a third "decoy" fleet would try to lure away Halsey's carriers. Meanwhile attacks would be made by a new force of Japanese "suicide planes." During October 23-26, in and around Leyte Gulf, there was fought a series of naval and aerial actions. The Japanese fleet to the north of Leyte was about to turn into the Gulf, when, perhaps scenting a trap, its commander decided to

Fifth Division Marines raising the flag on Mt. Suribachi, Iwo Jima, March 15, 1945

UNITED PRESS INTERNATIONAL

withdraw; the fleet to the south was driven off. The final result was a great American victory. The Japanese lost 4 battleships, 4 carriers, 10 cruisers and an unspecified number of planes, and suffered severe damage to at least 4 more battleships and 10 cruisers. The Americans lost the light carrier *Princeton*, 2 escort carriers, 3 destroyers, and over 100 planes.

MacArthur proceeded to the methodical conquest of Leyte, the first step in the Philippines campaign on which he had set his heart. "I have returned!" he said on landing. There were some 250,000 Japanese troops at different points in the islands under the command of General Yamashita, and most of them were soon fighting to maintain contact with one another against an enemy who had established absolute aerial and naval superiority. A long trail of wrecked and sunken transports and escort craft was all that was left of their persistent attempts to succor beleaguered survivors. At the last, precious loads of supplies were being run through the American blockade by sailboat. On December 15 American forces landed on Mindoro, and, on January 9, 1945, on Luzon. In February, they took Cavite and Corregidor, and the Japanese were making a last house-to-house stand in Intramuros, the ancient walled section of Manila. Meanwhile strong Australian forces, reinforced by a Dutch contingent, landed in Borneo.

On February 19, 1945, three divisions of American marines fought their way ashore on Iwo Jima, only 750 miles from Tokyo. This speck on the map was a tangle of dwarf rocks, lava ledges, sulphur pits, caverns and crevices – and no vegetation – and it had been seamed with the usual Japanese maze of blockhouses and bunkers. Gains at first were counted in yards, but in eighteen days, the Japanese defenses had been split in half, and the American flag at last was raised on March 15. Of the original 30,000 marines, 20,000 were casualties, including 4,189 killed. The Japanese lost 20,000 killed and 200 taken prisoner. Then, in the first week in March, four divisions of the United States Tenth Army were landed at Okinawa in the Ryukyus, only 350 miles from the southern tip of the Japanese mainland. The Japanese were again elaborately entrenched, and the fighting was the fiercest and most costly of the whole Pacific campaign. The island was not cleared till the end of June, at a loss to the Americans of 12,500 killed or missing and to the Japanese of nearly 110,000 killed, and 7,750 taken prisoner. General Simon B. Buckner, who led the original assault, was himself killed in the closing actions.

Japanese "suicide planes" had made their first appearance at Leyte, but had not been very effective. During and after the Okinawa operations, however, they constituted a formidable threat. The Kamikaze ("divine wind") squadrons, so named after the providential typhoon that shattered the attempted Mongol invasion of Japan in 1281, were composed of two types of aircraft. The more refined variety was a twenty-foot plane with a massive charge of TNT in its nose, which was launched from a "mother" bomber and guided to its objective by a single suicide pilot. Much more numerous was the improvised type, a single-engined fighter, laden with a maximum weight of explosive, designed to explode on contact. Aircraft carriers, with their flat, unarmored flight decks, were ideal targets for these weapons of desperation, especially if their gasoline-filled planes had not been flown off. The thin-skinned destroyer, too, was highly vulnerable. But even on the heavily armored battleships and cruisers, the Kamikazes could inflict, if not mortal injury, at least very serious damage. American losses from the Kamikazes amounted to 36 ships sunk, none larger than a destroyer, and 368 damaged, including 10 battleships and 13 carriers. Japanese losses have been estimated at 1,500 to 2,000 planes and pilots.

On April 5, 1945, the Soviet Government gave notice that it would denounce the Soviet-Japanese Neutrality Pact of 1941. With pointed defiance a new ministry was formed in Tokyo under Baron Suzuki, one of the admirals of the Russo-Japanese War of 1904-05. But the merciless erosion of Japanese strength did not wait upon Cabinet changes. The American air forces in the Pacific were reorganized under General Spaatz for the final assault. Since the taking of Saipan and Guam in the Marianas, Japan had been within range of the B-29 superfortresses. In the nine months from November 1944 to the surrender in September 1945, B-29's made 32,000 sorties against Japan – more than a hundred a day – dropped 169,000 tons of bombs, and lost 437 aircraft and over 3,000 personnel. With the taking of Iwo Jima and Okinawa, Japan could be systematically pounded with high explosive and fire bombs, paralyzing her inter-island transportation, her railroads and industries, and incinerating her inflammable and crowded cities. Her harbor mouths were sown with mines dropped from the air and outside this deadly barrier American and British fleets ranged with impunity within very sight of her coasts. Her remaining battleships were bombarded as they lay heavily camouflaged in harbor berths or river estuaries. The surrender of Germany, releasing further massive Allied naval and military resources for the Pacific, presaged the descent of new torrents of fire and steel. The Suzuki cabinet in Tokyo, however, was still temeritous enough to reject the Potsdam ultimatum of July 26 "as unworthy of public notice." It sought to enlist the Soviet Union as mediator in a negotiated peace. But the Soviet Union had other intentions in the Far East, and was patently preparing to implement its Yalta undertaking to enter the war.

The Potsdam ultimatum had not explicitly revealed the nature of that "complete and utter destruction" which was to befall Japan if she refused the alternative of surrender. But, as we have noted, the first nuclear explosion had been carried out in the deserts of New Mexico on July 16, 1945, the day before the Potsdam Conference began. As human discoveries go, "splitting the atom" had had a short, but intensive history. Ever since the early experiments with radioactivity before 1914, Western science had been haunted by the problem of releasing the vast stores of energy normally locked in the primary particles of the material universe. But it was not till the late 1930's that experiments with the isotopes of uranium, then being carried out simultaneously in Italy, France, Germany, and Britain, had opened up the tremendous possibilities of nuclear fission. By 1939 international competition for the development of an atomic weapon was already started. In October 1939, a letter from Albert Einstein was put in the hands of President Roosevelt to the effect that "extremely powerful bombs of a new type" could be achieved "in the immediate future." The French Government, just before the Fall of France, purchased the largest available quantity of heavy water from the Norsk Hydro Company of Norway, and subsequently British commandos raided heavy-water plants in Norway to prevent the precious fluid from falling into the enemy's hands. In April 1940, the Thomson Committee was set up by the British Air Ministry and, rather more than a year later, reported that the manufacture of an atom bomb was a feasible proposition. The basic material required was uranium 235, and the great difficulty was its isolation in sufficient amounts from ordinary uranium. The British War Cabinet set up a "Directorate of Tube Alloys" to implement the work of the Thomson Committee.

At the same time, reports were exchanged with American scientists, who had been conducting independent investigations. In October 1941, Roosevelt proposed to Churchill that all British and American efforts in this direction be combined and all research be concentrated in the United States. The Canadian Government was brought into the scheme, in view of the fact that Canada was one of the world's richest known sources of uranium ores and that Canadian hydroelectric engineering was peculiarly fitted for the production of the essential heavy water. A British-Canadian laboratory was set up in Montreal. The "master" American "Manhattan Project" was distributed between plants and laboratories at Oak Ridge, Tennessee; Richland near Pasco, Washington; and Los Alamos, New Mexico. Eventually the United States spent $2,500,000,000 over a period of four years on experiment and production processes for the manufacture of the atom bomb. In the final count, the credit for the preliminary theoretical research fell to many scientific workers of many different nationalities – some, ironically, were political refugees from Fascism and Nazism – but thereafter almost the whole of the huge technological burden was carried by the United States. At this point of time, no other nation could have expended the necessary industrial effort or recruited the necessary scientific personnel.

On August 6, the first atom bomb was dropped on Hiroshima from a solitary B-29 flying at high altitude. In the midst of this superhuman firespout, 78,000 persons were killed, 14,000 were missing, and 37,000 were injured, not counting thousands more who afterward developed curious disorders as the result of exposure to radiation. The American "divine wind" had blown, and there was no possible reply to it. On August 8 the Soviet Union declared war on Japan, and three army groups under Marshal Vasilevsky launched a converging offensive toward Harbin against the Japanese Kwantung Army in Manchuria. At any other time a Far Eastern war between the Soviet Union and Japan would have been a very considerable affair. The land forces of both powers were composed of picked troops, independently organized of homeland supplies, and long prepared for just such a conflict. But the Soviet Union was now fighting an enemy that was already in process of abandoning further resistance. The 750,000 men of the Kwantung Army, after a few days of fighting, broke up into isolated units, most of which proceeded to surrender in detail. On August 9, a second atom bomb, of different type but even greater destructive power, was loosed on the naval base at Nagasaki. The configuration of the city somewhat limited the area affected but, within that area, obliteration was absolute.

Even now, extreme Japanese militarists opposed a general capitulation, and it seemed for a moment as if the war would deteriorate into a disorganized scramble of guerrilla actions by individual Japanese chieftains at the head of such forces as would still bear them obedience. But, on the night of August 8, the Emperor held a meeting of the Cabinet and of Elder Statesmen and was advised to sue for peace. On August 10, the Japanese Government offered to accept the Potsdam ultimatum of July 26 "with the understanding that the said declaration does not comprise any demand which prejudices the prerogatives of the Emperor as a sovereign ruler." The Allied reply, transmitted by the United States Secretary of State, at once required that "from the moment of surrender the authority of the Emperor and the Japanese Government to rule the State shall be subject to the Supreme Commander of the Allied Powers." On August 14, the Suzuki cabinet accepted the Allied terms and, on the following day, resigned. Prince Higashikuni formed a new government. On August 28, the first American troops went ashore unopposed on Japanese soil in Sagami Bay.

On September 2, 1945, in Tokyo Bay, aboard the battleship *Missouri,* in the presence of General MacArthur, Admiral Nimitz, and ranking Allied officers, Japanese delegates signed the instrument of unconditional surrender. During the next three weeks, Japanese commanders formally surrendered in their respective areas in Harbin, Borneo, the Netherlands East Indies, Nanking, Singapore, and Hong Kong.

THE NATIONS IN THE SECOND WORLD WAR
WITH DATES OF ENTRY INTO THE WAR

The Axis Powers

Germany (September 1, 1939)
Italy (June 10, 1940)
Rumania (June 22, 1941)
Bulgaria (June 22, 1941)
Hungary (June 22, 1941)
Finland (June 22, 1941)
Japan (December 7, 1941)

The Allied Powers

Poland (September 1, 1939)
Britain (September 3, 1939)
France (September 3, 1939)
Australia (September 3, 1939)
New Zealand (September 3, 1939)
India (September 3, 1939)
South Africa (September 6, 1939)
Canada (September 10, 1939)
Norway (April 9, 1940)
Belgium (May 10, 1940)
Netherlands (May 10, 1940)
Greece (October 28, 1940)
Yugoslavia (April 6, 1941)
Soviet Union (June 22, 1941)
(including Ukraine and White Russia)
United States (December 7, 1941)
Brazil (August 22, 1942)

Also China (1937)
Czechoslovakia (1939)
Ethiopia (1939)

The twenty-one Allied Powers in the above list were those that had "actively waged war with substantial military forces against European enemy states." (See p. 614.)

The fifty "original" United Nations were those that attended the United Nations Conference at San Francisco in 1945 and that had previously declared war against Germany or Japan. Poland was subsequently allowed to count as one of the originals, thus making the fifty-first. (See pp. 840-41.)

Part Five

THE COLD WAR

We are destined, all of us here today, to live out most, if not all, of our lives in uncertainty and challenge and peril.

—JOHN F. KENNEDY

ATOMIC ENERGY COMMISSION

32. THE PEACE CONFERENCES AND THE PEACE TREATIES

The Foreign Ministers Council

At the end of the war in 1945 the grandiose precedent of the Peace Conference of Paris of 1919 was in everyone's mind. But the conditions of that conference did not now obtain. There were no dominating figures, such as President Wilson, Clemenceau, and Lloyd George. President Roosevelt was dead, Churchill out of office, and Stalin reluctant to leave Russia. The peacemaking of 1945-47 was conducted in the main not by heads of states, but by their foreign ministers, at *ad hoc* conferences convened at intervals in different places. The full-dress conference that did assemble in Paris in July 1946 was in all essentials still a foreign ministers' conference.

Discussions in regard to peace had taken place, and certain prospective lines of policy had been laid down, at the conferences at Teheran, Yalta, and Potsdam. At the Potsdam Conference in July 1945, the "Big Three" – the United States, Britain, and the Soviet Union – had agreed to delegate to a council of the foreign ministers of the United States, Britain, the Soviet Union, France, and China the task of preparing five peace treaties with the five Axis satellites – Italy, Rumania, Bulgaria, Hungary, and Finland. They had agreed furthermore that, for the discharge of that task, only those Powers should participate which had signed the armistices, except that, in the case of the treaty with Italy, France should be regarded as a signatory. Consequently, within the Foreign Ministers Council, four powers would draft the treaty with Italy, three the treaties with Rumania, Bulgaria, and Hungary, and two the treaty with Finland. This apparently innocent, entirely correct, and conveniently flexible "four-three-two" formula, however, was soon to create the first serious difficulty of the peacemaking.

The opening meeting of the new Foreign Ministers Council – attended by Byrnes, Bevin, Molotov, Bidault (representing France), and Wang Shih-chieh, the Chinese Foreign Minister – was held in London in September 1945. The Council agreed readily enough that the five treaties should include a Bill of Rights or other appropriate affirmation of the fundamental human freedoms lately set forth in the Charter of the United Nations. But thereafter the delegates were treated to their first outright exhibition of the Soviet's tactical methods in conference. Procedural questions, arising out of the "four-three-two" formula, eventually broke up the meeting, and the discussions upon the substantive peace terms were left to be continued in subcommittees. It was tacitly accepted by all parties that the Big Three should have the overriding decision in all matters of importance. But the Soviet delegate had probably not previously appreciated that the support of France – and no doubt that of China also – would be invariably weighted against the Soviet Union and on the side of the United States and Britain, and he thence embarked on a somewhat ungenerous campaign to try to obtain the exclusion of France and China from future discussions.

The impasse was partially resolved at a meeting of the Foreign Ministers in Moscow in December 1945, held without French and Chinese representatives. Byrnes at length secured adoption of a proposal – but not before he had dangled the hint of a loan before the Soviet Union – to the effect that those powers that had signed the armistices – including France, in the case of the treaty with Italy – should draw up the terms of peace and that these terms should then be considered at a general conference of all members of the United Nations which had "actively waged war with substantial military forces against European enemy states."

The second meeting of the Foreign Ministers Council – Byrnes, Bevin, Molotov, and Bidault – was held in Paris from April 25 to May 16, 1946. The atmosphere had grown still more tense. A crisis was mounting in Iran, where Soviet troops were in occupation. Several pressing problems were before the Council, namely Trieste, the Italian colonies and possessions overseas, reparations, the navigation of the Danube, the creation of democratic governments in the Balkans and in Eastern Europe, and the Franco regime in Spain. In all of these, the United States and Britain stood in sharp conflict with the Soviet Union, with France trying to steer a middle course. Molotov accused the Western Powers of seeking to form an "Anglo-Saxon bloc," and there were heated exchanges, notably between Molotov and Bevin. After nineteen days of inconclusive discussion, Byrnes asked for a recess "permitting each of us to give undivided attention to reexamination of our positions in the hope of finding means of reconciling them."

The Foreign Ministers Council reconvened in Paris between June 15 and July 12, 1946, for the continuation of its second meeting. The cleavages were manifest and undisguised. In the matter of Trieste, the Soviet Union demanded that the city and the surrounding area should be awarded to Yugoslavia; the Western Powers demanded that they and their predominantly Italian population should remain Italian. Clearly the Soviet Union was preferring the claims of its Slavic client; and clearly the Western Powers were seeking to deny an important Mediterranean base to a potentially unfriendly power. The problem was aggravated by the memory of the treatment of the adjacent Yugoslav territory during the recent Italian occupation. It recalled the Fiume crisis which had so disturbed the Peace Conference of 1919. (See p. 104.) A commission of investigation representing the Council was sent out to Trieste and drew up proposals for four different frontier demarcations, the American most favorable to Italy, the British rather less favorable to Italy, the Soviet most favorable to Yugoslavia, and the French again steering a middle course. In the end, the Council accepted the French proposal. Trieste, together with about 300 square miles of the surrounding area, was to become a Free Territory, whose independence "shall be assured by the Security Council of the United Nations." The remainder of Istria and the ports of Fiume and Pola would go to Yugoslavia. A governor for the Free Territory with full powers, who should not be "a citizen of either Italy, Yugoslavia, or the Free Territory," was to be nominated by the Security Council in consultation with the Italian and Yugoslav Governments. The compromise created a "second Danzig" and satisfied no party. When it was announced, the Yugoslavs declared that they would sign no such treaty with Italy nor withdraw Yugoslav troops from that part of Istria which was to be assigned to the Free Territory.

In the matter of the Italian colonies and possessions overseas, the Foreign Ministers Council decided that the Dodecanese Islands, in accordance with the wishes of the inhabitants, would be ceded to Greece and that Italy would renounce her sovereignty over her North African colonies, Libya (Tripolitania and Cyrenaica), Eritrea, and Italian Somaliland. But the problem of eventual disposal and trusteeship of these North African colonies was deferred. Molotov, perhaps not very seriously, claimed the trusteeship of Tripolitania for the Soviet Union. No decision was reached regarding the navigation of the Danube. (See pp. 108 and 112.)

The Peace Conference of Paris

The Peace Conference of those members of the United Nations that had "actively waged war with substantial military forces against European enemy states," assembled in the Luxembourg Palace in Paris between July 29 and October 15, 1946. The states numbered twenty-one in all – the United States, Britain, the Soviet Union, France, China, Australia, Belgium, Brazil, Canada, Czechoslovakia, Ethiopia, Greece, India, the Netherlands, New Zealand, Norway, Poland, South Africa, the Ukraine, White Russia, and Yugoslavia – and they were represented by over 1,500 delegates. Bidault represented France and was host and chairman of the Conference. Byrnes, the American Secretary of State, was accompanied by the American ambassadors to Britain and to the Soviet Union, respectively Averell Harriman and Bedell Smith, and by Senators Connally (Democrat) and Vandenberg (Republican). Attlee at first and then A. V. Alexander, First Lord of the Admiralty, represented Britain; Bevin, who was unwell, was present at the later stages of the Conference. Molotov, accompanied by Vyshinsky, represented the Soviet Union. As on the occasion of the Paris Peace Conference twenty-seven years before, some of the most remarkable and picturesque personalities belonged to the "smaller" states – Spaak of Belgium, Jan Masaryk of Czechoslovakia, Kardelj of Yugoslavia, and Manuilsky of the Ukraine. Field Marshal Smuts, the only delegate who had also been at Paris in 1919, represented South Africa, Mackenzie King represented Canada, and Evatt represented Australia. Among the enemy delegates who were permitted hearings at the Conference were De Gasperi, Saragat, and Bonomi of Italy, and Tatarescu of Rumania.

But in spite of the array of talent and distinction and the attempt to capture the spirit of high decision, the total result of the Paris Peace Conference of 1946 was meager and anticlimactic. Procedural questions continued to vex and harass the discussions. The machinery of the Conference included a General Commission – which actually never met – a Military Commission, a Legal and Drafting Commission, five Political Commissions for each of the five treaties, and two Economic Commissions, Plenary sessions were to be held at intervals. The smaller states were all represented on these bodies, but they objected that a proposed two-thirds majority ruling would virtually deprive them of a voice in the important decisions. The smaller states at the Conference indeed constituted a problem which, as once before, had sometimes to be very arbitrarily solved. (See pp. 97ff.)

The voting in the commissions repeatedly divided the "Soviet Six" – the Soviet Union, Czechoslovakia, Poland, the Ukraine, White Russia, and Yugoslavia – from the non-Soviet remainder. Some progress was made in regard to territorial adjustments (other than Trieste) and in regard to reparations. The Conference wound up its labors at a plenary session on October 15. The Yugoslav delegates, still disputing the Trieste settlement, absented themselves from the session.

The Peace Treaties with Italy, Rumania, Bulgaria, Hungary, and Finland

Elections in the United States in November 1946 resulted in a Congress largely dominated by Republicans. But the change in political color at home, it was evident, would make no difference to the country's foreign policy. It is probable that this display of the temper of the American people produced its salutary diplomatic repercussions, and the Foreign Ministers Council – Byrnes, Bevin, Molotov, and the French Deputy Foreign Minister, Couve de Murville, in the absence of Bidault – held its third meeting in an atmosphere of urgency in New York from November 4 to December 12, 1946. The texts of the five treaties were virtually completed before the end of the meeting.

Basically Trieste, reparations, and the Danube were still before the Council. Day after day was interminably absorbed in defining the powers of the future governor of the Free Territory of Trieste, especially for times of civil emergency, his relations with the proposed elected local council, and his responsibility to the Security Council of the United Nations. The Foreign Ministers reached agreements upon items of detail, such as the citizenship of the Free Territory and the management of its port and railroads. But the entire discussion over Trieste had an inevitable air of unreality as long as the Security Council of the United Nations was to be the competent authority for nominating the governor, and the Soviet Union could there resort to obstructive tactics to prevent that nomination from being made. Molotov argued strongly against any reference to the Danube in the treaties, but eventually agreed to the insertion of a clause to the effect that the navigation of the Danube should be "free and open for the nationals of all States . . . on a footing of equality." The Foreign Ministers issued a separate declaration that they would convene, within six months of the entry into force of the treaties, a further conference, at which they and the Danubian countries should be represented, to establish a Danube navigation authority.

The five treaties of peace with Italy, Rumania, Bulgaria, Hungary, and Finland were signed successively by Byrnes, Molotov, and Bevin in Washington, Moscow, and London, and then by Bidault and Allied and enemy delegates at a brief ceremony on February 10, 1947, at the Quai d'Orsay in Paris. Protests of one form or another against the treaties were lodged by Yugoslavia and Italy, and a campaign for revision was begun by all the enemy states except Finland. Upon his signature of the treaties, Byrnes resigned office and retired into private life.

Under the Italian treaty, Italy accepted the creation of the Free Territory of Trieste and the accompanying territorial and political readjustments which we have described. Certain small areas on the Franco-Italian frontier were ceded to France.[1] The Italo-Austrian frontier was left unchanged, and the southern Tirol and the Brenner Pass remained in Italian possession. As we have said, Italy renounced her sovereignty over her North African colonies, but their disposal was left to a future conference of the powers to be held within the coming twelve months. Ethiopia had already reverted to her former independent status of 1935. The Italian Army was not to exceed 250,000 men, the Navy 25,000, and the Air Force 25,000. All naval vessels, except two battleships, four cruisers, and some smaller ships were surrendered to the Allies. Italy restored all looted Allied property. She was to pay reparations, over a period of seven years, to the victims of her aggression – $100,000,000 to the Soviet Union, $125,000,000 to Yugoslavia, $105,000,000 to Greece, $25,000,000 to Ethiopia, and $5,000,000 to Albania – the sources of such reparations being factory equipment, war material and, after two years, current production. She was to assist in the apprehension and surrender of war criminals for trial by Allied tribunals.

Except for the territorial losses in North Africa and the enforced demilitarization, the Italian treaty could hardly be described as harsh. But Italy was a country of ancient civilization and of inexhaustible associations for all cultured people and, for all her recent Fascist follies, she had never acquired the sinister record of her German partner. The Italian resistance movement in the closing months of the war had materially contributed to the Allied victory, and it deserved its appropriate recognition. And, no doubt, the influence of Italian-born citizens of the United States helped somewhat to alleviate the final verdict. The provisions in the treaty regarding Trieste were largely inoperative. The Security Council failed to agree upon a choice of a governor. The Anglo-American occupation of the Free Territory meanwhile continued.

Under the Rumanian, Bulgarian, and Hungarian treaties, the whole of Transylvania was returned to Rumania; a rectification of the Hungarian frontier opposite Bratislava was made in favor of Czechoslovakia; and Rumania's cession of Bessarabia and northern Bucovina to the Soviet Union was confirmed. Bulgaria retained the southern Dobruja, but she failed to make good her claim to Western Thrace against Greece. Greece likewise failed to secure northern Epirus. All Allied looted property was restored, and reparations were to be paid to the Soviet Union, Czechoslovakia, and Greece. There were clauses providing for the reduction of army, navy, and air-force strengths and for the surrender of war criminals.

Under the Finnish treaty, the Finnish-Soviet frontiers of the treaty of March 1940 were restored, with the exception that the Petsamo area was now ceded to the Soviet Union. Porkkala was leased to the Soviet Union for fifty years as a naval base, and all communications thereto from Soviet territory were put under Soviet control. The Finnish Army was not to exceed 34,400 men, which was roughly the strength of the Finnish standing army of 1939, and Finnish naval and air-force units were to be proportionately reduced. Finland restored looted Soviet property and agreed to pay reparations to the Soviet Union to the amount of $300,000,000 in commodities, at the price level of 1938, over eight years. Again there was a clause for the surrender of war criminals. Certain political provisions forbade organizations of a "Fascist type" or organizations conducting anti-Soviet propaganda. They were provisions which clearly gave the Soviet Government considerable powers of interference in Finnish domestic affairs. (See p. 671.)

A later settlement at Trieste was reached on October 5, 1954. (See p. 706.) The peace treaty with Austria was signed in Vienna on May 15, 1955. (See pp. 654-55.) To date there has been no peace treaty with Germany. The peace treaty with Japan was signed in San Francisco on September 8, 1951. (See p. 757.)

33. THE UNITED NATIONS AND THE REORGANIZATION OF PEACE

The Origins of the United Nations

The joint Declaration of the United Nations was signed at Washington on January 1, 1942, by representatives of the twenty-six Allies pledging their full resources, military and economic, to the common struggle. The Declaration contained an explicit adherence to the "purposes and principles" of the Atlantic Charter. A permanent United Nations Organization to take the place of the League of Nations, "for the maintenance of world peace and security and the promotion of world economic and social advancement," was under serious discussion at high political levels during the ensuing year. The foreign ministers, in conference in Moscow in October 1943, formally recognized the necessity for establishing such an organization. Discussions were continued at the end of 1943 at the Cairo Conference between Roosevelt, Churchill, and Chiang Kai-shek and at the Teheran Conference between Roosevelt, Churchill and Stalin. Meanwhile the general plan, now fast maturing, was further prospered by the conference at Hot Springs, Virginia, in May and June 1943, which created the Food and Agriculture Organization (FAO), and the conference in Washington in November 1943, which created the United Nations Relief and Rehabilitation Administration (UNRRA), two organizations subsequently to become Specialized Agencies of the United Nations.

Representatives of the United States, Britain, the Soviet Union, and China – notably Stettinius, Cadogan and Halifax, Gromyko, and Wellington Koo – conferred at Dumbarton Oaks, near Washington, between August and October 1944, to make "tentative proposals" for the future organization. Soviet and Chinese representatives did not meet together, as the Soviet Union was not at war with Japan. A General Assembly and a Security Council were projected, somewhat on the lines of the similarly named bodies of the League of Nations, and in addition an International Court and an Economic and Social Council. But it was at Dumbarton Oaks that the first sharp differences arose over the voting procedure to be adopted in the Security Council. A working formula for that procedure was agreed upon at the Yalta Conference between Roosevelt, Churchill, and Stalin in February 1945 but, as we shall see, it remained thereafter a highly contentious issue. Thus primed and prepared, the representatives of fifty nations assembled at San Francisco on April 25, 1945, to draw up the Charter of the United Nations. At that time the Polish question was unsettled, and no Polish representative attended the San Francisco Conference, but under Article 3 of the Charter, as it was drawn up, Poland was afterward enabled to count herself an original member – the fifty-first.

The San Francisco Conference lasted two months in an atmosphere of high enthusiasm and hard work. The delegations were headed by a galaxy of political distinction and experience. Stettinius and Cordell Hull, and Senators Connally and Vandenberg represented the United States; Eden, Attlee, Cranborne, and Halifax represented Britain; Molotov and Gromyko represented the Soviet Union; Bidault represented France; T. V. Soong and Wellington Koo represented China; Spaak represented Belgium; Jan Masaryk, Czechoslovakia; Manuilsky, the Ukraine; Subasich, Yugoslavia; Mackenzie King represented Canada; Forde and Evatt, Australia; and Smuts, South Africa. The delegates had before them the Dumbarton Oaks proposals, and the Yalta agreement in regard to voting procedure in the Security Council, and the mass of their own amendments totaling some twelve thousand items. The work was divided among four commissions and their several subcommittees. The most lively discussions were over the trusteeship of non-self-governing territories, the registration and revision of treaties, regional arrangements and, of course, the voting procedure in the Security Council. All were questions which in one form or another had been controverted twenty-six years before when the League Covenant was drawn up. The final draft of the Charter was unanimously adopted at the Conference's ninth plenary session and signed by the delegates of the fifty nations on June 26, 1945.

The Charter came formally into force on October 24, 1945, since known as United Nations Day, when, under Article 110, ratifications had been deposited by the United States, Britain, the Soviet Union, France, China, and twenty-four of the other signatory nations. The General Assembly and Security Council met for the first time in London in January 1946. Trygve Lie, the Norwegian Foreign Minister, was elected Secretary General. He was succeeded in April 1953 by Dag Hammarskjöld, Swedish Minister of State, who was killed in an air crash in the Congo on September 18, 1961. To date (October 1961), the United Nations has 101 members.[1] As an indication of the immense size of the organization at the present time we could note the fact that its total annual expenditure amounted in 1961 to over $300,000,000, including its own Annual Budget and the costs of its Specialized Agencies, technical assistance, refugees, and the forces in Suez and the Congo.

The Constitution of the United Nations

The Preamble of the Charter recalls the lofty language and resolution of the League Covenant. Under Article 1 of the Charter, the purposes of the United Nations are the maintenance of international peace and security in economic, social, cultural, and humanitarian problems, the development of friendly relations among nations, and the achievement of international cooperation by means of effective collective measures. Under Article 2, the United Nations recognizes the sovereign equality of all its members and requires their good faith in the peaceful settlement of international disputes, their abandonment of the threat or use of force, and their assistance in any action which it shall deem necessary to take in accordance with the Charter. The United Nations is debarred from intervening in matters that fall within the domestic jurisdiction of its members.

The original members of the United Nations were those nations that had been signatories of the Declaration of January 1, 1942, or that had become signatories by March 1, 1945. Membership thereafter has been open to "all other peace-loving states" that accept the obligations of the Charter and are able and willing to carry them out, and the admission of such states requires "a decision of the General Assembly upon the recommendation of the Security Council" — and, as it eventually worked out, on the unanimous vote of the permanent members of the Security Council.

Constitutionally the United Nations functions through a General Assembly, a Security Council, and a Secretariat. The General Assembly consists of representatives of all the member nations. The Security Council consists of the representatives of eleven member nations, of whom the five Great Powers — China, France, the Soviet Union, Britain, and the United States — are permanent members, and the other six are elected by the General Assembly for two-year terms, three retiring every year. The Secretariat is a permanent body consisting of a Secretary General and staff, and acts as an international civil service. The headquarters of the United Nations is in New York and, since 1950, has been housed in a fine group of buildings overlooking the East River, a group financed by an interest-free loan from the United States. The ground on which it stands is "international" and technically is not part of New York State or City. A European office is maintained in the former League of Nations buildings in Geneva.

It had been hoped by its creators that the League of Nations would have superseded all the alliances of the old diplomacy, and the League Covenant had given a very grudging recognition of "regional understandings like the Monroe Doctrine." But the Charter appeared to encourage the formation of "regional arrangements," and the Security Council was prepared to make use of such arrangements for the pacific settlement of local disputes. The Pan American Union, the Western European Union, and the Atlantic Pact consequently could be regarded by their several sponsors as in no way repugnant to the ideals of the United Nations.

The Charter provides for a Trusteeship Council for the trust territories. It creates an International Court of Justice as the principal judicial organ of the United Nations. It also provides for an Economic and Social Council and for a series of Specialized Agencies, which we shall briefly discuss later in this chapter. The Charter requires the registration and publication of international treaties entered into by member nations, but it contains no article corresponding to Article 19 of the League Covenant, providing for the revision of treaties which have become inapplicable or obsolete. Amendments to the Charter require the votes of two-thirds of the members of the General Assembly and ratification by two-thirds of the members of the General Assembly including all the permanent members of the Security Council. But it is to be noted that to date, no amendments to the Charter have been made. Unlike the League Covenant, the Charter has remained an unchanged, cast-iron instrument.

The General Assembly and the Security Council

The General Assembly consists of all members of the United Nations. Each member may have five representatives, but only one vote. Decisions of the General Assembly "on important questions" are reached by a two-thirds majority. But under the Charter the General Assembly has few substantial powers. The Economic and Social Council and the Trusteeship Council are its subordinate organs, elected by it and responsible to it. But otherwise it may "consider general principles of cooperation . . . including the principles governing disarmament," "discuss any questions relating to the maintenance of international peace and security," "make recommendations with regard to such questions," "call the attention of the Security Council to situations which are likely to endanger international peace and security," "initiate studies for the purpose of promoting international cooperation," "receive and consider annual and special reports from the Security Council," and so forth. In effect, the General Assembly was intended to become the deliberative and consultative chamber and platform of the smaller states, even as the Security Council was intended to become the concert of the Great Powers. The General Assembly adopts its own rules of procedure and, for its regular functioning, refers a good part of its work to committees — to seven Main Committees and other subsidiary organs.

The Security Council is the body of "primary responsibility" in the United Nations. It was designed to have the authority, the respect, and the "teeth" which, in the view of many critics, the old League of Nations had so often lacked. In addition to its eleven members, it is entitled to invite a nation, not one of its members, or not even a member of the United Nations, to participate, without vote, in its discussion of any question affecting the interests of that nation. Under Articles 33-51, any member of the United Nations may bring to the attention of the Security Council a dispute likely to endanger international peace. The Security Council has power to call upon the parties to settle the dispute by negotiation, arbitration, recourse to the International Court, or by other peaceful means. It has the power to investigate the dispute itself and recommend appropriate procedures for settlement. It also has power "to determine the existence of any threat to peace, breach of peace, or act of aggression," and to decide first upon provisional measures to prevent an aggravation of the situation and then upon measures, not involving the use of armed force, such as the severance of economic or diplomatic relations. Finally, "should the Security Council consider that measures [so provided] would be inadequate . . . it may take such action by air, sea or land forces as may be necessary to maintain or restore international peace and security."

All members of the United Nations are under obligation to contribute to the maintenance of peace and to make available to the Security Council, "on its call and in accordance with special agreement," the necessary armed forces, assistance, and facilities, "including rights of passage." The Security Council is also to be responsible for establishing a system for the regulation of armaments. A Military Staff Committee, consisting of the chiefs of staff or other representatives of the five permanent members of the Security Council, is to advise the Security Council on its military requirements, on the employment of forces placed at its disposal, and on the regulation of armaments.

All these very considerable powers vested in the Security Council were intended not only to restore the peace already broken, but to anticipate threats to peace in the early stages, and to act quickly and decisively before any such threat lapsed into hostilities. Yet the exercise of these powers – and here is the rub – depends upon the unanimity of the five permanent members of the Security Council, the five Great Powers. Under Article 27 of the Charter, decisions on "procedural matters" are to be made by an affirmative vote of seven members, but decisions "on all other matters" are to be made by an affirmative vote of seven members, "including the concurring votes of the permanent members." This voting procedure was in accordance with the agreement made at the Yalta Conference, and as such it was a necessary concession to political realism. But it has resulted in practice in the so-called Great Power Veto. The League of Nations had sometimes been obstructed by its unanimity clause; but here was a unanimity clause that was to become even more insuperable and perverse.

The Trusteeship System

The trusteeship system of the United Nations is a virtual revival of the mandates system of the League of Nations. Generally that mandates system was acknowledged to have worked very well. The Mandatory Powers, most of whom already had a long tradition of responsible colonial administration behind them, had seldom abused their trust. But, in re-creating a body to correspond, and to act as successor, to the League's Mandates Commission, the opportunity was taken both for widening and for more closely defining its functions.

The Charter recognizes that certain members of the United Nations would have to assume responsibility for the administration of the former mandated territories, territories detached from enemy states as a result of the Second World War, and "territories voluntarily placed under the system by states responsible for their administration." The members in question must accept "as a sacred trust" the well-being and the political, economic, social, and educational advancement of the inhabitants of these territories. The administration of trust territories, as they were now to be called, by their respective administering authorities would then be in accordance with specific trusteeship agreements and would be supervised by a Trusteeship Council operating under the authority of the General Assembly.

The General Assembly at its first session, in February 1946, passed an interim resolution on "non-self-governing peoples" acknowledging that the trusteeship obligations of the Charter were already in force. The Trusteeship Council was established in December 1946 and met for its first session at Lake Success on March 26, 1947. It then consisted of representatives of the five administering authorities, namely, the former Mandatory Powers, Britain, Australia, New Zealand, France, and Belgium; the three other permanent members of the Security Council, namely, the United States, the Soviet Union, and China; and two other members, Iraq and Mexico, elected by the General Assembly. The Trusteeship Council meets twice annually, and appoints a President, Vice-President, and committees. The Secretary General of the United Nations and his staff act as its secretariat. It receives the annual reports of the administering authorities and presents to the General Assembly its own annual report on the discharge of its responsibilities. It accepts and examines petitions, presented orally or in writing, by the inhabitants of the trust territories or by other interested parties, and it sends representatives to inspect the trust territories.

By 1950, the peak year, eleven trusteeship agreements had been negotiated with seven administering authorities.[2] In addition the Security Council accepted an agreement entitling the United States to administer the former Japanese mandated islands in the Pacific as a "strategic trusteeship."

We shall discuss the question of Palestine in a later chapter. (See pp. 771-73 and 797ff.)

The International Court of Justice

The International Court of Justice, "the principal judicial organ of the United Nations," was an integral part of the League of Nations. Its Statute was expressly based upon the Statute of the former World Court, almost without amendment and was annexed to the Charter. Its fifteen judges are elected for nine-year terms by the General Assembly and Security Council. Its jurisdiction extends only to disputes of a specifically "legal" character voluntarily submitted to it by member nations. The former "Optional Clause" is retained and is still operative. Thirty-eight nations are now subscribers to the clause. At the same time the Charter expressly states that "each member of the United Nations undertakes to comply with the decision of the Court . . . in any case to which it is a party."

All members of the United Nations are automatically parties to the Statute of the Court. Other nations, not members of the United Nations, may become parties "on conditions to be determined in each case by the General Assembly upon the recommendation of the Security Council." At the present time there are three of these other states: Switzerland, Liechenstein, and San Marino. The General Assembly, the Security Council, and the Specialized Agencies may request the Court to give advisory opinions. The seat of the Court is The Hague. In April 1946, the former World Court was wound up and the new Court met for the first time. To date,[3] the Court has considered twenty-eight cases, including the Corfu Channel case in 1947 (see p. 681), the Anglo-Norwegian Fisheries case in 1949, the

Anglo-Iranian Oil Company case in 1951, and five cases arising out of aerial incidents, and it has handed down eleven advisory opinions, including three on South West Africa.

The Economic and Social Council (ECOSOC) and the Specialized Agencies

In 1939 the League of Nations had created a Special Committee for the Development of International Cooperation in Economic and Social Affairs, generally called the Bruce Committee after its chairman, the High Commissioner of Australia in London (later Lord Bruce of Melbourne). The Committee proposed an over-all integration of the League's economic and social work. Its further activities were prevented by the outbreak of war in that year, but the idea behind it was reborn in the Economic and Social Council of the United Nations (ECOSOC), formulated in the Charter. That Council consists of eighteen members of the United Nations, elected by, and responsible to, the General Assembly, six elected each year for a term of three years. It may initiate studies, prepare draft conventions for submission to the General Assembly, call international conferences on matters falling within its competence, and in particular it may make agreements with, and coordinate the activities of the Specialized Agencies.

At the time of writing the "Related Agencies," as they are sometimes called, are as follows: the International Labor Organization (ILO); the Food and Agriculture Organization (FAO); the United Nations Educational, Scientific, and Cultural Organization (UNESCO); the International Civil Aviation Organization (ICAO); the International Bank for Reconstruction and Development or World Bank; the International Monetary Fund (IMF); the Universal Postal Union (UPU); the World Health Organization (WHO); the International Telecommunication Union (ITU); the World Meteorological Organization (WMO); the International Finance Corporation (IFC); the Intergovernmental Maritime Consultative Organization (IMCO). The United National Relief and Rehabilitation Administration (UNRRA) and the International Refugee Organization (IRO) were wound up in 1947 and 1951 respectively. The International Trade Organization (ITO) never went into effect, but part of its intended functions have been taken over by the General Agreement on Tariffs and Trade (GATT). The International Atomic Energy Agency (IAEA), for the promotion of the peaceful uses of atomic energy, is classed as one of the Related Agencies, but is constituted separately from ECOSOC. The most recent creation, the International Development Association (IDA), reports to ECOSOC, but enjoys considerable freedom of action.

In addition ECOSOC has set up a number of commissions, such as the four regional Economic Commissions, respectively for Europe (ECE), for Asia and the Far East (ECAFE), for Latin America (ECLA), and for Africa (ECA); the Commission on Human Rights; the United Nations Children's Fund (UNICEF); and several other bodies, for instance on population, migration, stateless persons, crime, narcotics, and so forth.

We cannot possibly review this enormous humanitarian effort in our limited space. We can merely take separate note of some of the larger agencies.

The International Labor Organization (ILO)

The International Labor Organization (ILO) is the one League institution that has survived under its old name. Its origin and functions have been described elsewhere (see pp. 119-20). In 1940 it moved to Montreal, and it continued its work there throughout the Second World War. It resumed the regular sessions of its General Conference at Philadelphia in 1944. It sent representatives to Bretton Woods, to UNRRA, to the FAO, and to San Francisco. In deference to Soviet reservations, it was not expressly mentioned by name in the Charter of the United Nations.

An agreement defining the relationship between the ILO and the Economic and Social Council was approved by the ILO and the General Assembly at the end of 1946. The ILO operates through an annual Conference, a Governing Body, an Office, and a Director General, as he is now entitled. Since 1945, the Directors General have been, successively, Edward Phelan and David Morse. The ILO's headquarters are in Geneva, and it maintains branch offices in London, Paris, Washington, New York, Ottawa, and other cities. It now has 101 members. It continues all its former good work, its research, information services, reports and publications. To date, a total of 111 conventions and 111 recommendations have been adopted, and nearly 2,000 ratifications have been registered, covering such diverse subjects as employment, wages, hours of work, holidays, health, safety, the employment of women and children, the protection of the right to organize, and so forth.

The United Nations Relief and Rehabilitation Administration (UNRRA) and the International Refugee Organization (IRO)

As early as September 1941, under British initiative, an Allied conference was held in London to prepare estimates for the relief and rehabilitation of devastated Europe. The United States, then a neutral, was not represented, but the American ambassador in London gave the conference an assurance that American cooperation would be forthcoming. During 1942, plans for a vast economic reconstruction of Europe, partly financed and managed by Americans, was being freely discussed in the United States, and a somewhat premature start was made in the recruiting and training of American personnel for the task. In November 1943, at Washington, at a conference of the representatives of forty-four members of the United Nations, the United Nations Relief and Rehabilitation Administration (UNRRA) was created. Recent Allied military successes in Europe held out the prospect that the new organization would soon be called into action in the territories newly liberated from the Axis. Its first Director General was Herbert H. Lehman, former Governor of New York

State, and its second, from April to December 1946, Fiorello La Guardia, former Mayor of New York City.

UNRRA was a provisional organization for immediate needs. It worked in former Axis-occupied territories in Europe and Asia, among refugees and displaced persons and, on occasions, it supported whole populations. It provided food, clothing and footwear, medical stores, industrial and agricultural equipment, vehicles and rolling stock, and building materials. It provided livestock and feed for animals. It provided services in the form of hospitals and welfare centers, fully staffed and equipped. Its biggest recipients were the countries of Eastern Europe and the Balkans, including White Russia and the Ukraine, but it also sent supplies to China, Korea, and the Philippines. At one time it was feeding the entire city of Athens. It cared for two million Italian children. Five millions in Yugoslavia were wholly or partly dependent upon it.

Inevitably there were mistrust and friction. Usually UNRRA transferred its supplies in bulk to a receiving government at an agreed port or railhead. But it insisted on having observers with full freedom of movement in the country in question to check the distribution. It also insisted that no political discrimination should be exercised, and that all classes, parties, and creeds should share equally in its benefits. But often it seemed that the receiving government regarded the observers as the paid agents of "American imperialism," and there were several countries where UNRRA might have accomplished more, and more economically, but for local suspicion, obstruction, and graft. UNRRA officially brought its activities to an end in March 1949. In its six years it had expended over $4,000,000,000, of which $2,750,000,000 was contributed by the United States.

An International Refugee Organization (IRO) was proposed and its constitution approved by the General Assembly in December 1946. It was to be concerned with the repatriation of refugees, their legal and political protection, or their transport to, and resettlement in, countries willing and able to accept them. Like UNRRA, whose duties in this field of activity it inherited, it was a provisional organization, and it was wound up during 1951. It repatriated some 75,000 refugees and found new homes for over a million. Altogether it gave assistance to more than 1,600,000. The problem of refugees and of stateless persons, still a vast one, has now devolved on a United Nations High Commissioner for Refugees (UNHCR) with headquarters at Geneva.

The Food and Agriculture Organization (FAO)

The decision to create a Food and Agriculture Organization (FAO) was made at a conference of forty-four nations at Hot Springs, Virginia, in May and June 1943. The constitution of the FAO was drawn up by an Interim Commission and signed by the representatives of thirty nations at a conference at Quebec in October 1945. It is an advisory and consultative body. It operates through a Conference of members meeting at least once every two years, a World Food Council and other committees, and a Director-General and staff of experts. Its first Director-General was Sir John Boyd Orr of Britain. Its headquarters are now in Rome. It now has eighty-three members.

The FAO collects and disseminates information "relating to nutrition, food and agriculture" – and "agriculture" includes fisheries and forestry; it promotes research and education in its field and improved methods of agricultural production and marketing; it furnishes technical assistance and organizes missions of investigation and advice. Its work is acknowledged to be urgent and world-wide. The prevailing malnutrition even in many "advanced" countries and the long-term problems of soil exhaustion and soil erosion are all of unusual pertinence in the welfare of nations today. The good life which our social philosophers dream of will not be a reality so long as half the world's population lives below subsistence level. The FAO is already one of the great forces in international affairs, an example of what may be accomplished by voluntary, "functional" cooperation.

The United Nations Educational, Scientific, and Cultural Organization (UNESCO)

The United Nations Educational, Scientific, and Cultural Organization (UNESCO) reproduced in a much extended form the functions of the League's Committee on Intellectual Cooperation. (See p. 119.) Its first germ was conceived at a meeting of Allied ministers of education in London in 1942. Its constitution was signed by representatives of forty-four nations at a conference in London in November 1945. Its doctrine derives from the declaration that "since wars begin in the minds of men, it is in the minds of men that the defenses of peace must be constructed." It is an advisory and consultative body only. It operates through a biennial General Conference, an Executive Board, a Director-General, and secretariat. Its first Director General was Julian Huxley of Britain. Its headquarters is Unesco House, Paris. It now has 101 members and six associate members. It seeks to promote mutual knowledge and the understanding of peoples through all means of mass communication, to give fresh impulse to popular education and equality of educational opportunity, to suggest "educational methods best suited to prepare the children of the world for the responsibilities of freedom," to preserve the world's books and monuments, and to encourage the exchange of students and teachers.

The International Monetary Fund (IMF) and the World Bank

The long-term program for mending the chaotic monetary aftermath, not only of the war itself, but of the previous years of depression and totalitarianism, for financing industrial re-equipment, and for restoring international trade was put in the hands of various organizations largely created by American and British initiative. Thus a United Nations Monetary and Financial Conference, which was held in July 1944 at Bretton Woods in New Hampshire, created the International Monetary Fund (IMF), to which member nations should contribute according to adjustable quotas and which should be used to maintain exchange stability, avoid competitive exchange depreciation, cushion sudden fluctuations, and generally regulate a multilateral system of payments. Each national currency was to be assigned a value in terms of gold or of the American dollar, a value which the member in question was then obligated not to change without consultation with the Fund. Seventy-two nations are now members of the Fund and thirty-seven par values have so far been assigned. Unhappily, however, the basic obligation has already been disregarded, notably by France's devaluation of the franc in 1948 (see p. 694) — and, as some would argue, by Britain's devaluation of the pound in 1949 (see p. 726).

The same conference at Bretton Woods agreed simultaneously to set up an International Bank for Reconstruction and Development, or World Bank, as it came to be called, a long-term credit institution for the purpose of financing projects which have been unable to obtain private capital, in particular "the most useful and urgent projects, large and small." To date the World Bank has made over two hundred loans, totaling $4,250,000,000 to forty-nine countries. Since 1949, the Bank's President has been Eugene R. Black.

In 1955 an International Finance Corporation (IFC) was created, affiliated to the World Bank, though a separate legal entity, intended to provide loans to private enterprises.

The General Agreement on Tariffs and Trade (GATT)

During 1946 the Economic and Social Council set up a Preparatory Committee of representatives of nineteen states to prepare agenda and draw up a charter for consideration at an International Conference on Trade and Employment. The Preparatory Committee held meetings in London in the winter of 1946 and further meetings at Geneva from April to October 1947, when it adopted a draft Charter for an International Trade Organization (ITO), covering the flow of capital particularly to undeveloped countries, access to markets, reduction of tariff barriers, and the elimination of discriminatory and restrictive trade practices. In November 1947, at Havana, sixty nations, virtually the entire trading world outside the Soviet Union, met to discuss the draft Charter — or Havana Charter, as it came to be known — and the document was eventually signed on March 24, 1948, by fifty-three nations.

It seemed as if Articles 4 and 5 of the Atlantic Charter — and indeed Point 3 of the old Wilsonian Fourteen Points — were on the way to fruitful implementation. But the fifty-three nations in question showed no pronounced alacrity to ratify, by 1947 and 1948 interest in the main had already shifted to the European Recovery Program, and the great scheme lapsed. Better fortune however attended the somewhat less ambitious agreement, which had also grown out of the same discussions at Geneva, the General Agreement on Tariffs and Trade (GATT), signed on October 30,

1947, by twenty-three nations. To date thirty-seven nations, representing four-fifths of the world's trade have acceded to GATT.

The World Health Organization (WHO)

The constitution of the World Health Organization (WHO) was drawn up at a conference in Paris in March and April 1946, and was signed by the delegates of sixty-one nations, including the Soviet Union and the Ukrainian and White Russian Soviet Republics, at an International Health Conference in New York in the following July. It came officially into existence on April 7, 1948, since known as World Health Day. It operates through a World Health Assembly, an Executive Board, a Director General, and secretariat. Its headquarters are in Geneva, and it maintains six regional centers in Delhi, Alexandria, Manila, Washington, Brazzaville, and Copenhagen. It now has 106 members and three associate members. The Soviet Union and the Ukrainian and White Russian Soviet republics withdrew in 1949, but have recently rejoined.

The WHO has established itself as one of the influential bodies of the United Nations—in many ways the counterpart of the FAO. Its purpose is to act as the directing and coordinating authority in international health work, to help eradicate epidemic diseases, prevent accidental injuries, improve nutrition, housing, sanitation, and working conditions, promote maternal and child welfare, and promote mental health, especially "as affecting the harmony of human relations." It has undertaken numbers of special projects for combating malaria, treponemal diseases, tuberculosis, trachoma, and cholera.

Human Rights and Genocide

A Commission on Human Rights was set up by ECOSOC in February 1946 and began work early in 1947 under the chairmanship of Mrs. Franklin D. Roosevelt. The Universal Declaration of Human Rights, which it drafted, was adopted by the General Assembly in December 10, 1948, a day since known as Human Rights Day. The declaration was not a treaty and carried no legal obligations. It read as an expansion of the Preamble of the Charter, and it represented, in its own words:

> . . . A common standard of achievement for all peoples and all nations, to the end that every individual and every organ of society, keeping this Declaration constantly in mind, shall strive by teaching and education to promote respect for these rights and freedoms by progressive measures, national and international, to secure their universal and effective recognition and observance, both among the peoples of member states themselves and among the peoples of territories under their jurisdiction.

The Commission on Human Rights then turned to preparing detailed draft covenants for adoption by assenting member states.

On December 9, 1948, the General Assembly adopted a Convention on the Prevention and Punishment of the Crime of Genocide. The Convention defined genocide as an act committed "with intent to destroy, in whole or in part, a national, ethnical, racial, or religious group" — by killing members of the group or causing them serious bodily or mental harm, or by "deliberately inflicting on the group conditions of life calculated to bring about its physical destruction . . ."

The Military Staff Committee

The Military Staff Committee, which, under Article 47 of the Charter, was to advise the Security Council on its military requirements, met for the first time in London in February 1946, and thereafter continued its sessions in New York. It was instructed by the Security Council to prepare the special military agreements with the members of the United Nations in regard to the contributions to the proposed international force which, in accordance with the Charter, those members would be called upon to make. It submitted its report on this question to the Security Council in April 1947. Several articles in the report were not unanimously agreed by the delegates, the most contentious article being that on "over-all strength." The American, British, French, and Chinese representatives argued that the contributions which the five permanent members of the Security Council should be called upon to make should be "comparable" and logically apportioned to their respective technical and strategic situations; that, for example, one power might contribute the major part of the land forces, another might contribute the major part of the naval forces, and so forth. The Soviet representatives argued, on the contrary, that such an arrangement would give one power an undue advantage over another and would be inconsistent with the avowed equality of status of the powers under the Charter and that therefore the contributions of the five permanent members of the Security Council should be "not only of equal over-all strength but also of the same composition, that is, of equal number of land, sea and air forces."

The divergence of views, it is hardly necessary to say, was entirely academic — the realities of the situation lay in the atomic bomb. The Military Staff Committee nevertheless continued to meet, and it has never been formally dissolved. But it remains a virtually defunct body. Even so, it might be argued that some of its intended functions were carried out — although not in the way originally envisaged in the Charter — in the United Nations forces sent to Korea in 1950, to the Suez Canal in 1956, and to the Congo in 1960. (See pp. 783-84, 800-01, and 812.)

Disarmament

Under Article 11 of the Charter, "the General Assembly may consider the general principles of cooperation in the maintenance of international peace and security, including the principles governing disarmament and the regulation of armaments"; and under Article 26, "the Security Council shall be responsible for formulating . . . plans for the establishment of a system for the regulation of armaments." But the Charter was adopted at San Francisco some weeks before Hiroshima, and in consequence the disarmament problem in the United Nations started off under entirely unexpected conditions of difficulty and urgency.

The Atomic Energy Commission was set up by resolution of the General Assembly in January 1946 and held its first meeting in New York in the following June. It was composed of the members of the Security Council and of Canada – the inclusion of Canada being in deference to the part which she had played in atomic research during the Second World War and to the fact that some of the richest uranium deposits then known were located in the Dominion. At that moment the United States held a virtual monopoly of the atomic bomb. The United States in the main had developed and manufactured the bomb; the United States had first used it; the United States was therefore in a position to lead discussions for its future control – or total abolition.

But at the very first meeting of the Atomic Energy Commission the American representative, Bernard M. Baruch, and the Soviet representative, Andrei Gromyko, were in immediate and fundamental disagreement. Baruch proposed the establishment of an international Atomic Development Authority (ADA) for the managerial control or ownership of all atomic energy activities potentially dangerous to world security, for the inspection and licensing of all other atomic activities, for the promotion of the beneficial uses of atomic energy, and for research. When an adequate system of control had been agreed and put into effective operation, said Baruch, the United States would voluntarily renounce its present technical advantage, halt its manufacture of atomic bombs, destroy existing bombs, and put the ADA in possession of information "as to the know-how for the production of atomic energy." But, he added, there must be no veto in this case. "There must be no veto to protect those who violate their solemn agreements not to develop or use atomic energy for destructive purposes." The Soviet representative, Gromyko, proposed on the contrary the conclusion of a rigorous international agreement to prohibit the use of atomic weapons and to destroy all existing atomic weapons. He further proposed an international control commission "within the framework of the Security Council" – and therefore subject to the veto – with its own inspection system and with the necessary rights of information and access.

The Scientific and Technical Committee set up by the Atomic Energy Commission to examine the purely scientific and technical problems involved reported in September 1946 that effective control was "technologically feasible," and at once put the discussions upon a practical basis. Inspection was then a political, not a scientific problem. But inspection as such was soon seen to be the whole issue between the powers. Gromyko evinced no appreciation or gratitude for the United States' original generous gesture to share its technical knowledge with the world once adequate safeguards had been provided. For its own political and military good reasons, the Kremlin could not take kindly to the idea of Soviet territory being invaded by a corps of foreign inspectors prying at will into every Soviet mine and factory. Gromyko was entirely unimpressed by the argument that all states alike would have to submit to the same derogations of their privacies. But, at bottom, the Atomic Energy Commission was struggling with the same situation that bedeviled all the relations of the powers since their victory in 1945. Atomic energy with all its sinister implications was already an element in the universal Cold War.

In May 1948, the Atomic Energy Commission decided by 9 votes to 2 (the Soviet Union and the Ukraine) to suspend its work. "Agreement on international control is dependent . . . on cooperation in broader fields of policy, and failure to achieve it arises from a situation beyond the Commission's competence." On September 23, 1949, President Truman announced that an atomic explosion was known to have occurred recently in the Soviet Union, and that this development, though always foreseen, called all the more urgently for effective, enforceable international control.

A Commission for Conventional Armaments, a body complementary to the Atomic Energy Commission and of similar membership, was set up by the Security Council in February 1947. It devoted its first meetings to defining conventional armaments and then proceeded to discuss proposals for their reduction and verification. But, with or without Soviet opposition, it was soon clear that conventional and atomic armaments could not be considered separately. Discussions meanwhile were being harried by external events, notably the establishment of NATO in 1949 and the outbreak of the Korean War in 1950. In September 1951, the General Assembly recommended that a new Disarmament Commission be created under the Security Council, composed of the members of the Security Council and Canada, "for the regulation, limitation, and balanced reduction of all armed forces and all armaments." On November 1, 1952, the United States exploded a hydrogen bomb, and within a year the Soviet Union announced that it had done the same. During the "thaw" and period of "peaceful coexistence" that succeeded the death of Stalin in 1953, disarmament discussions were continued in a subcommittee of the Disarmament Commission, "consisting of the representatives of the powers principally involved" – namely the Soviet Union, Britain, Canada, France, and the United States – "which should seek in private an acceptable solution." Presumably it was hoped that something positive might emerge if the discussions could be moved away from the incessant pressure of publicity and propaganda. But the impasse continued. The arguments were uncommonly like those that we have noted in the disarmament conferences between the wars, but the stakes now were infinitely higher. They were spinning around in the same old vicious circle – no confidence without disarmament; no disarmament without confidence.

In December 1953, President Eisenhower sought to divert attention by bringing forward an "atoms for peace" plan, and he appealed to the nations in possession of atomic stockpiles to dedicate their strength "to the needs rather than the fears of mankind." In April 1954, the Disarmament Subcommittee was considering an Anglo-French plan for a three-phased disarmament and a "cut off" in the production of nuclear weapons. In May

1955 came the Malik Plan, so-called after the Soviet representative in the Disarmament Subcommittee, a plan which at first sight seemed to resemble the Anglo-French plan. In July 1955, President Eisenhower proposed an "open skies" plan, which would permit unrestricted aerial reconnaissance by any power anywhere in the world so as to spot preparations for surprise attack. Simultaneously came the Eden Plan for a trial inspection zone in Germany. In March 1956, the Disarmament Subcommittee was considering a revised Anglo-French plan and a new Soviet plan for partial disarmament. In April 1956, Harold Stassen presented an American plan for partial disarmament. In August 1957, the then American Secretary of State John Foster Dulles revived President Eisenhower's "open skies" plan and adapted it particularly for the area within the Arctic Circle. In December 1957 the Soviet representative, for reasons not yet clear, walked out of the Subcommittee, and the Disarmament Commission and Subcommittee virtually came to an end. During 1958 public discussion mainly centered around a proposal from the Polish Foreign Minister Adam Rapocki, a proposal called after him the Rapocki Plan, to create an "atom-free" zone covering Poland, Czechoslovakia, and East and West Germany. Then suddenly and unexpectedly, on March 31, 1958, Moscow announced that the Soviet Union would unilaterally stop tests of all nuclear weapons.

In July 1958, an eight-power conference of experts (of the United States, Britain, France, Canada, Poland, Czechoslovakia, Rumania, and the Soviet Union) met in Geneva to discuss methods for the detection of nuclear explosions and reported that it was technically feasible to establish "a workable and effective control system to detect violations of an agreement on the world-wide suspension of nuclear weapons tests." In October 1958, a three-power conference (of the United States, Britain, and the Soviet Union) opened at Geneva on the discontinuance of nuclear weapons tests. No formal agreement was reached, but a *de facto* nuclear holiday was observed, only to be broken in September and October 1961, when the Soviet Union resumed its tests — including one of a 50-megaton bomb.

"Uniting for Peace"

The League of Nations was criticized in its day for its weakness and for its eventual failure. In the last analysis its Covenant rested upon a moral code to which most of its members in practice were indifferent and to which many were even opposed. The United Nations was undeniably the stronger and more realistic organization and survived a far heavier buffeting. If nothing else, its extensive humanitarian and social work must justify it before the sharpest of its detractors. Its Secretariat and its agencies became a world's school of "functional" cooperation.

The outstanding problem of the United Nations was clearly the veto in the Security Council. Yet without the veto no modern power, jealous of its sovereignty, could have consented to membership of the organization. In the international relations of the twentieth century it was not that the veto was wrong so much as that it was abused — and abused by one power in particular. The legislative systems of most Western democracies provide for a veto to be used by the head of the state with extreme discretion and on very exceptional occasions. In the Security Council of the United Nations, however, the veto has been used to date (October 1961) 106 times—99 times by the Soviet Union.[4]

During 1950, after the outbreak of the Korean War, as the work of the United Nations was constantly stultified by the veto, the United States advanced proposals to strengthen the General Assembly and, if possible, to enable it to take over some of the functions of the Security Council. The result was the General Assembly's "Uniting for Peace" resolution of November 5, 1950. Under the essential clause of the resolution, if the Security Council, because of the veto, failed to exercise its primary responsibility in any case of a threat to peace or breach of peace, the General Assembly should meet in special emergency session within twenty-four hours of a vote by seven members of the Security Council or by a majority of the General Assembly. The members of the General Assembly would then survey their military resources and proceed as required to collective measures. The United Nations, without amending its Charter, thus effected perhaps the most considerable "constitutional" change in the first decade of its history.

34. GERMANY AND AUSTRIA: OCCUPATION AND RECOVERY

Allied Control in Germany

The capitulation of May 1945, signed by General Jodl and ratified by Field Marshal Keitel, was the last official act of the Third Reich. Total war had ended in total defeat. Germany had temporarily ceased to be a political organism. German troops placed themselves obediently under the nearest Allied commanders. U-boats one by one returned to their bases. There was no scuttling of ships. No armed opposition was encountered as the Allied forces proceeded without hitch to occupy their appointed zones. The "Werewolves," the much advertised Nazi guerrilla force in the "Bavarian Bastion," failed to materialize. The Nazi party leaders went into hiding or surrendered themselves; some committed suicide; but none resisted. The German population as a whole was stunned and prostrate or, at least in the Western zones, made a pathetic show of greeting the Allies as liberators.

In Germany whole cities were reduced to heaps of rubble and tangled iron. Roads were blocked by fallen buildings, and bridge after bridge had been blown up. Hitler's "scorched earth" policy was only partially carried out, but it was probably responsible for most of the last-minute demolition "in detail," especially of railways, harbors, and canals. A host of prisoners of war, foreign workers, and other "displaced persons," to the number of 10,000,000, suddenly released from organized duress, were roaming at large, trying to find their ways home, and levying a long deferred vengeance on their oppressors. But the most awful symbols of the fallen regime were the concentration camps, discovered by the advancing Allies in the last incredible horrors of overcrowding, filth, starvation, and disease.

It has been estimated that the war cost the *Wehrmacht* some 3,000,000 lives, and that 2,000,000 survived with various degrees of disablement. Some 300,000 of the civilian population died in air raids. Some 250,000 German nationals, mostly Jews, died in concentration camps. As for material losses, all manner of astronomical figures have been given out. Half the locomotives and rolling stock was unusable. Coal production in the Ruhr had declined from a prewar average of 400,000 tons a day to

25,000. Steel and other key industries had dropped to 5 per cent. Agricultural production was such that an average ration for the population would have worked out at 1,200 calories daily. Public debt had risen from 40,000,000,000 reichsmarks in 1938 to nearly ten times that figure in 1944. But, by contrast, much plant and machinery was found to be reparable; stocks of raw materials, replenished by systematic "looting," were often abundant. To complete the picture we would add that, on the cessation of hostilities, some 2,000,000 German prisoners of war in Allied hands were gradually repatriated; 10,000,000 refugees and expellees began to stream into Western Germany from the East.

The European Advisory Commission, whose formation we noted elsewhere, had worked out the detailed administrative machinery of the future Control Commission. (See p. 588.) It had also roughly delimited, as early as November 1944, three Allied zones of occupation. The decision to invite France to take over a fourth zone – though largely at the expense of the zone already allocated to the United States – was reached at the Yalta Conference. Further revisions were made at the Potsdam Conference in July 1945, where it was also agreed that Königsberg (afterward renamed Kaliningrad) should be assigned to the Soviet Union for eventual annexation and that a Polish "Administration" should be established up to the Oder and Neisse rivers. In the eventual allocation, the American zone comprised Bavaria, parts of Württemberg and Baden, and the enclave of Bremen. The British zone comprised northwestern Germany, the Ruhr, the Lower Rhine, "Lower Saxony," and Schleswig-Holstein. The French zone comprised the Palatinate, the Saar, and the remaining parts of Württemberg and Baden. The Soviet zone comprised central Germany. Contrary to the line traced at Potsdam, the district and port of Stettin on the Baltic was arbitrarily handed over to the Poles for inclusion in the Polish "Administration." Greater Berlin, within the Soviet zone, was divided into four sectors, severally occupied by the four Allies, and was made the seat of the Allied Control Council, the supreme Allied authority in Germany. The area itself was administered by a four-power body called the Kommandatura.

The Potsdam Conference furthermore had agreed upon "the political and economic principles to govern the treatment of Germany in the initial control period," namely the "five *d*'s" of future Allied occupation policy – demilitarization, denazification, deindustrialization, decentralization, and democratization. The Conference laid down that "so far as practicable, there shall be uniformity of treatment of the German population throughout Germany"; that all armed forces or paramilitary organizations should be disbanded, all arms and munitions and the facilities for their production destroyed; that Nazism and all its institutions should be extirpated, war criminals brought to trial, and education and law democratized; that democratic principles should be introduced into the provincial States or *Länder;* that, during the period of occupation, Germany should be treated as a "single economic unit"; that controls imposed on German economy should be such as to assure a production sufficient "to maintain in Germany average living standards not exceeding the average of the standards

CENTRAL EUROPE, POST-1945

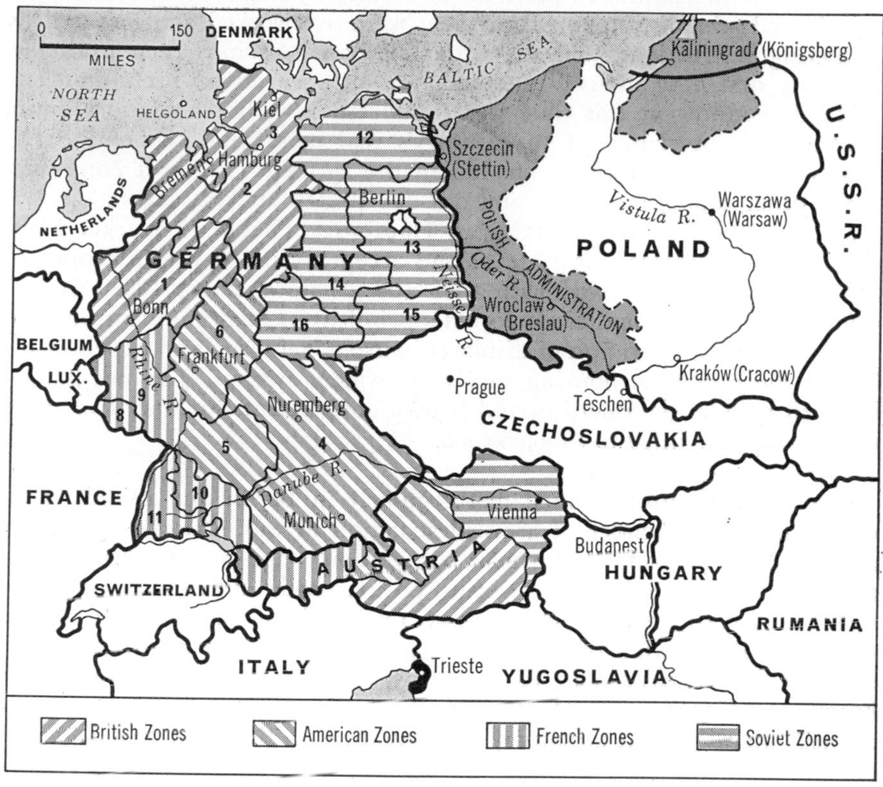

1 NORDRHEIN-WESTFALEN (North Rhine-Westphalia) 2 NIEDERSACHSEN (Lower Saxony) 3 SCHLESWIG-HOLSTEIN 4 BAVARIA 5 WÜRTTEMBERG-BADEN 6 HESSEN 7 BREMEN ENCLAVE 8 SAAR 9 RHEINLAND-PFALZ (Rhineland-Palatinate) 10 WÜRTTEMBERG 11 BADEN 12 MECKLENBURG 13 BRANDENBURG 14 SACHSEN-ANHALT 15 SACHSEN (Saxony) 16 THÜRINGEN (Thuringia)

of living of European countries"; that industrial capacity not so required should be demolished or removed; that reparations should be paid in part from capital equipment and in part from external assets – "current production," be it noted, was not mentioned in this context – and that such reparations "should leave enough resources to enable the German people to subsist without external assistance"; and, for the rest, that all industrial war potential should be eliminated, and cartels and syndicates broken up.

It is now a matter of history that many of these provisions failed. The East-West schism was not foreseen, nor was the extent of the German collapse realized. The Allied armies, the Control Commission, and UNRRA at first virtually had to govern the country. Roads, railroads, canals, docks, telegraph lines had to be cleared and repaired, and a start made on "reactivation" of the most essential mines and industries. In these days it was the policy of Allied governments to recruit "technical" experts for their personnel in Germany, and numbers of these men and women, who had never done a desk job in their lives, found themselves in the midst of a ravaged, chaotic country in positions of authority which would have taxed experienced administrators. All of them were overworked and harassed by conflicting instructions, and the little German assistance then available, hesitantly and obsequiously rendered, was of very mixed usefulness.

Allied planning at this time was conducted in a bureaucratic vacuum in total misappreciation of the country's real moral and economic state. Food was the prior problem, not less in the agricultural Soviet Zone than in the other zones. Food riots and one-day protest strikes occurred in different parts of Germany, notably in Hamburg. The black market flourished with the eternal cigarette as the accepted currency. Any house or building that had survived with roof and windows tolerably intact was overcrowded. Many families supported a primitive existence underground in cellars. The mass migration of displaced persons, refugees, and expellees bedeviled the rationing, housing, and employment systems. The net budget deficit in 1946 to the American and British governments for their two zones in Germany amounted to $500,000,000.

The Allied Control Council met regularly in Berlin and issued its directives on the surrender of arms, destruction of war material, demobilization of armed forces, employment registration, wages and working hours, food rationing, taxes, housing, census, police, repeal of Nazi laws and liquidation of Nazi organizations, and so forth. There was even a directive on the demilitarization of sport. But inevitably each one of the Allies interpreted these measures in its own way. The "five *d*'s" meant different things in different zones. As the demarcation lines hardened, the zones jealously guarded such autonomy and resources as they had and began to lead a life reflecting the attitude of the occupying power. "The Americans came to Germany as tourists," said a commentator, "the British as colonial governors, the Russians as freebooters, and the French as military police." By degrees four distinctive national characters were subtly stamped upon the quadrants of the country.

Demilitarization was relatively the least difficult part of the Allied program. The German army organization was already destroyed. Several ranking officers were held for trial as war criminals. Military installations, weapons and ammunition dumps, fortifications, air-raid bunkers, and self-evident industrial war plants which could not be allocated to reparations were dismantled or blown up. The process was lengthy and hampered by lack of Allied personnel, but at least the total occupation prevented the trickery and concealment which had formerly vitiated the Versailles settlement. It was hoped that the disarmament clauses of the future German peace treaty would merely serve to recognize the accomplished fact.

Denazification was again not difficult – relatively. Nazi organizations were dissolved, and all Nazi signs and emblems were prohibited. Here again the process was hampered by lack of Allied personnel. Hundreds of Nazi suspects were kept waiting in confinement for months while their *Fragebogen* (questionnaires) were worked through by the few Allied officers that could be assigned to the task. In the end whole classes of culprits, notably the younger Nazis, were amnestied in all zones. In 1946 denazification courts

The Nuremberg Trial, September, 1946: the accused in the dock

RADIO-TIMES HULTON

were set up in the *Länder*, conducted by Germans under Allied supervision. Denazification was generally considered to have been concluded by the end of 1947. War criminals and concentration-camp commandants were tried by Allied military courts in the zones or by courts in the particular country where the offenses had been committed.

Between November 1945 and October 1946, the trial of the German major war criminals took place before the International Military Tribunal at Nuremberg, the old medieval city and latterly the scene of Nazi party rallies. Arrangements had been elaborate. A mass of documentary evidence, itself a monument to German meticulousness and for all time a precious historical record, was garnered by Allied investigating teams throughout Germany and sifted and studied for months. A four-power agreement in London in August 1945, with its annexed charter defining procedure and jurisdiction, was the formal constitution of the Tribunal. Nineteen further members of the United Nations adhered to the agreement. Three categories of crime were laid down: crimes against peace, war crimes, and crimes against humanity. The Tribunal was conducted by four members, an American, a British, a French, and a Soviet, with four alternate members. The British member, Lord Justice Lawrence, was President. Every facility was given the accused to obtain counsel of their choice. In the courtroom itself, wired headphones enabled the proceedings to be followed in any one of four languages. A huge interpreting, secretarial, and photographic division was installed. Accommodation was provided for some 250 newspaper correspondents. The twenty-two accused were the chief surviving political and military leaders of Nazi Germany, impressive living representatives of the defeated regime, facing trial to answer, not only for their individual guilt, but for their collective guilt against the laws and usages of the civilized world. Of the twenty-two, six were condemned on all counts. Göring, Ribbentrop, Keitel, Jodl, Rosenberg, Frick, Seyss-Inquart, Sauckel, Bormann (*in absentia*), Kaltenbrunner, Frank, and Streicher were condemned to death by hanging; Raeder, Funk, and Hess to life imprisonment; Speer and Schirach to twenty years; Neurath to fifteen years; Doenitz to ten years; and Fritsche, Papen, and Schacht were acquitted. The Tribunal also condemned as "criminal organizations" the Nazi Leadership Corps, the Gestapo, the SS and SD. The Soviet member of the Tribunal, we should note, strongly protested against the acquittals and against the failure to condemn the German General Staff as a criminal organization. Fritsche, Papen, and Schacht were afterward tried by German denazification courts and condemned to periods of imprisonment.

The Nuremberg trial has been criticized on many grounds. The authority and competence of an international criminal court without precedent in international law, it has been argued, cannot be made to rest upon a charter drawn up by a coalition of victors for the purpose of punishing defeated enemies. The technical difficulties, the mass of evidence, and the complexity of the issues involved could not help but drag out the proceedings to unexpected length; public interest flagged; and the drama and effectiveness of a quick trial and quick sentence had to be foregone. But the crimes themselves and the need for making an example of their chief perpetrators were not denied. Outraged peoples of many nations would not have allowed the repeated pledges of Allied leaders to bring their tormentors to justice to go unfulfilled. The insulting farce at Leipzig after the First World War could not be repeated. (See p. 136.) At Nuremberg, the proceedings were conducted with scrupulous fairness, dignity, and discipline. There was no presumption of guilt; defending counsel suffered not the least suspicion of obstruction or intimidation; the vicious atmosphere of certain recent political trials was debarred; the individual prosecutors acted up to the ecumenical spirit of the trial and did not merely press for a narrow retribution for atrocities committed against their own people or on their own soil; the evidence submitted was painstakingly objective, cumulative, and overwhelming – by far the greater part of it consisted of documents of the defendants' authorship – and not even German historical casuistry is ever likely to succeed in calling it into question.

Demilitarization and denazification, we have said, were relatively easy. Deindustrialization, on the contrary, was difficult in the extreme. The Potsdam Conference had called for the treatment of Germany as "a single economic unit." But the joint administrations for communications, transport, finance, industry, and foreign trade, originally planned, were never set up. The French, who had not been signatories at Potsdam, objected to centralization of any sort, and the Russians soon showed that they had ideas of their own about these things. Eventually a Level of Industry Agreement was worked out, using steel as a yardstick, and, in March 1946, the Allied

Control Council announced that the steel level would be 5,800,000 tons per annum. But the figure for steel actually achieved in 1946 was less than half that amount.

It might have been more logical perhaps to have made coal, not steel, the basic commodity, for coal was at the center of all the interlocking vicious circles in German industry. For example, it was argued that coal production could be stepped up if the miners could be better housed. But housing required building materials, notably roofing tile and glass, which themselves required coal for their manufacture. However, by the end of 1946, partly as a result of better food rations for the miners, the output of the Ruhr coal pits rose to 200,000 tons a day, although this was still only half the output of 1939. At this time, about the only commodity in Germany not seriously reduced was electricity. It was curious, in the shattered cities, where so many public services were at a standstill, to see the streetcars and electric-lighting systems all operating normally. But here too coal was the basic, if indirect, agent of production. The electric power was brought in part from Switzerland, a former neutral undamaged by hostilities, but German coal was exported to Switzerland to pay for it.

Deindustrialization had its political as well as its technical aspects, and, as was soon seen, it was tied up with the last two of the "five *d*'s" – decentralization and democratization. Economic decentralization signified the breakup of the old cartels, notably the big combines in heavy industry, which had supported Germany's militarist regimes of 1914 and 1933. But, in this, the policies of the occupying powers were soon found to be sharply at variance. The Americans with their "trust-busting" traditions were at odds with the British, who were indifferent to decartelization as such; whereas the Russians, with quite another economic philosophy, were more interested in taking over German industries in their zone, ejecting their former owners and "reconcentrating" them on a communized basis. The Americans and British made a start bi-zonally to break up the big combines, such as Krupps, Stinnes, Siemens, the Farben Industries, and others. But, in the end, the process gradually lost its purpose and relevance. Within a few years, in the Western zones, most of the great German industrial magnates had been reinstated in their former properties.

Political decentralization and democratization were to be effected by the creation of new German states, or *Länder,* each with some degree of autonomy, although under Allied control, and each with a "democratic" constitution and elected Diet (*Landtag*). It was then the avowed policy of the occupying powers to transfer the local civil administration to these Diets, to induce in the German people a sense of responsibility for their own government and for their own economic recovery, and concurrently to cut down the numbers of the Allied administrative personnel in Germany. Meanwhile Greater Berlin formed a sort of separate *Land,* with an elected City Council of its own. On February 25, 1947, the Allied Control Council signed a law liquidating the state of Prussia. Henceforth the kingdom of Frederick the Great and the Hohenzollern Kaisers would cease to figure on the map of Europe.

But each zone was soon an operational field for the distinctive political philosophy of its occupying power. In each zone, inevitably, every German in office was *persona grata* with his Allied superiors. As no German political party could be formed in any zone without the authorization of the occupying power, it was soon seen that the Western powers would have ways and means of discouraging, and that the Soviet would have ways and means of encouraging, the German Communist party. In April 1946, in the Soviet zone, the Communists fused with the Social Democrats to form a German Socialist Unity party (SED, *Sozialistische Einheitspartei Deutschlands*), under Soviet sponsorship, to be the dominant party group in that zone. Elections for the new Diets were held in all zones during 1946 and early 1947. The SED won handsomely in the Soviet zone, and the "liberal" parties, mainly the Christian Democrats and the Social Democrats, won handsomely in the American, British, and French zones.

"Bizonia" and "Trizonia"

The East-West disagreement over Allied policy in Germany could no longer be concealed or denied. Early in 1946 issue had already been joined over reparations. The Soviet Government had begun to derive reparations from "current production." Evidently it had discovered that the dismantling and transport of heavy factory plant were expensive processes and that it was easier and cheaper to leave the plant *in situ* and put it to work. Reparations from "current production" were nowhere explicitly banned in any of the Allied agreements, but it had hitherto been assumed that reparations would take the form of capital equipment, and the recent Level of Industry Agreement had been based in part on that assumption. But even more troublesome was the persistent refusal of the Soviet authorities in Germany to furnish the Control Council with the information or with the bare statistical returns for a reasonable quadripartite administration. In May 1946, General Clay, the American commander, suspended reparations deliveries to the Soviet from the American zone.

During 1946 it was evident that the American and British zones were drawing together to the exclusion of the Soviet – with the French standing aside from all three, though for other reasons. In September 1946, James F. Byrnes, the American Secretary of State, speaking to a mixed audience of American and German officials at Stuttgart, made an important overall statement of American policy in Germany, defended the efforts that had been made to achieve a unified and balanced economy in the country, called in particular for a common currency reform to prevent "runaway inflation," and announced that the American and British Governments would shortly proceed to the economic fusion of their two zones. On December 2, 1946, with the ground thus prepared, an agreement for that fusion was signed by Byrnes and Bevin. The other two occupying powers, France and the Soviet Union, were invited to join "on identical terms at any time."

Meanwhile the Soviet zone was being converted step by step into a regulation Communist state. The business of living for all classes of the population was bureaucratically regimented. Such industry as could be "reactivated" operated to "norms" and "targets" under the so-called AG's (*Akti-*

engesellschaften). Land reforms broke up the East Prussian *Junker* estates and redistributed the land to peasants and smallholders. A "People's Police" was recruited and trained, and, against repeated protests from the Western powers, was armed as a paramilitary force. There were the usual tales of arbitrary arrests and imprisonments and the kidnapping of political undesirables. Above and within all these arrangements was the Soviet Military Administration in Karlshorst in suburban Berlin, first under Marshal Zhukov, and then under Marshal Sokolovsky. The stream of refugees, mainly into the Western sectors of Berlin, amounting sometimes to several thousand a day, indicated that the new state order was not happily accepted by all its citizens.

Four-power discussions for a prospective German peace treaty, therefore, did not begin too auspiciously. Preliminary soundings were made in London in January 1947 at a meeting of Foreign Ministers deputies, and the Foreign Ministers themselves – George C. Marshall (who had just succeeded Byrnes), Bevin, Bidault, and Molotov – met in Moscow in March with the German peace treaty on the agenda.

The first few days of the Moscow Conference were taken up with replies to accusations from Molotov regarding the slow progress of demilitarization and denazification in the Western zones. There were lively and inconclusive skirmishes over China, Austria, Albania, and the return of prisoners of war and displaced persons. The Foreign Ministers discussed the control of the Ruhr, they discussed a constitution for a federalized Germany, they discussed the German-Polish frontier, and they discussed a four-power treaty of guarantee to prevent the rearmament of Germany. But the crux of the discussions was reparations. Molotov brought up the story that the Soviet Union had been pledged $10,000,000,000 in German reparations in a secret protocol of the Yalta Conference, though the figure, he said, was a tenth of the Soviet Union's material losses in the war. It should be paid in part, he claimed, from German current production. But, inasmuch as the American and British Governments were already financing German food imports in their two zones, so Marshall and Bevin were careful to point out, the payment of reparations out of current production would mean little more than the transfer of American and British funds to the Soviet Union. The Foreign Ministers Council – Marshall, Bevin, Bidault, and Molotov – met again in London in November 1947. The conference lasted twenty-one days and, although there often seemed to be apparent agreement in matters of substance, disagreements arose over details so impossible as to rule out further discussion. Molotov read out elaborate allegations against the nefarious practices of the Western powers in Germany, allegations to which Marshall and Bevin made reply with increasing impatience. The main issue again was German reparations from current production. On December 15, 1947, the Foreign Ministers Council adjourned *sine die*.

Industrial progress in "Bizonia," it was clear, was now all of a piece with the current political and economic developments in the wider West European world. As we shall describe elsewhere, the European Recovery

Program was announced in June 1947. (See pp. 711-13.) In February 1948, an exploratory Three-Power conference (the United States, Britain, and France) was held in London to consider the inclusion of Germany in the European Recovery Program. On March 17, Britain, France, and the "Benelux" countries (Belgium, the Netherlands, and Luxembourg) signed the Treaty of Brussels. Three days later, on March 20, in Berlin, Marshal Sokolovsky, the Soviet Commander, who had taken umbrage over the recent Three-Power Conference in London and over the Treaty of Brussels, walked out of the Allied Control Council. In April 1948, the sixteen nations of the European Recovery Program, together with "Bizonia" and the French zone in Germany, created the Organization for European Economic Cooperation (OEEC). In the same April and May, a conference of the representatives of the United States, Britain, France, and the Benelux countries was held in London, and on June 1 it issued a series of recommendations, or the "London Decisions," as they were sometimes called, namely to associate the Benelux states in all discussions regarding Germany affecting their interests, to establish an International Authority for the Ruhr, to convene a Constituent Assembly for Western Germany, and to coordinate the economic policies of "Bizonia" and the French zone. The significance of the new agreement was the final alignment of United States, Britain, and France in Germany. "Bizonia" had become "Trizonia" and was linked with the European Recovery Program. On June 18, the much discussed and long heralded currency reform was put into operation in "Trizonia." A new Deutschemark replaced the former Reichsmark. On June 23, after acrimonious and inconclusive discussion in the Control Council in Berlin, the Deutschemark was also put into operation in the American, British, and French sectors in Berlin. Sokolovsky, in a proclamation, banned the Deutschemark in the Soviet zone and also in the Soviet sector in Berlin.

The currency reform was certainly long overdue. Without it, German economic rehabilitation was a mirage. Its effects were beneficial and immediate. Production began to rise; absenteeism among the German workers declined; consumer goods appeared in quantity in the shops; the farmer brought his produce to town; the black market for the moment seemed to be crippled. For the first time since the war Germans had money that bought something and was worth working for. For the first time since the war food ceased to be an obsession. Western Germany had made her first step to her "miraculous" recovery.

But, even before the introduction of the new currency in the Western zones and in the Western sectors of Berlin, the Soviet authorities had been resorting to "defensive" measures. Berlin lay entirely within the Soviet zone, and, toward the end of January 1948, American, British, and French traffic to and from Berlin passing through the Soviet zone was being stopped, delayed, searched, or otherwise obstructed. Protests of American, British, and French commanders in Berlin were all unavailing. By degrees a Soviet blockade of Berlin by road, railroad, and canal was established. The Western powers began to supply their troops and the German population of

The Berlin Airlift, 1948-49: Berliners watching the arrival of a relief plane

WALTER SANDERS-LIFE

their sectors in Berlin by the only means available to them – by air – and they gradually built up their famous "airlift," which eventually bore 3,000-4,000 tons per day of food, fuel, and other necessities of life to well over 2,000,000 persons.

It seemed that the Soviet authorities might even seek to interfere with the airlift. Soviet forces carried out parachute operations near the air corridors. In April 1948, a particularly ugly incident occurred, when a Soviet fighter collided in mid-air with a British transport plane over Gatow airfield in Berlin, killing the Soviet pilot and the British crew. In June, as the crisis mounted, sixty American superfortresses crossed the Atlantic and arrived at airfields in England, unmistakably advertising the intention of the United States to tolerate no further similar incidents.

Protests in Berlin were superseded by representations at diplomatic level. Beginning July 31, 1948, the American and French ambassadors and the British representative in Moscow were engaged in arduous discussions with Molotov and, on occasion, with Stalin himself. Throughout they made it plain that although their governments would be willing to accept the Soviet mark as the sole currency in all four sectors of Berlin, they would not allow the Soviet blockade of Berlin to blackmail them into evacuating the city. At the end of August, a draft directive on the currency for Berlin was finally hammered out, but when the four commanders met in Berlin, Sokolovsky disregarded the directive. In September, the United States, Britain, and France referred the entire dispute to the United Nations. In February 1949, the United States and Britain established a counterblockade and halted all traffic across the eastern frontier of their zones. Evidently Sokolovsky had had enough; at the end of March, he was succeeded by General Chuikov. In May 1949, nearly a year and a half after its first imposition, the Soviet government raised the blockade of Berlin.

Federal Republic and Democratic Republic

On September 1, 1948, at the height of the Berlin crisis, a German Parliamentary Council or Constituent Assembly of 65 delegates, nominated by the Diets of the *Länder* of the three Western zones in accordance with the London Decisions, met at Bonn under the presidency of Dr. Konrad Adenauer to draw up a Basic Law or provisional German constitution. By May 1949, after eight months of debates which were often reminiscent of the old German party asperities, the Basic Law was adopted by the Parliamentary Council, approved by the three Western Powers, ratified by the *Länder,* and on May 23, 1949, at Bonn, the Federal Republic of Germany was proclaimed.

The Basic Law started off with a declaration of fundamental human rights – freedom of conscience, freedom of speech and of "peaceful" assembly, equality before the law, respect for private property, and so forth – and then proceeded to describe the constitution of "a democratic and social Federal State." The Federal Parliament or Bundestag, elected for four years by universal, direct suffrage of the whole Federal Republic, formed the lower chamber. The Government consisted of a Chancellor, elected by the Bundestag and responsible to it, and the Federal Ministers. The Federal Council or Bundesrat, consisting of members of the *Länder* Diets, formed the second chamber. The President of the Republic, with largely ceremonial duties, was elected by majority vote of the Federal Assembly or *Bundesversammlung,* consisting of members of the Bundestag and Bundesrat. There was no article corresponding to Article 48 of the Weimar Constitution. (See pp. 135, 354, and 356.) The respective jurisdictions of the Federation and the *Länder* were carefully defined – foreign affairs, currency, customs, certain taxes, trade agreements, and so forth being reserved to the Federation. A Federal Constitutional Court was to be set up to interpret the Basic Law in the event of disputes, especially disputes between the Federal Government and the *Länder.*

Elections for the Bundestag were held in the three Western zones in August 1949 and returned – the Christian Democrats and their Bavarian affiliates, the Christian Social Union, with 139 seats; the Social Democrats with 131; the Free Democrats (Liberals) with 52; the right-wing German Party with 17; the Communists with 15; and five other parties with 48. In September, Theodor Heuss (Free Democrat), a former professor of political science and one of the authors of the Basic Law, was elected President. Konrad Adenauer was appointed Chancellor. He was leader of the Christian Democrats; he had been Burgomaster of Cologne, ousted by the Nazis in 1933, and had since lived in retirement. He now formed a coalition, consisting of his own party and the Free Democrats and the German Party. The opposition was formed by the Social Democrats under the leadership of Kurt Schumacher, a somewhat harsh, unrelenting man, crippled by his treatment in Nazi prison camps.

An Occupation Statute regulating the relations between the Federal Republic and three Western occupying powers had been announced in Washington in April 1949. It reserved to the three powers the fields of disarmament, reparations, occupation costs, foreign affairs, and displaced persons. Subject to such reservations the federal government would enjoy "full legislative, executive, and judicial powers in accordance with the Basic Law." Civilian control in the three Western zones would be exercised by three Allied High Commissioners, and military control by three Allied Commanders in Chief. On September 15, 1949, the Occupation Statute went into force, and military government as such in Western Germany terminated. Also in April 1949, the six powers of the London Decisions of June 1948 had drawn up a statute for the International Authority for the Ruhr, to be composed of the six powers and of Western Germany. Finally a new agreement was reached in the vexed question of reparations deliveries and the dismantling of industrial war plants.

In the Soviet zone opposed but complementary developments had been taking place. On May 15-16, 1949, elections were held for a "People's Congress." The "National Front" list of candidates, offered to the electorate, received nearly 8,000,000 votes or 66 per cent, but some 800,000 ballot papers had to be declared "invalid." The Congress met in the Berlin Opera House, where Hitler had formerly convened the *Reichstag,* and passed a constitution "for the whole of Germany." The legislature was to consist of an upper house or *Länderkammer* and a lower house or *Volkskammer,* and a Supreme Court was to be set up "to investigate and decide criminal cases of outstanding importance" and thereby "to protect the Republic from its enemies, internal and external." The German Democratic Republic was proclaimed on October 5, 1949, and its government took office with a rota of Communists in the principal posts – Wilhelm Pieck, President; Otto Grotewohl, Premier; and Walter Ulbricht, one of the Deputy Premiers.

The Democratic Republic quickly assumed characteristic features. A Five-Year Plan was announced, linked with the Soviet economy. The Communist party created a central Committee or Politburo, with Ulbricht as its Secretary. The "People's Police" now numbered about 50,000 men, organized into "alert squads" (*Bereitschaften*), equipped with artillery and tanks on the model of a Soviet motorized regiment, with Soviet officers in its higher commands; and there were also formations of "Sea Police" and "Air Police" – all trained as cadres for future expansion. In June 1950, after negotiations with the Polish Government, it was announced that the Oder-Neisse line would be the recognized eastern frontier of Germany. Grotewohl made repeated, and unsuccessful, appeals to Adenauer to meet to discuss the reunification of the country by means of all-German elections; but, in 1952, when the General Assembly of the United Nations appointed a commission to ascertain whether conditions existed in Germany "for holding genuinely free and secret elections," the commission was not permitted to enter the Democratic Republic.

The German scene by this time had acquired certain sharply drawn outlines. The division of the country seemed fixed and final. Each area had its appropriate political form – in the West, the Federal Republic, and in the East, the Democratic Republic. Reunification might be a hope, a fear, a propaganda issue, but it had ceased to be practical politics. The Iron Curtain lay across the former Reich, and only knaves or fools now supposed that it could be removed without a major, and extraneous, international transformation.

Ludwig Erhard, the West German Minister of Economics, as if he wished to sharpen his difference from the Communist East, was promoting a policy of old-fashioned orthodox liberalism, but it was a policy which, he claimed, was still mindful of its social responsibilities. At all counts West German economic recovery, whatever its methods, was now indeed the "miracle" it was so often described as being. Out of the fantastic devastation, which we described at the beginning of this chapter, rose as fantastic a prosperity. By 1953 industrial production was nearly double the figure for 1936; gold and dollar reserves stood at $2,000,000,000. In 1953 steel production, which in 1946 could not reach half the 5,800,000 tons permitted by the Level of Industry Agreement, was 15,000,000 tons. In the same year over 500,000 automobiles were produced, and 550,000 houses built. Some of the recovery was doubtless attributable to the fact that Western Germany had no burden of armaments. Dismantling of war factories had virtually ceased; decentralization continued but was obviously halfhearted. And there were some unpleasant patches. Erhard's economic philosophy was all to the benefit of ownership and management; labor disproportionately lagged behind. In 1953 unemployment in Western Germany was estimated to be over 1,500,000. Nevertheless we cannot detract from the total achievement. Traditional German habits of discipline and hard work had survived and overcome the catastrophe of 1945.

Rearmament

In less than a decade the "five *d*'s" of 1945 had been fulfilled or had ceased to be of practical interest. Indeed the first of the *d*'s, the problem of demilitarization, was passing into its opposite – the problem of remilitarization. If Western Germany was now achieving the status of a sovereign state, she had the elementary right of a sovereign state to the means of self-defense. Until she possessed that means, declared Adenauer in a statement in December 1949, her defense must be the responsibility of the Western powers. Western Germany, he said further, would be willing to make her contribution in the form of a German contingent under Allied High Command, but individual Germans would not be permitted to serve "as mercenaries" in foreign armies. But, on June 25, 1950, on the outbreak of the Korean War, the situation suddenly changed. Western Germany was in a panic; the Elbe might well become overnight "another 38th parallel."

Adenauer demanded at least a force to match the East German "People's Police." A conference of Western foreign ministers in New York authorized a West German security force of 30,000 men, armed and mobile.

West German rearmament thereafter was part of EDC and NATO – and of their economic counterpart, the Schuman Plan, and indeed of the entire Western European movement – and is best discussed in that larger context. (See pp. 716ff.) But we should note here the domestic reactions to the new development. Far from being eager to resume her place as a great armed power, Western Germany was now plunged into a severe public opinion crisis. Every Western nation at this juncture, called upon to rearm, found that it had some aversion to overcome; in Western Germany's case it was the disastrous double defeat in two World Wars. The youth of the country, after its hard international hectoring on the evils of militarism in general and of German militarism in particular, showed itself to be in no mood to volunteer for military service. Schumacher, the Social Democrat leader, was probably reflecting far more than his following when he came out in strong opposition to rearmament. There was still a good deal of the old pacifism in his party, as well as the iron of his own bitter experience. He was supported by the West German trade unions. But there was also at this time a more specific revulsion to Adenauer's policy. The Western powers, said Schumacher, must concede more "or else they must get along without me (*ohne mich*)." Western Germany was not to become an expendable buffer in an atomic war between East and West. Schumacher died in August 1952. He was succeeded by Erich Ollenhauer, a more cooperative, less acrimonious type of man; but Social Democratic thinking on the issue of German rearmament changed very slowly.

There was some revival at this time of former military organizations, such as the veterans' organization, the Stahlhelm. Otto Remer, who had helped to wreck the anti-Hitler putsch in 1944, was leader and figurehead of a Neo-Nazi "Socialist Reich Party." (See p. 587.) Nazi sympathizers were alleged to be strong in country districts and in the universities. A number of mushroom groups and parties were flaunting patriotic slogans; the words *"Deutsch"* or *"Reich"* tacked on to their name always carried an aggressive note. Whether all this was the inevitable lunatic fringe remained to be seen. But it was certainly opposed to the Adenauer government, and it certainly embarrassed that government's rearmament program.

On May 26, 1952, at Bonn, Adenauer and the Foreign Ministers, Acheson, Eden, and Schuman, signed the so-called Bonn Conventions, which were to terminate the Occupation Statute and establish Western Germany as a sovereign state. The Federal Republic would assume responsibility for its internal and external affairs, except as regards the Allied armed forces in Western Germany, the status of Berlin, and the reunification of Germany under a future peace treaty. The three Western Powers reserved to themselves certain emergency rights in the event of aggression against Western Germany or in the event of a failure of the democratic order in Western Germany. The next day, May 27, in Paris, the EDC (European Defense Community) Treaty was signed. Stormy debates on the ratification of the treaty continued in the Bundestag during the question of the constitutionality of the treaty to the Constitutional Court. To help ease tensions the Western Powers released a number of lesser war criminals, including Gustav Krupp.

In September 1953, Bundestag elections were held. The Christian Democrats gained a bare absolute majority with 244 seats; the Social Democrats gained 151 seats; the Free Democrats 48; the German Party 15; the small Catholic Center party gained 2 seats. The new refugee party (*BHE, Block Der Heimatvertriebenen und Entrechteten*) made its first electoral appearance with 27 seats. Neo-Nazis and Communists were unrepresented. Adenauer was confirmed in power. No doubt the country's prosperity had something to do with the result; but many voters were also becoming resigned to rearmament. The EDC Treaty was at last ratified, by the Bundestag on February 26, 1954, and by the Bundesrat on March 19, 1954. But on August 30, the treaty was rejected by France. (See p. 697-98.)

As we shall describe elsewhere, the collapse of EDC was quickly repaired by the London Agreement of October 3 and the Paris Agreements of October 23, 1954. (See pp. 697-98 and 719-20.) These agreements renewed the Bonn Conventions, notably as regards the Allied armed forces in Western Germany; the North Atlantic Treaty Organization (NATO) assumed the direction of West German rearmament; Western Germany gave an undertaking not to manufacture atomic weapons and missiles. The agreements were ratified by the Bundestag on February 27, and by the Bundesrat on March 18, 1955. As of May 5, 1955, the occupation regime ended, and in the same month the Federal Republic joined Western European Union (WEU) and NATO. In July, the Bundestag passed a Volunteers' Law to be replaced a year later, in July 1956, by a conscription act or Soldiers' Law. The new German Army had come into being.

In September 1957, Bundestag elections were again held. The Christian Democrats increased their absolute majority with 270 seats; the Social Democrats gained 169 seats; the Free Democrats 41; and the German Party 15. The election was remarkable for the decisive elimination of minor parties and splinter groups. For the first time in her parliamentary history Germany had the makings of a two-party political system. Adenauer, now in his eighty-first year, remained Chancellor. Erhard appeared in the new administration as Vice-Chancellor. In 1957 the German Army, or *Bundeswehr,* as it was now to be called, numbered 125,000 men. General Speidel, former Chief of Staff to Rommel, was Commander in Chief of the central sector of NATO in Europe. Discussion was already started over atomic weapons and bases in Western Germany.

The foregoing events were reflected in Eastern Germany. In his May Day speech of 1952 in Berlin, President Pieck declared that the military activities of the Western powers "compelled the Democratic Republic to organize its defense." But, for the moment, other political preoccupations had to come first. The death of Stalin in March 1953 was followed in the Soviet zone by general relief and relaxation. In May the Soviet Military Administration was wound up, and its former "political adviser," Vladimir Semyonov, a civilian, was appointed High Commissioner. Persecution of the churches suddenly ceased; religious teaching was permitted in schools;

Negotiating the Bonn Conventions, May 26, 1952: Adenauer, Acheson, Eden, and Schuman

RADIO-TIMES HULTON

requisitioned church properties were restored. In June the Politburo came out with a list of blanket cancellations of the more hateful decrees, notably in regard to rations, taxes, and interzonal travel. Such was the state of mind of the people of Eastern Germany that the first publication of these cancellations was believed to be a forgery or a cruel practical joke.

Unhappily the population was now tempted to take the bit between its teeth. Relaxation led to demands; the government's attempt to impose new "norms" was openly resisted. On June 17, 1953, the workers of East Berlin were staging mass demonstrations in the streets against the Soviet authorities and against the SED, and calling for free elections, increased rations, abolition of the People's Police – and the withdrawal of the Soviet occupation forces. The Soviet commander in Berlin ordered out tanks and truck-borne infantry, banned all public meetings, and imposed a curfew. Other disturbances occurred in Magdeburg, Leipzig, Dresden, Chemnitz, Jena, and elsewhere. But, face to face with steel, resistance collapsed. The death toll, due to rioting, was estimated at 25; but there were afterwards some 60 death sentences in the courts and some 25,000 imprisonments.

Once the Red Army had re-established the Republic's authority, relaxation in fact continued. Food restrictions were eased; minor nationalized enterprises and expropriated farms were returned to their owners; wages, pensions, and disability allowances were generally raised; reparations payments were canceled, and even occupation costs were reduced; hundreds of political prisoners and war criminals were released. But, during 1953,

300,000 refugees escaped, the great majority into West Berlin, whence they were flown to the Western zones. Such was the exodus that "incitement to flee the Republic" (*Republikflucht*) was made an indictable crime.

On March 25, 1954, the Soviet occupation regime was formally terminated, and the Soviet Government recognized the Democratic Republic as a sovereign, independent state. George Pushkin was appointed Soviet ambassador in Berlin. Thereafter the Democratic Republic settled down to a "normal" life. During 1955 its political and military status was confirmed in a series of pacts and enactments. In May 1955, the Republic was one of the signatories of the East European mutual assistance treaty, known as the Warsaw Pact. (See p. 666.) Grotewohl announced that the People's Police would be incorporated into a People's Army of about 90,000 men, though it would be recruited, he afterwards explained, by voluntary enlistment. In September, at a conference in Moscow the Soviet leaders Bulganin and Khrushchev on the one side and Grotewohl on the other agreed to a comprehensive treaty. The Soviet Union and the Democratic Republic recognized a mutual equality of rights and pledged a noninterference in each other's domestic affairs; but it appeared that Soviet troops would still be stationed in Eastern Germany "temporarily and with the approval of the Government of the Democratic Republic." At the end of the year, in December 1955, Grotewohl was visiting China and North Korea and signing a pact of friendship with the Chinese People's Republic.

Pieck remained President, and Grotewohl and Ulbricht Premier and Deputy-Premier respectively. In 1958 a second Five-Year Plan was announced, shortly to be absorbed into a Seven-Year Plan. Food rationing was at last abolished. In elections 98.87 per cent of the electorate voted, of which 99.87 per cent voted for the National Front list. An interesting constitutional amendment was made in the abolition of the upper house, the *Länderkammer*. As we write, Eastern Germany continues a somewhat gray, eventless existence, firmly tied to the Soviet Power, with little prospect of fundamental change.

The Saar

The territory of the Saar for the first years after the war lay somewhat outside the developments that we have been describing in this chapter. In 1945 it was incorporated in the French occupation zone. It had been much devastated; its chief city, Saarbrücken, had been heavily bombed and was about three-fourths destroyed. The French placed it under Military Governor, Gilbert Grandval, and proceeded to repair its damaged coal mines and attach them to the French economy. In short, the French established in the Saar the regime which they had attempted to establish there in 1919. It may be said that the Saarlanders showed little objection. They had always suffered by comparison with the richer, more fortunate territory of the Ruhr; their natural economic links were with iron mines of Lorraine; and, after their recent wartime experience, they had little heart for political decisions. At the Foreign Ministers' Conference at Moscow in May 1947, Marshall and Bevin agreed to Bidault's proposal that the Saar should become a semiautonomous area under French economic control—pending a German peace treaty. In elections in October 1947, the Saarlanders voted into being a Diet that approved, by 48 votes to 1, a French-made constitution for their territory. Johannes Hoffmann, leader of the local Catholic party, the Christian Populists, formed a coalition government composed of his own party and the local Social Democrats. Under French masters the Saarlanders set about to rebuild their shattered homes and industries.

After the setting up of the Federal Republic, Adenauer showed some apprehension over the possible definitive loss of the Saar. The Saar continued to be treated as an autonomous unit. In March 1950, at Paris, Robert Schuman, the French Foreign Minister, and Hoffmann signed a new agreement whose main clause stipulated a fifty-year control by France of the Saar mines, until and unless a German peace treaty restored the Saar to Germany. Some months later the Saar joined the Council of Europe as a separate member. In 1952, reflecting a similar change in the Federal Republic, the French Military Governor in the Saar, Grandval, became Ambassador. In November 1952, new elections showed that Hoffmann and his pro-French policies still had the support of two-thirds of the Saar electorate.

But the Saarlanders were changing their minds, and clearly the status of the Saar would have to be revised under the Schuman Plan then being discussed. (See p. 716.) Hoffmann had already been trying to ban the growing pro-German parties in the territory. The French Government was now proposing a "Europeanization" of the Saar, and a certain Jonkheer van Naters, at the instance of the Council of Europe, drew up a report in examination of such a proposal. At a conference in Paris in October 1954 a Saar Statute was drawn up, "a European Statute within West European Union," which, however, was to be submitted to a referendum of the Saarlanders. A year later, on October 23, 1955, the Saarlanders rejected the referendum by a vote of more than two to one, and in elections in the following December, the pro-German parties were generally successful, again by a vote of more than two to one. Hoffmann at once resigned, and the government of the Saar passed to Hubert Ney, a Christian Democrat, and a coalition of pro-German parties.

On January 1, 1957, the Saar returned to Germany as a *Land* of the Federal Republic. But France still retained certain rights for another twenty years to coal deliveries from the Wandt mines and to canal traffic on the Moselle.

Austria

By the end of April 1945, Vienna and the greater part of Austria had fallen to the Red Army. The Soviet set up a provisional Austrian government under Dr. Karl Renner, the former Social Democratic leader and Chancellor of 1919, and with a party composition of Social Democrats, Christian Socialists, and Communists in almost equal numbers. On May 14, 1945, a Soviet-sponsored declaration was broadcast from Vienna to the effect that the German *Anschluss* was dissolved and the Republic of Austria was reestablished according to the constitution of 1920.

During June and July 1945, Austria was divided into four Allied zones of occupation. The American zone comprised Upper Austria and Salzburg; the British zone, Styria and Carinthia; the French zone, Vorarlberg and the Tirol; the Soviet zone, Lower Austria and the Burgenland — with an over-all Allied Council in Vienna. Vienna itself, like Berlin, lay within the Soviet zone and was divided similarly into four sectors under an Allied Kommandatura. Austria in many ways took on the aspect of an occupied Germany writ small, with the difference that she had a provisional government of her own, albeit a weak and sadly encumbered one. However, that government was formally recognized by the four Allied Powers in October 1945. Elections shortly took place which returned a National Assembly composed of two preponderant moderate parties of almost equal strength — the People's Party and the Socialist party — and a very small Communist representation. Renner was elected President of the Republic, with Dr. Leopold Figl Chancellor (People's Party).

Demilitarization and denazification proceeded in all four zones. But, in general, it looked at this time as if the Allied occupation of Austria would not be too onerous and that the lapses of 1938 would not be too heavily charged to the largely innocent and defenseless Austrian people. For the first two years the country was in desperate straits, and most of the citizens of Austria were thanking UNRRA for their rations of 1,200 calories a day. Currency reforms were passed by the National Assembly in 1947 and, under the approval of the Allied Council, were introduced into all four zones, with much the same benefits as attended the similar currency reforms in Western Germany in 1948. Both the American and British governments were soon making grants towards Austrian recovery and foregoing occupation costs and reparations. But unhappily Soviet cooperation in the good work was not forthcoming.

During 1946 the Soviet authorities in the Soviet zone were already requisitioning factory plant, farm equipment, livestock, and even food and clothing, and they shortly turned their attention more particularly to German assets in Austria, such as oil refineries and river transport, on the ground that these were German and therefore available for reparations. The Austrian Government and the Western Powers protested and in vain demanded a proper designation and accounting of the seized properties. Here as elsewhere the growing disagreement between East and West was becoming a part of the established order of things. The one point, on which the Foreign Ministers Council did concur, was the one point most keenly resented by the Austrian people — the decision to leave the southern Tirol in Italian possession.

Meanwhile the conclusion of an Austrian peace treaty was held up by Soviet obstruction. The Soviet Government objected to the slow progress of denazification in Austria, or referred to the special danger at Trieste, or, after 1950, professed to fear an Austrian *Anschluss* with a rearmed Western Germany. It seemed that the divided country would continue indefinitely in this "twilight" condition. On the last day of 1950, President Renner died, and was later succeeded by General Koerner, Socialist Mayor of Vienna. Elections in 1953 confirmed the equivalence of the People's Party and the Socialists; the Communist strength stood at 4 seats. A new coalition was formed by Julius Raab (People's Party), who shortly appointed the former Chancellor, Figl, as his Foreign Minister.

Then, suddenly, in 1955, for no apparent reason, the Soviet Government changed its mind and expressed its willingness to conclude an Austrian peace treaty and to withdraw its occupation forces. On May 2, the Foreign Ministers of the four allied powers and the Austrian Foreign Minister, Figl, met in Vienna and signed the treaty on the 15th. Austria was re-established as "a sovereign, independent, and democratic state" with the frontiers of January 1, 1938. She accepted obligations to prevent political and economic union with Germany and to debar Fascist organizations. No limit was imposed on the size of the Austrian Army, but atomic weapons were disallowed. On October 25, all four occupation forces were withdrawn. The following day the Austrian President signed a constitutional law declaring Austria's perpetual neutrality.

35. RUSSIA: "PEACEFUL COEXISTENCE"

Devastation and Reconstruction

To discuss the Soviet Union in the immediate post-1945 period is to pass into the world of astronomic figures, both of devastation and reconstruction, figures that almost conceal the mass tragedy and triumph of the Russian people. About 500,000 square miles of Soviet territory were affected by the German invasion – an area about the size of New England, New York, and Pennsylvania, inhabited in 1941 by 88,000,000 persons and comprising some of the richest and most highly developed parts of the country. In four years of war this area had been "scorched" by the retiring Red Army, fought over – some localities more than twice – plundered during the German occupation, and then finally devastated with fanatic German thoroughness by the retiring German Army. It has been estimated that 1,700 towns and 70,000 villages were razed to the ground, and 25,000,000 persons made homeless. Coal mines were destroyed that produced 100,000,000 tons of coal per annum, iron mills that smelted 11,000,000 tons of iron per annum, oil installations in the Caucasus, the great Dnieper and Donetz power stations, and 30,000 other industrial enterprises employing 4,000,000 workers. Some 40,000 miles of railroad tracks were torn up, 13,000 railroad bridges demolished, and 15,500 locomotives and 425,000 wagons were destroyed or removed. From the farms, 135,000 tractors were destroyed or removed, as were 45,000 combine-harvesters, and 4,000,000 plows and other agricultural machinery. Loss of livestock included 7,000,000 horses and 17,000,000 cattle. Churches, monasteries, synagogues, museums, historical monuments were desecrated and burned down. Looting by soldiers of furniture, clothes, and other domestic articles was sometimes organized as a virtual military operation, especially in districts known to be inhabited by Jews. The total cost of material damage caused by the war has been put at $125,000,000,000 (1946 rate).

Loss of human life is scarcely imaginable. About 20,000,000 men were reported to have served at one time or another in the Soviet armed forces, and of this number 10,000,000 were killed or died in action. About 15,000,000 civilian deaths were directly attributable to the war – there were

600,000 deaths by starvation during the siege of Leningrad alone. To these figures we should add a fall in the birth rate and a rise in infant mortality. For the period of the war and the years immediately following, "The sum total of persons who would not have died plus those who would have been born" amounted to 45,000,000. The population of the Soviet Union in 1950 was about 180,000,000; but for the war, it should have been about 225,000,000, or 25 per cent more.[1] Catastrophe of this scale goes a long way to explaining Russian political behavior in the post-1945 period.

Some compensations and recoveries were effected during the war. Enormous quantities of industrial plant were successfully evacuated, much of it to areas beyond the Urals, and by 1943 it was claimed that Soviet industry was producing more arms and military equipment than in 1940. In 1944 and 1945, in the wake of the Red Army, peasants began to return to their farms. In the autumn of 1945 it was officially stated that three-fourths of the arable land in the Ukraine had been restored to cultivation. The great lack at this time was not only the shortage of man power, but the shortage of the elementary shelter for the man power to inhabit. By New Year's Day, 1946, it was reported that 2,500,000 persons "had been transferred from dugouts to dwellings" – but there were still millions in dugouts.

The political life of the Soviet Union was resumed in February 1946 with elections to the two chambers of the Supreme Soviet, and on March 12 the two chambers convened in Moscow. President Kalinin resigned on grounds of ill health. He was succeeded by the trade-union leader, Nicholai Shvernik, and died some three months later. Certain minor constitutional changes were made. The title Commissar was abolished, and the former Council of People's Commissars became the Council of Ministers – with Stalin as Premier or Chairman of the Council of Ministers, and Molotov as Deputy Premier, or Deputy Chairman, and Foreign Minister. Beria, Voroshilov, Mikoyan, Malenkov, Kaganovich, and Voznessensky were also Deputy Premiers. The former NKVD, accordingly, was now the MVD, and Beria could be described as Minister of the Interior. It is significant of the condition of the Soviet Union at this time that Kaganovich was also head of a newly created Ministry of Building Materials. The Politburo and the party organizations presumably were not affected and remained as before. New members of the Politburo at this time included Beria and Malenkov. A reform of the civil and criminal codes was projected; the death penalty was abolished.

On March 15, 1946, the first of three successive post-war Five-Year Plans was announced. The State Planning Commission (Gosplan) under Voznessensky was back to work. Targets for 1950 were modestly put at 25,400,000 tons of steel, 250,000,000 tons of coal, and 35,400,000 tons of oil, while the output of foodstuffs and consumer goods was to equal 1940 levels. As a supplement to industry huge removals of plant and machinery were made from occupied Germany, Austria, and Manchuria. But Russia's woes were not yet over. Drought and consequent crop failures in the summer of 1946 in the Ukraine and Volga districts were officially admitted to be as bad as in the great drought of 1921. The harvest beyond the Urals, however, was good, and a heroic repair of the roads and railroads enabled the most necessary supplies to be brought to the stricken areas. Nevertheless, with a sort of aggressive flourish, bread rationing was abolished in December 1947, probably for no better reason than that the black market was getting altogether out of hand. By that date, industry as a whole was hitting its targets; but agriculture was still 75 per cent behind.

Russia would not have been Russia if there had not been some purges at this time. But for the moment they were relatively mild affairs. There was some tightening up of collective farms where the perennial problem of discipline had once more become acute during the war and the recent drought. There was a revival of antireligious propaganda, which, however did not prevent the Orthodox Church from celebrating the 500th anniversary of its separate, autocephalous status in Russia. The most serious retributive incidents occurred among certain minority racial communities which, in the recent war, had shown themselves defective in patriotism. In 1946 the Tartars in the Crimea, the Chechens in the Caucasus, and the Kalmyks west of the Caspian were broken up as nationalities, and masses of them were deported to Siberia. There was also at this time and during the next two years a powerful ideological criticism of certain "degraded" artists and scientists. Well-known composers of the international caliber of Shostakovich and Prokofiev were warned that they "were losing touch with the masses," succumbing to "bourgeois tendencies," and producing music characterized by "atonality, dissonance, and neuropathic combinations." The biologist Orbeli was downgraded in the Biology Section of the Soviet Academy of Sciences for his "incorrect, anti-Socialist" theories of biology, and another biologist, Lysenko, was upgraded in the Soviet Academy of Agricultural Sciences presumably for his correct Socialist theories of biology. The persecution of certain physicists for "cosmopolitanism" had very definite anti-Semitic implications.

But by this time the Soviet Union was taking up its appropriate stand in the Cold War. We have already described some of the disputes in the Foreign Ministers Council over the peace treaties and in the Allied Control Council in Berlin over German reparations and German currency. (See pp. 613ff and 642ff.) Russian notions of military security, as well as an age-old temperamental secretiveness, may have contributed to the situation, but they also prevented the outside world from discovering and appreciating the Soviet's real straits. The facts of the loss of life and property, once withheld from the enemy, were now withheld from the Allies, and, only in after years, could a patient, deductive arithmetic make the terrible totals more generally known. In 1946 and 1947 all that the outside world was aware of was the Soviet's insatiable demand for reparations. At Soviet behest the peace treaties therefore included harsh reparations terms. The Allied occupation regimes in Germany, and to a less extent in Austria, were soon deadlocked over reparations. Yet, in June 1947, when Secretary of State George C. Marshall proposed his plan for economic aid from the United States to the war-stricken nations of Europe – the Marshall Plan, as it was often called, or the European Recovery Program – the Soviet

Union declined to accept and furthermore compelled its clients in Intermediate Europe to decline also. (See p. 713.)

In the next chapter we shall describe how, one by one, the states of Intermediate Europe — Poland, Czechoslovakia, Hungary, Albania, Bulgaria, and Rumania — were drawn into the Soviet economic and political orbit, and how narrowly Finland, Yugoslavia, and Greece escaped. At the end of September 1947 at Warsaw, as a counterblast to the European Recovery Program, a conference of the Communist parties of the Soviet Union, Poland, Czechoslovakia, Hungary, Bulgaria, Rumania, Yugoslavia — Yugoslavia then being still in the fold — and of France and Italy resolved to set up an Information Bureau, or Cominform as it came to be called, that would have its headquarters at Belgrade and would serve for "an exchange of experience and the coordination of activities." The chief architect of the organization appears to have been Andrei Zhdanov, successor to Kirov, the Party chief in Leningrad in 1934, lately chairman of the Allied Control Commission in Finland, perhaps the outstanding man of the moment in the party apparatus. In a long address to the conference on this occasion — the first of many like it that were to be reported to the Western world at large — Zhdanov roundly berated the United States for its predatory, expansionist aims and its designs to establish an imperialist supremacy, presumably in conspiracy with such malignant warmongers as Winston Churchill. The European Recovery Program, said Zhdanov, was clearly a part of the same nefarious design; but the Soviet Union and the Communist parties everywhere well knew how to uphold their honor and independence and prevent the enslavement of the world.

Affairs, Foreign and Domestic

The great difficulty facing the narrator of the events of these years — especially of events since the Second World War — is to decide into which contexts to put the various items in the huge multiplicity he must try to describe. History today not only has the whole world for its theater, but never has it seemed so wanting in convenient divisions. We are still far too near it for the normal arbitrary stops and sequences to have become generally accepted. Our "master" mention of the European Recovery Program, for instance, should rightly go into one of the European chapters, and perhaps be repeated in the American chapter. But, as the program touched the Soviet Union, even if indirectly, should it not be described here also? For that matter is there a chapter in this Part of the book where the program would not be relevant? However, for the moment, we are mainly concerned to sketch the Soviet scene since 1945 as it was played out against its accompanying international background, and the reader must be assured that our somewhat lavish use of cross references is only a means of saving him — and ourselves — from the labor of constant repetition.

By 1947 the Cold War was on. The Foreign Minister Council was jolting along to its final breakdown. (See p. 643.) In Germany the Allied Control Council was still functioning, but "Bizonia" had been set up, and the currency reforms were under discussion. (See p. 642.) Gromyko and Vyshinsky were accustoming the United Nations to the Soviet tactics with the veto. The Military Staff Committee and the Atomic Energy Commission were in the toils of their particular frustrations. (See pp. 630-33.) In Greece, civil war was raging between a British-sponsored Greek Government and Communist irregulars. In the Middle East, the Persian Government – with evident American support – rejected Soviet demands for oil concessions. (See p. 768.) Trouble of one sort or another, but always expressive of the selfsame East-West antagonism, seemed to be brewing everywhere. It was clear that 1948 would be a critical year. Accordingly, in January 1948, the Berlin blockade began. (See pp. 644-45.) In February a Communist coup carried out the "Second Revolution" in Czechoslovakia. (See p. 676.) In April elections in Italy established the Christian Democratic party in power, but, as it seemed at the time, another Communist coup was only narrowly averted. (See p. 706.) In June, in Germany, "Bizonia" became "Trizonia," and a new currency was introduced. (See p. 644.) Also, in June, the growing Soviet-Yugoslav dispute resulted in Yugoslavia's expulsion from the Cominform. (See pp. 679-80.) In the Far East, the Chinese Communists were evidently winning their long struggle with Chiang Kai-shek. In Malaya, Indochina, and the East Indies, "colonial" governments were fighting to suppress "native" Communist-inclined rebellions. (See pp. 777-78 and 788ff.)

On the Soviet home front for the time being there were relative peace and progress. The first of the postwar Five-Year Plans, according to the published statistics, was attaining its targets – sometimes with heavy overpluses – and was expected to go forward as per schedule to its official completion in 1950. Agriculture was still the most intractable of economic problems; but grain crops generally were back to 1940 levels. Huge afforestation schemes to prevent drought and soil erosion were started mainly in the lower Volga area. The Volga-Don Canal, power plants at Kuibyshev and Stalingrad, and buildings for Moscow University, all to be the pride of the Soviet Socialist State, were under construction. In September 1949 the first atomic explosion was carried out "somewhere in the Soviet Union."

Underneath the surface the old struggle for power was going on. Stalin was showing his years, and his death would instantly open the question of his successor. We have the strong sense of a secret war in progress reminiscent of that in Germany in 1932 round the aged Hindenburg. In August 1948 the mysterious death of Zhdanov was followed by a major purge of party chiefs, notably in Zhdanov's own city of Leningrad, a purge whose result was to confirm the now growing prominence of his former colleague – and rival – Georgy Maximilianovich Malenkov, a Deputy Premier and then also Minister for Electric Power. One figure to disappear was the economic planner Voznessensky. There was a slight flutter about this time when Stalin himself revived the ideological criticism of artists and scientists and condemned a certain Dr. Marr, an internationally known linguist, for errors in the theory of language. But, as was explained, Stalin, a former Commissar for Nationalities, had always been a student of linguistic problems and was perfectly well qualified to meet the Marrs of the learned world on their own ground. In January 1949, the death penalty was reintroduced.

Shuffling of ministerial posts brought forward new names and relegated old ones – and kept foreign observers busy at their guessing games. Early in March 1949 Molotov, Foreign Minister, was replaced by Andrei Vyshinsky, though he remained a Deputy Premier. Marshal Vassilievsky, Minister of Defense, was replaced by Marshal Bulganin, and Marshal Sokolovsky was brought back from Berlin to be Bulganin's Deputy. (See p. 646.) Perhaps not unconnected with those changes, the supreme defensive alliance between the United States, Britain, and ten other nations of the West against the Soviet Union, the North Atlantic Pact, was signed in Washington on April 4, 1949. (See pp. 715-16.) Nikita Sergeyevich Khrushchev, Secretary of the Urkrainian Party Committee, at this time was coming to the top at the center of affairs in Moscow. He was already a member of the Politburo, and, at the end of 1949, he was appointed Secretary of the Party. In May 1950, elections were held for the Supreme Soviet, at which 99.73 per cent of the votes were cast for the Soviet of the Union and 99.72 per cent for the Soviet of Nationalities – in both cases for the "Communist, non-Party Bloc."

In May 1949, shortly after the signature of the North Atlantic Pact, the Berlin blockade was raised. The quarrel between Yugoslavia and the Cominform continued. Perhaps these rebuffs to Soviet policy in Europe induced the Soviet Government to transfer its main international attention for the time being to the Far East. In January 1949, accordingly, the Soviet Government recognized the People's Republic of North Korea, in October the People's Republic of China, and in January 1950 Ho Chi-minh's regime in Indochina. At the end of 1949, Mao Tse-tung visited Moscow and was a feted guest at the celebrations of Stalin's seventieth birthday on December 21, 1949. A Soviet-Chinese treaty of mutual assistance followed in due course. Port Arthur and the Manchurian Railway were returned to Chinese possession. The Soviet Union's economic recovery was now so far advanced that the Soviet Government could grant its new Chinese friends credits to the amount of $300,000,000 over five years. On January 10, 1950, Yakov Malik, the Soviet delegate, protesting the failure of the United Nations to admit the People's Republic of China to membership, walked out of the Security Council, an action which, as it turned out, was a serious tactical error. The Korean War broke out in June 1950. (See p. 782.)

Malenkov to Khrushchev

In August 1952, it was announced that the Party would hold its Nineteenth Congress, constitutionally due in 1942, but postponed because of the war and the reconstruction. On October 5 in Moscow the Congress met, and the report, which at previous Congresses since the Revolution had been given by Lenin and then by Stalin, this time was given by Malenkov. The ageing Stalin presumably would now have been unequal to the physical strain of so important a keynote exercise, and he had graciously delegated the honor to the heir of his choice. Every aspect of domestic politics at this time reflected the struggle for the succession. Thus, by amendments to the Party's constitution, the former Politburo and Orgburo were abolished, and both were superseded by a Party Presidium of 25 permanent members and 11 alternate members – a numerous, incoherent flock, by which, so it was argued, Stalin could spread and weaken the opposition to himself – or to Malenkov.

At all events October 5 was Malenkov's day, and he made the most of it. His report took six hours to deliver; and he covered every possible aspect of Soviet policy to date. We have noted Zhdanov's speech to the Cominform in 1947; we now have Malenkov's report to the Nineteenth Party Congress in 1952; we shall be having Khrushchev's report to the Twentieth Party Congress in 1956. In the absence of other accessible records, the student of Soviet affairs may well be grateful for these periodic oratorical displays as a supplement to what must often be a somewhat empty story, more especially perhaps as they illustrate for him the workings of a regime where speech-making and policy-making were so closely associated. In any case it is important to be reminded occasionally of the content and tone of the official Soviet ideology.[2]

Malenkov began his report with foreign affairs. He reviewed the political consequences of the Second World War, notably the defeat and permanent weakening in the East of militarist Japan and in the West of Hitlerite Germany (mentioned by Malenkov in that order), and the weakening also of the powers France and Britain. But the Soviet Union had waxed stronger, and the "historic victory of the great Chinese people was a blow to the imperialist system." Today, said Malenkov, one-third of the human race had been delivered from oppression. And now, in the postwar period, two camps had emerged – the camp of peace and democracy, and the "aggressive anti-democratic camp headed by the United States."

Malenkov reviewed the postwar economic recoveries of the Soviet Union and claimed the annual production figures of 25,000,000 tons of pig iron, 35,000,000 tons of steel, 300,000,000 tons of coal, 47,000,000 tons of oil and 117,000,000,000 k.w.h. of electric power. He recalled the great expansion east of the Urals, and the development of Soviet science and research in all fields. The "grain problem" was solved, and plans were under consideration for similar progress in irrigation and afforestation. By contrast, said Malenkov, capitalism, especially American capitalism, was in deeper conflict with its fundamental contradictions and trying to prolong its last disastrous agonies by giving "aid" to its weaker clients. "Thus do the bloated tycoons of the United States, gamblers in the camp of the imperialist aggressors, seek to embroil the peoples in a sanguinary slaughter for the sake of their own profits." Malenkov adverted to the Soviet's efforts in the cause of peace, collective security, and disarmament, efforts which had met with constant rebuffs. He drew to a conclusion with a sharp criticism of the Party, its present state of discipline and organization, and with a careful reminder of its theoretical foundations in Marxist-Leninism. He rounded off finally with acclamatory honors to Comrade Stalin.

On January 13, 1953, Tass, the news agency, and Moscow Radio announced that a "terrorist group" of nine of the Kremlin doctors, six of them Jewish, "by means of harmful treatment had been shortening the lives of Soviet leaders." One such leader had been Zhdanov, and attempts were now to be made on the lives of two Marshals and other ranking officers of the Red Army. Certain members of the group were stated to belong to an international Jewish organization with headquarters in the United States, and others to British intelligence services. All the accused had already confessed their crimes by the time the disclosures were made. The affair recalled the hysteria of the treason trials of the late 1930's, and it seemed as if the Soviet Union was about to enter upon another round of purge and extermination. Evidently the old dragon in the Kremlin could still lash his tail.

But during the night of March 1, 1953, Stalin suffered a paralytic stroke. His death occurred on the evening of the 5th and was announced on the 6th. A joint statement by the Central Committee of the Communist Party, the Council of Ministers, and the Soviet Presidium called upon the Soviet people "to rally even closer to the great fraternal family under the tested leadership of the Communist Party." "The adamantine unity and monolithic cohesion of the Party's ranks are the chief requisites of the Party's strength." Stalin's body lay in state, after the manner of the Tsars, in the Hall of Columns in Moscow and was visited by massive crowds of the faithful for two days. He was interred beside Lenin in the Lenin Mausoleum at a ceremony that gathered together the leaders of the Communist world – Bierut, Gottwald, Rakosi, Gheorghiu-Dej, Chervenkov, Grotewohl, Ulbricht, Chou En-lai, Duclos, Togliatti, and Pollitt. Malenkov delivered the funeral oration and was followed in briefer speeches by Beria and Molotov.

On March 6, 1953, Malenkov became Premier and published the names of his colleagues. Beria, Molotov, Kaganovich, and Bulganin were Deputy Premiers. Beria was also Minister of the Interior; Molotov Foreign Minister; and Bulganin Minister of Defense, with Vassilievsky and Zhukov as his Deputies. Mikoyan was Minister of Home and Foreign Trade. Vyshinsky was named permanent Soviet representative at the United Nations. Marshal Voroshilov was President; Shvernik returned to his former chairmanship of the Council of Trade Unions. The Party Presidium was reduced to ten permanent members and four alternate members, and Khrushchev shortly became the Party's Senior Secretary. Malenkov in public made much of the principle of "collective leadership," which was now to replace Stalin's former dictatorial rule. The infamous "Doctors' Plot" was disavowed, and its victims released.

The transfer of power, it seemed, had been made with decision and dispatch. Fears that a struggle for the successorship would arise, similar to that which had followed the death of Lenin, were temporarily lulled. The world and the Soviet Union watched the course of events in Moscow with growing relief. One feature of new constellation was the strong rep-

Stalin's heirs at his lying in state, March 6, 1953: Molotov, Voroshilov, Beria, Malenkov

SOVFOTO

resentation of the army. Voroshilov, Bulganin, Vassilievsky, and Zhukov were all Marshals bearing names that had become well known to the West during the war and that still inspired confidence abroad. In a world of proliferating dictatorship, many argued that military dictatorship was often the mildest, safest, and least corrupt of the alternatives.

The transfer of power claimed one important victim – Lavrenty Beria. His position had been shaken as far back as 1948, when he had failed either to prove that Zhdanov had been murdered or to unmask the murderers. The recent arrests of the Kremlin doctors had been the work of his Ministry, and the doctors' subsequent rehabilitation had done him no good. Furthermore, it had become necessary to demonstrate by his removal that the worst features of the old police regime of the MVD – and the NKVD before it – would be abolished. In particular Beria had been responsible for the system of forced labor camps, and revolts in several of them had lately been reported. But probably the straw that broke Beria's back was the rising of the workers of East Berlin in June 1953 against their Soviet-sponsored masters. (See p. 651.) Beria was dismissed from Party and government on July 10, 1953. He was later arrested and accused of being a "vicious enemy of the Soviet people," a "bourgeois renegade," and a "hireling of foreign imperialism." On Christmas eve 1953, it was reported that he had been shot.

One of the surprises at this time was Malenkov's admission, in a statement soon after assuming office, that a nuclear war would be the end of both the socialist and capitalist halves of the world. This was the beginning of that "peaceful co-existence," which Khrushchev later was to make so much his own. But the statement momentarily was a novel assessment of the situation, and Malenkov, when he fell from power, was to be strongly criticized for it. It was totally at variance with orthodox Marxism. If the historically inevitable victory of the proletariat could be frustrated by a

Bulganin, Khrushchev, Kaganovich, and Mikoyan

gadget invented by scientists, then there must be something wrong with the entire doctrine.

The inevitable duel between Malenkov and Khrushchev was soon joined. One contestant was Premier, and the other was Party Secretary. The contest lay not only between two men, but between two offices. Neither contestant at first had seemed to be marked out for great leadership. Malenkov was a good chief of staff. The Stalinist regime had bred many such men; potential commanders it had destroyed. As for Khrushchev, he was then one of the least impressive of the Party's hierarchy. But, in the game of politics as it was now played in Moscow, fortune favored not so much the man of positive action as the man who bided his time and made no mistakes. In August 1953, the Supreme Soviet convened, and was regaled by another of Malenkov's speeches. He reviewed the country's economic progress in all fields; he remarked with satisfaction on the Korean armistice and on the resumption of relations with Yugoslavia and Greece; he announced that the Soviet Union was in possession of the hydrogen bomb. Malenkov's position seemed firm and unassailable. In September 1953, Khrushchev took the title of First Secretary of the Party.

But more serious than the party fracas was the basic policy disagreement that now developed over the allocation of the budget resources. Malenkov favored the higher production of consumer goods; Khrushchev favored agriculture and heavy industry. Agriculture, still suffering from the drought of 1946, was long overdue for new investments; the Red Army – in the person of Marshal Zhukov – needed heavy industry. The Old Guard – Molotov and Kaganovich – supported Zhukov. The Red Army, the Old Guard, and Khrushchev with the Party behind him in combination were too strong for Malenkov, and in February 1955, scarcely two years after Stalin's death, Malenkov was ousted from office. Bulganin succeeded Malenkov as Premier; Zhukov succeeded Bulganin as Minister of Defense.

A period of some confusion and uncertainty followed, during which the supreme authority was nominally vested in a "collective leadership" consisting of Bulganin, Molotov, Kaganovich, Mikoyan, and two newcomers to high office, Pervukhin and Saburov. Khrushchev pushed forward his agricultural policies — he was now advocating the wholesale cultivation of maize — and maintained a crisis atmosphere by constant changes in the Ministry of Agriculture and in the higher management of the state farms. Some relief of tensions, internationally, was effected by the Geneva "Summit" conference, by Khrushchev's visit on a mission of reconciliation to Yugoslavia, and by a general relaxation of rule in Eastern Germany and the satellite countries. (See pp. 652 and 680.) The Soviet Union had a "New Look"; the Cold War was turning into the "Big Thaw." Bulganin and Khrushchev were becoming well known abroad — "B and K," as they were called in the popular press of the West — a genial, convivial, plebeian pair, fond of trips to foreign parts — to India, China, France, and Britain. The Soviet satellites in Intermediate Europe meanwhile were quiet. The East Berlin rising of June 1953 was not repeated. In May 1955, the satellite defensive system was reorganized under a treaty of mutual assistance between the Soviet Union, Poland, Czechoslovakia, Eastern Germany, Hungary, Rumania, Bulgaria, and Albania, the Warsaw Pact. (See pp. 652 and 689.)

On February 25, 1956, at the Twentieth Party Congress, Khrushchev gave his celebrated speech attacking the memory of Stalin. Here was the "New Look" and the "Big Thaw" with a vengeance! Yet there are several questions regarding this extraordinary performance that are still unanswered. Did Khrushchev genuinely intend secrecy, or did he know very well that his every word would soon be international property? How far was he on the defensive and under the necessity of making a gesture on his own behalf? Was he attacking the Old Guard, still nostalgic for Stalin's autocracy? Or, for once, is the innocent interpretation the correct one — namely that Khrushchev, after years of indignity and dissimulation, felt that it was high time to expose the iniquities of the earlier regime? At any rate Khrushchev's hearers were very ready for the open admission of facts which they all knew and still hardly dared to utter.

Khrushchev's theme was the "cult of the individual," as he called it, in all its brutality and oppression. Stalin, he said, had ruled as a despot, destroying without mercy persons and often whole groups of persons on whom had lighted even the faintest suspicion of opposition to himself — suspicions which, of course, degenerates of the secret police like Yezhov and Beria had skillfully exploited. Stalin had been privy to the murders of Kivov in 1934 and of onetime colleagues and friends like Ordzhonikidze and Eikhe and, more recently, of Voznessensky. (See p. 433.) Voroshilov, Molotov, and Mikoyan had all been in danger of their lives at the time of his death. The trials and purges, the tortures and confessions, the mass deportations of whole populations during the 1920's and 1930's had been executed at his orders by his lieutenants. He had taken fiendish delight in humiliating prominent party leaders in public, and had deliberately

May Day Parade, Moscow, 1960: the "Showpiece" of the Soviet Union

SOVIET WEEKLY

surrounded himself with an atmosphere of hatred and rivalry. During the war his military incapacity had been manifest, and he had been personally responsible for the disaster at Kharkhov in 1941. Yet he had always caused the facts to be systematically distorted to create a legend of heroism and infallibility. Latterly the Cominform's quarrel with Tito and Yugoslavia had been entirely due to his intolerance and want of realism. And so forth. Yet, as one commentator pointed out, "in all the length of that marathon speech, there is not one word of criticism of the Soviet system itself—of the system which made Stalin possible, if not inevitable . . . Indeed the speech boils down to a stubborn defense of the system." [3] Khrushchev's peroration was a glorification of the verities and certitudes of the Marxist-Leninist creed, and the worst of Stalin's sins was his deviation therefrom.

Khrushchev's speech had a greater immediate effect abroad than in the Soviet Union. Foreign Communist parties were thrown into various attitudes of bewilderment or explanation. In Moscow the principle of "collective leadership" was kept up. But the struggle for the succession continued. Molotov was replaced by Dimitri Shepilov; Kaganovich took a lesser ministerial post. Unrest in the satellite countries, culminating in the Hungarian revolt in October 1956, probably persuaded Khrushchev that his

Peking, China, August 1958: meeting of Mao Tse-tung and Khrushchev

EASTFOTO

policy of leniency was turning against itself. (See pp. 674-75.) The end of 1956 and the beginning of 1957 was Khrushchev's most critical period. In July 1957, Marshal Zhukov became full member of the Party Presidium, the first – and last – professional soldier ever to be thus admitted to the inner circles of Soviet political power but for the time being Zhukov's support and that of the army were indispensable to Khrushchev. Thereafter demotions and dismissals came thick and fast. The "antiparty" group of Molotov, Kaganovich, and Malenkov were expelled from the Presidium. Molotov was ignominiously packed off as Soviet ambassador to Mongolia; and Malenkov was found remote exile as manager of a power station in Kazakhstan. Shepilov, Pervukhin, and Saburov were all demoted to minor positions. Andrei Gromyko became Foreign Minister. And then, in October 1957, Zhukov himself, having served his purpose and having perhaps aspired to still higher political honors, was summarily dropped and replaced by Malinovsky.

Khrushchev had won decisively. Only the ever neutral Mikoyan – and, for a time, Bulganin – survived his purge. All the more important offices of state and Party were staffed with his nominees. Success could hardly have smelled sweeter. But there was still more to come. On October 4, 1957, Sputnik I was launched into space to the vast admiration of the Soviet people and of the entire world. The hard struggle of industrial reconstruction since 1945, the decision to allocate precious national resources to scientific research, had all issued in a stupendous, symbolic triumph. For the first time in history Russia had taken the lead in a great technological advance. In March 1958, Khrushchev became Premier, remaining also First Secretary of the Party, thus uniting in himself the two highest offices in the Soviet Union. Some weeks later the loyal Bulganin paid for his loyalty and found himself relegated to the managership of an "economic council" in Stavropol in the Caucasus. Mikoyan remained as First Deputy Premier.

On April 12, 1961, the Soviet Union achieved the first manned orbital space flight, and on October 30, exploded a 50-megaton bomb.

36. INTERMEDIATE EUROPE: SATELLITE AND ANTI-SATELLITE

In Part Two we grouped together a series of thirteen states in an area to which we gave the name Intermediate Europe. (See p. 150.) In 1945 three of these states – Estonia, Latvia, and Lithuania – no longer existed; Austria we have now paired with Germany and described in Chapter 34. (See pp. 653-55.) But the post-1945 histories of the remainder – Finland, Poland, Hungary, Czechoslovakia, Yugoslavia, Albania, Bulgaria, Rumania, and Greece – should be related here. Throughout there is one dominant theme – the relationship of these states to the Soviet Union and their resistance to, or acceptance of, Soviet satellite status.

Finland

Finland had fought in the war against the Soviet Union; she had been defeated; she expected to suffer the consequences. We have already described the Finnish armistice of September 19, 1944, and the Finnish peace treaty of February 10, 1947. (See pp. 594 and 617.) Both had been harsh transactions. Marshal Mannerheim had become President just before the armistice, pledged to secure the best peace he could. His Premier was Juho Paasikivi at the head of a moderate coalition government. Elections were held for the Finnish Diet in March 1945, and, in the electoral composition that emerged, the Agrarians and Social Democrats each held about 25 per cent of the seats; the two right-wing parties, the Conservatives and the Liberals, held 15 and 5 per cent respectively; the Swedish People's party, representing the Swedo-Finnish minority, held 10 per cent; and the SKDL, the People's Democratic League, the extreme left-wing group of Communists and near-Communists, held 20 per cent. In three more elections in the next ten years, these proportions varied hardly at all.

Post-1945 Finland had four tasks: to wipe out the traces of the war; to find homes and livelihood for the 500,000 Finnish refugees and expellees from the former Finnish territory which, under the peace treaty, was now ceded to the Soviet Union; to pay reparations in products to the Soviet Union to the amount of $300,000,000 at the price level of 1938; and to maintain her national independence. Finland had all the disabilities of a defeated country. Former wartime leaders were under arrest, being tried or awaiting trial. The immediate domestic problems were inflation and its concomitant, labor unrest. On the credit side, there was some aid from UNRRA and from the United States. But public morale was extraordinarily sound, and the Finnish people set about putting their house in order in a mood of grim, cool determination. The Finnish Government declined the invitation to join the European Recovery Program, and its decision was made without pressure from the Soviet Union. Finland would not only rise above her difficulties, but she would do so, as her Premier said, "without involving herself in world political conflicts."

Mannerheim resigned the Presidency in March 1946, on grounds of ill health, and was succeeded by Paasikivi. The new Premier was Mauno Pekkala (SKDL), the only near-Communist Premier Finland was to have. He was Premier during the first half of the critical year 1948, and it is still not easy to explain how or why Finland, at this time and under such a leader, like so many of the other states of Intermediate Europe, did not submit to Soviet domination. On February 22, 1948 – at the moment that the fateful "Second Revolution" was taking place in Czechoslovakia – Stalin wrote a personal letter to President Paasikivi proposing the visit of a Finnish delegation to Moscow to conclude a treaty of mutual assistance. After some hesitation, the delegation went, and Pekkala went with it. Paasikivi stayed at home. The treaty was signed on April 6, 1948. But it was no capitulation to the Soviet interest. It bound Finland to oppose Germany, or any ally of Germany, attacking Finland or the Soviet Union; but Finland was obliged only to assist in military operations on Finnish soil. In July Karl-August Fagerholm (Social Democrat) formed a government based upon his own party and excluding the SKDL, and his first act in office was to clean up the police, which, under the former Minister of the Interior, Yrjö Leino, a Communist, had been steadily infiltrated with Communist officers. At the end of 1948, Finland was still an independent, democratic state.

Thereafter Fagerholm was under heavy attack, especially from Communist-inspired strikes. But his middle-of-the-road government, although based on a single party, stood the strain. In January 1950, Paasikivi was re-elected President. A new government was formed under Urho Kekkonen (Agrarian), again a minority government consisting of Agrarians, Liberals, and Swedes. The Soviet tactic now was to accuse the Finnish Government of harboring war criminals and to demand their surrender. The Finnish Government admitted the influx of refugees from the Soviet Union, but denied that they were war criminals and declined their surrender. This crisis also blew over. At the end of 1950, a new Soviet-Finnish trade agreement, freely negotiated, was signed. On January 27, 1951, occurred the death of Marshal Mannerheim, mourned and honored by the Finnish people.

In April 1952, Kekkonen on a visit to Stockholm declared in a public address that Finland had wiped out the traces of the war and she had found homes and livelihood for her 500,000 refugees and expellees; she had also paid reparations in full. Furthermore the original reparations account of $300,000,000 at the price level of 1938 had worked out nearer $600,000,000 at the price level of 1952. On August 29, 1952, the last trainload of reparations left Finland for the Soviet Union. And Kekkonen in his address might have added what was in everybody's mind, that Finland had preserved her independence. Appropriately the year 1952 was the year of the Olympic Games in Helsinki.

In September 1955, President Paasikivi and Kekkonen visited Moscow and signed a treaty for the return of the naval base at Porkkala to Finland. The Soviet Union released the last of Finnish prisoners of war still in its hands. Finland was admitted to the United Nations. All in all, Finland post-1945 makes a rare story of a great national struggle, a story all too rare in the world of the Cold War. As we shall see, other states in Intermediate Europe did not always fare so well.

Poland

The Polish question had been the first open breach between East and West in the newly developing phase of power politics, and in the closing months of the war the question had cast a deep gloom over Allied unity and over the hopes and ideals of the United Nations. (See pp. 580-81.) At the Teheran Conference, Churchill – and presumably Roosevelt – had acceded to Stalin's proposal that Poland's eastern frontier should be the Curzon Line and that she should receive territory in compensation towards the Oder, but the arrangement had been steadfastly rejected by Mikolajczyk and the Polish government in exile in London. At the Yalta Conference it was decided further that the Provisional Government, "now functioning in Poland," should be reorganized "on a broader democratic basis" as the Polish Provisional Government of National Unity, which should then be pledged "to the holding of free and unfettered elections (in Poland) as soon as possible." (See p. 598.) This government was eventually installed in Warsaw, with Edward Osóbka-Morawski of the former Provisional Government as Premier and Mikolajczyk of the government in exile in London as Deputy Premier, and was recognized by the United States and Britain. But the rump of the government in exile in London refused to dissolve itself, and numbers of men serving in Polish contingents in Britain, Italy, and the Near East who were faithful to it chose not to accept the option of returning home to Poland. No Polish representative attended the San Francisco Conference on the United Nations, but the new Polish Government in Warsaw afterwards joined the United Nations – albeit after an admitted legal equivocation.

The country itself was in a pitiable condition. It had been fought over by two great armies. Under the Nazi occupation it had suffered the treatment that we described in Chapter 30. Nazi extermination policies had fallen most heavily on those classes of education and technical skill which were now most needed for reconstruction. At the same time the Soviet Government now permitted the Polish occupation of Eastern Germany up to the Oder-Neisse line under the guise of a Polish "Administration," which was to all intents and purposes an annexation. In effect the Poland of 1919-39 was shifted bodily 150 miles westward. The new lands were fertile, and the native Germans inhabiting them were soon being expelled by the thousands to make room for Polish settlers.

It was all too clear that the Soviet Government was setting about unilaterally to shaping the new Polish state on the Communist pattern and was shortly destroying all elements of opposition. Some of the Polish underground leaders of the former Home Army were persuaded to reveal themselves on a promise of parleys and were whisked off to Moscow to be tried for "sabotage and treason." The Polish police, created afresh by the Provisional Government, were already well Communized and were now terrorizing the non-Communist parties. The promised elections were not held till January 1947, and then they were neither free nor unfettered. Numbers of candidates of Mikolajczyk's Peasant party were in jail on election day. Mikolajczyk afterward resigned and was succeeded as Deputy Premier by Ladislas Gomulka, a Communist. Boleslas Bierut, another Communist, was the new President of Poland. In October 1947, just after the establishment of the Cominform, Mikolajczyk fled to England. Later Osóbka-Morawski and Gomulka were themselves relieved of their posts for their alleged lukewarmness towards the Cominform and for other rightist deviations. The Polish United Workers' party (PZPR), Communist in all but name, with Bierut as its Secretary, was virtually the sole party in Poland, and its Politburo was the most powerful body in the state. The Polish economy was absorbed into a Three-Year Plan, followed by a Six-Year Plan, and tied to the Soviet Union. In November 1949, Marshal Rokossovsky, commander of the Soviet assault on Warsaw in 1944, himself Polish born, was created a Marshal of Poland and Minister of Defense, and accepted Polish citizenship. (See p. 594.)

The only power in Poland which resisted this progressive and inexorable sovietization was the Catholic Church. Cardinal Hlond, Primate of Poland, died in October 1946, and almost immediately the battle was joined. Government enactments confiscated Church lands and extended controls over charities and education. A new agreement between Government and Church was signed in 1950, but the Government evaded its terms from the start. In 1953 the Government assumed the right to make or unmake ecclesiastical appointments and demanded an oath of allegiance of all priests in the country. By the end of 1953 hundreds of church dignitaries were under arrest, including Hlond's successor, Cardinal Wyszinski.

Meanwhile in 1951, the Polish Government signed agreements with Eastern Germany and with the Soviet Union, delimiting the Polish frontiers – in the West, along the Oder-Neisse line, and in the East, with some minor rectifications, along the Curzon Line. (See p. 154.) In 1952 a new Polish constitution was adopted modeled on that of the Soviet Union. As the constitution had no provision for a President, Bierut was now named Premier. Rokossovsky was Vice-Premier. There seemed to be little more to do to complete the political transformation. The year 1955 was a gala year, punctuated by important foreign visits. The "Geneva spirit" was in the air. A great Trade Fair was drawing festive crowds to Poznan.

The jolt came in 1956. Bierut died early in the year, and with him went some of his arbitrary methods. Economic difficulties may have provided a further cause of disturbance. Industry was relatively prosperous, but agriculture had not maintained the pace; and then events in Hungary set off suppressed grievances. Rioting began in the Trade Fair city of Poznan. The Polish Government resorted to compromise — curiously out of character with the conduct of neighboring governments at the same time. The moderate Gomulka was hauled out of obscurity to become the new "strong man" of the Communist party — although he was given no government office. Rokossovsky went on extended leave; Cardinal Wyszinski was set at liberty. Elections in 1957, though returning huge majorities for the PZPR, were held to confirm Gomulka's policies. All-around amnesties followed; collectivization of the farms was halted; compulsory grain requisitions were abolished; even private ownership of land was occasionally permitted. Religious instruction was restored in the schools; Wyszinski called for Catholics to support the government. Somehow Gomulka contrived to guide the Polish state along lines of a socialism that observed "national features," while tempering the power of the police and the extreme bigotry of many of his own party members, and yet preventing evident popular discontent from breaking out into revolt.

Hungary

In April 1945, the Provisional National Government, whose formation at Debrecen under Soviet auspices we have already described, returned to Budapest, and the usual sovietization began. (See p. 595.) "People's courts" conducted purges of former collaborators and "reactionaries." Sweeping agrarian reforms broke up the old estates and redistributed the land to peasants in lots of 5 to 20 acres. A Soviet-Hungarian commercial treaty, negotiated in great secrecy, signified the virtual economic subjection of the country to the Soviet Union. However, elections for a Hungarian National Assembly, held in November 1945, resulted in a victory for the moderate agrarian Smallholders' party and a decisive Communist defeat. It was one of the few honest elections in Soviet-occupied territory — and probably the only honest election in the history of Hungary. Hungary was declared a republic with a constitution that read "like the Bill of Rights and the Four Freedoms rolled into one." Zoltan Tildy, a Smallholder, was elected first President, and Ferenc Nagy, another Smallholder, formed a coalition government largely composed of members of his party. Imre Nagy, a Communist, for a short time was Minister of the Interior.

But one of Ferenc Nagy's Vice-Premiers was Matyas Rákosi, Secretary of the Hungarian Communist party, and, from March 1946, his Minister of the Interior was the militantly fanatic Communist, Laszlo Rajk, who by virtue of his office controlled the police. The Hungarian peace treaty was signed in Paris in February 1947, but the Soviet commander, General Sviridov, was still in Hungary with Soviet forces at hand, when the expected crisis developed. Early in 1947, Rajk, claiming to have discovered a plot for Horthy's restoration, instituted a wave of arrests directed particularly against the Smallholders' party. Béla Kovács, the Smallholders' secretary, was one of the arrests and was afterward reported to have made confessions while in prison, implicating other members of his party. In May the government was remodeled. Ferenc Nagy, who happened to be in Switzerland, resigned by telephone and refused to return home. Lajos Dinnyés, a Smallholder, but a more pliant one, became Premier, with Rákosi Vice-Premier.

From 1948 onwards, by dint of purges, remodelings of the government, constitutional reforms, and new elections, Hungary was brought to approximate more closely to the Communist ideal. The schools were nationalized, and Cardinal Mindszenty, Primate of Hungary, protesting, was sentenced to life imprisonment after one of the most infamous trials of this time. The purge then suddenly turned on one of its instigators, Rajk himself, who was tried for espionage, confessed his sins, and was hanged. What was left of the Smallholders – identified inevitably with the *kulaks* – was gradually eliminated. Hungarian farming was completely subordinated to cooperatives and collectives. In 1952, as if to put the finishing touches to the process, Rákosi became Premier.

The death of Stalin and the emergence of Khrushchev, allegedly anti-Stalinist but otherwise an unknown quantity, may have encouraged the view that more lenient rule was to be introduced into Hungary. All the Soviet-dominated countries were restless, expectant, and then impatient, and they did not all have skillful Gomulkas to advise them in middle courses. During 1956 several Hungarian intellectual groups were criticizing Rákosi, and their attacks were reported at length in the Hungarian press. The food situation was bad; the harvest in all crops that year had failed, but it was common knowledge that nevertheless huge exports of agricultural produce were still going to the Soviet Union. There were student demonstrations in Budapest. Rajk's body was exhumed and was given a ceremonial funeral. Rákosi at last resigned; Imre Nagy, the moderate Minister of the Interior of 1945, was made, or made himself, Premier at the head of a coalition and undertook to negotiate with the Soviet Government the withdrawal of the Soviet occupying forces.

By the last week of October 1956, Budapest was in full revolt. Cardinal Mindszenty was released by hysterical, cheering crowds. But the Soviet Government quietly brought up troops, and, during the first week of November, the insurgent areas in Budapest and in other centers of population were being systematically reduced by artillery, tank, and bomber. Nagy escaped to the Yugoslav embassy, and Mindszenty to the American embassy. Some 150,000 Hungarian refugees fled into Austria. Janos Kádár was installed at the head of a new Hungarian Government with instructions to effect the pacification and reattachment of the erring country. Nagy at least was soon disposed of. He emerged from his refuge under promise of safe-conduct, was kidnaped, and was afterwards reported to have been secretly tried and sentenced to death. Mindszenty remained in the American embassy.

The Hungarian affair aroused the greatest indignation abroad. Action on the part of the Western Powers might have been more effective, had not the Suez Crisis occurred at the same time. An emergency session of the

Security Council convened on October 28; and, on November 4, the day before the installation of the Kádár government, the General Assembly, employing its "uniting for peace" machinery, passed a United States resolution by 50 votes to 8 – with 15 abstentions – calling upon the Soviet Union to withdraw its forces from Hungary. (See p. 634.) By the same resolution, United Nations observers were to be sent to Hungary, but Kádár gave out that they would be refused permission to enter the country. On December 10, the General Assembly somewhat unconvincingly discussed the application of sanctions against the Soviet Union, and then contented itself with a further resolution condemning Soviet action in Hungary and requesting the Secretary-General "to take any initiative he deems helpful in relation to the Hungarian problem in conformity with the principles of the Charter and the resolutions of the Assembly."

Czechoslovakia

Czechoslovakia's new phase of alignment with the Soviet Union had begun with the Czech-Soviet treaty of 1943. Recollections of "betrayal" by the Western Powers at Munich in 1938, the old fear and hatred of Germany, sentiments of Slavic solidarity, and the recent victories of the Red Army all operated in the same direction. Beneš visited Moscow in March 1945 in order to dramatize his return to Czechoslovakia from the East and, while in Moscow, he agreed to form a liberation government including Communists and Slovaks. In the first week of May 1945, General Patton with the United States First Army could have occupied Prague but was restrained by Eisenhower, who did not wish to prejudice his good relations with the Soviet High Command. Czech partisans, anticipating liberation, were fighting in the streets of Prague when, on May 9, 1945, the first units of the Red Army drove into the city.

On the whole, Czechoslovakia had escaped the worst ravages of the war. The Protectorate of the occupation years had been subject to the spoliations and persecutions we described in Chapter 30, but physical damage was relatively light; and Slovakia had been one of Hilter's showpieces. Prague in 1945 was in happy contrast to devastated Warsaw and Budapest. The country therefore settled down to the tasks of peace with distinct advantages. The liberation government took the form of a Provisional Assembly under the presidency of Beneš with a National Front of left-wing parties, pledged to call a Constituent Assembly to devise a new constitution. A purge of former collaborators was instituted. Hacha died in prison; Moravec committed suicide; Tiso was shot. Karl Hermann Frank, captured by the Americans, was handed over for trial in Prague and hanged. Meanwhile 3,000,000 Germans in the Sudetenland and 650,000 Magyars in southern Slovakia were being expelled. Teschen was occupied by Czech forces. Ruthenia was ceded to the Soviet Union.

Elections for the Constituent Assembly were held in May 1946. Of a heavy "compulsory" poll, 38 per cent of the votes went to the Communist party, and the remainder to seven other "National Front" and Catholic parties. The Assembly elected Beneš President of the Republic. On July

8, 1946, Klement Gottwald, the Communist leader, took office as Premier with eight members of his party in a cabinet of twelve. Jan Masaryk, of no party, was Foreign Minister; Vaclav Nosek, a Communist, Moscow-trained, was Minister of the Interior and, by virtue of that office, controlled the police. The new government at once showed its economic proclivities by launching a Two-Year Plan and signing a trade agreement with the Soviet Union.

There was perhaps no great difference between the subsequent political history of Czechoslovakia and that of other countries which were to find themselves within the Soviet bloc. But Czechoslovakia had always had well-wishers in the West, and especially in the United States, and during the interwar period she had been an exceptional and distinguished example of a modern democracy. Her present restoration under such well-known leaders as Beneš and Jan Masaryk seemed to be a happy assurance for a new future. But, in July 1947, it was already clear that all was not as it should have been in Czechoslovakia. On July 7, the Czech Government accepted the invitation to attend the conference on the Marshall Plan in Paris, and three days later suddenly and categorically withdrew. Evidently the satellites of the Soviet Union were not to be numbered with the nations of the European Recovery Program. (See p. 713.)

The year 1948 was to be one of the most critical years of the postwar period. The presence of the Cold War could no longer be denied. Berlin was under Soviet blockade; Yugoslavia had broken with the Cominform; in elections in Italy it was feared that the Italian Communist party would be widely successful; France was in the grip of Communist-inspired workers' strikes; Mao Tse-tung was triumphing in China. Early in 1948, the Czech Communist party was beginning to exert its characteristic pressures upon the Czech Government. It issued manifestos calling upon its members "to defend the regime" and to take "certain measures to forestall the dishonest plans of reaction." Nosek, Minister of the Interior, for some time had been dismissing "unreliable" police officers and replacing them with Communists, and on February 12, 1948, with similar intent, he dismissed eight police chiefs in Prague. The non-Communist ministers in the Czech Government at once instructed him to reinstate them, and, on February 20, when he refused, they resigned in a body. Gottwald and Nosek ignored the resignations and, in the absence of the ministers concerned, remodeled the government to suit themselves. Prague was now in the hands of Nosek's police. Zorin, Soviet Deputy Foreign Minister, who happened to be in Prague at the critical moment on a trade mission, supervised the transfer of power to the new masters of Czechoslovakia. On February 25, Beneš as President accepted Gottwald's reconstruction. On March 10, the body of Jan Masaryk, was found under one of the windows of the Czernin Palace, the Czech Foreign Ministry. He appeared to have committed suicide.

Czechoslovakia's "Second Revolution," as it was called, was speedily implemented. In April 1948, Gottwald's new government presented the Constituent Assembly with a ready-made Constitution, which that body obediently passed. This time Beneš refused his consent and resigned the presidency. He was succeeded by Gottwald with Antonin Zapotocky, the Communist trade union leader, as Premier. Elections in May returned sweeping majorities for the National Front; but 1,500,000 voting papers were blank or spoiled. "Action Committees" and "People's Courts" purged the country of intellectuals, journalists, army officers, and other "reactionaries," "imperialists," and "spies." In view of Czechoslovakia's strong Western links hitherto, the victims were numerous. But there was one distinct feature of the purge. It staged no spectacular trials of internationally prominent figures; and, in so far as it was directed against the Catholic Church, it only affected the obscurer priesthood. Nor – with the exception of the Slansky trial – was it followed by a second purge in the Communists' own ranks. Czechoslovakia in these years had no Petkovs, Rajks, or Mindszentys – but her experience was not less sinister for that. On September 3, 1948, occurred the death of the former President, Beneš.

A Czech Five-Year Plan was initiated in 1949, and, by means of Soviet-Czech trade agreements, the highly developed heavy industries of the Bohemian half of the country were effectively tied to the Soviet Union. Thereafter the economic history of Czechoslovakia was little more than an insistently pressed drive for the delivery of coal, steel products, and armaments to the Soviet alliance. The Czech workers were of a high level of intelligence, they had had a recent training in all the tricks of resistance, and it cannot be said that they took kindly to the new program. Their principal weapon was absenteeism, silent, apparently unorganized, but effective, especially in view of the fact that skilled labor was in short supply in any case. In accordance with the usual Soviet methods, failures in production had to be visited upon a selected scapegoat, and, during 1952, Rudolf Slansky, Secretary of the Czech Communist party, was brought to trial and executed. But the labor shortage was such that the government shortly introduced a virtual conscription of labor, including women and young persons over the age of 14 years. In 1953 the government was even trying to induce former Sudeten Germans to return to Czechoslovakia and offering them Czech citizenship.

On March 14, 1953, on his return from Stalin's funeral in Moscow, Gottwald died. He was succeeded in the presidency by Zapotocky.

Yugoslavia

The end of the war in 1945 found Yugoslavia gutted economically and rent asunder politically by the many-edged partisan war that had shed more of the nation's blood and energy than had the war against the Nazi invader. Ostensibly the Tito-Subasich Agreement of June 1944 was still in force. (See p. 585.) Under its terms and under the promptings of the Yalta Conference, Tito's Council for National Liberation was to be broadened so as to include as members Deputies of irreproachable record from the last prewar Yugoslav National Assembly. And accordingly, in Belgrade in March 1945, a provisional government took office with Josef Tito as Premier and Minister of National Defense, Ivan Subasich as Foreign Minister, and three other ministers hailing from the Yugoslav government in exile in London.

But, as was soon evident, Tito – and the Communist party – held the reins. His government clearly considered itself as something other than a neutral and interim custodian of authority until such time as elections could be held. During the resistance, the Communists had invariably dominated the regional committees of the Council for National Liberation, and these same Communists now occupied the chief political posts, especially outside Belgrade. The Communists as a party, however, did not yet come into the open but operated as usual behind a National Front of left-wing groups. As for Tito, the Marshal, he was now apostrophized by the journalists and poets of the land as the "greatest son of Mother Yugoslavia" and with other lyrical superlatives. The mass chanting that greeted him everywhere was disquietingly reminiscent of the salutations once practised in Rome and Berlin. King Peter, from London, denounced the developing dictatorship; Subasich delivered his contribution in a letter of resignation couched in strong language. But such protests were scarcely noticed in Yugoslavia.

In November 1945, elections were held for a Constituent Assembly. The National Front, according to the official count, won 90 per cent of the votes. The Constituent Assembly met forthwith, abolished the monarchy, and proclaimed the Federal People's Republic of Yugoslavia. On January 31, 1946, after a labor of two months, it unanimously adopted a constitution modeled on the Soviet Constitution of 1936. Thus Yugoslavia also became a Union of Socialist Republics, six in number – namely Serbia, Croatia, Slovenia, Montenegro, Bosnia-Herzegovina, and Macedonia. The new federalism, it was claimed, was the final and permanent solution of Yugoslavia's local nationalisms, whose former hostilities the war, the occupation, and the resistance had all so much intensified. The two chambers of the legislature represented respectively the citizens of the Union and the federal units. Tito was now Premier and Minister of Defense, with Kardelj as his Deputy Premier.

The liquidation of collaborators, rivals, and suspects of opposition followed in due course. In March 1946, the resistance leader Mihailovich was arraigned for his alleged war crimes and sentenced to be shot. In October of the same year Archbishop Stepinac, head of the Catholic hierarchy in Croatia, was arrested and tried, not so much for his active collaboration with the enemy, but rather for his passive connivance and repeated refusal to protest against the hardships of the occupation. He was sentenced to sixteen years' imprisonment. Whether the charges were justifiable or not, these trials and the arbitrary methods by which they were conducted created the greatest furor abroad. Mihailovich and Stepinac were men famous beyond their country's frontiers, and we can only guess at the numbers of lesser victims who paid forfeit without the slight consolation of foreign diplomatic protests or of international news dispatches.

Meanwhile Tito had set about repairing the country's economy. At the end of hostilities it was estimated that more than half the farming livestock had gone, almost every truck and automobile, and almost half the peasant carts. The human population had been reduced by 10 per cent. UNRRA provided immediate relief and spent at this time nearly 15 per cent of its total budget in Yugoslavia. Millions of Yugoslavs survived the winter of

1945-46 through its devoted efforts. Yugoslavia was one of the few countries of Soviet-dominated Europe in which UNRRA was permitted to function without obstruction – indeed with willing Soviet cooperation. The Yugoslav Government's own efforts, partly out of necessity, partly out of doctrinaire policy, took the form of the nationalization of industries, agrarian reforms, and the creation of state corporations for foreign trade, all supervised by a Federal Planning Commission. Trade agreements were sought, not only with neighboring regimes in Intermediate Europe, but with any foreign country which had machinery or raw materials to exchange or sell. In April 1947, Tito introduced an ambitious Five-Year Plan involving land reclamation, irrigation, industrialization, electrification, and improvements in transport to a total investment of $6,000,000,000.

Yugoslavia's foreign policy at this time was linked with the Soviet Union. It had been confirmed and typified by a Soviet-Yugoslav treaty of friendship, mutual assistance, and cooperation and by a concurrent trade agreement, both signed in Moscow in March 1945. Yugoslavia identified herself with the Soviet interest in the United Nations; she assisted the Greek guerrillas; she rejected the Marshall Plan; she joined the Cominform. At the same time she cultivated the friendship and cooperation of her Communist neighbors. In August 1947, Dimitrov of Bulgaria was invited to Belgrade to sketch out the general lines of a Yugoslav-Bulgarian defensive alliance and of an economic agreement which was eventually to include a customs union. In the November following, Dimitrov and Tito met again, this time in Sofia, to sign a treaty of friendship and mutual assistance amid much heady talk of Slavic unity in the Balkans. (See p. 683.)

But all this fraternalism was not the whole story. Even in 1944-45, despite the fervors of the liberation and of Slavic sentiment and despite the community of doctrine, there were already indications that the Soviet allegiance was going to be hard to maintain. Complaints were reaching Moscow from Yugoslavia regarding the conduct – or misconduct – of the Red Army in that country. Then further, in May 1945, Yugoslav forces advancing on Trieste had found their road blocked by the Western Allies, and subsequently, in the Foreign Ministers Council, Soviet diplomacy had failed to secure to Yugoslavia the greatly desired port. Yugoslav opinion was evidently fractious, and from time to time, Tito's public pronouncements carried a tone of something less than humble subservience to Moscow. In 1946, on the ground of the heavy expense, the Yugoslav Government requested the recall of 60 per cent of the Red Army officers attached to the Yugoslav Army.

In March 1948, matters at last came to a head. The Soviet Government complained of the "hostile attitude" and "lack of hospitality" being shown its officers and technicians in Yugoslavia. During the next three months an exchange of notes followed between Tito and Kardelj for the Yugoslav Communist party and Stalin and Molotov for the Soviet Communist party, the one side elaborately refuting the Soviet charges of party disloyalty and doctrinal deviation, and the other side repeating its grievances with rising wrath. Tito and Kardelj conceded every possible point short of complete abdication of all dignity, and they appealed for support to their comrades in the Cominform. But that body did not waver in its Soviet loyalties and duly handed down a verdict accusing the Yugoslav leaders of unfriendliness to the Soviet Union, of opposition to correct Marxism-Leninism, and "of boundless ambition, arrogance, and conceit." On June 28, 1948, the Cominform expelled Yugoslavia from membership. Shortly afterward the Cominform moved its headquarters from Belgrade to Bucharest.

Yugoslavia suffered immediate and total economic blockade from the East. But Stalin was wrong if he thought that she would now surrender – or collapse. The next few years were anxious enough, but Tito and his regime survived. Trade and aid developed from the West – in particular from the United States, Britain, France, Italy, and later Western Germany. After the famine and drought which afflicted the country in 1950, money grants and relief in kind poured in mainly from the United States and Britain to an eventual total of nearly $700,000,000. By an agreement concluded in November 1951, the United States provided war material at the rate of some $150,000,000 a year for seven years. A *rapprochement* with Greece, issuing in 1954 in a Yugoslav-Greek alliance, was another sign of the same trend of affairs. Tito meanwhile made not a single domestic political concession. His personal dictatorship continued unchanged. Indeed, in January 1953, a new constitution was adopted, which was claimed to be a reversion to pure Marxist doctrine. The federal system and the two chambers were retained, but the second chamber was now corporative in composition and represented workers' and peasants' organizations.

During 1955, Bulganin and Khrushchev, successors to Stalin, attempted to heal the Soviet-Yugoslav breach, and, during a visit to Belgrade, they issued a statement affirming the principle coexistence. The following year Tito visited the Soviet Union. Nevertheless Yugoslavia remained an uneasy neutral, between East and West, scrupulously avoiding irreparable involvement on either side. It was entirely consistent with Tito's middle-of-the-road policy that, in September 1961 in Belgrade, he should be host to the Conference of Uncommitted Nations.

Albania

In December 1944, under the Communist resistance leader Enver Hoxha, a provisional government took control in Albania bearing all the now familiar forms. The Communists operated behind a Democratic Front. Domestic reforms were proposed abolishing Albania's "feudalism," redistributing the land to needy peasants, and nationalizing mines and industries. Elections in December 1945 returned a Constituent Assembly composed almost wholly of members of the Democratic Front. A People's Republic was proclaimed, and a constitution was adopted largely modeled on that of Yugoslavia. Hoxha emerged as Premier, Foreign Minister, and Defense Minister of the new government.

Hoxha was vaguely anti-British and anti-American, and decidedly anti-Italian. British and American personnel – including UNRRA officials – were treated with unconcealed suspicion; Italians were sent packing. But the Soviet and all its works, of course, were popular. The Soviet Government from the first celebrated the new regime with a laudatory press campaign in Moscow, and accorded it unqualified diplomatic recognition. Thus Albania gave every possible support to her Soviet protector, assisted the Greek guerrillas, entered into the closest political and economic relations with Yugoslavia, and then, as obediently, despite her geographical and economic isolation, broke off these relations at the time of Tito's expulsion from the Cominform.

Meanwhile the deterioration of Anglo-Albanian relations had ended in an open dispute. In May 1946, Albanian coastal batteries fired on two British warships passing through the Corfu Channel. In October, while the Albanian Government was still evading settlement of the incident, two British destroyers struck mines in the same channel and suffered heavy injury and loss of life. The Albanian Government took the initiative in protesting to the United Nations against what it described as a flagrant violation of its territorial waters. In January 1947, the British Government, in turn, after more fruitless correspondence with the Albanian Government, brought the dispute before the Security Council. Two months later the Soviet delegate vetoed a resolution to assess Albania with indirect responsibility for laying the mine field, and the Security Council then resolved, with the Soviet Union and Poland abstaining, to refer the issue to the International Court of Justice.[1]

Bulgaria

Bulgarians dated the new era of their country from September 9, 1944, when, by the *coup d'état* which we described elsewhere, a Soviet-sponsored government and Regency Council had been installed in office in Sofia. (See p. 594.) The new Premier, Kimon Georgiev, and a number of his colleagues belonged to the Zveno, not a political party but rather a pressure group of army officers and substantial businessmen; the government as a whole was representative of the wartime alliance of left-wing parties known as the Fatherland Front. The Communists made one of the parties of the Fatherland Front, but, as usual, they were not at first overtly conspicuous. The Communist party giants, Georgi Dimitrov and Vasil Kalarov, were in Moscow and remained there for another two years awaiting the best psychological moment for their return. Tsola Dragoicheva at this time probably wielded more actual power than any other person in Bulgaria, but she was content to do so from a modest secretarial office.

On October 28, 1944, in Moscow, a Bulgarian armistice had been signed, and under its terms Bulgaria set about liquidating the errors of her war time record. She disgorged her territorial gains at the expense of Greece and Yugoslavia, but not of Rumania, and undertook to support a Soviet army of occupation and to bring war criminals to justice. In pursuance of this last laudable objective, the Fatherland Front set up 68 "people's courts," and, in the course of 1945, disposed of 3 regents, 22 ministers, 65 parliamentary deputies, 8 royal councilors, over a score of ranking army officers, and more than 1,500 other persons of varying degrees of eminence

– and perhaps ten times as many more of lesser citizens. Economic policy followed the usual Communist program. Larger landed holdings, still left over from earlier agrarian reforms, were broken up for redistribution and eventual collectivization. Trade agreements were signed with the Soviet Union and with friendly neighboring states. A Two-Year Plan was instituted in April 1947.

Elections for a national parliament were announced for August 1945, and, as the auspicious date approached, political parties were forced to reaffirm their membership in the Fatherland Front or else remain in vulnerable isolation outside. The United States and British Governments protested against these strange political maneuverings and momentarily secured a postponement of the elections. But the elections took place in mid-November 1945, and the Fatherland Front won the sweeping victory it had planned. Subsequent Anglo-American protests failed to obtain the inclusion of Opposition members in the new government, which was eventually formed in March 1946, under the peremptory personal intervention of Vyshinsky himself, the Soviet Deputy Foreign Commissar. Georgiev remained Premier, but he was now Premier of an all-Communist roster of ministers.

On September 8, 1946, the Government held a plebiscite to permit the Bulgarian people to choose between monarchy and republic. Out of 4,000,000 votes, fewer than 200,000, according to the official reckoning, were cast for the retention of the monarchy. Bulgaria accordingly was proclaimed a republic, and the six-year-old Tsar Simeon went to join his grandfather, Victor Emmanuel of Italy, in exile. Elections for a Constituent Assembly to draw up a republican constitution were held in the following October, and resulted in a win of 366 seats for the Fatherland Front, of which 279 were Communist. Georgi Dimitrov and Vasil Kalarov returned to Bulgaria from the Soviet Union, the former to take office as Premier and the latter as President.

Communism had once more triumphed. All that was left to be done was the final liquidation of surviving resisting elements in the country, notably the national Church, the minorities, and the Opposition. Nikola Petkov, leader of the former Agrarian party, was the defendant in one of the highly dramatized trials of these times and, despite fresh Anglo-American protests, was duly convicted and hanged. On December 4, 1947, the Constituent Assembly adopted a constitution closely modeled upon that of Yugoslavia. Bulgaria, in effect, was attired in the conventional vestments of a Communist Republic.

The foreign policy of the Fatherland Front began with a strong Slavic orientation. Despite old grievances against Serbia and Yugoslavia, which were seemingly part and parcel of Bulgaria's national tradition, despite Bulgaria's pariah-like status in the interwar years, and despite the Bulgarian spoliation of Yugoslavia in 1941, there was now a strong current of desire for an all-around reconciliation. The Yugoslavs were no less disposed toward a new start in neighborly relations. In January 1945, the Bulgarian Government issued a statement on its foreign policy covering a diversity of good intentions – toward the Soviet Union "eternal friendship," toward Yugoslavia "the closest possible alliance and fraternal collaboration," toward the rest of the world "friendly relations" — in other words, a practical *rapprochement* with Yugoslavia.

The Bulgarian peace treaty was signed in February 1947, but the *rapprochement* was not discouraged. In August 1947, Dimitrov paid a ceremonial visit to Yugoslavia, and, as we have already mentioned, he and Tito announced an expansive program of political and economic cooperation. In November, Tito made a return visit to Bulgaria and signed an alliance of friendship and mutual assistance, the basic provisions and language of which were now standard in agreements between the Communist-controlled states of Intermediate Europe. But in January 1948 it seems that Dimitrov, that very personification of Communism, in a moment of exuberance went beyond the bounds of discretion. He declared that, when the time was ripe, the countries of Eastern Europe and the Balkans intended to form a federation of states in alliance with the Soviet Union. A fortnight later *Pravda* struck down the fervid Dimitrov; the countries mentioned, it said, had no need for a "problematical and artificial federation or customs union"; their proper task was the protection of their independence and sovereignty through mobilizing their domestic democratic forces. A scramble of penitent denials issued from Sofia. Dimitrov himself, speaking before a Fatherland Front congress, admitted that the *Pravda*'s critical comments were "a timely, valuable, and useful warning against possible inappropriate infatuation harmful to the people's democracies."

In March 1948, Dimitrov took a delegation to Moscow and signed a comprehensive alliance with the Soviet Union. But apparently he was not forgiven. A year later he was again in Moscow on sick leave, and on July 2, 1949, it was given out that he had died there in a sanatorium. His place as Premier was taken by Kalarov who was now assisted by Vulko Chervenkov, Deputy Premier and party Secretary, probably the strongest man in the Bulgarian administrative machine. At the end of the year, in December 1949, the new Kalarov-Chervenkov combination demonstrated its power in another dramatized trial, this time of Traicho Kostov, a prominent member of the party Politburo and chairman of the government's Economic Committee. Kostov confessed to various doctrinal errors — but, surprisingly, refused to confess to treason — and duly went to his execution. In January 1950, Kalarov died, and Chervenkov became Premier and virtual dictator of Bulgaria.

Probably Bulgaria's was the most bigoted and ferocious of all the Sovietized regimes in Intermediate Europe. It was said that some 50,000 party "deviationists" were purged between 1948 and 1954, and the number is some measure of the situation. Chervenkov himself fell from grace in 1956, confessed his errors, and was succeeded by one of his former victims, Anton Yugov. But hopes of a liberalization of the regime were short-lived. After the Hungarian rising of that year, Yugov proved as hard a master in Bulgaria as Chervenkov. Indeed Chervenkov returned in 1957 as Minister of Education and became one of Yugov's most ruthless and efficient aides.

Rumania

General Sanatescu's government of August 1944, under King Michael, was composed in the main of his fellow army officers; but it also included the leaders of former moderate political parties. (See p. 594.) In cooperation with a somewhat moribund left-wing agrarian faction, the so-called Plowman's Front, and a group of bourgeois intellectuals, the Communist party resorted at once to the device of creating a National Democratic Front. Sanatescu was soon under pressure to remodel his government so as to include a stronger Communist representation. The Yalta Conference in February 1945 published its agreement regarding free elections in eastern Europe. But on February 24, within a fortnight of the Conference, when American and British members, in the interest of implementing the agreement, asked for a meeting of the Allied Control Commission in Bucharest, the Soviet chairman refused. On February 27 Vyshinsky, the Soviet Deputy Foreign Commissar, arrived in Bucharest and presented King Michael with a two-hour ultimatum demanding the formation of a government based "on the truly democratic forces of the country." It is reported that, to give point to his demands, he slammed the door as he left the royal presence, while Russian troops paraded in front of the palace grounds. Finally Vyshinsky was good enough to inform the King that Petru Groza, leader of the Plowman's Front, must be appointed Premier with a chosen list of ministers, or he (Vyshinsky) would not be responsible for the continuance of Rumania as an independent state.

Thus Groza became Premier on March 2, 1945. He was one of the wealthiest men in the country, a political opportunist of skill, experience, and no scruples, latterly working with the Communist party. His ministers included an ex-premier of dubious repute as a rigger of elections, a priest who had been a member of the Iron Guard, a general relegated for black-market operations, and others of as imposing biographies. But the realities of power rested with three high Communists who kept in the background, namely Ana Pauker, Vasile Luca, and Emil Bodnaras. The installation of Groza was followed by the retrocession of Transylvania to Rumania amid a great fanfare so as to make it appear as a special gift from the Soviet Union to Groza himself.

The Western Powers could little more than protest over these arrangements, but they protested vigorously. King Michael summoned Groza to the Palace and demanded his resignation; but Groza continued to govern on his own account. On the last day of December 1945, a three-power commission, composed of the American and British ambassadors in Moscow, together with Vyshinsky, arrived in Bucharest and obtained from Groza a formal pledge to hold free and early elections. On February 5, 1946, the United States and Britain somewhat hesitantly recognized the Rumanian Government. The elections were duly held, though after several delays, in November, and it was afterward announced that 80 per cent of the electorate had voted for the National Democratic Front.

The usual purges were already taking place. Antonescu was brought before a people's court in May 1946 for the crimes of his dictatorship, found guilty, and shot. A more systematic persecution of opposition parties during 1947 culminated in the arrest of the aged and ailing leader of the former Peasant party of the interwar years, Julius Maniu, on charges of conspiring to overthrow the government. His trial took place to the accompaniment of a violent press and radio campaign throughout the country, and he was finally condemned to a life sentence on the strength of confessions extorted from his imprisoned colleagues. He died in prison, four years later, in 1951. One by-product of his trial, however, was the damaging information elicited in regard to George Tatarescu, the Foreign Minister, one of the few non-Communist members of the Government, who consequently resigned. He was succeeded as Foreign Minister by that remarkable woman revolutionary, former Soviet citizen, Comintern official, and general of the Red Army, Ana Pauker. At the same time, Vasile Luca became Minister of Finance, and Emil Bodnaras Minister of War. The inner Communist triumvirate thus assumed open control.

On December 30, 1947, the last vestige of the old order disappeared when, without previous intimation to the public, King Michael announced his abdication in phrases bearing the stamp of Communism dictation. The government proceeded to the establishment of a Grand National Assembly on republican lines. Elections for this body were held in March 1948, and the National Democratic Front, in the official returns, was accorded 90 per cent of the votes and 405 of the 414 seats. A constitution was adopted, evidently inspired by the recent constitution in Yugoslavia. Thereafter we have the usual story of assimilation to the Soviet pattern – nationalization and collectivization, purges and trials, trade treaties and an overall Five-Year Plan, secularization of schools and persecution of churches. Nor was Rumania exempt from sharp revolutionary upheavals within the government and party. In 1952 Groza, who since 1948 had been living in some obscurity, was made President and was succeeded as Premier by George Gheorghiu-Dej, the party Secretary. Ana Pauker, Luca, and five other Ministers were dismissed. The triumvirate had collapsed. A new constitution was announced transforming Rumania into a "Workers' State," followed by elections in which a conventional 98 per cent of the votes went to the National Democratic Front. Bodnaras survived as Minister of War, and became Deputy Premier in 1953.

Greece

Of the states of Intermediate Europe, Greece – along with Finland, Austria, and Yugoslavia – did not succumb to Soviet domination. British influence was of primary importance, and Churchill, disappointed in his larger wartime Balkan ambitions, was determined that this territory at least should not be allowed to fall before the newly rising adversary of the East. It is interesting to note that while the greater part of Intermediate Europe approachable by land passed under Soviet domination, those areas escaped – notably Yugoslavia and the Greek peninsular – that could be succored from the sea. At all costs Trieste and the Dardanelles had to be held for the Western Powers. In these often forgotten corners of the maritime world, British strategic instinct was always on the alert.

Dimetrios Papandreou had returned to Athens in October 1944, in the wake of the British forces, pledged to form a government representative of the Greek parties. But he found the country in a state of civil war between the former partisan groups – notably the left-wing EAM and the more moderate EDES – and the immediate problem, for both Papandreou and his British sponsors, was the disarming and disbanding of these mutually hostile groups. (See p. 595.)

EAM and EDES were both represented in Papandreou's government. Each naturally was intent on the prior capitulation of the other. Nondiscriminatory orders to disarm and disband from General Scobie of the Allied Command in Athens were entirely ineffective. After scarcely two months of uneasy cooperation, EAM resigned from the government, and, in December 1944, open fighting broke out between ELAS, the militant arm of EAM, and the British occupation forces. Churchill and his Foreign Secretary, Eden, arrived in Athens on Christmas Day 1944, thereby advertising the importance the British Government attached to Greek affairs, but neither Churchill's pleas nor scoldings made the least impression on the unruly factions. ELAS still resisted Scobie's order, and EDES, pleased to have the British smite its enemy, saw no virtue in compromise. On the last day of 1944, Archbishop Damaskinos accepted an invitation to become Regent on behalf of the still exiled King George.

Early in 1945, in the face of a full-scale British offensive, ELAS surrendered under terms. The Greek Government promised an amnesty for political crimes and pledged itself to the maintenance of civil liberties. As an organization, ELAS faithfully dissolved itself and even delivered up more than its specified quota of arms. But some four thousand of its members on their own account took to the mountains or escaped into Yugoslavia, whence they could hatch further trouble for their homeland. The net result of this tangled course of events was to raise the prestige of the Right, the heirs of the former royalists, and thus to commit the British to the Right's support. Meanwhile EAM, discredited by the defeat of its militant arm, began to lose its wartime character as a union of left-wing national elements, leaving the always more powerful Communists dominant in its ranks.

In the circumstances, the next step in Greece, the holding of popular elections, was none too easy. Archbishop Damaskinos appointed successive premiers – Plastiras, Voulgaris, and Sophoulis – who could only postpone the critical date. But eventually, on March 31, 1946, under the eyes of over a thousand foreign observers, the Greek people went to the polls. The royalists, now headed by the Popular Party, won a landslide victory, gaining 231 of the 354 seats in the chamber. The results might have appeared to be satisfactory and convincing – the more so as they had been obtained without falsification or intimidation – until it was discovered that only 49 per cent of the registered electorate had voted, and this was enough to induce EAM to claim that the remaining 51 per cent consisted largely of its own supporters who had deliberately boycotted the election.

Nevertheless Sophoulis gave place to Tsaldaris, leader of the Popular Party, and Tsaldaris, rejecting British advice and paying little attention either to economic problems or to the activities of ELAS bands in the mountains, ordered a plebiscite on the monarchy. On September 1, 1946, the plebiscite was held; 69 per cent voted for the monarchy, and before the month was out King George had returned to his kingdom.

Greece by now might have been on the way to a general national rehabilitation. Relief from UNRRA and loans and gifts from Britain and the United States had been tiding over the worst of her economic difficulties. But the four thousand members of ELAS, who had escaped during the early months of 1945, had now become an organized guerrilla force operating from Yugoslavia, Albania, and Bulgaria in the Communist interest. The British, heavily committed in the Middle East, were finding the continued burden in Greece too much for them. The situation therefore was desperate, when President Truman, in the course of an address to a joint session of Congress in March 1947, announced the policy since named after him the Truman Doctrine for granting aid in particular to Greece and Turkey. (See p. 746.)

In December 1946, the Greek Government had already appealed to the Security Council of the United Nations and accused Yugoslavia, Albania, and Bulgaria of aiding the guerrillas. Early in 1947 the Security Council dispatched a commission to Greece which accumulated a formidable mass of evidence in confirmation of the Greek Government's case. On the basis of the commission's report the United States submitted a resolution to the Security Council condemning the activities of Greece's three northern neighbors and calling for a further commission of investigation and good offices to negotiate a peaceful settlement between the parties. In July 1947, the Soviet, supported by Poland, vetoed the resolution. In October the General Assembly, the larger forum where the veto was not operative, passed a comparable resolution submitted by the United States delegation. But the special committee which the Assembly now sent out to Greece did not include Soviet and Polish members. Just before Christmas 1947, there came the further news of the establishment of a defiantly self-styled "First Provisional Democratic Government of Free Greece" under the Communist guerrilla leader, "General Markos."

In November 1948, the General Assembly again called upon Yugoslavia, Albania, and Bulgaria to desist from aiding the guerrillas. The Greek General Staff announced success after success in its operations on Greek soil, but the defeated enemy could always escape across a "neutral" frontier and, in complete immunity, prepare to resume the struggle. Early in 1949 the quarrel between Yugoslavia and the Cominform spread its effects to Greece and led at last to the downfall of the elusive chieftain, General Markos. Tito closed the Yugoslav frontier, General Markos "retired" and was never heard of again. Civil war in Greece had come to a sudden and welcome end. In November 1949, British troops began to return home.

The reconstruction of the ravaged country began at once—largely with American aid—but was constantly obstructed by the usual political instability. Greek domestic history in those years consisted of complicated cabinet reshufflings, alternating on occasion with elections. Greece's Western orientation, however, was well established. A Greek contingent served in the Korean War in 1950-51; Greece joined the North Atlantic Pact in 1951; she entered into an alliance with Yugoslavia in 1954. During 1952, Field Marshal Papagos and his party, "The Rally," came to power by legitimate election, although that circumstance did not prevent the Field Marshal from treating the country to a dose of dictatorship reminiscent of that under General Metaxas in the 1930's. But, apart from serious earthquakes, the years of the dictatorship on balance were generally agreed to have been benevolent and beneficial. Papagos died on October 2, 1955, by which date Greece and Britain were in the toils of the dispute over Cyprus. (See pp. 801-02.)

The "Iron Curtain"

We have described very briefly the post-1945 histories of nine states of Intermediate Europe – Finland, Poland, Hungary, Czechoslovakia, Yugoslavia, Albania, Bulgaria, Rumania, and Greece. Three of these – Finland, Yugoslavia, and Greece – withstood the Soviet power. The other six succumbed in a process of extraordinary consistency. In these six the Soviet Union first sponsored a united "front," usually a coalition of left-wing elements, which was controlled by the local Communist party or else formed a screen behind which the local Communist party operated. The victory of this united front was then secured at elections which, far from being free and unfettered, were often shamelessly rigged. The emergent body was a People's Republic – or a constituent assembly whose function it was to draw up a constitution for a People's Republic – modeled ultimately on the Soviet Constitution of 1936. The procedure was carried out often under the leadership of returned Communist-trained exiles – Rajk, Nosek, Dimitrov, Ana Pauker – and, in specially difficult cases, was supervised by a Soviet emissary on the spot – Zorin, Sviridov, Vyshinsky. Details and nomenclature might vary in these arrangements, but the essentials were regular in the extreme.

The key post, both in the early provisional liberation government and in the subsequent People's Republic, was the Ministry of the Interior, which carried with it the control of the police and which, of necessity, was reserved to a ranking Communist. Purges were instituted by people's courts often in defiance of local public opinion or foreign censure. The trial and condemnation of prominent individuals – Petkov, Stepinac, Maniu, Mindszenty – who symbolized opposition parties, were deliberately dramatized for public edification and terrorization. Organized opposition was conspicuous by its absence. Even the national army bowed to the inevitable, and once-powerful political parties allowed themselves to be split or dissolved. Yet Soviet occupation forces – except in Rumania, Bulgaria, and Hungary – were not in open evidence and appeared to exert no pressure. On occasion the regime would need to be consolidated by the further purge of deviationists, such as Gomulka, Rajk, and Slansky.

The several People's Republics were bound together by a network of bilateral military alliances and trade agreements. Economic policy included state control of industry, nationalization, agrarian reform, and occasionally collectivization, and it was sometimes organized on the Soviet analogy as a Two-Year, Three-Year, or Five-Year Plan. All remained outside the European Recovery Program. There was, of course, no serious objection to trading with Western nations provided that such trade did not prejudice the collective independence, exclusiveness, and solidarity of the system. All the states – including Eastern Germany – signed the Warsaw Pact of May 1955, which virtually placed their armed forces under Red Army command. (See p. 666.) Later developments showed sometimes an alleviation, sometimes an aggravation of Soviet control – an alleviation, for example, in Poland, and very much the reverse, for example, in Hungary. Yet each state – and this was one of the curious features of the entire episode – retained its separate national individuality. With the possible exception of Rumania, which it was rumored at one time was to become a constituent republic of the Soviet Union, there was never any threat of Soviet annexation in any form, nor was there any attempt to amalgamate any two or more of the states into larger political units.

Yet Soviet control was, and remained, the paramount fact. In 1945, in the last year of the war, Churchill had insistently urged an Anglo-American campaign in the Balkans and Middle Danube precisely to prevent this unhappy result. His essential political foresight was not at fault. But it is difficult to see how Anglo-American control could afterward have been maintained. We have pointed out elsewhere that Intermediate Europe seems always to have been destined to fall under the domination of an external power. (See p. 150.) In the interwar period France had tried – unsuccessfully – to be that power. Could it have been seriously expected that the United States with far less interest and, geographically, much farther away would have done in this area what France had failed to do? As for Britain, she was unable to maintain a foothold even in Greece. Russia, granted her great military ascendency in the area, was the obvious and inevitable alternative. In 1945 the Iron Curtain descended on Intermediate Europe, and, at the time of writing, there seems little possibility of its being raised.

37. WESTERN EUROPE: FRANCE, ITALY, SPAIN, AND BENELUX

The Fourth Republic in France

On August 25, 1944, General de Gaulle arrived in liberated Paris to receive the acclamations of the French people. On August 30, the Provisional Government and Consultative Assembly, whose formation we described in another place, were transferred from Algiers to Paris. (See pp. 551 and 592.) De Gaulle took office as Premier, with Georges Bidault, former president of the Council of Resistance and leader of a new left-wing Catholic party, as Foreign Minister. For the moment it was assumed that the old Third Republic was restored; the Vichy Government and all its laws and ordinances were declared to be abolished. On October 23, the Provisional Government was recognized by the United States, Britain, and the Soviet Union. Whatever might be the present or future disabilities of France, it could at least be said that she was almost unique among liberated European nations in having thus achieved without friction the union of her former government in exile and her resistance movement at home.

The situation was of peculiar difficulty. The war still continued; fighting was in progress in eastern frontier districts. The turmoil left by the enemy's occupation and retreat had to be liquidated. American and British armies were now "in occupation," commandeering important buildings and public services, using the roads, railroads, and seaports. Considerable sums of money put into circulation by them aided inflation while giving the impression of prosperity. The Provisional Government, strictly speaking, had no constitutional status; it could style itself the trustee, but not the legal successor, of the Third Republic. The surviving civil service was short of personnel, and much of the personnel it had was politically suspect. The press – always so important and characteristic in France – appeared almost at once and, though its circulation was hampered by the transport shortage, it offered some reflection of the state of public feeling.

During the winter of 1944-45, political parties old and new, including Bidault's left-wing Catholic party, the MRP (*Mouvement républicain populaire*), held party congresses and organized themselves for electoral action.

Generally five political groups emerged: the Right; the former Radicals in the center; and three left-wing parties – the MRP, the Socialists, and the Communists. The Right was too much identified with collaboration to exert any considerable influence; the Radicals were too much identified with the fallen Third Republic. Consequently the real power resided in the three left-wing parties, the "tripartite coalition," which now constituted the main body of the Provisional Government.

After the first exhilaration of victory, the French people began more soberly to take stock of the physical and moral chaos of their country. Loss of life since 1939 from military operations, Allied bombing, and resistance was put at 500,000. Railroads, roads, bridges, rolling stock, canal and river shipping had been destroyed in the course of air attack and ground operations. The Atlantic seaports, where isolated forces of Germans had held out till well into 1945, were found on liberation to have been systematically demolished. The province of Normandy, as was to be expected, had suffered the worst damage, and here alone 500,000 persons were homeless. There were the usual shortages of food, clothing, fuel, and the other necessaries of life, especially in the towns. The long German servitude had left deep psychological scars. In particular it had bred a contempt for law and order. The heroes of the resistance, returning to civil life, had to learn the painful lesson that the qualities which had been virtues under the occupation now were almost antisocial. Young people who had grown up in a time of war in an atmosphere of fake identity cards, fake ration cards, black marketing, lying propaganda, betrayal, and terror could hardly be converted overnight into a citizenry fit for a newly redeemed democracy in time of peace.

The dilatory punishment of the former collaborators, the failure to wipe clean the disgrace and degradation of the occupation, were perhaps most exasperating and mortifying to the French people at this time. But the purge was hampered by the lack of legal personnel and the mountainous tasks of investigation. Accusations numbered over 100,000. Yet to the man in the street, who little appreciated the technical difficulties, delay seemed to follow delay, and still not one traitor had been shot. Many Vichy ministers and prefects were still at liberty, often in the same posts they had filled during the occupation. However, late in 1944, trials of collaborators, notably journalists, artists, and actors, made a beginning. In July and August 1945, Pétain himself was at last brought to trial and sentenced to death, the sentence being afterward commuted to life imprisonment. Laval, along with 600 others, suffered the supreme penalty. But the purge in France was very reminiscent of the denazification of Germany. It was neither thorough nor complete, nor was it always conducted even with ordinary dignity.

French military participation in the closing stages of the war compensated somewhat for the misfortunes of 1940. But French pride was in an abnormally sensitive state, and de Gaulle made the most of any and every circumstance or incident which could be used for the enhancement of French prestige. In December 1944, he visited Moscow and with Stalin signed a pact of mutual assistance. He demonstrated his diplomatic annoyance at not being invited to the Yalta Conference by refusing subsequently to meet President Roosevelt. But in August 1945, in company with Bidault, he visited Washington for a series of meetings with President Truman and Secretary Byrnes, and a communiqué was afterward issued emphasizing "the perfect harmony of views" of France and the United States "for the construction of the postwar world." France took a permanent seat in the Security Council of the United Nations; she was assigned a zone of occupation in Germany; a French representative – usually Bidault – attended the Foreign Ministers Council. In March 1947, at Dunkirk, France and Britain signed a treaty of alliance. In a word, France enjoyed complete diplomatic reinstatement and recovery of her former international status.

It obviously behooved the Provisional Government to proceed to a reestablishment of the old constitution or to the establishment of a new one. On July 12, 1945, in a broadcast, de Gaulle announced a forthcoming referendum to test the French electorate's preference for a return to the constitution of the Third Republic (of 1875) or for the election of a Constituent Assembly. The referendum in October 1945 – in which women in France voted for the first time – returned a Constituent Assembly with 161 Communists, 150 MRP, 150 Socialists, 28 Radicals, and 97 members of eight other parties. The MRP had been methodically organized and was believed to have been strongly supported by the new women's vote but, even so, its electoral success was remarkable. No less remarkable, in the opposite sense, was the collapse of the Radical party, the old party of the Third Republic. Of the total 586 men and women who composed the Assembly, over 400 were products of the resistance. One of the minor parties indeed had named itself after the resistance – UDSR (*Union démocratique et socialiste de la résistance*). De Gaulle, after fierce bickering with the Communists, became Head of the Government.

Political rivalries at this time centered around the person of de Gaulle and around his alleged dictatorial ambitions. The former Third Republic, from its very origins, had been burdened by a long history of controversy over the question of the presidential prerogatives. It had been founded as a reaction against dictatorship; all its old fears had lately been excited by the trend toward dictatorship in Europe. During the recent referendum the presidential prerogatives had again been the foremost issue. And de Gaulle, as now seemed all too likely, would be the President, a soldier who presumably might inherit the Napoleonic traditions and who already seemed to be drawing to himself right-wing elements strongly inclined towards authoritarian rule. De Gaulle assuredly was possessed of great personal force, not unmixed with vanity, intolerant and unbending, quite capable of creating a one-man *mystique*. At the opposite extreme were the Communists with a philosophy of dictatorship of their own. The prevailing chaos in France – the black market, inflation, rising prices, and the strikes – unless the moderate parties could resolve it, might easily play into the hands of the one or the other.

On January 20, 1946, after an altercation with the leftist parties over military appropriations, de Gaulle suddenly resigned. He was succeeded by the Socialist Félix Gouin, again at the head of a "tripartite coalition" of the three left-wing parties. A constitution committee drafted a new constitution, which proposed a single-chamber legislature and a presidential office of virtually no powers. This constitution was approved by the Constituent Assembly — the MRP voting against it — but was afterward rejected by a popular referendum. Elections for a second Constituent Assembly were held in June and resulted in a slight gain by the MRP. Bidault formed a new government. A second constitution was drawn up, this time proposing a bicameral chamber and a presidential office of stronger but still limited powers, and was approved by the new Constituent Assembly. De Gaulle came out of his retirement to make a series of speeches demanding the rejection of the constitution on the grounds of the presidential question. But the constitution was approved by a popular referendum in October 1946 — the third referendum in the course of the year — though with considerable "protest abstentions." The first elections under the new constitution were held in November 1946 and resulted in a general victory of the three left-wing parties — the Communists, the Socialists, and the MRP. The Fourth Republic was in being.[1]

Tripartism and the Third Force

If we are to look for a pattern in so complex a history as that of France since 1945, we could roughly distinguish four periods: the first, "Tripartism," 1945-46; the second, "the Third Force," 1946-51; the third, "Hexagonalism," 1951-58; and the fourth, from the Gaullist revolution of 1958 onward.

The first period, 1945-46, was the period of the "tripartite coalition" (*tripartisme*) of the three left-wing parties. It is the period in fact that we have been describing. The coalition broke down completely in May 1947, when the Communists went into permanent and uncompromising opposition. The somewhat unnatural alliance, born of the resistance and liberation, could not survive the onset of the Cold War and the organization of European recovery round American aid. Throughout this period Bidault was Foreign Minister and, in a sense, France's representative international statesman.

The second period, 1946-51, was marked by a series of governments of moderate composition, and all of them — with the exception of Blum's short-lived all-Socialist government, which began the series in December 1946 — were coalitions including Socialists. Tripartism had gone, and, as if by compensation, the period was marked by the revival of the Radical party, the great party of the Third Republic, which since 1940 had lain under a heavy cloud. It was the period of the "Third Force" (*la troisième force*) as it was called, which tried to hold a balance between the Gaullist extreme on the one side and the Communist extreme on the other. Finance as usual was the overriding problem, and the ups and downs of ministries recalled all the old permutations of French domestic politics. Characteristically every single ministry that fell during this period fell over a budgetary or other financial issue.[2] The country was evidently feeling the fully developed effects of the postwar economic aftermath, and yet it probably found a moral relief in meeting — or evading — the situation in ways that in the past had been normal and familiar.

In January 1947, the Monnet Plan was published, so called after its principal author, Jean Monnet, a plan for the fuller utilization of France's resources and for the modernization of her equipment. In July 1947, France was one of the sixteen nations of the European Recovery Program. (See p. 713.) But, despite evident improvements, France was compelled in January 1948 to devalue the franc — and to devalue it again, in sympathy with the devaluation of sterling, in September 1949. De Gaulle meanwhile made characteristic broadcasts to the effect that he would shortly return to active politics at the head of a "Rally of the French People" (*Rassemblement du peuple français, RPF*), but he indicated little of his political program beyond his usual repugnance for Communism. During 1947 and 1948 there were several workers' strikes that were not only for wage increases but that showed distinctive political objectives and showed also the extent of Communist infiltration into the trade unions, especially into the CGT (*Confédération générale du travail*). The pro-Socialist anti-Communist wing of the CGT broke away in the end to form a group known as the *Force ouvrière*. The coal miners' strike of October 1948 was the most serious industrial disturbance of the time, an avowed challenge to the government and to the regime. At the height of the strike several mining areas were being patrolled by regular troops.

In respect to imperial and foreign affairs this second period was more stable and promising. Under the Constitution of 1946 the French Union was composed of Metropolitan France and the overseas Departments and Territories. Syria and Lebanon had been lost to France in 1946; but thereafter the Union had become a practical and progressive reality. (See p. 770.) An insurrection in Madagascar in 1947 had been suppressed without much difficulty — although perhaps it was an omen of things to come. France was a founder state and member of the Dunkirk Treaty of 1947, of the Brussels Treaty of 1948, of the North Atlantic Pact of 1949, and of the Council of Europe of 1949. Her representative statesman of these years and the architect of her foreign policy was Robert Schuman, Premier from November 1947 to July 1948 and then Foreign Minister through nine successive governments till December 1952. In 1950 he first mooted the so-called Schuman Plan, out of which was to grow the European Coal and Steel Community (ECSC), later to be described. (See p. 716.) He was a Catholic, a leader of the MRP, born in Luxembourg, trained in law, a student at German universities, and Deputy for a Lorraine constituency in the interwar French Chamber. During his years as Foreign Minister he was the close associate of Adenauer in Germany and De Gasperi in Italy — all three Catholic and leaders of Catholic parties, all three speaking German.

Hexagonalism

The elections of June 1951 brought the second period to an end. The third period, 1951-58, was the period of "Hexagonalism." It was marked by stubborn and increasing external pressures. The Schumanesque

THE STRENGTH OF THE PARTIES IN THE FRENCH ELECTIONS, 1945-56 [3]

	Oct. 1945	*June 1946*	*Nov. 1946*	*June 1951*	*Jan. 1956*	*Nov. 1958*
Communists	161	153	183	101	150	10
Socialists	150	129	105	107	99	40
MRP (*Mouvement républicain populaire*)	150	169	167	96	84	57
Radicals	28	32	43	76	75*	35
UDSR (*Union démocratique et socialiste de la résistance*)	29	21	27	19	19	
Conservative Groups	64	67	71	98	97	132
RPF (*Rassemblement du peuple français*)				120	22†	(UNR)§188
Others	4	15	22	10	50‡	3
Totals	586	586	618	627	596	465

* Includes the RGR (*Rassemblement des gauches républicaines*).
† Includes the dissident Gaullists. ‡ Includes 42 Poujadists.
§ *Union pour la nouvelle république.*

PREMIERS OF THE FOURTH REPUBLIC [4]	*Foreign Minister*
De Gaulle, Sept. 26, 1944-Jan. 20, 1946	Bidault (MRP)
Gouin (Soc.) Jan. 26-June 12, 1946	Bidault (MRP)
Bidault (MRP) June 23-Nov. 28, 1946	Bidault (MRP)
Blum (Soc.), Dec. 12, 1946-Jan. 20, 1947	Blum (Soc.)
Ramadier (Soc.), Jan. 21-Nov. 19, 1947	Bidault (MRP)
Schuman (MRP), Nov. 22, 1947-July 19, 1948	Bidault (MRP)
Marie (Rad.), July 24-Aug. 27, 1948	Schuman (MRP)
Schuman (MRP), Sept. 1-7, 1948	Schuman (MRP)
Queuille (Rad.), Sept. 10, 1948-Oct. 6, 1949	Schuman (MRP)
Bidault (MRP), Oct. 28, 1949-June 24, 1950	Schuman (MRP)
Queuille (Rad.), July 1-4, 1950	Schuman (MRP)
Pleven (UDSR), July 11, 1950-Feb. 28, 1951	Schuman (MRP)
Queuille (Rad.), Mar. 9-July 10, 1951	Schuman (MRP)
Pleven (UDSR), Aug. 11, 1951-Jan. 7, 1952	Schuman (MRP)
Faure (Rad.), Jan. 17-Feb. 29, 1952	Schuman (MRP)
Pinay (Ind.), Mar. 6-Dec. 23, 1952	Schuman (MRP)
Mayer (Rad.), Jan. 7-May 21, 1953	Bidault (MRP)
Laniel (Ind.), June 26, 1953-June 12, 1954	Bidault (MRP)
Mendès-France (Rad.), June 18, 1954-Feb. 5, 1955	Mendès-France (Rad.)
Faure (Rad.), Feb. 23, 1955-Jan. 24, 1956	Pinay (Ind.)
Mollet (Soc.), Jan. 31, 1956-May 21, 1957	Pineau (Soc.)
Bourgès-Maunoury (Rad.), June 13-Sept. 30, 1957	Pineau (Soc.)
Gaillard (Rad.), Nov. 6-Apr. 16, 1958	Pineau (Soc.)
Pflimlin (MRP), May 13-28, 1958	Pleven (UDSR)
De Gaulle, June 1, 1958-	Couve de Murville (no party)

interlude was nearly over. France was now to come to terms as best she might with the development of NATO, German rearmament, Indochina, and eventually Algeria. The first two periods on balance, despite their confusions, could be said to have been periods of recovery and generally of optimism; the third period was one of steady retreat in all France's imperial and foreign relations. At home, not only was Tripartism long since dead, but so also was the Third Force. The elections of 1951 returned an Assembly in which six major parties were of substantially equivalent strength – Communists, Socialists, MRP, Radicals, Conservatives, and de Gaulle's new party, the RPF. In such a "Hexagonal Assembly," as it was called, government would be more difficult than it had ever been.

The greater international events of this period have been described in other contexts in other chapters. It is for us to note here their effects in France. Even before the elections of 1951, France had been shaken, as the whole of Western Europe had been shaken, by the outbreak of war in Korea in June 1950. The entire framework of her foreign policy – the Brussels Treaty, NATO, and the Council of Europe – seemed suddenly to have been exposed in all its weakness. In the next chapter we shall describe the discussions on a possible European Army and the immense pressures put upon France, mainly by the United States, to induce her to agree to the inclusion of a German contingent in that army. France's immediate reply took the form of the Pleven Plan of October 1950, named after her Premier of that date, proposing certain conditions for her agreement. (See p. 717.) Eventually, on May 26, 1952, under the so-called Bonn Conventions, Western Germany was to be restored to sovereignty, and on May 27, in Paris, the treaty to establish a European Defense Community (EDC) was signed by France, Western Germany, Italy, and the Benelux countries. But, undeniably, despite the arguments in favor of a German reinforcement and despite all the safeguards and controls in the treaty, public opinion in France could not but be dismayed and sickened at the thought of a Germany armed once more. Ratification of the treaty was delayed and delayed. The death of Stalin in March 1953 revived the hope that, after all, EDC might not be needed.

But, by 1953, EDC was no longer France's first major concern, or even her second. By 1953 her first major concern was Indochina, and her second was North Africa. For years the French people as a whole had hardly given a passing thought to the strange war in Indochina, albeit that it had continued on and off since 1945. (See p. 789.) After all, "colonial" wars of long duration and under atrociously difficult conditions were nothing new in France's experience. Moreover, the French forces in Indochina had been of mixed origins; most of them were native or colored, some were German, and few of them, except regular officers, hailed from Metropolitan France. Indochina therefore had not unduly disturbed public opinion in France – as yet. But, as time went on, the scale of the fighting increased, and so did the financial burden, and so did the general political significance. After the truce in Korea it was likely that Chinese reinforcements and supplies might go southward and that Indochina would become the next main theater of fighting in Asia. By 1954 Indochina had cost the lives of 19,000 Frenchmen and an estimated $8,000,000,000; and the end was not in sight. Dien

Bien Phu fell on May 7. (See p. 792.) It was clear that the policy of drift could not continue. On June 12, 1954, at the end of a debate on Indochina, Joseph Laniel, then Premier, was defeated in the Assembly, although by a narrow vote.

Pierre Mendès-France became French Premier and Foreign Minister on June 17, 1954, and he remained in office for nearly eight fervent, strenuous months till February 5, 1955. His cabinet was largely Radical, UDSR, and RPF, and it commanded only a minority in the Assembly, although the Socialists consistently voted for it. Mendès-France was a lawyer and a Jew, still a young man, with a fine, if stormy, political and military record. In the Second World War he had served in the Free French Air Force, and he had returned to politics in de Gaulle's government in 1945, in which he had interested himself mainly in economic questions. He has been described as the last democratic statesman in France to try, by democratic methods, to adjust France to the realities of the post-1945 world. He came to office at a moment of national desperation – like Clemenceau in 1917, or Poincaré in 1926, or Blum in 1936. In his investiture address on June 17, he virtually blackmailed the Assembly to adopt his policies or throw him out. He proposed a program of four items. First, he would obtain a cease-fire in Indochina, and he would do so, he declared, within thirty days. If successful, he would proceed, second, to comprehensive economic and fiscal reforms, such as, he declared, France had needed and neglected for years; third, to a solution of the problem of Germany's contribution to European defense; and fourth, to a peaceful settlement in North Africa. The first of these undertakings he carried out. The Geneva Conference on the Far East was still in session when he became Premier. He achieved his cease-fire in Indochina within the promised thirty days. (See p. 792.)

Events now moved at a furious pace. On July 31, 1954, Mendès-France flew to Tunis and, in his Carthage Declaration, gave out that he was ready to open negotiations with an all-Tunisian government for the immediate grant of independence to Tunisia. On August 10, the Assembly voted him virtually decree powers for his economic program in France. On August 19, he was in Brussels for a conference of EDC Powers to demand concessions intended to make EDC more acceptable in France; but they were concessions which in effect would have destroyed the supranational potentialities of EDC and reduced it to an ordinary military alliance of member governments controlling their respective national forces. The conference, impatient of French obstruction, broke down. (See p. 719.) Accordingly, on August 30, in a perfect demonstration of "hexagonal" politics, the ratification of EDC was decisively rejected by the French Assembly. EDC was dead and done with, and so also were the Bonn Conventions which had been made dependent upon it. But matters could not be allowed to rest there. In two months of confused, but strenuous negotiations, new proposals were put forward, emanating from the British Foreign Secretary, Eden, and this time found favor in the eyes of the refractory Republic. Conferences in London and Paris in September and October concluded in the so-called London Agreement and Paris Agreements. European defense would now be built around NATO and around a new organization to be called the Western European Union (WEU). (See p. 719.)

Mendès-France had been in office four months; of the four items of his program, he appeared to have succeeded brilliantly in three and to be about to succeed in the fourth. But already his original momentum was slowing down. Critics, recovering from his shock tactics, were beginning to chafe and complain. In particular his indulgence toward Tunisia, they argued, was typical of his policy of retreat and was encouraging "banditry" in Algeria. In January 1955, Mendès-France appointed one of de Gaulle's lieutenants, Jacques Soustelle, Governor General of Algeria. The appointment at once became a political issue and was interpreted as a maneuver to win RPF support. On February 5, 1955, in the early hours of the morning, after an uproarious two-day debate in the Assembly on North Africa – uproarious even by French parliamentary standards – Mendès-France and his government went down to defeat.

Historians will say that the fall of Mendès-France was really the fall of the Fourth Republic. It was not now just a question of resuming the old ministerial roundabout. The whole body politic of France seemed to be in dissolution. The major political parties themselves were breaking into splinter groups, and fresh government coalitions would now have to be constructed, not just from parties, but from factions of parties. The Radical party split into the so-called Mendésiste Radicals, led by Mendès-France, and the RGR (*Rassemblement des gauches républicaines*), led by Edgar Faure; the RPF was split into the Social Republicans, led by Soustelle, and the dissident Gaullists or ARS (*Action républicaine et sociale*). A new party made its appearance, the UDCA (*Union pour la défense des commerçants et artisans*), composed of shopkeepers and small businessmen, led by Pierre Poujade, himself a shopkeeper, and representing a sort of taxpayers' revolt.

Faure, Mendès-France's rival in the Radical party, became Premier on February 23, 1955, and for nine turbulent months held office against incessant motions of no confidence on the budget, the electoral system, and North Africa. He could claim some progress, however, in respect to Tunisia and Morocco, and both territories were shortly achieving independent status. But there was no similar progress to report in respect to Algeria, which was now emerging as the prior problem in the whole tangled web of French politics, domestic and foreign. On November 30, after a second defeat in the Assembly – this time on proposed new electoral laws – the exasperated Faure decided to invoke his constitutional privilege and dissolve the Assembly. New elections accordingly were held on January 2, 1956, and were contested by twenty-eight parties and sub parties. The Communists made big gains and were returned the strongest party in the Assembly with 150 seats. Poujade's UDCA won 52 seats – afterward reduced, as the result of inquiries into election irregularities to 42.

Three governments of declining effectiveness followed, beginning with that of the Socialist Guy Mollet – which, oddly enough, lasted sixteen months and was the longest-lived of all the governments of the Fourth

Republic – and the regime collapsed at last under the revolt of the French Army in Algeria in May 1958.

The French Army and the Fourth Republic

France's affairs since 1945 had been complicated and contradictory. In the beginning there had been the exhilaration of freedom and peace. The resistance and liberation, it seemed, had remade the country's morale and created a whole new cycle of national myths. But when the account was totted up, there was also the country's undeniable decline in terms of power in the modern international world. Nor was there any indication that the late experience of war, defeat, and victory had greatly affected the people's political habits. Rather it was almost as if the resumption of former ways was a conscious popular effort and a part of the psychological recovery. In two short years the Fourth Republic looked little different from the Third. Happy days were back again – with the familiar squabbles over the budget, inflation and deficit, taxation and evasion of taxation – all accompanied by the incessant rise and fall of ministries. The government reverted to the old *immobilisme* – a concentration on day-to-day parliamentary tactics and a scrupulous disregard of long-term reforms – while the people in general reverted to the old *incivisme* – an attitude of resentment, or just cynicism, toward all politics and political processes. *Immobilisme* and *incivisme* became a routine, with all the comfort of a routine, the baleful existence of which everyone admitted but was too afraid or too fatigued to want to change.

Throughout these years, however, one element in France had stood somewhat apart – namely the Army. English-speaking peoples have sometimes found it difficult to understand the enormous political and social importance of the "Continental" Army. In their own popular ideology nothing has been so abhorrent to them as militarism, of whatever shape or form, and in the course of their histories they have fought foreign wars and civil wars against militarisms that have threatened them. Latterly they had seen and destroyed the phenomenon in Germany and Japan. But France hitherto had been a "democratic" state possessed of an army which they had been disposed to accept in more kindly spirit. In 1940 that army had been defeated, and, not only had it contributed little to the subsequent resistance and scarcely more to the liberation, but it had thereafter suffered further repeated and humiliating defeats for which it felt it had not been responsible. The result was that the French Army was virtually estranged from the society of which it should have been an integral and honored part. The higher professional officers, a group with a strong corporate pride, eager to reestablish their former credit, resenting neglect even more than they resented injustice, were driven more and more into a sort of self-ostracism. Many of them were rough-hewn men, simple and direct, impatient of compromise, and by every feature of their temperament and training detesting the genus politician whose only stock in trade, it seemed to them, was talk, and talk, and then more talk. But this army, it is to be remembered, had *power*—a peculiar kind of power. It had not only physical power, but, like all modern "scientific" armies, it had precisely the technical and administrative resources, the facilities for secrecy, and the ready-made chain of command required for organizing a revolutionary coup. It was a cadre of all the talents. There was nothing, from running a railroad or a telegraph system to setting up an emergency civil service, that it could not do. And, with the men, the means, and the opportunity, naturally there sometimes came the temptation.

It is also to be remembered that this army tended to identify itself with France's territories overseas. It had found some of its hardest service, and thence the myths of its traditions, in Syria, Indochina, Madagascar, and above all in North Africa. But it was in these theaters, since 1945, that the French Army had been ignominiously and undeservedly treated. The crowning infamy had been Dien Bien Phu. And now, at all costs, Algeria must not be added to the list. By 1958 all the accumulated injury was piled into the war for the retention of this last stronghold of the empire and Union. The very Heavens might fall, but Algeria shall be French!

Morocco, Tunisia, Algeria and the Fifth Republic in France

There were three territories in North Africa in which France had an interest, Morocco, Algeria, and Tunisia, and we should briefly review the situation in each of these territories as it had now developed. Morocco and Tunisia, historically, had once been important Moslem states, though they were both in advanced decay in the nineteenth century by the time the French arrived. Morocco had formerly been part of the Sherifian Empire, dating from the sixteenth century, and nominally it continued to be ruled by the Sherifian Sultan from the ancient capital city of Fez. A "French Zone" had come under French military occupation in 1912, and it had been governed thereafter in the name of the Sultan by a French Resident General from the modern French capital of Rabat. Moroccan nationalism was slow to arise and did not properly emerge till the Second World War. One account has it that President Roosevelt met the Sultan during the Casablanca Conference in 1943 and "put ideas of American independence into his head." But the movement was complicated—as nationalist movements so often are—by the fact of mixed population. The urbanized Arabs, led by the Sultan Mohammed V, formed one party, the Istiqlal or United Independence party, which was anti-French; and the rural Berbers, led by their chieftain El Glaoui, the Pasha of Marrakesh, formed another party, which was pro-French. Moroccan political issues were soon hinging round the allegiances and rivalries of these two potentates.

The story of Morocco thereafter has a familiar ring—agitation, revolt, suppression, more agitation, more revolt, more suppression. By 1952 the situation had deteriorated to such an extent that the French encouraged their favorite, El Glaoui, to seize control, and they exiled the Sultan first to Corsica and then to Madagascar. But force in these matters was no more than a postponement of the inevitable. In 1955-56, the French Government reversed its Moroccan policy. Mohammed V returned to his kingdom in triumph, was reconciled to a contrite and humbled El Glaoui, and within the year had obtained a qualified independence, in treaty relations with France. In 1957 the former International Zone of Tangier reverted to the new Moroccan state, and the Sultan was making demands for the retrocession of the Spanish Zone. American air bases then established in Morocco, for the moment, were left unaffected by these changes.

Of the three territories in North Africa, Tunisia was of the greatest antiquity and, in modern times, the most "advanced." It had been the seat of the ancient Carthaginian empire, and it was correspondingly important in the Early Christian era. It had since succumbed to Arab and Turkish conquests, and, in the nineteenth-century European "scramble for Africa," it had been a choice bone of contention between France and Italy. It had fallen to French military occupation in 1881 and had since been governed by a French Resident General in the name of a weak, entirely anachronistic "sovereign," the Bey of Tunis. Tunisian nationalism, as would be expected, was older than the Moroccan and indeed predated the French occupation of 1881. The first nationalist party, the Destour, arose in the 1920's and was the contemporary of the Wafd in Egypt. The more extreme and revolutionary Neo-Destour arose in the 1930's under the nationalist leader Habib Bourguiba, but was broken up – or went underground – in 1938. Tunisian nationalism was complicated by the presence of 100,000 French settlers in the country, and almost as many Italians, and also by the presence of strong trade unions among the urbanized Arabs, reputedly infiltrated with Communism.

After the war in 1945, the nationalist movement, in the hands of the terrorist *fellaghas,* developed into an all-out resistance. Even the extreme Bourguiba was no longer extreme enough for his extreme partisans. On July 31, 1954, as we have said, Mendès-France made his Carthage Declaration, and set in train the negotiations which concluded in November 1955 in France's recognition of Tunisian independence. But France's relations with the new state were still unhappy. Several questions were left unsettled, notably the status of the French naval base at Bizerta. In November 1956, when Bourguiba's request for arms was rejected by the French Government, he obtained a "token" consignment from the United States and Britain, thereby sparking off a sharp protest from France. On February 8, 1958, as a climax to these various tensions, French planes bombed the Tunisian village of Sakiet, where it was alleged Algerian rebels had taken refuge. (See p. 703.)

Algeria was a territory entirely apart from Morocco or Tunisia. It had none of the historical distinction of its two neighbors. It was long famous – or infamous – as the lair of pirates, a sort of Mediterranean Port Royal, sometimes in shadowy allegiance to Fez or Tunis, and living in the main by its slave trade. It had touched American history twice in the naval expeditions of 1804 and 1815, under Decatur, sent to suppress its pirates. Algeria therefore had nothing creditable behind it when, in 1830, the French first occupied Algiers and found there a veritable sink of all the corruptions. The French were compelled to treat it as more than a colony, and they encouraged European settlement as the only solution for the derelict country. They organized it in "departments" on the French metropolitan pattern, and these, after 1875, were directly represented by their Deputies in the French parliament in Paris. Algeria, unlike Morocco or Tunisia, thus became an integral part of France. By the earlier half of the twentieth century, out of its population of 9,000,000, 1,000,000 were French *colons* whose families had been domiciled in Algeria for several generations, a class-conscious, politically sophisticated community, owning two-thirds of the country's arable land and controlling most of its commerce and industry. Between the wars several Moslem nationalist groups and factions appeared and enjoyed various degrees of importance and success, but none developed the prestige of the corresponding movements in Morocco and Tunis. They proselytized and quarreled, merged and split, wrecked and killed in bewildering fashion – and generally lived up to their country's unenviable historic record.

Algeria inaugurated the return to peace, on May 8, 1945, the day after the German surrender in Europe, in violent rioting against the European population, notably in Constantine. But thereafter the country was quiet, and, happily for France, it remained quiet throughout the worst period of the war in Indochina. Significantly, Mendès-France, in his investiture address in June 1954, had shown more concern for Morocco and Tunisia and had made the briefest reference to the Algerian Departments. The first serious Algerian uprising of any note or size occurred in November 1954, more than six months after Dien Bien Phu. But, from that date, Algeria was to be France's prior political problem.

In January 1956, the Socialist Guy Mollet became French Premier, full of earnest resolutions to find a solution in Africa. An outline law, or *loi-cadre,* was passed by the Assembly to provide for political evolution in all African territories still under French rule. Constitutional reforms and measures to Africanize the civil services were introduced in Togoland, the Cameroons, and Madagascar. For Algeria, an ambitious economic plan was worked out, covering especially the Saharan region where, as was now well known, immense reserves of oil had been discovered. But the situation did not improve. In February 1956, Mollet himself visited Algiers, hoping to imitate there Mendès-France's success two years before in Tunis. But he was met by gangs of *colons,* howling and throwing stones, and, astonished and terrified, he returned to France converted to a "tougher line" – "I came, I saw, I understood!" He announced that Robert Lacoste, a Socialist like himself, would be appointed "Minister Resident" in Algeria and would replace the somewhat invidious office of "Governor General." Come what might, he said, he would restore order and only then would he consent to negotiate with Algerian representatives a new institutional framework in Algeria which would respect the "Algerian personality" while maintaining "indissoluble links" with France.

There were now 400,000 French troops in Algeria, including nearly 300,000 conscripts, and France's contribution to NATO was being substantially depleted to reinforce them. The direct and indirect costs of the war to the French exchequer was estimated at 325,000,000,000 francs a year.

The Algerian nationalists had a well-equipped guerrilla army, organized by their FLN (*Front de la Libération nationale algérienne*), and they were receiving aid from Egypt, sometimes by sea and sometimes through Tunisia – to the steady accompaniment of incitement to violence over the Cairo Radio. French warships patrolling the coasts intercepted more than one boatload of arms destined for Algeria. Consequently the French Government was very ready to support Israel and to participate in the Suez campaign in October 1956 in the belief that the Egyptian source of supplies might be blocked up. French troops in Algeria were now resorting to the tactics of *"ratissage,"* the razing of entire Moslem villages suspected of harboring armed rebels, and cases of torture were being too often and too reliably reported to be denied. The war was spilling over into Metropolitan France, and Algerians, supposedly of rival factions, were terrorizing one another in the very streets of Paris. The French police were instituting night searches, detaining alleged sympathizers of Algerian nationalists, seizing publications. The wickedest days of the Nazi occupation, this time conducted by Frenchmen against Frenchmen, seemed to have returned.

On February 8, 1958, twenty-five French planes bombed the Tunisian border village of Sakiet, where, with the evident connivance of the Tunisian Government, Algerian rebels were believed to be in hiding. The attack, executed without the knowledge of the French Government in Paris, showed the extent to which French forces in Algeria could take the law into their own hands. French conspirative groups, military and civilian, were now active in Algeria, setting up "committees of public safety," and it was only a question as to what leadership or unified direction the inevitable insurrection would succeed in finding. Lacoste, the Minister Resident, reported that he no longer had any real authority. An invasion of Metropolitan France by the French Army in Algeria was said to be in preparation and would be prefaced by a parachute descent on Paris. On May 13, General Salan, Commander in Chief in Algeria, was in effective control and, from his balcony, was rallying the insurgent crowds with the cry, *"Vive la France! Vive l'Algérie française! Vive de Gaulle!"* At this spontaneous invocation of his name, de Gaulle stirred noncommittally in his rustic retreat at Colombey-les-Deux-Églises and, in a short proclamation arraigning the failure of party government, guardedly expressed his readiness "to assume the powers of the Republic." Pierre Pflimlin, the last Premier of the Fourth Republic, resigned on May 28 and three days later, on June 1, 1958, by the somewhat uncertain majority of 329 votes to 224, the Assembly invested de Gaulle with emergency powers for six months.

On September 28, 1958, by popular referendum a new constitution was accepted that gave wide powers to the President. Elections were held in November under the constitution and resulted in a Gaullist victory. In December de Gaulle was elected President for a term of seven years. The Fifth Republic was in being.

On February 13, 1960, France joined the world's "Nuclear Club" by exploding her first atomic device in the Sahara.

Italy

In Chapter 29 we described the formation of the Badoglio government and the Italian surrender. (See p. 556.) The Allied campaign against the Germans in Italy continued till May 1945, but, except for the Italian partisans in the north and some Italian recruited forces in the Allied armies, afterward known as the Corps of Liberation, the Italian people as a whole took no willing part in it. In Allied-occupied territory meanwhile, political Italy began to return to life. Six underground parties came out of hiding – the Liberal, Labor Democrat, Christian Democrat, Action, Socialist, and Communist. Intellectuals, like Benedetto Croce and Enrico De Nicola, emerged from semi-incarceration to take an active part in their country's affairs. Exiles returned – Count Carlo Sforza from the United States, Palmiro Togliatti from the Soviet Union, Luigi Einaudi from Switzerland, and Alcide De Gasperi from Vatican City. In April 1944, King Victor Emmanuel retired from public life – but did not abdicate – and was succeeded by Crown Prince Umberto as "Lieutenant General." Marshal Badoglio formed the first government of liberation, a coalition of the above-mentioned six parties, with Croce, Sforza, and Togliatti as ministers without portfolio.

In the north, under German occupation, Italian partisan forces were gradually organized into a Committee of National Liberation (*Comitato della Liberazione Nazionale* – CLN) in liaison with the Allies. As the Germans retired, and towns and villages were liberated, local units of the CLN took over administrative control till properly constituted authorities could be appointed. The assistance rendered the Allied cause by the CLN and the Corps of Liberation was far from contemptible, but unhappily it did not purchase the diplomatic respect of the Powers at the subsequent peace negotiations. Evidently there were deep psychological misconceptions on both sides. Italians generally were mortified at their treatment as "enemies" when they thought they should have qualified as Allied co-belligerents. The disappointed emotions of liberation, followed by the final retributive peace, inflicted perhaps a sharper injury to Italian national morale than all the physical devastations of the war.

Italy at this time resembled other liberated nations of Europe. Popularity lay with the Left. Former partisans of the CLN, now participating in politics, lent in addition a decided air of revolution. Of the six parties mentioned, three dominated Italy in 1945. The first was the Christian Democrat party, a clerical party, successor to the *Popolari* of 1919, led by De Gasperi. (See p. 235.) The second was the Socialist party, eventually to split into a moderate faction under Giuseppe Saragat and an extreme faction under Pietro Nenni. The third was the Communist party led by Togliatti. The three were "mass" parties and corresponded to the contemporary "tripartism" of the MRP, Socialist, and Communist parties in France. Of the other parties, the Liberal party, farthest to the right, was the party of "liberal" property owners and entrepreneurs and claimed as members such men as Croce, Nitti, and Einaudi; the Labor Democrat party was Socialist of the so-called Reformist group and was led by Ivanoe Bonomi; and the Action party was mainly a party of anti-Fascist and Socialist intellectuals, many of whom had been refugees abroad. There were a number of other parties, notably the Republican party, boasting a *risorgimento* ideology, led by Randolfo Pacciardi, former commander of a Republican brigade in the Spanish Civil War, and claiming as members such men as Sforza.

Italy postwar had two principal problems. The first was the problem of ministerial instability, unhappily reminiscent of the pre-Fascist era; and the second, connected with the first, was the problem of Communism. In regard to the first, it is perhaps enough to say that from Badoglio's government of April 1944 to April 1946, Italy had fourteen governments, and, from May 1948 to the time of writing (October 1961), she had another fourteen. As in France, the earlier governments were permutations of the moderate left, and, as in France, it was a time of constitution-building and popular referendums. Elections for a Constituent Assembly, coupled with a referendum on the monarchy, were held in June 1946. Women voted for the first time. The three "mass" parties swept the board; the referendum returned a narrow majority in favor of a republic. De Nicola was elected Head of the State. De Gasperi formed a government with Sforza as Foreign Minister, and later with Einaudi as Minister of Finance. In December 1947, after long debates, the Constituent Assembly passed the constitution of a "democratic Republic founded upon work," having a president and a central bicameral legislature and dividing the country locally into twenty-four semiautonomous regions. King Victor Emmanuel III died in exile in Egypt on December 28, 1947, the day after the promulgation of the new constitution.

The second problem, that of Communism, was the more important and the more serious internationally. The Italian people were impoverished by the war and humiliated by the peace, and by 1947 there were two million unemployed. Not surprisingly, therefore, Italy had the largest Communist party of any Western European country, and she quickly became one of the main domestic battlefields of the Cold War, anxiously watched by the whole Western democratic world. By the autumn of 1947, pressures were at bursting point, and it looked as if Trieste, disputed by East and West, would be selected as the symbol and the scene of the inevitable outbreak. (See pp. 613-15.) Relief was afforded by various American grants and by the "interim" aid of December 1947, and Italy was one of the sixteen nations of the European Recovery Program. But which way Italy was going to jump in the critical year 1948, whether she would remain in the Western camp or go Communist and drag down the entire European continent with her, this was still an open question.

Elections were due to be held under the new constitution. A wave of Communist-inspired strikes in the autumn months of 1947 appeared to be part of a regular subversive campaign. Extreme Socialists under Nenni were now collaborating with the Communists. New rightist parties emerged, and there was a monarchist party and a neo-Fascist party parading under the title of the "Italian Social Movement" or MSI (*Movimento Sociale Italiano*). As election fever mounted, the Congress of the Italian Communist party, meeting in Milan in January 1948, declared that the party would seize power by force if it lost the election. Rumors were flying concerning the formation of private militias and resistance brigades. Pacciardi, now Deputy Premier in De Gasperi's government, was made Minister of Public Order with the unenviable responsibility for the peaceful conduct of the elections. In February 1948 came the Communist seizure of power in Czechoslovakia, an incident which convulsed every neighbor and near neighbor of that country. On March 20, the United States, Britain, and France issued a joint proposal that Trieste should once more be restored to Italian sovereignty.

In the end the elections were held in April 1948 in relative calm. Over 90 per cent of the electorate voted. The result was a victory for De Gasperi exceeding all expectations. The Western democratic world need not have worried after all. Italy was safe. The Christian Democrat party won more than half the seats; the Communist, rather less than a third; the rightist parties made very small showing. In May 1948, the new parliament assembled. Einaudi was elected first President of the Italian Republic. De Gasperi continued as Premier.

De Gasperi indeed continued as Premier through eight governments — usually coalitions built around his Christian Democrat party — till July 1953, and he was succeeded by governments of much the same color. He died in August 1954. In two more elections — in 1953 and 1958 — the minor parties chopped and changed, but the major parties — the Christian Democrat, the two Socialist groups, and the Communist — varied surprisingly little. The monarchists and the MSI remained small and ineffective. After the tense situation in 1948, Italy made no further commotion and seemed almost content to bow herself out of the international scene. In October 1954, a last source of tension was happily removed, when, under strong American and British pressure, Italy and Yugoslavia at last agreed to a settlement in Trieste. By this settlement the city and port remained in Italian hands, and the frontier between the existing Italian and Yugoslav zones of occupation was adjusted a few miles to the advantage of Yugoslavia. (See pp. 613ff.)

Italy joined the European Recovery Program. She also joined the North Atlantic Pact, the Council of Europe, Western European Union, and the European Economic Community, and her external history thereafter was largely merged with the histories of these organizations.

Pope Pius XII died on October 9, 1958. He was succeeded by Cardinal Giuseppe Roncalli as Pope John XXIII.

Spain and Portugal

We return for a moment to Spain in 1939. (See p. 425.) Since his victory, General Franco had built up a modern totalitarian regime. He tried to wrap his own person about with the vestments of a Fascist dictator. He was El Caudillo, the Spanish Duce. His ideology was, however, peculiarly Spanish and was compounded of a fervent Spanish nationalism and a fervent Spanish Catholicism. He enacted the usual controls, censorships, and restrictions upon private liberties. He obliterated all the signs of Catalan and Basque autonomy. He suppressed Communism and Freemasonry. Subsequent reports of his cruelties to his late enemies were doubtless much exaggerated; but he declared no amnesty, and his police continued to hound the "Red hordes" and "Marxist rabble." Yet he claimed to base his authority on popular support and insisted always that "we belong to the people."

Meanwhile Franco set about the material and spiritual reconstruction of Spain, the building of the devastated areas, the promotion of social services, housing, and schools. But there was little agricultural or agrarian reform. Church lands and revenues were restored. Traditional religious ceremonies and festivals were revived in all their splendor. During the Second World War, profitable trade relations were established with Britain, Germany, and Italy. There was the usual story of shortages, inflation, and black market. Generally the country's recovery was rapid beyond expectation. On July 18, 1942, on the anniversary of the "Glorious Rebellion," as a sort of definitive consolidation of his regime, Franco announced the creation of a new Cortes, a distinctly corporative body composed of government nominees who had rendered "eminent services to the state." But despite occasional threatening moves, despite his declaration of nonbelligerency, Franco did not enter the Second World War. (See pp. 514-15.)

The Allied victories in North Africa and thereafter in Western Europe soon posed Franco with several delicate questions, including that of his very continuance in power. All the Spanish parties, at home and abroad, were maneuvering for position. In March 1945, the third son of Alfonso XIII, Don Juan, now pretender to the Spanish throne, issued a proclamation from his exile in Italy, calling for Franco's resignation and for a restoration of the monarchy. In October 1945, Franco adjusted himself to the altering political situation to the extent of withdrawing the Spanish troops that had occupied Tangier, and the international status of that territory was reestablished. (See p. 514.) Franco chose this particular moment to write a personal letter to Churchill virtually offering him an Anglo-Spanish alliance against the Soviet Union.

Allied governments exerted considerable diplomatic pressure to induce a change of government in Spain. At San Francisco, Spain was pointedly debarred from membership in the United Nations, and in February 1946 the General Assembly adopted a resolution to the effect that the existing Spanish Government, "by reason of its origins, its nature, its record, and its close association with aggressor states," did not possess the qualifications for membership. Spain was likewise excluded from the European Recovery Program. But mere protests never changed a totalitarian state, and Franco knew how to bide his time. After 1950, it was becoming clear that the alternative to Franco might be Communism, a view which Franco was naturally sedulous to propagate. Accordingly, in 1952 Spain was admitted to the FAO and UNESCO. In September 1953, by bilateral agreements with the United States, American bases were to be established at Cadiz, Cartagena, and other points in Spanish territory, and Spain accepted in return substantial economic and military aid. To all intents and purposes Spain, though not a signatory, was incorporated into NATO. Franco, now more kindly disposed toward the pretender Don Juan, agreed to allow the sixteen-year-old Infante Don Juan Carlos, Don Juan's eldest son, to receive his education in Spain – presumably in preparation for the eventual restoration of the monarchy. In 1955 Spain became a full member of the United Nations.

In Portugal, Salazar's dictatorship was one of the seemingly permanent features in a changing international situation. By 1961, out of seventy years of his life, he had spent nearly thirty as virtual head of his state. (See p. 427.) Apparently he was the only man who had ever been able to manage the Portuguese finances. He had made enemies – for instance, in the army, in the left-wing groups, and among surviving parliamentarians of previous regimes – but by none of them had his position ever been seriously threatened. In January 1961, one violent rival, a certain General Delgado, captured the Portuguese luxury liner *Santa Maria* while on a cruise in the Caribbean Sea and held the crew and six-hundred passengers as prisoners for a fortnight; but the precise purpose of this sensational act of piracy was never made very clear.

Salazar was neutral in the Spanish Civil War and neutral in the Second World War, and latterly he may be said to have followed a pro-Western but not too committed a foreign policy. Portugal was one of the original participants in the European Recovery Program and in NATO. But today, it would seem the Portuguese overseas empire has been giving Salazar more cause for concern than the affairs of Europe, the North Atlantic, or even Portugal at home. (See p. 812.)

Benelux

We have mentioned occasionally the affairs of the "Low Countries" in earlier chapters, notably the neutrality and involvement of Belgium and Luxembourg in the two World Wars, and the neutrality and involvement of the Netherlands in the Second World War. (See pp. 16, 19, and 509-10.) But in the post-1945 era these countries acquired an altogether new importance, and they call for a correspondingly fuller appreciation. They became, in fact, the nucleus of West European economic integration. Belgium and the Netherlands were also colonial powers that in the great "retreat from colonialism" of the mid-twentieth century were to lose their overseas possessions.

Belgium, for a small country, to some extent of artificial origins, was surprisingly well provided with national problems. A population of 8,500,000 was fairly equally divided between the Dutch-speaking Flemings, mainly in the northern provinces, and the French-speaking Walloons, in the southern. Although generalizations are odious, we could say that the Flemings were the more urbanized in their lives and occupations, and the Walloons were the more rural. Both communities were largely Catholic, but the Flemings were probably more so than the Walloons. There were also embittered and politically vigorous anticlerical Flemings and militantly secular anticlerical

Walloons. The parliamentary history of the country since 1945 has revolved around the opposition between two principal parties – a Catholic party, the Social Christians, and a Socialist party. Perhaps it is appropriate that Belgium's most distinguished citizen in recent years should have been Paul-Henri Spaak – with a Flemish father and a Walloon mother – himself a good Catholic and a Socialist, Foreign Minister and Premier for various periods in the 1930's, Foreign Minister of the Belgian government in exile in London in the Second World War, and after 1945 destined for an outstanding international career.

Belgium is a monarchy, but of its four kings since 1831, Leopold II and Leopold III have both been highly controversial figures. Leopold II, son of Leopold I, the first King of the Belgians and founder of the dynasty, was largely responsible for the acquisition of the Congo, a single territory that gave Belgium an empire surpassed in area only by the empires of Britain and France. His grandson, Leopold III, was the Leopold who surrendered to the Germans in May 1940. (See p. 510.) It is to be added that, in respect to the Royal Question, which rent the kingdom after 1945 – that is, the question of the return of Leopold bearing his dubious record in the war and in German captivity – the Flemings on the whole were royalist and the Walloons antiroyalist. In 1950, after a closely contested referendum on the issue, Leopold III renounced the throne, and his brother, Prince Charles, Count of Flanders, assumed the regency until such time as his son, Baudouin, was of age to succeed.

The Netherlands, with a population of 9,250,000 has at least a homogeneous people and a single language, and Netherlandish affairs are generally pitched on a lower, quieter note than the affairs of the southern neighbor. The Catholic and the Dutch Reformed Churches are of roughly equal following, but despite the importance of religion in the country's past, neither now stirs up serious political animus. Of the five or more political parties, two again are dominant – the Catholic People's party and the Socialist – and the country's recent parliamentary history has revolved around their opposition – or occasional coalition. The country is a monarchy, though without a Royal Question to divide it. Wilhelmina, Queen since 1890, abdicated in 1948 in favor of her daughter, Juliana, and both queens have been universally popular.

Finally, Luxembourg is a Grand Duchy of 999 square miles and a population of 300,000, with three official languages, French, German, and a local patois, constitutionally ruled by the Grand Duchess Charlotte, a reigning monarch since 1919.

The three countries, by reason of their proximity to one another, have had a long history of economic relationship. A Belgo-Luxembourg customs union was formed in 1921, and the union jointly concluded several trade agreements with the Netherlands during the 1930's. The three countries were small, but inhabited by thrifty, civilized peoples, and, with over 700 persons to the square mile, they represented the highest population density in Europe. They were industrially developed in a way that made them a natural viable unit. Something of their combined economic potential is indicated in Belgium's annual production of 27,500,000 tons of coal and 200,000 tons of textiles, and in Luxembourg's annual production of 3,500,000 tons of iron ore – a tenth that of France (1960). The Netherlands city of Rotterdam, razed by the Germans in 1940, was rebuilt to become, after New York, the second greatest port in the world.

A customs agreement between the three countries was under discussion by members of their governments in exile in London during the Second World War and was provisionally approved by them in 1944. The agreement was finally concluded in July 1947 and went into force as from January 1, 1948. Throughout, Spaak was the leading spirit in the discussions. We shall shortly describe how Benelux, as this economic condominium came to be known, developed into the European Coal and Steel Community (ECSC) and finally into the European Economic Community (EEC). (See pp. 713, 716, and 720-21.)

We shall describe the Netherlands East Indies and the Belgian Congo in later chapters. (See pp. 777-79 and 811-12.)

38. WESTERN EUROPE: ATLANTIC PACT, UNION, AND COMMON MARKET

The European Recovery Program (ERP)

The physical damage of the war was so extensive and so plain to see that it concealed at first the deeper, more serious, but less obvious injury to the economic system. Patching up the rubble of bombed cities was a small thing compared with making Europe once more a going concern. Agencies like UNRRA, or the American and Canadian loans to Britain in 1946, served only immediate and restricted purposes, and it was realized, if slowly and reluctantly, that genuine recovery was not going to be just a matter of *ad hoc* largesse or of ordinary financial mechanics. What was wanted was a much more comprehensive, long-term program under outside leadership. But it was also realized, if slowly and reluctantly, that such a program would have political implications and would have to come to terms with the Cold War.

The overwhelming political fact in 1946 and 1947 was the East-West schism. There had been premonitory signs of it at Yalta; it was in full evidence at Potsdam. In Western countries, a dutifully blinkered press and radio were keeping up the good spirit of the wartime alliance; but soon admiration and friendliness were turning to pained surprise and protest. Rational argument, it seemed, was lost on the Russians; international conferences regularly came to grief on the same old obstruction; the operative word in Molotov's vocabulary was always "No." On March 15, 1946, it was Churchill, then visiting the United States, who, in a speech at Fulton, Missouri, gave utterance at last to what many were beginning to feel and had not dared to say. He spoke as a private citizen "with full liberty to give my true and faithful counsel in these anxious and baffling times"; but the presence of President Truman as his chairman lent the occasion a special significance. He delivered a frank homily on "war and tyranny." The United States, he said, was at the pinnacle of power, but "with primacy in power is also joined an awe-inspiring accountability to the future." There was a shadow that had fallen upon scenes so lately lighted by the Allied victory, and no one could say what the Soviet Union and its Communist international intended to do or "what are the limits, if any, to their expansive proselytizing tendencies," and he thence dilated at length upon the "iron curtain" that had lately descended across the center of Europe.

Throughout 1946, wherever the forces of power politics met – in Iran, Greece, Germany, Trieste, Yugoslavia, Korea, to say nothing of the United Nations – by a seemingly inexorable logic, the Western Powers stood in absolute opposition to the Soviet Union. The "Cold War" was on. In December 1946 the United States and Britain merged their zones in Germany into a single "Bizonia" to the exclusion of the Soviet Union. Early in 1947 the five peace treaties with the former Axis satellites were concluded, as we have described, in circumstances reflecting the self-same conflict. In March 1947, the Foreign Ministers Council met in Moscow for their fruitless discussion of the German and Austrian settlements. (See pp. 643 and 654.)

In the United States the mood was one of perplexity and exasperation. In 1946 as in 1919 the American people were in psychological retreat. But it was beginning to look to them as if, having paid for the war, they were again to be asked to pay for the peace. "Interim aid" to Greece and Turkey had quickly followed upon the Truman Doctrine of March 1947, and then, while Congress was still giving legislative effect to that controversial measure, Undersecretary of State Dean Acheson had delivered a speech at Cleveland, appealing for further emergency assistance to Europe. On June 5, 1947, in a speech at Harvard University, Secretary of State Marshall broached the idea of the European Recovery Program (ERP). He referred to the visible destruction and to the more serious dislocation of the European economy, to the demoralization of the European people – and to the adverse consequences to the economy of the United States. He continued:

> . . . It is logical that the United States should do whatever it is able to do to assist in the return of normal economic health in the world, without which there can be no political stability and no assured peace. Our policy is directed not against any country or doctrine, but against hunger, poverty, desperation, and chaos . . .
>
> It is already evident that, before the United States Government can proceed much further in its efforts to alleviate the situation and help start the European world on its way to recovery, there must be some agreement among the countries of Europe as to the requirements of the situation and the part those countries themselves will take in order to give proper effect to whatever action might be undertaken by this Government . . . The initiative must come from Europe. The role of this country should consist of friendly aid in the drafting of a European program and of later support of such a program so far as it may be practical for us to do so. The program should be a joint one, agreed to by a number, if not all, European nations.

Under such auspices, Ernest Bevin, the British Foreign Secretary, called for an immediate conference of European nations, and for a moment it seemed as if Marshall's offer might succeed in breaking down the estrangement of the Soviet Union. A conference of twenty-five nations assembled in Paris. Molotov arrived with a numerous delegation giving every appearance of an intention to take part, but his opening speech, a compound of orthodox Marxism and undiluted economic nationalism, showed at once that Soviet cooperation was to be offered only on Soviet terms. He bluntly affirmed that the United States had reached the imperialist phase of its economic history, that it was extending credits in order to force its way into foreign markets, and that the mooted European Recovery Program was a desperate attempt to ward off the approaching crisis of American capitalism. Finally he withdrew not only the Soviet delegation but the delegations of the Soviet's East European satellites.

Britain and France therefore proceeded without Soviet participation and on July 12, 1947, sixteen nations – Austria, Belgium, Britain, Denmark, Eire, France, Greece, Iceland, Italy, Luxembourg, the Netherlands, Norway, Portugal, Sweden, Switzerland, and Turkey – set up in Paris a Committee of European Economic Cooperation (CEEC). The Committee's report, the Paris Report, as it was called, published in September, outlined a scheme for increasing the agricultural and industrial output of the sixteen nations and of Western Germany, controlling their exchanges and reducing their tariffs – and for special dollar credits from the United States. The scheme seemed already to be in process of implementation on a smaller scale when, during the same July, as we have already noted, the Benelux countries (Belgium, the Netherlands and Luxembourg) entered into a general customs agreement. (See p. 710.)

Counterdemonstration from the Soviet Union was not long in coming. In September 1947, a Communist Information Bureau, or Cominform, was set up in Belgrade. (See p. 659.) Communist parties began to consolidate their hold in Hungary, Poland, and in the Balkans. In February 1948 occurred the Communist coup in Czechoslovakia. Congress in the United States, startled and alarmed, responded by rushing through legislation to give effect to the ERP, and the Foreign Assistance Act was signed by President Truman on April 3, 1948. Under its terms, the United States undertook grants totaling over $6,000,000,000 for the first year. It would make for the economic rehabilitation of Western Europe and create, by mid-1952, a self-reliant, self-sufficient, and politically and militarily self-defensive, wholly viable unit. It would operate through an Economic Cooperative Administration (ECA) in Washington with branch missions in each participating European nation. Ostensibly the act had no "strings" but it was an open secret that the ECA would discontinue aid to any nation in the event of "changed conditions," notably in the event of that nation going Communist. On April 16, 1948, in Paris, representatives of the original sixteen nations of the CEEC signed a convention creating an Organization for European Economic Cooperation (OEEC) to act as the European counterpart of the ECA. Under the so-called London Decisions of June, the three Western-occupied zones of Germany were drawn into the scheme. (See p. 644.)

The Council of Europe

On March 4, 1947, at Dunkirk, Britain and France had concluded a treaty of alliance. A year later, on March 17, 1948, at Brussels, Britain, France, and the Benelux countries concluded a treaty of economic, social and cultural collaboration and of collective self-defense, to operate under a permanent Consultative Council of the five signatories and a Defense Committee. Both treaties were explicitly stated to be aimed at renewed German aggression, and the first at least was a reminder of the famous treaty of guarantee that France had failed to secure in 1919. (See p. 104.) But in the interval between their dates of signature, the entire strategic outlook in Europe had changed direction, and the second of the treaties, already the more comprehensive and flexible instrument, was now to become the basis of a close defensive confrontation to the Soviet Union and thus to form the political and military counterpart of the economic arrangements that we have just been describing.

Recent public discussion of a new European Union had provided indirectly a certain amount of ideological preparation. European Union had had a long and respectable history behind it. In the interwar years interest in it had been stimulated by such schemes as Coudenhove-Kalergi's Pan-Europa, Briand's European Federation, and, just before and during the Second World War, Federal Union, a British organization. The extraordinary success of Clarence Streit's *Union Now,* first published in 1939, suggested that the idea had a strong following in the United States. Churchill's offer of union with France in 1940 could be said to have had links with it; wartime resistance movements, especially in France, had declared for it – even Hitler's New Order could be described as a version of it. After the war, conferences were held by the European Union of Federalists at Montreux in 1947 and by the Congress of Europe at The Hague in 1948 – the latter meeting being notable for the attendance of Churchill. By this date discussions were reaching ministerial levels. The British Labor government, under Bevin's lead, had taken up the idea, though perhaps not very enthusiastically. The Scandinavian countries had already formed their own "pilot plant," the Nordic Council. In a world of declining nationalisms it was widely believed, nay hoped, that wider "regional arrangements" might become the pattern of the future international order. Western Europe, was obviously one such regional arrangement and was perhaps going through the same sort of growing pains as the American unification of 1787.[1]

In July 1948, at The Hague, the Consultative Council of the five nations of the Treaty of Brussels met to consider the creation of a European Assembly or, as it was shortly to be called, a Council of Europe. In January 1949, Field Marshal Montgomery was appointed Chief of the Defense Committee under the Treaty of Brussels and established his headquarters at Fontainebleau. On May 5, 1949, in London, the Statute of the Council of Europe was signed by the foreign ministers of Belgium, Britain, Denmark, France, Ireland, Italy, Luxembourg, the Netherlands, Norway, and Sweden. The Statute provided for a regular parliamentary type of constitution – a Committee of Ministers, to consist of the foreign ministers of the member nations; a Consultative Assembly, to consist of representatives appointed in such manner as their respective governments should decide; and a Secretariat. The first meetings of the Committee and Assembly of the Council of Europe were held at Strasbourg in the following August and September, and the first President of the Assembly was the Belgian Foreign Minister and international statesman, Paul-Henri Spaak, himself one of the chief designers and builders of the structure. The Committee of Ministers met again in Paris in November and agreed to admit Western Germany and the Saar to the Council of Europe as "associate members."

The North Atlantic Pact (NATO)

We have described American economic participation in Europe under ERP. (See also pp. 747-48.) The parallel American military participation was initiated in June 1948, when the Senate passed the Vandenberg resolution advocating the association of the United States with systems of collective defense. In December 1948, immediately after the presidential elections, exploratory talks were begun in Washington on a defensive pact between the United States, Canada, and the five Brussels Powers. Generally it was expected that France would provide the main ground forces of a future European Army, Britain the tactical air force, and the United States the strategic air force. There would be a joint command, joint use of bases, standardization of arms and equipment, and a new "Lend-Lease." Denmark and Norway were invited to accede. The missing links in the chain would then only be Ireland and Spain. Ireland presumably was still luxuriating in her recently acquired independence and neutrality; but Spain, despite her anomalous political regime, might yet discover ways of attaching herself to the new grouping. Sweden, too uncomfortably close to the Soviet Union, would avoid the faintest suspicion of involvement in either side.

The Soviet Union exerted itself against this fast maturing alliance. Norway, in reply to a Soviet warning in January 1949, protested that she would never take part "in a policy with aggressive aims" nor join in any agreement "to open bases for the military forces of foreign Powers in Norwegian territory, so long as Norway is not attacked or exposed to threats of attack." There was some talk of a "peace offensive" from the Kremlin. Stalin made use of an interview with an American journalist to suggest a personal meeting with President Truman in Poland or Czechoslovakia in order to discuss a world-peace pact and the disarmament of Germany. President Truman countered with an invitation to Washington, which Stalin declined "on doctor's advice." But there was no question now that the United States administration and the greater part of the American people were convinced of the necessity of some sort of Western Grand Alliance, and last lingering doubts were dispelled by the Communist progress in Intermediate Europe — and, indirectly, although no less forcibly, by the Communist progress in China.

The North Atlantic Pact was signed in Washington on April 4, 1949, by the foreign ministers of Belgium, Canada, Denmark, France, Iceland, Italy, Luxembourg, the Netherlands, Norway, Portugal, Britain, and the United States. In a carefully worded preamble, the signatories reaffirmed their faith in the purposes and principles of the Charter of the United Nations and "their desire to live in peace with all peoples and all governments." The core of the pact was contained in its Article 5:

> The Parties agree that an armed attack against one or more of them in Europe or North America shall be considered an attack against them all and consequently they agree that, if such an armed attack occurs, each of them, in exercise of the right of individual or collective self-defense recognized by Article 51 of the Charter of the United Nations, will assist the Party or Parties so attacked by taking forthwith, individually and in concert with the other Parties, such action as it deems necessary, including the use of armed force, to restore and maintain the security of the North Atlantic area.

The signatories further agreed to establish a Council and a Defense Committee. The whole was entitled the North Atlantic Treaty Organization, or NATO. Greece and Turkey adhered in 1951. (See pp. 688, 749-50, and 767.)

The European Defense Community (EDC) and Western European Union (WEU)

The Council of Europe, OEEC, and now NATO might well have been left to work out their several purposes. The European Recovery Program was already an acknowledged success. Production was rising; Western Europe bid fair to be economically viable by midsummer 1952, when the program would officially come to an end. The easing of tensions, particularly in France and Italy, indicated that the political objectives were being satisfied. Meanwhile OEEC was becoming less an agency for the distribution of American aid and more a directorate for long-term inter-European planning and especially for the "liberalization of trade." The three Benelux countries already had their customs union, a suggestive model for a larger association; and France, Italy, and the Benelux countries also had an agreement on monetary cooperation. In May 1950, Robert Schuman, then French Foreign Minister, announced the plan called after him the Schuman Plan, by which France and Western Germany would pool their coal and steel industries. Negotiations were shortly started between France, Western Germany, Italy, and the Benelux countries for the formation of a European Coal and Steel Community (ECSC), and on April 18, 1951, the ECSC Treaty was signed in Paris. But, by that date, the whole situation in Europe had already been transformed, on June 25, 1950, by the outbreak of war in Korea. (See pp. 781ff.)

Overnight whatever military planning or preparedness had been accomplished was obsolete. No one in Europe could blink the fact that there existed no adequate forces to resist the rapidly rearming Communist states of Intermediate Europe should they be induced to launch another "war by proxy" like the Korean War at the behest of the Soviet Union. Britain had small, well-trained, well-equipped forces of all arms, but their leadership was not "European minded," and, except for the contingent stationed in Germany, they were variously committed in Egypt, Malaya, and other distant parts of the world. France was then heavily involved in Indochina, domestically she was struggling with a large and obstructive Communist party, and all her governments were unstable and short-lived. In the circumstances simple military logic could hardly conclude otherwise than that the reinforcement so urgently required in Europe must come from Western Germany, and that this reinforcement must then be built into a well-coordinated European Army. But a rearmed Germany, scarcely five years after her unconditional surrender, was a terrible thing to contemplate. In August 1950, in the Consultative Assembly of the Council of Europe, at which Western Germany and the Saar appeared for the first time as associate members, the French representative, André Philip, accepted the thesis of a European Army, but he added that "even in the present danger, the German Army must not be reconstituted." Churchill, present on this occasion, spoke strongly in favor of the immediate creation of a European Army under unified command, without specifically mentioning Germany; but later, when pressed by a questioner, he admitted that he had intended to include Germany.

In September and December 1950, at meetings in New York and Brussels, the NATO Council, under strong pressure from the United States Joint Chiefs of Staff, agreed to establish an integrated European Defense Force containing a German contingent. General Eisenhower would be Supreme Allied Commander Europe (SACEUR) with his headquarters, Supreme Headquarters Allied Powers Europe (SHAPE), in Paris, and, early in the New Year, 1951, Eisenhower arrived to take up his command. Meanwhile, in October 1950, René Pleven, then French Premier, faced by the fearful prospect of German military resurgence, had hastily produced counterproposals in the form of the Pleven Plan, as it came to be known. Pleven described a European Army, under a European "Defense Minister," composed of "combat teams" of battalion or brigade strength – one German team to five non-German teams. Participating nations, which already possessed a national army, should retain absolute control over that part of it not incorporated into the European Army; German recruiting should be supervised by non-German officers, and, of course, there could be no German general staff and no German war ministry. (See p. 696.)

Months of agonized negotiations followed, and eventually a treaty for a European Defense Community was hammered out; but the European Army therein envisaged bore little resemblance to the Pleven Plan. In all these negotiations, of course, in the French view, France's vital interests were being consistently flouted – and flouted indeed by powers that perversely misunderstood her real position and that pretended to be her friends and allies. Germany, the public international enemy, twice defeated and twice disarmed, was almost being begged by panic-stricken neighbors to resume her former military predominance in Europe.

The diplomatic initiative was coming now in the main from the United States, not only on behalf of a European Army, but on behalf of European political and economic integration in general. Here indeed was a magnificent opportunity which might never come again for burying centuries of perpetual feud and for creating a powerful, viable European Super-State. The economic signs were favorable. The European Recovery Program was wound up according to plan in 1952, after having allocated $12,500,000,000 of American funds, and the Mutual Security Program was taking over. There was no question but that a self-reliant prosperity in Europe was on the way. The "German miracle" had happened. In Britain perhaps there were some doubts and hesitations. Britain, with her Commonwealth commitments, was in a unique position and was reluctant to align herself wholeheartedly with a new united Europe, though certainly the British Conservatives, who were returned to office in 1951, showed a little more sympathy toward such an alignment than their Labor predecessors had done.

On May 26, 1952, at Bonn, the Contractual Conventions — or the Bonn Conventions, as they were familiarly called — were signed by Adenauer and by the foreign Ministers, Eden, Schuman, and Acheson. By these instruments, Western Germany would be restored to sovereignty, and the Allied occupation terminated. A miscellany of detail followed regarding the stationing of "foreign forces" in Germany and the continuance of the Allied regime in Berlin. On May 27, at Paris, the European Defense Community (EDC) Treaty was signed by the foreign ministers of the six states — France, Italy, Belgium, the Netherlands, Luxembourg, and Germany — Schuman, De Gasperi, Van Zeeland, Stikker, Bech, and Adenauer. Britain was not a signatory, but, simultaneously, a treaty of guarantee was signed between Britain and EDC. A further Declaration was issued by Britain, France, and the United States to the effect that they would regard a threat to the security of EDC "as a threat to their own security" and that they would station such forces in Europe "as they deem necessary and appropriate to contribute to the joint defense of the North Atlantic Treaty area." Finally an agreement was published in Bonn prohibiting the manufacture of atomic weapons and missiles in Germany. The Bonn Conventions were made dependent on EDC and would come into force with the establishment of EDC.

In spite of the urgency behind the conclusion of the EDC Treaty, the six signatories were now most curiously tardy in their ratifications of it, and we now enter upon an interval of two years in which the affairs of Europe seemed to mark time. The Korean War had reached a stalemate, the fighting had died down, and armistice negotiations, interminably protracted, were going on. French public opinion, still fearful of German rearmament, had a worse worry in Indochina. Then, at one moment, the Saar was dragged into the discussions, and it seemed that France's ratification of EDC would be bargained against a more favorable agreement over that disputed territory. As for Britain, while glad to prod France into assuming European commitments, she was plainly "dragging her own feet." The approach of the presidential elections in the United States was delaying any political business in Europe with which the United States was connected. Eisenhower at SHAPE had been succeeded by Ridgway and had returned home to be groomed for candidacy by the Republican party. Then, in March 1953, Stalin died, and, if he was to have a more liberally disposed successor, EDC would lose its entire purpose. Meanwhile the Council of Europe, once hopefully founded as the instrument of a "European Political Community," felt itself being superseded by the newer organizations, EDC and ECSC, and was rather tamely trying to justify itself in debates on "social and cultural questions." In September 1952 Spaak, while remaining President of the Consultative Assembly of the Council of Europe, had become President of the ECSC Assembly, also at Strasbourg, the more interesting and promising body.

Between January and April 1954, Western Germany and the Benelux countries completed their ratifications of EDC. Italy's was proceeding. Mendès-France became Premier of France in June 1954, and, as we have related above, one of the four pledges of his investiture address, if not to effect France's long delayed ratification, was to find a solution of Germany's contribution to European defense. (See p. 697.) He tried to ease some of the more objectionable terms in the EDC treaty, and, to that end, in August 1954 he met the foreign ministers of the EDC Powers at a conference in Brussels. It seemed that Mendès-France was still thinking along the lines of the Pleven Plan, and the conference broke down. On August 30, 1954, the French Assembly wrote *finis* to EDC – and therewith to the Bonn Conventions also. The whole Western European system, which had been so painfully built, was on the brink of total collapse. Eden, the British Foreign Secretary, spent the first two weeks of September busily flying between Bonn, Rome, and Paris, in a heroic effort to save some of the pieces. John Foster Dulles, recently appointed American Secretary of State, arrived in London, bearing the full load of American threats and promises. The French Government and Assembly, having spectacularly made their point and now appalled at the havoc they had brought about, were manifestly contrite and conciliatory. (See pp. 697-98.)

At the end of September 1954, the foreign ministers of Britain, France, Italy, Belgium, the Netherlands, Luxembourg, Western Germany, Canada, and the United States – nine in all – among them Eden, Mendès-France, Spaak, Adenauer, Lester Pearson, and Dulles – met in London to remake the former Treaty of Brussels into a "focus of European integration" in place of the defunct EDC. Their meeting was resumed in Paris in October, simultaneously with a meeting of the NATO Council. Out of these deliberations emerged the London Agreement of October 3 and the Paris Agreements of October 23. The Bonn Conventions were reaffirmed. Western Germany was restored to sovereignty; the Allied occupation would be terminated as soon as possible, and the Allied High Commission abolished. Western Germany and Italy would join the Brussels Powers; in their newly extended form they would be known collectively as Western European Union (WEU). The Brussels Consultative Council would become a "Council with powers of decision." Western Germany would also join NATO and would contribute forces to be commanded by SACEUR and to be deployed "in accordance with NATO strategy." An agency would be set up for the control of armaments in Europe; the prohibition of the manufacture of atomic weapons and missiles in Germany was reaffirmed. Britain, Canada, and the United States gave fresh assurances concerning their forces in Europe. Eden, in a special pronouncement, pledged the British Government to continue to maintain forces in Europe equivalent to those already assigned to SACEUR.

The European Economic Community (EEC) and the European Free Trade Association (EFTA)

The European Coal and Steel Community (ECSC) was only the first step towards a far more comprehensive economic integration in Europe. In May 1955, the six member nations of ECSC, at a conference at Messina in Sicily, initiated conversations which eventually resulted in two treaties signed at Rome on March 25, 1957. The first of these treaties created the European Economic Community (EEC) or Common Market; and the second created the European Atomic Energy Community or Euratom. "The Six" – France, Western Germany, Italy, and the Benelux countries (Belgium, the Netherlands and Luxembourg) – were thus joined together in an attempt progressively to reduce all tariffs and other trade barriers between themselves and to abolish them altogether within a period of twelve to fifteen years; and they would also cooperate in their agricultural, transport, and social policies. But they would, as seemed necessary, present a common tariff to the outside world. With a population of 175,000,000 they would control one of the most highly developed concentrations of agriculture, commerce, and industry in the world. The European Economic Community would function through a Council of Ministers, a Parliamentary Assembly at Strasbourg, often called the "Parliament of Europe" (superseding the former ECSC Assembly), a Court of Justice to adjudicate disputes, and finally an independent executive European Commission. The president of the European Commission is now the German Dr. Walter Hallstein, former professor of law, with headquarters at Brussels.

The creation of so formidable an organization as EEC at once posed a problem for nonmembers in Europe, especially for the other nations of OEEC. Under Reginald Maudling, then British Paymaster-General, terms were gradually worked out for a European Free Trade Association (EFTA) to include "the Seven" – Britain, Austria, Denmark, Norway, Portugal, Sweden, and Switzerland. The association was created by a convention signed in Stockholm on November 20, 1959. EFTA was more negative in purpose than EEC. Its members agreed to reduce, and eventually to abolish tariffs and other trade restrictions between themselves, but not to adopt any common policy towards the outside world. Existing preferences or trade agreements between EFTA members and other countries – for instance between Britain and the Commonwealth – would remain unaffected.

As we write, EEC and EFTA are working out their twin destinies. Strong opposition to each has existed – and exists – notably from farming interests and from trade-unions, the one fearing for their prices and the other for their wages. Britain in particular has overriding difficulties in respect of her Commonwealth commitments. Unlike EEC, EFTA has no ulterior political motives – or at least had none originally. But economics is clearly not the only or the real issue. It is possible that in the classic manner, economic association will lead on to political association. Whatever else may have lain in the farseeing workmanship of the founders — Monnet, Schuman, and Spaak — some sort of political association is surely not to be excluded. If now the nations of EEC and EFTA — plus perhaps Spain and Portugal, despite their anomalous dictatorial regimes — should all come together, the total group would represent that part of Europe historically identifiable with Western civilization at its primary source, inhabited to-day by 250,000,000 people, of ancient traditions and with the most varied skills and resources. Such a group would compare comfortably with any Super-Power of the present or future.

39. BRITAIN: LABOR, WELFARE, AND CONSERVATISM

Labor and the Welfare State

A general election in July 1945, just after the end of the war in Europe, resulted in a heavy defeat for Winston Churchill and the Conservative party. It must be admitted that the British people afterward were a little pricked in conscience at having so served their great wartime leader; opinion abroad, especially in the United States, was stunned at the seeming ingratitude. But a great wartime leader is not always the best peacetime leader, and the country's decisive swing to the left at the first sign of peace was not wholly unexpected – nor wholly undesirable. The Labor majority in the election – 392 Labor seats to 216 Conservative – was certainly a very convincing demonstration of the electorate's hopes and wishes.

On July 27, 1945, Clement Attlee formed a Labor government, with Hugh Dalton as Chancellor of the Exchequer, Ernest Bevin as Foreign Secretary, Sir Stafford Cripps as President of the Board of Trade, and Aneurin ("Nye") Bevan as Minister of Health. It was the first Labor government in Britain with a clear majority, and it came to office with an explicit socialist program. Attlee himself had none of the color of his predecessor in office. He was the "safe" party man, eminently moderate, personally well liked and respected, an experienced administrative head, practical to a fault, and likely to be a good leader of a fractious, strong-willed cabinet. Attlee and Bevin represented Britain at the final sessions of the Potsdam Conference.

The country was not left long in doubt as to the new government's domestic policies. From the very opening of Parliament, in the speech from the throne, the King made mention of measures for the public ownership of key industries and services. Britain, under the new watchwords "planning" and "social justice," was to become a socialist state.

There was a curious, almost unreal optimism in the air. The British people had just been blessed by victory, a victory greater than that of 1918. Even amidst the physical devastation and disrepair, the full costs of the conflict were not yet realized. Responsive to the general confidence, Dalton's supplementary budget in October 1945 cheerfully reduced the income tax and even the Excess Profits Tax. These were the days when the bookshops blossomed out with volumes — attractively produced despite the paper shortage — describing the cities and housing schemes that were to adorn the face of Britain. Reports after the manner of the Beveridge Report delineated the country's future social and economic structure. Meanwhile, unlike 1919-20, wartime controls were not hastily abolished. Demobilization of man power and of industry was a deliberate, gradual process. Many supporters of the government indeed believed that the recent wartime regimentation had not been an unmixed evil and had prepared the country for an easy and painless translation into an era of planning. In the immense economic complexities of the modern world, it was argued, the old cutthroat chaos of private enterprise would never restore the nation's prosperity.

A first parliamentary session of fifteen months saw the passage of eighty-four acts, a mass of legislation unprecedented in British parliamentary history. It was something like the breakneck scramble of Roosevelt's "Hundred Days" in 1933. The Bank of England was nationalized. After intensive debate the coal industry was nationalized, and the long, grim story that had begun with the coal miners' strikes of the early 1920's after the First World War thus came to an end. Henceforth, nearly 2,000 British coal mines would be operated by a National Coal Board, appointed by the Minister of Fuel and responsible to him. The coal owners received about $750,000,000 in indemnities. A Transport Bill was proposed for the nationalization of railroads, canals, and long-distance road transport, and there were debates, bitter debates, on a bill for the nationalization of steel. Parliament repealed the Trades Disputes Act, passed shortly after the General Strike of 1926, an act which Labor had always regarded with particular dislike as a piece of punitive legislation. (See p. 269.)

The legislative surfeit continued into the second parliamentary session. To speed up the pace the government had recourse to the "guillotine" to cut short lengthening debates on several important measures during committee stage. Labor spokesmen argued that the government's program of reforms was already long overdue, and sufficient discussion of it had gone on, both inside and outside Parliament, for years past. The House of Lords, heretofore somewhat fallen in prestige, was restored to some of its historic eminence to become a chamber where debates could be continued in relative freedom and leisure. During 1947, Parliament passed the Transport Act and an Electricity Act nationalizing the electricity supply industry, and, early in 1948, an act nationalizing the gas industry. Finally, in 1948, under Bevan's guidance, came Labor's supreme domestic reform, the National Health Service Act, "nationalizing the doctors" and, partly supported by compulsory contributions, extending medical and hospital services to the entire population.

In September 1945, immediately after the Japanese surrender, the United States Government cancelled all outstanding contracts for Lend-Lease. The decision was proper, as Lend-Lease had been a wartime measure. But it was made without warning and came as a shock to former Lend-Lease beneficiaries, notably Britain. Lord Keynes and Lord Halifax were sent over to Washington to negotiate with the United States Treasury a financial arrangement that would tide over, in particular, the problems raised by the cessation of Lend-Lease and, in general, the longer-term problems of industrial reconversion from war to peace. Disagreement of experts over needs and principles was not serious. The main difficulty was to devise a plan acceptable to the legislatures and electorates of the two countries. Both sides were still far from realizing the extent of the dislocations of the war. American Congressional opinion was averse to reviving and perpetuating expenditures which were thought to have been brought to an end; British Parliamentary opinion was averse to contracting onerous new obligations. However, on December 7, 1945, the negotiators in Washington announced an agreement that would take the form of a loan of $3,750,000,000 from the United States to Britain at an interest of 2 per cent, the capital being repayable in fifty annual installments commencing December 31, 1951. In addition, the net liability of Britain with respect to Lend-Lease was reduced to $650,000,000, to be repaid to the United States simultaneously and on the same terms. The agreement was approved by the House of Commons and House of Lords in the face of strong opposition, and was approved by Congress after protracted debates and close voting in July 1946. A Canadian loan of $1,250,000,000 was provided under an agreement signed in Ottawa in March 1946. (See p. 745.)

The Labor government continued in office from 1945 to 1951. But, of these six years, the first two were unquestionably its most brilliant and successful. After the initial spate of legislation, what was its policy to be – to push on relentlessly in the same direction, or to pause to consolidate and reconsider? Revolutions, even peaceful ones, cannot always maintain their original momentum. Unlike certain European political movements, British Labor had never learned, nor wanted to learn, the technique of incessant crisis. On the contrary, in its own odd logic, as a party essentially inspired by grievance, it began to decline as a political force in proportion as it achieved its objects. Somehow the Welfare State in being was not nearly so exciting as the Welfare State in prospect, and once that state was established the zest of the struggle was followed by a feeling almost of anticlimax. By 1947 Labor's first fine careless rapture was over.

Already in April 1946, Dalton, introducing his budget, disclosed a deficit of £300,000,000 ($1,500,000,000). In July the Ministry of Food was forced to ration bread for some months. It was hardly to the credit of the socialist government, with all its "planning," that the one staple food of the people that had not been rationed during the war should have to be rationed upon the return of peace. During the summer and autumn of 1946 there were cuts in meat and fuels, the "basic" gasoline ration was abolished, a ban was imposed on holiday travel abroad, the import of foreign books and motion-picture films was restricted, and there were sharp shortages in cigarettes and tobacco. The winter of 1946-47 was one of the coldest and most uncomfortable on record and laid exceptional burdens on fuel stocks. A "switch-off" of electricity supply due to fuel shortage in February 1947 was estimated to have cost the country £200,000,000 ($1,000,000,000) in lost exports.

Meanwhile something had gone very wrong with the great spurt in the building industry which was to have repaired the bomb-devastated towns and provided thousands of new homes for returning servicemen and their families. Building materials, it was said, were in short supply – almost every building material but brick and cement had to be imported from abroad – the building-trades employees were slacking, the industry was clogged with bureaucratic controls, and so forth. In the daily press, at public meetings, in the Commons, the recurrent theme at this time was that of industrial "incentives" to supersede the more primitive economic incentives of the past which full employment had now removed. During 1947 the government intensively publicized the seriousness of the growing adverse balance of payments and called for a nation-wide drive to step up the export trade. The slogans "Export or Die" or "You are living on tick" were posted on billboards and railroad stations. Exhibitions, such as "Britain Can Make It" and the "British Industries Fair," were organized to bring British products to the notice of foreign buyers.

Then it appeared that the American and the Canadian loans of 1946 had been drawn upon far faster than had been expected, and both were exhausted by the end of 1947. A credit which, it had been hoped, would have lasted over a transitional gap of four to five years, lasted in fact rather less than two. There were various reasons suggested for this disastrous abbreviation. In particular, the inflationary rise of prices in the United States had sharply reduced the original value of the loans. Throughout these years, the prices of imported foods and raw materials rose faster than the prices of manufactured goods for export. Meanwhile the volume of Britain's exports had failed to maintain the promise of the initial postwar recovery, partly on account of the shortage of fuel required for manufacture. Inflation in Britain had tended to drive up production prices and had diverted goods intended for export to the home market, and too great a proportion of what had eventually been exported had gone to non-dollar destinations. Britain's former traditional compensations – in the shape of "invisible" exports, such as returns on overseas investments, shipping charges, banking, and insurance – were now reduced. The $40,000,000,000, for instance, held in 1939 by British investors abroad and yielding annual dividends of $1,000,000,000, had largely vanished. "Sterling balances" exceeding £3,500,000,000 ($14,000,000,000), namely debts incurred during the war for wartime supplies, mainly from the Dominions, India, Egypt, Argentina, and Portugal, had to be "frozen." But for the European Recovery Program in 1947, the state of Britain would have been serious indeed.

But also by 1947, problems other than purely domestic ones were in the offing. Britain could no longer remain a doctrinaire socialist vacuum, recking nothing of pressures from outside. In 1947 a new National Service

Act was passed conscripting men from 18 to 26, a stern reminder to the British people that in addition to their other cares they were not yet finished with the business of preparing for war. The year 1948 was a veritable *annus terribilis.* It was the year of the Berlin Blockade, the Czech crisis, the termination of the Palestine mandate, and the Communist triumph in China. Cripps had succeeded Dalton as Chancellor of the Exchequer in November 1947, as harsh a man as his predecessor had been genial, and he was quickly identified with a policy of "austerity," "cuts," and the "wage-freeze." A partial recovery followed, evidenced by increased production statistics and the derationing of certain commodities, such as clothing and shoes. A release of paint materials enabled houses and buildings, long neglected during the war years, to be repainted, and the consequent architectural refreshment was immensely heartening. Exports in the first quarter of 1949 rose to 150 per cent of their volume in 1938. But the situation suddenly worsened in the summer of 1949, partly because of a temporary recession in the United States and partly because of the increasing competition from other exporting countries which were now also recovering from the war. In the third quarter of 1949, British exports to the United States dropped by 30 per cent. On September 18, 1949, Britain devalued the pound from $4.03 to $2.80, and some weeks later the Prime Minister announced cuts in government expenditure amounting to £250,000,000.

In a general election in February 1950, Labor was again returned, though with a greatly reduced majority. Attlee remained Prime Minister, but two of his principal colleagues, Cripps and Bevin, were both sick men about to retire from public life. Cripps resigned in October 1950 and was succeeded by a comparative newcomer, Hugh Gaitskell; Bevin resigned in March 1951 and was succeeded by Herbert Morrison. It was soon clear that another election would have to be fought in 1951. Labor was not only losing some of its strongest leaders as well as its former majority in the country, but its setbacks were rousing discontents and recriminations within the party. Gaitskell, in his budget in April 1951, felt obliged to continue Cripps' austerity policy, one victim of which — as Bevan eloquently made out — was Bevan's great pride and joy, the National Health Service. Bevan, at that moment Minister of Labor, consequently resigned. As for Morrison's appointment as Foreign Secretary, it was admittedly little more than a stopgap. Morrison was next in seniority to Attlee in the Labor hierarchy, a grand party veteran, but quite unsuited for his new post. Unhappily he came to office just in time to run head on into the crises in Persia and Egypt. In May 1951, Mossadeq in Persia was rationalizing the oil industry; on October 8, 1951, Nahas in Egypt abrogated the Anglo-Egyptian treaty of 1936 — and in neither affair had Morrison experience or even much serious interest. (See pp. 793 and 795.)

The general election of October 1951 resulted in a Labor defeat. Churchill became Prime Minister with Eden as Foreign Secretary, and Butler as Chancellor of the Exchequer. Britain entered upon a period of Conservative rule. In two more elections, in 1955 and 1959, the Conservative lead was to be progressively increased.

Conservative Rise and Labor Fall

On February 6, 1952, King George VI died after a long illness. Princess Elizabeth and Prince Philip were then in East Africa on a tour that was to have taken them to Australia and New Zealand. They flew home at once, and the Princess succeeded to the throne as Queen Elizabeth II. Her coronation was celebrated in Westminster Abbey on June 2, 1953.

The new reign coincided with a moment of political transition. The Conservative party was changing, and even more so was the Labor. Older men were going, and younger were coming up. Winston Churchill was beginning to show his years – he was nearly eighty – and he was constantly rumored to be on the point of retiring. But Anthony Eden, whom many now acknowledged as his political heir, was seriously ill in 1953, and Churchill was persuaded to remain in office. He accepted the Order of the Garter and enjoyed two more years of his premiership as Sir Winston Churchill till April 1955, when he resigned and Eden seemed to be fit enough in health to succeed him. A new generation was arising in the Conservative party and in government office – Butler, Macmillan, Selwyn Lloyd, Thorneycroft, Monckton, Heathcoat Amory, Lennox-Boyd, Duncan Sandys.

Labor in these years lost almost the whole of its older leadership. Seldom indeed did a great parliamentary party go through so complete a personal transformation in so short a time. Bevin had died in 1951, a month after his resignation. Cripps died a year later in April 1952. Harold Laski, who for so many years had been Labor's intellectual mentor, had died in March 1950. Attlee resigned in December 1955 and went to the House of Lords with a Viscountcy. He was succeeded in the party leadership by Gaitskell. Bevan was still "in exile." Bevan died in 1960 – although, as we shall relate, his last five years were to be perhaps the most active and controversial of his career. As in the Conservative party, a new generation was arising – Hartley Shawcross, Robens, Pakenham, R. H. S. Crossman, Michael Foot, Denis Healey, Kenneth Younger – and, however vigorous the new generation might be, the loss of so many of the "Old Guard" could not but be weakening to the party as a whole.

Labor at this time, defeated at the polls – eventually thrice defeated – was not only rethinking its immediate future policy, but also its entire socialist philosophy. A deep-seated rift was appearing between its more orthodox leaders on the one hand – such as Gaitskell and, before his retirement, Attlee – and Bevan and his rebel following on the other. The rift was not new or unusual. All left-wing movements in Europe tended to split into "gradualist" and "revolutionary" factions. Such a situation had lately occurred in the left-wing movement in Western Germany, Austria, France, and, above all, Italy. The classic precedent and analogy was the Menshevik-Bolshevik breach of 1903, and British Labor from its first days at the beginning of the century had always harbored a similar dichotomy.

Disputes within the Labor party's leadership were reflected not only in the constant strikes at this time – notably of the railwaymen, dockers, and busmen – but in the fact that so many of the strikes were "unofficial" and were conducted by groups of workers in defiance of their trade unions. Discontent and indiscipline were playing upon each other, and the trade-unions, like the Labor party, seemed to be going through a crisis in loyalties. The big public questions of the moment were nationalization and rearmament, and naturally enough the orthodox calling in the party and the unorthodox rebels took opposite sides on both questions. As we have said, Labor's further policy after the initial spate of legislation in 1945-46 had already been in doubt even while the party was at the height of its power. How far should nationalization go? In terms of pure doctrine, nationalization should be total and absolute. Private enterprise of whatever kind and however small should yield to public ownership. But while the doctrine seemed incontestable, there were many who were beginning to fear certain unforeseen consequences. They feared in particular the extreme bureaucractic elaboration which the doctrine required when translated into practice and which might ultimately result in a tyranny infinitely more inefficient and inhuman than the capitalism it claimed to replace. And just as much many feared the increasing rigidity of the bigger trade unions which seemed to be converting themselves into privileged, self-interested, almost "conservative" bodies.

But more serious than its difficulties over nationalization were the Labor party's difficulties over rearmament. After Korea in 1950, all the NATO countries — including, eventually, Western Germany — were committed to rearmament. And here Labor had need to make a fundamental choice — a categorical Either-Or. It had to reaffirm or else renounce its former traditional pacifism — a pacifism now exacerbated by the supreme horror of the atom bomb. At the end of the war in 1945 Labor's sympathies in the main had been ranged alongside the kindred socialist state, the Soviet Union, and against the capitalist United States, and, despite the subsequent, unanswerable logic of the Cold War, Labor still wished neither to make too much an enemy of the one nor too much a friend of the other. But in addition, there had always been a strong, almost traditional distaste within the Labor party for foreign affairs as a whole. Labor, it used to be said, was not so much isolationist as "insulationist." Historically the Labor party had come into existence at the turn of the century in response to a domestic challenge, and it had since become the most domestic-minded of political parties. In its official pronouncements it subscribed to "International Socialism," and certain stock issues — for example, Russia and, within the Empire, India — were of undeniable and pressing concern. Now and then an international incident could rouse an entirely unpredictable degree of passion — Ethiopia in 1935, or Suez in 1956. But, in general, Labor's rank and file were largely uninterested in, often ignorant of, the outer world beyond the all-absorbing cares at home. Foreign affairs — with their cynical diplomacy and recurrent wars, all conducted by an all too ornamental, snob-ridden upper class of careerists — all this was a dirty imperialist-capitalist game and was in fact an integral part of the selfsame system which exploited the ordinary worker's daily livelihood. Yet in 1947, and even more so in 1950 — to say nothing of 1914 and 1939 — Labor was thrust willy-nilly into a world in which foreign affairs swallowed up domestic affairs and in which politics as formerly understood was left without any free or honest initiative.

These several problems and disputes within the Labor party soon centered around the person of Nye Bevan. In respect of nationalization, he and his "Bevanites" would have gone the limit. But, in respect of rearmament, curiously enough, the issues were not so black and white. Bevan, the one-time coal miner and local union organizer, the supreme example, if ever there was one, of domestic insularity, now used his years of self-imposed exile to acquaint himself with foreign lands and peoples. He visited Yugoslavia and, surprisingly, formed genuine friendships with Marshal Tito and other Yugoslavs; and he then returned home to groom himself as the future Labor Foreign Secretary! We may thence follow his career, through successive, extremely stormy annual Party Conferences, as the uncompromising – even if intensely reluctant – upholder of Britain's possession of the atom bomb and advocate of rearmament.

The above digression into the internal crisis of the Labor party in Britain is not irrelevant. In this book we are surely interested in the ideological agonies through which a great political movement of great importance to world affairs had to pass in these years. Labor again lost in the elections of 1955 and 1959, and each event was followed by even more searching self-examinations. Bevan, the protagonist of the crisis, died in July 1960, but the crisis survived him and as we write continues with increasing virulence and personal rancor.

The Conservative government meanwhile tried to reverse the nationalization policy of its predecessor. But unscrambling the accomplished fact was not easy, especially as part of the accomplishment was genuinely felt to be good, if not inevitable. In the end the government contented itself with legislation to denationalize steel and road transport. But the main preoccupations of the moment were imperial and foreign affairs. Unrest in Africa was growing, and it was growing particularly in those parts of the continent that hitherto had hardly ever been "in the news." In Kenya, for example, a new movement, known as Mau Mau, was active. There was some talk at official levels of a Central African Federation. Occasional episodes of popular appeal were favored by special publicity – for example, the public and private affairs of Seretse Khama, the young tribal chief who, since his marriage to a white woman, had been refused entry into his home in Bechuanaland. In South Africa, Dr. Malan had enunciated his policy of apartheid.

Everywhere in the world, it seemed, some sort of trouble was stirring – in the Middle East: Egypt and Cyprus; and in the Far East: Korea and Indochina. In Europe the government's chief concerns were EDC and NATO and, as we have seen, the attendant problem of rearmament. In May 1952, the European Defense Community Treaty had been signed in Paris. Britain was not a member of the new grouping, but she subscribed simultaneously to a treaty of guarantee between herself and EDC and to the joint American-Franco-British Declaration in support of EDC. In August 1954, however, as we have related elsewhere, EDC was rejected by France and lapsed. (See p. 719.) It fell to Eden to devise the subsequent London Agreement and

Paris Agreements, signed in October 1954, which superseded EDC and which provided for Germany's admission to NATO. It must be added perhaps that after initial misgivings, public opinion in Britain took all this somewhat technical and hypothetical diplomacy with remarkable placidity. There was neither any particular sympathy for France nor antipathy for Germany. It remained for the Suez Crisis of 1956 to raise up a much more general and disturbing problem.

Eden succeeded Churchill as Prime Minister in April 1955. His illness of two years earlier seemed to have left no aftereffects. He was now the obvious leader of Conservative Britain, a man at the peak of his powers, with an impeccable political record, widely experienced, especially in foreign affairs, respected by all shades of opinion at home and abroad. He came to office with high hopes of a long and prosperous tenure. He consolidated his position by a general election in October 1955, which returned his party with an increased majority. He gathered about himself a group of able and experienced colleagues. Harold Macmillan was Foreign Secretary, and R. A. ("Rab") Butler Chancellor of the Exchequer till December 1955, when Selwyn Lloyd became Foreign Secretary, and Macmillan Chancellor of the Exchequer. Butler was Leader of the House of Commons.

Eden found himself almost at once at grips with the restive Middle East. But it was an area with which he was well acquainted, and he welcomed both the opportunity to repair the loss of British prestige since the Iranian oil crisis — and to show his own mettle. During 1954, while he was still Foreign Secretary, SEATO, NATO's counterpart in the Pacific, had been negotiated and signed, and a similar organization in the Middle East would obviously complete the long line of defense against the Communist powers. Therefore, in discussions in Cairo, Karachi, and Baghdad, on his way to and from the first SEATO Council meeting at Bangkok in February 1955, Eden lent his strong support to the so-called Baghdad Pact, just then signed between Iraq and Turkey. Britain adhered to the Pact by means of a new treaty with Iraq in April 1955, a treaty that superseded the former Anglo-Iraqi treaty of 1930. Pakistan adhered to the Pact later in the year, in September, and Iran in October. (See pp. 193, 797, and 803.)

But, if there was one infallible law in the Middle East, it was that no diplomatic arrangement ever suited everybody. Colonel Nasser in Egypt was nursing his antipathy to Iraq and to Turkey — and to Britain. In July 1955, he made his "arms deal" with the Soviet Union. But he was simultaneously promoting his plan for a High Dam on the Nile, and he seemed to be on the point of reaching a financial agreement with the World Bank, and with Britain and the United States. To all intents and purposes he was bargaining skillfully and effectively with both sides, and he was clearly holding out for more substantial persuasion for the Baghdad Pact to become sufficiently attractive to him. In October 1955, he entered into an alliance with Syria and then into one with Saudi Arabia. There were now in effect two "Tiers" in the Middle East — a Northern Tier comprising the Baghdad Powers, Iraq, Turkey, Pakistan, Iran, and Britain, and a Southern Tier comprising Egypt, Syria, and Saudi Arabia — with Jordan wedged uncomfortably between them. The first meeting of the Council of the Baghdad

Pact took place in Baghdad in November 1955 and was attended by the Premiers of Iraq, Turkey, Pakistan and Iran, and by Macmillan, then British Foreign Secretary. The United States sent observers and generally advertised its good will toward the new grouping.

Meanwhile Parliament in Britain, almost in a waiting mood and deliberately self-blinkered, was somewhat meticulously debating such domestic issues as the death penalty, divorce, and automation. During March and April 1956, an interesting series of Russian visits occurred. Malenkov came to inspect British power stations and electrical plants; Bulganin and Khrushchev came for a rather more flamboyant tour and were appropriately entertained in London and Chequers, and in Oxford where, to their apparent satisfaction, they were "ragged" in the heartiest traditions of the undergraduate community. But, in the same March, the revolutionary situation blew up in Jordan; General Glubb, commander of the Jordanian "Arab Legion" and his British staff were expelled. (See p. 798.) In Israel, the Israelis were fighting raids by Egyptian *"fedayeen."* In Cyprus, now coming very much to the fore as a danger spot in the Middle East, terrorism and constitution-building were proceeding side by side. And then broke the Suez Crisis and the Hungarian Crisis.

The Suez Crisis

On July 19, 1956, Colonel Nasser in Egypt was bluntly informed by the United States State Department that the offer of American aid towards the High Dam would be withdrawn. Nasser's riposte came promptly. On July 26, in a speech at Alexandria, he declared the nationalization of the Suez Canal, which would provide revenues for the building of the High Dam. Next day, in the Commons in Westminster, Eden made only a brief reference to the Egyptian Government's unilateral act of expropriation in breach of existing agreements and in prejudice to the rights and interests of many nations. Gaitskell, for the Opposition, duly deplored "this high-handed and totally unjustifiable step." In the course of the next few days Eden consulted the French Government, the Commonwealth governments, and President Eisenhower. The arguments on his side seemed sound and simple, and concurrence could hardly be denied or delayed. The sanctity of treaties, Western prestige in the East, the free operation of an indispensable international utility, all these were under threat, not merely from Egyptian nationalism, but from a new upstart demagogue and dictator. Eden defined his position in a few words:

> No arrangements for the future of this great international waterway could be acceptable to Her Majesty's Government which would leave it in the unfettered control of a single power which could, as recent events have shown, exploit it purely for purposes of national policy.

At this stage Eden could surely be forgiven for believing that he had all the support, moral and material, that he needed. He could not have foreseen that the apparent sympathy accorded him by the Labor Party at home and by the United States abroad should have so quickly turned to hostility.

Gaitskell, after his first brave declaration in the Commons, had somewhat lamely climbed down, and he even seemed not averse from using the crisis for domestic political ends. Gaitskell had evidently not counted on his own back-benchers, among whom, as he soon discovered, there existed a vociferous faction unconditionally opposed to "imperialism" or to "gunboat diplomacy" in any shape or form. Eden could see no good purpose in referring the Egyptian dispute to the United Nations, especially in a situation which required immediate and decisive action. The Egyptian Government for the past four years had disregarded the Security Council's resolution to give Israeli ships the free passage of the Canal; and, if this were not enough, the Soviet Union always stood ready with its perpetual veto. But Labor now insisted that all the formalities of the United Nations Charter be faithfully carried out, and Labor could only applaud when the General Assembly, on November 2, 1956, by 64 votes to 5, adopted a resolution calling for an immediate cease-fire in Egypt and, by implication, condemned British and French policy. Throughout these weeks public opinion polls in Britain showed the country almost exactly bisected along party lines – with a surprisingly small percentage of "Don't Knows."

For Eden, the position was disastrous. At home he had a violently divided country behind him; and abroad only France was with him. In the United States President Eisenhower and his Secretary of State John Foster Dulles were in the midst of presidential elections and committed to noninvolvement. Dulles' policy in the Middle East had all the marks of Stimson's policy in the Far East twenty-five years before. He could preach, but he could not chastise – nor did he himself seem to have the wish to chastise. Dulles furthermore had the best reasons, as he thought, for seeing that no one else performed the chastisement. In the end Eden resolved on military action in Egypt without consulting Commonwealth governments – not even the Australian or the New Zealand – without consulting NATO or his allies of the Baghdad Pact, and without final notification to the United States. Herein perhaps was his most inexplicable and most inexcusable blunder. On October 31, 1956, British and French aircraft began bombing Egyptian airfields preparatory to landing operations in the Canal Zone. The Israeli invasion of Egypt was already in full career. The Hungarian Crisis had broken simultaneously; Soviet tanks and artillery at that moment were battering Budapest. (See p. 674.) But the Soviet Government was not therefore deterred from submitting a highly provocative resolution to the Security Council, under Article 42 of the Charter, proposing that the Soviet armed forces cooperate with the armed forces of other members of the United Nations, especially the United States, to halt Anglo-French aggression against Egypt. Moscow radio issued veiled threats of atomic retaliation on London and Paris.

We shall elsewhere describe events in Egypt and in the Middle East. (See pp. 795ff.) In Britain, Parliament reopened for its new session on November 6, 1956. The cease-fire in Egypt was agreed the same day, and Parliament was left somewhat anticlimactically to conduct its post-mortem on the crisis. By the curious logic or illogic of the democratic human being, public interest in the crisis was already subsiding. At a by-election at Chester on November 15, a safe Conservative seat, which might have been expected to serve as a test of feeling in the country, the Conservative vote fell by only 5 per cent. Opinion polls at this time were showing a slight pro-Eden upswing. The main weight of debate seemed to have been transferred to Washington and to the United Nations in New York, where Selwyn Lloyd, the British Foreign Secretary, was now battling for the good name of his maligned and misunderstood homeland. On November 19, Eden, suffering from "severe overstrain," left for a three-weeks' holiday in Jamaica. To all intents and purposes, except for its economic consequences – notably its effect on oil supplies – the Suez Crisis was over. Public bodies and employers' associations were then busy finding homes and jobs for the influx of Hungarian refugees.

Early in January 1957, under medical advice, Eden resigned office and went into complete retirement. He was suceeded by Macmillan as Prime Minister, with Butler as Home Secretary and Thorneycroft as Chancellor of the Exchequer. Selwyn Lloyd remained Foreign Secretary.

Britain now entered upon a period of extraordinary quiet. Harold Macmillan as Prime Minister, suave and unhurried, inspired increasing confidence and popularity. There was almost a new sense of normalcy in the air. Obviously crises might break from time to time – the world by now was used to trouble and expected it – and the Chancellor of the Exchequer periodically gave out warnings about the country's adverse trade balance. And then always in the background was the nagging ache of the existence of the atom bomb. But at least the Second World War and its most painful associations seemed to be receding into history. By 1958 young persons who had never seen a wartime ration card or clothes coupon were completing their education and entering workaday life. Meanwhile the familiar political round under a vaguely paternalistic government went on. Thorneycroft, the Chancellor of the Exchequer, resigned, presumably over government expenditure, and was succeeded by Heathcoat Amory. Discussions were started on joining a European Free Trade Association, to the great alarm of the trade unions and to the even greater alarm of the farming community. (See p. 720.) The public in general showed little interest in this economic tangle. At the moment Cyprus – a crisis compounded of Ireland, India, and Palestine, all in one – was much more important.

A general election was held in October 1959, and the Conservative party for the third time made gains at the expense of Labor. Shortly after the election, Lord Home became Foreign Secretary, and Selwyn Lloyd Chancellor of the Exchequer. In November Britain joined the European Free Trade Association. The Labor party resumed its agonizing self-examination, and some hopeful critics were predicting that it would shortly go into total dissolution, in which case, presumably, the Liberal party might revive. The press reported pockets of unemployment, especially in Scotland. But generally the economic barometer was fair. Perhaps the average British household was harried and worried by the increasing detail of modern civilized living. The tax burden and the bureaucratic overhead were atrocious. Nevertheless, not since 1928 – indeed not since 1914 – had the country as a whole been so prosperous, even if at times the prosperity seemed a little brittle. Macmillan's Conservative government was not far wrong in its election boast, "You have never had it so good!" If not the Welfare State, then the Affluent Society was coming to birth in Britain.

The British Commonwealth

The postwar years saw great changes in the British Commonwealth and Empire – or perhaps it would be truer to say that they saw the further and faster development of existing trends. The new Dominions of India, Pakistan, and Ceylon were formed; Burma became an independent republic. Newfoundland joined Canada. Events of the greatest importance took place in Egypt and the Sudan, Malaya, the British West Indies, and the tropical African colonies. The Palestine mandate was brought to an end. South Africa became an independent republic.

These changes and developments, at first sight, might seem to add up to a loosening of ties and an abdication of British power in the general line of the "Decline of the West." But they are not open to quite so facile an interpretation. The British Commonwealth and Empire in the postwar years was still a great field of experiment in human welfare. It was still served by some of the finest administrative talent that its many races could produce. In the world of postwar power politics, it had great strength and great weakness. We cannot hope, in a short section, to review even a fraction of this interesting piece of history. Sections on India, Burma, Malaya, Egypt, and Palestine in other chapters must suffice for a continuation of what we have written on these countries in earlier chapters of the book. (See pp. 771-73 and 773-77.) But it might be appropriate, in the present context, to discuss especially those aspects of post-1945 Commonwealth politics that were of "international" significance.

In Chapter 15 we described the growth of British imperial ideology during the interwar period. In 1939 the Dominions had severally entered the Second World War as sovereign powers according to their several constitutional procedures. Ireland had remained neutral. It is to be noted, for instance, that Canada's declaration of war on Germany in September 1939 followed that of Britain by some days and her declaration of war on Japan in December 1941 preceded that of Britain by some hours. The Dominions made their several contributions to the war effort, and they made them independently. They mobilized their own resources, recruited their own forces, appointed their own commanders, and participated as equals in high strategic discussions. Since 1945 the Dominions again advanced in international status. They were separately members of the United Nations and separately represented at the San Francisco Conference in 1945, at the Paris Peace Conference in 1947, and at other international conferences of the time. They increasingly made diplomatic appointments in foreign capitals.

In an age of rapid travel and communication the technical problems of imperial consultation were never easier, but a greater political decentralization was both sought and achieved. Mackenzie King, the Canadian Prime Minister, always emphasized his desire for complete informality in Commonwealth relations and urged that every care should be taken not only to leave each Dominion in unfettered control of its own affairs but to avoid even the appearance of an explicit and unified "Commonwealth point of view." Anything in the nature of a permanent imperial Secretariat, such as was sometimes proposed, would have been quite impossible. Except for existing official channels, the instrument of imperial consultation would continue to be the periodic conferences of Dominion Prime Ministers or of other ministers.

As for Britain herself, two World Wars left her with such diminished resources that she could hardly be expected to bear the same weight of responsibility as heretofore, and she was glad enough to relegate a greater share of the old imperial burden to her partners. The loans that she received from Canada and South Africa in 1946 and 1947 and the outright monetary gifts from Australia and New Zealand, gave a clear indication of her changed position. Furthermore, over the same period of the two World Wars, the entire demographic basis of the Commonwealth had shifted. With her falling birth rate, Britain had ceased to be one of the world's great exporters of men, and the white Dominions would now have to rely more and more on their own human resources or on non-British immigration for the peopling of their territories.

Within the "Dependent Empire" perhaps the most delicate of all political problems in these years was that of the transfer of power. Independence was the order of the day, but there were always the questions, When and How? Local independence leaders were often "difficult" men — they would hardly have followed their calling otherwise — and also they were often men of extreme simplicity, dedicated to one idea. Outside their careers of agitation or of the more violent forms of revolt, they had only the slightest political experience or understanding of the complexities of modern government. In their creed "freedom" was the universal solution — "Seek ye first the political kingdom and the rest shall be added unto you" [1] — and naturally enough delays in the achievement of their ambitions could only be blamed on the incorrigible wickedness of the imperial power. Yet Britain was probably as successful as any such imperial power in timing the great moment of independence and in ensuring that a minimum cadre of trained personnel existed to fill the adminstrative vacuum that might be left after her withdrawal. Moreover, both before and after independence, schemes for economic aid and technical collaboration were worked out — such as the Colombo Plan [2] — schemes which, however meager they seemed, might still help a little in territories of proverbial poverty and latterly of uncontrolled increase of population. (See pp. 773ff and 804ff.)

Canada came out of the Second World War with an impressive military and economic record and an enormously enhanced international importance. She had vast natural resources, and she had long been one of the principal food-exporting countries of the world, and the war had greatly expanded her industrial economy. After the United States, Britain, and the Soviet Union, she had been fourth largest producer of war materials for the United Nations. Her total war budget had exceeded $16,000,000,000 and, alone among the United Nations, she had received no Lend-Lease aid from the United States. Since 1945 it had become known that she possessed some of the richest uranium deposits in the world.

Canada's inclusion in the Security Council of the United Nations in 1947 was no more than an acknowledgment of her new position. She was an Atlantic, Pacific, American, and British Power. She was a naval and air power of no small consequence. Willy-nilly, she would have to take her part in the world's affairs. Two factors had always governed, and would now continue to govern, her international behavior, first her internal tensions, arising to a great extent out of her dual English and French nationalism, and second her contiguity to the United States. Big in area, she had less than one tenth the population of her southern neighbor, and it was inevitable that, despite French Canadian dislike of American influence, the events of 1941-45 would draw her to that neighbor. In August 1940 – before Pearl Harbor, be it noted – under the Ogdensburg Agreement, Canada and the United States had created a Permanent Joint Board of Defense at Washington. (See p. 534.) Though born of wartime emergency, the very title of the Board implied that military cooperation between the two powers would be prolonged beyond the close of hostilities. The United States retained the bases in Newfoundland acquired in the "Destroyers-for-Bases-Deal" in 1940. (See p. 534.) The continual exchange of service personnel, the standardization of arms, and the mutual availability of naval and air facilities, the Alaska Highway – and to some extent the St. Lawrence Seaway scheme – were all consequences of the implicit American alliance.

With the onset of the Cold War, Canada's Arctic territories assumed a new strategic importance. The Permanent Joint Board of Defense, aimed originally at Germany and Japan across the Atlantic and Pacific oceans, had now to reorientate itself to quite another direction. The Canada of the atomic age was no longer a "fireproof house" lying on the safe periphery of world events, but rather the buffer state of a Third World War. The shortest line from Moscow to New York lay across the Province of Quebec. In Alaska and British Columbia, moreover, was a still unforgotten tradition of Russian expansionism that the Soviet Union might at any time revive. Thus the United States planned a network of airfields and early warning stations from Alaska to Greenland. American and Canadian forces carried out expeditions and maneuvers to study the paralyzing effects of the awful temperatures in these far latitudes on human and mechanical efficiency.

Isolationist Canadians, particularly the French Canadians, no doubt resented this unexpected inversion of their onetime geographical immunity and the resulting intrusion of Americans in their affairs, just at a time when they were congratulating themselves on the widening gulf between their country and Britain. But whatever the views of these Canadians, they could not deny that for better or for worse they were now part and parcel of the strategic requirements of the Western Hemisphere, and the more realistic-minded Canadians of whatever race made a virtue of necessity and began to take the inevitable for granted. Then, during 1946, investigations by a Royal Commission revealed the existence of a Soviet spy ring, emanating from the Soviet military attaché in Ottawa, which had been trying to obtain information on atomic energy and radar from Canadian government employees and research workers and even from the Progressive-Labor

(Communist) Member of the Canadian House of Commons. If there was one thing that united Canadians, whether French-speaking or English, whether Catholic or Protestant, whether isolationist or nonisolationist, that thing was the detestation of Communism. In 1949 Canada was an initiator and founder member of the North Atlantic Pact, and all her parties and communities were agreed in support of it.

Canada's internal politics, meanwhile, consisted of the old rivalry between her Conservative and Liberal parties – the Conservative to some extent representing the English-speaking interest, and the Liberal the French-speaking interest. In 1947 Mackenzie King completed his twentieth year as Liberal Prime Minister of Canada. The following year he was succeeded by the Liberal Louis St. Laurent. In 1957 St. Laurent was defeated by the Progressive Conservative John Diefenbaker. But internationally, Canada's internal politics was of relatively minor importance. Except for pockets of unemployment, inevitable in a free and expanding economy, Canada's own affairs today are as prosperous as anywhere in the world, her two main communities are at peace with one another, and her future is as bright as the conditions of this critical mid-century allow.

Australia and New Zealand presented a wholly different set of circumstances and consequently a different attitude to Commonwealth relations. Their populations were predominantly of British origin, and their internal divisions arose, not from race or nationality, but from political partisanship. Australia had the old rivalry between Conservative (Country and Liberal parties) and Labor, and latterly she had both a strong Communist party and politically minded Catholic community; New Zealand had a simpler and less violent partisan division between her National and Labor parties. Consequently Australia and New Zealand were Dominions which, though more distant from Britain geographically, had closer ties with Britain than any other country of the Commonwealth. Both had come out of the war, as had Canada, with an impressive military record, considerable industrial development, and a greatly increased international importance. They were represented at international conferences by men well known for the force and candor of their views. But for all that they were too weak and isolated to stand alone in the new world of the Cold War.

The foreign policies of Australia and New Zealand post-1945 seemed a contradiction of assertiveness and uncertainty. Released from the overwhelming fear of foreign conquest – when British help at a critical moment had failed them – they hardly knew where their future security lay. They resented and welcomed the admitted American supremacy in the Pacific. Labor governments, first installed in Australia in 1941 and in New Zealand in 1935, continued in office till 1949. For the best part of the years 1945, say till 1948, the two Dominions – indeed like the United States, or, for that matter, Britain – could enjoy a momentary isolationism, devoted to domestic issues. Labor leadership gave them a somewhat "liberal" attitude towards international relations. For instance they participated – Australia actively, New Zealand by an observer only – in the Asian Conference in Delhi in January 1949, held to condemn "Dutch aggression in Indonesia."

But at the end of 1949, their Labor parties were defeated, and with the coming of more Conservative governments came also more militant and outward-looking foreign policies. Both Australia and New Zealand sent contingents to Korea in 1950, they joined with the United States in the ANZUS Pact of 1951, and they also joined in the weaker but more comprehensive SEATO in 1954. (See pp. 752, 779, 783-84, and 792.)

South Africa was the one Dominion which, even after 1949, could be said to have continued to enjoy relative strategic independence and consequently to indulge the luxury of a restive internal politics undisturbed by external menace. She regarded all African affairs as her affairs, and her cardinal policy was the security and *status quo* of the whole continent. The decline of French and Italian, and the disappearance of the German, influence in Africa had left herself and Britain – and perhaps Egypt – as the only countries with the pretensions of a power in her part of the world. But the growing divergence of view, as between her own Boer and British citizens, regarding the treatment of her colored peoples and concerning the part those colored peoples should be expected to play in their own future, infected her entire relationship with the British tropical African colonies, where far-reaching economic and political developments and liberal racial policies were about to be introduced. Her handling of her Indian minority was a matter of increasing protest in India and Pakistan, if not in all Asian countries, and of acute embarrassment to Britain.

In September 1939, General Smuts had formed a coalition government, and, for six years he had guided a loyal South African participation in the war. Smuts himself had played the role of a representative Allied statesman and cofounder of the United Nations. Nationalist parties under General Hertzog and Dr. Daniel F. Malan had tried, but failed, to form a united Opposition. Hertzog moreover had fouled his own nest with his pro-Nazi utterances. In 1942 he had died, and the extreme Malan found himself the Nationalist leader. Meanwhile the German invasion and treatment of Holland had clinched the sympathies of the Boers with the Allied cause. South African forces fought in Kenya, Ethiopia, North Africa, and afterward in Europe. But 1945 brought back the old-time rifts. The Indian question in Natal and the Transvaal was already to the fore before the war was over. Serious droughts and more serious soil erosion gave great distress to farmers. A cabinet reshuffle left Smuts and his United party alone in the government. The United Nations General Assembly declined to approve South Africa's incorporation of Southwest Africa and failed to obtain South Africa's consent to the transference of the territory to the new Trusteeship Council. In the spring of 1947, the King and the royal family made a state visit to South Africa, and the evident enthusiasm with which they were received perhaps concealed the approaching Nationalist swing of South African politics.

Meanwhile South Africa was immensely prosperous, but the benefits were hardly being equitably distributed among her people. The usual stresses and strains of an industrial revolution were now being increased beyond measure by the fact that the labor force was largely native and the managerial elite was exclusively white. Johannesburg had even worse slums in the middle twentieth century than any European city had had in the middle nineteenth. All political and economic alignments sharply reflected the dominant racial issue. In elections in May 1948, Smuts was defeated, and Malan formed a government with the declared platform of apartheid, or segregation. Under his administration new property acts and education acts were rushed through; the mobility of labor within the Union was restricted by various "Pass Laws"; mixed marriages were made illegal. Acts for the Suppression of Commission were obviously aimed at native unrest of any kind. An attempt by the government to remove 50,000 "colored" voters from the common roll, or common voters' registration, in Cape Province, where most of these voters lived, was disputed on constitutional grounds by the Supreme Court.[3] Smuts died on September 11, 1950, at the height of the Supreme Court controversy, and with the loss of Smuts, it seemed, went also the last hopes of liberal solutions in South Africa.

In elections in April 1953, Malan's Nationalists were returned with a slightly increased majority. Malan himself retired from politics in the following year and was succeeded by Johannes G. Strijdom, a Transvaaler and a Republican, a stronger supporter of apartheid – if that were possible – than Malan. South African policies and politics continued uncompromisingly along Nationalist lines – to a general chorus of protest from other Commonwealth countries, notably India and Pakistan, from the newly growing Afro-Asian bloc in the United Nations, and also from moderate South Africans – and to South African counterprotest, which was now taking the form of agitation to cut loose from the British connection and to declare South Africa an independent republic. In August 1958, after Strijdom's death, Dr. Hendrik F. Verwoerd, a man of similar convictions, became Prime Minister.

Bloodshed sooner or later was perhaps inevitable. It occurred on March 21, 1960, at Sharpeville, a township near Vereeniging, when the police shot down seventy anti-Pass Law demonstrators. Three weeks later an attempt was made upon the life of Verwoerd himself by a white farmer from Johannesburg. As we write, the future of South Africa would seem to be dismal indeed. The Afrikaner is now committed to a policy which he cannot change, even if he would. In March 1961, at the Commonwealth Prime Ministers Conference in London, in view of the "hostility and vindictiveness" shown to his country, Verwoerd "regretfully" withdrew South Africa's membership from the Commonwealth. On May 31, 1961, South Africa was proclaimed an independent republic.

Ireland

Finally there was Ireland.[4] There was always Ireland! Ireland had declared herself neutral in September 1939, and remained so throughout the war. Her Prime Minister, de Valera, refrained from raising controversial issues and made only occasional passing references to Partition, the "unnatural dismemberment" of Northern Ireland from the South which was the "obstacle to unified defense." Ireland suffered severe shipping shortages and consequent coal and gasoline shortages, and in general she was far from finding herself in the favored economic position she had enjoyed in the First World War. The use of her ports was strictly denied to the British and Allied navies. The diplomatic representatives of the Axis remained in Dublin, converting the city, as the British said, into a second Lisbon, a veritable hive of enemy espionage and propaganda. The government rejected requests for their expulsion in 1944 from the United States and Britain. In May 1945, de Valera expressed his formal condolences to the German minister in Dublin on the death of Hitler. Meanwhile, of course, Northern Ireland had entered the war as part of the United Kingdom and had played a full part in it. Londonderry somewhat compensated for the loss of the neutral Irish ports.

The end of the war in 1945 immediately revived an interest in Ireland's international status. De Valera was at pains to develop his thesis of "external association." "We are an independent Republic," he said, "associated as a matter of external policy with the States of the British Commonwealth." He reaffirmed his adherence to the External Relations Act of 1936. (See p. 275.) But generally, in the early postwar years, Ireland seemed to be more concerned with the usual contemporary problems of trade deficits and the dollar shortage. There were only occasional references to Partition in the debates in the Dail. Ireland applied for membership in the United Nations in 1946 and again in 1947, her application on each occasion being vetoed by the Soviet Union. However, Ireland was included in the European Recovery Program and was one of the first countries to receive assistance. It seemed at this time that Ireland had somewhat forsaken her fractious past and would lie quietly on the fringes of Commonwealth and international politics.

But at elections in February 1948, de Valera and his Fianna Fail party lost their absolute majority in the Dail, and a coalition of former antigovernment parties was formed by John A. Costello, leader of the Fine Gael party. The new government's platform was entirely domestic, and it was therefore a matter of some surprise, when suddenly, in the summer of 1948, Partition once more became a burning issue. "The continuance of this grave injustice," said Costello, "precludes us from taking our rightful place in the world." And, sure enough, in December 1948, the Dail passed a Republic of Ireland Act, repealing the External Relations Act and incidentally renaming the country the "Republic of Ireland," thus breaking the last tenuous tie with the British Crown.

Thereafter Ireland once more relapsed into domestic politics, occasionally enlivened by "incidents" by the "Irish Republican Army" across the border in Northern Ireland, incidents which the Irish Government strongly disavowed. She joined the United Nations in the "package deal" of 1955, but resolutely refused to prejudice her neutrality by joining NATO. Through the 1950's de Valera and Costello were in and out of the Premiership. De Valera was Premier in 1951, then Costello in 1954, then De Valera again in 1957. De Valera was elected President of the Irish Republic in June 1959.

Meanwhile Northern Ireland remained true to the British allegiance. In 1949 Sir Basil Brooke, the Prime Minister of Northern Ireland, stoutly reaffirmed his loyalty to the Crown and Commonwealth. Parliament in London passed an act declaring that Northern Ireland would not cease to be a part of His Majesty's dominions and of the United Kingdom "without the consent of the Parliament of Northern Ireland."

40. THE UNITED STATES: RESPONSIBILITY AND REARMAMENT

Postwar Reactions

Twice in one short generation had the United States been forced out of a traditional isolation to participate in world wars; twice had it made a major contribution to the victory of the side it had espoused; twice had it acquired an all but decisive leadership among its fellow nations. But the second occasion left it in a position very different from the first. After the Second World War, its economic power was relatively greater; it had only one chief partner, or rival, in the policies it intended to pursue; and its people had reached a state of political sophistication which made another isolationist relapse impracticable and unlikely. The conviction was general that with the Second World War, the old order was gone forever; that the growing range and deadliness of modern weapons made mock of any security that still relied on distance; that in the One World of the future, no nation could again live to itself alone; and that, in short, the fortunes of mankind, in war or peace, were henceforth indivisible.

From the middle 1930's to the middle 1940's the American economy had been stimulated by the demands of approaching or actual war. The national income, which had been $74,000,000,000 in 1937, was $182,000,000,000 in 1944. Despite the transfer of 12,000,000 men and women to the armed forces, industrial production rose by 80 per cent, and agricultural production by 36 per cent. The strong upward surge of agricultural prices raised the net farm income from $6,400,000,000 to $18,200,000,000. But after 1945, whatever was to happen to these massive figures – whether they rose, stood stable, or declined – would depend upon the wider state of world affairs. Prosperity was no longer a function of domestic supply and demand. Even in the latter 1930's full production had been increasingly dependent on the existence of foreign markets. By 1938 American exports had already exceeded those of every other country and amounted to 14 per cent of the total value of the world's international trade. The American people in 1945 were acutely aware that another "boom and bust" might cost them their newly won international position, and that their economic system — their very democracy — stood as an example to all the world and especially to that part of it that wanted and expected them to fail.

In the sphere of strategy, the long period of effortless and almost unconscious security had ended. In the nineteenth century, the main aggressive power centers of the world were to be found in Europe. The British Navy then dominated the Atlantic approaches to the New World. The United States and its hemispheric neighbors were safe from European encroachment, unless, as in 1812, the encroachment was made by Britain herself, or unless, as in 1861, it was made with her consent. Further, the European powers were otherwise absorbed by the tasks of national unification, economic development, and imperialist expansion in Africa and the East. On the Pacific approaches, Japan with her British alliance seemed more likely to become a counterpoise to Russian aggression than a threat to American tranquillity. In this isolationist Elysium, the United States was left largely unmolested to solve its own tasks of national unification, its expansion into the West, and its modest imperialist ventures in the Philippines and Caribbean Sea.

But from 1915 onward, a new weapon, the submarine, demonstrated the insufficiency of the old British naval cordon; in 1941 the bomber and torpedo plane penetrated the very bases of the American fleet; and in 1945 the atom bomb, the ultimate weapon of offense, roughly took away the last lingering vestiges of geographical security. Meanwhile the international primacy of Europe had fallen away, leaving the United States and the Soviet Union, two powers of profoundly different ways of life, whose peaceful or warlike relations would now be the main determinants in the future history of the world. The general situation as it faced the American people in 1945 was full of novelty, responsibility, and danger.

Yet, while their statesmen may warn, people are notoriously resistant to change, and the provocation must be obvious and constant if they are not to relax or slip back into their accustomed ways. After 1945 the American people at least showed a spirit of cooperation with the outer world. The United States was a member, indeed the dominating member, of the United Nations, the Specialized Agencies, the International Court, the Atomic Energy Commission, and the Control Councils in Germany and Austria. But the American people were still impatient and uncertain of the new policy. They had given their heads, but not their hearts. At home, their main object seemed to be to return to the old free economy that was their tradition, even if they did so more as a reaction from the irritations and inhibitions of the war than from a deep conviction that that economy was now, in fact, continuable. Thus industrial controls were lifted, armed forces were demobilized, ships laid up, airfields junked, despite the half-confessed mental reservation that, given a business recession of the too familiar type, or another threat of war, there might again be a need for all these unpleasant things. The American people in 1945-46 looked almost as if they were trying to make the most of an interval of unchallengeable supremacy before the full burdens of the future descended upon them. They alone held the grand secret of atomic energy, and they could indulge in a last furlough of normalcy while the monopoly lasted.

"The nation's release from the urgency of war," reported General Eisenhower in January 1946, "started an emotional wave to get men out of the army . . . This is wholly understandable . . . But I am frank to say that I never anticipated that this emotional wave would reach the proportions of near-hysteria." In round numbers, 5,000,000 had been demobilized by that date, 7,000,000 by April 1946, and 9,000,000 by July 1946. The War Department and the State Department were expressing some anxiety lest the country's armed strength should fall below the requirements of its occupation undertakings in Europe and the East and of its foreign policy in general. But it was the same with industry and labor. New technical equipment and increased capacity were waiting, nay straining, for the signal to go into full production of consumer goods. Businessmen, exasperated by wartime restrictions, rushed to take advantage of pent-up demands at home and of hungry foreign markets once served by Germany and Japan. Organized labor pressed no less insistently for the scrapping of wage controls. The general public, flushed by new earnings, and demobilized men with gratuities all demanded a carefree spending revel. There was in particular an acute housing shortage – over 1,000,000 moderate-priced dwelling units were required for returned veterans alone. Thus the War Production Board, which had regulated the production effort of the nation by a strict system of priorities and allocations, finished its business and ceased operations by December 1945. The Office of Price Administration (OPA), under Chester Bowles, fought a losing battle against inflation, and its powers, chipped away by Congress in response to ardent lobbies, were virtually defunct by midsummer 1946. Food prices, which had crept upward by 50 per cent since Pearl Harbor, jumped an additional 60 per cent between that July and October. Meanwhile the automobile, steel, and oil industries and the railroads were rent by strikes. John L. Lewis, the working man's hero of the hour, won successive wage increases for his United Mine Workers in the teeth of the government's threat to take over the strike-bound mines and of the Supreme Court's ruling against the illegality of his tactics.

In November 1946, in the Congressional elections, the Republicans won substantial minorities – 57 in the House and 6 in the Senate. One result was the Labor-Management Relations Act, more generally known as the Taft-Hartley Act, which became law over the President's veto in June 1947, and which allowed employers to sue unions for damages committed by their members in the course of industrial disputes, prohibited the use of union funds to support candidates for political offices, empowered the government to serve injunctions against strikes likely to disable the national economy, and outlawed the closed shop. Nonetheless, despite the worsening of labor relations and despite the warnings of the President himself against inflation and against Congressional obstruction, the plain fact was that civilian employment was good, and the market at home and abroad buoyant. At least the United States would now enter the Cold War with its domestic affairs going strong and true to form.

The "Cold War"

The first disturbing signs of the Cold War were appeals for aid from former allies. The Second World War had cost the American people over $300,000,000,000, and, if this was not enough, there now was UNRRA and the other philanthropic activities of the United Nations. In September 1945, Lend-Lease was terminated, and the very abruptness with which it was terminated showed how little Congressional opinion appreciated its indispensability to its recipients. Total Lend-Lease expenditures had amounted to $48,500,000,000, compared with $7,800,000,000 in reverse Lend-Lease. In a "master" settlement with Britain, British liabilities were scaled down from over $31,000,000,000 to $650,000,000, thus setting an example for similar settlements elsewhere. Yet, in that same September, despite these American generosities, Britain was requesting a loan of $3,750,000,000 to tide her over the transition from war to peace. (See p. 724.) In July 1946, after a discursive and occasionally acid debate, Congress gave a very dubious assent to the loan. But, by that date, almost every European country, with the conspicuous exceptions of Yugoslavia and the Soviet Union, had become recipients of new American loans amounting to $1,830,000,000. Once more the old isolationist resentment of the American people against Europe as the ancient breeding ground of wars and of distasteful, ungrateful ideologies was struggling with their humanitarian and missionary instinct to succor distress wherever it might be and however incontinently caused.

By 1946 the policies of cooperation and financial relief were becoming another name for "containment" of the Soviet Union. By imperceptible stages the work of world peace and recovery, to which the United States was now being committed, resolved itself into a species of warfare, the "Cold War," as it was called, of unlimited incidence and extent. On March 15, 1946, when Churchill made his "iron curtain" speech at Fulton, Missouri, there were many who protested that the incorrigible old "warmonger" was up to his tricks again and deplored his misuse of American courtesy to air his private prejudices against Russian Communism. But Churchill was not far wrong, and within the year, American aid was going to those countries particularly menaced by Soviet expansion – notably in the Balkans and Middle East, areas in which, it so happened, Churchill had once before tried to enlist American interest. (See p. 595.)

Greece, enfeebled by Axis invasion and occupation, had been kept in a state of uproar by Communist-led guerrillas constantly supplied and reinforced from Bulgaria, Yugoslavia, and Albania, all members of the Soviet bloc. A small British occupying force was trying to maintain the peace and loyalty of the harassed country. Late in 1946 the Greek Government asked the United States for a considerable sum for postwar reconstruction. Meanwhile, during 1946, Turkey had been confronted by repeated Soviet demands for a share in the defense of the Dardanelles and for the return of Kars and Ardahan, ceded by Russia to Turkey in 1918 under the Treaty of Brest Litovsk. The maintenance of a Turkish army of 650,000 men, mobilized in response to this persistent Soviet war of nerves, swallowed up half of Turkey's national budget. Then, during discussions in the Foreign Ministers Council on the Italian peace treaty, the Soviet Union had advanced claims for a trusteeship of Tripolitania. All in all, the Soviet's determination to break out of its strategic prison in the Black Sea was being very forcibly brought to the notice of its wartime allies. In January 1947, a mission of American economic experts was sent to Greece to study Greek requirements. The mission had not yet reported when the British Government informed the State Department that the economic and military support which Britain had been giving Greece and Turkey since 1945 would have to be discontinued after March 31, and, if necessary, the two countries would have to be abandoned to Soviet control. The economic situation in Britain which had dictated this decision must have been serious indeed to have thus driven her to renounce her century-old policy of excluding Russian influence from the Near East.

On March 12, 1947, in an address of exceptional urgency to a joint session of Congress, President Truman enunciated the policy called after him the "Truman Doctrine." He opened with a somber reflection on the gravity of the world situation and, in exemplification, made particular reference to Greece and Turkey. The very survival of Greece as a free nation, he said, was menaced by a militant, Communist-led minority which was exploiting human want and misery to create political chaos. And Turkey was in like straits. Truman continued:

> I believe that it must be the policy of the United States to support free peoples who are resisting attempted subjugation by armed minorities or by outside pressures. I believe that we must assist free peoples to work out their own destinies in their own way. I believe that our help should be primarily through economic and financial aid which is essential to economic stability and orderly political processes . . .
>
> The free peoples of the world look to us for support in maintaining their freedoms. If we falter in our leadership, we may endanger the peace of the world — and we shall surely endanger the welfare of our own nation. Great responsibilities have been placed upon us by the swift movement of events . . .

And he requested that $400,000,000 be applied for assistance to Greece and Turkey and that civilian and military missions be sent to instruct and train Greek and Turkish personnel.

American public opinion was still unprepared for a departure of policy so bold and comprehensive. Congress and people were far from convinced that all nations threatened by totalitarian penetration should automatically qualify for American assistance. It was argued that the sums represented an initial step toward unprecedented and incalculable commitments abroad, that the United States was entangling itself in the bankrupt traditions of Old World diplomacy, and that aid to needy countries should be internationally sponsored and disbursed through the United Nations. Nonetheless, the Greek-Turkish Aid Act was eventually passed by Congress, with respectable majorities, and was signed by the President on May 22, 1947.

President Truman greeting Secretary Marshall on his return from Paris and London, December 19, 1947, after negotiations over the European Recovery Program

UNITED PRESS INTERNATIONAL

But more was to come and to come soon. On May 8, 1947, while the Greek-Turkish Aid Act was still in its final stages, Undersecretary of State Dean Acheson, in a speech at Cleveland, pointed to the yawning gap between current American exports of $16,000,000,000 and imports of $8,000,000,000, and affirmed that the imbalance must be remedied by increased imports, a removal of trade barriers, and further loans – indeed that, until the countries of the world were once more self-supporting there could be no lasting peace or prosperity for anyone. The speech suggested that the new installment of aid to Europe should not be presented in the controversial form of an anti-Communist bribe, but as a comprehensive program of economic stabilization advantageous to the giver and the receivers alike. Thus, on June 5 at Harvard University, Secretary of State George C. Marshall laid down the principles that were shortly to be embodied in the European Recovery Program.

We have already described the European Recovery Program (ERP) as it appeared to its European beneficiaries. (See pp. 711-13.) In the United States, the implementation of the scheme was initiated on June 22, 1947, by Truman's announcement that he had submitted the proposals to three committees for advice. An official committee under Secretary of the Interior Julius A. Krug reported that the natural resources of the United States, agricultural land excepted, would not be inordinately depleted by the contemplated aid to Europe. The President's Council of Economic Advisers reported favorably on the capacity of the American economy to bear the burden of a further foreign aid program without creating hardships and restrictions at home. An unofficial committee under Secretary of Commerce Averill Harriman measured the availability of American resources against the needs of the sixteen nations. It whittled down the original estimate of $22,400,000,000 to an absolute maximum of $17,000,000,000. Meanwhile, two hundred congressmen of both parties were touring Europe to inform themselves at first hand of current conditions. In December 1947, Congress passed the Interim Aid Act, providing a "stopgap" aid of $597,000,000 to France, Italy, Austria, and China, while the larger ERP was still under debate.

The American people, on the whole, appeared to give a qualified approval to ERP. The political left still demanded loudly but vainly a nondiscriminatory program under the auspices of the United Nations. The Middle West, where isolationism lingered most stubbornly, disliked the idea of bearing continued taxation for the benefit of an incurably spendthrift Europe. But the great majority appreciated ERP as an indirect shoring-up of markets at home and abroad and therefore as an insurance against the postwar slump that many were still half-expecting "somewhere around the next corner" – and finally as a logical extension of the administration's now established bipartisan anti-Soviet policy. Even so the progress of the new legislation in Congress would have been slow and minutely contested if events in Europe had not played into its sponsors' hands, notably the collapse of the Foreign Ministers' conference in London in December 1947, the Communist coup in Czechoslovakia in February 1948, and finally the alarming situation in Italy, where the Communist party was campaigning to take power at the next elections. (See pp. 705-06.)

The Foreign Assistance Act, as it was called, passed both houses by a voice vote on April 2, 1948, and was signed by Truman the following day. It provided for a single package of $5,300,000,000 for the first year of ERP, $465,000,000 for China, and a further $275,000,000 for Greece and Turkey. Conditions were stiff and elaborate. The beneficiaries were to take steps to stabilize currencies, balance budgets, reduce tariffs, remove restrictive trade practices, control inflation, furnish the United States with strategic materials and, if required, deny the same materials to nonparticipant nations. Future aid would be voted annually, when presumably Congress would have the opportunity of periodic re-examination of the plan. President Truman nominated Paul Hoffman, president of the Studebaker Corporation, as chief of the Economic Cooperation Administration (ECA), which was to be the agency of the program in Washington, and nominated Harriman as "roving ambassador" and observer for the program in Europe. On April 16, as we have described elsewhere, the sixteen European nations created their counterpart Organization of European Economic Cooperation (OEEC). (See p. 713.)

Rearmament and the North Atlantic Pact

The political and economic policies of the Cold War were being matched, meanwhile, by the appropriate military preparedness. The country had become used to vast appropriations for defense and was not taken aback by the record-breaking peacetime outlay of $11,000,000,000 for the armed services in 1947. The National Security Act at the same time provided for reforms in the military establishment. The act created a single Department of Defense, to which the three Secretaries of the Army, Navy, and Air Force would be responsible, all three enjoying access to the President but not holding Cabinet rank. It also created a National Security Council, which would occupy itself with the interrelation of military, political, and research policies, and a Central Intelligence Agency, which would gather military and political information from abroad and make it available to government agencies concerned. The Joint Chiefs of Staff, created in 1942, remained the body responsible for strategy and for the broad planning of requirements.

In March 1948, President Truman requested Congress to adopt the principle of universal military training (UMT), which had already been debated in Congress in 1945 and since shelved. Discussions between the Department of Defense and the Joint Chiefs of Staff produced a compromise program for the expansion of the armed forces, and, in June 1948 Congress passed a bill compulsorily drafting men nineteen to twenty-five years of age for a service period of twenty-one months. A long schedule of exempt categories was intended to avoid undue interference with professional and technical education. The drafting of nearly 250,000 youths began promptly in August 1948. Universal military training; the prospective expansion of the armed forces to 2,000,000 men; a 70-group air force; the world's most powerful navy, patrolling the Atlantic, Pacific, and Mediterranean Seas, all seemed to indicate that the military burdens which had oppressed the nations of Europe from the Industrial Revolution to the Second World War had been permanently extended to the United States.

Debates in Congress on ERP had raised inevitably the further question of complementary military aid to Europe. By the Treaty of Brussels of March 1948, Western Europe had taken the initiative in an alliance which could come ready to the hand of the United States as an outpost of the American hemisphere against the Soviet menace. (See p. 714.) But the treaty might well compel the countries of Western Europe to misapply their benefits under ERP to heavy national rearmament programs. In June 1948, after a perfunctory debate, the Senate passed with only four dissenting votes a resolution of Senator Arthur Vandenberg, a one-time isolationist, advocating the association of the United States in systems of defense. The resolution indicated that the United States was turning away from the United Nations, veto-ridden and lacking effective force, and, like the Brussels Powers, was openly consulting its security in a regional pact – this time to be a North Atlantic Pact.

In November 1948 came the presidential election. In view of the reactionary trend of the Republican majority in Congress, a trend of which the recent Taft-Hartley Act had been the crowning example, all the political pundits forecast a victory for the Republican candidate, Governor Thomas E. Dewey. Nevertheless, Truman won – by a small margin – and Democratic majorities were returned at the same time to both Houses. This "greatest upset in American history" was a personal tribute to Truman; it was a public confirmation of the Administration's foreign policy and betrayed, perhaps, a lingering fear of the Republican party's traditional isolationism. It was also a declaration on the part of the "common people" – labor, farmers, foreign-born immigrants, and Negroes – that the Democratic party would now serve their interests best. At the same time, the crushing defeat of a third presidential candidate, Henry Wallace, showed very clearly that the electorate, for all its leftward swing, was far from any sympathy for a man tarred with pro-Soviet affiliations.

In December 1948, immediately after the presidential election, exploratory talks on a North Atlantic Pact were begun in Washington between the United States, Canada, and the five Brussels Powers. Other interested states were drawn in, and, as we have described elsewhere, the pact was signed in Washington on April 4, 1949, by the foreign ministers of Belgium, Britain, Canada, Denmark, France, Iceland, Italy, Luxembourg, the Netherlands, Norway, Portugal, and the United States. (See pp. 715-16.) Within the North Atlantic Treaty Organization (NATO) so formed, the signatories further agreed to establish a Council and a Defense Committee. The Consultative Council and Defense Committee of the Brussels Treaty would be superseded by these new bodies.

Diehard isolationists fought the pact to the bitter end. A war-torn, war-weary Russia, they argued, was unlikely to risk aggression, unless she reacted in alarm at the extension of American military aid to so many of her neighbors; or the new pact might be the first of a series unlimitedly committing American resources and prestige; or that military aid in any case was unfitted to meet the characteristic Communist methods of infiltration and "indirect aggression"; or that arms and dollars had not prevented the decomposition of Nationalist China. Yet on the other side were those who believed in a positive and dynamic American foreign policy. Soviet pressure had always increased at any sign of weakness or conciliation on the part of other nations and had correspondingly decreased at any demonstration of strength and unity. The United States had trodden the path of cooperation in 1945-46, only to meet frustration and abuse. A well-armed United States at the head of a North American–Western European Grand Alliance might better succeed in bringing the power-conscious Russians to the council table and to an agreement. Doubtless the cost of the policy would be formidable; but the alternative – to leave non-Communist Europe, and perhaps the world, to its fate – was unthinkable. Thus went the arguments in the Senate Foreign Relations Committee and in the country. The pact was ratified by the Senate on July 21, 1949, by 82 votes to 13.

On September 23, 1949, Truman announced that an atomic explosion was known to have occurred recently in the Soviet Union.

World-Wide Commitment

The isolationists were correct in one contention, that ERP and NATO – indeed the original Truman Doctrine – and all the complex political, economic, and military developments associated therewith, would cause a chain reaction that would thrust more and more responsibility upon the United States. Even as Europe no longer radiated her former power in the international order, so there was a corresponding social restlessness being released in European colonies overseas and indeed in all "backward" territories where European influence had reached. The non-European world was being swept by forces, some dangerous and all liable to get out of control, and it might soon be a small step before the United States would be forced to intervene protectively in this world and try to mobilize "counterforce" in any part of it, wherever the incessant activities of its Soviet rival appeared to be exploiting a weakness or lodging an entrance. On January 20, 1949, while NATO was still under discussion, President Truman had already defined the attitude of his administration in the famous "Fourth Point" of his inaugural address:

> We must embark on a bold new program for making the benefits of our scientific advances and industrial progress available for the improvement and growth of under-developed areas. More than half the people of the world are living in conditions approaching misery. Their poverty is a handicap and threat both to them and to more prosperous areas. In cooperation with other nations, we should foster capital investment in areas needing development. In due time, as our stability becomes manifest, I believe that those countries which now oppose us will abandon their delusions and join with the free nations of the world in a just settlement of international differences.

The American economic and military commitment was multiplying in every direction. Where was it all to end? The United States was becoming an Atlas supporting the entire non-Communist world. We need not relate all the details of the process. The principles behind the commitment were now established and widely accepted by the American people. The precise events and dates, the agreements and enactments by which the principles were implemented are of less concern to us. But perhaps we can give some kind of picture if we say that for the fiscal year ending June 1960, the total United States commitment of foreign economic aid, including capital assistance (grants and loans), technical assistance, and surplus food, amounted to $3,437,000,000 to seventy-six countries, and that over the same period the total commitment of foreign military aid amounted to $1,840,000,000 to fifty-one countries.[1]

PRINCIPAL MULTILATERAL DEFENSIVE TREATIES AND AGREEMENTS OF THE UNITED STATES

June 26, 1945

The United Nations Charter, signed at San Francisco.

September 2, 1947

Inter-American Treaty of Reciprocal Assistance, signed at Rio de Janeiro between the United States and—

Argentina	Dominican Republic	Nicaragua
Bolivia	Ecuador	Panama
Brazil	El Salvador	Paraguay
Chile	Guatemala	Peru
Colombia	Haiti	Uruguay
Costa Rica	Honduras	Venezuela
Cuba	Mexico	

April 30, 1948

Charter of the Organization of American States, signed at Bogotá, between the United States and the same Latin American states as in the Inter-American treaty of reciprocal assistance.

April 4, 1949

North Atlantic Treaty Organization (NATO), signed at Washington, between the United States and—

Canada	Iceland	Norway
Belgium	Italy	Portugal
Denmark	Luxembourg	United Kingdom
France	Netherlands	

together with Protocol, Oct. 17, 1951, signed at London, on the accession of Greece and Turkey.

and Protocol, Oct. 23, 1954, signed at Paris, on the accession of the Federal Republic of Germany.

December 23, 1950

Agreement for mutual assistance in Indochina, signed at Saigon, between the United States, Cambodia, France, Laos, and Viet-Nam.

September 1, 1951

Security treaty, signed at San Francisco, between the United States, Australia, and New Zealand (ANZUS Pact).

September 8, 1954

Southeast Asia Treaty Organization (SEATO), signed at Manila, between the United States and—

Australia	Pakistan	Thailand
France	Philippines	United Kingdom
New Zealand		

July 28, 1958

Declaration relating to the Baghdad Pact, signed at London, between the United States, Britain, Turkey, Iran, and Pakistan. (For the United States and the Baghdad Pact and CENTO see pp. 795, 797, and 803.)

The military commitment was represented in the main in the multilateral defensive treaties shown in the accompanying table. In addition, the United States was signatory to a whole array of bilateral treaties. With Canada alone there were the Ogdensburg agreement of August 18, 1940 (see p. 534), and other subsequent agreements on air bases, radar, early warning, the supply and standardization of arms, and communications (including the Alaska Highway). The American strategic system also covered the St. Lawrence Seaway. The United States was signatory to bilateral defensive treaties with the Philippines (August 30, 1951), South Korea (October 1, 1953), Nationalist China (December 2, 1954), and Japan (January 19, 1960). The United States was signatory to bilateral defensive agreements with some forty other countries and to various agreements on the supply and standardization of arms and on the loan of naval vessels with some thirty countries. The United States maintained military and/or naval bases, air fields and proving grounds in twenty countries, and accredited military, air force, and/or naval missions to twenty-four.

Latin America

In the postwar period the United States maintained its policy of the Good Neighbor toward the Latin-American states, despite the tendency of those states to throw up governments alien to the democratic spirit and even friendly to the United States' potential enemies. The Latin-American states – especially the larger of them – were becoming very well aware of their future importance. During the war their industries had expanded and their cities had boomed, and throughout the continent populations were multiplying. Traditional resentment against the "Yankee Colossus" could now be backed by real power. The years following 1945, therefore, in the United States–Latin-American relations were years of patience – at least on one side – and often of misunderstanding and disappointment, although in calmer moments it was generally realized by all parties that, after all, the hemisphere was bound together by undeniable common interests.

Argentina was at first the main trouble spot in Latin America. In November 1945, Uruguay, pleading "continental solidarity," demanded collective action on the part of her sister republics against Argentina, whose recent policies she construed as a threat to herself. Colonel Juan Perón, a colorful figure well versed in the latest refinements of demagogy, had held the substance of power in Argentina as the executive of a conservative-military clique since 1943. His ardent admiration for European Fascism had cooled toward the close of the war. His government had pledged good behavior at the Chapultepec Conference in Mexico City and had secured American support for the admission of Argentina into the United Nations. Perón persevered, nonetheless, in protecting Nazi agents and declined to expel or dissolve businesses blacklisted by the Allies. In February 1946, the State Department in Washington published the celebrated Blue Book, which demonstrated with the aid of captured German documents the extent of the wartime collaboration between Argentina and the Axis.

The Latin-American states, however, fearing a dangerous precedent, showed no enthusiasm for the Uruguayan appeal. At least the Perón imbroglio, while it lasted, was effective enough to prevent the Pan-American foreign ministers from again meeting in conference till 1947. But by that date it was not Germany but Russia that was the universal international menace, and, in the American view, the main trouble spot in Latin America had now shifted from the allegedly pro-Nazi Argentina to the allegedly pro-Communist Mexico. And by 1947 also, the hectic flush of wartime prosperity had begun to fade, and most of the republics were feeling conditions not dissimilar to those of contemporary Europe.

When, therefore, the Inter-American Conference for the Maintenance of Peace and Security assembled at Rio de Janeiro in mid-August 1947, it developed into a trading match between economic aid and political concessions. Out of the discussions emerged the Inter-American Treaty of Reciprocal Assistance, providing that assistance to a victim of unprovoked aggression should be a definite obligation decided by a two-thirds majority vote, but also providing that "no state should be required to furnish armed forces without its consent." Then, in March-April 1948 at Bogotá, the Colombian capital, a Pan-American conference drew up a Charter creating an Organization of American States to conduct inter-American relations as a "regional arrangement" within the United Nations. The Governing Board of the Pan American Union in Washington was to be the permanent Consultative Council of the new Organization. General policy was to be decided by the Inter-American Conferences, meeting at intervals of five years. The Conference of Foreign Ministers was retained "to consider problems of an urgent nature and of common interest to the American States." Inter-American disputes were to be settled by conciliation and arbitration. An Inter-American Defense Board would make recommendations in regard to collective action against aggression. A number of subsidiary Specialized Organizations were to be set up on questions of health, welfare, and agriculture.

Today, behind the political façade and the array of multilateral agreements, the old problems persist. Long established grievances battle with more enlightened self-interest for the mind of the Latin American. Governments are mostly of the military-authoritarian type, and they are apt to change violently and frequently. The oldest and greatest problem is peasant poverty, coupled with high birth rates and outdated land tenure systems. The newer but hardly lesser problem is the "colonial" status of industry – the dependence of industry on the export market. Brazilian coffee, Bolivian tin, Chilean copper, Peruvian lead, Guatemalan bananas, Cuban sugar have been all largely American financed, American managed, and American purchased, and naturally enough they are all highly sensitive to American business conditions and especially to American "recessions." Popular disturbances, accordingly, have often been revolts against "dollar imperialism." As for Communism, the situation would seem to be contradictory. To some extent Communism since 1945 has subsided and would probably have subsided with or without pressure from the United States. The revolutionary tradition in Latin America is prior to Communism and alien to it. Moreover, Moscow-directed Communism has made its deepest penetrations in the industrial cities, where it is both more easily organized and more easily suppressed, and has neglected the country estates and plantations where it could have been more elusive and dangerous. Finally, Catholicism remains the rock of social stability, and the primary source of Latin-American culture.

In 1958 two events showed all too clearly the state of feeling in the continent. The first, in May of the year, was Vice-President Nixon's "good will" tour of eight of the republics – and the hostile reception that was given him. He was heckled, jeered, and even stoned by students and street demonstrators, and at one point, Caracas, he escaped with his life from a mob that had recently run out the president of the country. Eisenhower from Washington threatened to dispatch American paratroopers and marines for his rescue. Meanwhile, the Soviet Vice-Minister of Foreign Affairs, Vasily Kuznetsov, was quietly visiting the republics assuring them of Soviet aid and trade, especially Soviet willingness to purchase their export commodities. American opinion at home, shocked out of its complacency, and indeed its ignorance, reacted with soul-searching and fact-finding surveys of the entire Latin-American relationship. President Eisenhower was now talking, not of the "Good Neighbor" policy, but of the "Good Partner" policy. President Kubitschek of Brazil seized the opportunity to press for increased economic aid and for a series of more meaningful inter-American conferences. The Cold War, he said, "is now presenting its symptoms on our continent."

The second important event of 1958 was Castro's revolution in Cuba. Since 1933 — with one interval (1944-52) — a certain Fulgencio Batista, originally an illiterate private in the Cuban Army, had been governing the country either as President or from behind a screen of Presidents of his nomination. Cuba, it seemed, was going through just another sordid dictatorial interlude. But in 1956, Fidel Castro and his brother raised the standard of revolt in the Sierra Maestra mountains in Oriente province and, from that inaccessible refuge, harassed and harried and at last overthrew Batista's forces. By the end of 1958, Batista was in flight and Castro was shortly in control in Havana as "Premier" of a new government.

Successful revolution against tyranny always has a popular appeal, and the new ruler of Cuba at first was sympathetically regarded abroad. The Castro government was immediately recognized by the United States, Britain, the Soviet Union, most of the Latin-American states, and the Holy See. But it was not long before Castro was laying about him as ruthlessly as any Batista, and, in three months of his administration, he caused to be summarily "executed" over five hundred of Batista's partisans. Moreover, he was repeating the old sinister pattern of governing from behind puppet presidents. Thereafter followed wholesale "nationalizations" of land and of foreign-owned properties, including American sugar plantations and American and British oil installations. The United States replied by cutting off its economic aid to Cuba and by reducing its quota on Cuban sugar imports. Meanwhile Castro's ulterior political predilections were being revealed in the overly cordial relations that he now cultivated with the Soviet Union and with the Chinese People's Republic and in the state visits — of Mikoyan to Havana, and of Castro's brother and fellow guerrilla fighter to Moscow. As we write, it still remains to be seen if Castro's revolution is an isolated incident or represents a wider "trend" affecting the whole of Latin America.

Purges, Deterrents, and Summits

The decade 1950-60 was a curious, almost schizophrenic period. At home, with occasional and temporary setbacks and rumors of setbacks, the nation enjoyed unprecedented prosperity; but the enjoyment was sullied by increasing frustration and fear from abroad. Halfway through the decade, in 1955, the gross national product (GNP) was about $400,000,000,000, or $2,500 per head of population, double the figure in any other country in the world. But out of this huge sum, the budget for the year was $65,000,000,000 of which $45,000,000,000 or 11.5 per cent of GNP went to defense. Armaments, especially nuclear and rocket armaments, were in continual development, and it seemed that no sooner was one monster born than it was swallowed by a bigger. In September 1949, as we have said, it was known that an atom bomb had been exploded in the Soviet Union. In November 1952, the first hydrogen bomb was exploded at Eniwetok in the Pacific. Less than a year later, in August 1953, a hydrogen bomb was exploded in the Soviet Union. In March 1954, another hydrogen bomb of greater power was exploded in the Marshall Islands, producting "total" devastation for a diameter of eight miles and "very serious" devastation for a diameter of sixteen, and, on this occasion, injuring twenty-three fishermen — one fatally — in a Japanese trawler, which, in consequence of a sudden change of wind, had sailed into the zone of radio-active fallout. In September 1954, the *Nautilus,* the first atomic-powered submarine, was commissioned. In October 1957, the first Soviet "sputnik" was successfully launched into orbit, and during 1959 the first American and Soviet "luniks" were shot at the moon. Among the groups of initials that now punctuated political and military talk, ICBM (inter-continental ballistic missile) had become one of the most familiar. In this new, modern race the former superfortress and the 60,000-ton supercarrier seemed puny and decrepit.

American defense policies had to be worked out against this darkening background. Secretaries of Defense and their aides and advisers, however tough and experienced they might be, were to be excused if sometimes they were human enough to break under their appalling responsibilities. The National Security Act of 1947 had already been passed to try to heal the growing rift between the three armed services — the Army, Navy, and Air Force. In February 1949, Eisenhower, who had lately become president of Columbia University, was induced to accept the "temporary" chairmanship of the Joint Chiefs of Staff and to attempt a new effort at conciliation. But Secretary of Defense James V. Forrestal, wearied of the months of bickering behind the scenes, resigned in March and two months later committed suicide. Eisenhower was then seriously ill. In July 1949, President Truman submitted to Congress amendments to the National Security Act designed to strengthen the authority of the Secretary of Defense. General Omar Bradley was appointed chairman of the Joint Chiefs of Staff. The services' dispute by now was public property and was being aired in congressional committees with what seemed utter disregard of military security or even conventional dignity. By 1950 the dispute had largely petered out, but while it lasted it signified much more than normal professional jealousy among top-level generals and admirals; it signified the extreme pressure to which the American technical and administrative genius was being subjected at this time.

Not surprisingly, the nation as a whole was laboring under the same kind of strain and finding relief in a near-hysterical "witch-hunt." President Truman, in response to the increasingly shrill demands of a Republican Congress, touched off the unhappy episode with his executive order of

March 21, 1947, calling for a loyalty investigation of all civilian government personnel. In July 1948, eleven leaders of the American Communist party were indicted for criminal conspiracy "to teach and advocate the overthrow and destruction of the United States Government by force and violence." David Lilienthal, chairman of the Atomic Energy Commission, was victimized by a scurrilous press campaign for alleged acts of negligence that had resulted in leakage of information, and he was forced to resign. During 1949 and 1950 Alger Hiss, formerly of the State Department, was twice tried and then convicted of perjury for denying that he had once been a Communist and a trafficker in official secrets. The McCarran Internal Security Act was passed over the President's veto requiring the registration of Communist groups and the tightening up of the immigration and naturalization laws. At this time Senator Joseph McCarthy of Wisconsin was taking upon himself the role of America's grand inquisitor. He startled the nation by charging that he could produce the names of card-carrying members of the Communist party in the State Department – he put their number on various occasions at 57, 205, and 81. Soon no one was too big or too little for McCarthy's suspicion or insolence – even such public figures as Acheson and Marshall. For the next two to three years the American people lived in the atmosphere of a totalitarian purge. There was not a government employee, university professor, school teacher, editor, broadcaster – or even film actor – but could be hauled off to Washington for a minute and harassing interrogation and consequent disgrace and loss of livelihood.

The outbreak and course of the Korean War will be described in some detail in Chapter 42 below. (See p. 780.) Dean Acheson had become Secretary of State early in 1949, and, from the midsummer of 1950, when it broke out, the war dominated his term of office. It was a "popular" war, in the sense that American public opinion never wavered in its support of American intervention, especially after the Chinese counteroffensive. American public opinion also strongly supported, indeed was largely responsible for, the resolution in the United Nations "branding" China the aggressor. General MacArthur returned to the United States in April 1951 and – although it was acknowledged that Truman's attitude toward him was only correct – the wild welcome that he received was clearly seen as an outburst of popular passion against China. (See p. 785.) Meanwhile – almost parenthetically – the Japanese peace conference of forty-nine nations met in San Francisco in September 1951, and despite the presence of a Soviet delegate, Acheson was able to steer it with the utmost skill to a prompt and successful conclusion.

Eisenhower was twice elected President of the United States – in 1952 and 1956. But on both occasions he found himself in a weak, anomalous position. He had won the first election decisively enough, and the second by the proverbial landslide vote; but Congress was returned in 1952 with a small Republican majority, and in 1954 with a small Democratic majority which successively increased in the elections of 1956 and 1958. President Eisenhower, the great "Father Figure" of his country, the symbol of the American people's craving for leadership, therefore had behind him a

Congress at no time very strong and, for six of his eight years, dominated by the opposing Democratic party. For his Secretary of State he had the forceful but highly controversial figure of John Foster Dulles. Into the bargain the President's health began to fail. In September 1955, he suffered a heart attack; in June 1956, he underwent a serious intestinal operation. His doctors, however, vouched for his complete recovery. His personal charm and approachability remained, but somehow the nerve had gone out of him, and more and more the load was being taken by Dulles and by Vice-President Richard Nixon. Dulles, latterly an ailing man also, resigned in April 1959 and died a month later. He was succeeded by Christian A. Herter, lately governor of Massachusetts.

Domestic affairs during the period were patchy and obviously subsidiary to foreign. McCarthy was still riding "high, wide, and not very handsome." He was now chairman of his own Permanent Subcommittee on Investigations and was probing the Voice of America and even the Army itself. He continued his extraordinary and symptomatic career till struck down at last by a Senate vote of censure in December 1954. For the rest, we might note the antisegregation movement in the South – although this too had its foreign repercussions and was much magnified abroad. It had an unfortunate simultaneity with apartheid in South Africa. During 1958 Little Rock, Arkansas, came to be as well known in the Soviet Union and in Afro-Asian countries as in the United States itself. Toward the end of Eisenhower's second term industry was giving some cause for concern. Between 1957 and 1959 unemployment rose from 3,000,000 to 5,000,000, and withdrawals of gold were increasingly serious. In 1959 the steel workers were out on a four-months' strike. But there was no trace of panic or failure of morale. The nation's main anxieties were concentrated not on affairs at home but on affairs beyond its borders.

In a lagging Europe, Dulles was trying once more to use American aid to promote the continent's political and military integration. In January 1953, when he took office, he gave warning that in the absence of "effective unity," there might have to be "a little re-thinking" of America's European policy. Later in the year, more impatient and more forthright, he was threatening "an agonizing reappraisal of basic United States policy." Presumably his candor helped to produce results. During 1954, as we have elsewhere described, Western European Union (WEU) was formed with pledges of support from the United States and Britain. (See p. 719.) In January 1954, with equal candor, Dulles enunciated for the ears of the Soviet Union his doctrine of "the deterrent of massive retaliatory power." But, then, in the face of sharp criticism both in the United States and in Western Europe, he afterwards explained in a typical Dullesian circumlocutory gloss that the doctrine did not preclude prior consultation among allies and that it was not necessarily to be applied "in every case of attack."

In the Far East, in China, the dust had settled, leaving the Chinese People's Republic in command and the United States hardened against its recognition and against its admission to the United Nations. The Korean War was brought to a precarious conclusion by the armistice of July 27, 1953. (See p. 786.) Communist pressure had thence been transferred to Indochina, but there too a long, agonizing struggle was brought to another precarious conclusion, at the Far Eastern Conference at Geneva, by the armistice of July 21, 1954. (See pp. 790-92.) Some weeks later, on September 8 at a conference at Manila in the Philippines, Dulles tried to repair his defenses with the creation of the Southeast Asia Treaty Organization (SEATO), which would stand in the East as the complement of NATO in the West. (See p. 792.) But then, as if this part of the world could never stay still, Communist pressure was transferred to the Formosa Straits, where, at the end of 1954, a new Communist assault appeared to be in preparation against the Chinese Nationalist forces occupying the "offshore" islands of Quemoy and Matsu. The assault did not develop; but, in this case, neither was there a concluding armistice or treaty.

On July 18-23, 1955, at Geneva, took place the first great "Summit Conference," on this occasion between Bulganin, Faure, Eden, Eisenhower, and their respective foreign ministers. The conference had been preceded by intensive discussions, initiated as far back as two years previously by Churchill. Stalin was gone, it was perhaps excusable to hope that a new, more liberal Russian leadership might be encouraged to reveal itself. The old Foreign Ministers Council had achieved so little, and, in the current "nuclear stalemate," an informal round-table meeting of the heads of the four Great Powers might conceivably contribute a little toward that "relaxation of tensions" so devoutly to be desired. The moment was well chosen. In May 1955, the Austrian Treaty had been signed; in June 1955, an array of statesmen from all over the world had been celebrating in San Francisco the tenth anniversary of the United Nations. NATO had just been balanced by the Warsaw Pact, signed on May 14, 1955, the day before the Austrian Treaty. The conference met in an outwardly cordial spirit – the "Geneva Spirit," as it was called. Such inflammatory items as self-determination in the Soviet satellite countries and the recognition of the Chinese People's Republic were carefully debarred. But even so, in an otherwise tactful agenda – on German unification, the control and inspection of armaments, and the improvement of East-West communications – there was still material enough for all the old arguments to be repeated, and in all of them the three Western Powers stood in unanimous opposition to the Soviet Union.

On January 16, 1956, an article in *Life* magazine quoted Secretary Dulles as saying that the United States had stood on the brink of war on three occasions during 1953 and 1954 and that his doctrine of deterrence had preserved the peace.[3] The first occasion had been in June 1953, when the Korean armistice negotiations were breaking down; the second had been in April 1954, at the time of the Far Eastern Conference at Geneva, when the Indo-chinese armistice negotiations were breaking down; and the third had been in December 1954, at the time of the threatened Communist assault on Quemoy and Matsu. Dulles was reported to have continued:

> You have to take chances for peace, just as much as you must take chances for war. Some say that we were brought to the verge of war. Of course we were

brought to the verge of war. The ability to get to the verge of war without getting into the war is the necessary art. If you cannot master it, you inevitably get into war. If you try to run away from it, if you are scared to go to the brink, you are lost. We've had to look it square in the face – on the question of enlarging the Korean War, on the question of getting into the Indochina War, on the question of Formosa. We walked to the brink, and we looked it in the face. We took strong action.

It took a lot more courage for the President than for me. His was the ultimate decision. I did not have to make the decision myself, only to recommend it. The President never flinched for a minute in any of these situations. He came up taut . . .

The article, as might have been expected, roused a fierce tempest in a teapot. Adlai Stevenson accused Dulles of "playing Russian roulette with the life of our nation" and Stevenson afterward added: "He flies now; we pay later!" President Eisenhower, ever loyal, came out strongly in defense of "the best Secretary of State I have ever known." Certainly by no stretch of the imagination could the article be described as being "in the Geneva spirit." We may dismiss the suggestion that the article was untrue or that Dulles was misreported. We may also dismiss the suggestion that in it Dulles had merely committed another of his famous *gaffes* – that he may have been a master of the art of brinkmanship but was a tyro in the art of public relations. Or we may argue that Dulles, honest to a fault, was trying to shock a peace-minded democracy into a greater awareness of the unpleasant facts of modern international life – and perhaps also into a greater sympathy and gratitude for the afflictions of a modern Secretary of State. The article remains nevertheless a revelation of the man and a still puzzling footnote to the history of these years.

The Summit Conference of 1955, which we have described, had passed off without concrete results but at least with proper diplomatic dispassion. The Summit Conference of 1960 was to be a much stormier episode. During the previous December 1959, President Eisenhower had gone on an eleven-nation good-will tour that had taken him from Italy to India. He was giving a reply in kind to a similar tour made not long since by the Bulganin-Khrushchev duumvirs, and he may also have been trying to assuage some of the lingering aftereffects of Dulles' recent brinkmanship in the East. In the course of the tour Eisenhower spent three days in Paris and Rambouillet for a "Western Summit" with de Gaulle, Macmillan, and Adenauer, and thence an invitation had been issued to Khrushchev for an "East-West Summit to be held in Paris in April 1960." After lengthy and tedious "pre-Summit maneuvering," the date for the historic meeting was at last agreed – May 16.

But on May 5 and 7, 1960, in speeches to the Supreme Soviet in Moscow, Khrushchev angrily announced that an American reconnaissance plane of the type known as U-2, flying from a base in Pakistan, had been shot down a few days before at Sverdlovsk some 1,000 miles within the Soviet Union. The pilot had parachuted to earth and had been interned. Strong Soviet notes followed to the United States, protesting against "aggression by American aircraft" and threatening "retaliatory measures," and also to Turkey,

Pakistan, and Norway, pointing out, in so many words, that the Soviet Union had the means for the instant elimination of foreign military bases in bordering territories. From Washington issued at first a somewhat inept denial and then full and frank admissions by Secretary Herter, recently successor to Dulles, and by President Eisenhower, to the effect that the flight of the U-2 had been part of an intelligence operation such as had been routine practice for some years.

Khrushchev, still smarting, arrived in Paris for the projected Summit Conference and at a preliminary private meeting at the Elysée on May 15 with de Gaulle, Macmillan, and Eisenhower, led off with a violent statement demanding an official apology from the United States for the action of its aircraft and an assurance that such action would not be repeated. Eisenhower made a patient and scrupulous point-by-point reply. But it was clear that the Summit had broken down before it had begun. The heads of states in Paris spent the next couple of days in confused, hurried, and fruitless bilateral talks. On May 19 after the usual valedictory courtesies, they departed to their several destinations. Later in the year, in August, the pilot of the luckless plane in question, after a spectacular trial in Moscow, was condemned to a ten-year term of imprisonment.

The U-2 incident had been referred to the United Nations Security Council, and on May 26, 1960, a Soviet resolution condemning the action of the United States had been rejected by 7 votes to 2, with 2 abstentions. The General Assembly of 1959 had already had before it various problems in Africa – Algeria, the Congo, and South Africa. The situation was therefore tense enough and full of potential drama when the Fifteenth General Assembly opened in New York on September 20, 1960. As if by prearrangement all the most important heads of states were present – including Macmillan, Diefenbaker, Menzies, Nash, Nehru, Nkrumah; Khrushchev, Gomulka, Novotny, Kadar; Tito, Nasser, King Hussein, Soekarno – and Castro of Cuba – many of them with numerous delegations in train. President Eisenhower and King Frederick of Denmark were both to give addresses. Seventeen new states, sixteen of them African, were to be admitted to membership. A few hours before the session assembled Khrushchev visited Castro in his Harlem hotel, spoke familiarly with pressmen, and posed for photographers.

The Assembly's debates lasted in the end for four months. Speeches were delivered by all the principal delegates, with the conspicuous exception of Couve de Marville of France. Khrushchev spoke for nearly two hours, violently attacking United Nations Secretary General Dag Hammarskjöld for "siding with the colonialists" in the Congo and demanding his replacement by a three-man Secretariat. Castro, attired in his usual revolutionary battle dress, spoke for four-and-a-half hours. Macmillan spoke for a modest one hour – with constant interruptions from Khrushchev. At one moment Khrushchev was thumping his table with his shoe. Incidental meetings took place behind the scenes, notably one between Khrushchev and Macmillan. Senior members present at this strange, theatrical occasion, comparing it reminiscently with other more sedate parliamentary procedures, must have shaken graying heads over the antics they were being called upon to endure;

and many Americans must have felt a twinge of regret over the turn of fate by which their original hospitality to the United Nations in their city of New York had made them the victims of a virtual conspiracy of insult in their own home at the hands of certain of their international guests. In order that something useful and concrete might emerge from the sessions, the leaders of five "neutral" states – Nehru, Tito, Nasser, Nkrumah, and Soekarno – submitted a draft resolution calling for an early meeting between Eisenhower and Khrushchev. But, after some discussion, this too was withdrawn.

Meanwhile Vice-President Richard M. Nixon and Senator John F. Kennedy were engaged in the presidential election campaign – as it turned out, an event of many historical superlatives. On November 8, 1960, after one of the toughest contests and by one of the closest votes in American history, the youngest President of the United States was elected. He was also the first Roman Catholic to hold that office.

41. ASIA: THE SETTLEMENT

"Western" and "Non-Western"

In this book we have confined our narrative in the main to Europe and to peoples of European origin. To use the vocabulary of certain modern historians, we have tried to describe the Western World, or the world of Western Man, and we have touched on other parts and peoples only insofar as they have seemed to us to affect our principal theme. Such has been the task and program with which we began and which we are now about to bring to a conclusion. It may be a fact that for some generations past Western Man has held, so to speak, the historical initiative. Since the Renaissance he has been the first history-maker of the human species. But it may also be a fact that at this particular moment, in mid-twentieth century, his one-time monopoly has been wearing thinner the more widely it has spread and that the future may find him more and more in competition most notably with those very peoples who, by his influence, have lately been discovering themselves and their national identity.

Probably nothing has contributed quite so much to Western Man's changing status as his own recent wars. The First World War was rightly named a World War, and more rightly so the Second – and again more rightly so the Cold War, in which we are now engaged. All wars destroy; but one thing they destroy is provincialism. Wars make contacts between peoples – between enemies and between allies. They induce travel and discovery, even if not under the happiest circumstances. Wars also have a way of spilling over into neutral territory and embroiling peoples who at first sight would seem to have no interest in the immediate issues – and this often without carrying open hostilities to their doors. Perhaps on those occasions when the main fronts or theaters of a war prove indecisive or deadlocked or too costly to break through, the combatants perforce probe out other fronts or theaters elsewhere. And the Cold War conforms precisely to the pattern. In its widening scope the Cold War has generated fronts and theaters all around it, and there is today no international problem or dispute, big or small, actual or potential, anywhere in the six continents, that cannot acquire an added significance by finding some linkage with it. As the main battle lines have hardened, so have pressures moved to the flanks, until the "indirect approach" has often become more important than the original war itself.

If now we are in the concluding chapters of this book – and in a Part that bears the title, "The Cold War" – what more appropriate subject could we have than the non-Western peoples who are no longer exempt from the great labor of history and who are so increasingly sharing with their Western brothers the fortunes of this third great world conflict of the century?

We could divide the peoples in question and their territories into six broad groups: the Middle East,[1] the Indian Sub-Continent, the Far East, Southeast Asia, and Africa. And, stretching a point, we might include Latin America. These all represent wide differences of latitude and climate, of land and language, of faith and custom. By contrast with them the Western World, despite its present geographical extent, at least shows peoples at a single general level of civilization, living for the most part in temperate climates and within easy access to the sea, inheriting a Christian culture, deriving their educational methods and standards from a common source, holding certain jealously guarded personal values – even if they do not always achieve those values – and possessing an indefinable but instantly recognizable intellectual outlook.

When, therefore, we say "Western" we know what we mean. We mean the European Continent (including Britain and European Russia), North America, and those parts of Central and South America, Australasia, and Africa (mainly South Africa) of European settlement. But no corresponding image answers to "Non-Western." Yet we are in need of a name for it. Toynbee has called it "Social Asia."[2] We could adopt the current, more restricted term "Afro-Asia," which moreover fits the contents of these chapters. Economically at least, Afro-Asia has certain distinctive qualities. It is by far the more populous, and it is, relatively, the Have-Not area of the world. And with these qualities go its relatively higher birth rates and death rates. Parts of it, like India, Japan, or Egypt, have adopted Western industries. Some have developed export trades in such materials as cotton, rubber, and above all oil. Here and there have arisen great cities with all the amenities of modern urban life – Cairo, Bombay, Calcutta, Singapore, Hong Kong – and here and there are to be seen exceptional wealth and luxury. But generally in Afro-Asia we are in the world of the peasant and the peasant's age-old domestic disabilities – land hunger, outdated tenure systems, fragmentation, indebtedness, soil deterioration, technical backwardness – and extreme poverty. Insofar as the peoples of this area are politically articulate and organized, they are strongly nationalist, "anti-colonial," and therefore often anti-Western. In the great modern arena of power politics they are also usually militarily weak. Finally, they are vulnerable to Communism, and theirs is the area in which, since 1945, Communism has made its principal advances. And herein indeed is the whole burden of the Cold War.

In the next two chapters we shall review the Afro-Asian countries. In the present chapter we shall describe them generally in Asia in the immediate post-1945 years. We have called this period "The Asian Settlement." The Cold War had not come to its fullest intensity, although, in the light of the afterknowledge, no one could fail to discern the growing evidences of it everywhere. In this sense, in this Chapter 41, we shall include the Middle East, Palestine and the First Israeli War, and the group of "colonial" territories from Pakistan and India to the Malay Peninsula and Indonesia. In the next chapter, Chapter 42, we shall pass on to "The Asian Revolt" from 1950 to 1960, namely the war in Korea, the oil crisis in Iran, the Suez Crisis and the Second Israeli War, and Iraq. From 1950 onwards, the Cold War had, so to speak, been unmistakably declared. In the second part of Chapter 42 we shall make a brief mention of Africa – East, West, and Central. North Africa has already been considered in Chapter 37, apropos of France, and South Africa in Chapter 39, apropos of Britain and the Commonwealth.

The Middle East

The Middle East had not been a battlefield in the Second World War as it had been in the First. It had been threatened by German invasion, and the threat had not been entirely removed till after the Battle of Alamein in October 1942. Except for the revolt in Iraq and the forcible occupation of Syria and Lebanon in 1941, there had been no actual hostilities in the area. Turkey and Germany had entered into a treaty of friendship in 1941; but Turkey had thereafter resisted pressures from both sides to join them, and she had entered the war against the Axis at last in February 1945, as did several other states about that time, not to participate actively, but to qualify for membership in the United Nations.

Although neutral in deed, the Middle Eastern peoples had not always been neutral in thought. Despite promises of union and independence in the First World War, many had suffered colonial or mandatory status, and their lands had been arbitrarily partitioned. They would have been less than human if sometimes they had not welcomed the Second World War and hoped for the defeat of their former masters, even at the hands of a Nazi Germany or a Fascist Italy. Egyptians, swayed by Italian propaganda, had accepted British protection with reluctance. Some of the educated elite were sympathetic to the democracies, but there were doubtless many who would have given Graziani or Rommel a fulsome reception in 1941, if either had reached Cairo. Ibn Saud in Saudi Arabia and Abdullah in Transjordan were pro-British throughout the Second World War, but it was a brittle loyalty. Only one group, the tiny Jewish minority in Palestine, was inescapably committed to the war for the destruction of Nazism, and its attitude was fixed whatever way that war might go.

One consequence of the war for the Middle Eastern peoples was the great increase in what might be called their regional self-consciousness. A wartime organization such as the Middle East Supply Center (MESC), set up in Cairo in 1941, at first British-sponsored and then Anglo-American, had imposed a measure of economic unity upon the area. (See p. 532.) It had been primarily a controlling agency, but it had also worked out a complex productive program, opened up sources of raw materials, allocated supplies, regulated imports and shipping, developed overland transport, and in general stimulated inter-Arab trade and communication. It had created, moreover, a certain habit of thought, so that even when wartime necessities had gone, the advantages of planning and cooperation were not forgotten. If nothing else, the war had shown the essential strategic unity of the Middle East as a whole. Its position astride East-West sea routes and air routes and its almost unlimited oil resources, all gave the territory a paramount importance in the new struggle for power in the world. Middle Eastern leaders could not have failed to appreciate the arguments for solidarity and collective action.

The big question was what political form this regional self-consciousness should now assume. One such form was an Arab League. It was an appropriate sequel to the entire Arab renaissance of the past half century. It was favorably viewed by outside powers, despite their opposition in years gone by. As early as May 1941 it had been given official British encouragement in a speech by Eden, the British Foreign Secretary. It took shape under the initiative and leadership of Nahas of Egypt and Nuri es-Said of Iraq. It eventually came into being on March 23, 1945, and included the seven Arab states – Egypt, Saudi Arabia, Iraq, Syria, Lebanon, Transjordan, and the Yemen – with headquarters and a secretariat in Cairo.

Another such form, at one time much canvassed, was a "Greater Syria" to comprise the states of the "Fertile Crescent" – Syria, Lebanon, Transjordan, and Iraq. Here would have been a "regional arrangement" well understood by members of the new United Nations. Another form would have revived the moribund Saadabad Pact of 1937. (See p. 205.) But the new regional self-consciousness, as it turned out, was not yet strong enough to overcome the undoubted disparities and rivalries of the Middle East. The Arab states themselves were of various political forms and of unequal political maturity. They were, moreover, of very unequal economies. An overpopulated, peasant country like Egypt, ruled by a Westernized constitutional monarch and bureaucracy, and exporting cotton, had little in common with a desert country of vast uninhabited areas like Saudi Arabia, a feudal theocratic kingdom, exporting oil.

The overriding political and international problem for the Middle East, and in particular for the Arab states, was Palestine. A common hatred is a powerful thing; and the "Jewish National Home" could have been the greatest of all unifying forces among its neighbors. Here was an alien, intrusive community, of evident enterprise and technical advancement, which, if not "a bridgehead for foreign imperialism," at least could call upon strong sympathies in a richer, larger outside world. Yet, as we shall shortly relate, it was upon the rock of the Israeli War in 1948 that Arab unity was almost shattered. The Arab League, untried and experimental at best, could hardly survive the defeat and humiliation of that encounter. The great Arab federation, envisioned in 1916, frustrated in 1920, in 1948 seemed further from realization than ever.

In their individual political arrangements the countries of the Middle East generally survived the Second World War with little change. Turkey, for example, was still the Turkey of Kemal Ataturk, and after the war she resumed the way of reform laid out by her great national leader. Early in 1946 an Opposition to the hitherto single Republican People's Party was permitted to appear in a new Democratic party. Certain police regulations, in force since 1940, were rescinded; Koranic teaching was reintroduced into Turkish schools. The general effect of these measures was to relax the harsh secularizing and totalitarian tendencies of the earlier Kemalist revolution, and they were warmly welcomed in the West. Militarily, Turkey had been a buffer state throughout the Second World War, a status not materially changed by her declaration of war on Germany in February 1945; and as a buffer state, although with Western sympathies – this time between the Soviet Union and the Middle East – her present leaders sought manfully to keep her. She stoutly rejected a Soviet demand that she should retrocede Kars and Ardahan to Soviet possession and permit Soviet bases to be established in the Dardanelles. In 1947 when her European neighbor, Greece, was fighting for national existence against Communist guerrillas, her government, with strong American and British diplomatic support, took the decisive step of accepting American aid offered her under the Truman Doctrine. This aid, which amounted to $100,000,000, she at once applied to her military budget. (See p. 746.)

In May 1950, in general elections in Turkey under a new electoral law, the new Democratic party defeated the People's Party. Celal Bayar, the Democratic party leader, became President, with Adnan Menderes as Premier. Menderes, a man of intense energy and conviction, saw himself as executor of the second phase of Turkey's Kemalist Revolution, but ambitious capital investments and social schemes quickly landed him in an unbalanced budget, and, as was soon to appear, the United States was not going to stand by every time to save him and his government from economic ruin. Elections in 1954 once more returned the Democratic party to power, but Menderes was already not averse to manipulating the polls. During 1954 he introduced a series of press laws that virtually protected him from public criticism. Meanwhile the Turkish Government carried on its unexceptionable foreign policy. In 1950 a Turkish contingent fought in Korea; in 1951 Turkey joined NATO; in 1954 she entered into a treaty of "friendly cooperation" with Pakistan, and in the same year she concluded a defensive alliance with Greece and Yugoslavia; in 1955 she joined the Baghdad Pact. Throughout she was in receipt of substantial American military aid.

In February 1959, while Menderes was on his way to the London conference on Cyprus, his plane crashed in foggy weather near Gatwick airport, Surrey. He himself miraculously survived, but the shock was said to have affected his mind. He now seemed to reck nothing of the opposition in Turkey to the Democratic party, an opposition now organizing itself round Ismet Inonu, leader of the People's Party, former president and successor to Kemal Ataturk. During 1959 student demonstrations were dispersed by troops – at a cost of over 100 casualties – the universities of Ankara and Istanbul were temporarily closed, and martial law was declared.

On May 27, 1960, a National Unity Committee, composed mostly of junior army officers, seized power in Turkey, ousted the Menderes government, and abolished the Assembly. A Provisional Government was set up under General Cemal Gursel, who at once reaffirmed his support of the Western alliance and pledged himself to restore a democratic constitution in Turkey as soon as possible. Members of the deposed government, including Bayar and Menderes, were taken into custody, and by the end of the year were on trial for their lives. Turkey, modern, progressive Turkey, the staunch ally who had always enjoyed a good press in the West, appeared to have joined the ranks of the military dictatorships.

Iran (Persia), after Turkey, was the second buffer state in the Middle East. But she first had to pass through a troubled period. She had suffered joint Allied occupation during the Second World War. She had been the "Persian Corridor" for the transit of Lend-Lease supplies to the Soviet Union, and her government had since virtually fallen into the hands of American military and economic advisers. Riza Shah had abdicated in 1942 and had left his young son, Mohammed Riza, to treat with Iran's new masters as best he could. In 1943 Iran had declared war upon the Axis, and the conference between Roosevelt, Churchill, and Stalin had taken place at Teheran. American and Soviet concessionaires were shortly competing for oil, and it looked as if the country would come out of the war divided into American and Soviet "spheres of influence" on the nineteenth-century pattern. A pro-Soviet radical party, the Tudeh (Masses), Communist in all but name, was at work in the chief urban centers.

In 1945 the war was over. British and American forces were duly withdrawn, but the Soviet forces remained in the northern provinces. Late in 1945 a Soviet-sponsored revolt broke out in Iranian Azerbaijan, a province in the Soviet zone, and a "Democratic" government was set up in Tabriz by members of the Tudeh party. All the maneuverings, soon to be familiar in the Soviet satellites of Eastern Europe, were in operation. Iranian Kurds, assisted by Soviet agents, issued a Kurdish declaration of autonomy and were joined by a contingent of their brethren from across the Iraqi borders. In January 1946, Iran's affairs were referred to the United Nations.

The Iranian crisis of 1946 was the first of the greater postwar crises and the first open sign of the East-West schism. It was also the first test of the new organization, the United Nations. Iran's case was argued out in the Security Council, and eventually, on April 4, 1946, Gromyko, the Soviet delegate in the Security Council, announced that the Soviet forces were being evacuated from the country. The Iranian Government and the United Nations thus emerged successfully from their contretemps with the Soviet Union. The Iranian Government went further. The legislative assembly, the Majlis, elected at the end of 1946, sensing the mood of triumph, consisted of a highly self-confident body of legislators, and, by an overwhelming vote – with the public encouragement of the American ambassador in Teheran – it declined to confirm the recent grant of a Soviet oil concession. Alleged violation was retorted on alleged violation. New revolts broke out in Azerbaijan, and it was not until 1948 that relative peace was restored and the Tudeh party was declared illegal and dissolved. A momentary peace descended upon Iran. But in 1950, as we shall describe later, disagreements between the Iranian Government and the Anglo-Iranian Oil Company developed into an open rupture. (See pp. 792-95.)

Iraq, Jordan, and Saudi Arabia were the three most stable of the Arab states of the Middle East in the immediate postwar years. In 1945 the Iraqi King Feisal II was a boy ten years old, and the country was being governed by a regent, his uncle, the Emir Abdul Illah, and his Premier, Nuri es-Said. Iraq had been the scene of a dangerous pro-Axis rising during the war in 1941 under Rashid Ali, leader of a local Fascist group. But British control had been re-established, and Iraq had returned to her British alliance. After the war, Nuri es-Said continued, with intervals, in the Premiership of Iraq, a confirmed Anglophile, widely respected abroad as one of the great elder statesmen of the Middle East.

One incident marred the otherwise even course of Iraqi affairs at this time. A new Anglo-Iraqi treaty, the Treaty of Portsmouth, intended to supersede the former treaty of 1930, was signed in January 1948. But provisions in it, which amounted to mutual military aid, were opposed by ardent Iraqi nationalists. Demonstrations against the treaty broke out in Baghdad, led in the main by students already excited by the Palestine issue and by Communist propaganda, and the Regent felt forced to announce that the treaty must be rejected. The incident served to show the extent of anti-British and pro-Communist feeling in Iraq and the insecurity of pro-British leaders like Nuri. Meanwhile, the country was relatively prosperous. The Iraq Petroleum Company was yielding a steady 50 per cent to the Iraqi exchequer. Except for the constant Communist threat and party rowdyism, Iraq's affairs seemed to be in fair condition.

Transjordan, hitherto an autonomous part of the British Palestine mandate, achieved her independence in 1946, her ruler, the Emir Abdullah, was crowned King, and the country was renamed the "Hashemite Kingdom of Jordan." A new treaty, virtually a mutual aid treaty, was signed with Britain in March 1948. The British Government was permitted to maintain air bases in Jordan. British officers, notably General Glubb, continued to hold appointments in the Jordanian "Arab Legion." Abdullah was a restless, scheming, ambitious character, not overpopular with his own people, disliked by his fellow neighboring monarchs, but, despite the Palestine issue, friendly to Britain. Even after Abdullah's assassination in 1951, Jordan, with all its poverty and geographical disabilities – and its refugee population – remained anchored to the Western interest.

Saudi Arabia's postwar history was almost lacking in outward events, except for the death in 1953 of her founder, the great Arab chieftain, King Ibn Saud. The country's economy and international position depended entirely upon oil. In 1945-50 the Gulf areas of Saudi Arabia produced 4 per cent of the world's petroleum and, together with Kuwait and Bahrain, were believed to possess 40 per cent of the world's petroleum reserves. The sole concessionaire in Saudi Arabia was Aramco, the Arabian American Oil Company, which, since an agreement of 1950, yielded 50 per cent of its profits, about $300,000,000 a year, to the national revenues of a population of 7,000,000. A once howling wilderness with a scattering of mean cities and Bedouin camps, barely supported upon a shepherd economy, had become as it were by accident in a single generation one of the wealthiest countries in the world. Roads, a railroad, hospitals, schools, and a university were soon under construction. The desert capital of Riyadh was redesigned by Western architects. Consequently Saudi Arabia was closely knit to her principal customer and benefactor, although as we write it would appear that an internal opposition to the reigning King Saud may be growing.

We pass now to the much stormier states of Syria and Lebanon, although it should be said in extenuation that they themselves were not entirely to blame for their condition. In 1940 the two countries, under their French governors, had adhered to Vichy, and in 1941 they had been forcibly occupied by British and Free French forces. (See p. 532.) Thereafter General de Gaulle, while seemingly agreeable to terminating the former French mandate, still hoped against hope that France's "pre-eminent and privileged position" in the two countries would be maintained. During 1943 and 1944 the two new republics of Syria and Lebanon were formed and were duly recognized by Britain, the United States, and the Soviet Union. But early in 1945, French troop "replacements" began to disembark at Beirut, and on May 27, in an atmosphere of increasing tension and without prior notice, the French opened an indiscriminate three-day bombardment of Damascus — just at the time that the United Nations was being organized at San Francisco. It was 1925 all over again. Winston Churchill sent a vigorous message to de Gaulle and ordered British troops into Syria to restore order. The French eventually withdrew their forces and most of their civilians, and effected thus the first of their postwar retirements from their overseas territories.

The stormiest of the Middle Eastern states at this time was Egypt. As the threat of invasion in 1942 receded, all the old party strifes started up again. Nevertheless, after elections in January 1945 the smaller parties seemed able to stay in power under a succession of premiers, Ahmed Maher, Nokrashy, and Sidky. The opposing Wafd party meanwhile was split between Nahas, a Moslem, and Makram Ebeid, a Coptic Christian. King Farouk was a symbol of growing unpopularity with his own people — and with his British supporters. Nationalist agitation cut across all party lines and generally found its objective in a revision of the Anglo-Egyptian Treaty of 1936 and also in a revival of the old issue, the "Unity of the Nile Valley," that is to say, the unification of Egypt and the Sudan under the Egyptian Crown. But the Sudanese now had their own ideas of independence and their own independence party, and they found little attraction in a possible Egyptian connection. In October 1946, Sidky went to London and obtained from Bevin, the British Foreign Secretary, the draft of a new treaty and a British pledge of complete withdrawal of British troops from Egypt. But the intemperate opposition of both Nahas and Makram Ebeid and threats from the powerful xenophobic organization, the Moslem Brotherhood, ended in the rejection of the new treaty, the resignation of Sidky, and the breakdown of Anglo-Egyptian negotiation. In December 1946, Nokrashy formed a government and made a brave attempt to divert a part of the national energy to urgent domestic problems — inflation and unemployment — but, in the eyes of all parties, the treaty and the Sudan were always more deserving of consideration.

Thus was the pattern set for Egyptian — and Sudanese — politics of the next few years. Needless to say, the British Government tried to conciliate the Sudanese factions and took the position that only the people of the Sudan should decide the future of the Sudan. In April 1947, Egypt brought the Anglo-Egyptian treaty dispute before the United Nations. The Security Council held over the dispute until that August, but by then the proposed partition of Palestine relegated every other dispute to a second place. In 1948 Egypt was fighting in the Israeli War.

In short, the Middle East at this time presents us with a remarkable political variety — six monarchies and three republics, all with a half-articulate regional self-consciousness, desperately nationalist, desperately needing internal reforms but generally little capable of achieving them, ready to admire or abhor, accept or reject the ever-present Western power and influence. But, as a part of this complex, we have still to consider Palestine.

Palestine

In an earlier chapter we left Palestine and her affairs somewhat in suspension. (See p. 200.) The British Government's White Paper of 1939 had been published and debated but not implemented when the Second World War broke out. But the provisions of the paper, although they had been appropriate in 1939, were soon outdated by the suddenly expanded pressure of Jewish immigration. Even during the war, whenever the means of transport was available, refugees in their thousands, often in unseaworthy boats and without quota assignments, left Europe to force their way into the country. The situation was reflected in the "Biltmore Program," adopted in May 1942 at a conference of American Zionists at the Biltmore Hotel in New York, repudiating the White Paper and demanding the creation of a Jewish State in Palestine and the transfer of immigration to the control of the Jewish Agency. Meanwhile, in Palestine during the war and immediately after, underground organizations, both Jewish and Arab, but particularly the Jewish Haganah, Irgun Zvai Leumi, and the Stern Gang, were increasingly active and were inflicting a new, Fascist-like terrorism on the country.

On August 31, 1945, in a letter to Attlee, the British Prime Minister, President Truman urged the immediate admission into Palestine of 100,000 Jews, mainly from Germany. The British Government declined the request "because of conditions in Palestine" and proposed a joint Anglo-American Committee of Inquiry into the Palestine question. The President continued to insist on his 100,000 Jews, and the British Government was persuaded to allow a temporary emergency quota of 1,500 a month, much to the alarm of the Arab states and the Arab League. The proposed Committee of Inquiry was appointed, went to work, and in April 1946 produced yet another in the long list of official Palestinian reports, all full of wise statesmanship and good will – and inacceptable to one or the other or both of the parties on the spot. But at least the new report, like the White Paper of 1939, recommended that Palestine should not be partitioned into separate Jewish and Arab states. In April 1947, the British Government referred the Palestine question to the United Nations and then gave formal notice that it would terminate the mandate in a year's time and withdraw all its troops by August 1948.

From this moment the situation in Palestine rapidly deteriorated. Irregular Jewish attacks of increasing scale and audacity were made on British personnel and British property. Some 100,000 British troops were in the country. Camps had already been set up in Cyprus to receive illegal Jewish immigrants intercepted out at sea. In April 1947, the General Assembly of the United Nations appointed another Special Committee of Inquiry, and in November, on the basis of its majority report, passed as a result of strong unofficial American and Zionist pressures, the General Assembly voted the partition of Palestine into separate Jewish and Arab states in economic union – with an internationalized Jerusalem enclave. But no one could say how the partition should be carried out, and no one was willing to lend the force to do it, if force was necessary. Certainly British troops, about to leave the country, could hardly be employed. Public opinion in Britain was sickened by the terrorism of Jewish armed gangs, which official Jewish organizations seemed to be doing nothing to restrain, and disappointed by the general lack of comprehension, outside Britain, of the British Government's years of painstaking effort in Palestine. It was now anxious only to wash its hands of the whole miserable affair. Meanwhile President Truman in the United States – in a presidential election year – was being subjected to an intense, nonstop fire from the Zionist lobby.

On May 15, 1948, the British mandate came to an end, and on the same day a Jewish Provisional Government proclaimed the State of Israel. Recognition by President Truman followed within minutes and by the Soviet Union a couple of days later. David Ben-Gurion was appointed Premier, and Dr. Chaim Weizmann was elected President of the Provisional Council.

The result was war. The Arab states went to the aid of the Arabs of Palestine, as they had warned they would do. Fighting was heaviest in and around Jerusalem, in the Negeb, and in Galilee. The Jordanian Legion occupied and held the Old City of Jerusalem. Surprisingly the State of Israel did not instantly collapse in a welter of massacre. An uneasy truce was agreed. Israeli terrorists assassinated the United Nations mediator, Count Folke Bernadotte of Sweden. The Israeli forces, by means of an air lift and in defiance of the truce terms, obtained arms and planes from sources on both sides of the Iron Curtain, notably from Czechoslovakia. By October, less than six months after the outbreak, Israeli forces had counterattacked and were deep in Arab territory. Early in 1949 under United Nations auspices, an armistice favorable to Israel was signed in Rhodes. King Abdullah of Jordan remained established in the Old City of Jerusalem, but 800,000 Arab refugees, driven from their homes in Palestine, were swarming into Jordan, a poor country which could not give them as much as a bare subsistence. The Arabs were left humiliated and revengeful. The Arab League's prestige was badly shaken. So ended the First Israeli War.

India, Pakistan, Ceylon, Burma, and Malaya

We have elsewhere described the rejection of the Cripps offer and the "Quit India" resolution of 1942. (See p. 543.) The Japanese threat was then at its height, and the Government of India was in no mood for risks. Gandhi and several of the leaders of the Indian National Congress consequently found themselves under detention. Outbreaks of violence and sabotage followed, notably in Bihar, along the army's lines of communication with the Assam front. The Moslem League under Jinnah was now fully committed to its plan for a separate Moslem state of Pakistan, while Hindu opinion was as adamant for "No Partition," and each side was trying to blackmail the British Government into acceptance of its particular thesis as the price of cooperation in the war. Nevertheless an Indian army of over 2,000,000, participating in campaigns of the Middle East, Africa, Italy, Burma, and Malaya, to a total cost of 180,000 casualties, would seem to have represented a war effort of no mean magnitude. In October 1943, Field Marshal Lord Wavell became Viceroy. At that moment the worst famine in India for forty years was raging in Bengal.

Gandhi was released from imprisonment in 1944 on grounds of ill health. His fellow Congress members were released in 1945, and the old fight was rejoined. The advent of the Labor government in Britain brought about no immediate change in British policy toward India. Government missions and leaders' conferences followed through 1945 and 1946. Differences between the National Congress and the Moslem League had now developed into an open struggle for political power. In October 1946, Wavell expanded the Viceroy's Executive Council into an "interim government," composed of Hindu and Moslem members, thus giving India her first responsible cabinet. By then both parties, Hindu and Moslem, were becoming alarmed at the current disturbances, which in Bihar and Bengal alone had cost over 10,000 lives. The British authorities in India were increasingly concerned over their inability to maintain law and order by the traditional methods and were clearly averse to risking the lives of British personnel in a conflict which Indians themselves were provoking.

In February 1947, Attlee, British Prime Minister, came out with the blunt pronouncement of a deadline – June 1948 – for the transfer of power in India from British to Indian hands, and India's future constitution, whatever it might be, would have to be completed by that date. At the same time Admiral Lord Mountbatten, lately Allied Supreme Commander in Southeast Asia, succeeded Wavell as Viceroy. The British Government's shock tactics and the immense personal ascendancy which the new Viceroy was able to establish over the Indian leaders, no less than the continual spread of riot and massacre, all had a sobering effect. The Viceroy was in London in June for Cabinet conferences and came back to India with a "procedural plan" providing for the immediate partition of India into separate Hindu and Moslem states. Attlee introduced an Indian Independence Bill into Parliament, and the two Dominions, India and Pakistan, were formally instituted on August 15, 1947. Mountbatten himself became the first Governor General of India, with Nehru as Prime Minister; Jinnah became the first Governor General of Pakistan.

On February 4, 1948, Ceylon likewise achieved Dominion status under a new constitution, creating a Ceylonese parliament with full powers.

Disturbances continued in India and Pakistan, but they were now the responsibility of the two new Dominions. The Sikh community, "betrayed" by a partition that cut right through its homeland, set out to exterminate the Moslems in the new province of Eastern Punjab, assigned to the Indian side of the line. Minorities in their thousands trecked from one Dominion to the other seeking security among their fellows. The total migration was estimated to have amounted to 5,000,000 persons. The Indian States, however, obliged to accede to the appropriate Dominion, usually did so peaceably and with good grace. But Hyderabad, with its Hindu majority and its Nizam, a Moslem ruler, stood out, and for a time it seemed that the Nizam was trying to create an independent state. Irregular Hyderabadi forces, allegedly led by Communist agents, were plundering and pillaging and even raiding across the Hyderabadi borders into India proper. Eventually, in 1948, Indian troops moved into Hyderabad and compelled the Nizam to declare his accession to India.

The state of Kashmir in the far north, however, with its Moslem majority and its Maharajah, a Hindu ruler, was not so readily settled. In 1947, immediately on the announcement of independence, Northwest Frontier tribesmen invaded Kashmiri territory, presumably on behalf of Pakistan. The Maharajah hurriedly acceded to India and appealed for Indian troops to protect his capital. Kashmir remained divided within herself and unattached to either Dominion, and fighting continued indecisively through 1948, when a United Nations commission, visiting the country, was at last able to arrange a cease-fire. As we write the Kashmir problem is still unsolved.

In 1948 both India and Pakistan lost their national leaders. On January 30 Gandhi was assassinated in Delhi; on September 11 Jinnah died in Karachi. Mountbatten, meanwhile, presuming that the transfer of power had now been effected, retired and was succeeded as Governor General of India by Rajagopalachari of Madras. Nehru was under strong pressure from his Indian associates to withdraw from the Commonwealth and from the entire British connection. In April 1949, at the Commonwealth Prime Ministers' Conference in London, he submitted, amicably but firmly, that he could only keep India within the Commonwealth if she became a republic, recognizing the British Crown "as the symbol of the free association of its independent members." And, upon his formula, the Indian Constituent Assembly, sitting in Delhi, completed its constitution for India. On January 26, 1950, the Republic of India was proclaimed. Rajendra

Prasad, former president of the Constituent Assembly, was elected first President of the Republic.

The subsequent history of the Republic of India (or simply India, as she must now be called) was extraordinarily even and steady. All the gloomy prognostications that she should relapse into the Mogul anarchy, from which the British had originally rescued her, turned out to be false. A great deal was due to her Prime Minister Nehru and to her Deputy Prime Minister, "strong man" Sardar Vallabhbhai Patel – and also to the trained Indianized civil service which the British left behind them in Delhi. On November 26, 1949, after two years' labor, the Constituent Assembly adopted a Constitution, a massive, highly detailed instrument, describing a Federal Republic with a President and Prime Minister, and a bicameral legislature at the Center (a Council of States and a House of the People) elected by adult franchise. The official language of India was to be Hindi.

India's foreign policy was at once aligned with "neutralism" between East and West, and remained so thereafter with absolute constancy. It was perhaps surprising that so big a country, with so many problems, should have subscribed to so simple and uncompromising a relationship with the rest of the world. But the choice was primarily Nehru's, and he was guided no doubt by the long pacifist tradition in Hindu India no less than by a frank, realistic recognition of the fact that India's military weakness gave him little alternative. Nehru, from his neutral stronghold, gradually emerged as a statesman of international stature, a veritable world consultant on mediation and conciliation, wielding indeed far more influence than his real power might suggest. But India's greatest problem, as we write, is not foreign but domestic. It is the problem she shares with her Asian neighbors – peasant poverty and overpopulation.

The subsequent history of Pakistan was very different from India's. The division of the Dominion into East and West Pakistan – the East more populous but a quarter the area of the West, with 1,000 miles of Indian territory between them – constituted a fundamental, insuperable disability. There was, for example, no obvious capital for the new state – although for the time being Karachi served the purpose well enough. Irrigation systems in the Punjab and in the Ganges Delta, once operating as self-contained wholes, were now arbitrarily cut by political boundaries. Primary products, like jute and cotton, if they were to be marketed, had to be processed as formerly in Bombay and Calcutta. Nor was the problem of a constitution quickly solved. A Constituent Assembly was set up in 1947 and acted temporarily as a legislature. But its discussions dragged on interminably, and in October 1954 the then Governor General, Ghulam Mohammed, deeming that the Assembly was no longer representative, summarily dissolved it. Shortly afterward, in September 1955, he resigned on grounds of ill health and was succeeded by General Iskander Mirza of the Pakistani Army. In February 1956, a constitution was at last adopted, and on March 23, 1956, the Federal Islamic Republic of Pakistan was duly proclaimed. But by then Pakistan was virtually a military dictatorship. In

October 1958, General Mohammed Ayub Khan, Commander in Chief of the Army, succeeded Mirza as President of the new Republic.

Again, in contrast with India, Pakistan's foreign policy was neither neutral nor pacifist. Pakistan looked outward upon the rest of the Moslem world and upon the Western alliance. In 1954 she entered into a treaty of "friendly cooperation" with Turkey. In the same year she began to receive substantial American military aid – greatly to the alarm of Indian opinion, which assumed that the armament was intended for aggression, if not against Kashmir, then against India herself. In 1955 Pakistan joined the Baghdad Pact, and in 1956 SEATO. (See p. 797.)

Burma, all this time, had stood apart from the above developments. The country had suffered Japanese occupation and was not liberated till the early months of 1945. Burma's problem, as in all liberated countries, was then to come to some accommodation with the wartime resistance, in this case the Anti-Fascist People's Freedom League (AFPFL), which now wished to constitute itself the national government. Eventually, early in 1947, Aung San, leader of the AFPFL, visited London and discussed with members of the British Government the election of a Constituent Assembly in Burma. He made it clear that Burmese opinion had gone too far to accept any sort of reversion to the British Commonwealth and that the country, if domestic peace was to be restored, must become a completely independent republic.

A Burmese Constituent Assembly was elected in April 1947, and Aung San and his AFPFL secured 173 out of 210 elective seats; in addition, 44 seats were allocated to Burma's minorities, the frontier peoples, the Shans, Kachins, and Chins. But Aung San unhappily was not to enjoy his office for long. On July 19, 1947, during a meeting of his cabinet, he and six of his colleagues were assassinated by a posse of gunmen, who had forced their way into the chamber and who were afterward proved to be connected with the collaborationists of the Japanese occupation. Aung San was succeeded by Thakin Nu, also of the AFPFL. A constitution was drawn up, somewhat recalling the Irish Constitution of 1937, and was approved by the Constituent Assembly. An Anglo-Burmese treaty, regulating the transfer of power, was signed in London by Attlee and Thakin Nu. The Union of Burma, an independent, republican sovereign state, came into existence on January 4, 1948.

But independence did not restore the domestic peace of Burma. Aung San's assassination was only one incident in what was now to be a long-drawn-out conflict. The former resistance groups, especially the two Communist wings of the AFPFL, were now turning to brigandage of a kind that had always been Burma's besetting sin. Also in the field were the Karen hillmen and, after 1948, units of Nationalist Chinese, which the Communist victory in China had left stranded in northern Burma. Industries, particularly those of British ownership or management, were at a standstill. But Burma in her misfortune was a good object lesson. As so often happened in these years, those former "colonial" countries made a better success of the great experiment of independence that did not, like

Burma, totally cut themselves loose, but retained some sort of link with the former metropolitan power.

Malaya completes the group of Asian territories which were formerly in British possession. Like Burma, Malaya had suffered Japanese occupation, and the fall of Singapore in 1942 had been, for Britain and the Allies, one of the key disasters of the war. Also like Burma, Malaya's postwar problem was centered in the wartime resistance groups, notably the Malayan People's Anti-Japanese Army (MPAJA), which refused to disband and, under a new political disguise, had taken to brigandage. The British, when they returned to Malaya, proposed a Malayan Union under a British Governor assisted by native councils. But this was far from the hopes and aspirations of the newly founded independence party, the United Malay Nationalist Organization (UMNO), which called for complete self-determination for Malaya. The titular rulers of the nine States, for their part, demanded the allegiance of their respective populations, not to a central Malayan Union, but to themselves.

The usual constitutional proposals and counterproposals followed in due course, but satisfied no party. Malaya was an uneasy assemblage of three ethnic communities – Malay, Indian, and Chinese – formerly divided into a loose federation of nine States and the city of Singapore; and now injected into this situation was the universal menace of Communism. The MPAJA, if it was anything, was Communist, and from its jungle hide-outs it conducted a guerrilla war against its enemies in the rubber plantations and tin mines. By 1948 50,000 British troops were in Malaya engaged in a long, difficult campaign against this elusive and resourceful force. Yet, nothing loth, the British Government proceeded with its political reforms. The Malayan Union was established in April 1946 and then superseded by a Federation of Malaya in February 1948 – Singapore, for the time being, remaining a crown colony. "Ministerial status" was achieved in 1953 with Abdul Rahman, leader of the UMNO as "Chief Minister," and full Dominion status on August 31, 1957.

Indonesia

Indonesia has always been somewhat of an anthropological, and thence a political, tangle. Even its name did not come into currency till the 1850's and was then used to denote the islands inhabited by the lighter-skinned peoples, south and east of Malaya. In European parlance hitherto the islands had been the "Spice Islands." Other common terms were "East Indies," "Further India," and "Malay Archipelago." The Dutch used to refer to their possessions in the area as "Netherlands India."

This very want of a name had its significance. Of all the "colonial" territories we have been describing in the present chapter, Indonesia had never developed a historic culture that its modern peoples, aspiring to independence, could look back upon. Except perhaps in Java and Bali, it had little in the way of an indigenous civilization to command respect or restoration. Earlier contacts with India had been rare and irregular. Islam arrived via India in the thirteenth century, but it built no empire. The Portuguese, Dutch, and British arrived in the sixteenth and seventeenth centuries and treated the islands as mere trading outposts. As we approach modern times Indonesia was a Dutch colonial possession, harshly but paternally administered, inhabited by a primitive and unsophisticated native people, speaking Malay, and mainly Moslem in religion, but grounded in no past – or future.

The Indonesian people, for all their cultural and political disabilities, were now producing a leadership and a nationalism. As early as 1908, educated Javanese had founded a local nationalist society under the flamboyant title of Boedo Oetomo or "Glorious Endeavor," and in 1918 the Dutch authorities, sensing signs of potential trouble, had set up a *Volksraad* or People's Council with advisory functions. In 1927 the National Indonesian party was organized by Achmad Soekarno, a Javanese schoolteacher, who like other "intellectuals" of his kind had completed his education in Holland. Indonesia's progress was very similar to that of many another colonial territory, when in 1941 she passed under Japanese occupation.

Early in August 1945, just before their surrender, the Japanese declared the independence of Indonesia in the name of the Japanese Emperor. They hoped no doubt to disembarrass themselves of local obstruction to their withdrawal – and incidentally to embarrass the returning Dutch or British. On August 17, 1945, Soekarno proclaimed the independence of the Indonesian Republic, not in the name of the Japanese Emperor, but in that of the Indonesian people. A British unit reached the former capital, Batavia, in September 1945 with orders to disarm and intern remaining Japanese troops. But then, in October, arrived the Dutch Governor General, Dr. van Mook, with a full complement of Dutch officials and armed forces. Negotiations opened between van Mook and a new Indonesian Premier, Sutan Sjahrir, who, though a Communist, had not compromised himself with the Japanese as had Soekarno. Van Mook returned to Amsterdam to induce the Dutch Government to take a more liberal line, and he conferred with Attlee, in London, who Labor-like, also urged drastic concessions.

Fighting had now broken out in different parts of Indonesia, fighting which often enough was conducted by terrorist gangs of no possible political allegiance, and for good measure the "Government" of a rebel Indonesian Republic had established a rival "capital" at Jogjakarta. In November 1946, partly as the result of British intervention, Dutch and Indonesians agreed to create a federal, democratic United States of Indonesia, linked with the Dutch Crown in a Netherlands-Indonesian Union. The scheme was pretentious and vague, and it soon broke down over the different "interpretations" put upon it by the different parties. Offers of mediation poured in from the United States, India, and Australia. The United Nations Security Council appointed a Committee of Good Offices. But in midsummer 1947 van Mook announced that Dutch forces would take such action as they deemed necessary to end an intolerable situation and set about a virtual reconquest of the island of Java. Indonesian Communists organized a "Soviet Republic" at Madiun. In 1948 Indonesia had three capitals – Batavia, Jogjakarta, Madiun – waging a triangular war against one another.

It is not necessary for our purpose to itemize all this incident. We have already had enough of this kind of history in this chapter. The eventual independence of Indonesia was brought about to some extent as the result of an Asian Conference convened at Delhi in January 1949, under the initiative of Nehru, and attended by the delegates or observers of nineteen countries, including India, Pakistan, Australia, and New Zealand. The conference condemned the Dutch military action in Java and forwarded its resolutions to the United Nations. This was the postwar period of colonial liberalism. The Indonesian settlement might have been otherwise had it been attempted at a date subsequent to the Korean War in 1950. After several further alarms and excursions, a full-dress conference of over a hundred Dutch and Indonesian representatives met at The Hague in August 1949, and on December 27, 1949, the Republic of Indonesia at last came into being with Soekarno as its first President and Batavia, renamed Jakarta, as its capital. Dutch New Guinea – or Irian, as the Indonesians called it – was excluded from these arrangements and remained under direct Dutch colonial administration.

It seemed as if the worst Dutch apprehensions would now be realized. Indonesia was not only a "power vacuum," as the modern phraseology has it, but also a culture vacuum. There was little to unite or stabilize the new national pride. Independence for a time was a chaos, in which the only enclaves of order were those under the control of individual leaders of various political colors, sometimes assisted by Dutch "volunteers." Small wonder that the Dutch Government in August 1954, on its own initiative, formally dissolved the Netherlands-Indonesian Union. By that date hardly any territory outside Java remained loyal to the government in Jakarta, and only gradually did Soekarno establish a somewhat precarious control over his far-flung republic.

42. ASIA AND AFRICA: THE REVOLT

The Korean War

In the last chapter we considered the "Asian Settlement" as we called it – although some of it, as we saw, seemed far from settlement. We now pass on to the Afro-Asian revolt. The key date is 1950. In Europe by that time there was a pause. The Berlin blockade was over; Intermediate Europe was quiescent; NATO had been established. The main weight of events now shifted to Asia and for three years was concentrated in the remote little country of Korea. In the first part of this chapter, accordingly, we shall consider the Asian Crises of 1950-60 as they arose: the Korean War, the war in Indochina, the Iranian Oil Crisis, the Suez Crisis and the Second Israeli War, and the Iraqi Revolution. In the last part of the chapter we shall consider Africa.

The Nationalist regime of Chiang Kai-shek in China had survived to the end of the Second World War in 1945, but it was undeniably corrupt, and it was fast losing the loyalty and respect of the Chinese people. General George C. Marshall, on a mission to China in 1946, could bring about no compromise or conciliation between it and its Communist rivals, then inaccessibly entrenched in the distant province of Yunan, and he returned home in January 1947 chagrined and pessimistic. During 1948 and 1949 Mao Tse-tung, the Communist leader, brought the whole of the Chinese mainland under his control. The Chinese People's Republic was proclaimed on October 1, 1949, with its capital at Peking. Chiang Kai-shek and the remnant of the Nationalist forces escaped to Formosa, which, together with the off-shore islands of Quemoy and Matsu, they continued to hold. Hong Kong remained a British colony.

Japan, meanwhile, was under Allied occupation – in the main, American occupation. The country was virtually subject to General Douglas MacArthur, Supreme Commander Allied Powers (SCAP), administering through a four-Power Control Council in Tokyo. A redefinition of the status of the Emperor, a new democratic constitution, extensive land reforms, and workers' unionization were all enacted during 1946 and were presumably accepted by the greater part of the Japanese people. The Japanese peace treaty was signed in San Francisco on September 8, 1951.

Given a chance "for the dust to settle" in China, as Dean Acheson put it, and for the Japanese to accustom themselves to their political reformation, the Far East should not again have troubled the world for many a long year. But in 1950, war broke out in Korea.

Geographically, Korea is a rugged, stumpy, semimountainous peninsula jutting out from the Manchurian mainland, about half the area of California, forming a natural "bridge" between Japan and China and historically more than once disputed by them. It is inhabited by a people ethnically mixed, but of distinctive language and of an ancient, homogeneous culture. Since 1895 – and formally since 1900 – it had passed under Japanese rule and thereafter had developed the usual characteristics of an oppressed nationalism – this time under an Asian oppression. During the Second World War, at the Cairo Conference in 1943, the United States, Britain, and China had declared that "in due course," Korea should once again become free and independent, and the declaration had been confirmed by implication at the Potsdam Conference in 1945.

However, the immediate fate of Korea was settled by events without reference to these prior diplomatic undertakings. During August 1945, after the surrender of Japan, Soviet forces entered Korean territory from the north, and, during September, American forces landed in the south; and the two forces, after some haphazard maneuvering, halted facing one another along the 38th parallel, a line virtually bisecting the country. A provisional military arrangement hardened into a static political division, and each Power – the Soviet to the north of the parallel and the American to the south – was shortly organizing its zone according to its lights. At the Moscow Conference at the end of 1945, proposals were made to set up a "Provisional Korean Democratic Government" to be assisted by a Soviet-American Joint Commission, pledged to consult "Korean democratic parties." In March 1946, the Joint Commission convened in Seoul – now in South Korea, although formerly the capital city of the whole country – but it was soon deadlocked over the definition of "democratic parties" and adjourned. In December 1946, in South Korea, under American auspices, a somewhat conservative legislative assembly came into being in Seoul. The United Nations debated the Korean situation in September 1947, and a United Nations commission was sent out to Korea to supervise elections for a new legislative assembly, but the members of the commission were refused admission into North Korea, the Soviet zone. Accordingly, in May 1948, to the accompaniment of widespread riots, elections were held in South Korea for a body which shortly constituted itself the Democratic Republic of Korea and which formally proclaimed the independence of Korea on August 15, 1948, with full American diplomatic recognition. Simultaneously, in North Korea, a People's Democratic Republic was set up in Pyongyang, with full Soviet diplomatic recognition.

By 1948 the celebrated 38th parallel had become an iron curtain as formidable as any in Intermediate Europe. On either side were two antagonistic political regimes, and their mutual isolation was broken only by the occasional passage of refugees or by sporadic frontier clashes. North Korea was Communist, with a hand-picked assembly of "workers" and "peasants"; South Korea was democratic, with a hand-picked assembly somewhat over-weighted by landlords and other "capitalist" elements. Economically the zones were further divided by the fact that North Korea contained most of the industries and the hydroelectric plants, and South Korea contained the main rice-bowl areas. An intense hostility developed between the zones. Each government claimed jurisdiction over the other; each constitution provided for eventual national reunification under itself; even in the respective legislative chambers, seats were left demonstratively vacant, awaiting absent members from the other side. The situation was soon matched by the creation of two military forces – in North Korea, a People's Militia, Soviet armed and trained, allegedly some 100,000 strong; and, in South Korea, a police, American armed and trained, allegedly some 50,000 strong. But whereas the militia was equipped as a fighting army, the police was only lightly armed, more after the manner of an internal security force. By this time the greater part of the American and Soviet occupation forces had been withdrawn.

The two zones were divided even by the character of their leaders. The President of the People's Republic was the legendary figure Kim Il-sung, still in his thirties, Moscow-trained, Secretary of the Korean Communist party, and since 1931 an underground resistance fighter against the Japanese. The President of the Democratic Republic was the equally legendary figure, Syngman Rhee, an elder statesman of over seventy years of age, who had fought the Japanese since the turn of the century, a graduate of Harvard and Princeton, a student and admirer of Woodrow Wilson, Methodist missionary, and head of the Korean governments in exile in the United States and China. Syngman Rhee, it may be added, was also one of that type of "difficult" nationalist leader with whom Western statesmanship in recent years so often had to deal, a man who represented in himself the stubborn, touchy dignity of a persecuted people, single-minded to the point of monomania, comprehending no arguments but his own, yet with undeniable heroism in his make-up.

Open warfare between the two zones in Korea started suddenly in the early morning of June 25, 1950 (Korean time), a Sunday. Informed journalists were not slow to recall that Pearl Harbor had been attacked on a Sunday, and that Hitler and Mussolini had favored Sundays for their surprises. The United Nations commission, which we mentioned earlier, was still in South Korea, and it reported within a few hours that South Korea had been invaded by North Korean forces. At an emergency meeting on June 25 (E.S.T.), the United Nations Security Council adopted an American resolution calling for an immediate cease-fire and the withdrawal of the North Korean forces to the 38th parallel. The Soviet delegate was then boycotting the Security Council, in protest against the presence in it of the Chinese (Nationalist) delegate, and was not at the meeting. The same afternoon and on the following day President Truman conferred with his advisers of the State and Defense Departments and of the Joint Chiefs of Staff in Washington, and, on the basis of their recommendations, he decided to give American support to the South Korean forces – first naval and air support and then ground forces. On June 27, the Security Council – again in the absence of the Soviet delegate – resolved that the members of the United Nations "furnish such assistance to the Republic of Korea as may be necessary to repel the armed attack and to restore international peace and security in the area."

Subsequent accusation and counteraccusation failed to shake the main facts of the case. The United Nations and Western opinion generally were satisfied that the North Koreans had launched "a well-planned, concerted, and full-scale invasion of South Korea" and moreover had done so with Soviet encouragement and cooperation. It could be argued that the North Koreans at first had intended only to liquidate the galling and dangerous situation along the 38th parallel. But the operation which now developed was no "Israeli raid"; it was war in all but name. The fact that the Soviet delegate was boycotting the Security Council and was not there to resort to his usual tactics with the veto also suggests that, even if the Soviet had wished the war, immediate events in Korea were not entirely according to Soviet calculations.

President Truman's decision to use American forces in Korea was entirely his own. He could have withdrawn behind a face-saving gesture. It was an open secret that the Joint Chiefs of Staff regarded Korea as militarily expendable. The logistic problems of fighting a war on the other side of the Pacific were stupendous. Nevertheless, the President resolved to act, and we have no reason to believe that he did not do so with the full consciousness of all the factors and consequences and with the highest motives. The North Korean challenge was flagrant and could hardly be shirked. As for the Soviet Union – if it was really behind the war – the motives were deeper and more disingenuous. Wars "by proxy" were already customary devices of the Soviet armory. Korea was not the first time that the Soviet Union had provoked a war among potential enemies – and, in Soviet eyes, all other powers were potential enemies – while it stood on the side lines and picked up whatever prizes might befall. Start a fight among other people, and keep out of it yourself. It was a dangerous game, but it had classical precedents. Cardinal Richelieu in the seventeenth century had played it. Soviet diplomacy in 1936 in respect to Spain, in 1939 in respect to Germany – and later in 1956 in respect to the Middle East – could in each instance bear such an interpretation. And now perhaps, in 1950, a Sino-American war would surely not come entirely amiss to the grand cynics of the Kremlin.

Forty member States of the United Nations associated themselves with the Security Council's resolution of June 27, 1950, and offered supplies, transport, hospital units and, in some cases, combat forces. But the main contribution came from the United States – and from South Korea. General MacArthur was designated Commander in Chief of the United Nations Forces in Korea. Chiang Kai-shek from Formosa, seeing an opportunity to recoup his fortunes, offered substantial forces, but the offer was firmly, though respectfully declined. Eventual casualties in the course of the war represent a gauge of military commitment and, incidentally, of political interest. By the end of 1951, after the Chinese intervention, when the front was once more stabilized, the United States had lost in killed, wounded and missing, over 100,000 men; the South Koreans had lost 200,000. Figures for the other participants were:

Britain	3,000	Greece	350
Turkey	2,000	Netherlands	350
France	850	Thailand	350
Australia	700	Philippines	300
Canada	650		

and lesser numbers for Belgium, Colombia, Ethiopia, New Zealand, and South Africa. North Korean and Chinese losses have been put at 1,500,000.[1]

The course of the Korean War fell into two phases – the first before, and the second after, the Chinese intervention. The first phase at once developed into a race against time – North Korean preparation versus American resilience and organization. American ground forces immediately available were occupation units in Japan, untrained for the fighting they were now called upon to undertake, and their initial casualties were disastrous. Reinforcements from the United States began to arrive in Korea within two weeks of the outbreak of hostilities – an incredible feat in itself – and the build-up continued thereafter. In the first month of the fighting the North Korean forces overran almost the entire South Korean territory, and were halted at last only 50 miles from the port of Pusan on the southern tip of the peninsula. Then, on September 14, 1950, an American army, covered by American and British naval forces, landed at Inchon and in twelve days retook the Korean capital, Seoul. The North Koreans, their communications severed, fell back in disorder. At the end of September, the United Nations forces once more stood along the 38th parallel. By all ordinary military reckoning the objectives of the war had been achieved. MacArthur promptly broadcast a surrender ultimatum to the North Korean commander.

But a second phase of the war, of far heavier fighting and more dangerous political complications, was now to come. The North Koreans refused to surrender, and the United Nations was faced with the decision of crossing the 38th parallel and defeating the enemy in his own territory. To cross or not to cross – that was the question. In the United Nations the main debate was now transferred to the General Assembly. The Soviet delegate, Yakov Malik, had returned to the Security Council, there to resume his policy of obstruction. Under the circumstances, the General Assembly, guided by Secretary Acheson, was taking over some of the responsibilities that the senior body had clearly shown itself unable to fulfill. Accordingly, on October 7, 1950, after long and agonizing discussions, the General Assembly of the United Nations resolved that "all constituent acts be taken . . . for the establishment of a unified, independent, and democratic government in the sovereign State of Korea." American forces crossed the 38th parallel the next day; South Korean forces, impatient of restraint, had already preceded them. Pyongyang, the North Korean capital, was quickly occupied; points on the Yalu River were reached on November 22.

Chou En-lai, the Communist Chinese Premier, declared from Peking that "the Chinese people will not tolerate aggression, nor stand aside while foreign imperialists savagely assault their neighbors," and a massive intervention on the part of the Chinese People's Republic was mounted in Korea by the end of the year. Seoul fell to the enemy early in January 1951, but was retaken by a counteroffensive under General Ridgway in March. By June, the anniversary of the outbreak of the war, the line was once more re-established along the 38th parallel.

The Korean War, especially in its present Sino-American phase, was strongly supported by wide sections of opinion in the United States and in Congress. The war had undoubtedly given psychological release to the national exasperation. Traditionally Americans had always had a deep affection for the Chinese people. American travelers had carried out much of the early exploration of the Chinese interior provinces; American museums housed some of the finest collections of Chinese art; American missions, schools, and hospitals had been built throughout the length and breadth of Chinese territory. But since the victory of Communism in China, all this philanthropy had been cast out. Insult had been heaped on injury. Missionaries, teachers, and nurses had been sent packing, some barely escaping with their lives, leaving their work in ruins. Americans were perhaps learning one of the lessons of their new international eminence in the world — that if there is one sentiment unknown to international relations, it is gratitude. The American temper was clearly demonstrated in the American-sponsored resolution in the United Nations General Assembly on February 1, 1951, by which Communist China was "branded" the aggressor.

American opinion was also shocked by the extreme ferocity of the war. The Koreans, a mild people by common repute, were found to be capable of incredible atrocities. The Chinese Communists, in their peculiar fanaticism, posed another problem quite beyond American military experience hitherto. Since the fighting in Europe in 1944-45, it had become accepted military doctrine that absolute command of the air could effectively immobilize an opposing army. But the Chinese Communists now exposed their sheer numbers to American air power and ground fire. By the "tactics of inundation" the defender was all but defied to exhaust his ammunition on the bodies of his assailants. For mass slaughter Korean battlefields were unprecedented even on the Western front in the First World War.

At the same time the war bore a curiously unreal aspect. All the greater powers and all the more forceful voices in the United Nations were unanimous that the war should not be extended beyond its Korean limits. Atomic weapons were not used, and even conventional bombing by American aircraft to the north of the Yalu River, where most of the Chinese supply depots were concentrated, was scrupulously avoided. Soviet submarines, operating from Vladivostok, could have instantly transformed the entire strategic position at sea. Soviet fighter planes appeared over Korea early in 1951, but otherwise there was no overt complicating Soviet intervention. MacArthur characteristically inveighed against "abnormal military inhibitions." But political caution prevailed. The Sino-American War remained localized.

MacArthur was evidently chafing under all these restrictions. Supreme Commander Allied Powers (SCAP), Commander in Chief Far East (CINCFE), and since June 1950 Commander in Chief of the United Nations Forces in Korea, General MacArthur had long been somewhat of a political problem child. Imperious in his administrative methods, fond of flamboyant statements in public, he had more than once sorely tried his superiors in Washington. He was now clearly using his unique authority to align himself with those elements in Congress that were pressing for more drastic action in Korea and, if necessary, in the entire Far East. On March 24, 1951, on his own initiative, he declared himself ready to confer with the enemy commander in North Korea on the terms of a political settlement "without being burdened by extraneous matters" and he coupled his offer with a covert threat to depart from the present "tolerant effort" to limit the war. Secretary Acheson hastened to explain that the General's statement was "unexpected and unauthorized." But on April 5 in the course of a debate in the House in Washington, Representative Joseph W. Martin, Leader of the Republican opposition, read a letter that he had received from MacArthur some days before, in which, in so many words, MacArthur had recommended the employment of the Chinese Nationalist forces from Formosa to open up a new front in China.

President Truman had no alternative. MacArthur had to be dismissed. MacArthur returned to the United States forthwith to participate in the political crisis that he had stirred up around himself. He enjoyed ticker-tape ovations in San Francisco, New York, Chicago, and his "home town" of Milwaukee; he addressed a joint session of Congress; he testified with force and brilliance before Senate committees; he did not deny that he had ambitions for the Presidency at the next elections.

The MacArthur affair belonged thereafter more to American history than to Asian. But it is right that we should mention it here. It served to crystallize American opinion towards the character and continuance of the Korean War. In the end the affair wore itself out. President Truman undoubtedly came out of it with immensely enhanced personal prestige. Then, on June 23, 1951, public interest was seized by a broadcast from Malik in Moscow appealing for a cease-fire in Korea. Armistice negotiations started, first at Kaesong in "No Man's Land," and then at Panmunjon. Large-scale fighting died down; but the armistice negotiations, often stormy and often interrupted, were to drag on for two years.

The crucial issue was over the repatriation of prisoners of war. Numbers of the North Korean and Chinese prisoners in the hands of the United Nations refused to be repatriated; several American prisoners in the hands of the North Koreans, it was alleged, had been "brain-washed" and some had signed "confessions" to the effect that they had taken part in bacteriological warfare. Eventually it was decided that a neutral "custodian force," in the main an Indian force and under the command of an Indian general, should supervise the task of interviewing the prisoners and returning them, without restraint, to the country of their choice. The armistice negotiations were concluded at last on July 27, 1953.

The Korean War was over – but only by an armistice that looked as thin as the paper it was written on. Syngman Rhee, headstrong as ever,

KOREA, 1945-53

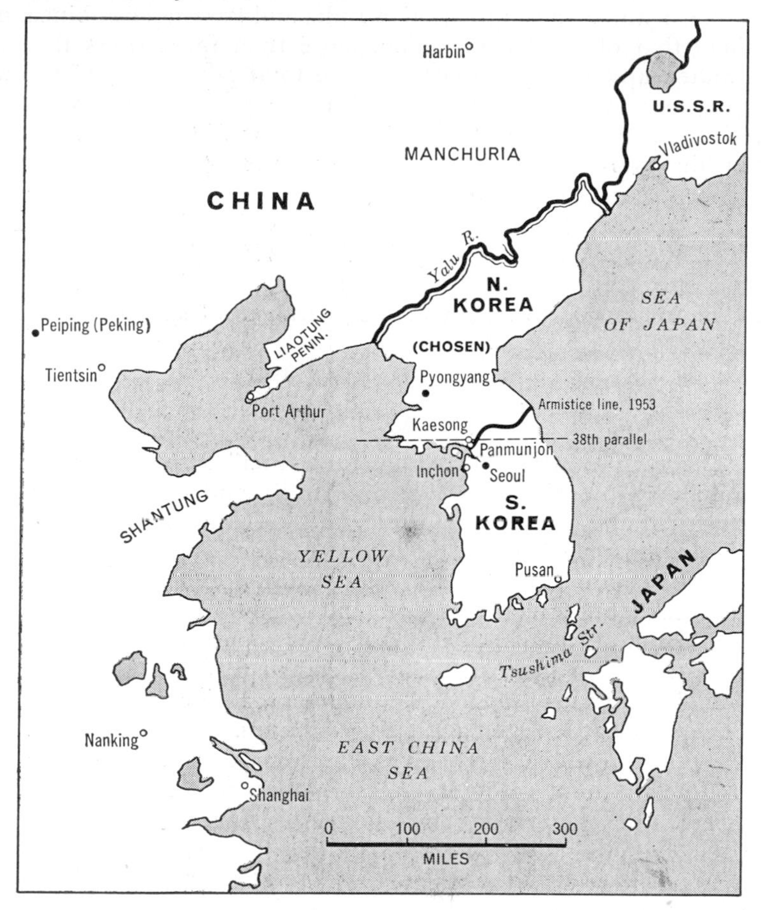

declared that it was a betrayal of all Korean aspirations for a United Korea and that the South Koreans, if necessary, would continue the war alone. As it happened, the South Koreans did not continue the war, but Syngman Rhee obtained some concessions, including a defensive treaty between South Korea and the United States, which was duly ratified by the Senate before the end of the year. In North Korea, characteristically, the armistice was celebrated with treason trials of prominent North Koreans, propaganda chiefs, and police officers accused of being in American pay. In China there appears to have been a simultaneous wave of arrests and death sentences.

The present section on this part of the Far East needs one postscript before we pass on to Indochina and then to the Middle East. In July 1953, about the same time as the conclusion of the Korean armistice, the National Bureau of Statistics in Peking, published its census of the population of China. The figure, long uncertain and often disputed, appeared at last to have been settled by an organized and accurate hard count. The population of the mainland of China (including Manchuria, but excluding

Formosa), as of June 1953, was given as 582,603,417 – that is to say, nearly half as much again as the population of India and Pakistan combined, nearly three times that of the Soviet Union, more than three times that of the United States, and nearly a quarter of the total population of the world. The figure, moreover, it is to be remembered, represented the residue from over half a century of continuous revolution and war. Since 1953, the population of China has risen by a net average rate of 10,000,000 a year and is now (1961) put at 650,000,000.

It was a staggering result. A population of this size, however "underdeveloped," had to count heavily in the world-wide contest for power. If nothing else, here was a crude mathematical fact which, in an era of mass destruction, amounted to an invincible guarantee of survival.

Indochina

The geographical expression "Indochina" designated mixed territories, inhabited by mixed peoples, historically and ethnically molded by contacts with India and China. Two large river basins and their deltas, the Red River or Song Koi in the north and Mekong in the south, separated by the massive S-shaped cordillera of Annam, formed its main physical features. French missionary and economic penetration had begun in the time of Louis XVI, and by the 1860's French political control had been generally established. Indochina thereafter had followed the usual history of a colonial territory – economic development, administrative experiment, and then, eventually, native nationalist resistance. Local revolt and mutiny had been touched off by Japan's victory over Russia in 1905 and by the Russian Revolution in 1917. Annamese coolies, who had served in labor battalions on the Western front in France during the First World War, returned home full of subversive ideas. In the interwar years Indochina could not help but react, as she had always reacted, to events then proceeding in India and China.

In 1939 French Indochina consisted of the colony of Cochin-China, the four protectorates of Cambodia, Annam, Tongking, and Laos, and the "leased" territory of Kwang-Chou. A king ruled in Cambodia by courtesy of the French Governor; an emperor ruled in Annam, by name Bao Dai, descendant of a former king of Cochin-China, a young man then completing his education in Paris. The capital of Indochina, the seat of the French Governor General, was in Saigon in Cochin-China.

Even without the Fall of France in 1940, Indochina was in no fit state, domestically or militarily, to resist the Japanese aggression; and, but for pressure from Berlin, which did not want to embarrass the Vichy government, Indochina would have fallen to Japan long before the decisive date of Pearl Harbor. As it was, the Japanese forced Admiral Jean Decoux, the French Governor General, a Vichy appointee since 1940, to close the ports in Tongking by which war materials were being sent inland to Nationalist China and to permit the construction of the bases, from which the Japanese assaults on Malaya and Siam were eventually made. In 1940-41 French and

Japanese troops combined to suppress a nationalist rising by a band of Annamese exiles operating from China. The rising was perhaps not very considerable, but it was the occasion of the first appearance of the Annamese revolutionary leader, Ho Chi-minh.

In March 1945, with defeat in sight, the Japanese acted in Indochina much as they acted in Indonesia. They declared the independence of Viet Nam (the "Peoples of the South"), a state composed of Cochin-China, Annam, and Tongking – under the Emperor Bao Dai. Bao Dai held his shaky throne through the summer months of 1945, and then, when the Japanese finally surrendered, he conveniently abdicated. Ho Chi-minh, still waging guerrilla war against Japan from the jungles of northern Tongking – and now in receipt of American supplies – proclaimed Viet Nam an independent democratic republic and declared all former treaties with France null and void.

In September 1945, a British-Indian force landed at Saigon with orders to disarm and intern Japanese found south of the 16th parallel, and to leave the similar task to the Chinese Nationalists north of the parallel. As in other territories in the same circumstances elsewhere, the inevitable struggle began between the returning colonial power and the local revolutionary nationalists. Ho Chi-minh, now styling himself leader of Viet Minh (abbreviation for the "Revolutionary League of Viet Nam"), was at first disposed to be cooperative. But fighting broke out when some 4,000 French troops, who had been interned by the Japanese, were released to protect French property in Saigon. In October negotiations opened and then stalled between the self-appointed Vietnamese government and Admiral Thierry d'Argenlieu, the newly arrived French High Commissioner. French reinforcements from France under General Leclerc began to land in Saigon. Ho Chi-minh withdrew to Hanoi in an embittered, belligerent mood.

A provisional cease-fire in Saigon was agreed in March 1946. The British-Indian force was under orders to return home. France formally recognized the Vietnamese Republic as a "Free State within the Indochinese Federation," and French forces were permitted to cross the 16th parallel to relieve the Chinese Nationalists. Conferences followed at Dalat and Fontainebleau to discuss more permanent arrangements when, on November 21, 1946, at Langsong in Tongking, a party of Vietnamese fired on French soldiers investigating the graves of French and Annamese killed in the war against Japan. It was the "Marco Polo Bridge" of Indochina. The incident could have been settled given the least modicum of good will; but, by now, the affairs of both sides were passing more and more into the hands of their respective extremists. Léon Blum, who became Premier of France on December 16, 1946, to enjoy five weeks in office, was pacific enough in his political convictions, but he had inherited a situation which was already out of control. General hostilities broke out in Tongking. Hanoi was captured by French forces after heavy house-to-house fighting. Ho Chi-minh escaped to his familiar jungle fastness in northern Tongking.

Ramadier, Blum's successor, sent out Émile Bollaert, a Senator with a distinguished record in the wartime resistance in France, to replace d'Argenlieu. Bollaert made a fresh attempt to negotiate with Ho Chi-minh, and he consumed most of the year 1947 flying back and forth between Saigon and Paris, bringing successive proposals. But, at this juncture, a new solution presented itself. Vietnamese *émigrés* in Nationalist China, together with "reactionary elements" from Cochin-China, put forward the claims of the former Emperor Bao Dai, then living in exile in Hong Kong. Bao Dai, at first sight a most unlikely candidate, had compromised himself by his former collaboration with the Japanese, and in exile he had earned something of the reputation of a playboy and gambler. But he was shrewd enough and showed little inclination to accept the role thus thrust upon him. The French, however, cottoning onto the scheme, proceeded to establish a "monarchist" government at Saigon under Nguyen Xuan, an Annamese who had become a French citizen and had risen to the rank of general in the French Army, and eventually, in June 1949, the reluctant Bao Dai was installed as Chief of State of Viet Nam with Nguyen Xuan as his Premier. Laos and Cambodia were "associated" with Viet Nam. Cochin-China became an "autonomous" territory. Outside these arrangements, and now openly at war against them, stood Ho Chi-minh and his Viet Minh, virtually a separate state in the hinterland of Tongking, with pockets of sympathizers deep in Annam and Cochin-China.

How long this strangely mixed regime would have lasted is an academic question. The situation had already been transformed by the Communist triumph in China. Fighting between Viet Nam and Viet Minh was now general. In January 1950, both the Chinese Republic and the Soviet Union recognized Viet Minh; in June 1950, the Korean War broke out. During the year Indochina took top priority in the debates of the National Assembly in Paris, debates which, even for France, were of exceptional rancor. The high rank of the soldiers now being sent out to Indochina – Marshal Juin and Generals de la Tour and de Lattre de Tassigny – was itself an index of French anxieties. At this time there were 70,000 French troops in Indochina, plus 20,000 Légionnaires, 40,000 Africans, and nearly 150,000 Vietnamese and other local auxiliaries, and the "war" in Indochina was costing over $1,000,000,000 annually, or about one-third of France's military budget.

Upon the conclusion of the Korean armistice, which we have described above, a general Far Eastern Conference was proposed principally to negotiate the final settlement, not only in Korea but in Indochina also. The conference, as it turned out, was one of the most important international conferences of these years and was attended by Dulles, Eden, Lester Pearson, Casey, Bidault, Molotov, Chou En-Lai – and later by Bedell Smith and Mendès-France. The press made the obvious joke out of the fact that Viet Nam representative was a certain Dinh, and the Viet Minh representative was a certain Dong. But never was there a conference so harried by shifting events outside its scope or control. It met at last at Geneva on April 26, 1954, for sessions which were to continue for some three confused, tedious months.

By that April the war in Indochina was going very badly. Since the Korean armistice, the Chinese had switched their interest southward and, by a prodigious logistic effort, they were supplying the Viet Minh forces with arms, especially artillery. Viet Minh forces were then approaching Luang Prabang, the royal capital of Laos, and had cut off a mixed French force

INDOCHINA, 1945-54

of 15,000 which they were closely besieging at Dien Bien Phu. Urgent discussions were proceeding in the United States at administration and staff levels and in the public press as to what kind or degree of intervention to attempt in order to save the French in Indochina from a major military disaster. For a time Dulles, the American Secretary of State, argued strongly for full-scale operations on the part of the United States to take the form of air raids – and using atomic weapons – against the staging bases in Indochina by which the Chinese had been transporting their guns, and he was supported by Admiral Arthur W. Radford, then Chairman of the Joint Chiefs of Staff. In the second week of April it became known that two American aircraft carriers – with tactical air groups and atomic weapons aboard – were cruising in the South China Sea. Congress, meanwhile, was perplexed and wavering, although, if it had come to the point, Congress – most certainly the Senate – would have voted heavily against intervention. But Dulles was afterward to claim that his very threat with atomic weapons had called the Communist powers to heel and had prevented

Geneva from degenerating into another useless, insulting endurance test like that at Panmunjon. (See p. 786.)

In Britain, the Government – of Churchill and Eden – came out against armed intervention in Indochina, and most categorically against the use of atomic weapons. In France, at that moment, Laniel's government was about to fall, and, if its views counted at all, it was much more interested in the growing crisis over Germany and EDC. (See pp. 696-97.) On May 7, 1954, after a bitter, heroic resistance, Dien Bien Phu at last surrendered. On June 17 Mendès-France became French Premier with a pledge to end the war in Indochina at whatever cost, and he shortly arrived in Geneva to press his case. (See p. 697.) Finally, on July 21, 1954, the conference put its signature to a cease-fire agreement, the main provision of which was an armistice line across the narrow waist of Indochina. Germany had her Iron Curtain; so had Korea; and now so also had Indochina.

None of the parties at the Far Eastern Conference could have claimed it a success – not even the Communists. For his part, Dulles was mainly interested afterward to mend the East Asian defenses for which the conference provided little more than a temporary patch. Once more he seems to have been persuaded by his British colleagues to strike a nice balance between unnecessary provocation and necessary security. The outcome, with all its inadequacies, was the Southeast Asia Defense Treaty, creating the Southeast Asia Treaty Organization (SEATO), signed at Manila on September 8, 1954, by the representatives of Britain, France, Pakistan, Siam, the Philippines, Australia, New Zealand, and the United States.

The essential clause in the treaty read as follows:

> Each Party recognizes that aggression by means of armed attack in the treaty area against any of the Parties or against any State or territory which the Parties by unanimous agreement may hereafter designate, would endanger its own peace and safety, and agrees that it will in that event act to meet the common danger in accordance with its constitutional processes.

After 1954 Viet Nam remained superficially stable and quiet. But persistent Communist infiltration took place into the neighboring state of Laos, and, as we write, an intermittent civil war has broken out in northern Laos, a war in which no side can claim a clean record and whose outcome is still uncertain.

The Iranian Oil Crisis

We return to Iran (Persia), whose affairs we discussed in the previous chapter and left in relative peace. (See pp. 768-69.) By 1949 the immediate Soviet menace had receded. Both Iran and her neighbor, Turkey, were safely lodged within the American "sphere of influence." The Soviet Union was then preoccupied with Germany and Intermediate Europe and was anxious to avoid distractions from elsewhere. Indeed the Soviet Union in 1949 was suddenly and almost suspiciously friendly towards Iran. But the release from external danger seemed now to rouse all Iran's domestic animosities. The country was very restless. Administrative corruption and the oppressions of the landlord system were long overdue for reform. On February 4, 1949, an attempt by a Communist was made upon the life of the Shah. The attempt failed, but it was a highly disturbing incident. Iran was the first country at this time to accept aid under President Truman's Point Four. (See p. 751.) But the Persian was a proud man, and there was always something humiliating in this foreign philanthropy. In June 1950, the Shah indicated the trend of affairs when he appointed a new Premier General Razmara, a professional soldier believed to be politically moderate and unambitious, much mentioned of late as the leader of a possible military dictatorship in Iran.

The feeling of resentment in the country was now finding an objective, not in the Soviet Union or the United States, but in Britain – and in particular in the Anglo-Iranian Oil Company (AIOC). That company, formerly the Anglo-Persian Oil Company, had operated a concession in Persia since 1909. The British Government had become its controlling shareholder in 1914. It had entered into a new agreement with the Persian Government in 1933. Its oil production, which before 1914 had amounted to 80,000 tons, was nearly 10,000,000 in 1933 and was now approaching 30,000,000, and was providing some two-thirds of the Persian national revenues. It controlled the largest tanker fleet in the world and had built at Abadan on the Persian Gulf the largest refinery in the world. A new agreement was mooted in 1948 and concluded in July 1949. Iran's royalties under this agreement were earmarked to finance a huge Five-Year Plan.

But strong opposition to the agreement was developing in the Majlis, the Iranian legislature, largely at the hands of a faction led by Mohammed Mossadeq, a pugnacious old patrician, nearly 70 years old, who had spent most of a long turbulent life in political opposition and who was now finding in oil an ideal field for his talents. In February 1951, the AIOC offered a further agreement on a fifty-fifty basis, such as was now becoming the accepted rule for all foreign oil concessions; but Mossadeq and his party would have none of it. On March 7, the moderate Premier, General Razmara, was assassinated by a Moslem fanatic, though it is doubtful if even Razmara at this stage could have kept the peace. On March 20, the Majlis passed an act "nationalizing" the oil industry of Iran; and on April 30 Mossadeq became Premier.

The Iranian case was very simple and very familiar: the AIOC was a monopoly exploiting the country's greatest natural asset and returned a miserable pittance for the millions it filched away. It was a conspicuous symbol of all that was worst in European imperialism. Its concessions – notably the concession of 1933 – had been extorted by fraud and maintained by force. In its day-to-day dealings with Iranians, high or low, it behaved with an arrogance insupportable to a people who had produced more than one great civilization in the past. It employed in its own plant and administration a minimum of Iranian personnel which, by contrast with its British personnel, it paid and housed contemptibly. We are in no doubt that the AIOC could have rebutted all these arguments in spirit and in detail and supplied plenty more in its own defense. It could have called attention to the many tangible benefits in Iran in public health, education, and general welfare, all consequences of its operations. But there came a stage in so many of the crises that we have been describing in this book when the feelings of one or both of the parties had passed beyond argument and had themselves become unalterably the prime factors in the situation.

Tactically, from the Iranian point of view, the crisis had been timed to a nicety. In Britain a Labor government was in office, a government disposed to be most ingeniously embarrassed by the issue of "nationalization." Ernest Bevin, the Foreign Secretary, a sick man, resigned on March 9, 1951, and he was succeeded by Herbert Morrison, admittedly a stopgap appointment until the General Elections of that October. British military action against Iran was impracticable, even had a Labor government been disposed to attempt it. Such action could have been mounted only from the very distant base at Suez – or from Karachi or Bombay, which since 1947 were no longer in British possession. British officials and technicians in Iran had no option but to evacuate the oil fields and the refinery at Abadan, but their departure left the industry at a standstill. The Iranians by themselves, as was soon to be shown, were quite unable to produce or to market their precious commodity. The crisis was referred to the Security Council, and by the Security Council to the International Court; but the International Court later decided, by 7 votes to 4, that it had no jurisdiction in the case. Anglo-Iranian diplomatic relations were broken off.

Mossadeq therefore followed his star with impunity. In the course of the next few months he rejected arbitration under the 1933 agreement; he rejected offers of independent American mediation; he visited the United States and rejected proposals from President Truman; he rejected proposals jointly drawn up by President Truman and Churchill. In Iran he was now finding support for himself in a National Front and in a revived Tudeh party – a party now admittedly Communist and taking orders direct from Moscow – and in a spate of excitable one-sided propaganda. Dictator-like, he was taking his revenge on his political opponents, several of whom were under arrest or in flight. His gangs terrorized the streets of Teheran – and incidentally the Shah's Palace. He was granted full powers by the Majlis over finance, economics, and justice, and for its pains, he threatened the Majlis with dissolution. It is difficult to imagine how much more could have been done to slake a man's hatred and vanity and to ruin a country. Meanwhile the world's journalism was kept agog with stories of Mossadeq's eccentricities, his various physical ailments, and his hysterical weeping fits.

The Iranian oil crisis lasted from 1951 through to 1953. In May 1953, Mossadeq appealed – unsuccessfully – to President Eisenhower for "prompt and effective aid." The end was then already in sight. The Iranian exchequer was bankrupt. Opposition was growing and rallying around General Zahedi and the army. Zahedi was arrested, but escaped, and for a time was in hiding actually in the Majlis building. On August 13, the Shah appointed him Premier, and then himself with the Queen left the country by air for Rome. A few days later the army revolted; the Shah and the Queen returned to Teheran in triumph; and it was now Mossadeq who was under arrest. Zahedi appealed – this time successfully – to President Eisenhower, whose aid was both prompt and effective. During November 1953, Mossadeq stood his trial for defying the Shah and seeking to overthrow the regime and was sentenced to three years' solitary confinement.

Anglo-Iranian diplomatic relations were resumed, and discussions for a settlement of the original oil dispute were opened in December 1953. An agreement was announced in August 1954 and signed by the Shah on October 29. Oil started to flow almost at once. Under the new terms, the Iranian oil industry would be operated by a consortium of eight companies, including the AIOC (renamed the British Petroleum Company), which would hold 40 per cent of the shares, and five American companies (Gulf Oil Corporation, Socony-Vacuum, Standard Oil of New Jersey, Standard Oil of California, and the Texas Company), which together would hold another 40 per cent of the shares; the profits would be divided between the Iranian Government and the consortium on a fifty-fifty basis. The inclusion of the American companies signified the growing American interest and influence in the Middle East and shared the former British monopoly with a power which, in Iranian eyes, was politically less compromised.

The Suez Crisis and the Second Israeli War

In Egypt the Israeli War of 1948 had left a trail of disorder and recrimination. Nokrashy, the Premier, under whom Egypt had entered the war, was assassinated on December 28, 1948, by a member of the Moslem Brotherhood. After a restless year, new elections in January 1950 installed the Wafd party in power with the Wafdist leader, Nahas, as Premier. The old anti-British agitation, somewhat in abeyance during the Israeli War, broke out with fresh force. In October 1951, Nahas denounced the Anglo-Egyptian Treaty of 1936 and prevailed upon King Farouk to declare himself King of the Sudan. He demanded the immediate withdrawal of all British forces from Egypt. He rejected proposals then being mooted that Egypt should become an equal partner in a new Middle East Defense Organization (MEDO), composed of Britain, France, Turkey, and the United States. (See p. 797.) National problems — the poverty of the worker and the peasant, and particularly the state of the Egyptian Army, whose inefficiency the recent campaign had so conspicuously exposed — all cried out for attention, but the Egyptian political genius seemed to be able to contribute nothing to them but the usual jobbery and partisan violence. Obstruction and nuisance were always easier. Egyptian authorities were now stopping Israeli ships in the Canal and even ships of other nationals sailing to or from Israeli ports.

On January 25, 1952, a serious clash occurred at Ismailia in the Canal Zone between British troops and Egyptian auxiliary police. The next day, "Black Saturday," riots broke out in Cairo; European premises were sacked; the well-known Shepheard's Hotel and several banks, shops, and offices were burned down; ten British nationals were murdered at the Turf Club. The Egyptian police made no attempt to interfere, and the King had to call out troops to restore order. He then dismissed the Wafdist Premier, Nahas, and a number of police officers. In March the King dissolved parliament. A series of moderate, anti-Wafdist premiers followed. The situation was now such that nothing short of external force or internal revolution could have altered it. On July 23, 1952, a bloodless military coup was carried out under General Mohammed Naguib and a group of younger army officers, most of whom had fought in the Israeli War and had seen for themselves the extent of their government's corruption. On July 26, King Farouk abdicated and went into exile, leaving his infant son Fuad to be proclaimed "King of Egypt and the Sudan."

For a time, as has happened in other revolutions, the new regime was remarkably moderate. There were several arrests, but no terrorism, and even obvious enemies of the revolution, like Nahas, were left at liberty. Naguib himself, cultured but politically inexperienced, governed with the aid of the army junta and a Council of Ministers composed of civilian experts. He introduced legislation for land reforms and industrial development, and for education and public health – all long overdue. The symbols of the old regime were removed. The titles of *pasha* and *bey* were abolished. Political parties and organizations, including the Wafd, were dissolved. On June 18, 1953, Egypt was declared a republic, with Naguib as President and Premier. Colonel Gamal Abdel Nasser, who was now emerging as the real force behind the revolution, was Deputy Premier.

For a time relations with Britain improved. Anglo-Egyptian discussions on the Sudan and on Suez were begun. The discussions on the Sudan concluded in an agreement in February 1953 which recognized the right of the Sudanese to self-determination. The discussions on Suez concluded in a new Anglo-Egyptian treaty in July 1954, which signified a total British withdrawal; but the treaty provided for the reavailability of the Suez base in case of future aggression, other than by Israel, against a member of the Arab League or against Turkey. Moreover Britain gave unqualified recognition of Egyptian sovereignty over the Canal in return for Egypt's guarantee to uphold the Convention of 1888 regarding freedom of passage through the Canal.

But, again as has happened in other revolutions, earlier moderation gave place to a more violent phase. Naguib and Nasser were embroiled in a struggle for power. There were arrests, censorships, and, temporarily, a closing of the universities. Late in October 1954, after an attempt on Nasser's life, the Moslem Brotherhood was dissolved and six of the Brotherhood terrorists were hanged. Naguib eventually retired, and, by the end of 1954, Nasser, much the abler but less attractive man, was in full control.

One complication to arise in the Egyptian issue, a complication from which the earlier Iranian oil crisis had been so surprisingly free, was the intervention of the Soviet Union. Except for pressure on Turkey in 1945 for the retrocession of Kars and Ardahan and except for the imbroglio in 1946 in Iran and Azerbaijan, the Soviet Union since the Second World War had shown little direct interest in the Middle East. (See pp. 767-68 and 794.) But in 1955, with the Korean armistice concluded and Intermediate Europe quiescent, the Kremlin might well turn its attention to the Arab countries and pick on Arab nationalism as a possible field for exploitation. At all events, in 1955 the Cold War shifted suddenly to the Middle East, and the local Egyptian issue became an issue for both blocs of world powers.

It is hard to say whether Western initiative anticipated or provoked the Soviet irruption. The earlier, partly American-sponsored Middle East Defense Organization (MEDO) of 1951, which was to have been an extension of NATO, had come to nothing, but it had not been entirely shelved, and the time now seemed ripe for reviving it. The Southeast Asia Treaty Organization (SEATO) had been created in September 1954, and a new MEDO, linking NATO with SEATO, looked like logical strategy. Here was "containment" with a vengeance! In the Middle Eastern states themselves there were recollections of the interwar Saadabad Pact of 1937, and Nuri es-Said of Iraq was now working actively for a similar combination. (See p. 205.) Turkey and Pakistan already had a treaty of "friendly cooperation," dating from early 1954, and in February 1955 at Baghdad, Turkey and Iraq entered into a general treaty of mutual defense. Then, in April 1955, Britain signed a special agreement with Iraq and simultaneously acceded to the Turkish-Iraqi treaty. Arguably Britain was seeking to restore her position in Iraq, still shaken by the Iraqi revolt of 1941, and to compensate for her recent reverses in Iran and Egypt. Before the year 1955 was out, Pakistan and Iran had also acceded to the treaty. The Baghdad Pact, as it was now generally known, thus had five members comprising the so-called Northern Tier of Middle Eastern states – Turkey, Iraq, and Iran – and Pakistan and Britain. The United States had originally given strong encouragement to the new combination. In May 1954, the United States had entered into a mutual defense pact with Pakistan. The United States did not now become a full member of the Baghdad Pact, but it joined the Economic and Counter-Subversive Committees of the pact, and later the Military Committee, and it was represented at meetings of the Council of the pact by observers. Meanwhile, a rival pact between the states of the so-called Southern Tier had come into existence by means of defense treaties, signed in October 1955, severally between Egypt and Syria and between Egypt and Saudi Arabia. (See pp. 730-31 and 803.)

The Soviet action now was of ingenious and devastating simplicity. On February 28, 1955, "one of the most fateful dates in Middle East history," in the midst of the diplomatic jockeying we have been describing, the Israeli Army had delivered a crushing "reprisal raid" against Egyptian forces in the Gaza Strip. Nasser at once applied to Britain and to the United States for arms, and was refused. In July Dimitri Shepilov, shortly to become Soviet Foreign Minister, then on a visit to Cairo for the third anniversary of the Egyptian revolution, and Nasser, meeting it is said at an embassy reception, soon found themselves on common ground, both seeking the maximum embarrassment of the Western Powers, and Shepilov there and then undertook to supply Nasser with the wanted arms. In October huge shipments – 300 tanks, 50 bombers, 100 fighters – from the Soviet Union and Czechoslovakia were on their way to Egypt together with Soviet officers to instruct the Egyptian Army in their use. For payment the Egyptian Government was to barter the Egyptian cotton crop. Similar and simultaneous deliveries were made to Egypt's ally, Syria.

In Israel the Soviet-Egyptian "Arms Deal" was at once interpreted as preparation for a new Arab aggression and a new Israeli war. Bands of Egyptian commandos or *fedayeen* were raiding across the Israeli-Egyptian borders. Irregular killings on both sides were occurring daily, and the general situation was about as tense as it had ever been. At the same time persistent rioting in Jordan, possibly Egyptian-inspired, caused the government of that country to dismiss several of its British advisers, including General Glubb, commander of the Arab Legion. Elections in Jordan some weeks later were to return overwhelming antimonarchist, anti-British – and, in the nature of the case, pro-Egyptian – majorities. Israel, hostilely encircled, appealed to France, and France in trouble with Arab unrest in Algeria and anxious to find an anti-Arab counterweight, lent a sympathetic ear. Algerian rebels, it was said, were being trained and armed in Cairo, and shortly French arms deliveries were reaching Israeli ports, Haifa and Tel Aviv. The Western Powers, Britain and the United States, which for so long had tried to insulate the Middle Eastern states from modern armaments – except those that they themselves produced and controlled – found themselves face to face with the prospect of a full-scale armaments race in the area – and of a most dangerous foreign intervention accompanying it.

Oddly enough, it was a domestic matter that fired the final international explosion. Nasser, while strengthening and reconstituting the Egyptian Army, had decided to press forward with a vast irrigation and hydroelectric project, the Aswan High Dam, a project first discussed in the early years of the Egyptian revolution. The dam would be three miles long, would cost some $300,000,000, and would take fifteen to twenty years to complete. It would need foreign aid. The World Bank was interested; so were the United States and Britain – and so also was the Soviet Union. But on July 19, 1956, the State Department in Washington bluntly announced that the American offer must be withdrawn. John Foster Dulles, Secretary of State, and Congress were under pressure from the cotton states and from the American Zionists, and both were irritated by Nasser's recent recognition of Communist China – no less than by his present pro-Soviet leanings. Some days passed while Nasser nursed his crushing double rebuke, a rebuke as much to his pride as to his economic policy, and then, in a speech on July 26 in Alexandria, he announced the nationalization of the Suez Canal, out of whose revenues, he declared, the High Dam would be built.

The story now becomes increasingly complicated and difficult to compress into a small space. It is also one in which several important details still remain to be explained. Probably no episode in recent years gives the commentator the feeling of dealing with so many unknowns. The crisis, moreover, was dominated by personalities and often by personal prejudices, prejudices which, however strongly felt, were never publicly admitted. Apart from Nasser, the main protagonists were Anthony Eden, the British Prime Minister, and John Foster Dulles, the American Secretary of State. Eden was the one-time champion of the League of Nations, of unrivalled diplomatic experience, still young, the protégé of Churchill, and the great hope of his country. He was assisted by Selwyn Lloyd, one of the ablest Foreign Secretaries in one of the ablest cabinets of any British government in recent times. But there were moments now when Eden's actions seemed to be entirely out of character. He was not strong enough to carry out the policy that he believed to be the right one. A more emotional man than he had allowed to appear hitherto, he seemed to be carried away by an almost personal obsession to destroy Nasser and to let everything else recede into second place. Also, it must surely be said, he was most shabbily served by his American ally and by his own parliamentary Opposition at home. As for Dulles, he was dealing with a part of the world where his countrymen had few traditional contacts and, till recently, few interests. His big fear was the Soviet Union. Otherwise he was emotionally uncommitted, even indifferent. His main purpose was to ride out of an awkward situation with as little damage as possible. He was always looking over his shoulder toward the domestic situation in the United States, where the presidential election was about to take place. At times he was shockingly inept, uncertain of his own mind, and guilty of *gaffes* in public that would have ruined a lesser man or one from a lesser country. Finally, it is to be remembered that both Eden and Dulles, throughout the crisis, were in very poor health.

The official British argument was that the nationalization was an arbitrary and indefensible breach of Egypt's international obligations, notably the basic Convention of 1888 and the more recent Anglo-Egyptian treaty of 1954. The French were perhaps even more concerned, since the Canal had originally been a French project, constructed by a French engineer, de Lesseps, and since the Suez Canal Company, although registered in Egypt, had always had its head office in Paris. Moreover, Egypt was now part of the entire North African complex, which, especially in French Algeria, was turning increasingly dangerous. The Canal was an indispensable international utility, open to the shipping of all nations, operated always with scrupulous efficiency and good faith, and defended at great cost in two World Wars. It was hard to believe that its record of service and its future development and security could now be entrusted to Egyptians, who up to now had shown so little technical, administrative, or military competence.

In London and Paris, after denunciations of Nasser's coup, the several parties consulted for action. On August 23, 1956, a conference, sponsored by the British and French governments, sent a mission to Egypt, headed by Menzies, the Australian Prime Minister then in London, to present to Nasser an "eighteen-nation plan" for the international control of the Canal – a plan which Nasser rejected. Military preparations were under way in Britain and France, and an expeditionary force was being built up in Cyprus and Malta. The next proposal, emanating from Dulles, was to form a Suez Canal Users' Association (SCUA); but whatever purpose this body could have had was effectively killed when Dulles unconditionally denied to it the essential recourse to force or even to economic sanctions. The United States, he said, "would not shoot its way through the Canal," and he hoped that no one else would. From that moment Nasser's attitude hardened, and the possibility of a compromise solution of the dispute vanished.

Britain and France then referred the issue to the United Nations Security Council and proposed principles for the "insulation of the Canal from politics"; but although Nasser this time agreed to the principles, further discussions in the Security Council were stalled by the Soviet veto. On October 16, 1956, Eden flew to Paris when, as far as is known, the fateful decision was taken to mount a joint Anglo-French attack on the Canal Zone. On October 29, Israeli forces, on their own account, invaded Egypt. The next day the British and French governments dispatched ultimatums to Israel and Egypt demanding the cessation of hostilities and the withdrawal of their forces to distances ten miles on either side of the Canal and further demanding that Egypt permit a temporary Anglo-French occupation of key positions in the Canal Zone. On the same day, in the Security Council, Britain and France vetoed an American resolution calling on Israeli forces to withdraw to their frontiers and on members of the United Nations to refrain from using or threatening force in the area. This was the first occasion of British use of the veto. On October 31, British and French aircraft began bombing Egyptian airfields and military installations around Port Said preparatory to landing operations. There was no prior notification to the United States or, in the case of Britain, to Commonwealth governments. President Eisenhower, in a nation-wide broadcast relayed to Europe, roundly upbraided "our friends," Britain and France, for their action in Egypt.

On November 1, the General Assembly, making use of its "Uniting for Peace" machinery, convened to debate the situation, and the next day, by 64 votes to 5, adopted an American resolution urging an immediate cease-fire. (See p. 634.) On the 4th, it adopted a Canadian resolution to set up an international United Nations Emergency Force to occupy the Canal Zone. At this moment the United Nations was considering the Hungarian crisis, and it was also on November 4, again using the "Uniting for Peace" machinery, that the General Assembly adopted an American resolution demanding the withdrawal of Soviet forces from Hungary. (See p. 675.) Meanwhile, the Israelis were deep in Sinai, but found that the bulk of the Egyptian Army had already withdrawn. On the 5th, British and French landings began at Port Said.

Egypt, Saudi Arabia, and Syria broke off relations with Britain and France; Iraq and Jordan broke off relations with France. The entire Middle East was in an uproar. The four Moslem members of the Baghdad Pact met demonstratively without Britain at Teheran and called for the withdrawal of all foreign forces from Egypt. In London and Paris financial panics were threatening. The British electorate was almost exactly bisected into pro- and anti-Eden factions. In debates in the normally sedate and austere House of Commons rules of order almost ceased to exist. There were similar violent party divisions in the Dominions — notably in Australia. The Soviet Union, it was said, was about to bombard London and other Western cities with rockets. Precisely what pressures the United States exerted on Britain and France are not yet known. But on November 7, 1956, British and French forces in Egypt halted, and the Israelis also began to fall back.

Egypt had suffered heavy casualties both in Sinai and Port Said. The Canal was blocked with sunken ships. But physical recovery was rapid. The United Nations Emergency Force (UNEF) began to arrive by the middle of November. British and French forces were evacuated in another month. The Canal was cleared and operating by April 10, 1957. The Egyptian Government sequestered all British businesses in Egypt, and most British nationals left the country. Nasser seemed more firmly established in power than before the crisis.

Cyprus

After Egypt, Cyprus. Two local Cypriot nationalist movements, both stirring in the 1930's and increasingly active since 1945, had now broken out into a confused guerrilla war and were providing the Middle East with the next crisis on its list. Here, in this once-Ottoman island in the Eastern Mediterranean, British power had been established in the late nineteenth century and confirmed by annexation in 1914. The population was 80 per cent Greek and Christian (of the Orthodox Church) and 20 per cent Turkish and Moslem. The Greek community demanded union (*enosis*) with Greece, and the Turkish community, perhaps more temperately but with equal determination, demanded union with Turkey. In Ottoman times the Church had always been the defender of Greek-Cypriot rights, and it was natural therefore that the leadership of the Greek movement should now have devolved upon Archbishop Makarios, Patriarch of the Orthodox Church in Cyprus. The military counterpart of the Greek movement was EOKA (National Organization of the Cypriot Struggle), under a certain Colonel Grivas. The Greek Government in Athens and the Turkish Government in Ankara each supported its respective group of compatriots.

The British Government, by now well acquainted with these tangled situations in its overseas territories, offered repeated constitutional proposals to the parties without success. The British Government's policy was clear. Although willing to concede all but total independence to the Cypriots, it required the right to maintain military bases in the island to offset the loss of its bases in Egypt, and, as the partition of so small a territory as Cyprus was scarcely practicable, it also required a settlement that would safeguard the liberties of both Cypriot communities.

In 1956, at the time of the Suez Crisis, Makarios was already suffering for his professions under a term of exile. But on his release, he was permitted to go to Athens, from where he at once resumed his political campaign. Terrorism in Cyprus was then at its worst. For two years it was all a weary, tragic repetition of Ireland, Malaya, and Palestine. Greece, a NATO member, was on the point of breaking off relations with Britain. But then, at the moment when prospects seemed darkest, a solution suddenly appeared. We still do not know what pressures were brought to bear upon the factions; presumably the NATO Powers had taken a hand behind the scenes. In February 1959, at a conference at Zurich in Switzerland, the Greek and Turkish Premiers agreed to compromise. A few days later, another conference was held in London, attended by Archbishop Makarios himself, now as conciliatory as formerly he had been hostile. A "Final Settlement" was signed by Macmillan, the British Prime Minister, and Karamanlis, the Greek Premier. Zorlu, the Turkish Foreign Minister, signed on behalf of Menderes, the Turkish Premier, then recovering from an air crash that had occurred at Gatwick airport in Surrey, while he was on his way to the conference. (See p. 767.)

Cyprus emerged from these discussions as an independent republic with a Greek President and a Turkish Vice-President; a Council of Ministers composed of seven Greeks and three Turks; and a House of Representatives of 70 per cent Greek membership and 30 per cent Turkish. The Cypriot civil service and defense forces would be similarly proportioned. The British Government would retain its bases on territory enjoying full British sovereignty.

The Iraqi Revolution

Upon the conclusion of the Suez Crisis, Egypt and Syria resumed the building up of their industries and armaments with Soviet aid, and their press and radio were loudly anti-Western and pro-Soviet. The United States — now that the presidential elections were over — moved to restore something of the lost Western position. On January 5, 1957, President Eisenhower asked a joint session of Congress to authorize the use of American forces to protect any Middle Eastern state that requested aid "against overt armed aggression from a nation controlled by international Communism." But the Eisenhower Doctrine, as this new policy was to be called, met with curiously little sympathy either in the United States or in those Middle Eastern states to which it was primarily addressed. Dulles, as if repenting of his former Suez equivocations, testified for six days on behalf of the doctrine before a joint session of the Senate Foreign Relations and Armed Services Committees. Perhaps more significant were the various state visits in 1957 among the monarchs of the Western bloc — King Saud to Baghdad and Amman; King Feisal to Teheran, Riyadh, and Ankara; King Saud and the Shah to Beirut — and King Saud to Washington.

Meanwhile Egypt and Syria, now feeling the draft themselves, moved closer together. On February 1, 1958, they were joined as the United Arab Republic (UAR), a new unitary state. On March 28 Yemen joined the UAR to form a federation, the United Arab States (UAS), which should be open to the membership of all Arab states. Of the UAR Nasser was elected President by plebiscite, and he formed his first government with two Vice-Presidents, one from the "northern region" (Syria) and one from the "southern region" (Egypt). Nasser shortly went to Moscow — apparently it was another state visit to dramatize a political friendship — but it was also to placate the Soviet Government, which had not looked too kindly upon the new Egyptian-Syrian union. In October 1958, the Soviet Government offered $100,000,000 toward financing the High Dam in Egypt. But that December Nasser inaugurated a general anti-Communist crusade in the Fertile Crescent and arrested some two hundred prominent Communists in both regions of the UAR.

On February 14, 1958, Iraq and Jordan countered the Egypto-Syrian union by forming one of their own — an Arab Federation, with Nuri es-Said as its President. Thus two blocs had come into existence in the Middle East — the anti-Western — but not pro-Soviet — UAR, and the pro-Western federation of Iraq and Jordan. Saudi Arabia stood aside from the federation; but, in any event, Saudi Arabia was attached to her American allegiance.

On July 14, 1958, in Baghdad, suddenly and with complete surprise, a group of Iraqi army officers, led by a Brigadier Abdul Karim Kassem, brought off a coup, seized the city and the palace, assassinated King Feisal, the Emir Abdul Illah, and several members of the royal family. Nuri tried to escape in disguise, but was captured and killed. A much more violent version of the Egyptian revolution of 1952, it seemed, was being re-enacted in Iraq. Kassem became Premier of a republican government, and set about the purge of his political predecessors and opponents. The Baghdad press and radio were virulently pro-Soviet. But Kassem went out of his way to show his independence of both the Soviet Union and the UAR, and to make friendly overtures to Western Powers. He disclaimed any intention of challenging the Iraq Petroleum Company. He was more interested, he declared, in eradicating corruption and promoting economic development, especially irrigation and land reform.

The immediate repercussions of the Iraqi revolt were felt in Jordan and Lebanon. The new Arab Federation, scarce five months old, collapsed, and King Hussein of Jordan, effectively isolated, at once appealed to the United States. In Lebanon a civil war was threatening between the Christian and Moslem populations, and the Lebanese President Camille Chamoun also appealed to the United States. Evidently the Eisenhower Doctrine was to be given its first practical trial. American marines from the Sixth Fleet landed at Beirut, and British paratroops were flown into Jordan. For the moment the situation was stabilized. But Kassem continued to be threatened by his own domestic opposition, and himself to threaten his weaker neighbors – notably the small but wealthy state of Kuwait.

One consequence of the Iraqi revolt was Iraq's withdrawal from the Baghdad Pact and the removal of the headquarters of the Pact to Ankara. The pact now had four full members – Turkey, Iran, Pakistan, and Britain – with the United States maintaining the same liaison as before. In August 1959, the name was changed to the Central Treaty Organization (CENTO). (See p. 797.)

The Middle East, as we survey it from the point we have now reached, is one of the most unsettled areas in an unsettled world. If stability is the greatest of political virtues, we see little pleasing in the prospect. There no longer exist those dependable figures like those of the past – Kemal Ataturk, Riza Shah, Feisal I, Nuri es-Said, Ibn Saud. Oddly enough, considering the vilification once heaped upon his head, Colonel Nasser of Egypt seems to have emerged as the staunchest friend of peace at the present moment. Whatever was left of British influence collapsed in 1956, and as yet no successor has come forward. Certainly the United States has commitments enough already without wanting to add to them. The United States would intervene in the Middle East only to deny intervention to the Soviet Union. As for the Soviet Union, its recent behavior suggests that its intervention would sooner take the form of "indirect aggression," and that it would then stand by to pick up the incidental advantages that dropped out of the chaos which it stirred up.

The great cause of Arab unity, for one reason or another, has not prospered. The UAR, and with it the UAS, have dissolved after rather more than three years of existence. Israel remains an anomaly in the Middle Eastern world, a challenge and an object of common hatred. But the biggest divisive factor in the Middle East is its economic disparity. Poverty and wealth never make good allies, and in the Middle East poverty and wealth in their most conspicuous forms exist side by side. National incomes vary from Egypt's $120 per capita to Kuwait's $2000. Except for oil and hydroelectric power, the Middle East is not richly endowed with the resources that count in modern international politics, and even these resources are eccentrically distributed. Foreign aid and domestic philanthropy can do much to help but never to cure the essential natural disability.

Africa

No area of the world entered contemporary history with such sudden impact as Africa. In the previous edition of this book (1950) – if we may be allowed to cite our own case as typical – we described Egypt, Ethiopia, and South Africa, but we barely referred to the middle area, "Black Africa," as it has been called, between the Sahara and the Kalahari, the area which, as we write now, has come to the forefront of the international scene. In 1950 this Africa was still the Africa of the late nineteenth century, modified only in respect to the former German colonies by the cessions of the Treaty of Versailles. Ethiopia had fallen to Italy in the Italo-Ethiopian War but in the Second World War had returned to her former status. In 1950 the whole continent lay under European rule, carved up into colonies, protectorates, or mandates – except for Ethiopia, Liberia, and South Africa – and except also for Egypt, nominally independent in treaty relations with Britain; the Sudan with a constitution defined by the Anglo-Egyptian Condominium of 1899; Algeria, a Department of France; Tangier, an International Zone; and the former Italian colonies of Libya, Eritrea, and Somaliland, then under Allied military government. But by 1960, in ten short years, the entire situation was transformed with national independence achieved or about to be achieved in every part of the continent.

As we look back on it now, it is easy to say that African nationalism was not the unexpected eruption it seemed to be. African nationalist leaders, like Kwame Nkrumah, Jomo Kenyatta, or Nnamdi Azikiwe, were active in their respective homelands, though not yet known abroad, as far back as the 1930's. During the Second World War, and notably after the Atlantic Charter, nationalist movements started up in the Gold Coast, Nigeria, the French Sudan, and Kenya. By 1950, even if the middle area of Africa was generally quiet, there was unrest, or the unmistakable likelihood of it, in North Africa – in Egypt, Morocco, Tunisia – but not yet in Algeria. (See pp. 700-02 and 770-71.) In South Africa, Malan's Nationalist government was putting into effect the policy of apartheid. (See p. 739.)

AFRICA, 1945

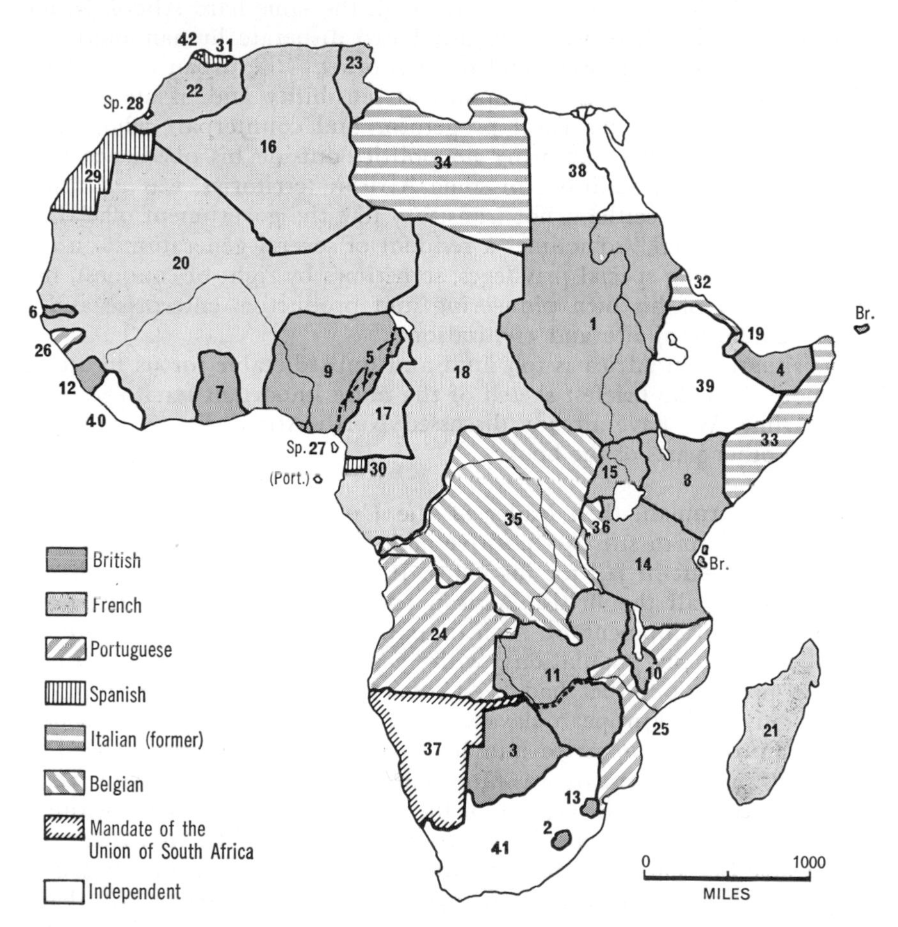

1 Anglo-Egyptian Sudan 2 Basutoland 3 Bechuanaland 4 British Somaliland 5 Cameroons (Mandate) 6 Gambia 7 Gold Coast 8 Kenya 9 Nigeria 10 Nyasaland 11 Rhodesia 12 Sierra Leone 13 Swaziland 14 Tanganyika (Mandate) 15 Uganda 16 Algeria 17 Cameroun (Mandate) 18 French Equatorial Africa 19 French Somaliland 20 French West Africa 21 Madagascar 22 Morocco 23 Tunisia 24 Angola 25 Mozambique 26 Portuguese Guinea 27 Fernando Po 28 Ifni 29 Rio de Oro 30 Rio Muni 31 Spanish Morocco 32 Eritrea 33 Italian Somaliland 34 Libya 35 Belgian Congo 36 Ruanda-Urundi 37 Southwest Africa 38 Egypt 39 Ethiopia 40 Liberia 41 Union of South Africa 42 Tangiers (International)

Meanwhile, in British Government circles cautious talks were beginning on African constitutional reforms and on "increased native participation" in African, especially West African, affairs.

But nationalism in Africa, as elsewhere, was soon seen to be part of a far greater problem, namely the development of a new polity, a polity of European provenance, probably quite alien to the African environment. Western Europe during the nineteenth century had learned all the lessons of the modern industrial revolution. East Asia and the Middle East, as we have seen, were undergoing an analogous educational process; and now presumably Africa was to be forced through the same hard school. In most African territories there were the usual two disparate human ingredients to be adjusted to the process, and to each other – the urban migrant with the beginnings of an articulate political sensibility and of an organized party leadership, and his rural progenitor and counterpart who, in this case, was the tribesman knowing no politics outside his obedience to his hereditary chief. In addition, in some African territories, was a third ingredient, the white settler – not transitory like the government official, but a genuine "national," sometimes a resident of several generations – a man, moreover, claiming special privileges, sometimes by right of conquest, more often by right of his own pioneering and productive enterprise and his higher standards of life and civilization.

The situation in Africa is too fluid and unpredictable for us to attempt here more than the briefest sketch of the more important territories at the present time. We have already discussed North Africa, Egypt, and South Africa in other parts of the book.

In 1950 Nkrumah, then leader of the United Gold Coast Convention Party, had begun to stir up "positive action" for "Dominion status *now!*" and had been put in jail for his pains. It was inevitable perhaps that the Gold Coast, of all the British African territories, should take the leadership in the development of African nationalism. Here were more "advanced" indigenous populations, with recollections of their own ancient cultures, populations that had been longest in contact with Europeans – even if only with European slavers – and that had since become beneficiaries of European commerce and had evolved a relatively educated and prosperous middle class. As was often said, cocoa created the West African nationalist consciousness. Here too, in the Gold Coast, was no white settler minority to complicate the issues. Here, accordingly, in 1948 was set up the first Legislative Council in British Africa to have an African majority. And here, on February 28, 1949, occurred the first clearly defined African nationalist revolt, when some thirty Africans were killed in street demonstrations in Accra and in the rioting which followed. But at this juncture, the British Governor, Sir Charles Arden-Clarke, instead of proceeding to a policy of repression, courageously released the nationalist leader Nkrumah from jail, and made him virtually the Prime Minister of the territory. And Nkrumah, for all his former seditions, not untinged with Marxism, now acted the statesman, curbed his naturally flamboyant personality, and for a transition period of six years cooperated in giving the Gold Coast a tranquil and trustful period of government. On March 6, 1957, the Gold Coast, with the friendliest of valedictory ceremonies in honor of the former colonial power, became the Dominion of Ghana within the British Commonwealth.

But within a year of this happy event, as if to show that she was not only precocious but was also to be typical of all African development hereafter, Ghana had to become embroiled in a domestic squabble with her proud and conservative Ashanti tribesmen who all along had opposed

AFRICA, 1961

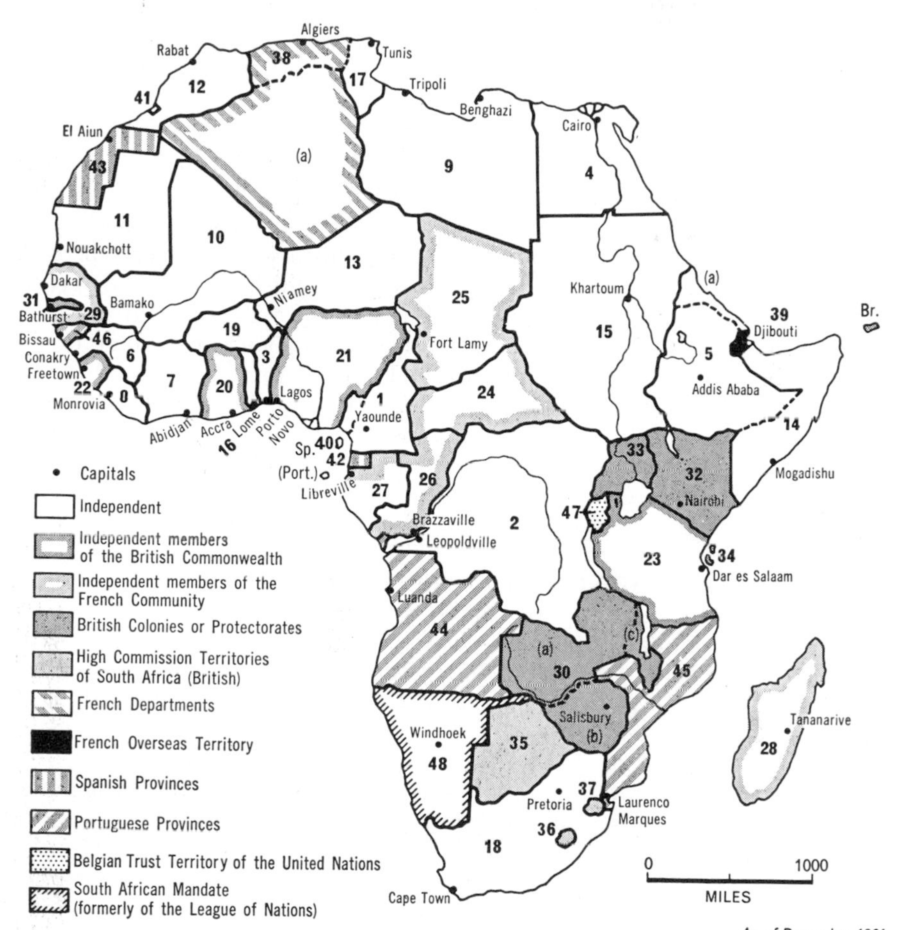

As of December 1961

1 Cameroun **2** Congo **3** Dahomey **4** Egypt **5** Ethiopia (Eritrea) **6** Guinea **7** Ivory Coast **8** Liberia **9** Libya **10** Mali **11** Mauritania **12** Morocco **13** Niger **14** Somalia **15** Sudan **16** Togo **17** Tunisia **18** Republic of South Africa **19** Upper Volta **20** Ghana **21** Nigeria **22** Sierra Leone **23** Tanganyika (As of Dec. 1961) **24** Central African Republic **25** Chad **26** Republic of the Congo **27** Gabon **28** Malagasy Republic **29** Senegal **30** Federation of Rhodesia and Nyasaland, (a) Northern Rhodesia, (b) Southern Rhodesia, (c) Nyasaland **31** Gambia **32** Kenya **33** Uganda **34** Zanzibar **35** Bechuanaland **36** Basutoland **37** Swaziland **38** Algeria, (a) French Sahara **39** French Somaliland **40** Fernando Po **41** Ifni **42** Rio Muni **43** Spanish Sahara **44** Angola **45** Mozambique **46** Portuguese Guinea **47** Ruanda-Urundi **48** South-west Africa

Southern Rhodesia is a British self-governing colony under the jurisdiction of the Commonwealth Relations Office. Northern Rhodesia and Nyasaland are British protectorates under the jurisdiction of the Colonial Office.

Nkrumah's type of nationalism and also doubtless felt that their particular community possessed a ready-made nationalism far more ancient and appropriate to Africa. Nkrumah struck back, outlawed all tribal and regional organizations, arrested and deported opposition leaders, instituted a series of trials and commissions of inquiry – and incidentally built up his own personal power. All the fine promise and promises of independence were disappointed, and arbitrary rule, corruption, and dictatorship, so it seemed, took Ghana for their own. But Nkrumah and Ghana, none the less, survived.

Nigeria was the largest in area of the British territories in Africa – four times the size of Britain herself. The three principal Regions of the territory differed widely in race, religion, and administration, and only by the "accident" of nineteenth-century imperial history had Nigeria become a state at all. In fact, not till 1946 was there established a central legislature, and not till 1954 a "federation." The Northern Region was the most populous, but was the poorest and most backward. It was the home of the Hausa tribes, Moslem in religion, ruled by a hierarchy of feudal emirs. The Western Region was the least populous, but was the richest and most cultivated. It was the home of the Beni and the Yoruba, at one time supporters of great African kingdoms. The Eastern Region was the home of the Ibo, formerly the least developed but now probably the most progressive of all the Nigerian peoples; it was also the home of Nnamdi Azikiwe, "Dr. Zik," leader of the nationalist party, the National Council of Nigeria and the Cameroons (NCNC). All Regions contained important minorities.

Out of this complex was now to be forged a modern independent nation. In 1957 regional self-government was introduced in the West and East, and in 1959 in the North. On October 1, 1960, Nigeria began her uncertain career as a Dominion within the British Commonwealth with Azikiwe as Governor General.

The British Protectorate Uganda was a land apart, at the headwaters of the White Nile, lying in the mountainous massif between the great lakes Albert and Victoria. It has been described as the "most African" of British African territories. Outside its Negroid stock, it had virtually no minorities, no color line, and no permanent white settlers. Incidentally, it was immensely prosperous, and its main cash crops, cotton and coffee, were almost wholly in African hands. But politically it was an anomaly and closely resembled, if anything, its neighbor Ethiopia. It consisted of four Kingdoms, each in separate treaty relations with Britain, the largest and most populous being Buganda, under the rule of a hereditary monarch, the Kabaka. And here, oddly enough, all the normal roles were reversed – the British Governor and the Colonial Secretary (in 1953, Oliver Lyttelton) seeking to introduce democratic reforms and the Kabaka clinging to his ancient feudal prerogatives. In the upshot a situation was created something like that at the same time in French Morocco. In 1953 the British decided to discipline the Kabaka by deposing him, and he was whisked off by plane to an exile in London.[2]

The British action was not just insult, but sacrilege. The Kabaka's court went into deep mourning; his sister died from the shock. In the end, after two years of commissions – and of surprising moderation on both sides – the Kabaka returned to his kingdom and to a hysterical welcome from his subjects. But he returned as a constitutional king, under a new agreement that clipped some of his former powers. As we write, Uganda's constitutional history is proceeding, still with the strongest opposition against change from the united opinion of the entire Baganda, or Buganda people.

The French colonial empire in Equatorial Africa covered territories eight times the size of Metropolitan France, inhabited by some 40,000,000 peoples of various races, cultures, and languages, mostly at tribal and pastoral levels – of little historical pride or of modern political sophistication – and, in the 1950's, by contrast with French Indochina and North Africa, all wrapped in peace and quiet. Here there were no white settlers, or *colons* – the climate was too impossible – and no native insurgents, or *fellagha* – it was too early – and the French colonial doctrines could be applied without complications or obstructions. The British had always tried to train their colonial peoples, in Africa as elsewhere, for eventual self-government; but they did not try to convert them into Britons. In the French system, an African was a potential Frenchman, capable of "evolving" into a citizen of the French Union (or Community). The French Government in Paris was now resolved that the transition to that high status should be effected quickly and painlessly, and surprisingly, within a few years, that result was legally accomplished.

In 1956 the Socialist government of Guy Mollet drafted the *Loi-cadre,* the basic instrument for the first stage of African suffrage. By then, African leaders and nationalist parties were in being, making mounting demands for independence – such as Houphouet-Boigny's RDA (*Rassemblement démocratique africain*) mainly in the central territories, and Senghor's MSA (*Mouvement socialiste africain*) in the western. In 1958, as one of the first acts of his presidency, General de Gaulle made a tour of French Africa – he was accompanied by Houphouet-Boigny – and represented himself as the great emancipator of Africa, except Algeria. On his return to France, he made the eighteen French overseas territories an offer of four options: first, to become Departments of France; second, to retain their present colonial status; third, to become independent members of the French Community; or fourth, to secede entirely. No territory chose the first option; certain Pacific and West Indian islands chose the second; twelve African territories, including Madagascar, chose the third. Guinea alone, under the ardent young patriot leader, Sekou Touré, chose the fourth, and was immediately cut off from French administration and French aid. On October 2, 1958, Guinea proclaimed herself a republic.

In the territories, British and French, which we have mentioned so far in this section, one factor was generally absent, namely the white settler. But the white settler constituted a problem, if not *the* problem, in Algeria – as we could also say in South Africa – and he constituted a problem in the British territories of Kenya and the Rhodesias.

Kenya could be described as the classic example of the multiracial state. Four communities were domiciled there, all originally immigrant, none with prior "rights" to the territory, each now filling a highly specialized social and economic role. Some 40,000 Europeans (mainly British) occupied the cities (Nairobi and Mombasa) and also the "White Highlands" where climate, altitude, and soil had combined to produce the ideal whiteman's farmland. Some 25,000 Arabs and 100,000 Asians (mainly Indians) were traders in the cities and on the coast. Some 6,000,000 Africans were partly urbanized and formed the main industrial labor force, but the greater number lived by their flocks and herds or by primitive agriculture in about forty tribes, of which the largest was the Kikuyu. Out of this complex, as if by a law of nature, developed the jealousies, fears, and terrors of a kind which has become all too familiar in this history.

Sometime before the Second World War, and with increasing and organized vehemence after it, Africans in Kenya had been demanding a betterment of their conditions, especially in regard to the ownership of land. In 1952 a rebellion broke out among the Kikuyu, led by the Mau Mau, a secret society of the tribe, a rebellion horrifying not only for its atrocities against the white settler community, but for the revolting witchcraft rites that the rebel initiates were reported to practice. The Government declared a state of emergency, army units were flown out, and the rebellion was gradually crushed at a total cost of several hundred lives. The local leader, Jomo Kenyatta, was tried and sentenced to seven years' imprisonment for his alleged part in the rebellion. In 1954 Oliver Lyttelton, the Colonial Secretary in London, proposed the creation of a multiracial council of ministers. Kenyatta's leadership devolved upon Tom Mboya, who of course demanded an African State *now*. A new constitution, giving a probable African majority, was devised to go into effect in 1961. But, as we write, Kenya's "transitional period" seems far from concluded, and Kenyatta's conditional release has found his followers violently at odds among themselves.

The Federation of Rhodesia and Nyasaland represented a partial solution of a similar multiracial tangle. This inland group of three British territories, Northern and Southern Rhodesia and Nyasaland, had little in common but their individual need to find a broader economic base. None of the three by itself was properly viable. Federation therefore had been discussed since the Second World War, planned in draft in 1951, and eventually established in 1953. From the point of view of the Rhodesian white settler, federation had contradictory objects. It protected his territory from the harsher policies now being pursued to the south in South Africa, but it might also secure him in his own position of relative superiority. From the African point of view, even if federation did not mean apartheid, it meant intolerable social and economic discrimination. All African parties were strongly opposed to it. Nor were they greatly impressed by somewhat pretentious talk of their "partnership" in the new political entity. In Northern Rhodesia, moreover, was a special regional problem created by the so-called Copper Belt, European-owned and operated, and

African-worked, an area of immense wealth under rapid development. Copper in Rhodesia, in fact, was producing much the same situation as oil in the Sahara.

It was therefore to be expected that a bitter struggle should result which, as we write, finds white interests supporting the Federation's Prime Minister, Sir Roy Welensky, and African interests supporting African leaders Kenneth Kuanda in Northern Rhodesia and Dr. Hastings Banda of Nyasaland — with parliamentary and official opinion in London, perplexed and divided, trying as usual to find the correct "British compromise." In 1959 the Federation's Governor, Sir Robert Armitage, announced that he had uncovered a plot on the part of African nationalists to massacre the white population, and for a moment it seemed that a new Mau Mau terror was about to break out in Africa.

But nowhere did the great African revolt find so tragic an outcome as in the Belgian Congo. By rights we should trace the history of this vast colony back to its beginnings under King Leopold II of the Belgians, for its history, even more than in other African countries, contributed to its subsequent condition. Before the First World War the "Congo Free State" had been a byword for atrocious maladministration, but thereafter, in repentant spirit, it had become "Africa's Welfare State." Nevertheless, paternalism and arbitrary rule continued side by side, all rigidly and absolutely controlled from Brussels. Nor had the white man, other than the official, a share — not even a vote — in the government of the territory; while the African, though encouraged to better himself economically, was denied the veriest elements of administrative training or responsibility. The most that the African was permitted was membership in social study groups, like the *Union des Intérêts sociaux congolais* (UNISCO), out of which was to emerge the first Congolese nationalist leader, Joseph Kasavubu, "King Kasa." By 1960, although the African *évolué* was beginning to creep into minor official posts, the Congolese civil service still only counted 600 Africans to nearly 10,000 Europeans, and the state police, the *Force publique,* was entirely officered by Belgians. The natural resources of the country, however, assured that the system produced the goods, whatever its type of administration, and it did so in fabulous quantity in almost every commercially useful mineral in the atomic table. Finally a very efficient propaganda service shielded the Congo from the least criticism of the outside world — including that of doubting Belgians in Belgium.

A trade recession in 1957 indicated that all was not well in this supposedly idyllic state. Nationalism was born of falling prices and unemployment. In 1958 de Gaulle's dramatic offer of independence to the neighboring French Congo was provocative, to say the least. Congolese nationalist leaders and parties sprang up as if from nowhere — notably Patrice Lumumba and his *Mouvement national congolais* (MNC). On January 4, 1959, unemployed rioters in the capital, Leopoldville, were dispersed by the *Force republique* with a loss of 49 lives; the Belgian Government panicked; colonial share prices on the Brussels Bourse broke; King Baudouin broadcast proposals for hastening the political evolution of the Congo. In

January 1960, a year after the Leopoldville riots, at a round-table conference of all parties in Brussels, plans were drawn up for the independence of the Congo in the next six months. Almost overnight, it seemed, this most autocratically governed of European colonies was to be given its independence, completely and unconditionally.

No one was prepared. The sudden achievement of independence at once aroused divisive forces. Lumumba and his party stood for a single unitary state; Kasavubu, more parochial – and probably more realistic – stood for the carving up of the Congo with its natural regions under a loose federation; Moise Tshombe, leader in the rich Katanga province, at one time a supporter of Kasavubu, talked of seceding from the Congo altogether and forming his province into a separate state. Nevertheless, on June 30, 1960, the Congolese Republic was proclaimed in Leopoldville, with Lumumba Premier and Kasavubu President.

The result was anarchy. African rioting and looting had begun before June 30. The *Force publique* mutinied and ran amok. Belgian nationals and their families escaped if they could – many of those in Leopoldville were ferried across the river to the safety of the French city of Brazzaville. Many that remained were the victims of savage atrocities. Troops were flown out from Belgium; Belgian warships bombarded Matadi, the Congo's only seaport. The new Congolese Government broke off relations with Belgium and demanded the withdrawal of all Belgian troops. Lumumba was at odds with Kasavubu, and the two leaders were soon "dismissing" each other from office. Tshombe declared the independence of Katanga, and another separatist movement flared up in Kasai, the "Diamond Province." The United Nations Security Council, hurriedly convened, authorized Secretary-General Hammarskjöld "to provide military assistance," and the first United Nations units from Ghana and Tunisia under the Swedish General von Horn began to arrive in Leopoldville on July 18. Colonel Mobutu, now commander of the Congolese Army, attempted a military coup in opposition to Lumumba and to the United Nations. Soviet aid to Lumumba in the shape of planes and trucks arrived during August. Lumumba himself seemed to be repeatedly under arrest, in hiding, or escaping. His death was subsequently reported.

After the Belgian Congo came the turn of Portuguese Angola, the oldest European possession in Africa. Under an amendment of the Portuguese Constitution in 1951 all Portuguese overseas territories were declared to be provinces of Portugal. But this legal quibble did not prevent a nationalist movement from arising in Angola, the neighbor of the Congo. Disturbances were touched off by a resolution of the United Nations General Assembly on December 15, 1960, calling upon Portugal to submit reports "without further delay" upon her colonial territories. Terrorist attacks on Europeans in Angola, allegedly organized by the revolutionary Union of Angolan Peoples, and by native workers rebelling against the forced labor system, broke out in February 1961 in the capital, Luanda, and then spread to other parts of the territory, especially to the northern areas bordering the Congo.

United Nations, New York, 1960: African delegates in conversation with Fidel Castro

SERGIO LARRAIN-MAGNUM

In February 1960, during his African tour, Macmillan, the British Prime Minister, addressed both Houses of the South African Parliament in Cape Town, and he uttered the statement that has since become famous:

> We have seen the awakening of national consciousness in peoples who for centuries have lived in dependence upon some other Power. Fifteen years ago this movement spread through Asia . . . Today the same thing is happening in Africa. In different places it may take different forms, but it is happening everywhere. The wind of change is blowing through the continent. Whether we like it or not, the growth of national consciousness is a political fact. We must accept it as a fact . . . I sincerely believe that, if we cannot do so, we may imperil the precarious balance of East and West on which the peace of the world depends.

In this section on Africa we have given the briefest sketch of this nationalist movement in some of the African territories. We have selected those territories that seemed to us the most important, and, through them, we have indicated the kind of problems which were common to them all. We ought perhaps to have extended our survey to include parallel events elsewhere at this time – for example in the West Indies. No part of the Non-Western world, as we called it in Chapter 41, was free from such developments. The final situation in Africa, as we write, is indicated on the accompanying map. (See p. 807.)

African leadership had sometimes played with the idea of a unification of the continent in a "United States of Africa." But there would seem to be a great gulf fixed between that ideal and its achievement. Moreover, each territory, as it became independent, characteristically grouped itself around a single leader – Nkrumah (Ghana), Azikiwe (Eastern Nigeria), Awolowo (Western Nigeria), Touré (Guinea), Senhor (Senegal), Houphouet-Boigny (Ivory Coast), Hastings Banda (Nyasaland), Nyerere (Tanganyika), Kenyatta (Kenya), and so forth. And to these names might be added that of the evergreen President Tubman of Liberia. As some commentators pointed out, Africa was exhibiting all the traits of a "personality cult," if not a "chieftainship cult," and, in all likelihood, existing divisions and diversities in Africa would always be sharpened by strong personal rivalries.

Nonetheless, an African consciousness, if not an Afro-Asian consciousness, was undeniably emerging among the one-time colonial peoples of Africa and Asia. Something of the sort, in its Asian expression, had been in evidence at the Delhi Conference of 1949 – attended also by representatives of Egypt and Ethiopia. (See p. 779.) It was very clearly formulated at the Afro-Asian Conference at Bandung in Indonesia in April 1955, a conference that was attended by representatives of twenty-nine states from Liberia to Japan, including Nasser, Nehru, and Chou En-lai of China, and which condemned colonialism in all its forms and singled out for specific reproof the French policy in North Africa, the Dutch policy in New Guinea, and of course apartheid in South Africa. A whole series of conferences between African nationalist leaders took place during 1960 – in January at Tunis, in February at Tangier, in April at Accra, in June at Addis Ababa, in August at Leopoldville, all serving to stimulate a corporate Pan-African spirit. At the same time the Afro-Asian countries were now forming a strong, self-conscious bloc in the United Nations General Assembly, so much so that we might also say that a virtual Afro-Asian conference in New York bade fair to become an annual event. Today the Afro-Asian bloc has tended to identify itself with the "Uncommitted Nations" and was again faithfully represented, for example, at the Conference of Uncommitted Nations at Belgrade in September 1961.

43. POSTSCRIPT

And so we bring this book to an end. In point of time the period it has covered is not very considerable — a half-century at most. In the number and significance of its events the period must surely be the most crowded of any equal period in human history. We have described two world wars, the fall of nine empires, the rise of several new nationalities, one revolution — the Russian Revolution — surpassing other lesser revolutions, and a Depression that confounded the economics of three centuries. We have also described two experiments in the organization of peace — the League of Nations and the United Nations — and three experiments in totalitarian government — Communism, Fascism, and Nazism. Whatever else may appear to have followed from these years, one consequence has been the deposition of Western Europe from the undoubted political and military supremacy that she enjoyed in 1914. At the same time, we have seen *first,* the corresponding growth in importance of two Super-Powers, so-called — the United States and the Soviet Union — each opposing to the other its particular philosophy of peace and human welfare, and *second,* the growth of new powers, as yet potential rather than actual, in the great periphery of Asia, Latin America, and Africa. Meanwhile, Western Europe now strives to compete in this situation by reconstructing herself as a new integral economic and political unit.

These years have also seen, outside the immediate field of politics but closely affecting it, the further extension of scientific techniques and their bifurcation into an ever-increasing command of wealth and into an ever-increasing destructiveness and terror. They have seen the discovery and development of new resources as well as the thoughtless "mining out" of older resources that are often more precious and irreplaceable. They have seen, despite the wars and revolutions, the unprecedented multiplication of the world's total population. They have seen the leveling and collectivization, so to speak, of society, the end of social privilege based on birth and culture, and correspondingly the triumph of mass man, mass social techniques, mass economics, mass communication, mass education, mass entertainment, and mass warfare.

But, in many ways, these nonpolitical developments have all been of European cause and origin. Paradoxically Western Europe's declension of power has not meant a declension of spiritual influence. Both the United

States and the Soviet Union, and even more so the lesser powers of the periphery, are still clients of European civilization. All the world today thinks with Europe's ideas and fights with Europe's weapons – and shares Europe's trials and tribulations.

We are constantly being told that something "went wrong" with European civilization perhaps at the turn of the century, perhaps in the last century, perhaps three centuries ago. But European civilization has never been static, and its present transformation is only a degree more complex and violent than other movements of the past. Our short-term destiny may be, in President Kennedy's words, "to live out our lives in uncertainty, challenge, and peril." Our longer-term hope is that human creativeness can again make all things new. For the wind bloweth where it listeth. History is always a preparation for the unpredictable. And so will be the next long episode in the incredible human drama.

NOTES

Chapter 1 (*pages* 4-18)

1. The British income tax in Lloyd George's budget of May 1914 was as follows:

9d on the pound for incomes	under £1,000,
10½d	between £1,000 and £1,500,
1/-	between £1,500 and £2,000,
1/2	between £2,000 and £2,500,
1/4	over £2,500.

There were other taxes and duties on certain imports, notably on tea and on wines and spirits.

2. The Belgian guarantee dated from 1839, and that of Luxembourg from 1867, Prussia being a guarantor in both cases.

3. The Triple Alliance was defensive. It guaranteed the *status quo* in the Balkans, and it was understood not to be directed against Britain.

4. The German *Burgfriede* and the French *Union Sacrée* in 1914 signified domestic peace, in particular the cessation of party politics. *Burgfriede* was the word used for the civic truces in the Middle Ages.

Chapter 2 (*pages* 19-33)

1. The Battle of Plevna, 1877, when the Turks held up the Russian invasion of the Balkans.

2. See Note 2, Chapter 1, above.

3. See Gerhard Ritter, *The Schlieffen Plan,* London, 1958.

4. Winston S. Churchill, *The Unknown War,* New York, 1931, Ch. XVI.

5. We shall use the term Central Powers in our chapters on the First World War to signify Germany and Austria-Hungary, and eventually all four members of the Quadruple Alliance: Germany, Austria-Hungary, Turkey, and Bulgaria.

6. The name "Anzac" was coined from the initials of the Australia and New Zealand Army Corps.

7. See Note 6, above.

8. See Note 5, above.

9. The Battle of Coruña, 1809, when a British army under General Sir John Moore, after a disastrous retreat, repulsed the French under Marshal Soult and succeeded in withdrawing by sea.

10. We shall use the term, Near East, in the earlier Parts of this book. The term, Middle East, became current during the Second World War, and we shall use it in Parts Four and Five. There is no general agreement as to the proper demarcation of either term.

Chapter 3 (*pages* 34-52)

1. See Note 4, Chapter 1, above.

2. The "making over" or "turning over" of clothes was turning them inside out and restitching them, a process at which the German housewife at this time became very skilful. The German word is *wenden.*

3. See Glossary, p. 830, for explanation of these official titles.

4. The Allies, of course, fought with heavy American financial assistance. But it is still arguable that they would have continued to fight, and would have somehow patched up their budgets, without that assistance. Germany bore a much greater financial burden alone.

5. It is to be noted that the conscription issue in Canada and Australia was over conscription for *overseas* service. There was no such issue over conscription for home defense. And it could be said that, in the case of Ireland in 1916, the issue again was essentially over conscription for service in France.

6. The Irish Volunteers, founded by John MacNeill in 1913; the Citizen Army, founded in Dublin by James Larkin and James Connolly, also in 1913; and Sinn Fein, founded by Arthur Griffith in 1900. All supported uncompromising political separation from England, in contradistinction to the Irish Nationalist party, led by John Redmond, which, for the time being, supported Asquith's Home Rule Bill of 1912.

7. F. E. Smith, mentioned earlier, was knighted in 1915. He was then Attorney General, and in that capacity he was prosecutor at the Casement trial. The historian we quote is H. G. Wells, *Outline of History,* Bk. VIII, Ch. XL, § 3.

8. The Committees of Zemstvos and Towns were unofficial philanthropic provincial and urban organizations, managed by civilians largely on a volunteer basis. See T. I. Polner, *Russian Local Government during the War and the Union of Zemstvos,* New Haven, 1930.

9. Sir Mark Sykes was a lieutenant colonel in the British Army, assigned to political duties with the French Foreign Ministry at the beginning of the First World War. François-Marie-Denis-Georges Picot was a representative of the French Foreign Ministry and onetime Consul General in Syria.

Chapter 4 (*pages* 53-81)

1. The French casualties at Verdun were 535,000; the German were 427,000. See an analysis of these figures in the British official *History of the Great War: Military Operations, France and Belgium, 1916,* London, 1932, Vol. I, Note II, pp. 496-97.

2. The writer acknowledges borrowing this very descriptive figure from B. H. Liddell Hart, *A History of the World War,* Boston, 1935, Chap. VI.

3. Winston S. Churchill, *The World Crisis: 1911-1918,* rev. ed. New York, 1931, p. 612.

4. "Unrestricted" (*uneingeschränkt*) meant the sinking without warning of *all* merchantmen, Allied and neutral. "Intensive" (*verschärft*) submarine warfare, practised by Germany for a few months in 1916, meant the sinking without warning of *armed* merchantmen only.

5. From the figures in Lord Hankey, *The Supreme Command,* London, 1961, Vol. II, p. 639.

6. See Note 4, Chapter 1, above.

7. In the American constitutional system members of the Cabinet are not, and must not be, members of Congress. But American readers should be reminded that this "separation of powers" is the reverse of the usual democratic procedure in Europe. In Germany, before 1918, "democratization" meant the granting of ministerial appointments to Reichstag Deputies, so as to bring the German constitutional system into line with the constitutional systems of Britain and France. In Prussia,

"democratization" meant reforms of the then existing discriminatory suffrage laws.

8. Franz Borkenau, *Austria and After,* London, 1938, p. 181.

9. J. W. Wheeler-Bennett, *The Forgotten Peace: Brest Litovsk,* New York, 1939.

Chapter 5 (*pages* 82-93)

1. During the entire war period German submarines succeeded in torpedoing only five American transports. Three of the five sank, two returned damaged to port. All five were on return voyages to the United States when struck, and were therefore carrying no troops. B. Crowell and R. F. Wilson, *How America Went to War: The Road to France,* New Haven, 1921, Vol. II, pp. 427-28.

2. Erich Ludendorff, *Meine Kriegserinnerungen, 1914-1918,* Berlin, 1919, p. 435.

3. American troops were put into a quiet section of the line near Nancy in October 1917 and suffered their first casualties on November 3, 1917. The first major action, however, took place in May 1918 at Cantigny in the Amiens salient. American divisions fought at Château-Thierry in June 1918. Fourteen American divisions were in the line in August 1918 at Ypres, Arras, Reims, Verdun, and St. Mihiel, and in Alsace. Three hundred thousand American troops fought in the Second Battle of the Marne, 550,000 in the action at St. Mihiel, and 1,200,000 in the Meuse-Argonne. About 1,200 participated in the Battle of Vittorio Veneto in Italy.

4. The United States never declared war on Bulgaria and did not withdraw its usual diplomatic representation in that country.

5. The Kaiser signed his abdication from his place of exile on November 28, 1918.

Chapter 6 (*pages* 96-111)

1. "Mr. Hughes, am I to understand," asked Wilson on this occasion, "that if the whole civilized world asks Australia to agree to a mandate in respect to these islands, Australia is prepared to defy the appeal of the whole civilized world?" "That's about the size of it, President Wilson," replied Hughes. Paul Birdsall, *Versailles Twenty Years After,* New York, 1941, p. 72.

2. Harold Nicolson, *Peacemaking, 1919,* New York, 1939, pp. 58-59.

3. D. Lloyd George, *The Truth about the Peace Treaties,* London, 1938, Vol. I, p. 237.

4. The Powers at the Peace Conference in plenary session were:

The United States	5 seats	
Britain	5	British Empire 14 seats in all
Canada	2	
Australia	2	
South Africa	2	
New Zealand	1	
India	2	
France	5	
Italy	5	
Japan	5	

The following 3 seats each: Belgium, Brazil, Yugoslavia (Serbia).

The following 2 seats each: China, Czechoslovakia, Greece, Hejaz, Poland, Portugal, Rumania, Siam.

The following 1 seat each: Bolivia, Cuba, Ecuador, Guatemala, Haiti, Honduras, Liberia, Nicaragua, Panama, Peru, Uruguay.

The delegates of the five principal powers included, in addition to those mentioned in our text: for France, Marshal Foch, André Tardieu, Jules Cambon, Léon Bourgeois; for Britain, Bonar Law, G. N. Barnes, Viscount Milner, Winston Churchill, Lord Robert Cecil, Lord Hardinge, Sir Maurice Hankey, J. M. Keynes, Philip Kerr; for Italy, Salandra and Scialoja, and later Nitti and Tittoni; for the United States, Colonel House, Henry White, General Tasker H. Bliss, Norman H. Davis, Thomas W. Lamont, Bernard M. Baruch, Vance McCormick, Herbert Hoover, George Louis Beer, Joseph Clark Grew, Samuel Gompers; and for Japan, Viscount Chinda. Also for India, the Maharajah of Bikaner and Lord Sinha.

5. The Commission on the League of Nations seemed to include the most illustrious names of the Conference: President Wilson, Colonel House, Lord Robert Cecil, General Smuts, Léon Bourgeois, Orlando, Hymans, Venizelos, Dmowski, Kramář, Vesnich, Makino, and Chinda.

6. G. P. Gooch, *Germany,* New York, 1925, pp. 214-15. But, on this question of the continuation of the blockade of Germany after the Armistice, see Note 1, Chapter 10, below.

Chapter 7 (*pages* 112-28)

1. Spain and Brazil resigned from the League of Nations over the altercation in 1926 when Germany was given a permanent seat in the League Council. Spain returned in 1928. Brazil never returned, but she remained in the ILO and from time to time joined other agencies. Costa Rica also resigned because she could not pay the annual contribution.

2. Paul Birdsall, *Versailles Twenty Years After,* New York, 1941, p. 9.

3. Owing to frequent cancellations and renewals, it is difficult to determine the status of the Optional Clause in any one year. The figures quoted are from M. O. Hudson, *The World Court, 1921-1938,* 5th ed., Boston, 1938, pp. 14-15, 30-31.

4. Professor James T. Shotwell.

5. The fifteen Powers which signed the Pact of Paris on August 27, 1928, were the United States, Australia, Belgium, Britain, Canada, Czechoslovakia, France, Germany, India, Irish Free State, Italy, Japan, New Zealand, Poland, and South Africa. By the end of 1931, forty-five more states had adhered.

6. February 1778, treaty of alliance between France and the United States, signed in Versailles for the United States by Benjamin Franklin.

7. The Litvinov Protocol was signed in Moscow on February 9, 1929, by the Soviet Union, Poland, Latvia, Estonia, and Rumania. Lithuania and Turkey adhered on April 1, Danzig on April 30, and Persia on July 4, 1929.

8. We might translate these words by using those of George Washington in his first annual address to both houses of Congress on January 8, 1790: "To be prepared for war is one of the most effectual means of preserving peace."

Chapter 8 (*pages* 129-49)

1. See Note 4, Chapter 1, above.

2. J. W. Wheeler-Bennett, *Nemesis of Power,* London, 1953, pp. 20-21.

3. The facts concerning the continuation of the blockade after the Armistice are given in: F. M. Surface and R. L. Bland, *American Food in the World War and Reconstruction Period,* Stanford, 1931, pp. 189 ff; H. W. V. Temperley, *A History of the Peace Conference of Paris,* London, 1920, Vol. I, pp. 313 ff; Lindley Fraser, *Germany between Two Wars,* Oxford, 1944, pp. 30-36; J. H. Morgan, *Assize of Arms,* Vol. I, London, 1945, pp. 187-90.

4. We now know a good deal about German-Soviet relations during the 1920's. See Lionel Kochan, *Russia and the Weimar Republic,* London, 1954; Ruth Fischer, *Stalin and German Communism,* Cambridge, Mass., 1948; and J. W. Wheeler-Bennett, *Nemesis of Power,* London, 1953.

5. J. M. Keynes, *The Economic Consequences of the Peace,* London, 1919, p. 124.

6. These figures are from *Verhandlungen der verfassunggebenden Deutschen Nationalversammlung,* Berlin, 1920; *Verhandlung des Reichstags,* Berlin, 1920-25; and *Verzeichnis der Mitglieder des Reichstags,* Berlin, 1925-33.

Chapter 9 (*pages* 150-60)

1. *Trümmerzone,* or "Debris Zone," was a term used by the German geopoliticians. See Karl Haushofer, *e.g.* in his *Weltpolitik von Heute,* Berlin, 1934, p. 111. Richard Hartshorne used the term "Shatter Zone" in a chapter in Hans W. Weigert and Vilhjalmur Stefansson, *Compass of the World,* New York, 1944, p. 203.

Chapter 10 (*pages* 161-79)

1. We are using the term, Christian Social, rather than Christian Socialist, which strictly is a mistranslation. The full German name of the party is *Christlich-Soziale Partei Oesterreichs.*

2. See Note 1, above.

Chapter 11 (*pages* 180-206)

1. See Note 10, Chapter 2, above.

2. The Ottoman Sultan-Caliph played a dual role in the Islamic world. As Sultan, he was military and civil head of the Ottoman Empire. As Caliph, he was "Commander of the Faithful" and titular (theoretical) and spiritual head of all Moslems. The title Caliph was assumed by Selim, the Osmanli Sultan who conquered Egypt in 1517. Thereafter the Sultan was *de facto* (if not *de jure*) successor of the Arab Caliphs who had succeeded Mohammed. The Sultan-Caliph represented the indivisible union of the temporal and spiritual powers of Islam, vested in the person of a single supreme ruler.

3. The Capitulations were special treaties, some dating as far back as the sixteenth and seventeenth centuries, which granted extraterritorial rights and privileges to nationals of "Capitulatory" Powers.

4. See Note 3, above.

Chapter 12 (*pages* 207-33)

1. "Great Russia" appears on the pre-1914 maps of Russia. It was the core, so to speak, of European Russia and included an area roughly within a 200-mile radius of Moscow, as distinct from West Russia, Little Russia, South Russia, and Kazan.

2. On December 23, 1917, Milner for Britain and Clemenceau for France signed a convention for dividing Russia into "zones of influence." See Louis Fischer, *The Soviets in World Affairs,* London, 1930, Vol. II, App., p. 836.

3. The requisitions under the system of War Communism took everything and then turned over a residue for the peasant's food and sowing. The grain tax was a levy, by which the peasant gave up a part of his produce to the authorities — much along the lines of the old-fashioned tithe — and kept the remainder to use as he pleased. See L. E. Hubbard, *The Economics of Soviet Agriculture,* London, 1939, pp. 79-82.

4. The State would "wither away." This famous phrase is from Engels and occurs in his *Anti-Dühring.* But Marx has something like it, almost on the last page of his *Misère de la Philosophie:* "There will then be no more political power properly

speaking, since political power is precisely the official expression of (class) conflict in the social system."

5. See N. Berdyaev, *Origin of Russian Communism,* London, 1937, Ch. I.

6. Quoted in W. H. Chamberlin, *Russian Revolution,* London, 1935, Vol. II, p. 77.

7. See N. A. Timasheff, *The Great Retreat,* New York, 1946.

8. Compare these figures with American production for the peak year, 1929: 550,000,000 tons of coal; 138,000,000 tons of oil (crude petroleum); 43,000,000 tons of pig iron; 57,000,000 tons of steel; 771,000 trucks, etc.; 4,587,000 automobiles. (The tons are metric tons.) *Statistical Year-Book of the League of Nations, 1938-39,* Geneva, 1939.

9. See Naum Jasny, *The Socialized Agriculture of the USSR: Plans and Performance,* Stanford, 1949, pp. 311-312, 323, 553; App., pp. 709-14.

***Chapter* 13 (*pages* 234-51)**

1. The *fasces* was the Latin name for a bundle of rods tied around the haft of an ax. It was an emblem of unity and authority, and was carried by the Roman lictors, who attended the magistrates.

2. The *Guardia Regia* was a special force, numbering 25,000, which had been created by Nitti during his premiership in 1919 to assist the police in maintaining order. The force was disbanded by Mussolini soon after he came to power.

3. The reference is to the withdrawal of the plebeians of the city of Rome to the Aventine Hill in 493 B.C.

4. Requoted from H. Finer, *Mussolini's Italy,* London, 1935, p. 191.

5. B. Mussolini, article on Fascism in the *Enciclopedia Italiana,* requoted from H. Finer, *ibid.,* pp. 173, 174, and 222.

6. Requoted from H. W. Schneider, *Making the Fascist State,* New York, 1928, p. 253.

7. Also from H. W. Schneider, *ibid.*

8. At the consistory of 1953 Pope Pius XII created fourteen non-Italian cardinals — two French, two Spanish, and one each from Germany, Poland, Yugoslavia, Ireland, the United States, Canada, Brazil, Colombia, Ecuador, and India. Pius XII died in 1958 and was succeeded by Cardinal Angelo Giuseppe Roncalli as Pope John XXIII.

***Chapter* 14 (*pages* 252-62)**

1. We shall use the terms Radical for Radical Socialist, and Radical party for Radical Socialist party.

2. It should be remembered that the French word, *réparation,* means repair or making good. In English, reparation also has the sense of the French *indemnité,* the payment of monetary compensation. Much misunderstanding has arisen from this verbal difficulty.

3. So says General de Gaulle, *France and Her Army,* London, 1945, the last page.

4. The presidential question in France has been keenly debated since the Constitution of 1875, which deliberately reduced the President's powers. The question was still very much alive in the constitutional plebiscites after 1945 — and still is. (See pp. 692-93.)

***Chapter* 15 (*pages* 263-91)**

1. The results of the General Election of December 1918 were unusually complex. The London *Times* gave the following analysis:

Coalition Parties

Conservatives (Unionists)	338	seats
Liberals	136	
National Democratic party	10	
	484	

Non-Coalition Parties

Labor	59	seats
Conservatives (Unionists)	48	
Liberals	26	
National party	2	
Independents	7	
Sinn Feiners	73	
Irish Nationalists	7	
	122	

In the ensuing government, Lloyd George was the Liberal Prime Minister of the Coalition. Asquith remained a non-Coalition Liberal. The election signified a division of the old Liberal party which broke up as one of the great political parties of Britain.

2. The authenticity of the famous "Red Letter" is still in doubt. Lord Vansittart, who was in a position to know, says it was "probably genuine," but he derides Zinoviev and regards the whole incident as "a more than ridiculous thing to fight about." See his *Mist Procession,* London, 1958, pp. 330-31. Herbert Morrison, *Government and Parliament,* London, 1959, pp. 64-66, says, "To this day one cannot be absolutely sure about it."

3. Sir Austin Chamberlain, Chancellor of the Exchequer (1903-06 and 1919-21) and Foreign Secretary (1924-29), was the younger half brother of Neville Chamberlain, Chancellor of the Exchequer (1923-24 and 1931-37) and Prime Minister (1937-40). Their father was Joseph Chamberlain, the Victorian statesman and "Liberal Unionist."

4. Arcos Ltd. (from the initials of the Anglo-Russian Co-operative Society) was the trading company in London representing the Soviet Co-operative Societies.

5. Land purchase has had a long history in Ireland. In some ways it was analogous to the agrarian reforms in European peasant countries, designed to buy out the landlords (often absentee landlords) for the benefit of landless and indigent tenants; but it was complicated by the peculiar nature of Irish landlordism. However, by a series of acts (the Land Act of 1923 being the last), provision was made for the issue of bonds, out of which compensation to the landlords would be made, and which were guaranteed by the British Government. The purchasers of land paid off their debts in part by means of annuities and in part by government bonus. After the establishment of the Free State, Cosgrave agreed to collect and pay to the British Government the full amount of the annuities. See Dorothy Macardle, *The Irish Republic,* London, 1937, App. II, 36, pp. 1026-28.

6. See Note 5, Chapter 3, above.

7. Readers of this book will recall the old controversy over the selection of Washington, D.C., as the capital of the United States.

8. The Indian census was taken every ten years. The figures were: 1901, 294,000,000; 1911, 315,000,000; 1921, 320,000,000; 1931, 353,000,000; 1941, 388,000,000. Since 1947 the figures have been:

	1951	*1961*
India	357,000,000	438,000,000
Pakistan	76,000,000	94,000,000

9. Purdah, by definition, is a screen or veil. It refers (a) to the secluded life of Moslem women, and (b) to the veil worn by Moslem women when in public. Some Hindu castes adopted purdah, for instance in Rajputana.

10. The name "Congress" is misleading, especially to Americans. The Indian National Congress, it must be remembered, was a political party, membership being open to both Hindus and Moslems on payment of a small subscription.

11. Hindus and Moslems are referred to as "communities," and their joint affairs and problems are "communal." In Indian parlance, therefore, a "communal" riot is always a riot between Hindus and Moslems.

Chapter 16 (*pages* 292-311)

1. Senator Lodge's "Round Robin" was a resolution signed by thirty-seven Republican senators (including Lodge, Knox, Borah, Lenroot, and Johnson) and inserted in the Congressional Record on March 4, 1919, the last day of Congress. It was to the effect that the peace terms with Germany should first be negotiated, and only then should the proposal for a League of Nations be taken up for consideration, and that "the constitution of the League of Nations in the form now proposed to the Peace Conference should not be accepted by the United States."

2. Had the war continued into 1919 a considerable expeditionary force from Brazil would have fought on the Western front. Brazil's contribution to the war was recognized when she received three seats in the plenary sessions of the Peace Conference. See Note 4, Chapter 6, above.

3. In February 1901, Orville Hitchcock Platt, chairman of the Committee on Cuban Relations, introduced the amendment (to an army appropriations bill) which bears his name. It provided for American military intervention in Cuba in certain contingencies, and forbade Cuba to enter into any treaty with a foreign Power to the prejudice of her independence.

4. The Clark Memorandum was drafted by J. Reuben Clark, Assistant Secretary of State, in 1928, and made public in 1930. It repudiated unofficially the "Theodore Roosevelt Corollary" of 1904 to the Monroe Doctrine, which had asserted that "chronic wrongdoing" in a Latin-American state "may force the United States, however reluctantly, in flagrant cases of such wrongdoing . . . to the exercise of an international peace power."

5. Brokers' loans may be made on a "time" basis or on a "call" or "demand" basis. Rate of interest on a "time" loan is usually agreed between the broker, who borrows, and the bank, which lends, and it continues unchanged for the duration (30 days to 1 year) of the agreement. The "call" or "demand" loan, as its name implies, may be terminated "at call" by borrower or lender at any time, and the rate of interest is on a day-to-day basis. "Call money," or the call loan rate, depends on the state of the market and may change during the day as new loans are made.

Purchases of stock may be made by a broker on behalf of a client against a deposit of a percentage of the purchase price, the broker holding the stock as security. In effect, this is a loan from broker to client. Before 1929, the New York Stock Exchange informally required of its member firms that this percentage, or margin, should be at least 17 per cent of the market value of the stocks. In the spring of 1929, the percentage was increased to 20 per cent. The margin itself, of course, was usually more stock – and so also was the broker's collateral. And this is where the trouble began.

See Raymond Vernon, *The Regulation of Stock Exchange Members,* New York, 1941.

Chapter 17 (*pages* 314-34)

1. Winston S. Churchill, *The World Crisis, 1918-1928: The Aftermath,* New York, 1929, Ch. XX.
2. See H. G. Moulton and L. Pasvolsky, *War Debts and World Prosperity,* New York, 1932, pp. 5-6.
3. In 1929 France's gold reserve was over 40,000,000,000 francs; in 1930 it was over 80,000,000,000 francs. See Paul Einzig, *France's Crisis,* London, 1934, p. 130.
4. Three premiers: MacDonald, Brüning, and Laval; six foreign ministers: Henderson, Curtius, Briand, Stimson, Grandi, and Hymans; four financial ministers: Snowden, Flandin, Mellon, and Mosconi. All of which was sufficient indication of the importance of the occasion.

Chapter 18 (*pages* 335-49)

1. The Kuomintang began as the Association for the Regeneration of China, founded in 1894. In 1905 it was merged into the larger Revolutionary Alliance, out of which sprang the present Kuomintang. The Revolutionary Alliance was a network of secret societies, opposed to the Manchu dynasty and kept together mainly by the unremitting activity of Dr. Sun Yat-sen. Propaganda was spread chiefly by young Chinese educated in the United States, Europe, and Japan. Generous subscriptions were obtained from well-to-do Chinese scattered throughout the Pacific area. It was claimed that the alliance had a membership of 300,000 in 1912. It was reorganized as the Kuomintang (National People's party) in 1912.
2. See T. E. Lafargue, *China and the World War,* Stanford, 1937; and P. E. Eckel, *The Far East since 1500,* New York, 1947, pp. 391-93.
3. The scramble for monopolistic concessions in China at the end of the nineteenth century prompted Britain and the United States to take the lead in formulating a doctrine designed to assure Western Powers equal trading opportunities throughout China. The first of the "Open Door" proposals, embodying this doctrine, was made by John Hay, Secretary of State, in 1899, since when the "Open Door" in China has been a cardinal principle of United States foreign policy. See P. E. Eckel, *The Far East since 1500,* New York, 1947, pp. 353-55.
4. The whole of this very controversial incident has been re-examined in the light of available documents by Sara R. Smith in *The Manchurian Crisis, 1931-1932: A Tragedy in International Relations,* New York, 1948.

Chapter 19 (*pages* 350-75)

1. See Fritz Tobias, "Stehen Sie auf, van der Lubbe!" *Der Spiegel,* Hamburg, October 21-December 2, 1959. But we have not yet had the last word on this incident.
2. Konrad Heiden, *Der Führer,* London, 1945, p. 147.
3. H. Rauschning, *The Voice of Destruction,* New York, 1940, pp. 109-10.
4. Adolf Hitler, *Mein Kampf,* New York, 1939, p. 313. But, in fairness, we must note that this well-known passage accuses Germany's enemies of the "Big Lie." But the passage is revealing for all that.
5. It is a common mistake to regard *Mein Kampf* as a "program." It is a confession of faith. And not all of it, by any means, was fulfilled as the Führer hoped, even up to 1941.
6. Winston S. Churchill, *The World Crisis,* rev. ed., New York, 1931, p. 848.
7. Leopold Schwarzschild, *World in Trance,* London, 1943, p. 190.
8. Papal Encyclical, *Mit brennender Sorge,* 1937, Paras. 25 and 28.
9. S. H. Roberts, *The House That Hitler Built,* New York, 1939, Chap. IV.

***Chapter* 20 (*pages* 376-97)**

1. See Note 1, Chapter 10, above.

***Chapter* 22 (*pages* 413-27)**

1. The Civil Guard (*Guardia Civil*) corresponded to the French gendarmerie and were organized on semimilitary lines. The Republicans changed their name to *Guardia Nacional Republicana.*

2. The Assault Guards (*Guardias de Asalto*) were the shock brigades, a second semimilitary police, formed in the first year of the Republic in 1931.

3. The Carlists were extreme monarchists and took their name from the brother of Ferdinand VII, Don Carlos, whose claim to the throne was contested in the Carlist wars of the early nineteenth century.

4. These groups are described in A. J. Toynbee, *Survey of International Affairs* for 1937, Oxford, Vol. II, pp. 88 ff.; and in Hugh Thomas, *Spanish Civil War,* London, 1961, Bk. II, pp. 184-97.

5. Non-Spanish intellectuals in one way or another involved in the Spanish Civil War make a remarkable list:

British: W. H. Auden, Fred Copeman, John Cornford, J. B. S. Haldane, C. Day Lewis, George Nathan, George Orwell, Esmond Romilly, Tom Wintringham
American: Ernest Hemingway, Herbert Matthews
French: Louis Aragon, André Malraux
German: Ludwig Renn
Italian: Pietro Nenni, Randolfo Pacciardi
Hungarian: Mata Zalke ("General Lukacz")

And we might add "General Kléber," Milovan Djilas, and Tito. See Hugh Thomas, *ibid.,* Bk. IV, pp. 324-27 and 389-93; and Bk. V, pp. 495-96.

6. For details of foreign intervention, see Hugh Thomas, *ibid.,* Bk. IV, pp. 324-28, 389-93; and App. iii, pp. 634-43.

***Chapter* 23 (*pages* 428-40)**

1. The literature on the Soviet purges of the 1930's is considerable. Walter Duranty's account is still one of the most credible. See his *Kremlin and the People,* New York, 1941. It is now pretty well established that Stalin was privy to Kirov's assassination.

2. Antinomianism, so called after the Antinomians, members of a German sect of the sixteenth century, is the doctrine which holds that the moral law is independent of theological sanction. In short, it is "ethics without religion."

3. Joseph Stalin, "The Foundations of Leninism" and "The Problems of Leninism," *Problems of Leninism,* Moscow, 1947, pp. 41, 65-66, 78, 162.

4. Khrushchev's report was generally available in 1956. See Note 3, Chapter 34, below.

***Chapter* 24 (*pages* 441-49)**

1. The "distressed" or "special" areas in England at this time were those in the coal fields, or the shipbuilding or other industrial districts, whose recovery was never expected to take place. These areas were particularly bad in South Wales and Durham.

2. Winston S. Churchill, *The Second World War: The Gathering Storm,* Boston, 1948, Bk. I, pp. 201 and 220.

3. Chamberlain himself wrote of his first meeting with Hitler at Berchtesgaden: "In spite of the hardness and ruthlessness I thought I saw in his face, I got the im-

pression that here was a man who could be relied upon when he had given his word." – Keith Feiling, *Life of Neville Chamberlain,* London, 1947, Bk. IV, p. 367.

4. The League of Nations Union was founded in London in 1919 as a society whose aims were "to secure the whole-hearted acceptance by the British people of the League of Nations as the guardian of international right . . ." Lord Grey, Lord Robert Cecil, Gilbert Murray, and other distinguished men were active in it. Its successor today is the United Nations Association.

5. Baldwin's famous "appalling frankness" speech of November 12, 1936, still provokes discussion. See R. Bassett, "Telling the Truth to the People," Cambridge, England, *Journal,* Vol. II, No. 2, November 1948.

Chapter 25 (*pages* 450-58)

1. The French municipal pawnshops are mentioned briefly in the article on "Pawnbroking" in the *Encyclopaedia Britannica.* See also F. Astier, *Des Monts-de-Piété en France,* Paris, 1913.

Chapter 26 (*pages* 459-73)

1. We have already forgotten the fierce conviction with which these views were once held. See, for instance, H. L. Engelbrecht and F. Hanighen, *Merchants of Death,* New York, 1934, which was so widely read.

2. The Reconstruction Finance Corporation was established under President Hoover by act of Congress in January 1932. Provided with an initial grant of $2,000,000,000 it sought to restore the American financial structure by furnishing credits to banks, railroads, and industrial corporations.

3. Cordell Hull, *Memoirs,* New York, 1948, Vol. I, pp. 535-41.

Chapter 27 (*pages* 474-99)

1. Lord Halifax, formerly Baron Irwin, Viceroy of India (1926-31). Succeeded to the Viscountcy of Halifax in 1934. Foreign Secretary, 1938-41. British ambassador to the United States, 1941-45.

2. Winston S. Churchill, *The Second World War: The Gathering Storm,* Boston, 1948, Bk. I, pp. 251-55; and Sumner Welles, *The Time for Decision,* New York, 1944.

3. Kurt von Schuschnigg, *Austrian Requiem,* London, 1947, Chs. I-II and XII-XIV.

Chapter 28 (*pages* 502-28)

1. Winston S. Churchill, *The Second World War,* Boston, 1948-53, 6 vols., Vol. III, pp. 113, 119, 141; Vol. IV, pp. 110, 128; Vol. V, pp. 11, 12, 14; Vol. VI, p. 725.

Chapter 29 (*pages* 529-64)

1. General Karl Heinrich von Stuelpnagel succeeded General Otto von Stuelpnagel as Military Governor of Occupied France in February 1942. He was afterwards implicated in the plot to assassinate Hitler in July 1944. There was also a General Siegfried von Stuelpnagel who does not appear in our history. All were of the same Prussian family.

2. Walter Millis, *This Is Pearl!,* New York, 1947, p. 342 n.

Chapter 30 (*pages* 565-87)

1. See A. J. Toynbee, *Survey of International Affairs* for 1939-46, "Hitler's Europe," London, 1950, p. 192.

2. Shirer gives a résumé of these figures. See William L. Shirer, *The Rise and Fall of the Third Reich,* London, 1960, Bk. 5, pp. 967-74. See also A. J. Toynbee, *ibid.,* pp. 153-64.

Chapter 32 (*pages* 612-17)

1. The areas ceded to France under the Italian Treaty were the Little St. Bernard Pass, the Mont Cenis Plateau, the Mont Thabor-Chaberton area, and the Tenda-Briga area.

Chapter 33 (*pages* 618-34)

1. In this chapter "to date" signifies up to October 1961.

2.

Trust Territory	*Administering Authorities*
Cameroons (British)	Britain
Cameroons (French)	France
Nauru	Australia (for New Zealand and Britain)
New Guinea	Australia
Pacific Islands	United States
Ruanda-Urundi	Belgium
Samoa (Western)	New Zealand
Somaliland	Italy
Tanganyika	Britain
Togoland (British)	Britain
Togoland (French)	France

3. See Note 1, above.
4. See Note 1, above.

Chapter 35 (*pages* 656-68)

1. See Warren W. Eason, "The Soviet Population Today," *Foreign Affairs,* July 1959.

2. Malenkov's report to the Nineteenth Party Congress is given in full in Martin Ebon, *Malenkov: Stalin's Successor,* New York, 1953, App., pp. 162-262.

3. Edward Crankshaw, "Khrushchev's Oration," the London *Observer,* June 17, 1956. The speech was published by the London *Observer,* June 10, 1956. The Manchester *Guardian* at the same time brought out a full text in pamphlet form.

Chapter 36 (*pages* 669-89)

1. The International Court took up the case – its first – in February 1948 and rendered its verdict in April 1949. The Court overwhelmingly vindicated the British claim to the right of innocent passage through the Corfu Channel, but it found that the British mine-sweeping operations, undertaken after the explosions, had violated Albania's sovereignty. By a vote of eleven to five the judges held Albania responsible for the fact that the British destroyers ran into the mines.

Chapter 37 (*pages* 690-710)

1. Strictly speaking the Fourth Republic was not in being till December 24, 1946, the date of the inaugural session of the Council of the Republic (the upper chamber under the new constitution) in the Luxembourg Palace, Paris. Vincent Auriol was elected President of France on January 14, 1947.

2. See Philip Williams, *Politics in Post-War France,* London, 1958, pp. 22-23.

3. French election records are most unsatisfactory. Even standard authorities differ. The present table has been compiled in the main from Philip Williams, *ibid.,* App. III, p. 440, and App. V, pp. 446-47.

4. Strictly speaking, as the Fourth Republic officially dated from December 24, 1946, the first Premier was Blum. See Note 1, above.

Chapter 38 (*pages* 711-21)

1. For the early history of the movement for European union see for example Andrew and Frances Boyd, *Western Union,* London, 1949, Ch. II.

Chapter 39 (*pages* 722-41)

1. Inscription on the base of President Nkrumah's statue in Accra.

2. It is impossible in a book of this kind, where so much has to be condensed, to give an account even of such interesting and attractive topics as the Colombo Plan. However a considerable literature, official and unofficial, on the plan is available. See F. C. Benham, *The Colombo Plan and Other Essays,* London, 1956.

3. Under the "entrenched" sections of the South Africa Act, passed by the British Parliament in 1909, the white and nonwhite voters of Cape Province shared a "common roll," and these sections of the Act could not be amended by the South African Parliament except by a two-thirds majority of both houses of the South African Parliament sitting together.

4. Strictly speaking we should be using the name "Eire" at this point. Under the Irish Constitution of 1937 the name of Ireland was changed to Eire. (See p. 275.) The name "Republic of Ireland" was adopted in 1948, and to date remains the country's official name.

Chapter 40 (*pages* 742-62)

1. See *U. S. Foreign Assistance and Assistance from International Organizations, July 1, 1945 through June 30, 1960,* International Cooperation Administration, Washington, D.C., 1961.

2. See *Treaties in Force: A List of Treaties and Other International Agreements of the United States in Force on January 1, 1961.* Office of the Legal Adviser, Department of State, Publication 7132, Washington, D.C.

3. Interview by James Shepley, *Life,* January 16, 1956.

Chapter 41 (*pages* 763-79)

1. See Note 10, Chapter 2, above.

2. Toynbee used the term "Social Asia" or "Greater Asia" in a broadcast. See A. J. Toynbee, "The Impact of the West on Asia," *The Listener,* London, May 24, 1951.

Chapter 42 (*pages* 780-814)

1. *Year-Book of the United Nations* for 1950, United Nations Publications, pp. 224-28; and for 1951, pp. 249-58.

2. In the local syntax, Buganda is the name of the country — Kiganda is the adjective; Muganda is the citizen — Baganda is the plural; and Luganda is the language. The Kabaka is the ruler; and the Great Lukiko is the parliament. — James Cameron, *The African Revolution,* London, 1961, pp. 71-72.

Glossary

The following words and terms of common diplomatic usage appear in the text:

Casus belli. An event or incident which may be a cause of, or justification for, war.
Démarche. "Faire une démarche" is to make representations, usually involving a revision or change of policy.
Détente. A relaxation of strained relations.
Fait accompli. An accomplished fact, action or event, presumably irrevocable.
Rapprochement. A drawing together of two nations or governments, especially after a period of strained relations.
Refroidissement. A cooling of relations between two nations or governments, formerly warmly disposed toward one another.
Status quo (ante bellum). The state or condition existing (before a war), used especially of the restoration of former existing frontiers.

See Chap. X on "Diplomatic Language" in Harold Nicolson, *Diplomacy,* New York, 1939.

The following names of British Cabinet offices appear in the text:

The Chancellor of the Exchequer corresponds to the American Secretary of the Treasury. The First Lord of the Admiralty corresponds to the Secretary of the Navy; he is usually, but not always, a civilian. The senior officer of the Admiralty is the First Sea Lord. He is always a high naval officer, but is not a member of the Cabinet; he would correspond to the American Chief of Naval Operations.
The Lord President of the Council, the Lord Privy Seal, and the Chancellor of the Duchy of Lancaster are old, honorific titles. They provide a means of giving a man a cabinet post without departmental duties, very much on the lines of a Minister without Portfolio.

The Chief of the Imperial General Staff (C.I.G.S.) is the senior officer of the British Army and corresponds to the Chief of Staff of the United States Army.

APPENDIXES

THE REICHSTAG PEACE RESOLUTION, JULY 19, 1917

The Reichstag Peace Resolution, July 19, 1917 – passed by the German *Reichstag* by 212 votes to 126.

As on the fourth of August so also now on the threshold of a fourth year of war, the words of the speech from the throne hold true: "We are not impelled by the lust of conquest." Germany has taken up arms in defense of her freedom, her independence, and the integrity of her soil.

The Reichstag strives for a peace of understanding and a lasting reconciliation among peoples. Violations of territory and political, economic, and financial persecutions are incompatible with such a peace. The Reichstag rejects every scheme which has for its purpose the imposition of economic barriers or the perpetuation of national hatreds after the war. The freedom of the seas must be secured. Economic peace alone will prepare the ground for the friendly association of peoples. The Reichstag will actively promote the creation of international organizations of justice.

But so long as the enemy governments dissociate themselves from such a peace, so long as they threaten Germany and her allies with conquest and domination, then so long will the German people stand united and unshaken, and fight till their right and the right of their allies to live and grow is made secure. United thus, the German people is unconquerable. The Reichstag knows that in that sentiment it is at one with the men who battle heroically to protect the Fatherland. The imperishable gratitude of our people goes out to them.

PRESIDENT WILSON'S FOURTEEN POINTS

The Wilsonian Code, as we have called it, consisted of a series of pronouncements made by President Wilson during 1918:

The Fourteen Points, January 8, 1918,
The Four Principles, February 11, 1918,
The Four Ends, July 4, 1918,
The Five Particulars, September 27, 1918.

Space prevents us from quoting these pronouncements in this Appendix, except the Fourteen Points. The full texts are available in H. W. V. Temperley, *A History of the Peace Conference of Paris,* London, 1920, Vol. I, pp. 431-48, and Alma Luckau, *The German Delegation at the Paris Peace Conference,* New York, 1941, pp. 137-39.

The Fourteen Points are as follows:

1. Open covenants of peace, openly arrived at, after which there shall be no private international understandings of any kind, but diplomacy shall proceed always frankly and in the public view.

2. Absolute freedom of navigation upon the seas, outside territorial waters, alike in peace and in war, except as the seas may be closed in whole or in part by international action for the enforcement of international covenants.

3. The removal, so far as possible, of all economic barriers and the establishment of an equality of trade conditions among all the nations consenting to the peace and associating themselves for its maintenance.

4. Adequate guarantees given and taken that national armaments will be reduced to the lowest point consistent with domestic safety.

5. A free, open-minded, and absolutely impartial adjustment of all colonial claims, based upon a strict observance of the principle that in determining all such questions of sovereignty the interests of the populations concerned must have equal weight with the equitable claims of the government whose title is to be determined.

6. The evacuation of all Russian territory and such settlement of all questions affecting Russia as will secure the best and freest co-operation of the other nations of the world in obtaining for her an unhampered and unembarrassed opportunity for the independent determination of her own political development and national policy and assure her of a sincere welcome into the society of free nations under institutions of her own choosing; and, more than a welcome, assistance also of every kind that she may need and may herself desire. The treatment accorded Russia by her sister nations in the months to come will be the acid test of their good will, of their comprehension of her needs as distinguished from their own interests, and of their intelligent and unselfish sympathy.

7. Belgium, the whole world will agree, must be evacuated and restored without any attempt to limit the sovereignty which she enjoys in common with all other free nations. No other single act will serve as this will serve to restore confidence among the nations in the laws which they have themselves set and determined for the government of their relations with one another. Without this healing act the whole structure and validity of international law is forever impaired.

8. All French territory should be freed and the invaded portions restored, and the wrong done to France by Prussia in 1871 in the matter of Alsace-Lorraine, which has unsettled the peace of the world for nearly fifty years, should be righted, in order that peace may once more be made in the interest of all.

9. A readjustment of the frontiers of Italy should be effected along clearly recognizable lines of nationality.

10. The peoples of Austria-Hungary, whose place among the nations we wish to see safeguarded and assured, should be accorded the freest opportunity of autonomous development.

11. Rumania, Serbia, and Montenegro should be evacuated; occupied territories restored; Serbia accorded free and secure access to the sea; and the relations of the several Balkan states to one another determined by friendly counsel along historically established lines of allegiance and nationality; and international guarantees of the political and economic independence and territorial integrity of the several Balkan states should be entered into.

12. The Turkish portions of the present Ottoman Empire should be assured a secure sovereignty, but other nationalities which are now under Turkish rule should be assured an undoubted security of life and absolutely unmolested op-

portunity of autonomous development, and the Dardanelles should be permanently opened as a free passage to the ships and commerce of all nations under international guarantees.

13. An independent Polish state should be erected which should include the territories inhabited by indisputably Polish populations, which should be assured a free and secure access to the sea, and whose political and economic independence and territorial integrity should be guaranteed by international covenant.

14. A general association of nations must be formed under specific covenants for the purpose of affording mutual guarantees of political independence and territorial integrity to great and small states alike.

A MEMORANDUM OF OBSERVATIONS

A Memorandum of Observations by the Allied Governments accompanying the American note to Germany on November 5, 1918.

The Allied Governments have given careful consideration to the correspondence which has passed between the President of the United States and the German Government. Subject to the qualifications which follow, they declare their willingness to make peace with the Government of Germany on the terms of peace laid down in the President's address to Congress of January 1918, and the principles of settlement enunciated in his subsequent addresses. They must point out, however, that Clause Two relating to what is usually described as the Freedom of the Seas, is open to various interpretations, some of which they could not accept. They must therefore reserve to themselves complete freedom on this subject when they enter the peace conference.

Further, in the conditions of peace laid down in his address to Congress of January 8, 1918, the President declared that invaded territories must be restored as well as evacuated and freed. The Allied Governments feel that no doubt ought to be allowed to exist as to what this provision implies. By it they understand that compensation will be made by Germany for all damage done to the civilian population of the Allies and their property by the aggression of Germany by land, by sea and from the air.

THE BALFOUR DECLARATION

The Balfour Declaration — conveyed in a letter from Balfour, then British Foreign Secretary, to Lord Rothschild.

Foreign Office
November 2nd, 1917

DEAR LORD ROTHSCHILD,

I have much pleasure in conveying to you, on behalf of His Majesty's Government, the following declaration of sympathy with Jewish Zionist aspirations which has been submitted to, and approved by, the Cabinet.

"His Majesty's Government view with favour the establishment in Palestine of a national home for the Jewish people, and will use their best endeavours to facilitate the achievement of this object, it being clearly understood that nothing shall be done which may prejudice the civil and religious rights of existing non-Jewish communities in Palestine, or the rights and political status enjoyed by Jews in any other country."

I shall be most grateful if you will bring this declaration to the knowledge of the Zionist Federation.

Yours sincerely

ARTHUR JAMES BALFOUR.

THE COVENANT OF THE LEAGUE OF NATIONS

For the sake of saving space only those Articles are quoted which are discussed in this book. The full text of the Covenant is easily available, notably in the *Encyclopaedia Britannica.*

The Amendments in force in 1938 are printed in italics, with the date of their adoption in brackets.

ARTICLE 8.

1. The Members of the League recognise that the maintenance of peace requires the reduction of national armaments to the lowest point consistent with national safety, and the enforcement by common action of international obligations.

2. The Council, taking account of the geographical situation and circumstances of each State, shall formulate plans for such reduction for the consideration and action of the several Governments.

3. Such plans shall be subject to reconsideration and revision at least every ten years.

4. After these plans shall have been adopted by the several Governments, the limits of armaments therein fixed shall not be exceeded without the concurrence of the Council.

5. The Members of the League agree that the manufacture by private enterprise of munitions and implements of war is open to grave objections. The Council shall advise how the evil effects attendant upon such manufacture can be prevented, due regard being had to the necessities of those Members of the League which are not able to manufacture the munitions and implements of war necessary for their safety.

6. The Members of the League undertake to interchange full and frank information as to the scale of their armaments, their military, naval and air programmes and the condition of such of their industries as are adaptable to warlike purposes.

ARTICLE 10.

The Members of the League undertake to respect and preserve, as against external aggression, the territorial integrity and existing political independence of all Members of the League. In case of any such aggression, or in case of any threat or danger of such aggression, the Council shall advise upon the means by which this obligation shall be fulfilled.

ARTICLE 11.

1. Any war or threat of war, whether immediately affecting any of the Members of the League or not, is hereby declared a matter of concern to the whole League, and the League shall take any action that may be deemed wise and effectual to safeguard the peace of nations. In case any such emergency should arise, the Secretary-General shall, on the request of any Member of the League, forthwith summon a meeting of the Council.

2. It is also declared to be the friendly right of each Member of the League to bring to the attention of the Assembly or of the Council any circumstance whatever affecting international relations which threatens to disturb international peace or the good understanding between nations upon which peace depends.

ARTICLE 12.

1. The Members of the League agree that, if there should arise between them any dispute likely to lead to a rupture they will submit the matter either to arbi-

tration *or judicial settlement* or to enquiry by the Council, and they agree in no case to resort to war until three months after the award by the arbitrators *or the judicial decision,* or the report by the Council.

2. In any case, under this Article the award of the arbitrators *or the judicial decision* shall be made within a reasonable time, and the report of the Council shall be made within six months after the submission of the dispute. [September 26, 1924]

ARTICLE 13.

1. The Members of the League agree that, whenever any dispute shall arise between them which they recognise to be suitable for submission to arbitration *or judicial settlement,* and which cannot be satisfactorily settled by diplomacy, they will submit the whole subject-matter to arbitration *or judicial settlement.*

2. Disputes as to the interpretation of a Treaty, as to any question of international law, as to the existence of any fact which, if established, would constitute a breach of any international obligation, or as to the extent and nature of the reparation to be made for any such breach, are declared to be among those which are generally suitable for submission to arbitration *or judicial settlement.*

3. *For the consideration of any such dispute, the Court to which the case is referred shall be the Permanent Court of International Justice, established in accordance with Article* 14, *or any tribunal agreed on by the parties to the dispute or stipulated in any Convention existing between them.* [September 26, 1924]

4. The Members of the League agree that they will carry out in full good faith any award *or decision* that may be rendered, and that they will not resort to war against a Member of the League which complies therewith. In the event of any failure to carry out such an award *or decision,* the Council shall propose what steps should be taken to give effect thereto. [September 26, 1924]

ARTICLE 14.

The Council shall formulate and submit to the Members of the League for adoption plans for the establishment of a Permanent Court of International Justice. The Court shall be competent to hear and determine any dispute of an international character which the parties thereto submit to it. The Court may also give an advisory opinion upon any dispute or question referred to it by the Council or by the Assembly.

ARTICLE 15.

1. If there should arise between Members of the League any dispute likely to lead to a rupture, which is not submitted to arbitration *or judicial settlement* in accordance with Article 13, the Members of the League agree that they will submit the matter to the Council. Any party to the dispute may effect such submission by giving notice of the existence of the dispute to the Secretary-General, who will make all necessary arrangements for a full investigation and consideration thereof. [September 26, 1924]

2. For this purpose the parties to the dispute will communicate to the Secretary-General, as promptly as possible, statements of their case with all the relevant facts and papers, and the Council may forthwith direct the publication thereof.

3. The Council shall endeavour to effect a settlement of the dispute, and, if such efforts are successful, a statement shall be made public giving such facts and explanations regarding the dispute and the terms of settlement thereof as the Council may deem appropriate.

4. If the dispute is not thus settled, the Council, either unanimously or by a majority vote, shall make and publish a report containing a statement of the facts

of the dispute and the recommendations which are deemed just and proper in regard thereto.

5. Any Member of the League represented on the Council may make a public statement of the facts of the dispute and of its conclusions regarding the same.

6. If a report by the Council is unanimously agreed to by the members thereof, other than the representatives of one or more of the parties to the dispute, the Members of the League agree that they will not go to war with any party to the dispute which complies with the recommendations of the report.

7. If the Council fails to reach a report which is unanimously agreed to by the members thereof, other than the representatives of one or more of the parties to the dispute, the Members of the League reserve to themselves the right to take such action as they shall consider necessary for the maintenance of right and justice.

8. If the dispute between the parties is claimed by one of them, and is found by the Council to arise out of a matter which by international law is solely within the domestic jurisdiction of that party, the Council shall so report, and shall make no recommendation as to its settlement.

9. The Council may in any case under this Article refer the dispute to the Assembly. The dispute shall be so referred at the request of either party to the dispute provided that such request be made within fourteen days after the submission of the dispute to the Council.

10. In any case referred to the Assembly, all the provisions of this Article and of Article 12, relating to the action and powers of the Council, shall apply to the action and powers of the Assembly, provided that a report made by the Assembly, if concurred in by the representatives of those Members of the League represented on the Council, and of a majority of the other Members of the League, exclusive in each case of the representatives of the parties to the dispute, shall have the same force as a report by the Council concurred in by all the members thereof other than the representatives of one or more of the parties to the dispute.

ARTICLE 16.

1. Should any Member of the League resort to war in disregard of its Covenants under Articles 12, 13 or 15, it shall *ipso facto* be deemed to have committed an act of war against all other Members of the League, which hereby undertake immediately to subject it to the severance of all trade or financial relations, the prohibition of all intercourse between their nationals and the nationals of the Covenant-breaking State, and the prevention of all financial, commercial or personal intercourse between the nationals of the Covenant-breaking State and the nationals of any other State, whether a Member of the League or not.

2. It shall be the duty of the Council in such case to recommend to the several Governments concerned what effective military, naval or air force the Members of the League shall severally contribute to the armed forces to be used to protect the Covenants of the League.

3. The Members of the League agree, further, that they will mutually support one another in the financial and economic measures which are taken under this Article, in order to minimise the loss and inconvenience resulting from the above measures, and that they will mutually support one another in resisting any special measures aimed at one of their number by the Covenant-breaking State, and that they will take the necessary steps to afford passage through their territory to the forces of any of the Members of the League which are co-operating to protect the Covenants of the League.

4. Any Member of the League which has violated any Covenant of the League may be declared to be no longer a Member of the League by a vote of the

Council concurred in by the representatives of all the other Members of the League represented thereon.

ARTICLE 17.

1. In the event of a dispute between a Member of the League and a State which is not a Member of the League, or between States not Members of the League, the State or States not Members of the League shall be invited to accept the obligations of membership in the League for the purposes of such dispute, upon such conditions as the Council may deem just. If such invitation is accepted, the provisions of Articles 12 to 16 inclusive shall be applied with such modifications as may be deemed necessary by the Council.

2. Upon such invitation being given, the Council shall immediately institute an enquiry into the circumstances of the dispute and recommend such action as may seem best and most effectual in the circumstances.

3. If a State so invited shall refuse to accept the obligations of membership in the League for the purposes of such dispute, and shall resort to war against a Member of the League, the provisions of Article 16 shall be applicable as against the State taking such action.

4. If both parties to the dispute, when so invited, refuse to accept the obligations of membership in the League for the purposes of such dispute, the Council may take such measures and make such recommendations as will prevent hostilities and will result in the settlement of the dispute.

ARTICLE 18.

Every Treaty or international engagement entered into hereafter by any Member of the League shall be forthwith registered with the Secretariat, and shall, as soon as possible, be published by it. No such Treaty or international engagement shall be binding until so registered.

ARTICLE 19.

The Assembly may from time to time advise the reconsideration by Members of the League of Treaties which have become inapplicable, and the consideration of international conditions whose continuance might endanger the peace of the world.

ARTICLE 21.

Nothing in this Covenant shall be deemed to affect the validity of international engagements, such as Treaties of Arbitration, or regional understandings like the Monroe doctrine, for securing the maintenance of peace.

ARTICLE 22.

1. To those colonies and territories, which as a consequence of the late war have ceased to be under the sovereignty of the States which formerly governed them, and which are inhabited by peoples not yet able to stand by themselves under the strenuous conditions of the modern world, there should be applied the principle that the well-being and development of such peoples form a sacred trust of civilisation, and that securities for the performance of this trust should be embodied in this Covenant.

2. The best method of giving practical effect to this principle is that the tutelage of such peoples should be entrusted to advanced nations who, by reason of their resources, their experience, or their geographical position, can best undertake this responsibility, and who are willing to accept it, and that this tutelage should be exercised by them as Mandatories on behalf of the League.

3. The character of the Mandate must differ according to the stage of the de-

velopment of the people, the geographical situation of the territory, its economic conditions and other similar circumstances.

4. Certain communities formerly belonging to the Turkish Empire have reached a stage of development where their existence as independent nations can be provisionally recognised subject to the rendering of administrative advice and assistance by a Mandatory until such time as they are able to stand alone. The wishes of these communities must be a principal consideration in the selection of the Mandatory.

5. Other peoples, especially those of Central Africa, are at such a stage that the Mandatory must be responsible for the administration of the territory under conditions which will guarantee freedom of conscience and religion, subject only to the maintenance of public order and morals, the prohibition of abuses such as the slave trade, the arms traffic and the liquor traffic, and the prevention of the establishment of fortifications or military and naval bases, and of miltary training of the natives for other than police purposes and the defence of territory, and will also secure equal opportunities for the trade and commerce of other Members of the League.

6. There are territories, such as South-West Africa and certain of the South Pacific Islands, which, owing to the sparseness of their population, or their small size, or their remoteness from the centres of civilisation, or their geographical contiguity to the territory of the Mandatory, and other circumstances, can be best administered under the laws of the Mandatory as integral portions of its territory, subject to the safeguards above mentioned in the interests of the indigenous population.

7. In every case of Mandate, the Mandatory shall render to the Council an annual report in reference to the territory committed to its charge.

8. The degree of authority, control or administration to be exercised by the Mandatory shall, if not previously agreed upon by the Members of the League, be explicitly defined in each case by the Council.

9. A permanent Commission shall be constituted to receive and examine the annual reports of the Mandatories and to advise the Council on all matters relating to the observance of the Mandates.

ARTICLE 23.

Subject to and in accordance with the provisions of international Conventions existing or hereafter to be agreed upon, the Members of the League—

(*a*) Will endeavour to secure and maintain fair and humane conditions of labour for men, women and children, both in their own countries and in all countries to which their commercial and industrial relations extend, and for that purpose will establish and maintain the necessary international organisations.

(*b*) Undertake to secure just treatment of the native inhabitants of territories under their control.

(*c*) Will entrust the League with the general supervision over the execution of agreements with regard to the traffic in women and children, and the traffic in opium and other dangerous drugs.

(*d*) Will entrust the League with the general supervision of the trade in arms and ammunition with the countries in which the control of this traffic is necessary in the common interest.

(*e*) Will make provision to secure and maintain freedom of communications and of transit and equitable treatment for the commerce of all Members of the League. In this connection, the special necessities of the regions devastated during the war of 1914-18 shall be borne in mind.

(*f*) Will endeavour to take steps in matters of international concern for the prevention and control of disease.

THE ATLANTIC CHARTER

The Atlantic Charter — Statement issued by President Roosevelt and Prime Minister Churchill, after their meeting "at sea," on August 14, 1941.

The President of the United States and the Prime Minister Mr. Churchill, representing His Majesty's Government in the United Kingdom, being met together, deem it right to make known certain common principles in the national policies of their respective countries on which they base their hopes for a better future for the world.

First: Their countries seek no aggrandizement, territorial or otherwise;

Second: They desire to see no territorial changes that do not accord with the freely expressed wishes of the peoples concerned;

Third: They respect the right of all peoples to choose the form of government under which they will live; and they wish to see sovereign rights and self-government restored to those who have been forcibly deprived of them;

Fourth: They will endeavor, with due respect for their existing obligations, to further the enjoyment by all states, great or small, victor or vanquished, of access, on equal terms, to the trade and to the raw materials of the world which are needed for their economic prosperity;

Fifth: They desire to bring about the fullest collaboration between all nations in the economic field, with the object of securing for all improved labor standards, economic adjustment and social security;

Sixth: After the final destruction of the Nazi tyranny, they hope to see established a peace which will afford to all nations the means of dwelling in safety within their own boundaries, and which will afford assurance that all the men in all the lands may live out their lives in freedom from fear and want;

Seventh: Such a peace should enable all men to traverse the high seas and oceans without hindrance;

Eighth: They believe that all of the nations of the world, for realistic as well as spiritual reasons, must come to the abandonment of the use of force. Since no future peace can be maintained if land, sea or air armaments continue to be employed by nations which threaten, or may threaten, aggression outside of their frontiers, they believe, pending the establishment of a wider and permanent system of general security, that the disarmament of such nations is essential. They will likewise aid and encourage all other practicable measures which will lighten for peace-loving peoples the crushing burden of armaments.

MEMBERSHIP OF THE UNITED NATIONS (as of October 1961)

The twenty-five United Nations of the Declaration of January 1, 1942, in italics. Poland made the twenty-sixth.

*The original fifty nations at the San Francisco Conference. June 1945. Poland became a member of the United Nations on October 24, 1945, and counted as an original member, the fifty-first.

Afghanistan
Albania
*Argentina
**Australia*
Austria

**Belgium*
*Bolivia
*Brazil
Bulgaria
Burma

Cambodia
Cameroun
**Canada*
Central African Republic
Ceylon
Chad
*Chile
**China (Nationalist)*
*Colombia
Congo (formerly Belgian Congo)
Congo (Republic)
**Costa Rica*
**Cuba*
Cyprus
**Czechoslovakia*

Dahomey
*Denmark
**Dominican Republic*

*Ecuador
*Egypt
**El Salvador*
*Ethiopia

Finland
*France

Gabon
Ghana
**Greece*
**Guatemala*
Guinea

**Haiti*
**Honduras*
Hungary

Iceland
**India*
Indonesia
*Iran (Persia)
*Iraq
Ireland
Israel
Italy
Ivory Coast

Japan
Jordan

Laos
*Lebanon
*Liberia
Libya
**Luxembourg*

Malagasy Republic
Malaya
Mali
*Mexico
Morocco

Nepal
**Netherlands*
**New Zealand*
**Nicaragua*
Niger
Nigeria
**Norway*

Pakistan
**Panama*
*Paraguay
*Peru
*Philippines
**Poland*
Portugal

Rumania

*Saudi Arabia
Senegal
Sierra Leone
Somalia
**South Africa*
**Soviet Union (U.S.S.R.)*
Spain
Sudan
Sweden
*Syria

Thailand (Siam)
Togo
Tunisia
*Turkey

*Ukraine
**United Kingdom (Britain)*
**United States*
Upper Volta
*Uruguay

**Venezuela*

*White Russia (Byelorussia)

Yemen
**Yugoslavia*

***Total* 101**

BIBLIOGRAPHY

This bibliography is not intended to be a specialist's bibliography, nor is it a bibliography of sources used in this book. The author has assumed that the specialist will find his own way into his field, and that this book is of too general a kind to need an elaborate bibliographical apparatus. The author's object is to give a short "further-reading list" of accessible, useful material, well worn in the estimation of acknowledged authorities. Official publications and institutional literature are occasionally included, but periodicals not at all. The list for the Cold War must necessarily be very provisional.

GENERAL AND REFERENCE

Annual Register: A Review of Public Events at Home and Abroad. London, 1758-1960.

Langer, William L., ed., *Foreign Affairs Bibliography, 1919-1932.* New York, 1933, for Council on Foreign Relations.

Langsam, Walter Consuelo, and J. M. Eagan, *Documents and Readings in the History of Europe since 1918.* Philadelphia, 1939.

Toynbee, Arnold J., and others, *Survey of International Affairs.* London, 1921-1956. Annual surveys published under the auspices of the Royal Institute of International Affairs.

Wheeler-Bennett, J. W., *Documents on International Affairs.* London, 1928-1958. A companion to the Toynbee, above.

Woolbert, Robert Gale, ed. *Foreign Affairs Bibliography, 1932-1942.* New York, 1945, for the Council on Foreign Relations. A sequel to the Langer, above.

Pre-1914 and the First World War

Albertini, Luigi. *The Origins of the War of 1914.* Trans. Isabella M. Massey, London, 1952-53. 3 vols. Massive, fully documented.

Bouton, S. Miles. *And the Kaiser Abdicates: The Story of the Death of the German Empire.* New Haven, 1920. An account of the collapse of Germany in 1918.

Chambers, Frank P. *The War Behind the War, 1914-1918: A History of the Political and Civilian Fronts.* New York, 1939.

Churchill, Winston S. *The World Crisis, 1911-1918.* Rev. ed. New York, 1931.

———. *The World Crisis, 1918-1928: The Aftermath.* New York, 1929.

———. *The Unknown War: The Eastern Front.* New York, 1931.

Cruttwell, C. R. M. F. *A History of the Great War, 1914-1918.* Oxford, 1936. A general history.

Dickinson, G. Lowes. *The International Anarchy, 1904-1914.* New York, 1926. A liberal thinker deplores the state of the international world before 1914.
Falls, Cyril. *The First World War.* London, 1960. A condensed military history.
Florinsky, Michael T. *The End of the Russian Empire: A Study in the Economic and Social History of the War.* New Haven, 1931.
Hankey, Lord. *The Supreme Command, 1914-1918.* London, 1961. 2 vols. The inner story of the British wartime cabinet.
Hart, Basil Henry Liddell. *A History of the World War.* Boston, 1935. A military history.
Hendrick, Burton J. *The Life and Letters of Walter H. Page.* Garden City, N.Y., 1927. The recognized biography of Walter Hines Page, American ambassador to Britain.
Jaszi, Oscar. *The Dissolution of the Hapsberg Monarchy.* Chicago, 1929.
Kennan, George F. *Russia Leaves the War.* Princeton, N.J., 1956. Soviet-American relations at the end of the war.
Lawrence, T. E. *Seven Pillars of Wisdom.* New York, 1935. Colonel Lawrence's account of the Arab Revolt.
Lloyd George, David. *War Memoirs.* 6 vols., Boston, 1933-37. A record of the war years and of his wartime government.
Ludendorff, Erich. *My War Memories: Ludendorff's Own Story.* New York, 1919. By the commander of the German Army in the last two years of the war. Indispensable for an appreciation of the German position.
Mansbergh, Nicholas. *The Coming of the First World War: A Study of the European Balance, 1878-1914.* London, 1949. A recent reconsideration of the old material.
Millis, Walter. *Road to War: America 1914-1917.* Boston, 1935. An isolationist view of America's neutral period.
Moorehead, Alan. *Gallipoli.* London, 1956. Grand descriptive writing of the campaign.
Pares, Bernard. *The Fall of the Russian Monarchy.* New York, 1939.
Rodzianko, M. V. *The Reign of Rasputin: An Empire's Collapse.* London, 1927. The end of Tsarist Russia as related by the president of the Duma.
Ropp, Theodore. *War in the Modern World.* Durham, N.C., 1959. Contains an excellent chapter on the First World War.
Rosenberg, Arthur. *The Birth of the German Republic, 1871-1918.* London, 1931. A political history of Germany during the war.
Tuchman, Barbara W. *The Zimmermann Telegram.* New York, 1958. Lively reconstruction of an important incident.
Wheeler-Bennett, J. W. *The Forgotten Peace: Brest Litovsk, 1918.* New York, 1939.

The Peace Conference of Paris and the Peace Treaties, 1919-20

(See also the section on Reparations, Debts, and the Depression, below.)

Birdsall, Paul. *Versailles Twenty Years After.* New York, 1941. Versailles rethought and redocumented. Favorable to Wilson.
Keynes, John Maynard. *The Economic Consequences of the Peace.* New York, 1920. A vehement, highly controversial attack, especially on the reparations clauses of the Treaty of Versailles.
Lloyd George, David. *Memoirs of the Peace Conference.* New Haven, 1939. 2 vols. Published in England (1938) as *The Truth about the Peace Treaties.* Lloyd George's apologia for the Peace Conference.
Mantoux, Étienne. *The Carthaginian Peace.* London, 1946. A French reply to Keynes, above.

Nicolson, Harold. *Peacemaking, 1919.* Boston, 1945. A personal commentary.
Seymour, Charles. *Intimate Papers of Colonel House.* Boston, 1926-28. 4 vols. Informative on President Wilson's diplomacy and the work of the American delegation at Paris.
Temperley, Harold W. V. *A History of the Peace Conference of Paris.* London, 1921-24. 6 vols. Ranks almost as the official history.

The League of Nations and the Quest for Peace in the Interwar Period

Carr, Edward Hallett. *The Twenty Years' Crisis, 1919-1939: An Introduction to the Study of International Relations.* London, 1939.
Cecil, Viscount (Lord Robert Cecil). *A Great Experiment: An Autobiography.* London, 1941. An account of the League by one of its creators.
Hudson, Manley O. *The Permanent Court of International Justice.* New York, 1934.
Madariaga, Salvador de. *Disarmament.* New York, 1929. A personal exposition of the whole problem.
Miller, David Hunter. *The Drafting of the Covenant.* New York, 1928. Complete historical record.
———. *The Peace Pact of Paris: A Study of the Briand-Kellogg Treaty.* New York, 1928.
Myers, Denys P. *Handbook of the League of Nations: A Comprehensive Account of Its Structure, Operation, and Activities.* Boston, 1935.
———. *World Disarmament: Its Problems and Prospects.* Boston, 1932.
Phelan, E. J. *Yes and Albert Thomas.* London, 1936. A popular account of the International Labor Organization and of its first director.
Rappard, William E. *The Quest for Peace Since the World War.* Cambridge, Mass., 1940.
Shotwell, James T. *War as an Instrument of National Policy and Its Renunciation in the Pact of Paris.* New York, 1929. The ideology and history of the Pact of Paris by one of its originators.
Walters, F. P. *A History of the League of Nations.* London, 1952. 2 vols. The standard history.
Wheeler-Bennett, J. W. *The Disarmament Deadlock.* London, 1934. A history of the Disarmament Conference at Geneva.
Wolfers, Arnold. *Britain and France Between Two Wars: Conflicting Strategies of Peace Since Versailles.* New York, 1940. A study of Anglo-French diplomacy in Europe, 1919-39.
Zimmern, Alfred. *The League of Nations and the Rule of Law, 1918-1935.* New York, 1939.

Reparations, Debts, and the Depression in the Interwar Period

Arndt, H. W. *Economic Lessons of the Nineteen Thirties.* London, 1944.
Day, J. P. *An Introduction to World Economic History Since the Great War.* London, 1939.
Galbraith, John Kenneth. *The Great Crash, 1929.* Boston, 1955.
Hodson, H. V. *Slump and Recovery, 1929-1937.* London, 1938.
Lloyd George, David. *The Truth about Reparations and Debts.* New York, 1932. Lloyd George's defense of the Versailles reparations clauses.
Robbins, Lionel. *The Great Depression.* London, 1934.
Wheeler-Bennett, J. W. *The Wreck of Reparations: Being the Political Background of the Lausanne Agreement, 1932.* New York, 1933.

The United States and Latin America

Allen, H. C. *Great Britain and the United States: A History of Anglo-American Relations.* London, 1954.

Bailey, Helen Miller, and Abraham P. Nasatir. *Latin America: The Development of a Civilization.* Englewood Cliffs, N.J., 1960.

Bailey, Thomas Andrew. *A Diplomatic History of the American People.* New York, 1958.

———. *Woodrow Wilson and the Great Betrayal.* New York, 1945. President Wilson and the rejection of the Treaty of Versailles in the United States.

Beard, Charles A. *American Foreign Policy in the Making, 1932-1940: A Study in Responsibilities.* New Haven, 1946. A polemic dissertation on presidential and party attitudes to European entanglements.

———. *President Roosevelt and the Coming of the War.* New Haven, 1948. Severe criticism of Roosevelt's foreign policy.

Brogan, Denis W. *The Era of Franklin D. Roosevelt.* New Haven, 1951.

Byrnes, James F. *Speaking Frankly.* New York, 1947. By the former Secretary of State.

Dulles, Foster Rhea. *China and America: The Story of Their Relations Since 1784.* Princeton, N.J., 1946.

———. *The Road to Teheran: The Story of Russia and America.* Princeton, N.J., 1944.

Hull, Cordell. *Memoirs.* New York, 1948. By the former Secretary of State.

Humphreys, Robin A. *The Evolution of Modern Latin America.* Oxford, 1946.

Lippmann, Walter. *U.S. Foreign Policy: Shield of the Republic.* Boston, 1943. Effective polemics by a leading American publicist.

Millis, Walter. *This Is Pearl! The United States and Japan, 1941.* New York, 1947. An account of the events immediately preceding Pearl Harbor.

Osgood, Robert Endicott. *Ideals and Self-Interest in America's Foreign Relations: The Great Transformation of the Twentieth Century.* Chicago, 1953. The conflict of power and moral purpose in American foreign policy today.

Schlesinger, Arthur M. *The Age of Roosevelt.* Boston, 1957-60. 3 vols. Contemporary historical writing at its best.

Sherwood, Robert E. *Roosevelt and Hopkins: An Intimate History.* New York, 1948. Published in England (1949) as *The White House Papers of Harry L. Hopkins.*

Smith, Sara R. *The Manchurian Crisis.* New York, 1948. Re-examination of a controversial episode.

Stettinius, Edward R., Jr. *Lend-Lease: Weapon for Victory.* New York, 1944. By the chief administrator of Lend-Lease and former Secretary of State.

———. *Roosevelt and the Russians: The Yalta Conference.* New York, 1949.

Stimson, Henry L. *The Far Eastern Crisis: Recollections and Observations.* New York, 1936. The Secretary of State describes the Manchurian crisis.

———. *On Active Service in Peace and War.* New York, 1948. The latter part of the book covers the author's activities as Secretary of War during the Second World War.

Strausz-Hupé, Robert. *The Balance of Tomorrow: Power and Foreign Policy in the United States.* New York, 1945. A tractate against isolationism.

———, and others. *Protracted Conflict.* New York, 1959. A symposium on foreign policy in the nuclear age.

Truman, Harry S. *Memoirs.* New York, 1955. 2 vols.

The United States in World Affairs, 1945– . New York, 1947– . Annual surveys published for the Council on Foreign Relations.

Welles, Sumner. *The Time for Decision.* New York, 1944.

Welles, Sumner. *Seven Decisions That Shaped History*. New York, 1951. Published in England as *Seven Major Decisions*. The former Undersecretary of State describes episodes of his term of office.

Britain and the British Commonwealth (Including Ireland, India, and South Africa)

Bishop, Donald. *The Administration of British Foreign Relations*. Syracuse, 1961.
Brady, Alexander. *Democracy in the Dominions: A Comparative Study in Institutions*. Toronto, 1958.
Chamberlin, William Henry. *Canada, Today and Tomorrow*. Boston, 1942.
Churchill, Winston S. *The World Crisis, 1918-1928: The Aftermath*. New York, 1929. Account of the 1920's from an English – and Churchillian – viewpoint.
Coupland, R. *The Indian Problem, 1833-1935; Indian Politics, 1936-1942; The Future of India*. London, 1942-43.
Eden, Anthony. *Memoirs*. London, 1960. 2 vols.
Elliott, W. Y. *The New British Empire*. New York, 1932. Imperial ideology and inter-imperial relations.
Epstein, Leon D. *Britain: Uneasy Ally*. Chicago, 1955. An excellent account of Britain post-1945.
Feiling, Keith. *The Life of Neville Chamberlain*. London, 1946.
Garratt, G. T. *An Indian Commentary*. London, 1928.
Gretton, R. H. *A Modern History of the English People*. London, 1930.
Gwynn, Denis. *The Irish Free State, 1922-1927*. London, 1928.
Hancock, W. K. *Survey of British Commonwealth Affairs*. London, 1937-58. 5 vols.
Hartog, Lady (Mabel Hélène). *India in Outline*. Cambridge, England, 1944.
Hinden, Rita. *Empire and After: A Study of British Imperial Attitudes*. London, 1949. The history of imperial ideology.
Kennedy, John F. *Why England Slept*. New York, 1940. An account of Britain during her appeasement and rearmament phase.
Kiewiet, C. W. de. *A History of South Africa: Social and Economic*. Oxford, 1941.
Knaplund, Paul. *Britain: Commonwealth and Empire, 1901-1955*. London, 1956.
MacCormac, John. *Canada, America's Problem*. New York, 1940.
Macleod, Ian. *Neville Chamberlain*. London, 1961.
Mansergh, Nicholas. *The Commonwealth and the Nations: Studies in British Commonwealth Relations*. London, 1948.
———, and others. *The Multi-Racial Commonwealth*. London, 1955.
Marquard, Leo, *The Peoples and Policies of South Africa*. London, 1960.
Mason, Philip. *The Men Who Ruled India*. London, 1954. 2 vols. A sympathetic account of the British Raj.
Medlicott, W. N. *British Foreign Policy since Versailles*. London, 1940.
Miller, J. D. B. *The Commonwealth in the World*. London, 1958.
Moraes, Frank. *Jawaharlal Nehru: A Biography*. New York, 1956.
Mowatt, Charles Loch. *Britain between the Wars, 1918-1940*. London, 1955.
Nehru, Jawaharlal. *Toward Freedom*. New York, 1941. Published in England (1936) as *An Autobiography*.
Nicolson, Harold. *King George V*. London, 1952.
Parkin, G. Raleigh. *India Today: An Introduction to Indian Politics*. New York, 1946.
Phillips, W. Alison. *The Revolution in Ireland, 1906-1923*. London, 1923.
Priestley, J. B. *English Journey*. London, 1934. A travelogue of the Depression.
Wade, Mason. *The French-Canadian Outlook: A Brief Account of the Unknown North Americans*. New York, 1946.
Walker, Eric A. *A History of Southern Africa*. London, 1957.
Young, G. M. *Stanley Baldwin*. London, 1952.

France

Aron, Robert. *The Vichy Régime, 1940-44.* London, 1958.

Brogan, D. W. *France Under the Republic, 1870-1939.* New York, 1940. Published in England as *The Development of Modern France.*

Earle, Edward Mead, and others. *Modern France.* Princeton, N.J., 1951. A series of chapters by recognized scholars on social, economic, and political issues.

Furniss, Edgar S. *France: Troubled Ally: De Gaulle's Heritage and Prospects.* New York, 1960.

Maritain, Jacques. *France My Country: Through the Disaster.* London, 1941. Reflections on the Fall of France.

Maurois, André. *Tragedy in France.* New York, 1940. Published in England (1941) as *Why France Fell.*

Micaud, Charles A. *The French Right and Nazi Germany, 1933-1939: A Study of Public Opinion.* Durham, N.C., 1943.

Munro, Katharine. *France, Yesterday and Today: A Short Survey.* London, 1945.

Peel, George. *The Economic Policy of France.* London, 1937. Expert study of French finance.

Pickles, Dorothy M. *The French Political Scene.* London, 1938. A handbook on interwar French politics.

———. *France Between the Republics.* London, 1946. A sequel to the foregoing.

———. *The Fifth French Republic.* London, 1960.

Siegfried, André. *France: A Study in Nationality.* New Haven, 1930.

Stokes, Richard L. *Léon Blum: Poet to Premier.* New York, 1937. A biography.

Taylor, Edmond. *The Strategy of Terror.* Boston, 1940. An account of the "war of nerves" in France between 1938 and 1940.

Thomson, David. *Democracy in France: The Third and Fourth Republics.* London, 1958.

Werth, Alexander. *The Twilight of France, 1933-1940.* New York, 1942. Published in England as *A Journalist's Chronicle.* Description of France in the 1930's.

———. *The Strange History of Pierre Mendès-France.* London, 1957.

———. *The De Gaulle Revolution.* London, 1960.

Williams, Philip. *Politics in Post-War France.* London, 1958.

Germany

(See also the section on The Approach of the Second World War, below.)

Bruck, W. F. *Social and Economic History of Germany from William II to Hitler, 1888-1938.* Cardiff, Wales, 1938.

Bullock, Alan L. C. *Hitler: A Study in Tyranny.* New York, 1953.

Crankshaw, Edward. *Gestapo: Instrument of Tyranny.* London, 1956.

Fraser, Lindley. *Germany Between Two Wars: A Study of Propaganda and War Guilt.* London, 1944. The interwar mentality of Germany.

Fried, Hans Ernest. *The Guilt of the German Army.* London, 1942. The responsibility of the German Army for the militarist tradition and armament policy in Germany.

Gatzke, Hans W. *Stresemann and the Rearmament of Germany.* Baltimore, 1954.

Gooch, G. P. *Germany.* New York, 1925. A general history.

Grosser, Alfred. *Western Germany: From Defeat to Rearmament.* London, 1955.

Heiden, Konrad. *Der Führer: Hitler's Rise to Power.* Boston, 1944. An early biography of Hitler and history of the Nazi party. Still invaluable.

Hitler, Adolf. *Mein Kampf.* New York, 1940.

———. *My New Order.* New York, 1941. A collection of Hitler's speeches, with a running commentary.

Horne, Alistair. *Back into Power: A Report on the New Germany*. London, 1955.
Kogon, Eugen. *The Theory and Practice of Hell: The German Concentration Camps and the System Behind Them*. London, 1950.
Micklem, Nathaniel. *National Socialism and the Roman Catholic Church*. London, 1939.
Morgan, J. H. *Assize of Arms: The Disarmament of Germany and Her Rearmament, 1919-1939*. London, 1945. A former Control Commission officer describes his experience of German evasion and duplicity.
Reveille, Thomas. *The Spoil of Europe: The Nazi Technique in Political and Economic Conquest*. New York, 1941.
Roberts, Stephen H. *The House That Hitler Built*. New York, 1937. History and analysis of the Nazi movement.
Rosenberg, Arthur. *A History of the German Republic*. London, 1936. An account of the Weimar Republic.
Rosinski, Herbert. *The German Army*. New York, 1940. Historical and political background.
Schuman, Frederick L. *The Nazi Dictatorship: A Study in Social Pathology and the Politics of Fascism*. New York, 1936.
Schwarzschild, Leopold. *World in Trance: From Versailles to Pearl Harbor*. New York, 1942. A sustained indictment of Germany and the German people.
Shirer, William L. *The Rise and Fall of the Third Reich*. New York, 1960.
Stolper, Gustav. *German Economy, 1870-1940*. New York, 1940. By an economist and former Deputy of the *Reichstag*.
Trevor-Roper, H. R. *The Last Days of Hitler*. London, 1956.
Wallich, Henry C. *Mainsprings of the German Revival*. New Haven, 1955. Germany's economic recovery since 1945.
Wheeler-Bennett, J. W. *The Wooden Titan: Hindenburg in Twenty Years of German History, 1914-1934*. New York, 1936.
——. *The Nemesis of Power: The German Army in Politics, 1918-1945*. New York, 1956.

The following are appended as a separate list. Our generation has been well served by its newspaper correspondents, and these books are all fine examples of their labors.

Deuel, Wallace R. *People Under Hitler*. New York, 1942.
Miller, Douglas. *You Can't Do Business with Hitler*. Boston, 1941.
Mowrer, Edgar Ansel. *Germany Puts the Clock Back*. New York, 1939.
Reed, Douglas. *The Burning of the Reichstag*. London, 1934.
Shirer, William L. *Berlin Diary*. New York, 1941.
Smith, Howard K. *Last Train from Berlin*. New York, 1942.
Tolischus, Otto. *They Wanted War*. New York, 1940.

The following books are also appended as a separate list. There is now a considerable literature on the philosophy, ideology, and prehistory of Nazism, and these books represent a selection.

Butler, Rohan D'O. *The Roots of National Socialism, 1783-1933*. New York, 1942.
Cobban, Alfred. *Dictatorship: Its History and Theory*. New York, 1939.
Foerster, F. W. *Europe and the German Question*. New York, 1940.
McGovern, William Montgomery. *From Luther to Hitler: The History of Fascist-Nazi Political Philosophy*. Boston, 1941.
Meissner, Erich. *Confusion of Faces: The Struggle Between Religion and Secularism in Europe*. London, 1946.

Neumann, Franz. *Behemoth: The Structure and Practice of National Socialism.* London, 1942.
Oakeshott, Michael. *Social and Political Doctrines of Contemporary Europe.* Cambridge, England, 1939.
Paul, Leslie. *The Annihilation of Man: A Study of the Crisis in the West.* London, 1944.
Rauschning, H. *The Revolution of Nihilism: Warning to the West.* Chicago, 1939. Published in England (1939) as *Germany's Revolution of Destruction.*
———. *The Voice of Destruction.* New York, 1940. Published in England (1939) as *Hitler Speaks.*
Stirk, S. D. *The Prussian Spirit: A Survey of German Literature and Politics, 1914-1940.* London, 1942.
Taylor, A. J. P. *The Course of German History: A Survey of the Development of Germany Since 1815.* New York, 1945.
Viereck, Peter. *Metapolitics: From the Romantics to Hitler.* New York, 1941.

Italy

Binchy, D. A. *Church and State in Fascist Italy.* London, 1941.
Boveri, Margaret. *Mediterranean Cross-Currents.* London, 1938. History and strategy of the Mediterranean.
Finer, Herman. *Mussolini's Italy.* London, 1935. History and description of Fascist Italy.
Grindrod, Muriel. *The New Italy: Transition from War to Peace.* London, 1947. A short account of post-1945 Italy.
Gwynn, Denis. *The Vatican and War in Europe.* London, 1940. A general history of the Papacy in its international relations since 1914.
Macartney, Maxwell H. H., and Paul Cremona. *Italy's Foreign and Colonial Policy, 1914-1937.* London, 1938.
Matthews, Herbert L. *The Fruits of Fascism.* New York, 1943. A description of Italy, especially at the beginning of the Second World War.
Monroe, Elizabeth. *The Mediterranean in Politics.* Oxford, 1938.
Mussolini, Benito. *The Political and Social Doctrine of Fascism.* New York, 1935. A translation of Mussolini's well-known article on Fascism in the *Enciclopedia Italiana.*
Salvemini, Gaetano. *Under the Axe of Fascism.* New York, 1936. A refugee from Fascism speaks his mind.
———. Prelude to World War II. New York, 1953.
Schneider, Herbert W. *Making the Fascist State.* New York, 1928. History and description of the Fascist movement.
Sprigge, Cecil J. S. *The Development of Modern Italy.* New Haven, 1943.
Webster, Richard A. *Christian Democracy in Italy, 1860-1960.* London, 1961.
Young, W. Hilton. *The Italian Left: A Short History of Political Socialism in Italy.* London, 1949.

The Middle Danube

(See also the section on The Approach of the Second World War, below.)
Ball, M. Margaret. *Post-War German-Austrian Relations: The Anschluss Movement, 1918-36.* Stanford, 1937.
Borkenau, Franz. *Austria and After.* London, 1936.
Bullock, Malcolm. *Austria, 1918-1938: A Study in Failure.* London, 1939.
Gedye, G. E. R. *Betrayal in Central Europe: Austria and Czechoslovakia, the Fallen Bastions.* New York, 1939. Published in England as *Fallen Bastions.* An eyewitness narrative of Nazi aggression in Austria and Czechoslovakia.

Macartney, C. A. *Hungary*. London, 1934.
———. *Hungary and Her Successors*. London, 1937.
———. *The Social Revolution in Austria*. Cambridge, England, 1926.
Machray, Robert. *The Struggle for the Danube and the Little Entente, 1929-38*. London, 1938.
Roucek, Joseph S., and others. *Central Eastern Europe: Crucible of World Wars*. New York, 1946. A historical and general compendium.
Seton-Watson, Hugh. *Eastern Europe Between the Wars, 1918-1941*. Cambridge, England, 1945.
Seton-Watson, R. W. *A History of the Czechs and Slovaks*. London, 1943. The last chapter gives a review of interwar Czechoslovakia, Munich, and the Nazi occupation.
Wiskemann, Elizabeth. *Czechs and Germans: A Study of the Struggle in the Historic Provinces of Bohemia and Moravia*. London, 1938. History and description of an ancient nationalist conflict.

Intermediate Europe
(*The Baltic, Poland, and the Balkans*)

Information Department, Royal Institute of International Affairs. *The Baltic States: Estonia, Latvia, and Lithuania*. London, 1938. A survey of Baltic politics and economics.
Buell, Raymond Leslie. *Poland: Key to Europe*. New York, 1939.
Frankel, Henry. *Poland: The Struggle for Power, 1772-1939*. London, 1946.
Jackson, J. Hampden. *Finland*. London, 1940.
Machray, Robert. *The Poland of Pilsudski*. London, 1936.
McNeill, William Hardy. *The Greek Dilemma: War and Aftermath*. Philadelphia, 1947.
Mitrany, David. *The Effect of the War in Southeastern Europe*. New Haven, 1936. Balkan problems, especially economic, in the 1920's.
Pribichevich, Stoyan. *World without End: The Saga of Southeastern Europe*. New York, 1939. On the social life, agrarian problems, and the cooperative movement in the Balkans.
Rose, William John. *Poland Old and New*. London, 1948.
Rouček, Joseph S. *The Politics of the Balkans*. New York, 1939.
———. *Balkan Politics: International Relations in No Man's Land*. Stanford, 1948.
Royal Institute of International Affairs. *South-Eastern Europe: A Political and Economic Survey*. Oxford, 1939.
Schevill, Ferdinand. *The History of the Balkan Peninsula: From the Earliest Times to the Present Day*. New York, 1933. The historical background of the Ottoman Empire and its dissolution.
Seton-Watson, Hugh. *Eastern Europe Between the Wars, 1918-1941*. Cambridge, England, 1945.
———. *The East European Revolution*. London, 1956.
Wolff, Robert Lee. *The Balkans in Our Time*. Cambridge, Mass., 1956.

Spain

Brenan, Gerald. *The Spanish Labyrinth: An Account of the Social and Political Background of the Civil War*. Cambridge, England, 1943.
Madariaga, Salvador de. *Spain*. New York, 1931. Introduction to modern Spanish history and politics.
Peers, E. Allison. *The Spanish Tragedy 1930-1936: Dictatorship, Republic, Chaos*. London, 1936. An account of the Revolution and outbreak of the Civil War.

Peers, E. Allison. *Spain in Eclipse, 1937-1943*. London, 1943. A sequel to the foregoing.
Thomas, Hugh. *The Spanish Civil War*. New York, 1961.

The Soviet Union

Beloff, Max. *The Foreign Policy of Soviet Russia, 1929-1941*. London, 1948. 2 vols.
Berdyaev, Nicolas. *The Origin of Russian Communism*. London, 1937. The philosopher tries to show that the Soviet adaptation of Marx is in the Russian tradition.
———. *The Russian Idea*. London, 1947. Contemporary Russian thought against its Christian background.
Borkenau, F. *The Communist International*. London, 1938. An account of the activities of the Communist International in different countries.
Carr, Edward Hallett. *The Soviet Impact on the Western World*. London, 1947.
———. *The Bolshevik Revolution*, London, 1950- . Incomplete, but already a standard work.
Chamberlin, William Henry. *The Russian Revolution, 1917-1921*. New York, 1935. 2 vols. An early work, but still invaluable.
Crankshaw, Edward. *Russia and the Russians*. London, 1947.
Deutscher, Isaac. *Stalin: A Political Biography*. London, 1949.
———. *Trotsky*. Vol. I, *The Prophet Armed;* Vol. II, *The Prophet Unarmed*. Oxford, 1954, 1959.
Duranty, Walter. *USSR: The Story of Soviet Russia*. Philadelphia, 1944.
Fischer, Louis. *The Soviets in World Affairs: A History of the Relations between the Soviet Union and the Rest of the World*. London, 1951. 2 vols.
Florinsky, Michael T. *Toward an Understanding of the U.S.S.R.: A Study in Government, Politics, and Economic Planning*. New York, 1939.
Harper, Samuel N. *The Government of the Soviet Union*. New York, 1937. More than its title indicates. A general review of the Soviet state.
Koestler, Arthur. *The Yogi and the Commissar*. London, 1945. A personal account and condemnation of Soviet Communism.
Laski, Harold J. *Communism*. New York, 1927.
Pares, Bernard. *A History of Russia*. London, 1955.
Reed, John. *Ten Days That Shook the World*. London, 1929. Vivid, eye-witness report of the Bolshevik Revolution.
Rosenberg, Arthur. *A History of Bolshevism from Marx to the First Five Years' Plan*. London, 1934.
Schapiro, Leonard. *The Communist Party of the Soviet Union*. New York, 1960.
Shubb, David. *Lenin: A Biography*. New York, 1948.
Taracouzio, T. A. *War and Peace in Soviet Diplomacy*. New York, 1940. Soviet foreign policy through its many phases and changes up to 1939.
Timasheff, Nicholas S. *The Great Retreat: The Growth and Decline of Communism in Russia*. New York, 1946.
Towster, Julian. *Political Power in the U.S.S.R., 1917-1947: The Theory and Structure of Government in the Soviet State*. New York, 1948.
Trotsky, Leon. *The History of the Russian Revolution*. New York, 1932. 3 vols. Trotsky's own classic account of the revolution.

Near and Middle East
(Including Turkey and Iran)

Antonius, George. *The Arab Awakening in The Story of the Arab National Movement*. Philadelphia, 1939.
Bentwich, Norman. *Palestine*. London, 1940.

Bentwich, Norman. *Israel Resurgent.* London, 1960.
Caroe, Olaf. *Wells of Power: The Oilfields of Southwestern Asia: A Regional and Global Study.* London, 1951.
Elwell-Sutton, L. P. *Modern Iran.* London, 1941.
———. *Persian Oil: A Study in Power Politics.* London, 1955. A controversial but important book, especially on the Iranian Oil Crisis of 1950.
Gibb, H. A. R., and Harold Bowen. *Islamic Society and the West: A Study of the Impact of Western Civilization on Moslem Culture in the Near East.* Oxford, 1957.
Glubb, John Bagot. *Britain and the Arabs: A Study of Fifty Years, 1908-1958.* London, 1959.
———. *A Soldier with the Arabs.* London, 1957. The Arab Legion by its British commander.
Grant, Christina Phelps. *The Syrian Desert: Caravans, Travel, and Exploration.* New York, 1938. Including the post-1918 development of transport and communications over the land bridge.
Hourani, A. H. *Minorities in the Arab World.* London, 1947.
———. *Syria and Lebanon: A Political Essay.* London, 1946.
Howard, Harry N. *The Partition of Turkey: A Diplomatic History, 1913-1923.* Norman, Oklahoma, 1931.
Ireland, Philip Willard. *Iraq: A Study in Political Development.* London, 1937.
Kedourie, Elie. *England and the Middle East: The Destruction of the Ottoman Empire, 1914-1921.* London, 1956.
Kirk, George E. *A Short History of the Middle East, from the Rise of Islam to Modern Times.* London, 1948.
Laquer, Walter Z. *Communism and Nationalism in the Middle East.* New York, 1956.
Lawrence, T. E. *Seven Pillars of Wisdom: A Triumph.* New York, 1936.
———. *Revolt in the Desert.* Garden City, N.Y., 1927. An abridgment of *Seven Pillars.*
Lenczowski, George. *Oil and State in the Middle East.* Ithaca, N.Y., 1960.
———. *Russia and the West in Iran, 1918-1948: A Study in Big-Power Rivalry.* Ithaca, N.Y., 1949.
Lilienthal, Alfred M. *What Price Israel.* Chicago, 1953. Forthright and authoritative criticism of the Zionists.
Little, Tom. *Egypt.* New York, 1958. Masterly summary of recent history.
Longrigg, Stephen Hemsley. *Oil in the Middle East: Its Discovery and Development.* London, 1961.
Marlowe, John. *Arab Nationalism and British Imperialism.* London, 1961.
———. *The Seat of Pilate: An Account of the Palestine Mandate.* London, 1959.
The Middle East: A Political and Economic Survey. London, 1958. Published for the Royal Institute of International Affairs.
Monroe, Elizabeth. *The Mediterranean in Politics.* London, 1938.
Neguib, Mohammed. *Egypt's Destiny.* New York, 1955.
Philby, H. St. J. B. *Arabia.* New York, 1930. Account of the Wahhabis, Ibn Saud, and the Ikhwan Movement, and of Anglo-Arab relations during and after the First World War.
———. *Arabian Jubilee.* London, 1952. A biography of King Ibn Saud.
Stark, Freya. *The Arab Island: The Middle East, 1939-1943.* New York, 1945.
Storrs, Sir Ronald. *Memoirs.* New York, 1937. Published in England as *Orientations.* The author was for nine years Governor of Jerusalem, first Military Governor, later Civil Governor.
Warriner, Doreen. *Land and Poverty in the Middle East.* London, 1948.
Watt, D. C. *Britain and the Suez Canal.* London, 1956.

Webster, Donald Everett. *The Turkey of Ataturk: Social Process in the Turkish Reformation*. Philadelphia, 1939.
Weizmann, Chaim. *Trial and Error: The Autobiography of Chaim Weizmann*. New York, 1949.
Wilber, D. N. *Iran, Past and Present*. Princeton, N.J., 1948.
Wint, Guy, and Peter Calvocoressi. *Middle East Crisis*. London, 1957. An excellent short account of the Suez Crisis of 1956.

Africa

(For Algeria, etc. see section on France; and for South Africa, see section on Britain and the British Commonwealth.)
Cameron, James. *The African Revolution*. London, 1961.
Gunther, John. *Inside Africa*. New York, 1955. Now dating very fast, but still one of the best of the Gunther series.
Hailey, Lord. *An African Survey: A Study of the Problems Arising in Africa South of the Sahara*. London, 1957.
Haines, C. Grove, and others. *Africa Today*. Baltimore, 1955.
Kimble, George H. T. *Tropical Africa*. New York, 1960. 2 vols.

The Far East and Southeast Asia

Ball, W. Macmahon. *Nationalism and Communism in East Asia*. Melbourne, 1952.
Benedict, Ruth. *The Chrysanthemum and the Sword: Patterns of Japanese Culture*. Boston, 1946.
Brimmell, J. H. *Communism in South East Asia: A Political Analysis*. New York, 1959.
Chiang Kai-shek. *China's Destiny*. New York, 1947.
Eckel, Paul E. *The Far East since 1950*. New York, 1947.
Emerson, Rupert, and others. *Government and Nationalism in Southeast Asia*. New York, 1942.
Jones, F. C. *Manchuria since 1931*. London, 1949.
Kenneth Scott Latourette. *A Short History of the Far East*. New York, 1957.
Lattimore, Owen. *The Making of Modern China: A Short History*. New York, 1945.
Mao Tse-tung. *China's New Democracy*. New York, 1944.

The Approach of the Second World War and the Second World War

(See also the sections on the United States, Britain, France, Germany, etc.)
Ansel, Walter. *Hitler Confronts England*. Durham, N.C., 1960. An American admiral assesses the chances of the German invasion of Britain in 1940.
Bryant, Arthur. *The Turn of the Tide, 1939-1943; Triumph in the West, 1943-1946*. London, 1957, 1959. Based on the diaries of Field Marshal Viscount Alanbrooke.
Churchill, Winston S. *The Second World War*. Boston, 1948-53. 6 vols.
Clark, Mark W. *Calculated Risk*. New York, 1950. General Clark's account of the campaigns in North Africa and Italy.
Deane, John R. *The Strange Alliance: The Story of Our Efforts at Wartime Economic Co-operation with Russia*. New York, 1947.
Eisenhower, Dwight D. *Crusade in Europe*. New York, 1948.
Falls, Cyril. *The Second World War: A Short History*. London, 1948.
Feis, Herbert. *The Road to Pearl Harbor: The Coming of the War Between the United States and Japan*. Princeton, N.J., 1950.

Fleming, Peter. *Invasion 1940*. London, 1957. German preparations and British counterpreparations.
Gafencu, Grigore. *Prelude to the Russian Campaign: From the Moscow Pact to the Opening of Hostilities in Russia*. London, 1945.
Gantenbein, James W., ed. *Documentary Background of World War II, 1931 to 1941*. New York, 1949.
Langer, William L., and S. Everett Gleason. *The Undeclared War, 1940-1941*. New York, 1953. World events up to Pearl Harbor as seen from the United States.
Leahy, William D. *I Was There*. New York, 1950. Admiral Leahy's account as President Roosevelt's Chief of Staff.
McNeill, William Hardy. *America, Britain, and Russia: Their Cooperation and Conflict, 1941-1946*. London, 1953.
Namier, L. B. *Diplomatic Prelude, 1938-1939*. London, 1948.
———. *Europe in Decay: A Study in Disintegration, 1936-1940*. London, 1950.
Snyder, Louis L. *The War: A Concise History, 1939-1945*. New York, 1960.
Spears, Edward. *Assignment to Catastrophe*. London, 1954. 2 vols. A British general with the French Army in 1940.
Toynbee, Arnold, and Frank T. Ashton-Gwatkin, eds. *The World in March 1939*. London, 1952.
Voices of History, 1941-42, 1942-43, 1943-44 ed. by Franklin Watts; 1944-45, 1945-46 ed. by Nathan Ausubel, New York. Speeches and papers of national wartime leaders.
Wheeler-Bennett, J. W. *Munich: Prologue to Tragedy*. New York, 1948.
Wilmot, Chester. *The Struggle for Europe*. New York, 1952. A fine military history of the European theater.
Wiskemann, Elizabeth. *The Rome-Berlin Axis: A History of the Relations Between Hitler and Mussolini*. London, 1949.

The United Nations, the Peace Treaties, and the Cold War

Boyd, Andrew, and Frances Boyd. *Western Union*. London, 1949. An account of the European Union movement.
Bull, Hedley. *The Control of the Arms Race: Disarmament and Arms Control in the Missile Age*. London, 1961.
Davison, Walter Phillips. *Berlin Blockade: A Study in Cold War Politics*. Princeton, N.J., 1958.
Feis, Herbert. *Between War and Peace*. Princeton, N.J., 1960. The Potsdam Conference and its background.
Goodrich, Leland M. *Korea: A Study of U.S. Policy in the United Nations*. New York, 1956.
———. *The United Nations*. New York, 1959.
Goodwin, Geoffrey L. *Britain and the United Nations*. London, 1957. For the Carnegie Endowment for International Peace.
Ismay, Lord. *NATO: The First Five Years*. n.d.
Lie, Trygve. *In the Cause of Peace: Seven Years with the United Nations*. New York, 1954. By the former Secretary General.
McInnis, Edgar. *The Atlantic Triangle and the Cold War*. Toronto, 1959.
Opie, Redvers, and others. *The Search for Peace Settlements*. Washington, D.C., 1951. An account of the peace negotiations and the treaties.
Scott, William A., and Stephen B. Withey. *The United States and the United Nations, The Public View*. New York, 1958. One of the series prepared for the Carnegie Endowment for International Peace.
Seton-Watson, Hugh. *Neither War nor Peace: The Struggle for Power in the Post-War World*. London, 1960. Reflections on the Cold War.

INDEX

Ranks and titles listed are the most familiar or the latest contemporary with our text. Subsequent ranks and titles are shown in parentheses. The names of European aristocracy are sometimes simplified. For the full names the reader should consult the books of reference, *Almanach De Gotha, Debrett's Peerage,* etc.

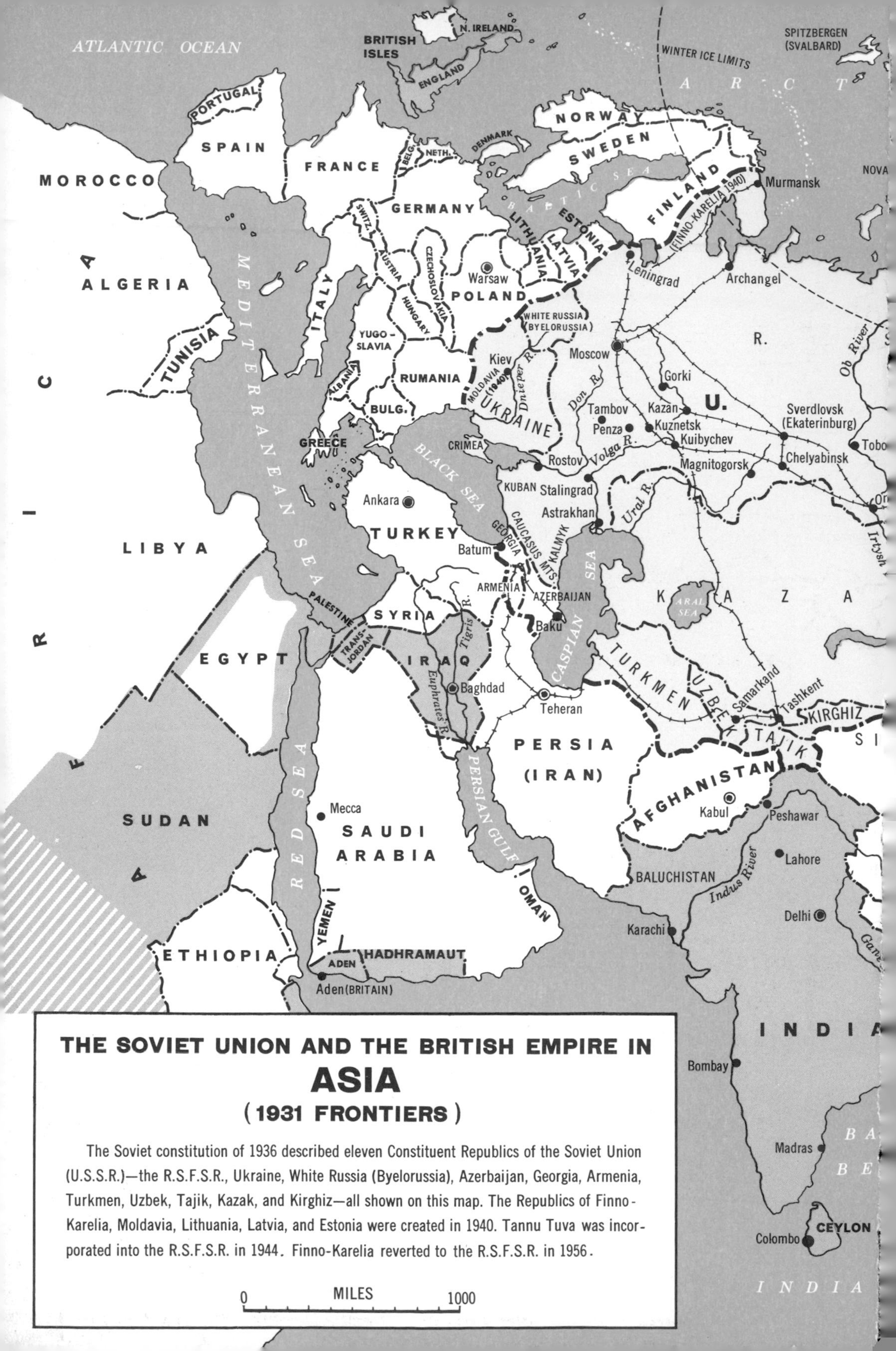

THE SOVIET UNION AND THE BRITISH EMPIRE IN

ASIA

(1931 FRONTIERS)

The Soviet constitution of 1936 described eleven Constituent Republics of the Soviet Union (U.S.S.R.)—the R.S.F.S.R., Ukraine, White Russia (Byelorussia), Azerbaijan, Georgia, Armenia, Turkmen, Uzbek, Tajik, Kazak, and Kirghiz—all shown on this map. The Republics of Finno-Karelia, Moldavia, Lithuania, Latvia, and Estonia were created in 1940. Tannu Tuva was incorporated into the R.S.F.S.R. in 1944. Finno-Karelia reverted to the R.S.F.S.R. in 1956.

0 MILES 1000